EQ

EQ

Encyclopaedia of the Qurʾān

VOLUME FOUR

P – Sh

Jane Dammen McAuliffe, *General Editor*

Brill, Leiden – Boston

2004

Koninklijke Brill NV incorporates the imprints Brill Academic
Publishers, Martinus Nijhoff Publishers and VSP.

ISBN 90 04 12355 5

Printed in The Netherlands on acid-free paper.

ABBREVIATIONS

AI = *Annales islamologiques*
AIUON = *Annali dell' Istituto Universitario Orientale di Napoli*
AO = *Acta orientalia*
AO-H = *Acta orientalia (Academiae Scientiarum Hungaricae)*
Arabica = *Arabica. Revue d'études arabes*
ARW = *Archiv für Religionswissenschaft*
AUU = *Acta Universitatis Upsaliensis*
BASOR = *Bulletin of the American Schools of Oriental Research*
BEO = *Bulletin d'études orientales de l'Institut Français de Damas*
BGA = *Bibliotheca geographorum arabicorum*
BIFAO = *Bulletin de l'Institut Français d'Archéologie Orientale du Caire*
BO = *Bibliotheca orientalis*
BSA = *Budapest studies in Arabic*
BSOAS = *Bulletin of the School of Oriental and African Studies*
Der Islam = *Der Islam. Zeitschrift für Geschichte und Kultur des islamischen Orients*
EI[1] = *Encyclopaedia of Islam*, 1st ed., Leiden 1913-38
EI[2] = *Encyclopaedia of Islam*, new ed., Leiden 1954-2002
ER = *Encyclopedia of religion*, ed. M. Eliade, New York 1986
ERE = *Encyclopaedia of religion and ethics*
GMS = *Gibb memorial series*
HO = *Handbuch der Orientalistik*
IA = *Islâm ansiklopedisi*
IBLA = *Revue de l'Institut des Belles Lettres Arabes, Tunis*
IC = *Islamic culture*
IJMES = *International journal of Middle East studies*
IOS = *Israel oriental studies*
IQ = *The Islamic quarterly*
Iran = *Iran. Journal of the British Institute of Persian Studies*
JA = *Journal asiatique*
JAL = *Journal of Arabic literature*
JAOS = *Journal of the American Oriental Society*
JE = *Jewish encyclopaedia*
JESHO = *Journal of the economic and social history of the Orient*
JIS = *Journal of Islamic studies*
JNES = *Journal of Near Eastern studies*
JRAS = *Journal of the Royal Asiatic Society*
JSAI = *Jerusalem studies in Arabic and Islam*
JSS = *Journal of Semitic studies*
MFOB = *Mélanges de la Faculté Orientale de l'Université St. Joseph de Beyrouth*
MIDEO = *Mélanges de l'Institut Dominicain d'études orientales du Caire*
MO = *Le monde oriental*
MSOS = *Mitteilungen des Seminars für orientalische Sprachen, westasiatische Studien*
Muséon = *Le Muséon. Revue des études orientales*
MW = *The Muslim world*
OC = *Oriens christianus*

OLZ = *Orientalistische Literaturzeitung*
Orientalia = *Orientalia. Commentarii periodici Pontificii Instituti Biblici*
Qanṭara = *al-Qanṭara. Revista de estudios arabes*
QSA = *Quaderni de studi arabi*
RCEA = *Répertoire chronologique d'épigraphie arabe*
REI = *Revue des études islamiques*
REJ = *Revue des études juives*
REMMM = *Revue du monde musulman et de la Méditerranée*
RHR = *Revue de l'histoire des religions*
RIMA = *Revue de l'Institut des Manuscrits Arabes*
RMM = *Revue du monde musulman*
RO = *Rocznik Orientalistyczny*
ROC = *Revue de l'orient chrétien*
RSO = *Rivista degli studi orientali*
SIr = *Studia iranica*
SI = *Studia islamica*
WI = *Die Welt des Islams*
WKAS = *Wörterbuch der klassischen arabischen Sprache*
WO = *Welt des Orients*
WZKM = *Wiener Zeitschrift für die Kunde des Morgenlandes*
ZAL = *Zeitschrift für arabische Linguistik*
ZDMG = *Zeitschrift der Deutschen Morgenländischen Gesellschaft*
ZGAIW = *Zeitschrift für Geschichte der arabisch-islamischen Wissenschaften*
ZS = *Zeitschrift für Semitistik*

AUTHORS OF ARTICLES

VOLUME IV

Khaled M. Abou El Fadl, University of California at Los Angeles
Asma Afsaruddin, University of Notre Dame
M. Shahab Ahmed, Harvard University
Michael W. Albin, Library of Congress, Washington, DC
Mohammed A. Bamyeh, Macalester College
Meir M. Bar-Asher, Hebrew University, Jerusalem
Herbert Berg, University of North Carolina at Wilmington
Hartmut Bobzin, University of Erlangen
Michael Bonner, University of Michigan
Maurice Borrmans, Pontificio Istituto di Studi Arabi e d'Islamistica, Rome
Issa J. Boullata, McGill University
Gerhard Böwering, Yale University
William M. Brinner, University of California, Berkeley
Jonathan E. Brockopp, Pennsylvania State University
Angelika Brodersen, University of Gottingen
Patrice C. Brodeur, Connecticut College
Ahmad Salim Dallal, Georgetown University
F.C. de Blois, University of London
Majid F. Fakhry, Georgetown University
Reuven Firestone, Hebrew Union College, Los Angeles
Dmitry V. Frolov, Moscow University
Anna M. Gade, Oberlin College
Avner Giladi, University of Haifa
Valerie Gonzalez, School of Architecture, Marseille-Luminy
William A. Graham, Harvard University
Beatrice Gruendler, Yale University
Gerald R. Hawting, University of London
Paul L. Heck, Georgetown University
Sherman A. Jackson, University of Michigan
Alan Jones, University of Oxford
Shigeru Kamada, University of Tokyo
N.J.G. Kaptein, University of Leiden
Philip F. Kennedy, New York University
Richard Kimber, University of St. Andrews
Leah Kinberg, Tel-Aviv University
Alexander D. Knysh, University of Michigan
Kathryn Kueny, Fordham University
Paul Kunitzsch, University of Munich
Arzina R. Lalani, Institute of Ismaili Studies, London
Frederik Leemhuis, University of Groningen
Franklin D. Lewis, Emory University

Jean-Yves l'Hôpital, University of Rennes II
Shari Lowin, Stonehill College, Easton, PA
Joseph Lowry, University of Pennsylvania
Daniel A. Madigan, Pontifical Gregorian University, Rome
Louise Marlow, Wellesley College
David Marshall, Lambeth Palace, London
Jane Dammen McAuliffe, Georgetown University
Christopher Melchert, University of Oxford
Josef W. Meri, Institute of Ismaili Studies, London
Mustansir Mir, Youngstown State University
John A. Nawas, Catholic University, Leuven
Angelika Neuwirth, Free University, Berlin
Kathleen M. O'Connor, University of South Florida
Matthias Radscheit, Bonn, Germany
Bernd R. Radtke, University of Utrecht
Wim Raven, University of Frankfurt
Andrew Rippin, University of Victoria
Uri Rubin, Tel-Aviv University
Zeki Saritoprak, John Carroll University
Robert Schick, Henry Martyn Institute of Islamic Studies, Hyderabad
Arie Schippers, University of Amsterdam
Sabine Schmidtke, Free University, Berlin
Marco Schöller, University of Köln
Irfan Shahid, Georgetown University
Moshe Sharon, Hebrew University, Jerusalem
Paul Stenhouse, Sacred Heart Monastery, Kensington, NSW
Devin J. Stewart, Emory University
Mark N. Swanson, Luther Seminary, St. Paul, MN
Liyakat Takim, University of Denver
Roberto Tottoli, Università degli Studi di Napoli "L'Orientale"
Nargis Virani, Washington University
Earle H. Waugh, University of Alberta
Bernard G. Weiss, University of Utah
Brannon M. Wheeler, University of Washington
Lutz Wiederhold, University Halle-Wittenberg
Clare Wilde, The Catholic University of America
A.H. Mathias Zahniser, Asbury Theological Seminary
Kate P. Zebiri, University of London

SHORT TITLES

Abbott, *Studies II*
N. Abbott, *Studies in Arabic literary papyri. II. Qur'ānic commentary and tradition,* Chicago 1967

ʿAbd al-Bāqī
Muḥammad Fuʾād ʿAbd al-Bāqī, *al-Muʿjam al-mufahras li-alfāẓ al-Qurʾān al-karīm,* Cairo 1945

ʿAbd al-Jabbār, *Mutashābih*
ʿAbd al-Jabbār b. Aḥmad al-Asadābādī al-Qāḍī al-Hamadhānī, *Mutashābih al-Qurʾān,* ed. ʿAdnān M. Zarzūr, 2 vols., Cairo 1969

ʿAbd al-Jabbār, *Tanzīh*
ʿAbd al-Jabbār b. Aḥmad al-Asadābādī al-Qāḍī al-Hamadhānī, *Tanzīh al-Qurʾān ʿan al-maṭāʿin,* Beirut 1966

ʿAbd al-Raḥmān, *ʿAṣrī*
ʿĀʾisha ʿAbd al-Raḥmān, *al-Qurʾān wa-l-tafsīr al-ʿaṣrī,* Cairo 1970

ʿAbd al-Raḥmān, *Tafsīr*
ʿĀʾisha ʿAbd al-Raḥmān, *al-Tafsīr al-bayānī lil-Qurʾān al-karīm,* 3rd ed., Cairo 1968

ʿAbd al-Razzāq, *Muṣannaf*
ʿAbd al-Razzāq b. Hammām al-Ṣanʿānī, *al-Muṣannaf,* ed. Ḥabīb al-Raḥmān al-Aʿẓamī, 11 vols., Beirut 1390/1970; 2nd ed. Johannesburg 1983; ed. Muḥammad Sālim Samāra, 4 vols. (with indices of ḥadīth), Beirut 1408/1988

ʿAbd al-Razzāq, *Tafsīr*
ʿAbd al-Razzāq b. Hammām al-Ṣanʿānī, *al-Tafsīr,* ed. Muṣṭafā Muslim Muḥammad, 3 vols. in 4, Riyadh 1410/1989; ed. ʿAbd al-Muʿṭī Amīn Qalʿajī, 2 vols., Beirut 1411/1991; ed. Maḥmūd Muḥammad ʿAbduh, 3 vols., Beirut 1419/1999

Abū Dāwūd
Abū Dāwūd Sulaymān b. al-Ashʿath al-Sijistānī, *Sunan,* ed. Muḥammad Muḥyī l-Dīn ʿAbd al-Ḥamīd, 4 vols., Cairo 1339/1920; ed. Kamāl Yūsuf al-Ḥūt, 2 vols., Beirut 1988

Abū l-Futūḥ Rāzī, *Rawḥ*
Abū l-Futūḥ Ḥusayn b. ʿAlī Rāzī, *Rawḥ al-jinān wa-rūḥ al-janān,* 12 vols., Tehran 1282-7/1962-5; 5 vols., Qumm n.d.

Abū Ḥayyān, *Baḥr*
Abū Ḥayyān al-Gharnāṭī, *Tafsīr al-baḥr al-muḥīṭ,* 8 vols., Cairo 1328-9/1911; repr. Beirut 1983; ed. ʿĀdil Aḥmad ʿAbd al-Mawjūd and ʿAlī Muḥammad Muʿawwaḍ, 8 vols., Beirut 1993

Abū l-Layth al-Samarqandī, *Tafsīr*
Abū l-Layth Naṣr b. Muḥammad b. Aḥmad al-Samarqandī, *Baḥr al-ʿulūm,* ed. ʿAbd al-Raḥīm Aḥmad al-Zaqqa, 3 vols., Baghdad 1985-6; ed. ʿAlī Muḥammad Muʿawwaḍ et al., 3 vols., Beirut 1413/1993

Abū Shāma, *Murshid*
ʿAbd al-Raḥmān b. Ismāʿīl Abū Shāma, *Kitāb al-Murshid al-wajīz ilā ʿulūm tataʿallaq bi-l-kitāb al-ʿazīz,* ed. Ṭayyar Altikulaç, Istanbul 1968

Abū ʿUbayd, *Faḍāʾil*
Abū ʿUbayd al-Qāsim b. Sallām, *Faḍāʾil al-Qurʾān,* ed. Wahbī Sulaymān Khāwajī, Beirut 1411/1991

Abū ʿUbayd, *Gharīb*
Abū ʿUbayd al-Qāsim b. Sallām, *Gharīb al-ḥadīth,* ed. Muḥammad ʿAbd al-Muʿīd Khān, 4 vols., Hyderabad 1384-7/1964-7; 2 vols., Beirut 1406/1986; ed. Ḥusayn Muḥammad M. Sharaf et al., 4 vols., Cairo 1404-15/1984-94; ed. Masʿūd Ḥijāzī et al., Cairo 1419/1999

Abū ʿUbayd, *Nāsikh*
Abū ʿUbayd al-Qāsim b. Sallām, *Kitāb al-Nāsikh wa-l-mansūkh,* ed. J. Burton, Cambridge 1987

Abū ʿUbayda, *Majāz*
Abū ʿUbayda Maʿmar b. al-Muthannā al-Taymī, *Majāz al-Qurʾān,* ed. F. Sezgin, 2 vols., Cairo 1954-62

Akhfash, *Maʿānī*
Abū l-Ḥasan Saʿīd b. Masʿada al-Akhfash al-Awsaṭ, *Maʿānī l-Qurʾān,* ed. Fāʾiz Fāris al-Ḥamad, 2nd ed., 2 vols., Kuwait 1981; ed. ʿAbd al-Amīr Muḥammad Amīn al-Ward, Beirut 1405/1985; ed. Hudā Maḥmūd Qurrāʿa, Cairo 1990

Allard, *Analyse*
M. Allard, *Analyse conceptuelle du Coran sur cartes perforées,* Paris 1963

Ālūsī, *Rūḥ*
Maḥmūd b. ʿAbdallāh al-Ālūsī, *Rūḥ al-maʿānī fī tafsīr al-Qurʾān al-ʿaẓīm wa-l-sabʿ al-mathānī,* 30 vols. in 15, Cairo 1345/1926; repr. Beirut n.d.

ʿĀmilī, *Aʿyān*
Muḥsin al-Amīn al-ʿĀmilī, *Aʿyān al-shīʿa,* 56 parts, Damascus 1935-63; 11 vols., Beirut 1986

Anbārī, *Bayān*
Abū l-Barakāt ʿAbd al-Raḥmān b. Muḥammad b. al-Anbārī, *al-Bayān fī gharīb iʿrāb al-Qurʾān,* ed. Ṭāhā ʿAbd al-Ḥamīd and Muṣṭafā al-Saqqā, 2 vols., Cairo 1969-70

Anbārī, *Nuzha*
Abū l-Barakāt ʿAbd al-Raḥmān b. Muḥammad al-Anbārī, *Nuzhat al-alibbāʾ fī ṭabaqāt al-udabāʾ,* Cairo 1294; Stockholm 1963; ed. Ibrāhīm al-Sāmarrāʾī, Baghdad 1970

Arberry
A.J. Arberry, *The Koran interpreted,* London 1955

Arkoun, *Lectures*
M. Arkoun, *Lectures du Coran,* Paris 1982

ʿAyyāshī, *Tafsīr*
Muḥammad b. Masʿūd al-ʿAyyāshī, *Tafsīr,* 2 vols., Tehran 1380/1961

Baghawī, *Maʿālim*
al-Ḥusayn b. Masʿūd al-Shāfiʿī al-Baghawī, *Tafsīr al-Baghawī al-musammā bi-Maʿālim al-tanzīl,* ed. Khālid ʿAbd al-Raḥmān al-ʿAkk and Marwān Sawār, 4 vols., Beirut 1983

Baghdādī, *Farq*
Abū Manṣūr ʿAbd al-Qāhir b. Tāhir al-Baghdādī, *al-Farq bayna l-firāq,* ed. Muḥammad Badr, Cairo 1328/1910; ed. Muḥammad Muḥyī l-Dīn ʿAbd al-Ḥamīd, Cairo n.d.

Baghdādī, *Taʾrīkh Baghdād*
Abū Bakr Aḥmad b. ʿAlī al-Khaṭīb al-Baghdādī, *Taʾrīkh Baghdād,* 14 vols., Cairo 1349/1931

Baḥrānī, *Burhān*
Hāshim b. Sulaymān al-Baḥrānī, *Kitāb al-Burhān fī tafsīr al-Qurʾān,* ed. Maḥmūd b. Jaʿfar al-Mūsawī al-Zarandī et al., 4 vols., Tehran 1375/1995; repr. Beirut 1403/1983

Baljon, *Modern*
I.M.S. Baljon, *Modern Muslim Koran interpretation (1880-1960),* Leiden 1961, 1968

Bāqillānī, *Iʿjāz*
al-Qāḍī Abū Bakr Muḥammad b. al-Ṭayyib al-Bāqillānī, *Iʿjāz al-Qurʾān,* ed. al-Sayyid Aḥmad Ṣaqr, Cairo 1954

Bāqillānī, *Intiṣār*
al-Qāḍī Abū Bakr Muḥammad b. al-Ṭayyib al-Bāqillānī, *Nukat al-intiṣār li-naql al-Qurʾān*, ed. Muḥammad Zaghlūl Salām, Alexandria 1971

Bayḍāwī, *Anwār*
ʿAbdallāh b. ʿUmar al-Bayḍāwī, *Anwār al-tanzīl wa-asrār al-taʾwīl*, ed. H.O. Fleischer, 2 vols., Leipzig 1846; Beirut 1988

Beeston, *CHAL*
A.F.L. Beeston et al., eds., *The Cambridge history of Arabic literature*, 4 vols. to date, Cambridge 1983-

Bell, *Commentary*
R. Bell, *A commentary on the Qurʾān*, ed. C.E. Bosworth and M.E.J. Richardson, 2 vols., Manchester 1991

Bell, *Qurʾān*
R. Bell, *The Qurʾān. Translated, with a critical re-arrangement of the sūras*, 2 vols., Edinburgh 1939; repr. 1960

Beltz, *Mythen*
W. Beltz, *Die Mythen des Koran. Der Schlüssel zum Islam*, Düsseldorf 1980

Bergsträsser, *Verneinungs*
G. Bergsträsser, *Verneinungs- und Fragepartikeln und Verwandtes im Ḳurʾān*, Leipzig 1914

Biqāʿī, *Naẓm*
Burhān al-Dīn Ibrāhīm b. ʿUmar al-Biqāʿī, *Naẓm al-durar fī tanāsub al-āyāt wa-l-suwar*, 22 vols., Hyderabad 1969-84; repr. Cairo 1992

Birkeland, *Lord*
H. Birkeland, *The Lord guideth. Studies on primitive Islam*, Oslo 1956

Birkeland, *Opposition*
H. Birkeland, *Old Muslim opposition against interpretation of the Koran*, Oslo 1955

Blachère
R. Blachère, *Le Coran. Traduit de l'arabe*, Paris 1966

Blachère, *Introduction*
R. Blachère, *Introduction au Coran*, Paris 1947

Bobzin, *Koran*
H. Bobzin, *Der Koran. Eine Einführung*, Munich 1999

Bobzin, *Reformation*
H. Bobzin, *Der Koran im Zeitalter der Reformation. Studien zur Frühgeschichte der Arabistik und Islamkunde in Europa*, Beirut/Stuttgart 1995

Bouman, *Conflit*
J. Bouman, *Le conflit autour du Coran et la solution d'al-Bāqillānī*, Amsterdam 1959

Bouman, *Gott und Mensch*
J. Bouman, *Gott und Mensch im Koran. Eine Strukturform religiöser Anthropologie anhand des Beispiels Allāh und Muḥammad*, Darmstadt 1977

Böwering, *Mystical*
G. Böwering, *The mystical vision of existence in classical Islam. The qurʾānic hermeneutics of the Ṣūfī Sahl at-Tustarī (d. 283/896)*, Berlin 1980

Brockelmann, *GAL*
C. Brockelmann, *Geschichte der arabischen Litteratur*, 2nd ed., 2 vols. and 3 vols. suppl., Leiden 1943-9; with new introduction, Leiden 1996

Buhl, *Das Leben*
F. Buhl, *Das Leben Muhammeds*, trans. H.H. Schaeder, Leipzig 1930; 1931 (3rd ed.)

Bukhārī, *Ṣaḥīḥ*
Abū ʿAbdallāh Muḥammad b. Ismāʿīl al-Bukhārī, *Kitāb al-Jāmiʿ al-ṣaḥīḥ*, ed. L. Krehl and T.W. Juynboll, 4 vols., Leiden 1862-1908; 9 vols., Cairo 1958

Burton, *Collection*
J. Burton, *The collection of the Qurʾān*, Cambridge 1977

Chabbi, *Seigneur*
J. Chabbi, *Le seigneur des tribus. L'islam de Mahomet*, Paris 1997

Creswell, *EMA*
K.A.C. Creswell, *Early Muslim architecture*, 2 vols., Oxford 1932-40; 2nd ed., London 1969

Dāmaghānī, *Wujūh*
al-Ḥusayn b. Muḥammad al-Dāmaghānī, *al-Wujūh wa-l-naẓāʾir li-alfāẓ Kitāb Allāh al-ʿazīz*, ed. Muḥammad Ḥasan Abū l-ʿAẓm al-Zafītī, 3 vols., Cairo 1412-16/

1992-5; ed. ʿAbd al-ʿAzīz Sayyid al-Ahl (as *Qāmūs al-Qurʾān*), Beirut 1970

Damīrī, *Ḥayāt*
Muḥammad b. Mūsā al-Damīrī, *Ḥayāt al-ḥayawān al-kubrā,* 2 vols., Cairo 1956

Dānī, *Muqniʿ*
Abū ʿAmr ʿUthmān b. Saʿīd al-Dānī, *al-Muqniʿ fī rasm maṣāḥif al-amṣār maʿa Kitāb al-Naqṭ = Orthographie und Punktierung des Koran,* ed. O. Pretzl, Leipzig/Istanbul 1932; ed. Muḥammad al-Ṣadīq Qamḥawī, Cairo n.d.

Dānī, *Naqṭ*
Abū ʿAmr ʿUthmān b. Saʿīd al-Dānī, *al-Muḥkam fī naqṭ al-maṣāḥif,* ed. ʿIzzat Ḥasan, Damascus 1379/1960

Dānī, *Taysīr*
Abū ʿAmr ʿUthmān b. Saʿīd al-Dānī, *Kitāb al-Taysīr fī l-qirāʾāt al-sabʿ = Das Lehrbuch der sieben Koranlesungen,* ed. O. Pretzl, Leipzig/Istanbul 1930

Dāraquṭnī, *Muʾtalif*
Abū l-Ḥasan ʿAlī b. ʿUmar al-Dāraquṭnī, *al-Muʾtalif wa-l-mukhtalif,* ed. Muwaffaq b. ʿAbdallāh b. ʿAbd al-Qādir, 5 vols., Beirut 1986

Dārimī, *Sunan*
ʿAbdallāh b. ʿAbd al-Rāḥmān al-Dārimī, *Sunan,* Cairo 1966

Darwaza, *Tafsīr*
Muḥammad ʿIzzat Darwaza, *al-Tafsir al-ḥadīth,* 12 vols., Cairo 1381-3/1962-4

Dāwūdī, *Ṭabaqāt*
Muḥammad b. ʿAlī al-Dāwūdī, *Ṭabaqāt al-mufassirīn,* ed. ʿAlī Muḥammad ʿUmar, 2 vols., Beirut 1983

Dhahabī, *Mufassirūn*
Muḥammad Ḥusayn al-Dhahabī, *al-Tafsīr wa-l-mufassirūn,* 2 vols., Cairo 1976

Dhahabī, *Qurrāʾ*
Shams al-Dīn Muḥammad b. Aḥmad al-Dhahabī, *Maʿrifat al-qurrāʾ al-kibār ʿalā l-ṭabaqāt wa-l-aʿṣār,* ed. Sayyid Jad al-Ḥaqq, n.p. 1969

Dhahabī, *Siyar*
Shams al-Dīn Muḥammad b. Aḥmad al-Dhahabī, *Siyar aʿlām al-nubalāʾ,* ed. Shuʿayb al-Arnaʾūṭ et al., 25 vols., Beirut 1981-8

Dhahabī, *Tadhkira*
Shams al-Dīn Muḥammad b. Aḥmad al-Dhahabī, *Tadhkirat al-ḥuffāẓ,* 4 vols., Hyderabad 1375/1955

Dhahabī, *Taʾrīkh*
Shams al-Dīn Muḥammad b. Aḥmad al-Dhahabī, *Taʾrīkh al-Islām,* ed. ʿUmar ʿAbd al-Salām Tadmurī, 52 vols. to date, Beirut 1989-; 4 vols. (years 601-640), ed. Bashshār ʿAwwād Maʿrūf et al., Beirut 1408/1988

van Ess, *TG*
J. van Ess, *Theologie und Gesellschaft im 2. und 3. Jahrhundert Hidschra. Eine Geschichte des religiösen Denkens im frühen Islam,* 6 vols., Berlin/New York 1991-7

Fārisī, *Ḥujja*
Abū ʿAlī al-Ḥasan b. ʿAlī al-Fārisī, *al-Ḥujja lil-qurrāʾ al-sabʿa,* ed. Badr al-Dīn al-Qahwajī et al., 6 vols., Damascus 1984-92

Farrāʾ, *Maʿānī*
Abū Zakariyyāʾ Yaḥyā b. Ziyād al-Farrāʾ, *Maʿānī l-Qurʾān,* ed. Aḥmad Yūsuf Najātī and Muḥammad ʿAlī l-Najjār, 3 vols., Cairo 1955-72

Fīrūzābādī, *Baṣāʾir*
Majd al-Dīn Muḥammad b. Yaʿqūb al-Fīrūzābādī *Baṣāʾir dhawī l-tamyīz fī laṭāʾif al-kitāb al-ʿazīz,* ed. Muḥammad ʿAlī l-Najjār, 6 vols., Cairo 1964-73; repr. Beirut n.d.

GAP
W. Fischer and H. Gätje, eds., *Grundriss der arabischen Philologie,* 3 vols., Wiesbaden 1982-92

Gardet and Anawati, *Introduction*
L. Gardet and M.M. Anawati, *Introduction à la théologie musulmane,* Paris 1948, 3rd ed., 1981

Gilliot, *Elt*
C. Gilliot, *Exégèse, langue, et théologie en Islam. L'exégèse coranique de Ṭabarī (m. 310/923),* Paris 1990

Gimaret, *Jubbāʾī*
D. Gimaret, *Une lecture muʿtazilite du Coran. Le tafsīr d'Abū ʿAlī al-Djubbāʾī (m. 303/915) partiellement reconstitué à partir de ses citateurs,* Louvain/Paris 1994

Goldziher, *GS*
I. Goldziher, *Gesammelte Schriften,* ed. J. Desomogyi, 6 vols., Hildesheim 1967-73

Goldziher, *MS*
I. Goldziher, *Muhammedanische Studien,* 2 vols., Halle 1888-90; trans., C.R. Barber and S.M. Stern, *Muslim studies,* London 1967-72

Goldziher, *Richtungen*
I. Goldziher, *Die Richtungen der islamischen Koranauslegung,* Leiden 1920; repr. 1970

Graham, *Beyond*
W.A. Graham, *Beyond the written word. Oral aspects of scripture in the history of religion,* Cambridge and New York 1989

Grimme, *Mohammed, I-II*
H. Grimme, *Mohammed. I, Das Leben nach den Quellen. II, Einleitung in den Koran. System der koranischen Theologie,* Münster 1892-5

Grünbaum, *Beiträge*
M. Grünbaum, *Neue Beiträge zur semitischen Sagenkunde,* Leiden 1893

Ḥājjī Khalīfa, *Kashf*
Muṣṭafā ʿAbdallāh Ḥājjī Khalīfa, *Kashf al-ẓunūn,* ed. and trans. G. Flügel, 7 vols., Leipzig 1835-58; ed. Şerefettin Yaltkaya and Kilisli Rifat Bilge, 2 vols., Istanbul 1941-3; repr. Beirut 1992-3

Hawting, *Idolatry*
G.R. Hawting, *The idea of idolatry and the emergence of Islam. From polemic to history,* Cambridge 1999

Hawting and Shareef, *Approaches*
G.R. Hawting and A.A. Shareef (eds.), *Approaches to the Qurʾān,* London 1993

Ḥawwā, *Tafsīr*
Saʿīd Ḥawwā, *al-Asās fī l-tafsīr,* 11 vols., Cairo 1405/1985

Horovitz, *KU*
J. Horovitz, *Koranische Untersuchungen,* Berlin/Leipzig 1926

Hūd b. Muḥakkam, *Tafsīr*
Hūd b. Muḥakkam/Muḥkim al-Huwwārī, *Tafsīr,* ed. Balḥājj Saʿīd Sharīfī, 4 vols., Beirut 1990

Ibn ʿAbbās, *Gharīb*
ʿAbdallāh b. ʿAbbās (attributed to), *Gharīb al-Qurʾān,* ed. Muḥammad ʿAbd al-Raḥīm, Beirut 1993

Ibn Abī l-Iṣbaʿ, *Badīʿ*
Ibn Abī l-Iṣbaʿ al-Miṣrī, *Badīʿ al-Qurʾān,* ed. Ḥifnī Muḥammad Sharaf, Cairo n.d.

Ibn Abī Uṣaybiʿa, *ʿUyūn*
Aḥmad b. al-Qāsim b. Abī Uṣaybiʿa, *ʿUyūn al-anbāʾ fī ṭabaqāt al-aṭibbāʾ,* ed. A. Müller, 2 vols., Cairo 1299/1882; 3 vols., Beirut 1957

Ibn al-Anbārī, *Īḍāḥ*
Abū Bakr Muḥammad b. al-Qāsim b. al-Anbārī, *Īḍāḥ al-waqf wa-l-ibtidāʾ fī Kitāb Allāh,* ed. Muḥyī l-Dīn ʿAbd al-Raḥmān Ramaḍān, 2 vols., Damascus 1391/1971

Ibn al-ʿArabī, *Aḥkām*
Muḥammad b. ʿAbdallāh Abū Bakr b. al-ʿArabī, *Aḥkām al-Qurʾān,* 2nd ed., Cairo 1392/1972

Ibn al-ʿArabī, *Tafsīr*
Muḥammad b. ʿAbdallāh Abū Bakr b. al-ʿArabī, *Tafsīr al-Qurʾān,* 2 vols., Beirut 1968 (see Qāshānī)

Ibn ʿAsākir, *Taʾrīkh*
ʿAlī b. al-Ḥasan b. ʿAsākir, *Taʾrīkh madīnat Dimashq,* abridged ed. ʿAbd al-Qādir Bardān and Aḥmad ʿUbayd, 7 vols., Damascus 1329-51/1911-31; facsimile ed., 19 vols., Amman n.d.; 29 vols., Damascus 1404-8/1984-8; ed. Muḥyī l-Dīn ʿUmar b. Gharāma al-ʿAmrāwī, 80 vols., Beirut 1995-2000

Ibn ʿĀshūr, *Tafsīr*
Muḥammad al-Ṭāhir b. ʿĀshūr, *al-Tafsīr al-taḥrīrī wa-l-tanwīrī,* 30 vols., Tunis 1984

Ibn ʿAskar, *Takmīl*
Muḥammad b. ʿAlī al-Ghassānī b. ʿAskar, *al-Takmīl wa-l-itmām li-Kitāb al-Taʿrīf wa-l-iʿlām,* ed. Ḥasan Ismāʿīl Marwa, Beirut/Damascus 1418/1997 (see Suhaylī)

Ibn al-Athīr, *Kāmil*
ʿIzz al-Dīn ʿAlī b. al-Athīr, *al-Kāmil fī l-taʾrīkh*, ed. C.J. Tornberg, 14 vols., Leiden 1851-76; corrected repr. 13 vols., Beirut 1385-7/1965-7

Ibn al-Athīr, *Nihāya*
Majd al-Dīn al-Mubārak b. al-Athīr, *al-Nihāya fī gharīb al-ḥadīth wa-l-athar*, ed. Ṭāhir Aḥmad al-Zāwī and Maḥmūd al-Ṭanāḥī, 5 vols., Cairo 1963-6

Ibn ʿAṭiyya, *Muḥarrar*
Abū Muḥammad ʿAbd al-Ḥaqq b. Ghālib b. ʿAṭiyya al-Gharnāṭī, *al-Muḥarrar al-wajīz*, ed. ʿAbd al-Salām ʿAbd al-Shāfī Muḥammad, 5 vols., Beirut 1413/1993

Ibn Ḍurays, *Faḍāʾil*
Muḥammad b. Ayyūb b. Ḍurays, *Faḍāʾil al-Qurʾān*, ed. Ghazwa Budayr, Damascus 1988

Ibn Ḥajar, *Tahdhīb*
Ibn Ḥajar al-ʿAsqalānī, *Tahdhīb al-tahdhīb*, 12 vols., Hyderabad 1325-7/1907-9; Beirut 1968

Ibn Ḥanbal, *Musnad*
Aḥmad b. Ḥanbal, *Musnad*, ed. Muḥammad al-Zuhrī al-Ghamrāwī, 6 vols., Cairo 1313/1895; repr. Beirut 1978; ed. Aḥmad Muḥammad Shākir et al., 20 vols., Cairo 1416/1995

Ibn Ḥazm, *Milal*
ʿAlī b. Aḥmad b. Saʿīd b. Ḥazm, *al-Fiṣal fī l-milal wa-l-ahwāʾ wa-l-niḥal*, ed. Muḥammad Ibrāhīm Naṣr and ʿAbd al-Raḥmān ʿUmayra, 5 vols., Beirut 1995

Ibn al-ʿImād, *Shadharāt*
ʿAbd al-Ḥayy b. Aḥmad b. al-ʿImād, *Shadharāt al-dhahab fī akhbār man dhahab*, 8 vols., Cairo 1350-1/1931-2; repr. Beirut n.d.

Ibn Isḥāq, *Sīra*
Muḥammad b. Isḥāq, *Sīrat rasūl Allāh* (recension of ʿAbd al-Malik b. Hishām), ed. F. Wüstenfeld, Göttingen 1858-60; repr. Beirut n.d.; ed. Muṣṭafā al-Ṣaqqā et al., 4 vols. in 2, 2nd ed., Cairo 1955

Ibn Isḥāq-Guillaume
Muḥammad b. Isḥāq, *The life of Muhammad. A translation of Ibn Isḥāq's* Sīrat rasūl Allāh, trans. A. Guillaume, Oxford 1955; repr. Karachi 1967

Ibn al-Jawzī, *Funūn*
Abū l-Faraj ʿAbd al-Raḥmān b. ʿAlī b. al-Jawzī, *Funūn al-afnān fī ʿajāʾib ʿulūm al-Qurʾān*, ed. Rashīd ʿAbd al-Raḥmān al-ʿUbaydī, Baghdad 1408/1988

Ibn al-Jawzī, *Muntaẓam*
Abū l-Faraj ʿAbd al-Raḥmān b. ʿAlī b. al-Jawzī, *al-Muntaẓam fī taʾrīkh al-mulūk wa-l-umam*, ed. Muḥammad and Muṣṭafā ʿAbd al-Qādir ʿAṭā, 19 vols., Beirut 1412/1922; ed. Suhayl Zakkār, 11 vols. in 13, Beirut 1995-6

Ibn al-Jawzī, *Nuzha*
Abū l-Faraj ʿAbd al-Raḥmān b. ʿAlī b. al-Jawzī, *Nuzhat al-aʿyun al-nawāẓir fī ʿilm al-wujūh wa-l-naẓāʾir*, ed. Muḥammad ʿAbd al-Karīm Kāẓim al-Rāḍī, Beirut 1404/1984

Ibn al-Jawzī, *Zād*
Abū l-Faraj ʿAbd al-Raḥmān b. ʿAlī b. al-Jawzī, *Zād al-masīr fī ʿilm al-tafsīr*, intr. Muḥammad Zuhayr al-Shāwīsh, 9 vols., Damascus 1384-5/1964-5; annot. Aḥmad Shams al-Dīn, 8 vols., Beirut 1414/1994

Ibn al-Jazarī, *Ghāya*
Shams al-Dīn Abū l-Khayr Muḥammad b. Muḥammad b. al-Jazarī, *Ghāyat al-nihāya fī ṭabaqāt al-qurrāʾ = Das biographische Lexikon der Koranleser*, 3 vols. in 2, ed. G. Bergsträsser and O. Pretzl, Leipzig/Cairo 1933-5

Ibn al-Jazarī, *Munjid*
Shams al-Dīn Abū l-Khayr Muḥammad b. Muḥammad b. al-Jazarī, *Munjid al-muqriʾīn wa-murshid al-ṭālibīn*, ed. Muḥammad Ḥabīb Allāh al-Shanqīṭī et al., Cairo 1350/1931; Beirut 1980

Ibn al-Jazarī, *Nashr*
Shams al-Dīn Abū l-Khayr Muḥammad b. Muḥammad b. al-Jazarī, *Kitāb al-Nashr fī l-qirāʾāt al-ʿashr*, ed. ʿAlī Muḥammad al-Ḍabbāʿ, 2 vols., Cairo 1940; repr. Beirut n.d.

Ibn Jinnī, *Muḥtasab*
Abū l-Fatḥ ʿUthmān b. Jinnī, *al-Muḥtasab fī*

tabyīn wujūh shawādhdh al-qirāʾāt wa-l-īḍāḥ ʿanhā, 2 vols., ed. ʿAlī al-Najdī Nāṣif et al., Cairo 1386-9/1966-9; repr. 1994

Ibn Kathīr, *Bidāya*
ʿImād al-Dīn Ismāʿīl b. ʿUmar b. Kathīr, *al-Bidāya wa-l-nihāya*, 14 vols., Beirut/Riyadh 1966; repr. Beirut 1988

Ibn Kathīr, *Faḍāʾil*
ʿImād al-Dīn Ismāʿīl b. ʿUmar b. Kathīr, *Faḍāʾil al-Qurʾān*, Beirut 1979

Ibn Kathīr, *Tafsīr*
ʿImād al-Dīn Ismāʿīl b. ʿUmar b. Kathīr, *Tafsīr al-Qurʾān al-ʿaẓīm*, ed. ʿAbd al-ʿAzīz Ghunaym et al., 8 vols., Cairo 1390/1971; 4 vols., Cairo n.d.; repr. Beirut 1980

Ibn Khālawayh, *Ḥujja*
Abū ʿAbdallāh al-Ḥusayn b. Aḥmad b. Khālawayh, *al-Ḥujja fī l-qirāʾāt al-sabʿ*, ed. ʿAbd al-ʿĀl Salīm Mukarram, Beirut 1971

Ibn Khālawayh, *Iʿrāb*
Abū ʿAbdallāh al-Ḥusayn b. Aḥmad b. Khālawayh, *Iʿrāb thalāthīn sūra min al-Qurʾān al-karīm*, Baghdad 1967

Ibn Khālawayh, *Iʿrāb al-qirāʾāt*
Abū ʿAbdallāh al-Ḥusayn b. Aḥmad b. Khālawayh, *Iʿrāb al-qirāʾāt al-sabʿ wa-ʿilaluhā*, ed. ʿAbd al-Raḥmān b. Sulaymān al-ʿUthaymīn, 2 vols., Cairo 1413/1992

Ibn Khaldūn, *ʿIbar*
ʿAbd al-Raḥmān b. Khaldūn, *Kitāb al-ʿIbar*, ed. Naṣr al-Ḥūrīnī, 7 vols., Būlāq 1284/1867

Ibn Khaldūn-Rosenthal
ʿAbd al-Raḥmān b. Khaldūn, *The Muqaddimah*, trans. F. Rosenthal, 3 vols., New York 1958; 2nd rev. ed., Princeton 1967

Ibn Khallikān, *Wafayāt*
Shams al-Dīn b. Khallikān, *Wafayāt al-aʿyān wa-anbāʾ abnāʾ al-zamān*, ed. F. Wüstenfeld, 4 vols., Göttingen 1835-50; ed. Iḥsān ʿAbbās, 8 vols., Beirut 1968-72; trans. M. De Slane, *Ibn Khallikān's biographical dictionary*, 4 vols., Paris 1842-71; repr. New York 1961

Ibn Māja
Muḥammad b. Yazīd b. Māja, *Sunan*, ed. Muḥammad Fuʾād ʿAbd al-Bāqī, 2 vols., Cairo 1952-3

Ibn Mujāhid, *Sabʿa*
Abū Bakr Aḥmad b. Mūsā b. Mujāhid, *Kitāb al-Sabʿa fī l-qirāʾāt*, ed. Shawqī Ḍayf, Cairo 1979

Ibn al-Nadīm, *Fihrist*
Muḥammad b. Isḥāq b. al-Nadīm, *Kitāb al-Fihrist*, ed. G. Flügel, 2 vols., Leipzig 1871-2; ed. Riḍā Tajaddud, Tehran 1971; 2nd ed., Beirut 1988

Ibn al-Nadīm-Dodge
Muḥammad b. Isḥāq b. al-Nadīm, *The Fihrist of al-Nadīm*, trans. B. Dodge, 2 vols., New York/London 1970

Ibn al-Naqīb, *Muqaddima*
Abū ʿAbdallāh Muḥammad b. Sulaymān al-Naqīb, *Muqaddimat al-tafsīr fī ʿulūm al-bayān wa-l-maʿānī wa-l-badīʿ wa-iʿjāz al-Qurʾān*, ed. Zakariyyāʾ Saʿīd ʿAlī, Cairo 1415/1995

Ibn Qayyim al-Jawziyya, *Tibyān*
Muḥammad b. Abī Bakr b. Qayyim al-Jawziyya, *al-Tibyān fī aqsām al-Qurʾān*, Beirut 1982

Ibn al-Qifṭī, *Ḥukamāʾ*
Abū l-Ḥasan ʿAlī b. Yūsuf b. al-Qifṭī, *Taʾrīkh al-ḥukamāʾ*, ed. J. Lippert, Leipzig 1903; repr. Baghdad 1967

Ibn Qutayba, *Gharīb*
Abū Muḥammad ʿAbdallāh b. Muslim al-Dīnawarī b. Qutayba, *Tafsīr gharīb al-Qurʾān*, ed. al-Sayyid Aḥmad Ṣaqr, Cairo 1958; Beirut 1978

Ibn Qutayba, *al-Shiʿr*
Abū Muḥammad ʿAbdallāh b. Muslim al-Dīnawarī b. Qutayba, *Kitāb al-Shiʿr wa-l-shuʿarāʾ*, ed. M.J. de Goeje, Leiden 1900

Ibn Qutayba, *Taʾwīl*
Abū Muḥammad ʿAbdallāh b. Muslim al-Dīnawarī b. Qutayba, *Taʾwīl mushkil al-Qurʾān*, ed. al-Sayyid Aḥmad Ṣaqr, Cairo 1954; Cairo 1973; Medina 1981

Ibn Qutayba-Lecomte
G. Lecomte, *Le traité des divergences du hadīt d'Ibn Qutayba*, Damascus 1962

Ibn Saʿd, *Ṭabaqāt*
Muḥammad b. Saʿd, *al-Ṭabaqāt al-kubrā*, ed. H. Sachau et al., 9 vols., Leiden 1905-40; ed. Iḥsān ʿAbbās, 9 vols., Beirut 1957-8

Ibn Taymiyya, *Daqāʾiq*
Taqī l-Dīn Aḥmad b. ʿAbd al-Ḥalīm b. Taymiyya, *Daqāʾiq al-tafsīr. al-Jāmiʿ li-tafsīr al-Imām Ibn Taymiyya*, ed. Muḥammad al-Sayyid al-Julaynid, 6 vols. in 3, Jedda/Beirut/Damascus 1986

Ibn Taymiyya, *Muqaddima*
Taqī l-Dīn Aḥmad b. ʿAbd al-Ḥalīm b. Taymiyya, *Muqaddima fī uṣūl al-tafsīr*, Beirut 1392/1972; Riyadh 1382/1962

Ibn Wahb, *al-Jāmiʿ*
ʿAbdallāh b. Wahb, *al-Ǧāmīʿ. Die Koranswissenschaften*, ed. M. Muranyi, Wiesbaden 1992

Ibyārī, *Mawsūʿa*
Ibrāhīm al-Ibyārī and ʿAbd al-Ṣabūr Marzūq, *al-Mawsūʿa al-qurʾāniyya*, 6 vols., Cairo 1388/1969; 11 vols., Cairo 1405/1984

Ihsanoglu, *Translations*
E. İhsanoğlu (ed.), *World bibliography of translations of the meanings of the holy Qurʾān. Printed translations* 1515-1980, Istanbul 1406/1986

Iṣfahānī, *Aghānī*
Abū l-Faraj al-Iṣfahānī, *Kitāb al-Aghānī*, 21 vols. in 7, Cairo 1323/1905; 25 vols., Beirut 1955-62

Iṣfahānī, *Muqaddima*
Abū l-Ḥasan al-ʿĀmilī al-Iṣfahānī, *Muqaddimat tafsīr mirʾāt al-anwār wa-mishkāt al-asrār*, ed. Maḥmūd b. Jaʿfar al-Mūsawī al-Zarandī, Tehran 1374/1954

Iṣlāḥī, *Tadabbur*
Amīn Aḥsan Iṣlāḥī, *Tadabbur-i Qurʾān*, 8 vols., Lahore 1967-80

ʿIyāḍ b. Mūsā, *Shifāʾ*
al-Qāḍī Abū l-Faḍl ʿIyāḍ b. Mūsā, *al-Shifāʾ bi-taʿrīf ḥuqūq al-muṣṭafā*, 2 vols. in 1, Damascus 1978; ed. Muḥammad Amīn Qarah ʿAlī et al., Amman 1407/1986

Izutsu, *Concepts*
Toshihiko Izutsu, *Ethico-religious concepts in the Qurʾān*, Montreal 1966

Izutsu, *God*
Toshihiko Izutsu, *God and man in the Koran*, New York 1964; repr. 1980

Jāḥiẓ, *Bayān*
ʿAmr b. Baḥr al-Jāḥiẓ, *al-Bayān wa-l-tabyīn*, ed. ʿAbd al-Salām Muḥammad Hārūn, 4 vols., Cairo 1948-50; repr. Beirut n.d.

Jalālayn
Jalāl al-Dīn Muḥammad b. Aḥmad al-Maḥallī and Jalāl al-Dīn al-Suyūṭī, *Tafsīr al-Jalālayn*, Damascus 1385/1965

Jansen, *Egypt*
J.J.G. Jansen, *The interpretation of the Koran in modern Egypt*, Leiden 1974, 1980

Jaṣṣāṣ, *Aḥkām*
Abū Bakr Aḥmad b. ʿAbdallāh al-Jaṣṣāṣ al-Rāzī, *Aḥkām al-Qurʾān*, 3 vols., Istanbul 1335-8/1916-19

Jawālīqī, *Muʿarrab*
Abū Manṣūr Mawhūb b. Aḥmad al-Jawālīqī, *al-Muʿarrab min al-kalām al-ʿajamī ʿalā ḥurūf al-muʿjam*, ed. Aḥmad Muḥammad Shākir, Cairo 1361/1942

Jeffery, *For. vocab.*
A. Jeffery, *Foreign vocabulary of the Qurʾān*, Baroda 1938

Jeffery, *Materials*
A. Jeffery, *Materials for the history of the text of the Qurʾān. The Kitāb al-Maṣāḥif of Ibn Abī Dāwūd together with a collection of the variant readings from the codices of Ibn Masʿūd, etc.*, Leiden 1937

Jeffery, *Muqaddimas*
A. Jeffery, *Two muqaddimas to the Qurʾānic sciences. The muqaddima to the* Kitab al-Mabani *and the muqaddima of Ibn ʿAtiyya to his* Tafsir, Cairo 1954

Jurjānī, *Asrār*
ʿAbd al-Qāhir al-Jurjāni, *Asrār al-balāgha*, ed. H. Ritter, Istanbul 1954

Jurjānī, *Dalāʾil*
ʿAbd al-Qāhir al-Jurjānī, *Dalāʾil iʿjāz al-*

Qurʾān, Cairo 1372; ed. Maḥmūd Muḥammad Shākir, Cairo 1404/1984
Justi, *Namenbuch*
F. Justi, *Iranisches Namenbuch*, Marburg 1895
Kaḥḥāla, *Muʿjam*
ʿUmar Riḍā Kaḥḥāla, *Muʿjam al-muʾallifīn*, 15 vols. in 8, Beirut n.d.; Damascus 1957-61
Kaḥḥāla, *Nisāʾ*
ʿUmar Riḍā Kaḥḥāla, *Aʿlām al-nisāʾ fī ʿālamay al-ʿArab wa-l-Islām*, 5 vols., Damascus 1379/1959
Kāshānī, *Minhaj*
Mullā Fatḥ Allāh Kāshānī, *Minhaj al-ṣādiqīn fī ilzām al-mukhālifīn*, 10 vols., Tehran 1347[solar]/1969
Kāshānī, *Ṣāfī*
Mullā Muḥsin Fayd Kāshānī, *al-Ṣāfī fī tafsīr kalām Allāh al-wāfī*, ed. Ḥusayn al-Aʿlamī, 5 vols., Beirut 1399/1979
Khāzin, *Lubāb*
ʿAlāʾ al-Dīn al-Khāzin, *Lubāb al-taʾwīl fī maʿānī l-tanzīl*, Cairo 1381/1961
Khwānsārī, *Rawdāt*
Muḥammad Bāqir al-Mūsawī al-Khwānsārī, *Rawdāt al-jannāt*, ed. Asad Allāh Ismāʿīlīyān, 8 vols., Tehran 1392/1972
Kisāʾī, *Mutashābih*
ʿAlī b. Ḥamza al-Kisāʾī, *Kitāb Mutashābih al-Qurʾān*, ed. Ṣabīḥ al-Tamīmī, Tripoli 1994
Kisāʾī, *Qiṣaṣ*
Muḥammad b. ʿAbdallāh al-Kisāʾī, *Vita prophetarum auctore Muḥammed ben ʿAbdallāh al-Kisāʾī*, ed. I. Eisenberg, 2 vols., Leiden 1922-3
Kulaynī, *Kāfī*
Abū Jaʿfar Muḥammad b. Yaʿqūb al-Kulayn, *Rawḍat al-kāfī*, ed. ʿAlī Akbar al-Ghifārī, Najaf 1395/1966; repr. Beirut n.d.
Kutubī, *Fawāt*
Ibn Shākir al-Kutubī, *Fawāt al-wafayāt*, 2 vols., Cairo 1299/1882; ed. Iḥsān ʿAbbās, 5 vols., Beirut 1973-4
Lane
E.W. Lane, *An Arabic-English lexicon*, 1 vol. in 8 parts., London 1863-93; New York 1955-6; repr. 2 vols., Cambridge 1984
Lecker, *Muslims*
M. Lecker, *Muslims, Jews and pagans. Studies on early Islamic Medina*, Leiden 1995
Le Strange, *Lands*
G. Le Strange, *The lands of the eastern caliphate*, 2nd ed., Cambridge 1930
Lisān al-ʿArab
Muḥammad b. al-Mukarram b. Manẓūr, *Lisān al-ʿArab*, 15 vols., Beirut 1955-6; ed. ʿAlī Shīrī, 18 vols., Beirut 1988
Lüling, *Ur-Qurʾān*
G. Lüling, *Über den Ur-Qurʾān. Ansätze zur Rekonstruktion der vorislamisch-christlichen Strophenlieder im Qurʾān*, Erlangen 1972; 2nd ed. 1993
Makkī, *Ibāna*
Makkī b. Abī Ṭālib al-Qaysī, *Kitāb al-Ibāna ʿan maʿānī l-qirāʾāt*, ed. Muḥyī l-Dīn Ramaḍān, Damascus 1979
Makkī, *Kashf*
Makkī b. Abī Ṭālib al-Qaysī, *al-Kashf ʿan wujūh al-qirāʾāt al-sabʿ wa-ʿilalihā wa-ḥujajihā*, ed. Muḥyī l-Dīn Ramaḍān, 2 vols., Damascus 1974
Makkī, *Mushkil*
Makkī b. Abī Ṭālib al-Qaysī, *Mushkil iʿrāb al-Qurʾān*, ed. Yāsīn M. al-Sawwās, Damascus 1974
Mālik, *Muwaṭṭaʾ*
Mālik b. Anas, *al-Muwaṭṭaʾ*, ed. Muḥammad Fuʾād ʿAbd al-Bāqī, Cairo 1952-3; Beirut 1985; ed. ʿAbd al-Majīd Turkī, Beirut 1994
Masʿūdī, *Murūj*
Abū ʿAlī b. al-Ḥusayn al-Masʿūdī, *Murūj al-dhahab*, ed. C. Barbier de Meynard and Pavet de Courteille, 9 vols., Paris 1861-77; ed. and trans. Ch. Pellat, *Les prairies d'or*, 7 vols. text and 4 vols. translation, Paris-Beirut 1962-89; ed. Qāsim al-Shamāʿī al-Rifāʿī, 4 vols., Beirut 1989

Māturīdī, *Taʾwīlāt*
Abū Manṣūr Muḥammad b. Muḥammad al-Māturīdī, *Taʾwīlāt ahl al-sunna,* ed. Ibrāhīm and al-Sayyid ʿAwadayn, Cairo 1391/1971; ed. Jāsim Muḥammad al-Jubūrī, Baghdad 1404/1983

Māwardī, *Nukat*
ʿAlī b. Muḥammad al-Māwardī, *al-Nukat wa-l-ʿuyūn fī l-tafsīr,* ed. al-Sayyid b. ʿAbd al-Maqṣūd b. ʿAbd al-Raḥīm, 6 vols., Beirut 1412/1992

McAuliffe, *Qurʾānic*
J.D. McAuliffe, *Qurʾānic Christians. An analysis of classical and modern exegesis,* Cambridge 1991

Mir, *Dictionary*
M. Mir, *Dictionary of Qurʾānic terms and concepts,* New York 1987

Mir, *Verbal*
M. Mir, *Verbal idioms of the Qurʾān,* Ann Arbor, MI 1989

Mufaḍḍaliyyāt
al-Mufaḍḍal b. Muḥammad al-Ḍabbī, *al-Mufaḍḍaliyyāt,* ed. Aḥmad Muḥammad Shākir and ʿAbd al-Salām Muḥammad Hārūn, Cairo 1942

Muir, *Mahomet*
W. Muir, *The life of Mahomet. With introductory chapters on the original sources of the biography of Mahomet, I-IV,* London 1858-61

Mujāhid, *Tafsīr*
Abū l-Ḥajjāj Mujāhid b. Jabr, *al-Tafsīr,* ed. ʿAbd al-Raḥmān b. Ṭāhir b. Muḥammad al-Suwartī, Qatar 1976; ed. Muḥammad ʿAbd al-Salām Abū l-Nīl, Cairo 1989

Mukarram, *Muʿjam al-qirāʾāt*
ʿAbd al-Āl Salīm Mukarram, *Muʿjam al-qirāʾāt al-qurʾāniyya,* 8 vols. to date, Kuwait 1982-

Muqātil, *Ashbāh*
Abū l-Ḥasan Muqātil b. Sulaymān al-Balkhī, *al-Ashbāh wa-l-naẓāʾir fī l-Qurʾān al-karīm,* ed. ʿAbdallāh Maḥmūd Shiḥāta, Cairo 1975

Muqātil, *Khams miʾa*
Abū l-Ḥasan Muqātil b. Sulaymān al-Balkhī, *Tafsīr al-khams miʾat āya min al-Qurʾān,* ed. I. Goldfeld, Shfaram 1980

Muqātil, *Tafsīr*
Abū l-Ḥasan Muqātil b. Sulaymān al-Balkhī, *al-Tafsīr,* ed. ʿAbdallāh Maḥmūd Shiḥāta, 5 vols., Cairo 1980-7

Muslim, *Ṣaḥīḥ*
Muslim b. al-Ḥajjāj, *Ṣaḥīḥ*, ed. Muḥammad Fuʾād ʿAbd al-Bāqī, 5 vols., Cairo 1955-6

Nāfiʿ, *Masāʾil*
Masāʾil al-Imām ʿan asʾilat Nāfiʿ b. al-Azraq wa-ajwibat ʿAbd Allāh b. ʿAbbas, ed. ʿAbd al-Raḥmān ʿUmayra, Cairo 1413/1994

Nagel, *Einschübe*
T. Nagel, *Medinensische Einschübe in mekkanischen Suren,* Göttingen 1995

Nagel, *Koran*
T. Nagel, *Der Koran. Einführung-Texte-Erläuterungen,* Munich 1983

Naḥḥās, *Iʿrāb*
Abū Jaʿfar Aḥmad b. Muḥammad al-Naḥḥās, *Iʿrāb al-Qurʾān,* ed. Zuhayr Ghāzī Zāhid, 2nd ed., 5 vols., Beirut 1985, 1988

Nasafī, *Tafsīr*
ʿAbdallāh b. Aḥmad b. Maḥmūd al-Nasafī, *Madārik al-tanzīl wa-ḥaqāʾiq al-taʾwīl,* ed. Zakariyyāʾ ʿUmayrāt, 2 vols. Beirut 1415/1995

Nasāʾī, *Faḍāʾil*
Aḥmad b. Shuʿayb al-Nasāʾī, *Faḍāʾil al-Qurʾān,* ed. Samīr al-Khūlī, Beirut 1985

Nasāʾī, *Sunan*
Aḥmad b. Shuʿayb al-Nasāʾī, *al-Sunan al-kubrā,* ed. ʿAbd al-Ghaffār Sulaymān al-Bundārī and al-Sayyid Kisrawī Ḥasan, 6 vols., Beirut 1411/1991

Nawawī, *Sharḥ*
Abū Zakariyyāʾ Yaḥyā b. Sharaf al-Nawawī, *Sharḥ Ṣaḥīḥ Muslim,* 18 vols. in 9, Cairo 1349/1929-30; ed. Khalīl Muḥammad Shīḥā, 19 vols. in 10, Beirut 1995

Neuwirth, *Studien*
A. Neuwirth, *Studien zur Komposition der mekkanischen Suren,* Berlin 1981

Nīsābūrī, *Tafsīr*
Niẓām al-Dīn al-Ḥasan b. Muḥammad b.

al-Ḥusayn al-Qummī al-Nīsābūrī al-Aʿraj, *Tafsīr gharāʾib al-Qurʾān wa-raghāʾib al-furqān,* on the margin of Ṭabarī, *Jāmiʿ al-bayān,* 30 vols., Cairo 1323-9/1905-11; repr. Beirut 1392/1972; ed. Ibrāhīm ʿAṭwa ʿAwaḍ, 13 vols., Cairo 1962-4

Nöldeke, *GQ*
T. Nöldeke, *Geschichte des Qorāns,* new edition by F. Schwally, G. Bergsträsser and O. Pretzl, 3 vols., Leipzig 1909-38

Nwyia, *Exégèse*
P. Nwyia, *Exégèse coranique et langage mystique. Nouvel essai sur le lexique technique des mystiques musulmans,* Beirut 1970

Paret, *Kommentar*
R. Paret, *Der Koran. Kommentar und Konkordanz,* Stuttgart 1971; 1977; Kohlhammer 1980

Paret, *Koran*
R. Paret, *Der Koran. Übersetzung,* Stuttgart 1962

Paret (ed.), *Koran*
R. Paret (ed.) *Der Koran,* Darmstadt 1975

Penrice, *Dictionary*
J. Penrice, *A dictionary and glossary of the Koran,* London 1873; repr. 1971

Pickthall, *Koran*
M.M. Pickthall, *The meaning of the glorious Koran,* London 1930; New York 1976

Qāshānī, *Taʾwīl*
ʿAbd al-Razzāq al-Qāshānī, *Taʾwīl al-Qurʾān,* 2 vols., Beirut 1968 (see Ibn al-ʿArabī)

Qāsimī, *Tafsīr*
Muḥammad Jamāl al-Dīn al-Qāsimī, *Maḥāsin al-taʾwīl,* 18 vols., Cairo 1957-70

Qasṭallānī, *Laṭāʾif*
Aḥmad b. Muḥammad b. Abī Bakr al-Qasṭallānī, *Laṭāʾif al-ishārāt li-funūn al-qirāʾāt,* ed. ʿĀmir al-Sayyid ʿUthmān and ʿAbd al-Ṣabūr Shāhīn, Cairo 1972

Qasṭallānī, *Mawāhib*
Aḥmad b. Muḥammad b. Abī Bakr al-Qasṭallānī, *al-Mawāhib al-laduniyya bi-l-minaḥ al-muḥammadiyya,* ed. Ṣāliḥ Aḥmad al-Shāmī, 4 vols., Beirut/Damascus/Amman 1412/1991

Qummī, *Tafsīr*
Abū l-Ḥasan ʿAlī b. Ibrāhīm al-Qummī, *Tafsīr,* ed. Ṭayyib al-Mūsāwī al-Jazāʾirī, 2 vols., Najaf 1387/1967; Beirut 1991

Qurṭubī, *Jāmiʿ*
Abū ʿAbdallāh Muḥammad b. Aḥmad al-Qurṭubī, *al-Jāmiʿ li-aḥkām al-Qurʾān,* ed. Aḥmad ʿAbd al-ʿAlīm al-Bardūnī et al., 20 vols., Cairo 1952-67; Beirut 1965-7

Qushayrī, *Laṭāʾif*
Abū l-Qāsim ʿAbd al-Karīm b. Hawāzin al-Qushayrī, *Laṭāʾif al-ishārāt,* ed. Ibrāḥim Basyūnī, 6 vols., Cairo 1968-71

Quṭb, *Ẓilāl*
Sayyid Quṭb Ibrāhīm Ḥusayn Shādhilī, *Fī ẓilāl al-Qurʾān,* 6 vols., Beirut 1393-4/1973-4; rev. 11th ed., Cairo 1993

al-Rāghib al-Iṣfahānī, *Mufradāt*
Abū l-Qāsim al-Ḥusayn al-Rāghib al-Iṣfahānī, *Muʿjam mufradāt alfāẓ al-Qurʾān,* Beirut 1392/1972

Rashīd Riḍā, *Manār*
Muḥammad Rashīd Riḍā and Muḥammad ʿAbduh, *Tafsīr al-Qurʾān al-ḥakīm al-shahīr bi-Tafsīr al-Manār,* 12 vols., Beirut n.d.

Rāzī, *Tafsīr*
Fakhr al-Dīn al-Rāzī, *al-Tafsīr al-kabīr (Mafātīḥ al-ghayb),* ed. Muḥammad Muḥyī l-Dīn ʿAbd al-Ḥamīd, 32 vols. in 16, Cairo 1352/1933; Tehran n.d.; Beirut 1981

Rippin, *Approaches*
Andrew Rippin (ed.), *Approaches to the history of the interpretation of the Qurʾān,* Oxford 1988

Rummānī et al., *Rasāʾil*
ʿAlī b. ʿĪsā al-Rummānī, Ḥamd b. Muḥammad al-Khaṭṭābī and ʿAbd al-Qāhir al-Jurjānī, *Thalāth rasāʾil fī iʿjāz al-Qurʾān,* ed. Muḥammad Khalaf Allāh Aḥmad and Muḥammad Zaghlūl Sallām, Cairo 1976

Rūzbihān al-Baqlī, *ʿArāʾis*
Rūzbihān b. Abī Naṣr al-Baqlī, *ʿArāʾis al-bayān fī ḥaqāʾiq al-Qurʾān,* 2 vols., Cawnpore 1301/1884

Ṣābūnī, *Tafsīr*
Muḥammad ʿAlī Ṣābūnī, *Ṣafwat al-tafāsīr. Tafsīr lil-Qurʾān al-karīm,* 3 vols., Beirut 1981
Ṣafadī, *Wāfī*
Khalīl b. Aybak al-Ṣafadī, *al-Wāfī bi-l-wafayāt. Das biographische Lexikon des Ṣalāḥaddīn Ḫalīl ibn Aibak aṣ-Ṣafadī,* ed. H. Ritter et al., 24 vols. to date, Wiesbaden-Beirut-Damascus 1962-
Sakhāwī, *Jamāl*
ʿAlam al-Dīn ʿAlī b. Muḥammad al-Sakhāwi, *Jamāl al-qurrāʾ wa-kamāl al-iqrāʾ,* ed. ʿAlī Ḥusayn al-Bawwāb, 2 vols., Mecca 1408/1987
Ṣaliḥī, *Subul*
Shams al-Dīn Muḥammad b. Yūsuf al-Ṣāliḥī, *Subul al-hudā wa-l-rashād,* ed. ʿĀdil Aḥmad ʿAbd al-Mawjūd and ʿAlī Muḥammad Muʿawwaḍ, 12 vols., Beirut 1414/1993
Samʿānī, *Ansāb*
ʿAbd al-Karīm b. Muḥammad al-Samʿānī, *Kitāb al-Ansāb,* facsimile ed., D.S. Margoliouth, Leiden 1912; ed. Muḥammad ʿAbd al-Muʿīd Khān et al., 13 vols., Hyderabad 1382-1402/1962-82
Schawāhid-Indices
A. Fischer and E. Bräunlich (eds.), *Indices der Reimwörter und der Dichter der in den arabischen Schawāhid-Kommentaren und in verwandten Werken erläuterten Belegverse,* Leipzig 1934-45
Schwarzbaum, *Legends*
H. Schwarzbaum, *Biblical and extra-biblical legends in Islamic folk-literature,* Wallford-Hessen 1982
Sezgin, GAS
F. Sezgin, *Geschichte des arabischen Schrifttums,* 9 vols., Leiden 1967-84
Shāfiʿī, *Aḥkām*
Muḥammad b. Idrīs al-Shāfiʿī, *Aḥkām al-Qurʾān,* 2 vols. in 1, Beirut 1980
Shāfiʿī, *Mufassirān*
Muḥammad Shāfiʿī, *Mufassirān-i shīʿah,* Shiraz 1349[solar]/1970
Shahrastānī, *Milal*
Abū l-Fatḥ Muḥammad al-Shahrastānī, *al-Milal wa-l-niḥal,* ed. W. Cureton, 2 vols., London 1846; ed. Muḥammad Fatḥ Allāh Badrān, 2 vols., Cairo 1947-55; ed. Fahmī Muḥammad, Beirut 1992
Shawkānī, *Tafsīr*
Abū ʿAbdallāh Muḥammad b. ʿAlī al-Shawkānī, *Fatḥ al-qadīr al-jāmiʿ bayna fannay l-riwāya wa-l-dirāya fī ʿilm al-tafsīr,* 5 vols., Cairo 1349/1930; repr. Beirut 1973
Sibṭ Ibn al-Jawzī, *Mirʾāt*
Shams al-Dīn Abū l-Muẓaffar Yūsuf b. Qizoğlu Sibṭ Ibn al-Jawzī, *Mirʾāt al-zamān fī taʾrīkh al-aʿyān,* ed. Iḥsān ʿAbbās, Beirut 1405/1985
Speyer, *Erzählungen*
Heinrich Speyer, *Die biblischen Erzählungen im Qoran,* Gräfenhainich 1931; repr. Hildesheim 1961
Sprenger, *Moḥammad*
A. Sprenger, *Das Leben und die Lehre des Mohammad,* 3 vols., 2nd ed., Berlin 1869
Storey, PL
C.A. Storey, *Persian literature. A bio-bibliographical survey,* 2 vols. in 5, London 1927
Sufyān al-Thawrī, *Tafsīr*
Abū ʿAbdallāh Sufyān al-Thawrī, *al-Tafsīr,* ed. Imtiyāz ʿAlī ʿArshī, Beirut 1403/1983
Suhaylī, *Taʿrīf*
Abū l-Qāsim ʿAbd al-Raḥmān b. ʿAbdallāh al-Suhaylī, *al-Taʿrīf wa-l-iʿlām fī mā ubhima fī l-Qurʾān min al-asmāʾ wa-l-aʿlām,* ed. ʿAbdallāh Muḥammad ʿAlī al-Naqrāṭ, Tripoli 1401/1992
Sulamī, *Ziyādāt*
Abū ʿAbd al-Raḥmān Muḥammad b. al-Ḥusayn al-Sulamī, *Ziyādāt ḥaqāʾiq al-tafsīr,* ed. G. Böwering, Beirut 1995
Suyūṭī, *Durr*
Jalāl al-Dīn al-Suyūṭī, *al-Durr al-manthūr fī l-tafsīr bi-l-maʾthūr,* 6 vols., Beirut 1990
Suyūṭī, *Ḥuffāẓ*
Jalāl al-Dīn al-Suyūṭī, *Ṭabaqāt al-ḥuffāẓ,* ed. ʿAlī Muḥammad ʿUmar, Cairo 1973

Suyūṭī, *Itqān*
Jalāl al-Dīn al-Suyūṭī, *al-Itqān fī ʿulūm al-Qurʾān,* ed. Muḥammad Abū l-Faḍl Ibrāhīm, 4 vols. in 2, Cairo 1967
Suyūṭī, *Khaṣāʾiṣ*
Jalāl al-Dīn al-Suyūṭī, *al-Khaṣāʾiṣ al-kubrā,* Hyderabad 1320/1902; repr. Beirut n.d.
Suyūṭī, *Mufḥamāt*
Jalāl al-Dīn al-Suyūṭī, *al-Mufḥamāt al-aqrān fī mubhamāt al-Qurʾān,* ed. Muṣṭafā Dīb al-Bughā, Damascus and Beirut 1403/1982
Suyūṭī, *Muhadhdhab*
Jalāl al-Dīn al-Suyūṭī, *al-Muhadhdhab fī mā waqaʿa fī l-Qurʾān min al-muʿarrab,* ed. al-Tihāmī al-Rājī al-Hāshimī, Rabat n.d.; in *Rasāʾil fī l-fiqh wa-l-lugha,* ed. ʿAbdallāh al-Jubūrī, Beirut 1982, pp. 179-235
Suyūṭī, *Ṭabaqāt*
Jalāl al-Dīn al-Suyūṭī, *Ṭabaqāt al-mufassirīn,* ed. ʿAlī Muḥammad ʿUmar, Cairo 1976
Suyūṭī, *Taḥbīr*
Jalāl al-Dīn al-Suyūṭī, *al-Taḥbīr fī ʿilm al-tafsīr,* ed. Fatḥī ʿAbd al-Qādir Farīd, Cairo 1406/1986
Suyūṭī, *Tanāsuq*
Jalāl al-Dīn al-Suyūṭī, *Tanāsuq al-durar fī tanāsub al-suwar,* ed. ʿAbd al-Qādir Aḥmad ʿAṭā, Beirut 1406/1986
Ṭabarānī, *Awsaṭ*
Abū l-Qāsim Sulaymān b. Aḥmad al-Ṭabarānī, *al-Muʿjam al-awsaṭ,* ed. Ṭāriq b. ʿAwaḍ Allāh b. Muḥammad and ʿAbd al-Muḥsin Ibrāhīm al-Ḥusaynī, 10 vols., Cairo 1415/1995
Ṭabarānī, *Kabīr*
Abū l-Qāsim Sulaymān b. Aḥmad al-Ṭabarānī, *al-Muʿjam al-kabīr,* ed. Ḥamdī ʿAbd al-Majīd al-Salafī, vols. i-xii, xvii-xx and xxii-xxv, Baghdad 1398-1404/1977-83; Mosul 1401/1983
Ṭabarī, *Tafsīr*
Abū Jaʿfar Muḥammad b. Jarīr al-Ṭabarī, *Jāmiʿ al-bayān ʿan taʾwīl āy al-Qurʾān* [up to Q 14:27], ed. Maḥmūd Muḥammad Shākir and Aḥmad Muḥammad Shākir, 16 vols., Cairo 1954-68; 2nd ed. for some vols., Cairo 1969; ed. Aḥmad Saʿīd ʿAlī et al., 30 vols., Cairo 1373-77/1954-7; repr. Beirut 1984
Ṭabarī, *Taʾrīkh*
Abū Jaʿfar Muḥammad b. Jarīr al-Ṭabarī, *Taʾrīkh al-rusul wa-l-mulūk,* ed. M.J. de Goeje et al., 15 vols., Leiden 1879-1901; ed. Muḥammad Abū l-Faḍl Ibrāhīm, 10 vols., Cairo 1960-9
Ṭabarsī, *Majmaʿ*
Abū ʿAlī l-Faḍl b. al-Ḥasan al-Ṭabarsī, *Majmaʿ al-bayān fī tafsīr al-Qurʾān,* intr. Muḥsin al-Amīn al-Ḥusaynī al-ʿĀmilī, 30 vols. in 6, Beirut 1380/1961
Ṭabāṭabāʾī, *Mīzān*
Muḥammad Ḥusayn Ṭabāṭabāʾī, *al-Mīzān fī tafsīr al-Qurʾān,* 20 vols., Beirut 1393-4/1973-4; vol. xxi, Beirut 1985
Tāj al-ʿarūs
Muḥibb al-Dīn al-Sayyid Muḥammad Murtaḍā al-Zabīdī, *Sharḥ al-qāmūs al-musammā Tāj al-ʿarūs min jawāhir al-Qāmūs,* 10 vols., Cairo 1306-7; ed. ʿAbd al-Sattār Aḥmad Faraj et al., 40 vols., Kuwait 1965-2001
Thaʿālibī, *Iʿjāz*
ʿAbd al-Malik b. Muḥammad al-Thaʿālibī, *al-Iʿjāz wa-l-ījāz,* ed. Iskandar Āṣāt, Constantinople 1897; Beirut 1983
Thaʿālibī, *Iqtibās*
ʿAbd al-Malik b. Muḥammad al-Thaʿālibī, *al-Iqtibās min al-Qurʾān al-karīm,* ed. Ibtisām Marhūn al-Ṣaffār and Mujāhid Muṣṭafā Bahjat, 2 vols. in 1, Cairo 1412/1992
Thaʿālibī, *Yatīma*
ʿAbd al-Malik b. Muḥammad al-Thaʿālibī, *Yatīmat al-dahr fī maḥāsin ahl al-ʿaṣr,* 4 vols., Damascus 1304/1886-7; ed. Muḥammad Muḥyī l-Dīn ʿAbd al-Ḥamīd, 4 vols., Cairo 1375-7/1956-8
Thaʿlabī, *Qiṣaṣ*
Aḥmad b. Muḥammad b. Ibrāhīm al-Thaʿlabī, *Qiṣaṣ al-anbiyāʾ al-musammā bi-ʿArāʾis al-majālis,* Cairo 1322; repr. Beirut 1980

Thaʿlabī-Goldfeld
I. Goldfeld, *Qurʾānic commentary in the eastern Islamic tradition of the first four centuries of the hijra. An annotated edition of the preface to al-Thaʿlabī's "Kitāb al-Kashf wa-l-bayān ʿan Tafsīr al-Qurʾān,"* Acre 1984

Tirmidhī, *Ṣaḥīḥ*
Abū ʿĪsā Muḥammad b. ʿĪsā al-Tirmidhī, *al-Jāmiʿ al-ṣaḥīḥ*, ed. Aḥmad Muḥammad Shākir et al., 5 vols., Cairo 1937-65

Ṭūsī, *Fihrist*
Muḥammad b. al-Ḥasan al-Ṭūsī, *al-Fihrist*, Najaf 1356/1937; Beirut 1983

Ṭūsī, *Tibyān*
Muḥammad b. al-Ḥasan al-Ṭūsī, *al-Tibyān fī tafsīr al-Qurʾān*, intr. Āghā Buzurk al-Ṭihrānī, 10 vols., Najaf 1376-83/1957-63

Tustarī, *Tafsīr*
Sahl b. ʿAbdallāh al-Tustarī, *Tafsīr al-Qurʾān al-ʿaẓīm*, Cairo 1329/1911

ʿUkbarī, *Tibyān*
Abū l-Baqāʾ ʿAbdallāh b. al-Ḥusayn al-ʿUkbarī, *al-Tibyān fī iʿrāb al-Qurʿān*, ed. ʿAlī Muḥammad al-Bajāwī, 2 vols., Cairo 1396/1976

Wagtendonk, *Fasting*
K. Wagtendonk, *Fasting in the Koran*, Leiden 1968

Wāḥidī, *Asbāb*
Abū l-Ḥasan ʿAlī b. Aḥmad al-Nīsābūrī al-Wāḥidī, *Asbāb al-nuzūl*, Cairo 1968

Wāḥidī, *Wasīṭ*
Abū l-Ḥasan ʿAlī b. Aḥmad al-Nīsābūrī al-Wāḥidī, *al-Wasīṭ fī tafsīr al-Qurʾān*, ed. ʿĀdil Aḥmad ʿAbd al-Mawjūd et al., 4 vols., Beirut 1415/1994

Wansbrough, *QS*
J. Wansbrough, *Quranic studies. Sources and methods of scriptural interpretation*, Oxford 1977

Wāqidī, *Maghāzī*
Muḥammad b. ʿUmar al-Wāqidī, *Kitāb al-Maghāzī*, ed. M. Jones, 3 vols., London 1966

Watt-Bell, *Introduction*
W.M. Watt, *Bell's introduction to the Qurʾān*, Edinburgh 1970, 1991

Wensinck, *Concordance*
A.J. Wensinck et al., *Concordance et indices de la tradition musulmane*, 8 vols., Leiden 1936-79; repr. 8 vols. in 4, 1992

Wensinck, *Handbook*
A.J. Wensinck, *A handbook of early Muhammadan tradition*, Leiden 1927

Wild, *Text*
S. Wild (ed.), *The Qurʾān as text*, Leiden 1996

Yaḥyā b. Sallām, *Tafsīr*
Yaḥyā b. Sallām al-Baṣrī, *al-Taṣārīf. Tafsīr al-Qurʾān mimmā shtabahat asmāʾuhu wa-taṣarrafat maʿānīhi*, ed. Hind Shalabī, Tunis 1979

Yaʿqūbī, *Buldān*
Aḥmad b. Abī Yaʿqūb b. Wāḍiḥ al-Yaʿqūbī, *Kitāb al-Buldān*, ed. M.J. de Goeje, Leiden 1892, 1967

Yaʿqūbī, *Taʾrīkh*
Aḥmad b. Abī Yaʿqūb b. Wāḍiḥ al-Yaʿqūbī, *Ibn Wādhih qui dicitur al-Jaʿqubi historiae*, ed. M.T. Houtsma, 2 vols., Leiden 1883; repr. 1969

Yāqūt, *Buldān*
Yāqūt b. ʿAbdallāh al-Ḥamawī, *Muʿjam al-buldān*, ed. F. Wüstenfeld, 6 vols., Leipzig 1863-6; 5 vols., Beirut 1374-6/1955-7; ed. Farīd ʿAbd al-ʿAzīz al-Jundī, 7 vols., Beirut 1990

Yāqūt, *Irshād*
Yāqūt b. ʿAbdallāh al-Ḥamawī, *Irshād al-arīb ilā maʿrifat al-adīb. Muʿjam al-udabāʾ*, ed. D.S. Margoliouth, 7 vols., London and Leiden 1923-6; ed. Iḥsān ʿAbbās, 7 vols., Beirut 1993

Zajjāj, *Maʿānī*
Abū Isḥāq Ibrāhīm b. Muḥammad b. al-Sarī l-Zajjāj, *Maʿānī l-Qurʾān wa-iʿrābuhu*, ed. ʿAbd al-Jalīl ʿAbduh Shalabī, 5 vols., Beirut 1408/1988

Zamakhsharī, *Asās*
Maḥmūd b. ʿUmar al-Zamakhsharī, *Asās al-balāgha*, Beirut 1979

Zamakhsharī, *Kashshāf*
Maḥmūd b. ʿUmar al-Zamakhsharī, *al-*

Kashshāf ʿan ḥaqāʾiq ghawāmiḍ al-tanzīl wa-ʿuyūn al-aqāwīl fī wujūh al-taʾwīl, 4 vols., Beirut 1366/1947; ed. Muḥammad ʿAbd al-Salām Shāhīn, 4 vols., Beirut 1995

Zambaur, *Manuel*
E. de Zambaur, *Manuel de généalogie et de chronologie pour l'histoire de l'Islam*, Hanover 1927; repr. Bad Pyrmont 1955

Zarkashī, *Burhān*
Badr al-Dīn al-Zarkashī, *al-Burhān fī ʿulūm al-Qurʾān*, ed. Muḥammad Abū l-Faḍl Ibrāhīm, 4 vols., Cairo 1957; Beirut 1972; ed. Yūsuf ʿAbd al-Raḥmān al-Marʿashlī et al., 4 vols., Beirut 1994

Zayd b. ʿAlī, *Musnad*
Zayd b. ʿAlī Zayn al-ʿĀbidīn, *Musnad*, ed. Bakr b. Muḥammad ʿĀshūr, 1328/1910; Beirut 1983

Ziriklī, *Aʿlām*
Khayr al-Dīn al-Ziriklī, *al-Aʿlām. Qāmūs tarājim li-ashhar al-rijāl wa-l-nisāʾ min al-ʿArab wa-l-mustaʿribīn wa-l-mustashriqīn*, 10 vols., Damascus 1373-8/1954-9; 8 vols., Beirut 1979

Zubaydī, *Ṭabaqāt*
Abū Bakr Muḥammad b. al-Ḥasan al-Zubaydī, *Ṭabaqāt al-naḥwiyyīn wa-l-lughawiyyīn*, ed. Muḥammad Abū l-Faḍl Ibrāhīm, Cairo 1373/1954

Zubayrī, *Nasab*
Muṣʿab al-Zubayrī, *Nasab Quraysh*, ed. E. Lévi-Provençal, Cairo 1953

Zurqānī, *Sharḥ*
Muḥammad b. ʿAbd al-Bāqī al-Miṣrī al-Mālik, *Sharḥ al-mawāhib al-laduniyya*, ed. Muḥammad ʿAbd al-ʿAzīz al-Khālidī, 12 vols., Beirut 1417/1996

P

Pact see COVENANT

Paganism see AGE OF IGNORANCE; IDOLATRY AND IDOLATERS; SOUTH ARABIA, RELIGION IN PRE-ISLAMIC

Pages see SHEETS; SCROLLS

Pairs and Pairing

Any aspect of the language and style of the Qur'ān in which pairs are perceived as a structural element in the composition of the Qur'ān (see FORM AND STRUCTURE OF THE QUR'ĀN), such as any form of parallelism or repetition, pairs of synonymous, synthetic or antithetic terms or concepts, double divine epithets (see GOD AND HIS ATTRIBUTES) as well as aspects of the number two or use of the dual form (see NUMBERS AND ENUMERATION).

Ethical dualism

Throughout the Qur'ān, an antithetic or dual parallelism is observable in the admonitions to humankind (see EXHORTATIONS), in the descriptions of an individual's fate on the day of judgment (see LAST JUDGMENT) as well as of the two possible final destinations for people, paradise (q.v.) and hell (see HELL AND HELLFIRE).

Admonitions to believe in and obey God and his apostle (see BELIEF AND UNBELIEF; MESSENGER; OBEDIENCE), to repent (see REPENTANCE AND PENANCE), to enjoin what is right and to prohibit what is wrong (see VIRTUES AND VICES, COMMANDING AND FORBIDDING), to be grateful (see GRATITUDE AND INGRATITUDE), to do right and to follow the right path as revealed to humankind are usually presented as a promise followed by a corresponding threat: "He who follows the right path (see PATH OR WAY) does so for himself, and he who goes astray (q.v.) errs against himself" (Q 10:108; cf. also Q 17:15; 39:41); "Those who disbelieve and obstruct (others) from the way of God will have wasted their deeds. But those who believe and do the right, and believe what has been revealed to Muḥammad (see REVELATION AND INSPIRATION), which is the truth (q.v.) from their lord, will have their faults pardoned by him and their state improved" (Q 47:1-3; cf. also Q 5:9-10; 35-6, 40-2; 9:67-72; 10:7-9; 22:50-1; 32:18-20; 35:7; 48:5-6; 57:19); "Whoever does good does so for himself, and whoever does wrong bears the guilt thereof" (Q 41:46; cf. also Q 16:90; 40:39-40; 45:15; 92:5-11); "If you obey, God will give you a good reward; but if you turn back… he will punish you with grievous affliction" (Q 48:16; cf. also Q 13:18; 48:17; see REWARD AND PUNISHMENT); "It is better for you to repent. If you do not, remember that you cannot elude (the grip of) God" (Q 9:3; cf. also Q 4:141-7); "Remember, your lord proclaimed: 'If you are grateful I shall give you more; but if you are thankless, then surely my punishment is very great'" (Q 14:7; cf. also Q 2:152; 39:7).

The choices that human beings face are described as one between two paths, the path of rectitude *(sabīl al-rushd)* or the straight path *(sabīl mustaqīm)*, on the one hand, and the path of error (q.v.; *sabīl al-ghayy*), on the other: "Did we not give him [i.e. humans] two eyes, a tongue, and two lips, and show him the two highways?" (*al-najdayn;* Q 90:8-10; cf. also Q 7:146; 76:3). As a norm of distinction, the believers are described as the "people of the right hand" *(aṣḥāb al-maymana/aṣḥāb al-yamīn)* whereas the unbelievers are described as the "people of the left hand" (*aṣḥāb al-mash'ama/aṣḥāb al-shimāl,* Q 56:8-9, 27-56; 90:17-9; see LEFT HAND AND RIGHT HAND). By the same token, the believer is compared to one who can hear and see whereas the unbeliever is said to resemble a person who is deaf and blind (e.g. Q 11:24; 40:58; cf. also Q 30:52-3; 35:19; 43:40; 47:23; see SEEING AND HEARING; VISION AND BLINDNESS; HEARING AND DEAFNESS). In those qur'ānic passages where human responsibility appears to be completely eclipsed and where human destiny is said to depend on the will of God, it is God who either guides individuals rightly or leads them astray (Q 6:39; 7:30, 178; 14:4; 16:93; 35:8; 39:36-7), decreases or increases people's fortunes (*rizq,* Q 13:26) and means (*rizq,* Q 30:37), has mercy (q.v.) on people or punishes them (Q 5:18, 40; 17:54; 29:21; 41:43; 48:14; see FREEDOM AND PREDESTINATION).

Similar dual parallelisms are to be observed when it comes to the reckoning of an individual's deeds on the day of judgment. "On that day people will be separated so that he who disbelieves will bear the consequence of his unbelief; and he who does the right will straighten out the way for his soul, so that God may reward those who believed and did what was good, by his grace. Surely he does not love unbelievers" (Q 30:43-5; cf. also Q 11:105-8; 20:74-6; 22:56-7; 30:14-6; 33:73; 39:71-4; 42:7); "[Only] those whose scales are heavier in the balance will find happiness. But those whose scales are lighter will perish and abide in hell forever" (Q 23:102-3; cf. also Q 7:8-9; 101:6-9; see WEIGHTS AND MEASURES); "[Many] faces will that day be bright, laughing and full of joy; and many will be dust-begrimed, covered with the blackness (of shame)" (Q 80:38-41; see JOY AND MISERY).

On the day of judgment, the evil-doer will receive the book (q.v.; *al-kitāb*) containing the record of his deeds in his left hand or from behind his back, whereas the obedient will be given it in his right hand (Q 69:18-32; 84:7-12). The *sijjīn,* the books where the deeds of the evil-doers are listed, is contrasted with the *'illiyyūn,* the book where the deeds of the pious are listed (Q 83:7 f.; see HEAVENLY BOOK). An exception to this strict dual parallelism is to be found in Q 56 where humankind is said to be separated at the last judgment into three classes, the "people of the right side" *(aṣḥāb al-maymana),* the "people of the left side" *(aṣḥāb al-mash'ama)* and "those preceding" *(al-sābiqūn).* "Those are the ones brought near *(al-muqarrabūn),* in gardens of delight, a multitude from the former (times) and a few from the later (times)" (Q 56:11-4). Those who belong to this class — the first converts to Islam, the prophets (see PROPHETS AND PROPHETHOOD) or any person of outstanding virtue according to al-Zamakhsharī (d. 538/1144; *Kashshāf,* ad loc.) and al-Bayḍāwī (d. prob. 716/1316-7; *Anwār,* ad loc.) — are given the highest reward in paradise.

Qurʾānic descriptions of humanity's two final destinations also evidence a pair structure. A description of the joys of paradise or the torments of hell is, as a rule, followed by the antithetic description of the respective other. For example, "Certainly hell lies in wait, the rebels' abode where they will remain for eons, finding neither sleep *(bard)* nor anything to drink except boiling water and benumbing cold: a fitting reward. They were those who did not expect a reckoning, and rejected our signs (q.v.) as lies (see LIE). We have kept account of everything in a book. So taste (the fruit of what you sowed), for we shall add nothing but torment. As for those who preserve themselves from evil and follow the straight path *(al-muttaqīna),* there is attainment for them: orchards and vineyards, and graceful maidens of the same age (see HOURIS), and flasks full and flowing. They will hear no blasphemies (see BLASPHEMY) there or disavowals: A recompense from your lord, a sufficient gift" (Q 78:21-36). The parallelism is, however, at times, asymmetric. Depending on the context, either the description of hell or of paradise is more detailed. Such an asymmetric antithesis is to be observed in Q 55, where the fate of the unbelievers in hell is described in four verses (Q 55:39, 41, 43, 44), whereas the fate of the believers in paradise is described in eight verses (Q 55:46, 48, 50, 52, 54, 56, 58, 60), whereupon there follows another description of the garden of the same length (Q 55:62, 64, 66, 68, 70, 72, 74, 76; cf. Gilliot, Parcours exégétiques, 91-111). Having two sets of gardens for two classes of believers would seem to be confirmed by the parallel two classes of gardens in Q 56:10-38 (Abdel Haleem, Context, 91 f.; see GARDEN).

Pairs of concepts and terms

Pairs of synonymous as well as synthetic concepts are to be found in the description of Muḥammad and earlier prophets as "bearers of warnings and bringers of happy news" *(mubashshir[wa-] mundhir/mubashshir nadhīr/bashīr [wa-]nadhīr;* Q 2:119, 213; 4:165; 5:19; 6:48; 7:188; 10:2; 11:2; 17:105; 18:56; 25:56; 33:45; 34:28; 35:24; 41:4; 48:8; see WARNER; GOOD NEWS); of the book of Moses (q.v.; *kitāb Mūsā*) as a "way-giver and a grace" (q.v.; *imām wa-raḥma;* Q 11:17; 46:12; see IMĀM); of the Torah (q.v.) and the Gospel (q.v.) as containing "guidance and light" *(nūran wa-hudan/hudan wa-nūrun)* for humans (Q 5:44, 46; 6:91; cf. 42:52); and of the earlier revelations and the Qurʾān as a "guidance and grace" *(hudā wa-raḥma)* for those who believe (Q 6:154; 7:52, 154, 203; 10:57, et al.; *hudā wa-bushrā,* Q 27:2; *hudā wa-shifāʾ,* Q 41:44; *hudā wa-dhikrā,* Q 40:54). To the prophets God gave "wisdom (q.v.) and knowledge" (*ḥukm wa-ʿilm,* Q 12:22; 21:74, 79; 28:14; see KNOWLEDGE AND LEARNING). Another pair of terms frequently referred to in the context of earlier revelations is "scripture and wisdom" (*al-kitāb wa-l-ḥikma,* Q 2:231; 4:54, 113; 5:110; see SCRIPTURE AND THE QURʾĀN). The pair of terms "wealth and (male) children" *(māl wa-banūn/amwāl wa-banūn/amwāl wa-awlād/māl wa-walad/anʿām wa-banūn)* signifies wealth of this world (e.g. Q 9:55, 69; 17:6; 18:46; 23:55; 26:88, 133; 34:35, et al.; see CHILDREN). As a pair of antithetic concepts, the verses to be understood clearly *(muḥkamāt)* are contrasted with the parabolic verses of the Qurʾān *(mutashābihāt)* as mentioned in Q 3:7 (see AMBIGUOUS).

Contrasting pairs such as "heaven (see HEAVEN AND SKY) and earth (q.v.)," "sun (q.v.) and moon (q.v.)," "day and night" (q.v.; see also DAY, TIMES OF), "east and west," "land and sea," "known and unknown (see HIDDEN AND THE HIDDEN)," "before and after," "life (q.v.) and death (see DEATH AND THE DEAD)" — all signifying the entirety of creation (q.v.) or "all" — are employed to describe God's unicity, omnipotence (see POWER AND IMPOTENCE) and omniscience. To God belongs all that is in the heavens and the earth (*mā fī l-samāwāt wa[-mā fī] l-arḍ,* Q 2:116, 284; 10:55, 68; 14:2; 16:52; 18:14, et al.; cf. also Q 35:44); his kingdom extends over the heavens and the earth (Q 7:158, 185; 9:116; 10:66; 13:16; 24:42, et al.); God holds the keys of the heavens and the earth (*maqālīd al-samāwāt wa-l-arḍ;* Q 39:63; 42:12); he is the light *(nūr)* of the heavens and the earth (Q 24:35); his are the armies of the heavens and the earth (*junūd al-samāwāt wa-l-arḍ,* Q 48:4, 7; see RANKS AND ORDERS), and his seat extends over heavens and earth (*wasiʿa kursiyyuhu al-samāwāt wa-l-arḍ,* Q 2:255; see THRONE OF GOD); and he provides people with food and sustenance [from the heavens and the earth] (Q 10:31; 16:73; 27:64; 31:20; 34:24; 35:3; 45:5, 13). The fact that God created the heavens and the earth (Q 2:117; 9:36; 10:3; 11:7; 12:101; 14:10, 19, 32, et al.; variation: God created the heavens and the earth and all that lies between them *[wa-mā baynahumā],* Q 15:85; 21:16; 25:59; 30:8; 32:4; 37:5; 38:27; 44:38; 46:3; 50:38) and that he brings to light what is hidden in the heavens and the earth (Q 27:25) indicate his omnipotence, whereas his omniscience is indicated by his knowledge which encompasses all that is in the heavens and the earth (Q 5:97; 11:123; 14:38; 16:77; 17:55; 18:26; 21:4, et al.) — there is not the weight of an atom "on the earth and in the heavens" that is hidden from him (Q 10:61; 31:16). His omniscience is further indicated by the fact that he knows "what is hidden and what is evident" (*al-ghayb wa-l-shahāda,* Q 6:73; 9:94, 105; 13:9; 23:92; 32:6; 39:46; 59:22; 62:8; 64:18), what humans "hide and disclose" (i.e. Q 2:33, 77; 16:19, 23; 21:110; 27:25, 74; 28:69; 33:54; 36:76; 60:1; 64:4; 87:7), and what was before humans and what lies behind them (*mā bayn aydīhim wa-mā khalfahum,* Q 2:255; 20:110; 21:28; 22:76). God's unicity is indicated by the fact that all things that move on the earth and in the heavens bow down before him (Q 13:15; 16:49; 22:18; 24:41; 57:1; 59:1, 24; 61:1; 62:1; 64:1; see BOWING AND PROSTRATION) and that his semblance is the most sublime in the heavens and the earth (Q 30:27). By the same token, the gods of the unbelievers are said to be without any power over the heavens and the earth, nor do they have any share in them (Q 34:22; 38:10; see POLYTHEISM AND ATHEISM). Moreover, God is the first and the last *(al-awwal wa-l-ākhir),* the transcendent and the immanent (*al-ẓāhir wa-l-bāṭin,* Q 57:3). God's omnipotence is further evident in that he created "the sun and the moon" (Q 10:5; 13:2; 16:12; 21:33; 22:61, et al.), and made "the day and the night" an alternation (Q 10:6, 67; 13:3; 16:12; 17:12; 23:80; 24:44; 25:47, 62, et al.), that he enables people to travel over "land and sea" (*fī l-barr wa-l-baḥr,* Q 10:22; 17:70; cf. also Q 27:63), that he gives life and death (Q 9:116; 10:31, 56; 23:80; 30:19; 40:68; 44:8; 45:26; 50:43; 53:44; 57:2), makes happy and morose (Q 53:43), and that he is the lord of the east and the west (*rabb al-mashriq wa-l-maghrib,* Q 26:28; 73:9; *rabbu l-mashriqayn wa-rabb al-maghribayn,* Q 55:17; *rabbu l-mashāriq wa-l-maghārib,* Q 70:40; *wa-lillāhi l-mashriq wa-l-maghrib,* Q 2:115, 142).

Pairs of contrasts such as "sky and earth," "sun and moon," "day and night," as well as of similar terms such as "fig and olive" are also encountered in oaths: "I call to witness the rain-producing sky and the earth which opens up" (Q 86:11-2); "I call to witness the sun and its early morning splendor, and the moon as it follows in its wake, the day when it reveals its radiance, the night when it covers it over, the heavens and its architecture, the earth and its spreading out" (Q 91:1-6); "I call the night to witness when it covers over, and the day when it shines in all its glory" (Q 92:1-2); "I call to witness the fig and the olive" (Q 95:1). Idols are described as those who can neither harm nor profit their worshippers (*mā lā yaḍurruhu wa-mā lā yanfaʿuhu*, Q 22:12; cf. also Q 5:76; 6:71; 10:18, 106; 20:89; 21:66; 25:55; 26:72 f.; 34:42; see IDOLS AND IMAGES).

Contrasting this ephemeral world with the enduring hereafter serves to admonish humankind to concentrate on the latter (see ESCHATOLOGY). "O people, the life of this world is ephemeral; but enduring is the abode of the hereafter" (Q 40:39); "Whatsoever has been given you is the stuff this life is made of, and (only) its embellishment. What is with your lord is better and abiding. Will you not understand?" (Q 28:60; cf. also Q 8:67; 16:96; 30:7; 33:28-9; 42:20; 57:20).

The contrasting pair of "light and darkness" describes the benefit which the Prophet and the revelation bring to humankind: "An apostle who recites before you the explicating revelations of God that he may bring those who believe and do the right out of darkness (q.v.) into light" (Q 65:11; cf. also Q 14:5); "It is he who sends down resplendent revelations to his votary, that he may take you out of darkness into light" (Q 57:9; cf. also Q 14:1).

Double divine epithets

Double divine epithets occur frequently at the end of verses, particularly in the longer sūras. At times, these have little or no relevance to the verses they are attached to; in other instances the phrases are appropriate to the context. Numerous pairs of terms describing God consist of synonyms, such as the double epithet *al-raḥmān al-raḥīm* "most benevolent, ever-merciful" of the *basmala* (q.v.) formula which occurs in five further instances (Q 1:3; 2:163; 27:30; 41:2; 59:22); "all-forgiving and ever-merciful" (*ghafūr raḥīm*, Q 2:173, 182, 192, 199, 218, 226; 3:31, 129; 4:23, 25, et al.; *al-raḥīm al-ghafūr*, Q 34:2; *al-ghafūr dhū l-raḥma*, Q 18:58; see FORGIVENESS); "all-forgiving and forbearing" (*ghafūr ḥalīm*, Q 2:225, 235; 3:155; 5:101; *ḥalīm ghafūr*, Q 17:44; 35:41); "all-forgiving and loving" (*al-ghafūr al-wadūd*, Q 85:14); "benign and forgiving" (*ʿafuww ghafūr*, Q 4:43, 99; 22:60); "forgiving and ever-merciful" (*tawwāb raḥīm*, Q 4:16, 64; 49:12; cf. 9:104, 118); "compassionate and ever-merciful" (*raʾūf raḥīm*, Q 2:143; 9:117, 128; 16:7, 47; 22:65; 57:9; 59:10); "ever-merciful and loving" (*raḥīm wadūd*, Q 11:90); "just and merciful" (*al-barr al-raḥīm*, Q 52:28); "all-knowing, all-wise" (*ʿalīm ḥakīm*, Q 4:11, 17, 26, 92, 104, 111, 170; 8:71, et al.; *ḥakīm ʿalīm*, Q 6:83, 128, 139; 15:25; 27:6; 43:84; 51:30); "all-knowing and cognizant" (*ʿalīm khabīr*, Q 4:35; 31:34; 49:13; 66:3); "all-wise and cognizant" (*al-ḥakīm al-khabīr*, Q 6:18, 73; 34:1); "sublime and great" (*[al-]ʿaliyy [al-]kabīr*, Q 4:34; 22:62; 31:30; 34:23; 40:12); "great and most high" (*al-kabīr al-mutaʿāl*, Q 13:9); "sublime and supreme" (*al-ʿaliyy al-ʿaẓīm*, Q 2:255; 42:4); "powerful and mighty" (*[al-]qawiyy [al-]ʿazīz*, Q 11:66; 22:40, 74; 33:25; 42:19; 57:25; 58:21); "worthy of praise and glory" (*ḥamīd majīd*, Q 11:73). Moreover, God is humankind's only friend and advocate (*waliyy shafīʿ*, cf. Q 6:51, 70; *mawlan naṣīr*, cf. Q 22:78; *waliyy naṣīr*, cf. Q 4:123, 173; 29:22; 33:17; 42:8, 31; 48:22; see CLIENTS AND CLIENTAGE; FRIENDS AND FRIENDSHIP; INTERCESSION).

Other combinations of adjectives referring to God complement each other, such as "all-hearing and all-knowing" (*[al-]samīʿ [al-]ʿalīm*, Q 2:127, 181, 224, 227; 3:34, 35, 121; 4:148; 5:76; et al.); "all-hearing and all-seeing" (*[al-]samīʿ [al-]baṣīr*, Q 4:58, 134; 17:1; 22:75; 31:28; 40:20, 56; 42:11; 58:1); "[God is] near and answers" (*qarīb mujīb*, Q 11:61); "all-hearing and all-near" (*samīʿ*

qarīb, Q 34:50); "judge and all-knowing" (*al-fattāḥ al-ʿalīm,* Q 34:26); "the one and the omnipotent" (*al-wāḥid al-qahhār,* Q 13:16; 14:48). Other pair epithets describe different aspects of God, such as "mighty and all-wise" (*[al-]ʿazīz [al-]ḥakīm,* Q 2:129, 209, 220, 228, 240, 260; 3:6, 18, 62, 126, et al.); "mighty and all-knowing" (*[al-]ʿazīz [al-]ʿalīm,* Q 6:96; 27:78; 36:38; 40:2; 41:12); "mighty and worthy of praise" (*al-ʿazīz al-ḥamīd,* Q 14:1; 34:6; 85:8); "mighty and ever-merciful" (*[al-]ʿazīz [al-]raḥīm,* Q 26:9, 68, 104, 122, 140, 159, 175, 191, 217; 30:5; 32:6; 36:5; 44:42); "mighty and all-forgiving" (*[al-]ʿazīz [al-]ghafūr,* Q 35:28; 67:2; *al-ʿazīz al-ghaffār,* Q 38:66; 39:5; 40:42); "all-knowing and all-powerful" (*[al-]ʿalīm [al-]qadīr,* Q 16:70; 30:54; 35:44; 42:50); "all-knowing and forbearing" (*ʿalīm ḥalīm,* Q 22:59; 33:51); "infinite and all-knowing" (*wāsiʿ ʿalīm,* Q 2:115, 247, 261, 268; 5:54; 24:32); "infinite and all-wise" (*wāsiʿ ḥakīm,* Q 4:130); "responsive to gratitude and all-knowing" (*shākir ʿalīm,* Q 4:147); "all-forgiving and rewarding" (*ghafūr shakūr,* Q 35:30, 34; 42:23); "rewarding and forbearing" (*shakūr ḥalīm,* Q 64:17); "benign and all-powerful" (*ʿafuww qadīr,* Q 4:149); "self-sufficient and forbearing" (*ghaniyy ḥalīm,* Q 2:263); "self-sufficient and praiseworthy" (*ghaniyy ḥamīd,* Q 2:267; 4:131; 14:8; 22:64; 31:12, 26; 57:24; 60:6; 64:6; see PRAISE); "living self-subsisting (or: sustaining)" (*al-ḥayy al-qayyūm,* Q 2:255; 3:2); "the creator and all-knowing" (*al-khallāq al-ʿalīm,* Q 15:86; 36:81); "compassionate and all-wise" (*tawwāb ḥakīm,* Q 24:10); "all-wise and praiseworthy" (*ḥakīm ḥamīd,* Q 41:42); "all-high and all-wise" (*ʿaliyy ḥakīm,* Q 42:51).

Aspects of the number two and uses of dual forms

The Qurʾān frequently mentions that God created pairs of everything — humans, beasts and even fruits (Q 6:143-4; 13:3; 35:11; 36:36; 42:11; 43:12; 51:49; 53:45; 55:52; 75:39; 78:8; see ANIMAL LIFE; AGRICULTURE AND VEGETATION); he also commanded Noah (q.v.) to take a pair of every species into the ark (q.v.; cf. Q 11:40; 23:27). At the end of days God will create people a second time: "We created you from the earth and will revert you back; and raise you up from it a second time" (*tāratan ukhrā,* Q 20:55; cf. with variations Q 10:4, 34; 21:104; 27:64; 29:19, 20; 30:11, 27; 50:15; 85:13); "They say: 'O lord, twice you made us die, and twice you made us live. We admit our sins (see SIN, MAJOR AND MINOR). Is there still a way out?'" (Q 40:11).

Those who believe in God and his apostle are said to receive twice as much of his bounty and their reward will be duplicated: "What you give on interest to increase (your capital) through other people's wealth (see USURY) does not find increase with God; yet what you give in alms and charity (*zakāt,* see ALMSGIVING) with a pure heart (q.v.), seeking the way of God, will be doubled" (Q 30:39; cf. with variations Q 2:245, 261, 265; 4:40; 28:54; 34:37; 57:11, 18, 28; 64:17). By the same token, the punishment of those who commit acts of shamelessness will be doubled: "O wives of the Prophet (q.v.), whosoever of you commits an act of clear shamelessness, her punishment will be doubled. That is easy for God [to do]. But whoever of you is obedient to God and his apostle, and does right, we shall give her reward to her twofold; and we have prepared a rich provision for her" (Q 33:30-1; cf. with variations Q 9:101; 11:20; 17:75; 25:69). Similarly, the unbelievers call for those who led them astray to suffer double punishment: "They will say: 'O lord, give him who has brought this upon us two times more the torment of hell'" (Q 38:61; cf. also Q 7:38; 33:68).

The number two also occurs in numerous legal regulations (see LAW AND THE QURʾĀN). A borrower deficient of mind or infirm or unable to explain requires two male witnesses to draw up a debt contract

(Q 2:282; see DEBT). The same number of witnesses is proscribed when one dictates his last will (Q 5:106-7; see INHERITANCE) as well as in the case of divorce (Q 65:2; see MARRIAGE AND DIVORCE). Divorce is revocable two times after pronouncement; thereafter the husband has either to keep the wives honorably or part with them in a decent manner (Q 2:229). Following divorce, mothers should suckle their babies for a period of two years if both parents agree on this (Q 2:233; cf. also Q 31:14; see WET-NURSING; FOSTERAGE). Two honorable men are required to determine a livestock of equivalent value as atonement for the one who purposely kills game during pilgrimage (q.v.; Q 5:95; see also HUNTING AND FISHING). The share of the male child in inheritance is equivalent to that of two female children (Q 4:11).

The number two also plays a role in some of the qurʾānic parables such as the parable (q.v.) of the two men, one of whom owns two gardens (Q 18:32-44); the story of the two gardens of the Sabaeans (Q 34:15-7; see SHEBA), or the parable of the two men (Q 16:76). Furthermore, we have the episode of the two men who feared God (Q 5:23) as well as those passages where God is said to have made two bodies of water flow side by side *(maraja l-baḥrayn),* one fresh and sweet, the other brine and bitter, and to have placed a barrier (q.v.) between them (cf. Q 25:53; 27:61; 35:12; 55:19 f.; see BARZAKH). The number two also occurs in the creation account given in Q 41:9-12, which differs from the other qurʾānic accounts of the creation of the world in saying that God created the earth in two days rather than the more usual six; the creation of firm mountains and the means of growing food was completed in four days and the creation of the seven heavens in two days.

Contrast and dualism feature obviously throughout Q 55. The frequent use of the dual has baffled commentators and scholars alike, who often argued that the dual forms were demanded by the scheme obtaining there for verse juncture (Nöldeke, *Neue Beiträge,* 10; Horovitz, *Paradies,* 55; Müller, *Untersuchungen,* 132; see LANGUAGE AND STYLE OF THE QURʾĀN; LITERARY STRUCTURES OF THE QURʾĀN). Wansbrough [*QS,* 26-7] argued that there was a "juxtaposition in the canon of two closely related variant traditions, contaminated by recitation in identical contexts or produced from a single tradition by oral transmission." In their respective investigations of Q 55, Neuwirth (Symmetrie und Paarbildung) and Abdel Haleem (Context) have shown that most dual forms are to be explained by the grammatical context of the sūra (see GRAMMAR AND THE QURʾĀN). The addressees of the challenging question of the refrain in the dual, for example, "Which, then, of your lord's bounties do you deny?" — which is repeated thirty-one times throughout the sūra — are humans and jinn (q.v.), introduced in verses 14 and 15 (for the pair of humans and jinn see also Q 7:38; 32:13; 41:25, 29; 46:18; 72:5-6; 114:6). There are only two dual forms that are not to be explained by the immediate context. The use of duals in Q 55:17, "The lord of the two easts and the two wests," refers to the two extreme points on the horizon where the sun rises in the winter and in the summer, and where it sets in the winter and in the summer. As for the dual form "two gardens" (*jannatān,* Q 55:46 and 62), which is also not to be explained by the immediate context, Neuwirth and Abdel Haleem follow the suggestion of al-Farrāʾ (d. 207/822) that the notion of two gardens represents perfect eternal bliss (cf. Farrāʾ, *Maʿānī,* iii, 118).

Verse pairs

Pairs of verses which either together form complete sentences or can be identified on the basis of exact parallelism or strict metrical regularity (see RHYMED PROSE) are the smallest stylistic entities of the Qurʾān (Neuwirth, *Studien*, 176 f.). Examples of pairs of verses characterized by strict parallelism and a metrical regularity are to be found in oaths (q.v.; Q 81:15-6, 17-8; 86:11-2; 100:4-5), in eschatological scenes (Q 52:9-10; 70:8-9; 89:21-2; 101:4-5), in descriptions of the last judgment (Q 89:25-6), and in ethical admonitions (Q 89:17-8, 19-20; see ETHICS AND THE QURʾĀN). Other pairs of verses fulfill only one function such as metrical regularity or strict parallelism. In another type of verse pair the second verse consists of a mere repetition of the first verse: "Surely with hardship there is ease. With hardship there is ease" (Q 94:5-6; cf. also 74:19-20; 75:34-5; 78:4-5; 82:17-8; 102:3-4). Other verse pairs consist of antitheses: "But no, you prefer the life of the world. Though the life to come is better and abiding" (Q 87:16-7; cf. also Q 51:54-5; 75:20-1; 86:13-4; 91:9-10; 95:4-5). Pairs of verses in which the second verse repeats or complements a portion of the first verse are to be classified as synthetic parallelism: "Read in the name of your lord who created, created man from an embryo" (Q 96:1-2; cf. also Q 2:149-50, 184-5; 37:20-1; 106:1-2; see BIOLOGY AS THE CREATION AND STAGES OF LIFE). Numerous pairs of verses that are characterized by synthetic parallelism also show grammatical and semantic parallelism: "Some of them listen to you: But can you make the deaf hear who do not understand a thing? Some of them look toward you: But can you show the blind the way even when they cannot see?" (Q 10:42-3). Parallel style is also found within one verse: "Bad women deserve bad men, and bad men are for bad women; but good women are for good men, and good men for good women" (Q 24:26); "Men should not laugh at other men, for it may be they are better than they; and women should not laugh at other women, for they may perhaps be better than they" (Q 49:11; see LAUGHTER; MOCKERY). Other pairs of verses, although not characterized by antithetic parallelism themselves, constitute antithetic parts of larger groups of verses: "Then he whose scales [of good deeds] shall weigh heavier will have a tranquil life. But he whose scales [of good deeds] are lighter will have the abyss for an abode" (Q 101:6-9). An example of an entire sūra being characterized by parallelism is Q 109: "Say: 'O you disbelievers, I do not worship what you worship, nor do you worship what I worship. Nor am I a worshiper of what you worship, nor are you worshipers of what I worship. To you your way *(dīnukum)*, to me my way *(dīnī)*'" (see RELIGION; WORSHIP; RELIGIOUS PLURALISM AND THE QURʾĀN).

Sūra-pairs

The Indian Qurʾān commentator Amīn Aḥsan Iṣlāḥī (b. 1906), who, like most twentieth-century Muslim thinkers (see EXEGESIS OF THE QURʾĀN: EARLY MODERN AND CONTEMPORARY) considers the sūras as organic unities, proposes that most of the Qurʾān consists of "sūra-pairs" that have closely related themes and complement each other. With this, he further developed the idea of his teacher, Ḥamīd al-Dīn al-Farāhī (1863-1930), who had argued that each sūra has a central theme, called *ʿamūd*, around which the entire sūra revolves. Iṣlāḥī holds that only adjacent sūras may form pairs and, given that the notion of complementarity underlies his concept of sūra-pairs, he identifies several types of complementarity, such as brevity and detail, principle and illustration, different types of evidence, difference in emphasis, premise and conclusion, and unity of opposites. These pairs are then said to constitute seven "sūra groups" (for a critical appraisal, cf. Mir, Iṣlāḥī's concept of sura-pairs).

Sabine Schmidtke

Bibliography
Primary: Bayḍāwī, *Anwār;* Farrā', *Ma'ānī;* A.A. Iṣlāḥī, *Tadabbur-i Qur'ān,* Lahore 1967-80; Zamakhsharī, *Kashshāf.*
Secondary: M.A.S. Abdel Haleem, Context and internal relationships. Keys to qur'ānic exegesis. A study of *Sūrat al-Raḥmān* (Qur'ān chapter 55), in Hawting and Shareef, *Approaches,* 71-98; Fr. Buhl, Über Vergleichungen und Gleichnisse im Qur'ān, in *Acta orientalia* 2 (1924), 1-11; Chr. Daxelmüller, Dualismus, in K. Ranke (ed.), *Enzyklopädie des Märchens. Handwörterbuch zur historischen und vegleichenden Erzählforschung,* Berlin 1975-2003, 11 vols., iii, 903-18; Ṣ. El-Ṣaleḥ, *La vie future selon le Coran,* Paris 1971, 1986[2]; C. Gilliot, Parcours exégétiques. De Ṭabarī à Rāzī (sourate 55), in *Etudes arabes. Analyses-théorie.* [Section d'arabe, Université Paris VIII] (1983), 86-116; J. Horovitz, Das koranische Paradies, in *Scripta universitatis atque bibliothecae Hierosolymitanarum* [Orientalia et Judaica] 1 (1923), 1-16 [article no. VI]; L. Kinberg, *Muḥkamāt* and *mutashābihāt* (Koran 3/7). Implication of a kor'ānic pair of terms in medieval exegesis, in *Arabica* 35 (1988), 143-72; M. Mir, *Coherence in the Qur'ān,* Indianapolis 1987; id., Iṣlāḥī's concept of sura-pairs, in *MW* 73 (1983), 22-32; id., The sūrahs as a unity. A 20th-century development in Qur'ān exegesis, in Hawting and Shareef, *Approaches,* 211-24; F.R. Müller, *Untersuchungen zur Reimprosa im Kor'ān,* Diss., Bonn 1969; A. Neuwirth, Symmetrie und Paarbildung in der koranischen Eschatologie. Philologisch-stilistisches zu *Sūrat ar-Raḥmān,* in *Mélanges de l'Université Saint-Joseph* 50 (1984), 447-80; Th. Nöldeke, *Neue Beiträge zur semitischen Sprachwissenschaft,* Strasburg 1910; S.J. O'Shaughnessy, Three pairs of men in the *Spiritual exercises* and the Qur'ān, in *Philippine studies* 29 (1981), 535-48; R. Paret, 'Illiyyūn, in *EI*[2], iii, 1132-3; V. Vacca/ed., Sidjdjīn, in *EI*[2], ix, 538; A.T. Welch, Ḳur'ān, in *EI*[2], v, 400-29; id., Sūra, in *EI*[2], ix, 885-9; H. Zirker, *Der Koran. Zugänge und Lesarten,* Darmstadt 1999, 148-52.

Palms

see DATE PALM; AGRICULTURE AND VEGETATION

Parable

An illustrative story teaching a lesson. The word for parable, *mathal* (pl. *amthāl,* often used with a form of the verb *ḍaraba/yaḍribu,* "to strike," "to coin"), occurs numerous times in the Qur'ān and evidences a much broader semantic range than does the English word "parable." For Arabic literature in general, *mathal* can be translated by such terms as simile, similitude, example, parable, allegory, proverb, motto, apothegm, aphorism, fable and maxim (see also SIMILES; LITERARY STRUCTURES OF THE QUR'ĀN). This range of meaning for *mathal* also characterizes other Semitic languages, e.g. Hebrew *māshāl;* Aramaic *matlā.* Although *mathal* generally describes any item of discourse featuring one object or event illuminating another (usually) less tangible reality by comparison, some *amthāl* in the Qur'ān do not involve comparison at all (e.g. Q 25:8-9; 36:78). Furthermore, some exegetes have included as *amthāl* stories involving the supernatural and paranormal, such as Adam naming the animals (Q 2:30-4; see ADAM AND EVE; ANIMAL LIFE), a crow instructing Adam's son about the burial of his brother (Q 5:27-31; see CAIN AND ABEL) and Jesus (q.v.) calling down a table (q.v.) from God (Q 5:112-5).

In their complex of meaning, *amthāl* comprise one of the most significant categories of qur'ānic discourse (see FORM AND STRUCTURE OF THE QUR'ĀN; LANGUAGE AND STYLE OF THE QUR'ĀN). A prophetic ḥadīth (tradition) includes *amthāl* among the five main categories of qur'ānic revelation (see REVELATION AND INSPIRATION; ḤADĪTH AND THE QUR'ĀN). A statement attributed to 'Alī b. Abī Ṭālib (q.v.; d. 41/661) says that *sunan,* "patterns of behavior" and *amthāl* comprise a fourth of the Qur'ān (see SUNNA). The legal theorist al-Shāfi'ī (d. 204/820) held that valid legal analysis *(ijtihād)* requires knowledge of the *amthāl* of the Qur'ān (cf. Suyūṭī, *Itqān,* chap. 63, iv, 44; see LAW AND THE QUR'ĀN).

Al-Suyūṭī (d. 911/1505) notes that, for some, *amthāl* serve to clarify and support doctrines and laws by making them concrete through comparison with known events and objects in the everyday life of the receptor (Suyūṭī, *Itqān,* iv, 45). They assist in giving advice, in motivating and restraining behavior, and in reflecting upon and determining truth by bringing to mind something that can be pictured and sensed. The Qurʾān insists, however, that only the knowledgeable will fully grasp their meaning (Q 29:43; see KNOWLEDGE AND LEARNING; SCHOLAR).

If parable in its qurʾānic context can be defined to include similitudes (extended explicit comparisons), example stories (featuring positive or negative characters to be emulated or avoided), parables (metaphors extended in a narrative; see METAPHOR; NARRATIVES) and allegories (featuring a series of related metaphors), then the following *amthāl* can be classified as parables: the fire [at night] (Q 2:17; see FIRE); the downpour (Q 2:19); the deaf, dumb, and blind (Q 2:171; see SEEING AND HEARING; VISION AND BLINDNESS; HEARING AND DEAFNESS); the sprouting seed (Q 2:261); the rock with thin soil (Q 2:264); the hilltop garden (Q 2:265; see GARDENS); the freezing wind (Q 3:117; see AIR AND WIND); the panting dog (q.v.; Q 7:176); the harvested bounty (Q 10:24; see GRACE; BLESSING; SUSTENANCE; AGRICULTURE AND VEGETATION); senses: dead and alive (Q 11:24); the futile reach (Q 13:14); the smelting foam (Q 13:17); the good and the corrupt trees (Q 14:24-7); the slave and the free man (Q 16:75; see SLAVES AND SLAVERY); the mute slave and the just master (Q 16:76; see JUSTICE AND INJUSTICE); the complacent town (Q 16:112; see PUNISHMENT STORIES); the man with two gardens (Q 18:32-44); the water and vegetation (Q 18:45); the light (q.v.) of God (Q 24:35; treated allegorically by exegetes); the desert mirage (Q 24:39); the darkness on the sea (Q 24:40); the spider's (q.v.) house (Q 29:41); the master and his slaves (Q 30:28); stark contrasts (Q 35:19-22; see PAIRS AND PAIRING); the unbelieving town (Q 36:13-29); the slave with several masters (Q 39:29); the verdure that withers (Q 57:20); the upright crops (Q 48:29); the book-laden donkey (Q 62:5); and the blighted garden (Q 68:17-34).

The most significant narrative parables include "the man with two gardens," "the unbelieving town" and "the blighted garden." Each occupies a prominent place in its respective sūra. The first (Q 18:32-44) is clearly identified as a *mathal*. God provides one of two men with two prosperous gardens supplied with abundant water. The fortunate man turns greedy and brags to his apparently landless colleague about his garden's produce, exuding confidence that his future is secure. He fears neither God nor the last judgment (q.v.; see also PIETY; FEAR). The other man, who professes never to have associated anything with God, warns him that his arrogance (q.v.) amounts to unbelief (see BELIEF AND UNBELIEF; GRATITUDE AND INGRATITUDE). Though poor in this world, this good man will receive God's reward in the next (see REWARD AND PUNISHMENT). He warns his wealthy counterpart that his gardens could be destroyed. When the gardens are suddenly destroyed, the hand-wringing proprietor expresses regret that he trusted in anything but God. The moral of the tale becomes explicit in Q 18:46: "Wealth (q.v.) and sons (see CHILDREN) are the adornment of the present world; but the abiding things, the deeds of righteousness (see GOOD DEEDS), are better with God in reward, and better in hope." Al-Suhaylī (d. 581/1185) transmitted a tradition in which the historical details of this story are given, including the names of the two men, Tamlīkhā and Fūṭīs (Suhaylī, *Taʿrīf*, 185).

The "unbelieving town" (Q 36:13-29) also starts out as a clearly labeled *mathal*. The people of a city reject the messengers (see MESSENGER) God sends, saying they are simply citizens like themselves and not prophets (see PROPHETS AND PROPHETHOOD). The people associate an evil omen with the messengers and threaten to stone them (see PORTENTS; FORETELLING). An obedient citizen from the margins of the city comes and affirms the mission of the messengers. He urges the people of the city to obey their message since the messengers serve without reward and have received God's guidance (see OBEDIENCE; ASTRAY). He then rehearses his own good fortune in believing in the one God. He enters paradise (q.v.) praying for his people (see INTERCESSION; PRAYER). The city ends in destruction while the thematic unit containing the parable ends with God's lamentation over the people's rejection of his messengers (Q 36:30-2). Two traditions connect this parable with the city of Antioch and name the three messengers. One tradition makes the messengers disciples of Jesus: Simon, John and Paul (see APOSTLE). It names the obedient citizen Ḥabīb and reports that he was stoned to death (see STONING).

While "the blighted garden" (Q 68:17-34) is not specifically designated a *mathal,* its comparison is explicit: God has tried Muḥammad's opponents as he tried "the people of the garden" (Q 68:17). These people confidently resolve to get up in the morning and harvest their garden, resolving to leave nothing for the poor (see POVERTY AND THE POOR). But when they approach their garden, they find it devastated. A just person among them chides the others for not praising God (see PRAISE; LAUDATION; GLORIFICATION OF GOD). They respond by confessing their guilt and blaming each other. In the end they express hope for a restoration of an even better garden from God. The thematic unit containing the parable concludes with Q 68:34, "Surely for the godfearing shall be the gardens of bliss with their lord." Exegetes have cited reports that the garden actually existed in Yemen (q.v.).

Some typical features of qurʾānic parables follow. The truths they illustrate are usually stated explicitly. Taken largely from the agricultural and commercial worlds of seventh-century Arabia, they tend to be related by exegetes to historical events (see HISTORY AND THE QURʾĀN). Many are based on natural phenomena (see NATURE AS SIGNS). Their themes include justice and communal responsibility (see JUSTICE AND INJUSTICE; COMMUNITY AND SOCIETY IN THE QURʾĀN), the proper stewardship of wealth (see PROPERTY), the protection of the disadvantaged, the fleeting nature of this world's blessings, the certainty of divine judgment, and the importance of acknowledging the oneness and sovereignty of God. God is a prominent player in most of the parables and they frequently stress the oneness of God (see GOD AND HIS ATTRIBUTES) — even when it is not the main point of the comparison.

A.H. Mathias Zahniser

Bibliography

Primary: Ibn Kathīr, *Tafsīr,* ed. Ghunaym; Ibn Qayyim al-Jawziyya, *Amthāl al-Qurʾān,* ed. M.B. ʿAlwān al-ʿAlīlī, Baghdad 1987; Suhaylī, *Taʿrīf;* Suyūṭī, *Itqān,* chap. 63, iv, 44-52 (for *amthāl*); Zarkashī, *Burhān,* Cairo 1957.
Secondary: Bell, *Commentary;* F. Buhl, Über Vergleichungen und Gleichnisse im Qurʾān, in *AO* 59 (1924), 1-11; M.A. Khalaf Allāh, *Al-fann al-qaṣaṣī fī l-Qurʾān,* Cairo 1965; Neuwirth, *Studien;* L.I. Ribinowitz, Parable, in C. Roth and G. Wigoder (eds.), *Encyclopaedia judaica,* 16 vols., Jerusalem 1971-, xiii, 71-7; R. Sellheim, Mathal, in *EI²*, vi, 815-25; M. Sister, Metaphern und Vergleiche im Koran, in *Mitteilungen des Seminars für Orientalische Sprachen zu Berlin.* 2 Abt. *Westasiatische Studien* 34 (1931), 103-54; K.R. Snodgrass, Parable, in J.B. Green, S. McKnight and I.H. Marshall (eds.), *Dictionary of Jesus and the Gospels,* Downers Grove, IL 1992, 592-601; Speyer, *Erzählungen,* 426-38 *(Das Gleichnis im Qoran);* J. al-Subḥānī, *Mafāhīm al-Qurʾān. Tafsīr mawḍūʿī*

lil-Qurʾān. ix. Dirāsat al-amthāl wa-l-aqsām fī l-Qurʾān al-karīm, Qom 2000 (very useful); A.T. Welch, Ḳurʾān, in *EI²*, v, 400-29.

Paraclete

see MUḤAMMAD; NAMES OF THE PROPHET; CHRISTIANS AND CHRISTIANITY; POLEMIC AND POLEMICAL LANGUAGE

Paradise

The abode of the souls of the righteous after their death, heaven; also, the garden of Eden. In the Qurʾān, descriptions of the hereafter appear in relation to the arrival of a day, "the hour" *(al-sāʿa),* "reckoning day" *(yawm al-ḥisāb),* "the day of judgment" *(yawm al-dīn)*, "the last day" *(al-yawm al-ākhir),* or "the day of resurrection" *(yawm al-qiyāma),* in which every individual is resurrected and has to face up to his or her deeds and be judged accordingly (Q 52:21, "... Every man shall be pledged for what he earned..."). The descriptions of heaven and hell, which are very often adduced as opposites, are interwoven with descriptions of deeds that lead to reward or punishment; together they contribute to an understanding of the way divine providence operates: the righteous are rewarded and directed to the good abode, while the evil doers are punished and find themselves tortured in hell. All will happen when "the day" or, "the hour," comes (Q 19:75-6; 79:35-41; and more; see GOOD DEEDS; EVIL DEEDS; REWARD AND PUNISHMENT; LAST JUDGMENT).

The hereafter is portrayed in the Qurʾān as an eternal physical abode (see ETERNITY), and its permanent dwellers are presented as living, sensible human beings. The descriptions use worldly concepts, of the kind that can be readily understood by humans. These, among more general aspects related to Islamic eschatology (q.v.), are partially found in general books about Islam or in the few studies dedicated to the subject. They are widely described in early Islamic sources, either in the form of ḥadīths, dreams or theological and mystical inquiries (see THEOLOGY AND THE QURʾĀN; ṢŪFISM AND THE QURʾĀN). The following survey, however, is limited to the Qurʾān and focuses on the qurʾānic verses that treat the blessed part of the hereafter. Emphasis has been put on philological aspects insofar as the image of the qurʾānic paradise is depicted through its names. The edifying purpose of the heavenly delights is represented by listing the groups that will reside in paradise, the deeds that lead their performers to the ultimate bliss and the pleasures bestowed upon the blessed. Following these lines, no comparison has been made between the Meccan and Medinan sūras (see CHRONOLOGY AND THE QURʾĀN).

The names of the gardens

Janna: In the Qurʾān the term used most frequently for paradise is *janna* (cf. the Hebrew *gan, Gen* 2:8: "And the lord God planted a garden *[gan]* in Eden"; see also Katsh, *Judaism,* 34, especially note 2). The word *janna* means literally garden (q.v.) and Muslim philologists and commentators treated it as an Arabic word, derived from the root *j-n-n,* which means "to cover, to conceal, to protect." Al-Rāghib al-Iṣfahānī (fl. early fifth/eleventh cent.; *Mufradāt,* 204) defines *janna* as any garden, the trees of which hide the soil (a similar explanation is offered by Abū l-Walīd Marwān Ibn Janāḥ [d. 441/1050] in *Sepher Haschoraschim,* 96). Al-Rāghib al-Iṣfahānī further suggests that the word *janna* was chosen to indicate paradise either because it resembles worldly gardens or because its bliss is hidden from people's eyes, as stated in Q 32:17: "No soul knows what comfort is laid up for them secretly, as a recompense for that they were doing" (Arberry, ii, 18). The word *janna* also appears in the Qur'ān with reference to the primordial garden, the dwelling place of Adam (Q 2:35; see ADAM AND EVE) and also in the meaning of a worldly garden (Q 2:264-5).

Although most commonly used (over eighty times), *janna* is not the only word in the Qur'ān that conveys the idea of paradise. Its plural form, *jannāt,* appears over forty times, of which about half occur in combination with other terms: *jannāt ʿadn* (six times), *jannāt al-naʿīm* (seven times), *jannāt firdaws/al-firdaws* (once each), *jannāt/jannat al-maʾwā* (once each). Other words presented in the commentaries as indicating paradise are *dār al-salām* (twice), *dār/jannat al-khuld* (once each), *dār al-muqāma* (once), *maqām amīn* (once), *maqʿad al-ṣidq* (once), *dār al-muttaqīn* (once), *dār al-qarār* (once), *ṭūbā* (once), *ʿilliyyūn/ʿilliyyīn* (once each), *rawḍa/rawḍāt jannāt* (once each), *ḥusnā* (four times), as well as numerous verses in which *al-dār al-ākhira/al-ākhira* is interpreted to mean paradise. This variety of names underlies the numerous traditions presented in the exegetical literature concerning the different facets of paradise.

Firdaws: According to words ascribed to al-Farrāʾ (d. 207/822), *firdaws* is an Arabic word (quoted in Jawharī [d. 398/1007], *Ṣiḥāḥ,* iii, 959; cf. *Tāj al-ʿarūs,* viii, 392). This is, however, an exceptional opinion. The commentaries on Q 18:107 focus on the foreign origin of the name, which means garden in Greek or Syriac (Suyūṭī, *Durr,* iv, 279; *Tāj al-ʿarūs,* viii, 392), and Ibn Janāḥ (*Sepher Haschoraschim,* 419) connects it with the Hebrew *pardes* (see FOREIGN VOCABULARY). Various commentaries also present a prophetic tradition, according to which the *janna* consists of a hundred levels, among which the *firdaws* is the best. God's throne (see THRONE OF GOD) is situated above the *firdaws* and from it spurt the rivers of paradise (Ṭabarī, *Tafsīr,* xvi, 30; Qurṭubī, *Jāmiʿ,* xi, 68; Suyūṭī, *Durr,* iv, 279; and see Zaghlūl, *Mawsūʿa,* iii, 363; iv, 514). Another prophetic tradition states that the *firdaws* consists of four gardens, two made of gold and two of silver (Ṭabarī, *Tafsīr,* xvi, 30; cf. Zaghlūl, *Mawsūʿa,* iv, 502, and the commentaries on Q 55:62 mentioned below).

ʿAdn: The biblical name Eden *(Gen 2)* is treated in Islamic sources as deriving from the root *ʿ-d-n,* which means "to be firmly established and have a long duration" (al-Rāghib al-Iṣfahānī, *Mufradāt,* 553; cf. Qurṭubī, *Jāmiʿ,* x, 396; Ibn Qayyim al-Jawziyya, *Ḥādī l-arwāḥ,* 142; see also the detailed study of *ʿadn* in the meaning of a mineral *[maʿdan]* in Tamari, *Iconotextual studies,* chaps. 1 and 2). The plural form *(jannāt ʿadn)* is used to indicate width (Qurṭubī, *Jāmiʿ,* x, 396). Fakhr al-Dīn al-Rāzī (d. 606/1210; *Tafsīr,* xx, 25, ad Q 16:31) says that *jannāt* denotes the palaces and the gardens, whereas *ʿadn* conveys its eternity. Commentaries on Q 13:23 cite a prophetic tradition proclaiming that in the *janna* there is a palace, the name of which is *ʿadn.* It is surrounded by towers and meadows, and has five thousand (or ten thousand) doors. Each door opens onto five thousand gardens (or twenty-five thousand beautiful women), and only prophets (see PROPHETS AND PROPHETHOOD), righteous people, martyrs (q.v.; *shuhadāʾ;* see also WITNESSING AND TESTIFYING) and upright imāms (see IMĀM) are allowed to enter it (Qurṭubī, *Jāmiʿ,* ix, 311; Suyūṭī, *Durr,* iv, 65). As stated about the *firdaws, ʿadn* is also defined as the center of the *janna* (Qurṭubī, *Jāmiʿ,* ix, 311; x, 396; Suyūṭī, *Durr,* iv, 65; cf. Zaghlūl, *Mawsūʿa,* iv, 502). Other verses that mention *ʿadn* emphasize the luxuries it offers. Q 18:31, for example, reads: "Those — theirs shall be gardens of Eden, underneath which rivers flow; therein they shall be adorned with bracelets of gold (q.v.), and they shall be robed in green garments of silk (q.v.) and brocade, therein reclining upon couches — O, how excellent a reward! and O, how fair a resting place!"

'Illiyyūn/'illiyyīn (Q 83:18-21): Most commentaries deal with the location of the *'illiyyūn,* and combine it with the basic meaning of the root of the word, namely height and glory. Thus *'illiyyūn* appears as lofty degrees surrounded by glory; as the seventh heaven (see HEAVEN AND SKY), where the souls of the believers stay; as the lotus tree in the seventh heaven (see ASCENSION; AGRICULTURE AND VEGETATION); as a green chrysolite tablet containing the deeds of people that hangs beneath the throne; as the most elevated place, the dwellers of which can be seen only as sparkling stars up in the sky; as the residence of the angels (see ANGEL), or the celestial host (Ṭabarsī, *Majma',* xxx, 71; Qurṭubī, *Jāmi',* xix, 262-3). Other terms derived from the same root that indicate high degrees in paradise are *al-darajāt al-'ulā* (Q 20:75) and *janna 'āliya* (Q 69:22; 88:10).

Jannat/Jannāt al-ma'wā, "garden/s of the refuge": the abode of Gabriel (q.v.; Jibrīl) and the angels, or of the souls of the *shuhadā'* (both in Wāḥidī, *Wasīṭ,* iv, 198, ad Q 53:15), or of green birds that contain the souls of the *shuhadā'* (Ibn Qayyim al-Jawziyya, *Ḥādī l-arwāḥ,* 142), or yet, the residing place of the believers in general (Wāḥidī, *Wasīṭ,* iii, 454, ad Q 32:19; see BELIEF AND UNBELIEF). Nothing is said about its location.

Dār al-salām (Q 6:127; 10:25): the abode *(dār)* of everlasting security and soundness *(salāma),* or the *janna (= dār)* of God, *salām* being one of God's names (see GOD AND HIS ATTRIBUTES; PEACE), derived from his immunity from any kind of evil (Wāḥidī, *Wasīṭ,* ii, 322; cf. al-Rāghib al-Iṣfahānī, *Mufradāt,* 421-2; Ibn Qayyim al-Jawziyya, *Ḥādī l-arwāḥ,* 142; see GOOD AND EVIL). Similar is the meaning given to the term *maqām amīn* (Q 44:51), presented as the future dwelling of the righteous, and interpreted to mean the eternal world of security and immunity from fear (q.v.) and death (Muqātil, *Tafsīr,* iii, 825; cf. Ibn Qayyim al-Jawziyya, *Ḥādī l-arwāḥ,* 145-6; see HOUSE, DOMESTIC AND DIVINE).

Dār al-khuld occurs in Q 41:28 in the meaning of hell (see HELL AND HELLFIRE), whereas *jannat al-khuld* is mentioned in Q 25:15 in the meaning of paradise, both aiming at an eternal existence. Muqātil (d. 150/767) gives the same meaning to *dār al-muqāma* (Q 35:35). He defines the latter as *dār al-khulūd,* the place where people stay forever (Muqātil, *Tafsīr,* iii, 558; cf. Ibn Qayyim al-Jawziyya, *Ḥādī l-arwāḥ,* 141).

Maq'ad al-ṣidq (Q 54:55), the place of goodness promised to the righteous: Ibn Qayyim al-Jawziyya (d. 751/1350; *Ḥādī l-arwāḥ,* 146-7) considers it, as well as the term *qadam al-ṣidq* (Q 10:2), as one of the names of paradise.

Jannāt/jannat na'īm/al-na'īm: The name conveys the variety of pleasures *(ni'am)* offered in paradise (Ibn Qayyim al-Jawziyya, *Ḥādī l-arwāḥ,* 145; see BLESSING). The commentaries that deal with the term concentrate mainly on the issue of compensation. Fakhr al-Dīn al-Rāzī (*Tafsīr,* xxii, 49, ad Q 5:65) deals with two kinds of happiness (see JOY AND MISERY). One is the removal of sins (see SIN, MAJOR AND MINOR; REPENTANCE AND PENANCE) and the other is the bestowal of reward. *Na'īm,* in al-Rāzī's opinion, is to be understood as the latter. In several cases *na'īm* is identified with *firdaws* (for example, Wāḥidī, *Wasīṭ,* iii, 356, ad Q 26:85).

Dār al-ākhira appears mostly in contrast with the present world *(al-dunyā).* Q 40:39 juxtaposes the transience of the present world with the stability of the hereafter *(al-ākhira),* and defines the latter as *dār al-qarār.* Q 16:30-1 mentions *dār al-ākhira* together with *dār al-muttaqīn* and *jannāt 'adn,* and Q 29:64 defines it as the abode of life (q.v.; *ḥayawān*), meaning either the abode of eternal life, or the eternal abode (Wāḥidī, *Wasīṭ*, iii, 425-6; cf. Ibn Qayyim al-Jawziyya, *Ḥādī l-arwāḥ*, 144).

Ṭūbā (Q 13:29): A common tradition, cited by most commentators, states that *ṭūbā* is a tree in *janna* (Wāḥidī, *Wasīṭ*, iii, 15, 16; Jawharī, *Ṣiḥāḥ*, i, 173; cf. Zaghlūl, *Mawsūʿa*, iii, 360). An attempt to show a foreign origin may explain the statement that *ṭūbā* means *janna* in the Ethiopian/Indian language (Wāḥidī, *Wasīṭ*, iii, 16; Suyūṭī, *Durr*, iv, 67). Other explanations, however, treat *ṭūbā* as an Arabic word, meaning good, the eternal ultimate stage in *janna* (al-Rāghib al-Iṣfahānī, *Mufradāt*, 528; *Tāj al-ʿarūs*, ii, 189; for the usage of *ṭūbā* in Persian poetry, see Schimmel, Celestial garden, 18-9).

(Al-)ḥusnā is often interpreted to mean *janna* (for example Wāḥidī, *Wasīṭ*, ii, 104, 544; iii, 13, 68, ad Q 4:95; 10:26; 13:18; 16:62), but also as the ultimate good and as the vision of God (*Tāj al-ʿarūs*, xvii, 142; see FACE OF GOD).

The number of the gardens

Q 55:46 mentions two gardens awaiting those who fear God. The commentators offer several ways to distinguish one garden from another. Al-Qurṭubī (d. 671/1272; *Jāmiʿ*, xvii, 177) cites the following explanations: one garden was created especially for the individual, the other was inherited; one garden is for the destined, the other for his wives (see MARRIAGE AND DIVORCE); one garden is his home, the other his garden; one has the lower palaces, the other the upper ones. Abū Ḥayyān (d. 745/1344; *Baḥr*, x, 67) adduces similar ideas, among which he suggests that one garden is for those who obey God (see OBEDIENCE), the other for those who refrain from sin; one is for the jinn (q.v.), the other for people. Al-Ṭabarsī (d. 548/1154; *Majmaʿ*, vi, 101) mentions one garden inside the palace and another outside. Al-Suyūṭī (d. 911/1505; *Durr*, vi, 163) presents a prophetic tradition, according to which both gardens reach the width of a hundred years walking distance (cf. Q 3:133, which compares the width of the *janna* to that of heaven and earth; for Jewish parallels see Katsh, *Judaism*, 214), and both gardens have fruitful trees, flowing rivers, and wonderful fragrances. Al-Wāḥidī (d. 468/1076; *Wasīṭ*, iv, 225) cites al-Ḍaḥḥāk as saying that one garden is for the believers who worshiped God secretly and the other for those who worshiped him openly. Verse 62 of the same sūra (Q 55) also mentions two gardens. Most commentaries refer to these two as additional gardens, assuming altogether the existence of four gardens: two gardens of trees and two of plants and seeds; two gardens for the "foremost in the race" *(sābiqūn)* and "those brought near" *(al-muqarrabūn)*, two for the "people of the right hand" (*aṣḥāb al-yamīn;* see LEFT HAND AND RIGHT HAND); the first two (v 46) are *ʿadn* and *naʿīm*, the other pair (v 62) the *firdaws* and *dār al-maʾwā;* the first two are of gold and silver, the others are of sapphire and emerald (Qurṭubī, *Jāmiʿ*, xvii, 183-4; cf. Ṭabarī, *Tafsīr*, xvii, 89-91; Suyūṭī, *Durr*, vi, 161-3; for a stylistic analysis of these verses, see Nöldeke, Koran, 45; Schimmel, Celestial garden, 17-8; Abdel Haleem, Context, 89-93).

The inhabitants of paradise

Sūrat al-Wāqiʿa ("The Event," Q 56), which describes the day of resurrection (q.v.), mentions three groups of people as the future inhabitants of paradise: (1) "the people of the right hand" (*aṣḥāb al-maymana*, Q 56:8), who are more commonly referred to as *aṣḥāb al-yamīn* (Q 56:27, 38, 90, 91; cf. *The Babylonian Talmud*, Tractate Shabat, 63a); (2) "the foremost in the race" (*al-sābiqūn*, Q 56:10); and (3) "those brought near" (*al-muqarrabūn*, Q 56:11).

Aṣḥāb al-yamīn/al-maymana: Q 56:28-38

give a picturesque description of the rewards awaiting the *aṣḥāb al-yamīn:* "Mid thornless lote-trees and serried acacias, and spreading shade and outpoured waters, and fruits abounding unfailing, unforbidden, and upraised couches, perfectly we formed them, perfect, and we made them spotless virgins, chastely amorous, like of age for the companions of the right hand." The commentaries explain their name in three ways: those who, on the day of judgment, will receive the record of their deeds in their right hand (cf. Q 17:71; 69:19; 84:7; see BOOK), those who are strong, and those whose belief is illuminated by the light of God (all in Rāzī, *Tafsīr,* xxix, 143, 163).

Al-sābiqūn: Q 9:100 reads: "And the outstrippers *(sābiqūn),* the first of the emigrants and the helpers (see EMIGRANTS AND HELPERS), and those who followed them in good doing, God will be well pleased with them and they are well pleased with him; and he has prepared for them gardens underneath which rivers flow therein to dwell forever and ever." The common identifications of the *sābiqūn,* adduced in the commentaries, are of two kinds: those who lived prior to the arrival of Muḥammad (Rāzī, *Tafsīr,* xxix, 149) and those who contributed to Islam in its first stages. Among the latter, the following are mentioned: those who prayed toward both *qibla*s (see QIBLA), those who participated in Badr (q.v.), those who took part in Ḥudaybiya (q.v.) or, more generally, those who lived during Muḥammad's lifetime (all in Wāḥidī, *Wasīt,* ii, 520). Fakhr al-Dīn al-Rāzī, who prefers to identify the *sābiqūn* as those who performed the emigration (q.v.) with Muḥammad, states that the *sābiqūn* are the most elevated in paradise (Rāzī, *Tafsīr,* xvi, 172, ad Q 9:100). In his commentary on Q 56:10-1, al-Rāzī (*Tafsīr,* xxix, 147) defines the *sābiqūn* as the most exalted among the *muqarrabūn,* higher than *aṣḥāb al-yamīn,* the most elevated among the *muttaqūn* (ibid., 148), and those who will reach paradise without judgment (ibid., 144).

Muqarrabūn: in Q 3:45 Jesus (q.v.; ʿĪsā) is considered one of the *muqarrabūn.* In Q 4:172 the angels are the *muqarrabūn,* while in Q 56:10-26 the *muqarrabūn* are identified as *sābiqūn,* and the description of the rewards bestowed upon them seems the most highly detailed in the Qurʾān: "In the gardens of delight ... upon close-wrought couches reclining upon them, set face to face, immortal youths going round about them with goblets, and ewers, and a cup from a spring (see CUPS AND VESSELS), no brows throbbing, no intoxication (see INTOXICANTS; WINE), and such fruits as they shall choose, and such flesh of fowl as they desire, and wide-eyes houris (q.v.) as the likeness of hidden pearls, a recompense for that they labored. Therein they shall hear no idle talk (see GOSSIP), no cause of sin, only the saying peace."

Other verses promise heavenly delights to additional groups: Two groups often mentioned (over fifty times each), are (1) "the godfearing" *(al-muttaqūn/alladhīna ttaqū)* and (2) "those who believed and performed righteous deeds" (*alladhīna āmanū wa-ʿamilū l-ṣāliḥāt;* for detailed descriptions of the bliss bestowed upon each of the groups see Q 44:51-7 and Q 2:25 respectively). Also mentioned are "the inhabitants of paradise" (*aṣḥāb al-janna,* over ten times; see e.g. Q 2:82; 10:26), and the "pious" (*abrār,* six times; see PIETY).

Deeds that lead their performers to paradise

The general term "righteous deeds" *(ṣāliḥāt)* is mentioned about sixty times in the Qurʾān, always as a guarantee to entry into paradise. Q 4:122-4 read: "But those that believe, and do deeds of righteousness, them we shall admit to gardens underneath which rivers flow, therein dwelling for ever and ever ... and whosoever does deeds of righteousness, be it male or female (see GENDER), believing — they shall enter paradise ..." (cf. Q 3:195, and see also the description of the *mu'minūn* in Q 8:2-4). Q 7:157-8, among other verses, emphasize the belief in God and his messenger as a guarantee of prosperity. Q 2:112 restricts good fate to "those who submit their will to God," namely Muslims, and implicitly excludes Jews and Christians from being potential dwellers in paradise (see JEWS AND JUDAISM; CHRISTIANS AND CHRISTIANITY). Q 13:20-3 and Q 70:22-35 mention a list of conditions, the fulfillment of which is necessary to gain entry into paradise. Other verses focus on particular deeds that ensure reaching paradise, such as praying (Q 2:277; 4:162; 27:3; see PRAYER), almsgiving (q.v.; Q 3:134; 27:3), belief in the last day (Q 58:22; 65:2), fear of the last day (Q 76:10), obedience (Q 3:132; 4:13), gratitude (Q 3:144; see GRATITUDE AND INGRATITUDE), patience (Q 76:12; see TRUST AND PATIENCE; TRIAL), restraint of rage and forgiving the evil of other people (Q 3:134; see ANGER; FORGIVENESS), fulfillment of vows (Q 76:7; see VOW; BREAKING TRUSTS AND CONTRACTS; CONTRACTS AND ALLIANCES), support of the needy (Q 76:8; see POVERTY AND THE POOR), participation in the emigration (*hijra*, Q 3:195), in Ḥudaybiya (cf. Q 48:18), and in jihād (q.v.; i.e. Q 2:218; 3:195; 4:95; 8:74; 9:20; 61:11-2).

Rewards in paradise

The bliss bestowed upon the dwellers of paradise may be divided into two types: sensual pleasures and spiritual ones.

Spiritual pleasures: Here one can find general expressions, such as God's pleasure (*riḍwān*, Q 3:15; for the personification of *riḍwān* in Persian poetry to mean the heavenly doorkeeper of paradise, see Schimmel, Celestial garden, 16-8; see PERSIAN LITERATURE AND THE QUR'ĀN), forgiveness (Q 3:136), acquittal of evil deeds (Q 3:195; 48:5), divine protection from the evil day (cf. Q 76:11), praise of God (see LAUDATION; PRAISE) and greetings of peace (Q 10:9-11; cf. 56:26). Q 10:26 promises *al-ḥusnā* and *ziyāda* "to the gooddoers" *(lilladhīna aḥsanū)*. *Al-ḥusnā* is interpreted to mean paradise and *ziyāda* is interpreted to mean looking at God's face (al-Rāghib al-Iṣfahānī, *Mufradāt*, 386; Wāḥidī, *Wasīṭ*, ii, 344-5; Suyūṭī, *Durr*, iii, 331-2). The ability to look at the face of the lord can be drawn from additional verses. Q 83:15 proclaims that those who do not believe will be "veiled from their lord." In the commentaries on this verse several traditions are adduced to indicate that if veiling is a sign of divine anger, unveiling, namely the permission to see God, is a sign of divine contentment (Wāḥidī, *Wasīṭ*, iv, 446; see VEIL). A more straightforward verse is Q 75:22-3: "Upon that day (resurrection day) faces shall be radiant, gazing upon their lord." (The issue of permission to see God became controversial and was widely discussed in theological and mystical circles; see Ibn Qayyim al-Jawziyya, *Ḥādī l-arwāḥ*, 402-77; Ājurī, *Taṣdīq;* Gimaret, Ru'yat Allāh; Baljon, 'To seek the face of God,' 254-66; Schimmel, *Deciphering*, 238.) Further aspects of spiritual pleasures can be drawn from the verses that deal with the fate that awaits the martyrs *(shuhadā'):* "Count not those who were slain in God's way as dead (see PATH OR WAY; EXPEDITIONS AND BATTLES; FIGHTING), but rather living with their lord, by him provided, rejoicing in the bounty that God has given them, and joyful in those who remain behind and have not joined them, because no fear shall be on them, neither shall they sorrow, joyful in blessing and bounty from God...."

Sensual pleasures: The most frequently mentioned reward (over fifty times) focuses on rivers flowing beneath gardens. Q 47:15 describes four rivers flowing in paradise:

"… Rivers of water unstaling, rivers of milk (q.v.) unchanging in flavor, and rivers of wine — a delight to the drinkers, rivers, too, of honey (q.v.) purified. …" (Schimmel, Celestial garden, 15, points out that "The idea of the four rivers which flow through Paradise may have helped late architects to conceive the canals as they flow through the gardens of Iran and Mughal India, for it was said by the court poets of this time that every part of the royal garden was in some way a similitude of Paradise." See also Tamari, *Iconotextual studies,* chap. 3.)

Thoroughly studied, but also criticized in non-Islamic circles, is the topic of the women granted the faithful as a celestial reward in the qurʾānic paradise (see the bibliographical references mentioned in the notes of Wendell, Denizens of paradise). Compared to the carnal, sensuous, highly detailed descriptions of women awaiting the righteous adduced in ḥadīth literature, the qurʾānic text is restrained (see ḤADĪTH AND THE QURʾĀN). It mentions purified women (*azwāj muṭahhara,* Q 2:25; 3:15; 4:57), "wide-eyed houris" (*[bi-]ḥūr ʿīn,* Q 44:54; 52:20; 56:22; but see the exegesis of these verses for the various understandings of the phrase), maidens with swelling breasts, equal in age (*kawāʿib atrāban,* Q 78:33) and amorous virgins equal in age (*abkār ʿuruban atrāban,* Q 56:36-7).

Other rewards that await one in heaven are young boys serving wine (*wildān mukhalladūn,* Q 56:17; 76:19; *ghilmān,* Q 52:24), sofas to lean against (*surur,* Q 15:47; 37:44; 43:34; 52:20; 56:15; 88:13; *furush,* Q 55:54; 56:34; *al-arāʾik,* Q 18:31; 36:56; 76:13; *rafraf,* Q 55:76), green garments of silk and brocade (Q 18:31; 76:21), gold/silver bracelets (Q 18:31; 22:23; 35:33; 76:21), fruit (*thamara,* Q 2:25; *fākiha,* Q 36:57; 38:51; 43:73; 44:55; 52:22; 55:11, 52, 68; 56:20, 32; 80:31; *fawākih,* Q 37:42; 77:42, especially dates and grapes; see DATE PALM), wine that does not intoxicate (*khamr,* Q 47:15; *kaʾs,* Q 37:45; 52:23; 56:18; 76:17; 78:34; *sharāb,* Q 38:51; 76:21), vessels of silver and goblets of crystal (Q 76:15), plates/trays of gold (Q 43:71), pleasant weather (Q 76:13), shade (Q 4:57; 36:56; 56:30; 76:14; 77:41), provision (*rizq,* Q 37:41; 65:11; cf. 40:40), palaces (Q 25:10), and whatever the souls desire and in which the eyes delight (Q 43:71; cf. 50:35). Such pleasures and those like them are often defined as "[the great] triumph" (*fawz,* Q 4:13; 5:119; 9:72, 89, 100; 45:30; 48:5; 57:12; 61:12; 64:9; 85:11), mostly with emphasis on their eternal existence.

These heavenly delights became an issue that has often been used for polemical purposes against Islam. These descriptions "angered theologians for centuries … the large-eyed virgins, the luscious fruits and drinks, the green couches and the like seemed too worldly to most non-Muslim critics" (Schimmel, *Deciphering,* 238, especially note 44). The following words, ascribed to the so-called ʿAbd al-Masīḥ al-Kindī (probably third/ninth cent.), may give an idea about the nature of the non-Muslim reaction: "All these [descriptions of paradise in the Qurʾān] suit only stupid, ignorant and simple-minded people, who are inexperienced and unfamiliar with reading texts and understanding old traditions, and who are just a rabble of rough Bedouins accustomed to eating desert lizards and chameleons" (cited in Sadan, Identity and inimitability, 338, from al-Kindī's book, which, "transcribed by Jews into Hebrew characters and translated from Arabic into Latin, taught the Spanish Christians how to fight Islam in the most vigorous and harsh way"; see also notes 12 and 39).

Conclusion

Although comparison between the Meccan and Medinan sūras appears as one of the central features in the examination of the Qurʾān, as it relates to paradisiacal descriptions, such a comparison seems superfluous. The components that comprise the descriptions of paradise of both periods are similar, and even though the issue of the last day is less prominent in the sūras of Medina (q.v.), one common concept underlies all the descriptions. This is the idea of a direct proportion between deeds and rewards that furnishes the eschatological status of the individual. It can be considered the *leitmotiv* of all the celestial descriptions found in the Qurʾān and the key to understanding the spirit of Islam.

Leah Kinberg

Bibliography

Primary (Although each of the ḥadīth collections has a chapter of paradisiacal descriptions, always with references to qurʾānic verses, there are also collections dedicated solely to the subject; the following list includes only these specialized collections.): ʿAbd al-Mālik b. Ḥabīb (d. 238/853), *Waṣf al-firdaws*, Beirut 1987 (a ḥadīth collection dedicated solely to paradise); Abū Ḥātim al-Rāzī, Aḥmad b. Ḥamdān, *Kitāb al-Zīna fī l-kalimāt al-islāmiyya al-ʿarabiyya*, ed. Ḥ.b.F. al-Hamdānī, 2 vols., Cairo 1957-8, ii, 196-205; Abū Nuʿaym al-Iṣfahānī, *Waṣf al-janna*, Beirut 1988 (a ḥadīth collection dedicated solely to paradise); al-Ājurī, Abū Bakr (d. 360/970), *al-Taṣdīq bi-l-naẓar ilā llāh taʿālā fī l-ākhira*, Riyadh 1985; Aṭafayyish, Muḥammad b. Yūsuf, *al-Junna fī waṣf al-janna*, Oman 1985 (a ḥadīth collection dedicated solely to paradise); Bukhārī, *Ṣaḥīḥ*, ed. Krehl, ii, 314-7; iv, 239-45, 247-50, trans. O. Houdas and W. Marçais, *El-Bokhâri. Les Traditions islamiques*, 4 vols., 1903-14; ii, 306-13, 315-8, 438-43; al-Ghazālī, Abū Ḥāmid Muḥammad, *al-Durra al-fākhira*, ed. and trans. L. Gautier, *La perle précieuse* (ad-dourra al-fâkhira) *de Ghazālī. Traité d'eschatologie musulmane*, Geneva 1878, repr. Amsterdam 1974; id., *Iḥyāʾ ʿulūm al-dīn*, 4 vols., Būlāq 1289/1872, repr. Cairo 1933, iv, 455-67 (Book XL); trans. T.J. Winter, *Al-Ghazālī. The remembrance of death and the afterlife.* Kitāb Dhikr al-mawt wa-mā baʿdahu. *Book XL of The revival of the religious sciences,* Iḥyāʾ ʿulūm al-dīn, Cambridge, UK 1989, 232-61; Ibn Abī al-Dunyā (d. 281/894), *Waṣf al-janna wa-mā aʿadda llāh min al-naʿīm*, Amman 1997 (a ḥadīth collection dedicated solely to paradise); Ibn Janāḥ, *Sepher Haschoraschim*, Berlin 1896; Ibn Qayyim al-Jawziyya, *Ḥādī l-arwāḥ ilā bilād al-afrāḥ aw waṣf al-janna*, Beirut 1991; al-Jawharī, Ismāʿīl b. Ḥammād, *al-Ṣiḥāḥ*, Beirut 1956; Muqātil, *Tafsīr;* Muslim, *Ṣaḥīḥ*, iv, 2174-2206; Qurṭubī, *Jāmiʿ;* al-Rāghib al-Iṣfahānī, *Mufradāt*, Beirut 1992; Rāzī, *Tafsīr;* Suyūṭī, *Durr;* Ṭabarī, *Tafsīr;* Ṭabarsī, *Majmaʿ; Tāj al-ʿarūs;* Wāḥidī, *Wasīṭ;* M. Wolff, *Muhammedanische Eschatologie. ʿAbd al-Rahim b. Ahmad al-Qadi, Kitab ahwal al-qiyama*, Leipzig 1872, 105-15 (Arabic text), 185-205 (Ger. trans.); Abū Hājir Zaghlūl (ed.), *Mawsūʿat aṭrāf al-ḥadīth*, Beirut 1989.

Secondary: M.A.S. Abdel Haleem, Context and internal relationships. Keys to qur'anic exegesis. A study of Sūrat al-Raḥmān (Qurʾān chapter 55), in Hawting and Shareef, *Approaches*, 71-98; Arberry; *The Babylonian Talmud*, Jerusalem 1979, Tractate *Shabat;* M.S. Baljon, 'To seek the face of God' in Koran and ḥadīth, in *AO* 21 (1953), 254-66; J.E. Bencheikh, *Le voyage nocturne de Mahomet*, Paris 1988, 81-119; van Ess, *TG*, iv, 543-61 (on eschatology); L. Gardet, Djanna, in *EI²*, ii, 447-52, and the bibliography there; D. Gimaret, Ruʾyat Allāh, in *EI²*, viii, 649; J. Horovitz, Das koranische Paradies, in *Scripta universitatis atque bibliothecae Hierosolymitanarum* [Orientalia et Judaica] 1 (1923), article no. VI [pp. 1-16]; A.I. Katsh, *Judaism and the Koran*, New York 1954 (repr. 1962); L. Kinberg, Interaction between this world and the afterworld in early Islamic traditions, in *Oriens* 29/30 (1986), 285-308 (for bibliography concerning eschatological themes in the Qurʾān see note 2; for the issue of life after death, notes 3 and 5); T. Nöldeke, The Koran, in Ibn Warraq (ed.), *The origins of the Koran*, Amherst, NY 1998, 36-63; F. Rahman, *Major themes of the Qurʾān*, Chicago 1980; J.B. Rüling, *Beiträge zur Eschatologie des Islam*, Inaugural-Dissertation, Leipzig 1895, 32-40 (qurʾānic discussion), 64-8 (extra-qurʾānic discussion); J. Sadan, Identity and inimitability. Contexts of inter-religious polemics and solidarity in medieval Spain, in the light of two passages by Moše Ibn ʿEzra and Yaʿaqov Ben Elʿazar, in *IOS* 16 (1994), 325-47; A. Schimmel, The celestial garden in Islam, in E.B. Macdougall and R. Ettinghausen (eds.), *The Islamic garden*, Washington, DC 1976, 13-39; id., *Deciphering the signs of God*, Albany, NY 1994; H. Stieglecker, *Die Glaubenslehren des Islam*, Munich 1959-62, 768-73; S. Tamari, *Iconotextual studies in the Muslim vision of paradise*, Wiesbaden/Ramat Gan 1999; C. Wendell, The denizens of paradise, in *Humaniora islamica* 2 (1974), 29-59 (notes 3, 9, 13 and 16 mention some of the most prominent studies of the first half of the twentieth century that deal with the qurʾānic paradise, such as those of J. Horovitz, E. Berthels, D. Künstlinger, and E. Beck).

Parchment see WRITING AND WRITING MATERIALS; SHEETS; SCROLLS

Pardon see FORGIVENESS

Parents

Those who beget or bring forth children. Terms designating "parents" in the Qurʾān are *wālidāni* and *abawāni,* respectively the dual form of *wālid,* "father, one who begets a child" (the passive *al-mawlūd lahu* indicates "to whom the child is borne"; *wālida,* "mother, one who brings forth a child," appears in both the singular and the plural; *umm/ummahāt* also designate "mother"), and the dual form of *ab,* "father" (the singular means "nurturer," see Robertson-Smith, *Kinship and marriage,* 142; Lane, 10; in certain verses the plural *ābāʾ* means "ancestors").

Natural aspects of parenthood are particularly identified throughout the Qurʾān with maternal functions, pregnancy, giving birth (q.v.), breastfeeding and weaning (e.g. Q 16:78; 39:6; 53:32; 58:2; see also BIOLOGY AS THE CREATION AND STAGES OF LIFE). Q 2:232-3 calls upon divorced mothers to fulfill their natural role as nurses whereas the role of fathers is limited to supplying the nursing mother and the nursling with economic support (see LACTATION; MAINTENANCE AND UPKEEP). Moreover, maternal emotions of love (q.v.) and solicitude find emphatic expression in the qurʾānic story of Moses (q.v.; Q 28:7-13; 20:38-40; cf. Stowasser, *Women,* 57-8; Giladi, *Infants,* 14-5). In two verses, Q 7:150 and 20:94, Aaron (q.v.; Hārūn) calls his brother *"Mūsā ibn umma,"* thus attributing him to their mother ("to implore his mercy," cf. Ṭabarī, *Tafsīr;* Zamakhsharī, *Kashshāf;* Ibn Kathīr, *Tafsīr,* ad loc.) rather than to their father as could have been expected in a patrilineal system (see e.g. Q 8:75; 33:6 where blood relatives are referred to as *ūlū l-arḥām, arḥām* being the plural of *raḥim,* "womb"; see also PATRIARCHY; FAMILY). When, in Q 31:14 and 46:15, Muslims are commanded to honor both parents (see below), it is the (biological) role of the mother that is emphasized ("His mother beneath him in weakness upon weakness"; cf. Pickthall, *Koran*; Ibn Kathīr, *Tafsīr,* ad loc.), implying that it serves best to justify or explain the commandment.

As reproduction is (implicitly) presented as the goal of marriage (Q 4:1; 7:189; see MARRIAGE AND DIVORCE; SEX AND SEXUALITY; CHILDREN), both parents are depicted as bringing up their children (Q 17:24,... *kamā rabbayānī ṣaghīran*); fathers are described as having intimate knowledge of their sons (Q 6:20) and seeking comfort from their descendants as well as from their wives (Q 25:74).

Several verses from the second Meccan period onwards (see e.g. Q 4:36; 6:151; 17:23-4; also Q 31:13-4; cf. Ibn Kathīr, *Tafsīr,* ad Q 4:36: "For God made parents the reason for the servants to come into existence.") contain a recurring formula in which the commandment "to be good to one's parents" *(wa-bi-l-wālidayni iḥsānan)* is presented as second in importance only to the commandment "to worship no god but Allāh" (cf. *Lev* 19:2-4; Q 2:83; on the apparent influence of the Hebrew decalogue on the Qurʾān in this regard, see Roberts, *Social laws,* 46-9; see also IDOLATRY AND IDOLATERS; POLYTHEISM AND ATHEISM; SCRIPTURE AND THE QURʾĀN). Nevertheless, in cases of conflict, that is, when one's parents "strive hard with you that you may associate with me that of which you have no knowledge" (Q 29:8), and submission to God prevails, the duty to obey parents becomes void (see also Q 31:13-5 from the third Meccan period [Nöldeke] or early Medinan [Bell]). This is exemplified particularly through qurʾānic references from the second Meccan period onwards to the conflict between Abraham (q.v.; Ibrāhīm) and his people, including his pagan father (e.g. Q 9:114; 19:41-8; 37:83-98). Q 21:51-70 describes a dramatic clash in which Abraham uses the expression of exasperation *uffin lakum* ("fie on you," Q 21:67) which, according to Q 17:23, Muslims are never to direct at their parents (cf. Q 46:17). In several verses (e.g. Q 14:41; 26:86) Abraham is depicted as praying for his father, but unable to evoke divine response (Q 60:4). Noah (q.v.; Nūḥ) prays similarly, to no avail, for his sinful son (Q 11:45-6).

In contrast to the tension between him and his (polytheist) father, Abraham's relationship with his own (believing) son is harmonious. Abraham is depicted as asking God to give him "[one] of the righteous" *(mina l-ṣāliḥīna)* and is indeed granted a "mild-tempered" *(ḥalīm)* son who, being "one of the enduring ones" *(mina l-ṣābirīna;* see TRUST AND PATIENCE), is ready to obey God's command and be sacrificed for his sake (Q 37:100-7; see OBEDIENCE; ISAAC; ISHMAEL).

Thus, Muslims are guided to prefer loyalty to God above the fulfillment of filial duties, "to be witnesses for God, even though it be against yourselves, or your parents and relatives..." (Q 4:135). In any case, they are warned, "neither their relations nor their [polytheist; cf. *Jalālayn,* ad loc.] children will profit them on the day of resurrection" (the Medinan Q 60:3; cf. Ibn Kathīr, *Tafsīr,* ad loc.; see also the Meccan Q 70:11-2; 80:34-5). On the other hand, "those who believe and whose progeny have followed them in belief" are assured that God will "cause their progeny to be united with them [in paradise; cf. *Jalālayn,* ad loc.]" (Q 52:21; for a detailed discussion see Ṭabarī, *Tafsīr;* ad loc.; also Q 13:23; 40:8; and Motzki, Das Kind, 399 n. 42; see also REWARD AND PUNISHMENT; PARADISE; BELIEF AND UNBELIEF).

Attitudes of parents towards their children are also reflected in the Qurʾān, some of whom are strongly criticized from the point of view of monotheist morality (see CHILDREN). Although sons (and property) are acknowledged as signs of divine benevolence (see GRACE; BLESSING), they are also regarded as temptation for the believers (Motzki, Das Kind, 398). For example, there is a legend in which one of God's servants, al-Khiḍr (cf. Ṭabarī, *Tafsīr,* ad Q 18:74), kills a youth: "Have you taken an innocent life, not in return for a life?" Moses asks, adding: "Surely you have committed a thing unheard of" (Q 18:74). The unnamed servant of God then explains the act by saying that "his [i.e. the youth's] parents were believers and we feared that he might impose upon them arrogance (q.v.) and unbelief" (Q 18:80; cf. Ibn Kathīr, *Tafsīr,* ad loc.: "Their love for him might make them follow him in disbelief;" see KHAḌIR/KHIḌR).

In Mecca (q.v.), the Qurʾān had frowned on help based on ties of kinship (see O'Shaughnessy, Qurʾānic view, 37-8), but in the Medinan period, when blood ties and the duties they impose are again emphasized (see BLOOD AND BLOOD CLOT), a few verses were dedicated to parent-descendant relationships from the viewpoint of mutual socioeconomic responsibilities (see COMMUNITY AND SOCIETY IN THE QURʾĀN; ETHICS AND THE QURʾĀN; ECONOMICS). Reciprocal inheritance rules find a relatively detailed formulation in Q 2:180 and 4:7, 11 (see also INHERITANCE). In Q 2:215 Muslims are encouraged to support their parents economically, as well as relatives and such members of the community as are in need, e.g. "orphans (q.v.), the poor (see POVERTY AND THE POOR) and the follower of the way (see JOURNEY)."

Prohibitions of marriage between, among others, males and their own mothers (as well as their non-maternal wet nurses, see LACTATION; WET NURSING), and between males and their own daughters (as well as their own wives' daughters, see FOSTERAGE) are enumerated in Q 4:23 (see PROHIBITED DEGREES). Q 33:6, wherein the Prophet's wives (see WIVES OF THE PROPHET) are referred to as the "mothers" of the believers, was understood to mean that they were not allowed to remarry after Muḥammad's death (*wa-azwājuhu ummahātuhum* = *wa-ḥurmat azwājihi — ḥurmat ummahātihim ʿalayhim,* cf. Ṭabarī, *Tafsīr,* ad loc.). See also GUARDIANSHIP.

Avner Giladi

Bibliography

Primary: Ibn Kathīr, *Tafsīr,* Riyadh 2000 (abr.); *Jalālayn;* Ṭabarī, *Tafsīr;* Zamakhsharī, *Kashshāf.*

Secondary: M.H. Benkheira, Donner le sein c'est *comme* donner le jour. La doctrine de l'allaitement dans le sunnisme médiéval, in *SI* 92 (2001), 5-52; A. Giladi, *Infants, parents and wet nurses. Medieval Islamic views on breastfeeding and their social implications,* Leiden 1999; H. Motzki, Das Kind und seine Sozialisation in der islamischen Familie des Mittelalters, in J. Martin and A. Nitschke (eds.), *Zur Sozialgeschichte der Kindheit,* Munich 1986, 391-441; Th. J. O'Shaughnessy, The qurʾānic view of youth and old age, in *ZDMG* 141 (1991), 33-51; R. Roberts, *The social laws of the Qurʾān,* London 1925; W. Robertson Smith, *Kinship and marriage in early Arabia,* London 1907; B. Stowasser, *Women in the Qurʾān, tradition and interpretation,* Oxford 1994.

Parody of the Qurʾān

Literary composition attempting to imitate the language and style of the Qurʾān. Parodies of the Qurʾān (sing. *muʿāraḍat al-Qurʾān*) have been known in Islamic history, but no authentic and complete texts of them have come down to us. What Islamic sources have recorded of them in snippets shows imitation that is obviously weak, grossly ludicrous and vastly inferior to the Qurʾān in language, style and content (see LANGUAGE AND STYLE OF THE QURʾĀN; FORM AND STRUCTURE OF THE QURʾĀN; LITERARY STRUCTURES OF THE QURʾĀN), making the parodies themselves the object of ridicule.

When the qurʾānic challenge to disbelievers to produce a discourse like it (Q 52:33-4) or to fabricate ten sūras (q.v.; Q 11:13) or even one sūra (Q 10:38) like it was not met, the Qurʾān affirmed that, even if humans and jinn (q.v.) combined their efforts, they would be unable to produce a similar Qurʾān (Q 17:88; see PROVOCATION). Islamic doctrine holds that the Qurʾān is God's speech (q.v.) and, as such, it is characterized by inimitability (q.v.; *iʿjāz*) and is thus the prophet Muḥammad's miracle (q.v.; *muʿjiza*) and evidence of his prophecy (see PROPHETS AND PROPHETHOOD; WORD OF GOD; BOOK; CREATEDNESS OF THE QURʾĀN).

In Muḥammad's lifetime, the most famous parodist of the Qurʾān was Musaylima (q.v.). Known in Muslim writings as "the liar" *(al-kadhdhāb),* he claimed prophecy in Yamāma and held authority in eastern Arabia until he was killed in 11/633 in the war against apostates (see APOSTASY) waged by the first caliph (q.v.), Abū Bakr. As recorded in al-Ṭabarī (d. 310/923) and other Muslim sources, Musaylima's parody consisted of rhyming prose verses of unequal lengths (see RHYMED PROSE), in which oaths (q.v.) were often made, reference was made to the wonders of life and nature (see NATURE AS SIGNS), a God called Allāh and al-Raḥmān was invoked (see GOD AND HIS ATTRIBUTES) and very few regulations were posited (see VIRTUES AND VICES, COMMANDING AND FORBIDDING). The parody has a hollow ring to it, even when echoing a qurʾānic turn of phrase, because it lacks a sublime subject. It has been suggested, however, that the Islamic tradition has handed down "weak" examples of Musaylima's prowess in order to make him look ridiculous. This argument contends that the Islamic tradition would not have termed him the "Liar" and expended the energy to make him the object of ridicule if he had been incapable of producing good verses or good rhymed prose in the style of the soothsayers, that could reasonably be compared to the Qur᾽ān (cf. Gilliot, Contraintes, 24-5).

Ibn al-Muqaffaʿ (executed in 139/756), whose acclaimed prose writings and translations attest to his command of Arabic, is said to have tried to imitate the Qur᾽ān but apparently abandoned the attempt, acknowledging its difficulty (cf. van Ess, *TG*, ii, 35-6). Fragments of his polemic against Islam and the Qur᾽ān are quoted in the refutation of the Zaydī Imām, al-Qāsim b. Ibrāhīm (d. 246/860) and citations from the parody of the Qur᾽ān attributed to him are quoted by the Zaydī Imām, Aḥmad b. al-Ḥusayn al-Mu᾽ayyad-bi-llāh (d. 411/1020).

Another early attempt to imitate the Qur᾽ān is attributed to Nashī l-Akbar (d. 239/906), a Murji᾽ite who was close to the Muʿtazilīs (q.v.): he is said to have died while trying to write an imitation of the Qur᾽ān (cf. van Ess, *TG*, iv, 146). Yet another early parodist was the renowned poet Abū l-Ṭayyib Aḥmad b. al-Ḥusayn (d. 354/965), known as al-Mutanabbī, "the would-be prophet." He parodied the Qur᾽ān in his youth and led some beguiled Syrian Bedouins (see BEDOUIN) in a revolt that ended in his imprisonment in 322/933 and his recantation. In adult life, he often dismissed that experience as a youthful escapade.

The skeptical, blind poet Abū l-ʿAlā᾽ al-Maʿarrī (d. 449/1057) was falsely accused of parodying the Qur᾽ān in his *al-Fuṣūl wa-l-ghāyāt,* a work which praises God and offers moral exhortations. Only volume one of this book is extant, displaying a masterful style in rhyming prose disposed in chapters *(fuṣūl),* with paragraphs that have endings *(ghāyāt)* with a regular rhyme. In this work's rhyme scheme, these paragraphs all end in one letter of the alphabet, which is different for each chapter; additionally, each paragraph has sentences that rhyme or partly rhyme in other letters. This elaborate rhyming scheme, however, is not that of the Qur᾽ān.

It is interesting to note that we have attestations of Muslims admitting the possibility of compositions better than the Qur᾽ān up through the third/ninth century. Ibn al-Rawāndī (d. ca. 298/910-1) wrote in his *Kitāb al-Zumurrud,* "In the words of Aktham al-Ṣayfī, we find better than: "Lo! We have given you al-kawthar [Q 108:1]" (cf. van Ess, *TG,* vi, 472-3; Gilliot, L'embarras). In the traditional Islamic perspective, Q 108 is considered a great marvel (cf. Gilliot, L'embarras; see MARVELS). Further, the Persian Muʿtazilī Murdār (d. 226/821) refused the inimitability of the Qur᾽ān (van Ess, *TG,* iii, 608) and said that "people are able to bring something similar to this Qur᾽ān, or even more eloquent than it" (cf. van Ess, *TG,* v, 33, text 12 for the Arabic; see also Abdul Aleem, 'Ijazu'l-Qur'an for the names of some poets who denied the linguistic inimitability of the Qur᾽ān, or who criticized it and tried to surpass it in composition and style).

The attempt at imitating the Qur᾽ān has continued up until the present day. In 1995, unknown individuals anonymously offered four "sūras" on the Internet to meet the Qur᾽ān's challenge but, after Muslim protest, their website was closed by the server in the United States, although it continues in the United Kingdom.

Issa J. Boullata

Bibliography
Primary: al-Maʿarrī, Abū l-ʿAlāʾ Aḥmad b. ʿAbdallāh b. Sulaymān, *al-Fuṣūl wa-l-ghāyāt fī tamjīd Allāh wa-l-mawāʿiẓ*, ed. M.Ḥ. Zanātī, Beirut [1938]; Ṭabarī, *Taʾrīkh*, ed. Ibrāhīm (1979[4]), iii, 272-3, 283-4, 300.
Secondary: Abdul Aleem, ʿIjazu'l-Qur'an, in *IC* 7 (1923), 64-82, 215-33 (see esp. 228-33 for parodies and critics of the Qurʾān); J. van Ess, Some fragments of the *Muʿāraḍat al-Qurʾān* attributed to Ibn al-Muqaffaʿ, in W. al-Qāḍī (ed.), *Studia arabica et islamica. Festschrift for Iḥsān ʿAbbās*, Beirut 1981, 151-63; id., *TG;* C. Gilliot, L'embarras d'un exégète musulman face à un palimpseste. Māturīdī et la sourate de l'Abondance (*al-Kawṯar*, sourate 108). Avec une note savante sur le commentaire coranique d'Ibn al-Naqīb (m. 698/1298), in *Festschrift G. Endress*, Peeters (forthcoming); id., Muḥammad, le Coran et les "contraintes de l'histoire," in Wild, *Text*, 3-26; Goldziher, *MS*, trans. C.R. Barber and S.M. Stern, ii, 363-5; http://members.aol.com/suralikeit/(as of 2004 this site has an index page from which the [now five] "sūras" may be accessed separately, under the following titles: Surat ad-Du'a [new]; Surat al-Iman; Surat at-Tajassud; Surat al-Muslimoon; Surat al-Wasaya).

Parties and Factions

Divisions within groups. The Qurʾān has a relatively rich and varied, but not precisely differentiated, vocabulary which refers to parties or factions within larger communities or groups (see COMMUNITY AND SOCIETY IN THE QURʾĀN). Although the words and phrases concerned are sometimes used in the Qurʾān in an apparently neutral way, for example, with reference to groups among the believers themselves (see BELIEF AND UNBELIEF), they are often employed there in a derogatory sense or in polemic against opponents. The opponents are accused of dividing their religion (q.v.) into factions, and a contrast is often made with the actual or ideal unity of the believers (see RELIGIOUS PLURALISM AND THE QURʾĀN). The value of the united community *(umma)* of the believers is stressed; in some passages believers are urged not to take intimates or friends among outsiders (e.g. Q 3:118; 5:51; see FRIENDS AND FRIENDSHIP) and marriage relationships with outsiders are regulated (see MARRIAGE AND DIVORCE; SOCIAL RELATIONS).

We do not receive the impression that the parties and factions that are referred to exist in any formal or organized sense and their identity is usually not specified precisely. For instance, Q 3:23 mentions a faction *(farīq)* among "those who have been given a part *(naṣīb)* of the book (q.v.)," whereas two other passages which use this latter phrase (Q 4:44, 51) lump them all together as "idolaters" (see IDOLATRY AND IDOLATERS) and followers of error (q.v.). In other passages factions are alleged to exist among opponents designated generally as "idolaters" (*mushrikūn;* see also POLYTHEISM AND ATHEISM) or "hypocrites" (*munāfiqūn;* see HYPOCRITES AND HYPOCRISY). Although the Qurʾān does contain the names of groups such as the "Emigrants" *(muhājirūn)*, "Helpers" (*anṣār*, see EMIGRANTS AND HELPERS), and "believers" *(muʾminūn)*, they are not generally referred to using the vocabulary of party and faction.

Among the words indicative of divisions and distinctions, the most obvious are *ḥizb* (pl. *aḥzāb*, which Nöldeke postulated as a loan word from Ethiopic; see FOREIGN VOCABULARY), *ṭāʾifa*, *shīʿa* (pl. *shiyaʿ*) and derivatives of the root *f-r-q*. All can be understood with the general meaning of "party" or "faction." Other words occur less frequently and sometimes their exact meaning is unclear: for example, the plural form *zubur* in Q 23:53 is sometimes interpreted as "sects" or "factions" *(firaq, ṭawāʾif)* but how the word, which is understood as the plural form of *zabūr*, comes to mean that is a problem (see PSALMS). In some passages the different words appear to be used interchangeably and randomly — *ḥizb* being a variant of *ṭāʾifa*, *zubur* of *shiyaʿ*, etc.

Ḥizb in its singular, dual and plural forms appears nineteen times. The party of God *(ḥizb Allāh)* is victorious or successful (Q 5:56; 58:22) while the party of Satan (*ḥizb al-shayṭān*, see DEVIL) is lost (Q 58:19). The single *umma* of the believers is contrasted with the splits among their opponents who have made their affair into *zubur*, each *ḥizb* rejoicing in what it has (Q 23:52-3). Similarly, Q 30:31-2 appeals to the believers not to be like the opponents called *mushrikūn* who divided their religion and became parties *(shiyaʿ)*, each *ḥizb* rejoicing in what it has. Q 38:13 identifies the *aḥzāb (ūlāʾika l-aḥzāb)* as a series of peoples who had rejected the prophets sent to them (see PROPHETS AND PROPHETHOOD), and the context of "the day of the *aḥzāb*" in Q 40:30 suggests the same reference although it is frequently understood as an allusion to the "battle of the ditch" in the year 5/627 (cf. Paret, *Kommentar*, 233, wherein he posits that in Q 38:11-3 and 40:5, 30-3, the expression "*aḥzāb*" is used in the Ethiopic sense of "pagans"; see also PEOPLE OF THE DITCH).

Sūra 33, Sūrat al-Aḥzāb ("The Clans"), is explained in the commentaries and *sīra* reports (material on the life of the Prophet; see SĪRA AND THE QURʾĀN) as containing a number of allusions to the events associated with the battle of the ditch when various parties *(aḥzāb)* among the opponents of the Prophet, are said to have united to facilitate an attack on the Muslims in Medina (q.v.). The Quraysh (q.v.) of Mecca (q.v.), the Arab tribe of Ghaṭafān, and the Jewish tribe of Qurayẓa (q.v.) within Medina are especially mentioned (see TRIBES AND CLANS; WAR; POLITICS AND THE QURʾĀN). Q 33:20 is often understood as referring to some hypocrites *(munāfiqūn)* who tried to persuade the followers of the Prophet that the *aḥzāb* had not really retreated and that they would come again, while Q 33:22 reflects the believers' recognition that the coming of the *aḥzāb* was simply what the Prophet had promised them.

Shīʿa (q.v.) and *shiyaʿ* occur eight times. It sometimes seems to be a fairly neutral expression: Moses (q.v.) had a *shīʿa* (Q 28:15) and there was a *shīʿa* of Noah (q.v.; Q 37:83). On the other hand, the believers are contrasted with opponents who have "divided their religion and become parties" (Q 6:159 and 30:32: *farraqū dīnahum wa-kānū shiyaʿan;* in the latter passage the opponents are referred to as *mushrikūn*, cf. Q 30:31).

Similarly, derivatives of *f-r-q*, which occur frequently, sometimes appear with reference to the believers. The one occurrence of *firqa*, which in Islamic literature is a common term for a "sect," refers to a unit among the believers: "the believers should not all go out together to fight; of every *firqa* of them a *ṭāʾifa* should remain behind to acquire religious knowledge" (Q 9:122; see KNOWLEDGE AND LEARNING; FIGHTING). Q 9:117, too, refers to God's having turned in forgiveness to *(tāba ʿalā)* "the Prophet and the Emigrants and Helpers who followed him in the hour of difficulty *(sāʿat al-ʿusra)* after the hearts of a *farīq* among them had almost turned away" (see HEART; FORGIVENESS). There are many passages containing formations from *f-r-q*, however, which call upon the believers to avoid division and disagreement in religion and which show those as characteristics of the opponents (e.g. Q 6:159 and Q 30:32 cited above; also Q 3:103, 105; 6:153; 42:13; see OPPOSITION TO MUḤAMMAD).

Ṭāʾifa and its dual forms appear twenty-three times. It may be a more neutral expression, used more or less randomly to refer to groups or parties among the People of the Book (q.v.; Q 3:69, 72), the believers (Q 3:154; 4:102, etc.), the hypocrites (4:81, 113; 9:66; 33:13, etc.) and others, in the past and the present.

Stress on the divided nature of the opponents, therefore, may be seen as part of the polemical language characteristic of the Qurʾān. In non-qurʾānic and post-qurʾānic Arabic, too, *shīʿa, firqa,* and *ṭāʾifa* often reflect the negative implications of fragmentation and division contrasted with the positive value of unity *(umma, jamāʿa).* They are the product of *fitna* (strife within the community) and in modern Arabic *al-ṭāʾifiyya* is a common translation of "sectarianism." It may be that this echoes Sunnī values in particular, since among the Shīʿīs one does find *al-shīʿa* and *al-ṭāʾifa* (the latter also among the Ṣūfīs), sometimes qualified by an epithet such as *al-muḥaqqiqa,* used in expressions of self-designation (see SHĪʿISM AND THE QURʾĀN; ṢŪFISM AND THE QURʾĀN). In the reports about early Islam, too, the word *shīʿa* is used quite neutrally to indicate the supporters of a particular individual: not only was there a *shīʿa* of ʿAlī (see ʿALĪ B. ABĪ ṬĀLIB), but also of ʿUthmān (q.v.), Yazīd and others. As for *hizb* (party), the Khārijīs (q.v.) referred to their non-Khārijī opponents as the parties (*aḥzāb;* on their derivation of this negative connotation of *aḥzāb* from the Qurʾān itself, see van Ess, *TG,* ii, 462; see also POLEMIC AND POLEMICAL LANGUAGE; OPPOSITION TO MUḤAMMAD). The usage of *ḥizb* (party) has been influenced not only by the qurʾānic *ḥizb Allāh* (which has become the self-designation of the modern Shīʿī activist group, Hizbollah) but also by modern concepts of political parties.

The typical allusiveness of the qurʾānic style (see LANGUAGE AND STYLE OF THE QURʾĀN) combines with its use of polemic to make identification of the groups concerned, specification of their characteristics and even confirmation of their existence, difficult. Polemic involves distortion and exaggeration of the opponents' positions and standard polemical accusations, such as idolatry, following error, distortion of scripture (see SCRIPTURE AND THE QURʾĀN; FORGERY), and inventing lies about God (see LIE), are transferable between different opponents. Furthermore, the terminology is not specific to the contemporaries of the Qurʾān. As is evident from the examples cited above, words like *aḥzāb* and *shīʿa* are used in the Qurʾān with reference to groups in the past as well as the present and the same is true of designations like *muhājirūn* ("emigrants") and *anṣār* ("helpers"). In the Qurʾān, Lot (q.v.) describes himself as "a *muhājir* to my lord" (q.v.; Q 29:26) and the apostles of Jesus (q.v.) call themselves "*anṣār* of God" (Q 3:52; 61:14; see APOSTLE). "Hypocrite," the usual understanding of *munāfiq,* is a common term in monotheist polemic (e.g. *Matt* 23 passim).

In the commentaries on the Qurʾān (see EXEGESIS OF THE QURʾĀN: CLASSICAL AND MEDIEVAL) and other traditional Islamic literature such as the material on the life of the Prophet (*sīra* material), nevertheless, the parties and factions alluded to in the Qurʾān are identified in the context of Muḥammad's career. For example, the *aḥzāb,* as already indicated, are associated with the battle of the ditch, while the Emigrants and Helpers are identified as groups among the supporters of the Prophet.

The frequent occurrence and relative richness of the relevant vocabulary, the several accusations that opponents have divided their religion, the emphasis on the unity of the believers, and the measures designed to distinguish the believers from outsiders may reflect the appearance of the qur'ānic materials in a situation of intense religious fragmentation and division. To the extent that parties and factions really existed beyond the realm of polemic, they could be understood as indicative of a religious society prone to the generation of numerous groups with the character of nascent sects. John Wansbrough *(Sectarian milieu)* identified the proliferation of barely distinguishable confessional groups as characteristic of the sectarian milieu out of which he considered Islam to have emerged to become eventually a major distinct tradition within monotheism.

In certain historical situations the tendency towards internal divisions and splits, which is a characteristic of the monotheistic (and perhaps other) religious traditions, may be intensified. The situation in Palestine around the beginning of the Christian era perhaps offers a parallel and the tendency to fragmentation, observable in certain modern right- and left-wing political movements, may also be relevant. Social and political circumstances as well as the character of the religious movement within which the divisions are generated are important for understanding the phenomenon of sectarianism.

The literary description in works other than the Qur'ān — for example works of qur'ānic commentary and prophetic biography — of the society in which the Prophet lived does not explicitly support the thesis of the sectarian milieu. To the extent that groups within it are identified, they are classified by their relationship and attitude to the Prophet *(muhājirūn, anṣār, munāfiqūn)* or as monotheists (Muslims, Jews, ḥanīfs; see ḤANĪF; JEWS AND JUDAISM; see also CHRISTIANS AND CHRISTIANITY) contrasted to idolaters *(mushrikūn)*. With some exceptions, we do not generally find in this literature reports about the Prophet arguing fine points of monotheist doctrine or behavior with groups in his environment or those groups being associated with one or more identifying doctrines or practices. This is in contrast with the way in which parties like the Pharisees and Sadducees appear in the gospels and other sources from the early Christian period.

In contrast, the Qur'ān itself contains numerous references to, and statements about, typical monotheist issues such as the validity of intercession (q.v.), belief in the last day (see LAST JUDGMENT; ESCHATOLOGY; APOCALYPSE), the status of Jesus (see TRINITY; ANTHROPOMORPHISM; POLYTHEISM AND ATHEISM) and questions of ritual purity (q.v.). This material can be seen as indicative of a situation in which these issues were topics of argument and polemic between parties and factions with common concerns and concepts. While we should be careful about transforming the qur'ānic polemic too readily into statements of fact, its language and ideas do seem consistent with a society particularly subject to sectarian tensions.

Gerald R. Hawting

Bibliography

Primary: Ibn Isḥāq-Guillaume; Ṭabarī, *Tafsīr* (on the verses referred to in the article); Wāqidī, *Maghāzī*.
Secondary: van Ess, TG; Horovitz, KU, 19; D.B. MacDonald, Ḥizb, in EI², iii, 513-4; Th. Nöldeke, *Neue Beiträge zur semitischen Sprachwissenschaft*, Strassburg 1990, 59 n. 8; Th. F. O'Dea, Sects and cults, in *International encyclopedia of the social sciences*, 17 vols., New York 1968, xiv, 130-6; Paret, *Kommentar*, 233-4 (on Q 11:17); R. al-Sayyid, *Mafāhīm al-jamā'āt fī l-islām*, Beirut 1984, 25-44 (for the qur'ānic terminology, see esp. 30-1, *shī'a, fāriq, ṭā'ifa;* 34-5, 39, *ḥizb/aḥzāb*); J. Wansbrough, *The sectarian milieu*, Oxford 1978; W.M. Watt, *Muhammad at Medina*, Oxford 1956.

Partisan

see FRIENDS AND FRIENDSHIP; PARTIES AND FACTIONS

Partition

see VEIL; BARRIER; BARZAKH

Partners [of God] see POLYTHEISM AND ATHEISM

Party of God see PARTIES AND FACTIONS; FRIENDS AND FRIENDSHIP

Party of Satan see PARTIES AND FACTIONS; ENEMIES

Path or Way

That along which one passes to reach a destination. The concept of the path or way (of God) — expressed by derivatives of several roots *(sabīl, ṣirāṭ, ṭarīq, minhāj)* — pervades the Qurʾān and is related to several basic notions of Islam such as right guidance (*hudā* or *hidāya;* see ASTRAY), the religious law (*sharīʿa;* see LAW AND THE QURʾĀN) and jihād (q.v.). When the Qurʾān uses this last notion (which connotes "struggle" and is often rendered as "holy war") in conjunction with the concept of the path or way of God, it is expressed exclusively by the term *sabīl* and only in a set phrase, "in the way of God" *(fī sabīli llāhi)*. This phrase — with or without *"jihād"* — occurs only in Medinan sūras (q.v.; see also CHRONOLOGY AND THE QURʾĀN) and comprises about one-third of the occurrences of *sabīl*. The analysis of the contexts related to jihād shows that all the basic aspects of the concept of "holy war" had already been laid down in the earlier qurʾānic passages (see also FIGHTING; WAR).

The frequency of the above-mentioned terms varies greatly — *sabīl*, 176 occurrences; *ṣirāṭ*, forty-five; *ṭarīq* (or *ṭarīqa*), nine; *minhāj*, once — but, as a rule, they are treated as synonyms by the Arabic lexicographers and commentators who explain the meaning of any given one of these terms through another. The only term that expresses virtually nothing but the notion of "the way of God" is *ṣirāṭ* (the sole exception being Q 7:86), while only five occurrences of *ṭarīq* are related to the notion in question (see Q 4:168, 169; 46:30; 72:16, *al-ṭarīqa*). About thirty occurrences of *sabīl* are unrelated to this notion, the most frequent phrase being "a man of the road" *(ibn al-sabīl),* a traveler who should be helped (see JOURNEY).

Several points are worth mentioning about this group of terms. First, only one occurrence of *sabīl* (Q 80:20) can be positively attributed to the early Meccan period and it has nothing to do with the notion of "the way of God." All other occurrences of such terms are divided equally between the later Meccan and Medinan sūras. Second, two of them *(sabīl, minhāj)* belong to common Semitic stock and some scholars suggest that they are loan words from Aramaic or Hebrew (see FOREIGN VOCABULARY). A third term *(ṣirāṭ)* is an established loan word from Latin (i.e. *strata*). Third, three of them (*sabīl, ṣirāṭ* and *minhāj*) are the only qurʾānic utilizations of the corresponding root letters, an uncommon event in Arabic (which generally uses multiple derivatives of the triliteral roots), and *ṭarīq (ṭarīqa),* too, very nearly falls into this category. All three observations point in one direction, namely, that the notion of the way, or path, is a late addition to the vocabulary of the Qurʾān (see LANGUAGE AND STYLE OF THE QURʾĀN; FORM AND STRUCTURE OF THE QURʾĀN), most probably a replica of the analogous biblical and post-biblical concept (see SCRIPTURE AND THE QURʾĀN).

Let us now follow more closely the process of the formation of the concept of "the way of God" in the qurʾānic message. The first stage is Meccan. If we take the majority of the Meccan contexts, the notion in question appears within the concept of the prophetic mission as the realization of the lord's (q.v.) guidance of his creatures. The phrase "the way of God" has several lexical manifestations (e.g. *ṣirāṭ Allāh,* Q 42:53; *sabīl Allāh,* passim; *ṣirāṭ rabbika,* "the way of your lord," Q 6:126). Additionally, one finds "the ways of your lord" (*subul rabbika,* Q 16:69) and "the way of the mighty, the glorious one" (*ṣirāṭ al-ʿazīzi l-ḥamīdi,* Q 14:1; 34:6). It is also used with personal pronouns, as in "your way" (*ṣirāṭaka,* Q 7:16; *sabīlika,* Q 10:88; *sabīlaka,* Q 40:7), "his way" (*sabīlihi,* Q 6:117, 153; 14:30), or "my way" (*ṣirāṭī,* Q 6:153; *sabīlī,* Q 12:108).

There are several aspects of the notion introduced in the later Meccan sūras. The "way of God" is the result of the lord's guidance (cf. Q 14:12; 16:15; 28:22; 29:69; 76:3). It is the "way of righteousness" (*sabīl al-rushd* or *rashād;* cf. Q 7:148; 40:38) and also the "straight" or "even" path. Of the two synonymous epithets, the first *(mustaqīm)* is more frequent in the Qurʾān, being used either with *ṣirāṭ* (twenty-one occurrences; cf. especially the contexts of Q 6:126, 153; 7:16) or with *ṭarīq* (Q 46:30). The second epithet is used either in the attributive phrase *ṣirāṭ sawiyy* (cf. Q 19:43; 20:135), or in the genitive phrase: *sawāʾ al-ṣirāṭ* (Q 38:22) or *sawāʾ al-sabīl* (Q 28:22; 60:1). Being originally "the way of God," it connotes the path of the true believers, of the righteous or the blessed, an idea which is also expressed in several other basically synonymous ways (Q 1:7; 31:15). All these themes are continued in the Medinan sūras as well, the only addition being that "the way of God" is equated with the sunna (q.v.) and the law (Q 5:48), which accords with the general character of these sūras, in which legal prescriptions are given (see FORBIDDEN; BOUNDARIES AND PRECEPTS; PROHIBITED DEGREES; ETHICS AND THE QURʾĀN).

The set of basic qurʾānic notions is characterized by a kind of conceptual dualism, in which almost every positive term has its negative counterpart (see PAIRS AND PAIRING). This feature applies also to "the way of God," which is contrasted to the other way, the way of the *ṭāghūt,* usually interpreted by Muslim commentators as Satan (*shayṭān;* see DEVIL). This latter way is opposed to the way of God (cf. Q 4:76; see ENEMIES), and is the way to hell (cf. Q 37:23; 4:169; see HELL AND HELLFIRE). It is the path of error (q.v.; *ghayy*) opposed to the path of righteousness (as in Q 7:146: "If they see the path of righteousness, they shall not choose it for [their] path; but if they see the path of error, they shall choose it for [their] path, because they disbelieved our signs *[āyāt]*"; see BELIEF AND UNBELIEF), as well as the way of the ignorant (Q 10:89; see IGNORANCE), of the wrongdoers (Q 7:142; see EVIL DEEDS) and of the wicked (Q 6:55; see SIN, MAJOR AND MINOR). It is noteworthy that a number of contexts show the interplay of the singular and plural forms, an interplay which embodies the opposition of the single straight path and many corrupt ways (see, for instance, Q 6:153: "And that this my path is straight *(ṣirāṭ mustaqīman);* so follow it, and follow not [other] paths *(subul)* lest they scatter you from his path" (*ʿan sabīlihi;* see RELIGIOUS PLURALISM AND THE QURʾĀN).

Yet, the concept of the two opposing ways, one of God and the other of Satan, one leading to paradise (q.v.) and the other to hell, or of the one right path contrasted with many wrong ways, is second in the Qurʾān to another concept, that of the right way and deviating from it, or, in other words, losing it *(ḍalāla).* This latter concept is devoid of even the slightest trace of dualism. This deviation is the result of one and the same will, that of the lord, who guides *(yahdī)* whom he pleases and leads astray *(yuḍillu)* whom he pleases. At the same time, unbelievers and Satan can block *(ṣadda)* people from the right path. The exact understanding of the reasons which govern human choice between the right path and the wrong path rests on one's interpretation of the complicated problem of the relation between predestination and human free will in the Qurʾān (see FREEDOM AND PREDESTINATION).

The second stage is Medinan. The new idea generated in the Medinan sūras is the notion of fighting or struggling "in the way of God" *(fī sabīli llāhi),* for God's cause or the idea of holy war *(jihād).* In literary Arabic the phrase *fī sabīli,* "in the way of..." (which has a parallel in post-biblical Hebrew *bi-shᵉbīl*), acquires the same technical prepositional meaning as "for the sake of, because of" (cf. Jastrow, *Dictionary,* s.v.). It is not accidental, then, that in the Meccan sūras the preposition, *"fī,"* is used — instead of the phrase *"fī sabīli"* (see Q 29:69: "Those who fight/struggle *[jāhadū]* for our cause *[fīnā],* we will surely guide *[nahdī]* to our paths *[subulanā]*"). Nonetheless, as it is used in the Qurʾān almost exclusively in the above expression, it has become inseparable from the concept of holy war in Muslim tradition. The only exception relates to the conceptual dualism mentioned above, as it juxtaposes holy war with its opposite (see Q 4:76: "The believers fight *[yuqātilūna]* in the way of God and the unbelievers fight in the way of the *ṭāghūt.* Fight therefore against the friends of Satan *[shayṭān];* surely the guile of Satan is ever feeble.").

The phrase "in the way of God"/"in his way" occurs in the Qurʾān forty-nine times. The verbs most frequently used with it connote "fighting": *qātala* (fifteen occurrences, e.g. Q 2:190; 3:13; 4:75; 9:111; 61:4; 73:20) as well as *jāhada* and its derivatives (fourteen occurrences, e.g. Q 2:218; 5:35; 8:74; 9:20; 61:11). It is worth mentioning that both substantives derived from this latter root, *jihād* and *mujāhid,* which are so full of symbolic meaning in subsequent Muslim tradition, are already used in the Qurʾān in this context (see for the former Q 9:24; 60:1; for the latter Q 4:95).

The qurʾānic usage stresses the readiness to give one's own life for the cause of God as one of the most important aspects of the concept of jihād and assures that those who are killed "in the way of God" go straight to paradise (see Q 2:154: "And say not of those slain *[man yuqtalu]* in the way of God, 'They are dead'; rather they are living, but you are not aware"; cf. also Q 3:157, 169, 195; 22:58; 47:4; see MARTYRS).

At the same time, the qurʾānic message specifies another possible way of participating in jihād, namely, by giving money and everything one possesses for the cause of God; the verb *anfaqa* "to spend" occurs seven times in this context (Q 2:195, 261, 262; 8:60; 9:34; 47:38; 57:10). There is even a synthetic formula coined in the Medinan sūras which joins the two ways of jihād in a unified concept, "to fight in the way of God by one's wealth and one's life" (*jāhada fī sabīli llāhi bi-amwālihi wa-nafsihi;* cf. Q 8:72; 9:41, 81; 49:15).

These are the qurʾānic formulations of the concept of jihād, from which Muslim scholars developed an impressive theory of holy war that was, in some variants of Muslim doctrine, subsequently raised to the status of the sixth "pillar" *(rukn)* of Islam, next to the famous five (*shahāda* [see WITNESS TO FAITH], prayer [q.v.], fasting [q.v.], almsgiving [q.v.] and pilgrimage [q.v.]; see also FAITH).

Summing up, the concept of "the way of God" has two distinct meanings in the Qurʾān, that of obedience (q.v.) to the revealed law which governs all aspects of the life of a true believer and that of fighting and giving one's wealth and life for the cause of God which assures martyrs direct access to paradise without waiting for the day of resurrection (q.v.) and without passing through the purgatorial stage of the "suffering of the grave" (*ʿadhāb al-qabr*, see LAST JUDGMENT; DEATH AND THE DEAD; ESCHATOLOGY).

Dmitry V. Frolov

Bibliography
Primary (For the classical Muslim exegesis of the concept, see the commentaries noted below to the passages cited in the article. The chapters on jihād in the major collections of ḥadīth, in expositions of Islamic law and in treatises on Muslim doctrine also give a sense of the emergence of the concept of "struggle" in the "way of God."): ʿAbd al-Bāqī (s.vv. for further details on the usage and meaning of the terms); Abū Ḥātim al-Rāzī, Aḥmad b. Ḥamdān, *Kitāb al-Zīna fī l-kalimāt al-islāmiyya al-ʿarabiyya*, 2 vols. in 1, ed. Ḥ.b.F. al-Hamdānī, Cairo 1957-8, ii, 215-8; Bayhaqī, *Shuʿab al-īmān*, 7 vols., Beirut 1990, iv, 3-64 (for jihād in Muslim doctrine); Bukhārī, *Ṣaḥīḥ*, ed. Krehl, ii, 198-270; Fr. trans. O. Houdas and W. Marçais, *El-Bokhâri, Les traditions islamiques*, 4 vols., Paris 1903-14, 281-379; Eng. trans. M.M. Khan, 9 vols., New Delhi 1984[5], iv, 34-276 (chapter on jihād; this collection of ḥadīth, available in many editions, is an English translation with parallel Arabic text); Ibn Kathīr, *Tafsīr*; *Jalālayn*; *Lisān al-ʿArab* (s.vv. for further details on the usage and meaning of the terms); Muslim, *Ṣaḥīḥ* (see the chapter on jihād); Shāfiʿī, *al-Umm*, Beirut 1988, 8 vols. in 4, 159-69 (for jihād in Islamic law); Suyūṭī, *Durr*; Ṭabarī, *Tafsīr*; Zamakhsharī, *Kashshāf*.
Secondary: C.E. Bosworth, Sabīl. 1. As a religious concept, in *EI²*, viii, 679; M. Jastrow, *Dictionary of the targumim. Talmud Babli and Yerushalmi and midrashic literature*, 2 vols., New York 1950, ii, 1514; M. Khadduri, *War and peace in the law of Islam*, Baltimore 1955; Ch. A. Mawlawi, *A critical exposition of popular jihad*, Calcutta 1985; A. Morabia, *Le gihâd dans l'Islam médiéval*, Paris 1993; A. Noth, *Heiliger Krieg und Heiliger Kampf in Islam und Christentum*, Bonn 1966; R. Peters, Djihād. War of aggression or defense? in *Akten des VII Kongresse für Arabistik und Islamwissenschaft*, Göttingen 1976, 282-9; id., *Jihad in medieval and modern Islam*, Leiden 1977; F. Schwally, Der heilige Krieg des Islam in religionsgeschichtlicher und staatsrechtlicher Bedeutung, in *Internationale Monatsschrift für Wissenschaften, Kunst und Technik* 11 (1916), 678-714; E. Tyan, Djihād, in *EI²*, ii, 538-40.

Patience and Self-Restraint

see TRUST AND PATIENCE

Patriarchs

see PROPHETS AND PROPHETHOOD; CHILDREN OF ISRAEL; NOAH; ABRAHAM; MOSES

Patriarchy

A social structure characterized by the supremacy of the father in the clan or family. References to patriarchy in the Qurʾān cluster around three concerns: (1) the roles of patriarchal authority in ordinary social relations (see SOCIAL INTERACTIONS), i.e. roles circumscribed in various ways (see FAMILY; PARENTS); (2) the patriarch as an ideal religious figure, expressed through narratives (q.v.) and allegories drawn from the biblical tradition (see LITERARY STRUCTURES OF THE QURʾĀN; SCRIPTURE AND THE QURʾĀN); and (3) the question as to whether divinity could possess patriarchal attributes (see GOD AND HIS ATTRIBUTES; ANTHROPOMORPHISM).

Patriarchal authority in ordinary social relations

While the Qurʾān highlights patriarchy as a desired status, it also surrounds it with limits. On more than one occasion the Qurʾān mentions progeny in the same sequence in which it lists other aspects of worldly material wealth (q.v.; cf. e.g. Q 3:10, 116; 8:28; 9:69, 85; 19:77; 34:35; see also CHILDREN; GRACE; BLESSING). Clearly patriarchal kinship (q.v.) structures are privileged. Not having progeny, especially male (see GENDER), is a sign of misfortune, and in the stories of patriarchs such as Zechariah (q.v.) or Abraham (q.v.), God reveals his merciful nature by offering sons to his pious followers in their old age, when they had despaired of the possibility (Q 19:2-7; 11:71-3). Muḥammad himself was of course without a male heir and in the Qurʾān God compensates the Prophet for this lack of proper patriarchal status with a special domicile within paradise (q.v.;

Q 108; see also FAMILY OF THE PROPHET; PEOPLE OF THE HOUSE).

The value of male progeny, as explicitly stated in Zechariah's case, is clearly connected to the need to assure the welfare of the house of the patriarch after his passing away. This obligation is evident in the many edicts on honoring both parents, which permeate the qur'ānic text (Q 2:180; 4:11; 31:14). Likewise, when the social roles of patriarchy are detailed (as in Sūrat al-Nisā', "The Women," e.g. Q 4:1-42, 127-30), the discussions deal with such central concerns to family law (see LAW AND THE QUR'ĀN) as rules of inheritance (q.v.), marriage, polygamy (see MARRIAGE AND DIVORCE), property (q.v.) rights and the status of orphans (q.v.).

While the important passages in the fourth sūra admit of a variety of interpretations (see FEMINISM AND THE QUR'ĀN), it is impossible to understand them apart from a conception of patriarchy as a type of authority (q.v.) justified by social responsibilities, rather than simply by privilege. Polygamy, for example, is discussed only in connection with the need to protect orphans' trusts (Q 4:3; see also CONCUBINES; WIVES OF THE PROPHET). Similarly, the edicts on the prerogatives of men over women are conditional on the ability of men to maintain more exacting virtue (q.v.; see also VIRTUES AND VICES, COMMANDING AND FORBIDDING) and sustained financial support for the family (Q 4:34, 24-5; 65:6; see MAINTENANCE AND UPKEEP): the man is forbidden to expel his wife, separate from her or claim their common domicile without good cause, which is usually understood to be verifiable sexual infidelity (*fāḥisha*, Q 4:15-6; 65:1-2; see CHASTITY).

As it sanctified the property of women, the Qur'ān explicitly prohibits a man from unlawfully claiming any part of a woman's inheritance or even claiming back his "gifts" to her (see BRIDEWEALTH), all of which automatically become an inviolable part of the woman's property (Q 4:19-20). Generally, men are expected to be in control of their temper (see ANGER); and all further discussions of patriarchy which detail social obligations beyond faith (q.v.) itself make patriarchal authority dependent on its ability to uphold domestic justice (see JUSTICE AND INJUSTICE), as well as to dispose income and charities responsibly.

The patriarch as an ideal religious figure

Patriarchy also appears in the Qur'ān in an idealized form, a form associated most directly with the requisites of transmitting common wisdom (q.v.) and proper religion (q.v.). Allegorized in the stories of pre-Islamic patriarchs (see PRE-ISLAMIC ARABIA AND THE QUR'ĀN), the prototypical character in this regard is the sage Luqmān (q.v.). He instructs his son to adopt monotheism (see POLYTHEISM AND ATHEISM), honor his parents, seek out rightful company, appreciate the divine source of all life, worship (q.v.), bear adversity with fortitude (see TRIAL; TRUST AND PATIENCE) and stand up to derogation, while at the same time maintaining modesty (q.v.) throughout life (Q 31:13-9).

Likewise, the Qur'ān portrays several biblical prophets, such as Abraham, Noah (q.v.), Jacob (q.v.), Zechariah and others as having served mainly as transmitters of monotheistic faith to their sons specifically and to kin generally (e.g. Q 2:130-5; 14:35-7). The authority of patriarchy is assaulted, however, when it conveys the "wrong" wisdom. For example, the Qur'ān frequently denounces habitual, unthinking worship of idols (see IDOLS AND IMAGES; IDOLATRY AND IDOLATERS), which their worshippers justified by the fact that the idols had been passed on to the tribe by their forefathers (cf. e.g. Q 2:170; 5:101-4).

This dual approach to patriarchy as both

a vehicle for and obstacle to disseminating divine messages suggests that patriarchal hierarchy could even be reversed, in accordance with the principle of progress in human knowledge (see KNOWLEDGE AND LEARNING). This is evident in Abraham's assertion of a pedagogic posture toward his own father. In that case, Abraham leaves home as he asks God to forgive his idol-worshipping father (Q 19:41-7; cf. 14:41; see ĀZAR). A late qurʾānic sūra further shows Abraham disavowing intercession (q.v.) and disowning his father (Q 9:114). The possibility of the son showing the way to the patriarch is likewise evident in the story of Joseph (q.v.), which culminates in a complicated image of the prophet raising his parents to the throne while they simultaneously prostrate themselves in front of their young son (Q 12:100; see BOWING AND PROSTRATION).

Patriarchal attributes and divinity

As it distinguishes Islam (q.v.) from both Christianity (see CHRISTIANS AND CHRISTIANITY) and pre-Islamic paganism, the Qurʾān affirms from its earliest verses and consistently thereafter a highly abstract conceptualization of divinity. This requires rejecting the notion that God can be apprehended with references to experienced realities, including fatherhood. Indeed, one of the main early theological differences between Islam and Christianity (see THEOLOGY AND THE QURʾĀN; POLEMIC AND POLEMICAL LANGUAGE) concerns the Qurʾān's denunciation of the concept of "God the father" and its vehement assertion of the humanity of Jesus (q.v.), who is regarded as a mere messenger (q.v.) rather than God's son (esp. Q 4:171; 5:17, 75; 9:30; 19:34-5, 88-93; 112). This stance can likewise be understood in the context of Islam's early battle against paganism, which was defined by immediacy to divinity. From an early point the Qurʾān affirms as a logical precept that an appropriate concept of a high God means that God could not possibly be apprehended in terms of human relations. Thus if God is eternal (see ETERNITY), the divine could not have been "born," and if God is omnipotent (see POWER AND IMPOTENCE), there is no need for God to emulate the human methods of bringing forth life, e.g. begetting progeny (cf. Q 112). The divine simply brings being out of nothingness (Q 19:35; cf. 16:40; 40:68; see COSMOLOGY). Therefore patriarchal attributes, while meaningful in terms of social relations, social responsibilities and the requisites of knowledge transmission (see COMMUNITY AND SOCIETY IN THE QURʾĀN), could, when applied to God, only dilute or render inconsistent the necessarily abstract conceptualization of the divine.

Mohammed A. Bamyeh

Bibliography

Primary: Ibn Taymiyya, *Fiqh al-nisāʾ*, Beirut 1989; al-Manṣūr bi-llāh ʿAbdallāh b. Ḥamza, *Risālat al-thabāt fī mā ʿalā l-banīn wa-l-banāt*, Ṣaʿda 2000; Māwardī, *Kitāb al-Nafaqāt*, Beirut 1998; al-Ṭurṭūshī, Abū Bakr Muḥammad b. al-Walīd, *Birr al-wālidayn*, ed. M. ʿAbd al-Ḥakīm al-Qāḍī, Beirut 1986.

Secondary: A. Degand, *Geschlechtsrollen und familiale Strukturen im Islam*, Frankfurt-am-Main 1988; M. Shaḥrūr, *Naḥwa uṣūl jadīda lil-fiqh al-islāmī. Fiqh al-marʾa*, Damascus 2000.

Patron
see CLIENTS AND CLIENTAGE

Pauses
see RECITATION OF THE QURʾĀN

Peace

State of tranquility or quiet. Peace *(al-salām)* plays an important role in the Qurʾān and in Muslim life, yet as a term and a concept it is most commonly paired with religious warfare, commonly termed *jihād* (q.v.). This is unfortunate, since the word "peace" and related cognates from the Arabic root *s-l-m* reflect a semantic field of considerable depth and sophistication. Indeed, much of the emphasis and language of the Qurʾān mirrors a similar complexity found in Christian and Jewish scripture (see SCRIPTURE AND THE QURʾĀN). In order to indicate the principal dimensions within this semantic field, four distinctive foci need to be examined: the theological, eschatological, prophetic and social.

Theologically, the justification for the conceptual position of peace in Islam rests finally and ultimately in the character of God (see GOD AND HIS ATTRIBUTES): it is a spiritual quality attributed to his very nature (*al-salām*, Q 59:23). Hence, God provides an inner peace to those whom he guides (cf. Q 6:125-7) and welcomes the true believer to the garden (q.v.) of righteousness (see PARADISE) with "Enter it in peace" (cf. Q 50:31-4). God also bids greetings to be made to the Prophet with peace (Q 33:56). In a series of parallelisms on peace designed for intensification (see LANGUAGE AND STYLE OF THE QURʾĀN; LITERARY STRUCTURES OF THE QURʾĀN), God begins peace with Noah (q.v.), delegates it to Abraham (q.v.), imparts it to both Moses (q.v.) and Aaron (q.v.), instills it in Elijah (q.v.) and concludes, with a heightened flourish, by including all messengers as the beneficiaries of the divine bestowal of peace (Q 37:79-181). Moreover, peace itself attends the coming down of the Qurʾān on the Night of Power (q.v.; Q 97:1-5; see also REVELATION AND INSPIRATION) and tranquility (*sakīna;* see SHEKHINAH) is a spiritual gift sent down by God (cf. Q 9:26, 40; 48:4, 18). In short, the text gives ample justification for the Muslim claim that peace is a fundamental component in God's relationship with humans.

Second, the Qurʾān elaborates considerably on peace in its language dealing with matters of the end-time (see ESCHATOLOGY; APOCALYPSE): At the end of time, the heavens will be rolled up like a scroll (Q 21:104), angels (see ANGEL) will descend and God will reign (Q 25:25-6). Then will come the day when the book of deeds will be opened (cf. Q 17:71; see HEAVENLY BOOK) and each soul will stand on its own before God in judgment (i.e. Q 30:14-6; 82:1-15; see LAST JUDGMENT; INTERCESSION); believers will no longer fear (q.v.; Q 7:49) nor experience terror (Q 27:88-90) nor suffer grief (Q 21:97-103; see BELIEF AND UNBELIEF). Significantly, they will have joy (see JOY AND MISERY) and peace (Q 36:55-8) because, as believers in the book (q.v.), all will be judged by its standard (Q 28:85-7). The Qurʾān insists that peace must be assumed to be the wish of all people, even if it is quite possible they might use it deceitfully (Q 8:61-2). Such language underscores the key role that peace played in qurʾānic notions of the future (cf. Q 7:96).

Third, a functional notion of peace played a role both in defining Muḥammad's career and in shaping his attitude towards the people with whom he had to deal. This is often reflected in the sūras that treat his dealings with tribal peoples (see ARABS; BEDOUIN). In the late Medinan period (see CHRONOLOGY AND THE QURʾĀN), the Bedouins are castigated for their ignorance of the Prophet's purposes (Q 9:97); they itch for a fight and then evaporate when the Prophet decides to negotiate the submission of the enemy (cf. Q 48:17), as if fighting (q.v.) was an end in itself. The urban wealthy, who make journeys in winter and summer to other places (see CARAVAN; SEASONS), should acknowledge that they could not do this without God providing them both plenty and peacefulness (Q 106:1-5; see GRACE;

BLESSING). Like all Muslims, Muḥammad was enjoined to make peace between quarreling believers (Q 49:9), a requirement made even more telling by the fact that God is delighted with the believers when a treaty replaces conflict with the unconverted Meccans (Q 48:18). As a governing policy, the dictum, "But if the enemy incline toward peace, do you also so incline" (Q 8:61) must have posed difficult choices for the Prophet, especially in determining what "incline" might mean in any given context. His decisions must have also been made with one eye on the available history of the prophets who went before him (see NARRATIVES; PROPHETS AND PROPHETHOOD), for they are deemed examples (Q 43:28, 56, 57). Indeed, it is evident that the Prophet's relationship to this provisional peace shifted considerably throughout his career. In the first Meccan period, he appears as a warner (q.v.) and teacher (Q 71:10, 25; see TEACHING); his role then shifts to that of a deliverer à la Moses (Q 20:44, 47, 77) in order to face the forces that militate against the truth (Q 16:120) in the third Meccan period. In the late Meccan period, he reacts against violence, and, finally, moves to military jihād during the Medinan period (Q 4:95-6).

Finally, peace operates in a social and political milieu (see COMMUNITY AND SOCIETY IN THE QUR'ĀN; POLITICS AND THE QUR'ĀN). Peace is a matter of public policy, as Q 4:91 implies: "If they do not back away from you, and offer you peace, and temper their hands, then seize and kill them." This justifies fighting those who attack (Q 22:39), those who fight against Muslims (Q 2:190), but requires proper intelligence about the motives of those against whom war (q.v.) is carried out (Q 4:94). Judging from the Qur'ān, the principles that guided the use of jihād indicate that it had no universally perceived meaning; it functioned against a background of peace as one of the tools for bringing about the formation of the community of believers (*umma;* see BELIEF AND UNBELIEF) and was applied contextually by the Prophet. Hence it is probable that it functioned primarily within the community's task of establishing the *umma.* Only later would it develop into a sophisticated military element of state policy, which carried it in quite different directions, and added several other layers of legal and political interpretation to its history. Still, enough has been said to indicate that qur'ānic peace was of such complexity that it could give rise to that history after the time of the Prophet.

Earle H. Waugh

Bibliography
Y. Friedmann, *Tolerance and coercion in Islam,* Cambridge 2003; M. Khadduri, *War and peace in the law of Islam,* Baltimore 1975; G. Mensching, *Toleranz und Wahrheit in der Religion,* Heidelberg 1955; trans. H.J. Klimkeit, *Tolerance and truth in religion,* Mobile, AL 1971; I.H. Qureshi, *The religion of peace,* New Delhi 1930; E.H. Waugh, *Peace as seen in the Qur'ān,* Jerusalem 1986.

Pearls see METALS AND MINERALS

Pen see WRITING AND WRITING MATERIALS

Penalty see REWARD AND PUNISHMENT; CHASTISEMENT AND PUNISHMENT

Penance see REPENTANCE AND PENANCE

Pentateuch see TORAH

People of Midian see MIDIAN

People of Scripture see PEOPLE OF THE BOOK; SCRIPTURE AND THE QUR'ĀN; BOOK

People of the Book

People of the Book [i.e. scripture] is the literal translation of *ahl al-kitāb,* a qurʾānic term used to designate both Jews and Christians (see JEWS AND JUDAISM; CHRISTIANS AND CHRISTIANITY) — collectively or separately — as believers in a revealed book (q.v.).

When *ahl* appears in a construction with a person it means his blood relatives (see FAMILY; KINSHIP; PEOPLE OF THE HOUSE), but with other nouns it acquires wider meanings, for instance, *ahl madhhab* are those who profess a certain doctrine or follow a particular school of law; *ahl al-islām* are the Muslims (see LAW AND THE QURʾĀN; COMMUNITY AND SOCIETY IN THE QURʾĀN). The term *ahl al-qurʾān,* which appears in the ḥadīth literature (see ḤADĪTH AND THE QURʾĀN), refers, according to Ibn Manẓūr (*Lisān al-ʿArab,* s.v. *ahl*) to those who memorize and practice the Qurʾān. He adds that "these are the people of God and his elect," in other words, the Muslims; as such, the term may at first glance seem synonymous to *"ahl al-kitāb."*

The term has also alternative forms that do not change its fundamental meaning, that is to say, people who possess a "book" presumably of a divine origin or to whom such a book or part of it "was given" (*alladhīna ūtū l-kitāb* or *alladhīna ūtū naṣīban mina l-kitābi,* e.g. Q 2:144-5; 3:19-20, 23; 4:44, 47,131; 5:5, 57; 6:20 and similar expressions: e.g. Q 2:146; 42:14). The idea is implied also in narratives (q.v.) wherein the circumstances in which "the book" was given to its respective recipients are mentioned (e.g. Q 6:91-2, 154-7; 35:25). In all these cases, the "giving" or "sending down *(tanzīl)*" of the book means a special act of grace (q.v.) on the part of God who chose certain people, or communities, to be the recipients and custodians of his word (see WORD OF GOD; REVELATION AND INSPIRATION). The actual act of the transmission of the book to its recipients was made through the mediation of a prophet-messenger (see PROPHETS AND PROPHETHOOD; MESSENGER). In the case of the Jews this was Moses (q.v.; Mūsā, Q 6:91; 11:110) and in the case of the Christians it was Jesus (q.v.; ʿĪsā, Q 3:44-8). It is possible to regard other prophets, especially David (q.v.; Dāwud, Q 4:163; 17:55), as instrumental in delivering a book to the Jews (cf. Q 2:87; see also CHILDREN OF ISRAEL). Sometimes the books are specified by their names (*tawrāt, injīl, zabūr,* respectively; see TORAH; GOSPEL; PSALMS) in addition to being identified as "the book" (*al-kitāb,* e.g. Q 4:105; 5:68, 110; 41:45).

According to the Qurʾān, since the Jews and Christians were chosen to be the recipients of the book, they were expected to follow its contents and to be worthy of being its custodians (Q 5:68; 40:53). On the whole, however, the Qurʾān regards the "People of the Book" as unworthy of this particular divine attention and benevolence (see also BLESSING). This is chiefly because they intentionally ignored the revelation given to Muḥammad, of which they should have good knowledge (Q 5:19, 41-4). If the People of the Book were to refer to the true book that was given to them, they would find that it confirms (*muṣaddiq,* Q 5:48; 6:91-2; 46:12) Muḥammad's message. Acting obstinately, however, they "concealed," "changed" and "substituted" (Q 2:174; 4:46; 5:13, 41) the true information in their book, in order to justify their opposition to the Prophet, thus joining hands with the polytheists (*mushrikūn,* e.g. Q 98:1; see FORGERY; POLEMIC AND POLEMICAL LANGUAGE).

The term *ahl* that the Qurʾān uses in order to describe a group of people — a family, a tribe, a community (see TRIBES AND CLANS; COMMUNITY AND SOCIETY IN THE QURʾĀN) — is used in the case of *ahl al-kitāb* in an almost unique way, conveying the idea of a religious community which is identified by its scriptures. The usual usage of the term, which denoted people of a certain locality (Yathrib, Medina, Madyan; cf. Q 33:13; 9:101, 120; 15:67; 20:40; 28:45; see MIDIAN) or mode of settlement (*ahl al-qurā,* Q 7:96-8; see CITY) or family (*ahl [al-] bayt,* Q 11:73; 28:12; 33:33), was borrowed by the Qurʾān to indicate a group of people who follow the teaching of a book, a scripture of divine origin. This is made very clear when the Qurʾān refuses to accept the exclusive claim of the Jews to the ancestry of Abraham (q.v.; Ibrāhīm): "Abraham was not a Jew nor was he a Christian but he was a *ḥanīf* (q.v.), a Muslim, and he was not one of the polytheists (see POLYTHEISM AND ATHEISM; IDOLATRY AND IDOLATERS). Surely the people who are nearest to Abraham are those who followed him and this Prophet, and those who have believed..." (Q 3:67-8).

Although the Qurʾān attributes the ancestry of the Jews to Abraham's grandson Jacob (q.v.; or son, Q 11:71), the text is far more interested in their and the Christians' affiliation to the revealed scriptures. These revealed scriptures are in the form of a *kitāb,* a "book." This term must have been well known to the people of western Arabia long before the time of the Prophet, since it is used freely in the Qurʾān (see ORALITY AND WRITING IN ARABIA; PRE-ISLAMIC ARABIA AND THE QURʾĀN; SOUTH ARABIA, RELIGION IN PRE-ISLAMIC). In the light of recent scholarship that indicates a fair degree of interaction of Arabic-speaking peoples with other Semitic linguistic communities, it is likely that the word itself, *kethāb hak-kāthūb* in Hebrew and *kethābah* in Aramaic, would also have been well known in some circles there. The Jews in Yemen (q.v.) and Babylonia as well as the Aramaic (Syriac) speaking Christians may even have used it to denote the Bible in general. The Jews used the term *torah she-bi-ketāb* to identify the written law, the Pentateuch. Both parts of this term were likely known in the Arabian environment, and the Qurʾān refers to them separately, *kitāb* and *tawrāt,* in almost interchangeable fashion. It is clear in the Qurʾān that the *kitāb* was actually a written text and it is possible to read some qurʾānic references as indicating that its revelation differs from the former "books" only by the fact that it was orally transmitted and not written down (see ORALITY; RECITATION OF THE QURʾĀN). The majority of qurʾānic references, however, make clear that its message cannot be different from that of its predecessors and that it also had to be recorded in a book, identical with, and also confirming and bringing to perfection, the former books (Watt-Bell, *Introduction,* 142 f.). "[God] has sent down to you the book with the truth confirming what was sent before it, and he sent down the Torah and the Gospel aforetime as guidance for the people, and he sent down the *furqān*" (Q 3:3-4; see CRITERION). Nevertheless, in spite of this clear identification, the term *ahl al-kitāb* is still reserved in the Qurʾān for the followers of the Torah and the Gospel *(injīl).* In one instance, the text is more specific, when it identifies the Christians by the term *ahl al-injīl* (Q 5:47).

Thus, the holy book of the Jews and the Christians, the *kitāb,* assumed the place of the locality or blood relations as the primary point of identification for a particular group of people. By doing so, the Qurʾān followed its main doctrine of the community of believers, namely the overarching structure created by the bond of religion (q.v.). Just as the community of Muḥammad's followers was that of *muʾminūn* (and, less frequently, *muslimūn*) bound together by its revelation, the Jews and Christians were religious communities as well, bound together by their respective revelations.

Since the divine origin of these revelations was not questioned (though in their present state these texts represent only a defective version of the original), it follows that *ahl al-kitāb* deserve special treatment by the community of believers. Exegesis of Q 9:5 and 9:29 has elaborated upon a seeming qurʾānic distinction between the treatment of "People of the Book" and "polytheists" *(mushrikūn)* as defeated military opponents of the believers (see FIGHTING; EXPEDITIONS AND BATTLES). Rather than the polytheists' choice between death and "submission," the believers may accept a settlement from the "People of the Book" that allows them to live within the Muslim polity without necessarily converting to Islam. But it is incumbent upon the community of believers to use force of arms, if necessary, in order to compel *ahl al-kitāb* to settle into the legal status fixed for them (Q 9:29; Kister, ʿAn yadin).

Most references to *ahl al-kitāb* in the Qurʾān are polemical. These peoples (or, frequently, the "disbelievers" from among them) are basically the enemies of the Muslims, who wish that the former accept their revelation in the Qurʾān. They are jealous of the Muslims because God had chosen to send them a prophet as well (Q 2:105-9). On the other hand, the Qurʾān also seeks common ground between Muslims and *ahl al-kitāb*. In Q 2:62 we find the assertion that "Jews, Christians and the Ṣābiʾīn (see SABIANS), whoever has believed in God and the last day (see LAST JUDGMENT; APOCALYPSE), and has acted uprightly (see GOOD DEEDS; VIRTUES AND VICES, COMMANDING AND FORBIDDING), have their reward with their lord (q.v.): fear (q.v.) rests not upon them, nor do they grieve (see JOY AND MISERY)." The search for common ground with the People of the Book reflected in this verse appears even more clearly in Q 3:64: "O People of the Book, come to a word (that is) fair between us and you, (to wit) that we serve only God, that we associate nothing with him...."

The later qurʾānic revelations, given at the time of intensive polemical encounters at Medina, reduced the base for such common ground with the Jews and the Christians to two: pure monotheism and belief in the day of judgment (or the "last day"). It seems, however, that these two principles, even if the People of the Book acknowledged them, were not enough to outweigh the doctrinal differences between the parties. The Qurʾān accuses both Jews and Christians of polytheism, because of the Christian doctrines of the Trinity (q.v.) and of the divine sonship of Jesus and the Jewish claim that ʿUzayr (see EZRA) was the son of God. The latter accusation is enigmatic and no satisfactory explanation has yet been offered for it. The name of ʿUzayr does not appear in this form in any Jewish text, and the idea of God having a son is not only completely alien to rabbinic thought of the time, but it was also the major area of conflict between mainstream Judaism and Christianity. But since the Qurʾān speaks about the sonship of ʿUzayr as an apparently known and accepted fact (Q 9:30: "The Jews say that ʿUzayr is the son of God and the Christians say that the Messiah *[al-masīḥ]* is the son of God..."), it might mean that there was a concrete group of people who called themselves Jews and attributed sonship to a person called ʿUzayr. The fact that the context of this assertion is the sonship attributed by the Christians to the Messiah *(al-masīḥ),* is likely significant. The preceding verse (Q 9:29) calls on the believers to fight against those "who do not believe in God or in the last day... of those who have been given the book" *(min alladhīna ūtū l-kitāb)*. Following immediately is the verse about the polytheistic doctrines of the Jews and the Christians. It is clear first, that the Prophet is absolutely sure about the issue of ʿUzayr and second, that this passage does not speak about a difference of doctrine between the two communities but about the difference in the appellation that each one of them used for the son of God. The Christians call him *al-masīḥ*, the Jews ʿUzayr. The solution of the riddle is rather simple: The likely source of the name ʿUzayr is the Hebrew word *ʿOzēr*, rather than an Arabic diminutive. Taking into consideration that the only way to render the long *ē* in Hebrew is by the diphthong *ay* in Arabic, ʿUzayr would represent the transliteration of the Hebrew ʿOzēr into Arabic. ʿOzēr in Hebrew means "helper," or even "savior." The word appears in biblical and post-biblical sources alone and together with words derived from the root *y-sh-ʿ* denoting salvation, too. (At the beginning of the 18 Benedictions, the most important Jewish prayer, God is called: "king *[mēlek]*, helper *[ʿozēr]*, savior *[moshīʿa]*, protector *[magen]*.") In other words, the Qurʾān, when speaking about Jews and Christians as those to whom the book was given, speaks about two similar groups, both of whom believed in the son of God as the savior, with only one difference: each referred to him under a different title, the Jews called him *ʿozēr* and the Christians *masīḥ* (see SALVATION).

The problem of ʿUzayr has a wider implication in regard to the question of the identity of the Jews in the Medinan context (see MEDINA; CHRONOLOGY AND THE QURʾĀN). Based on the qurʾānic material alone it is very possible that at least some of these Jews (if not all of them) represented a sect with a distinct messianic doctrine, who regarded the Messiah as the son of God and called him "the savior," "the helper" *(ʿozēr, ʿuzayr)*. This could well be the reason why many times the term *ahl al-kitāb* refers to both Jews and Christians, and one cannot always be sure if a certain reference in the Qurʾān refers to Jews, to Christians or to both. In all the thirty-one verses of the Qurʾān with a direct reference to *ahl al-kitāb* there are only two references that can be identified as referring specifically to Jews and to Christians, respectively. In Q 4:153-5, the People of the Book ask the Prophet to bring down to them a book from heaven (see PROVOCATION; OPPOSITION TO MUḤAMMAD); in doing so they follow the example of their forefathers who, even after they were given the evidence *(bayyināt)*, made the golden calf (see CALF OF GOLD) and persisted with the rebellion (q.v.) against God, and his prophets. The other case is Q 4:171, where *ahl al-kitāb* are clearly Christians. Here the Qurʾān urges them to speak about God with truth, and not to exaggerate in their religion. Jesus (ʿĪsā) was only a messenger of God, even though he was created when God cast his spirit (q.v.) into Jesus' mother (see MARY). He is ʿĪsā son of Maryam, that is to say, not ʿĪsā son of God. But even in these two cases one cannot be sure that the Prophet is not speaking about two very similar groups, each of whom exalted Jesus as a messianic figure and "son of God," but under two different titles: "Masīḥ" (Messiah) and ʿOzēr" (Savior). From the qurʾānic references, it appears that the "Naṣāra" were those who termed him the "Messiah," while the "Yahūd" called him "Savior." Both are attacked in the qurʾānic discourse for saying that God has a son; they differ only in the name which they use to identify him. From this reading of the qurʾānic references to the "Yahūd," it would appear that they should not be equated with post-exilic Judaism which had categorically rejected any association with Jesus.

In what follows, the qurʾānic verses dealing strictly with *ahl al-kitāb* will be summarized without reference to either ḥadīth or commentary, i.e. without exegetical interference. To begin, the second and third sūras contain a number of references.

Q 2:105 — those who disbelieve from *ahl al-kitāb* and the polytheists *(mushrikūn)* do not like the fact that the believers receive God's goodness and favor. Q 2:109 — many *ahl al-kitāb* are jealous of the Muslims and wish they would become unbelievers. Q 3:64 — the Qurʾān calls on *ahl al-kitāb* to accept monotheism as a common ground of belief with the Muslims. Q 3:65 — *ahl al-kitāb* cannot claim Abraham for themselves since the Torah and the Gospel were revealed only after his time. (Since Abraham plays a major part in both Judaism and Christianity, the verse cannot be identified with either one.) Q 3:69 — a group of *ahl al-kitāb* wish to lead the Muslims astray (q.v.), but they mislead only themselves. Q 3:70-1 — *ahl al-kitāb* are asked why they disbelieve in the signs (q.v.) of God and confuse truth (q.v.) with falsehood (see LIE). Q 3:75 — there are some individuals from *ahl al-kitāb* who are trustworthy, others who are not. These even lie about God himself. Q 3:98-100 — *ahl al-kitāb* disbelieve in God's signs and turn the believers away from his path. The believers are warned that some of those "to whom the book has been given" wish to render them unbelievers. Q 3:100-14 — it would have been much better if *ahl al-kitāb* were to believe but most of them are transgressors. The Muslims will defeat them. They are destined to permanent humiliation because they disbelieved in God's signs and killed the prophets. But not all *ahl al-kitāb* are the same: some recite God's revealed verses while prostrating in the night (see BOWING AND PROSTRATION; VIGILS) and believe in God and the last day. (Only the commentaries identify either Jews or Christians with these verses.) Q 3:199 — among *ahl al-kitāb* there are those who believe in God and in what was revealed to them as well as in what was revealed to the Prophet. God will properly reward them. Q 4:123-4 — reward and punishment (q.v.) depend on one's actions. They are not dependent on the convictions of either *ahl al-kitāb* or the Muslims.

The fourth sūra, al-Nisāʾ ("The Women"), includes three significant and lengthy paragraphs. Q 4:153-9 — *ahl al-kitāb* ask the Prophet to bring down for them a book from heaven. This is a sign of their audacity, for in the past they asked Moses to give them a clear sign of God, and even after they were struck by lightening they made the calf *(al-ʿijl)*. God lifted the mountain over them, ordered them to keep the sabbath (q.v.), and took from them "a firm compact" (see COVENANT). They will be punished for violating the compact, for their disbelief in the signs of God, for their killing of the prophets, speaking against Mary and for claiming to have killed the Messiah, ʿĪsā. In fact, they never killed or crucified him (see CRUCIFIXION); instead, God caused him to ascend to him: "And there are no People of the Book but will surely believe in him before his death, and on the day of resurrection (q.v.), he will be regarding them a witness (see INTERCESSION; WITNESSING AND TESTIFYING)." (This is the only clear reference to Jewish material, though it is not clear whether the reference here is to the events of the past or to some current controversy. Q 4:157 contains a reference to those who have differences of opinion about Jesus or have doubts concerning him, and, having no clear knowledge about him, they follow uncertain opinions. This verse cannot be attributed to either Jews or Christians but, unlike the other verses of a historical nature, this one seems to refer to the present and reflect differences of opinions regarding the nature of Christ among Christians and Judeo-Christian groups.) Q 4:171 — *ahl al-kitāb* are warned not to exaggerate in their religion and regard Jesus only as a messenger (q.v.) of God and his word conveyed to Mary from a spirit which God cast into her. God is one, he is exalted above having a son (see GOD AND HIS ATTRIBUTES; ANTHROPOMORPHISM); he has all that is in heaven and earth (see POWER AND IMPOTENCE). (The verse seems to refer to the Christians but could well hint at a controversy concerning the nature of Christ among local Christian or pseudo-Christian groups, perhaps a distant echo of the debate in the institutionalized Byzantine church.)

In the first relevant reference in the fifth sūra (Q 5:15), *ahl al-kitāb* are informed that God's messenger has arrived revealing all that they had been concealing from the "book." God sent the light (q.v.) to them and a "clear book." Q 5:19 — *ahl al-kitāb* are told that God's messenger came to make things clear for them and as a bringer of good tidings (see GOOD NEWS) and a warner (q.v.). Q 5:59 — *ahl al-kitāb* are asked if they reproach the Muslims for their belief in what has been sent to them and what was sent before and for their belief in God. The implication is that whatever God has sent to them is identical with whatever was sent aforetime. Q 5:65 — if *ahl al-kitāb* were to become believers God would forgive their sins (see FORGIVENESS; SIN, MAJOR AND MINOR) and cause them to enter paradise (q.v.). Q 5:68 — *ahl al-kitāb* are called upon to keep the Torah and the Gospel; the Prophet's revelation causes many of them to increase their arrogance (q.v.) and disbelief. Q 5:77 — *ahl al-kitāb* are urged not to exaggerate in their religion, to speak only the truth about God, and to beware of following the ways of those who in the past have strayed from the straight path. (The verse is reminiscent of Q 4:171, but without the apparently Christian references.)

In Q 29:46-7, the Muslims are to debate with *ahl al-kitāb* in a positive manner (see DEBATE AND DISPUTATION) and stress the common belief in the one God and in what had been revealed to *ahl al-kitāb* (in the past) and the Muslims (at present). A book *(kitāb)* was revealed to the Prophet similar to the other book that was revealed in the past and in which *ahl al-kitāb* believe. Some of them will believe in this book, too. Only the unbelievers deny the signs of God (see GRATITUDE AND INGRATITUDE). Q 33:26 — God caused the Muslims to be victorious over *ahl al-kitāb*, who were compelled to forsake their towers *(ṣayāṣīhim)*. (According to tradition the verse and its context has to do with the "battle of the trench [or ditch]" and *ahl al-kitāb* here refers to the Jews who fought against the Prophet; see PEOPLE OF THE DITCH.) Q 57:29 — *ahl al-kitāb* have no power over any part of the bounty of God who is the sole possessor of all his bounty, which he bestows on whomsoever he wishes.

Q 59:2 is a somewhat ambiguous passage which deserves more extended attention: The believers were victorious over some *ahl al-kitāb* by the grace of God and caused them (i.e. the disbelievers from the People of the Book) to evacuate their homes and forts after they had thought that these were impregnable (and Muslims did not think that the People of the Book could be defeated). God put fear in their hearts and they destroyed their homes with their own hands. For the Muslims this victory came unexpectedly. (The verse is usually understood to refer originally to the expulsion of the Jews of the Banū Qaynuqāʿ [q.v.] which was revised and extended after the expulsion of the Jews of the Banū al-Naḍīr [see NAḌĪR, BANŪ AL-; cf. Bell, *Commentary*, ii, 363-4]. The verse speaks about those of the "People of the Book who have disbelieved." They were the ones whom God expelled from their dwellings. The attribution of the reference to a certain clan of Jews is a reasonable assumption; the Qurʾān does not, however, use the word *"yahūd,"* but the more general term *ahl al-kitāb*. It is clear that the verse does not speak about doctrinal differences but about physical confrontation, which was given a religious garb. The group of *ahl al-kitāb* who took part in this confrontation are defined only as "unbelievers" and there is no other hint about their identity.)

Q 59:11 is also one of those verses that refer to *ahl al-kitāb* in the context of the Prophet's physical confrontation with his opponents. It speaks about the hypocrites *(alladhīna nāfaqū)* who promise "their brothers" from "those who disbelieve from among *ahl al-kitāb*" that they will go into exile with them if expelled and assist them if attacked (see HYPOCRITES AND HYPOCRISY). The passage adds that they are liars. (Again, according to the standard histories, this verse refers to the hypocrites of Medina before the expulsion of the Banū al-Naḍīr. There is nothing in the verse itself to back this presumption. Again, the verse uses the general term "the unbelievers from among the People of the Book" which, without any polemical context, is far from being specific. Yet, it is clear from the context and from the verses immediately following this verse, that the Qurʾān is speaking about a war [q.v.] in which their opponents fought the Muslim faithful "in fortified towns and behind walls" [Q 59:14].)

Sūra 98 is completely dedicated to the "unbelievers of the People of the Book" and the polytheists. The eight verses of the sūra speak about the union between these two groups, who were given the opportunity for salvation when the "evidence" *(bayyina)* of a true Prophet came to them "reciting pure scrolls (or sheets)" (*yatlū ṣuḥufan muṭahharatan*, see SHEETS; SCROLLS). Those who were given the book *(alladhīna ūtū l-kitāba)* separated (or had differences of opinion?) only after the evidence had come to them. They were ordered to worship God exclusively and observe the prayer (q.v.) and the payment of *zakāt* (see ALMSGIVING). Those of *ahl al-kitāb* (who disbelieved) and the polytheists are the worst of all creatures and are destined to abide in the fire of hell (*jahannam;* see HELL AND HELLFIRE). In comparison, those of them who do believe and do good deeds are the best of all creatures and are to dwell eternally in the garden (q.v.) of Eden wherein the rivers flow. (The sūra represents a summary of the Qurʾān's attitude to *ahl al-kitāb:* those who believe share the good fortune of all other believers. By believing the Qurʾān means acceptance of the Prophet as one who recites holy writing, as the evidence *(ḥujja)* and the practice of the two main ordinances of Islam: prayer *[ṣalāt]* and the prescribed payment of *zakāt*. Humanity is thus divided into two camps: the saved ones are the believers who are also the best of all creatures *[khayr al-bariyya]* — they inherit heaven; and the worst of all creatures, who are the unbelievers of *ahl al-kitāb* and the polytheists, who inherit hell).

Except for a few cases, therefore, *ahl al-kitāb* in the Qurān does not necessarily refer to either Jews or Christians. Even if such identification can be made, especially in the case of Jews, it is not clear to what kind of Jews or Christians the text refers, unless there is clear reference to past history. It is very possible that, in addition to rabbinic Jews (from Yemen and Babylonia?), the Prophet came into contact with messianic groups who identified themselves as *yahūd*. Based on the qurʾānic text it is impossible to be more specific about the identity of *ahl al-kitāb* with whom the Prophet had ideological, doctrinal and physical confrontations. Part of them he succeeded in making believers while against others he had to fight to the end. The main subjects of the doctrinal confrontations were, first, the validity and truth of Muḥammad's prophecy and, second, the meaning and true nature of monotheism. Whether defined as Jews or Christians, *ahl al-kitāb* were, by the end of the Prophet's lifetime, accused of having forsaken the true monotheistic religion of old prescribed in their books and of having adopted polytheistic doctrines that put them in the same camp as the *mushrikūn* (cf. McAuliffe, Persian exegetical evaluation, 104-5). See also BELIEF AND UNBELIEF; FAITH; CHILDREN OF ISRAEL; RELIGIOUS PLURALISM AND THE QUR'ĀN.

M. Sharon

Bibliography
Primary: *Lisān al-'Arab;* Ṭabarī, *Tafsīr,* Beirut 1984 [the following is a list of references to *ahl al-kitāb* in al-Ṭabarī's *Tafsīr* indicating the cases of their identification as Jews (J), Christians (C), or neither (N): Q 2:105 (N); 2:109 (J); 3:64 (C,J) 3:65 (C,J); 3:69 (J,C and J only); 3:70 (N); 3:71 (C,J); 3:72 (J of Medina); 3:75 (C,J); 3:98 (C,J or J only); 3:99 (C,J, or J only); 3:110 (C,J); 3:113 (J who converted to Islam); 3:199 (C,J); 4:123 (C,J); 4:153 (J); 4:159 (C,J); 4:171 (C,J or C only); 5:15 (C,J); 5:19 (N); 5:59 (J) 5:65 (C,J); 5:68 (J); 5:77 (C,J) 29:46 (C); 33:26 (J); 57:29 (N or J); 59:2 (J of B. Naḍīr); 59:11 (J of B. Naḍīr); 98:1 (C,J) 98:6 (N)].
Secondary: Z. Abedin, Al-dhimma. The non-believers' identity in Islam, in *Islam and Christian-Muslim relations* 3 (1992), 40-57; M. Ayoub, Dhimmah in Qur'ān and ḥadīth, in *Arab studies quarterly* 5 (1983), 172-82 (stresses that the term *ahl al-dhimma* is not qur'ānic, and that the usage of *ahl al-kitāb* for Jews and Christians may suggest a certain level of equality of faith between the People of the Book and the Muslims; cf. esp. 178); id., 'Uzayr in the Qur'ān and Muslim tradition, in W.M. Brinner and S.D. Ricks (eds.), *Studies in Islamic and Judaic traditions,* 2 vols., Atlanta 1986, i, 3-18; Bell; id., *Commentary;* I. Goldziher, Ahl al-kitāb, in *EI*[1], i, 184-5; M.J. Kister, *'An yadin* (Qur'ān IX.29). An attempt at interpretation, in *Arabica* 11 (1964), 272-8; H. Lazarus-Yafeh, 'Uzayr, in *EI*[2], x, 960; J.D. McAuliffe, Persian exegetical evaluation of the *ahl al-kitāb,* in *MW* 73 (1983), 87-105; A.A. Sachedina, Jews, Christians and Muslims according to the Qur'ān, in *Greek Orthodox theological review* 31 (1986), 105-20 (especially pp. 105, 107-8, 114, 118); G. Vajda, Ahl al-kitāb, in *EI*[2], i, 264-6; W.M. Watt, *Muhammad at Medina,* Oxford, 1962, 192 f.; Watt-Bell, *Introduction,* 141 f.

People of the Cave

see MEN OF THE CAVE

People of the Ditch

The Qur'ān mentions the mysterious People of the Ditch *(aṣḥāb al-ukhdūd)* saying that "slain were the People of the Ditch — the fire abounding in fuel — when they were seated over it and were themselves witnesses of what they did with the believers" (Q 85:4-7). The Qur'ān adds that they were tortured in this way only because they believed in God "to whom belongs the kingdom of the heavens and the earth, and God is witness over everything" (Q 85:8-9).

The expression "People of the Ditch" is the single detail of this whole passage that has been subject to differing interpretations. Consequently, most exegetical works contain an interpretation of this phrase. Some are based on a long ḥadīth (see ḤADĪTH AND THE QUR'ĀN) in which Muḥammad tells the story of a boy who is learning magic (q.v.) from a magician. But, after meeting a monk (see MONASTICISM AND MONKS), the boy became a true believer in God. Subsequently, the boy was tortured by the king in order to make him abandon his faith, and after his death the king had ditches dug and burned those who followed the boy's religion (Muslim, *Ṣaḥīḥ,* iv, 2299-301, no. 3005).

In contrast, some other reports consider this passage an allusion to the martyrdom of the Christians of Najrān (q.v.) by order of the king Dhū Nuwās, which, according to Christian sources, took place around 523 C.E. (see CHRISTIANS AND CHRISTIANITY). Dhū Nuwās, the last Ḥimyarite king, converted to Judaism and changed his name to Joseph (see JEWS AND JUDAISM; SOUTH ARABIA, RELIGION IN PRE-ISLAMIC). When he learned that there were some Christians in Najrān, he went there, intent upon forcing them to convert to Judaism. At their refusal, Dhū Nuwās had one or more ditches dug, in which wood was put and a fire was lit. All of the Christians, numbering in the thousands (eight, twenty or even seventy), refused to renounce their faith and adopt that of the king, so they were thrown into the fire alive. According to certain reports, only one of the people of Najrān, named Daws Dhū Thaʿlabān, was able to escape. He reached the Byzantine court where he sought assistance. Some reports refer to the dimensions of the ditch or of the fire, or add that among the people slain there was a woman with a two-months-old baby who miraculously spoke and convinced her to accept the torment (Muqātil, *Tafsīr,* iv, 648).

According to some interpretations, the expression "People of the Ditch" alludes instead to three kings, Dhū Nuwās in Yemen, Antiochus in Syria and Nebuchadnezzar in Iraq or Persia. A tradition explains the qurʾānic passage as referring to an Abyssinian prophet who summoned his people to faith but the people, who refused to listen to the prophet, dug a ditch and threw the prophet and his followers in it (Majlisī, *Biḥār,* xiv, 439-40). A report attributed to ʿAlī b. Abī Ṭālib (q.v.; d. 40/661) includes another version: the ditch was dug by a Mazdean king who decided to permit incestuous marriages, but when his people opposed this innovation, the king, failing to convince them, had them thrown into the burning ditch.

Modern research has proposed other interpretations. The story of the People of the Ditch mentioned in the Qurʾān could be an allusion to the men in the furnace in Daniel 3:15 f., as already suggested by al-Ṭabarī (d. 310/923; *Tafsīr,* xxix, 132-3) and other exegetes. Alternatively, it may refer to the members of Quraysh (q.v.) slain by the Prophet's army at Badr (q.v.). It may also simply be a generic allusion to those damned to hell (Paret, *Kommentar,* 505-6; see REWARD AND PUNISHMENT; HELL AND HELLFIRE).

Roberto Tottoli

Bibliography

Primary: ʿAbd al-Razzāq, *Tafsīr,* ii, 362-4; Ibn Ḥabīb, Muḥammad b. Ḥabīb Abū Jaʿfar, *Kitāb al-Muḥabbar,* ed. I. Lichtenstaedter, Hyderabad 1942, 368; Ibn Isḥāq, *Sīra,* ed. al-Saqqā, i, 34-7; Ibn Kathīr, *Bidāya,* ii, 129-32; id., *Tafsīr,* 4 vols., Beirut n.d., iv, 777-81; al-Majlisī, Muḥammad Bāqir, *Biḥār al-anwār,* Beirut 1983, xiv, 438-44; Maqdisī, al-Muṭahhar b. Ṭāhir, *al-Badʾ wa-l-taʾrīkh,* ed. C. Huart, 6 vols., Paris 1899-1919, iii, 182-3; Mujāhid, *Tafsīr,* ed. Abū l-Nīl, 718-9; Muqātil, *Tafsīr,* iv, 647-8; Muslim, *Ṣaḥīḥ,* iv, 2299-301, no. 3005; Qummī, *Tafsīr,* Beirut 1991, ii, 442; Suyūṭī, *Durr,* 8 vols., Cairo 1983, viii, 465-70; Ṭabarī, *Tafsīr,* Cairo 1968, xxx, 131-6; id., *Taʾrīkh,* ed. de Goeje, i, 919-26; Ṭabarsī, *Majmaʿ,* 10 vols., Beirut 1986, x, 593-4; Thaʿlabī, *Qiṣaṣ,* 393-6.

Secondary: Horovitz, *KU,* 12, 92-3; A. Moberg, *Über einige christliche Legenden in der islamischen Tradition,* Lund 1930, 18-21; R. Paret, Aṣḥāb al-ukhdūd, in *EI*², i, 692; id., *Kommentar,* Kohlhammer 1980, 505-6; Speyer, *Erzählungen,* 424.

People of the Elephant

The phrase in the first verse of Q 105 (Sūrat al-Fīl, "The Elephant"), from which *al-fīl* ("the elephant") provides the term by which that sūra is known. The verse is addressed directly to the prophet Muḥammad: "Have you not seen how your lord has dealt with the People of the Elephant *(aṣḥāb al-fīl)?*" The short sūra of five verses is early Meccan (see CHRONOLOGY AND THE QURʾĀN) and it describes an expedition in which one of the mounts was an elephant and which was miraculously annihilated by God, who sent flocks of birds against the invading host. The sūra leaves unknown both the identity of the People of the Elephant, the objective of the invading force, and the motives behind the expedition.

What was left obscure in the sūra was illuminated with great precision by the Arabic Islamic historical and exegetical tradition. *Aṣḥāb al-fīl* were Abyssinians (see ABYSSINIA); the leader was Abraha (q.v.); the target was Mecca (q.v.) and the Kaʿba (q.v.); the name of the elephant was Maḥmūd, its "driver" *(sāʾis)* was Unays; the guide of the expedition was Abū Righāl; the elephant stopped at al-Mughammas and would not proceed towards Mecca; the route of the elephant, *darb al-fīl,* was charted from Yemen (q.v.) to al-Mughammas; the Prophet's grandfather, ʿAbd al-Muṭṭalib, was involved in negotiating with Abraha; and even Quraysh (q.v.), as Ḥums, were associated with the failure of the expedition of the People of the Elephant against the Kaʿba; Abraha died a dolorous death and was carried back to Yemen.

It is equally difficult to accept or reject any of the above data as provided by the Arabic Islamic tradition. Yet a modicum of truth may be predicated since, as is clear from the first verse of the sūra, the episode was a recent one and was probably still remembered by the Prophet's older Meccan contemporaries, who might well have been the first tradents of the later historical and exegetical tradition. Indeed, the so-called "Year of the Elephant," *ʿām al-fīl,* marked the inception of one of the Arab pre-Islamic eras (see PRE-ISLAMIC ARABIA AND THE QURʾĀN). The Islamic profile of the episode consisted in associating the year of the expedition with the birth date of Muḥammad; Umm Ayman, Muḥammad's nurse, was said to have been a captive from the defeated Abyssinian host; and Muslims were expected to stone the tomb of Abū Righāl at al-Mughammas. The sūra itself yields only the following: the expedition of the People of the Elephant was a serious and important event; the destruction of the invading host was theologically presented, effected by God himself; and since the sūra was addressed to the Prophet, the implication is that he or his city or Quraysh benefited from this divine intervention on their behalf. Hence, the failure of the expedition of the People of the Elephant sheds much light on the pre-Islamic history of Quraysh and on the pre-prophetic period of Muḥammad's life.

Attempts to invoke the epigraphic evidence from south Arabia to shed light on the People of the Elephant have failed. The Murayghān inscription commemorated a victory, not a defeat, for the Ethiopians and the site of the battle was very far from Mecca. Additionally, these attempts have been gratuitously plagued by the involvement of the Prophet's birth date — traditionally considered 570 C.E. — with the date of the expedition, mounted by the People of the Elephant. An alternative approach towards negotiating the imprecision of the sūra, namely, the exegesis of the Qurʾān by the Qurʾān *(tafsīr al-Qurʾān bi-l-Qurʾān),* has been more fruitful and successful. Many medieval Muslim scholars considered Q 106 ("Quraysh") not a separate sūra but a continuation of Q 105. The unity of these two sūras, however, had not been seriously considered until the present writer published an article to that effect in 1981. Accepting the unity of the two sūras *al-Fīl* and *Quraysh,* and setting them against the background of the history of western Arabia in the sixth century, based on authentic contemporary sources, yield the following conclusions on the People of the Elephant and their expedition:

They were Abyssinians, not Arabs, the *fīl* being an African not an Arabian animal; their leader was either Abraha or one of his two sons who succeeded him, Yaksūm or Masrūq; the destination no doubt was Mecca and the Kaʿba, referred to in verse Q 106:3; the destruction of the Ethiopian host may be attributed to the outbreak of an epidemic or the smallpox. Its destruction was Mecca's commercial opportunity in international trade, now that it could safely conduct the two journeys (see CARAVAN; JOURNEY): the winter journey to Yemen and the summer one to Syria (q.v.; *bilād al-shām*); let the Meccans, therefore, worship the lord of the "house" (the Kaʿba; see HOUSE, DOMESTIC AND DIVINE), who made all this possible (Q 106:3-4). The true motives behind the expedition remain shrouded in obscurity but they must be either or both of the following: (1) Retaliation for the desecration of the cathedral/church, built by Abraha in Ṣanʿāʾ; or (2) the elimination of Mecca as an important caravan city on the main artery of trade in western Arabia.

Whatever the motive behind the expedition of the People of the Elephant was, the qurʾānic revelation that refers to them in Q 105 remains the sole reliable evidence for the importance of Mecca in the sixth century, clearly implied in the fact that the ruler of south Arabia found it necessary to mount a major military offensive against it. The destruction of the Ethiopian host is also the sole reliable evidence that explains the enhanced prosperity of Mecca as a result of long-distance international trade, through which the future Prophet of Islam benefited, materially and otherwise, in the fifteen years or so, during which he led the caravans before his prophetic call (see PROPHETS AND PROPHETHOOD; REVELATION AND INSPIRATION) around 610 C.E.

Irfan Shahīd

Bibliography
Primary: Ibn Isḥāq, *Sīra,* ed. M. ʿAbd al-Ḥamīd, 4 vols., Cairo 1937, i, 46-65; Rāzī, *Tafsīr,* Beirut 1985, xxxii, 96-110; Ṭabarī, *Taʾrīkh,* trans. C.E. Bosworth, *The history of al-Ṭabarī. v. The Sāsānids, the Byzantines, the Lakhmids, and Yemen,* New York 1999, 212-32 (cf. T. Nöldeke's earlier translation and commentary, *Geschichte der Perser und Araber zur Zeit der Sasaniden,* repr. Graz 1973, 195-220).
Secondary: A.F.L. Beeston, Notes on the Muraighan expedition, in *BSOAS* 17 (1954), 389-92 (has been invalidated by ʿAbdel Monem Sayed, Emendations to the Bir Murayghan inscription, in *Seminar for Arabian studies* 18 [1988], 131-43); L.I. Conrad, Abraha and Muhammad, in *BSOAS* 50 (1987), 225-140; P. Crone, *Meccan trade and the rise of Islam,* Princeton 1987; A. al-Nasser and A. al-Ruwaite, A preliminary study of *darb al-feel,* Route of the Elephant, in *Aṭlāl* 11 (1988), 145-72; A.-L. de Prémare, Les éléphants de Qādisiyya, in *Arabica* 45 (1998), 261-9; V. Saḥḥāb, *Īlāf Quraysh. Riḥlat al-shitāʾ wa-l-ṣayf,* Beirut 1992; I. Shahīd, Two qurʾānic sūras. Al-Fīl and Quraysh, in W. al-Qāḍī (ed.), *Studia Arabica et Islamica. Festschrift for Iḥsān ʿAbbās,* Beirut 1981, 429-36.

People of the Heights

Qurʾānic eschatological designation for people not destined for hell. The term *al-aʿrāf* (pl. of *ʿurf*) in Q 7:46 and Q 7:48 (where it appears in the construct, *aṣḥāb al-aʿrāf:* "the companions — or people — of *al-aʿrāf*") has been variously understood as "elevated place, crest, to distinguish between things, or to part them." *Al-aʿrāf* (the name of the seventh sūra of the Qurʾān) also signifies "the higher, or the highest," and "the first or foremost," hence the source of the English term "[the People of] the Heights," and of M.H. Shakir's (*Holy Qurʾān,* 140-1) translation as "the Elevated Places." Finally, the exegetical tradition has indicated a connection with the triliteral Arabic root for "knowledge" (ʿ-r-f; see e.g. Ṭabarī, *Tafsīr,* xii, 450, ad Q 7:46, reporting a tradition from al-Suddī: "It is named *"al-aʿrāf"* because its companions 'know' — *yaʿrifūna* — humankind.").

The classical works of exegesis (see EXEGESIS OF THE QURʾĀN: CLASSICAL AND MEDIEVAL) list a number of interpretations of both *"al-aʿrāf"* and "the people of *"al-aʿrāf."* Al-Ṭabarī (d. 310/923) reports a tradition that identifies the "veil" (q.v.; *ḥijāb*) of Q 7:46 that separates those destined for heaven (see GARDEN) from those destined for hell (see HELL AND HELLFIRE) as both "the wall" *(al-sūr)* and "the heights" (*al-aʿrāf;* Ṭabarī, *Tafsīr,* xii, 449, ad Q 7:46; cf. Muqātil, *Tafsīr,* ii, 38-9, ad Q 7:46; see ESCHATOLOGY). A slight variation of this tradition is that *"al-aʿrāf"* is the "wall" or, alternately, the "veil," "between the garden and the fire" (q.v.; ibid.; see also BARRIER).

The exegetical tradition regarding the identity of the "men" *(rijāl)* or the "companions" *(aṣḥāb)* of *al-aʿrāf* is also multivalent: while some have posited angels (q.v.; cf. i.e. Ṭabarī, *Tafsīr,* xii, 459, ad Q 7:46), the majority has maintained that these individuals are human beings (children of Adam: Ṭabarī, *Tafsīr,* xii, 452, ad Q 7:46) — be they martyrs (i.e. those who "were killed in the path of God"; cf. Ṭabarī, *Tafsīr,* xii, 457, ad Q 7:46; see MARTYRS; PATH OR WAY), or virtuous humans or people whose good and evil works are equal (see GOOD DEEDS; EVIL DEEDS). This latter understanding is arguably the dominant one, as the "men" on *al-aʿrāf* (Q 7:46) have been understood to be those who "have not [yet] entered [paradise]" (Q 7:46): "the people of *al-aʿrāf" (aṣḥāb al-aʿrāf)* have been viewed as persons whose good and evil works are of equal quality (see WEIGHTS AND MEASURES). Thus, they should not merit paradise by the former or hell by the latter (cf. e.g. Ṭabarī, *Tafsīr,* xii, 452, ad Q 7:46) — nor merit it as prophets or angels (see PROPHETS AND PROPHETHOOD; ANGEL; cf. Rāzī, *Tafsīr,* xiv, 93, where the argument is put forth that the People of the Heights cannot be martyrs, as the description found in Q 7:46, that "they will not have entered [heaven], but they have an assurance" is explained as not applying to prophets, angels or martyrs; also, ibid., 94, where mention is made of the view, attributed to al-Ḥudhayfa and others, that the People of the Heights will be the last people to enter heaven; see THEOLOGY AND THE QURʾĀN; MUʿTAZILA). They are thus in the "intermediate" state between salvation (q.v.) and damnation, for Q 7:47 ("When their gaze will be turned towards the companions of the fire they will say, 'Our lord, do not put us with the wrongdoing people'") is also understood to refer to these people of *al-aʿrāf* (cf. Ṭabarī, *Tafsīr,* xii, 452-4, ad Q 7:46; see JUSTICE AND INJUSTICE; FREEDOM AND PREDESTINATION; DESTINY; FATE). Finally, Ṣūfī mystics have used the term to express a condition of the mind and soul when meditating on the existence of God in all things (see ṢŪFISM AND THE QURʾĀN).

Modern scholarship reflects the range of interpretations to be found in the classical exegetes. T. Andrae (*Der Ursprung,* 77) wrote that they were probably dwellers in the highest degree of paradise "who are able to look down on hell and on paradise." Bell (Men, 43), however, finds no linguistic justification for this claim, unless an unusual metathesis of the Arabic root letters of the verb "to raise up" (*r-f-ʿ* < *ʿ-r-f,* of *"al-aʿrāf"*) is assumed. Some interpreters imagined that *al-aʿrāf* was a sort of limbo, using the term *barzakh* (q.v.) for the patriarchs and prophets, or for the martyrs, and those whose eminence gave them sanctity.

Western translations of the Qurʾān reflect the lack of exegetical consensus regarding the phrase *"al-aʿrāf."* While some translators of the Qurʾān prefer to retain the

Arabic *"al-aʿrāf"* as the title of Q 7, others have attempted to translate the term, and have used their translations as the title of Q 7: e.g. Arberry (176-7) used "The Battlements" and "The Ramparts," and Pickthall (*Koran,* 121) "The Heights" (cf. Dawood, *Koran,* 112-3). Some rather more involved translations are the "Wall Between Heaven and Hell" (Ahmad Ali, *Qurʾān,* 137; e.g. his rendition of Q 7:46: "On the wall will be the men (of *al-aʿrāf*)..."; and of Q 7:48: "The men of *al-aʿrāf* will call [to the inmates of Hell]...."). Two earlier writers, Sale (*Koran,* 151) and Rodwell (*Koran,* 297-8), had simply used *al-aʿrāf* as the title. Sale named Q 7 "Al Araf" and did not divide the sections. He wrote, "... men shall stand on al araf who shall know every one of them..."; and "... those who stand on al araf shall call unto certain men...." Rodwell called it "Al Araf": "and on *the wall* Al Araf shall be men..." (Q 7:46; cf. his footnotes: "On this wall [the name of which is derived from *Arafa,* 'to know', with allusion to the employment of those upon it] will stand those whose good and evil works are equal, and are not, therefore, deserving of either Paradise or Gehenna..."; Q 7:48: "... and they who are upon Al Araf shall cry to those whom they know..."). The French scholar Kasimirski also retained the name *"al-aʿraf"*, as the title of Q 7, and he rendered the relevant phrase of Q 7:46: "... sur l'Alaraf...."

William M. Brinner

Bibliography
Primary: Muqātil, *Tafsīr;* Rāzī, *Tafsīr;* Ṭabarī, *Tafsīr.*
Secondary: A. Ali, *Al-Qurʾān. A contemporary translation,* Princeton, NJ 1984/1994; T. Andrae, *Der Ursprung des Islams und das Christentum,* Uppsala 1926; Arberry; Bell, *Commentary,* i, 232-3; id., The men of the Aʿrāf, in *MW* 22 (1932), 43-8; B. Carra de Vaux, Barzakh, in *EI²,* i, 1071-2; N.J. Dawood, *The Koran. With parallel Arabic text,* London 1956¹, 1990; J. Horowitz, Das Koranische Paradies, Jerusalem, in *Scripta Universitatis atque bibliothecae Hierosolymitanarum* (Orientalia et Judaica) (1923), 1-16 (no. VI); Th.P. Hughes, *A dictionary of Islam,* New York 1885, 20-1; M. Kasimirski, *Le Koran,* Paris 1844; Lane, 2015 [pt. v]; R. Paret, al-Aʿrāf, in *EI²,* i, 603-4; id., *Kommentar,* 160; Pickthall, *Koran;* J.M. Rodwell, *The Koran,* intr. G. Margoliouth, London 1973³ (1861), 297-8; G. Sale, *The Koran... the Alkoran of Mohammed,* London 1734 (notes by F.M. Cooper, prefixed *A life of Mohammed,* 1885); M.H. Shakir, *Holy Qurʾān,* Elmhurst, NY 1992; M.M. Zaki, Barzakh, in *EQ,* i, 204-7.

People of the House

Literally, "(the) people of the house" *(ahl al-bayt),* a family, a noble family, a leading family and, most probably, also those who dwelt near the house of God (see HOUSE, DOMESTIC AND DIVINE), the Kaʿba (q.v.). Without the definite article *"al-,"* it means "household" (see FAMILY; KINSHIP; COMMUNITY AND SOCIETY IN THE QURʾĀN). In Shīʿī (see SHĪʿISM AND THE QURʾĀN) as well as Sunnī literature the term *ahl al-bayt* is usually understood to refer to the family of the Prophet (q.v.). In the Qurʾān the term appears twice with the definite article (Q 11:73; 33:33) and once without it (*ahl bayt,* Q 28:12).

According to the lexicographers, when *ahl* appears in a construction with a person it refers to his blood relatives (see BLOOD AND BLOOD CLOT), but with other nouns it acquires wider meanings: thus the basic meaning of *ahl al-bayt* is the inhabitants of a house (or a tent). They used to call the inhabitants of Mecca (q.v.; *ahl makka*) "the people of God" as a sign of honor (for them), in the same way that it is said "the house of God" *(bayt Allāh). Ahl madhhab* are those who profess a certain doctrine; *ahl al-islām* are the Muslims, and so on (see for additional examples, *Lisān al-ʿArab,* s.v. *ahl*).

The Qurʾān frequently uses *ahl* to denote

a certain group of people. Sometimes the word is connected with the name of a place, and in these cases the term refers to the inhabitants of that place, such as: *ahl yathrib,* "the people of Yathrib" (Q 33:13) or *ahl al-madīna,* "the people of Medina" (q.v.; Q 9:101); *ahl madyan,* "the people of Midian" (q.v.; Q 20:40; 28:45). Sometimes the term is used to denote the people of unidentified locations such as *ahl qarya,* "the inhabitants of a town or village" (Q 18:77; cf. 29:31, 34), *ahl al-qurā,* "townspeople, dwellers of the villages" (Q 7:96-8; 12:109; 59:7; see CITY). At other times the word *ahl* refers to certain groups of people typified or identified by some ethical or religious characteristics, as in *ahl al-dhikr,* "people of the reminder" (Q 21:7; see MEMORY) or *ahl al-nār,* "people of the (hell-) fire" (Q 38:64; see HELL AND HELLFIRE). Or it has the meaning of "fit for," in which case the word describes an individual, not a group, such as *ahl al-taqwā,* "(a person) fit for piety" (q.v.; Q 74:56), or *ahl al-maghfira,* "(a person) fit for forgiveness" (q.v.; Q 74:56).

The term *ahl al-bayt* falls into one or more of these categories, namely people who belong to a certain house in the literal or socio-political meanings of the word. At least in one case (Q 33:33), however, its identification with the Prophet turned the term into a major issue in qur'ānic exegesis and tradition literature (see EXEGESIS OF THE QUR'ĀN: CLASSICAL AND MEDIEVAL; ḤADĪTH AND THE QUR'ĀN).

The qur'ānic usage of *ahl al-bayt* is as follows:

In Q 11:73 — the story of Abraham (Ibrāhīm) and the divine messengers. When the patriarch's wife is informed that she is going to give birth to Isaac (Isḥāq) and Jacob (Yaʿqūb), she reacts by saying: "Alas! Shall I bring forth when I am old and my husband here an old man? Verily this is a thing strange" (Q 11:72). The angels respond: "Do you think the affair of God strange? The mercy and blessing of God be upon you, O people of the house..." *(raḥmatu llāhi wa-barakātuhu ʿalaykum ahla l-bayti).*

In Q 28:12 — situated in the story of the rescue of the infant Moses (Mūsā) by Pharaoh's (Firʿawn) wife. The phrase appears without the definite article: Moses' sister asks, "Shall I direct you to a household who will take charge of him (the infant Moses) for you?..." *(hal adullukum ʿalā ahli baytin yakfulūnahu lakum).*

In Q 33:33 — "God simply wishes to take the pollution from you, O people of the house and to purify you thoroughly" *(innamā yurīdu llāhu li-yudhhiba ʿankumu l-rijsa ahla l-bayti wa-yuṭahhirakum taṭhīran).*

The first two verses, Q 11:73 and Q 28:12, were understood by almost all Muslim commentators to mean family, in the first case Abraham's family and in the second the prophet Moses' family. In the case of Q 33:33, however, the word *bayt* most probably means not a family but the Kaʿba, the house of God; thus the term *ahl al-bayt* would seem to mean the tribe of Quraysh (q.v.) or the Islamic community in general, as suggested by R. Paret (Der Plan, 130; cf. Bell, *Qur'ān,* ii, 414 n. 3; *Lisān al-ʿArab*).

The tribe of Quraysh was explicitly called *ahl al-bayt* in an early Islamic tradition recorded by Ibn Saʿd: "Quṣayy said to his fellow tribesmen, 'You are the neighbors of God and people of his house'" *(innakum jīrān Allāh wa-ahl baytihi;* Ibn Saʿd, *Ṭabaqāt,* i/1, 41, l. 16). In this sense the term assumes an even wider meaning: it includes all those who venerated the Kaʿba. This original meaning was neglected in favor of the more limited scope of the Prophet's family, and Q 33:33 became, consequently, the cornerstone for both Shīʿī and ʿAbbāsid claims to the leadership of the Muslim community (see POLITICS AND THE QUR'ĀN). The Shīʿa (q.v.) claimed that the verse speaks about the divine choice of the ʿAlid family and their preference to all the other relatives of the Prophet. To be sure, the idea of divine selection was accepted also by the so-called non-Shīʿī, or Sunnī, tradition. Thus the Prophet is made to say: "God created human beings, divided them into two parties, and placed me in the better one of the two. Then he divided this party into tribes (see TRIBES AND CLANS) and placed me in the best of them all, and then he divided them into families (*buyūt*, lit. "houses") and placed me in the best of them all, the one with the most noble pedigree" (*khayruhum nasaban;* Fīrūzābādī, *Faḍā'il*, i, 6). Within this concept of selection, there is a wide area of variation. The tendency of the Shīʿa has always been to carry the list of the divine selection further down, so as to achieve maximum exclusivity.

One of the most widespread traditions quoted by Shīʿī as well as Sunnī sources in relation to the interpretation of Q 33:33 is the so-called *ḥadīth al-kisā'*. Through the many variations on this ḥadith, the idea of the "holy five" was established. The Prophet is reported to have said: "This *āya* was revealed for me and for ʿAlī (see ʿALĪ B. ABĪ ṬĀLIB), Fāṭima (q.v.), Ḥasan and Ḥusayn." When the verse was revealed, the tradition goes on to say, the Prophet took a "cloak" or "cape" (*kisā'*, meaning his robe or garment; see CLOTHING), wrapped it around his son-in-law, his daughter and his two grandchildren and said: "O God, these are my family *(ahl baytī)* whom I have chosen; take the pollution from them and purify them thoroughly." The clear political message in this tradition was stressed by additions such as the one in which the Prophet says: "I am the enemy of their enemies (q.v.)," or invokes God, saying: "O God, be the enemy of their enemies" (authorities quoted in Sharon, Ahl al-bayt, 172 n. 6).

To the same political category belong the various traditions which consider assistance and love for the *ahl al-bayt* a religious duty and enmity towards them a sin. "He who oppresses my *ahl bayt*," the Prophet says, "or fights against them or attacks them or curses them, God forbids him from entering paradise (q.v.)." In another utterance attributed to the Prophet he says: "My *ahl bayt* can be compared to Noah's (q.v.) ark (q.v.), whoever rides in it is saved and whoever hangs on to it succeeds, and whoever fails to reach it is thrust into hell" (Fīrūzābādī, *Faḍā'il*, ii, 56-9; 75-87).

Once the idea of the "chosen five" or the selected family was established as the main Shīʿī interpretation of the term *ahl al-bayt*, there was no reason why the idea of purification (see CLEANLINESS AND ABLUTION; RITUAL PURITY), which appears in the qur'ānic verse, should not be connected in a more direct way to the divinely selected family. In addition to *ahl al-bayt*, one therefore finds terms such as *al-ʿitra al-ṭāhira* and *al-dhuriyya al-ṭāhira*, "the pure family," or also "the pure descendents," an expression that is more than reminiscent of the holy family (i.e. Jesus [q.v.], Mary [q.v.] and Joseph) in Christianity. And as if to accentuate this point, Fāṭima and Mary are explicitly mentioned together as the matrons of paradise and Fāṭima is even called *al-batūl*, "the virgin" (see SEX AND SEXUALITY; ABSTINENCE; CHASTITY), a most appropriate description for the female figure in the Islamic version of the holy family (see McAuliffe, Chosen).

When the ʿAbbāsids came to power, they, too, based the claim for the legitimacy of their rule on the fact that they were part of the Prophet's family. Concurrently, therefore, the meaning of the term *ahl al-bayt* underwent modifications in opposite directions. While the Shīʿa moved towards the formulation of the idea of the "holy five," or the "pure family" described above, the ʿAbbāsids strove to widen the scope of this family to include ʿAbbās, the Prophet's uncle, stressing that women, noble and holy as they may be, could not be regarded as a source of *nasab* and that the paternal uncle in the absence of the father was equal to the father (see GENDER; INHERITANCE). The extension of the boundaries of *ahl al-bayt* under the ʿAbbāsids followed an already existing model. The ḥadīths speaking about the process of God's selection stop at the clan of Hāshim to include all the families in this clan, the Ṭālibids as well as the ʿAbbāsids. Such traditions can be even more explicit, specifying that the families included in the Prophet's *ahl al-bayt* are *"āl ʿAlī wa-āl Jaʿfar wa-āl ʿAqīl wa-āl al-ʿAbbās"* (Muḥibb al-Dīn al-Ṭabarī, *Dhakhāʾir al-ʿuqbā,* 16).

Not all the commentators accepted the idea that the term *ahl al-bayt* in Q 33:33 is associated with the Prophet's family in the sense that the contending parties wished. Alongside the above-mentioned interpretations, one finds the neutral interpretation that *ahl al-bayt* means simply the Prophet's wives (*nisāʾ al-nabī;* see WIVES OF THE PROPHET). And as if to stress the dissatisfaction with the political and partisan undertones of the current exegesis, one of the commentators stresses that *ahl al-bayt* are the Prophet's wives, "and not as they claim" (Wāḥidī, *Asbāb,* 139-40; Sharon, Ahl al-bayt, 175 n. 15).

As may be expected, a harmonizing version also exists which interprets the term *ahl al-bayt* in such a way that both the Prophet's family and his wives are included. To achieve this end, the term *ahl al-bayt* was divided into two categories: the one, *ahl bayt al-suknā,* namely those who physically lived in the Prophet's home, and *ahl bayt al-nasab,* the Prophet's kin. The qurʾānic verse, according to this interpretation, primarily means the Prophet's household, namely, his wives. But it also contains a concealed meaning (see POLYSEMY), which the Prophet himself revealed by his action, thus disclosing that *ahl al-bayt* here included those who lived in his home, such as his wives, and those who shared his pedigree. They were the whole (clan) of Banū Hāshim and ʿAbd al-Muṭṭalib. Another version of this interpretation states that the Prophet's *ahl al-bayt* included his wives and ʿAlī *(Lisān al-ʿArab).*

In Arabic literature the term *ahl bayt* is used generically to specify the noble and influential family in the tribe or any other socio-political unit, Arab and non-Arab alike (see ARABS). The nobility attached to the term is sometimes stressed by connecting it to the word *sharaf.* The word *bayt* on its own could mean nobility *(wa-bayt al-ʿarab ashrafuhā)* says Ibn Manẓūr (*Lisān al-ʿArab,* s.v. *bayt*). The usage of *ahl al-bayt* for denoting leading families in the Age of Ignorance (q.v.; *jāhiliyya*) as well as under Islam was very extensive. Two examples will suffice to make the point. Ibn al-Kalbī (d. ca. 205/820) says that Nubāta b. Ḥanẓala, the famous Umayyad general, belonged to a noble family of the Qays ʿAyalān "and they are *ahl bayt* commanding strength and nobility" *(wa-hum ahlu baytin lahum baʾs wa-sharaf).* The same is said about non-Arabs. Speaking about the Byzantine dynasties (see BYZANTINES), Ibn ʿAsākir (d. 571/1176) mentions ten *ahl buyūtāt.* The Barmakids are referred to as "from the noble families of Balkh" (*min ahl buyūtāt Balkh;* references in Sharon, Ahl al-bayt, 180-1).

It is noteworthy that the usage of the phrase "people of a/the house" (Ar. *ahl bayt*) to denote the status of nobility and leadership is not unique to the Arabic language (q.v.) or Arab culture. It is rather universal: the ancient Romans spoke about the *patres maiorum gentum,* namely, the elders of the major clans or houses. The tradition concerning this Roman expression goes back to the early days of the Roman monarchy, when the Roman senate was composed of 100 family elders: Tarquinius Priscus, the fifth king of Rome (r. 616-578 B.C.E.), enlarged the number of senate members by another 100 elders who were called "the elders of the minor houses" (*patres minorum gentium;* Elkoshi, *Thesaurus,* 279). In the Bible, the usage of the word "house" *(bāyit)* to denote a family is very common. Moreover, in many cases, the "house" is named after an outstanding personality, and has a similar meaning as the Arabic *ahl al-bayt* (e.g. *Gen* 17:23, 27; *Num* 25:15; cf. Brown et al., *Lexicon,* 109b-110a). The most famous of such "houses" is the "house of David" *(bēth David).* When used in this way, the word has the same meaning as the English "house" in reference to a royal family or a dynasty in general.

It is only natural that under Islam the members of the caliphs' families were called *ahl al-bayt.* ʿAbdallāh, the son of Caliph ʿUmar, referring to his sister's son (the future caliph) ʿUmar b. ʿAbd al-ʿAzīz, says: "He resembles us, *ahl al-bayt,"* which means to say that the Umayyads referred to themselves as *ahl al-bayt.* In a letter written by Marwān II to Saʿīd b. ʿAbd al-Malik b. Marwān during the rebellion against Caliph Walīd II (125-6/743-4), the future caliph referred twice to the Umayyad family as *ahl bayt* and *ahl al-bayt* (for the reference see Sharon, Ahl al-bayt).

It may be concluded that once the caliphate had been established, the pre-Islamic Arabic *(jāhilī)* practice of calling the leading and noble families of the tribes *ahl al-bayt* was extended to each of the four families of the first caliphs. But since ʿAlī's caliphate was controversial, the definition of his family as *ahl al-bayt* was not shared by the whole Muslim community. The Umayyads and their Syrian supporters (see SYRIA) questioned the legitimacy of ʿAlī's rule, with the result that his Iraqi partisans (see IRAQ) and the Shīʿa not only emphasized the *ahl al-bayt* status of ʿAlī's descendents but also gave the term a specific and exclusive meaning. In this way, *ahl al-bayt* acquired a religious overtone, and in time lost its generic meaning. Once the term was attached to the Prophet's person, the road was open for qurʾānic exegesis, originating in Shīʿī circles, to establish its origin in the Qurʾān itself. All the politically charged interpretations of the qurʾānic phrase *ahl al-bayt* emerge because its original meaning was either deliberately or unintentionally forgotten. Yet one should also take into account that such interpretations of the term in connection with the Prophet's family would have been impossible had the term not been used generally as meaning family or kinsfolk.

On the other hand, it is doubtful whether in the Qurʾān the term *ahl al-bayt* (with the definite article) means family. R. Paret, who differentiates between the general term *ahl al-bayt* and the specific one, suggests that it literally meant "the people of the house," namely those who worshipped at the Kaʿba. In all cases in which the term *al-bayt* appears in the Qurʾān, it refers only to the Kaʿba sanctuary (Q 2:125, 127, 158; 3:97; 5:2, 97; 8:35; 22:26, 29, 33; 52:4; 106:3). *Al-bayt* may appear on its own or with an adjective, such as *al-bayt al-ʿatīq* (Q 22:29, 33), *al-bayt al-maʿmūr* (Q 52:4) or *al-bayt al-ḥarām* (i.e. Q 5:97). Paret goes on to suggest that the fact that the *ahl al-bayt* under discussion (Q 33:33) is mentioned in the context of cleaning from pollution falls well within the idea of the purification of the Kaʿba by Abraham and Ishmael (q.v.; Ismāʿīl), which can be found elsewhere in the Qurʾān. One may therefore quite safely conclude, Paret continues, that in the two cases where *ahl al-bayt* appears in this form in the Qurʾān, the original meaning must have been the "worshippers of the house," the Ka'ba, as prescribed by Islam (Paret, Der Plan, 128: *"Anhänger des islamischen Ka'ba-Kultes"*). Along this line of thought, it would not be far-fetched to suggest that the original meaning of the term before Islam was the tribe of Quraysh in general and that this is what is meant in Q 33:33. As to Q 11:73 the connection with the Ka'ba is less certain.

To sum up, the meaning of *ahl al-bayt* in the Qur'ān follows the accepted usage of the term in pre- and post-Islamic Arab society. It denotes family and blood relations as well as a noble and leading "house" of the tribe. Only in the case of Q 33:33 does the term seem to have another, more specific meaning.

M. Sharon

Bibliography

Primary: Abū 'Ubayda, Ma'mar b. al-Muthannā al-Taymī, *Tasmiyat azwāj al-nabī wa-awlādihi,* ed. K.Y. al-Ḥūt, Beirut 1985; M.Ḥ. Fīrūzābādī, *Faḍā'il al-khamsa,* 2 vols., Beirut 1393/1973; Ḥākim al-Ḥaskānī, 'Ubayd Allāh b. 'Abdallāh, *Shawāhid al-tanzīl li-qawā'id al-tafḍīl fī l-āyāt al-nāzila fī ahl al-bayt,* ed. M.B. al-Maḥmūdī, 2 vols. in 1, Beirut 1974; Ibn Abī l-Dunyā, 'Abdallāh b. Muḥammad, *al-Ishrāf fī manzil al-ashrāf,* ed. N.'A. Khalaf, Riyadh 1990; Ibn Sa'd, *Ṭabaqāt,* ed. Sachau; *Lisān al-'Arab;* al-Maqrīzī, Aḥmad b. 'Alī, *Ma'rifat mā yajibu li-āl al-bayt al-nabawī min al-ḥaqq 'alā man 'adāhum,* ed. M.A. 'Āshūr, Cairo 1973; Suyūṭī, *Iḥyā' al-mayyit bi-faḍā'il ahl al-bayt,* ed. K. al-Fatlī, Beirut 1995; al-Ṭabarī, Muḥibb al-Dīn Abū l-'Abbās Aḥmad b. 'Abdallāh, *Dhakhā'ir al-'uqbā fī manāqib dhawi l-qurbā,* Beirut 1973, 16; Wāḥidī, *Asbāb.*

Secondary: 'A.A. 'Abd al-Ghanī, *al-Jawhar al-shaffāf fī ansāb al-sāda al-ashrāf. Nasl al-Ḥusayn,* 2 vols., Damascus 1997; M.M. Bar-Asher, *Scripture and exegesis in early Imami Shiism,* Leiden 1999 (see 94-7 for discussion of Q 55:31, a classical locus for Shī'ī exegesis of the *ḥadīth al-thaqalayn,* i.e. the two things of "weight" that Muḥammad left with his community: the Qur'ān and either the sunna [q.v.] of Muḥammad or the People of the House); Bell, *Qur'ān;* F. Brown, S.R. Driver, C.A. Briggs, *A Hebrew and English lexicon of the Old Testament,* Oxford 1959, 109b-110a; G. Elkoshi, *Thesaurus proverbiorum et idiomatum latinorum,* Jerusalem 1981, 279; I. Goldziher, C. van Arendonk and A.S. Tritton, Ahl al-bayt, in *EI*², i, 257-8; M.A. Isbir, *Ahl bayt rasūl Allāh. Fī dirāsa ḥadītha,* Beirut 1990, 1993; W. Madelung, *The succession to Muḥammad. A study of the early caliphate,* Cambridge 1997, esp. 13-5; J.D. McAuliffe, Chosen of all women. Mary and Fatima in qur'anic exegesis, in *Islamochristiana* 7 (1981), 19-28; M.T. Mudarrisī, *al-Nabī wa-ahl baytihi. Qudwa wa-uswa,* 2 vols., Beirut 1993; R. Paret, Der Plan einer neuen, leicht kommentierten wissenschaftlichen Koran¸bersetzung, in E. Littmann, *Orientalische Studien Enno Littman,* ed. R. Paret, Leiden 1935, 121-30; M. Sharon, *Ahl al-bayt* — People of the House, in *JSAI* 8 (1986), 169-84 (contains further references); id., *Black banners from the east,* Jerusalem/Leiden 1983, 75-82; id., The development of the debate around the legitimacy of authority, in *JSAI* 5 (1986), 121-41 (contains additional bibliography on the topic); id., The Umayyads as *ahl al-bayt,* in *JSAI* 14 (1991), 116-152 (also contains additional bibliography).

People on the Left

see LEFT HAND AND RIGHT HAND; LAST JUDGMENT; BOOK

People on the Right

see LEFT HAND AND RIGHT HAND; LAST JUDGMENT; BOOK

People of the Thicket

An English rendering of the Arabic phrase *aṣḥāb al-ayka* that occurs in four Meccan sūras (Q 15:78; 26:176; 38:13; 50:14). No consensus exists about the identity of these people who suffered the fate of punishment by destruction for their unbelief (see BELIEF AND UNBELIEF; PUNISHMENT STORIES). There are at least five different theories about the identity of these people who are associated with the prophet Shu'ayb (q.v.). Some exegetes consider them to have been the inhabitants of a place called Madyan (see MIDIAN) or, secondly, a subgroup of a people called Madyan; it is also posited that they are another people altogether, a second people to whom the prophet Shu'ayb was sent (i.e. in addition to Madyan), while a fourth alternative suggests that *al-ayka* was a village *(balad),* namely, the village of al-Ḥijr (which is also the title of a qurʾānic sūra, Q 15; see ḤIJR). The fifth theory that is put forward suggests that they are simply Bedouins (*ahl al-bādiya*, people of the desert; see BEDOUIN). Lexicographers define *ayka* and its plural *ayk* as tangled vegetation or a dense forest or wood, hence the English "thicket" or, in Muḥammad Asad's translation, "wooded dales." Others add that it consisted of a particular palm tree, *al-dawm* in Arabic (see DATE PALM). The early exegete Muqātil b. Sulaymān (d. 150/767; see EXEGESIS OF THE QURʾĀN: CLASSICAL AND MEDIEVAL) explains that *al-dawm* is in fact *al-muql* (Theban palm; *Tafsīr,* ii, 434).

This inability to identify precisely the People of the Thicket is further complicated by the variant readings for *al-ayka* (see READINGS OF THE QURʾĀN). Al-Farrāʾ (d. 207/822) discusses the disappearance of the *alif* in two of the four verses which mention the *aṣḥāb al-ayka*. According to him, al-Ḥasan al-Baṣrī (d. 110/728), ʿĀṣim (d. 127-8/745) and al-Aʿmash (d. 148/765) all read *al-ayka* with an *alif* throughout the entire Qurʾān. The people of Medina (q.v.), however, read in two cases (in Q 26:176 and Q 38:13) *layka* instead of *al-ayka* (Farrāʾ, *Maʿānī,* ii, 91; see also RECITATION OF THE QURʾĀN; ORALITY AND WRITING IN ARABIA). Abū Ḥayyān (d. 745/1344) neatly summarizes this discussion, referring to the analogy of Mecca (q.v.) as *makka* in Q 48:24 and *bakka* at Q 3:96, adding that *"layka"* was rejected by the major exegetes. Abū Ḥayyān explains that the *alif* of the definite article was not written down, and that caused the *fatḥa* (the vowel "a") to be shifted to the letter *lām*. As a consequence, the *hamza* (the glottal stop) was dropped completely in these two verses (see ARABIC LANGUAGE). This resulted in some scholars' thinking that *layka* was derived from the radicals *l-y-k* (instead of *ʾ-y-k*). That suggestion, in turn, gave rise to the notion that Layka was a village located in the larger area of al-Ayka (Abū Ḥayyān, *Baḥr,* vii, 36).

Whatever the identification or the linguistic meaning of the word *al-ayka* may be, the qurʾānic importance of the People of the Thicket reflects their exemplification of a typical Meccan theme: a people who disregarded their prophet and who consequently perished. The People of the Thicket are but one of such peoples whose plight ended in destruction for not heeding God's message. The leading classical exegete al-Ṭabarī (d. 310/923) narrates that these people received a particularly harsh punishment since God first sent fire on the People of the Thicket for seven days, from which there was no refuge. After the fire, God sent a cloud as if to protect them and to offer them relief by the suggestion of water, but, in the end, they were annihilated by the fire that came out of the cloud (Ṭabarī, *Tafsīr,* vii, 530-1; likewise the Khārijī Hūd b. Muḥakkam, *Tafsīr,* ii, 354 and the Shīʿī al-Ṭūsī, *Tibyān,* 350; see KHĀRIJĪS; SHĪʿISM AND THE QURʾĀN). Beeston ("Men of the Tanglewood") provides some evidence that they were members of the Dusares cult of ancient northwestern Arabia, a vegetation deity (see PRE-ISLAMIC ARABIA AND THE QURʾĀN). Speyer (*Erzählungen,* 253), on the other hand, suggests that *ayka* may refer to the tamarisk that Abraham (q.v.) had planted near Beersheba (*Gen* 21:33; see AGRICULTURE AND VEGETATION).

John Nawas

Bibliography

Primary: Abū Ḥayyān, *Baḥr,* ed. Beirut; Farrāʾ, *Maʿānī;* Hūd b. Muḥakkam, *Tafsīr;* Kisāʾī, *Qiṣaṣ,* trans. W.M. Thackston, *The tales of the prophets of al-Kisaʾi,* Boston 1978, 204-8; al-Rāghib al-Iṣfahānī, *Mufradāt;* al-Samīn al-Ḥalabī, Aḥmad b.

Yūsuf, *ʿUmdat al-ḥuffāẓ fī tafsīr ashraf al-alfāẓ*, ed. M.B. ʿUyūn al-Sūd, 4 vols., Beirut 1996, i, 144; Ṭabarī, *Tafsīr*, Beirut 1992, vii, 530-1; ix, 471; Thaʿlabī, *Qiṣaṣ*, trans. W.M. Brinner, *Lives of the prophets*, Leiden 2002, 274-7; Ṭūsī, *Tibyān*. Secondary: A.F.L. Beeston, The "Men of the Tanglewood" in the Qur'an, in *JSS* 13 (1968), 253-5; C.E. Bosworth, Madyan Shuʿayb in pre-Islamic and early Islamic lore and history, in *JSS* 29 (1984), 53-64; Horovitz, *KU*, 93-4, 119-20; id., The qurʾānic prophet Shuʿaib and Ibn Taimiyya's epistle concerning him, in *Muséon* 87 (1974), 425-40; Speyer, *Erzählungen*.

People of Tubbaʿ

see TUBBAʿ; PUNISHMENT STORIES

Permitted

see FORBIDDEN; LAWFUL AND UNLAWFUL

Persecution

see CORRUPTION; DISSENSION

Perseverance

see TRUST AND PATIENCE

Persian Literature and the Qurʾān

The influence of the Qurʾān on Persian language and literature has been pervasive but at the same time, diffuse and often mediated, making it difficult, in the absence of methodologically rigorous studies of the matter, to quantify or assess precisely. Persian poetry and prose *belles lettres* of the fourth/tenth to fifth/eleventh centuries, though of "Islamicate" expression, looked for the bulk of its subject matter to the pre-Islamic Middle Persian traditions of minstrelsy and lyric poetry, advice literature *(andarz),* epic and romance (which typically assert the values of the old Sasanian nobility over and above, or in addition to, Islamic ones) as well as translations of Sanskrit and Parthian tales. Persian poetry did, of course, adapt particulars from Arabic literary models: for example, the imitation of the *nasīb* and *raḥīl* of the pre-Islamic Arabic *qaṣīda* (see POETS AND POETRY; ORALITY AND WRITING IN ARABIA) by Manūchihrī (d. ca. 432/1041) and, later on, the reworking of the *Majnūn-Laylā* cycle by Niẓāmī (d. 605/1209) and scores of subsequent Persian, Turkish and Urdu poets (see LITERATURE AND THE QURʾĀN).

The Arabic Qurʾān, being in another language and in an inimitable category (see INIMITABILITY; ARABIC LANGUAGE; LANGUAGE AND STYLE OF THE QURʾĀN) above literature, rarely provided the initial inspiration for Persian literary texts, though it did help shape the lexical, stylistic and moral contours of the emerging literature of Islamicate expression in greater Iran, especially through Persian translations and *tafsīr*s of the text beginning in the fourth/tenth century or even earlier (see TRANSLATIONS OF THE QURʾĀN; EXEGESIS OF THE QURʾĀN: CLASSICAL AND MEDIEVAL; TRADITIONAL DISCIPLINES OF QURʾĀNIC STUDY; GRAMMAR AND THE QURʾĀN). The practice, however, of professional poetry within the milieu of the princely courts — the source of most literary patronage — was often regarded as inherently secular or even un-Islamic, which initially discouraged the extensive incorporation of scriptural or religious subjects in literature. Some early Persian poetry, patronized by the eastern Iranian feudal nobility *(dihqāns),* evinces a strong concern with *sukhun* (modern *sukhan*), well-considered and carefully crafted speech of philosophical or ethical nature (see PHILOSOPHY AND THE QURʾĀN; ETHICS AND THE QURʾĀN). In the fifth/eleventh century religious poetry, of either popular expression (e.g. the quatrains of the Ṣūfī saint Abū Saʿīd-i Abī l-Khayr [d. 440/1049]; see ṢŪFISM AND THE QURʾĀN) or sectarian bent (the *qaṣīda*s of the Ismāʿīlī preacher Nāṣir-i Khusraw [d. ca. 470/1077]; see SHĪʿISM AND THE QURʾĀN), achieved canonical status within specific textual communities. Sanāʾī of Ghazna (d. ca. 525/1131), appealing consciously to the example of Ḥassān b. Thābit (d. before 40/661), managed to attract the patronage of the mystically-minded religious scholars *(ʿulamā)* in Khurasān. Here Sanāʾī achieved a reputation for combining the practice of poetry *(shiʿr)* with the preaching of religion *(sharʿ)* and was subsequently able to secure the patronage of Bahrāmshāh to pursue such mystico-didactic poetry at the Ghaznavid court (Lewis, *Reading,* 171-87; see TEACHING AND PREACHING THE QURʾĀN). The tension between court and cloister nevertheless remained a concern two hundred years later, as revealed in the belabored distinction that Sulṭān Walad of Konya (d. 712/1312) makes between the poetry of professional poets and the poetry of saints (*Mathnawī-yi waladī,* 53-5 and 211-2; see SAINT).

By the end of the sixth/twelfth century, allusions *(talmīḥāt)* and quotations *(iqtibās)* from Qurʾān and ḥadīth (see ḤADĪTH AND THE QURʾĀN) jostled with Greek philosophy and Iranian mythopoesis for authority, as indicated in the following verse *(bayt)* of Jamāl al-Dīn-i Iṣfahānī (d. 588/1192): *rah bi Qurʾān ast kam khwān harza-yi Yūnāniyān/aṣl akhbār ast mashnaw qiṣṣa-yi Isfandiyār,* "The path is through Qurʾān; do not read the nonsense of the Greeks so much!/The source is *akhbār;* do not listen to the story of Esfandiyar." The conscious and direct appeal to qurʾānic authority in Persian poetry reached its peak in the seventh/thirteenth to eighth/fourteenth centuries. Subsequent to this, qurʾānic motifs tend to assume more metaphorical and elastic qualities, in part because of the aesthetic ideals of the "Indian" style of poetry but also because the Qurʾān had so thoroughly permeated the tradition that qurʾānic allusions might evoke famous secondary or tertiary literary texts in Persian, rather than pointing the reader to the Qurʾān itself. From the Safavid era onwards, Shīʿī sacred history and ritual, as embodied in the mythopoetics of Ḥusayn's martyrdom (see PEOPLE OF THE HOUSE; FAMILY OF THE PROPHET; MARTYRS) and the passion play *(taʿziya),* informs the poetry of religious expression whereas the gradually secularizing literary canon of the late nineteenth and twentieth centuries reflects nationalist and modernist agendas as well as the influence of European letters (see also POLITICS AND THE QURʾĀN).

The Arabic element in Persian language and literature

The bulk of the Iranian nobility appear to have converted to Islam in the third/ninth century, until which time Zoroastrians (see MAGIANS) continued composing works in Middle Persian, an Indo-European language written in a script derived from Aramaic. By the fourth/tenth century (neo-) Persian had itself emerged as a vibrant literary language, written in the Arabic script (q.v.) and widely patronized throughout the eastern areas of greater Iran (Khurasan, Afghanistan and Transoxania).

The frequency of occurrence of lexemes of Arabic origin in Persian has been calculated (though on the basis of a rather limited corpus) at only about 10% in the fourth/tenth-century and 25% in the sixth/twelfth-century. The ratio of Arabic loanwords to native Persian lexemes in the entire lexicon has, however, been calculated for texts of the fourth/tenth century at about 25 to 30% and for the sixth/twelfth century at around 50% (Jazayery, Arabic element, 117). The increased penetration and use of loanwords from Arabic reflects at least in part the influence of the Qurʾān on Persian literature and society, though this naturally depends a great deal on the topic and genre of writing. During the Safavid era Arabisms come into vogue in bureaucratic language and the volumes of religious writing (in which the vocabulary of Arabic and the Qurʾān are proportionally higher) while Arabic itself paradoxically waned as a living literary language in Persia (Perry, Persian in the Safavid period, 272, 276). In the middle of the twentieth century, it was estimated that words of Arabic origin occur at an average frequency of approximately 45%, though the percentage is far below this in poetry and higher for technical subjects relating to religion, philosophy or law (Jazayery, Arabic element, 118). Since that time, however, conscious efforts to use Persian roots for calques and new coinages (e.g. *Qurʾān-pazhūhī*, or "Qurʾānic studies," a term from the 1980s), encouraged by the Persian Academy of Language *(Farhangistān)* in Iran, have gradually led to a perceived (though as yet seemingly undocumented) decrease in this percentage.

Since lexical and morphological borrowing from Arabic occurred through a variety of social nexuses and institutions (military garrisons, government administration and registers, princely courts, religious courts, mosques and Ṣūfī lodges, the Niẓāmiyya colleges, etc.; see MOSQUE), this does not measure the direct influence of the Qurʾān, per se. Persian poetry borrowed from Arabic poetry the obligatory use of rhyme (see RHYMED PROSE), the conventions and terminology of rhetoric (see RHETORIC AND THE QURʾĀN) and prosody and the basic categories and thematics of the *qaṣīda* and the *ghazal* (which latter, however, Persian poets adapted from a thematic into a specific fixed-form genre). Likewise, certain metaphors, motifs or rhetorical conceits can be traced to particular literary models or Arabic proverbs (see the catalogues in Shamīsā, *Farhang-i talmīḥāt,* and Dāmādī, *Maḍāmīn-i mushtarak;* see METAPHOR). Among the most influential Arabic models for classical Persian literature we may note the panegyric *qaṣīda*s of al-Mutanabbī (d. 354/965); the wine (q.v.) odes of Abū Nuwās (d. 198/810); the literary anthologies of al-Thaʿālibī (d. ca. 427/1038); the artistic prose works of Ibn al-Muqaffaʿ (d. 142/760) and Badīʿ al-Zamān al-Hamadhānī (d. 398/1008); the philosophic and scientific treatises of Abū ʿAlī Ibn Sīnā (d. 428/1037) and al-Bīrūnī (d. 443/1051; see SCIENCE AND THE QURʾĀN; POPULAR AND TALISMANIC USES OF THE QURʾĀN); and works of mystico-didactic orientation by authors such as al-Qushayrī (d. 464/1072) or especially al-Ghazālī (d. 505/1111). It should be noted that several of these figures were ethnic Iranians and/or composed some of their works in Persian, a fact that doubtless played a role in facilitating the assimilation of Arabic literary traditions into Persian.

Arabic courtly literature may therefore have played a larger role than the Qurʾān itself in the Arabicization of Persian literature. Nevertheless, adoption of the Arabic script, adaptation of Arabic literary forms and the acceptance of a large body of Arabic-origin lexemes into both literature and everyday speech may all be read as indices of the oblique influence of the Qurʾān on Persian, insofar as the Qurʾān created the prerequisite conditions for Arabic to become an administrative, religious, scientific and literary lingua franca in greater Persia.

Translations of the Qurʾān in Persia

Though some poets of the seventh/thirteenth century, such as Saʿdī and Rūmī, would routinely compose original macaronic verse in Arabic and Persian, those literate in Persian (including Persophilic Turks, Mongols and Indians as well as ethnic or native Persian-speakers; see TURKISH LITERATURE AND THE QURʾĀN; SOUTH ASIAN LITERATURE AND THE

QUR'ĀN) might nevertheless remain imperfectly tutored in the Arabic of the Qur'ān. We are told that Shaykh Aḥmad of Jām (*Spiritual elephant,* 31-2), before his repentance at the age of twenty-two (ca. 463/1070), was unable to recite even the *al-ḥamd* (a familiar name in Iran for Q 1, Sūrat al-Fātiḥa; see PRAISE; FĀTIḤA). In one *ghazal,* Sanā'ī portrays a beautiful boy who, though newly repentant and celibate, previously spent his time at the taverns (the *kharābāt,* often associated with the Magians/*mughān*), had never before managed to memorize a short sūra like Q 95 and had in fact been so debauched that he would even invent short pseudo-sūras to declaim as if by heart (Sanā'ī, *Dīwān,* 1021-2; see MEMORY; RECITATION OF THE QUR'ĀN).

We may infer from such statements that, while a basic knowledge in Arabic of at least some sūras of the Qur'ān was expected of literate Persian-speaking Muslims (to say nothing of the large number of Persian scholars of religion and law, many of whom trained in Arabic in the Niẓāmiyya and other *madrasa*s from the fifth/eleventh century onward; see LAW AND THE QUR'ĀN; THEOLOGY AND THE QUR'ĀN), there was nevertheless a need to translate the Qur'ān for Persian Muslims. Many Persians apparently preferred to encounter the text in Persian, with the help of Persian commentaries and bilingual dictionaries/guides such as the *Wujūh-i Qur'ān* written in 558/1163 by Abū l-Faḍl Ḥubaysh of Tiflis. Abū Bakr-i Nayshābūrī, who wrote his *Tafsīr-i sūrābādī* circa 470-80/1077-87 in simple, fluent Persian prose, indicates that had he written it in Arabic, it would have needed a teacher to give an accurate and agreeable Persian translation (*targum,* Sajjādī, *Guzīda'ī,* 199). Abū l-Futūḥ-i Rāzī indicates in his voluminous Qur'ān commentary, *Rawḍ al-jinān wa-rūḥ al-janān* (composed over the years 510-56/1116-61) that he chose to write a commentary in Persian and one in Arabic but began with the former, for which there was more demand (Sajjādī, *Guzīda'ī,* 205). From Sulṭān Walad's remark in 700/1301 (*Rabābnāma,* 414) that all the legal schools allow the ritual prayers *(namāz)* to be recited in Persian and that the Ḥanafīs allow this even for a person who is capable of reciting them in Arabic, it would seem that Persian was preferred even for rote liturgical situations (see PRAYER; RITUAL AND THE QUR'ĀN).

Medieval sources attribute the first Persian translation of a portion of the Qur'ān — the Fātiḥa, for use in the *ṣalāt* prayers (see PRAYER FORMULAS) — to the first Persian believer, Salmān-i Fārsī, who supposedly attained the Prophet's tacit approval for this practice (see COMPANIONS OF THE PROPHET). Salmān is said to have translated the Arabic *basmala* (q.v.) using an entirely Persian lexicon, as *bi nām-i yazdān-i bakhshāyanda.* However apocryphal the Salmān story may be, Abū Ḥanīfa, whose eponymous legal tradition was dominant in pre-Safavid Iran, did permit translation of the Qur'ān for those who did not know Arabic well and although this position was not universally accepted, a large number of Persian translations of the Qur'ān exist from both the medieval and modern periods.

A fragmentary Persian translation (of Q 10:61 through Q 14:25) tentatively dated to the early fourth/tenth century documents an intermediate stage in the transition from popular accentual to the new quantitative Persian metrics. This translation (Rajā'ī, *Pulī*) presents the Arabic text of the Qur'ān broken into blocks (perhaps paragraphs or pericopes), each followed by the corresponding passage in a sonorous Persian that alternates between rhymed prose, quasi-accentual and quantitative metrics. This translation does not demonstrate a strong concern for consistency in the Persian, ranging from an exact rendering in some places, to paraphrase in others, to a somewhat free interpretation in still others. Indeed, in another very early interlinear Persian translation (Riwāqī, *Qurʾān-i quds*), which is otherwise quite accurate, the Persian of the *basmala* often changes from sūra to sūra, becoming variously:

bi nām-i khudā-yi mihrbān-i raḥmat-kunār
bi nām-i khudā-yi rūzī-dādār-i raḥmat-kunār (e.g. Q 7)
bi nām-i khudā-yi mihrbānī-yi bakhshāyanda (e.g. Q 61)
bi-nām-i khudā-yi rūzī-dahanda-yi bakhshāyanda (e.g. Q 34)

We might predict lexical variety from one Persian translation of the Qurʾān to another on the basis of regional or dialectical idiosyncrasies but such internal variation quite possibly reflects the fluidity of the Islamic homiletic tradition and the authority of orally delivered, or perhaps even prompt-book Persian "targums" for individual sūras, as delivered by different popular preachers in Iran. Al-Jāḥiẓ (d. ca. 254/868) tells of a contemporary, the popular bilingual preacher Mūsā b. Sayyār al-Aswārī, who would read a verse of the Qurʾān aloud to his class and then comment upon it in Arabic to the Arabs, sitting together at his right, and then turn to the Persians, sitting at his left, and repeat his comments for them in Persian (*Bayān,* i, 368).

In addition to stand-alone translations, many Persian works of exegesis also contain translations of the Qurʾān. The mid-fourth/tenth century *Tarjuma-yi tafsīr-i Ṭabarī,* a loose adaptation of material from al-Ṭabarī's (d. 310/923) commentary and his history, which might be more accurately described as "the Samanid Persian Commentary project," also includes an elegant and accurate Persian translation of the Qurʾān. The Samanid ruler, Manṣūr b. Nūḥ (r. 350-66/961-76), received a forty-volume manuscript in Arabic of al-Ṭabarī's works from Baghdād but finding it difficult to read it, commissioned several Transoxanian scholars to translate it to Persian. Probably because it was an official state project, and to avoid any theological objections, al-Manṣūr sought and received *fatwa*s declaring the permissibility of translating the book for those who do not know Arabic. This "translation" of al-Ṭabarī's *tafsīr* remained prestigious and influential but did not by any means end the market for new Persian *tafsīr*s, scores of which — from various theological standpoints — survive from the medieval and early modern period (see Muḥammad-Khānī, Tafsīr-i Qurʾān; see EXEGESIS OF THE QURʾĀN: CLASSICAL AND MEDIEVAL), some of them consisting primarily of a Persian rendering of the qurʾānic text, such as the *Tafsīr* of Abū Ḥafṣ Najm al-Dīn-i Nasafī (d. 538/1143). Mention should be made of Maybudī's popular Ṣūfī *tafsīr, Kashf al-asrār wa-ʿuddat al-abrār* (written 520/1126), which incorporates the commentary of his teacher, Anṣārī of Herat (see below), and features a three-step exegesis: first a literal translation of the sūra in question, then a traditional grammatico-lexical analysis and explanation of the circumstances of revelation (see OCCASIONS OF REVELATION) and, finally, a mystical-esoteric reading (see POLYSEMY; LITERARY STRUCTURES OF THE QURʾĀN).

Many theoretical works on *fiqh,* lay manuals about ritual observance (not a few in verse) and compilations of *fatwa*s were composed in or translated to Persian, beginning no later than the Ghaznavid period but becoming especially important in the Safavid era, when they assisted in the Shīʿīfication of the populace. Such works often contain translations and glosses of some Qurʾān verses (see Barzigar, Fiqh, 1048-51). Though the Islamic Republic of Iran has placed greater emphasis on the study of Arabic in the curriculum, perhaps a dozen new Persian translations of the Qurʾān appeared in the 1980s and 1990s.

Formal features and imagery of the Qurʾān in Persian poetry

Persian prose texts of the fourth/tenth to fifth/eleventh centuries generally ignore rhetorical artifice and ornamentation. By the seventh/thirteenth century, however, rhymed prose *(sajʿ)* became *de rigeur* in Persian *belles lettres,* largely inspired by the secular example of Hamadhānī's *Maqāmāt,* and relying heavily on the morphological parallels of loanwords from Arabic. The application of *sajʿ* to devotional texts, such as the *Munājāt* (intimate prayers) of ʿAbdallāh Anṣārī of Herat (d. 481/1088), may also reflect the stylistic inspiration of the Arabic Qurʾān or a Persian translation (e.g. Rajāʾī, *Pulī*) which tried to create similar prose cadences and rhymes in Persian.

Persian narrative poems conventionally begin with a section *(ḥamd)* of several lines invoking and praising God. These doxologies, especially in the early period, tend not to emphasize the terminology of specific Islamic doctrine and theology but to expound God's transcendence in a generalized Persian vocabulary. It had, in fact, already been the practice to begin Middle Persian texts with the formula "In the name of God" *(pat nām-i Yazdān),* though the practice received further authority from the Qurʾān as well as the specific wording of the Arabic *basmala,* which usually appeared as a prefatory formula on the opening page of Persian texts. Niẓāmī moved the conventional *basmala* from its place at the head of the text as a disconnected prose formula and embedded it, with some metrical elasticity, as a quotation *(taḍmīn)* into the opening line of verse in his *Makhzan al-asrār* (ca. 572/1176?): *bism-i a[ ]lāhi l-raḥ[a]māni l-raḥīm/hast kilīd-i dar-i ganj-i ḥakīm,* "In the name of God, the merciful, the compassionate/is the key to the door of the treasure of the wise one." This practice was frequently emulated by subsequent poets composing in this same meter *(sarīʿ),* some of whom repeat the phrase as a litany throughout ten or more opening lines of the poem (Khazānadārlū, *Manẓūma,* 15-25).

Immediately following the opening invocation and doxology, the poet typically includes sections in praise *(naʿt)* of the Prophet (an additional section dedicated to the imāms often appears in the works of Shīʿī authors; see NAMES OF THE PROPHET; IMĀM; IMPECCABILITY; PROPHETS AND PROPHETHOOD) and a subsequent section recalling the Prophet's *miʿrāj* (see ASCENSION). These sections occasionally reference or allude to phrases in the Qurʾān (e.g. *qāba qawsayn,* Q 53:9), though they draw in the main on extra-qurʾānic elaborations. Illumination and illustration (see ICONOCLASM; ORNAMENTATION AND ILLUMINATION) were an integral feature of the Persian literary tradition, at least for manuscripts produced by royal courts, and some themes from the Qurʾān and its associated lore regularly recur in the miniature tradition, including the prophet Muḥammad riding Burāq on the *miʿrāj* and Joseph (q.v.) being rescued from the pit (see BENJAMIN; BROTHERS AND BROTHERHOOD). Though illustrations of the Prophet and ʿAlī do occur (e.g. Mīrzā ʿAlī's depiction of the Prophet and ʿAlī with Ḥasan and Ḥusayn in the ship of faith, ca. 1530, included in the Houghton/Shāh Ṭahmāsp *Shāhnāma;* see ʿALĪ B. ABĪ ṬĀLIB), the scenes depict extra-qurʾānic material, probably to avoid the iconic representation of sacred scripture.

Furthermore, one may point to specific

images or concepts which stem from the Qurʾān but occur in various literary contexts, both sacred and profane, without necessarily evoking a specific verse of the Qurʾān. Examples of this might include allusions to Isrāfīl and the blast of the trumpet of resurrection (q.v.; multiple qurʾānic references, e.g. Q 50:20; see also APOCALYPSE). The generative letters *kāf* and *nūn,* which joining together form the divine command *kun,* "Be!" as e.g. in the phrase *kun fa-yakūn* in Q 2:117 (see CREATION; COSMOLOGY), are evoked in the opening line of Asadī's *Garshāspnāma* (written 458/1066), as follows: *sipās az khudā īzad-i rahnamāy/ki az kāf wa nūn kard gītī bi-pāy,* "Thanks to God, the guiding lord/who by the letters B and E set up the world." Discrete ideas and images from the Qurʾān are most commonly used as complementary terms in similes and metaphors. Niẓāmī's Majnūn, for example, finds himself in a garden with flowing rivers, like Kawthar, reminiscent of Q 108 and the definitions of *al-kawthar* elaborated in the ḥadīth and *tafsīr* literature (see GARDENS; SPRINGS AND FOUNTAINS).

Historical and exegetical works, such as the so-called translation of al-Ṭabarī's *tafsīr,* provided details about the lives of the qurʾānic prophets in Persian from at least the middle fourth/tenth century. Nevertheless, Persian panegyric poetry through the fifth/eleventh century contains infrequent mention of the prophets, with the exception of Nāṣir Khusraw's poetry in praise of ʿAlī and the Fāṭimid imāms, which alludes often to the stories of the prophets (Pūrnāmdārīān, *Dāstān-i payāmbarān,* 7-35). Persian imitations of the Arabic "stories of the prophets" *(qiṣaṣ al-anbiyāʾ)* genre are common, the most popular being the fifth/eleventh century prose work of Abū Isḥāq Ibrāhīm of Nayshābūr, though there are also some in verse. Entire poems are also dedicated to single prophetic figures, such as Moses (q.v.), Solomon (q.v.), etc. Niẓāmī's portrayal of Alexander (q.v.) in his *Iskandarnāma* draws upon the qurʾānic Dhū l-Qarnayn (Q 18:83 f.) for the image of Alexander as explorer/conqueror, but also relies on the Alexander romance of pseudo-Callisthenes and medieval Persian literature of Zoroastrian provenance for the image of Alexander as philosopher and prophet.

The depiction of Jesus (q.v.) in Persian poetry derives primarily from the Qurʾān and *tafsīr* as well as from the *qiṣaṣ al-anbiyāʾ* literature and Arabic poetry (Aryān, *Chihra-yi masīḥ,* 11, 96). It is worth noting the existence of a complete Judeo-Persian translation of the Pentateuch from 1319 C.E. (there are also earlier fragmentary versions), and Judeo-Persian poems in praise of Moses, Solomon and other Hebrew prophets from the fourteenth century onward; Jewish Persian scholars appear to have been consulted by Bīrūnī and others and may constitute an independent source of *Isrāʾīliyyāt* (i.e. Jewish and Christian lore; see JEWS AND JUDAISM; CHRISTIANS AND CHRISTIANITY; CHILDREN OF ISRAEL; PEOPLE OF THE BOOK) for Persian literature (Rypka, *History,* 737-8). Despite their familiarity with all these ancillary sources, Persian mystical poets nevertheless continued to think of the Qurʾān as the *Ur*-source for human knowledge of the prophets. The qurʾānic encounter between Moses and an unnamed servant (later identified with Khiḍr; see KHAḌIR/KHIḌR) endowed by God with knowledge that gives him superior insight (Q 18:65-82; see KNOWLEDGE AND LEARNING) is often upheld as a paradigm of the relationship of a disciple to his Ṣūfī master. Sulṭān Walad (*Mathnawī-yi waladī,* 41-2) compares the relationship between Jalāl al-Dīn Rūmī (d. 672/1273) and Shams-i Tabrīzī (disappeared ca. 645/1248) in terms of Moses and Khiḍr. Rūmī, meanwhile, sees the

Qurʾān as primarily a vehicle to attain similar prophetic insight, when he speaks (*Mathnawī*, i, 1537-8) of the mystic "states of the prophets, those fish of the pure sea of divine majesty... When you escape into the true Qurʾān, you mix with the soul of the prophets."

The Joseph narrative, described as "the best of stories" *(aḥsan al-qaṣaṣ)* in Q 12:3 (see NARRATIVES), was the primary qurʾānic narrative reflected in longer poems in Persian. In the late fifth/eleventh century two renditions of the story of Joseph (Yūsuf) and Potiphar's wife (invariably named Zulaykhā in the Persian texts, drawing on extra-qurʾānic lore) appeared: a prose version doubtfully attributed to ʿAbdallāh Anṣārī in the *Anīs al-murīdīn wa-shams al-majālis* and a verse recitation, formerly attributed to Firdawsī but perhaps by Amānī (fl. fifth/eleventh cent.). That this story was not thought of as a literary adaptation of the Qurʾān text but rather as an elaboration of the *Isrāʾīliyyāt* and a springboard for the poet's imagination can be seen in both the famous mystical elaboration by Jāmī (d. 898/1492), which goes far beyond and changes the focus of the "best of stories," and the politically progressive rendition of 1239/1823 by the Tajik poet, Hoziq of Bukhara.

Direct references to the Qurʾān in Persian literature

From the seventh/thirteenth century, mystico-didactic poetry became the dominant (though not exclusive) genre of Persian poetry, frequently presenting the stories of the prophets (including the biography of Muḥammad; see SĪRA AND THE QURʾĀN) and the saints (*aqṭāb* or *abdāl*) in verse. Such poetry might be thought of as the most intense locus of qurʾānic influence on Persian, though it draws as much, if not more, upon ḥadīth and *sīra*, the *Isrāʾīliyyāt*, the homiletic traditions of official preachers *(khaṭīb)*, street preachers *(wāʿiẓ)* and story-tellers *(quṣṣāṣ)*, Ṣūfī manuals and other vernacular and oral sources, however much these may all have seen the Qurʾān as their ultimate locus of inspiration.

Ritual use of the Qurʾān is, naturally, attested in Persian literature, especially with respect to healing and funerals (e.g. Shaykh Aḥmad, *Spiritual elephant*, story 13; see BURIAL; MEDICINE AND THE QURʾĀN). Saʿdī (*Gulistān*, 132) tells several jokes about muezzins and others reciting the Qurʾān poorly or in an ugly voice. One man with a particularly bad voice explains he receives no salary but chants for the sake of God; for God's sake, don't chant, he is told. Ḥāfiẓ (d. 792/1391), who claims the ability to recite the Qurʾān by heart in all fourteen canonical recitations (*chārdah riwāyat*, *Dīwān*, i, 202; see READINGS OF THE QURʾĀN), documents the still very common practice of swearing an oath upon the Qurʾān in everyday speech (Ḥāfiẓ, *Dīwān*, i, 892; see OATHS): *nadīdam khwushtar az shiʿr-i tu ḥāfiẓ/bi-Qurʾān-ī ki andar sīna dārī*, "I have never seen poetry more beautiful than yours, Ḥafiẓ!/By the Qurʾān which you carry within your heart!" Elsewhere, humorously consoling himself over the inability of pious ascetics to comprehend his debauchery *(rindī)*, Ḥāfiẓ alludes to the belief that demons flee from people who recite the Qurʾān (*Dīwān*, i, 392; see DEVIL; JINN; ASCETICISM). Recitation of the verse *wa-in yakād* (Q 68:51) was believed to act as a prophylactic to the effects of the evil eye (see EYES), as a line of Humām-i Tabrīzī (d. 714/1314) attests: *dar ḥāl wa-in yakād bar khwānd har kas ki naẓar fikand bar way*, "Immediately whenever anyone cast a glance upon him, he would recite *wa-in yakād*."

Poetry and secular prose attest a Persian vocabulary for the uttering of pious formulas, which though perhaps derived from the exegetical or theological literature, assumed a vernacular form of expression (see EVERYDAY LIFE, THE QURʾĀN IN). We find phrases such as *istirjāʿ-kunān* (Bayhaqī, *Tārīkh*, 953), meaning "while reciting the verse *innā lillāh wa-innā ilayhi rājiʿūn*," as per Q 2:156. Rūmī's *Mathnawī* (i, 50) argues the primacy of intention when it comes to the utterance of the *istithnā*, a term derived from *lā yastathnūna* (Q 68:18), meaning the recitation of *in shāʾ Allāh* as enjoined in Q 18:23-4: *ay basī n-āwarda istithnā bi guft/ jān-i ū bā jān-i istithnā-st juft*, "The soul of many a person is one with *istithnā* even without verbalizing the *istithnā* aloud."

The word *qurʾān* itself appears frequently in Persian poetry, pronounced, of course, according to Persian phonology (e.g. *qorʾān*) and behaving as a nativized Persian word, without the Arabic definite article *(al-)*. Shīʿī translators of the text into Persian, following the descriptive adjective given in Q 50:1 and Q 85:21 typically title it *Qurʾān-i majīd*. A Middle Persian word, however, meaning book or document, *nubī* (the medial labial consonant is unstable, appearing also as *nupī* or *nawī*), also appears in classical Persian poetry as an alternate proper name for the Qurʾān ("the scripture"; see BOOK; NAMES OF THE QURʾĀN). In 485/1092 Asadī-yi Ṭūsī writes in his *Garshāspnāma* (3): *nubī muʿjiz ūrā zi īzad payām*, "The scripture inimitable, his message from God." Sanāʾī (*Dīwān*, 1061) says: *jamʿ kard īn rahī-t shiʿr-i tu rā/cun nubī rā guzīda ʿuthmān kard*, "This servant of yours gathered your poetry, just as ʿUthmān compiled the scripture" (see COLLECTION OF THE QURʾĀN). Several lines of Rūmī's *Mathnawī* begin with the phrase *dar nubī...*, "In the scripture...," such as this line (vi, 656) which glosses the phrase *yuḍillu bihi kathīran wa-yahdī bihi kathīran* from Q 2:26 as follows: *dar nubī farmūd k-īn Qurʾān zi dil/hādi-yi baʿḍī u baʿḍī rā muḍill*, "In the scripture [God] said that this Qurʾān, with respect to the heart (q.v.)/guides some and misleads some" (see ASTRAY; ERROR; FREEDOM AND PREDESTINATION).

Quotations from the Qurʾān in Persian literature

Perhaps because of the difficulty of setting quotations from Arabic of more than a word or two within one of the established Persian meters, poets frequently allude to particular verses of the Qurʾān by an abbreviated name, often deriving from the commentary tradition, though Persian poetry does not always use qurʾānic verses in a particularly pious context. In an early poem about the virtues of ʿAlī, Kisāʾī of Marw (b. 341/953) refers in one line to the *āyat-i qurbā* (Q 17:26 and Q 30:38) and in another to the *āyat al-kursī*, a conventional name for Q 2:255 (but sometimes alluding to Q 57:4; see VERSES; THRONE OF GOD). He even quotes a few phrases from the Qurʾān in Arabic (*Kisāʾī*, 93, 95). Saʿdī (*Būstān*, 76) writes around 654/1256: *basā kas bi rūz āyat-i ṣulḥ khwānad/chu shab āmad sipah bar sar-i khufta rānad*, "Many a person will read the peace (q.v.) verse in the daytime/ When night comes, he'll charge the army against the sleeping [foe]." This allusion to the *āyat-i ṣulḥ*, or "peace verse," has been identified with Q 49:9-10 (e.g. *fa-aṣliḥū bayna akhawaykum*), though Q 4:128 *(al-ṣulḥ khayrun)* has also been suggested (see also ENEMIES; FIGHTING; DAY AND NIGHT). Nāṣir-i Khusraw seems to intend two separate verses, Q 48:10 and Q 48:18, by his reference to the *āyat-i bayʿat* in the following line: *yik rūz bikhwāndam zi Qurʾān āyat-i bayʿat/k-īzad bi Qurʾān guft ki bud dast-i man az bar*, "One day I read the verse of allegiance from the Qurʾān how God said in the Qurʾān that my hand was the upper one." The Perso-Arabic phrase *yār-i ghār*, "the friend in the cave (q.v.)," alluding to Q 9:40 as well as the extra-qurʾānic amplifications of the story of Abū Bakr accompanying the prophet Muḥammad on his migration to Medina (q.v.; see also EMIGRATION; OPPOSITION TO MUḤAMMAD), is proverbially and hyperbolically used in Persian poetry to describe exemplary friendship or discipleship (see FRIENDS AND FRIENDSHIP).

As noted above, Arabic prosody differs considerably from Persian and it requires some versatility to set extended Arabic phrases within the metrical constraints of Persian verse. Poets nevertheless managed to find ways to do this without altering the qurʾānic text, except for slight licenses (such as elision of the definite article *al-*), and, of course, vocalizing the words according to Persian phonology and prosody. The first to include citations from the Qurʾān extensively was Sanāʾī, who in the context of discussing the *miʿrāj,* for example, embeds *mā zāgha l-baṣar* from Q 53:17 in one poem (*Dīwān,* 568), and weaves the words *alladhī asrā* and *aqṣā* from Q 17:1 into another (Sanāʾī, *Ḥadīqa,* 195). ʿAṭṭār (d. ca. 617/1221) manages within a Persian hemistich of only fifteen syllables (*Dīwān-i ʿAṭṭār,* 774) to incorporate two Arabic quotations, of six and of five syllables in length, respectively, from the "light (q.v.) verse" (*āya-yi nūr,* Q 24:35): *ay chirāgh-i khuld az īn miskhāt-i muẓlim kun kinār/tā shawī nūrun ʿalā nūrin ki lam tamsas-hu nār,* "O lamp (q.v.) of the highest heaven, avoid this gloomy niche/That you may become "light upon light" though "no fire (q.v.) touched it." In part due to the subject matter, but also in part due to the fact that it constitutes two perfect feet of the *ramal* meter, Rūmī quotes the phrase *mā ramayta idh ramayta* from Q 8:17 in at least ten separate places in his *Mathnawī.*

Persian poems quoting extensively from the Qurʾān or focusing on qurʾānic themes came to be seen tongue-in-cheek as Persian scripture. An illuminated manuscript of Jāmī's *Haft Awrang* copied probably in Mashhad between 1556-65, introduces the poem *Yūsuf u Zulaykhā* (folio 84b-85a) with three lines inset in a roundel, including the following hemistich: *naẓm-īst ki mīrisānad az waḥy payām,* "It is verse that conveys a message of revelation." Sanāʾī's *Ḥadīqat al-ḥaqīqa* incorporates many Arabic phrases quoted from the Qurʾān and for this reason has even been described as *Qurʾān-i pārsī,* the "Persian Qurʾān." The *Mathnawī* of Rūmī has likewise been styled as such, in lines variously ascribed to Jāmī or Shaykh Bahāʾī (Nicholson, *Mathnawī,* vii, xi, and Schimmel/trans. Lahouti, *Shukūh-i shams,* 846-7) and the following or similar lines are frequently included as a frontispiece or title-page to nineteenth century printings of the *Mathnawī:*

man chi gūyam waṣf-i ān ʿālī-jināb/nīst
payghambar walī dārad kitāb
mathnawī-yi mawlawī-yi maʿnawī/hast
Qurʾān-ī bi lafẓ-i pahlawī
How suitably to praise his eminence?/Not
prophet, yet he has revealed a book!
The mystic *Mathnawī* of Mawlawī/is a
Qurʾān expressed in Persian tongue!

A variant reading of this line appears playfully blasphemous: *man namīgūyam ki ān ʿālī-jināb/hast payghambar walī dārad kitāb,* "I am not saying of his eminence/he is a prophet. Yet he has a book (q.v.)!"

Rūmī's *Mathnawī* often performs a nontraditional exegesis of the Qurʾān by juxtaposing various qurʾānic verses together. In discussing Ḥamza, the Prophet's uncle, and his bravery in battle, the *Mathnawī* (iii, 3422) poses this question: *Na tu lā tulqū bi-aydīkum ilā/tahluka khwāndī zi payghām-i khudā,* "Have you not read 'Do not cast yourselves by your own hands in/ruin' from the message of God?" A few lines further on, Rūmī alludes to this same verse Q 2:195, as *tahluka* (obviously for the hapax legomenon *al-tahluka,* "ruin"), and quotes a conjugated Arabic verb *(lā tulqū)* from it, while alluding in the following line to another verse (Q 3:133) from an entirely different sūra, by quoting its initial Arabic verb *(sāriʿū): ānki murdan pīsh-i chashm-ash "tahluka"-st/amr-i "lā tulqū" bigīrad ū bi dast//w-ānki murdan pīsh-i ū shud fatḥ-i bāb/"sāriʿū" āyad mar ū rā dar khatāb* (*Mathnawī*, iii, 3434): "He whose eyes see dying as 'ruin'/Will seize hold of the command 'do not be cast'//And he who sees dying as an opening door/'Vie with one another' will be addressed to him."

The mystical ethos infecting much of Persian poetry for the last 750 years contrasts the restrictive and prescriptive outlook of the ascetic (*zāhid;* see ASCETICISM), the preacher *(wāʿiẓ),* the jurisprudent (*faqīh;* see LAW AND THE QURʾĀN), the judge *(qāḍī),* the vice officer *(muḥtasib)* and other figures of qurʾānic and Islamic authority, with the more expansive attitude of the lover (*ʿāshiq;* see LOVE), the mystic *(ʿārif),* the rogue *(rind)* and so on. By and large, it is the latter group whose interpretation and daily implementation of the Qurʾān is recommended as closer to the inner meaning *(maʿnā),* in contradistinction to the outward form *(ṣūra).* For this reason, one must read the Qurʾān with spiritual insight and open eyes (*Mathnawī,* vi, 4862). Rūmī compares the meaning of the Qurʾān to a human body — the soul of both are hidden within and might not be discovered by people who live in very close proximity to it, even for a lifetime (*Mathnawī,* iii, 4247-9). Thus, literalists see only words in the text of the Qurʾān, remaining blind to the illumination of the scriptural sun (*Mathnawī,* iii, 4229-31). Ḥāfiẓ (*Dīwān,* i, 34) rails against the hypocritical use of religion and the Qurʾān, urging us to drink wine and act disreputably, but not to wield the Qurʾān as a weapon, as others do in their duplicity *(dām-i tazwīr ma-kun chun digarān Qurʾān rā).* A work of expressly ethico-didactic intent, Saʿdī's *Gulistān,* does quote from the Qurʾān and ḥadīth more than forty times but also argues that "the purpose of the revelation of the Qurʾān is the acquisition of a good character, not the recitation of the written characters" (*Gulistān,* 184; see PIETY). Thus, canonical works of classical Persian literature which frequently cite and appeal to the authority of the Qurʾān argue on the whole for an interiorization of the Qurʾān in the life of the believer as opposed to a rigid or institutional imposition of scriptural laws.

Franklin Lewis

Bibliography

Primary: Shaykh Aḥmad-i Jām, *Maqāmāt-i zhandih pīl,* ed. H. Moayyad, Tehran 1340 Sh./1961, 1345 Sh./1966[2]; trans. and ed. H. Moayyad and F. Lewis, *The spiritual elephant and his colossal feats. Shaykh Ahmad-e Jâm,* Costa Mesa, CA: Mazda Publishers (forthcoming); Asadī-yi Ṭūsī, *Garshāspnāma,* ed. H. Yaghmāʾī, Tehran 1316 Sh./1937; ʿAṭṭār-i Nayshābūrī, Farīd al-Dīn, *Dīwān-i ʿAṭṭār,* ed. T. Tafaḍḍulī, Tehran 1345 Sh./1966; al-Bayhaqī, Abū l-Faḍl Muḥammad, *Tārīkh-i Bayhaqī,* ed. ʿA.A. Fayyāḍ, Mashhad 1971; Ḥāfiẓ, Shams al-Dīn Muḥammad, *Dīwān-i Ḥāfiẓ,* ed. P.N. Khānlarī, 2 vols. Tehran 1359 Sh./1980, 1362 Sh./1983[2]; Jāḥiẓ, *Bayān;* Kisāʾī-yi Marwazī, *Kisāʾī-yi Marwazī. Zindigī, andīsha wa shiʿr-i ū,* ed. M. Amīn Rīāḥī, Tehran 1367 Sh./1988; ʿA. Riwāqī (ed.), *Qurʾān-i quds. Kuhantarīn bar-gardān-i Qurʾān bi fārsī,* 2 vols., Tehran 1364 Sh./1985; Jalāl al-Dīn Rūmī, *Kulliyyāt-i shams, yā dīwān-i kabīr,* ed. B. Furūzānfar, 10 vols., Tehran 1957-67; id., *The Mathnawī of Jalālu'ddīn Rūmī,* ed. R. Nicholson, 8 vols., Cambridge 1925-40 (cited by book number, verse number); Saʿdī, *Būstān-i Saʿdī. Saʿdīnāma,* ed. G.Ḥ. Yūsufī, Tehran 1989; id., *Gulistān,* ed. G.Ḥ. Yusūfī, Tehran 1365 Sh./1986; Sanāʾī, *Dīwān-i ḥakīm Abū l-Majd Majdūd b. Ādam. Sanāʾī-yi Ghaznawī,* ed. M.T. Mudarris-i Raḍawī, Tehran 1341 Sh./1962, 1362 Sh./1983[2]; Sulṭān Walad, *Mathnawī-yi waladī. Inshāʾ-i Bahā al-Dīn b. Mawlānā Jalāl al-Dīn Muḥammad b. Ḥusayn-i Balkhī. Mashhūr bi Mawlawī,* ed. J. Humāʾī, Tehran 1316 Sh./1937; id., *Rabābnāma,* ed. ʿA.S. Gurdfarāmarzī, Tehran 1369 Sh./1980.

Secondary: Ā. Ādharnūsh, *Tārīkh-i tarjuma az ʿarabī bi fārsī (az āghāz ta ʿaṣr-i Ṣafawī). i. Tarjuma-hā-yi Qurʾānī,* Tehran 1373 Sh./1994; Q. Āryān, *Chihra-yi masīḥ dar adabiyyāt-i fārsī,* Tehran 1369 Sh./1990; Ḥ. Barzigar-i-Kishtlī, Fiqh dar adab-i fārsī, in Ḥ. Anūsha (ed.), *Dānishnāma-yi adab-i fārsī. ii. Farhangnāma-yi adabī-yi fārsī,* Tehran 1376 Sh./1997, 1043-56; id., Ḥadīth dar adab-i fārsī, in Ḥ. Anūsha (ed.), *Dānishnāma-yi adab-i fārsī. ii. Farhangnāma-yi adabī-yi fārsī,* Tehran 1376 Sh./1997, 514-23; S.M. Bayghi, The first available Persian interpretation of the Qurʾān known as the *Tarjumah Tafsīr-i-Ṭabarī* (the Persian translation of al-Ṭabarī's interpretation of the Qurʾān), in *Hamdard Islamicus* 19/4 (1996), 31-44; R. Bulliet, *Conversion to Islam in the medieval period. An essay in quantitative history,* Cambridge 1979; J.C. Bürgel, Conquérant, philosophe et prophète. L'image d'Alexandre le Grand dans l'épopée de Nezāmi, in C. Balaÿ et al. (eds.), *Pand-o Sokhan. Mélanges offerts à Charles-Henri de Fouchécour,* Tehran 1995, 65-73; id., *The feather of Simurgh. The "licit magic" of the arts in medieval Islam,* New York 1988; id., Die Profanierung sakraler Sprache als Stilmittle in klassischer arabischer Dichtung, in *Ibn an-Nadīm und die mittelalterliche arabische Literatur. Beiträge zum I. Johann Wilhelm Fück-Kolloquium,* Wiesbaden 1996, 64-72; S.M. Dāmādī, *Maḍāmīn-i mushtarak dar adab-i fārsī wa ʿarabī,* Tehran 1379 Sh./2000; M. Dānish-pazhūh and S.H. Sādāt-Nāṣirī (comps. and eds.), *Hizār sāl-i tafsīr-i fārsī. Sayrī dar mutūn-i kuhan-i tafsīrī-yi pārsī. Bā sharḥ wa-tawḍīḥāt,* Tehran 1369 Sh./1990; ʿA.A. Ḥalabī, *Taʾthīr-i Qurʾān wa ḥadīth dar adabiyyāt-i fārsī,* [Tehran] 1371 Sh./1992; S.ʿA. Ḥayrat-i Sajjādī, *Guzīdaʾī az taʾthīr-i Qurʾān bar naẓm-i fārsī,* Tehran 1371 Sh./1992; ʿA.A. Ḥikmat, *Amthāl-i Qurʾān. Faṣl-ī az tārīkh-i Qurʾān-i karīm,* Tehran 1332 Sh./1954; M.T. Jaʿfarī, *Az daryā bi-daryā. Kashf al-abyāt-i Mathnawī,* [Tehran] 1364-5 Sh./1985-6; M.A. Jazayery, The Arabic element in Persian grammar. A preliminary report, in *Iran. Journal of the British Institute of Persian Studies* 8 (1970), 115-24; M.ʿA. Khazāna-dārlū, *Manẓūma-hā-yi fārsī,* Tehran 1375 Sh./1996; B. Khurramshāhī (ed.), *Dānishnāma-yi Qurʾān wa Qurʾān-pazhūhī,* Tehran 1377 Sh./1998; R. Levy, A prose version of the Yūsuf and Zulaikhā legend. Ascribed to Pīr-i Anṣār of Harāt, in *JRAS* n.s. (1929), 103-6; F. Lewis, Golestān-e Saʿdi, in E. Yarhsater (ed.), *Encyclopædia Iranica,* xi, fasc. 1 (2001), 78-86; id., Hafez and *rendi,* in E. Yarhsater (ed.), *Encyclopædia Iranica,* xi, fasc. 5 (2002), 482-91; id., *Reading, writing and recitation. Sanāʾī and the origins of the Persian ghazal.* Ph.D. diss., U. Chicago 1995; id., *Rumi. Past and present. East and west,* Oxford 2000; W. Madelung, *Religious trends in early Islamic Iran,* Albany, NY 1988; R. Milstein, K. Rührdanz and B. Schmitz, *Stories of the prophets. Illustrated manuscripts of Qiṣaṣ al-anbiyāʾ,* Costa Mesa 1999; ʿA.M. Muʾādhdhinī, *Dar qalamraw-i āftāb. Muqaddimaʾī bar taʾthīr-i Qurʾān wa-ḥadīth dar adab-i pārsī,* Tehran 1372 Sh./1993; ʿA.A. Muḥammad-Khānī, Tafsīr-i Qurʾān dar adab-i Fārsī, in Ḥ. Anūsha (ed.), *Dānishnāma-yi adab-i fārsī.* ii. *Farhangnāma-yi adabī-yi fārsī,* Tehran 1376 Sh./1997, 383-94; S.B. Muzhdahī, Qurʾān wa adab-i fārsī, in Ḥ. Anūsha (ed.), *Dānishnāma-yi adab-i fārsī.* ii. *Farhangnāma-yi adabī-yi fārsī,* Tehran 1376 Sh./1997, 1080-119; J. Perry, Persian in the Safavid period. Sketch for an *état de langue,* in C. Melville (ed.), *Safavid Persia,* London 1996, 269-83; T. Pūrnāmdārīān, *Dāstān-i payāmbarān dar kulliyyāt-i shams. Sharḥ wa tafsīr-i ʿirfānī-yi dāstān-hā dar ghazal-hā-yi mawlawī,* Tehran 1364 Sh./1995; A.ʿA. Rajāʾī (ed.), *Pulī miyān-i shiʿr-i hijāʾī wa ʿarūḍī-yi fārsī dar qurūn-i awwal-i hijrī. Tarjuma-ī āhangīn az du juzw-i Qurʾān-i majīd,* Tehran 1353 Sh./1974; J. Rypka (ed.), *History of Iranian literature,* Dordrecht 1968; C. Saccone, *Viaggi e visioni di re, sufi, profeti. Storia tematica della letterature persiana classica,* Milan 1999; S. Ḍiyā l-Dīn-i Sajjādī (comp.), *Dībācha-nigārī dar dah qarn,* Tehran 1372 Sh./1993; J. Salmāsī-zāda, *Tārīkh-i tarjuma-yi Qurʾān dar jahān,* Tehran 1369 Sh./1980; A. Schimmel, *The triumphal sun. A study of the works of Jalaloddin Rumi,* London 1980, Albany 1993[2]; ed. and (Pers.) trans. H. Lahouti, *Shukūh-i Shams,* Tehran 1367 Sh./1988, 1382 Sh./2003[4]; S. Shamīsā, *Farhang-i talmīḥāt. Ishārāt-i asaṭīrī, dāstānī, tārīkhī, madhhabī dar adabiyyāt-i fārsī,* Tehran 1366 Sh./1987; M.J. Yāḥaqqī, et al. (eds. and comps.), *Farhangnāma-yi Qurʾānī. Farhang-i barābar-hā-yi fārsī-yi Qurʾān bar asās-i 142 nuskha-yi khaṭṭī-yi kuhan-i maḥfūẓ dar kitābkhāna-yi markazī-i āstān-i quds-i raḍawī,* 5 vols., Mashhad 1372-1375 Sh./1993-96.

Pharaoh

Title of the ancient rulers of Egypt. Pharaoh (Ar. *firʿawn*) means literally "(the) Great House" in Egyptian and was perhaps pronounced something like *pārĕō* or *pār*^{e}*ō*ʿ. It designated part of the palace complex at Memphis and came, through metonymy, by the mid-second millennium B.C.E., to refer to the king of Egypt himself, just as "the Porte" came to refer to the Ottoman sultan some three millennia later. The Arabic rendering, *firʿawn,* corresponds most closely to the Syriac *ferʿōn* and because current scholarship considers it unlikely that pre-Islamic poetic references to Pharaoh are authentic, the term seems to have entered Arabic literary culture through the Qurʾān. According to the traditional chronology of the qurʾānic revelations, the term appears as early as the first Meccan period (see CHRONOLOGY AND THE QURʾĀN; FOREIGN VOCABULARY).

The term occurs in the Qur'ān seventy-four times; it never appears in Sūrat Yūsuf (Q 12, "Joseph"), the Joseph (q.v.) narrative, where "king" is used instead (see KINGS AND RULERS), but occurs repeatedly in the many references to Moses (q.v.; and Aaron [q.v.] and the Children of Israel [q.v.]) in Egypt (q.v.). The story of Moses and Pharaoh takes its place among the many in the qur'ānic corpus that depict former human civilizations refusing to believe their divinely sent prophets or revelations, as a result of which they were destroyed (see PUNISHMENT STORIES; PROPHETS AND PROPHETHOOD; REVELATION AND INSPIRATION). The lesson for Muḥammad's contemporaries is that they, like Pharaoh's people *(āl firʿawn* or *qawm firʿawn)* and the people of ʿĀd (q.v.) or Thamūd (q.v.), the peoples of Noah (q.v.), Lot (q.v.), Midian (q.v.) and others, will be destroyed by God if they continue refusing to believe their prophet (see GRATITUDE AND INGRATITUDE; LIE; BELIEF AND UNBELIEF).

Pharaoh is an evil king but his people as a whole are condemned in more than a dozen verses. The "people of Pharaoh," or "house of Pharaoh" *(āl firʿawn),* did not believe God's signs (Q 3:11; 8:52, 54). They imposed upon the Israelites *(banū isrāʾīl)* the worst of punishments: destroying their sons while allowing the women to live (Q 7:141; 14:6). In Q 7:127, however, it is Pharaoh himself who sets this policy in response to the complaints of his notables *(al-malaʾu min qawmi firʿawna).* As a result, the "people of Pharaoh" suffer the most severe punishment of the fire (q.v.; Q 40:45-6). This eternal fate (see ETERNITY; REWARD AND PUNISHMENT) does not contradict their destruction by drowning (q.v.; Q 8:54; 10:90; 17:103; 20:78; 28:40).

The ubiquitous qur'ānic paradigm of the destroyed or "lost/past peoples" *(al-umam al-khāliya)* who did not obey God (see OBEDIENCE; GENERATIONS) did not hinder developments in plot and detail in the various renderings of the theme within the Qur'ān. In Q 10:90, Pharaoh declares at the moment of his doom in the sea: "I believe that there is no god aside from the one in which the Children of Israel believe, and I am a submitter *(wa-anā mina l-muslimīna).*" Despite his submission, however, according to Q 11:98, Pharaoh will lead his people to hellfire (see HELL AND HELLFIRE) on the day of resurrection (q.v.). The example of Pharaoh's profession of belief was used in the *kalām* discussions of whether the conversion of a sinner on the point of death was possible (cf. Q 4:18; with relation to the case of Pharaoh, see van Ess, *TG,* iv, 581; see THEOLOGY AND THE QUR'ĀN). Although most classical exegetes judged his conversion to be too late, others, such as Ibn al-ʿArabī (d. 638/1240), deemed Pharaoh to have been saved through his final act of conversion (see Gril, Personnage, 39, 49-50, 52). In the Qur'ān, Pharaoh is cruel and arrogant, transgressing limits (Q 20:24, 43; see ARROGANCE; BOUNDARIES AND PRECEPTS). He considers Moses bewitched *(masḥūr,* Q 17:101), or mad *(majnūn,* Q 26:27; see INSANITY; JINN). When his advisors set out to prove Moses and his signs wrong, they are quickly convinced of the reality and unity of God, as a result of which Pharaoh threatens to mutilate and crucify them (Q 7:124; 20:71; 26:49). Pharaoh accuses Moses of being ungrateful for having grown up in the royal court (Q 26:18-9) and threatens anyone who will choose a god aside from himself (Q 26:29).

In Q 28:4, Pharaoh's sins are enumerated (see SIN, MAJOR AND MINOR): he exalted himself overly much, divided the people into groups or castes, tried to weaken one of these by killing their sons, and generally caused corruption. Hāmān (q.v.; cf. biblical book of Esther) is Pharaoh's only named advisor (Q 28:8, 38) but Moses comes to

Korah (q.v.; Qārūn; cf. *Num* 16:1-35) along with Pharaoh and Hāmān with divine signs and proofs (Q 29:39; 40:23-4). Pharaoh commands Hāmān to build a tower that will reach into heaven so that Pharaoh can prove Moses' claims about God false (Q 28:38; 40:36-7). Pharaoh's claim to power is associated with the power and sustenance of the Nile (Q 43:51). He proclaims in Q 79:24, "I am your highest lord" *(anā rabbukum al-aʿlā)*. His wife, however, unlike the wives of Noah and Lot, demonstrates her righteousness by praying that God deliver her from Pharaoh and his sinful people and build her a house in "the garden" (q.v.; Q 66:10-1). As these examples illustrate, there is a great deal of variety in the qurʾānic accounts of Pharaoh; there is need for much further research into the qurʾānic intertextuality of the many renditions and references to the story of Moses and Pharaoh in Egypt.

The exegetical literature expands these brief qurʾānic references and mini-narratives into long and wonderful tales in which both known (scriptural) and other, surprising (i.e. non-scriptural) characters and personages and themes extend the breadth and depth of the story. In later Islamic literatures, especially Arabic literature, Pharaoh became a symbol of arrogance and evil.

Reuven Firestone

Bibliography
Primary: Ibn Kathīr, *Qiṣaṣ;* Kisāʾī, *Qiṣaṣ;* Ṭabarī, *Tafsīr,* Beirut 1984, by verses; id., *Taʾrīkh,* ed. de Goeje, 444-58, 467-82; Thaʿlabī, *Qiṣaṣ,* Beirut n.d., 147-77.
Secondary: van Ess, *TG;* D. Gril, Le personnage coranique du Pharaon d'après l'interprétation d'Ibn ʿArabi, in *AI* 14 (1978), 37-57; Horowitz, *KU;* Jeffery, *For. vocab.;* A.H. Johns, "Let my people go." Sayyid Quṭb and the vocation of Moses, in *Islam and Christian Muslim relations* 1 (1990), 143-70 (on the modern use of the image of Pharaoh); D. Redford, Pharaoh, in D.N. Freedman (ed.), *The Anchor Bible dictionary,* 6 vols., New York 1992, v, 288-9.

Philosophy and the Qurʾān

Introduction

Although not a philosophical document in the strict sense, the Qurʾān has been at the center of the most heated philosophical and theological controversies in Islam. Now, if by philosophy is meant wisdom *(sophia)* or rather love of wisdom, as understood by Pythagoras, who coined the term *philo-sophos,* the Qurʾān itself attests to the merit of acquiring wisdom (q.v.; *ḥikma*) as a gift from God. For as Q 2:269 puts it: "He [God] gives wisdom to whomever he wills," adding that indeed "whoever receives wisdom has received an abundant good" (see GIFT-GIVING; GRACE; BLESSING).

More specifically, *ḥikma* refers in a number of verses to the Qurʾān itself as a divine revelation (see REVELATION AND INSPIRATION; NAMES OF THE QURʾĀN) to Muḥammad (Q 4:113; 54:5; 62:2) or to his predecessors, such as Luqmān (q.v.; Q 31:12), David (q.v.; Q 38:20) and Jesus (q.v.; Q 3:48; 5:110). In the latter two verses, Jesus is said to have been taught by God the Torah (q.v.) and the Gospel (q.v.) as well as the *ḥikma,* which appears to refer to the "sapiential" books of the Hebrew Bible (i.e. "wisdom literature"), generally attributed to Solomon (q.v.). In one verse (Q 43:63), Jesus is simply reported to have said: "I have come to you with the wisdom," and to have brought "the clear proofs" (see PROOF).

The broader meaning of the term philosophy in ordinary usage may be said to correspond to the activity of speculation, reflection or rational discourse in general. Thus, the *Oxford dictionary* defines "to philosophize" as "to speculate, theorize, moralize," whereas Aristotle tended to describe wisdom *(sophia)* as the study of certain principles and causes, and first philosophy (i.e. metaphysics) as the study of first principles and causes (*Metaphysics,* 14 f.: bk. A.981b ln.29 f.).

In the Qurʾān, the terms reflecting *(tafakkur),* considering *(naẓar),* pondering *(iʿtibār)* and reasoning *(ʿaql)* are frequently used in what can only be described as a teleological context, intended to illustrate God's creative power (see CREATION), his sovereignty (q.v.; see also KINGS AND RULERS) and the rationality of his ways (see INTELLECT), as we will see in the next section, which deals with philosophical methodology and the Qurʾān.

There is thus a *prima facie* case for the correlation of philosophy and the Qurʾān, as this article proposes to show. As a matter of history, however, there were from the earliest times vast differences of opinion among Muslim exegetes (see EXEGESIS OF THE QURʾĀN: CLASSICAL AND MEDIEVAL), jurists and other scholars, on the justifiability of applying rational discourse, the paramount expression of philosophical methodology, to the text of the Qurʾān, whether in the form of exegesis *(tafsīr)* or interpretation *(taʾwīl).* Al-Ṭabarī (d. 310/923), one of the earliest and most learned commentators of the Qurʾān, prefaces his commentary by referring to those scholars who were reluctant to engage in exegesis "out of fear of error (q.v.), inadequacy or liability to sin" (Ṭabarī, *Tafsīr,* i, 46). He then quotes a saying of Ibn ʿAbbās (d. 68/687), cousin of the Prophet, to the effect that "he who discusses the Qurʾān by recourse to opinion *(raʾy),* let him occupy his place in hell." Without endorsing this opinion in full, al-Ṭabarī (*Tafsīr,* i, 42) comments that this prohibition bears on "exegesis *(tafsīr)* by recourse to reprehensible but not praiseworthy opinion." He, then, invokes the authority of Ibn Masʿūd (d. 32/652-3) and other scholars in support of the permissibility of *tafsīr* and quotes Q 38:29, which reads: "It is (i.e. the Qurʾān) a blessed book that we have sent down to you, that they may ponder its verses and that those possessed of understanding may remember" (see MEMORY; REMEMBRANCE; REFLECTION AND DELIBERATION). This is followed by Q 39:27, which reads: "We have given humankind every kind of parable (see PARABLES) in this Qurʾān that perchance they might remember." These verses, al-Ṭabarī comments, show that "the knowledge of *tafsīr* and the exposition of its senses is obligatory." For, "pondering, taking stock, remembrance and piety (q.v.)," he adds "are not possible without the knowledge of the meanings of the [qurʾānic] verses, grasping and understanding them." He then speaks of the two varieties of sound *tafsīr:* (1) that which rests on the traditions of the Prophet, provided they are well-accredited and sound (see SUNNA; ḤADĪTH AND THE QURʾĀN); and (2) that which meets the rules of the soundest demonstration *(burhān)* and is grounded in the knowledge of the meaning of words (see GRAMMAR AND THE QURʾĀN; ARABIC LANGUAGE), poems (see POETRY AND POETS), proverbs and different dialects (q.v.) of the Arabs (q.v.). To this doubly logical and linguistic criterion should be added, according to al-Ṭabarī, material derived from the ancients *(salaf),* including the Companions of the Prophet (q.v.), their immediate successors and other learned scholars (see SCHOLAR).

On the second question of interpretation *(taʾwīl),* al-Ṭabarī reviews the conflicting interpretations of Q 3:7, which refers to those parts of the Qurʾān which are precise in meaning *(muḥkamāt)* and those which are ambiguous (q.v.; *mutashābihāt*), then goes on to state: "As for those in whose heart there is vacillation, they follow the ambiguous in it, seeking sedition and intending to interpret. No one, however, except God knows its interpretation. Those well-grounded in knowledge say, we believe in it; all is from our lord." Whether the phrase "those well-grounded in knowledge" should be conjoined to God raises a serious grammatical question that was at the center of the controversy which pitted liberal and conservative scholars against each other (see KNOWLEDGE AND LEARNING). According to al-Ṭabarī (*Tafsīr*, i, 214), Mālik b. Anas (d. 179/795) and ʿĀʾisha, wife of the Prophet (see WIVES OF THE PROPHET; ʿĀʾISHA BINT ABĪ BAKR), chose the reading which stops at God; whereas Ibn ʿAbbās and Mujāhid b. Jabr (d. 104/722) allowed for the conjunction of God and those well-grounded in knowledge. Al-Ṭabarī himself appears to opt for the first reading, reserving the knowledge of the ambiguous parts of the Qurʾān to God. As for the distinction between the *muḥkamāt* and *mutashābihāt* parts, he holds the view that *al-muḥkam* is that of which the learned know the interpretation; whereas *al-mutashābih* is that of which no one but God has any knowledge, which is essentially a restatement of what Q 3:7 explicitly states. The only clarification he offers is that "ambiguous" references bear on such questions as "the time of the (second) coming of Jesus, son of Mary (q.v.), the coming of the hour, the end of the world and such like" (Ṭabarī, *Tafsīr*, i, 209; see LAST JUDGMENT; APOCALYPSE).

Philosophical methodology and the Qurʾān

The investigation of the relation of philosophy to the Qurʾān compels us to distinguish between two aspects of this relation, the methodological and the substantive. As regards the latter, any correspondence of the qurʾānic teaching with the classical philosophical tradition on such questions as the origin of the world (see COSMOLOGY), the nature of God (see GOD AND HIS ATTRIBUTES), human destiny (q.v.; see also FATE; REWARD AND PUNISHMENT) and the nature of right and wrong (see GOOD AND EVIL), is purely accidental; the method(s) used by traditional philosophers to arrive at these conclusions is entirely different. The crux of the methodological relation, on the other hand, consists in the degree to which the Qurʾān calls upon the believers to "consider, reflect on, or ponder" the creation, as a means of discovering the secrets of this creation, leading up to the knowledge of God, his omnipotence, his wisdom, and his sovereignty in the world. Thus, Q 7:185 asks: "Have they not considered the kingdom of the heavens (see HEAVEN AND SKY) and the earth (q.v.) and all things that God has created?" In Q 88:17 f., it is asked: "Will they not consider the camels, how they were created (see CAMEL); heaven how it was raised up, the mountains, how they were hoisted and the earth, how it was leveled?" (see ANIMAL LIFE; AGRICULTURE AND VEGETATION; NATURE AS SIGNS).

In these and similar verses, a teleological message is more explicitly preached: by reflecting on the creation of the heavens and the earth, "people of understanding" are said to perceive that the creation of the heavens and the earth is not in vain (Q 3:190-1). In Q 2:164, it is stated that: "Indeed, in the creation of the heavens and the earth, the alternation of night and day (see DAY AND NIGHT); in the ships that sail the seas with what profits humankind; in the water (q.v.) which God sends down from the sky to bring the earth back to life (q.v.) after its death [...] — surely in these are signs (q.v.) for people of understanding" (see also PAIRS AND PAIRING).

In a number of verses, such as Q 59:2 (cf. Q 39:21), people of "understanding" or of "perception" are urged to "ponder" or take stock *(fa-ʿtabirū)* of the wonders of creation and the calamities which befall the unbelievers (see PUNISHMENT STORIES; CHASTISEMENT AND PUNISHMENT), by recourse to the God-given light of reason. In token of this divine light, God is said in Q 2:31-2 to have taught Adam (see ADAM AND EVE), his deputy on earth (see CALIPH), the names of which the angels themselves were ignorant (see ANGEL).

The Qurʾān also speaks of people who reason *(yaʿqulūn),* and accordingly are capable of obeying God or worshiping him (see OBEDIENCE; WORSHIP). In fact, the expressions "they reason" or "you reason" occur forty-six times in the Qurʾān. In this context, it is assumed that, prior to revelation, as a well-known tradition of the Prophet (ḥadīth) has it, humankind partook of a natural religion *(dīn al-fiṭra)* into which they were born and were subsequently made Jews, Christians or Muslims by their own parents (see RELIGIOUS PLURALISM AND THE QURʾĀN; RELIGION; PARTIES AND FACTIONS).

No wonder, then, that the Qurʾān has defined the rules of debate between rival groups in terms of rational argument or good counsel (see DEBATE AND DISPUTATION). Thus, the Prophet is urged in Q 16:125 to "call to the way of your lord (q.v.) with wisdom and mild exhortation and argue with them in the best manner" (see INVITATION; EXHORTATIONS). It is this call, which, following the period of conquest, was historically at the basis of the debates with Christians. The earliest such instance is the debate between a Christian and a "Saracen" on the question of free will and predestination (see FREEDOM AND PREDESTINATION). This debate is attributed to Theodore Abū Qurra (d. 210/826), Bishop of Ḥarrān, or his teacher, St. John of Damascus (d. 130/748), the last great doctor of the Orthodox Church (cf. Sahas, *John of Damascus*). Another instance is the debate in which Abū Yaʿqūb b. Isḥāq al-Kindī (d. ca. 252/866) has given a "Refutation of the Christian Trinity," which has survived in the rebuttal of the Jacobite Yaḥyā b. ʿAdī (d. 363/974). The Muʿtazilī (see MUʿTAZILĪS) al-Jāḥiẓ (d. 255/868-9), al-Kindī's contemporary, has pursued the same theme in his own "Refutation of the Christians." An anti-Islamic polemical tract which pitted the Nestorian (see CHRISTIANS AND CHRISTIANITY) ʿAbd al-Masīḥ al-Kindī against the well-known Muslim scholar, ʿAbdallāh al-Hāshimī, had a broader impact, since it denigrated the Islamic rites of pilgrimage (q.v.), the qurʾānic account of the pleasures reserved to the righteous in paradise (q.v.) and the expeditions of the Prophet against Quraysh (q.v.; cf. Muir, *Apology;* see EXPEDITIONS AND BATTLES; FIGHTING; WAR).

Apart from his anti-Trinitarian polemic (see TRINITY; POLEMIC AND POLEMICAL LANGUAGE), Abū Yaʿqūb b. Isḥāq al-Kindī was the first Muslim philosopher to espouse the cause of the total compatibility of philosophy and Islam. For him, philosophy is the highest human art, which seeks "the knowledge of the first or true one *(al-ḥaqq)* who is the cause of every truth (q.v.)." Now, in so far as the aim of both philosophy and revelation, embodied in the Qurʾān, is the pursuit of truth, it follows, according to al-Kindī, that the "seeker of truth" should be willing to look for it from whatever source, even if that source was "races (q.v.) distant from us and nations different from us," by whom he undoubtedly meant the Greeks (Fakhry, *History,* 70; see STRANGERS AND FOREIGNERS). He concedes, however, that although religious truths belong to an order of "divine wisdom," which is higher than "human wisdom," the truths preached by the prophets (see PROPHETS AND PROPHETHOOD) are not different from those taught by the philosophers.

Contrary to the claims of his predecessors or contemporaries, such as Mālik b.

Anas (d. 179/796) and Aḥmad b. Ḥanbal (d. 241/845), al-Kindī then goes on to argue that the Qurʾān itself, which embodies that higher divine wisdom, is not averse to the use of reasoning or argument which is the core of the method used by the philosophers. To illustrate this point, he refers to a passage in the Qurʾān which bears on the mystery of resurrection (q.v.), questioned by the infidel (see UNCERTAINTY) who asks: "Who brings the flowers back to life, once they are withered?" In response the Qurʾān states: "He who originated them the first time and has knowledge of every creation" (Q 36:79) and goes on to add: "It is he who produces fire from green trees for you" and as such is able to bring the contrary from its contrary, fire (q.v.) from green trees, life from its opposite, and is accordingly able to create or re-create as he pleases. Thus, al-Kindī concludes, "the truth to which Muḥammad, the truthful, may God's blessings be upon him, has summoned, added to what he has received from God almighty," can be demonstrated by recourse to rational arguments, which only the fool can question. "People of sound religion and intelligence" cannot, therefore, doubt the need to resort to rational discourse or interpretation *(taʾwīl)* in the attempt to understand the ambiguous passages of the Qurʾān. He then illustrates this point by referring to Q 55:6, which reads: "And the stars and trees prostrate themselves" to God, to show how everything, including the outermost sphere, referred to in this verse as the stars, submits to God (Fakhry, *History*, 81; see BOWING AND PROSTRATION).

The earliest theological controversies

Al-Kindī, who was known for his Muʿtazilī sympathies, lived at a time when theological controversies had defined to some extent the course which philosophy and theology *(kalām)* were to take (see THEOLOGY AND THE QURʾĀN). In concrete historical terms, the earliest controversies centered on such questions as grave sin (*kabīra;* see SIN, MAJOR AND MINOR), faith (q.v.; *īmān*) and free will and predestination *(qadar)*. Although those controversies had definite political undertones, the arguments that bolstered them were ultimately grounded in the qurʾānic text (see POLITICS AND THE QURʾĀN). The first of these questions was raised by the Khārijīs (q.v.), who split from the main body of the army of ʿAlī, the fourth caliph (d. 40/661; see ʿALĪ B. ABĪ ṬĀLIB), charging him with committing a grave sin *(kabīra),* by exposing his legitimate claims to the caliphate to question, upon consenting to the so-called arbitration (q.v.), following the battle of Ṣiffīn (q.v.; 37/657). The Khārijīs' charge against ʿAlī was later generalized to apply to any Muslim who committed a grave sin, political or other: such an individual was considered to become thereby an apostate deserving of death (ʿAlī himself was killed by a Khārijī at the mosque of Kūfa in 40/661; see APOSTASY). In the heat of ensuing controversy, the Murjiʾīs trod a moderate path, arguing that genuine faith cannot be determined in this life but should be deferred — hence their name of Murjiʾīs or "Deferrers" — and accordingly should be left to God (see DEFERRAL). Almost simultaneously, the Qadarīs raised the question of free will and predestination, designated by the ambiguous term of *qadar,* meaning human or divine power (see POWER AND IMPOTENCE).

This last question had a profound political significance during the early Umayyad period. The early Qadarīs, such as Maʿbad al-Juhanī (d. after 83/703) and Ghaylān al-Dimashqī (d. 116/743), challenged the Umayyad caliphs' claims that their actions, however vile or cruel, were part of the divine decree *(qaḍāʾ wa-qadar)* and could not for that reason be questioned. Although both Maʿbad and Ghaylān were killed by the order of the caliphs, ʿAbd al-Malik (r. 65-86/685-705) and Hishām (r. 105-25/724-43), respectively, the former ruler, assailed perhaps by understandable doubts, is reported to have put the whole question of *qadar* to the eminent religious scholar, al-Ḥasan al-Baṣrī (d. 110/728), whose response has survived in a famous "Treatise on *qadar*" (cf. Fakhry, *Fikr,* i, 17-28). In this treatise, al-Ḥasan al-Baṣrī draws extensively on the Qurʾān, which, according to him, supports unquestionably the thesis of free will, or human *qadar,* as a prerequisite of religious obligation *(taklīf)* — a thesis which is also endorsed by reason or sound commonsense. For "God almighty," he writes, "is too just and equitable (see JUSTICE AND INJUSTICE) to cause the human servant to be blind and then order him to see, then tell him: 'Or else, I would punish you'; cause him to be deaf and then say to him: 'Hear or else I will torture you'" (see VISION AND BLINDNESS; SEEING AND HEARING). For "this is too obvious," al-Baṣrī adds, "to be misunderstood by any reasonable person" (Fakhry, *Fikr,* i, 24). He then proceeds to inveigh against the false interpretations, proposed by those who continue to question these propositions, by whom he undoubtedly meant the "determinists" *(jabriyya),* such as Jahm b. Ṣafwān (d. 128/745), Ḍirār b. ʿAmr (of the middle second/eighth century) and others.

The significance of this treatise, despite the doubts concerning its authenticity, is that it is the earliest instance of recourse to the Qurʾān in the attempt to resolve the controversy over the question of *qadar,* destined to become one of the pivotal issues in philosophical and theological circles. Interestingly enough, al-Ḥasan al-Baṣrī, who quotes the Qurʾān extensively, does not refer to the ḥadīth in this treatise but supplements the qurʾānic quotations by commonsense or rational arguments.

Other scholars of the period, such as Mālik b. Anas (d. 179/795), founder of one of the four Sunnī creeds *(madhhabs;* see CREED; LAW AND THE QURʾĀN), tended to reject absolutely the application of deduction or independent reasoning to qurʾānic questions. Asked once what he thought of the qurʾānic references to God's sitting on the throne (as in e.g. Q 7:54; 10:3; 13:2; see THRONE OF GOD; ANTHROPOMORPHISM), Mālik is reported to have answered "The sitting is well-known; its modality is unknown. Belief in it is a duty and questioning it is a heresy [or innovation] *(bidʿa).*"

This rigid traditionalism and deference to the authority of the revealed text was outstripped in the next century by Ibn Ḥanbal (d. 241/855), founder of another one of the four creeds, when in 212/827 the ʿAbbāsid caliph al-Maʾmūn (r. 198-218/813-33) proclaimed two doctrines to be official — i.e. the preeminence of ʿAlī (see SHĪʿISM AND THE QURʾĀN; SHĪʿA) and the createdness of the Qurʾān (q.v.; *khalq al-Qurʾān*) — a pronouncement that set the stage for the notorious *miḥna* or inquisition (q.v.). When the concurrence of all the religious judges and scholars in the Muʿtazilī thesis of the creation of the Qurʾān was demanded, Ibn Ḥanbal rejected this thesis with utter single-mindedness. Jailed, scourged and humiliated in a variety of ways, he refused to change his stand that the Qurʾān was the "eternal and uncreated speech (q.v.) of God" (see also WORD OF GOD; INIMITABILITY).

By Ibn Ḥanbal's time, however, the impact of Greek philosophy was beginning to be felt in theological and philosophical circles. The translation of the first three parts of Aristotle's *Organon,* i.e. the *Categories,* the *Interpretations* and the *Prior analytics,* as early as the eighth century by ʿAbdallāh b. al-Muqaffaʿ (d. 139/756) — or his son Muḥammad, presumably from Persian — had opened the door wide for theological and philosophical discussions in an unprecedented manner. (Some time after, even the grammarians felt compelled to jump into the fray and question the authority of Aristotelian logic as superfluous.)

Greek philosophy and Aristotelian logic had been at the center of theological controversies among Syriac-speaking Jacobites and Nestorians centuries before at Antioch, Edessa, Qinnesrin and Nisibin, and contacts between Muslim and Christian scholars had been common since at least the time of the above-mentioned St. John of Damascus. Not surprisingly, the first theological movement in Islam was spawned as early as the second/eighth century by Wāṣil b. ʿAṭāʾ (d. 131/748), disciple of the illustrious al-Ḥasan al-Baṣrī. This rationalist movement was fully developed by the great theologians of the third/ninth century, Abū l-Hudhayl (d. ca. 235/849), al-Naẓẓām (d. ca. 226/845), al-Jubbāʾī (d. 303/915) and others. Even contemporary philosophers, like the aforementioned al-Kindī, were sympathetic to the Muʿtazilī cause. The teaching of that school centered around the two principles of divine unity and justice, which the Muʿtazilīs supported by recourse to reason, which they, like the philosopher al-Kindī, believed to be perfectly compatible with the teaching of the Qurʾān. They also believed, like the philosophers in general, that right and wrong can be determined by reason and are not, as their opponents contended, matters of divine injunction or prohibition (see COMMANDMENTS; FORBIDDEN). Divine revelation, embodied in the Qurʾān, simply confirms the validity of such principles and this confirmation is a divine grace or favor *(luṭf)* that God "dispenses to humankind, so that whoever perishes would perish after a clear proof [had been given] and those who survive would survive after a clear proof" (Q 8:42).

The Ashʿarī onslaught on the philosophers

Some of the philosophers who succeeded al-Kindī did not evince the same deference to the revealed text. Thus, Abū Bakr al-Rāzī (d. ca. 318/930) rejected the whole fabric of revelation as superfluous and held that the God-given light of reason was sufficient for solving human philosophical, moral and practical problems (see ETHICS AND THE QURʾĀN). The source of all wisdom was, for him, Greek philosophy, as expounded particularly by Plato, "the master and leader" of all the philosophers. Al-Rāzī substituted, on essentially philosophical (Platonic) grounds, five co-eternal principles, i.e. the creator *(bāriʾ)*, the soul, space, matter and time, for the unique God of the Qurʾān.

By the fourth/tenth century, the philosophical scene was dominated by the names of the great system-builders and Neoplatonists, al-Fārābī (d. 339/950) and Ibn Sīnā (Avicenna) (d. 428/1037), who constructed an elaborate metaphysical and cosmological scheme, which they presented as an alternative to the Islamic system of beliefs. This Neoplatonic scheme had a remote resemblance to the qurʾānic worldview and was received from the start with suspicion by the traditional scholars and the masses at large.

The arch-enemies of the Neoplatonists during this period were the Ashʿarī theologians, whose leader, Abū l-Ḥasan al-Ashʿarī (d. 324/935) had been, up to the age of forty, a Muʿtazilī theologian of profound erudition. His disenchantment with the Muʿtazila, we are told, was inspired by a call of the Prophet to tend to the (Muslim) community *(irʿa ummatī)*. Without abandoning the Muʿtazilī methodology of rational discourse, al-Ashʿarī was thoroughly committed to Ḥanbalī traditionalism. The leading Ashʿarī theologians of the fifth/eleventh and sixth/twelfth centuries, such as al-Bāqillānī (d. 403/1013), al-Baghdādī (d. 429/1037), al-Juwaynī (d. 478/1085) and al-Ghazālī (d. 505/1111) pursued al-Ashʿarī's line of anti-Muʿtazilism and Neoplatonism in an unabated manner.

Al-Ghazālī and al-Juwaynī, his master, were the most notable standard-bearers of the Ashʿarī onslaught on the Muslim philosophers, represented by al-Fārābī and Ibn Sīnā, with Aristotle as their master. Al-Ghazālī accuses those philosophers of irreligion *(kufr)* on three scores: the eternity (q.v.) of the world, God's knowledge of particulars and bodily resurrection. Thus, when they profess to prove the existence of God as creator of the world, the philosophers, according to him, are guilty of dissimulation *(talbīs)* since an eternal universe does not require a creator. They also impugn the perfection of God when they limit his knowledge to that of universals and are finally unable to demonstrate the resurrection of the body. On all those scores, none of the arguments of the philosophers are convincing or conclusive and the only recourse left to the conscientious searcher, according to al-Ghazālī, is the Qurʾān, whose authority on all these questions is indisputable. For the Qurʾān stipulates in unmistakable terms that God is the sovereign and all-knowing creator of the world in time (q.v.) and *ex nihilo,* who is able to do whatever he pleases. He is, in addition, the sole agent, who operates directly and miraculously in the world without reference to secondary or natural causes (Ghazālī, *Tahāfut,* question 17).

Ibn Rushd's anti-Ashʿarī polemic and the defense of Aristotle

The philosopher who pursued those questions relentlessly and confronted al-Ghazālī's onslaught head-on was the great Aristotelian philosopher and Mālikī judge, Ibn Rushd (Averroes; d. 595/1198) of Cordoba, Spain. In his *Faṣl al-maqāl,* "Decisive treatise," Ibn Rushd begins by defining philosophy as the art of "investigating entities and considering them in so far as they manifest the maker; I mean in so far as they are made." From this premise, he draws the inference that "existing entities actually manifest the maker… and the more complete their status as made *(maṣnūʿa)* is known, the knowledge of their maker is more complete" (Ibn Rushd, *Faṣl,* 27). After reviewing a series of qurʾānic verses, which call on humankind to "consider" or "reflect on" creation, he concludes that scripture *(al-sharʿ),* by which he clearly means the Qurʾān, has not only exhorted humankind to investigate "existing entities" but has actually regarded such investigation as obligatory.

As a good jurist, to whom we owe a major juridical treatise, *Bidāyat al-mujtahid,* the "Primer of the accomplished scholar," Ibn Rushd proceeds next to draw a close analogy between juridical and rational deduction *(qiyās)* and to defend the use of the latter as perfectly legitimate. In fact, rational deduction is more appropriate than juridical. For, as he asks, who indeed is more worthy of our esteem than he who investigates the very nature of existing entities insofar as they manifest their maker — by whom he obviously meant the philosopher.

Now, whoever wishes to know God, as the maker of existing entities, must begin by mastering the rules of deduction and distinguishing between the three modes of deduction, the demonstrative used by the philosophers, the dialectical used by the theologians *(al-mutakallimūn)* and the rhetorical used by the masses at large. These rules, as everybody knows, are embodied in Aristotle's logical treatises, especially the *Posterior analytics,* known in Arabic sources as *Kitāb al-Burhān,* the "Book of Demonstration." Ibn Rushd is emphatic that, of these modes, the demonstrative is the highest. Fully conscious of the aversion to the study of logic and the other so-called "foreign sciences" in theological and popular circles, Ibn Rushd proceeds to defend such a study on the ground that the conscientious searcher cannot dispense with the assistance of his predecessors, "regardless of whether they share in our religion or not" (Ibn Rushd, *Faṣl,* 31). Moreover, logic, being simply a tool or "instrument of thought," has no specific religious character or national affiliation. Accordingly, it is our duty, he states, to look into the books of the ancients (by whom he meant the Greeks; see GENERATIONS; ORALITY AND WRITING IN ARABIA), and to examine what they have said about existing entities, and then determine the extent to which it conforms with the "principles of demonstration." "If we find," he writes, "that some of it is accordant with the truth, we should receive it gladly from them and thank them. If, on the contrary, it is not accordant with truth, we should draw attention to it, warn against it and excuse them" (ibid., 33). In stressing the "formal" character of deduction or logical discourse, Ibn Rushd cites the example of the lawful slaughter (q.v.) of animals, which is entirely independent of the instrument *(āla)* used (see also LAWFUL AND UNLAWFUL; CONSECRATION OF ANIMALS; SACRIFICE).

It is to be noted that, in drawing a parallel between juridical and rational deduction, Ibn Rushd exploits skillfully the ambiguity of the term *qiyās,* which derives from a root meaning "to measure" and does not occur in the Qurʾān at all (see MEASUREMENT). Juridical *qiyās* had been used from earlier times as a means of enunciating legal decisions on matters on which the Qurʾān was silent, by recourse to the method of analogy, accurately denoting resemblance *(shabah)* rather than deduction. What justified analogy in legal decisions was actually the reason *(ʿilla)* which the parallel cases had in common. Thus, jurists, on the whole, were not willing to proceed beyond particular cases. Their procedure was, in other words, purely inductive; whereas rational *qiyās* was deductive and conformed to the syllogistic rules Aristotle and the Greek logicians had laid down. Al-Kindī, the first genuine Islamic philosopher, had used a more accurate term to translate the Greek *syllogismos,* i.e. *al-jāmiʿa,* which, over time, fell out of use and was replaced by the ambiguous term *qiyās.*

Deduction or *qiyās* was thus recommended by the philosophers who, like the Muʿtazilīs, were willing to apply the rational canons of proof to the qurʾānic text. Faced with the anthropomorphisms and incongruities of that text, the two groups felt compelled to resort to another rational device, interpretation *(taʾwīl),* which, as we have seen, the Qurʾān had allowed where "ambiguous" verses were concerned.

Of the philosophers, no one exploited the method of interpretation in his theological treatises as thoroughly as Ibn Rushd. After explaining that by interpretation is meant eliciting the real meaning underlying the figurative connotation of scriptural terms, Ibn Rushd proceeds to argue that this method is explicitly recommended in that famous passage (Q 3:7) which speaks of the Qurʾān as a revelation from God, "with verses which are precise in meaning *(muḥkamāt)* and which are the mother of the book (q.v.) and others which are ambiguous *(mutashābihāt).*" The latter are then said to be the object of interpretation by "those in whose heart there is vacillation" and are in quest of sedition. Contrary to al-Ṭabarī's already-mentioned reading, however, Ibn Rushd proposes the conjunction of both "God and those well-grounded in knowledge," referred to in the last part of the verse, as equally competent to undertake the interpretation of the ambiguous parts.

By those well-grounded in knowledge, Ibn Rushd is categorical: only the philosophers, or "people of demonstration" as he calls them, are meant. That definitely excludes the two lower classes: that of the theologians, the "dialectical," and the masses at large, the "rhetorical" class.

In his other theological treatise, *al-Kashf ʿan manāhij al-adilla,* the "Exposition of the methods of proof," written in 576/1180 as a sequel to the *Faṣl,* Ibn Rushd lays down the rules or "canon of interpretation," as he calls it, in a systematic way. The texts of scripture *(sharʿ),* he explains, fall into two major categories: (1) Those which are perfectly explicit and do not need any interpretation, corresponding to that part the Qurʾān has called "precise in meaning" *(muḥkamāt);* and (2) Those in which the intent of the scripture is one of allegory or representation and which fall into four parts: (a) in which the allegory or representation *(mithāl)* is too abstruse to be understood by any except the especially gifted; (b) which is the opposite of the former and in which the allegory or representation is readily understood; (c) which is readily recognized to be an allegory, but the significance of that allegory is known with difficulty; and (d) which is the opposite of the former, or that in which the significance of the allegory is readily recognized. The sense in which it is an allegory is, however, only known with difficulty (see POLYSEMY).

The first part (a), Ibn Rushd goes on to explain, should be accepted at face value by the theologians and the masses at large. The second part (b) may be interpreted but its interpretation should not be divulged to the public (see SECRETS; HIDDEN AND THE HIDDEN). The third part (c) may be divulged as a means of explaining the allegorical intent of scripture and the reason why it is expressed in the form of an allegory. The fourth part (d) may not be interpreted for fear that such interpretation may lead to "wild opinions," such as those in which the Ṣūfīs and their ilk are liable to indulge (see ṢŪFISM AND THE QURʾĀN).

Logic as an instrument of thought

In matters of both interpretation and deduction, it is clear that logic plays a preponderant role. Ẓāhirī scholars, however, such as Ibn Ḥazm (d. 456/1064), Ibn Qudāma (d. 620/1223) and Ibn Taymiyya (d. 728/1328) were averse to the use of logic or deduction in any form or guise. Some commentators of the Qurʾān, such as al-Zamakhsharī (d. 538/1144), tended to accord grammar a more preponderant role than logic in their qurʾānic exegesis. The Ashʿarīs, despite their anti-Muʿtazilī and anti-philosophical sympathies, did not exclude the use of deduction or logical methods of proof in theological disputations altogether. This is illustrated by al-Ashʿarī's own treatise, *Istiḥsān al-khawḍ fī ʿilm al-kalām,* "Vindication of the use of theological discourse" and al-Ghazālī's own attitude to logic in his anti-philosophical works. Here, as is explicitly stated in *Tahāfut al-falāsifa,* the "Incoherence of the philosophers," a clear-cut distinction is made between logic as an "instrument of thought" and the philosophical sciences, such as physics and metaphysics (see SCIENCE AND THE QURʾĀN). The former is perfectly innocuous from a religious viewpoint; whereas the latter contains the bulk of the philosophers' pernicious propositions which are "in conflict with the fundamentals of religion (i.e. Islam)."

In fact, apart from this friendly concession, al-Ghazālī bequeathed to posterity a very lucid and systematic treatise on Aristotelian logic entitled the *Miʿyār al-ʿilm,* "Criterion of knowledge." Even more to the point, he developed in another treatise, *al-Qusṭās al-mustaqīm*, the "Straight balance," a variety of logic which may be termed qur'ānic, which, according to him, was proposed by God, taught by Gabriel (q.v.) and used by both Abraham (q.v.) and Muḥammad (Ghazālī, *Qusṭās*, 12).

This qur'ānic logic rests on three principles, according to al-Ghazālī: (1) the principle of parallelism; (2) that of concomitance; and (3) that of disjunction. He illustrates the first principle by referring to Abraham's challenge in the Qur'ān to Nimrod (q.v.), who arrogated to himself the title of divinity in these words (Q 2:258): "God brings the sun (q.v.) from the east, so bring it up from the west!" Being unable to meet this challenge, Nimrod's arrogation of divinity is logically confuted.

The second principle of concomitance is illustrated by reference to the qur'ānic dictum, "Were there in them both [i.e. the heaven and earth] other gods than God, they would surely have been ruined" (Q 21:22). Since they have not been ruined, we are justified in concluding that there is no god but God. The logical form of this argument, according to al-Ghazālī, is that of the conditional syllogism: If A then B; but not-B, therefore not-A. An instance of the third principle of disjunction is the question asked in the Qur'ān: "Say, who provides for you (see SUSTENANCE) from the heaven and the earth?" followed by the answer: "Say, God and you or we are either rightly guided or in manifest error" (Q 34:24). From this, we are justified in inferring that God is the provider and we, as well as the infidels who question this proposition, are in manifest error.

It is not without interest to note that, in developing this system of qur'ānic logic, al-Ghazālī actually refers to his two other treatises of conventional logic, *Mi'yār al-'ilm*, the "Criterion of knowledge" and the shorter *Miḥakk al-naẓar*, the "Touchstone of speculation," in which, he says, he had refuted the ten deceptions of Satan (see DEVIL), which he does not list (*Qusṭās*, 42 f.). The chief advantage of the principles he has given in *al-Qusṭās* consist, according to him, in the fact that they are bound to confirm our faith in Muḥammad as the infallible teacher (see IMPECCABILITY), as against the Shī'ī imām (q.v.), who is in temporary occultation, as al-Ghazālī has also asserted in his autobiography, *al-Munqidh*, the "Deliverance from error." Moreover, the logic of the *Qusṭās*, he goes on to argue, will be found to be suitable "for measuring (or testing) the arithmetical, poetical, physical, juridical and theological sciences, as well as any real science, which is not purely conventional" (ibid., 53).

Notwithstanding this wild claim, it is clear, we believe, that a careful analysis of this alleged qur'ānic logic would reveal that it differs little formally from the traditional, Aristotelian scheme al-Ghazālī himself had expounded in the "Criterion of knowledge" and elsewhere. The only difference between the two systems consists simply in the type of qur'ānic instances he cites to illustrate his specific logical points. The syllogistic rules in both cases are really the same.

God, his existence and his attributes

The most overwhelming impression the Qur'ān leaves on its reader is God's utter uniqueness, his omniscience and his sovereignty or lordship. In the prefatory or opening sūra (Sūrat al-Fātiḥa; see FĀTIḤA), God is described as the "Lord of the worlds… master of the day of judgment" (Q 1:2, 4) and in the near-final Sūrat al-Ikhlāṣ (Q 112), God is said to be "the only one, the everlasting, who did not beget and is not begotten. None is his equal"

(Q 112:1-4). This last point is stated more dramatically in these words: "Nothing is like unto him" (Q 42:11).

As regards God's existence, the Qur'ān provides its readers with ample evidence which later theologians and philosophers were able to exploit to the full in formulating systematic proofs of his existence. In the process, they were divided into three groups: (1) Those who favored the argument from temporal creation *(ḥudūth)* or the argument *a novitate mundi;* (2) those who favored the argument from contingency *(jawāz)* or possibility *(imkān);* and (3) those who favored the teleological proof, or the argument from providence, as Ibn Rushd was later to call it.

The Ashʿarīs and the Muʿtazilīs, who believed the world to consist of compounds of atoms and accidents, which do not endure for two instants of time, argued that the world was created by an act of divine fiat *(amr),* which the Qur'ān has expressed in these words: "Be and it [the world] comes to be" (Q 2:117, etc.). Al-Kindī, who was the first philosopher to formulate the first argument, held that both the world and its temporal duration are finite, and accordingly must have a beginning *(muḥdath).* As such, the world, being *muḥdath,* must have an originator, *muḥdith,* who created it in time.

The argument from contingency was developed by Ibn Sīnā, who argues in his *al-Shifā',* the "Book of healing" (and that of *al-Najāt,* "Salvation"), that the series of existing entities, being contingent or possible, terminates in a being who is non-contingent or necessary, whom he calls for that reason the necessary being; otherwise that series would go on *ad infinitum,* which is absurd (*Najāt,* 271 f.). The Ashʿarī al-Juwaynī opted for this argument in his lost *Nizāmiyya* treatise, as we are told by Ibn Rushd.

Ibn Rushd favored the teleological argument, which is supported by the most overwhelming evidence and is truly characteristically qur'ānic. This argument, which is the most accordant with the precious book, as Ibn Rushd has put it, rests on the premise that everything in the world is necessarily ordered in accordance with the dictates of divine wisdom, so as to serve the existence of humankind and their well-being on earth. Thus, he invokes verses Q 78:6-14, which ask: "Have we not made the earth as a wide expanse, and the mountains as pegs and [have we not] created you in pairs?... Have we not built above you seven mighty heavens; and created a shining lamp (q.v.); brought down from the rain-clouds abundant water?" Similarly, he invokes Q 25:61, which reads: "Blessed is he who placed in the heavens constellations (see PLANETS AND STARS) and placed therein a lamp and an illuminating moon (q.v.)." He finally cites verses Q 80:24-32, which read: "Let humankind consider its nourishment. We have poured the water abundantly; then we split the earth wide open; then caused the grain to grow therein, together with vines and green vegetation... for your enjoyment and that of your cattle" (cf. Ibn Rushd, *Kashf,* 152, 198 f.; see GRASSES; AGRICULTURE AND VEGETATION).

All these and similar verses prove, according to Ibn Rushd, the existence of a wise creator, who has determined willfully that the world and everything in it was intended to be subservient to the existence and well-being of humankind.

A closely related argument that is embodied in the Qur'ān, according to Ibn Rushd, is that of invention *(ikhtirāʿ).* This argument is supported by a series of verses, such as Q 22:73 which reads: "Surely, those upon whom you call, beside God, will never create a fly, even if they band together" (see POLYTHEISM AND ATHEISM; IDOLS AND IMAGES), or Q 7:185, which reads: "Have they not considered the kingdom of the heavens and the earth and all the things God has created?" Having been invented or created, Ibn Rushd concludes, the world must have an inventor or creator, who brought it into being, in the first instance.

For these and other reasons, Ibn Rushd was critical of the first two traditional arguments. To begin with, the argument from the temporal creation of the world as formulated by the Ashʿarī in particular and the *mutakallimūn* in general, rests on the two premises of temporality *(ḥudūth)* and the atomic composition of existing entities. Now, neither of these premises is demonstrable in a conclusive way and each is too abstruse to be readily understood by the learned, let alone the masses at large. As a good Aristotelian, Ibn Rushd was opposed to the thesis of atomic composition of substance as well as the creation of the world in time, expressed in the Arabic sources as temporality *(ḥudūth)*, the antithesis of eternity.

Secondly, the argument from contingency or possibility runs counter to the incontrovertible maxim that everything in the world is causally determined by its wise creator, or maker, who did not abandon it to the vagaries of chance (*ittifāq;* Ibn Rushd, *Kashf,* 200 f.). Here and elsewhere, Ibn Rushd inveighs on two fundamental grounds against al-Ghazālī and the Ashʿarīs in general for repudiating the concept of causality: That whoever repudiates the necessary causal correlation between existing entities (a) repudiates divine wisdom, and (b) repudiates the very concept of reason, which is nothing but the faculty of apprehending causes (Ibn Rushd, *Tahāfut,* 522).

As for the attributes of God, the Muslim philosophers and theologians alike were inspired by the qurʾānic verse which states: "Were there other deities than God, they [i.e. the heavens and the earth] would have indeed been ruined" (Q 21:22); as well as Q 23:91, which reads, "God did not take to himself a child and there was never another god with him; or else each god would have carried off what he created, and some of them would have risen against the others."

The anti-Trinitarian implications of the first part of the second verse are not difficult to see. Accordingly, as mentioned above, many of the debates with, or polemical writing against, the Christians, turned on the question of the Trinity. The Neoplatonists among the philosophers, such as al-Fārābī and Ibn Sīnā, inspired by the teaching of Plotinus (d. 270 C.E.), built their cosmology and metaphysics around the pivotal concept of "the one" or "the first" [being]. Thus, al-Fārābī, the founder of Muslim Neoplatonism, opens his *opus magnum, al-Madīna al-fāḍila,* the "Virtuous city," with a discourse on the first (being), who is the first cause of all existing entities, is free from all imperfections and is entirely distant from everything else. In addition, he has no equal or partner *(sharīk),* has no opposite and is therefore utterly unique. His uniqueness, al-Fārābī goes on to argue, follows from the fact that "his existence, whereby he is distinct from all other existing entities, is nothing other than that whereby he exists in himself" (Fārābī, *Madīna,* 30). In short, God's uniqueness is synonymous with his existence, which is identical with his essence.

Another sense of unity, as applied to the first being, is then given as indivisibility, from which al-Fārābī infers that he is indefinable since the parts of the *definiendum* are reducible to the causes of its existence or its components, which in the case of the first being is impossible.

Other Neoplatonists, including Ibn Sīnā,

followed al-Fārābī's example in asserting the unity, indivisibility and indefinability of the first being, whom Ibn Sīnā calls the necessary being. Ibn Sīnā, however, denied that the necessary being has an essence, exposing himself to the vehement strictures of Ibn Rushd, Aquinas and others, who regarded the identity of existence and essence in God as incontrovertible. That identity was in a sense the hallmark of God's uniqueness.

The other attributes, known collectively as the seven attributes of perfection, consisted of knowledge, life, power, will, speech, hearing and sight. Those attributes were regarded by the philosophers and the Muʿtazilīs, despite allegations by their opponents to the contrary, as identical with the divine essence *(dhāt)*, whereas the Ashʿarīs regarded them as distinct from that essence. The most heated controversy raged around the two active attributes of speech and will. With respect to the first attribute, the controversy centered on the question of how God's eternal speech can be embodied in a temporal document, i.e. the Qurʾān. With respect to the second attribute, the question was asked: How can God will the creation of the universe in time, without a change in his essence?

In response to the first question, the Muʿtazilīs simply asserted that the Qurʾān, as God's speech, was created in time — rejecting the rival Ḥanbalī thesis of its eternity — on the ground that this would entail a multiplicity of eternal entities. For them, the only eternal entity is God, who is entirely one and whose attributes are identical with his essence. For that reason, the Muʿtazilīs labeled themselves as the "people of divine unity and justice." The Ḥanbalīs and the Ashʿarīs, relying on the qurʾānic references to the Qurʾān as the "preserved tablet" (q.v.; Q 85:22) and the "mother of the book" (Q 3:7; 13:39; 43:4) insisted that, as Aḥmad b. Ḥanbal put it: "The Qurʾān is God's eternal *(qadīm)* and uncreated speech," a position to which he stuck adamantly, despite the persecution and vilification to which he was exposed, in the wake of the afore-mentioned inquisition *(miḥna)* imposed by the caliph al-Maʾmūn.

Faced with the problems which the creation of the world in time raised, the Ḥanbalīs took an entirely agnostic line, whereas the Ashʿarīs took the more sophisticated line of proposing that God created the world in time by an act of eternal will. That thesis was rejected by the philosophers on the ground that, as Ibn Rushd was to argue in his rebuttal of al-Ghazālī, God's eternal will entails logically an eternal creation, which the Ashʿarīs rejected. For the world to come into being in time, subsequent to God's willing it from all time, entails the absurdity that an infinite lapse of time intervened between his willing and his action due to some outward impediment or some deficiency on his part. It follows, as Ibn Rushd argues, that the world, as the product of God's willing and doing, must be supposed to have existed from all time, or as the Latin scholastics were later to put it, to be the product of God's *creatio ab aeterno*, or eternal creation. For, of the two modes of creation or origination of the world, the "continuous" and the "discontinuous" *(dāʾim* and *munqaṭiʿ)*, as Ibn Rushd calls them, the former — continuous — creation *(iḥdāth dāʾim)* is more appropriately predicated of God, whose creative designs can never be thwarted by any impediment or deficiency (Ibn Rushd, *Tahāfut*, 162).

Notwithstanding, Ibn Rushd was never fully reconciled to the concept of eternal will, as predicated of God. He accuses al-Ghazālī of conceiving of divine will as analogous to human will and asserts that the modality of God's will, like the modality of his knowledge, is unknowable (ibid., 149).

The other attributes of life, power and knowledge, asserted so dramatically in the Qurʾān, did not, on the whole, raise serious problems. Hearing and sight were likewise asserted on the authority of the Qurʾān which speaks of God as all-seeing *(baṣīr)* and all-hearing *(samīʿ)*. For the philosophers, such as al-Kindī and Ibn Rushd, those two attributes are predicable of God on the ground that his knowledge encompasses all objects of cognition, whether intelligible or perceptible.

The creation of the world

The Qurʾān speaks of God's creative power in the most dramatic terms. He created the world in six days and then sat upon the throne (Q 7:54; 10:3; 32:4: 57:4); he creates by a sheer act of divine fiat, for if he wills anything, he bids it to be and it comes to be (Q 2:117; 16:40; 36:82; 40:40). He has created "everything in truth" (Q 45:22; 46:3), for "we have not created the heavens and the earth and what lies between them as sport," as Q 44:38 puts it. What the purpose of creation is, is left undefined but in Q 51:56, it is stated, "I have not created the jinn (q.v.) and humankind except to worship me." The *mutakallimūn,* almost without exception, interpreted the Qurʾān to mean that God created the world *ex nihilo* and in time. A variety of terms are used in the Qurʾān to highlight God's creative might, such as creator *(khāliq)*, cleaver *(fāṭir)*, originator *(badīʿ, mubdiʿ)*, fashioner *(bāriʾ)* and so on.

Although the philosophers did not question the fact of creation or bringing the world into being, they tended to steer clear of the term *khāliq* (creator) and *khalq* (creation) and to substitute for the first such terms as *bāriʾ* (al-Rāzī), *ṣāniʿ* (Ibn Rushd), *muḥdith* (al-Kindī) and for the second *ibdāʿ* (Ibn Sīnā), *iḥdāth* or *ījād* (Ibn Rushd), and so on. Al-Kindī went so far as to coin the two terms *muʾayyis* — "maker," from *aysa* (to be), the antonym of *laysa* — and the parallel term *muhawwi* — from the Arabic pronoun *huwa,* "he," or its Syriac equivalent — to express God's role as the creator of the world out of nothing.

The Neoplatonists, as we have seen, substituted for the concept of creation that of emanation *(ṣudūr, fayḍ),* derived ultimately from Plotinus, founder of Greek Neoplatonism, and his successor, Proclus. The universe, according to the emanationist view, is not the product of God's creative power or will, in the strict sense, but an eternal and necessary emanation or procession from God's very substance. According to this emanationist view, God (the one or first, i.e. being) generates, by an eternal act of overflowing, the first intellect *(nous),* followed by a series of intellects, culminating in the tenth or active intellect, followed by the soul *(psyche)* and finally matter. The lower world consists of an infinite variety of compounds of form and matter, whose simplest ingredients are the four elements of Aristotelian physics, fire, air (see AIR AND WIND), water and earth.

The philosophers questioned whether the Qurʾān explicitly supports the *mutakallimūn*'s concept of creation *(khalq), ex nihilo* and in time. Ibn Rushd, who rejected the Avicennian thesis of emanation while retaining the concept of eternal creation *(iḥdāth dāʾim),* as we have seen, argues that a number of verses in the Qurʾān, such as Q 11:7, imply, on the surface, the eternity of the universe. That verse reads: "It is he who created the heavens and the earth in six days, and his throne was upon the water," which implies the eternity of water, the throne and the time that measures their duration. Similarly, verse Q 41:11, which states that "he arose to heaven while it was smoke," implies that the heaven was created out of a pre-existing matter, which is smoke, rather than out of nothing as the *mutakallimūn* claim (Ibn Rushd, *Faṣl,* 42 f.).

What rendered the concept of eternity entirely nefarious from the Ashʿarī point of view in particular and that of the *mutakallimūn* in general was the contention that it appeared to entail a limitation of God's power to act freely, to create or not create the world at any time of his own choosing. The philosophers, including Ibn Rushd, as we have seen, rejected this contention on the ground that eternal creation was more in keeping with God's perfection. It ensured that creating the world involved no change in his essence and that his power, being infinite, could not be barred by some impediment or deficiency from bringing the world into being from all time.

Contrary to the philosophers, God's creation of the world, like his other actions or decisions, was represented by the *mutakallimūn* as miraculous, or independent of any conditions other than the divine will, spoken of in the Qurʾān as the divine command *(amr)*. For this reason, they were led to reject the Aristotelian concept of necessary causation, insofar as it entailed that other causes or agents, whether voluntary or involuntary, operated in the world beside God. For al-Ghazālī (*Tahāfut*, 276), who held that God is the sole agent, that claim runs counter to the consensus of the Muslim community that God is able to do whatever he pleases in a miraculous way.

On the question of the end of the world, the philosophers tended to assert the post-eternity *(abadiyya)* of the world, as a counterpart to its pre-eternity *(azaliyya, qidam)*. They were charged on this account by al-Ghazālī with heresy (q.v.) or innovation (q.v.; *tabdīʿ*), rather than the more serious charge of irreligion (*takfīr;* see BELIEF AND UNBELIEF). For the philosophers, whether Neoplatonists, like Ibn Sīnā, or Aristotelians, like Ibn Rushd, the post-eternity of the world was a consequence either of the eternity of prime matter and time (as Aristotle held) or the eternal procession of the universe from the one (as Plotinus held). The two major exceptions were al-Kindī, who adhered, as we have seen, to the qurʾānic view of creation in time and *ex nihilo (ḥudūth)* and al-Rāzī, who maintained a central metaphysical conception of five coeternal principles (see above: matter, space, time, the soul and the creator; cf. Fakhry, *History*, 121). Al-Rāzī adhered to a picturesque view of the creation of the world by the creator *(al-bāriʾ)* out of the three co-eternal principles of space, time and matter to serve as the stage upon which the soul's infatuation with a sister co-eternal principle, matter, could be requited. Once the union of these two sister-principles is achieved, the soul is led eventually to rediscover its original essence as a denizen of the intelligible world, through the therapeutic function of philosophy; the material world will then, according to al-Rāzī, cease to exist and the soul will in Platonic fashion regain its original abode in the higher world (Fakhry, *History*, 101).

The *mutakallimūn* without exception rejected the thesis of post-eternity as inimical to God's unlimited creative power. Their position was in line with those qurʾānic verses, such as Q 55:26-7, which explicitly indicate that nothing remains forever: once the world is destroyed or ceases to exist, all perishes except the "face of your lord" (see FACE OF GOD).

Ethics and eschatology

The Muʿtazilīs were the first genuine moral theologians of Islam. Their ethical speculation bore, from the start, on such fundamental issues as the justice of God, the nature of right and wrong, the capacity *(istiṭāʿa)* or power of the agent to act freely and the genuine meaning of responsibility (q.v.) or accountability, as a logical corollary of free will.

The precursors of the Muʿtazilīs in the first/seventh century, known as the Qadarīs, were the first to challenge the traditionalist view that all human actions are predetermined by God, for which the human agent cannot be held responsible. The early Umayyad caliphs, as we have seen, welcomed the determinists' view as a means of justifying their repressive policies, contending that, however cruel or heinous, their crimes or transgressions were part of the divine decree *(qadāʾ)*, which cannot be questioned.

For the Muʿtazilīs, who rationalized what was in part a natural response to the political excesses of the Umayyads, God, who is just and wise, cannot perpetrate or sanction actions which are morally wrong. To substantiate this claim, they undertook to demonstrate that God was truly just, that human actions are known to be right or wrong in themselves, and that the human agent is both free and responsible for his deeds and misdeeds.

Despite their rationalist stand on these issues, the Muʿtazilīs sought a basis for these propositions in the Qurʾān. Apart from this, a careful perusal of the qurʾānic verses which bear on all three questions would reveal that the textual evidence is equally weighted in favor of both indeterminism and determinism and allows for divergent interpretations, as in fact the history of Islamic theology *(kalām)* shows.

Although justice is not predicated in positive terms of God, there are numerous verses in the Qurʾān, which assert that: "God [or your lord] is not unjust to the [human] servants" (cf. Q 3:182; 41:46). In Q 28:50, 46:10, etc., God is said "not to guide the unjust people [aright]," and in Q 16:90, God is said to "enjoin justice, charity and giving to kinsmen (see KINSHIP)," reinforced by the statement that "he forbids indecency (see MODESTY; ADULTERY AND FORNICATION), wrongdoing and oppression (q.v.)."

Overwhelmed by the parallel spectacle of God's absolute power and majesty, as depicted in the Qurʾān, the determinists *(jabriyya)* and traditionalists could not reconcile themselves to the notion of God submitting, like human agents, to a higher canon of right and wrong. In fact, they adhered to the maxim that right is precisely what God commands, evil what he has prohibited, and accordingly his actions cannot be described as either just or unjust. As al-Ghazālī has put it, to predicate justice or injustice of God is as frivolous as predicating playing or frolicking of the wall or the wind.

The Muʿtazilīs insisted from the start, however, that responsibility entailed the ability of the agent to discriminate between good and evil, right and wrong. In addition to such discrimination, the agent should be able to choose freely; otherwise no merit would attach to his actions, which would be no different from mechanical or involuntary reactions, such as convulsions, trembling or the like.

The two qurʾānic terms on which the Muʿtazilīs seized to describe the intrinsic property of goodness or badness predicated of human actions were *al-maʿrūf*, "approved," and *al-munkar*, "disapproved." Demanding or commanding the "approved" and prohibiting the "disapproved" were then posited as one of their five fundamental principles (see VIRTUES AND VICES, COMMANDING AND FORBIDDING).

If we turn to the qurʾānic text, we will find that right actions are, in general, spoken of as acts of obedience *(ṭāʿāt)*, vicious actions as acts of disobedience (q.v.; *maʿāṣin*). The term applied frequently to the first category of action is *birr*, "righteousness," *khayr*, "goodness," *qisṭ*, "equity," or *maʿrūf*, "approved," whereas the term applied to the second category is *ithm,* "wickedness," *wizr,* "burden, sin," or *munkar,* "disapproved" (see GOOD DEEDS; EVIL DEEDS).

In a number of verses, the Qur'ān speaks in laudatory terms of people who discriminate between those two categories. Thus, Q 3:104 reads: "Let there be among you a nation calling to goodwill *(al-khayr),* bidding the right *(al-ma'rūf)* and forbidding the wrong *(al-munkar)*. These are the prosperous." In Q 3:114, the People of the Book (q.v.) are commended as those "who believe in God and the last day, bid the right and forbid the wrong, hastening to do the good deeds." In the next verse, it is stated "that whatever good they do, they will not be denied it. God knows well the godfearing" (see FEAR). The deontological implications of this and similar verses are clear; the distinction between good and evil, right and wrong is explicit and God's pleasure or displeasure consequently is explicit, too.

As for human responsibility for freely chosen actions or, as the Qur'ān puts it, what an individual has "earned" or "acquired" (*kasaba* and *iktasaba*), the Qur'ān is categorical that the righteous and the wicked are bound to meet with their appropriate punishment or reward in the hereafter (see ESCHATOLOGY). Thus, Q 42:30 reads: "Whatever calamity might hit you is due to what your hands have earned *(kasabat)*." Q 2:281 reads: "Fear a day when you will be returned to God; then each soul will be rewarded [fully] for what it has earned, and none shall be wronged." Similarly, Q 2:286 reads: "God does not charge any soul beyond its capacity. It will get what it has earned and will be called to account for what it has acquired."

Set against these and similar verses, there are numerous verses in the Qur'ān which support the contrary or determinist thesis, according to which God's decrees are irreversible and unquestionable. Thus, Q 54:49 reads: "We have created everything in measure *(bi-qadarin)*" and Q 13:8, which reads: "Everything with him is according to a certain measure." Finally, Q 64:11 reads, "No disaster befalls you on earth or in yourselves but is in a book before we created it."

The concepts of measure and book in these and other verses clearly indicate that human actions, as well as their consequences, are part of the divine decree and will not escape God's ineluctable reckoning on the day of judgment. The book in question appears to be identified with the "preserved tablet" (Q 85:22), on which the Qur'ān was originally inscribed and is the embodiment of the divine decree, which admits of no alteration (see HEAVENLY BOOK; REVISION AND ALTERATION). This is forcefully brought out in Q 85, called appropriately Sūrat al-Burūj, "The Constellations," which asks rhetorically in verse 9: "To whom belongs the dominion of the heavens and the earth?" adding "God is witness of everything" (see WITNESSING AND TESTIFYING). Then, after assuring the righteous of their well-earned reward in heaven, and the unbelievers of their eventual consignment to hell, the supreme prerogative of God, "the lord of the glorious throne," is reasserted and the wicked are reminded that "the vengeance (q.v.) of your lord is surely terrible." (Q 85:12).

As far as the theological controversy is concerned, the early determinists, such as Jahm b. Ṣafwān (d. 128/745) and al-Ḥusayn b. Muḥammad al-Najjār (d. middle of the third/ninth century), as well as the whole class of Ash'arīs, adhered to a theodicy in which God's creative power was absolute and his decrees irreversible. Thus, al-Ash'arī writes in *Kitāb al-Ibāna,* the "Book of clarification":

> We believe that God Almighty has created everything by bidding it to be, as he says [in Q 16:40]: "Indeed, when we want a thing to be, we simply say to it 'Be' and it comes to be; that there is nothing good or evil on earth except what God has pre-ordained;... that there is no creator but God and that the deeds of the creatures are created and pre-ordained by God, as he says [in Q 37:96]: "God created you and what you make."

As regards the universal sway of providence, al-Ashʿarī continues:

> We believe that good and evil are the product of God's decree and pre-ordination *(qaḍāʾ wa-qadar)*... and we know that what has missed us could not have hit us, or what has hit us could not have missed us and that the creatures are unable to profit or injure themselves without God's leave (Ashʿarī, *Ibāna*, 23 f.; McCarthy, *Theology*, 238 f.).

The leading Ashʿarī doctors of the next two centuries, such as al-Bāqillānī (d. 403/1013), al-Baghdādī (d. 429/1037), al-Juwaynī (d. 478/1085) and al-Ghazālī (d. 505/1111), developed and systemized the teaching of the master. To rationalize this deterministic view, they developed an "occasionalist" theory according to which the world consists of indivisible particles (atoms) and accidents, which God continuously creates and recreates as long as he wishes their compounds to endure. When God wishes them to cease to exist, he just stops the process of continuous creation or, as some Ashʿarīs had put it, he creates the accident of annihilation *(fanāʾ)* but in no substratum and then the world would cease to exist at once. Justice and injustice, as al-Ashʿarī had taught, consisted in what God commands or prohibits, and humans have no share in the production of their actions, which the Muʿtazilīs had attributed to them, considering people to be free agents. To moderate the extreme determinism of Jahm b. Ṣafwān and his followers, however, they made a purely verbal concession, based on those qurʾānic verses, which, as already mentioned, speak of acquisition or earning *(kasaba, iktasaba)* the merits or demerits of the actions by the agent. They continued to hold, nonetheless, that God creates both the choice and the action.

In the field of eschatology, the Qurʾān had depicted the fate of humans in the hereafter in such dramatic terms, especially in the Meccan sūras, that pious souls, especially among ascetics and mystics (see ASCETICISM; SAINT), were later obsessed with the spectacle of hell and its horrors drawn in these sūras; while others, especially poets, dwelt on the delectable pleasures of the garden (q.v.), reserved for the righteous in the life to come. Thus, a number of sūras bear such expressive titles as "The Earthquake" (Sūrat al-Zalzala, Q 99), "The Calamity" (Sūrat al-Qāriʿa, Q 101), "Worldly Increase" (Sūrat al-Takāthur, Q 102), "The Chargers" (Sūrat al-ʿĀdiyāt, Q 100), "The Clear Proof" (Sūrat al-Bayyina, Q 98) and "The Overwhelming Day" (Sūrat al-Ghāshiya, Q 88) to highlight the picture of hell and its horrors (see HELL AND HELLFIRE). People on the last day are said to be "like scattered butterflies and the mountains like tufted wool" (Q 101:4-5) and "faces on that day shall be downcast, laboring and toiling; roasting in a scorching fire; given to drink from a boiling spring" (Q 88:2-5; see SPRINGS AND FOUNTAINS). By contrast, the righteous are promised the most bounteous rewards in glowing terms, as in Q 88:8-16: "Faces on that day shall be blissful; well-pleased with their endeavor; in a lofty garden; wherein no word of vanity is heard (see GOSSIP); wherein is a flowing spring; wherein are upraised couches, and cups passed round (see CUPS AND VESSELS), and cushions in rows, and carpets spread out."

For the Muslim philosophers, life after death raised the most acute questions (see DEATH AND THE DEAD; BURIAL; SALVATION). Some, like al-Kindī, concurred with the *mutakallimūn* in adhering to the thesis of bodily resurrection and the attendant pleasures or tortures of paradise or hell, as embodied in the Qur'ān. In support of this thesis, al-Kindī quotes Q 36:78 f., which refer to God's supreme power to "bring the bones back to life, once they are withered and to bring opposites from opposites," as he does in causing fire to come from green trees (Q 36:80).

Other philosophers, such as al-Fārābī and Ibn Sīnā, while conceding the immortality of the soul, were embarrassed by the qur'ānic thesis of bodily resurrection. Accordingly, they tried to interpret this resurrection in a variety of ways, which the *mutakallimūn* found unacceptable. For al-Fārābī, the soul's fate after leaving the body will depend on the degree of its apprehension of true happiness and its vocation as an inhabitant of the intelligible world. Upon separation from their bodies, souls will partake of a growing measure of happiness, as they join successive throngs of kindred souls in the intelligible world. Those souls, however, whose happiness consisted in clinging to bodily pleasures in this world, will continue to pass from one body to the other endlessly. Wayward souls will continue to be embodied in lower material forms until they have degenerated to the bestial level, whereupon they will simply perish. What adds to the misery of such wayward souls, as they pass through this cycle of transmigration, is the perpetual agony which they will suffer upon separation from the body and its pleasures, for which they will continue to yearn, until they perish completely (Fārābī, *Ahl al-madīna,* 118).

Al-Fārābī's spiritual disciple and successor, Ibn Sīnā, was committed to the view, adhered to by almost all the Muslim philosophers, especially the Neoplatonists among them, that the soul's perfection consists in achieving "conjunction" *(ittiṣāl)* with the active intellect. This is the precondition of true happiness and the warrant of the soul's becoming, once it fulfilled its intellectual vocation, a replica of the intelligible world to which it originally belonged, prior to its descent into the body. Those souls which have fallen short of this condition, by virtue of their attachment to the body and its cares, will suffer misery consequent upon the unwanted separation from the body. But once they are freed from this misery by attaining the level of apprehension proper to them, they will be able to partake of that intellectual pleasure which is "analogous to that blissful condition proper to the pure, living entities (i.e. spiritual substance) and is greater and nobler than any other pleasure" (Ibn Sīnā, *Najāt,* 330).

Ibn Sīnā, however, recognizes in addition to this intellectual condition of which the soul will partake upon separation from the body a scriptural *(sharʿī)* one, that resurrection "which is received from scripture *(sharʿ)* and can only be demonstrated by recourse to the holy law *(sharīʿa)* and assent to prophetic reports" (ibid., 326). "Thus, the true law," Ibn Sīnā writes, "which Muḥammad our Prophet has brought us, has set forth the nature of the happiness and misery in store for the body" (ibid., 326; see JOY AND MISERY). Ibn Sīnā does not call into question this bodily happiness but continues to hold that there is a higher intellectual happiness which the "metaphysical philosophers" are intent on seeking in "proximity to God," which the mystics (Ṣūfīs) have placed at the center of their teaching and which is confirmed, according to Ibn Sīnā, by the "true holy law" of Islam.

Ibn Rushd, despite his divergence from Ibn Sīnā and the Neoplatonists generally, tended to agree with this conciliatory position. Resurrection or survival after death *(maʿād),* as he prefers to call it, is a matter on which "all the religious laws or creeds are in agreement and which the demonstrations of the philosophers have affirmed." After distinguishing three Islamic views of happiness and misery, which although generically different only in point of duration, degree of corporality or spirituality, he goes on to argue that the crass corporal resurrection entertained by the vulgar is untenable. According to that view, the soul, upon resurrection, will be reunited to the same body it dwelt in during its terrestrial existence. How is it possible, he then asks, for the same body which was reduced to dust upon death, then changed into a plant on which another man has fed, and then turned into semen which gave rise to another person, to enter into the makeup of a resurrected person? It is more reasonable, Ibn Rushd holds, to assert that the risen soul will be united on the last day to a body, which is analogous, but not identical, with its original body (Ibn Rushd, *Tahāfut,* 586). In fact, religious creeds are in agreement regarding the reality of survival after death, he goes on to explain, but are nevertheless in disagreement on its modality *(ṣifa).* Some creeds, by which he probably meant the Christian, regard it as spiritual, whereas others, by which he meant Islam, regard it as doubly corporeal and spiritual. If, however, we probe the difference between the various creeds on this question, we will find, he argues, that they are reducible to the mode of "representation" *(tamthīl)* or idiom used by each one of them in describing the misery or happiness reserved to the wicked or righteous in the life to come. To the extent that corporeal representations are more effective in commanding the assent of the masses at large, they are preferable to purely spiritual representations that are appreciated only by the intellectually gifted, including the philosophers in general. Thus it appears, he writes, "that the (corporeal) representation found in this our own region (i.e. Islam) is more effective in leading to understanding, where the majority of humankind are concerned, and in moving their soul in that direction... whereas spiritual representation is less effective in moving the souls of the masses" (Ibn Rushd, *Kashf,* 244). Illuminationist (Ishrāqī) philosophers, such as al-Shīrāzī (d. 1050/1641), who recognized the harmony of philosophy and mysticism (Ṣūfism) for the first time in Islamic history, tended to follow the lead of Ibn Sīnā on this and similar questions.

Conclusion

This article has shown that the Qur'ān speaks in the first place of wisdom *(ḥikma),* both in the Greek sense of *sophia* and the Semitic or biblical sense of divine revelation to Muḥammad, Jesus and the Hebrew prophets. In the second place, it urges the believers to contemplate the wonders of creation, to reflect, to consider and ponder the mysterious ways of God. Such contemplation, reflection, consideration and pondering are the hallmarks of the philosophical method as it was applied to the theological and ethical questions which preoccupied the *mutakallimūn* and the philosophers from the earliest times.

The major problems around which controversy in theological and philosophical circles turned centered on such questions as the existence of God, the creation of the world, the destiny of humans in the hereafter and the rationality and justice of God's ways as creator and providential ruler of the world. As the controversy between the philosophers and the theologians intensified, the latter split into two rival groups, the pro-philosophical, led by the Muʿtazilīs, and the anti-philosophical, led by the Ḥanbalīs and the Ashʿarīs. Naturally enough, both groups sought support in the Qurʾān for their conflicting interpretations of those ambiguous passages which bear directly or indirectly on the problems in question. Some theologians and jurists confined the prerogative of interpreting the so-called "ambiguous" passages of the Qurʾān to God; others, including some philosophers, extended this prerogative to the learned or specially gifted, as Ibn Rushd has done.

The status of the Qurʾān itself and whether it was created in time *(makhlūq)* or was eternal *(qadīm)* raised, from the third/ninth century on, the most acute questions and led to endless recriminations between some theologians, such as the Muʿtazilīs, and those jurists and tradition-mongers *(muḥaddithūn),* such as Ibn Ḥanbal and his followers, who insisted that the Qurʾān was "the eternal and uncreated word of God," relying in the last analysis on those passages in the Qurʾān itself which speak of the "mother of the book" and the "well-preserved tablet," in reference to the original codex on which the Qurʾān was inscribed since all time. The Ashʿarīs, who sought an intermediate position between the Muʿtazilīs and the Ḥanbalīs, tried to resolve the conflict by distinguishing between the "significations" *(dalālāt)* of the words in which the Qurʾān is expressed and the actual words themselves, written (see TEXTUAL CRITICISM OF THE QURʾĀN; COLLECTION OF THE QURʾĀN; MUṢḤAF; CODICES OF THE QURʾĀN) or recited (see RECITATION OF THE QURʾĀN), which could not as such be eternal or uncreated, since they belonged to the category of perishable accidents. Some philosophers, including Ibn Rushd, subscribed to this view. In popular Muslim consciousness, however, it is fair to say that the Ḥanbalī view, which stresses the sanctity and inimitability *(iʿjāz)* of the qurʾānic text, may be said to have triumphed, and the Qurʾān continues today to be regarded by the vast majority of Muslims as the miraculous word of God (see MIRACLES; MARVELS). Contemporary scholars, such as the late Pakistani Fazlur Rahman (d. 1988) and the Egyptian Naṣr Ḥāmid Abū Zayd, who attempted to draw a line of demarcation between the human and divine aspects of the qurʾānic text, or to apply the canons of literary or "higher criticism" to that text (see CONTEMPORARY CRITICAL PRACTICES AND THE QURʾĀN), have been either reprimanded or declared infidel (*kāfir;* see EXEGESIS OF THE QURʾĀN: EARLY MODERN AND CONTEMPORARY; POST-ENLIGHTENMENT ACADEMIC STUDY OF THE QURʾĀN). This has served as a warning to other contemporary liberal scholars or philosophers to avoid this highly sensitive subject altogether.

Majid Fakhry

Bibliography

Primary: Aristotle, *Metaphysics,* ed. and trans. H.G. Apostle, Bloomington 1966, 1973[3]; al-Ashʿarī, Abū l-Ḥasan ʿAlī b. Ismāʿīl, *al-Ibāna ʿan uṣūl al-diyāna,* ed. F. Ḥusayn Maḥmūd, Cairo 1997; Eng. trans. R.J. McCarthy, *The theology of al-Ashʿarī,* Beirut 1953; al-Fārābī, Abū Naṣr Muḥammad b. Muḥammad, *Ārāʾ ahl al-madīna al-fāḍila,* ed. A. Nader, Beirut 1959; al-Ghazālī, Abū Hāmid Muḥammad b. Muḥammad, *al-Qusṭās al-mustaqīm,* ed. M.A. al-Zuʿbī, Beirut 1973; id., *Tahāfut al-falāsifa,* ed. M. Bouyges, Beirut 1927; al-Ḥasan al-Baṣrī, Abū Saʿīd b. Abī l-Ḥasan, *Risāla fī l-qadar,* in M. Fakhry, *al-Fikr al-akhlāqī l-ʿarabī,* 2 vols., Beirut 1978, 1986, i, 17-28; Ibn Rushd, Abū l-Walīd Muḥammad b. Aḥmad, *Bidāyat al-mujtahid wa-nihāyat al-muqtaṣid* [English]. *The distinguished jurist's primer,* trans.

A.Kh. Nyazee, 2 vols., Doha 1994-6, Reading 2000; id., *Faṣl al-maqāl,* ed. A. Nader, Beirut 1961; id., *al-Kashf ʿan manāhij al-adilla,* ed. M. Qāsim, Cairo 1961; id., *Tahāfut al-tahāfut,* ed. M. Bouyges, Beirut 1930; Ibn Sīnā, Abū ʿAlī al-Ḥusayn b. ʿAbdallāh, *Kitāb al-Najāt,* ed. M. Fakhry, Beirut 1985; al-Jāḥiẓ, al-Radd ʿalā l-naṣārā, in A.S.M. Hārūn (ed.), *Rasāʾil al-Jāḥiẓ,* 4 vols., Cairo 1979, iii, 301-51; Ṭabarī, *Tafsīr,* Cairo 1954-68. Secondary: I. Bello, *The medieval Islamic controversy between philosophy and orthodoxy. Ijmāʿ and taʾwīl in the conflict between al-Ghazālī and ibn Rushd,* Leiden 1989; D. Black, *Logic and Aristotle's rhetoric and poetics in medieval Arabic philosophy,* Leiden 1990; H. Corbin, *History of Islamic philosophy,* trans. L. Sherrard, London 1993; van Ess, *TG;* M. Fakhry (ed.), *al-Fikr al-akhlāqī l-ʿarabī,* 2 vols., Beirut 1986; id., *A history of Islamic philosophy,* New York 1983; id. (trans.), *The Qurʾān. A modern English version,* Reading 1998; O. Leaman, *A companion to the philosophers,* ed. R. Arrington, Oxford 1999; id., *Key concepts in eastern philosophy,* London 1999; P. Morewedge (ed.), *Islamic philosophical theology,* Albany 1979; id. (ed.), *Islamic philosophy and mysticism,* New York 1981; W. Muir, *The apology of al-Kindī,* London 1882; S. Nasr and O. Leaman (eds.), *History of Islamic philosophy,* London 1996; K. Reinhart, *Before revelation. The boundaries of Muslim moral thought,* Albany 1995; N. Rescher, *The development of Arabic logic,* Pittsburgh 1964; Rippin, *Approaches;* D. Sahas, *John of Damascus on Islam,* Leiden 1972; W.M. Watt, *Islamic philosophy and theology. An extended survey,* Edinburgh 1985; H. Wolfson, *The philosophy of the kalam,* Cambridge, MA 1976.

Piety

Exhibiting loyalty to parents (i.e. filial piety) or manifesting devotion to God. The concept of piety in Arabic can be conveyed by the non-qurʾānic terms *waraʿ* and *zuhd,* and the qurʾānic words *birr, taqwā* and *iḥsān.* (For *zuhd* as ethics, see Kinberg, Zuhd; see also ETHICS AND THE QURʾĀN. *Iḥsān* is often used to express filial piety and understood by the commentators as *birr;* see Rahman, *Major themes,* 42.) The following focuses on the terms *birr* and *taqwā,* which are treated in the Qurʾān as crucial components of true belief (see BELIEF AND UNBELIEF).

Those who practice *birr,* the *abrār,* and those who have *taqwā,* the *muttaqūn,* or *alladhīna ttaqū,* are mentioned among the future dwellers of paradise (q.v.; Q 82:13; 68:34). The most comprehensive definition of the term *birr* is given in Q 2:177: "It is not piety *(al-birr)* that you turn your faces to the east and to the west. [True] piety is [this]: to believe in God and the last day (see LAST JUDGMENT; APOCALYPSE; ESCHATOLOGY), the angels (see ANGEL), the book (q.v.), and the prophets (see PROPHETS AND PROPHETHOOD), to give of one's substance, [however cherished,] to kinsmen (see KINSHIP), and orphans (q.v.), the needy (see POVERTY AND THE POOR), the traveler (see JOURNEY), beggars, and to ransom the slave (see SLAVES AND SLAVERY), to perform the prayer (q.v.), to pay the alms (see ALMSGIVING). And they who fulfil their covenant (q.v.), when they have engaged in a covenant, and endure with fortitude misfortune, hardship and peril (see TRUST AND PATIENCE; TRIAL), these are they who are true in their faith (q.v.), these are the truly godfearing (*al-muttaqūn;* see also FEAR)." This list touches upon interpersonal relationships as well as human-divine relationships, and in this sense it agrees with the definition of piety as it appears in *Webster's new twentieth century dictionary:* (1) devotion to religious duties and practices; (2) loyalty and devotion to parents, family, etc.

For a more profound understanding, however, of the references to piety in the Qurʾān, one should examine the qurʾānic correlation between *birr* and *taqwā.* The ending of Q 2:177 mentions the *muttaqūn,* "the godfearing," and refers to them as those who fulfill all the duties presented in the first part of the verse, namely those who practice *birr.* Q 2:189 is even clearer about the similitude between *birr* and *taqwā:* "... Piety *(al-birr)* is not to come to the houses from the backs of them (see PRE-ISLAMIC ARABIA AND THE QURʾĀN); but piety is to be godfearing *(al-birru mani ttaqā);* so come to the houses by their doors, and fear God; haply so you will prosper."

In both verses cited above, comparisons are made between the true believers and the others, either Jews and Christians (see JEWS AND JUDAISM; CHRISTIANS AND CHRISTIANITY) or the pre-Islamic Arabs (*jāhilīs*; see AGE OF IGNORANCE; SOUTH ARABIA, RELIGION IN PRE-ISLAMIC) and the early Muslims who did not have the *sharīʿa* (see PATH OR WAY; LAW AND THE QURʾĀN) to follow (Qurṭubī, *Jāmiʿ*, ii, 237, 345). *Birr,* in both verses, presents duties, the performance of which indicates true belief, defined as being godfearing or possessing *taqwā*. Furthermore, Q 5:2 mentions *birr* and *taqwā* as two complementary elements of proper conduct: "... Help one another to piety *(al-birr)* and fear of God *(al-taqwā);* do not help each other to sin and enmity (see SIN, MAJOR AND MINOR; ENEMIES). And fear God; surely God is terrible in retribution" (see also Q 58:9). The commentators on this verse distinguish one term from the other by stating that *birr* implies duties one should perform whereas *taqwā* refers to actions from which one should refrain (Wāḥidī, *Wasīṭ*, ii, 150). This may be used to illuminate the way the two terms relate to each other and to clarify the way the Qurʾān understands piety. *Birr* is the inclusive term for ethics; it underlies the pleasing conduct in daily communal life; it is anchored in and stimulated by the feeling of fear of the one God *(taqwā),* which is fear of the consequences of actions that violate the values included under *birr* (see also VIRTUES AND VICES, COMMANDING AND FORBIDDING).

Leah Kinberg

Bibliography
Primary: Ibn al-Jawzī, *al-Birr wa-l-ṣila,* Beirut 1993; Qurṭubī, *Jāmiʿ*; Wāḥidī, *Wasīṭ*.
Secondary: Arberry; Izutsu, *Concepts;* id., *God and man in the Koran,* Tokyo 1964; L. Kinberg, What is meant by *zuhd,* in *SI* 61 (1985), 27-44; F. Rahman, *Major themes of the Qurʾān,* Chicago 1980.

Pig see ANIMAL LIFE

Pilgrimage

A journey to a holy place, and the religious activities associated with it. The words most often translated as pilgrimage, both in the Qurʾān and with regard to Muslim ritual (see RITUAL AND THE QURʾĀN), are *ḥajj* and *ʿumra*. The word *ḥajj* occurs nine times in five different verses (in Q 2:189, three times; in Q 2:196, three times; and once each in Q 2:197, Q 9:3 and Q 22:27), *ʿumra* twice in one verse only (Q 2:196) but there are also a number of related nominal and verbal forms for each. With reference to Muslim practice, *ḥajj* is sometimes distinguished as the major pilgrimage, *ʿumra* as the minor, but whether one is speaking of the Qurʾān or of Muslim practice, the word pilgrimage is not really an adequate indication of what *ḥajj* and *ʿumra* involve. The English word commonly suggests a journey to a sacred place made as a religious act. The focus is on the journey itself, even though the pilgrim may participate in religious ceremonies and rituals once the object of the pilgrimage has been reached. Those who make *ḥajj* and *ʿumra,* it is true, have nearly always traveled long distances to Mecca (q.v.) in order to do so, and a substantial part of the journey has to be made in the sacral state known as *iḥrām,* but it is the rites and ceremonies that are performed after arriving that really constitute the *ḥajj* or the *ʿumra*. If consideration is restricted to the relevant qurʾānic passages without reference to Muslim practice, it is questionable how far they evoke the idea of pilgrimage as journey, although it could not be ruled out that traveling to perform *ḥajj* or *ʿumra* is envisaged.

The traditional Arabic lexicographers associate the verbal forms *ḥajja* and *iʿtamara* with the idea of travelling to a place (especially the sanctuary; see KAʿBA) for the purpose of a visit *(ziyāra)* but that possibly reflects standard Muslim practice and may not be an accurate guide to the basic meaning of the words. The roots *ḥ-j(-j)* (or *ḥ-w-j*) and *ʿ-m-r* occur in other Semitic languages apart from Arabic but it is difficult to determine basic meanings for them. The use of cognate words to elucidate the meaning of *ḥajj* and *ʿumra* is complicated by the fact that Semiticists sometimes use Arabic materials influenced by Islam to attempt to clarify the vocabulary of, say, Hebrew or south Arabian. *Ḥ-j(-j),* it has been suggested, has a number of possible meanings including procession, round, dance or festival. It has been argued that basically it refers to the act of dancing or processing around an altar or other cultic object, and that that relates to the ritual of the circumambulation *(ṭawāf)* of the Kaʿba, which is an important part of both *ḥajj* and *ʿumra*. In the Bible the Hebrew *ḥaj* is usually translated simply as festival or feast, although it could involve the participants in journeying to the place, Jerusalem or elsewhere, where the *ḥaj* was to be held (e.g. *Exod* 23:14-7; *Deut* 16:16). In that light the Arabic *ḥajj* might be understood as a "pilgrim festival." The root *ʿ-m-r* is harder to document in any sense securely related to the Arabic *ʿumra*.

As well as the nine qurʾānic attestations of *ḥajj,* Q 3:97 proclaims *ḥijj* (sic) *al-bayt* (*bayt* referring to the house or sanctuary associated with Abraham; see ABRAHAM; HOUSE, DOMESTIC AND DIVINE) as a duty owed to God for anyone who can find a way to it *(mani staṭāʿa ilayhi sabīlan)*. This is the verse that is understood as establishing the obligation *(farḍ)* for every Muslim to make *ḥajj* at least once in his lifetime; possible justifications for failing to meet the obligation are discussed in commentary on the phrase "for anyone who can find a way to it." Generally, *ḥijj* is seen as no more than a dialectical variant of *ḥajj* without significance as to meaning, although there are some attempts to make distinctions in meaning between the two vocalizations. Q 2:158 uses the verbal forms *ḥajja* and *iʿtamara (man ḥajja l-bayta awi ʿtamara)*. Q 9:19 has the noun *ḥājj,* apparently indicating someone making *ḥajj,* in the context of a rhetorical question: "Do you count providing water for him who makes *ḥajj,* and habitation of *al-masjid al-ḥarām* (see PROFANE AND SACRED), as comparable with believing in God and the last day and making jihād (q.v.) in the way of God (see PATH OR WAY; LAST JUDGMENT; FAITH)?" The references to *ḥajj* and *ʿumra* sometimes occur in the context of more extended passages which contain regulations for those making them or which relate in some way to the sanctuary at which they take place. The qurʾānic verses do not, however, contain sufficient detail to enable us to use them as a blueprint even for those rituals to which they allude, and there are many aspects of the Muslim sanctuary and its pilgrimage ceremonies to which no allusion is made in the Qurʾān. The detailed Islamic regulations regarding these pilgrimages, therefore, do not depend primarily upon qurʾānic passages.

Furthermore, it sometimes seems that there is a degree of tension between Muslim practice or legal doctrines and some of the qurʾānic materials. The commentators, naturally, attempt to interpret the verses and the more extended passages, and to address the problems which they raise, with the Muslim forms of *ḥajj* and *ʿumra* in mind. They assume that the passages are concerned with the Kaʿba at Mecca and its related sacred places and that they not only refer to, but to some extent provide a warrant for, the *ḥajj* and the ʿ*umra* as we know them from Muslim law and practice (see LAW AND THE QURʾĀN).

In some cases, however, the qurʾānic materials are problematical from that point of view, and much of the interest in reading the commentaries on the verses relating to *ḥajj* and ʿ*umra* consists in observing how the texts are accommodated to later Muslim assumptions. In general, it seems that while there are definite points of contact (e.g. in terminology and some proper names) between the qurʾānic passages and the pilgrimages as we know them from Muslim law and practice, it cannot be said that all the scriptural passages fit easily with the normative Muslim forms of *ḥajj*, ʿ*umra*, and the sanctuary with which they are associated. The following examples illustrate some apparent disjunctions and some of the interpretative strategies that seem to be adopted in order to overcome them.

Q 2:158 reads: "Al-Ṣafā and al-Marwa (see ṢAFĀ AND MARWA) are among the signs *(shaʿāʾir)* of God. Whoever makes *ḥajj* of the sanctuary *(al-bayt)* or ʿ*umra*, no wrong attaches to him if he makes circumambulation of the two *(lā junāḥa ʿalayhi an yaṭṭawwafa bi-himā)*. Whoever performs something good voluntarily *(wa-man taṭawwaʿa khayran)*, God recognizes and knows (it)." Commentators here unanimously identify al-Ṣafā and al-Marwa as the two small elevations known by those names in Mecca, the former just to the south-east, the latter to the north-east, of the mosque which contains the Kaʿba, about 400 yards apart. The ritual of the Muslim *ḥajj* and ʿ*umra* includes a seven-times-repeated passage between al-Ṣafā and al-Marwa, part of which has to be covered at a faster than walking pace. For that reason the ritual is ordinarily referred to as the *saʿy* (literally, "run"). The commentators, usually without discussion, identify the Islamic *saʿy* with the circumambulation implied in the Qurʾān's *an yaṭṭawwafa bi-himā* even though the Islamic ritual here can only questionably be described as a circumambulation. In discussions of the ritual in ḥadīth (see ḤADĪTH AND THE QURʾĀN) and jurisprudence *(fiqh)* it is usually referred to as *saʿy* but *ṭawāf* is not infrequent. The major issue discussed in connection with this verse, however, is why it is stated that "no wrong attaches to" *(lā junāḥa ʿalā)* the person who makes the *ṭawāf* of al-Ṣafā and al-Marwa when it is virtually unanimously accepted in Islam that the ritual is an integral part of both *ḥajj* and ʿ*umra*. A well-known report tells us that ʿUrwa b. al-Zubayr asked ʿĀʾisha (see ʿĀʾISHA BINT ABĪ BAKR) whether it meant that no wrong accrued to a person who did not make the *ṭawāf* between them, an interpretation which she strongly rejected.

There are several variant reports intended to explain how something which is regarded as meritorious, and by most as obligatory, should be described as incurring no wrong (*junāḥ* is often glossed as *ithm*, "sin"; see SIN, MAJOR AND MINOR). Most attempt to do so by referring, with variant details, to a group, which before Islam avoided al-Ṣafā and al-Marwa because they were associated with idolatry (see IDOLATRY AND IDOLATERS; POLYTHEISM AND ATHEISM) and therefore had qualms about making the *ṭawāf* of them in Islam. The wording of the verse was intended to reassure them that God did not disapprove of the rite once its idolatrous associations had been removed. Another "occasion of revelation" (see OCCASIONS OF REVELATION) report refers to a group that did make this *ṭawāf* before Islam and were puzzled when God ordered the *ṭawāf* of the Kaʿba (Q 22:29 is understood to mean that) but did not mention the two hills. They asked the Prophet whether there was anything wrong in making the *ṭawāf* of al-Ṣafā and al-Marwa and then the verse was revealed.

Some claimed that the passage between the two elevations is not an obligatory part of the ritual of *ḥajj* and *ʿumra* and, in addition to suggesting that the verse may be read "there is no harm in not making circumambulation of the two," wanted to see its concluding words, "whoever voluntarily does something good, God is thankful and cognizant," as a reference to the voluntary nature of this *saʿy/ṭawāf.* That was rejected by the majority who insisted that the ritual is an integral part of both *ḥajj* and *ʿumra,* and said that the concluding words of the verse allude to those who make a voluntary *ḥajj* or *ʿumra* — it has nothing to do with al-Ṣafā and al-Marwa. Among those who insisted that the ritual was obligatory, there were differences of opinion about the consequences of failing to perform the passage between al-Ṣafā and al-Marwa when making the obligatory once-in-a-lifetime *ḥajj* *(ḥijjat al-islām):* can missing it be compensated for by a recompense *(fidya)* of a blood offering (see SACRIFICE) like some of the other rites, or does it require a return to Mecca in person to perform it? There are conflicting views on this point.

Similar problems arise concerning the command at the beginning of the long verse Q 2:196: "Complete the *ḥajj* and the *ʿumra* for God." Commentary on this phrase is fundamentally concerned to establish the distinction between *ḥajj* and *ʿumra* (what rituals each involves) and with the issue of whether, as the wording might imply, the *ʿumra* is obligatory *(farḍ wājib)* like the *ḥajj,* or merely voluntary as the majority view in Islam holds.

Some proponents of the voluntary nature of *ʿumra* read that word in the nominative case, giving the sense, "complete the *ḥajj* but the *ʿumra* is for God...." Others who hold this understanding of the voluntary nature of *ʿumra* maintained the standard reading, with *ʿumra* in the accusative, but argued that "complete" *(atimmū)* means "complete it when you have undertaken to perform it." To the accusation that that could mean that the *ḥajj* also is voluntary, they responded by arguing that it is Q 3:97 and not this verse which establishes the obligatory nature for every Muslim of at least one *ḥajj*. Those who held the *ʿumra* to be obligatory preferred the standard reading and supported their argument with ḥadīths in which the Prophet included *ʿumra* among the obligatory things required of a Muslim. Their opponents rejected the validity of those ḥadīths and countered with ones proclaiming the opposite.

The continuation of Q 2:196 then presents a different problem regarding the accommodation of the text to extra-qurʾānic considerations. One immediately noticeable and surprising feature in the commentaries is the amount of attention given to the meaning of the expression "if you are detained" *(fa-in uḥṣirtum)* in the regulations about what should be done if you are unable to fulfil the verse's initial command to "complete the *ḥajj* and the *ʿumra* for God." Generally it is agreed that this means, "if you are detained when you have undertaken to make *ḥajj* or *ʿumra*." In that case, according to the verse, the person prevented from fulfilling the injunction made at its opening must make "a convenient [animal] offering" (*mā staysara mina l-hady;* see CONSECRATION OF ANIMALS) and must remain in the sacral state of *iḥrām* ("do not shave your heads") until the animal offerings arrive at the time and place for slaughter (q.v.; *ḥattā yablugha l-hadyu maḥillahu*). There is, however, quite complex discussion about the circumstances that may lead to detention. Does it mean only such things as illness (see ILLNESS AND HEALTH), injury to one's mount, and financial difficulties (see POVERTY AND THE POOR); does it refer only to detention by an enemy (see ENEMIES) or a human agent such as a ruler; or does it cover all of these possible causes? Those questions are related to the fact that it is widely accepted that this verse was revealed at the time when the Prophet and his companions were prevented by his Meccan opponents from completing an intended *ʿumra* on which they had started (see OPPOSITION TO MUḤAMMAD). Most of the reports about that incident say that the Prophet ordered his companions to slaughter the animal offerings *(hady)* at al-Ḥudaybiya (q.v.) where they had been stopped. Most agree that al-Ḥudaybiya was outside the sacred territory (the *ḥaram;* see SACRED PRECINCTS), that the Prophet did not imply that he and his companions had any further obligations once the *hady* had been slaughtered, but that in the following year he went to Mecca and performed an *ʿumra* (known as *ʿumrat al-qaḍāʾ* or *ʿumrat al-qaḍiyya,* "the *ʿumra* of completion"). This tradition seems to conflict with the regulations set out in Q 2:196 concerning someone who is "detained" from completing *ḥajj* or *ʿumra* — that abandoning the sacred state should not take place until the animal offerings reach their time and place for slaughter. The complex and detailed discussions in the commentaries on this verse display varying attitudes as to whether priority should be accorded to the tradition about the Prophet's behavior at al-Ḥudaybiya, to the regulations set out in the verse (and further elaborated by some of the scholars), or to practicality. Generally the Mālikīs emphasize the importance of the tradition about al-Ḥudaybiya as a model for someone intending to make *ʿumra* but who is then prevented from completing it through detention by an enemy. Anyone detained by any other cause must not leave the consecrated state (except in the case of an illness the treatment of which necessitates this) until he has reached Mecca and performed an *ʿumra.* Al-Ṭabarī's (d. 310/923; *Tafsīr,* ad loc.) account of the Mālikī understanding of Q 2:196 and of the way in which they relate it to their doctrine is, however, hard to understand and does not seem completely logical. Others give priority to the wording of the verse and some attempt to harmonize it with the Ḥudaybiya tradition by excluding detention by an enemy from the cases covered by *fa-in uḥṣirtum.* In general, the complex arguments of the commentators on this part of the verse may be understood as the result of their attempts to interpret it in the light of existing practice, law and other material regarded as relevant for determining practice.

A further example of the difficulties which arise when attempting to interpret the qurʾānic material with the Muslim rituals in mind is provided by Q 2:198-9. Q 2:198 tells believers that after making *ifāḍa (fa-idhā afaḍtum)* from ʿArafāt (q.v.) they should remember God by *al-mashʿar al-ḥarām;* the next verse orders them to "then" make *ifāḍa* from where the people make it *(thumma afīḍū min ḥaythu afāḍa l-nāsu).* In the Muslim *ḥajj* rituals, ʿArafāt, a hill about twenty-five kilometers to the east of Mecca, is the site of the ceremony of the *wuqūf,* without which, according to several traditions and legal authorities, *ḥajj* is invalid. The *wuqūf,* the "standing" ritual, takes place on the flat ground on the side of the hill towards Mecca on the 9th of Dhū l-Ḥijja. Outside the Qurʾān the name of the hill often occurs in the form ʿArafa, and the commentators discuss and offer various explanations for the seemingly feminine plural form of the name in the Qurʾān and for its etymology: associating it with the verb *ʿarafa,* "to know, to recognize," they relate various stories involving earlier prophets (especially Adam or

Abraham) who recognized people or things there (see ADAM AND EVE).

The attempted identification of *al-mashʿar al-ḥarām* is more complex and, to some extent, inconsistent. *Al-mashʿar* is understood to mean the same as *al-maʿlam*, "a place in or by which something is known, a place in which there is a sign" — here, a place in which rituals of the *ḥajj* take place. Statements attempting to locate *al-mashʿar al-ḥarām* give various specifications. Common to many of them is the idea that it is associated with al-Muzdalifa, the destination of a procession *(ifāḍa)* from ʿArafa in the Muslim *ḥajj*. The simplest statement is of the form "all of al-Muzdalifa is *al-mashʿar al-ḥarām*." Others are more specific but at the same time more confusing, while some seem to indicate a much wider area. For example, Ibn ʿUmar is reported to have said when he stood "at the furthest part of the hills *(jibāl)* adjoining ʿArafāt" that "all of it is *mashāʿir* to the furthest point of the *ḥaram*." In notable reports cited by al-Ṭabarī, Ibn Jurayj seems not to know the location of al-Muzdalifa while ʿAbd al-Raḥmān b. al-Aswad said that he could not find anybody who could tell him about *al-mashʿar al-ḥarām*. Al-Ṭabarī comments on these traditions in ways which limit their apparent significance. The verbal noun *ifāḍa*, literally a "pouring out" or "pouring forth," is understood as referring to a sort of hasty procession when the pilgrims pour forth from one place, where they have been gathered together, to another. The name is given to various "processions" involved in the *ḥajj* ceremonies, but it most commonly refers to that to al-Muzdalifa from the plain in front of the hill of ʿArafa. At al-Muzdalifa the pilgrims spend the night before going to Minā on the next day. It may be this which leads to the attempts to identify *al-mashʿar al-ḥarām* in connection with al-Muzdalifa. There is then a problem with the command, "then make *ifāḍa* from where the people make *ifāḍa,*" at the beginning of Q 2:199, since it comes after the phrase "when you have made *ifāḍa* from ʿArafāt" in Q 2:198. Some understand the same *ifāḍa*, i.e. that from ʿArafāt to al-Muzdalifa, to be referred to in both passages and see the latter command as addressed specifically to the Quraysh (q.v.) of Mecca who, in the Age of Ignorance (q.v.; *jāhiliyya*), belonged to a group called the Ḥums. The Ḥums, we are told, regarded it as beneath them to go outside the *ḥaram* at the time of the *ḥajj*. Since ʿArafāt lies outside the sacred area, they would not go to join in the *ifāḍa* thence like the rest of the people. That explains the apparent difficulty of having the command introduced after the allusion which suggests that the duty had already been fulfilled.
Another approach is to see the *ifāḍa* commanded in the second passage as different from that in the former: while the former is that from ʿArafa to al-Muzdalifa, the latter is that from al-Muzdalifa to Minā (sometimes called the *daffāʿ*). The command is understood as addressed to the Muslims generally while "the people" *(al-nās)* is interpreted as a reference to Abraham. Al-Ṭabarī himself prefers this second possibility even though it is a minority one and even though it involves explaining how the collective *nās* could refer to a single individual. His reasoning is that he does not think that God would say "when you have made the *ifāḍa*" in the previous verse and then begin this one with the words "then make *ifāḍa*" if the same *ifāḍa* was meant both times.

In Q 2:203 the "numbered days" *(ayyām maʿdūdāt)* on which we are commanded to remember God are generally identified as the so-called *ayyām al-tashrīq* of the Muslim *ḥajj*, the three days spent at Minā following the slaughter of the animal offerings there. The following statement that no sin *(ithm)* is incurred by those who "make haste in two days" *(man ta'ajjala fī yawmayn)* nor by those who "delay" *(man ta'akhkhara),* so long as there is fear (q.v.) of God, is generally understood to mean that there is nothing wrong with departing from Minā after two days nor with doing so after three. Since the latter is the normal accepted practice, however, that raises the same question which we have seen asked about the qur'ānic reference to al-Ṣafā and al-Marwa: why would God say that no sin is incurred by doing something regarded as a normal part of the *ḥajj* rituals? An alternative way of interpreting this verse — that it is alluding to the Muslim belief that a properly accomplished *ḥajj* frees the pilgrim from some or all of his sins, and that that applies whether one cuts short the *ayyām al-tashrīq* or remains at Minā until they have finished — is probably to be understood as an attempt to avoid the difficulty inherent in the previous interpretation.

The mention in Q 3:96 of the "first house *(bayt)*... at Bakka," which is naturally understood as a reference to the Ka'ba at Mecca (Makka), involves the commentators in variant explanations as to why the Qur'ān uses the form Bakka. It seems obvious that all of the suggested explanations are simply attempts to account for something of which the commentators had no real knowledge, and the way in which it is done — e.g. by reference to the crowding (*izdiḥām,* a word the root of which is said to have the same meaning as that of *bakka*) of the people in the circumambulation of the Ka'ba — again illustrates the way in which the commentators attempt to relate the qur'ānic material to the Muslim pilgrimage rituals.

Finally in this connection there may be noted the difficulties the commentators have with the expression *al-ḥajj al-akbar,* "the greater *ḥajj,*" in Q 9:3 ("a proclamation from God and his messenger to the people on the day of *al-ḥajj al-akbar*"). Here there is considerable diversity in interpretation of the phrase: some wish to explain it as referring to a particular day or particular days of the *ḥajj* rituals — the day of the "standing" at 'Arafa, the day of the slaughter of the victims, etc.; most associate it with the *ḥajj* led by Abū Bakr immediately following the conquest of Mecca by the Prophet, but some with the "Farewell Pilgrimage" (q.v.) led by the Prophet himself in the last year of his life, and they give variant explanations of why the one or the other should be called *al-ḥajj al-akbar;* yet others explain it by reference to the distinction between the "major" pilgrimage (the *ḥajj*) and the "minor" pilgrimage (the *'umra* which may, allegedly, be called *al-ḥajj al-aṣghar*), or between a *ḥajj* combined with an *'umra* and a *ḥajj* performed alone. Again it seems obvious that the commentators have no real understanding of the phrase but try to make sense of it by aligning it with Muslim practice and, in this case, with traditions relating to the life of the Prophet.

It might be argued that, in spite of disjunctions of the sort illustrated above, the qur'ānic materials nevertheless reflect institutions and practices that are not radically different from those of Islam. Much of the qur'ānic terminology, after all, is used also in Muslim law and ritual practice, and the few proper names that occur (al-Ṣafā, al-Marwa, 'Arafāt) are those of places in or near Mecca. On the other hand, it might be thought that the relative paucity and lack of detail of the qur'ānic verses concerning *ḥajj* and *'umra* make it impossible to judge the extent to which they envisage the same rites in the same places as does classical Islam. Not only are some rites and places which are of major importance in Muslim practice (e.g. Zamzam, Minā, the *wuqūf,* the stoning ritual; see STONING; SPRINGS AND FOUNTAINS) not mentioned at all in the Qur'ān, those names which do occur may not indicate the same things as they do in classical Islam. The traditional accounts of how the Meccan sanctuary and the rites associated with it came to be incorporated into Islam assume a basic continuity. According to tradition, the Prophet took over the Kaʿba and the other places in the vicinity of Mecca and did not radically change the rituals which at the time constituted the *ḥajj* and the *ʿumra*. He cleansed them of the idolatry which polluted them and restored the pristine monotheism which had existed when Abraham built the Kaʿba and summoned humankind to make *ḥajj* and *ʿumra*, but apart from that he made only minor and marginal alterations (see ḤANĪF).

Some scholars have suggested that the changes involved in the identification of the Meccan sanctuary as the Muslim sanctuary were more significant. Following Snouck Hurgronje and Wellhausen, many have argued that the evidence points to a unification of a number of originally distinct and independent holy places and rituals in a way that focused them on the Kaʿba at Mecca. According to that view, the *ḥajj* originally had nothing to do with Mecca or the Kaʿba but concerned Mount ʿArafa and other holy places at some distance from Mecca. It was the *ʿumra* which was originally the ritual associated with the Kaʿba.

The phrasing of Q 2:158 with its apparent concern to reassure the hearers that *ṭawāf* of al-Ṣafā and al-Marwa was an acceptable part of *ḥajj* or *ʿumra* has sometimes been explained by reference to that idea: it reflects an early stage in the process in which the rituals of the *ʿumra* came to be incorporated in the *ḥajj* and perhaps mirrors the objections of those who questioned the validity of that incorporation. (For a different approach, see Burton, *Collection*, 12, 16, 30-1.)

A particularly difficult passage in Q 2:196 might also reflect such a development. Following the section, discussed above, which establishes rules for those "detained" from meeting the command to "complete the *ḥajj* and the *ʿumra* for God," we then read: "and when you are in security, then whoever enjoys/benefits from the *ʿumra* to/for/until the *ḥajj (man tamattaʿa bi-l-ʿumrati ilā l-ḥajji)*, then [there is incumbent upon him] a convenient [animal] offering *(mā staysara mina l-hady)*."

"When you are in security" *(fa-idhā amintum)* is understood as meaning "when the circumstances which detained you no longer pertain." Commentary then concerns itself with the knotty issue of what is meant by the *tamattuʿ* referred to in the following phrase. In their discussions commentators and other traditional scholars also use the forms *mutʿa* and *istimtāʿ* and they reflect a variety of understandings of what the phrase means. The relevant phrase in Q 2:196 *(man tamattaʿa bi-l-ʿumrati ilā l-ḥajji)* is difficult to translate, and attempts to interpret it reflect ideas current in Islamic practice or legal theory.

What most interpretations have in common is that *tamattuʿ* (or *istimtāʿ* or *mutʿa*) involves a premature abandonment of the consecrated state on the part of the pilgrim. For example, one of the most common understandings of the concept is that the pilgrim has begun by intending to perform both *ʿumra* and *ḥajj* and has stated that intention when he adopted *iḥrām*. On arriving at Mecca before the *ḥajj* has started he performs an *ʿumra* and then leaves the state of *iḥrām*, thus removing restrictions regarding such things as toilet, dress and sexual activity (see SEX AND SEXUALITY; RITUAL PURITY). He remains in this normal, desacralized state until the time for the *ḥajj* arrives, when he once more enters *iḥrām* and remains in the sacralized state until the *ḥajj* is over. For that break in *iḥrām* he is liable to the penalty of an offering or something in lieu of it.

The issue is a contentious one and the traditions report disputes about it among the Companions and Successors (see COMPANIONS OF THE PROPHET). In spite of this qurʾānic verse which treats *tamattuʿ* in a rather matter-of-fact way even though it does say that an offering must be made by anyone who takes advantage of it, and in spite of traditions which tell us that the Prophet told his Companions to avail themselves of *mutʿa* (but one often involving a different understanding of it to that just summarized) at the time of the Farewell Pilgrimage, there are reports that some Companions and caliphs (see CALIPH) disapproved of and even forbade it. The caliph ʿUmar figures prominently in such reports. Nevertheless, the Sunnī schools of law *(madhhabs)* all recognize the validity of the procedure and the Shīʿīs (see SHĪʿISM AND THE QURʾĀN) even recommend it as the preferred way of performing *ḥajj*.

A related verbal form occurs in Q 4:24 *(mā stamtaʿtum bihi minhunna),* where it clearly refers to the sexual enjoyment of women by men, and the word *mutʿa* is more widely known as the name of a form of temporary marriage (q.v.), where the contract specifies for how long the marriage will last (see also MARRIAGE AND DIVORCE). This form of marriage, as is well known, is generally rejected by Sunnī Islam but it is accepted as valid by the Shīʿa. In order to distinguish between it and the *mutʿa* that may be involved in making pilgrimage it is sometimes called *mutʿat al-nisāʾ* and the latter *mutʿat al-ḥajj*. Traditional scholarship and many modern scholars have insisted on the essential distinctness of the two forms of *mutʿa*. ʿAṭāʾ b. Abī Rabāḥ is quoted as insisting that the *mutʿa* connected with *ḥajj* is so called because it involves making *ʿumra* during the months of the *ḥajj* and "enjoying" or "benefiting from" the *ʿumra* for (or until?) the *ḥajj;* it is not so called, he insists, because it makes permitted the enjoyment of women *(wa-lam tusamma l-mutʿa min ajli annahu yuḥallu bi-tamattuʿi l-nisāʾ)*. Some modern scholars, however, have argued that the two *mutʿa*s were originally closely connected, essentially that the premature abandonment of *iḥrām* in the case of *mutʿat al-ḥajj* was intended to allow the pilgrim to resume normal sexual activity and that the temporary liaisons allowed by *mutʿat al-nisāʾ* were associated with the making of *ḥajj*. The evidence and competing views have been extensively investigated by Arthur Gribetz.

It may be that this qurʾānic passage also reflects the merging in early Islamic times of the previously distinct rituals of *ḥajj* and *ʿumra*. The preferred way of performing *ḥajj* and *ʿumra* — whether both separately, both combined, or one of them only — is much discussed and variously evaluated in Muslim law. A few scholars have gone further and envisaged more radical discontinuities in the development of the Muslim sanctuary and the rituals associated with it. Some have suggested the transference not only of ideas but also of ritual practices and nomenclature from other places to Mecca at a time in the emergence of Islam considerably later than the death of the Prophet. The qurʾānic materials are not inconsistent with such theories which, however, really depend on other evidence regarding the development of the sanctuary and the rituals associated with it in early Islam.

Gerald Hawting

Bibliography

Primary: Bukhārī, *Ṣaḥīḥ*, ed. Krehl, 384-443, 443-51; Fr. trans. O. Houdas and W. Marçais, *El-Bokhâri. Les Traditions islamiques,* 4 vols., Paris 1903-14, i, 493-567, 568-78; Ibn Abī Zayd al-Qayrawānī, *La risâla ou épître sur les éléments du dogme et de la loi de l'islâm selon le rite mâlikite,* trans.

L. Bercher (with Ar. text), Algiers 1948², chap. 28, 140-51; Ṭabarī, *Tafsīr*.
Secondary: Burton, *Collection;* N. Calder, The *saʿy* and the *jabīn*. Some notes on Qurʾān 37:102-3, in *JSS* 31 (1986), 17-26; P. Crone, *Meccan trade and the rise of Islam,* Princeton, NJ 1987, 168-99; M. Gaudefroy-Demombynes, *Le pèlerinage à la Mecque,* Paris 1923; A. Gribetz, *Strange bedfellows.* Mutʿat al-nisāʾ *and* mutʿat al-ḥajj. *A study based on Sunnī and Shīʿī sources of tafsīr, ḥadīth and fiqh,* Berlin 1994; G.E. von Grunebaum, *Muhammadan festivals,* New York 1951; G.R. Hawting, The origins of the Muslim sanctuary at Mecca, in G.H.A. Juynboll (ed.), *Studies on the first century of Islamic society,* Carbondale, IN 1982, 23-47; H. Lazarus-Yafeh, The religious dialectics of the Ḥadjdj, in id. (ed.), *Some religious aspects of Islam,* Leiden 1981, 17-37; C. Pansera, Alcuni precisazioni sull'espressione *al-mašʿar al-ḥarām,* in *RSO* 24 (1949), 74-7; F.E. Peters, *The hajj. The Muslim pilgrimage to Mecca and the holy places,* Princeton, NJ 1994; J. Rivlin, *Gesetz im Koran. Kultus und Ritus,* Jerusalem 1934, 21-49; U. Rubin, The great pilgrimage of Muḥammad. Some notes on sūra ix, in *JSS* 27 (1982), 241-60; id., The Kaʿba. Aspects of its ritual functions and position in pre-Islamic and early Islamic times, in *JSAI* 8 (1986), 97-131; C. Snouck Hurgronje, *Het Mekkaansche Feest,* Leiden 1880; part. Fr. trans.: Le pèlerinage à la Mecque, in G.-H. Bousquet and J. Schacht (eds.), *Selected works of C. Snouck Hurgronje,* Leiden 1957, 171-213; It. trans.: *Il pellegrinaggio alla Mecca,* Turin 1989; J. Wellhausen, *Reste arabischen Heidentums,* Berlin 1897².

Pit

Deep abyss. The qurʾānic term *hāwiya,* the "pit, abyss," is related to the verb *hawā, yahwī,* "to fall," and is generally understood as one of the names of hell (see HELL AND HELLFIRE). It occurs once in Sūrat al-Qāriʿa ("The Great Calamity," Q 101), a text which depicts the cataclysmic events of the apocalypse (q.v.; Q 101:1-5) and the weighing of humankind's deeds on the day of judgment (Q 101:6-11; see LAST JUDGMENT; GOOD DEEDS; EVIL DEEDS; WEIGHTS AND MEASURES; REWARD AND PUNISHMENT). Two parallel conditional sentences describe the fate of humankind as a result of this weighing: Whoever's deeds weigh heavy will enter paradise (q.v.; Q 101:6-7) and whoever's deeds weigh light will enter hell (Q 101:8-11). While the overall purport of the sūra (q.v.) seems clear, verse 9 and the term *hāwiya* in particular have puzzled commentators. It reads *fa-ummuhu hāwiya,* which may be construed as "Then his mother will be *hāwiya* (adj.)"; "Then his mother will be a *hāwiya* (indefinite noun)"; or "Then his mother will be *Hāwiya* (definite proper noun)," alternatively "Then *Hāwiya* will be his mother." In recognition of the difficulty of rendering the verse accurately, Bell (*Qurʾān,* ii, 674 n. 6) retains the term *hāwiya,* then explains it in a footnote. Paret describes the passage as "a bizarre play on words" (Paret, *Kommentar,* 518).

There are three main explanations of this verse in Islamic tradition (see Ṭabarī, *Tafsīr,* xxx, 282-3; Ṭabarsī, *Majmaʿ,* x, 679-80; Zamakhsharī, *Kashshāf,* ad loc.). The most widely accepted is that *hāwiya* is a proper noun, one of several names of hell, and that *umm* here is used metaphorically to mean "refuge," as in Q 5:72: *wa-maʾwāhu l-nāru,* "Then his refuge will be hell." According to the second interpretation, attributed to the Companion Abū Ṣāliḥ (see COMPANIONS OF THE PROPHET), *umm* here means *umm al-raʾs,* "the crown of the head," and the verse as a whole, "The crown of his head will fall," referring to sinners' being pitched into hell head first. The third interpretation, attributed to Qatāda (d. ca. 117/735), connects the verse with the idiomatic expression *hawat ummuhu,* literally, "his mother has fallen," said of a man in a dire situation, something like the English expression "his goose is cooked." Al-Zamakhsharī (d. 538/1144) adds that *hawat ummuhu,* "May his mother fall!" is a curse (q.v.) wishing for a man's demise. This is similar to the more common curse *thakalatka ummuka,* "May your mother be bereft of you!" According to this interpretation, the verse would mean,

"Then his mother will fall," figurative for "Then he will perish."

Sprenger (*Moḥammad*, ii, 503) held that this last interpretation was the correct explanation of the word. Fischer (Qorān-Interpolation; Zu Sūra 101,6) also adopts this view and further suggests that the sūra originally ended with Q 101:9. In his view, a later reader, puzzled by verse 9 and interpreting *hāwiya* as referring to hell, added the following two verses to make this clear: *wa-mā adrāka māhiya — nārun ḥāmiya*, "But how should you know what that is?! A scorching fire." Goldziher (*Introduction*, 29 n. 37) endorses Fischer's interpretation and remarks that a true, critical edition of the Qurʾān should note such interpolations. C. Torrey (Three difficult passages, 466-7) rejects Fischer's explanation for several reasons. It is unlikely, in his view, that the Companions or early Muslims would have been mystified by the Arabic usage of this passage, as opposed to being puzzled by its content or interpretation. The attention to rhyme and rhetorical construction throughout the sūra (see RHETORIC AND THE QURʾĀN; LANGUAGE AND STYLE OF THE QURʾĀN; FORM AND STRUCTURE OF THE QURʾĀN), including the odd modifications to produce a rhyme in *-iya*, paralleled in the forms *kitābiya* (Q 69:19, 25) and *sulṭāniya* (Q 69:29), also in rhyme position — and, we may add, *ḥisābiya*, Q 69:20, 26 and *māliya*, Q 69:28 — suggests that the final passage is not incongruous with the rest of the sūra (ibid., 467-68). Torrey interprets the phrase as an intentional pun, rather than an interpolation designed to explain a misunderstood expression, drawing both on the expression *hawat ummuhu* but at the same time interpreting *hāwiya* as a name for hell. Torrey (Three difficult passages, 470), holding that the most probable hypothesis when an odd theological term appears in the Qurʾān is that it is a foreign, borrowed term, suggests that *hāwiya* is a borrowing from Hebrew *hōwā*, "disaster" (*Isa* 47:11; *Ezek* 7:26; see FOREIGN VOCABULARY; THEOLOGY AND THE QURʾĀN). Bell (*Qurʾān*, ii, 674 n. 6) accepts Torrey's analysis, minus the Hebrew connection, adding a note to his translation explaining the untranslated term *hāwiya:* "i.e. childless; a phrase implying that the man will perish, or at least meet misfortune. The added explanation, however, takes *hāwiya* as a designation for Hell." Paret agrees with the first part of Torrey's interpretation but considers the link with Hebrew questionable. Jeffery objects to Torrey that the biblical passages in question do not describe hellfire specifically and are therefore unlikely to have served as a basis for this text. On the argument that this is a very early passage, he considers it unlikely to be related to the Jewish tradition but to the Christian tradition instead (see JEWS AND JUDAISM; CHRISTIANS AND CHRISTIANITY). He proposes, tentatively albeit, two Ethiopian words from the root combination *ḥ-w-y*, *ḥewāy*, meaning "the fiery red glow of the evening sky," or *ḥwe*, meaning "fire, burning coal" (Jeffery, *For. vocab.*, 285-6). These are both unlikely because the Ethiopic *ḥ* corresponds to the Arabic *ḥ* and not *h*. Jeffery also notes that Mainz suggested the Syriac *ḥewāyeh*, "his life," referring to the Messiah (cf. Mainz, Review, 300; see JESUS); this is also unlikely, for the same reason.

Bellamy *(Fa-ummuhū)* proposes an emendation of Q 101:9, suggesting that it should read *fa-ummatun hāwiya*, meaning, "Then a steep course downward" (sc. into hell shall be his). In other words, he understands *hāwiya* here to mean "falling" or "dropping off precipitously." This emendation is implausible for several reasons. First, it upsets the parallelism between the two conditional sentences in Q 101:6-9. Just as the pronoun *huwa* ("he") in the apodosis of the first conditional sentence (verse 7) refers back to *man* ("whoever") in the protasis (verse 6), so does the attached pronoun *-hu* in *ummuhu* ("his mother") in the apodosis of the second conditional sentence (verse 9) refer back to *man* ("whoever") in the protasis (verse 8). Removing the pronoun upsets the balance between the two. Second, from the perspective of form criticism, the emendation would render this passage odd in comparison with similar oracular texts in the Qurʾān.

The construction *X * mā X * wa-mā adrāka mā X: * Y,* "X. What is X? And how do you know (lit. 'what made/let you know') what X is? (X is) Y" (see Sells, Sound and meaning, 410-3) is a standard form in the oracular stylistic repertoire of pre-Islamic soothsayers (q.v.). The full form consists of (1) the mention of an obscure or ambiguous term, (2) a rhetorical question concerning that term, (3) a second, more emphatic, rhetorical question concerning that term, and (4) a definition or explanation of that term. Repetition of the initial term necessarily creates a strong rhyme and rhythmical pattern. In the Qurʾān, the full form occurs only three times (Q 69:1-3; 82:14-9; 101:1-3). In other passages, (2) is omitted, producing the pattern *X * wa-mā adrāka mā X: * Y* (Q 74:26-7; 83:7-8; 83:18-9; 86:1-2; 90:11-2; 97:1-2; 104:4-5). In yet other passages, (3) is omitted, producing the pattern *X * mā X: * Y* (Q 56:8, 9, 27, 41). The passage under examination exhibits a reduced form of the *mā adrāka* construction: *fa-ummuhu hāwiya * wa-mā adrāka mā-hiya * nārun ḥāmiya,* "And how should you know what that is?! A scorching fire" (Q 101:9-11). It differs from other instances of the *mā adrāka* construction in that it does not actually repeat the ambiguous term *(hāwiya),* substituting the pronoun *hiya,* "she, it," instead: *wa-mā adrāka mā-hiya.* This feature probably helped suggest to Fischer (Qorān-Interpolation) that verses 10-11 represent an interpolation. The use of reduced forms of this construction is, however, quite common, and the use of the pronoun here may be due to the presence of the same construction in full at the beginning of the sūra (verses 1-3).

This construction is characterized by what Sells (Sound and meaning) terms semantic openness: The initial term, which is then defined, is necessarily ambiguous. For this reason, Sells leaves *qāriʿa* and *hāwiya* untranslated in his discussion of this sūra. Bellamy's emendation renders the initial term *ummatun hāwiya,* "a descending path," or "a steep course downward." An indefinite noun modified by an adjective would be an anomaly with regard to this oracular form in the Qurʾān. Most initial terms occurring in the *mā adrāka* construction are definite nouns, unmodified: *al-ḥāqqa* (Q 69:1-3), *al-ṭāriq* (Q 86:1-2), *al-ʿaqaba* (Q 90:12), *al-qāriʿa* (Q 101:1-3), *al-ḥuṭama* (Q 104:4-5). Other terms are nouns without the definite article but nevertheless definite and unmodified: *saqar* (Q 74:26-7), *sijjīn* (Q 83:7-8), *ʿilliyyūn* (Q 83:18-9). Ambiguous terms that consist of two words are all constructs: *aṣḥāb al-maymana* (Q 56:8), *aṣḥāb al-mashʾama* (Q 56:9), *aṣḥāb al-yamīn* (Q 56:27), *aṣḥāb al-shimāl* (Q 56:41; see LEFT HAND AND RIGHT HAND), *yawm al-faṣl* (Q 77:13-4), *yawm al-dīn* (Q 82:17-8), *laylat al-qadr* (Q 97:1-2; see NIGHT OF POWER). It is unlikely that the ambiguous phrase presented, questioned and then defined would be a noun modified by an adjective. Adjectives are circumscribing, narrowing modifiers and most often occur in the definitions that follow the rhetorical question rather than in the ambiguous terms themselves. For example, *sijjīn* and *ʿilliyyūn* are both defined as *kitābun marqūm...,* "an engraved book" (q.v.; Q 83:7-9, 18-20); *al-ṭāriq* is defined as *al-najmu l-thāqib,* "the piercing star" (Q 86:1-3; see PLANETS AND STARS); *al-ḥuṭama* is defined as *nāru llāhi l-mūqada,* "the kindled fire (q.v.) of God" (Q 104:4-6) and, here, the term in question *(al-hāwiya)* is defined as *nārun ḥāmiya*, "a scorching fire" (Q 101:11). The emendation is thus probably wrong: *hāwiya* is not an adjective modifying the previous noun but a predicate; the ambiguous initial term is the final word *hāwiya* alone. It is worth adding that several of the other ambiguous terms in such passages also have the form *fāʿila* (see GRAMMAR AND THE QURʾĀN), such as *al-ḥāqqa* (Q 69:1-3) and *al-qāriʿa;* as do ambiguous terms occurring in oracular passages which do not exhibit the *mā adrāka* construction, such as *al-wāqiʿa* (Q 56:1), *al-ṭāmma* (Q 79:34) and *al-ghāshiya* (Q 88:1). Three other terms that occur in this construction and are devoid of the definite article all appear to be proper nouns. The terms *saqar* (Q 74:26-7) and *sijjīn* (Q 83:8) are names for hell and *ʿilliyyūn* (Q 83:19) is a name for heaven. The term *hāwiya* is likely to be a proper noun referring to hell.

It is well known that many verse-final words in the Qurʾān are modified in form to fit the rhyme scheme (see RHYMED PROSE; Suyūṭī, *Itqān,* ii, 214-7; Müller, *Untersuchungen;* Stewart, Sajʿ) and Ibn al-Ṣāʾigh al-Ḥanafī (d. 776/1375) cites *hāwiya* as an example of this phenomenon. In his view, *hāwiya* is an instance of a rare or odd word's being used in place of a common one for the sake of rhyme (Suyūṭī, *Itqān,* ii, 216). In my view, *hāwiya,* literally "falling (fem.)," is a cognate substitute understood as equivalent to *huwwa, mahwan,* or *mahwā,* all meaning, "pit, chasm, abyss." Many such cognate substitutes appear frequently in the Qurʾān: *taḍlīl* (Q 105:2) for *ḍalāl* (Müller, *Untersuchungen,* 46-50; see ERROR; ASTRAY); *lāghiya* (Q 88:11) for *laghw* (ibid., 24-6; see GOSSIP); *amīn* (Q 44:51; 95:3) for *āmin* (ibid., 54-59), and so on. Modifications for the sake of rhyme are evident in several verses of Sūrat al-Qāriʿa (Q 101) itself. As Sells (Sound and meaning) has shown in detail, rhyme and rhythm are crucial features of the sūra, so it is reasonable to suggest that such modifications occur. In verse 7, the active participle *rāḍiya,* literally "approving, pleased," appears with the meaning of the cognate passive participle *marḍiyya,* "approved, pleasant." The pronoun *hiya* occurs as *hiyah* in final position in verse 10; the two words *mā* and *hiyah* are also joined here to form one rhythmic unit or foot: *mā-hiyah. Hāwiya* would be an additional cognate substitute. Moreover, the morphological pattern of *hāwiya* — *fāʿila* — occurs frequently in such cognate substitutions: *kāshifa* (Q 53:58) for *kashf* (Müller, *Untersuchungen,* 26-8); *kādhiba* (Q 56:2) for *kadhib* (ibid., 20-4; see LIE); *bi-l-ṭāghiya* (Q 69:5) for *bi-ṭughyānihim* (ibid., 16-20); and *al-rājifa* (Q 79:6) for *al-rajfa* (ibid., 30-3). A parallel example is the term *al-ḥuṭama*, also a name for hell, that occurs in a *mā adrāka* construction (Q 104:4-5). It appears to be a cognate substitute for a form such as *al-ḥāṭima* or *al-ḥaṭṭāma* and conveys the general meaning of "the crusher."

The most plausible interpretation of the term *ummuhu* is that which takes *umm* as a metaphorical term for (destined, final) refuge or abode (see FATE; DESTINY; FREEDOM AND PREDESTINATION). This interpretation is in keeping with other passages of the Qurʾān that state that while heaven is the dwelling place of those who have faith (q.v.) and do good works, hell is the refuge or final place of the evildoers (see GOOD AND EVIL). The most common term used in this fashion is *maʾwā,* "refuge," which refers to the abodes of humankind in the afterlife: heaven in Q 32:19, 53:15; 79:41 and hell in Q 3:151, 162, 197; 4:97, 121; 5:72; 7:16; 9:73, 95; 10:8; 13:18; 17:97; 24:57; 29:25; 32:20; 45: 34; 57:15; 66:9; 79:39. Similar terms include *mathwā,* "abode," which refers to hell in Q 3:151; 6:128; 16:29; 29:68; 39:32, 60, 72; 40:76; 41:24; 47:12; *mihād,* "cradle, bed," which can also refer to hell (cf. Q 2:206; 3:12, 197; 7:41; 13:18; 38:56); and *ma'āb*, "end, goal, place where one ends up," which refers to hell in Q 78:22, 38:55. Torrey (Three difficult passages, 469) states that the use of the term "contained the grimly ironical assurance that (the hearer's) acquaintance with Hāwiya would not be merely temporary; she would be his permanent keeper and guardian." In any case, perhaps closest to *umm* in this context is *mawlā*, "master," used to refer to hell in Q 57:15: "Your refuge is hell *(al-nār)*; it will be your master, and what an evil destiny it is!"

Devin J. Stewart

Bibliography

Primary: Suyūṭī, *Itqān;* Ṭabarī, *Tafsīr*, ed. ʿAlī; Ṭabarsī, *Majmaʿ;* Zamakhsharī, *Kashshāf;* Zarkashī, *Burhān*.

Secondary: Bell, *Qur'ān;* J. Bellamy, *Fa-ummuhū hāwiyah*. A note on sūrah 101:9, in *JAOS* 112 (1992), 485-7; T. Fahd, *La divination arabe*, Strasbourg 1966; id., Sadjʿ. 1. As magical utterances in pre-Islamic Arabian usage, in *EI*², viii, 732-4; A. Fischer, Eine Qorān-Interpolation, in C. Bezold (ed.), *Orientalische Studien Theodor Noeldeke zum siebzigsten Geburtstag (2. Marz 1906)*, 2 vols., Giessen 1906, i, 33-55; id., Zu Sūra 101,6, in *ZDMG* 60 (1906), 371-74; I. Goldziher, *Introduction to Islamic theology and law*, trans. A. and R. Hamori, Princeton 1981 (trans. of *Vorlesungen über den Islam*, Heidelberg 1910); Jeffery, *For. vocab.;* E. Mainz, Review of C.C. Torrey, *The Jewish foundations of Islam*, in *Der Islam* 23 (1936), 299-300; F.R. Müller, *Untersuchungen zur Reimprosa im Koran*, Bonn 1969; Paret, *Kommentar;* M. Sells, Sound and meaning in *Sūrat al-qāriʿah*, in *Arabica* 40 (1993), 403-30; Sprenger, *Moḥammad;* D.J. Stewart, *Sajʿ* in the Qur'ān. Prosody and structure, in *JAL* 21 (1990), 101-39; C.C. Torrey, Three difficult passages in the Koran, in T.W. Arnold and R.A. Nicholson (eds.), *A volume of Oriental studies presented to E.G. Browne*, Cambridge 1922, 457-71, esp. 464-71.

Place of Abraham

A location in Mecca (q.v.) at which Abraham (q.v.) is believed to have stood and/or prayed. The station or place of Abraham *(maqām Ibrāhīm)* is cited twice in the Qur'ān. Q 2:125, "Take the station of Abraham as a place of prayer" (q.v.; *wa-ttakhidhū min maqāmi Ibrāhīma muṣallan*) and Q 3:97, "In it [the house of God, i.e. the *ḥaram* sanctuary in Mecca] are clear signs (q.v.), the station of Abraham." Most have read Q 2:125 as an imperative (referring to the Muslim community), rather than in the past tense *wa-ttakhadhū*, "and they took."

Opinions vary about the area to be considered as the station, whether, for example, it is all of the sacred territory of Mecca or, more narrowly, the *ḥaram* (see PROFANE AND SACRED; FORBIDDEN). Most, however, have identified the station with a stone bearing the footprints of Abraham located within the *ḥaram* a short distance from the Kaʿba (q.v.). Identifying the station with a stone, however, leaves a grammatical awkwardness due to the preposition *min*, "from," in Q 2:125. The verse could be rendered "Take within the station of Abraham a place of prayer," or "Take a part of the station of Abraham as a place of prayer."

For those who identify the station as a stone, there are a number of stories about how Abraham's footprints came to be impressed on it. For some, Abraham stood on a stone (or a water jug) when Ishmael's (q.v.) dutiful second wife once washed Abraham's head. But following a more commonly held story, while Abraham and Ishmael were building the Kaʿba, Abraham stood on the stone in order to reach the upper parts of the Kaʿba walls. According to a third story, Abraham stood on the stone when he called upon humankind to perform the pilgrimage (q.v.; Q 22:27). A fourth version has Abraham praying at the stone as his *qibla* (q.v.), turning his face to the Kaʿba door (see especially Firestone, *Journeys*).

A ḥadīth (Bukhārī, *Ṣaḥīḥ*, 8, *Ṣalāt*, 32; ed. Krehl, i, 113; trans. Khan, i, 395) links the revelation of Q 2:125 to ʿUmar b. al-Khaṭṭāb who, during the Prophet's farewell pilgrimage (q.v.), said, "O messenger of God, if only we were to take the station of Abraham as our place of prayer." Shortly thereafter Q 2:125 was revealed (see ḤADĪTH AND THE QURʾĀN; OCCASIONS OF REVELATION). Other ḥadīths (Bukhārī, *Ṣaḥīḥ,* 8, *Ṣalāt,* 30; ed. Krehl, i, 113; trans. Khan, i, 389, 390; ii, 670) report that the Prophet performed the circumambulation *(ṭawāf)* around the Kaʿba and offered a two-*rakʿa* prayer (see BOWING AND PROSTRATION; RITUAL AND THE QURʾĀN) behind the station (of Abraham) and then performed the traversing *(saʿy)* of Ṣafā and Marwa (q.v.).

The stone identified as the station is some 60 cm wide and 90 cm high and has been placed in different locations within the *ḥaram* in the course of the centuries. For a time it was placed in a box on a high platform to keep it from being swept away in floods. The stone cracked in 161/778 and the ʿAbbāsid caliph al-Mahdī (r. 158-69/775-85) had it repaired with gold braces. In 256/870 the broken pieces of the stone were thoroughly restored (as reported in detail by al-Fākihī, an eyewitness [see Kister, A stone]; al-Fākihī noted some Ḥimyar letters on the stone; see SOUTH ARABIA, RELIGION IN PRE-ISLAMIC; ARABIC SCRIPT).

In the nineteenth century the station was a little building with a small dome, while the Saudi reconstructions of the *ḥaram* in the mid-twentieth century have replaced that building with a small hexagonal glass-enclosed structure, within which the stone can be seen. (For photographs of the station as it was about one hundred years ago, see Nomachi and Nasr, *Mecca,* 19, 50, 190-1; Wensinck and Jomier, Kaʿba, plates ix and x; Frikha and Guellouz, *Mecca,* 32-3, 44-5.)

Robert Schick

Bibliography
Primary: Bukhārī, *Ṣaḥīḥ,* ed. Krehl; trans. M.M. Khan, Medina 1971.
Secondary: R. Firestone, *Journeys in holy lands. The evolution of the Abraham-Ishmael legends in Islamic exegesis,* Albany 1990; A. Frikha and E. Guellouz, *Mecca. The Muslim pilgrimage,* New York 1979; M. Gaudefroy-Demombynes, *Le pèlerinage à la Mekke,* Paris 1923, 102-9; G. Hawting, The origins of the Muslim sanctuary at Mecca, in G.H.A. Juynboll (ed.), *Studies on the first century of Islamic society,* Carbondale, IN 1982, 23-47; M. Kister, Maḳām Ibrāhīm, in *EI²,* vi, 104-7; id., Maḳām Ibrāhīm. A stone with an inscription, in *Muséon* 89 (1971), 477-91; A.K. Nomachi and S.H. Nasr, *Mecca the blessed, Medina the radiant. The holiest cities of Islam,* New York 1997; A.J. Wensinck/J. Jomier, Kaʿba, in *EI²,* iv, 317-22.

Plagues

Supernatural events inflicted upon the Egyptian Pharaoh (q.v.; *firʿawn*) and his nation and delivered by Moses (q.v.). Reference to the Egyptian plagues appears in the Qurʾān approximately twenty times. Identification of the actual plagues themselves appears only once (Q 7:133).

The most detailed qurʾānic accounts of Moses' interaction with the Egyptian Pharaoh appear in Q 7:100-41 and Q 20:1-77. These largely resemble the account in the biblical book of Exodus (*Ex* 7:14-12:30), in which God sends Moses to free the Israelites from slavery in Egypt; when Pharaoh refuses to acquiesce, God sends down ten plagues as punishment and as enticement for him to relent. In the Qurʾān, the plagues appear not as "plagues" but as "signs" (q.v.; *āya,* pl. *āyāt*). The difference in nomenclature points to the Qurʾān's understanding of their function, a function different than that in the Bible. In the Qurʾān it seems the main purpose of these *āyāt* is not to punish Pharaoh for refusing to free the Israelites (see CHILDREN OF ISRAEL). Rather, these events are first and foremost signs attesting to God's omnipotence and omnipresence, which Pharaoh has previously refused to acknowledge. In fact, the account of Q 20:1-77 suggests that the freeing of the slaves is itself punishment; Pharaoh, we are told in Q 20:43, had become exceedingly rebellious (see DISOBEDIENCE; ARROGANCE) against God and so God sent Moses and his brother (see AARON) to him with God's signs. Other qur'ānic references to Moses and the signs mention neither the slaves nor their redemption at all. This omission indicates that the bringing of signs that would prove God's power (see POWER AND IMPOTENCE) to Pharaoh, and not the freeing of the slaves per se, was Moses' main charge (Q 7:103; 10:75; 11:96-7; 23:45; 28:4, 32; 29:39; 40:23; 43:46; one exception to this appears in Q 14:5).

Because of this different understanding of the purpose of these events, some decidedly non-plague events are included in the Islamic lists. The Qur'ān, in Q 17:101, puts the number of signs at nine but does not specify what they are. In Q 7:133, the Qur'ān identifies five of these, though without any further elaboration, as wholesale death, locusts, lice, frogs and blood (cf. the ten plagues in the Bible). Qur'ānic exegetes present various explanations of the remaining four. Some scholars identify these with four other signs mentioned in the Egyptian context: famine (q.v.), dearth of everything (Q 7:130), Moses' hand turning white and his staff turning into a serpent (Q 7:107-8; Ṭabarī, *Tafsīr,* ix, 30-40; Ibn Kathīr, *Tafsīr,* iv, 357; see ROD). Others maintain that the four are Moses' hand, staff, and tongue — presumably a reference to his speech impediment — and the sea — presumably a reference to its splitting and allowing the Israelites to walk through unharmed while the Egyptians drowned (Ṭabarī, *Tafsīr,* xv, 171-2). Yet others replace Moses' tongue with generalized obliteration (ibid.).

Horovitz (*KU,* 20) points out that Psalms 105:25-36 and the first century C.E. Jewish historian Josephus (in his *Antiquities,* book 2, chapter 14) recount only nine plagues, as in the Qur'ān, rather than Exodus' ten. Both lists differ from the Qur'ān's list as well as from each other.

Shari L. Lowin

Bibliography

Primary: Ibn Kathīr, *Tafsīr,* 7 vols., Beirut 1966; al-Kisā'ī, *The tales of the prophets of al-Kisa'i,* trans. W.M. Thackston, Boston 1978, 226-32; Ṭabarī, *Tafsīr,* 30 vols., Beirut 1984; id., *Ta'rīkh,* ed. de Goeje, i, 459-68, trans. W.M. Brinner, *The history of Ṭabarī. iii. The Children of Israel,* Albany 1991, 43-53; Tha'labī, *Qiṣaṣ,* trans. and annot. W.M. Brinner, *'Arā'is al-majālis fī qiṣaṣ al-anbiyā' or "Lives of the prophets,"* Leiden 2002, 316-26.

Secondary: Horovitz, *KU;* A. Jeffrey, Āya, in *EI²,* i, 773-4; Speyer, *Erzählungen,* 278-81; R. Tottoli, *Vita di Mosé secondo le tradizioni islamiche,* Palermo 1992, 41-9.

Planets and Stars

Celestial bodies. Not unexpectedly, references to celestial phenomena in the Qur'ān were influenced by the contemporary knowledge of these phenomena in the Arabian peninsula. The ancient Arabs, prior to their contacts with Persian, Indian and Greek science (beginning in the second/eighth century), had developed over the centuries their own popular rather than "scientific" knowledge of the sky and celestial phenomena (see PRE-ISLAMIC ARABIA AND THE QUR'ĀN; SCIENCE AND THE QUR'ĀN). From the third/ninth century onward, Arabic lexicographers collected this astronomical information in special monographs, the so-called *anwā'*-books. The ancient Arabs knew the fixed stars and the planets, though the current words for "star," *kawkab* and *najm,* were used indiscriminately and with no distinction between the two. Several hundred stars were known by name (cf. Kunitzsch, *Untersuchungen*) and there were indigenous names also for the planets (cf. Eilers,

Planetennamen). Seasons (q.v.) and periods of rain and drought were connected with the observation of the acronychal settings and simultaneous heliacal risings of certain stars or asterisms, the so-called *anwāʾ* (cf. Pellat, Anwāʾ), while the stars were used for orientation *(ihtidāʾ)* in the migrations of the Bedouins (see BEDOUIN) by night (see DAY AND NIGHT; MONTHS). But from all this lore only one star is mentioned in the Qurʾān by name, *al-shiʿrā* (see below, under "Defined stars"; see also SIRIUS).

Vocabulary

It is noteworthy that many words used in the Qurʾān in connection with celestial phenomena later became part of the technical vocabulary in Arabic-Islamic "scientific" astronomy. Such words are *burj* (pl. *burūj*), "the constellations," or "signs," of the zodiac (Q 15:16; 25:61; 85:1; in Q 4:78 *[fī burūjin mushayyadatin]*, however, *burūj* is used in the sense of "towers"); *fajr*, "dawn" (Q 2:187, etc.; see DAY, TIMES OF); *falak*, "sphere, orbit" (Q 21:33; 36:40; cf. Hartner, Falak); *gharaba*, "to set" (i.e. Q 18:17, 86), and derivations (*ghurūb*, "setting": Q 20:130; 50:39; and *maghrib*, "place of setting, west": Q 2:115, etc.); *khasafa*, the moon (q.v.) "is eclipsed" (Q 75:8); *kawkab* (pl. *kawākib*), "star" (Q 6:76, etc.); *manāzil*, "stations," or "mansions" of the moon (Q 10:5; 36:39; cf. Kunitzsch, al-Manāzil); *mashriq*, "east" (Q 2:115, etc.); *najm* (pl. *nujūm*), "star" (Q 16:16, etc.; also in Q 55:6, where the preferred interpretation of *al-najm* is "star[s]" rather than "plants," or "grasses" [q.v.]; cf. Paret, *Kommentar*, 465); *al-qamar*, "the moon" (Q 6:77, etc.); *al-shams*, "the sun" (q.v.; Q 2:258, etc.); *shihāb* (pl. *shuhub*), "fire" (Q 15:18; 37:10; 72:8-9; but in context rather more specifically "shooting star, meteor"); *ṭalaʿa*, "to rise" (i.e. Q 18:17, etc.) and derivations (*ṭulūʿ*, "rising": Q 20:130; 50:39; and *maṭlaʿ*, "rising" of the dawn: Q 97:5; also *maṭliʿ*, "place of rising" of the dawn: Q 18:90); and *ufuq* (pl. *āfāq*), "horizon" (Q 41:53; 53:7; 81:23).

Items of astronomical interest

The order of the universe

God has created the heavenly abode as "seven heavens," *samāwāt* (Q 2:29; 17:44; 23:86; 41:12; 65:12; 78:12), which are arranged in layers one above the other, *ṭibāqan* (Q 67:3; 71:15), or in paths or courses, *ṭarāʾiq* (Q 23:17; see HEAVEN AND SKY). While, on the one hand, this strongly reminds one of Greek cosmology (q.v.) with the famous spheres superimposed above each other, it is, on the other hand, unlikely that any echo of this Aristotelian-Ptolemaic theory had ever come to the knowledge of seventh-century Arabia. Also, the Greek system needs eight spheres for the sun, moon, the five planets and the fixed stars, whereas the Qurʾān speaks of only seven. So the qurʾānic seven heavens do not seem to belong to cosmology or astronomy, but rather to theological speculation and may be compared to the seven heavens mentioned in the "Testament of the XII Patriarchs" (*Lev* 3) and in the Talmudic literature (see THEOLOGY AND THE QURʾĀN). Similarly it remains an open question whether the courses *(ṭarāʾiq)* of Q 23:17 really refer to the courses of the sun, the moon and the five planets. Very interesting in this connection is also Q 21:33: "[God created] ... and the sun and the moon, each of them moving in a sphere" (... *wa-l-shamsa wa-l-qamara wa-kullun fī falakin yasbaḥūn;* cf. also Q 36:40). This seems like an echo of Greek cosmology: each celestial body moves in its own sphere. But here again we hesitate to understand the Qurʾān's statement in such a strict scientific sense. The sun, moon and the stars are, at his command, "made to serve [humans]" (*musakhkharāt*, Q 7:54; cf. 14:33; 16:12; 31:20; 45:13). Sun and moon were created as a means for calculating time (q.v.) by years and months (*ḥusbānan,* Q 6:96; or *bi-ḥusbān,* Q 55:5; cf. 10:5). For this purpose, God divided the moon's course into "mansions" (*manāzil,* Q 10:5; 36:39) and the heavens into "constellations," or, more specifically, "the zodiacal signs" (*burūj,* Q 15:16, 25:61). It remains undetermined whether the Qurʾān here refers to the complete system of the twenty-eight lunar mansions as developed in later Arabic writings or to some unspecified mansions only. The oldest known text showing the complete list of the twenty-eight lunar mansions is reported by ʿAbd al-Malik b. Ḥabīb on the authority of Mālik b. Anas (d. 179/795-6; cf. Kunitzsch, ʿAbd al-Malik). As far as the constellations are concerned, what evidence we have for seventh-century Arabia indicates an awareness of only some of the constellations of the — originally Babylonian — zodiac. The complete system of twelve constellations or, respectively, signs, became known only after contact with Greek science (cf. Hartner-Kunitzsch, Minṭaḳa).

Further qurʾānic citations indicate that observation of the new moons *(al-ahilla)* was used to determine time and the date for pilgrimage (q.v.; Q 2:189). The stars served for orientation by night *(ihtidāʾ)* on land and sea (i.e. Q 6:97; 16:16; cf. also Q 6:63; 27:63; see JOURNEY). Mention is frequently made of a "fire" (*shihāb,* pl. *shuhub*) in the sky, which is thrown at some satans trying to listen secretly to the discourse of the angels (Q 15:17-8; 37:6-10; 67:5; 72:8-9; see ANGEL; DEVIL). It is quite probable that this "fire" in the sky describes shooting stars, i.e. meteors. *Shihāb* later became the still current Arabic term for "shooting star." The "myth of the shooting stars" (*Sternschnuppenmythus;* cf. Ullmann, *Neger,* 73-6) became a favorite motif in post-classical Arabic poetry.

Unspecified stars

In several of the oldest sūras (see CHRONOLOGY AND THE QURʾĀN), oath formulas (see OATHS; LANGUAGE AND STYLE OF THE QURʾĀN) appear — such as "By the heaven with its constellations" (*wa-l-samāʾi dhāti l-burūj,* Q 85:1), "By the sun and its light in the morning" (*wa-l-shamsi wa-ḍuḥāhā,* Q 91:1), "By the moon when it is full" (*wa-l-qamari idhā ttasaqa,* Q 84:18) — which are all easily understandable. In some cases, however, an oath is sworn by some star which remains undefined, as in "by the heaven and the one coming by night" (*wa-l-samāʾi wa-l-ṭāriqi,* Q 86:1), where the ambiguous phrase, "the one coming by night" *(al-ṭāriq),* may refer to a star or, as some say, to the morning star, which would be Venus. But *al-ṭāriq* is explained in Q 86:3 as "the star brightly shining" *(al-najmu l-thāqibu),* which — by analogy to Q 37:10, where *thāqib* is the epithet of *shihāb,* a shooting star — may also here describe a shooting star or meteor. The setting of any star could be meant by Q 53:1: "By the star when it sinks" *(wa-l-najmi idhā hawā);* alternatively, it could specifically refer to the setting of the Pleiades (*al-najm* is reported as an Arabic name for the Pleiades; cf. Kunitzsch, *Untersuchungen,* no. 186), or — if *hawā* is interpreted as a sudden, quick, falling — as a meteor shooting down. Q 56:75, "I swear by the *mawāqiʿ* of the stars" *(fa-lā uqsimu bi-mawāqiʿi l-nujūmi),* is also ambiguous: *mawāqiʿ* could be the places where the stars set on the western horizon, or places where meteor showers come down. Further undefined celestial phenomena are the star *(kawkab)* seen in the night by Abraham (q.v.; Q 6:76; see Gilliot, Abraham) and the eleven stars *(kawkab)* seen by Joseph (q.v.), together with the sun and the moon (Q 12:4; on this topic cf. Joseph's dream in *Gen* 37:9; see also DREAMS AND SLEEP; VISIONS).

Defined stars

Only once is a star mentioned in the Qurʾān by its old Arabic name: "Has the one who turned away [from God's message] not been informed that (Q 53:33) ... and that he is the lord of *al-shiʿrā?*" (*wa-annahu huwa rabbu l-shiʿrā,* Q 53:49). *Al-shiʿrā* is the star alpha Canis Maioris, Sirius, the brightest fixed star in the sky. The implication is that Sirius was adored by some Arab tribes in the Age of Ignorance (q.v.; *jāhiliyya*), the time before Islam (cf. Kunitzsch, al-Shiʿrā); here it is now stressed that God, the creator of all beings, is also the lord of Sirius, so that the adoration of stars has come to an end (see POLYTHEISM AND ATHEISM; IDOLS AND IMAGES; CREATION). A clear case is also Q 81:15-6, where an oath is sworn by the five planets (i.e. Mercury, Venus, Mars, Jupiter and Saturn; cf. Ibn Qutayba, *Anwāʾ*, 126, 6-8; Ibn Sīda, *Mukhaṣṣaṣ*, ix, 36,14-5; Ibn al-Ajdābī, *Azmina*, 90-4): "I swear by the [stars] retrograding,/travelling [and] hiding" *(fa-lā uqsimu bi-l-khunnas/al-jawārī l-khunnas)*. These three epithets refer to the characteristic qualities of the planets: retrogradation, their travelling (as opposed to the fixed stars, which always keep their position relative to each other; similar terms are sometimes found in later literature: *al-kawākib al-jāriya*, WKAS, i, 580 [col. b, ll. 29-30]; *al-nujūm al-jāriyāt*, Ullmann, *Naturwiss.*, 387) and their "hiding" in the light of the sun when they come near it (cf. Ibn al-Ajdābī, *Azmina*, 94,11).

Paul Kunitzsch

Bibliography

Primary: Ibn al-Ajdābī, Abū Isḥāq Ibrāhīm b. Ismāʿīl, *al-Azmina wa-l-anwāʾ*, ed. ʿI. Ḥasan, Damascus 1964; Ibn Qutayba, *Kitāb al-Anwāʾ*, ed. M. Hamidullah and Ch. Pellat, Hyderabad 1956; Ibn Sīda, Abū l-Ḥasan ʿAlī b. Ismāʿīl al-Mursī, *Kitāb al-Mukhaṣṣaṣ fī l-lugha*, 17 vols. in 9, Būlāq 1316-21/1898-1903, vol. ix.

Secondary: W. Eilers, *Sinn und Herkunft der Planetennamen*, München 1976; C. Gilliot, Abraham eut-il un regard peccamineux? in E. Chaumont et al. (eds.), *Mélanges Gimaret. Autour du regard*, Leuven 2003, 33-51; W. Hartner, Falak, in EI², ii, 761-3; id. and P. Kunitzsch, Minṭaḳat al-burūdj, in EI², vii, 81-7; P. Kunitzsch, ʿAbd al-Malik ibn Ḥabīb's *Book on the stars*, in ZGAIW 9 (1994), 161-94; 11 (1997), 179-88; id., al-Manāzil, in EI², vi, 374-6; id., al-Shiʿrā, in EI², ix, 471-2; id., *Untersuchungen zur Sternnomenklatur der Araber*, Wiesbaden 1961; Paret, *Kommentar*; Ch. Pellat, Anwāʾ, in EI², i, 523-4; M. Ullmann, *Die Natur- und Geheimwissenschaften im Islam*, Leiden 1972; id., *Der Neger in der Bildersprache der arabischen Dichter*, Wiesbaden 1998; WKAS.

Plant(s) see AGRICULTURE AND VEGETATION

Play see HUMOR; LAUGHTER

Pledge

Something given as security for the satisfaction of a debt or other obligation; the contract incidental to such a guaranty. The term commonly translated as "pledge" appears three times in the Qurʾān in three different forms: *rahīn* (Q 52:21), *rahīna* (Q 74:38) and *rihān* (Q 2:283). Al-Qurṭubī (d. 671/1272), in his *Jāmiʿ*, reports that the term in Q 2:283 is also read by Ibn Kathīr and Ibn ʿAmr as *ruhun*, by ʿĀṣim b. Abī al-Najūd as *ruhn* and by Abū ʿAlī al-Fārisī as *rahn* (see READINGS OF THE QURʾĀN; RECITATION OF THE QURʾĀN; ORTHOGRAPHY OF THE QURʾĀN).

Exegetes interpret the uses of "pledge" in Q 52:21 and Q 74:38 as being parallel. In his *Tafsīr*, Abū l-Layth al-Samarqandī (d. 375/985) interprets both verses to refer to the day of resurrection (q.v.) on which all souls will be pledged and weighed for the works of each person (see GOOD DEEDS; EVIL DEEDS; LAST JUDGMENT). Ibn Kathīr (d. 774/1373; *Tafsīr*, ad loc.) says the meaning of both verses is that a person cannot carry the sins of another with his good deeds (see SIN, MAJOR AND MINOR). Modern interpretations (see EXEGESIS OF THE QURʾĀN: EARLY MODERN AND CONTEMPORARY) also stress that these verses militate against the idea of saintly or prophetic intercession (q.v.; see also SAINT; PROPHETS AND PROPHETHOOD).

Q 2:283 is the focus for exegesis about the legality of giving a pledge or "pawn" in the case of an exchange when no witness or writer is present to draw up a document of the exchange (see WITNESSING AND TESTIFYING; CONTRACTS AND ALLIANCES). Al-Qurṭubī (*Jāmiʿ*, ad loc.) defines a pledge as the legal retention of a specific object, in lieu of a document, until the price is paid. Legal theorists raise several points of dispute beyond this basic characterization (see LAW AND THE QURʾĀN).

In his *Aḥkām* on Q 2:283, Ibn al-ʿArabī (d. 543/1148) reports that Mujāhid, based on a literal reading of Q 2:283, is of the opinion that a pledge can only be used when an exchange is made while traveling (see JOURNEY). Ilkiyā l-Harrāsī (d. 504/1110; *Aḥkām al-Qurʾān*, ad loc.) cites a report that the prophet Muḥammad once made a pledge to a Jew (see JEWS AND JUDAISM) in Medina (q.v.), thus demonstrating that pledging while not traveling is permitted.

There is also disagreement over the legal status of the pledge once it is in the hands of the party receiving it. According to al-Shāfiʿī (d. 204/820), the pledge is only in lieu of a document of contract. The recipients of the pledge, therefore, are not responsible for its upkeep; but neither are they allowed usufruct or confiscation of the pledge if the contract for which the pledge is made is not fulfilled by the giver of the pledge. The Ḥanafīs and Mālikīs hold that the party receiving the pledge is responsible for its upkeep, may use and benefit from the pledged item, and is entitled to keep the pledge if the giver of the pledge does not fulfill the contract in the specified time (see BREAKING TRUSTS AND CONTRACTS).

Other areas of dispute include: whether an item jointly owned may be pledged by only one of the owners or by both of them for different transactions; whether a debt (q.v.) can be pledged; to whom the pledge can be entrusted; the circumstances in which a slave or a slave's manumission may be pledged (see SLAVES AND SLAVERY); and what happens when the person receiving the pledge dies before the fulfillment of the contract (see INHERITANCE). See also COVENANT for "pledge" in the sense of testament, commitment or covenant.

Brannon M. Wheeler

Bibliography

Primary: Abū l-Layth al-Samarqandī, *Tafsīr;* Ilkiyā l-Harrāsī, *Aḥkām al-Qurʾān,* 4 vols., Beirut 1984-5; Ibn al-ʿArabī, *Aḥkām;* Ibn Kathīr, *Tafsīr;* Qurṭubī, *Jāmiʿ*.

Secondary (for brief, synthetic discussions of the pledge in legal theory): E. Sachau, *Muhammedanisches Recht,* Berlin 1897, 319-35, and Index, 868, s.v. "Pfandrecht"; D. Santillana, *Istituzioni di diritto musulmano malichita,* 2 vols., Rome 1938, ii, 464-83, and Index, 763, s.v. "rahn"; J. Schacht (ed.), *G. Bergsträsser's Grundzüge des islamischen Rechts,* Leipzig 1935; id., *An introduction to Islamic law,* Oxford 1964.

Poetry and Poets

Composition in metrical and rhymed language; and those who compose such compositions. By the time the Prophet was born, Arabic poetry had long been the key cultural register of the language. Other literary forms, particularly oratory and story telling, had important cultural roles but it was poetry that dominated (see PRE-ISLAMIC ARABIA AND THE QURʾĀN; LITERARY STRUCTURES OF THE QURʾĀN; ORALITY AND WRITING IN ARABIA). It is uncertain when this poetry *(shiʿr),* which has no functional parallel in any of the other Semitic languages (see RHYMED PROSE), first came into being, but it is reasonably clear that its original forms, rhyme patterns, meters and thematic conventions were largely fixed by the early part of the fifth century C.E. (the time of the earliest surviving pieces). There were to be developments after that, but they built on the foundations already in place. In later times the overarching themes were thought to be panegyric, lampoon, lament, love, description, self-glorification and aphoristic sayings; but such broad categorizations give little idea of the detailed thematic richness we find in the surviving corpus.

It is clear that most of this poetry is essentially tribal poetry; that the tribes were nomadic and dependent on their camels and, to a lesser extent, on their horses, sheep and goats (see CAMEL; ANIMAL LIFE); that they lived in the desert and semi-desert and the surrounding mountains (see ARABS; BEDOUIN; NOMADS); that the tribes frequently fought each other (see FIGHTING; WAR; EXPEDITIONS AND BATTLES); that life was at all times perceived as hard and dangerous; that intratribal and intertribal relationships had led to a complex code of conduct both for men and for women (see COMMUNITY AND SOCIETY IN THE QURʾĀN; SOCIAL INTERACTIONS); that there was an ethical code based on the notion of *muruwwa* (see ETHICS AND THE QURʾĀN); but that, in contrast, with few exceptions, religious ideas were relatively little developed (see RELIGION; SOUTH ARABIA, RELIGION IN PRE-ISLAMIC), with the vagaries of a rarely benevolent fortune and the ever-present menace of death and, particularly, untimely death consuming the tribesman's thoughts (see FATE). There was an ambivalent view of settlements (see CITY): they were the source of necessities not found in the desert and of imported luxuries such as wine (q.v.; see also INTOXICANTS); but they were thought to be unhealthy places.

There were also poets in the settlements themselves; for example, al-Samawʾal b. ʿĀdiyā at Taymāʾ, ʿAdiyy b. Zayd at al-Ḥīra, and an older contemporary of the Prophet, Umayya b. Abī l-Ṣalt at al-Ṭāʾif. None of the poets of the settlements, however, achieved the fame and status of the great Bedouin poets. It was to the latter that the Lakhmid rulers of al-Ḥīra and their rivals the Ghassānids of southern Syria turned when they wanted some panegyric (see BYZANTINES; CHRISTIANS AND CHRISTIANITY). By the beginning of the seventh century C.E. their patronage enabled successful poets such as Maymūn b. Qays al-Aʿshā to become itinerant troubadours. Al-Aʿshā was not the only master poet to be a contemporary of the Prophet. Others were Zuhayr b. Abī Sulmā, Labīd b. Rabīʿa, ʿĀmir b. al-Ṭufayl and Durayd b. al-Ṣimma. There were many more not of the highest rank.

Some seventy-five years ago, Gibb (*Arabic literature*) succinctly summed up some of the key reasons for the success of pre-Islamic poetry:

[But] its appeal lies far more in the fact that, in holding the mirror up to life, it presented an image larger than life. The passions and emotions and portrayals were idealized in content and expression — in content because it presented the Arabs to themselves as they would have liked to be, immeasurably bold and gallant and openhanded, and in expression because these ideal images were clothed in rich, sonorous and evocative language, and given emotional intensity by the beating rhythms and ever-recurring rhyme (p. 25).... All of these subserved [the poet's] main purpose, so to stimulate the imaginative response of his audience that the poem becomes a dialogue between them, a dialogue in which the audience are alert to grasp the hints and allusions compressed within the compass of his verse and to complete his portrait or thought for themselves (p. 26).

Factors such as these were instrumental not only in ensuring the success of the poetry in its own time but in providing it with an appeal that still grips Arabic-speaking hearers today.

None of this is likely to have troubled the Prophet greatly, but there were two aspects of poetry that must have been deeply disturbing to him. The first is that it was a short step from lampoon to obscenity or, much worse, to the uttering of curses (see CURSE). Poets' invective was common and caused much ill will. The second aspect is more complex and more serious. From the beginning the Arabs had linked their poets with magic (q.v.) or, at least, preternatural, non-human forces (see DEVIL; JINN; INSANITY). There is ample evidence that poets (and likewise *kāhin*s, soothsayers [q.v.]) were believed to have a preternatural driving force, given various names: *khalīl* (euphemistic "friend, companion"; see FRIENDS AND FRIENDSHIP), *jinn* and even *shayṭān* — the Greek *daimōn*. We do not rely on late sources for evidence on this. Al-Aʿshā, for example, several times refers to his demonic alter ego by the pet name *misḥal*, "the eloquent tongue."

It is against this background of the preternatural and of magic that one should view what the Qurʾān has to say about poetry and the poets. The key words found in the text are *shāʿir*, "poet" (Q 21:5; 37:36; 52:30; 69:41), *shiʿr*, "poetry" (Q 36:69), *majnūn*, "possessed by a jinn" (Q 15:6; 26:27; 37:36; 44:14; 51:39, 52; 52:29; 54:9; 68:2, 51; 81:22), *jinna*, "possession by a jinn" (Q 7:184; 23:25, 70; 34:8, 46) and also *kāhin*, "soothsayer" (Q 52:29; 69:42). Because of overlapping (Q 37:36, for example, has the phrase *shāʿir majnūn*), they involve nineteen passages, which fall into two kinds: (1) Those in which unbelievers are depicted as declaring that a prophet is a poet, a soothsayer, or possessed; and (2) those in which there is a strong denial of such claims.

Most of the passages are found in sūras thought to be early or middle Meccan, though there are also three from the late Meccan period (see CHRONOLOGY AND THE QURʾĀN). They are obviously of a polemical kind, though a surprising number are linked to eschatological material (see ESCHATOLOGY). There is no Medinan passage of this kind. The objections are normally put into the mouths of Muḥammad's Meccan opponents (see OPPOSITION TO MUḤAMMAD), though in the case of *majnūn*, two of the passages refer to Pharaoh (q.v.) and Moses (q.v.), and two to Noah (q.v.) and his opponents. The general picture is therefore that Muḥammad is not alone as a prophet in facing such objections. The passages specifically referring to *shāʿir* (and also *kāhin*), however, relate to Muḥammad rather than anyone else. The objections of the Prophet's opponents are vividly summed up in Q 21:5: "No! They say, 'Tangled nightmares. No! He has invented it. No! He is a poet. Let him bring us a sign, just as the ones of old were sent with signs'."

The slightly earlier Q 52:29-31 is a particularly striking passage. First, there is a firm denial that Muḥammad is either a *kāhin* or *majnūn*. This is then countered by a suggestion by his anonymous opponents that he is a *shāʿir*: "So give the reminder (q.v.). By the grace of your lord you are neither a soothsayer nor one possessed. Or they say, 'A poet for whom we await the ill-doings of fate.' Say, 'Wait. I shall be one of those waiting with you'." In addition to using three of the key words, the passage has *rayb al-manūn,* "the ill-doings of fate," a phrase that has various parallels in pre-Islamic poetry.

The conclusion to be drawn from such passages is that there was a great deal of verbal sparring and polemic on both sides in Mecca (q.v.) and that the Prophet's opponents did not hesitate to call him "a poet," a "soothsayer," "one possessed" (and much else that is of no direct concern here). This makes good sense if the words are being used because of their pejorative background. The alternative suggestion that Muḥammad's opponents could not differentiate between poetry, the utterances of *kāhin*s and passages from the Qur'ān does not bear close scrutiny.

The Qur'ān also makes it clear that poetry is not an appropriate vehicle for the transmission of God's message by the Prophet. Q 36:69-70 runs: "We have not taught him poetry. That is not proper for him. This is only a reminder and a recitation that is clear, that he might warn those who are alive and that the word may be proved true against the unbelievers." In short, not only was the Prophet not possessed, either as a poet or anything else; in addition, poetry was not suitable as the register of the revelation (see REVELATION AND INSPIRATION; RECITATION OF THE QUR'ĀN).

These passages thus determine the position of the Prophet and the revelation vis-à-vis poetry but they say nothing about other poets. For that we must turn to the final section of Q 26 and in particular to Q 26:224, which gives the sūra its name — "The Poets." Verses 224-7 are usually thought to be Medinan (whereas the rest of the sūra is considered to be middle Meccan) but there is no cogent reason for this view, apart from the final verse.

"Shall I tell you of those on whom the satans descend? They descend on every sinful liar (see LIE). They listen, but most of them are liars. And [there are] the poets, those who go astray (q.v.) follow them. Have you not seen how they wander in every valley, and how they say what they do not do? That is not the case with those who believe and do righteous deeds and remember God often and help themselves after they have been wronged. Those who do wrong will surely know by what overturning they will be overturned" (Q 26:221-7).

The passage is usually thought of as beginning at Q 26:224 but in view of the verses on *shāʿir* and *majnūn* mentioned above, it seems likely that the reference to *al-shayāṭīn,* "satans," in verse 221 is a typically oblique introduction to verse 224. Clearly poets are denounced but, as the passage is rhetorical (see RHETORIC AND THE QUR'ĀN), the strength of the comment is very much a matter of interpretation. The view that it is a severe one seems to rely to some extent on views formed on the passages already discussed. If, however, one takes the view that Q 26:225-6 refer to the poets rather than to "those who go astray," one may reasonably take the view that it exempts at least some poets from stricture.

The possibility offered by Q 26:227 that some poets might be or become righteous fits in with the evidence of the *sīra,* the biography of the Prophet (see SĪRA AND THE QUR'ĀN), and stories about the poets themselves, though there is much that cannot be taken at face value. It would appear that the well established, though minor, poet Ḥassān b. Thābit, of the Medinan tribe of Khazraj, composed poetry for the new community from the year 5/627 onwards (though quite what material this was is now difficult to determine: at a conservative estimate 70% of his *Dīwān* is spurious). Also active on behalf of the Muslims was Bujayr b. Zuhayr b. Abī Sulmā, who eventually persuaded his brother Kaʿb b. Zuhayr to drop his opposition to Islam. Kaʿb then came to the Prophet, submitted and recited his eulogy *Bānat suʿād*, much to the delight of Muḥammad. Bujayr is alleged to have warned Kaʿb that at the conquest of Mecca Muḥammad had ordered the execution of "some of those who had satirized and insulted him" (cf. Ibn Isḥāq-Guillaume, 597). On the other hand, the Prophet appears to have taken no action against other hostile poets. Thus ʿĀmir b. al-Ṭufayl, who was implacably opposed to Islam, came on a deputation from the Banū ʿĀmir to visit the Prophet in 9/630. Despite being rumored to be involved in a plot to kill Muḥammad, he was allowed to leave Medina, though he died on the way back to his tribe, probably through an illness picked up in Medina. We may also note that somewhat later, when ʿĀmir's fellow legate, Arbad b. Qays, was killed by lightning, Arbad's half-brother Labīd, apparently by then a devout Muslim, saw nothing wrong in composing a series of laments for him.

On this basis the simple interpretation of Q 26:224-7, to wit that it shows some disapproval of poets, though with a let-out clause in Q 26:227, seems the most reasonable. That did not stop many commentators in later periods from taking a much dimmer view. This is not surprising as poets regularly got themselves into trouble for foul-mouthed satire or even inadvertently offending those in temporal or religious authority.

Alan Jones

Bibliography
(in addition to the EI² articles on the poets named in the article): R. Blachère, La poésie dans la conscience de la première génération musulmane, in AI 4 (1963), 93-103; Cl. Gilliot, Poète ou prophète? Les traditions concernant la poésie et les poètes attribuées au prophète de l'islam et aux premières générations musulmanes, in F. Sanagustin (ed.), *Paroles, signes, mythes. Mélanges offerts à Jamal Eddine Bencheikh*, Damascus 2001, 331-96; H.A.R. Gibb, *Arabic literature*, Oxford 1963², chaps. 2 and 3; A. Jones, *Early Arabic poetry*, Reading 1992-6, introduction; I. Shahid, A contribution to koranic exegesis, in G. Makdisi (ed.) *Arabic and Islamic studies in honor of Hamilton A.R. Gibb*, Cambridge, MA 1965, 563-80; id., Another contribution to koranic exegesis. The sura of the Poets (XXVI), in JAL 14 (1983), 1-21; M. Zwettler, A Mantic manifesto. The sūra of "The Poets" and the qurʾānic authority, in J.L. Kugel (ed.), *Poetry and prophecy. The beginnings of a literary tradition*, Ithaca 1990, 75-119.

Polemic and Polemical Language

Discussion of controversial [religious] matters or allusion to them. Polemic in the Qurʾān consists primarily of argumentation directed against pagans (see POLYTHEISM AND ATHEISM and IDOLATRY AND IDOLATERS), Jews and Christians (see JEWS AND JUDAISM; CHRISTIANS AND CHRISTIANITY). Yet, polemical language may also be employed in other contexts, for example when addressing erring or recalcitrant Muslims (see ERROR; ASTRAY).

Polemic in the sense of argumentation or the refutation of others' beliefs is a prominent element in the Qurʾān since in the course of his mission Muḥammad encountered various types of opposition and criticism (see OPPOSITION TO MUḤAMMAD). It is easy, however, to underestimate the extent to which the Qurʾān contains polemical language since certain words or passages, if taken literally or at face value, would cease to be polemical (see next section; see LANGUAGE AND STYLE OF THE QURʾĀN; RHETORIC AND THE QURʾĀN; POLYSEMY).

Such an underestimation could be the consequence of preferring a literal reading as more in keeping with the solemnity and sacrosanct nature of scripture; nevertheless, elements such as hyperbole and lampooning are undeniably present in the Qurʾān (see LITERARY STRUCTURES OF THE QURʾĀN; HUMOR).

The process of refuting others' beliefs is often inseparable from the parallel process of defending one's own. For religious groups, this activity is an important part of identity-formation and boundary-drawing to the extent that a group defines itself by dissociating itself from others. In relation to the chronology of revelation (the traditional account of Muḥammad's life is here accepted in its broad outlines; see CHRONOLOGY AND THE QURʾĀN), this process is progressive. Thus, the arguments against pagans mainly in the Meccan period might constitute common ground with other monotheistic faiths, whereas the arguments deployed against Jews and Christians in the Medinan period are by definition more distinctive, serving to reinforce an Islamic identity over and against Judaism and Christianity. Among scriptures, the Qurʾān offers a particularly good example of this process since it reflects the fluctuating relations which Muḥammad and his followers had with the pagans, mainly in Mecca (q.v.), and with the Jews and Christians, mainly in Medina (q.v.). Furthermore the Qurʾān appears to have interacted in a very direct manner with its environment to the extent that it reflects a response to questions addressed to Muḥammad by specific individuals (see OCCASIONS OF REVELATION).

The nearest qurʾānic equivalents to the word "polemic" are the third-form verbs derived from the roots *jadala* and *ḥajja* (the former being rather more prevalent), both meaning to argue or dispute (see DEBATE AND DISPUTATION). Argument or disputation are activities usually attributed to Muḥammad's opponents and generally considered blameworthy (e.g. Q 3:20; 6:25; 8:6); in these instances both verbs might best be translated as "wrangling" (but it should be noted that *jadal* — or "debate" — does not necessarily have negative connotations; indeed, a treatise on the qurʾānic modes of *jadal,* i.e. the rhetorical devices employed in debating or disputing, was written by the Ḥanbalite Najm al-Dīn al-Ṭūfī [d. 716/1316]; cf. Suyūṭī, *Itqān,* iv, 60; Zarkashī, *Burhān,* ii, 24; McAuliffe, Debate with them). Disputing about God or his signs (q.v.) is considered particularly reprehensible (e.g. Q 2:139; 13:13; 40:69; 42:35). The Qurʾān says that every people *(umma)* disputed with the messenger (q.v.) who was sent to them (Q 40:5) and many of the arguments which are reported as having taken place between former prophets and their peoples (see e.g. Q 11:84-95; see PROPHETS AND PROPHETHOOD) have a bearing on Muḥammad's disputes with his contemporaries, whether they be doctrinal (e.g. relating to the oneness of God or the final judgment; see LAST JUDGMENT) or moral (e.g. exhorting to honesty [q.v.] in transactions; see ETHICS AND THE QURʾĀN; VIRTUES AND VICES, COMMANDING AND FORBIDDING). They are therefore to be considered an integral part of the qurʾānic polemic. The polemical function of these passages is reinforced by the frequent references to the punishment, whether temporal or otherworldly (see CHASTISEMENT AND PUNISHMENT; REWARD AND PUNISHMENT), which was visited on the recalcitrant disputants.

The relationship between the qurʾānic polemic and pre-Islamic monotheistic polemic is of interest but rather too complex to be explored in any detail here (see SOUTH ARABIA, RELIGION IN PRE-ISLAMIC;

PRE-ISLAMIC ARABIA AND THE QURʾĀN). John Wansbrough has sought to situate the qurʾānic polemic, along with the polemical material in the *sīra* literature (i.e. the "biography of the Prophet"; see SĪRA AND THE QURʾĀN), within the broader Judeo-Christian tradition (see SCRIPTURE AND THE QURʾĀN). To this end he identified twelve main themes and their pre-Islamic antecedents: prognosis of Muḥammad in Jewish scripture; Jewish rejection of that prognosis; Jewish insistence upon miracles (see MIRACLE) for prophets; Jewish rejection of Muḥammad's revelation (see REVELATION AND INSPIRATION); Muslim charge of scriptural falsification (see FORGERY); Muslim claim to supersede earlier dispensations (see ABROGATION); the direction of prayer (see QIBLA); Abraham (q.v.) and Jesus (q.v.) in sectarian soteriology (see ESCHATOLOGY; SALVATION; HISTORY AND THE QURʾĀN); Solomon's (q.v.) claim to prophethood; sectarian Christology; the "sons of God"; and the "faith [q.v.] of the fathers" (Wansbrough, *Sectarian milieu*, 40-3; see BELIEF AND UNBELIEF; GENERATIONS; ḤANĪF).

Language and style

The form and style of the Qurʾān is integral to its import and impact (see FORM AND STRUCTURE OF THE QURʾĀN), and polemic by definition seeks to have an impact on those whom it addresses. Elements of polemic are not confined to any particular sections of the Qurʾān, and there is a constant interplay and overlap between polemic and other elements such as eschatology, signs controversies and narrative (see NARRATIVES), as has been demonstrated by Robinson with reference to the early Meccan sūras (q.v.; Robinson, *Discovering*, 99-124). Polemical elements in the Qurʾān, which are often parenthetical, may incorporate any one or more of the following:

— exhortation (see EXHORTATIONS), e.g. Q 2:40: "O Children of Israel (q.v.)! Remember my favor I bestowed upon you (see GRACE; BLESSING); fulfill your covenant (q.v.) with me and I shall fulfill my covenant with you, and fear (q.v.) none but me";

— rebuke or criticism, e.g. Q 5:61: "When they come to you, they say: 'We believe,' but in fact they enter with disbelief and they go out the same";

— arguments, e.g. Q 16:103: "We know indeed that they say: 'It is a man that teaches him.' [But] the tongue of him they mischievously refer to is foreign, while this is a clear, Arabic tongue" (see ARABIC LANGUAGE; INFORMANTS);

— challenges, e.g. Q 2:111: "They say: 'None shall enter paradise (q.v.) unless he be a Jew or a Christian;' those are their vain desires. Say: 'Produce your proof (q.v.) if you are telling the truth'" (see PROVOCATION);

— refutations of accusations against Muḥammad, e.g. Q 53:2-3: "Your companion has neither gone astray nor erred, nor does he speak out of his own desire";

— discrediting opponents by means of a critical aside or by declaring them to be liars (see LIE), e.g. Q 37:151-2: "Behold they say, out of their own invention: 'God has begotten children'; but they are liars!";

— threats or warnings of temporal or otherworldly punishment, e.g. Q 9:61: "Those who molest the Prophet will have a grievous chastisement";

— declarations of woe, e.g. Q 2:79: "Woe to those who write the book (q.v.) with their own hands and then say: 'This is from God'";

— curses, e.g. Q 2:161: "Those who disbelieve and die in a state of unbelief, on them is God's curse (q.v.) and the curse of

angels (see ANGEL) and of all humankind";
— satire, e.g. Q 7:176: "His similitude (see PARABLES) is that of a dog (q.v.): if you attack him, he lolls out his tongue, and if you leave him alone, he lolls out his tongue. That is the similitude of those who reject our signs";
— rhetorical or hypothetical questions, e.g. Q 84:20: "What is wrong with them, that they do not believe?";
— exclamations, e.g. Q 7:10: "We have placed you on the earth and given you therein a provision for your livelihood, but little do you give thanks!";
— emphatic denials or denunciations, e.g. Q 104:3-4: "He thinks his wealth (q.v.) will give him immortality (see ETERNITY). By no means! He will certainly be thrown into the consuming one (see HELL AND HELLFIRE)!".

The range of qurʾānic terminology associated with polemic is too broad to be treated here. As far as the content of the polemic is concerned, this terminology could perhaps most usefully be analyzed in terms of clusters of words related to central concepts such as being astray/turned away (from guidance or the truth [q.v.]); immorality and unrighteousness; enmity and hostility (to God, Muḥammad and/or the Muslims; see ENEMIES); hypocrisy (see HYPOCRITES AND HYPOCRISY); haughtiness and pride (q.v.; see also ARROGANCE); rebellion (q.v.; see also DISOBEDIENCE) or stubbornness (see INSOLENCE AND OBSTINACY); and stupidity or ignorance (q.v.).

A striking feature of the qurʾānic polemic, particularly in its admonitory or exhortatory passages, is the regular occurrence of paired opposites: believers and unbelievers, truth and falsehood, guidance and error, paradise and hell (e.g. Q 2:2-7; 47:1-3; 59:20; see PAIRS AND PAIRING). These binary oppositions serve to confront the listener with a stark choice, and generally incorporate an implicit or explicit warning about the consequences of making the wrong one. Another common feature is a reciprocity or parallelism between the attitude of unbelievers or hypocrites to God and his attitude to them; thus they seek to deceive God but in fact he deceives them (Q 4:142); they forget him and so he forgets them (Q 9:67); they plot but so does God (Q 3:54; 8:30), and so on.

Polemical passages may be directed at particular groups of people (see headings below) or at particular beliefs or forms of behavior. Far from being a dispassionate discourse on morals, the qurʾānic condemnation of a given behavior often constitutes an accusation that such behavior is being engaged in, and the emphasis falls as much on the perpetrators as on the behavior itself. This is in accordance with the Qurʾān's tendency to emphasize the practical and the concrete rather than the abstract. It may, for example, describe those who are engaging in a particular form of morally reprehensible activity as "those in whose hearts there is a disease" (*alladhīna fī qulūbihim maraḍun*, e.g. Q 8:49; see HEART; ILLNESS AND HEALTH), or it may declare or call down God's curse on them, or refer to their unenviable destiny in the hereafter. The eschatological dimension shows the qurʾānic concern not just to describe or condemn, but also to motivate humans to avoid or desist from such behavior.

As indicated above, polemic is not necessarily to be taken at face value, as is clear from its frequent association with elements such as satire, encompassing features like hyperbole and caricature, and from its frequent use of metaphorical language (see METAPHOR). The Qurʾān contains many examples of the use of irony or satire to ridicule opponents: those who were charged with the prescriptions of the

Torah (q.v.) but failed to carry them out are compared to "a donkey laden with huge tomes" (Q 62:5); poets (see POETRY AND POETS), with whom Muḥammad's opponents sought to identify him, are described as "wandering distractedly in every valley" (Q 26:225); the pagans who attribute daughters to God prefer sons for themselves, and are grief-stricken when they receive tidings of a baby girl (Q 43:16-7; see INFANTICIDE; CHILDREN; GENDER); those who are reluctant to fight have rolling eyes or almost swoon at the mention of battle (Q 33:19; 47:20; see FIGHTING; EXPEDITIONS AND BATTLES; JIHĀD); and there is probably a lampooning element in the accusation that, for Christians, God is not just one of a trinity or tritheism but "the third of three" (Q 5:73; see TRINITY). Examples of the use of metaphorical language include the description of the unbelievers as deaf, dumb and blind (e.g. Q 2:18; see SEEING AND HEARING; VISION AND BLINDNESS; HEARING AND DEAFNESS; SPEECH), or as having a veil, seal or lock on their hearts (e.g. Q 17:46; 2:7; 47:24).

The classification of parts of the Qurʾān as polemical may require identifying those passages where particular terms are not intended as a straightforward objective description. For example, the term *ʿaduw*, "enemy," would not be considered polemical when used to describe a military opponent, but becomes so when the situation is rather more ambiguous, or when the foremost aim is condemnation, as where particular persons are branded as, for instance, "enemies of God" (e.g. Q 41:28; cf. 58:19, the "party of Satan"; see DEVIL; PARTIES AND FACTIONS). If one applies the same principle to a central religious concept such as "polytheism/polytheist" *(shirk/mushrik)*, it becomes apparent that an analysis of polemic in the Qurʾān could have considerable significance for the interpretation of particular terms or concepts.

Polemic against polytheists, unbelievers and hypocrites

The terms "polytheist" and "unbeliever" correspond closely to the qurʾānic terms *mushrik* and *kāfir* (the latter term also incorporating the sense of ingratitude, i.e. in the face of God's favors; see GRATITUDE AND INGRATITUDE). These terms and their cognates, however, sometimes appear to be used interchangeably (e.g. Q 6:1; 40:12), and on occasion both terms have a more comprehensive semantic application. For example, both are at times applied to Christians or Jews (see next section). In these cases, as in subsequent Muslim tradition, the accusation of "polytheism" *(shirk)* or "unbelief" *(kufr)*, is directed at self-professed monotheists, the point being not that they are literally to be equated with outright idolators or polytheists but that certain aspects of their belief or practice are seen as compromising the divine oneness. *Kufr* is sometimes closely associated with various types of reprehensible behavior, in fact certain types of behavior may be taken as an indication that the perpetrator is an unbeliever; Izutsu (*Ethical terms*, 113-67) has shown how central this concept is, and how closely related to almost all other negative ethical values or qualities. It is therefore inappropriate to try to define these terms too narrowly or precisely; an *a priori* assumption of absolute precision or consistency in qurʾānic usage would lead to difficulties and apparent contradictions.

For obvious reasons, it is mainly in the Meccan portions of the Qurʾān that the objections raised by Muḥammad's pagan opponents are reported and refuted. The major themes in the qurʾānic argumentation at this stage are: the insistence on the oneness of God and the corresponding denial of any associates; the affirmation of the last day (see APOCALYPSE), bodily resurrection (q.v.) and the final judgment; and the denial of various accusations made against Muḥammad.

Some of the arguments employed are fairly simple. For example, in the face of the pagans' denial of bodily resurrection, the Qurʾān frequently argues that if God were able to create them in the first instance, then he is capable of bringing them back to life for the purpose of judgment (q.v.; e.g. Q 6:94-5; 17:51; see CREATION; DEATH AND THE DEAD). In support of the oneness of God, the Qurʾān asserts, "if there were in them [i.e. the heavens and the earth] deities other than God, both would have been ruined" (Q 21:22). Other cases provide examples of fairly extended or multifaceted arguments. For example, in the face of demands for a miracle on the part of Muḥammad's detractors, several arguments are employed in defense of Muḥammad's alleged failure to produce one. In the Qurʾān, God declines to appease the critics by effecting miracles for various reasons: because they still would not believe (e.g. Q 6:109); in order to emphasize Muḥammad's human, non-divine status (Q 17:90-3; see IMPECCABILITY); and because the Qurʾān should be sufficient for them (Q 29:50-1). Muslims have traditionally linked this theme with the phenomenon of the "challenge" contained in several qurʾānic passages (e.g. Q 2:23-4; 10:38), which call on Muḥammad's critics to produce something comparable to the Qurʾān. Muslims understood this as implying that the Qurʾān itself constituted Muḥammad's miracle, as later elaborated in the doctrine of qurʾānic inimitability (q.v.; *iʿjāz*).

The Qurʾān reserves some of its harshest strictures for unbelievers and polytheists, especially the latter. For example, *shirk* is described in the Qurʾān as the only sin which cannot be forgiven (Q 4:48, 116; see FORGIVENESS; SIN, MAJOR AND MINOR) and the *mushrikūn* are described as "unclean," and are therefore prohibited from entering the sacred mosque (q.v.) in Mecca (Q 9:28). Unlike Jews and Christians, unbelievers and polytheists appear to have no redeeming features. Frequently, God's curse is pronounced on them and/or allusion is made to their destination in hell (e.g. Q 33:64).

The term *munāfiqūn*, "hypocrites," is almost exclusively Medinan and over time is increasingly used to denote a specific group of people. At Medina these people come to be numbered among Muḥammad's staunchest opponents, along with unbelievers and polytheists; indeed, they are sometimes explicitly paired with one of these categories (e.g. Q 4:140; 48:6), or with "those in whose hearts there is a disease" (Q 8:49; 33:12, 60). As with unbelievers, their destiny in hell is frequently proclaimed (e.g. Q 4:138; 66:9). The terms *nifāq* and *riʾāʾ* are both used to denote the abstract quality of hypocrisy, but by and large the main function of the term *munāfiqūn* appears to be to serve as a condemnatory label to draw attention to a group of people in Medina who are opportunistic and therefore fickle in their support of the Muslims. The Qurʾān is, in effect, warning the Muslims of this as well as warning the hypocrites of the consequences of their actions; actual hypocrisy and dissembling is only one of several reprehensible forms of behavior for which they are criticized in the Qurʾān.

Polemic against Jews and Christians

In the Medinan period the Qurʾān increasingly recognizes the followers of Judaism and Christianity as communities in their own right (see RELIGIOUS PLURALISM AND

THE QURʾĀN; RELIGION; COMMUNITY AND SOCIETY IN THE QURʾĀN). This is not the place to speculate on precisely which groups of Christians and Jews (although in the case of the latter the picture is somewhat clearer) may have been present in the Arabian peninsula in Muḥammad's time (see SOUTH ARABIA, RELIGION IN PRE-ISLAMIC; PRE-ISLAMIC ARABIA AND THE QURʾĀN); but the Qurʾān does appear at times to have been addressing particular, possibly heretical, groups of Jews or Christians (e.g. Q 9:30 attributes to Jews the belief that ʿUzayr/Ezra [q.v.] is the son of God, a belief to which no Jewish or other extra-qurʾānic attestation has been found), and at others to reflect the beliefs of particular groups (e.g. the Nestorian emphasis on Jesus' humanity or the Docetists' denial that he was really crucified). Attempts to demonstrate any direct influence of specific groups, however, remain highly speculative.

The qurʾānic material relating to Judaism and Christianity or Jews and Christians is not all polemical, and indeed there are some verses that could be described as conciliatory; but a sizeable proportion of it, probably the majority, is. Certain criticisms are directed at both Jews and Christians, sometimes under the rubric People of the Book (q.v.; *ahl al-kitāb* or *alladhīna ūtū l-kitāb*), a category which denotes primarily but not exclusively Jews and Christians, while others are directed at one to the exclusion of the other. References to the People of the Book generally consist of exhortations (e.g. Q 4:171; 5:15), didactic questions (e.g. Q 3:98, 99), or criticisms of their behavior (e.g. Q 3:19, 69). Although some verses appear to distinguish between good and bad People of the Book (e.g. Q 3:75, 110), the prevailing opinion appears to be that most of them are unrighteous (e.g. Q 5:59; see GOOD AND EVIL; JUSTICE AND INJUSTICE). Yet other verses speak of "those who disbelieve from among the People of the Book" (e.g. Q 2:105; 59:2; 98:1), showing that the categories of *kāfirūn* and People of the Book are not mutually exclusive. There is some ambiguity concerning the question of whether conversion to Islam is expected or demanded of the People of the Book. Their respective scriptures and faiths are at least implicitly affirmed (e.g. Q 5:44, 46-7; 10:94), but at times there seems to be an expectation that People of the Book should believe in the Qurʾān, and verses expressing a desire for this vary from the wistful (e.g. Q 3:110) to the threatening (e.g. Q 4:47). This ambiguity, and the use of terms such as *kufr* and *shirk* in connection with Jews and Christians, has given rise to disagreement among Muslim interpreters as to whether, in fact, Jews and Christians who remain in their respective faiths can attain salvation, despite the apparent confirmation of this in Q 2:62 and Q 5:69. Criticisms which are directed at both Jews and Christians, although not necessarily to the same degree, include distorting, forgetting, misinterpreting or suppressing parts of their scriptures (e.g. Q 2:75, 101; 5:15, 41; see REVISION AND ALTERATION); desiring to lead Muslims astray (e.g. Q 2:109; 3:100); failing to believe in Muḥammad's message (e.g. Q 3:70; 5:81); being religiously complacent or exclusivist (e.g. Q 2:80; 5:18); being divided amongst themselves (e.g. Q 5:14; 98:4); elevating their religious leaders to quasi-divine status (e.g. Q 9:31; see LORD); and failing to follow their own religious teachings properly (e.g. Q 5:47).

In general, the qurʾānic polemic against Jews is harsher in tone and more *ad hominem* than that against Christians. The most sustained passage on the Children of Israel (*banū Isrāʾīl*, the most common designation of the Jews) takes up about half of the longest sūra in the Qurʾān (beginning from Q 2:40). Commencing with exhortation, the passage becomes increasingly condemnatory, recalling the Jews' past (and by implication present) stubbornness, disobedience and ingratitude. Just as stories of the former prophets and their opponents (see PUNISHMENT STORIES) are clearly targeting Muḥammad's contemporaries in their criticisms of those opponents, so this passage dissolves the distance between past and present by directly associating Muḥammad's Jewish contemporaries with the misdeeds of Jews almost two millennia previously. Thus, in a passage generally believed to refer to an event recorded in Deuteronomy 21:1-9 and Numbers 19:1-10, the Qurʾān declares: "Remember when you killed a man and fell into dispute among yourselves about it.... Thenceforth were your hearts hardened: they became like rocks or even harder" (Q 2:72-4; see McAuliffe, Assessing). In one of the more strongly worded passages concerning Jews it is stated that "those of the Children of Israel who disbelieved were cursed... evil indeed were the deeds which they committed... God's wrath is on them, and in torment will they abide forever," and it is concluded that Jews, along with polytheists, are "strongest in enmity to the believers" (Q 5:78-82).

Arguments directed at Christians often concern religious doctrine. The Qurʾān appears to refute the Trinity (e.g. Q 5:73, although strictly speaking the verses in question refute tritheism); the divine sonship of Jesus (e.g. Q 4:171); the divinity of Jesus (e.g. Q 5:17); and the crucifixion (q.v.; Q 4:157-8). Some of these doctrines are declared tantamount to *kufr* or *shirk* (e.g. Q 4:171; 5:17, 72-3), thus blurring the distinction between Christians and polytheists/unbelievers in much the same way that the distinction between People of the Book and unbelievers is blurred in the verses cited above.

Even more than in the case of polemic against unbelievers, it is important to observe the chronology of revelation when assessing passages relating to Jews and Christians. An example of this is the apparent denial of the crucifixion, often cited in Muslim-Christian polemic but in fact revealed in the early Medinan period when Jews, not Christians, were considered to be the main opponents of the Muslims. This denial is therefore to be understood primarily as a reproach to the Jews and a refutation of their claim to have killed Jesus. A few (e.g. Ayoub, Islamic Christology, 116-7; Zaehner, *Sundry times,* 212) conclude that this leaves open the possibility of interpreting the verse as affirming the role of God, while denying that of the Jews, in bringing the crucifixion to pass.

The fact that the Qurʾān contains conciliatory as well as polemical material relating to Jews and Christians raises the hermeneutical question of the relationship between the two types of passages. In view of the fact that the chronological progression in the Qurʾān is generally in the direction of greater hostility towards and criticism of these groups, many of the classical scholars (see EXEGESIS OF THE QURʾĀN: CLASSICAL AND MEDIEVAL) took the later, more confrontational verses as abrogating the earlier, more conciliatory ones (e.g. Q 9:29, among other verses, was generally taken to abrogate Q 2:256; see VERSES). Furthermore, the dividing line between good and bad People of the Book was generally taken to coincide with the dividing line between those who either accept Islam or would do so if they were to hear about it and those who do not or would not. In the modern period (see EXEGESIS OF THE QURʾĀN: EARLY MODERN AND CONTEMPORARY), exegetes tend to place rather less emphasis on abrogation, so other approaches emerge. Those who continue to hold an overwhelmingly negative view of Christians and Christianity may distinguish between an ideal, meta-Christianity posited in the Qurʾān and the actual Christianity with which Muḥammad and other Muslims down to the present have come into contact (see McAuliffe, *Qurʾānic*). Modernists (e.g. Ayoub, Nearest in amity, 162) prefer to take the more positive verses (e.g. Q 2:256) as of universal application while interpreting the negative verses as having limited and temporary application, for example in conditions of warfare (see WAR) or hostility between Muslims and others.

Because of its ongoing relevance throughout history, polemic against Jews and Christians raises another hermeneutical question, namely that of how far or in what respects the qurʾānic material applies to a changed environment. If individual qurʾānic verses respond to the particular beliefs of Muḥammad's Jewish and Christian contacts, as appears to be the case in at least some instances, then the question arises as to how far it is appropriate to apply those verses to later Jewish or Christian groups. Some have suggested that the Qurʾān refutes heretical Christian beliefs (e.g. tritheism, adoptionism, the physical generation of the Son) rather than the orthodox doctrines of the Trinity, Incarnation, etc. In practice, however, the vast majority of Muslim commentators have assumed that the Qurʾān does refute the Trinity, the Incarnation, and the Christian doctrine of divine sonship, especially as these are understood to contradict the central Islamic tenet of the oneness of God.

Post-qurʾānic polemic

The Qurʾān has had an immeasurable impact on subsequent Islamic literature (see LITERATURE AND THE QURʾĀN). It would be impossible to quantify the stylistic influence of the polemical material in the Qurʾān but it is safe to assume that it has been extensive; Muslim polemical writings often echo or reproduce qurʾānic vocabulary and phrases. This section will be confined to religious polemic, where the qurʾānic influence has been most in evidence.

Heresiographical and other types of work incorporate various accusations against those outside the Jewish and Christian traditions, for example charges of atheism *(ilḥād)*, heresy (q.v.)/Manicheanism *(zandaqa)* or materialism *(dahriyya)*. It is Christians who, however, have been the target of the bulk of Muslim polemical literature. This is in part because of the shared border with Christendom and the resulting fact that the Muslims' most significant military opponents were generally Christians, right down to the modern period. Christians also formed the most numerically significant communities under Muslim rule, in the case of many of the central Islamic lands evolving from a majority to a minority over the course of a few centuries. In addition, from the earliest period it was often Christians, such as John of Damascus (d. ca. 132/749), who initiated religious debates, thereby prompting a response from Muslims. Many refutations of Christianity were composed, often under the rubric *al-radd ʿalā l-naṣāra*. There was also a lesser amount of anti-Jewish polemic, and some overlap between the two in that biblical criticism, insofar as it pertained to the Hebrew Bible or the Old Testament, could be directed equally at both communities.

The Muslim polemic, although not devoid of *ad hominem* and, from about the ninth century, rational and philosophical arguments based on Greek (especially Aristotelian) philosophical categories (see PHILOSOPHY AND THE QURʾĀN), was heavily dependent on the Qurʾān, a dependence which accounts for a high degree of consistency in this literature. Thus the main areas of criticism were scriptural integrity and the related accusation of suppressing predictions of Muḥammad and conveying false doctrine, and the overriding claim was that of abrogation (generally in the sense of Islam abrogating or superseding previous religions, but also applied internally to the biblical text). There was, however, also some knowledge and criticism of empirical Christianity, i.e. the actual practices of various Christian groups and the doctrinal and other differences between them. The polemic is not to be found in any one genre; aside from polemical works proper, treatments of other religions can be found in Qurʾān and ḥadīth commentaries (see ḤADĪTH AND THE QURʾĀN), theological treatises (see THEOLOGY AND THE QURʾĀN), works of *fiqh* (jurisprudence; see LAW AND THE QURʾĀN), heresiography, historical and geographical compendiums (see GEOGRAPHY AND THE QURʾĀN), belles lettres, and poetry.

Not surprisingly, the majority of those who undertook systematic refutations of Christianity were theologians. Among them, Muʿtazilīs (q.v.) were especially prominent (e.g. Abū ʿĪsā al-Warrāq, d. ca. 246/860, al-Jāḥiẓ, d. 255/869 and ʿAbd al-Jabbār, d. 415/1025), and instrumental in introducing more sophisticated, philosophically based arguments. Unfortunately earlier works by some of the founding figures of Muʿtazilism have not survived, for these might have given a clearer picture of the influence of Muslim-Christian controversies on the development of Islamic theology. What is clear is that certain Christian doctrines had a bearing on internal Muslim disputes. There was, for example, a parallel between the Christian concept of the Logos and the Muslim doctrine of the uncreated Qurʾān (see CREATEDNESS OF THE QURʾĀN), and between the hypostases of the Trinity and the question of the independent existence of the attributes of God (see GOD AND HIS ATTRIBUTES). While Muʿtazilī tenets had the effect of distancing Islam from those Christian doctrines, the mainstream Ashʿarī theology, which was formed in reaction to the Muʿtazila, considerably narrowed this distance.

One of the most significant figures for both the anti-Christian and anti-Jewish polemic is the Andalusian Ẓāhirī theologian Ibn Ḥazm (d. 456/1064), whose major work, *Kitāb al-Fiṣal fī l-milal wa-l-ahwāʾ wa-l-niḥal,* has continued to be influential down to the present. This work is notable for being the first Muslim source to incorporate a thorough, systematic treatment of the biblical text. His relatively detailed knowledge of the text (although it is likely that he relied on secondary sources to some extent) enabled him to list alleged contradictions, absurdities, errors, lewdness, and anthropomorphisms (see ANTHROPOMORPHISM) in the Bible. He argued strongly for the view that *taḥrīf* (scriptural corruption; see CORRUPTION) entailed extensive textual alteration, and not just misinterpretation as some other scholars had held. Like others before him, however (notably ʿAlī b. Rabbān al-Ṭabarī; d. ca. 241/855?), in his *Kitāb al-Dīn wa-l-dawla,* he claimed to be able to identify biblical predictions of Muḥammad in the extant text. Despite his considerable knowledge of both the biblical text and Islamic sciences (see TRADITIONAL DISCIPLINES OF QURʾĀNIC STUDY) Ibn Ḥazm lacked philosophical sophistication and, not surprisingly for a Ẓāhirī, had an extremely literalistic approach to scripture. With few exceptions, the writings of later polemicists such as Ibn Taymiyya (d. 728/1328) and Ibn Qayyim al-Jawziyya (d. 751/1350) were largely derivative, often relying heavily on Ibn Ḥazm.

The Muslim anti-Christian polemic was mainly intended for a Muslim audience and (as with the Christian anti-Muslim polemic) was unlikely to convince the opponent because it relied on internal (i.e. Islamic) categories, in particular the doctrine of *taḥrīf* which presupposed a different understanding of revelation from the Christian one. This is seen most clearly in the qurʾānic assumption that God revealed the gospel (q.v.; *injīl*) to Jesus in the same way that he revealed the Qurʾān to Muḥammad, which posits an Aramaic gospel consisting purely of God's own words.

Contemporary Muslim polemic tends to draw more on sources external to the Qurʾān, in particular higher biblical criticism which can be used to demonstrate that the Bible is not "revealed" in the sense that Muslims generally understand revelation, i.e. the verbatim word of God (q.v.) preserved without any alterations. Two works which have been particularly influential in the modern period are Rahmat Allah Kayranawi's *Izhar ul-haqq*, which emerged from the nineteenth-century Indian Christian-Muslim public debates *(munāẓarāt)*, and the twentieth-century Egyptian scholar Muḥammad Abū Zahra's *Muḥāḍarāt fī l-naṣrāniyya*. Despite benefiting from higher criticism, however, the modern polemic is not demonstrably superior to the classical works and indeed often shows an inferior knowledge of empirical Christianity. See also APOLOGETICS.

Kate Zebiri

Bibliography

Primary: Suyūṭī, *Itqān;* id., *Muʿtarak al-aqrān fī iʿjāz al-Qurʾān*, ed. ʿA.M. al-Bajāwī, 3 vols., Cairo 1969-72, ii, 56-7 (definition of *jadal* in the Qurʾān); al-Ṭūfī, Najm al-Dīn al-Ḥanbalī, *ʿAlam al-jadhal fī ʿilm al-jadal. Das Banner der Fröhlichkeit über die Wissenschaft vom Disput*, ed. W. Heinrichs, Wiesbaden 1987; Zarkashī, *Burhān*.

Secondary: C. Adang, *Muslim writers on Judaism and the Hebrew Bible. From Ibn Rabban to Ibn Ḥazm*, Leiden 1996; G. Anawati, Polémique, apologie et dialogue islamo-chrétiens, in *Euntes docete* 22 (1969), 375-451; M. Ayoub, Nearest in amity. Christians in the Qurʾān and contemporary exegetical tradition, in *Islam and Christian-Muslim relations* 8 (1997), 145-64; id., Towards an Islamic Christology II. The death of Jesus, reality or delusion? in MW 70 (1980), 91-121; S.M. Behloul, *Ibn Hazm's Evangelienkritik. Eine methodische Untersuchung*, Leiden 2002; A. Charfi, La fonction historique de la polémique islamochrétienne à l'époque Abbasside, in S. Khalil Samir and J. Nielsen (eds.), *Christian Arabic apologetics during the Abbasid period* (750-1258), Leiden 1994, 44-56; R. Ettinghausen, *Antiheidnische Polemik im Koran*, Gelnhausen 1934; E. Fritsch, *Islam und Christentum im Mittelalter*, Breslau 1930; H. Goddard, *Muslim perceptions of Christianity*, London 1996; G. Hawting, *The idea of idolatry and the emergence of Islam. From polemic to history*, Cambridge 1999, esp. 46-7, 67-87; id., Shirk and "idolatry" in monotheist polemic, in IOS 17 (1997), 107-26; J. Henninger, *Spuren christlicher Glaubenswahrheiten im Koran*, Schöneck/Beckenried 1951, 45-56; ʿA. Ḥifnī, *Uslūb al-sukhriyya fī l-Qurʾān al-karīm*, Cairo 1978; T. Izutsu, *The structure of the ethical terms in the Koran. A study in semantics*, Tokyo 1959; J. Jomier, *Bible et coran*, Paris 1959; id., *The great themes of the Qurʾān*, London 1997; M.A. Khalaf Allāh, *Mafāhīm qurʾāniyya*, Kuwait 1984; Kh.A. Khalīl, *Jadaliyyat al-Qurʾān*, Beirut 1977; H. Lazarus-Yafeh, *Intertwined worlds. Medieval Islam and Bible criticism*, Princeton 1992; A. Ljamai, *Ibn Hazm et la polémique islamo-chrétienne dans l'histoire de l'islam*, Leiden 2003; D. Marshall, *God, Muhammad and the unbelievers. A qurʾānic study*, London 1999; J.D. McAuliffe, Assessing the *Isrāʾīliyyāt*. An exegetical conundrum, in S. Leder (ed.), *Story-telling in the framework of non-fictional Arabic literature*, Wiesbaden 1998, 345-69; id., Debate with them in the better way. The construction of a qurʾanic commonplace, in B. Embaló et al. (eds.), *Myths, historical archetypes and symbolic figures in Arabic literature*, Beirut 1999, 163-88; id., *Qurʾānic;* id., The qurʾānic context of Muslim biblical scholarship, in *Islam and Christian-Muslim relations* 7 (1996), 141-58; M. Mir, Humor in the Qurʾān, in MW 81 (1991), 179-93; M. Perlmann, The medieval polemics between Islam and Judaism, in S.D. Goitein (ed.), *Religion in a religious age*, Cambridge, MA 1974; F. Rahman, *Major themes of the Qurʾān*, Chicago 1980; N. Robinson, *Discovering the Qurʾān. A contemporary approach to a veiled text*, London 1996; Ḥ. Sharqāwī, *al-Jadal fī l-Qurʾān*, Alexandria 1986; M. Sherif, *A guide to the contents of the Qurʾān*, Reading 1995; M. Steinschneider, *Polemische und apologetische Literatur in arabischer Sprache, zwischen Muslimen, Christen und Juden, nebst Anhängen verwandten Inhalts*, Leipzig 1877, repr. Hildesheim 1965; J.W. Sweetman, *Islam and Christian theology. A study of the interpretation of theological ideas in the two religions,* 2 vols., London 1945-67; D. Thomas, *Anti-Christian polemic in early Islam. Abū ʿĪsā al-Warrāq's "Against the Trinity",* Cambridge 1992; J. Waardenburg, Types of judgment in Islam about other religions, in G. de la Lama (ed.), *Middle East,* 2 vols., Mexico City 1982, i, 135-44; M. Waldman, The development of the concept of *kufr* in the Qurʾān, in *JAOS* 88 (1968), 442-55; J. Wansbrough, *The sectarian milieu. Content and composition of Islamic salvation history,* Oxford 1978; W.M. Watt, The Christianity criticized in the Qurʾān, in *MW* 57 (1967), 197-201; R.C. Zaehner, *At sundry times. An essay in the comparison of religions,* London 1958; K. Zebiri, *Muslims and Christians face to face,* Oxford 1997.

Political Science see SOCIAL SCIENCES AND THE QURʾĀN

Politics and the Qurʾān

This article will discuss the use of the Qurʾān to justify or contest rule. Three areas will be considered: (1) quasi-political themes in the Qurʾān; (2) the politicization of the Qurʾān in early Islam; and (3) the possibility and limitations of human rule alongside or in addition to the Qurʾān as divine communication.

Some preliminaries: As an institution governing a territory, administering its peoples and resources and legislating a socio-political order, the state as organ of rule came into being in early Islam not from qurʾānic directive but from the experience and consensus of the first Muslims (see COMMUNITY AND SOCIETY IN THE QURʾĀN; LAW AND THE QURʾĀN). Strong emphasis is given in the Qurʾān to obedience (q.v.) to God and the messenger (q.v.) of God (and, at one place, to those in power, *ūlū l-amr* [Q 4:59], a heavily exploited phrase which early exegetes understood as those with knowledge and intelligence, not political authority, e.g. Mujāhid, *Tafsīr,* i, 163; see KNOWLEDGE AND LEARNING; SCHOLAR; INTELLECT). The Qurʾān makes enough mention of struggle between the followers of Muḥammad and his opponents (see OPPOSITION TO MUḤAMMAD) to suggest that politics was at play in the first attempts to announce its message. Moreover, the Prophet was awarded authority (q.v.) in the form of an oath of allegiance (*bayʿa,* e.g. Q 48:10, 18; see OATHS; CONTRACTS AND ALLIANCES), in which his followers promised to fight for the cause of God (see PATH OR WAY; EXPEDITIONS AND BATTLES) until death (*bayʿat al-riḍwān;* Ibn Isḥāq, *Sīra,* iii, 236) and early writers of history, such as Ibn Saʿd (d. 230/845; *Ṭabaqāt*), do depict the Prophet as a regional hegemon, receiving delegations and tribute in exchange for protection (see CLIENTS AND CLIENTAGE; SĪRA AND THE QURʾĀN; HISTORY AND THE QURʾĀN).

Those who succeeded Muḥammad as leaders of the Muslim community worked to consolidate and expand the domain of Islam, e.g. Abū Bakr (r. 11-13/632-4) in the wars of apostasy (q.v.) and ʿUmar b. al-Khaṭṭāb (r. 13-23/634-44) in the conquest of Byzantine and Sasanian lands. It was conquest (q.v.) that led to the formation of a state ruled by a caliph (q.v.) and local governors and administered by magistrates and functionaries (judges and secretaries). None of this, however, can be said to bear a clear connection to qurʾānic inspiration (see REVELATION AND INSPIRATION) or even a loose one in the manner in which the Israelite monarchy was viewed through the words of Deuteronomy 16:18-18:22. The interest of theological literature in the leadership of the Muslim community was limited to sectarian debate (*kalām* or *ʿilm al-firaq;* see Madelung, Imāma; see THEOLOGY AND THE QURʾĀN; IMĀM; KHARAJĪS; SHĪʿISM AND THE QURʾĀN); and the collections of prophetic reports (*ḥadīth;* see ḤADĪTH AND THE QURʾĀN) and law *(fiqh),* while speaking to the moral parameters of Islamic rule (e.g. Bukhārī, *Ṣaḥīḥ,*

Kitāb al-Aḥkām; Muslim, *Ṣaḥīḥ, Kitāb al-Imāra*), say nothing about the concept or details of political organization. The formulation of a theory connecting rule and religion was left to a genre of literature of Greek and Persian provenance known as "mirrors-for-princes," i.e. advice literature, in which it was argued that salvation (q.v.) in the next world was contingent upon socio-political prosperity in this one, mainly for two reasons. First, socio-political chaos was not conducive to performing the religious obligations by which one attained salvation and, secondly, the revealed law — the commands and prohibitions of God that define the Muslim community — could only be enforced by well-established rule, including various organs of governance and bureaus of administration. It was al-Māwardī (d. 450/1058), above all, who articulated this vision of Islamic rule, both its theory and form of governance, in *Tashīl al-naẓar wa-taʿjīl al-ẓafar* ("Raising awareness and hastening victory") and *al-Aḥkām al-sulṭāniyya* ("The laws of Islamic governance"), respectively. It should be mentioned, however, that such connections between governance *(siyāsa)* and revelation *(sharīʿa)* were never above suspicion, playing a role in Sunnī-Shīʿī debate (see Heck, *Construction,* ch. 4).

Quasi-political themes in the Qurʾān

There is no agreement that the Qurʾān even has a political message. For Qamaruddin Khan *(Political concepts)* the qurʾānic message is not political but moral (see ETHICS AND THE QURʾĀN), a summons to submit to the one God and a life of faith (q.v.). He claims that the Qurʾān in no way sanctions one political form (i.e. monarchy, theocracy, democracy, etc.) and that those who derive a political message from the Qurʾān exploit its verses out of context for their own goals. In contrast, for Muḥammad ʿIzzat Darwaza the Qurʾān speaks to all aspects of human life, including the state and its financial, judicial, military and missionary tasks (see INVITATION) — a specifically qurʾānic political program implied, as he sees it, in the reference of Q 57:25 to the book (q.v.) and iron, i.e. divine justice and the coercive force needed to ensure public order (Darwaza, *al-Dustūr al-qurʾānī,* 50 f.; cf. Muqātil, *Tafsīr,* v, 4, 245, who associates iron with warfare; and al-ʿĀmirī, *Iʿlām,* 152, who characterizes both prophecy and human rule as divine endowment *[mawhiba samāwiyya];* see WAR; JUSTICE AND INJUSTICE; PROPHETS AND PROPHETHOOD). To that end, he adduces a number of verses (q.v.) purported to have called for political leadership after the death of the Prophet (Darwaza, *al-Dustūr al-qurʾānī,* 56 f.) and marshals forth in the body of the work an array of verses on the basis of which he constructs a qurʾānic vision of political organization.

Despite the range of opinion about its political content, the Qurʾān is clear about the connection between socio-political prosperity and obedience to the message of God as conveyed by his messengers. Denial of the divine message leads to destruction at the hands of God (e.g. Q 25:37; see PUNISHMENT STORIES). This is the way of God (*sunnat Allāh,* Q 40:85), to bring to naught those who sow corruption (q.v.) on earth (e.g. Q 28:4, 43). By underscoring the demise of former nations *(umam khāliya)* that failed to heed God's messengers (e.g. Q 40:21-2, 82; see GENERATIONS; WARNING; GEOGRAPHY), the Qurʾān signals rhetorically (see RHETORIC AND THE QURʾĀN) to its audience the consequence they will suffer if they fail to respond gratefully to the prophet Muḥammad (see GRATITUDE AND INGRATITUDE). The prophetic mission is God's claim upon a people to live in gratitude and faithfulness, making it a matter of survival to comply with prophecy once announced (Q 28:58-9). It is no exaggeration to say that the example of former nations has considerably influenced Muslim political consciousness through the centuries (e.g. Māwardī, *Aʿlām*, 65: *wa-qaṣaṣ man ghabara min al-umam wāʿiẓ*), ensuring religion a central place in formulations of political prosperity (e.g. Juwaynī, *Ghiyāth al-umam*).

The terms traditionally used for political governance *(siyāsa)* and political order *(niẓām)* are absent from the Qurʾān but all things in heaven and earth are subject to God's administering command (Q 32:5, *yudabbiru l-amra mina l-samāʾi ilā l-arḍi;* cf. Q 10:3, 31; 13:2; see POWER AND IMPOTENCE; COSMOLOGY). Responsibility for living in conformity to God's administration (*tadbīr,* equated with governance *[siyāsa]* in classical Islamic political thought) has been divinely entrusted to humankind, signified in the idea of *khalīfa* — e.g. Q 6:165 and Q 10:14, verses which indicate that this idea, whether understood as successor to former nations or delegate of God on earth, implies a test of fidelity to the will of God (for the different interpretations of this term by the early exegetes, see al-Qāḍī, Khalīfa; for its political appropriation by Umayyad and ʿAbbāsid rulers, see Crone and Hinds, *Caliph,* and al-Qāḍī, Foundation; for an historical overview of the institution of the caliphate, see Sourdel et al., Khalīfa).

This responsibility, now on Muslim shoulders, was foreshadowed in (1) God's plan for Adam to be caliph on earth (Q 2:30; see ADAM AND EVE) and (2) the divine trust *(al-amāna)* accepted by humankind prior to creation (q.v.; Q 33:72, its rejection by the rest of the created order making it the distinctive mark of human beings) in recognition of God as their sovereign lord (q.v.; Q 7:172). Since, however, humankind was destined to be subject to Satan's temptations (see DEVIL; FALL OF MAN), there was need for warning and guidance (see ASTRAY; ERROR; FREEDOM AND PREDESTINATION): Prophecy thus stands at the heart of the proper ordering of human affairs, serving to orient humankind not only to its final destiny in the next world (see ESCHATOLOGY; REWARD AND PUNISHMENT) but to prosperity in this one, as summarized by Muqātil b. Sulaymān (d. 150/767; *Tafsīr,* ii, 42): "When God sends a prophet to humankind and they obey him, the land and its people prosper *(ṣalaḥati l-arḍ wa-ahluhā)*. Disobedience [results in] the corruption of sustenance (q.v.; *fasād al-maʿīsha*) and the destruction of the land's people." A moral society is, after all, a blessing from God (Q 3:104): "That there be [made] of you a nation that calls for the good, commanding the right and forbidding the wrong. Those are the ones who thrive (*al-mufliḥūn;* see VIRTUES AND VICES, COMMANDING AND FORBIDDING)."

This is not to imply that prophets are to exercise rule themselves; Muḥammad is reminded on several occasions that he is merely a bearer of good tidings (see GOOD NEWS) and a warner (e.g. Q 25:56). Rather, prophets are to witness to the rule of God, the main instrument of which is scripture (*kitāb;* see BOOK), along with rule *(ḥukm)* and prophecy (*nubuwwa,* e.g. Q 3:79; 6:89; 45:16). Muqātil (*Tafsīr,* i, 289, 574) understands *ḥukm* as knowledge and understanding, which, by arbitrating human differences (cf. Q 2:213), bring about sociopolitical harmony under divine truth (q.v.) — a qurʾānic idea first embodied tangibly in the Constitution of Medina, which recognizes differing communal norms within one polity (see Zein al-Abdin, Political significance).

All dominion is envisioned as God's (*lillāhi mulku l-samāwati wa-l-arḍi,* e.g. Q 3:189; 5:17-8; less frequently *malakūt,* e.g. Q 6:75, 23:88, 36:83). It is in that sense that the political program of the Qurʾān is essentially other-worldly or eschatological, i.e. oriented to the final day when all judgment (q.v.) will be truly divine (Q 25:26; see Ḥāmid, *Uṣūl,* 56, for whom the eschatological message of the Meccan verses forms a necessary backdrop to the divinely — i.e. other-worldly — oriented polity of the Medinan ones; see MECCA; MEDINA; CHRONOLOGY AND THE QURʾĀN). While dominion is God's alone (Q 17:111; 25:2), he distributes it as he wishes (Q 3:26), for instance to Saul (q.v.; Q 2:247) and David (q.v.; Q 2:251). Dominion in human hands cannot, however, be reduced merely to power over others but is conceived as the application of divinely bestowed knowledge (e.g. Q 2:251; 12:101; 85:9) that will lead humankind to the religious and moral life ordained by God and destined to be fully realized on judgment day (Q 22:56; cf. 40:16; see LAST JUDGMENT). Humans may have been entrusted with rule (e.g. Q 5:20; 12:43) but God alone is true king (*al-malik al-ḥaqq,* e.g. Q 20:114; see KINGS AND RULERS).

The qurʾānic depiction of dominion as divine kingship recalls the imagery of the Psalms (q.v.), which are themselves shaped by conceptions of kingship of the ancient Near East. In the Psalms, it is the temple that represents God's heavenly throne as symbol of ultimate authority (e.g. *Ps* 11:4-5). In the Qurʾān, God is the final judge *(ḥakam),* seated on his throne and ruling his creation from its inception (cf. Q 7:54). He strikes those who transgress his order (cf. Q 6:124; see BOUNDARIES AND PRECEPTS; CHASTISEMENT AND PUNISHMENT), sets a path to be followed (Q 6:153), ensures the just settlement of dispute (Q 6:57; cf. 5:48), is the enemy of unbelievers (Q 2:98), lord of east and west (Q 2:115, 142), and his rule protects his subjects from the chaotic forces of unbelief (cf. Q 2:286; see BELIEF AND UNBELIEF).

It is in this sense that the prophet Muḥammad acts as emissary *(rasūl)* from the heavenly court, sent to give warning of impending judgment (e.g. Q 10:15) similar to that meted out to former nations. There is thus no break between divine and prophetic authority (e.g. Q 4:80; cf. 4:153), making obedience to the prophetic message *(risāla)* the singular means of avoiding doom. Following that message will result in true rule and prevent strife and corruption in the land, thereby ensuring prosperity rather than the destruction that former nations met as their fate for failing to heed God's messengers (Q 10:13) and choosing instead to follow the command of earthly potentates (Q 11:59). Human beings, custodians of divine communication, are worthy of rule (Q 4:59; cf. 4:83; 27:33): Indeed God uses human rulers to restrain humankind from sowing corruption in the land through mutual aggression (Q 2:251, a theme taken up vigorously in classical Islamic political thought; see Heck, Law) and even allows a human hierarchy regardless of moral standing (cf. Q 6:165). Rule in itself, however, is no guarantee of success, for even the wicked rule over one another (cf. Q 6:129). Humans, as problematic creatures given to strife and factionalism, need recourse to a higher standard to establish socio-political harmony. Although offering no details of political organization, the Qurʾān is quite clear that the processes of rule and arbitration are never to ignore the designs of God.

Thus, human beings, created weak (Q 4:28), must be reminded of their divinely entrusted responsibility, which happens periodically through prophetically established covenants (*mīthāq,* Q 5:7; with the Israelites, Q 2:63, 93; 5:12; with the Christians, Q 5:14; with the prophets, Q 3:81, 33:7; see CHILDREN OF ISRAEL; CHRISTIANS AND CHRISTIANITY; COVENANT). Such covenants are never limited to monotheistic worship (q.v.) but include socio-moral norms (e.g. Q 2:83, where the covenant with Israel demands honoring one's parents [q.v.] and relatives, care for orphans [q.v.] and the dispossessed *[al-masākīn]* and kindly speech to others; cf. Q 4:154; see POVERTY AND THE POOR). These covenants, accompanied by divine knowledge (e.g. scripture and prophetic wisdom), impose upon their recipients an obligation to carry out God's program, an obligation neglected with grave consequences (Q 3:187; 5:70-1; 7:169). Rejecting covenant results not only in unbelief and infidelity (Q 4:155) but also in a disregard for God's interest in human welfare, ultimately bringing about corruption in the land (*fasād fī l-arḍ*, cf. Q 2:27; 13:25, a phrase denoting the very antithesis of the qurʾānic vision of socio-political prosperity). Human welfare, ordained by God, nevertheless depends on human willingness to bring it about by cooperating with God's revelation.

It will be important to recount briefly the mythic narratives of the Qurʾān (see MYTHS AND LEGENDS IN THE QURʾĀN), i.e. the stories of former nations, which highlight the clash between godly and human rule — the central political theme of the Qurʾān that provides meaning for Muḥammad's own struggle with the peoples of his day who rejected or did not fully accept his message and who are negatively characterized in various ways: faithless ingrate *(kāfir)*, polytheist (*mushrik;* see POLYTHEISM AND ATHEISM), recipient of previous scripture (*ahl al-kitāb*, i.e. "people of the book [q.v.]," usually identified as Jews and Christians; see JEWS AND JUDAISM) and, more generally, hypocrite (*munāfiq;* see HYPOCRITES AND HYPOCRISY), transgressor *(ẓālim)* and sinner (*fāsiq;* see SIN, MAJOR AND MINOR). They, too, like the former nations, are destined to perish for refusing the message of God conveyed to them by the prophecy of Muḥammad. This is not to discount the rhetorical purpose of such narrative, i.e. a literary technique to encourage acceptance of the recited message. Rather, it is to say that the Qurʾān is not naive about the use of power to shape human society for a godly end *(fī sabīl Allāh)*. The former nations' rejection of prophecy justifies struggle *(jihād),* even armed struggle, against the opponents of Muḥammad (see JIHĀD). In turn, the Muslims, whom God has chosen as final successors to former nations, must prosper by struggling for the way of God against those who mock or deny him (see MOCKERY; LIE), making prosperity, i.e. political success, the litmus test of obedience to God.

In other words, socio-political prosperity is a heavy burden, envisioned by the Qurʾān not only as the performance of moral and religious obligations but also as a ritual performance meant to recall and resonate with the mythic narrative of the Qurʾān. The political ritual of Islam — *ʿibāda mulkiyya* in the words of al-ʿĀmirī (d. 381/992; *Iʿlām,* 148-50) — has been diversely imagined by Muslims: eschatologically (Khārijīs), legally (Sunnīs), hierarchically (Shīʿīs), esoterically (Ismāʿīlīs), ideally (the vision of philosophers such as al-Fārābī; see PHILOSOPHY AND THE QURʾĀN) and sociologically (the position of state-aligned intellectuals, e.g. Qudāma b. Jaʿfar, al-Māwardī, Ibn Khaldūn; see SOCIAL SCIENCES AND THE QURʾĀN). But, for all, it is the means of sanctifying the Muslim community by recalling God's promise of sustenance and support until the end of time (Māwardī, *Naṣīḥat al-mulūk,* 67), in contrast to the former nations that he brought to ruin — the mythic narrative recorded in the scrolls (q.v.) of previous scripture as a reminder (*dhikrā,* see MEMORY; REMEMBRANCE) to all and heeded by some (*ahl al-dhikr,* Q 16:43;

21:7). The qur'ānic narrative thus makes of politics — the quest for socio-political success — a salvifically driven drama that re-enacts the revealed message. Failure to imagine socio-political prosperity in recollection of the mythic narrative puts divine favor at risk and, for some, may demand acts of heroic sacrifice, i.e. martyrdom (see MARTYRS), by which to restore what is understood to be a relation with God gone awry (for an example of a martyr culture in opposition to the world, see Sharāra, *Dawla,* esp. 291 f.). Alternatively, it may demand a re-reading of the Qur'ān such that political reality be understood in light of qur'ānic narrative. An example of this from the classical period can be found in the work of Abū Ḥayyān al-Tawḥīdī (d. 414/1023; *Imtā'*, ii, 33), who at a time of political flux in the Islamic world made the claim on the basis of Q 2:247 that the ruler *(malik),* no less than prophet, is heaven-sent *(mab'ūth),* and that to the great astonishment of the vizier *(ka'annī lam asma' bi-hādhā qaṭṭ).* Of the many examples of this in the modern period, one can point to the work of the Syrian sheikh and parliamentarian, Muḥammad al-Ḥabash, who places emphasis on the benefits *(maṣāliḥ)* and prosperity to accrue to Muslims from a greater engagement with the modern world, as a qur'ānic mandate (see Heck, Religious renewal; cf. al-Ḥamd, *al-Siyāsa*).

At play throughout the Qur'ān, the political drama of former nations is more or less coherently narrated across its seventh, eighth and ninth chapters: the first revealed in Mecca, the last two in Medina. Accounts begin in Q 7 (Sūrat al-A'rāf, "The Heights") as follows: God alone is protector (Q 7:3), since it is he who arbitrates on judgment day (Q 7:8-9). Unbelievers seek out the protection of demons (*shayāṭīn,* Q 7:27), a theme recalling the fall of Adam and Eve (Q 7:22-4) and the resulting human struggle to resist demonically inspired temptation (Q 7:16-7) and strife (Q 7:24). Those who do sin and transgress God's decrees fail to recognize his exclusive authority (Q 7:33, *an tushrikū bi-llāhi mā lam yunazzil bihi sulṭānan* — *sulṭān* identified as God's book by Muqātil, *Tafsīr,* ii, 34); they are the nations of jinn (q.v.) and humans occupying hell (Q 7:38, *umam... mina l-jinni wa-l-insi fī l-nār;* see HELL AND HELLFIRE). God as lord of all (Q 7:54) wills that there be no corruption in the land after it has been made good (Q 7:56, *lā tufsidū fī l-arḍi ba'da iṣlāḥihā;* cf. Q 7:85), having sent a series of messengers to various peoples for that purpose (to call them to monotheism *[tawḥīd]* according to Muqātil, *Tafsīr,* ii, 43): Noah (q.v.; Nūḥ), Hūd (q.v.), Ṣāliḥ (q.v.) and Shu'ayb (q.v.). In each case, the worldly leaders of the day (*mala',* a tribal term that Muqātil, *Tafsīr,* ii, 45, 49, identifies with the arrogant, *al-kubarā', alladhīna takabbarū 'an al-īmān;* see ARROGANCE) reject the purported messenger (Q 7:60, 66, 75, and 88, respectively) for speaking against the beliefs of the community (e.g. *milla* in the case of Shu'ayb, Q 7:88; on such community-identifying terms, see Aḥmed, Key). Each in turn (Q 7:61-2, 67-8, 79 and 93) responds that he is a messenger of God, sent to convey his message and offer counsel (*naṣīḥa,* for the reform of the affairs of the nation in question, e.g. Q 7:85 in the case of Shu'ayb; *'ulamā'* would later claim this role of socio-political counsel, called *nuṣḥ,* e.g. Ibn Taymiyya, *Siyāsa,* 1). The people, led by their arrogant leaders (Muqātil, *Tafsīr,* ii, 45, see this as oppression [q.v.] of the weak *[ḍu'afā']* by the strong, i.e. preventing them from the benefits of God's message; cf. Q 40:47, where, in hell, the weak ask the arrogant why they misled them), inevitably disavow the messengers of God and are destroyed by his judgment (understood by Muqātil, ibid., 47, as a fitting punishment), which, however, creates the possibility of successor nations (*khulafā',*

Q 7:69, 74, understood by Muqātil, ibid., 43, as successors in punishment *[ʿadhāb]*). Up to this point, however, the settled peoples of the world (*ahl al-qurā;* see CITY) refuse to believe, thus foregoing the material blessings (*barakāt)* that accompany fidelity to God (Q 7:96).

Such narration (*al-qaṣaṣ*, Q 7:176; cf. 7:7; see NARRATIVES), mytho-historical staging for Muḥammad's own prophetic mission, culminates in the account of Moses (q.v.) and Pharaoh (q.v.): the archetypical clash of godly and worldly power. Moses is God's messenger to Pharaoh and his court (*malaʾ*, Q 7:103). Pharaoh takes on the characteristics of God, accusing Moses of sowing corruption in the land and claiming to be the one who subdues the world (cf. Q 7:127): The problem here is not human rule itself but denial of God's ultimate sovereignty. Moses convinces the reluctant Israelites that God will destroy their enemy and make them the latest successors to custodianship of God's message (Q 7:129). Indeed, after the destruction of Pharaoh and his folk, the Israelites do inherit the earth, east and west (suggesting the entire earth, Q 7:137). It is they, finally, who form a community *(umma)* of truth and justice (Q 7:160) and yet they, too, eventually divide into twelve tribes or nations and do wrong (Q 7:159), signaling the judgment to be passed against the Israelites as against former nations (Q 7:168). The religious divisions of humankind in general and the Israelites specifically are attributed by al-Ṭabarī (d. 310/923) to political aspiration *(ṭalab al-riʾāsa)* and the desire of humans to subject one another (*istidhlāl min baʿḍihim li-baʿḍ,* Ṭabarī, *Tafsīr,* i, 650-1, where it is explained that the Muslims, on account of divine guidance *[hidāya],* refrain from these differences and on judgment day will serve as witness against the former nations for rejecting the messengers sent to them; see RELIGIOUS PLURALISM AND THE QURʾĀN; WITNESSING AND TESTIFYING). The belief that religious divisions are the product of political ambition is echoed in the fourth/tenth-century letters of the Ikhwān al-Ṣafā ("Brethren of Purity"; *Rasāʾil Ikhwān al-Ṣafā,* iii, 151-6; cf. also Māwardī, *Adab al-dīn,* 169-70, where weak rule is shown to be the source of religious innovation and division, and id., *Naṣīḥat al-mulūk,* 70-6, where the ruler is expected to defend creedal orthodoxy against theological innovations understood as breaches of socio-political harmony; see HERESY; INNOVATION).

The turn has now fallen to Muḥammad, as foreshadowed in previous scriptures, who legislates by commanding the right and proscribing the wrong (*al-amr bi-l-maʿrūf wa-l-nahy ʿan al-munkar;* cf. Cook, *Commanding right,* 13-31) and by establishing the lawful *(ḥalāl)* and unlawful (*ḥarām*, see LAWFUL AND UNLAWFUL), making of Muḥammad the messenger to all people from the one God to whom belongs sovereignty over the heavens and the earth (cf. Q 7:157-8). As if to bring the story full circle, the Qurʾān has Muḥammad declare that God alone is his protector (Q 7:196 in echo of Q 7:3; see PROTECTION), presumably in the face of those groups who, as we see in the following two chapters, have set themselves against him.

That the account of Muḥammad's struggles in Q 8 (Sūrat al-Anfāl, "The Spoils") and Q 9 (Sūrat al-Tawba, "Repentance") is to be read as fulfillment of the historical narration of Q 7 is confirmed by Q 9:70, which queries whether the news (q.v.; *nabaʾ*) of former nations had not reached the ears of Muḥammad's opponents. The themes of Q 7 are thus reworked into the context of Muḥammad's own mission, helping to explain the nature of the opposition. There is a call to obey God and his messenger (Q 8:46; cf. 8:26 where people are reminded not to betray the trust *[amāna]* given to them and Q 9:63, where hell is the judgment upon those who oppose God and his messenger). The enemies of Muḥammad are compared to Pharaoh (Q 8:52). In the end it is God who rules all through his book (cf. Q 8:68, 75). Strife — the seduction of the devil and source of religious division — will be avoided once all opposition has been subdued and all religion has been handed over to God (Q 8:39). Thus is a godly nation born out of struggle with ungodly opposition, both polytheists (i.e. *mushrikūn* or at least those polytheists who have broken a treaty made with Muḥammad [Q 9:3-4, cf. 8:56]; see BREAKING TRUSTS AND CONTRACTS) and recipients of previous scriptures who neither believe nor recognize the lawful and unlawful in their own scriptures (Q 9:29), making them tantamount to *mushrikūn* by associating other lords with God in denial of his singular sovereignty (Q 9:30-1; see IDOLATRY AND IDOLATERS). In other words, failure to heed one's scripture leads to socio-moral breakdown. This new nation is composed of people who believe, command right and forbid wrong, are committed to both prayer (q.v.) and the payment of alms (Q 9:71; see ALMSGIVING), leave their homes (i.e. separate from the wayward) and care both for one another (Q 8:72) and for the weaker members of society (cf. Q 8:41 and 9:60 on the distribution of spoils and alms, respectively, and Q 7:75 and 7:137 on concern for the downtrodden *[mustaḍʿaf]*; see BOOTY; OPPRESSED ON EARTH, THE).

It is worth noting the resemblance of such qurʾānic narrative to the biblical oracles against the nations and oracles of restoration (*Ezek* 25:1-32:32 and 33:1-39:29 and *Jer* 25:13-38 and 46:1-51:64), where judgment was passed against the nations, including Israel, for cultic, not political, deviance and hope was offered for a new Israel and even a new temple and cult (*Ezek* 40:1-58:35). Is, then, the qurʾānic concern for unity under God's rule as mediated by the prophet Muḥammad a socio-political concern or a cultic one? Is it for political or cultic reasons that God has sent his final messenger to a nation destined to succeed all previous ones (Q 13:30)? Q 22:67 mentions dispute over ritual *(mansak;* see RITUAL AND THE QUR'ĀN), Q 16:124 and Q 39:3 over the Sabbath (q.v.) and Q 5:45 over bodily injury. Does the rule of God as announced by the Qurʾān include the political or is it more properly limited to ritual *(ʿibādāt),* social affairs (*muʿāmalāt,* e.g. commercial, criminal and family law; see MARRIAGE AND DIVORCE; FAMILY) and morals *(akhlāq)?*

At least one group in early Islam, the Khārijīs, made no separation between the political and the ritual. In a context in which revelation is believed to be operative, differences must be mitigated or removed for the sake of a communal purity that is itself a pre-condition for further revelation. In other words, when a nation fails to carry out the work *(ʿamal)* commanded of them by God, the possibility of further divine communication is jeopardized and previous communication is rendered suspect. Hence, qurʾānic charges of scriptural distortion (see FORGERY; POLEMIC AND POLEMICAL LANGUAGE) against recipients of previous scripture were also accusations of socio-moral impropriety. Parallels to this can be found in the Judeo-Christian tradition: The Israelites had to undergo purification in anticipation of God's manifestation on Mount Sinai (*Exod* 19:1-24:18, especially 19:8-19); and the community at Qumran — for whom prophecy was not at all closed — maintained a strict code of ritual and legal purity as a pre-condition for further divine communication. The Qurʾān, for its part, states that the *mushrikūn* are a pollutant *(najas)* and are not to go near the sacred mosque (q.v.; Q 9:28). Pollution (*rijs,* Q 9:125; see CLEANLINESS AND ABLUTION; RITUAL PURITY) — construed as transgression of ritual practice, dietary laws (see FOOD AND DRINK), sexual norms (see SEX AND SEXUALITY), etc. — poses a problem for further disclosure of revelation (Q 9:127, *wa-idhā mā unzilat sūratun naẓara baʿḍuhum ilā baʿḍin, hal yarākum min aḥadin…*). This suggests that qurʾānic reference to the rule or reign of God has nothing to do with political decision-making but implies rather the unity of communal purpose that the cultic maintenance of God's presence amidst his people entails.

Still, scripture is God's mode of decision-making, which is not limited to the book sent to Muḥammad (see SCRIPTURE AND THE QURʾĀN), but includes both the Torah (q.v.) and Gospel (q.v.; Q 5:44-7). The claim is made by one exegete (Ṭabarī, *Tafsīr*, iii, 243) that these verses were revealed in response to a group of Jews who questioned Muḥammad about two adulterers and thus failed to follow the judgment — stoning (q.v.) — that their own scripture called for (Ṭabarī, *Tafsīr*, iii, 233-5): Those who do not make decisions according to God's revelation are ingrates, transgressors, wicked (Q 5:44, *wa-man lam yaḥkum bi-mā anzala llāhu fa-ūlāʾika humu l-kāfirūn;* Q 5:45 uses *ẓalīmūn* and Q 5:47, *fāsiqūn*).

The political potential of such verses was certainly not lost on al-Ṭabarī (d. 310/923), who narrates a story of a group of Khārijīs who inquire of Abū Mijlaz whether Q 5:44-6 could be applied to the political leaders of the Muslims *(umarāʾ wa-wulāt al-muslimīn),* considered to be in sin simply for their assumption of rule, which in Khārijī opinion belongs only to God. Clearly aware of the Khārijī angle of their inquiry (as was al-Ṭabarī who explains it), Abū Mijlaz responds by saying that Islam (q.v.) is their religion even if they sin and that the verses in question were revealed in reference to Jews, Christians and polytheists. The question is not settled, however, since faithless ingratitude *(kufr)* does not properly apply to these groups, leading al-Ṭabarī to demonstrate that Q 5:44 *(kāfirūn)* applies to lapsed Muslims, while Q 5:45 *(ẓālimūn)* and Q 5:47 *(fāsiqūn)* applies to Jews and Christians, respectively, and that the unbelief into which lapsed Muslims have fallen is not of the kind necessitating excommunication, which would make it licit to take their life (ibid., iii, 237-8; see MURDER) — an argument that has not swayed Islamist groups today from using such verses to justify attacks against Muslim leaders who fail to implement the rule of God to Islamist satisfaction.

It cannot be denied that God alone decrees the final fate of his creatures (Q 40:48) as the most just of judges (Q 11:45) but this capacity is shared by prophets and humans in general, who are called to judge with justice (*al-ʿadl*, e.g. Q 4:58 and 5:95; or *al-qisṭ*, Q 5:42) and truth *(ḥaqq)* without partiality (*hawā*, Q 38:26), as a check against transgression (*baghy*, Q 38:22). Such standards are associated with the scripture itself (*ḥukm al-kitāb*, cf. Q 3:23 and 4:105), which, as the highest standard of arbitration, serves to reconcile differences and to end conflict (e.g. Q 2:213; cf. 3:23 and 45:17), while all quarrels are to be settled by God's final verdict on judgment day (Q 22:68-9). If it is indeed the word of God (q.v.; *kalām Allāh*) that must rule, to prevent strife and ensure prosperity, then the extent to which humans are capable of interpreting the divine will and thus meriting a share in rule remains the central if elusive question for politics and the Qurʾān.

The politicization of the Qurʾān in early Islam

The ideological use of the Qurʾān for political purposes, i.e. its politicization, occurred early. As the word of God, the Qurʾān is the emblem of Islamic legitimacy par excellence and has been used to that end by standing governments and rebels alike, by activists and theorists, and in defense of both hereditary rule and elected politics. Given its divine origin, scripture acts as an alternative authority, making it an interest of a state with a religious dispensation to supervise the text, as can be seen in both the earliest and more recent periods of Islamic history, e.g. (1) the establishment of a single recension of the qurʾānic text (*muṣḥaf* [q.v.]) by the third caliph, ʿUthmān (r. 23-35/644-56), who outlawed variant versions (see COLLECTION OF THE QURʾĀN; CODICES OF THE QURʾĀN; READINGS OF THE QURʾĀN) to the resentment of the so-called Qurʾān reciters (*qurrāʾ*; see RECITERS OF THE QURʾĀN), a decision that, according to Sayf b. ʿUmar (d. 180/796), led them to seek his assassination (Sayf b. ʿUmar, *Kitāb al-Ridda*, 49-52); and (2) the decision by ʿAbd al-Ḥamīd II (r. 1876-1909) to make the printing of the Qurʾān (q.v.) an Ottoman state monopoly and to set up a commission under the highest religious office of the state (*shaykh al-islām*) for the inspection of all printed copies. Even states without a religious dispensation may seek to manage the Qurʾān, as seen in the Turkish Republic's interest in promoting a Turkish translation of the Qurʾān with commentary (Albayrak, The notion; see TRANSLATIONS OF THE QURʾĀN).

The diverse political ends that the Qurʾān has served, from earliest Islam until today, have been possible simply because it is, as the word of God, beyond human control. Can the Qurʾān be subordinated to human interpretation? To what extent can it accommodate human decision-making? Is the Qurʾān itself to determine political rule or is it to be located within a constellation of human conceptions of rule? Is the Qurʾān to shape the political order or is it to be placed at the service of the political order? On the one hand, the qurʾānic announcement of the absolute sovereignty of God has been taken very seriously by some Muslims, especially those with Khārijī leanings. On the other, the absence of any qurʾānic details on political organization has made apparent to most Muslims the need for non-revealed guidance in the realm of politics. The politicization of the Qurʾān, from its beginning, centered upon the possibility of its interpretation and thus subordination to human judgment — a vast topic which here can only be glimpsed in the traces left to us in the chronicle written by the third/ninth-century historian, al-Ṭabarī (*Taʾrīkh*).

The death of the Prophet gave rise to a struggle over the nature of Islamic society and leadership, imagined variously as succession to the Prophet and as delegated agent of God on earth. The extent to which the Muslim community was to be politically organized under central rule was also in question. All parties involved, both recognized caliphs and their opponents, cited qurʾānic verse in support of their cause. In his letter to a group of apostates, the first successor to the Prophet, Abū Bakr, couched in abundant qurʾānic citation his argument that Islam will survive the death of its Prophet (Ṭabarī, *Taʾrīkh*, 1882; trans. x, 55-60), while one of his supporters, Abū Ḥudhayfa, mobilized military enthusiasm against the apostates by calling out to the Muslims as the people of the Qurʾān (ibid., 1945, trans. 121). Later, the widow of the Prophet, ʿĀʾisha (see ʿĀʾISHA BINT ABĪ BAKR), in a letter to the people of Kūfa, reportedly argued for Medinan hegemony against the emerging center of power in southern Iraq under the leadership of ʿAlī b. Abī Ṭālib (q.v.; r. 35-40/656-61), the cousin and son-in-law of the Prophet and fourth of the rightly-guided caliphs, by calling the people to uphold the book of God against the killers of ʿUthmān, quoting Q 3:102-3 and Q 3:23 on the importance of communal unity (ibid., 3133; trans. xvi, 74-6). In response, ʿAlī is reported to have asserted his adherence to the book (i.e. of God) as arbiter and imām (ibid., 3141; trans. xvi, 83), unsuccessfully attempting to use a copy of the Qurʾān as a symbol of reconciliation *(iṣlāḥ)* for the divided community (ibid., 3186, 3189; trans. xvi, 126, 129-30).

The real test for the relation of the Qurʾān to Islamic rule came at the battle of Ṣiffīn (q.v.) between the partisans of ʿAlī (see SHĪʿA) and those of Muʿāwiya, founder of the Umayyad dynasty (r. 41-60/661-80) who based his claim to lead the Muslim community on his right to avenge the blood of ʿUthmān as closest kin (see BLOOD MONEY; KINSHIP). In the course of the battle, which had swayed in favor of ʿAlī, the soldiers of Muʿāwiya reportedly raised copies of the Qurʾān *(maṣāḥif)* on the tips of their spears as a symbol of their desire for arbitration (q.v.; Ṭabarī, *Taʾrīkh*, 3329; trans. xvii, 78). ʿAlī hesitated at first, claiming that Muʿāwiya and his followers were without religion and without Qurʾān (here in the indefinite — perhaps alluding to one of many recitations *[qirāʾāt]* of the Qurʾān) and that he had fought them in the first place so that they might adhere to rule by "this book" *(li-yadīnū bi-ḥukm hādhā l-kitāb,* ibid., 3330; trans. xvii, 79). Eventually, a group within his partisans, the vociferous advocates of rule by the Qurʾān later known as Khārijīs, urged him to respond to this offer of judgment by the book of God (ibid., 3332; trans. xvii, 86). While the trick played by Muʿāwiya to get the better of ʿAlī is well-known, the story of the arbitration between the two raised significant issues about the relation of the Qurʾān to Islamic rule.

After calling ʿAlī to submit to the rule of the Qurʾān, these first Khārijīs challenged his claims to personal charismatic authority, especially his attempts to associate himself with the character and prestige of the Prophet (ibid., 3336; trans. xvii, 85; cf. Mubarrad, *Kāmil,* ii, 540; Sayf b. ʿUmar, *Kitāb al-Ridda,* 357), protesting that their oath of allegiance to him did not imply special privilege (cf. 1 *Chron* 21 and 1 *Kings* 10:23-11:13, where David and Solomon, respectively, are rebuked for pursuing lordly status based on worldly power); rather, he was like them in all respects, acting as their recognized leader and not in any way an inspired figure. With the arbitration between ʿAlī and Muʿāwiya exposed as a hoax, this group withdrew from ʿAlī's partisans, accusing him of failing to submit fully to the rule of the Qurʾān and of permitting human judgment over the book of God (Mubarrad, *Kāmil,* ii, 539-40; Ṭabarī, *Taʾrīkh,* 3360-2, esp. 3362, where one Khārijī ends his accusation of ʿAlī with the following: "Our lord is not to be set aside or dispensed with. O God, we take refuge in you from the introduction of things of this world into our religion, a smearing *[idhān]* of the affairs of God and a disgrace *[dhull]* that brings down his wrath upon his people.").

Their position crystallizing in opposition to ʿAlī, whom they attack — on the basis of Q 49:9 — for his failure to repent, the Khārijīs would go on to proclaim a highly pietistic, strongly individualistic and qurʾānically centered religiosity (Ṭabarī, *Taʾrīkh,* 3349; trans. xvii, 99): Considering themselves the only true Muslims for their freedom from sin (i.e. defined as the use of human judgment in the affairs of God; see IMPECCABILITY), they dispensed with — at least in principle — the need for a leader (i.e. human rule; cf. Crone, Statement); authority was for them to be purely consultative among their members (see CONSULTATION), all of whom, it is to be presumed, were entirely faithful to the voice of the Qurʾān, while their oath of allegiance, to God alone, required them to adhere strictly to the principle of commanding the right and forbidding the wrong.

Ibn ʿAbbās (d. ca. 68/686-8), dispatched

by ʿAlī to the Khārijī rebels, was faced with a stubborn refusal to listen to his use of analogical reasoning to justify the arbitration (on the basis of Q 4:35, which calls for arbitration to reconcile a couple in conflict; Ṭabarī, *Taʾrīkh,* 3351; trans. xvii, 100-1; Mubarrad, *Kāmil,* ii, 528-9). The Khārijīs responded by insisting that, while human discretion is permissible where God has delegated authority, it is not for his servants to judge what he has decreed, namely that Muʿāwiya and his party should repent or be killed, a judgment based on Q 9:5 which calls for the killing of those who do not repent of their failure to acknowledge the singular sovereignty of God.

At stake here are essentially two very different notions of qurʾānic interpretation with consequences for political authority. For these first Khārijīs, no human interpretation of the Qurʾān was possible, ensuring its unequivocal if problematic status as final arbiter and leader of human society (see Ibn Abī Shayba, *Muṣannaf,* viii, 729-43, nos. 2, 3, 38-40, 48, where the Prophet is made to predict the coming of the Khārijīs as a people whose engagement with revelation is limited to an oral recitation unmediated by human judgment; see also no. 33, which describes Khārijī insistence that communal differences be decided solely by the rule of the book of God *[ḥukm al-kitāb];* nos. 27 and 51, which explain their defense of divine rule alone as a ploy to do away with human governance [*imra* or *imāra*]; and no. 22, which cites Khārijī neglect of ambiguous [q.v.; *mutashābih*] verses of the Qurʾān as evidence of their rejection of interpretation). For ʿAlī and his partisans, the human being formed the cognitive link between the Qurʾān and communal decision-making, as exemplified in Ibn ʿAbbās' use of analogy and ʿAlī's own argument that the Qurʾān is merely dead script between two covers and that it does not speak but rather that humans speak through it (Ṭabarī, *Taʾrīkh,* 3353; trans. xvii, 103; see SPEECH). For that, he was accused of giving authority over the book of God to humans (ibid., 3361; trans. xvii, 111), an accusation he recognized but defined as a failure of judgment, not sin, while accusing the Khārijīs in turn of disrupting the governance necessary for Muslims to fulfill their pact with God (citing Q 16:91-3) by making of the Qurʾān something it was not intended to be (citing Q 39:65, essentially accusing the Khārijīs of polytheism). Both sides cite the Qurʾān (ibid., 3362; trans. xvii, 113) as proof texts to justify two different conceptions of scripture, one subject to human interpretation and the other effective without it.

The Khārijīs, in a later encounter with Ibn al-Zubayr, accused ʿUthmān of having introduced innovations into the religion and of opposing the rulings of the book (Ṭabarī, *Taʾrīkh,* 516; trans. xx, 99-100), a transgression they identify with ʿUthmān's attempt to create a dynastic rule officiated by his close kin and based on central control of the proceeds of the Islamic conquests. In short, the corruption that the Qurʾān so vehemently denounces is understood by both the representatives of the nascent Islamic state and their Khārijī opponents as disobedience (q.v.) to God, the difference being that for the former disobedience to God included disobedience to properly constituted and divinely endowed human authority.

This first debate over the relation of the Qurʾān to human rule must be seen in the context of changing social conditions, especially the emergence of an increasingly centralized state with control over the material wealth of the community, which meant in the case of early Islam the considerable proceeds of conquest which had turned many of the first Muslims into landowners of vast estates (see Kenney,

Emergence), while depriving others from a share of the spoils of victory according to seniority in the cause of Islam, as had been the case under the Prophet and his first two successors. One report claims that it was ʿAlī's refusal to permit the Muslim fighters to plunder the property of conquered peoples that first provoked Khārijī resentment (Sayf b. ʿUmar, *Kitāb al-Ridda,* 357). Under ʿAlī's policy, conquered lands were to be administered and taxed by state officials and not distributed as tribal booty to Muslim fighters, who were now to receive a salary fixed by the state. It was thus partly the consolidation of Islamic rule in worldly terms that brought about the politicization of the Qurʾān, the strongly eschatological (other worldly) coloring of its verses serving as a platform for opponents of the state to protest its policies: How could there be worldly rule in light of the rule of God as inaugurated and announced by the Qurʾān? It was not merely a question of the qurʾānic narrative of former nations but the presence of the Qurʾān itself in the midst of the believing community. If revelation — God's word and not human effort — was to be the effective agent of grace (q.v.) and guidance, any other rule would be automatically disqualified on the grounds of being worldly: Those whom the rapidly changing social conditions of early Islamic society had marginalized from an increasingly centralizing power and dispossessed of a share in the growing wealth of the Muslim community found a strong ally in the Qurʾān. In short, Khārijī shame at being marginalized in a changing socio-political order came to be associated with qurʾānic condemnations of sinful worldliness and human governance identified as the object of God's wrath, transforming scriptural rhetoric into a political program. Human governance, now defined as godless, is to be attacked in order to ensure avoidance of the historical catastrophe that beset former nations. Social marginalization becomes imagined as religious anxiety over the possibility of suffering the horrifying consequences of human dismissal of the prophetic message. Amidst such developments, the only way to display piety (q.v.) is by attacking the state and those who award it authority, now depicted in eschatological terms as the foes of God (see ENEMIES), as seen in an early Khārijī poem (ʿAbbās, *Shiʿr al-khawārij,* no. 258):

I did not want a share from him, only aspiring in killing him that I succeed and relieve the earth of him and those who wreak havoc and turn from the truth. Every tyrant *(jabbār)* is stubborn. I consider him to have abandoned the truth and to have legislated misguidance *(sannat al-ḍalāl).* Verily do I sell myself to my lord, quitting their hollow words, selling my family and wealth, in the hopes of a place and possessions in the gardens of eternity (q.v.; see also GARDEN).

It would not be totally inaccurate to dismiss Khārijī use of the Qurʾān as a means to defend their material interests, as Muʿāwiya did (Ṭabarī, *Taʾrīkh,* 2913, 2930), but it is still important to link their material interests to their conception of revelation and its corresponding view of all worldly goods as sacrificial offering to God (see SACRIFICE). It was not just a matter of control of communal resources but also of the divine consumption of the lands and property of the conquered peoples as preparation for the rule of God signaled by revelation, as suggested by Q 27:91-3, which Sālim b. Dhakwān (*Epistle,* 64; cf. 50) cites in support of fighting against any association *(ishrāk)* of the worldly with the divine. By comparison, this attitude is well illustrated in the book of Joshua, where the voice of God commands the Israelites not only to conquer the land but to plunder its wealth and kill its inhabitants — men, women and children — as a holocaust offering to the lord (e.g. *Josh* 6:17-21; 8:2, 24-6; 10:28-40; 11:6-14; see also *Num* 21:33-5 and *Deut* 3:1-7). The rule of God is to be prepared by the elimination of all that stands in its way, a mission contingent upon the uncompromised purity of a community consecrated to the sacralizing, sanctifying, all-consumptive and annihilating voice of God as announced by the book of the law of Moses (*Josh* 8:34-45; 23:6-8). The qur'ānically inspired militancy of the early Khārijīs served as an expression of vengeance on the worldly powers of the day, now Muslims and not merely forces hostile to Islam, who were both an affront to the reign of God and a threat to socio-political harmony, as expressed by the proto-Khārijī Ibn Budayl as grounds for fighting Muʿāwiya (Ṭabarī, *Ta'rīkh,* 3289-90, citing Q 9:123-7). Q 4:66-78, a rhetorical foil to encourage listeners to choose the way of God over that of Satan (*ṭāghūt;* see IDOLS AND IMAGES), speaks of fighting (q.v.) and killing as a religious activity (associated with prayer and fasting), a scriptural theme that became a way of life for the early Khārijīs, who passed sleep-deprived nights reciting the Qur'ān and long days in battle until death (Ṭabarī, *Ta'rīkh,* 3286-7), both activities understood as a means of drawing closer to God by lowering the barrier between this world and the next.

Recent studies on the Khārijī phenomenon (see Donner, Piety and eschatology; al-Jomaih, Use of the Qur'ān; Higgins, Qur'ānic exchange; Heck, Eschatological scripturalism) have raised important questions about their conception of revelation, their eschatological point of view and their desire to die in battle against the enemies of God. The reports about them as well as their own point of view as represented in their poetry (ʿAbbās, *Shiʿr al-khawārij*) suggest that their rejection of any mediating barrier between the voice of God and its reception by humans worked to create an inherently antagonistic relation between the divine and the human, in which violence against the world was the only form piety might take and in which one's death in battle against the enemies of God — lethal martyrdom — is considered a fair exchange *(shirā')* for a place in eternity absolved of the sinful impurities of this world. Martyrdom as a pure offering to God in an act of violence — the desire to die in battle — becomes an effective means of winning God's favor by disassociating oneself from the sinful ways of a Muslim community that, having established itself as a worldly power, now falls into the category of former nations that rejected the rule of God.

In pursuit of their Islamic utopia, the Khārijīs separated from what they viewed as a wayward Muslim community (Ṭabarī, *Ta'rīkh,* 518-9; trans. xx, 103-4) and pursued a campaign of terror against those who admitted sin by refusing to condemn ʿUthmān's rule, killing at random men, women and children, even ripping open the wombs of pregnant women (Ṭabarī, *Ta'rīkh,* 755-6; trans. xxi, 125) and crucifying villagers (ibid., 760; trans. 129). Such violence may reflect gang tactics (Khārijī initiates were required to kill *[istiʿrāḍ]* as a test of loyalty and, when asked by state authorities to hand over the guilty, claimed collective responsibility — e.g. Ṭabarī, *Ta'rīkh,* 3377; trans. xvii, 127: "All of us were their killers and all of us consider your and their blood to be licit"). Violence (q.v.) does, however, serve to promote protest (e.g. the American and French revolutions). Indiscriminate violence can also serve to define the boundaries of a scripturally based community (cf. the New England Puritans who in 1637 carried out genocide against the Pequot Indians in order to, in their own words, eradicate their memory from the face of the earth). Whatever the case may be, it would seem that the Khārijī conception of revelation, free of human mediation, motivated them to purify the Muslim community of its sinful turn to human authority and protection (*wilāya*, e.g. ʿUthmān, cf. Ṭabarī, *Taʾrīkh*, 516; trans. xx, 101; or ʿAbd al-Malik, cf. Ṭabarī, *Taʾrīkh*, 821-2, trans. xxi, 199). The Qurʾān had declared that no such protection should be sought in anyone other than God (Q 7:3) and in imitation of the Prophet, the early Khārijī leader, Nāfiʿ b. Azraq, declared that one should seek protection only in God (Ṭabarī, *Taʾrīkh*, 518; trans. xx, 103). Those who did not have a negative opinion of the leaders of the nascent Islamic state stood in sin for seeking protection in human beings. Sin for the Khārijīs, then, meant any positive association with human governance.

It is difficult to make sense of Khārijī activism without assuming an open-ended conception of revelation, in which the word of God continues to command and guide. Indeed, the Qurʾān depicts itself as open-ended (Q 25:32-3, see Madigan, *Qurʾān's self-image*). This does not mean a completely oral definition of the Qurʾān but a scriptural corpus that was not entirely fixed — cf. Khārijī accusations against ʿUthmān of having torn up books of the Qurʾān, a reference to his destruction of versions of the Qurʾān that differed with his official recension, to which ʿAlī responded with the claim that the decision was made after consultation (*shūrā*, a principle of human decision-making based on Q 3:159) among the Companions of the Prophet (q.v.; Ṭabarī, *Taʾrīkh*, 747; trans. xxi, 114). Notwithstanding the theological diversity in early Khārijism, its earliest form illustrates how scriptural rhetoric, originally a gloss on a community's self-understanding of survival amidst hostile forces, is transformed into a historical record of battle and bloodshed on behalf of God — scriptural rhetoric as litmus test of militancy (see Donner, Piety and eschatology, 16; cf. Ṭabarī, *Taʾrīkh*, 517; trans. xx, 102 and Ibn ʿAbd Rabbihi, *ʿIqd*, i, 217-9, esp. 219, which culminates in the report of Mirdās Abū Bilāl al-Khārijī, "There was no sect or innovating group with more penetrating insight than the Khārijīs, nor greater effort [*ijtihād*], nor more reconciled to death. Among them there was one who was stabbed, and the spear went through him, and he continued to make his way toward his killer, saying, 'I have hastened to you, O lord, that you might be pleased'"). This aspect of the Khārijī phenomenon — political re-enactment of scriptural rhetoric — remains current today. For example, Sayyid Quṭb (d. 1966) passionately sought to persuade Muslims to listen to qurʾānic recitation (see RECITATION OF THE QURʾĀN) as its first audience did and imagine themselves to be faced with the choices the first Muslims faced in meeting the enemies of the Qurʾān (e.g. *Ẓilāl*, i/3, 115-27; cf. Arjomand, Unity and diversity). While such qurʾānic commentary served Quṭb's purposes of associating his enemies, particularly the Egyptian state, with those of the Prophet, his words do show this very important connection between the experience of direct revelation and political empowerment against political injustice, whether real or perceived. Later echoes of the Khārijī mindset include the culture of martyrdom and jihād on the Islamic-Byzantine frontier during the second/eighth and third/ninth centuries (see Bonner, *Aristocratic violence;* Heck, Jihad revisited) and the contemporary phenomenon of self-sacrificial violence, also known as suicide attacks, advocated by contemporary extremist groups that use terrorist means to achieve their goals.

The interpretation of qurʾānic narrative as primarily a clash between worldly and godly rule first came to play in the assassination of ʿUthmān. Having penetrated the inner confines of his house in Medina, his assassins found him alone with a copy of the Qurʾān as his only defense (Ṭabarī, *Taʾrīkh*, 3023-5; trans. xv, 221-3). They are reported to have refrained from killing him immediately, choosing instead to debate with him about the nature of legitimate rule. For ʿUthmān, rule was legitimate in itself, having been established by God. As for his status as a Muslim ruler, ʿUthmān declares himself a believing Muslim, who, according to Islamic law, may be put to death only in three cases — apostasy, unlawful sexual relations and the killing of an innocent Muslim (see BLOODSHED), none of which ʿUthmān had committed. Most importantly, he argues, rebellion (q.v.) instead of reform — even in the name of correcting innovations made in the rulings of the Qurʾān — jeopardizes the enforcement of the law upon which political order, stability and socio-moral cohesion stand. The rebels, for their part, also couch their argument in legal and scriptural terms, although it is clear that their dissatisfaction lay in their marginalization from power and wealth at a time when the concerns of a centralizing state increasingly trumped the egalitarian ones of Islam (see Marlow, *Hierarchy*). They understood the worldly character of ʿUthmān's reign as a form of injustice, tyranny and the failure to rule competently, which put at risk the well-being of society as a whole and robbed the people of the sound government necessary for peace and prosperity. Quoting Q 5:33-4, which calls for the death of those who sow corruption on earth, the rebels labeled ʿUthmān as a brigand or highway robber (see THEFT) who had disrupted the peace, terrorized the innocent and deprived people of their right to life and unhindered pursuit of their affairs. In short, ʿUthmān represented for them worldly rule as opposed to the godly rule called for by the Qurʾān and followed under the leadership of the Prophet.

Notwithstanding the connection this account has to later legal discussions over the laws of rebellion (*aḥkām al-bughāt;* see Abou El Fadl, *Rebellion*), it does demonstrate the potential of the Qurʾān as a tool of protest against the state, regardless of the actual complaints of the opposition. This is further illustrated in the rebellions of the Umayyad period (41-132/661-750). The reasons behind the revolt of al-Mukhtār (d. 67/687) may have included vengeance (q.v.) for the blood of the family of the Prophet (q.v.; i.e. Ḥusayn's death at Karbala; see also PEOPLE OF THE HOUSE) and defense of the weak (manumitted slaves; see SLAVES AND SLAVERY) but it was announced as a summons to rule by the book of God and sunna (q.v.) of the Prophet (Ṭabarī, *Taʾrīkh*, 607, 609-20, 633; trans. xx, 191, 194, 217), in addition to messianic claims (the Islamic *mahdī* also featured prominently in early rebellions but is not a qurʾānic term). Similarly, the rebellion of Ibn al-Ashʿath (d. 82/701), while motivated by the state's treatment of the army under his command, resorted to the Qurʾān as a cloak of legitimacy. The first oath of allegiance given to Ibn al-Ashʿath by his soldiers is set alongside complaints against incompetent leadership, unfair distribution of spoils, disavowal of the arch-representative of state concerns, al-Ḥajjāj (d. 95/714), and support of Ibn al-Ashʿath's effort to expel him as governor of Iraq (Ṭabarī, *Taʾrīkh*, 1054-5; trans. xxiii, 5-6), but the second one includes a summons to the book of God and sunna of the Prophet, disavowal of the imāms of error and struggle against those who violate what is sacred (ibid., 1058; trans. xxiii, 8).

Finally, although colored by the concerns of a settled and culturally diverse society (see Sharon, *Revolt*), the ʿAbbāsid revolution that brought an end to Umayyad rule was ideologically inspired by an oath of allegiance to the Hāshimī family in terms of fidelity to the book of God and sunna of the Prophet along with the chosen one *(al-riḍā)* from the family of the messenger of God (Ṭabarī, *Taʾrīkh,* 1989, 1993; trans. xxviii, 97, 101).

This invocation of the Qurʾān by rebels against the state encouraged an official response that properly constituted rule was part of God's design for humankind, even apart from the prophetic heritage. To do this, rulers and their ideologues turned primarily to the genre known as "mirrors-for-princes" to account for the existence of the Islamic state. In short, non-qurʾānic arguments were advanced to demonstrate that political rule was a necessary part of the Muslim responsibility to meet the qurʾānic directive to be prosperous in contrast to former nations.

With no clear outline of political organization in the Qurʾān and ḥadīth, early Muslim rulers — Umayyad and ʿAbbāsid alike — were compelled to construct non-qurʾānic arguments for political rule: as divinely determined *(jabr)* and thus worthy of obedience in the case of the Umayyads (see al-Qāḍī, Religious foundation) or as the effective agent of a just *(ʿadl)* and harmonious association *(iʾtilāf)* in the case of the ʿAbbāsids (see Heck, Law). Such non-qurʾānic arguments for rule did, however, draw widely upon qurʾānic material, as well as reports of early Arabo-Islamic history. It was, then, this state-sponsored genre of literature that did much to bring the revealed and non-revealed into a single epistemological framework of Islamic civilization, e.g. al-Māwardī, *Naṣīḥat al-mulūk,* i.e. "advice to rulers." This title echoes the advisory mission of the prophets of Q 7, thereby suggesting that it and similar works offered to the rulers of the day — like prophets to former nations — wisdom (q.v.) that led to prosperity. In his introduction, the author claims that he is right in drawing upon a variety of sources of knowledge, both revealed and non-revealed, even the wisdom of former nations, to show the legitimacy of political rule:

> We are not, however, singular in our use of our own ideas in our book, nor do we rely in anything we say on our own opinion *(hawā)* but justify *(naḥtajj)* what we say by the revealed word of God *(qawl Allāh al-munazzal),* the majestic and exalted, and the reports of his messenger *(aqāwīl rasūlihi)* that narrate his practices *(sunan)* and precedents *(āthār),* and then the ways of kings of old *(siyar al-mulūk al-awwalīn),* past imāms and the rightly-guided caliphs, [along with the wisdom of] ancient philosophers *(al-ḥukamāʾ al-mutaqaddimīn)* of former nations *(al-umam al-khāliya)* and past days, since their words are worthy to be imitated, their traces to be followed and their model to be emulated (Māwardī, *Naṣīḥat al-mulūk,* 46).

Human wisdom, then, could be harnessed for the revealed goal of socio-political prosperity.

Similarly, the Umayyad al-Walīd II (r. 125-6/743-4), in a letter designating his two sons to succeed him, argued that prophecy and rule are two divinely ordained institutions (Ṭabarī, *Taʾrīkh,* 1757-64; trans. xxvi, 106-15), suggesting that the ruling office of caliph is part of God's plan in its own right (comparable in that sense to pre-modern European arguments for a divine right of kings) and drawing out in detail, including qurʾānic citation, the reasons for considering rule a necessary pillar of socio-political prosperity, not least of which is its function as effective agent of legal order, both religious and public (ibid., 1758; trans. xxvi, 108; for Umayyad use of qurʾānic material in state letters, see al-Qāḍī, Impact of the Qurʾān; cf. Dähne, Qurʾānic wording).

For their part, the ʿAbbāsids drew upon the Sasanian heritage to articulate a theory of political authority *(sulṭān)* and sovereignty (q.v.; *mulk*), understood, along with the Qurʾān, as the basis of legitimate Islamic rule. Long before the appearance of Islam, the Sasanians coined the adage that "there can be no rule without religion (q.v.) and no religion without rule" *(lā mulka illā bi-dīn wa-lā dīna illā bi-mulk)*. It is this fundamental link between religion and rule that informs the testimony of the ʿAbbāsid al-Manṣūr (r. 136-58/754-75) to his son and successor al-Mahdī (r. 158-69/775-85), particularly its emphasis on strong rule as a combination of political authority *(sulṭān)* and holy writ *(qurʾān)*. He says that for the protection of authoritative rule, God has ordered in the Qurʾān double the penalty on those who stir up corruption in the land (quoting Q 5:33), and that sovereignty is the strong rope of God, a firm bond and the unshakeable religion of God (in reference to Q 2:256 and Q 3:103); in short, he encourages his son to protect and defend an Islamic sovereignty as buttressed by the revealed law (Ṭabarī, *Taʾrīkh*, 447; trans. xxix, 153-4). The idea of the essential role of political sovereignty in ordering the affairs of the world so suited the tastes and needs of ʿAbbāsid caliphs that the idea became current that God worked to arrange worldly order by political power *(sulṭān)* even more so than by revelation (*qurʾān*, e.g. Qudāma b. Jaʿfar, *Siyāsa min kitāb al-kharāj*, 56; Māwardī, *Adab al-dīn*, 169: *inna llāh la-yazaʿu bi-l-sulṭān akthar mimmā yazaʿu bi-l-Qurʾān*). That idle and rebellious humans had to be coerced by a strong power to live in political order was considered by the ruling powers through the ʿAbbāsid period and beyond as essential to God's designs of ordering his creation, willingly or not (i.e. either out of longing or fear, Q 21:90), in function of his quality of subduing *(qahhār)* all forces to his will (e.g. Q 12:39; for this connection of God's coercive power to political sovereignty, see Heck, Law). This attempt to link religious and political authority is nowhere more clear than in the chapter of early ʿAbbāsid history known as the Inquisition (q.v.; *al-miḥna*), in which elevation of the human authority of al-Maʾmūn (r. 198-218/813-33) depended on reduction of the Qurʾān to a created, rather than uncreated, status (see Nawas, *al-Maʾmūn;* cf. Cooperson, *Biography*, 24-69; see CREATEDNESS OF THE QURʾĀN).

The possibility of human rule alongside the Qurʾān

The themes discussed in the previous section recur in various ways throughout Islamic history, especially the recognition of the need for non-revealed sources of decision-making in the political arena — i.e. how to understand human judgment *(raʾy)* as an Islamically sanctioned agent of political organization, as well as pre-Islamic local custom *(ʿurf)* in public administration, like methods of tax-collection, that Muslim rulers had left intact (see POLL TAX). It was not only a matter of granting a share in Islamic rule to the human intellect *(ʿaql)*, which, in "mirrors-for-princes" works, was seen as the partner of religion in preserving justice and socio-political prosperity, but also of claiming, as works of jurisprudence did, that Islam did not abrogate all pre-Islamic custom (see ABROGATION), which was given a legal value of its own (e.g. *al-sharʿ min qablinā*, a source of law used to justify the claim that the five principles *[panchasila]* at the heart of Indonesian political organization not only approximate but actually meet the requirements of Islam's revealed law; see Mujiburrahman, Indonesia), not to mention a panoply of other jurisprudential devices, such as discretion *(istiḥsān),* that allowed rulers to enact law without insult to the final authority of the Qur᾽ān.

Explications centered upon the question of human judgment *(ra᾽y).* Was it to be permitted in areas concerning public good *(maṣlaḥa)* about which the Qur᾽ān was silent? At stake was not only the relation of the divine to human society but also that of political to religious authority. Given the Qur᾽ān's reminder to carry out God's design for creation, the Muslims' centuries-long struggle to formulate rule has had to maneuver between social recognition of the need for and benefit of human rule and scriptural recognition that all rule belongs ultimately to God. While a host of factors are at play in conceptions of rule, specific to Islam is this interplay between the social and scriptural (see Jadʿān, *Miḥna,* esp. 291 f.). The rule of the last Shah of Iran, for example, was contested partly on grounds of his preference for the social (i.e. the Persian heritage of monarchy) over the scriptural (identified in the Iranian case with Shīʿī notions of clerical jurisdiction over public affairs; see Arjomand, Shiʿite jurisprudence; and Calder, Accommodation and revolution). Likewise, in Egypt, Anwar Sadat's alliance with the West clashed violently with increasingly bold notions among Islamists of a sovereignty *(ḥākimiyya)* that belonged to God alone (see Faraj, *Farīḍa,* trans. esp. 1-34).

The tension between the social and scriptural cannot, however, be limited to the post-colonial clash between secular nationalism and religious fundamentalism, since it was recognized very early that political governance cannot stand on the texts of revelation alone. Among the first to treat this question was Ibn al-Muqaffaʿ (d. 139/756) in an epistle to the ʿAbbāsid al-Manṣūr (r. 136-58/754-75). To establish the legal authority of political leadership *(ra᾽y al-imām),* Ibn al-Muqaffaʿ (*Risāla,* 120-2), a state official and convert to Islam, had to navigate between two groups: (1) those claiming to be released from obedience to the ruler when it involved disobedience to God (i.e. a political ruling contrary to scripture; *la ṭāʿata lil-makhlūq fī maʿṣiyat al-khāliq*), a position essentially placing sovereign authority *(sulṭān)* in the hands of the people by awarding them the choice to decide which ruler to obey and which of his commands to follow, in the end rendering all equals *(naẓā᾽ir)* in political decision-making with destructive consequences for rule itself (a likely reference to the Khārijī position, resurrected by Sayyid Quṭb, see below); and (2) those advocating complete submission to the ruler in all matters without concern for obedience or disobedience to God, with the claim that the ruler alone is privileged with knowledge of and competence in such things (a position essentially placing the command of the ruler above that of the revealed text, reformulated by Ayatollah Khomeini in contemporary Iran, see below). To resolve these two positions — the first representing the scriptural, the second the social — Ibn al-Muqaffaʿ drew an important distinction which was to echo in Islamic politics through the centuries: that the ruler is not to be obeyed in anything that goes against clear scriptural directives in the Qur᾽ān and sunna, such as prayer, fasting, pilgrimage (q.v.), penal sanctions *(ḥudūd)* or dietary restrictions but must be obeyed in all his rulings where no scriptural precedent *(athar)* exists.

Although treated extensively by theorists in the classical period, such as Abū Yūsuf (d. 182/798), Qudāma b. Jaʿfar (d. 337/948) and al-Māwardī (d. 450/1058), this question remains a concern today. On the

Sunnī side, Yūsuf al-Qaraḍāwī — a Qatar-based *muftī* with associations to the Muslim Brotherhood — argues, like Ibn al-Muqaffaʿ, that God mercifully did not disclose clear and decisive rulings for all human affairs, an action that would have rendered human intelligence useless (Qaraḍāwī, *Siyāsa,* 72). Indeed, most of Islamic law requires human judgment, while the clear and decisive rulings *(qaṭʿiyya)* of revelation are very limited (Qaraḍāwī, *Siyāsa,* 77). Thus, in matters where no revealed text exists, the governing ruler can apply his judgment *(raʾy al-ḥākim al-siyāsī)* for the sake of the public good *(al-maṣāliḥ al-mursala)*. His argument, an explanation of the fifth of the twenty principles expounded by Ḥasan al-Bannā (d. 1949), the founder of the Muslim Brotherhood, demonstrates that there is an area of life, namely governance, that God has left to humans and that can thus change with circumstance and custom. The result is a division of the world's affairs into religious ones *(al-umūr al-taʿabbudiyya)* that are ruled by the revealed texts and customary ones *(al-umūr al-ʿādiya)* that fall to human judgment. He does, however, part ways with Ibn al-Muqaffaʿ — who justified human judgment alongside revelation by awarding a privileged status to the ruler's intellect *(ʿaql al-imām)* — by binding valid use of human judgment to the consultation *(shūrā)* of religious scholars, whose immersion in the study of revealed law *(al-sharīʿa)* guarantees that the ruler's judgment conforms with its intentions (*maqāṣid,* an important concept in modern Islamic political thought; see Heck, Religious renewal). Thus does al-Qaraḍāwī offer an updated version of traditional Sunnī jurisprudence and its use of analogical reasoning *(qiyās)* to apply revelation to political problems with no textual precedent: Worldly rule, although informed by human judgment, remains subordinate to godly authority.

Strikingly, al-Qaraḍāwī, using Q 4:60-5, views human judgment — illuminated by revealed texts — as the means for reconciling differences among Muslims, whereas in the Qurʾān it was the book above all that arbitrated human differences. He claims, like Ibn al-Muqaffaʿ, to be navigating between two extremes (Qaraḍāwī, *Siyāsa,* 49), those who say the ruler's judgment abrogates divine rulings *(aḥkām sharʿiyya)* and those who refuse to acknowledge any human rule not explicitly designated by a revealed text. Rather, for al-Qaraḍāwī (Qaraḍāwī, *Siyāsa,* 63-7), although different degrees of correct judgment exist, there is a need for human judgment — no matter how much one has memorized textual precedents *(aḥādīth wa-āthār)* — for the sake of governance and justice *(idārat shuʾūn al-bilād wa-tadbīr amr al-ʿibād wa-iqāmat al-ʿadl baynahum)* since Islam is both a religious and political order *(iqāmat al-dīn wa-siyāsat al-dunyā)*.

Similarly, while couching his words in qurʾānic verse, Ayatollah Khomeini, the first supreme leader of the Islamic Republic of Iran, argues for governance by the book as determined by the authority of the Shīʿī jurist (*wilāyat al-faqīh;* see Khomeini, Islamic government). Another leading cleric at the time of the Islamic revolution, Ayatollah Montazeri, drew a distinction, like al-Qaraḍāwī, between religious ruling *(hukumat-i sharʿi)* and the customary ruling *(hukumat-i ʿurfi)* — the difference being that Montazeri judges non-religious rulings to be non-binding without the endorsement of the jurists who represent the hidden but infallible Imām of Twelver Shīʿism (see Arjomand, Shiʿite jurisprudence), while al-Qaraḍāwī ties the validity of such rulings to the intentions of the revealed law. In fulfillment of this theory, the Constitution of the Islamic Republic of Iran, while replete with qurʾānic citation, essentially puts all authority in the hands of the jurists and Khomeini in particular, as spelled out in principles 5 and 107 (see Mayer, Fundamentalist impact; cf. Abū l-Fawāris, *Risāla,* for an early Ismāʿīlī use of Islamic scripture to justify infallible human leadership). In one of his last acts before his death in 1988, Khomeini amended the Constitution to further enhance the authority of the human, even if privileged, judgment of the jurist over all affairs of state and society.

In contrast, elevation of the Qurʾān over human affairs has been promoted in post-colonial times by the Muslim Brotherhood. The Muslim Brotherhood's political thought and activity, since its founding in 1928, ranges from militant fundamentalism to participation in elected politics (for their history, see the pioneering but now limited work of Mitchell, *Society of Muslim Brothers*). Moreover, other, more violent, contemporary extremist groups that use violence to achieve their goals (such as al-Jamāʿa l-Islāmiyya and al-Jihād, which latter merged in 1998 with al-Qāʿida) were inspired partly by Muslim Brotherhood rhetoric and its promotion of a qurʾānically shaped society, as witnessed in the writings of the group's founder, Ḥasan al-Bannā (see *Five tracts*), and its most celebrated figure, Sayyid Quṭb (see Haim, Sayyid Quṭb; Haddad, Qurʾānic justification; Carré, *Mystique,* 342-3 [trans. text on the Islamic economic and political model, ad Q 59:7], 325 [on the *shūrā*]). The writings of these two figures promote a qurʾānically-based divine sovereignty for the sake of a greater egalitarianism which, in the writings of Quṭb, takes a revolutionary form against the perceived tyranny of Nasserist rule (i.e. the pan-Arabist and left-leaning socialist ideology of the Egyptian president Gamal Abdel Nasser, r. 1956-70). The goal was socio-political coherence and identity — especially against post-colonial secularizing/westernizing tendencies in Egypt and the Islamic world — through scriptural adherence.

Drawing upon the work of the Islamist ideologue and founder of the Pakistan-based Jamāʿat-e Islāmī, Abū l-Aʿlā l-Mawdūdī (whose formulation of an Islamic political constitution contributed to the Islamization of Pakistani politics; see, for example, his *First principles,* parts of which became law under Ziyā l-Ḥaqq's military dictatorship in the 1980s; for the legacy of Mawdūdī, see Zaman, *Ulama,* 87-110), Quṭb insisted that sovereignty belongs to God alone (*ʿAdāla,* trans. 105). In general, he does not seek to accommodate human judgment but envisions a fundamental clash between revealed sovereignty *(ḥākimiyya)* and non-revealed rule, which he labels as human ignorance (q.v.; *jāhiliyya;* Quṭb, *ʿAdāla,* trans. 107; see also AGE OF IGNORANCE). Human interpretation of scripture and thus the possibility of human rule must be accordingly reduced; religion *(dīn)* becomes the system *(niẓām)* of rule (Quṭb, *ʿAdāla,* trans. 110). In echo of Q 5:48-50, frequent references are made to God's program *(manhaj)* and way (*shirʿa,* cf. Ṭabarī, *Tafsīr,* iii, 246, for a discussion of the scope of this way, i.e. whether in reference to the many ways revealed by God to different communities or the way of the Muslim community specifically, etc.), the conclusion being that association of Islam with any human system, such as democracy, socialism, monarchy, etc., is entirely unacceptable (Quṭb, *ʿAdāla,* trans. 108, 112). Rulers are only to be obeyed to the extent that they themselves submit to the sovereignty of God and apply his revealed law (Quṭb, *ʿAdāla,* trans. 113-4), departure from which deprives them of the right to obedience (Quṭb, *ʿAdāla,* trans. 114): "... hearing and obeying is conditional upon following the book of God Almighty." The result is a marked restriction on the employment of human judgment in rule (Quṭb, *ʿAdāla,* trans. 114-5): "... he becomes a ruler only by the absolutely free choice of the Muslims [a reference to Mawdūdī's idea of theo-democracy]... after that his authority derives from his undertaking to enforce the revealed law of God without claiming for himself any right to initiate legislation by an authority of his own." Consultation *(shūrā),* limited to those learned in religion, does, however, remain a principle of Islamic governance (Quṭb, *ʿAdāla,* trans. 116). Also, in echo of Ibn al-Muqaffaʿ, permission is given to the leader whose authority is based on the revealed law of God to make new decrees for the sake of the common good, provided such decrees do not violate a revealed text *(naṣṣ),* e.g. the imposition of taxes not mentioned in the Qurʾān, which, however, are not to be collected for maintaining state institutions but in service of a greater social justice in line with qurʾānic principles (Quṭb, *ʿAdāla,* trans. 119; see TAXATION).

From such pointed rhetoric has emerged a call for jihād against all worldly rule, epitomized in the work of ʿAbd al-Salām Faraj (d. 1982), who was executed with the four assassins of Egypt's president, Anwar Sadat, killed after he had signed a peace treaty with Israel. Faraj's now famous treatise, *al-Farīḍa al-ghāʾiba,* "The neglected duty," begins by quoting Q 57:16, which calls for the submission of believing hearts (see HEART) to divinely revealed truth in contrast to former nations, whose hearts had hardened against the book of God. He claimed that the Egyptian state had come to be ruled by laws of unbelief, a reference to the adoption of western law (see Faraj, *Farīḍa,* trans. 162), making of its rulers apostates deserving of death. What is new here is not the insistence on an Islamic state as a necessary condition for the performance of God's precepts or the identification of Muslim rulers with the pre-Islamic Age of Ignorance but rather the intensely militant rejection of any humanly tinged rule. In the manner of the first Khārijīs, Faraj quotes Q 5:44: "Those who do not rule by what God has revealed are infidels," as prelude to his identification of the Muslim rulers of his day with the Mongols, who ruled without sufficient attention to Islamic law (Faraj, *Farīḍa,* trans. 167-8). There is simply no room for human governance in Faraj's treatise but an insurmountable gap between political rulings *(al-siyāsāt al-mulkiyya)* and qurʾānic rulings (*aḥkām;* Faraj, *Farīḍa,* trans. 49, commenting on Ibn Kathīr's exegesis of Q 5:50).

There is thus, for Faraj, no action — not charity, not participation in elected politics, not the Islamic education of society — that can take precedence over jihād (understood by him solely as armed struggle) against worldly rulers, for the worldly must be subdued, the godly exalted. Given that human governance is a contradiction in terms for this militant brand of Islamism, accommodation is impossible. War, not merely Islam, is the solution, and Faraj devotes the latter half of his work to Ibn Taymiyya's position on jihād. Picking up the theme of Q 9 (Sūrat al-Tawba, "Repentance"), Faraj declares that in the Islamic age, worldly power must be brought to an end not through natural phenomena, as God has done in the case of former nations, but through the armed struggle of belief against unbelief (Faraj, *Farīḍa,* trans. 162, 190). In other words, it has now become the duty of Muslims to act on behalf of God and annihilate those nations that fail to heed his message. Seen in that light, it is hardly surprising that

Sadat's assassins claimed to have killed Pharaoh.

In light of Islamist esteem for the writings of Ibn Taymiyya (d. 728/1328), it is necessary to ask how closely his thought corresponds to Islamist goals today. He does give an elevated status to scripture as guarantor of Muslim identity after the fall of the caliphate to the Mongols in 656/1258; but, unlike Faraj, he was a jurist who worked within the framework of traditional Islamic jurisprudence. As will be outlined, his post-Mongol protest, unlike Faraj's post-colonial one, was not against human rule per se but communal heterodoxy that he viewed as a threat to the unity of a Muslim community bereft of the office of caliph.

In his most famous work, *al-Siyāsa al-sharʿiyya,* Ibn Taymiyya recognizes the social dimension of rule, arguing that political office *(wilāya)* is a religious necessity (*Siyāsa,* 172-80) since the social chaos resulting from its absence would prevent people from performing the precepts of the religion. He supports his position philosophically by claiming that only via human congregation *(ijtimāʿ)* can human welfare be attained, since humans are mutually dependent for their survival, and that human congregation most effectively serves the good when it is ordered under and enforced by political rule (Ibn Taymiyya, *Siyāsa,* 172-3). Ibn Taymiyya thus affirms the necessity of human rule even when not in complete conformity to the divine will. His model of public administration, while aspiring to justice as based upon the Qur᾿ān and sunna (*al-ʿadl alladhī dalla ʿalayhi al-kitāb wa-l-sunna;* Ibn Taymiyya, *Siyāsa,* 13), is not based on scripture alone. The work begins by quoting Q 57:25, which states that God sent down not only the book and balance (see WEIGHTS AND MEASURES), by which humans might act in accordance with the divine will, but also iron as a mighty power for the benefit of humankind, i.e. rule as the effective agent by which human society in its diversity might be made, even coerced, to live in political harmony.

The work's self-stated goal is to explain Q 4:58-9, which calls for justice in arbitrating human affairs and obedience to those holding command *(ūlī l-amri).* Ibn Taymiyya argues on the basis of qur᾿ānic citation for a complementary notion of God's guidance, embodied in scripture, and political rule. Hence, although he draws heavily upon the Qur᾿ān and the sunna, his words are directed to state officials (e.g. provincial governors, tax-collectors, military commanders, state ministers and secretaries, etc.; Ibn Taymiyya, *Siyāsa,* 5). While revelation is meant to shape the socio-political order, the qualifications for election *(ikhtiyār)* to office are ambiguous. They essentially boil down to two criteria (Ibn Taymiyya, *Siyāsa,* 12-4): (1) strength *(quwwa),* meaning effectiveness, e.g. in war, and (2) trust *(amāna),* meaning pious commitment to govern justly in accordance with revelation *(sharʿ).* Since, however, these two criteria so rarely coexist in a single person, effectiveness may trump pious commitment, depending on the office in question, making it preferable to appoint an effective military commander or judge even if he is personally immoral (*fājir,* Ibn Taymiyya, *Siyāsa,* 14, 18) or does what the Prophet has forbidden (*yaʿmal mā yunkiruhu al-nabī,* ibid., 15) — in other words, offends against divine revelation. Ibn Taymiyya cites in support of this examples from the first community of Muslims and a saying of the Prophet (*Siyāsa,* 15), "Indeed God supports this religion with an immoral man."

Ibn Taymiyya's call to jihād is not, then, aimed against impious individuals entrusted with the governance of Muslim society. Constituted authority, even if straying from Islamic perfection, is validated by its end: social harmony and human welfare. Jihād is directed not at political rule but heterodox Islam, particularly the Nuṣayrī sect. Ibn Taymiyya's concern with Mongol rule must be seen within the context of the ritual pluralism of post-Mongol Islam, which had long existed in Islam but became a more significant concern in the absence of the caliphate. For him, the Mongol invasions were providential (Ibn Taymiyya, *Rasā'il*, 53 f.), a test by which God separates hypocrites from true believers, as he tested the first Muslims by external attack (illustrated in Q 3:152; again, the attempt to relate political developments to qur'ānic narrative). Such external hostility was, he claimed, to be welcomed as part of the divine plan to expose Muslim groups given to ritual innovation *(bid'a)*, which posed the greatest threat to the religion, making it necessary to identify not religiously imperfect political authorities but ritually heterodox Muslims, along with infidels *(kuffār)*, as legitimate objects of jihād (Ibn Taymiyya, *Siyāsa*, 131; id., *Fiqh al-jihād*, 100). Reading this concern alongside his vision of political rule as described in the previous paragraph, it is possible to conclude that the use of Ibn Taymiyya by radical Islam today grossly distorts his thought, which must be seen as a legal development aiming to articulate the theory of jihād anew in the midst of altered social circumstances where Islamic identity was no longer imagined and guaranteed in terms of political authority but by means of ritual and communal practice. The main thrust behind his work is not eschatological violence against worldly power in witness to the rule of God symbolized by Islamic scripture, nor is it political rebellion against constituted authority in the name of an Islamic rule based exclusively on scripture, but rather the unity of religious and communal identity in the face of its own ritually pluralistic membership (see Heck, Jihad revisited).

The Qur'ān has been drawn upon no less effectively in support of democracy and even secularism (see Esposito and Voll, Islam's democratic essence). New concepts of authority, based upon an individual's encounter with scripture *(ijtihād)* apart from traditional authority, are at play in the modernizing exegesis of such figures as Muḥammad 'Abduh (d. 1905), who was himself aware of the political consequences of his work (see Jomier, La revue "al-'Orwa al-Wothqa"). His tabling of tradition, while meant to spur a legal and religious dynamism necessary to meet the challenges of modernity, widened the scope of qur'ānic interpretation for political ends, opening the door to both fundamentalist and reformist uses of Islamic scripture. The contemporary use of the Qur'ān by fundamentalist Islam having been given above, here the reformist point of view will be illustrated by the writings of three Egyptian thinkers.

Amidst much controversy (Enayat, *Modern political thought*, 62-8), 'Alī 'Abd al-Rāziq (d. 1966) argued in *al-Islām wa-uṣūl al-ḥukm* (135-64, chapter 3 of book 2, entitled *Risāla lā ḥukm, dīn lā dawlā*) that the mission of the Prophet was limited to a message (i.e. to bear good news and to warn, citing several qur'ānic verses to that effect, e.g. Q 17:105; 24:54; 25:56; 33:45-6) and did not include the creation of a polity: Muḥammad may have struggled to defend his message, even using force to do so, but never did he undertake to coerce people into a polity, there being no evidence for such — 'Abd al-Rāziq challenges his audience to find any — between the two covers of the Qur'ān or in the sunna. Since governance is a worldly affair (here 'Abd al-Rāziq inverts traditional arguments for religious supervision of worldly affairs), God has given it to human minds to manage their worldly affairs according to what they see best in light of their knowledge, interests and tendencies. ʿAbd al-Rāziq certainly recognizes the necessity of government (on the basis of Q 43:32 and Q 5:48) but denies that it is an article of faith or that it is limited to the forms known to Islamic history — caliphate and despotic government in his opinion. Even if the installation of the state is viewed as an act of political wisdom, Islamic ideals can still be guaranteed by the spiritual message of the Prophet and not control of the state (Enayat, *Modern political thought,* 68).

ʿAbd al-Rāziq's ideas came at a chaotic moment for Muslim identity — the collapse of the Ottoman empire and the height of colonial domination along with largely unsuccessful attempts to develop a pan-Islamic institution to deal with Muslim affairs globally. His thought must be seen as an attempt to facilitate an Islamic reconciliation with the strongly modernizing tendencies of his day. In contrast, the writings of Muḥammad Saʿīd al-ʿAshmāwī (b. 1932) are a counter to the increasingly bold fundamentalism of a post-colonial Egypt in search of national identity and civil society. He maintains in *al-Islām al-siyāsi* (175-92), against fundamentalist condemnations of Egyptian rule as apostate, that Egyptian law is in point of fact in full harmony with the principles of the revealed law of Islam. For him, the paucity of legal norms enshrined in the Qurʾān — only 200 of some 6,000 verses have a legal character, he claims — supports the original meaning of *sharīʿa* at the time of qurʾānic revelation as a way and not as a collection of legal details. It has thus been left to the Egyptian state to work out a rule of law, and as a high-ranking judge, al-ʿAshmāwī displays his intimate knowledge of Egyptian law, which, he argues, in no way contradicts the dictates of the Qurʾān. He says at one point that the Islamist position that truly Islamic rule must be limited to the book of God confuses revelation *(al-sharīʿa),* i.e. the qurʾānic way, with law *(fiqh),* which is a process by which jurists and judges apply their own efforts of judgment *(ijtihād)* to legal matters. Indeed, for al-ʿAshmāwī, Islamist exploitation of the Qurʾān for political ends is a danger for Islam and should cease since Egyptian law has not been tainted by any innovation *(bidʿa)* but remains consistent with Islamic revelation.

Finally, Muhammad Khalaf Allāh (d. 1997) presses the qurʾānic theme of consultation (*shūrā,* citing Q 3:159) in *al-Qurʾān wa-l-dawla* (55-79) as the Islamic mode of political decision-making. Drawing on Muḥammad ʿAbduh, Khalaf Allāh insists that those in authority (*ūlū l-amr,* cf. Q 4:59) should be identified with those to whom the Muslim community has entrusted responsibility for making laws and overseeing the governance of society. But this should not be done, however, in the manner of divinely constructed offices held by figures claiming a personal right to rule, but by political officials chosen by the community — and thus removable by the community — who govern not religious but worldly affairs after the manner of the Prophet and his Companions, namely through consultation (a position reminiscent of the Indonesian Nurcholish Madjid's idea that the oneness of God *[tawḥīd]* should actually prevent Muslims from viewing the state in sacred terms; see Madjid, Islamic roots of pluralism). In this light, religious leaders have no inherent right to this legislative role. Their task — as was the Prophet's — is to explain beliefs *(ʿaqāʾid),* worship *(ʿibādāt)* and the norms of social affairs *(muʿāmalāt)* but they, like the Prophet, enjoy no mandate to legislate worldly affairs on the basis of revelation.

Khalaf Allāh, it should be added, is perhaps most known for his employment of literary methodology in scriptural exegesis, by which he argues that the Qurʾān is not a record of historical facts (see INIMITABILITY; HISTORY AND THE QURʾĀN) but an exhortation to the Islamic faith (see EXEGESIS OF THE QURʾĀN: EARLY MODERN AND CONTEMPORARY). His entire oeuvre, then, confirms the thesis that Muslim recognition of the role of human (i.e. non-revealed) decision-making in the political organization of society's affairs follows closely upon willingness to allow human interpretation of the Qurʾān. It is thus the possibility and parameters of exegesis (see EXEGESIS OF THE QURʾĀN: CLASSICAL AND MEDIEVAL), as debated across Islamic history from ʿAlī b. Abī Ṭālib to Muḥammad Khalaf Allāh, that stand at the heart of politics and the Qurʾān.

Paul L. Heck

Bibliography

Primary: I. ʿAbbās (ed.), *Shiʿr al-khawārij*, Amman 1982[4]; A. ʿAbd al-Rāziq, *al-Islām wa-uṣūl al-ḥukm*, ed. M. Ḥaqqī, Beirut 1966 (reprint); Abū l-Fawāris Aḥmad b. Yaʿqūb, *Risāla fī l-imāma. The political doctrine of the Ismāʿīlīs*, ed. and trans. S.N. Makārim, Delmar, NY 1977; Abū Ḥayyān al-Tawḥīdī, *al-Imtāʿ wa-l-muʾānasa*, ed. A. Amīn and A. al-Zayn, 3 vols. in 1, Beirut [1970]; al-ʿĀmirī, Abū l-Ḥasan Muḥammad b. Yūsuf, *Kitāb al-Iʿlām bi-manāqib al-Islām*, ed. A. ʿAbd al-Ḥamīd Ghurāb, Cairo 1967; M.S. al-ʿAshmāwī, *al-Islām al-siyāsī*, Cairo 1987; Ḥ. al-Bannā, *Five tracts*, trans. C. Wendell, Berkeley 1978; Bukhārī, *Ṣaḥīḥ;* M.ʿI. Darwaza, *al-Dustūr al-qurʾānī fī shuʾūn al-ḥayāt*, Cairo 1956; ʿA. Faraj, *al-Farīḍa al-ghāʾiba*, ed. J. al-Bannā, Cairo 1984; trans. J.J.G. Jansen, *The neglected duty. The creed of Sadat's assassins and Islamic resurgence in the Middle East*, New York 1986; Ibn ʿAbd Rabbihi, *al-ʿIqd al-farīd*, ed. A. Amīn et al., 7 vols., Cairo 1949-65; Ibn Abī Shayba, Abū Bakr ʿAbdallāh b. Muḥammad, *al-Muṣannaf*, ed. S. Laḥḥām, 9 vols., Beirut 1989; Ibn Isḥāq, *Sīra*, ed. al-Ṣaqqā et al.; Ibn al-Muqaffaʿ, *Risāla fī l-ṣaḥāba*, in M. Kurd ʿAlī (ed.), *Rasāʾil al-bulaghāʾ*, Cairo 1946[2], 118-34; Ibn Saʿd, *Ṭabaqāt;* Ibn Taymiyya, *Fiqh al-jihād*, ed. Z. Shafīq al-Kabbī, Beirut 1992; id., *al-Siyāsa al-sharʿiyya fī iṣlāḥ al-rāʿī wa-l-raʿiyya*, Cairo 1951; id., *Thalāth rasāʾil fī l-jihād*, ed. M. Abū Ṣuʿaylīk and I. al-ʿAlī, Amman 1993; Ikhwān al-Ṣafā, *Rasāʾil*, Qumm 1985; al-Juwaynī, Abū l-Maʿālī ʿAbd al-Malik, *Ghiyāth al-umam fī ltiyāth al-ẓulam*, Alexandria 1990; M. Khalaf Allāh, *al-Qurʾān wa-l-dawla*, Cairo 1973; R. Khomeini, Islamic government, in H. Algar (trans.), *Islam and revolution. Writings and declarations of Imam Khomeini*, Berkeley 1981; N. Madjid, Islamic roots of modern pluralism. Indonesian experiences, in *Studia Islamika* 1 (1994), 55-77; Māwardī, *al-Aḥkām al-sulṭāniyya wa-l-wilāyat al-dīniyya*, al-Manṣūra 1989; Eng. trans. A. Yate, *The laws of Islamic governance*, London 1996; id., *Aʿlām al-nubuwwa*, ed. Kh.ʿA. al-ʿAkk, Beirut 1994; id., *Kitāb Adab al-dīn wa-l-dunyā*, ed. M.F. Abū Bakr, Cairo 1988; id., *Naṣīḥat al-mulūk*, ed. Kh.M. Khiḍr, Kuwait 1993; id., *Tashīl al-naẓar wa-taʿjīl al-ẓafar fī akhlāq al-malik wa-siyāsat al-mulk*, ed. R. al-Sayyid, Beirut 1997; A.A. Mawdūdī, *First principles of the Islamic state*, trans. Kh. Ahmad, Lahore 1978 (reprint); al-Mubarrad, Abū l-ʿAbbās Muḥammad b. Yazīd, *al-Kāmil*, ed. W. Wright, 2 vols., Leipzig 1864; Mujāhid, *Tafsīr;* Muqātil, *Tafsīr;* Muslim, *Ṣaḥīḥ;* Y. al-Qaraḍāwī, *al-Siyāsa al-sharʿiyya fī ḍawʾ nuṣūṣ al-sharīʿa wa maqāṣidihā*, Cairo 1998; Qudāma b. Jaʿfar, *al-Siyāsa min kitāb al-kharāj wa-ṣināʿat al-kitāba*, ed. M. al-Ḥiyārī, Amman 1981; S. Quṭb, *al-ʿAdāla al-ijtimāʿiyya fī l-islām*, trans. W.E. Shepard, *Sayyid Quṭb and Islamic activism. A translation and critical analysis of social justice in Islam*, Leiden 1996; id., *Ẓilāl;* Sālim b. Dhakwān, *The Epistle of Sālim b. Dhakwān*, ed. P. Crone and F. Zimmerman, Oxford 2001; Sayf b. ʿUmar, *Kitāb al-Ridda wa-l-futūḥ*, ed. Q. al-Sāmarrāʾī, Leiden 1995; R. Shafīq Shunbūr, *Dustūr al-ḥukm wa-l-sulṭa fī l-Qurʾān wa-l-sharāʾiʿ*, Beirut 1954; Ṭabarī, *Tafsīr*, ed. Ṣ.ʿA. al-Khālidī, 7 vols., Damascus 1997; id., *Taʾrīkh*, ed. de Goeje; annot. Eng. trans. *The history of al-Ṭabarī*, 39 vols., Albany 1989-98, esp. vols. x, xv, xvi, xvii, xx, xxi, xxiii, xxvi, xxviii, xxix (various translators).

Secondary: Kh. Abou El Fadl, *Rebellion and violence in Islamic law*, Cambridge 2001; M. Aḥmed, Key political concepts in the Qurʾān, in *Islamic studies* 10 (1971), 77-102; I. Albayrak, The notion of *muḥkam* and *mutashābih* in the commentary of Elmalı'lı, Muḥammad Ḥamdī Yazır, in *Journal of qurʾanic studies* 5 (2003), 19-34; S.A. Arjomand, Shiʿite jurisprudence and constitution making in the Islamic Republic of Iran, in M.E. Marty and R.S. Appleby (eds.), *Fundamentalisms and the state*, Chicago 1993, 88-110; id., Unity and diversity in Islamic fundamentalism, in M.E. Marty and R.S. Appleby (eds.), *Fundamentalisms comprehended*, Chicago 1995, 179-98; M. Bonner, *Aristocratic violence and holy war. Studies in the jihad and the Arab-Byzantine frontier,* New Haven 1996; C.E. Bosworth et al., Siyāsa, in *EI²*, ix, 693-6; N. Calder, Accommodation and revolution in Imami Shiʿi jurisprudence. Khumayni and the classical tradition, in *Middle Eastern studies* 18 (1982), 3-20; O. Carre, *Mysticism and politics. A critical reading of* Fī ẓilāl al-Qurʾān *by Sayyid Quṭb (1906-1966),* Leiden 2003, *Mystique et politique. Le Coran des islamistes. Lecture du Coran par Sayyid Quṭb, Frère musulman radical (*1906-1966*)*, Paris 2004²; M. Cook, *Commanding right and forbidding wrong in Islamic thought,* Cambridge, UK 2000; M. Cooperson, *Classical Arabic biography. The heirs of the prophets in the age of al-Maʾmūn,* Cambridge, UK 2000; P. Crone, A statement by the Najdiyya Khārijites on the dispensability of the imamate, in *SI* 88 (1998), 55-76; id. and M. Hinds, *God's caliph. Religious authority in the first centuries of Islam,* Cambridge 1986; S. Dähne, Qurʾānic wording in political speeches in classical Arabic literature, in *Journal of qur'anic studies* 3 (2001), 1-14; F. Donner, The formation of the Islamic state, in *JAOS* 106 (1986), 283-96; id., Piety and eschatology in early Kharijite poetry, in I. al-Saʿʿāfīn (ed.), *Fī miḥrāb al-maʿrifa. Festschrift für Iḥsān ʿAbbās,* Beirut 1997, 13-9; H. Enayat, *Modern Islamic political thought,* Austin 1982; J.L. Esposito and J.O. Voll, Islam's democratic essence, in *Middle East quarterly* 1/3 (September 1994), 3-11; Y.Y. Haddad, The qurʾānic justification for an Islamic revolution. The view of Sayyid Quṭb, in *Middle East journal* 37 (1983), 14-29; S.G. Haim, Sayyid Qutb, in *Asian and African studies* 16 (1982), 147-56; T. al-Ḥamd, *al-Siyāsa bayn al-ḥalāl wa-l-ḥarām. Antum aʿlam bi-umūr dunyākum,* London 2003³; ʿAbd al-Qādir Ḥāmid, *Uṣūl al-fikr al-siyāsā fī l-Qurʾān al-makkī,* Amman 1995; P.L. Heck, *The construction of knowledge in Islamic civilization,* Leiden 2001; id., Eschatological scripturalism and the end of community. The case of early Kharijism, in *Archiv für Religionswissenschaft* 7 (2004) (forthcoming); id., Jihad revisited, in *Journal of religious ethics* 32 (2004), 95-128; id., Law in ʿAbbāsid political thought from Ibn al-Muqaffaʿ (d. 139/756) to Qudāmah b. Jaʿfar (d. 337/948), in J.E. Montgomery (ed.), *ʿAbbasid studies. Occasional papers of the School of ʿAbbasid Studies. Cambridge, 6-10 July 2002,* Leuven 2004, 81-107; id., Religious renewal in Syria. The case of Muḥammad al-Ḥabash, forthcoming in *Islam and Christian-Muslim Relations* 15 (2004); A. Higgins, *The qurʾānic exchange of the self in the poetry of the* shūrāt *(Khārijī) political identity* 37-132 *A.H.*/657-750 *A.D.*, Ph.D. diss., Chicago 2001; F. Jadʿān, *al-Miḥna. Baḥth fī jadaliyyat al-dīn wa-l-siyāsa fī l-Islām,* Amman 1989; I. al-Jomaih, *The use of the Qurʾān in political argument. A study of early Islamic parties (35-86 A.H./656-705 A.D.),* Ph.D. diss., UCLA 1988; J. Jomier, La revue "al-ʿOrwa al-Wothqa" (13 mars-16 octobre 1884) et l'autorité du Coran, in *MIDEO* 17 (1986), 9-36; J.T. Kenney, The emergence of the Khawārij. Religion and social order in early Islam, in *Jusūr* 5 (1989), 1-29; Q. Khan, *Political concepts in the Qurʾān,* Karachi 1973; W. Madelung, Imāma, in *EI²*, iii, 1163-9; D. Madigan, *The Qurʾān's self image. Writing and authority in Islam's scripture,* Princeton 2001; L. Marlow, *Hierarchy and egalitarianism in Islamic thought,* Cambridge 1997; Kh. Masud, The doctrine of siyasa in Islamic law, in *Recht van de Islam* 18 (2001), 1-29; A.E. Mayer, The fundamentalist impact on law, politics, and constitutions in Iran, Pakistan, and the Sudan, in M.E. Marty and R.S. Appleby (eds.), *Fundamentalisms and the state,* Chicago 1993, 110-51; R.P. Mitchell, *The Society of Muslim Brothers,* Oxford 1969; Mujiburrahman, Islam and politics in Indonesia. The political thought of ʿAbdurrahman Wahid, in *Islam and Christian-Muslim relations* 10 (1999), 339-52; J.A. Nawas, *al-Maʾmūn.* Miḥna *and caliphate,* Ph.D. diss., Nijmegen 1992; W. al-Qāḍī, The impact of the Qurʾān on the epistolography of ʿAbd al-Ḥamīd, in Hawting and Shareef, *Approaches,* 285-313; id., The religious foundation of late Umayyad ideology and practice, in *Saber religioso y poder politico en el Islam. Actas del simposio internacional, Granada, 15-18 octubre 1991,* Madrid 1994, 231-74; id., The term "Khalīfa" in early exegetical literature, in *WI* 27 (1988), 392-411; M.F. Rahman, *The qurʾānic foundation and structure of Muslim society,* 2 vols., Karachi 1973; W. Sharāra, *Dawlat Ḥizb Allāh. Lubnān. Mujtamaʿan islāmiyyan,* Beirut 1998³; M. Sharon, *Revolt. The social and military aspects of the ʿAbbāsid revolution. Black banners from the east II,* Jerusalem 1990; D. Sourdel et al., Khalīfa, in *EI²*, iv, 937-53; M.Q. Zaman, *The ulama in contemporary Islam. Custodians of change,* Princeton 2002; A. Zein al-Abdin, The political significance of the constitution of Medina, in R.L. Bidwell and G.R. Smith (eds.), *Arabian and Islamic studies. Articles presented to R.F. Sergeant,* London 1983, 146-52.

Poll Tax

A tax per head, usually levied on every adult male of a given age. The Arabic term, *jizya,* used for the poll tax levied on non-Muslims, specifically the People of the Book (q.v.) living under Muslim rule (*ahl al-kitāb,* also identified eventually as "protected people," *ahl al-dhimma*), does have a qurʾānic origin (Q 9:29: … *ḥattā yuʿṭū l-jizyata ʿan yadin wa-hum ṣāghirūn,* i.e. "… until they pay the *jizya* from their wealth [lit. from hand], submissively"). There is no evidence in the Qurʾān, however, of a tax per head *(ʿalā l-raʾs)* as assumed by later jurists (e.g. Mālik, *Muwaṭṭaʾ,* 187-9; Abū ʿUbayd, *Amwāl,* 23-56). The tax per capita as finally established in Islamic law seems to have derived from a Sassanian practice (*khāk bar sar,* Abū ʿUbayd, *Amwāl,* 29, no. 61; cf. Ṭabarī, *Taʾrīkh,* i, 2371; see Lokkegaard, *Islamic taxation,* 128-43; for the adoption of the Byzantine poll tax in Egypt, see al-Dūrī, *Nuẓum,* 79) developed by Muslims through the course of the conquests, first being applied to all members of a conquered locale — men, women and children (Abu ʿUbayd, *Amwāl,* 31, no. 66) — and then limited to mature males (*ḥālim,* ibid., 33, no. 72; 39, no. 93; see LAW AND THE QURʾĀN). The poll tax varied according to the terms of the treaty between the Muslims and the local peoples (see Ṭabarī, *Taʾrīkh,* i, 2051; cf. Morony, *Iraq,* 584-8), was assessed according to one's wealth (q.v.; see Cahen, Djizya), was first applied to non-Muslim Arabs and then gradually extended, by the Prophet's example (*sunna,* Abū ʿUbayd, *Amwāl,* 38, no. 88), to non-Arab non-Muslims living in the conquered lands (ibid., 25, no. 53), including Zorastrians (*majūs;* see MAGIANS) as well as Jews (*yahūd;* see JEWS AND JUDAISM) and Christians (*naṣārā;* see CHRISTIANS AND CHRISTIANITY). There also seems to have been a connection, at least initially, between the payment of this tax and socio-professional status, for it is reported that the large Christian tribe (see TRIBES AND CLANS), the Banū Taghlib, refused to pay the *jizya* on the grounds that they were Arabs (q.v.), not farmers; presumably to avoid the humiliation *(ṣaghār)* of being classified with those who work the land, they were granted the right to pay, instead, the Muslim tax *(ṣadaqa),* although at twice the normal rate (ibid., 32; cf. Mālik, *Muwaṭṭaʾ,* 189, who explains the distinction in religious terms: "The Muslim tax was levied on Muslims as a means of purifying them *[taṭhīran lahum]* … and the *jizya* was levied on the People of the Book as a means of subordinating them [*ṣaghāran lahum,* i.e. to Muslim rule]).

It has been demonstrated rather persuasively that the exegetical tradition on Q 9:29 bears no relation to the historical conditions of the verse (see Rubin, Qurʾān and tafsīr; see SĪRA AND THE QURʾĀN); the verse does seem to have been used by later exegetes as a point of departure for elaborating differences — theological and legal — between Muslims and non-Muslims (e.g. Ibn al-Jawzī, *Zād,* 420, for whom the verse is a confirmation of the abrogation of previous religions with the appearance of Muḥammad's religion *[dīn Muḥammad];* see also McAuliffe, Fakhr al-Dīn al-Rāzī; see RELIGIOUS PLURALISM AND THE QURʾĀN). Nevertheless, the rationale generally given for the poll tax — a compensation *(jazāʾ)* in exchange for enjoying the protection *(dhimma)* of Muslim rule — does demonstrate a certain conceptual continuity with the qurʾānic term *jazāʾ* (cf. Ṭabarī, *Taʾrīkh,* i, 2470: … *maʿa l-jazāʾ ʿan aydīhim ʿalā qadri ṭāqatihim,* i.e. "… with compensation from their wealth [lit. from their hands] according to their ability [to pay]"). Claims for continuity, however, between the qurʾānic sense of the term and its later legal and exegetical use rest on the identity of those people specified as being obligated to pay the *jizya,* namely those who have been given the book *(min alladhīna ūtū l-kitāb),* widely assumed to be non-Muslim recipients of God's revelation (i.e. People of the Book) in contrast to those who are without knowledge of God's oneness (*mushrikūn,* see Rāzī, *Tafsīr,* ad Q 9:30; see POLYTHEISM AND ATHEISM).

Rubin *(Barā'a)* has concluded that *jizya* at Q 9:29 connotes financial compensation for the loss of income sustained by the rupture of commercial relations with non-Muslim traders who are prohibited, at Q 9:28, from approaching Mecca (q.v.). This does seem to be borne out in Q 9:29 itself, the opening words of which claim that the people obliged to pay the *jizya* do not believe in God or judgment day (*lā yu'minūna bi-llāh wa-lā bi-l-yawmi l-ākhir;* see LAST JUDGMENT). Book (q.v.; *kitāb*), while connoting divine knowledge (see KNOWLEDGE AND LEARNING) and authority (q.v.), can also serve as a metonymy for treaty, the terms of which were fixed in writing (a *kitāb*) and included some kind of payment of tribute (see CONTRACTS AND ALLIANCES). *Jizya,* in fact, occurs in such a context in Ibn Saʿd's history (*Ṭabaqāt,* i, 257 f.), where the term for the missives *(kutub)* sent by Muḥammad to other groups and rulers connotes both letter and pact. Were, then, the people named in Q 9:29 the so-called People of the Book *(ahl al-kitāb)* or merely tribal groups of varied character which had entered into alliance with the tribal overlordship of Muḥammad and his Muslim partisans while not sharing their monotheistic beliefs? Simonsen (*Studies,* 47-61) argues — on the basis that there is no qur'ānic connection between *dhimma* and *jizya* — that Q 9:29 applies to all non-Muslims dwelling within the reach of Medinan hegemony, whether monotheists or not (see MEDINA).

In favor of the identification of the *jizya*-payers of Q 9:29 with the People of the Book, support can be drawn from the verses subsequent to Q 9:29, which serve a doctrinal polemic against the claim of Jews that Ezra (q.v.; ʿUzayr) is the son of God and that of Christians who say that Jesus (q.v.) is (Q 9:30), and against the undue attribution of divine authority awarded by both groups to their religious leaders (*ittakhadhū aḥbārahum wa-ruhbānahum arbāban min dūni llāh,* Q 9:31). Later exegetes understood Q 9:29 to indicate the failure of Jews and Christians to affirm fully God's oneness (e.g. Muqātil, *Tafsīr,* ii, 166; Zamakhsharī, *Kashshāf,* iii, 32; Ibn al-Jawzī, *Zād,* iii, 419; see POLEMIC AND POLEMICAL LANGUAGE). Moreover, the fact that the concept of the protection *(dhimma)* of God and his Prophet was not limited in the earliest period to the People of the Book, as Simonsen demonstrates, need not negate the more specific application of *jizya* to them apart from the *mushrikūn.* Finally, the usage of *min alladhīna ūtū l-kitāb* elsewhere in the Qur'ān does indeed suggest recipients of previous revelation (e.g. Q 4:47; see REVELATION AND INSPIRATION).

The occasion for the revelation of Q 9:29 (see OCCASIONS OF REVELATION) is thought to have been the Prophet's expedition in 9/30 to Tabūk (Ṭabarī, *Tafsīr,* xiv, 200) in the northwestern region of the Arabian peninsula (cf. Bakhit, Tabūk), conducted in anticipation of a Byzantine-sponsored attack (see EXPEDITIONS AND BATTLES). While the attack never materialized, the Prophet took the opportunity to conclude pacts with tribal groups near the Gulf of ʿAqaba. The use of *jizya* for non-Muslim and specifically Jewish, Christian and Zoroastrian groups only after the expedition to Tabūk seems to be confirmed by the reports of Ibn Saʿd (d. 230/845; cf. Simonsen, *Studies,* 47-61). The suggestion has been made that the appearance of *jizya* was linked to the Medinan policy towards tribes already accustomed to payment of tribute (q.v.) to Byzantine and Sassanian overlords (Schmucker, *Untersuchungen,* 74 f.), and it is in that sense that this tribute became a sign of obeisance (*wa-hum ṣāghirūn,* cf. Q 27:37) to the growing socio-political hegemony of Islam (see COMMUNITY AND

SOCIETY IN THE QUR'ĀN; POLITICS AND THE QUR'ĀN).

Most significantly for our understanding of the Qur'ān, it must be noted that the concept of *jizya* at Q 9:29 does serve a program of Muslim confessional definition vis-à-vis other groups, in both the formative and classical periods of Islam. The qur'ānic occurrence of the verse in a Medinan context (Q 9: Sūrat al-Tawba, "Repentance"), where concerns for the formation of the Muslim polity and corresponding confessional demarcations of religio-political identity were urgent, suggests that the qur'ānic *jizya* can best be understood in terms of a confessional tax levied upon tribal and other groups unwilling to meet the requirements of membership in Islam (it is also used in this sense in the rules of jihād [q.v.], where those refusing the call of Islam are offered the chance to pay the *jizya* in exchange for cessation of hostilities). Such boundaries were embodied in both religious and fiscal terms, and it is in this sense that taxation (q.v.) of other groups served Islam in its definition of such confessional lines. The context in which Q 9:29 occurs is quasi-creedal in coloring (see CREEDS). The exegetes understood it in this way, although they developed its original connotation (see above). In addition, the administrative history of the term also confirms its confessional orientation: While *jizya* was used interchangeably in the earliest period with the term for the land-tax (*kharāj*, e.g. "*jizya* on the land" or "*kharāj* on the head"; see Cahen, Djizya), the two terms became gradually disassociated when ownership of the lands of conquest — through conversion of the tenants to Islam or sale of their land to Muslims — was no longer solely identifiable with non-Muslims (a policy believed to have first been instituted by the Umayyad 'Umar b. 'Abd al-'Azīz, r. 99-101/717-20; see Gibb, Fiscal rescript).

Paul L. Heck

Bibliography

Primary: Abū 'Ubayd, *Kitāb al-Amwāl*, ed. M. Khalīl Harrās, Cairo 1981³, 23-56; Abū Yūsuf, Ya'qūb b. Ibrāhīm al-Anṣārī, *Kitāb al-Kharāj*, ed. I. 'Abbās, Beirut 1985; Ibn al-Jawzī, *Zād*, ed. Beirut 1965, iii, 419-21; Ibn Qayyim al-Jawziyya, *Aḥkām ahl al-dhimma*, ed. Ṣ. al-Ṣāliḥ, Beirut 1983³; Ibn Sa'd, *Ṭabaqāt*, ed. I. 'Abbās; *Jalālayn*, ad Q 9:29; Mālik, *Muwaṭṭa'*, ed. A.R. 'Armūsh, Beirut 1977³, 187-9; Muqātil, *Tafsīr*, ii, 166-7; Rāzī, *Tafsīr*; Ṭabarī, *Tafsīr*, ed. Shākir, xiv, 198-201; id., *Ta'rīkh*, ed. De Goeje; Ṭūsī, *Tibyān*, ed. A.Ḥ. Quṣayr al-'Āmilī, 10 vols., Beirut n.d., v, 202-4; Zamakhsharī, *Kashshāf*, ed. 'A.A. 'Abd al-Mawjūd and 'A.M. Mu'awwaḍ, 6 vols., Riyadh 1998, iii, 32-3.

Secondary: A. Abel, La *djizya*. Tribut ou rançon? in *SI* 32 (1970), 5-19; M.A. al-Bakhit, Tabūk, in *EI²*, x, 50-1; Cl. Cahen, Djizya (i), in *EI²*, ii, 559-62; D.C. Dennett, *Conversion and the poll tax in early Islam*, Cambridge, MA 1950; 'A.'A. al-Dūrī, *al-Nuzum al-islāmiyya*, Baghdad 1950; A. Fattal, *Le statut légal des non-musulmans en pays d'islam*, Beirut 1958; H.A.R. Gibb, The fiscal rescript of 'Umar II, in *Arabica* 2 (1955), 1-16; S.M. Hasanuz Zaman, *Economic functions of an Islamic state (the early experience)*, Leicester 1990²; P.L. Heck, *The construction of knowledge in Islamic civilization. Qudāma b. Ja'far (d. 337/948) and his* Kitāb al-kharāj wa-ṣinā'at al-kitāba, Leiden 2002 (esp. chapter four); K.-E. Ismail, *Das islamische Steuersystem vom 7. bis 12. Jahrhundert n. Chr. unter besonderer Berücksichtigung seiner Umsetzung in den eroberten Gebieten*, Köln 1989; F. Lokkegaard, *Islamic taxation in the classic period*, Copenhagen 1950, 128-43; J.D. McAuliffe, Fakhr al-Dīn al-Rāzī on *ayat al-jizyah* and *ayat al-sayf*, in M. Gervers and R.J. Bikhazi (eds.), *Conversion and continuity. Indigenous Christian communities in Islamic lands. Eighth to eighteenth centuries*, Toronto 1990, 104-19; M. Morony, *Iraq after the Muslim conquests*, Princeton 1984, 584-8 (summary of literature on the poll tax); U. Rubin, *Barā'a*. A study of some qur'ānic passages, in *JSAI* 5 (1984), 13-32; id., Qur'ān and tafsīr. The case of *'an yadin*, in *Der Islam* 70 (1993), 133-44 (excellent source for exegetical references); W. Schmucker, *Untersuchungen zu einigen wichtigen bodenrechtlichen Konsequenzen der islamischen Eroberungsbewegung*, Bonn 1972; J.B. Simonsen, *Studies in the genesis and early development of the caliphal taxation system*,

Copenhagen 1988 (esp. 47-61); A.S. Tritton, *The caliphs and their non-Muslim subjects,* London 1930.

Pollution see CONTAMINATION

Polygamy see MARRIAGE AND DIVORCE; PATRIARCHY; WOMEN AND THE QURʾĀN

Polysemy in the Qurʾān

The plurality of senses that words can have. It is the property of words in all natural languages to have more than one meaning, for polysemy is an essential condition of a language's efficiency: a finite set of lexical elements is used to express a potentially infinite set of situations. Arabic words in the Qurʾān also have this property and many words in the Qurʾān have been classified as polysemous in the exegetical tradition (see EXEGESIS OF THE QURʾĀN: CLASSICAL AND MEDIEVAL). In fact, some exegetes suggest that all words in the Qurʾān contain several meanings or levels of meaning (see LANGUAGE AND STYLE OF THE QURʾĀN; LITERARY STRUCTURES OF THE QURʾĀN).

The possibility of ambiguity or equivocation is, however, a counterpart of polysemy — although contextual, syntactic and lexical clues in practice reduce this possibility. For example, mutual appropriateness reduces a word's semantic pertinence so that only part of the semantic field of a word is used; the remainder is excluded or repressed. The Qurʾān, however, inhibits this reduction. It is a referential text that often does not provide a great deal of context. This difficulty was alleviated somewhat by biographical materials (*sīra;* see SĪRA AND THE QURʾĀN), the circumstances of revelation literature (*asbāb al-nuzūl;* see OCCASIONS OF REVELATION) and other narrative texts that offered historical explanations or allusions that emphasized monosemy and, by providing a context frequently missing in the Qurʾān itself, word sense disambiguation. Early works on the *gharīb,* i.e. difficult words such as *hapax legomena,* foreign and dialectal words (see FOREIGN VOCABULARY; DIALECT), also emphasized monosemy by providing mostly simple glosses.

On the whole, the Islamic exegetical tradition embraced polysemy in the Qurʾān. Although the Qurʾān was thought to have a divine origin and Arabic came to be viewed as a divine language, not a "natural" one, polysemy was not considered a defect (see REVELATION AND INSPIRATION; ARABIC LANGUAGE). Rather, polysemy in the Qurʾān became one of its miraculous features (see MIRACLE; INIMITABILITY). The issue was not whether the Qurʾān was polysemous but rather how to express and limit the polysemy. As a result, polysemy has been represented or imposed in several different but overlapping ways throughout the history of reading and interpreting the Qurʾān (see READINGS OF THE QURʾĀN). The question remains whether the polysemes discovered by the exegetes are deliberate or merely imposed upon the Qurʾān for theological and other reasons (see THEOLOGY AND THE QURʾĀN).

Wujūh al-Qurʾān

The most obvious works dealing with polysemy are those of *wujūh* (polysemes and homonyms) and *naẓāʾir* (synonyms or analogues). *Wujūh* refers to words employed several times in the Qurʾān but with at least two and perhaps as many as forty different meanings (Abdus Sattar, Wujūh, 138). The distinction between homonymy, which refers to words of different origins or roots that coincide phonetically, and polysemy, which refers to words of related origin but whose roots or derived forms have several discernable senses, is essentially arbitrary. Synchronically, homonymy is a kind of polysemy but even diachronic homonymy can become polysemy and vice versa because the criteria for distinguishing between homonymy and polysemy are themselves somewhat arbitrary. In any case, it is a distinction that those qur᾿ānic exegetes who discussed *wujūh* did not generally make. *Wujūh* is a branch of the sciences of the Qur᾿ān (*ʿulūm al-Qur᾿ān;* see TRADITIONAL DISCIPLINES OF QUR᾿ĀNIC STUDY) and finds sanction in several prophetic ḥadīths (see ḤADĪTH AND THE QUR᾿ĀN): "The Qur᾿ān… conveys [many] meanings *(wujūh);* so impute to it the best of its meanings" (Zarkashī, *Burhān,* ii, 163). And, "a jurisprudent's *(faqīh)* jurisprudence is not comprehensive until he sees many *wujūh* in the Qur᾿ān" (Suyūṭī, *Itqān,* i, 299; see LAW AND THE QUR᾿ĀN).

Muqātil b. Sulayman (d. 150/767) is credited with authoring the first *wujūh* and *naẓā᾿ir* work (cf. Nwyia, *Exégèse,* 109-16; Gilliot, *Elt,* 118-20). His methodology, largely followed by later authors in this genre, is to provide a gloss or brief definition for each of the meanings *(wujūh)* of a word and then to list other analogous qur᾿ānic passages *(naẓā᾿ir)* — that is, those in which the word is employed with the same meaning. Important early *wujūh* works are those of Ibn Qutayba (d. 276/889), al-Dāmaghānī (d. 478/1085), and Ibn al-Jawzī (d. 597/1200). Of course, the subject is treated by al-Zarkashī (d. 794/1391) and al-Suyūṭī (d. 911/1505) in their works on the sciences of the Qur᾿ān. None of these works are systematic examinations of qur᾿ānic vocabulary. Rather, the words chosen by these exegetes are religiously significant ones. It should also be noted that in these works, the terms *wujūh* and *naẓā᾿ir* are themselves somewhat polysemous (Rippin, Lexicographical texts, 167-71). By the time of al-Zarkashī, the existence of *wujūh* in the Qur᾿ān had acquired its most important theological implication: it is one "of the miracles *(muʿjizāt)* of the Qur᾿ān since one word imparts twenty aspects (sing. *wajh*), or more or less; and one does not find that in the speech of mankind" (Zarkashī, *Burhān,* i, 102).

Polysemy in the Qur᾿ān has, at least at times, been created by the exegetical tradition itself, which even has the Qur᾿ān "inventing" new meanings for some words. See, for example, the development of the association of "sleep" with *bard,* "cold," in order to "solve intra-qur᾿ānic and Qur᾿ān versus dogma conflict" (Rippin, Qur᾿ān 78/24, 311-20; see DREAMS AND SLEEP; HOT AND COLD). If such is the case, one can legitimately ask whether the exegetes' rich tradition of finding polysemes in the Qur᾿ān is more a product of the exegetes' ingenuity than a deliberate feature of the Qur᾿ān. Certainty may well be restricted to those words for which there are other reasons for assuming polysemy, such as the use of puns in the Qur᾿ān (see HUMOR).

Levels of meaning in the Qur᾿ān

As a technical term *wujūh* connotes that category of words that are used in different ways in different passages of the Qur᾿ān, but proved to be an inadequate rubric under which to discuss words, expressions and phrases, which have multiple meanings within a single passage. Several other overlapping rubrics were developed and employed in various ways by Sunnī, Shīʿī and Ṣūfī exegetes (see SHĪʿISM AND THE QUR᾿ĀN; ṢŪFISM AND THE QUR᾿ĀN). Generally, all the methods that they developed were based on the premise that the passages of the Qur᾿ān had several levels of meaning, though the deeper levels should not be allowed to negate the single, literal meaning.

One of the more significant ways of accounting or allowing for polysemy (at least at the level of expressions and phrases as opposed to individual words) was introduced by using the distinction between the *muḥkamāt* and *mutashābihāt* given in Q 3:7. Whether these two words are polysemous in the Qurʾān is uncertain but in the explanations of later exegetes they are certainly understood to be. Some argued, Abū ʿUbayd (d. 224/838) for instance, that they refer to the abrogating and regulative passages, and to the abrogated and non-regulative passages, respectively (see ABROGATION), while others saw them as the clear and unclear passages, respectively (see AMBIGUOUS). Of more immediate significance is that *mutashābihāt* came to mean verses that were polysemous. For instance, al-Jaṣṣāṣ (d. 370/981) states that the *muḥkamāt* permit only one meaning but the *mutashābihāt* may have several. The meanings and aspects *(wujūh)* of the latter must be understood in reference to the former, though not all of them could be known (Jaṣṣāṣ, *Aḥkām,* ii, 3-4).

Tafsīr and *taʾwīl* are another pair of terms employed to convey the notion of several levels of meaning (see EXEGESIS OF THE QURʾĀN: CLASSICAL AND MEDIEVAL). *Tafsīr* came to mean the exegesis that was concrete, exoteric, and/or based on tradition. *Taʾwīl* came to mean exegesis that was abstract, esoteric, and/or based on personal opinion *(raʾy)*. Thus, al-Ṭabarī's (d. 310/923) exegesis is *tafsīr* and al-Qushayrī's (d. 465/1072) *Laṭāʾif al-ishārāt* is *taʾwīl*. The distinction between terms was only theoretical, however, since exegetes such as the Ṣūfī al-Sulamī (d. 412/1021) labeled their works as *tafsīr*s and al-Ṭabarī's work was originally entitled as *taʾwīl* — again the terminology of polysemy is itself polysemous. Also for some exegetes, *tafsīr* permitted only one meaning *(la-yaḥtamilu illā wajhan wāḥidan),* whereas *taʾwīl* allowed more (Suyūṭī, *Itqān,* ii, 381). Thus, *taʾwīl* allowed for unrestricted polysemy. In practice, however, even *tafsīr* was polysemous. Al-Ṭabarī cites a tradition from Ibn ʿAbbās in which he states, "*Tafsīr* has four aspects: an aspect which is known to the Arabs (q.v.) through their speech, a *tafsīr* of which no one can plead ignorance, a *tafsīr* which the learned know, and a *tafsīr* known only to God" (Ṭabarī, *Tafsīr,* i, 57; Eng. trans. i, 34). Furthermore, al-Ṭabarī's *tafsīr,* though based on traditions, often accepts that all the diverse opinions found in the earlier exegetes are correct (cf. Gilliot, *Elt,* 112-33).

The most prominent binary distinction that allowed for polysemy is the one between *ẓāhir* and *bāṭin*. In his discussion of the seven *ḥarf*s, al-Ṭabarī cites a tradition in which Muḥammad says "Each of the *ḥarf*s has an outward meaning *(ẓahr)* and an inward meaning *(baṭn)*. Each of the *ḥarf*s has a border, and each border a lookout" (Ṭabarī, *Tafsīr,* i, 35-6; Eng. trans. i, 16; cf. Gilliot, *Elt,* 112 f.). Generally, *ẓāhir* refers to the exoteric, outer, obvious, or literal meaning and *bāṭin* to the esoteric, inner, concealed, or symbolic meaning. Theoretically, *ẓāhir* had but one meaning and was associated with *tafsīr,* while *bāṭin* could be multivalent and it, along with everything else that was not *ẓāhir,* was subsumed under *taʾwīl*. Shīʿīs and Ṣūfīs placed a great deal of emphasis on *bāṭin*. The Imāmī Shīʿī exegete al-Ṭabāṭabāʾī (d. 1981) expanded the levels of polysemy by suggesting that inner meaning itself could have up to seven inner meanings (Ṭabāṭabāʾī, *Mīzān,* i, 7). The classical formulation, however — which seems to incorporate the tradition from Ibn ʿAbbās and the *ẓāhir-bāṭin* distinction — recognized that *every* qurʾānic verse had, not two, but four separate meanings. The Ṣūfī Sahl al-Tustarī (d. 283/896) lists *ẓāhir* (literal), *bāṭin* (symbolic), *ḥadd* (prescriptive) and *maṭla*ʿ (anagogical). "The *ẓāhir* is the recitation; the *bāṭin* the understanding; the *ḥadd* the permitted and forbidden (q.v.; things in the verses); the *maṭla*ʿ the control of the heart (q.v.) over what is intended by them by way of comprehension from God" (Tustarī, *Tafsīr,* 3; cf. Böwering, Scriptural senses, 350; see INTELLECT; KNOWLEDGE AND LEARNING; RECITATION OF THE QURʾĀN). These four levels of meaning came to be accepted in various forms by Sunnī scholars also. For example, al-Zarkashī states: "The outward interpretations *(ʿibārāt)* are for the general public; they are for the ear. The allusions *(ishārāt)* are for the special ones; they are for the intellect. The subtleties *(laṭāʾif)* are for the friends [of God; see FRIENDS AND FRIENDSHIP]; they are glimpses. And the essences *(ḥaqāʾiq)* are for the prophets (see PROPHETS AND PROPHETHOOD); they are the submission [to God]" (Zarkashī, *Burhān,* ii, 153-4). Similarly, the benefits of hearing the Qurʾān are fourfold and suit the listeners' capabilities. Those who hear it merely from a reciter benefit from the knowledge of its precepts; those who hear as though from the Prophet benefit from his admonitions (see WARNING) and the demonstrations of his miracles so that the heart delights in the subtleties of his oration; and those who hear it as though from Gabriel (q.v.) glimpse hidden things (see HIDDEN AND THE HIDDEN) and promises disclosed in it (to the Prophet); those who hear as though from God are extinguished by it and their attributes effaced — they gain the attributes of truth *(taḥqīq)* through glimpsing the knowledge, source, and truth of certainty (Zarkashī, *Burhān,* ii, 154).

Despite these fourfold levels of meaning, most exegetes essentially recognized only two such levels. Even al-Tustarī, in practice if not in theory, uses the typical literal-allegorical distinction; he combines *ẓāhir* and *ḥadd,* and *bāṭin* and *maṭla*ʿ (Böwering, Sahl al-Tustarī, 841). In any case, none of these various ways of constructing polysemy in the Qurʾān need be considered mutually exclusive. *Muḥkam* versus *mutashābih, tafsīr* versus *taʾwīl, ẓāhir* versus *bāṭin,* in each of these binary oppositions it is theoretically only the latter which is open to multiple (levels of) meanings (Wansbrough, *QS,* 243-4).

Herbert Berg

Bibliography
Primary: Dāmaghānī, *Wujūh,* ed. al-Zafītī; Ibn al-Jawzī *Nuzha;* Ibn Qutayba, *Taʾwīl;* Jaṣṣāṣ, *Aḥkām;* Muqātil, Abū l-Ḥasan Muqātil b. Sulaymān al-Balkhī, *al-Ashbāh wa-l-naẓāʾir fī l-Qurʾān al-karīm,* ed. ʿA.M. Shiḥāta, Cairo 1975; Suyūṭī, *Itqān,* Beirut 1995; Ṭabarī, *Tafsīr,* 30 vols. in 12, Beirut 1992, abr. Eng. trans. J. Cooper, *The commentary on the Qurʾān,* Oxford 1987-, i; Ṭabāṭabāʾī, *Mīzān,* Beirut 1973-4; Tustarī, *Tafsīr;* Zarkashī, *Burhān.*
Secondary: M. Abdus Sattar, Wujūh al-Qurʾān. A branch of tafsīr literature, in *Islamic studies* 17 (1978), 137-52; A.J. Arberry, Synonyms and homonyms in the Qurʾān, in *IQ* 13 (1939), 135-9; M. Ayoub, *The Qurʾān and its interpreters,* Albany 1984 (vol. i); G. Böwering, Sahl al-Tustarī, in *EI*², viii, 841; id., The scriptural "senses" in medieval Ṣūfī Qurʾān exegesis, in J.D. McAuliffe, B.D. Walfish, and J.W. Goering (eds.), *With reverence for the word,* New York 2003, 346-65; Gilliot, *Elt;* id., Les sept "lectures." Corps social et écriture révélée, in *SI* 61 (1985), 5-25 (Part I); 63 (1986), 49-62 (Part II); Nwyia, *Exégèse;* A. Rippin, Lexicographical texts and the Qurʾān, in Rippin, *Approaches,* 158-74; id., Qurʾān 78/24. A study in Arabic lexicography, in *JSS* 28 (1983), 311-20; Wansbrough, *QS.*

Polytheism and Atheism

The worship of many gods; the belief in no god. Although the concept of atheism was unknown to the qurʾānic audience, the human tendency to ascribe divine tendencies to something other than the one, true God was not. The qurʾānic allusions to "polytheism" have been variously understood: idolatry on the part of pre-Islamic

Arabian tribes; the pre-Islamic Arabs' ascription of divine attributes to lesser beings, perhaps even within a monotheistic framework; or, alternatively, a polemical accusation that Jews and Christians had distorted aspects of their earlier revelations. The following is an overview of the qurʾānic attitude towards these two aspects of human denial of God's omnipotence — the ultimate act of ingratitude.

Polytheism

The qurʾānic Arabic term for polytheism is *shirk*. The central dogma affirmed in the Qurʾān is that of monotheism *(tawḥīd)*, and *shirk*, as its antithesis, takes the brunt of qurʾānic doctrinal criticism. The Qurʾān's rejection of *shirk* is categorical and absolute (a concise statement is found in the short Q 112). It is the only sin for which, even theoretically, there is no forgiveness (q.v.): "God will not forgive the act of associating [anything] with him, though he might forgive anyone he likes anything other than that" (Q 4:48, 116; see SIN, MAJOR AND MINOR). The Arabic phrase for "anything other than that," *mā dūna dhālika*, also connotes "anything less than that" — again implying that *shirk* is the greatest of all sins, all other sins being "less" than it. The ancient Arabian sage Luqmān (q.v.) is represented in the Qurʾān, in a sūra (Q 31) named after him, as admonishing his son against committing *shirk:* he calls *shirk* "a great wrong indeed" (Q 31:13). The same sūra exhorts one to respect and obey one's parents (q.v.) but forbids one to commit *shirk* should one's parents put pressure on one to do so (Q 31:14-5; see also Q 29:8). *Shirk* nullifies good deeds (q.v.): on the day of judgment (see LAST JUDGMENT) the polytheists (*mushrikūn;* sing. *mushrik*) will discover that any good deeds they might have done have been wiped out (Q 6:88; 39:65).

Definition

The literal meaning of *shirk* is association. As a technical term in the Qurʾān, therefore, *shirk* means to set up associates or partners of God — the one true God — such that they are taken to be equal or comparable to the godhead. This definition would cover the positing of any deities besides God, whether they are one or many in number, whether they are believed to partake of his essence *(shirk fī l-dhāt)* or share his attributes (*shirk fī l-ṣifāt*, see GOD AND HIS ATTRIBUTES) and whether they are held to be equal to or less than him. And it would cover both crass idolatry (see IDOLATRY AND IDOLATERS) and metaphysical dualism. According to the Qurʾān, *shirk* can be both conceptual and practical. Actually, to hold the belief that deities other than God exist and that the universe and its workings cannot be explained until more than one God are taken to exist or possess the attributes that properly belong to him alone — that is, to reject monotheism in principle and affirm polytheism in principle — is conceptual *shirk*, whereas to regard any being or power other than God as being worthy of receiving obedience (q.v.) that is rightfully due only to God and to do so even when one affirms belief in monotheism in principle, would be practical *shirk*.

Forms

A number of pre-Islamic nations come under strong criticism in the Qurʾān for their polytheistic beliefs (see PRE-ISLAMIC ARABIA AND THE QURʾĀN; SOUTH ARABIA, RELIGION IN PRE-ISLAMIC). For example, the nation of Abraham (q.v.) counted heavenly bodies like the sun (q.v.), the moon (q.v.), and the stars (see PLANETS AND STARS) among deities, and these and other deities were represented by statues that were worshipped (see IDOLS AND IMAGES). Q 6:74-81 recounts Abraham's debate with his polytheistic nation, in which he refuses to accept such heavenly bodies as deities. Another debate of Abraham's, which is followed by his demolition of temple idols, is reported in Q 21:52 f. The pagans of Arabia proudly called themselves the descendents of Abraham and the qurʾānic reference to Abraham's uncompromising opposition to idolatry therefore gave a particular pungency to the qurʾānic criticism of Arabian polytheism. Other nations besides Abraham's that are criticized in the Qurʾān are those of Noah (q.v.; Q 11:26; see also Q 71:23), ʿĀd (q.v.; Q 11:50-5) and Thamūd (q.v.; Q 11:61-2). The Egyptian Pharaoh (q.v.) of Moses' (q.v.) time claimed to be a god (Q 26:29) and so did the king with whom Abraham debated (Q 2:258). According to certain qurʾānic verses (Q 25:43; 45:23), following one's base desires to such an extent that one becomes their slave also amounts to *shirk* (see ABSTINENCE).

The Arabian polytheism of Muḥammad's time is sometimes called henotheism, which is belief in the existence of many deities alongside a supreme God. The Arabs believed that there was a supreme God who had created the universe: "If you were to ask them, 'Who created the heavens and the earth?' they would assuredly say, 'God'" (Q 39:38; see CREATION; NATURE AS SIGNS). The Arabs thought, however, that God could be approached only through a number of lesser deities. "We worship them [other deities] only so that they may bring us close to God" (Q 39:3). "Say, 'Who gives you sustenance (q.v.) from the heavens and the earth (q.v.; see also FOOD AND DRINK; AGRICULTURE AND VEGETATION; HEAVEN AND SKY) — or who has power over hearing and vision (see HEARING AND DEAFNESS; VISION AND BLINDNESS; SEEING AND HEARING; EARS; EYES), and who brings the living from out of the dead and the dead from out of the living (see DEATH AND THE DEAD; RESURRECTION; LIFE), and who administers things?' At this they will say, 'God'" (Q 10:31; see also Q 29:61). A distinctive feature of Arabian *shirk* was angel worship. The Arabs believed that the angels (see ANGEL) were the daughters of God through whom God might be approached and persuaded to bless the devotees; and on the last day (see LAST JUDGMENT), the angels were expected to intercede with God on their devotees' behalf. Q 53:19-20 mentions three such goddesses by name (al-Lāt, al-ʿUzzā, and Manāt; see SATANIC VERSES).

The Qurʾān is critical of the Christian Trinitarian belief (see CHRISTIANS AND CHRISTIANITY; TRINITY): "Those people have certainly committed an act of disbelief who have said, 'God is one member of a trinity'" (Q 5:73; also Q 4:171; for an understanding of the *mushrikūn* of the Qurʾān as Christians who had transgressed the tenets of their religion, see Hawting, *Idea of idolatry*, esp. chaps. 2 and 3; see also IDOLATRY AND IDOLATERS). It seems that some Jews (see JEWS AND JUDAISM), in their exaggerated veneration of Ezra (q.v.), deified the reformer-prophet, and Q 9:30 refers to this. The same verse refers to the deification of Jesus (q.v.) by Christians and the next verse accuses the People of the Book (q.v.) of setting up their scholars (see SCHOLAR) and monks (see MONASTICISM AND MONKS) as "lords (see LORD) besides God." According to qurʾānic commentators, the accusation refers to the fact that the Jews and Christians had, at certain times in their history, come to regard their scholars and monks as a more authoritative source of legislation or guidance (see ASTRAY; ERROR) than the revealed scriptures (see BOOK; SCRIPTURE AND THE QURʾĀN) themselves and this amounted to *shirk*, or was seen as a form of *shirk*, since they thereby accorded their scholars and saints the position of legislator that belongs to God (see LAW AND THE QURʾĀN; JUSTICE AND INJUSTICE). It should be noted, however, that while the Qurʾān accuses the People of the Book of committing certain acts of *shirk*, it does not call them *mushrikūn*. The distinction derives from the fact that the People of the Book in principle reject polytheism and avow monotheism *(tawḥīd)* as their fundamental belief, and the Qurʾān accepts that avowal. It is for this reason that Islamic law treats the People of the Book as a category by itself. Incidentally, many Muslim scholars point out that sometimes Muslims themselves commit acts of *shirk* (saint worship in some Muslim societies is cited as an example; see SAINTS; BELIEF AND UNBELIEF).

Causes

There are, the Qurʾān suggests, several causes of *shirk*. Power — especially absolute power — leads some to think that they are God-like, and they have been accepted as such by those subject to them (see POWER AND IMPOTENCE). The king with whom Abraham debated declared himself to be god "because God had given him kingly power" — that is, instead of being grateful for the gift, he set himself up as a deity because he had, he thought, absolute, god-like power (Q 2:258; see KINGS AND RULERS). Certain phenomena of nature inspire feelings of awe, wonder or admiration, leading people to regard them as deities; examples are the sun, the moon and the stars (Q 6:74-81; see COSMOLOGY). And, as noted above, people may become slaves of their base desires and passions, seeking always to satisfy them; in so doing they commit a kind of *shirk*. No matter what its cause, *shirk* represents the human beings' failure, caused by ignorance (q.v.) or perversity (see REBELLION; DISOBEDIENCE; INSOLENCE AND OBSTINACY), to see the truth, evidenced in all of existence, that there is only one God.

Arguments against shirk

The Qurʾān offers several arguments against *shirk*. First, the stability and order prevailing throughout the universe is proof that it was created and is being administered by one God and that no one has any share in his power (e.g. Q 28:70-2). In Q 27:60-4, which contains a series of arguments against *shirk*, the polytheists are repeatedly asked after every argument: "Is there a god alongside God?" An impartial reflection on the universe leads one to the conclusion that "He is the one who is God *(ilāhun)* in the heavens and God *(ilāhun)* in the earth" (Q 43:84); "Had there been several gods in them [heavens and earth], these would have been disrupted" (Q 21:22). Second, human beings have an instinctive distaste for *shirk*, which is borne out by the fact that at times of crisis they forget the false deities and call upon the one true God for help. Thus, even idolaters, while traveling on the high seas, would, when their ship is overtaken by a storm, call upon the one God, forgetting their other deities. But as soon as they reach the safety of the shore, they start associating other beings with God (Q 29:65; see also Q 7:189-90; 10:22-3; see GRATITUDE AND INGRATITUDE). Third, *shirk* takes away from human dignity. Human beings have been honored by God, who has given them charge of the physical world, and for them to commit shirk would be to disgrace their position in the world. "Do you worship what you sculpture?" — that is, would you worship something you carve out with your own hands? Finally, there is the combined evidence of the prophetic messages throughout human history, for the essential doctrine preached by all the prophets was that of *tawḥīd* (cf. Q 7:59 [Noah; q.v.]; 7:65 [Hūd; q.v.]; 7:73 [Ṣāliḥ; q.v.]; 7:85 [Shuʿayb; q.v.]). Here it should be pointed out that prophecy in Islam begins with Adam (see PROPHETS AND PROPHETHOOD; ADAM AND EVE). This means that, as prophet, Adam preached monotheism, so that *tawḥīd* is not a later discovery made by the human race but the very first lesson that God taught human beings. Q 7:172-3 recounts the event that took place in pre-existence and according to which God brought forth all human beings who were ever to be born, making them testify that he alone was their lord (see COVENANT).

Atheism

Q 45:24 is sometimes cited as referring to atheism. The verse reads: "And they say, 'This worldly life of ours is all there is — we die and we live, and nothing but time destroys us.' But they have no knowledge of it; they are only speculating." Yet the view that there existed, at the time of the prophet Muḥammad, individuals or groups of people who denied the existence of divinity altogether, is highly implausible. The verse is best interpreted as referring to the pre-Islamic view of the Arabs (q.v.) that the rise and fall of nations is governed not by any definite moral laws, as the Qurʾān maintained, but by the impersonal hand of fate (q.v.; see also DESTINY). In criticizing this view, the verse is affirming, by implication, that societies rise and prosper or decline and perish, strictly in accordance with moral laws laid down by God (see ETHICS AND THE QURʾĀN). Denying the relevance of morality to prosperity and success in the world, the Arabs claimed that the rise and fall of nations was due to the perpetually moving wheel of fortune that first raised a nation to the top and then brought it down. On this view, the Quraysh (q.v.) of Mecca (q.v.) could ward off the qurʾānic criticism that their affluence (which, according to the Qurʾān, was really a gift from God; see GIFT AND GIFT-GIVING; WEALTH) was meant to put them to the test (see TRIAL) and that they were expected to make responsible use of the resources put at their disposal.

But even though Q 45:24 may not be cited to prove the existence of atheists in Arabia, the qurʾānic concept of *tawḥīd* would, by definition, negate atheism: just as the Qurʾān rejects the idea that there can be two or more gods, so it would reject the idea that there is no god; the Islamic declaration of faith (see WITNESS TO FAITH) as cited in several places in the Qurʾān does not stop at *lā ilāha,* "there is no god," but goes on to affirm the existence of one God, *illā llah,* "except God." See also PRE-ISLAMIC ARABIA AND THE QURĀN.

Mustansir Mir

Bibliography
Amīn Aḥsan Iṣlāḥī, *Ḥaqīqat-i dīn. The true essence of Islam* [in Urdu], Lahore 1973; C. Brockelmann, Allah und die Götzen. Der Ursprung des islamischen Monotheismus, in *Archiv für Religionswissenschaft* 21 (1922), 99-121 (discussion of the traditional information about pre-Islamic Arab idolatry); T. Fahd, *Le panthéon de l'Arabie centrale à la veille de l'hégire,* Paris 1968 (discussion of the traditional information about pre-Islamic Arab idolatry); D. Gimaret, Shirk, in *EI*[2], ix, 484-6 (on *shirk* in the Qurʾān and in Muslim usage); G.R. Hawting, *The idea of idolatry and the emergence of Islam. From polemic to history,* Cambridge 1999, esp. chaps. 2 and 3; M.I.H. Surty, *The qurʾānic concept of al-shirk (polytheism),* London 1982 (on *shirk* in the Qurʾān and in Muslim usage); J. Waardenburg, Un débat coranique contre les polythéistes, in *Ex orbe religionum. Studia Geo Widengren oblata,* Leiden 1972 (on *shirk* in the Qurʾān and in Muslim usage); J. Wansbrough, *The sectarian milieu,* London 1978 (for idolatry as a topic of polemic); A.T. Welch, Allah and other supernatural beings. The emergence of the qur'anic doctrine of tawhid, in *JAAR* 47/4s (1979), 733-58.

Pomegranates see GARDEN; AGRICULTURE AND VEGETATION

Pool see BILQĪS

Poor see POVERTY AND THE POOR

Popular and Talismanic Uses of the Qurʾān

Several terms (*ṭilasm*, pl. *ṭalismāt* or *ṭalāsim; ruqya*, pl. *ruqā; siḥr*) connote this topic and the subject itself includes a wide range of practices all based on the materialization/actualization of the Qurʾān, whether tapping the power inherent in verbal performance or creating physical renderings of divine speech. These materializations and actualizations of the Qurʾān are often designated para-liturgical, that is, those uses of the Qurʾān outside the contexts of formal Islamic rites (*ṣalāt, tajwīd;* see PRAYER; RECITATION OF THE QURʾĀN). They include the range of personal prayer (*duʿāʾ*, see PRAYER FORMULAS); spells, incantations and verbal charms *(ruqya);* physical talismans *(ṭilasm)* and amulets (q.v.; *taʿwīdh*) and other healing applications of the Qurʾān conveyed by using liquids *(maḥw, nushra);* divining *(istikhāra, faʾl)* through interpretation of the qurʾānic text, as well as divining through the incubation of dreams *(ruʾyā)* which are interpreted *(taʿbīr)* using the qurʾānic text (see DREAMS AND SLEEP); and physical representations of qurʾānic contents in calligraphic arts (stone and plaster bas relief, metal engraving, mosaic and inlay of *objets d'art* and decoration of objects in daily use, painted murals, textile embroidery, wall hangings and carpets, poster art and other ephemera; see MATERIAL CULTURE AND THE QURʾĀN; EVERYDAY LIFE, THE QURʾĀN IN; EPIGRAPHY AND THE QURʾĀN). The para-liturgical uses of the Qurʾān are most often applied for protection from disease, accident, or conscious malefic intention; protection and blessing of interior and exterior physical space (especially the domicile or place of business; see HOUSE, DOMESTIC AND DIVINE); success in defensive as well as aggressive warfare (see VICTORY; WAR; FIGHTING); material well-being and accrual of wealth (q.v.); fertility (human, animal, and agricultural); individual, familial, and communal welfare, particularly that of children; and knowledge of the meaning and outcome of specific events or the destiny of a given life within the unfolding of sacred history (see HISTORY AND THE QURʾĀN; FATE; DESTINY; FREEDOM AND PREDESTINATION).

The Qurʾān and spiritual mediation (wasīla) *and intercession* (shafāʿa)

Talismanic and popular uses of the Qurʾān find their meaning within the framework of spiritual mediation in Islam. Spiritual mediation or intercession (q.v.) by God with himself and by the prophet Muḥammad and the *ahl al-bayt*, the "People of (the Prophet's) House" (see PEOPLE OF THE HOUSE; FAMILY OF THE PROPHET), through God's permission (*wasīla*, Q 5:35; 17:57; *shafāʿa*, e.g. Q 2:255; 10:3; 20:109; 21:28; 34:23; 43:86), to improve, ameliorate, and sustain one's circumstances in life is a belief which had currency throughout medieval Islam and continues at the popular level into the modern era (Padwick, *Muslim devotions*, 37-47, 235-44). Muslims having recourse to spiritual mediation operate within a specific context of divine blessing (q.v.; *baraka*), which can be conveyed and absorbed by association with sacred persons (prophets, saints, etc.; see PROPHETS AND PROPHETHOOD; SAINT) and through objects which have absorbed the holiness of persons (clothing, hair and bodily detritus, personal belongings or objects of ritual use), as well as contact with places of birth, habitation, or death which become objectified in devotion as sanctuaries and sites of pilgrimage (see FESTIVALS AND COMMEMORATIVE DAYS). Popular and talismanic uses of the Qurʾān draw upon both the reifying power of qurʾānic speech (q.v.; its ability to cause and maintain all things in existence; see WORD OF GOD; COSMOLOGY) and the physical transmissibility of qurʾānic *baraka* (O'Connor, Prophetic medicine, 52-3). The verbal and material object which is perhaps the most universally accessible vehicle of divine blessing and amelioration to Muslims, of course, is the Qurʾān itself. It is at the same time a vehicle of worship and of spiritual and material action, encompassing parameters most often inappropriately segregated by scholarship as religion (q.v.) and magic (q.v.).

Magic (siḥr) *and the uses of the Qurʾān: Licit and illicit "magic" in Islam*

Based on qurʾānic references and other early accounts (such as Ibn al-Kalbī's *Kitāb al-Aṣnām,* "Book of idols"), *siḥr,* or "magic/sorcery," in pre-Islamic belief and practice seems to have included invocation of spirits or demons *(jinn),* spirit possession, exorcism of such spirits, soothsaying and divining by arrows and lots and geomantic omens, talismanry, cursing and healing by verbal, gestural, and material action (see SOOTHSAYERS; JINN; INSANITY; DIVINATION; FORETELLING; CURSE; PRE-ISLAMIC ARABIA AND THE QURʾĀN). The range of activities associated with the word *siḥr* in Islamic times include active and practical magic (spells, tying of knots, invocations, talismans, cursing and healing; see ILLNESS AND HEALTH) as well as intuitive systems of extraordinary knowledge (soothsaying, divining, and geomancy; Fahd, *Divination,* 214-45, 363-7). All the activities of *siḥr* were the proper role of the poetesses/poets (*shāʿir/a, shuʿarāʾ;* see POETS AND POETRY) and priestesses/priests *(kāhin/a, kahana)* of the pre-Islamic era and, in the transition to the rise of Islam, came to be circumscribed by its new dispensation (Serjeant, Islam, 216-21). Recast in the mould of Islam, these arts flourished without any marked discontinuity, and only later would be characterized by the fourth/tenth-century proto-Ismāʿīlī authors of the *Rasāʾil Ikhwān al-Ṣafāʾ* as "permitted" or licit magic *(al-siḥr al-ḥalāl),* those arts which served Islam, such as the permission to perform magic accorded by God to various prophetic figures in the Qurʾān (e.g. Solomon's God-given power to command the winds and the armies of the jinn, Q 21:81-2, 34:12-3; see SOLOMON; AIR AND WIND) and "forbidden" or illicit magic *(al-siḥr al-ḥarām),* those arts which opposed Islam, or attempted to operate independently of Islam, such as malefic magic, cursing, and other evils (Bürgel, *The feather,* 28-37; Ikhwān al-Ṣafāʾ, *Rasāʾil,* iv, 327-8, 345).

> ... This is the licit or permitted magic *(al-siḥr al-ḥalāl)* which is the mission toward God, may he be praised, by means of the truth and the speech of sincerity. And false magic is that which is the opposite, such as the works of the opponents of the prophets and the enemies of the sages... whose laws protected the weak among men and women against the fascination *(siḥr)* of their minds by falsehood.... This is illicit or forbidden magic *(al-siḥr al-ḥarām)* which has no stability in it, nor continuance, and is that which is without proof or trustworthy demonstration... (ibid., iv, 348-9).

Examples of such forbidden practices would be widespread belief in or use of the "evil eye," whether the source is human malice or that of the jinn, and other forms of cursing, as well as preventing malefic magic, or counter-magic (Q 68:51, Q 113, Q 114; for medieval examples see Ibn Qayyim al-Jawziyya [d. 751/1350], *Ṭibb*, 119-21, 124; Ibn Bisṭām [fl. third/ninth century], *Ṭibb*, 43, 49-53, 161, 177, 185-6; Ṣuyūṭī [d. 911/1505], *Ṭibb*, 164-72; and for the modern Muslim world, see Ibrahim, *Assaulting with words*, chap. 4 [Arabic *siḥr*]; Flueckiger, The vision, 255; Ewing, Malangs, 369; Bowen, Return to sender).

The Qurʾān groups a variety of practices all loosely associated with pre-Islamic or foreign religion (see RELIGIOUS PLURALISM AND THE QURʾĀN; SOUTH ARABIA, RELIGION IN PRE-ISLAMIC) under the category of magic or "sorcery" (Q 2:102 for "the devils…, who taught sorcery *[siḥr]* to people, which, they said, had been revealed to the angels of Babylon, Hārūt and Mārūt [q.v.]"). Although classical definitions of "magic" in Islam are focused on the qurʾānic proscriptions against the "sorcery" of "knot-tying," "soothsaying," and demonic possession as in the style established by pre-Islamic oracular/gnomic poets and priests, an interrelated group of more or less licit magical and theurgic disciplines were categorized as the "occult sciences" *(al-ʿulūm al-ghaybiyya)* by their practitioners. These magical sciences recoded the Greek or foreign sciences (philosophy, mathematics, celestial mechanics, physical and natural law, and medicine) within an Islamic creationist universe (see PHILOSOPHY AND THE QURʾĀN; SCIENCE AND THE QURʾĀN; MEDICINE AND THE QURʾĀN; KNOWLEDGE AND LEARNING; INTELLECT; CREATION). Included are beliefs in the inherent power of sacred places and objects pre-Islamically expressed in divine images, shrines, altars, and sacred trees, wells, stones, and Islamically expressed in the use of talismans (qurʾānic and other) and the cult of saints (Schimmel, *Mystical dimensions;* Eaton, Political and religious authority; Hoffman, *Ṣūfism;* Ernst, *Eternal garden*). Pre-Islamic star worship (see PLANETS AND STARS) will become the Islamic interpenetration of astrology with many medieval "occult" and physical sciences, such as astrological medicine, the twin disciplines of astronomy-astrology, astrological talismanry and amuletry *(ʿilm al-khawāṣṣ wa-l-ṭalāsim)*, astrological alchemy *(al-kīmiyāʾ)*, astrologically coded numerology (q.v.) and geomancy (*ʿilm al-jafr* and *ʿilm al-raml;* Nasr, Alchemy; id., *Introduction;* id., Spiritual message; Savage-Smith/Smith, *Islamic geomancy*). Pre-Islamic divination by arrows and animal remains (Q 3:44; 5:90) becomes Islamic divining with the Qurʾān *(istikhāra, faʾl)*, dream incubation, and interpretation (*taʿbīr al-ruʾyā;* Donaldson, The Koran; Lamoreaux, *Early Muslim tradition;* Glassé, *Concise encyclopedia*, s.v. Istikhārah). The pre-Islamic poetic/priestly role of spirit possession and mediumship is channeled through Islamic manipulation, conjuring, and exorcism of spirits, angels, and demons *(jinn)* through qurʾānic spells used with material substances, especially physical representations of the Qurʾān and the divine names (*al-asmāʾ al-ḥusnā;* see GOD AND HIS ATTRIBUTES) from the Qurʾān (Ibn Qayyim al-Jawziyya, *Ṭibb;* Ṣuyūṭī, *Ṭibb;* Ibn Bisṭām, *Ṭibb*). Pre-Islamic cursing and malefic action by spells, such as the tying of knots, become Islamic verbal charms *(ruqya)* for healing and protection from the evil eye drawn from qurʾānic contents accompanied by knot-tying and other gestures like spitting and blowing (Ibn Qayyim al-Jawziyya, *Ṭibb;* Ṣuyūṭī, *Ṭibb;* Ibn Bisṭām, *Ṭibb;* also Robson, Magical use).

In the realm of "popular" devotion, the sources for "magic" in Islam strongly overlap with those for talismanic and popular uses of the Qurʾān, since most "licit" magic in Islam centers on magical and material uses of the Qurʾān, particularly in medieval Sunnī and Shīʿī texts (see SHĪʿISM

AND THE QURʾĀN) on prophetic medicine *(al-ṭibb al-nabawī)* and books of qurʾānic material efficacy (*kutub khawāṣṣ al-Qurʾān,* cf. Ḥājjī Khalīfa, *Kashf,* iii, 180, no. 4814; Ghazālī, *al-Dhahab al-ibrīz*) and popular medieval and modern chapbooks or manuals on qurʾānic devotions, dream divination, prophetic medicine and qurʾānic healing (handbooks of medicines and treatments of illness reported by the Prophet, such as *Luqaṭ al-amān fī l-ṭibb* (or, *Luqaṭ al-manāfiʿ fī l-ṭibb,* "Beneficial selections from medicine") by Ibn al-Jawzī (d. 597/1200), and two works simply entitled *al-Ṭibb al-nabawī* ("Prophetic medicine") by al-Dhahabī (d. 784/1348) and Ibn Qayyim al-Jawziyya (d. 751/1350); and the early Shīʿī compendium, *Ṭibb al-aʾimma* ("Medicine of the Imāms") by Ibn Bisṭām (ca. third/ninth century; see O'Connor, Prophetic medicine, 48-64; Fahd, Khawāṣṣ). The Qurʾān in Muslim life and practice is, thus, the central arena for observing the permeability of "licit magic" in Islam. As Islam's most religiously authoritative, rigorously liturgical, and legally conservative source (see THEOLOGY AND THE QURʾĀN; LAW AND THE QURʾĀN), the Qurʾān also comes down to the present as Islam's most intimately negotiated, vernacularly creative, and magically effective venue of religious action (Primiano, Vernacular religion, 44-51).

Paraliturgical uses of the Qurʾān: Expressions of kufr *or* tawḥīd?

The liturgical and paraliturgical uses of the Qurʾān are not as easily separable. Often, the methods, material, and purposes of the paraliturgical uses of the Qurʾān overlap with those of its liturgical uses. The distinction tends to be made when the physical form of the Qurʾān, or any part of its verbal contents, is used as an object of inherent power, to achieve either superhuman faculties (such as foreknowledge) or to invoke divine mediation as in physical protection (q.v.) and healing. The difference is in the style, context, and intention of performance, as well as the ritualization of objects, rather than in the contents, which are often the same or similar (see RITUAL AND THE QURʾĀN). The essential qurʾānic justification for the amuletic and talismanic use of the Qurʾān refers to its God-given purpose as a healing and a mercy (q.v.; *shifāʾun wa-raḥmatun,* Q 17:82; cf. Owusu-Ansah, *Islamic talismanic tradition,* 122), and that "no human deed [is] more effective in escaping God's wrath than the recounting of the *dhikr* of God," i.e. divine speech in the Qurʾān (Nana Asmaʾu, Medicine, 118-9; see MEMORY; REMEMBRANCE). Muslim qurʾānic spell- and talisman-makers, although bracketed by ongoing medieval legal debate (Owusu-Ansah, *Islamic talismanic tradition,* 25-40) and modern rationalist dismissal (see CONTEMPORARY CRITICAL PRACTICES AND THE QURʾĀN), draw upon the range of positive juristic and popular opinion that it "cannot be the act of unbelieving *(kufr),* if the process brings benefit and especially if the content is from the Qurʾān" (El-Tom, Drinking the Koran, 33-4; see BELIEF AND UNBELIEF). The rationalist and reformist orientation of much contemporary public Muslim discourse draws on such staunch late medieval legal authorities as Ibn Taymiyya (d. 728/1328), whose *Kitāb Iqtiḍāʾ al-sirāṭ al-mustaqīm mukhālafat aṣḥāb al-jaḥīm,* "Book of the necessity of the straight path against the people of hell," portrays qurʾānic "intercession" and other paraliturgical uses of the Qurʾān as "human distortions… and deformations of true *tawḥīd*" (Waardenburg, Official and popular religion, 340-2; see PATH OR WAY). A century or so later, al-Ṣuyūṭī wrote his own version of the already established talismanic genre, *al-Ṭibb al-nabawī,* "Prophetic medicine," in which he draws a fine line between faithful recitation and recitation that lapses into *shirk,* "associating anything with God" (see POLYTHEISM AND ATHEISM).

The *umm al-Qurʾān* ["mother of the Qurʾān," i.e. Sūrat al-Fātiḥa, the opening chapter] is the most useful of all to recite, because it contains glorification of God (q.v.), together with worship of him alone, and calling on him for help. It is said that the exact point at which the cure is actually effected when reciting the *āyāt* is at the words, "Only you do we worship, and only you do we ask for help" (Q 1:5).
The Prophet, may God bless him and grant him peace, said, "Combining the recitation of *āyāt* [qurʾānic verses] with charms is *shirk.*" The reason for this statement is that in this case, *shirk* is being associated with the recitation of the *āyāt.* And so indeed it is. But when the recitation of *āyāt* is free from *shirk,* then it is *ḥalāl* ["permitted/lawful"] for Muslims to do so (see LAWFUL AND UNLAWFUL). There is nothing to prevent the recitation of *āyāt* over a sick man, provided that there is no *shirk* involved....
It is probably that this prohibition of something that was known to work was because some people believed that the cure came from the very nature of the words themselves. At a later stage, this prohibition was lifted. When Islam and the search for truth became established in their hearts, then he gave them permission to use such recitation, provided that they understood that it was God who effected the cure — or not... (Ṣuyūṭī, *Ṭibb,* 133).

Despite this juristic dissonance and the fact that talismanic and popular uses of the Qurʾān have declined greatly due to the rise in education and literacy, and the impact of secularism, westernization, and modernization in the post-colonial Muslim world, the need for an affective and immediate experience of God through materializations/actualizations of his speech continues to express itself among Muslims today in a variety of living responses to the qurʾānic text. Contemporary male and female Muslim religious healers (frequently but not exclusively Ṣūfīs, who are both likely to command the written technology of the Qurʾān and knowledge and experience of its talismanic applications; see ṢŪFISM AND THE QURʾĀN; TRADITIONAL DISCIPLINES OF QURʾĀNIC STUDY) have used virtually the same sources (qurʾānic verses, the divine names or attributes of God in the Qurʾān, and ḥadīth which support qurʾānic talismanry/spellmaking; see ḤADĪTH AND THE QURʾĀN) to justify popular and talismanic use of the Qurʾān as have those Muslims who disapprove or disavow such activities (Flueckiger, The vision; Bowen, *Muslims through discourse;* El-Tom, Drinking the Koran; Ewing, Malangs of the Punjab; Eaton, Political and religious authority; Hoffman, *Ṣūfism*).

Popular, folk, and vernacular religion and the uses of the Qurʾān

Before addressing specific aspects of the talismanic and popular uses of the Qurʾān, some discussion of method in the study of people's religion is appropriate. Although the use of the term "popular" as in "popular religion" is invoked in the very title of this article, its academic use continues to spark divergent reflections on the nature of religion as a social phenomenon. It usually is the second of a pair of opposite or complementary terms implying a hierarchical and dichotomized view of religion, such as official and popular religion, or normative and popular religion, paralleling other dichotomizations, such as orthodox and heterodox religion (see HERESY), and elite and folk religion. "Official, normative, orthodox, elite" all yield meanings which place the religion and people who practice it so identified at the center of authority and legitimacy, and their complementary opposites "popular, heterodox, folk" at the margins, without authority or tinged with the flavor of illegitimacy (Waardenburg, Official and popular; Lewis, *Saints and Somalis;* id., The power of the past; Patai, Folk Islam). There is an implicit assumption in both scholarly and popular awareness of religion that there is some central, institutionalized, and validated form which is "real" religion, and then there are all the subversive things that ordinary believers think and do. "Real religion" for scholars has been overwhelmingly re-posited in the texts of religion, particularly those texts said to be divinely revealed, accompanied by the authoritative commentary, legal, and moral literature derived from revealed or inspired religion (see SCRIPTURE AND THE QURʾĀN; EXEGESIS OF THE QURʾĀN: CLASSICAL AND MEDIEVAL). One of the inherent consequences of the tendency of these dichotomous terms to elevate textual/institutional religion and the hierarchy of religious professionals to a centrist, even megalithic, dimension is the corresponding devaluation of the religion of ordinary believers and everyday life. Focus upon the Qurʾān in everyday life, however, tends to break down this dichotomization of religion by seeing the intersection of official and folk or normative and popular, orthodox and heterodox, in the objectification and materialization of the divine speech of the Arabic Qurʾān (see also INIMITABILITY). The function and meaning of the Qurʾān in everyday life and everyday speech (see ARABIC LANGUAGE; LITERATURE AND THE QURʾĀN; SLOGANS FROM THE QURʾĀN), as well as its more technical uses in para-liturgical devotions and talismanic practices, render the heart of Islam visible to view, that is, the intimate and personal bond between every individual believer, their immediate community, and the *umma* as a whole, with the substance of divine "healing and mercy," as the Qurʾān describes itself (Q 17:82). The vernacular religious creativity and interpretive negotiations of actual believers in the para-liturgical uses of the Qurʾān, include the *ʿulamāʾ* or Islam's religious hierarchy (Primiano, Vernacular religion, 46; see SCHOLAR). It is medieval and modern Muslim "scholars" who make "elite" materials available to the masses, interpreting primary sources — Qurʾān and the ḥadīth which discuss its uses in everyday life (see EXEGESIS OF THE QURʾĀN: EARLY MODERN AND CONTEMPORARY) — and channeling them into "popular" devotional literature, like prayer manuals, prophetic medical texts, charm- and talisman-making booklets, as well as editions of the Qurʾān marked with methods for divination and dream interpretation (Donaldson, The Koran, 258; El-Tom, Drinking the Koran, 429; Perho, *The Prophet's medicine;* see MANUSCRIPTS OF THE QURʾĀN; TEACHING AND PREACHING THE QURʾĀN).

Literature on popular and talismanic uses of the Qurʾān

Throughout the Islamic middle ages and into the modern era, as the above examples have shown, vernacular qurʾānic healing practices have been widely and fervently espoused in Muslim practice (if not theory) and have generated an extensive body of "how-to" literature. This instructional literature informed and guided local practitioners on the procedures and methods of interpretation of all these qurʾānic arts and included a variety of sub-genres such as encyclopedias of dream interpretation, chapbooks of qurʾānic prayers/spells for magical effect and manuals on the creation of qurʾānic talismans and "erasures." The use of qurʾānic speech

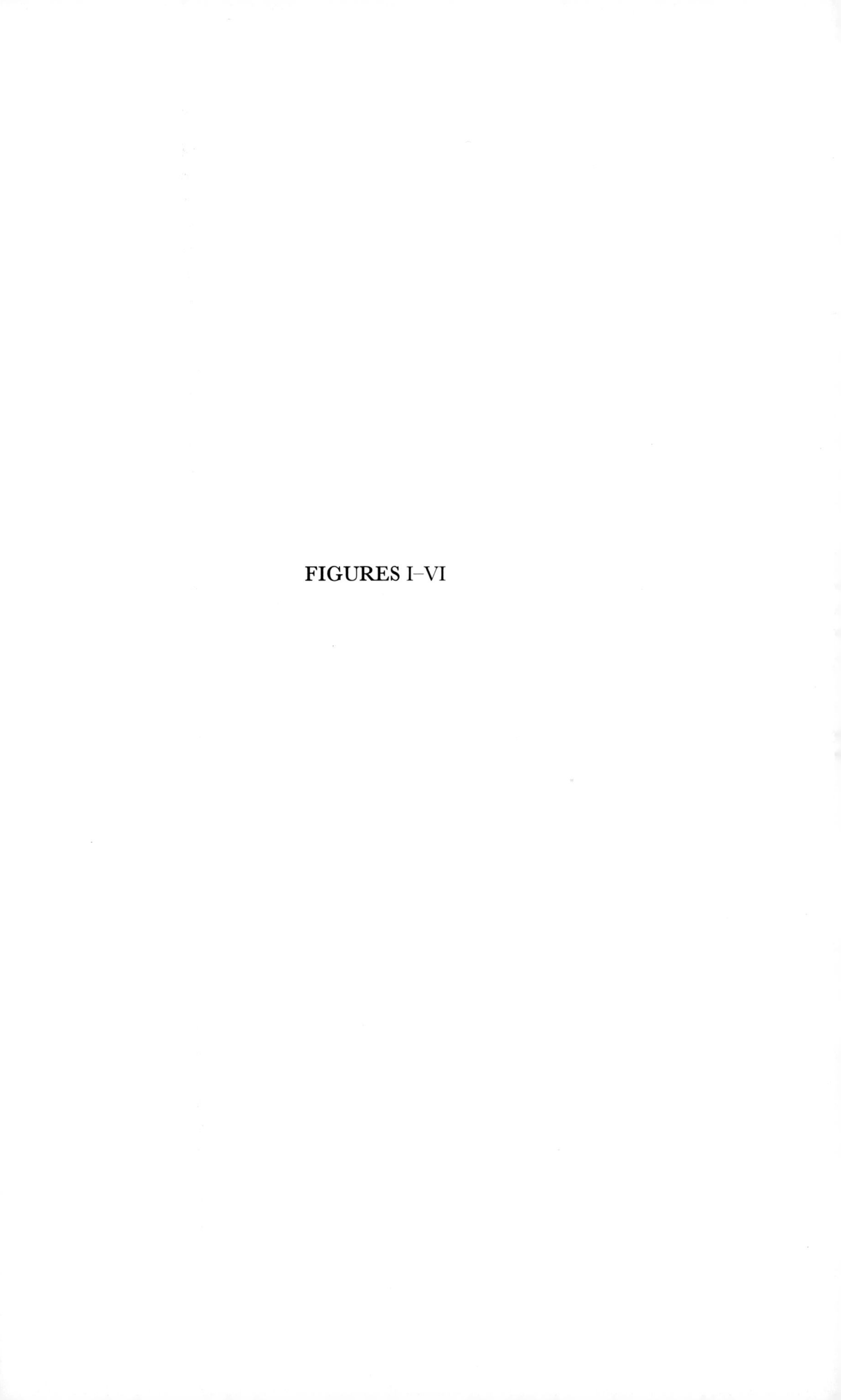

FIGURES I–VI

[I] Magic medicine bowl, back (lead): unknown provenance, second/eighth or third/ninth centuries. The center is inscribed with a portion of the *basmala*, "In the name of God" and, below it, "God suffices me" (Q 9:129; 39:38). Courtesy of the Nasser D. Khalili Collection (MTW 621).

[II] Magic medicine bowl (bronze): Iran, eleventh/seventeenth century. The interior of the bowl, depicted here, is filled with invocations and prayers in Arabic and Persian. Three of the four roundels contain prayers, the *shahāda* and invocations, while the fourth contains Persian and Arabic titles and formulas typical of Ṣūfī dervish orders. The attached cartouches contain additional formulas and titles that indicate a Ṣūfī context, as well as verses from Q 109, 113 and 114. Other qur'ānic citations are found throughout. Courtesy of the Nasser D. Khalili Collection (MTW 1444).

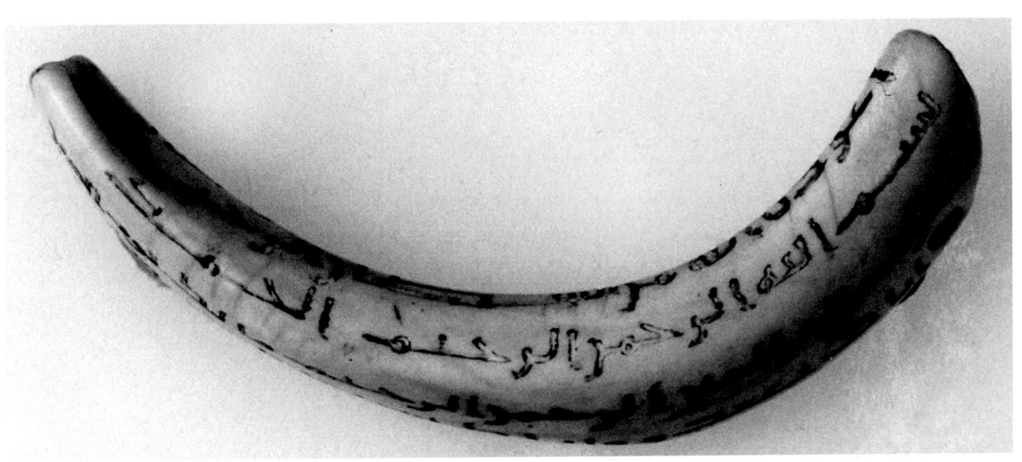

[III] Amulet (tusk): Iran, ca. third/ninth century. Q 1:1-7 form part of the six lines of Kūfic text inscribed on this object. Courtesy of the Nasser D. Khalili Collection (TLS 2466).

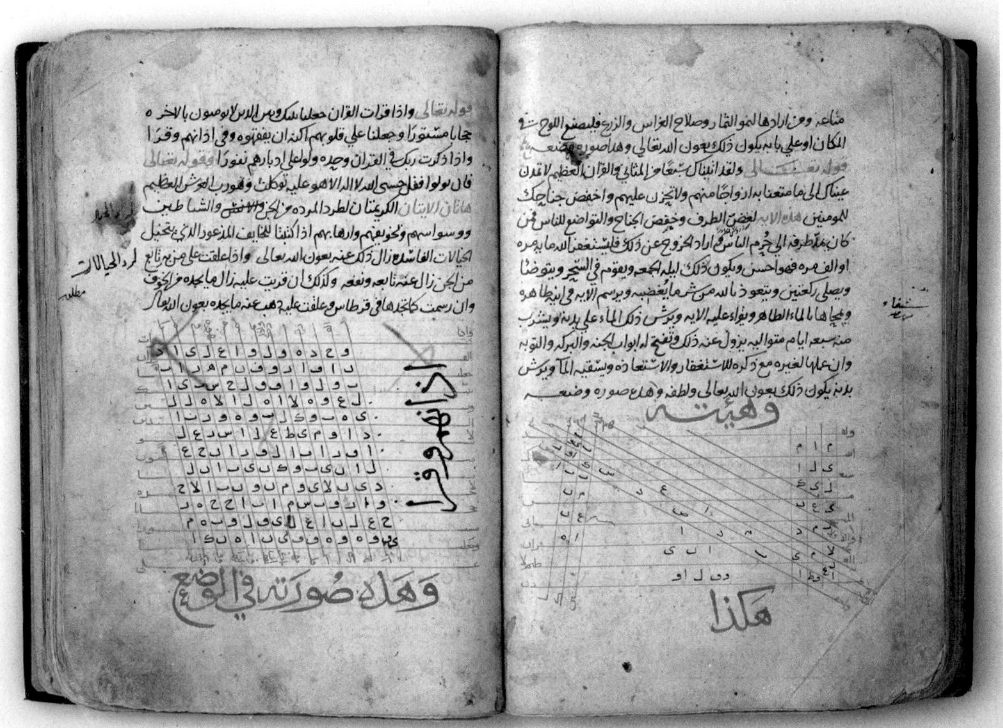

[IV] Talismanic book with chart: Iraq?, 828/1425. This manuscript contains the earliest recorded copy of a treatise (five of the six parts of which discuss the magical uses of the names of God) written by Abū l-ʿAbbās Aḥmad b. ʿAlī b. Yūsuf al-Būnī l-Qurashī (d. ca. 622/1225). The sixth section provides specific talismans employing the divine names, individual verses of the Qurʾān and their talismanic uses, and a general discussion of magical alphabets. The folios shown here, which are taken from the sixth section, discuss Q 15:87-8, 17:45-6, and 9:129. Courtesy of the Nasser D. Khalili Collection (MSS 300, folios 62b-63a).

[v] Talismanic shirt, front (cotton): Iran?, tenth/sixteenth or eleventh/seventeenth centuries. The shirt is comprised of two large rectangular pieces, joined at the shoulders, while six smaller pieces form the sleeves and under-arm areas. Each piece of material is framed by a wide band containing prayers, invocations and qurʾānic quotations (e.g. Q 2:255; 24:35; 110; 112). Courtesy of the Nasser D. Khalili Collection (TXT 77).

[VI] Talismanic chart (parchment): Iran, 1919. The bulk of this chart (i.e. most of the lower two-thirds) is a 100X100 magic square composed of 10,000 individual cells, each of which contains a numeral. The border of each of the four large circles in the upper third of the chart contains the Throne Verse (Q 2:255); the lower two circles frame two 16X16 magic squares that flank a 10X10 Latin square (*wafq majāzī*) composed of the "mysterious letters" that open a number of qur'ānic sūras. Courtesy of the Nasser D. Khalili Collection (MSS 755).

in magical images of power and blessing, as talismans against harm and amulets for sickness, forms part of a range of vernacular expression encompassing a diverse popularly disseminated talismanic literature and practice, leaving an extensive manuscript and print record in recipe books and how-to manuals into the eighteenth and nineteenth centuries which have been reprinted or lithographed up until the present day. Books of instruction, such as the *Majmaʿ al-dawāt*, as well as professional practitioners of these extra-canonical qurʾānic "sciences" were numerous throughout medieval Islam and into the modern era. Special Qurʾāns have been published with marginal notation on methods of divination and apposite verses for magical or talismanic use. Treatises on the preparation and use of qurʾānic talismanry and prophetic medicine interacted with and were influenced by the variety of "occult" works of magical medicine such as ʿAlī b. Sahl al-Ṭabarī's *Firdaws al-ḥikma*, "Paradise of wisdom," one of the earliest works of Arabic medicine, completed in 235/850, as well as the magical cures included in larger works such as Muḥammad b. Zakariyyāʾ al-Rāzī's tenth-century "Book of the magician" *(Kitāb al-Ḥāwī)* and his "Book of natural sciences" *(Maqāla fī mā baʿd al-ṭabīʿa)*, as well as the genre of occult medicine, the *kutub al-mujarrabāt*, "books of the tested," that is, magical techniques "tested" by experience, such as the *Mujarrabāt* of Aḥmad al-Dayrabī (d. ca. 1151/1739) and Abū ʿAbdallāh Muḥammad b. Yūsuf al-Sanūsī (d. 895/1490).

This genre of medieval literature and chapbooks *(al-mujarrabāt)* on the paraliturgical uses of the Qurʾān evolved, analyzing the text according to its extraordinary properties *(khawāṣṣ)* and applying those properties to talismanic uses of the divine names and other materials in the Qurʾān (see Fig. IV). A variety of subcategories were established in these texts: *ʿilm al-khawāṣṣ*, for the knowledge derived from the extraordinary qualities inherent in the divine names and other materials in the Qurʾān; *ʿilm al-ruqā*, for qurʾānic spell magic; *ʿilm al-faʾl*, for the reading of omens using the Qurʾān; manipulations of number and letter, known either as *ʿilm al-jafr* or *ʿilm al-ḥurūf*, and applied to the divine names or other words or letters of the Arabic in the Qurʾān; and finally, *ʿilm al-taʿbīr*, or the incubation and interpretation of dreams and visions *(ruʾyā)*. Dictionaries and encyclopedias of dream symbolism and poetic expositions of divining through their systematic interpretation were generated from the early Islamic middle ages, such as those ascribed to Ibn Sīrīn (d. 110/728), Ibrāhīm b. ʿAbdallāh al-Kirmānī (fl. late second/eighth cent.), and extant manuscripts of Ibn Qutayba (d. 276/889), and Aḥmad al-Sijistānī (d. 399/1008), as well as late medieval manuals by al-Qayrawānī and al-Dīnawarī (fl. late fifth/eleventh cent.), the Ṣūfī al-Kharkūshī (d. ca. 406/1015), and the philosopher Ibn Sīnā (d. 428/1037). These medieval divining and dream sources were used into modern times (Westermarck, *Ritual and belief*, 46-57; Fahd, *Divination*, 330-67; Lamoreaux, *Early Muslim tradition*, 15-78).

Qurʾānic talisman recipes: The magic square

A specific example of talismanic literature falling under the heading of *ʿilm al-ḥurūf* is that detailing recipes for "magic squares" in which Arabic phrases, words, and letters from the Qurʾān, especially the names or attributes of God, angels (see ANGEL), prophets or their numerological equivalents are placed in a grid of squares, or other geometric shapes (Ibn Bisṭām, *Ṭibb*, 88-9; Lane, *Manners and customs*, 278-84; Westermarck, *Ritual and belief*, i, 141-7; Doutté, *Magie et religion*, 190 f.; for an example of a talismanic chart containing such magic squares, see Fig. vi). Magic squares, and other number/letter talismans, were a popular expression of the learned systems of Islamic alchemy (*ʿilm al-mīzān,* or science of "balance," and *mīzān al-ḥurūf/mīzān al-lafẓ,* or "balance of letters/speech," in the alchemical corpus of Jābir b. Ḥayyān; see Kraus, *Jābir,* ii, 117-8, 187-230, 236-69). Magic squares were also a part of Ṣūfī and Shīʿī texts which connect the cosmogonic nature of divine speech and Arabic orthography (see ARABIC SCRIPT) with mystical numerology (*ʿilm al-ḥurūf,* also called *al-sīmiyāʾ,* in Ibn Khaldūn, *Muqaddima,* 422-46; abr. trans. Rosenthal, *The Muqaddimah,* 396 f.; cf. number/letter correspondences in Ikhwān al-Ṣafāʾ, *Rasāʾil,* iv, 304-5). Finally, texts of neo-Pythagorean philosophy and magical talismanry also created systems of mystical numerology and magic square recipes (*ʿilm al-jafr* in Ibn Sīnā, *al-Risāla al-nayruziyya;* see Nasr, *Introduction,* 209-12; and Aḥmad al-Dīn al-Būnī [d. 622/1225], *Shams al-maʿārif wa-laṭāʾif al-ʿawārif*).

Nineteenth-century qurʾānic talismanry manuscripts of the Asante in west Africa (now Ghana), and the Sokoto caliphate (now northwestern Nigeria), incorporate verbal performance, or incantational prayer, along with visual/physical representations of divine speech in magic squares, or "seals/rings" (*khawātim,* sing. *khātim;* Lane, *Manners and customs,* 269-70, 279; Robson, Magical use, 35; Owusu-Ansah, *Islamic talismanic tradition,* 96-8; Nana Asma'u, Medicine, 102-19). The *khātim* serves a variety of purposes and is immediately effective upon the written execution of the square. When inscribed with God's names, these "seals" command effect, whereas with other qurʾānic passages they only supplicate, indicating a hierarchy of power in the different forms of divine speech privileging divine names (*al-asmāʾ al-ḥusnā,* the "beautiful names," as well as the *ism akbar,* the "great" or secret name of God), as most powerful and magically efficacious. Magic squares, employing divine names or other qurʾānic materials, continue as vernacular healing and protection devices into the modern era and are still reported to be present in some contemporary Muslim healing rituals where they are used as both diagnostic tool and talismanic prescription (Flueckiger, The vision, 251, 257-8). Emphasis on number/letter mysticism in recent Ṣūfī devotional texts published in the West continues the medieval legacy of esoteric interpretation (see POLYSEMY) and application of the powers of the divine names and alphabetic components of divine speech. Contemporary manuals of qurʾānic spells or talisman making, and other books of magical healing in the *mujarrabāt* genre are in print and available for consultation by contemporary male and female professional and lay practitioners throughout the Muslim world (Robson, Magical use; Donaldson, The Koran; El-Tom, Drinking the Koran; Hunzaʾi, *Qurʾānic healing;* Flueckiger, The vision; Chisti, *Ṣūfī healing*).

Uses of the Qurʾān in historical and living contexts: Oral uses of the Qurʾān

Qurʾānic talismanry and popular uses of the Qurʾān begin with para-liturgical uses of the spoken and performed Qurʾān such as *tajwīd* (melodic recitation of the Qurʾān), *dhikr* (recitation of divine names and brief qurʾānic phrases), *ruqya* (qurʾānic spell-casting and spoken charm-making), *nushra* (performance of qurʾānic verses or chapters accompanied by spitting and/or blowing of their essence onto the client), and the endemic use of qurʾānic phrases in daily speech. What makes these performances "popular" or "talismanic" is not their contents, but the context and purpose, which is traditionally for protection/prevention of illness or accident, healing, fertility, and material abundance. In pre-modern Islamic culture, illness, for example, was attributed to physical and metaphysical (spiritual/magical) causation. Regarding the relationship between the "heart" (q.v.) and the body, God's messenger (q.v.) said:

Every disease has a cure... the illnesses of the body and those of the heart are alike.... For every illness of the heart God created, he also created a cure that is its opposite. When someone whose heart is sick recognizes his disease and counters it with it opposite, he will recover, by God's leave" (Ibn Qayyim al-Jawziyya, *Ṭibb*, 14).

Healing is a manifestation of divine mercy and provides a vehicle for repentance and gratitude (see REPENTANCE AND PENANCE; GRATITUDE AND INGRATITUDE). These texts on prophetic medicine define two basic types of illness: those of the body and those of the heart. Bodily illnesses can be treated in practical ways (through cleansing, abstaining from food and drink or purging, or use of curative or restorative herbs/simples) and also in spiritual ways (through interior prayers, invocations of the divine names of God, verbal spells, and physical charms).

Illnesses of the heart, on the other hand, are spiritual, emotional, and mental both in origin and in cure. They are caused by heart sickness, defined as emotional and mental states such as suspicion (q.v.), doubt (see UNCERTAINTY), and loss of faith, or they can be caused by sins of commission (see SIN, MAJOR AND MINOR) such as desire or allurement (Ibn Qayyim al-Jawziyya, *Ṭibb*, 3-13). "Spiritual" illness included what modern western medicine would identify as mental or emotional illness, since in Islamic understanding the ultimate causation of mental or emotional unease (anxiety, depression, stress, doubt, uncertainty) is lapses or weakening in faith and, correspondingly, health and well-being rest upon "spiritual" nourishment (Suyūṭī, *Ṭibb*, 172-7).

The Prophet says: "I dwell with my lord (q.v.), and he gives me my food and drink (q.v.)." The Qurʾān is the largest repository of spiritual nourishment... the stronger one's faith, love for his lord, joy and gratitude to be in his presence — the more ardent and fervent his yearning to meet his lord — the stronger becomes his certitude *(yaqīn)*, contentment and satisfaction with his lord's will.... Such renewed spiritual strength compensates immeasurably for the patient's needs (Ibn Qayyim al-Jawziyya, *Ṭibb*, 62).

Ḥadīth literature collected in a genre of medieval texts entitled "prophetic medicine" prescribed using the Qurʾān for the prevention and healing of disease, especially for "spiritual illness." The prophet Muḥammad is said to have recommended: "Make use of two remedies: honey (q.v.) and the Qurʾān," which is "a cure for [the disease of] the hearts" (Q 10:57; cf. Ibn Qayyim al-Jawziyya, *Ṭibb*, 27). Shīʿī medical texts also invoke the power of the Qurʾān in the healing and protection of the faithful. Related from ḥadīth of the sixth imām, Jaʿfar al-Ṣādiq (d. 148/765), who replied regarding a query as to the use of a charm for scorpion and snakebite, as well as the spell *(nushra)* for the insane and enchanted who are in torment:

...there is no objection to the charm and invocation and spell if they are taken from the Qurʾān. Whomsoever the Qurʾān does not cure, God does not cure him. Is there anything more effective in these matters than the Qurʾān [citing Q 17:82; 59:21]?... Ask us, we will teach you and acquaint you with the verses of the Qurʾān for every illness" (Ibn Bisṭām, *Ṭibb,* 54).

Even physical illness was often categorized as having non-physical causality, such as ascribing the condition of epilepsy to spirit possession which required an exorcism using qurʾānic verses to accomplish "the rehabilitation of one's sanity and the revival of his faith" (Ibn Qayyim al-Jawziyya, *Ṭibb,* 46-7). "Spiritual remedies" are the antidote to spiritual disease, and the "light" (q.v.) of the Qurʾān (Q 24:35) is the "antithesis of darkness (q.v.) and gratitude is the opposite of denial" (*kufr;* ibid., 91; see PAIRS AND PAIRING).

Qurʾānic recitation, or *tajwīd,* in which Muslims "adorn the Qurʾān with their voices" has both informal curative as well as more formal ritual performance contexts. "It is speech and intonation to which God the almighty has added perfume" (Suyūṭī, *Ṭibb,* 127). Support for auditory use of the Qurʾān makes listening to recitation the cure of infants, beasts, and all those distressed in spirit: "So give good news (q.v.) to my servants (see SERVANT) those who listen to the word and then follow the best of it" (Q 39:17-8). Listening to recitation is described in the prophetic medical texts as the "calmer of hearts, food of the spirit. It is one of the most important psychological medicines. It is a source of pleasure, even to some animals" (Suyūṭī, *Ṭibb,* 127). *Dhikr* (recitation of divine names and phrases from the Qurʾān) is recommended as a specific remedy against pre-Islamic sorcery *(siḥr)* by the Prophet as "faith and nearness to his lord is the divine medicine *(dawāʾ ilāhī)* that no disease can resist... invoking the divine attributes *(dhikr)* will sharpen one's hearing and sight and sustain his faculties" (Ibn Qayyim al-Jawziyya, *Ṭibb,* 91-2). The divine attribute whose recitation will guarantee health is reported to be "the absolute living one" (*al-ḥayy al-qayyūm,* cf. Q 2:255; 3:2; 20:111), which the Prophet describes as "the opposite of all ailments and sufferings... therefore, calling upon his attribute, the living controller, will surely cure the illness" (Ibn Qayyim al-Jawziyya, *Ṭibb,* 165). The active performance of reciting whole sūras is considered efficacious as well, and can be classed in the same category as qurʾānic spell-making, since frequent repetition and ritual preparation are involved. Medieval and early modern talismanic texts prescribe sūra recitation for fertility (Q 89), protection from the evil eye and the like (Q 48, 75, 85, 87), providence (Q 56), forgiveness (q.v.) for sins/spiritual healing (Q 62, 81), peaceful sleep (q.v.; Q 92), finding/restoring what is lost/forgotten (Q 93; Nana Asmaʾu, Medicine).

The repetitive chanting of qurʾānic formulae and particularly the divine names becomes a normative institution in Ṣūfī practice throughout the Islamic middle ages and into modern times. Individual Ṣūfī teachers who became founders of Ṣūfī communities often recommended a particular form of *dhikr* practice (silent or voiced, individual or group recitation, usually male-only or female-only groups; see Schimmel, *Mystical dimensions;* Netton, *Ṣūfī ritual;* Raudvere, *Book and roses*). The melodic nature of qurʾānic recitation is amplified in *dhikr* to increase and intensify the emotional impact and transformative nature of its performance and its audition (sometimes including rhythmic music, then known as *samāʿ,* and sometimes with voices alone). It often takes a call/response pattern of group performance, with the Ṣūfī master or a *munshid,* or "song" specialist, leading and the community following either at the Ṣūfī lodge or in private homes (Waugh, *Munshidun of Egypt*). In south Asia, a sub-genre of *dhikr* in the form of devotional "song" is the *qawwālī,* sung in Persian or Urdu interspersed with Arabic phraseology from the Qur'ān. *Qawwālī* sessions function similarly to *dhikr* sessions, although the group attending may be a lay Muslim audience as well as members of the Ṣūfī community (Qureishi, *Ṣūfī music*). Contemporary Ṣūfī literature, particularly in the West, has a strong emphasis on the textual interpretation of the Qur'ān as a form of spiritual healing. Books on Ṣūfī healing as well as audio tapes of *dhikr* by Ṣūfī communities intended for a broad popular Muslim audience (and potential converts to the mystic path; see MEDIA AND THE QUR'ĀN), illustrate the spiritual message of the qur'ānic script and create analogies between the orthography (q.v.) of the Qur'ān when linked to the bodily postures of prayer and *dhikr* practice (Nasr, Spiritual message; Chisti, *Ṣūfī healing;* see also Bawa Muhaiyaddeen on prayer in Banks and Green, *Illuminated prayer*).

Among the spoken uses of the Qur'ān applied to healing is the use of specific short chapters or verses of the Qur'ān as a form of spell *(ruqya)* and charm. For example, the recitation aloud of the Fātiḥa (q.v.), or opening chapter of the Qur'ān, accompanied by "blowing them on the affected person, followed by his spittle upon the victim — God willing, such reading will incur the reaction of evil spirits and cause the elimination of their evil act" (Ibn Qayyim al-Jawziyya, *Ṭibb,* 139; Suyūṭī, *Ṭibb,* 132-3, 180; Robson, Magical use, 38-9). Regarding the basic question of the lawfulness of such uses of the Qur'ān, a Muslim asks the Prophet: "You see all these amulets *(ruqā)* we carry, prayers we recite, medicine we take, and other preventive routines we use for recovering from illness — Do any of them obstruct God's decree?" And the Prophet replied, "They are part of God's decree" (Ibn Qayyim al-Jawziyya, *Ṭibb,* 11). The Prophet is also reported to have similarly recited the Throne Verse (Q 2:255; see THRONE OF GOD) and the two "refuge-taking" chapters (Q 113, 114), and blown into his hands and wiped his face and body so as to physically spread the healing benefit of the sūras over his person for protection (Suyūṭī, *Ṭibb,* 158-9, 180). The phrases of refuge-taking in the final two chapters of the Qur'ān are universally applicable to all purposes of protection whether against accident, illness, acts of nature, demonic powers, the evil eye, spiritual dangers from the lower self *(nafs),* the evil which God has created, and finally from God himself: "I take refuge with thee from thyself" (Padwick, *Muslim devotions,* 83-93). The Prophet recommended further the combination of recitation of qur'ānic prayers as spells *(ruqya)* along with plant/mineral materials to form compound "natural and spiritual cures" (Ibn Qayyim al-Jawziyya, *Ṭibb,* 145-6). The *basmala* (q.v.) which opens every chapter of the Qur'ān but one is also a focus of prayerful invocation: "I beseech thee by virtue of every mystery which thou has set in 'In the Name of God the Merciful, the Compassionate'" (Padwick, *Muslim devotions,* 99; see also Ibn Bisṭām, *Ṭibb,* 6). Ṣūfīs have delved into the components of these qur'ānic phrases and created a system of visualization and meditation which isolates and emphasizes each individual letter and orthographic sign and grammatical function of the written Arabic of the Qur'ān (see GRAMMAR AND THE QUR'ĀN). From a collection of prayers on the *basmala* is this interiorization of every element of the phrase, starting with its first letter, by ʿAbd al-Qādir al-Jīlānī: "O God, I ask thee by virtue of the *bā'* of thy name, the letter of 'withness,' the conjunction with the greatest Object of Desire, and the finding of all that was lost and by the point beneath the *bā'* guiding to the secrets of thy everlastingness and thy pre-eternal and sole Being..." (Padwick, *Muslim devotions,* 100). Belief in their power and efficacy by generations of Muslims seems to have provoked even magical applications of them, such as the belief in "laying on" the divine names. "Thy names of moral beauty *(al-asmāʾ al-ḥusnā)* to which all things upon which they are laid are subdued" (from *Khulāṣat al-maghnam* of ʿAlī Ḥasan al-ʿAttās); and "All thy names of moral beauty which, falling upon anything cause its body to be subdued" (from Aḥmad b. ʿAlī l-Būnī, *Majmuʿāt al-aḥzāb;* see Padwick, *Muslim devotions,* 106, 109).

Another application of the physical transmissibility of qurʾānic *baraka* is the technique of *nushra,* which involves qurʾānic recitation over water that is then used by the sick person for washing him/herself (Ibn Qayyim al-Jawziyya, *Ṭibb,* 142; Ṣuyūṭī, *Ṭibb,* 172, Robson, Magical use, 34) or it can be recited over food that is then eaten and the qurʾānic virtue is absorbed by the body as well as the soul (Nana Asmaʾu, Medicine, 112-3, 117). Although not necessarily involving oral recitation of the sacred text, yet another method of "imbibing the Qurʾān" is through the use of "magic medicine bowls," vessels on which qurʾānic verses are inscribed and from which the believer drinks to accrue their benefit (see Figs. I and II). *Nushra* relies upon the materialization of the *baraka* of recitation as a physical "residuum" of qurʾānic *baraka.* Although this practice is reported in the context of disapproval, such reports clearly indicate a living practice and can be understood in relation to the Companions of the Prophet (q.v.) who are said in the ḥadīth and *sīra* (hagiographical) literature (see SĪRA AND THE QURʾĀN) to have collected the Prophet's washing water, fingernail and hair clippings, for their traces of *baraka.* The residual *baraka* of this prophetic "wash" and qurʾānic "wash" are clearly connected to the larger phenomenon of qurʾānic erasure *(maḥw).* The extension of this *baraka* from physical traces of blessing to that conveyed by the verbal articulation (and breath) of qurʾānic recitation is found in its use when accompanied by magical gestures conveying the personal life force or essence of the performer (such as spitting and blowing) which the Qurʾān itself disallows as pre-Islamic/pagan magic. The inclusion within the body of the *sunna* of traditional magical methods regardless of their forbidden status in the Qurʾān is a paradoxical aspect of the "magical" use of the Qurʾān. Through recitation/prayer, the Qurʾān seems to invest the breath of the Prophet physically with its essence or *baraka* which is transmitted via touch. "The messenger used to recite Sūrat al-Ikhlāṣ ["God's oneness"; Q 112]... and then blow into the palms of his hands and wipe his face and whatever parts of his body his hands could reach" (Ibn Qayyim al-Jawziyya, *Ṭibb,* 142; Ibn Bisṭām, *Ṭibb,* 40). In another report, it is blowing the essence of Sūrat al-Fātiḥa, the opening chapter, which is believed to convey the healing virtue of the whole Qurʾān. Via words, breath, and saliva of the believing lay healer, following the example of the Prophet, this medicinal recitation is an exorcism of evil spirits encompassing both spiritual and physical efficacy:

If one's faith, soul (q.v.) and spirit (q.v.) are strong, and if he adapts himself to the essence of the opening chapter, and by God's leave, by reciting its holy words and blowing them on the affected person followed by his spittle upon the victim, God willing, such reading will incur the reaction of evil spirits and cause the elimination of their evil act" (Ibn Qayyim al-Jawziyya, *Ṭibb,* 139).

Somewhat later, Ibn al-Qayyim cites a statement from the Prophet that combines the application of saltwater with blowing his "blessed breath" and reciting the

Qurʾān to heal a wound. A contemporary south Indian Muslim woman healer marshals her spiritual "medicine" in exorcising patients possessed by spirits (manifested as loss of speech, rational capacity, deep depression, and immobility, or conversely, unnatural physical strength) using qurʾānic recitation accompanied by "blowing" *duʿāʾ*, or personal prayers, for healing intercession which include qurʾānic formulae, verses, or divine names, over the person and even inside the mouth (Flueckiger, The vision, 259-60).

Uses of the Qurʾān in historical and living contexts: Written uses of the Qurʾān

The divine names, their component parts, and the phrases in which they occur in the Qurʾān become part of a medieval "science of letters," or number/letter mysticism, and a "science of names" (*ʿilm al-ḥurūf, jafr, abjad, sīmiyāʾ;* Massignon, *Essay,* 68-72; Canteins, Hidden sciences, 448-63; Nasr, Spiritual message, 30-4), and, at the same time, objects of devotion as prayerful litanies *(wird),* elements of ritual practice *(dhikr),* and, above all, items in a rich visual field (Nasr, Spiritual message), in Ṣūfī and Shīʿī "calligrammes" such as those employed by the Ḥurūfiyya and Bektāshiyya (Wilson, *Sacred drift,* 6, 66-9, 130; Safadī, *Islamic calligraphy,* 31, 136-7; Dierl, *Geschichte und Lehre,* 1985).

He who loves God empties his heart of all but him: the *alif* [first letter of the Arabic alphabet, and first letter of the name of God] of Allah pierces his heart and leaves no room for anything else.... One need only "know" this single letter in order to know all that is to be known, for the Divine Name is the key to the Treasury of Divine Mysteries and the path to the Real. It is that Reality by virtue of the essential identity of God and his sanctified Name. That is why in Ṣūfīsm meditation upon the calligraphic form of the Name is used as a spiritual method for realizing the Named (Nasr, Spritual message, 31; see CALLIGRAPHY).

Beyond its ritual and devotional importance, qurʾānic calligraphy spans the formal Islamic arts of qurʾānic manuscript illumination (Lings, *Quranic art;* see ORNAMENTATION AND ILLUMINATION), it defines formal architecture and public buildings as Islamic space (see ART AND ARCHITECTURE AND THE QURʾĀN), and it enters into the diversity of "folk" or vernacular arts. Qurʾānic vernacular art forms include sewing and embroidery, such as the *kiswa,* the house-sized black cloth draped over the Kaʿba that is embroidered in qurʾānic phrases in black and gold, and smaller wall hangings embroidered with divine names or qurʾānic verses that are used in Muslim homes or businesses, as well as such unique regional expressions as the *ḥajj* (see PILGRIMAGE) murals which adorn the outside of Egyptian homes (and some apartments), which developed at the turn of the twentieth century and are found from Cairo to the villages of upper Egypt (Campo, *Other sides,* 139-65, 170-9; Parker and Avon, *Ḥajj paintings*). This use of qurʾānic calligraphy protects the physical space and the members of the household from external evils by framing the entryway, the outside walls which face the street, around windows, and along outside staircases leading to and surrounding the front door (in the case of apartments).

The religious meaning of Muslim space, whether private or public, has been established by the presence and elaboration of traditional qurʾānic calligraphy on the outside, as well as the use of divine names and/or phrases/verses from the Qurʾān in textile wall-hangings, poster art and other ephemera on the inside (Metcalf, *Making Muslim space*). Unlike the Sunnī mainstream, contemporary Ṣūfī and Muslim sectarian communities in North America have begun to make extensive use of their own new and unique forms of qurʾānic iconography, that is, qurʾānic calligraphy and image-making as doctrinal teaching and meditation tools, a kind of "visual" *dhikr,* which is disseminated through their devotional texts and journals and can be purchased as poster art for home use. Medieval Ṣūfī and Shīʿī "calligrammes" from the Arabic, Persian, and Turkish styles of qurʾānic calligraphy are re-invented and elaborated with a religious use of representational images unknown in earlier Islamic visual arts. A whole new wedding of word and image can be seen in the colorful poster art by Bawa Muhaiyaddeen for his Philadelphia-based Ṣūfī Fellowship, and ʿĪsā Muḥammad for his originally Brooklyn-based African-American Muslim group, the Ansarullah Community, first known as the Ansar Pure Sufis (see Bawa Muhaiyaddeen's "Heartswork" posters and companion commentary texts, published by the Bawa Muhaiyaddeen Fellowship; also poster art published by the Ansarullah in their devotional journal, *The Truth: Nubian bulletin,* and in the founder's extensive commentary literature; see O'Connor, Islamic Jesus; id., Nubian Islamic Hebrews).

Qurʾānic amulets and talismans are written on diverse materials (e.g. leather, parchment, paper); embroidered on cloth (see Fig. v); or engraved, for example, on clay, bone, or stone (see Fig. III), and selected from verses which address profound needs or desires. Traditional categorizations of qurʾānic verses are found in Arabic talismanic manuals: *āyāt al-ḥifẓ,* "verses of protection," such as the Throne Verse (Q 2:255); *āyāt al-shifāʾ,* "verses of healing," such as Q 1; *futūḥ al-Qurʾān,* "verses of opening or victory," such as the first verse of the sūra of victory (Q 110:1); *āyāt al-ḥarb,* "verses of war or overpowering enemies"; *āyāt al-laṭīf,* "verses of kindness" which protect against enemies; and verses which contain all the letters of the Arabic alphabet (Q 3:148; 48:29) against all fear and sorrow and all disease (Robson, Magical use, 53-6; id., Islamic cures, 34-43; Donaldson, The Koran). Medieval compendia of prophetic medicine, extracted ḥadīth (Sunnī and Shīʿī) advising on healing uses and benefits of written qurʾānic amulets and talismans (Ibn Qayyim al-Jawziyya, *Ṭibb;* Suyūṭī, *Ṭibb;* Ibn Bisṭām, *Ṭibb*) and texts as late as the nineteenth-century include references gleaned and organized from these earlier medieval authorities (Owusu-Ansah, *Islamic talismanic tradition;* Nana Asmaʾu, Medicine).

The metaphor of "qurʾānic tincture" can be used to describe the infusion of qurʾānic contents and methods of discourse throughout not only the religious sciences of qurʾānic study proper but the philosophical and occult sciences as well. The phenomenon of qurʾānic "erasure," an amuletic use of writing all or part of the Qurʾān, is another type of "qurʾānic tincture" of an altogether more medicinal nature found documented in the prophetic medical corpus and texts on qurʾānic magic and healing, as well as manifested in the living practice of religious healers throughout every region of the Muslim world (O'Connor, Prophetic medicine, 56-8). Medieval prophetic medical texts state that "there is no objection to writing qurʾānic verses, washing the contents in water, and giving it to the sick person to drink" (Ibn Qayyim al-Jawziyya, *Ṭibb,* 124; Ibn Bisṭām, *Ṭibb,* 9, 25, 55). The Berti, as a contemporary example of this form of qurʾānic healing, are a modern Muslim people of the northern Sudan, whose leaders or *faki*s (from the Arabic *faqīh,* or learned jurisprudent) perform the traditional Islamic social and educational roles in a society with little general knowledge of Arabic and incomplete Islamic acculturation (Holy, *Religion and custom;* El-Tom, Drinking the Koran). These social and educational roles are complemented and even subsumed by their functions as healers, diviners, dream interpreters, and providers of amulets based upon qur'ānic magic. It is in this socio-religio-magical milieu that qur'ānic "erasure" has meaning.

"… Another important activity of the *faki* is to write some Koranic verses on both sides of a wooden slate *(loh)* using a pen made of a sharpened millet stalk and ink *(dawai)* made of a fermented paste of soot and gum arabic. The written text is then washed off with water which is drunk by the *faki*'s clients. The water is referred to as *mihai* (from the verb *yamḥa,* to erase) and, following al-Safi [*Native Medicine in the Sudan* 1970:30], I have translated this term as 'erasure'" (El-Tom, Drinking the Koran, 415).

Although the Berti's only partial knowledge of Arabic may produce an "occultation" of the Arabic text of the Qur'ān and encourage an instrumental approach to it by the believer, the process of interpretation of the text through the agency of the *faki* is as much an Islamic one as any found in other more fully acculturated (i.e. Arabized) settings. The interpretation is one which operates relatively innocent of received tradition, however, and returns to the text unencumbered by previously established meanings. The example of an erasure created and prescribed to induce pregnancy in a woman who has not borne children shows a magical qur'ānic application in which human creation of life via the power of divine speech is possible. This fertility erasure is based upon writing a single verse from Q 3, Sūrat Āl 'Imrān, "The Family of 'Imrān," because it invokes the creative act of conception and God's absolute power of realization (see BIOLOGY AS THE CREATION AND STAGES OF LIFE): "It is he who forms you *(yuṣawwirukum)* in the wombs *(al-arḥām)* as he wishes. There is no god but he, the almighty and all-wise" (Q 3:6; El-Tom, Drinking the Koran, 419; cf. Donaldson, The Koran, 266).

Two nineteenth-century collections of Islamic talisman texts in Arabic using the Qur'ān — one group from the Asante on the Guinea coast of west Africa (Owusu-Ansah, *Islamic talismanic tradition*), and another from the daughter of Shaykh Usman dan Fodio, Nana Asma'u, writing in what is now northwestern Nigeria — recommend the use of erasure — called here "text water/writing water" — of specific verses in order to call upon their divine powers (Nana Asma'u, Medicine). The erasure of the following verses is recommended to the Asante: Q 9:1-2 for travel, Q 19:1-7 for blessing, Q 67:1-2 for sovereignty, Q 48:1-2 for victory, Q 55:1-7 for beneficence (cf. Owusu-Ansah, *Islamic talismanic tradition,* 47-8, 86, 109/note 33). Sūrat Yā' Sīn (Q 36) and other specific sūras used in both talismanry and erasure, employ diverse materials for magical writing (stone, clay, iron, silver, copper, cloth, animal bones, particularly shoulder blades and neck vertebrae — used in their own right as a form of divining called scapulomancy) and the liquids for "erasure" (rose water, musk, saffron, ink, honey, mint juice, grape juice, grease; cf. Donaldson, The Koran, 258-63, 266; Robson, Magical use, 40). Nana Asma'u surveyed existing manuals of prophetic medicine in her day and created a poetic list of suitable amuletic and talismanic uses, simply entitled "Medicine of the Prophet," including erasure of certain sūras into water (Q 76, 90, 92), the recitation of other sūras over food (Q 105), and the preparation of written amulets/talismans from others to be worn on the person (Q 53, 77, 90, 101, 108).

These texts and contemporary anthropological accounts of qurʾānic talismanry and erasure report not only drinking the remedy but incorporating it into food — by, for example, inscribing it directly onto unleavened bread — and eating it oneself or giving it to one's animals to eat for fertility, ease in calving, recovery from illness (Owusu-Ansah, *Islamic talismanic tradition,* 79; see Flueckiger, The vision, 251, 257, for feeding a qurʾānic charm written on a chapati to dogs as surrogates for "errant husbands or disobedient children"). Qurʾānic amuletry/talismanry and spell-making were often applied to animal illness and infertility of the herds/flocks. Shīʿī collections of Imāmī medicine directly paralleled Sunnī prophetic medical texts, only being drawn from medical ḥadīth ascribed to the *ahl al-bayt,* the People of the [Prophet's] House, namely the Prophet and his descendants through ʿAlī (see ʿALĪ B. ABĪ ṬĀLIB) and Fāṭima (q.v.). From one such early collection (ca. second/eighth cent.) comes a talisman for the relief in labor and safe delivery for a mare of her foal.

Write this invocation for an old and noble mare at its time of delivery on the parchment of a gazelle and fasten it to her at her groin: "O God, dispeller of grief and remover of sorrow, the merciful and compassionate of this world and the next, have mercy on [the owner of the mare], son of so and so, the owner of the mare, with a mercy which will make him free of mercy from other than you. Dispel his grief and sorrow, relieve his anxiety, keep his mare from harm, and make easy for us its delivery (Ibn Bisṭām, *Ṭibb,* 125).

Such an amulet resonates and paraphrases several qurʾānic contexts which affirm that the popular use of the Qurʾān is not *shirk,* or associating anything with God, since the power to heal comes only from him (cf. e.g. Q 3:49; 5:110; 26:80). With such qurʾānic charms and erasure for the benefit of animals, however, are also found the un-Islamic practices of inscribing qurʾānic words or letters on living animals and sacrificing them as a form of magical transference and expiation, or "scapegoating," often associated with malefic or cursing magic (Owusu-Ansah, *Islamic talismanic tradition,* 58; Flueckiger, Vision; see CONSECRATION OF ANIMALS; SACRIFICE).

Divinatory uses of the Qurʾān: Dream incubation and dream interpretation

Another type of recitation of the qurʾānic text which most jurists have judged as transgressing the legal limits of the Qurʾān is the "reading" of the Qurʾān associated with forms of divination which attempt to "read" the future. The Qurʾān is used in "popular" practice for two types of divination: the incubation of dreams by performing special *rakʿās*, or additional personal prayers before sleeping while asking for God's guidance in the form of *faʾl,* a sign or omen; and "cutting" the Qurʾān, or *istikhāra,* "asking for the best choice" or "seeking goodness" from God (Lane, *Manners and customs,* 270-1; Westermarck, *Ritual and belief,* ii, 2-3, 46-57; Donaldson, The Koran, 256-7; Fahd, *Divination,* 363-7). Dream interpretation rests on a single qurʾānic proof text, saying that believers will receive "glad tidings *(al-bushrā)* in the life of this world and in the next" (Q 10:64), which the Qurʾān distinguishes as true dreams versus *aḍghāth aḥlām,* or "confused dreams" (Q 21:5 of [jinn-inspired] poets, and Q 12:44 referring to Pharaoh's [q.v.] dreams; Lamoreaux, *Early Muslim tradition,* 107-34). Dream experiences in Islam are modeled on prophetic characters in the Qurʾān, Abraham (q.v.; Ibrāhīm), who receives the message from God to sacrifice his son, understood to be Ishmael (q.v.; Ismāʿīl; Muslims are spiritual descendents of Ishmael, not Isaac [q.v.]), in a dream (Q 37:102, 105); the prophet Joseph (q.v.; Yūsuf), who possesses the faculty of dream interpretation and knowledge of the "unseen" (*al-ghayb;* see HIDDEN AND THE HIDDEN), "revealed by inspiration" (*waḥy;* see REVELATION AND INSPIRATION) by God (Q 12:101-2; also Q 12:6, 21); and Muḥammad, who receives during sleep dreams *(manām)* and visions (q.v.; *ruʾyā*) which are listed as among God's "signs" (q.v.; *āyāt* in Q 30:23; cf. 39:42, 48:27) and what is assumed by some Muslim theologians to be his dream night journey and ascension (q.v.), the *isrāʾ/miʿrāj* (Q 17:1, 60; Fahd, *Divination,* 255-330; Lamoreaux, *Early Muslim tradition,* 108-11). The importance of dreams and visions are, thus, established for Muslims by the qurʾānic prophets, and are enshrined as part of the interpretive tradition of the Qurʾān by the subsequent generations of early Muslim Qurʾān and ḥadīth scholars. From a scholarly point of view, divinatory literature becomes a legitimate form of Qurʾān commentary with ḥadīth collections devoting chapters to the interpretation and meaning of dreams (*taʿbīr al-ruʾyā;* Lamoreaux, *Early Muslim tradition,* 116-7). The popular techniques which mine the Qurʾān for its guidance about hidden truths are founded on the evolution of popular manuals of dream divining and encyclopedias of dream interpretation (see Lamoreaux, *Early Muslim tradition,* 175-81 for his appendix on early Islamic dream manuals) and are called *istikhāra,* "cutting the Qurʾān," and *faʾl,* "divination" or omens. Readers of the Qurʾān, in the sense of divination, are often women, but in urban contexts may be professional "readers" who combine other techniques (e.g. astrology, numerology) with divining the Qurʾān in order to assist believers with the decisions facing them. According to practitioners, "cutting" the Qurʾān allows believers to access the hidden knowledge and guidance inherent in revelation: "And with him are the keys of the secret things; none know them but he: he knows whatever is on the land and in the sea" (Q 6:59). The basics of the technique allow one to open the text of the Qurʾān spontaneously, and "randomly" select a verse by pointing and not looking. The client's query regarding any serious matter — a prospective journey, an upcoming business or employment situation, a health question, the timing of an event, be it a medical or surgical treatment, a marriage, a divorce, a partnership, etc. — guide the "reader's" interpretation of the qurʾānic verse(s). *Faʾl* seems to be similar to *istikhāra* but more detailed, being the reading of whole passage for the purpose of learning the final outcome. Although medieval texts on the special characteristics *(khawāṣṣ)* of the Qurʾān include brief reference to these divining techniques, the literature on divining mentions that even some Qurʾāns were edited and published with marginal notations which would guide its use for divination and dream interpretation (Donaldson, The Koran, 256-7). Although "fortune-telling" was clearly part of the anti-magic and anti-sorcery statements of the Qurʾān, the focus on dream incubation and dream interpretation associated divination with categories of prophetic and inspired experience. Dream messages could be divinely inspired, but required careful analysis to sift the true guidance from false and misleading images. Popular practitioners of this type of consultative use of the Qurʾān were often, but not exclusively, at least persons with a basic command of Islam's written technology and knowledge of the manuals of popular practice and encyclopedias of dream interpretation drawn from earlier medieval sources (Nana Asmaʾu, Medicine; Flueckiger, The vision; Bowen, Return to sender).

Popular and talismanic uses of the Qurʾān in the modern Muslim world

Ḥadīth and the devotional prayers of 1400 years of Islamic culture have generated a wide ranging modern popular print literature in diverse Islamic languages grounded in medieval Islamic source texts (primarily in Arabic and Persian) on prophetic medicine *(al-ṭibb al-nabawī)* and qurʾānic "magic," i.e. the instrumental use of the Qurʾān as recitation and written text, performed/embodied in Islam's religious material culture. Examples of qurʾānic instrumentality have been observed since the nineteenth century and through the twentieth by ethnographers, anthropologists, and scholars of prophetic medicine and qurʾānic healing among Middle Eastern Muslims (Doutté, Westermarck, Lane, Robson, Donaldson, and Maghniyya), and throughout the larger Muslim world (Ewing, Hoffman, Owusu-Ansah, Mack and Boyd, Padwick, El-Tom, Holy, Flueckiger, Bowen, Campo, and Hunzāʾī), as well as among immigrant, expatriate, and indigenous Muslims in the West (Metcalf, O'Connor). These include qurʾānic medallions worn on the person engraved with names of God, the Throne Verse (*āyat al-kursī,* Q 2:255) or other particular verses for protection (*āyāt al-ḥifẓ,* or *āyāt al-laṭīf,* verses of divine "kindness" as protection from one's enemies) and success or victory in any endeavor *(futūḥ al-Qurʾān)*. In contemporary Muslim communities, qurʾānic talismans are hung from taxi-cabs' rearview mirrors or a miniature Qurʾān is mounted on the dashboard, or, more often, in the rear window spaces to protect against accident. Posters or woven hangings with qurʾānic verses or names of God are used inside or in storefront windows both for protection/blessing and, in the West, for advertisement to attract Muslim customers. From a younger generation of contemporary Muslims comes a variety of popular and talismanic uses of the Qurʾān, frequently as a legacy of their mothers and grandmothers. A recent example is a highly educated and professionally employed Iranian living in the United States of America whose mother keeps a Qurʾān suspended above the refrigerator so that the food will not spoil. Equally, the protective value of qurʾānic medallions in Muslim belief still holds true even among those who are otherwise highly secularized.

These and untold other examples are continuing testament to contemporary belief in the power of the Qurʾān as divine speech and in its efficacy to create, sustain, and direct the world. The most pervasive influence of the instrumentality of the Qurʾān is its impact on everyday speech (see Piamenta, *Islam in everyday Arabic,* for the impact of qurʾānic expressions on native Arabic speakers, also applicable to the use of Arabic qurʾānic expressions by non-Arabic speakers). Devout Muslims invoke God's name in the *basmala* when entering a room or house, opening a book, starting a trip, upon drinking or eating, before getting into bed, when entering the market or the mosque, in fact, as a blessing on any everyday act of life (Padwick, *Muslim devotions,* 94-6). Equally common is performing the *taṣliya,* or "calling down blessings," on the prophets of Islam, especially Muḥammad and his family, and the Ṣūfī saints and Shīʿī imāms (ibid., 152-72; see IMĀM). Perhaps, greater than any qurʾānic response in daily life is that of giving praise (q.v.; *taḥmīd;* see also LAUDATION) and glory (q.v.) to God *(takbīr)*. Each of these accompanies the ups and downs of daily life as acts of humility and gratitude, keeping believers grounded in their relationship with God as creatures to creator (ibid.,

35-6). Varieties of commonly performed talismanic uses of the Qurʾān stem not from a deviation from the Islamic tradition but arise at the center of its religious authority. Whether as oral performance in spoken invocations, verbal formulae, or supplicatory prayers, or as material representation in medallions, wall plaques, written amulets or their residuum (the "erasures"), the verbal and material images of the Qurʾān have the ability to manifest constantly the protective and providential powers of divine speech. See also SCIENCE AND THE QURʾĀN.

Kathleen Malone O'Connor

Bibliography

Primary: Bawa Muhaiyaddeen, Heartswork Posters, Bawa Muhaiyaddeen Fellowship, Philadelphia 1979 (1999)-85 (The four religions; Four steps to pure iman, with companion text, 1999/1979; The rocky mountain of the heart; Asma ul-husna: The 99 beautiful names of God, with companion text, 1979; The inner heart; The tree of the prophets; Come to the secret garden, companion text: Come to the secret garden: Ṣūfī tales of wisdom, 1985); al-Būnī, Muḥyi l-Dīn Abū l-ʿAbbās Aḥmad b. ʿAlī, *Shams al-maʿārif wa-laṭāʾif al-ʿawārif,* Cairo 1962; al-Dayrabī, Aḥmad b. ʿUthmān, *al-Mujarrabāt,* Cairo n.d.; Dhahabī, *al-Ṭibb al-nabawī,* Beirut 1981; al-Ghazālī, Abū Ḥāmid Muḥammad, *Kitāb al-Dhahab al-abraz (al-ibrīz) fī asrār khawāṣṣ kitāb Allāh al-ʿazīz,* ed. ʿA.Ṣ. Ḥamdān, Cairo [2000]; Ḥājjī Khalīfa, *Kashf,* ed. Flügel; Ibn Bisṭām, al-Ḥusayn and ʿAbdallāh b. Bisṭām, *Ṭibb al-aʾimma,* Beirut 1994; Ibn al-Jawzī, *Luqaṭ al-amān fī l-ṭibb [Luqaṭ al-manāfiʿ fī l-ṭibb],* ed. A.Y. al-Daqqāq, Damascus 1987; Ibn al-Kalbī, Abū l-Mundhir Hishām b. Muḥammad, *Kitāb al-Aṣnām,* Cairo 1965; Ibn Khaldūn, *al-Muqaddima,* Beirut 1879; trans. F. Rosenthal, *The Muqaddimah,* ed. and abr. N.J. Dawood, Princeton 1969, 1989[9]; Ibn Qayyim al-Jawziyya, *al-Ṭibb al-nabawī,* Cairo 1978; Ibn Talḥā, Kamāl al-Dīn Abū Sālim Muḥammad, *Kitāb al-Jafr al-jāmiʿ wa-l-nūr al-lāmiʿ,* Beirut 1987; Ibn Taymiyya, *Kitāb Iqtiḍāʾ al-sirāṭ al-mustaqīm mukhālafat aṣḥāb al-jaḥīm,* Cairo 1907; Ikhwān al-Ṣafāʾ, *Rasāʾil Ikhwān al-Ṣafāʾ wa-khillān al-wafāʾ,* 4 vols., Beirut 1957; Nana Asmaʾu, Medicine of the Prophet, in B. Mack and J. Boyd (eds. and trans.), *One woman's jihād. Nana Asmaʾu, scholar and scribe,* Bloomington, IN 2000, 102-19; al-Rāzī, Abū Bakr Muḥammad b. Zakariyyāʾ, *Kitāb al-Ḥāwī fī l-ṭibb,* Hyderabad 1955; al-Suyūṭī, *al-Ṭibb al-nabawī,* Beirut 1986; al-Ṭabarī, Abū l-Ḥasan ʿAlī b. Sahl Rabban, *Firdaws al-ḥikma,* ed. M.Z. al-Ṣiddīqī, Berlin 1928, repr. Frankfurt 1996; al-Tilimsānī, Muḥammad b. al-Ḥājj, *Shumūs al-anwār wa-kunūz al-asrār al-kubrā,* Tunis 1964; al-Yāfiʿī, Abū Muḥammad ʿAbdallāh b. Asad al-Yamānī, *Kitāb al-Durr al-naẓīm fī khawāṣṣ al-Qurʾān al-ʿaẓīm,* Cairo n.d.

Secondary: C. Banks and M. Green, *The illuminated prayer. The five-times prayer of the Ṣūfīs as revealed by Jellāludīn Rūmī and Bawā Muḥaiyaddeen,* New York 2000; J.R. Bowen, *Muslims through discourse. Religion and ritual in Gayo society,* Princeton 1993, chapter 4; id., Return to sender. A Muslim discourse of sorcery in a relatively egalitarian society. The Gayo of northern Sumatra, in C.W. Watson and R. Ellen (eds.), *Understanding witchcraft and sorcery in southeast Asia,* Honolulu 1993, 179-90; Brockelmann, *GAL;* J.C. Bürgel, *The feather of Simurgh. The "licit magic" of the arts in medieval Islam,* New York 1988; J. Campo, *The other sides of paradise. Explorations into the religious meanings of domestic space in Islam,* Columbia, SC 1991; J. Canteins, The hidden sciences in Islam, in S.H. Nasr (ed.), *Islamic spirituality. Manifestations,* New York 1997, 447-68; H.M. Chisti, *The book of Ṣūfī healing,* Rochester, VT 1991; A. Christensen, *Xavāṣṣ-i-āyāt. Notices et extraits d'un manuscrit Persan traitant la Magie des versets du Coran,* Copenhagen 1920; J. Dierl, *Geschichte und Lehre des anatolischen Alevismus-Bektasismus,* Frankfort 1985; B.A. Donaldson, The Koran as magic, in *MW* 27 (1937), 254-66; id., *The wild rue. A study of Muḥammadan magic and folklore in Iran,* London 1938; E. Doutté, *Magie et religion dans l'Afrique du Nord,* Algiers 1909; R.M. Eaton, The political and religious authority of the shrine of Bāba Farīd, in B.D. Metcalf (ed.), *Moral conduct and authority. The place of adab in south Asian Islam,* Berkeley 1984, 333-56; A.O. El-Tom, Drinking the Koran. The meaning of koranic verses in Berti erasure, in J.D.Y. Peel and C. Stuart (eds.), *Popular Islam south of the Sahara,* Manchester 1985, 414-31; C.W. Ernst, *Eternal garden. Mysticism, history, and politics at a south Asian Ṣūfī center,* Albany, NY 1992; K. Ewing, Malangs of the Punjab. Intoxication or adab as the path to God? in B.D. Metcalf (ed.), *Moral conduct and authority. The place of adab in south Asian Islam,* Berkeley 1984, 357-71; T. Fahd, Khawāṣṣ al-Ḳurʾān, in *EI²*, iv, 1133-4; id., *La divination arabe. Études religieuses, sociologiques et folklorique sur le milieu natif de l'Islam,* Leiden 1966; J. Flueckiger, The vision was of written words. Negotiating authority as a female Muslim healer in south

India, in D. Shulman (ed.), *Syllables of sky. Studies in south Indian civilization,* Delhi 1995, 249-82; C. Glassé, *The concise encyclopedia of Islam,* San Francisco 1991, 201 (s.v. "Istikhārah"); V. Hoffman, *Ṣūfism, mystics, and saints in modern Egypt,* Columbia, SC 1995 (for discussion of the mosque and the cult of the saint); L. Holy, *Religion and custom in Muslim society. The Berti of Sudan,* Cambridge, UK 1991; N.N. Hunzaʾi, *Qurʾānic healing,* trans. F.M. Hunzaʾi, Karachi 1987; A.A. Ibrahim, *Assaulting with words. Popular discourse and the bridle of the sharīʿah,* Evanston, IL 1994; P. Kraus, *Jābir ibn Ḥayyān,* 2 vols., Cairo 1942; J.C. Lamoreaux, *The early Muslim tradition of dream interpretation,* Albany, NY 2002; E.W. Lane, *An account of the manners and customs of the modern Egyptians,* London 1895, chapters 10-12; I.M. Lewis, The power of the past. African "survivals" in Islam, in id., *Religion in context. Cults and charisma,* Cambridge, UK 1986, 94-107; id., *Saints and Somalis. Popular Islam in a clan-based society,* Lawrenceville, NJ 1998; M. Lings, *Quranic art of calligraphy and illumination,* Westerham, Kent, UK 1996 (London 1976); M.Ḥ. Maghniyya, *Mujarrabāt al-imamiyya fī l-shifāʾ bi-l-Qurʾān wa-al-duʿāʾ,* Beirut 1996; L. Massignon, *Essay on the origins of the technical language of Islamic mysticism,* Notre Dame, IN 1997; É. Mauchamps, *La sorcellerie au Maroc,* Paris n.d.; B.D. Metcalf (ed.), *Making Muslim space in North America and Europe,* Berkeley 1996; S.H. Nasr, Alchemy and other occult sciences, in id., *Islamic science. An illustrated study,* London 1976, 193-208; id., *An introduction to Islamic cosmological doctrines,* Boulder 1978; id., The spiritual message of Islamic calligraphy, in id., *Islamic art and spirituality,* Ipswich, UK 1987, 17-36; I.R. Netton, *Ṣūfī ritual. The parallel universe,* Richmond, Surrey 2000; K.M. O'Connor, The Islamic Jesus. Human divinity and messiahhood in the exegesis of African American Muslim groups, in *JAAR* 66 (1998), 493-532; id., The Nubian Islamic Hebrews, Ansaaru Allah Community. Jewish teachings of an African American Muslim community, in Y. Chireau and N. Deutsch (eds.), *Black Zion. African-American religious encounters with Judaism,* New York 1999, 118-50; id., Prophetic medicine and qurʾānic healing in medieval Islam and today, in J.W. Brown and R. Barlow (eds.), *Studies in Middle Eastern health,* Ann Arbor 1999, 39-77; D. Owusu-Ansah, *Islamic talismanic manuscripts among the Asante. History of Islam in Africa,* Athens, GA 2000, 477-88; id., *Islamic talismanic tradition in nineteenth-century Asante,* Lewiston, NY 1991; C. Padwick, *Muslim devotions. A study of prayer-manuals in common use,* London 1961; A. Parker and N. Avon, *Ḥajj paintings. Folk art of the great pilgrimage,* Washington, DC 1995; R. Patai, Folk religion. Folk Islam, in *ER,* v, 382-5; I. Perho, *The Prophet's medicine. A creation of the Muslim traditionalist scholar,* Helsinki 1995; M. Piamenta, *Islam in everyday Arabic speech,* Leiden 1979; L.N. Primiano, Vernacular religion and the search for method in religious folklife, in *Western folklore* 54/1 (1995), 37-56; R. Qureishi, *Ṣūfī music of India and Pakistan. Sound, context and meaning in Qawwālī,* Chicago 1986, 1995[2]; C. Raudvere, *The book and the roses. Ṣūfī women, visibility and zikir in contemporary Istanbul,* Istanbul 2002; J. Robson, Islamic cures in popular Islam, in *MW* 24 (1934), 34-43; id., The magical use of the Koran, in *Transactions* 6 (1929-33), 53-60; J. Sadan, Genizah and Genizah-like practices in Islamic and Jewish tradition, in *Bibliotheca orientalis* 43 (1986), 36-58; Y.H. Safadī, *Islamic calligraphy,* Boulder, CO 1979; E. Savage-Smith and M.B. Smith, *Islamic geomancy and a thirteenth-century divination device,* Malibu, CA 1980; A. Schimmel, *Mystical dimensions of Islam,* Chapel Hill, NC 1975; R.B. Serjeant, Islam, in M. Loewe and C. Blacker (eds.), *Oracles and divination,* Boulder, CO 1981, 215-32; S.J. Tambiah, The magical power of words, in *Man* 3 (1968), 175-209; J.D. Waardenburg, Official and popular religion as a problem in Islamic studies, in P.H. Vrijhof and J.D. Waardenburg (eds.), *Official and popular religion. Analysis of a theme for religious studies,* Paris 1979, 340-86; E.H. Waugh, *The Munshidun of Egypt. Their world and their song,* Columbia, SC 1989; E. Westermarck, *Ritual and belief in Morocco,* 2 vols., New York 1926; P.L. Wilson, *Sacred drift. Essays on the margins of Islam,* San Francisco, CA 1993.

Popular Media and the Qurʾān see MEDIA AND THE QURʾĀN

Pork see LAWFUL AND UNLAWFUL; FOOD AND DRINK

Portents

Anticipatory sign, warning or threat; also, marvel. While the Qurʾān is explicit in its condemnation of any belief that an impersonal fate (q.v.), rather than God, controls human destiny (q.v.; see also FREEDOM AND PREDESTINATION), and does not condone the efforts of soothsayers (q.v.) and other pre-Islamic "fortunetellers" (see DIVINATION; FORETELLING; PRE-ISLAMIC

ARABIA AND THE QURʾĀN; SOUTH ARABIA, RELIGION IN PRE-ISLAMIC), it is adamant that there are signs that humans must heed. Perhaps the most notable of these exhortations (q.v.) is the warning to heed the "signs of the hour" (*ashrāṭ al-sāʿa;* cf. Q 47:18; see LAST JUDGMENT; ESCHATOLOGY; APOCALYPSE; TIME).

Although it has no root in Arabic, *āyāt* (sing. *āya;* prob. borrowed from Syriac or Aramaic; see Jeffery, *For. vocab.,* 72-3; for biblical uses of the Heb. cognate, cf. Numbers 2:2; Joshua 4:6; Exodus 8:19; Deuteronomy 4:34; Psalms 78:43; I Samuel 10:7; see FOREIGN VOCABULARY) is a multivalent term for "portents" that appears 383 times in the Qurʾān, and may connote "signs" (q.v.), "miracles" (see MIRACLE) and "verses" (q.v.). Such qurʾānic utterances serve to signal the wonders (see MARVELS) or omens God bestows upon the world to demonstrate his power, wisdom (q.v.), judgment (q.v.) or wrath (see ANGER). As natural marvels, such as the rain that sustains life (q.v.; Q 30:24; see also WATER; SUSTENANCE), the fruits of the palm and vine (Q 16:67; see AGRICULTURE AND VEGETATION; DATE PALM), or the ships (q.v.) that appear like mountains on the seas (Q 42:32), portents elicit the awe-provoking magnitude of God's creation (q.v.). These tokens not only appear as cosmic and natural wonders but also as the extraordinary works of prophets and messengers through whom God guides his creation (see COSMOLOGY; PROPHETS AND PROPHETHOOD; MESSENGER; ASTRAY; ERROR). Examples of this type of portent include demonstrations of Moses' (q.v.) white hand and slithering staff (Q 7:106-8; see ROD), and Jesus' (q.v.) enlivening of the clay bird (Q 3:49). The verses *(āyāt)* of the Qurʾān that relay such portents also call humans to recognize God's power and might (see POWER AND IMPOTENCE). Left unnoticed or worse, rejected, these same portents, whether embedded in nature (see NATURE AS SIGNS), prophetic action or revelation itself (see REVELATION AND INSPIRATION), will bring forth terrifying demonstrations of divine wrath (see ANGER) upon those who fail to interpret what the sign truly signifies. The Qurʾān recounts numerous tales of individuals and communities pummeled for their neglect or denial of those clear signs a merciful God bestows upon his creation (see CHASTISEMENT AND PUNISHMENT; PUNISHMENT STORIES). In turn, the denunciations and punishments themselves serve as portents for those tempted to follow the same course of action. One might say the entire Qurʾān, from a single verse to the broader images it provokes, stands as a sign signifying simultaneously divine glory and wrath.

The Qurʾān emphasizes repeatedly the abundance and clarity of divine portents available for those who wish to see them (see SEEING AND HEARING). What is not clear, however, is whether one must "believe" or "understand" already in order to fathom the true meaning of the sign (see BELIEF AND UNBELIEF; KNOWLEDGE AND LEARNING; IGNORANCE; REFLECTION AND DELIBERATION). The portents manifest "for those who understand," or for "those who believe" (Q 13:3; 16:79; 30:21) are presumably the same signs rejected by those who already disbelieve (Q 37:14; 39:63; 41:15), which suggests the signs themselves have demonstrative, rather than persuasive, value.

Kathryn Keuny

Bibliography

Primary: Ṭabarī, *Tafsīr,* ed. Shākir.
Secondary: W. Graham, 'The winds to herald his mercy,' and other 'Signs for those of certain faith.' Nature as token of God's sovereignty and grace in the Qurʾān, in S.H. Lee et al. (eds.), *Faithful imaginings. Essays in honor of Richard R. Niebuhr,* Atlanta 1995, 18-38; Jeffery, *For. vocab.;*

H.E. Kassis, *A concordance of the Qurʾān*, London 1983; Lane; Pickthall, *Koran*.

Possession and Possessions

Ownership, the act of holding something or someone as property; the enjoyment or acquisition of the right to exercise control over something, and the objects thus controlled. In the Qurʾān, the idea of possession is frequently conveyed by the verb *malaka*, "to possess, to have, to own, to exercise sovereignty over," and its nominative derivatives, such as *mulk/malakūt*, "property, dominion, fiefdom," and, by extension, "sovereignty"; *mālik*, "owner, possessor"; and *malik*, "sovereign, ruler, king" (see KINGS AND RULERS). Similar meanings are associated with the word *rabb*, "lord (q.v.), master," that is applied to God throughout the Qurʾān either independently or in conjunction with the object of his sovereignty, e.g. "lord of the heavens (see HEAVEN AND SKY) and lord of the earth (q.v.), lord of the worlds" (Q 45:36; cf. 13:16; 17:102; 18:14; 19:65; 51:23, etc.), "lord of Sirius" (q.v.; Q 53:49), "lord of the mighty [heavenly] throne" (Q 9:129; see THRONE OF GOD), "lord of the east and the west and what is between them" (Q 26:28), "lord of the daybreak" (Q 113:1; see DAWN) and "lord of humankind" (Q 114:1). Also common are constructions with the possessive particle *li/la*, "to [God belongs], his is…" (see e.g. Q 2:255; 5:18; 42:4). As one may expect, in the Qurʾān, possession is essentially the prerogative of God, although he may occasionally grant it to his servants (see SERVANT), be they human beings or angels (e.g. Q 2:258; 3:26; see ANGEL).

Possession is one of the principal manifestations of God's absolute power (see POWER AND IMPOTENCE) over the universe and its inhabitants. In many passages these divine attributes (see GOD AND HIS ATTRIBUTES) go hand in hand and are, to some extent, interchangeable. God's power inevitably implies his uncontested ownership of all created beings and vice versa (see CREATION). While God can bestow possession of a certain property or rank upon individual creatures, as the ultimate ruler of his worldly domain (*mālik al-mulk*, Q 3:26; cf. 36:83; 39:6; 64:1; 67:1), he can also dispossess them at will in order to remind them of the transitory status of worldly possessions and of their true source (Q 3:26; see GRACE; BLESSING). The Qurʾān never tires of throwing these ideas into sharp relief: "lord of the worlds" (Q 1:2); "to him belongs whatsoever is in the heavens and whatsoever is in the earth" (Q 42:4); "glory be to him in whose hand is the dominion of everything" (Q 36:83); "you give the dominion to whom you will and you seize the dominion from whom you will" (Q 3:26), etc. God's sovereignty is not limited to this world. He is the wielder of the judgment day (*mālik yawm al-dīn*, Q 1:4; cf. 25:26; see LAST JUDGMENT) and, according to many exegetes, also of the hereafter (Ṭabarsī, *Majmaʿ*, i, 100; see ESCHATOLOGY; REWARD AND PUNISHMENT).

In several eloquent passages the Qurʾān condemns polytheists for their misguided belief that their deities possess the power to hurt or benefit their worshippers (see POLYTHEISM AND ATHEISM; IDOLATRY AND IDOLATERS). Unlike God, who owns life (q.v.), death (see DEATH AND THE DEAD) and the ability to effect the resurrection (q.v.) of decomposed bodies and moldering bones, these pagan deities have no power to give or take life. Nor are they capable of raising human beings from the dead. These are the exclusive prerogatives of God, who has created both the pagan deities and their worshipers. He alone has "no associate" *(sharīk)* in his absolute and uncontestable sovereignty (q.v.) over this world (Q 25:2-3). He alone is the possessor of the "most beautiful names" (Q 7:180; 17:110; 20:8), whose perfection sets him apart from his imperfect creatures. This message is brought home in a memorable passage from Q 35:13, which presents God as the absolute and undisputed master of reality: "That is God, your lord; to him belongs the dominion/possession *(al-mulk);* and those you call upon, apart from him, possess not so much as the skin of a date-stone!" The same idea is reiterated in Q 4:53: "Have they [the unbelievers] a share in the dominion? [Certainly not!] They can give not a single date-spot to the people!"

While human beings are allowed by God to enjoy their earthly possessions — "heaps of gold (q.v.) and silver, horses of mark, cattle and tillage" and the sensual delights of this world (see ANIMAL LIFE; NATURE AS SIGNS; AGRICULTURE AND VEGETATION) — they are constantly reminded that this life is but a respite granted to them by God, who will eventually become their "fairest resort" (Q 3:13). When the day of reckoning comes, their wealth (q.v.) and relatives will be of no avail to them (see KINSHIP; INTERCESSION); only their obedience (q.v.) or disobedience (q.v.) to God will count. According to Q 16:75, the ungrateful evildoer (see GRATITUDE AND INGRATITUDE; EVIL DEEDS) is like "a servant possessed by his master *(mamlūk),* having no possession of his own *(lā yaqdiru ʿalā shayʾin)*"; the righteous person, on the other hand, is like one "whom we [God] ourselves have provided with a provision fair." In a passage reminiscent of Psalm 37:29, God promises to reward his faithful servants in the hereafter by bequeathing to them "the [entire] land" (usually understood as paradise [q.v.]; cf. Q 39:74).

In this life, human beings are God's "vicegerents *(khalāʾif)* on the earth" (see CALIPH) and their possessions and social ranks (see COMMUNITY AND SOCIETY IN THE QURʾĀN) are a means by which God tests their loyalty (q.v.) to their maker (Q 6:165). Thus, human possession is distinct from that of God by its transience and inconstancy. Ancient Arabian tribes (see TRIBES AND CLANS; ARABS; PRE-ISLAMIC ARABIA AND THE QURʾĀN) were given abundant wealth and splendid palaces, but their ungodly ways and stubborn belief in their self-sufficiency vis-à-vis God brought divine wrath upon them (see ANGER). Following their refusal to amend their ways, God withdrew his favor from the wrongdoers, dispossessed them and wiped them from the face of the earth (see PUNISHMENT STORIES). Their tragic end serves as a reminder to later generations (q.v.) that God's bounty and solicitude for the well-being of his human subjects call for continual gratitude. This idea is eloquently stated in Q 36:71-3: "Have they not seen how we have created for them of what our hands wrought cattle that they own *(lahā mālikūna)?* We have subdued them to them, and some of them they ride and some they eat; other uses they have in them, and beverages (see HIDES AND FLEECE; FOOD AND DRINK). What, will they not be thankful?"

In elaborating on the meaning of the phrase "they own" *(mālikūna),* the Yemeni exegete al-Shawkānī (d. 1250/1839) explains that it means that God has granted humankind full and coercive control *(ḍābiṭūna qāhirūna)* over their domestic animals. This is viewed by the commentator as a sign of God's benevolence toward his human servants, for he could have created the animals wild so that "they would run away from them [the people] and they would have been unable to subdue them." Instead, argues al-Shawkānī, God has made the animals part and parcel of human beings' estate/possession *(ṣārat fī amlākihim),* over which they exercise full sovereignty (*mulk;* Shawkānī, *Tafsīr,* iv, 382; cf. Ṭabarī, *Tafsīr,* xxiii, 28-9). This idea is reiterated over and over again throughout the Qurʾān, as in e.g. Q 31:20: "Have you not seen that God has subjected to you whatsoever is in the heavens and the earth, and he has lavished upon you his benefits *(niʿamahu),* outward and inward" (cf. Q 2:29; 22:65).

Possession of worldly goods by people entails responsibilities, which are stipulated in the numerous passages of the Qurʾān that constitute the foundation of the legal norms pertaining to property rights under Islam (see LAW AND THE QURʾĀN). The rich are enjoined by God to share their wealth with the poor (see POVERTY AND THE POOR) generously but not to squander it either: "And give the kinsman his right, and the needy, and the traveler (see JOURNEY); and never squander; the squanderers are brothers of the satans" (Q 17:26-7). Wives, "those of weak intellect," and orphans (q.v.) are entitled to their share in the property of their husbands and guardians (see MARRIAGE AND DIVORCE; FAMILY; MAINTENANCE AND UPKEEP; GUARDIANSHIP), who are commanded to treat them equitably (Q 4:4-6; see JUSTICE AND INJUSTICE). In one instance, the injunction to share one's wealth with others appears alongside the two principal articles of the Islamic creed — an eloquent evidence of its importance for the nascent faith: "Believe in God and his messenger (q.v.), and expend what he has made you stewards of; for those of you who have believed and expended is (in store) a great reward" (Q 57:7; cf. 24:33; see BELIEF AND UNBELIEF; JIHĀD). Statements such as this one make it abundantly clear that all worldly possessions held by human beings ultimately belong to and come from God, who lends them to his servants for appointed terms. Therefore, hoarding what is effectively God's property for one's private gain is strongly condemned: "Those who hoard gold and silver and do not expend them in the way of God (see ALMSGIVING; USURY) — to them give the good tidings of a painful chastisement (see CHASTISEMENT AND PUNISHMENT), the day they shall be heated in the fire of *jahannam* (see HELL AND HELLFIRE) and therewith their foreheads and their sides and their backs shall be branded: 'This is what you hoarded for yourselves: therefore taste you now what you were treasuring!'" (Q 9:34-5).

The Qurʾān contains a number of stipulations regarding the proper relations between male and female slaves ("those whom your right hands own") and their masters, in everyday life and at manumission (see SLAVES AND SLAVERY; GENDER; WOMEN AND THE QURʾĀN). Within the household, the masters are commanded to treat their human property kindly (Q 4:3, 25, 36; 16:71; 24:33, 59, etc.; see SOCIAL RELATIONS). At manumission, the owners are enjoined to "contract them [freed slaves] accordingly… and give them of the wealth of God that he has given you" (Q 24:33). Again, the idea is that, in the final account, all wealth and possessions come from God, who lends them temporarily to his servants.

In the later exegetical tradition (see EXEGESIS OF THE QURʾĀN: CLASSICAL AND MEDIEVAL) pertaining to passages that deal with divine sovereignty over the world, one finds a debate over the semantic nuances of *mālik,* "owner, possessor," as opposed to *malik,* "sovereign, king." At issue with medieval commentators was the respective scope of each of these terms. Some (Abū ʿUbayd, d. 224/838, and al-Mubarrad, d. 285/898) argued that the latter was more encompassing *(ablagh),* as the king's *(malik)* writ overrules the sovereignty of any individual owner *(mālik)* within his realm *(mulk).* Others (al-Zamakhsharī,

d. 538/1144) considered the word "owner" *(mālik)* to be more comprehensive when applied to God, in so far as he can be regarded as the ultimate "owner" of all human beings, be they kings or commoners. Hence, the title "owner" is more comprehensive than "king" when applied to God, while the title "king" is more comprehensive than "owner" when applied to human beings (Ṭabarsī, *Majmaʿ*, i, 97-8). According to al-Shawkānī, each term carries connotations that are unique to it and missing from its counterpart; therefore the dispute around their respective scope is futile. From the viewpoint of the Ashʿarī doctrine (see THEOLOGY AND THE QURʾĀN) of divine attributes, however, the term *mālik*, "owner," when it is applied to God, should be regarded as his attribute of action *(ṣifa li-fiʿlihi)*. The term *malik* ("king, sovereign"), on the other hand, should be seen as an attribute of the divine essence (*ṣifa li-dhātihi;* Shawkānī, *Tafsīr*, i, 71).

In his "rationalist" commentary on the Qurʾān the great Muslim theologian and exegete Fakhr al-Dīn al-Rāzī (d. 606/1210) argues that God's status as the "sovereign" *(malik)* of the universe indicates that he is located outside it, since he cannot be "sovereign of himself." This conclusion, in his view, is corroborated by Q 19:93, according to which "None is there in the heavens and earth, but comes to the all-merciful as a worshipper *(ʿabd)*." If, argues al-Rāzī, everything on earth and in heaven worships God, he of necessity should be located outside and above it, for otherwise he would have been the worshipper of himself, which is logically impossible (cf. Rāzī, *Tafsīr*, xxi, 255-6). For the accusation of the "possession" of humans by malevolent forces, see JINN; INSANITY; OPPOSITION TO MUḤAMMAD.

Alexander D. Knysh

Bibliography

Primary: Ibn Kathīr, *Tafsīr*, ed. S. al-Salāma, 8 vols., Riyadh 1997, esp. i, 131-4; Rāzī, *Tafsīr*, Beirut 1981; Shawkānī, *Tafsīr*, Cairo 1930, esp. i, 322-4; iii, 180-2; iv, 60-2, 340-3, 381-2; Ṭabarī, *Tafsīr*, ed. ʿAlī, iii, 199-205; xiv, 148; xviii, 126-32, 181; xxii, 124-5; xxv, 7-8 (in addition to the pages cited in the article); Ṭabarsī, *Majmaʿ*, Beirut 1986.

Secondary: ʿAlī al-ʿAfīf, *al-Milkiyya fī l-sharīʿa al-islāmiyya*, Beirut 1990; J. Botterweck and H. Ringgren (eds.), *Theological dictionary of the Old Testament*, trans. J.T. Willis, 11 vols., Grand Rapids, MI 1974-2001, vi, 368-96; x, 144-8 (for comparative materials).

Post-Enlightenment Academic Study of the Qurʾān

The modern study of the Qurʾān, meaning thereby "the critical dispassionate (i.e. non-polemical) search for knowledge, unconstrained by ecclesiastical institutional priorities" (Rippin, *Qurʾan. Style and contents*, xi n. 2), insofar as it is a living tradition of learning and the basis of all contemporary research, cannot be assessed in its entirety in a single entry. Rather, the present entry can merely aim at specifying the major trends of research and the overall development of modern scholarship. The selective bibliography below is limited to writings of a general character, collections of papers and literature dealing specifically with the modern study of the Qurʾān and its methodology.

The study of the Qurʾān has never ceased being a primary concern in the realm of Islamic studies during the past two centuries. Given the outstanding importance of the Qurʾān in Islam, it is likely to remain so in the future. The interest of scholars in the Qurʾān, however, has shifted its center of attention from time to time, depending on the prevailing *Zeitgeist* as well as on the ensuing challenges and results of ongoing research.

Nineteenth century

The academic study of the Qurʾān in the West around the middle of the nineteenth century was largely stimulated and influenced by two German works, G. Weil's *Historisch-kritische Einleitung* (1844[1]) and Th. Nöldeke's *Geschichte des Qorāns* (1860[1]). Both writings, but above all Nöldeke's, set new standards for future research and went beyond the achievements of previous literature. As an illustration of the contemporary state of the art in Europe, suffice to say that, in 1846, Solvet's *Introduction à la lecture du Coran* merely offered to the French public a new translation of G. Sale's *Preliminary discourse* (this discourse was part of Sale's influential book *The Koran commonly called Alcoran of Mohammed… to which is prefixed a preliminary discourse,* which had already been published in London in 1734; see PRE-1800 PREOCCUPATIONS OF QURʾĀNIC STUDIES). The treatise of Sale offers a general overview of the contents of the Qurʾān, the basic tenets of the Muslim faith (q.v.; see also CREEDS) and a rough sketch of pre-Islamic Arabia and the developments of early Islam (see PRE-ISLAMIC ARABIA AND THE QURʾĀN; AGE OF IGNORANCE). In itself, it draws mainly on material contained in E. Pococke's *Specimen historiae arabum* (1650) but more importantly, and in marked difference to the accounts of Weil and Nöldeke, Sale does not yet treat the text of the Qurʾān in its own right nor does he deal in detail with the formal, linguistic and stylistic elements of the text.

G. Weil in his *Historisch-kritische Einleitung,* which is only a short treatise that devotes some forty pages to the Qurʾān as such, took up the Muslim division between Meccan and Medinan sūras (see CHRONOLOGY AND THE QURʾĀN; MECCA; MEDINA) in order to establish a chronological framework of revelation (see REVELATION AND INSPIRATION; OCCASIONS OF REVELATION). In doing so, he became the first to attempt a reassessment of the traditional dating of the sūras and to divide the Meccan material into three further periods, something which was then fully elaborated and improved upon by Nöldeke. Although Weil and Nöldeke considered matters of content while establishing a chronological order of revelation for the Meccan sūras — e.g. similarity of content and terminology in individual sūras was seen as evidence for their mutual correlation and their approximate time of origin — both scholars also stressed the importance of formal and linguistic elements of the qurʾānic text for defining the criteria according to which the three Meccan periods could be distinguished (see e.g. FORM AND STRUCTURE OF THE QURʾĀN; OATHS; RHETORIC AND THE QURʾĀN; EXHORTATIONS). This four-period dating system, consisting of three Meccan periods and the Medinan period, proved influential for decades to come. It considerably influenced the future conceptual analysis of the Meccan segments of the Qurʾān and even led to the re-arrangement of the Meccan sūras in a number of twentieth-century translations of the Qurʾān in western languages (cf. Blachère, *Introduction,* 247 f.) and was also initially adopted for the French translation by R. Blachère. The idea of re-arranging the text of the Qurʾān, including the division of single sūras into unities of differing chronological status, ultimately led to the complex undertaking of R. Bell in his translation of the Qurʾān "with a critical re-arrangement of the Surahs" (1937-9; see also below; see TRANSLATIONS OF THE QURʾĀN).

Of the studies mentioned so far, Nöldeke's *Geschichte des Qorāns (GQ),* since its appearance in a second enlarged edition in the first decades of the twentieth century — considerably augmented by three other scholars — has proven to be the decisive standard text to which all modern scholars interested in the Qurʾān must refer. It is still a helpful tool today, especially as many of its shortcomings have been detected, discussed and revised. The elaboration of the four-period dating system is presented in the first volume of GQ. The second volume, written by Nöldeke's pupil F. Schwally, contains a detailed analysis of the collection of the Qurʾān (q.v.; see also CODICES OF THE QURʾĀN; MUṢḤAF). The third volume, by G. Bergsträsser and O. Pretzl, treats the history of the qurʾānic text and is mainly concerned with variant readings and the later-established "readings" *(qirāʾāt)* known from Islamic tradition (see READINGS OF THE QURʾĀN).

In some sense, the third volume of GQ can be considered as the indispensable preliminary to the final task of an edition of the Qurʾān according to the most exacting standards of the philological method, that is, an edition based on ancient manuscripts, the entire available Islamic literature on the subject (see TRADITIONAL DISCIPLINES OF QURʾĀNIC STUDY) and, most importantly, accompanied by a critical apparatus that would list all known variant readings and orthographical peculiarities (cf. Bergsträsser, Plan eines Apparatus Criticus). Nothing, however, has come of this and an edition of the Qurʾān that follows the above-mentioned critical methodology remains a desideratum. The final contribution of research in this direction, pre-dating the publication of the third volume of GQ by one year, is Jeffery's *Materials for the history of the text of the Qurʾān* (1937). Since then, individual contributions for the history of the text have been made in a number of articles but no major work has been published which would offer a synthesis of the material. Also, ancient manuscripts of the Qurʾān, going back to the first and second Islamic centuries, and which have become known in the meantime, have not yet been published properly and still await detailed analysis (cf. Puin, Observations). It is noteworthy, however, that in his multi-volume Arabic-German edition of the Qurʾān (Gütersloh 1990 f.) A.Th. Khoury decided to include many variant readings in the commentary, although he made no effort to be comprehensive (the contributions of Antoine Isaac Silvestre de Sacy, the first European to study al-Dānī, and those of Edmund Beck for the study of the variant readings of the Qurʾān should likewise not be overlooked).

Nöldeke's GQ and the work of Schwally, Bergsträsser and Pretzl shaped in any case much of the modern study of the Qurʾān in its later developments, directing it mainly towards the study of the formal, stylistic and linguistic aspects of the text, as well as towards the study of the terminology of the Qurʾān and to its semantic and conceptual analysis. Yet many topics of future research were, as seems natural, not yet raised in the GQ. It is also important to note that Nöldeke's pioneering work, notwithstanding its undeniable scientific merits, is littered with less-than-sympathetic remarks about what he (as well as other Orientalists of his formation and generation) thought of the scripture to which he devoted his studies, in particular its aesthetic qualities (see Wild, Die schauerliche... Öde). In this respect, his generation stood too much under the spell of ancient literature which pervaded the minds of nineteenth-century European philologists and which made them incapable of truly appreciating texts stemming from different cultural contexts. The nearest Nöldeke came to esteeming the Arabic literary heritage was in his fondness for pre-Islamic poetry, in which he discovered a likeness between the Bedouin (q.v.) worldview and that of the ancient Germanic tribes (see also POETRY AND POETS; ARABS). In many of their judgments on the Qurʾān, however, Nöldeke and his successors come perilously close to T. Carlyle's famous statement, "it is a toilsome reading as I ever undertook. A wearisome confused jumble, crude, incondite; endless iterations, long-windedness, entanglement (...). Nothing but a sense of duty could carry any European through the Koran" (*On heroes*, 86 f.). The modern study of the Qurʾān during the last part of the twentieth century has contributed much to changing this attitude, yet the works of the nineteenth- and early twentieth-century scholars were chiefly responsible for the fact that only in the recent past did it become widely acknowledged in the West that the Qurʾān could be esteemed as a piece of highly artful literature, possessing considerable and distinctive aesthetical qualities, as well as beauty of expression.

Another shortcoming of the *GQ*, and perhaps the one that most limits its merits from our viewpoint, is the relatively marginal role accorded to Islamic learning and heritage. This is not to be seen as an entirely negative factor, or only as a drawback, because, for one thing, to begin to treat the Qurʾān as a text in its own right and to attempt to judge and evaluate it on its own premises, independently of what the Islamic scholarly tradition had to offer, was a great step forward in the understanding of the Qurʾān. Furthermore, the Arabic literature available to nineteenth- and early twentieth-century scholars was very limited and simply insufficient, if compared to today's wealth of accessible material. Yet this method of setting aside or overriding, if necessary, the data of the Islamic tradition in favor of the intrinsic evidence of the qurʾānic text manifests a major methodological flaw. The reason for that is the eclectic, and therefore often arbitrary, use made of the Islamic tradition. On the one hand, the *GQ* authors often did not follow the Islamic tradition concerning the origin, chronology, order and semantic value of the textual constituents of the Qurʾān but, on the other hand, in trying to establish an independent framework and in attempting a fresh interpretation of the qurʾānic event, they did take the Islamic tradition into account. Within the context of this latter approach, the tradition was especially consulted on two accounts: for the qurʾānic depictions of the historical circumstances of the revelation (viz. the life of the Prophet and the vicissitudes of his community; see SĪRA AND THE QURʾĀN) and for the details found in classical Islamic works elucidating the emergence of the Qurʾān as a document in a historically definable context. Nöldeke himself had become aware of this problem through his acquaintance with the studies by H. Lammens, whose writings emphasize the non-historicity of the Islamic tradition and, consequently, the futility of making use of it at all. Nöldeke thus felt compelled to defend the value of the Islamic tradition in historical matters and stressed that the Medinan period, at least, was "in the clear light of history" ("mit der Übersiedlung nach Jathrib betreten wir hell historischen Boden," Die Tradition, 165). The methodological flaw involved here is, however, undeniable. Disclosing this weakness and its wide-reaching implications was to become a distinctive feature of the modern study of the Qurʾān during the twentieth century.

The latter half of the nineteenth century is marked by an increasing number of treatises produced in the wake of Weil and Nöldeke. Many of those are distinguished by the fact that they adopt the principles of research developed by the German Orientalists but reach different conclusions. This is the case — to name but a few — with the respective writings of W. Muir, A. Rodwell, H. Grimme and H. Hirschfeld. Although these scholars came to different and conflicting conclusions, all (with the debatable exception of Rodwell) certainly enhanced the critical study of the Qurʾān along the lines of philological research. Muir and Rodwell, in their treatises of 1878, each developed a chronological sequence and re-arrangement of the sūras. Muir's re-arrangement distinguishes six different periods, proposing five Meccan periods, which he defined by recourse to the successive stages of Muḥammad's career as a prophet (see PROPHETS AND PROPHETHOOD). Grimme, on the contrary, attempted to order the sūras on the basis of doctrinal characteristics, with only two Meccan periods and one Medinan (cf. Watt-Bell, *Introduction*, 112). Finally, Hirschfeld, in his *New researches into the composition and exegesis of the Qoran* (1902) introduced still another sequence of the qurʾānic passages. This scheme is likewise based on the content of the sūras and their respective messages, which were assigned by Hirschfeld to one of six "modes" (confirmatory, declamatory, narrative, descriptive, legislative, parable).

In contrast to the preceding studies, in which the sūras (q.v.) were largely taken for granted as textual unities and thus as entities of the same origin and chronological status, Rodwell and Hirschfeld also tried to identify single passages within the sūras that belong together thematically and hence also chronologically. This idea was then carried forward and implemented, in varying degrees, by R. Bell and R. Blachère. In Bell's re-arrangement of the sūras, incorporated into his translation of the Qurʾān, he not only tried to break the sūras up into short coherent passages but even into single verses (q.v.) or verse groupings. This was done according to his famous hypothesis that all sūras had undergone various processes of revision and that during the collection of the Qurʾān the leaves or papers that contained the text were partially disordered. He also suggested that something written on the back of these papers was then, by mistake as it were, inserted in the context of a sūra to which it did not belong (see Watt-Bell, *Introduction*, 101-7; also Merrill, Bell's critical analysis; Bell's evidence for his dissections of the single sūras is available in greater detail in his posthumously published *Commentary*). Less radically, Blachère in the first edition of his translation of the Qurʾān (1947-51) adopted, with minor modifications, the chronological scheme of the Meccan sūras as laid down in GQ and thus produced his own "reclassement des sourates." This scheme, however, was abolished in the second edition (1956) and Blachère retained the traditional (Islamic) order.

It needs to be emphasized that none of the studies carried out during the second half of the nineteenth century ever reached the influence of Nöldeke's GQ in modern scholarship; nor were their results accepted as easily and widely. This is doubtless because Nöldeke's initial periodization and the ensuing evaluation of the qurʾānic text on the basis of his chronology steers the middle course between being too indiscriminate on the one hand and being too sophisticated on the other. Compared to that, Muir's six periods or Hirschfeld's six "modes" seem somewhat over-detailed and thus of difficult application in further research. Another reason for the dominance of Nöldeke's scheme in modern scholarship has been the fact that the second edition of GQ appeared only after the publication of the late nineteenth-century treatises and thus already includes the critical discussion or even refutation of rival accounts. What is more, given the hypothetical nature of every such reconstruction of the origin of the Qurʾān, which is based on circumstantial evidence drawn primarily from formal, linguistic and stylistic features, the more detailed the proposed partition of the qurʾānic text, the more difficult it is to argue for both its accuracy and its ability to do justice to other sorts of reasonable hypotheses. Having proposed a dissection of the qurʾānic text into tiny passages of accidental sequence and thus rendering a meaningful reconstruction of its internal chronology virtually impossible, R. Bell then faced this problem in its most extreme form.

From the present point of view, therefore, the late nineteenth-century and early twentieth-century attempts at rearranging the qurʾānic text do not seem very convincing. The character of most such rearrangements is too hypothetical to be assessed properly. Also, there is essentially no evidence that is extra-qurʾānic but contemporaneous with the period of qurʾānic origins that could validate or refute the proposed hypotheses. We are thus left with the impression that much of what was said in favor of a certain rearrangement of the qurʾānic text often does not appear improbable — but neither is there any compelling evidence for its validity. One final drawback of first establishing a chronological order of the qurʾānic textual material and then attempting its interpretation on the very basis of this scheme has been summarized by A. Rippin (*Qurʾan. Style and contents,* xxii) as follows:

Using the chronological framework produces a systematic picture of the development of semantic information which may then be used to re-date elements which do not fit into the basic scheme. Certainly such a method has its circularity (...), but it is often held out that such a study might prove persuasive if it combined a number of such thematic and semantic elements to produce a single cohesive and coherent pattern; a study of this type, however, has not yet been undertaken.

It is not by accident, therefore, that the majority of studies pertaining to the form and structure of the Qurʾān and to single sūras conducted since the second half of the twentieth century no longer try to establish a fixed chronological order or rearrangement of sūras, on whatever basis. Rather, such studies tend to limit themselves to phenomenological description of the qurʾānic wording (Müller, *Untersuchungen*), re-propose the unity of the Meccan sūras as distinctive and not incidentally composed entities (Neuwirth, *Studien*) or attempt to solve problems of textual coherence by recourse to the vast Islamic literature on the subject (Nagel, *Einschübe;* see TEXTUAL CRITICISM OF THE QURʾĀN).

Before concluding the survey of nineteenth-century scholarship, it must be stressed that the dominant trend in qurʾānic studies, namely the reconstruction of the textual history of the Qurʾān chiefly on the basis of its internal features and with the assistance of the Islamic tradition for its historical context, is less noticeable in works concerned with the history of early Islam, in particular the life of the Prophet. Clearly, the Qurʾān plays a major role in this field too, being the foundational document of the new religion. The best example of such scholarship, one that drew upon the Islamic tradition and the bulk of the exegetical material (as far as it was known at the time and much more than was done in the works reviewed above) is probably A. Sprenger's three-volume biography of Muḥammad (1869). Here, Sprenger went a long way towards combining the qurʾānic data with the lore of tradition. In this, he was much assisted by the sources at his disposition in Indian libraries. Although both form and content of the Qurʾān are not to the fore in Sprenger's study, it nevertheless contains much that directly pertains to the study of the Qurʾān. Sprenger's study is thus, in this respect, far ahead of other writings of his time but his work was never granted the place in the modern study of the Qurʾān it justly deserves.

The heritage of Western nineteenth-century scholarship on the Qurʾān was to determine the course that modern research took during the first half of the twentieth century. Some lines of continuity and lasting influence have already been mentioned: for example, the quest for the role of Islamic tradition in establishing the external and contextual framework for the historical process of the revelation, or Bell's fragmentation of the qurʾānic text as the ultimate consequence of applying formal and stylistic criteria in detecting coherent, if minute, passages of textual and thematic unity. The main thrust, however, behind nineteenth-century research was towards the philological treatment of the text, its individual constituents and the interest in both the significance and origin of single terms or concepts. It is along these lines that much of the ensuing research evolved.

First half of the twentieth century

Topics dominant in early twentieth century-scholarship were the linguistic aspects of the qurʾānic wording, its variant readings (see READINGS OF THE QURʾĀN) and its foreign (i.e. of non-Arabic origin) vocabulary (see FOREIGN VOCABULARY; LANGUAGE AND STYLE OF THE QURʾĀN), the significance of single qurʾānic terms and concepts, the order and chronology of the textual parts and their integrity (see FORM AND STRUCTURE OF THE QURʾĀN; LITERARY STRUCTURES OF THE QURʾĀN), and the influence of the older monotheistic faiths upon the content and message of the Qurʾān (including the pivotal role of biblical and apocryphal lore; see NARRATIVES; SCRIPTURE AND THE QURʾĀN; JEWS AND JUDAISM; CHRISTIANS AND CHRISTIANITY).

One topic that aroused the interest of numerous scholars during much of the twentieth century was the significance of the so-called "mysterious letters" (q.v.) which were first dealt with in Nöldeke's *GQ*. Many hypotheses as to their possible meaning were then advanced, starting with O. Loth and leading to the extensive articles by H. Bauer and E. Goossens. Before that, we find the remarks made by H. Hirschfeld in his *New researches*, and further contributions were added by A. Jones, M. Seale and J. Bellamy. It is fair to say, however, that no truly convincing solution to the origin and relevance of the "mysterious letters" has yet been found, although many hypotheses which were advanced do not lack ingenuity and demanded much effort in order to establish them. Interest in this subject abated in recent years and few new hypotheses have been put forward since (cf. Massey, Mystery letters).

Another thread of research which had its origins in the late nineteenth century and was then carried on for many decades in the twentieth century concerns the language used in the Qurʾān and, by implication, the language originally spoken by the Prophet. The subject was raised to prominence by K. Vollers who in his *Volkssprache und Schriftsprache im alten Arabien* argued that the Qurʾān was first recited in colloquial Arabic lacking the case-endings, whereas the known text of the Qurʾān was a result of the work of later philologists trying to purge the wording from all traces of dialect and to generate a text conforming to the rules of classical Arabic, the language used by the ancient poets. This view found some adherents (P. Kahle, G. Lüling) but was more often rejected (e.g. R. Geyer, Th. Nöldeke, F. Schwally). Since then it has been largely agreed upon, following a number of further articles and discussions in monographs exploring the ramifications of this argument (e.g. R. Blachère [*Histoire*, i, 66-82], C. Rabin, J. Fück [*Arabiya*]), that the original language of the Qurʾān, in accordance with what we find in the standard text, consists more or less of the so-called *koinè* used in inter-tribal communication and ancient poetry, with some traces of the Meccan dialect left in the peculiarities of the qurʾānic orthography (see ORTHOGRAPHY; DIALECTS; ARABIC LANGUAGE; ORALITY AND WRITING IN ARABIA).

Both the detailed study of the "mysterious letters" as well as the quest for the original language of the Qurʾān clearly betray the language-oriented direction of much of modern research after the beginning of the twentieth century. The outcome of both fields of study may seem, especially if one considers the intellectual labor involved, rather disappointing: the "mysterious letters" have remained mysterious, though less unfamiliar, and the present linguistic form of the Qurʾān is widely accepted as being that from the time of its origin onwards. Much more promising, therefore, proved the interest twentieth-century scholars took in the terms used in the Qurʾān. Here a field of study was opened, yet not without having antecedents during the late nineteenth century, which offered the possibility of combining interest in linguistic features with a closer study of the message of the Qurʾān, as both are inevitably linked to each other in the semantic potential of single terms. Among the first writings in this field, preparing the way for further research in the twentieth century, were the Arabic-English glossary of the Qurʾān by J. Penrice (*Dictionary*, 1873) and the analysis of commercial terms used in the Qurʾān and their relation to qurʾānic theology by Ch. Torrey (*Commercial-theological terms*, 1892; see TRADE AND COMMERCE; THEOLOGY AND THE QURʾĀN). The studies which then appeared in the first half of the twentieth century shifted their interest to the etymological background of qurʾānic key-terms, their connections to the use in earlier monotheist religions and the proper names found in the Qurʾān. The most influential and stimulating writings in this regard are the relevant passages in J. Horovitz's *Koranische Untersuchungen* (1926), as well as A. Mingana's "Syriac influence" (1927), K. Ahrens's *Christliches im Qoran* (1930) and A. Jeffery's *Foreign vocabulary* (1938).

Interestingly, the shift in the study of terms and concepts towards their possible origin in Jewish, Christian or Judaeo-Christian usage reflects the growth of an area of study which might be said to be the true novelty of early twentieth-century scholarship on the Qurʾān. Turning away from a purely language-centered approach or the attempt to understand the qurʾānic message intrinsically on the sole basis of its textual constituents and stylistic phenomena, the qurʾānic terms, narrations, legal prescriptions (see COMMANDMENTS; LAW AND THE QURʾĀN), elements of eschatology (q.v.) and theology were now increasingly compared to, and set into relation with, corresponding items in the Jewish and Christian traditions. Although the problem of the exact relationship of emergent Islam and its Prophet with Judaism and Christianity had already been raised by A. Geiger (*Was hat Mohammed*), A. Sprenger (Moḥammad's Zusammenkunft), and Th. Nöldeke (Hatte Muḥammad christliche Lehrer), no immediate attempt had been made to trace the tokens of Jewish and Christian influence on nascent Islam in the Qurʾān. Beginning with Hirschfeld's *Jüdische Elemente* (1878) and Schapiro's (incomplete) *Haggadische Elemente* (1907), however, this approach soon developed into a major area of study through the monographs by W. Rudolph (1922), H. Speyer (1931), J. Walker (1931) and D. Sidersky

(1933). More importantly still, the field of qurʾānic studies at this point merged with the more generally-oriented and less Qurʾān-centered history of early Islam, a field in which two influential writings had appeared just at that time, namely R. Bell's *The origin of Islam in its Christian environment* (1926) and Ch. Torrey's *The Jewish foundation of Islam* (1933).

Without exaggeration, the research into the supposed Jewish or Christian roots of early Islam and hence of its scripture may be said to be the lasting heritage of early twentieth-century qurʾānic studies, having had by far the most wide-reaching influence until the present day. Although only few would today claim either that Islam came into being in a predominantly Christian environment or that its foundations are predominantly Jewish, the research carried out in order to support these assertions did indeed produce much evidence for the actual relationship between the monotheistic faiths. In addition, the studies generated during the first decades of the twentieth century drew attention to the great amount of biblical lore which we find in the Qurʾān and sharpened our view of how biblical and apocryphal material is adapted and presented in the Qurʾān. With much-reduced claims as to the origin of Islam and its scripture or its historical indebtedness towards Judaism and Christianity, the study of the interrelatedness of the three great monotheistic religions and their scriptures has never stopped, producing many writings in the 1950s (D. Masson, J. Henninger, J. Jomier, A. Katsh) and beyond (K. Cragg, M. Seale, U. Bonanate). This approach was accompanied by research into the connection of the qurʾānic message to Near Eastern realms of a more marginal nature (Qumran, Samaritan Judaism) and to the pre-Islamic pagan Arab religion (see POLYTHEISM AND ATHEISM; PILGRIMAGE; IDOLATRY AND IDOLATERS). In the latter half of the twentieth century, a number of monographs were published concerning various biblical figures — such as Adam (see ADAM AND EVE), Abraham (q.v.) and Mary (q.v.) and, above all, Jesus (q.v.) — as portrayed in the Qurʾān (M. Hayek, H. Michaud, G. Parrinder, H. Räisänen, N. Robinson *[Christ in Islam]*, O. Schumann). The quest for the presence of Jewish and Christian elements in the Qurʾān is likely to continue in the time to come under the aegis of an increasingly active inter-confessional dialogue.

Reviewing the field of Western qurʾānic studies in the first half of the twentieth century, one will become aware of the fact that, with the notable exception of the aforementioned study of Jewish and Christian elements in the Qurʾān and the revised edition of *GQ*, no syntheses or all-encompassing monographs were produced. Rather, scholarship followed different tracks of research which either led to a great number of interconnected articles, as in the case of the mysterious letters or the quest for the original language of the Qurʾān, or to monographs dealing with a particular subject such as the study of the origin and etymology of qurʾānic terms. In this vein, the first half of the twentieth century was chiefly a period of research into problems of limited range and of a fervent collection of data. Putting it somewhat more positively, one could also say that in this time tools for further study were devised in a number of thematically defined fields which, however, all have their bearing on the whole. Another good example of this type of approach is A. Spitaler's *Verszählung des Koran* (1935). Therefore, during this period — despite the waging of two world wars in the geographic center of the academic study of the Qurʾān — time was not lost in modern qurʾānic studies. The 1920s and 1930s can thus be considered a period of the most intense and prodigious research concerning the Qurʾān, although the majority of its results lay scattered in learned journals, academy transactions, miscellanea and collections of studies. The true amount of what was achieved step by step in this period only became apparent in post-World War II scholarship, after a certain tendency towards the accumulation of the widely-dispersed material had set in among French and British scholars.

Second half of the twentieth century

This period is, at its beginning, distinguished by the publication of three influential general works dealing with the phenomenon of the Qurʾān as a whole, namely R. Blachère's introduction to the first edition of his translation (1947, independently published in 1959), A. Jeffery's *The Qurʾān as scripture* (1952) and R. Bell's *Introduction to the Qurʾān* (1953, rev. ed. by W.M. Watt in 1970: Watt-Bell, *Introduction*). Thus there were now three comprehensive and up-to-date monographs available which, in many respects, brought together the manifold results of scholarship from the earlier half of the twentieth century. At the same time, the gist of GQ became known to the non-German speaking world via these writings. For decades to come, the books by Bell, Blachère and Jeffery remained, together with the GQ, the standard reference texts for everybody involved in qurʾānic studies.

Curiously, but perhaps not surprisingly, the monographs by Blachère, Bell and Jeffery drew upon much of the earlier twentieth-century research and offer in many ways a synthesis of the previous achievements, yet at the same time their writings also mark the end of a still homogeneous tradition of scholarship. The hallmarks of that tradition were the importance of the philological approach and its relative independence, or isolation, from many other fields of related interest such as anthropology, religious studies, social studies and literary criticism. The biggest contribution to qurʾānic studies had been made, up to that time, only by the methods of biblical and theological studies. It is true that most of the fields like anthropology and religious studies were newcomers to Western scholarship in the twentieth century and could not be expected to be immediately adopted or acknowledged by the modern study of the Qurʾān. Yet up to the present day, Islamic studies generally tends to lag behind the developments in fields of related interest, something which might, in part, be excused by the fact that the rather impenetrable and boundless mass of material of all sorts that confronts the scholars of Islam does not easily permit them to turn their attention towards cognate disciplines. As it is, however, the increasing influence of relevant disciplines and a steadily growing array of new methods, perspectives and approaches has characterized the modern study of the Qurʾān since the second half of the twentieth century.

Another novel feature of post-war qurʾānic studies has been a new interest in the actual content of the qurʾānic text and a changed understanding of how to elucidate the semantics of qurʾānic terms and concepts. Both approaches disentangled themselves, to varying degrees, from similar attempts that were made earlier in the twentieth century and showed their provenance to be the then dominant philological mode of research. As to the first point, i.e. the new examination of the contents of the Qurʾān, one could refer to the writings of T. O'Shaughnessy, whose studies of qurʾānic theology appeared from 1948 onwards. Similarly, a number of scholars set about examining the ethical doctrines of the Qurʾān (M. Draz, S. al-Shamma,

M.D. Rahbar, D. Bakker, I. Zilio-Grandi; see ETHICS AND THE QUR'ĀN), its eschatology (R. Eklund, S. El-Salih, T. O'Shaughnessy) or its inherent anthropology (J. Bouman, T. Izutsu, J. Jomier, S. Wild). Others researched details of communal life and ritual (K. Wagtendonk) as present in the Qur'ān, albeit the first influential study of that kind appears to be R. Robert's *Social laws of the Qur'ān* (1927; see *inter alia* SOCIAL INTERACTIONS; RITUAL AND THE QUR'ĀN; RAMAḌĀN; FASTING). As to the second point, i.e. a changed understanding of the semantics of qur'ānic terms and concepts, it is largely agreed upon that the pioneering works of T. Izutsu brought major progress in the field of semantic studies, especially as his approach takes up methods of modern linguistics. Izutsu aims at analyzing the meaning of terms in context and does not look for a meaning inherent in the terms themselves. In doing so, he superseded the earlier research carried out in the field of semantic studies, although Izutsu's method is only seemingly in direct opposition to the former philological method and its stress on etymology (cf. Rippin, *Qur'an. Style and contents,* xvi f.).

A third, particularly important novelty of twentieth-century qur'ānic studies consists in the discovery of the general contextuality of the qur'ānic wording, that is, the difficulty of drawing a line between the meaning of the text in itself — a concept now considered by many as erroneous in principle — and the creation of its meaning(s) in the process of interpretation and exegesis (see EXEGESIS OF THE QUR'ĀN: CLASSICAL AND MEDIEVAL; EXEGESIS OF THE QUR'ĀN: EARLY MODERN AND CONTEMPORARY). The only meaning a text is considered to possess is thus the meaning which is accorded or ascribed to it in the process of actual reception and exegesis. From around the middle of the twentieth century, therefore, scholars in the field of qur'ānic studies tended, hesitantly at first, to develop a contextual view of the Qur'ān. Consequently, less stress was laid on the intrinsic character of the text, the meaning of individual terms and the question of the origin of its material, as had been the case during the first half of the twentieth century. Rather, attention was devoted to the ways in which the Qur'ān was embedded in the wider realm of Islamic learning and the emergence of its meaning(s) from Islamic tradition and the endeavors of the exegetes. This increasingly led scholars to analyze the close ties between the Qur'ān and exegesis, Islamic tradition (see ḤADĪTH AND THE QUR'ĀN), Islamic theology and Arabic philological studies devoted to the terminology and vocabulary of the Qur'ān. This clearly signified a major step forward, with the result that many elements of the qur'ānic wording were understood more thoroughly and in greater detail by making use of the vast quantity of Muslim scholarship dealing with all facets of the text (see TRADITIONAL DISCIPLINES OF QUR'ĀNIC STUDY).

The first immediate outcome of the change of perspective in the modern study of the Qur'ān towards its contextuality and the significance of Muslim exegesis was the growing interest in qur'ānic exegesis. This field, of prime importance as it always was in the culture of Islam, was up to the second half of the twentieth century almost wholly, and inexplicably, missing from the agenda of Western scholars, with the notable exception of I. Goldziher's pioneering *Richtungen der islamischen Koranauslegung* (1920) and some dispersed comments in the writings of early twentieth-century Orientalists. The concentrated and still ongoing effort, however, of a large number of scholars, especially after the work of J. Wansbrough (see below), has resulted in considerably more research being done in the vast field of Muslim exegesis than in the field of qurʾānic studies proper. But as said before, it would by now be practically impossible to differentiate between the study of the Qurʾān and the study of its exegesis, both being so closely related as to permit no meaningful separation between these two fields of research. On the contrary, one could even argue that, in contrast to the traditional self-perception of modern scholarship, the academic quest for the understanding of the Qurʾān is in itself nothing but a further continuation of Muslim exegesis, which, to a certain extent, uses different means and is stimulated by other guiding principles. The more that becomes known of Muslim exegesis, however, the closer we are brought to admit that there is actually little of what modern qurʾānic scholarship claims as its own achievement that was unknown beforehand or is original to the "modern post-enlightenment academic" approach.

Recognizing the importance of Muslim exegesis for the modern study of the Qurʾān is also part of a larger discussion among scholars. This discussion revolves around the question of what role the Islamic scholarly tradition can, or should, play in the study of the Qurʾān and early Islam in general, one of the chief matters of debate in research of the last quarter of the twentieth century. From late nineteenth-century and early twentieth-century scholarship, the modern study of the Qurʾān inherited an approach that tended to set the Islamic tradition aside or use it only in closely circumscribed areas, such as reconstructing the historical context in which the revelation took place (see above). In contrast to that, later twentieth-century research has shown that in Islamic tradition and learning, all fields are closely interrelated and that it might prove difficult, if not impossible, to single some of its parts out as valuable or historically reliable and others as irrelevant. Rather, as a matter of principle, there is no irrelevant or non-valuable notice which might not further our understanding of the whole. This is not to say that some parts of that tradition may not indeed be more valuable or historically accurate than others but, as most scholars would admit, we are lacking the necessary means to decide in the majority of cases whether this is true of a certain piece of tradition or not.

The growing familiarity of Western scholars with the immense wealth of material stemming from the formative and classical periods of Islam and pertaining more or less directly to the historical context of early Islam and the coming into being of the Qurʾān has also generated another important insight: namely, that only a small part of the available material, if collated and seen together with all relevant bits and pieces, seems to allow a single historical reconstruction which might be considered reasonably more certain than others. M. Cook (*Early Muslim dogma,* 155 f.) has called this the "indefinite tolerance of the source-material for radically different historical interpretations," which is why we "know how to *maintain* rival theories; but we can do little to decide *between* them." The methodologies, however, which are capable of discerning the value, or tendency, of the source material have become more refined in the past years and the study of early Islamic tradition is a vivid topic in recent research. It is here that qurʾānic studies has come into close contact with the study of the life of the Prophet and the history of his community. Given that the Qurʾān as a historical document cannot be understood irrespective of the setting of its genesis, this merging of qurʾānic studies with the quest for the evolution of early Islam is bound to remain an important element of future research.

In some sense, the perceived need to confront the qurʾānic data with everything that is known from the Islamic tradition about the historical context of revelation in order to elucidate the significance and meaning of the Qurʾān runs parallel to the urge towards incorporating data from the exegetical tradition. For this latter trend aims at the elucidation of the Qurʾān's significance and meaning via the semantic universe created by the Muslim exegetes. Although the implications of the studies of J. Wansbrough, A. Rippin and U. Rubin have still to be worked out fully, their work shows that the exegetical tradition may eventually prove vital for establishing the very textual history of the Qurʾān during the first decades of Islam and for understanding the origin of Islam itself. Both these developments — the turn towards tradition and towards Muslim exegesis — in the modern study of the Qurʾān are ultimately the result of the basic insight within later twentieth-century scholarship, that a non-contextual understanding of the Qurʾān will prove impossible and its attempt futile. One is obliged to add that the opposite attempt has been made — to clarify the material of Islamic tradition and its depiction of early Islam by starting with the qurʾānic data and not vice versa, notably by R. Paret and W.M. Watt. Yet this has merely shown that the "historical" references contained in the Qurʾān and those which might tell us something about the context of its revelation are too limited and ambiguous in meaning to permit a large-scale use of the Qurʾān for the reconstruction of the setting and context of its origination.

Apart from the exegetical tradition and the source material concerning the life of the Prophet and the history of early Islam, later twentieth-century qurʾānic studies also drew attention to the relations between the Qurʾān and the fields of jurisprudence and legal theory (J. Burton, M. Schöller). In this respect, it is hoped that the attitudes of early Muslim legal scholars towards the qurʾānic text and the use they made of it may tell us something about the role of the Qurʾān in early Islamic society and hence allow the formation of an idea of the function(s) it fulfilled in its original setting. This could also bear upon the problem of its presumed time and place of origin, a matter which has been put into question in twentieth-century scholarship (see below). In the same vein, the modern study of the Qurʾān in the second half of the twentieth century returned to the philological study of the Qurʾān, yet with more stress on the aspects of grammar and syntax and less on the semantic properties of the text (A. Ambros, M. Chouémi, Cl. Gilliot [Les citations], F. Leemhuis, W. Reuschel, R. Talmon, C. Versteegh; see GRAMMAR AND THE QURʾĀN; LANGUAGE AND STYLE OF THE QURʾĀN; but cf. also the ground-breaking work of A. Neuwirth, who focuses less on a philological/atomistic approach than on philological analysis of individual sūras as paralleling elements of monotheistic liturgy; cf. FORM AND STRUCTURE OF THE QURʾĀN; RHETORIC AND THE QURʾĀN); a computer-aided analysis of the entire text of the Qurʾān along morphological, grammatical and syntactical features is presently in preparation (cf. Edzard, Perspektiven, 350 f.; see COMPUTERS AND THE QURʾĀN). In returning to the linguistic analysis of the qurʾānic wording, a huge advance was made over the achievements of early twentieth-century scholarship. This is not only because the wealth of relevant Arabic literature now available compares so favorably with that of the earlier part of the twentieth century. Rather, it is chiefly because the vast Arabic grammatical and philological tradition, still largely unexplored and virtually inaccessible to the non-specialist, has now become the object of serious scrutiny. This thread of research also serves as an important corrective to recent work which, under the weight of theoretical models, new approaches and methodological premises, carries the risk of losing touch with the linguistic side of the Qurʾān whose study is, after all, a basic requirement for its adequate understanding and interpretation.

Unresolved proposals

The last novelty of later twentieth-century qurʾānic studies to mention is the publication of some hypotheses regarding the origin of the Qurʾān which contest the Islamic tradition as well as the results of modern scholarship. The value of these hypotheses, some of which had a greater influence on the academic discussion than others, is still a matter of debate and is likely to remain so. Most scholars of Islam, however, presently concur that none of these hypotheses will eventually prove correct. Yet it must be admitted that, to date, no large-scale refutation of any of them has been produced; nor can all the arguments put forward be dismissed very easily. The positive effect, in any case, of the proposed hypotheses has been one of resuscitating the modern study of the Qurʾān and stimulating increased efforts in that direction. The current state of affairs, perhaps even the very fact of this encyclopedia, is the welcome result of this stimulus.

The first study to challenge the conventional view regarding the origin of the Qurʾān was published in 1974 by G. Lüling as a reworking and enlargement of his Ph.D. dissertation of 1970. He has since repeated and pursued his basic claims in a number of other studies. Put succinctly, he comes to the conclusion that the qurʾānic text consists of different layers which were subjected to several redactions. The basic layer of the text, the so-called "two-sense layer," was originally of Christian provenance and hymnic in character, representing the *"Ur-Qurʾān"* and proclaiming the message of Muḥammad's Judeo-Christian mission. It was then changed, in the processes of redaction, to conform to the later orthodox, post-prophetic Islamic views. Another layer, the so-called "one-sense layer," was of post-prophetic Islamic provenance from the outset and should serve to turn the meaning of the "two-sense layer" towards the later views by being inserted at appropriate places in the text. Much of what is proposed by Lüling is astute and based on broad learning. His general thesis, however, remains unconvincing to most scholars primarily for two serious weaknesses which neither Lüling nor anyone else is likely to remove in the future.

First, Lüling's reconstruction requires the consequent assertion that the entire Islamic tradition pertaining to the history of early Islam is a gigantic fabrication created to cover up a different story. Given what we know and considering the enormous amount of preserved information, this assumption is most unlikely and strains credulity. The second drawback, equally decisive, derives from the fact that in his reconstruction of the text of the presumed *"Ur-Qurʾān"* Lüling not only changed, in many instances, the vocalization of the text but also its consonantal structure, its word sequence and entire words (something to which he resorted to an even greater extent in later writings). Although this was done with great ingenuity, the obvious risk in tampering with a text in order to fit a theory was carefully formulated by G.R. Hawting in his review of another of Lüling's books (rvw. of *Die Wiederentdeckung des Propheten Muhammad,* in *JSS* 27 [1982], 111): "It seems to me that the argument is essentially circular and that since there is no way of controlling or checking the recomposed *Ur-Qurʾān,* there is a danger that it will be recomposed to suit one's own preconceptions about what one will find in it." In other words, anyone familiar with how easy it is to change the meaning of an Arabic consonantal text by systematically modifying vocalization and/or consonant markings will admit that this may open the gates of semantic hell, so to speak. Taken to extremes, one could as well replicate the Cairo phone-book as a Ṣūfī chain of mystical succession. Applying such textual modification to the Qurʾān can be done but, in the absence of supporting evidence from contemporary documents, it can neither be confirmed nor falsified. Therefore, the value of Lüling's hypothesis, whatever its merits in matters of detail, depends upon how much weight modern scholarship is willing to concede to conspiracy theories that do not admit of falsification.

In 2000 a study was published with the title *Die syro-aramäische Lesart des Koran. Ein Beitrag zur Entschlüsselung der Koransprache,* whose author writes under the pseudonym Ch. Luxenberg. Similar to Lüling's hypothesis but without recourse to his work, the meaning of many terms and passages of the Qurʾān is here traced back to an original Syriac wording, in the process of which the original meaning of the respective qurʾānic terms and passages, lost or suppressed in the Islamic tradition as we know it, is "rediscovered" (see SYRIAC AND THE QURʾĀN). Although it seems too early to venture a decisive judgment upon this publication which was accorded a methodically rigorous review (cf. Gilliot, Langue et Coran, 381-93), it is clear that Luxenberg's proposal suffers from the same weaknesses as does Lüling's account: the complete silence of the Islamic tradition with respect to his proposed origin of the Qurʾān and his resort to the modification of the consonantal text in both vocalization and consonant marking (for a positive appraisal of Luxenberg's thesis, see Gilliot, Langue et Coran; id., Le Coran. Fruit d'un travail collectif?; cf. also van Reeth, L'évangile du prophète).

With Lüling's 1974 study having remained largely unknown outside the German-speaking academic world, the major watershed in the modern study of the Qurʾān occurred in 1977 when three highly controversial monographs were published, namely J. Burton's *Collection of the Qurʾān,* M. Cook's and P. Crone's *Hagarism,* and J. Wansbrough's *Quranic studies.* These studies all present a novel reading and/or reconstruction of early Islam and the history of its scripture. For the study of the Qurʾān, Burton's and Wansbrough's monographs are of particular importance, especially as the conclusions reached by these two British scholars are diametrically opposed to each other. In Wansbrough's account we are told that the canonical form of the Qurʾān, i.e. the text in its present form, was not established prior to the end of the second/eighth century and does not entirely go back to the time of the Prophet. From Burton's study, on the other hand, it can be inferred that the collection of the canonical text predates the death of the Prophet and was known in this form ever since. Both claims, albeit entirely irreconcilable with each other, contradict the mainstream Islamic tradition which states that the canonical text of the Qurʾān was eventually ratified only during the two decades following the death of the Prophet and up to the caliphate of ʿUthmān (q.v.; r. 23-35/644-56). Together with the strongly original theses of *Hagarism* which was published at the same time, the monographs by Burton and Wansbrough created the first major impetus to qurʾānic studies in many decades.

An important difference between the accounts of Burton and Wansbrough and the aforementioned hypotheses of Lüling and Luxenberg lies in the fact that neither

Burton nor Wansbrough set about modifying the qurʾānic text. Rather, in the case of Burton it is precisely the fact that the Qurʾān contains some difficult and seemingly contradictory passages that are hard to understand which serves as argument against any later redaction (that easily could have done away with all such difficulties; see ABROGATION; AMBIGUOUS; DIFFICULT PASSAGES). In the case of Wansbrough, the belief that the present text of the Qurʾān achieved canonical status during the first Islamic centuries is questioned, yet no attempt is made to question the accuracy of the transmitted text beyond the variant readings current in the Islamic tradition. A greater difficulty faced both Burton and Wansbrough with regard to the Islamic tradition concerning the origin of the Qurʾān, although Burton's hypothesis seems to be easier to reconcile with what the sources tell us than does Wansbrough's. Nevertheless, both negate the historicity of much of the traditional material on Islamic origins and thus constitute variants of conspiracy theories. The early Islamic biographical literature, for example, is called by Wansbrough (*QS*, 140) a "pseudo-historical projection." Yet, both Burton and Wansbrough make valid points, which cannot be side-stepped in research, and there is indeed some evidence in the Islamic tradition which supports their hypotheses. The general, somewhat paradoxical, effect upon many readers of their studies appears to be that much of what Burton and Wansbrough present in order to reach their respective conclusions is admitted by most to be sound and important for the course of future scholarship, yet their conclusions are not.

J. Wansbrough's hypothesis, being more contentious and radical, has received more attention from the scholarly community than Burton's proposal. The consensus reached after an initial analysis of Wansbrough's study praised his method and his recourse to typology and criteria of biblical and literary criticism. His conclusions about the origin of the Qurʾān were, however, received with great skepticism or outright denial. Few were convinced that the generation of the Qurʾān was protracted until the end of the second/eighth century. Indeed, especially considering the evidence of qurʾānic epigraphy from the first two centuries of Islam (see EPIGRAPHY AND THE QURʾĀN; ARCHAEOLOGY AND THE QURʾĀN; ART AND ARCHITECTURE AND THE QURʾĀN), it is hard to see how the history of early Islam could have evolved if its scripture was still in the making and the product of a gradual evolution. His inability to offer an alternative scenario is a weakness of Wansbrough's hypothesis (cf. rvw. of *QS* by A. Neuwirth, in *WI* 23-4 [1984], 540 f.) and in his second treatise — which further expounds his basic proposal — Wansbrough explicitly denies any attempt at historical reconstruction: "My purpose... is not historical reconstruction, but rather, source analysis" (*Sectarian milieu*, ix). For the understanding of the Qurʾān, however, Wansbrough's hypothesis signifies that the text in its present form cannot be traced back to the Prophet or to any single individual. Rather, in this view, the Qurʾān consists of the redaction and collection of material ("logia"), dealing with Islamic "salvation history" (see SALVATION; HISTORY AND THE QURʾĀN) that was first generated in various sectarian communities, and finally accorded canonical status as an authoritative text. Passages or logia which were not included in that canon remained part of the various fields of the Islamic tradition, chiefly prophetic biography *(sīra)*, ḥadīth and commentary *(tafsīr)*. Wansbrough maintains that, with virtually no evidence about the details of the presumed redaction and collection at our disposal, every attempt at trying to establish a chronology of the individual parts of the qurʾānic text, or at reconstructing the *Formgeschichte* of the Qurʾān, is impossible in principle; the actual origins of the qurʾānic data must remain unknown. The stylistic features and the literary form of the qurʾānic text itself are of no help in determining its date of origin and its authenticity (cf. Wansbrough, *QS*, 147). Finally, with the Qurʾān offering almost no material useful for historical purposes, the chronological framework known from the Islamic tradition appears merely as an historical order "introduced into what was essentially literary chaos" (Wansbrough, *QS*, 177).

Notwithstanding the controversial validity of Wansbrough's overall thesis concerning the genesis of the Qurʾān as scripture and its evolution in time, his treatise opened up many ways of research for the first time which then heavily influenced the ensuing efforts of scholarship. He was the first to use the exegetical commentaries of the second/eighth century systematically and to conceive of a typology and terminology in order to better understand what the early Muslim exegetes were actually doing. Or put differently, he pushed the contextual approach to the Qurʾān to its limits, making the notion of "the Qurʾān" as a body of texts which can be interpreted and analyzed within the traditional paths of "historical criticism," almost meaningless. A. Rippin, who in a number of articles defended the merits of Wansbrough's approach, rightly observed of Wansbrough's work that "the theories proffered about the origins of the Qurʾān have tended to overshadow the others" (id., Methodological notes, 39), resulting in an ultimate misconception of his approach and the dismissal of his method and its achievements for the sake of denying the validity of his overall conclusion. Indeed, it might be supposed, and there is some rumor to that effect among contemporary scholars of early Islam, that Wansbrough's hypothesis of a cumulative creation of the Qurʾān and its gradual evolution into scripture in a sectarian setting of broadly Near Eastern monotheistic stamp might still be safeguarded if the period of the Qurʾān's origin is no longer placed in the first Islamic centuries but ante-dated to the time prior to the Prophet's mission (see ḤANĪF). It then would also become compatible with Burton's well-argued hypothesis that the Qurʾān had already reached its present form and structure in the time of the Prophet. To clarify this issue will be a major challenge for the modern study of the Qurʾān in the years to come. In doing so, it will be imperative to work with all the literary sources at one's disposal, yet at the same time avoid the temptation of creating new texts out of those presently known in order to fit one's own theories.

Prospects of further research

Many of the aforementioned research trends as they developed in the second half of the twentieth century will undoubtedly determine the further course of the study of the Qurʾān in the foreseeable future. The seminal works of Burton and, above all, Wansbrough are especially likely to exert ever more influence upon qurʾānic studies and the methods used therein. The contextual approach towards the Qurʾān, placing its study in close connection to the study of the various related fields of Islamic learning (Tradition, exegesis, law, grammar), will probably continue to dominate most academic efforts. There is still much optimism and vigor in qurʾānic studies, and justly so. Illustrative of this is the fact that 1999 witnessed the publication, after some 150 years of modern Western scholarship on the Qurʾān, of the first volume of the first periodical devoted exclusively to qurʾānic matters, *Journal of qurʾanic studies;* it is noteworthy that in the editorial of its first issue, the field of qurʾānic studies is called, albeit somewhat disrespectfully towards the achievements of the past, "an evolving discipline."

Apart from the trends inherited from late twentieth-century scholarship, however, there are a number of areas in qurʾānic studies whose importance has not yet been fully recognized and whose status remains unsatisfactory in the wider realm of the modern study of the Qurʾān. Mention could be made here of the obvious connections of the Qurʾān and the origin of Islam to the pre-Islamic, Arab pagan world and the ties with the non-monotheistic population of south Arabia (see SOUTH ARABIA, RELIGION IN PRE-ISLAMIC). Although some important work has been done in this field (M. Bravmann, R.B. Serjeant, S. Noja, G.R. Hawting), it seems that not everything of relevance has yet come to light. There is still, one is led to think by the available evidence in Islamic tradition, a slight overstating of the influence of monotheistic religions on the formation of the Qurʾān and early Islam and a possible underestimation of the impact of the indigenous, non-monotheistic Arabic culture. This, of course, is partly inherited from the quest for the origins of Islam as conducted in the first half of the twentieth century, but also stems in part from the weight accorded to the monotheistic background in the more recent works of J. Wansbrough, A. Rippin and others. At any rate, archaeological fieldwork and the data of epigraphy, not yet fully exploited in qurʾānic studies, does yield some distinctive evidence about the impact of the Arab pagan culture upon early Islam. Another field to stimulate research in this direction, also until now insufficiently explored, is the study of Muslim eschatology and the rich imagery pertaining to the nether world as known from the Qurʾān and early tradition. Here, many elements lead the observer towards Arab pagan notions and even to concepts current in ancient Egypt, yet away from the patterns of thought normally considered to be part of the monotheistic groups of the Near East in early Islamic times (cf. PARADISE; GARDEN; HELL AND HELLFIRE).

The last, but not the least, area of qurʾānic studies which possesses considerable potential for further research is the role and place of the Qurʾān in Islam as a token of piety, symbol of faith and liturgical document. Little work has been done so far on the art of qurʾānic recitation (K. Nelson; cf. Sells, *Approaching;* see RECITATION OF THE QURʾĀN; EVERYDAY LIFE, THE QURʾĀN IN; ORALITY) and the related field of Islamic learning as a subject of study in its own right (see TEACHING AND PREACHING THE QURʾĀN). The pioneering study of the recited Qurʾān seen as a "phonetic phenomenon" in its various religious and liturgical uses is, for the time being, N. Kermani's *Gott ist schön. Das ästhetische Erleben des Koran* (1999; the work of A. Neuwirth has also contributed to the understanding of the Qurʾān as a liturgical document; cf. RHETORIC AND THE QURʾĀN; FORM AND STRUCTURE OF THE QURʾĀN). In addition, the role of the qurʾānic text in calligraphy (q.v.; see also MANUSCRIPTS OF THE QURʾĀN) and epigraphy (above all in inscriptions on buildings and tombstones) has never been researched systematically nor has the presence of qurʾānic terms and allusions in Arabic poetry and language (see LITERATURE AND THE QURʾĀN), in particular in Arabic phraseology and daily speech, received proper attention (cf. Piamenta, *Islam in everyday Arabic speech;* see also SLOGANS FROM THE QURʾĀN; MATERIAL CULTURE AND THE QURʾĀN; for some discussion of the impact of the Qurʾān on non-Arabic Islamic literature, see AFRICAN LITERATURE; PERSIAN LITERATURE AND

THE QURʾĀN; TURKISH LITERATURE AND THE QURʾĀN; SOUTH ASIAN LITERATURE AND THE QURʾĀN; SOUTHEAST ASIAN LITERATURE AND THE QURʾĀN). The degree to which the culture of Islam is being pervaded by the wording of its scripture is remarkable and sets it apart from most other comparable systems of high culture. The more remarkable, then, that this realization has yet to enter the agenda of Western qurʾānic studies. It is hoped that this hitherto neglected area of research within qurʾānic studies, as a part of the wider phenomenology of Islamic culture and religion, will be developed more quickly in the future than it has been in the past.

Marco Schöller

Bibliography

K. Ahrens, Christliches im Qoran. Eine Nachlese, in ZDMG 9 (1930), 15-68, 148-90; M. Allard, *Analyse conceptuelle du Coran sur cartes perforées,* 2 vols., The Hague 1963; A.A. Ambros, Lākin und lākinna im Koran, in ZAL 17 (1987), 21-30; id., Syntaktische und stilistische Funktionen des Energikus im Koran, in WZKM 79 (1989), 35-56; M. Arkoun, Comment lire le Coran? in *Le Coran. Traduit de l'arabe par Kasimirski,* Paris 1970, 11-36; id., *Lectures du Coran,* Paris 1982; D. Bakker, *Man in the Qurʾān,* Amsterdam 1965; H. Bauer, Über die Anordnung der Suren und über die geheimnisvollen Buchstaben im Qoran, in ZDMG 75 (1921), 1-20; E. Beck, Arabiyya, Sunna und ʿĀmm in der Koranlesung des zweiten Jahrhunderts, in *Orientalia* 15 (1946), 180-224; id., Die ʿuṯmānischen Varianten bei al-Farrāʾ, in *Orientalia* 23 (1954), 412-35; id., Die b. Masʿūdvarianten bei al-Farrāʾ, in *Orientalia* 25 (1956), 353-83; 28 (1959), 186-205, 230-56; id., Die dogmatisch religiöse Einstellung des Grammatikers Yaḥyā b. Ziyād al-Farrāʾ, in *Muséon* 54 (1951), 187-202; id., Die Kodizesvarianten der Amṣār, in *Orientalia* 16 (1947), 353-76; id., Studien zur Geschichte der Kufischen Koranlesung in den beiden ersten Jahrhunderten, in *Orientalia* 17 (1948), 326-55; 19 (1950), 328-50; 20 (1951), 316-28; 22 (1953), 59-78; Bell, *Commentary;* id, *Introduction to the Qurʾān,* Edinburgh 1953; id., *The origin of Islam in its Christian environment,* London 1926; id., *Qurʾān;* J. Bellamy, The mysterious letters of the Koran. Old abbreviations of the *basmalah,* in JAOS 93 (1973), 267-85; id., Some proposed emendations to the text of the Koran, in JAOS 113 (1993), 562-73; G. Bergsträsser, Plan eines Apparatus Criticus zum Koran (1930), repr. in Paret (ed.), *Koran,* 389-97; J. Berque, *Relire le Coran,* Paris 1993; Frankfurt-am-Main 1995 (Ger. trans.); W.A. Bijlefeld, Some recent contributions to qurʾānic studies. Selected publications in English, French, and German, 1964-1973, in MW 64 (1974), 79-102, 172-9, 259-74; Blachère; id., *Histoire de la littérature arabe,* 3 vols., Paris 1952; id., *Introduction;* H. Bobzin, *Der Koran. Eine Einführung,* Munich 1999; U. Bonanate, *Bibbia e corano. I testi sacri confrontati,* Turin 1995; I. Boullata (ed.), *Literary structures of religious meaning in the Qurʾān,* Richmond 2000; J. Bouman, *Gott und Mensch im Koran,* Darmstadt 1989[2]; P. Branca, *Il Corano,* Bologna 2001; M. Bravmann, *The spiritual background of early Islam,* Leiden 1972; M. Buitelaar and H. Motzki (eds.), *De Koran. Ontstaan, interpretatie en praktijk,* Muiderberg 1993; Burton, *Collection;* T. Carlyle, *On heroes, hero-worship, and the heroic in history,* London 1897; M. Chouémi, *Le verbe dans le Coran. Racines et formes,* Paris 1966; M. Cook, *Early Muslim dogma,* Cambridge 1981; id., *The Koran. A very short introduction,* Oxford 2000; Turin 2001 (It. trans.); K. Cragg, *The event of the Qurʾān. Islam in its scripture,* Oxford 1971[1], 1994[2]; id., *The mind of the Qurʾān. Chapters in reflection,* London 1973; id. (ed.), *Readings in the Qurʾān,* London 1988; P. Crone and M. Cook, *Hagarism. The making of the Islamic world,* New York 1977; D. DeSmet, G. de Callatay and J. van Reeth (eds.), al-Kitāb. *La sacralité du texte dans le monde de l'Islam. Actes du Symposium international tenu à Leuven et Louvain-la-Neuve du 29 mai au 1 juin 2002* [Acta orientalia belgica. Subsidia III], Brussels 2004; M. Draz, *Initiation au Koran,* Paris 1951 (Eng. trans. *Introduction to the Qur'an,* New York 2000); id., *La morale du Koran,* Paris 1951; id., *Les hommes à la découverte de Dieu = Ad dîn. Prologue à une histoire des religions. Suivi de Le regard de l'islam sur les autres religions révélées,* Beirut/Paris 1999; L. Edzard, Perspektiven einer computergestützten Analyse der qurʾānischen Morpho-Syntax und Satz-Syntax in kolometrischer Darstellung, in *Arabica* 50 (2003), 350-80; R. Eklund, *Life between death and resurrection according to Islam,* Inaugural dissertation, Uppsala 1941; Ṣ. El-Ṣaleḥ, *La vie future selon le Coran,* Paris 1971; J. Fück, *Arabiya,* Berlin 1950; id., *Die arabischen Studien in Europa bis in den Anfang des 20. Jahrhunderts,* Leipzig 1955; H. Gätje, *Koran und Koranexegese,* Zurich 1971; Eng. trans. A.T. Welch, *The Qurʾān and its exegesis,* Berkeley 1976; A. Geiger, *Was hat Mohammed aus dem Judenthume aufgenommen?* Bonn 1833; R.E. Geyer, Review of Vollers, *Volkssprache,* in *Göttingische gelehrte Anzeigen* 171 (1909), 10-55; id., Zur Strophik des Qurâns, in *WZKM* 22 (1908), 265-86; Eng. trans. The strophic structure of the Koran, in Ibn Warraq (ed. and trans.), *What the Koran really says. Language, text, and commentary,* Amherst 2002, 625-46; C. Gilliot, *Elt;* id., Langue et Coran (see below, under Luxenberg); id., Le Coran. Fruit d'un travail collectif? in D. DeSmet, G. de Callatay and J. van Reeth (eds.), al-Kitāb. *La sacralité du texte dans le monde de l'Islam. Actes du Symposium international tenu à Leuven et Louvain-la-Neuve du 29 mai au 1 juin 2002* [Acta orientalia belgica. Subsidia III], Brussels 2004, 185-231; id., Les citations probantes *(šawāhid)* en langue, in *Arabica* 43 (1996), 297-356; Goldziher, *Richtungen;* E. Goossens, Ursprung und Bedeutung der koranischen Siglen, in *Der Islam* 13 (1923), 191-226, repr. in Paret (ed.), *Koran,* 336-73; H.C. Graf von Bothmer et al., Neue Wege der Koranforschung, in *Magazin Forschung* 1 (1999), 33-46; H. Grimme, *Mohammed. Zweiter Teil. Einleitung in den Koran,* Münster 1895; R. Hartmann, Die Welt des Islam im Lichte des Quran, in *Moslemische Revue* 6/4 (1930), 105-6; id., Zur Erklärung von Sūre 18,59 ff., in *Zeitschrift für Assyriologie und Verwandte Gebiete* 24 (1910), 307-15; G.R. Hawting, *The idea of idolatry and the emergence of Islam. From polemic to history,* Cambridge 1999; id. and Shareef, *Approaches;* G.R. Hawting and J. Wansbrough, Islam and monotheism, in *Method and theory in the study of religion* 9 (1997), 23-38; M. Hayek, *Le Christ de l'Islam,* Paris 1959; J. Henninger, *Spuren christlicher Glaubenswahrheiten im Koran,* Schöneck 1951 (articles published originally in *Neue Zeitschrift für Missionswissenschaft,* 1945-51); H. Hirschfeld, *Beiträge zur Erklärung des Korāns,* Leipzig 1886; id., *Jüdische Elemente im Korān,* Berlin 1878; id., *New researches into the composition and exegesis of the Qoran,* London 1902; Horovitz, *KU;* Ibn Warraq (ed.), *The origins of the Koran. Classic essays on Islam's holy book,* Amherst 1998; id., *What the Koran really says. Language, text and commentary,* Amherst, NY 2002; Izutsu, *Concepts;* id., *God;* id., *The structure of the ethical terms in the Koran. A study in semantics,* Tokyo 1959; Jeffery, *For. vocab.;* id., *Materials;* id., The mystic letters of the Koran, in *MW* 14 (1924), 247-60; id., The present status of qurʾānic studies, in *Middle East Institute. Report on current research* (Spring 1957), 1-16; id., Progress in the study of the Qurʾān text, in *MW* 25 (1935), 4-16; id., *The Qurʾān as scripture,* New York 1952; J. Jomier, *The Bible and the Koran,* New York 1964; id., *Dieu et l'homme dans le Coran,* Paris 1996; id., *Les grand thèmes du Coran,* Paris 1978; London 1997 (Eng. trans.: *The great themes of the Qur'an,* London 1997); A. Jones, The language of the Qurʾān, in *The Arabist* 6-7 (1994), 29-48; id., The mystical letters of the Qurʾān, in *SI* 16 (1962), 5-11, repr. in Paret (ed.), *Koran,* 379-85; id., Narrative technique in the Qurʾān and in early poetry, in *JAL* 25 (1994), 185-91/*The Arabist* 8 (1994), 45-54; id., The oral and the written. Some thoughts about the qur'anic text, in *The Arabist* 17 (1996), 57-66; P.E. Kahle, The Arabic readers of the Koran, in *JNES* 8 (1949), 65-71; repr. in Ibn Warraq (ed. and trans.), *What the Koran really says. Language, text, and commentary,* Amherst 2002, 201-10; id., *The Cairo Geniza,* Oxford 1959[2] (London 1941, 1947), 141-9, 345-6 (ed. of a text of al-Farrāʾ); id., The Qurʾān and the ʿarabīya, in S. Loewinger and J. Somogyi (eds.), *Ignace Goldziher memorial volume,* Budapest 1948, 163-8; A. Katsh, *Judaism in Islam. Biblical and Talmudic backgrounds of the Koran and its commentaries,* New York 1954; N. Kermani, *Gott ist schön. Das ästhetische Erleben des Koran,* Munich 1999; M. Khalifa, *The sublime Qurʾān and orientalism,* London 1983; J. Koren and Y.D. Nevo, Methodological approaches to Islamic studies, in *Der Islam* 68 (1991), 87-107; F. Leemhuis, About the meaning of nabba'a and 'anba'a in the Qur'an, in A. Dietrich (ed.), *Akten des VII. Kongresses für Arabistik und Islamwissenschaft, Göttingen, 15 bis 22 August 1974,* Göttingen 1973, 244-9; id., *The D and H stems in koranic Arabic. A comparative study of the function and meaning of the faʿʿala and afʿala forms in koranic usage,* Leiden 1977; id., A koranic contest poem in Sūrat aṣ-Ṣāffāt, in G. Reinink et al. (eds.), *Dispute poems and dialogues in the ancient and medieval Near East,* Leuven 1991, 165-77; id., Qur'anic siǧǧīl and Aramaic sgyl, in *JSS* 27 (1982), 47-56; G. Lüling, *Die Wiederentdeckung des Propheten Muhammad. Eine Kritik am "christlichen" Abendland,* Erlangen 1981 [Review by G. Hawting, in *JSS* 27 (1982), 108-12]; id., *Über den Ur-Qurʾān. Ansätze zur Rekonstruktion vorislamischer christlicher Strophenlieder im Qurʾān,* Erlangen 1974; Ch. Luxenberg, *Die syro-aramäische Lesart des Koran. Ein Beitrag zur Entschlüsselung der Koransprache,* Berlin 2000 [Review by C. Gilliot, Langue et Coran. Une lecture syro-araméenne du Coran, in *Arabica* 50 (2003), 381-93]; D.A. Madigan, *The Qurân's self-image. Writing and authority in Islam's scripture,* Princeton 2001; id., Reflections on some current directions in qurʾānic studies, in *MW* 85 (1995), 345-62; G. Mandel, *Corano senza segreti,* Milan 1991; S. Parvez Manzoor, Method against truth. Orientalism and qurʾānic studies, in *Muslim world book review* 7 (1987), 33-49, repr. in A. Rippin (ed.), *The Qurʾān. Style and contents,* Aldershot 2001, 381-97; D. Marshall, *God, Muhammad and the unbelievers. A qurʾānic study,* Richmond 1999; R.C. Martin, Understanding the Qur'an in text and context, in *History of religions* 21 (1982), 361-84; K. Massey, A new investigation into the "mystery letters" of the Qurʾān, in *Arabica* 43 (1996), 497-501;

D. Masson, *Le Coran et la révélation judéo-chrétienne. Études comparées,* 2 vols., Paris 1958; McAuliffe, *Qurʾānic;* J.E. Merrill, Dr. Bell's critical analysis of the Qurʾan, in *MW* 37 (1947), 134-48, repr. in Paret (ed.), *Koran,* 11-24; H. Michaud, *Jésus selon le Coran,* Neuchâtel 1960; A. Mingana, Syriac influence on the style of the Ḳurʾān, in *Bulletin of the John Rylands Library* 11 (1927), 77-98; Y. Moubarac, *Le Coran et la critique occidentale,* Beirut 1972; W. Muir, *The Corān. Its composition and teaching,* London 1878; F.R. Müller, *Untersuchungen zur Reimprosa im Koran,* Bonn 1969; Nagel, *Einschübe;* id., Vom "Qurʾān" zur "Schrift" — Bell's Hypothese aus religionsgeschichtlicher Sicht, in *Der Islam* 60 (1983), 143-65; K. Nelson, *The art of reciting the Qurʾān,* Austin 1985; A. Neuwirth, Koran, in *GAP,* ii, 96-135; id., *Studien;* id., Vom Rezitationstext über die Liturgie zum Kanon, in Wild, *Text,* 69-111; id., Zum neueren Stand der Koranforschung, in F. Steppat (ed.), *ZDMG Suppl.* 5 (1983), 183-9; S. Noja, *L'Islàm e il suo Corano,* Milan 1988; Nöldeke, Die Tradition über das Leben Muhammeds, in *Der Islam* 5 (1914), 160-70; id., *GQ;* id., Hatte Muḥammad christliche Lehrer? in *ZMDG* 12 (1858), 699-708; T. O'Shaughnessy, *Creation and the teaching of the Qur'an,* Rome 1985; id., Creation from nothing and the teaching of the Qur'an, in *ZDMG* 120 (1970), 274-80; id., *The koranic concept of the word of God,* Rome 1948; rev. ed. *Word of God in the Qur'an,* Rome 1984[2]; id., *Muhammad's thoughts on death. A thematic study of the qur'anic data,* Leiden 1969; R. Paret, Der Koran als Geschichtsquelle (1961), repr. in id. (ed.), *Koran,* 137-58; id., *Grenzen der Koranforschung,* Stuttgart 1950; id. (ed.), *Koran;* id., *Mohammed und der Koran,* Stuttgart 1980[5]; G. Parrinder, *Jesus in the Qur'an,* London 1965, Oxford 1995; Penrice, *Dictionary;* M. Piamenta, *Islam in everyday Arabic speech,* Leiden 1979; D.S. Powers, *Studies in Qurʾān and ḥadīth,* Berkeley 1986; O. Pretzl, Aufgaben und Ziele der Koranforschung (1940), repr. in Paret (ed.), *Koran,* 411 f.; G.-R. Puin, Observations on early Qurʾān manuscripts in Ṣanʿāʾ, in Wild, *Text,* 107-11; C. Rabin, *Ancient west-Arabian,* London 1951; id., The beginnings of classical Arabic, in *SI* 4 (1955), 19-37; M. Radscheit, *Die koranische Herausforderung. Die taḥaddī-Verse im Rahmen der Polemikpassagen des Korans,* Berlin 1996; M.D. Rahbar, *God of justice. A study on the ethical doctrine of the Qurʾān,* Leiden 1960; F. Rahman, *Major themes of the Qurʾān,* Minneapolis 1994[2]; H. Räisänen, *Das koranische Jesusbild. Ein Beitrag zur Theologie des Korans,* Helsinki 1971; id., *The idea of divine hardening. A comparative study of the notion of divine hardening, leading astray and inciting to evil in the Bible and the Qur'an,* Helsinki 1976; J.M.F. van Reeth, L'évangile du prophète, in D. DeSmet, G. de Callatay and J. van Reeth (eds.), al-Kitāb. *La sacralité du texte dans le monde de l'Islam. Actes du Symposium international tenu à Leuven et Louvain-la-Neuve du 29 mai au 1 juin 2002* [Acta orientalia belgica. Subsidia III], Brussels 2004, 155-74; W. Reuschel, *Aspekt und Tempus in der Sprache des Korans,* Leipzig 1969, Frankfurt 1996; A. Rippin, Literary analysis of Qurʾān, *tafsīr,* and *sīra.* The methodologies of John Wansbrough, in R.C. Martin (ed.), *Approaches to Islam in religious studies,* Tucson 1985, 151-63; id., *The Qurʾān and its interpretative tradition,* Aldershot 2001; id. (ed.), *The Qurʾan. Formative interpretation,* Aldershot 1999; id. (ed.), *The Qurʾan. Style and contents,* Aldershot 2001; id., Quranic Studies, Part IV: Some methodological notes, in *Method and theory in the study of religion* 9 (1997), 39-46; id., Reading the Qurʾān with Richard Bell, in *JAOS* 112 (1992), 639-47; R. Roberts, *The social laws of the Qurʾān,* London 1927; N. Robinson, *Christ in Islam and Christianity,* Albany, NY 1991; id., *Discovering the Qurʾan. A contemporary approach to a veiled text,* London 1996; A. Rodwell, *The Korān,* London 1876[2]; U. Rubin, Abū Lahab and sūra CXI, in *BSOAS* 42 (1979), 13-28; id., *The eye of the beholder. The life of Muḥammad as viewed by the early Muslims. A textual analysis* [Studies in late antiquity and early Islam, 5], Princeton, NJ 1995; id., The great pilgrimage of Muḥammad. Some notes on sura IX, in *JSS* 27 (1982), 241-60; id., The īlāf of Quraysh. A study of sūra CVI, in *Arabica* 31 (1984), 165-88; id., Meccan trade and qurʾānic exegesis (Qurʾān 2:198), in *BSOAS* 53 (1990), 421-8; K. Rudolph, Neue Wege der Qoranforschung? in *Theologische Literaturzeitung* 105 (1980), 1-19; W. Rudolph, *Die Abhängigkeit des Korans von Judentum und Christentum,* Stuttgart 1922; T. Sabbagh, *La métaphore dans le Coran,* Paris 1943; I. Schapiro, *Die haggadischen Elemente im erzählenden Teile des Korans,* Leipzig 1907; M. Schöller, *Exegetisches Denken und Prophetenbiographie. Eine quellenkritische Analyse der Sīra-Überlieferung zu Muḥammads Konflikt mit den Juden,* Wiesbaden 1998; O. Schumann, *Der Christus der Muslime. Christolog. Aspekte in d.arab.-islam. Literatur,* Gütersloh 1975; id., Quraninterpretation und Bibelexegese, in *Evangelisches Missionsmagazin* 109 (1965), 20-39; M. Seale, *Muslim theology. A study of origins with reference to the church fathers,* London 1964; id., The mysterious letters in the Qur'an, in H. von Franke (ed.), *Akten des vierundzwanzigsten Internationalen Orientalisten-Kongresses (24th International Congress of Orientalists). München 28. August bis 4. September 1957,* Wiesbaden 1957, 276-9; id., *Quran and Bible,* London 1978; M. Sells, *Approaching the Qurʾān. The early revelations,* Ashland, OR 1999; R.B. Serjeant, Hud and other pre-Islamic prophets of Hadramaut, in *Muséon* 67 (1954), 121-79; id., *Studies in Arabian history and civilization,* London 1981;

S. al-Shamma, *The ethical system underlying the Qur'ān,* Tübingen 1959; id., The source of morality in the Meccan period of the Qur'an, in *Bulletin of the College of Arts (Baghdad)* 7 (1964), 43-54; D. Sidersky, *Les origines des légendes musulmanes dans le Coran et dans les vies des prophètes,* Paris 1933; A. Silvestre de Sacy, Du manuscrit arabe n° 239 de la Bibliothèque Impériale [... etc.], in *Notices et extraits des manuscripts de la Bibliothèque Impériale* 8 (1810), 290-362 (5 articles); id., Mémoire sur l'origine et les anciens monuments de la littérature parmi les Arabes, in *Mémoires tirés des registres de l'Académie royale des inscriptions et belles letters* 50 (1785), 247-441; Ch. Solvet, *Introduction à la lecture du Coran ou Discours préliminaire de la version anglaise du Coran de G. Sale. Traduction nouvelle,* Algiers/Paris 1846; H. Speyer, *Die biblischen Erzählungen im Qoran,* Hildesheim 1961²; A. Spitaler, *Die Verszählung des Koran nach islamischer Überlieferung,* Munich 1935; A. Sprenger, *Das Leben und die Lehre des Moḥammad,* 3 vols., Berlin 1869²; id., Moḥammad's Zusammenkunft mit dem Einsiedler Bahyrâ, in *ZDMG* 12 (1858), 238-49; R. Talmon, *Arabic grammar in its formative age. Kitāb al-ʿAyn and its attribution to Ḫalīl b. Aḥmad,* Leiden 1997; Ch.C. Torrey, *The commercial-theological terms in the Koran,* Leiden 1892; id., *The Jewish foundation of Islam,* New York 1933; C.H.M. Versteegh, *Arabic grammar and qurʾānic exegesis in early Islam,* Leiden 1993; K. Vollers, *Volkssprache und Schriftsprache im alten Arabien,* Straßburg 1906; K. Wagtendonk, *Fasting in the Koran,* Leiden 1968; J. Walker, *Bible characters in the Koran,* Paisley 1931; Wansbrough, *QS* [Review by A. Neuwirth, in *WI* 23-4 (1984), 539-42]; id., *The sectarian milieu,* Oxford 1978; W.M. Watt, The dating of the Qurʾān. A review of Richard Bell's theories, in *JRAS* n.s. (1957), 46-56; id., *Muḥammad's Mecca. History in the Qurʾān,* Edinburgh 1988; Watt-Bell, *Introduction;* G. Weil, *Historisch-kritische Einleitung in den Koran,* Bielefeld 1844, 1878²; A.T. Welch, Introduction. Quranic studies — Problems and prospects, in id. (ed.), Studies in Qurʾān and tafsir, in *JAAR* 47 (1980) [Thematic issue], 619-758 (620-31 for Introduction); id., "Die schauerliche... Öde des heiligen Buches." Westliche Wertungen des koranischen Stils, in A. Giese and J.Ch. Bürgel (eds.), *Gott ist schön und Er liebt die Schönheit (FS A. Schimmel),* Berlin 1994, 429-47; id., (ed.), Studies in Qurʾān and tafsir, in *JAAR* 47 (1980) [Thematic issue], 619-758; S. Wild, *Mensch, Prophet und Gott im Koran,* Münster 2001; id., *Text;* I. Zilio-Grandi, *Il Corano e il male,* Milan 2002; H. Zirker, *Der Koran. Zugänge und Lesarten,* Darmstadt 1999.

Potter

see CLAY; CREATION

Poverty and the Poor

The quality or state of being indigent and, often, in need of material assistance in order to survive; those who are indigent. While modern discussion has concentrated on qurʾānic almsgiving (q.v.) and its voluntary or involuntary character (see bibliography below), the broader themes of poverty and the poor reveal the image of a community of believers bound together in a network of generosity and benefaction (see COMMUNITY AND SOCIETY IN THE QURʾĀN).

Feeding the poor (lit. "hungry"; see FAMINE) is a trait of the "companions of the right hand" (Q 90:13-18; see LEFT HAND AND RIGHT HAND) and of the righteous who "give food, though it be dear to them" (Q 76:8). Prescribed for the pilgrimage sacrifice (Q 22:28; see PILGRIMAGE; SACRIFICE), feeding the poor is also a way to expiate sins (Q 5:89, 95; 58:4; see SIN, MAJOR AND MINOR; REPENTANCE AND PENANCE). Medieval lexicography and modern philology have both connected *zakāt* with "purification" *(z-k-y);* and purification (see RITUAL PURITY; CLEANLINESS AND ABLUTION) similarly figures in the qurʾānic requirement for alms (Q 9:103, here *ṣadaqa*). But not only must goods be purified, they must circulate, vertically and downwards (cf. esp. Q 59:7). At Q 30:39, *ribā* (lit. "usury" [q.v.]) refers to some kind of bad circulation, contrasted with a good kind called *zakāt.* The exegetes identified *ribā* here as a gift given in the hope of receiving a greater gift in return, a practice of Arabia before Islam (Ibrāhīm al-Nakhaʿī in Ṭabarī, *Tafsīr,* ad. loc.; cf. Qurṭubī, *Jāmiʿ,* xiv, 36-9 on the ambiguity here between the vocabularies of sale and gift; see TRADE AND COMMERCE; GIFT-GIVING).

The Qurʾān lists the recipients of various benefactions, including alms (Q 9:60, *ṣadaqāt*); distribution of spoils (Q 8:41; see BOOTY); presents made at the division of an inheritance (q.v.; Q 4:8); and generosity *tout court* (Q 4:36, *iḥsān;* Q 2:215, *khayr*). Most of the recipients named in these lists are, in effect, types of poor, including orphans (q.v.), sojourners (see JOURNEY), prisoners (q.v.), slaves (see SLAVES AND SLAVERY), debtors (see DEBT) and (aspiring) warriors (see FIGHTING; WAR; EXPEDITIONS AND BATTLES). The most frequently recurring categories, however, are kin (*dhū l-qurbā;* see KINSHIP), the poor *(al-miskīn)* and the wayfarer *(ibn al-sabīl)*. This triad constitutes a spectrum of persons who are known and those who are unknown, with the poor *(miskīn)* as the ambiguous case. By contrast, *faqīr/fuqarāʾ* ("poor, destitute") can refer to the neediness of the human condition, contrasted with God's self-sufficiency (Q 47:38), and to humanity's need for God (Q 35:15). Elsewhere, the *fuqarāʾ* are at the center of the community (*al-fuqarāʾ al-muhājirīn,* Q 59:8; see Décobert, *Le mendiant,* on the *fuqarāʾ* as the "inner" and the *masākīn* as the "outer" poor; see POLYSEMY). Finally, they are deemed the meritorious poor who, because they do not reveal their condition, are worthy recipients of charity (Q 2:271, 273).

In pre-Islamic Arabia there was a belief that the owner of surplus property (q.v.) must give all or part of it away (Bravmann, The surplus; id., *Spiritual background;* see PRE-ISLAMIC ARABIA AND THE QURʾĀN). In the Qurʾān, *faḍl,* usually understood as "grace" (q.v.; see also BLESSING), sometimes retains this sense of surplus wealth (q.v.; e.g. Q 9:28; 24:22; 62:9-10). Where it does, we find exhortations to reciprocate the divine *faḍl* through human generosity. This occurs in the one place where an individual — usually understood as Muḥammad himself — is addressed as "poor" (*ʿāʾilan,* Q 93:8).

Radical conclusions have been drawn from the qurʾānic teachings on poverty. It is the ḥadīth (see ḤADĪTH AND THE QURʾĀN) and the legal literature (see LAW AND THE QURʾĀN) which introduce the notion of a core of wealth which one may not give away. Moreover, the qurʾānic *ḥaqq,* "claim, right, duty," seems, when it comes to donations, to inhere in the object given. So the community of believers consists of "Those upon whose wealth there is a recognized right *(ḥaqq maʿlūm)* for the beggar and the deprived" (Q 70:24-5; cf. 51:19). Poverty and the poor appear intermittently in the "biography of the Prophet" literature (*sīra;* see SĪRA AND THE QURʾĀN) and that on the military exploits of the early Muslims (*maghāzī;* see EXPEDITIONS AND BATTLES), especially regarding the earliest community at Mecca (q.v.) and the military expeditions at the end of Muḥammad's life, when individuals provided arms, mounts and supplies to those who lacked the means to join the fight. Emphasis is placed on these themes in some modern discussions of earliest Islam (i.e. Watt, *Muhammad at Mecca* and *Muhammad at Medina,* and Ibrahim, *Merchant capital*). Finally, it should be added that Islam arose at a time when, as Brown *(Poverty and leadership)* has now shown, poverty had a new significance for the urban, Christian Mediterranean and Near East (see CHRISTIANS AND CHRISTIANITY; CITY; RELIGIOUS PLURALISM AND THE QURʾĀN; ASCETICISM; MONASTICISM AND MONKS).

Michael Bonner

Bibliography

Primary: Qurṭubī, *Jāmiʿ;* Ṭabarī, *Tafsīr.*
Secondary: S. Bashear, On the origins and development of the meaning of *zakāt* in early Islam, in *Arabica* 40 (1993), 84-113; M. Bonner, Definitions of poverty and the rise of the Muslim urban poor, in *JRAS* [ser. 3] 6/3 (1996), 335-44; M.M. Bravmann, *The spiritual background of early Islam,* Leiden 1972, 229-53; id., The

surplus of property. An early Arab social concept, in *Der Islam* 38 (1962), 28-50; P. Brown, *Poverty and leadership in the later Roman empire*, Hanover 2002; C. Décobert, *Le mendiant et le combattant. L'institution de l'islam*, Paris 1991; M. Ibrahim, *Merchant capital and Islam*, Austin, TX 1990; J. Schacht, Zakāt, in *EI*[1], iv, 1202-5; W.M. Watt, *Muhammad at Mecca*, Oxford 1953; id., *Muhammad at Medina*, Oxford 1956; T.H. Weir/A. Zysow, Ṣadaḳa, in *EI*[2], viii, 708-16.

Power and Impotence

Ability to act or the possession of controlling influence over others; the lack of either of these capacities. In the Qurʾān, the notion of power revolves around two principal foci: (a) the possession of control, authority and influence over others; (b) the capacity to act, to create, to destroy, to fight, to win and to impose one's will. The lack of these qualities results in impotence. These various connotations of the English word "power" are conveyed in the Qurʾān and qurʾānic commentaries by such Arabic terms as *sulṭān, mulk, qahr, ʿizza, nufūdh, quwwa, ghalaba, istiṭāʿa, ṭāqa, baʾs*, and a few others (cf. Dāmaghānī, *Wujūh*, i, 412-6 for *sulṭān;* ii, 206 for *mulk;* ii, 64-5 for *ʿizza;* ii, 161-2 for *quwwa;* ii, 99 for *ghalaba;* i, 101-2 for *istiṭāʿa* and *ṭāqa;* i, 171 for *baʾs*). For those that fall under rubric (a), i.e. the possession of authority over others, see the article AUTHORITY. The present entry will focus primarily on meanings covered under rubric (b) as listed above.

In the qurʾānic text, the ability to give and take life (q.v.; see also DEATH AND THE DEAD), to exert power and control over nature (see NATURE AS SIGNS; CREATION) and human beings, to vanquish one's enemy (see ENEMIES; VICTORY) and to impose one's will on others is attributed primarily to God. As the ultimate wielder of power, he can delegate this ability to those of his creatures whom he chooses, especially to prophets and kings (see PROPHETS AND PROPHETHOOD; KINGS AND RULERS). The enemies of the qurʾānic prophets are routinely humbled and destroyed by God, who unleashes against them the destructive powers of nature (see PUNISHMENT STORIES). The prophets, on the other hand, are miraculously protected by God's superior power against the rage of their adversaries, be they individuals or entire tribes (see e.g. ABRAHAM; MOSES; HŪD; ṢĀLIḤ, etc.). God can "empower" or "enable" (*ʿazzaza, aʿazza, makkana*) certain nations, rulers and kings as a reward for their righteousness (Q 3:26; 7:10; 12:21; 16:6; 36:13; 46:26, etc.; see REWARD AND PUNISHMENT; CHASTISEMENT AND PUNISHMENT). Thus, God gave Alexander the Great "power in the earth and bestowed upon him a way of access to every thing" (Q 18:84; see ALEXANDER). Alexander then used this power to construct a rampart of iron and brass to protect an oppressed people from the depredations of Gog and Magog (q.v.). Likewise, God granted Solomon (q.v.) power over natural forces and the evil ones (*shayāṭīn;* see DEVIL) in order to elevate him above the other worldly rulers of his age (cf. Q 38:34-40). God's bestowal of power on certain rulers, however, may infuse them with false pride (q.v.) and arrogance (q.v.) and eventually lead them to destruction (see e.g. PHARAOH; KORAH; HĀMĀN). Therefore, the Qurʾān repeatedly emphasizes that whatever power these individuals may have possessed was always derivative, ephemeral and subject to withdrawal without notice, as demonstrated by the story of Moses and Pharaoh (Q 2:50; 7:135-6).

In and of themselves, rulers and kings have no power whatsoever. As in the Jewish and Christian exegetical traditions, impotence is a distinguishing feature of the human race, especially those among its representatives who seek to arrogate the rights that belong to God alone, such as

Pharaoh, Nimrod (q.v.), Goliath (q.v.), and so on. When Nimrod claimed the power to give life by copulating with his concubines (q.v.), and to take it away by executing his subjects (see MURDER), Abraham challenged him to bring the sun (q.v.) from the west and "the unbeliever was confounded" (Q 2:258). Likewise, when Pharaoh, in his inordinate arrogance and vain pride attempted to weaken and denigrate the Children of Israel (q.v.), God empowered them *(numakkin lahum fī l-arḍ)* by giving their leader, Moses, the ability to upset Pharaoh's cruel designs (Q 28:3-6).

God and his messengers will always triumph over their misguided opponents, for "Surely, God is all-strong, all-mighty" (Q 58:21) and there is "nothing in the heavens (see HEAVEN AND SKY) or the earth (q.v.) that he is incapable of doing" (*mā kāna llāhu li-yuʿjizahu min shayʾin,* Q 35:44). In addition to God's singular capacity to punish, test and protect his creatures, he alone has the power to provide them with the right guidance (see ASTRAY; ERROR). Neither humans nor jinn (q.v.), even if they were to join forces, are capable of producing "the like of this Qurʾān" (Q 17:88), which God revealed through his Prophet (see INIMITABILITY; PROVOCATION; LANGUAGE AND STYLE OF THE QURʾĀN). At the same time, God's prophets are impotent, like their fellow human beings, unless God decides to empower them. For example, in Q 19:8 Zechariah (q.v.) bemoans his decrepitude and consequent inability to produce a child (cf. also Q 42:49-50, in which God's absolute sovereignty over earthly existence is expressed in his ability to give male and female children [q.v.] to whom he pleases, while rendering other people barren). The idea of God's absolute power over the destinies of his human servants is brought into sharp relief in Q 30:54: "God [is he who] has created you of weakness, then after weakness has appointed strength, then after strength appointed weakness and gray hairs; he creates what he wills, he is the one who wills and has power" (see the commentary of al-Shawkānī, *Tafsīr,* iv, 230-2; see BIOLOGY AS THE CREATION AND STAGES OF LIFE). In Q 3:26-7 we find an illuminating summary of the various manifestations of divine omnipotence: "You give the power to whom you will, and withdraw the power from whom you will; you exalt whom you will and abase whom you will (see OPPRESSED ON EARTH, THE); verily you have power over all things. You cause the night to interpenetrate the day, and the day to interpenetrate the night (see DAY AND NIGHT); you bring forth the living from the dead and the dead from the living; you provide for whom you will without reckoning (see GRACE; BLESSING)." Here, as in many other passages of the Qurʾān (e.g. Q 67:1-3, 15-6, 21, 23; 86:5-12, etc.), God's ability to bestow life and take it away at will is often mentioned alongside his capacity to create natural objects and phenomena for the benefit of humankind. Thus, he makes the crops grow and winds (see AIR AND WIND) blow; he has studded the firmament with stars (see PLANETS AND STARS) to guide travelers (see JOURNEY); he has subdued the sea and made it a source of sustenance (q.v.) and finery for men and women (see METALS AND MINERALS); he has created domestic animals which serve human beings as nourishment (see FOOD AND DRINK; HIDES AND FLEECE) and means of transportation, etc. God's capacity as creator of the universe, giver of life, sustainer of human beings, and eventually their judge (see LAST JUDGMENT; JUSTICE AND INJUSTICE) is used throughout the Qurʾān as an argument against the pagan opponents of the Prophet (see POLYTHEISM AND ATHEISM; OPPOSITION TO MUḤAMMAD): "Have they not considered that God, who created the heavens and earth without being exhausted by the creation of them, has [the] power to bring the dead to life? Yea, verily over everything he has power" (Q 46:33).

As one of God's critical attributes (see GOD AND HIS ATTRIBUTES), which is reflected in such divine epithets as "the powerful" (*al-qawī*, cf. Gimaret, *Noms divins*, 237-8), "the overpowering" (*al-qahhār*, cf. Gimaret, *Noms divins*, 241-2), "the dominator" (*al-ghālib*, cf. Gimaret, *Noms divins*, 242-3), "the [all-] mighty" (*al-qādir*, cf. Gimaret, *Noms divins*, 235-7), "the great" (*al-ʿazīz*, cf. Gimaret, *Noms divins*, 243-6), etc., power has loomed large in Muslim exegetical tradition since its inception (see EXEGESIS OF THE QURʾĀN: CLASSICAL AND MEDIEVAL). References to God's exclusive ability to grant power *(al-mulk)* to whomever he wishes (Q 3:26) were construed by some Muslim exegetes as a prediction of the later Muslim conquest of the Byzantine and Sasanian empires (see e.g. Ṭabarī, *Tafsīr*, iii, 222; Ṭabarsī, *Majmaʿ*, iii, 50-1; Qurṭubī, *Jāmiʿ*, iii, 52; cf. Ibn Kathīr, *Tafsīr*, iii, 42; see POLITICS AND THE QURʾĀN; BYZANTINES). In elaborating on this verse, some modern Muslim commentators — for instance, Muḥammad al-Shaʿrāwī (d. 1998), former minister of Pious Endowments of the Republic of Egypt — pointed out that unjust and despotic rulers (see OPPRESSION) were deliberately appointed by God to punish a given Muslim community for abandoning the principles of "true Islam," as well as the inability of its scholars (see SCHOLAR; KNOWLEDGE AND LEARNING) to provide proper guidance to their followers (Shaʿrāwī, *Tafsīr*, xvii, 1404, 1418). According to al-Shaʿrāwī, God's absolute and unrestricted power to provide for whomsoever he wills "without reckoning" (Q 3:27), explains why certain Arab nations were blessed with oil riches, even though they may not have deserved them due to their indolence (ibid., 1418). Such interpretations are readily embraced by certain Islamic parties and movements, which advocate the removal of some contemporary Middle Eastern regimes as morally "corrupt" and, therefore, religiously "illegitimate."

In the classical exegetical tradition, Q 3:26 was sometimes used as an occasion to debunk the Christian doctrine of the divinity of Jesus (q.v.). Thus, according to al-Ṭabarī (d. 310/923), while God indeed empowered Jesus to perform certain miraculous deeds, like raising people from the dead (see MIRACLES), healing various diseases, breathing life into clay birds and predicting future events, he nevertheless withheld from him such a uniquely divine prerogative as the absolute and unrestricted power over the created world, including both its sustenance and the natural phenomena therein, e.g. the ability to change night into day and vice versa (Ṭabarī, *Tafsīr*, iii, 227). In a similar vein, al-Suyūṭī (d. 911/1505; *Durr*, vi, 531) used Q 31:34 to vindicate God's exclusive ability to know things that are concealed from all his creatures (see HIDDEN AND THE HIDDEN), including the prophets, namely, the day and time of the resurrection (q.v.) and final judgment; the ability to foresee the falling of rain, to divine the contents of the womb and to predict the destiny of the human fetus as well as its final resting place (see FORETELLING; DIVINATION; PORTENTS). See also FREEDOM AND PREDESTINATION; FATE.

Alexander D. Knysh

Bibliography

Primary: Dāmaghānī, *Wujūh*, ed. al-Zafītī; Ibn Kathīr, *Tafsīr*, ed. Muṣṭafā Sayyid Muḥammad et al., 15 vols., Cairo 2000; Qurṭubī, *Jāmiʿ*, Beirut

1965-7; M. al-Shaʿrāwī, *Tafsīr al-Shaʿrāwī,* 40 vols., Cairo 1991-3; Shawkānī, *Tafsīr,* Beirut 1973; Suyūṭī, *Durr,* 8 vols., Beirut 1982; Ṭabarī, *Tafsīr,* ed. ʿAlī; Ṭabarsī, *Majmaʿ,* Beirut 1961.
Secondary: M. Barnes, *The power of God,* Washington, DC 2001 (for some illuminating parallels with the Jewish and Christian notions of divine/human power); G.J. Botterweck and H. Ringgren (eds.), *Theological dictionary of the Old Testament,* trans. J.T. Willis, 11 vols., Grand Rapids, MI 1974-2001 (s.v. "*ʿzz*" and "*mlk*"); T.J. de Boer/R. Arnaldez, Ḳuwwa, in *EI²,* v, 576; T. Dozeman, *God at war,* Oxford 1996; D. Gimaret, *Les noms divins en Islam,* Paris 1988, 236-51 ("Tout-Puissant"); P. Gräbe, *The power of God in Paul's letters,* Tübingen 2000; R. Kearsley, *Tertullian's theology of divine power,* Carlisle 1998; A. Miller, Power, in *ER,* xi, 467-76.

Praise

To express approbation of, or to glorify (especially God); also, to magnify, as in song. A number of qurʾānic lexemes convey this concept, but with varying nuances; derivatives of the following triliteral roots are the most prominent qurʾānic terms connoting "praise": *ḥ-m-d, sh-k-r, s-b-ḥ, ʾ-w-b* — although, generally, *sh-k-r* denotes thanking or thankfulness, and *s-b-ḥ,* glorification or exaltation, rather than "praise" proper. Occasionally, however, the second verbal form of *s-b-ḥ* is used in conjunction with the verbal noun, *ḥamd,* a combination that may be rendered in English as "to proclaim praise" — i.e. Q 2:30; 40:7. With the exception of *sh-k-r,* God is never the active agent: i.e. God is the object of praise, rather than the one praising. For example, God is the "all-thankful," *shakūr* (Q 35:30 or also *shākir,* Q 2:158) — but the "all-laudable," *ḥamīd* (Q 11:73; but cf. Gimaret, *Noms,* 351-3 and 222-3 for a range of the classical exegetes' understandings of these divine names; see GOD AND HIS ATTRIBUTES). As *sh-k-r* and *s-b-ḥ* have been dealt with elsewhere (see GRATITUDE AND INGRATITUDE and GLORIFICATION OF GOD, respectively), the following discussion shall focus on derivatives of *ḥ-m-d* and the hapax legomenon, *awwiba* (Q 34:10; for the name of the qurʾānic Prophet, which is derived from *ḥ-m-d,* see NAMES OF THE PROPHET).

In the Qurʾān, praise is closely related to other proper human responses to God, such as gratitude and glorification. God is the only one worthy of praise *(ḥamd),* being the lord (q.v.) of the worlds/all existence (*rabb al-ʿālamīn,* Q 39:75) and of the heavens (see HEAVEN AND SKY) and the earth (q.v.; Q 45:36; cf. 3:188, wherein people who want to be praised for things they have not done are promised a painful doom; see REWARD AND PUNISHMENT; HELL AND HELLFIRE; cf. Bravmann, *Spiritual background,* 116-9, for a discussion of the attribution of *ḥamd* to human heroes in early Arabic literature; see PRE-ISLAMIC ARABIA AND THE QURʾĀN). He is the originator *(fāṭir)* of the heavens and earth who uses angels as his messengers (Q 35:1; see MESSENGER; ANGEL; CREATION; COSMOLOGY), and who has not taken a son (Q 17:111; see POLYTHEISM AND ATHEISM). He has revealed the book (q.v.; i.e. the Qurʾān to Muḥammad; Q 18:1; see REVELATION AND INSPIRATION), kept his promise and bequeathed the earth to humankind (Q 39:74; see COVENANT). He saved Noah's (q.v.) people from those who would oppress them (Q 23:28; see OPPRESSION), he preferred David (q.v.) and Solomon (q.v.) over many of his believing servants (Q 27:15), and he takes grief away from those in paradise (q.v.; Q 35:34; see also JOY AND MISERY). God should be praised evening (q.v.) and day (Q 40:55; 30:17; see DAY, TIMES OF; NOON; DAWN), and "when you arise" (Q 52:48). He is praised both in the heavens and on the earth (Q 30:18) and in the hereafter (Q 34:1; see ESCHATOLOGY).

Q 9:112 includes "those who praise [God]" *(al-ḥāmidūn)* in a list of descriptors put in apposition to the believers to whom the good news (q.v.) is to be announced. Also in this list are "the repentant" (*al-tāʾibūn;* see REPENTANCE AND PENANCE), "the worshippers" (see WORSHIP), "those who fast" (see FASTING), "those who bow," "those who prostrate" (see BOWING AND PROSTRATION), "those who command the good and forbid the evil" (see GOOD AND EVIL; VIRTUES AND VICES, COMMANDING AND FORBIDDING) and "those who keep the limits of God" (see BOUNDARIES AND PRECEPTS). And Q 15:98 indicates that to be among those who proclaim God's praise is to be among those who prostrate themselves. Although the manner in which humans should praise God is not specified, the seeming specification of times of praise (morning and evening — although this mention of day and night may also be a figure of speech indicating that there is no time that God should *not* be praised; see PAIRS AND PAIRING) and the indication that bowing or prostration was associated with the proclamation of God's praise evoke Jewish and Christian liturgical practices (cf. i.e. Jammo, *Structure,* 58 f., for an overview of the east Syrian liturgy and its relations to Jewish practices; cf. esp. the "La<u>h</u>u Māra," instances of bowing and prostration, and the attribution of singing God's praises to cherubim and servants of God, but the proclamation of his holiness to seraphim; also Codrington, Syrian liturgy, 135-48 indicates that the "praise" of God, esp. Psalm 116, is included in the morning, evening and night recitations of the divine office). Certain qurʾānic passages in which praise of God is evoked are also reminiscent of Jewish and Christian scriptural and/or liturgical formulae: "He is God. There is no god but he. His is the praise in the beginning and the end. And his is the judgment; to him you will return" (Q 28:70); "All in heaven and earth exalt God; his is the kingdom and his is the praise; and he has power over everything" (Q 64:1; see i.e. the aforementioned *Ps* 116: "Praise God all you nations; glorify him, all you peoples…"; cf. *Gal* 1:5; and the final doxology of the Lord's prayer, as contained in the fourth century C.E. *Apostolic Constitutions* "For yours are the kingdom, the power and the glory forever"; cf. *Catechism of the Catholic church,* pt. 4, sect. 2, no. 2760; see also FORM AND STRUCTURE OF THE QURʾĀN; RHETORIC AND THE QURʾĀN; PRAYER; PSALMS).

If the object of praise is often God (or, alternatively, the lord, e.g. Q 40:55), those who should be engaged in the act of praise are God's servants (q.v.) — humankind. Like the glorification of God, however, the praise of the lord is not restricted to humans: in fact, there is nothing that does not proclaim his praise (*wa-in min shayʾin illā yusabbiḥu bi-ḥamdihi,* Q 17:44) — even thunder (Q 13:13) and the angels (i.e. Q 39:75) do so. In Q 34:10, the mountains and the birds are ordered to praise God *(awwibī)* along with David. Although the exegetical consensus on the signification of *awwiba* is "glorification" (*sabaḥa,* in the sense of "return" — i.e. repeat, respond; cf. Muqātil, *Tafsīr,* iii, 526; Ṭabarī, *Tafsīr,* xx, 356-9; Rāzī, *Tafsīr,* xxv, 246), al-Ṭabarī (d. 310/923) reports a variant reading that is given the understanding of "behave" instead of "praise/repeat" (*Tafsīr,* xx, 357). He also includes a tradition that attributes the word to Abyssinian origins (ibid.; see FOREIGN VOCABULARY). Al-Rāzī (d. 606/1210) reports that a "special movement" may be involved in this action (*Tafsīr,* xxv, 246).

Post-qurʾānic developments

"To God belongs the praise" (*al-ḥamdu lillāhi,* i.e. Q 1:2) is a frequent qurʾānic refrain. Like the *basmala* (q.v.) and the qur'ānic glorification formula (*subḥān Allāh*, Q 21:22), this *ḥamdala* (see LAUDATION) often appears in Muslim prayer formulas (q.v.), and has entered the common language of Arabic speakers (and non-Arab Muslims; see SLOGANS FROM THE QUR'ĀN; EVERYDAY LIFE, THE QUR'ĀN IN). Finally, indicative of its centrality to Muslim spirituality, "praise" of God is an important part of the ritual formulations of the Ṣūfī *dhikr* ("remembrance [of God]"; see MEMORY; ṢŪFISM AND THE QUR'ĀN; REMEMBRANCE).

Clare E. Wilde

Bibliography

Primary: Muqātil, *Tafsīr;* Rāzī, *Tafsīr;* Ṭabarī, *Tafsīr.*

Secondary: A. Baumstark, Jüdischer und christlicher Gebetstypus im Koran, in *Der Islam* 16-18 (1927-9), 229-48; M.M. Bravmann, *The spiritual background of early Islam,* Leiden 1972; *Catechism of the Catholic church,* on http://www.vatican.va/archive/ccc_css/archive/catechism/p4s2.htm (for the concluding doxology to the Lord's prayer); H.W. Codrington, The Syrian liturgy. VI. The divine office, in *The eastern churches quarterly* 1 (1936), 135-48 (esp. 140-3 for the specific Psalms and types of prayer recited at each time); G. Elmore, Hamd al-hamd. The paradox of praise in Ibn al-ʿArabi's doctrine of oneness, in S. Hirtenstein (ed.), *Praise. Foundations of the spiritual life according to Ibn ʿArabi,* Oxford 1997, 59-93; id., A selection of texts on the theme of praise from some gnomic works by Ibn al-ʿArabi, in *Journal of the Muhyiddin Ibn ʿArabi Society* 23 (1998), 58-85; D. Gimaret, *Les noms divins en Islam,* Paris 1988; D. Gril, 'There is no word in the world that does not indicate his praise,' in S. Hirtenstein (ed.), *Praise. Foundations of the spiritual life according to Ibn ʿArabi,* Oxford 1997, 31-43; S.Y.H. Jammo, *La structure de la messe chaldienne* [Orientalia christiana analecta 207], Rome 1979; Jeffery, *For. vocab.;* C.A. Keller, Praise as a means to mystical advancement, according to Ibn ʿArabi and other religious traditions, in S. Hirtenstein (ed.), *Praise. Foundations of the spiritual life according to Ibn ʿArabi,* Oxford 1997, 19-29; D.B. MacDonald, Ḥamdala, in *EI*², iii, 122-3; D. Madigan, *The Qurʾān's self-image. Writing and authority in Islam's scripture,* Princeton 2001, esp. 193-203.

Prayer

Islam presents three primary terms for prayer, *ṣalāt* (ritual prayer), *duʿāʾ* (personal supplication) and *dhikr* (mystical recollection; see REMEMBRANCE; MEMORY; ṢŪFISM AND THE QUR'ĀN), all of which are rooted in the qur'ānic language. These qur'ānic terms were eventually chosen to designate principal Muslim prayer practices which derive many of their characteristic features from the encounter of Islam with the cultural environment of the Middle East, particularly in the early centuries of its development, as well as that of territories Islam eventually conquered. This article will concentrate upon the concepts and practices of prayer that can be traced in the Qur'ān as read against the background of Muḥammad's biography, while disregarding the analysis of post-qur'ānic developments in the very rich and variegated tradition of prayer in Islam (see PRAYER FORMULAS; RITUAL AND THE QUR'ĀN; EVERYDAY LIFE, THE QUR'ĀN IN). Muḥammad's proclamation of the Islamic scripture occurred in an environment that was fully familiar with ways of worship rooted in the Arab tribal cult and in some measure aware of normative and sectarian forms of prayer practiced in the organized religions of the Middle East (see SOUTH ARABIA, RELIGION IN PRE-ISLAMIC; PRE-ISLAMIC ARABIA AND THE QUR'ĀN). In addition to a variety of gnostic, esoteric, magic (q.v.) and mystical rituals, these included organized rites of prayer, whether performed as individual duties or communal liturgies, that were perceptible in the general religious environment in which Muḥammad's own awareness of worship (q.v.) and prayer emerged (see RELIGION; RELIGIOUS PLURALISM AND THE QUR'ĀN). These obligatory prayer rites of organized religions included (1) the three daily prayers, recited at dawn (q.v.), in the afternoon (q.v.) and in the evening (q.v.) by the followers of rabbinic Judaism privately or in assemblies (see JEWS AND JUDAISM); (2) the prayer rhythm of eastern Christian monasticism whose monks observed seven offices each day in their assemblies or churches (see MONASTICISM AND MONKS; CHURCH; SYRIA; ABYSSINIA); (3) the five prayers offered individually at fixed times of the day by the followers of Mazdaean Zoroastrianism (see MAGIANS); and (4) the four times of prayer and prostration (see BOWING AND PROSTRATION) prescribed for the daily ritual of adoration by the ordinary followers of Manicheanism. Marked by fixed times (see DAY, TIMES OF), these forms of prayer had many other characteristic manifestations, such as sacred space for worship (see PROFANE AND SACRED; FORBIDDEN; HOUSE, DOMESTIC AND DIVINE), cosmic orientation of the actual performance of prayer (see QIBLA), purification in preparation for prayer (see CLEANLINESS AND ABLUTION; RITUAL PURITY), solemn recitation of passages from sacred texts or chanting of hymns, invocative or meditative use of prayer formulas, bodily postures of standing and bowing in adoration, and conformity of the repetitive performance of prayer to the natural rhythm described by night and day (see DAY AND NIGHT).

The personal prayer of Muḥammad

Prayer is one of the most central features of the Qurʾān. It forms the core of Muḥammad's experience of God and is the foundation of his qurʾānic proclamation. Prayer was practiced daily by the nascent Muslim community and included recitation and characteristic gestures of standing and bowing in adoration. Eventually developed as a consistent communal ritual, it has come to constitute an essential part of everyday Muslim life throughout the ages. Both as a foundation of the qurʾānic message and an ongoing practice, it encapsulates the personal prayer of Muḥammad at its core. Prior to his prophetic call, the orphan and merchant Muḥammad (see ORPHANS; CARAVAN) shared the religious ideas of his clan (see KINSHIP; TRIBES AND CLANS): his uncle, Abū Lahab ʿAbd al-ʿUzzā, was a staunch adherent of the Arab tribal religion (cf. Q 111:1) and his guardian and protector, Abū Ṭālib, never adopted Islam. Muḥammad himself took part in the pagan rites at the Kaʿba (q.v.; cf. Q 108:2) and sacrificed a white sheep at the shrine of the goddess al-ʿUzzā (Q 53:19-20; cf. Macdonald and Nehmé, al-ʿUzzā, 968; see POLYTHEISM AND ATHEISM). He believed in the world of demons (*jinn*, Q 72:1; 55:15) whom the Arabs (q.v.) of Mecca (q.v.) believed to be God's comrades and next of kin (6:100; 37:158), to whom they offered sacrifices (cf. Q 6:128) and from whom they sought protection (q.v.; Q 72:6; see also JINN; SACRIFICE).

As can be judged from the earliest layers of the qurʾānic proclamation, Muḥammad's personal prayer was based on ecstatic inspiration and visions (q.v.) by night (Q 17:1; cf. 53:1-8; 81:19-25). He had to defend himself against the accusation of being one of the soothsayers (q.v.; sing. *kāhin*) possessed by the alter ego of a demon (Q 52:29; 68:2; 69:42; 7:184; see INSANITY). The utterances of his prayer were cast in rhymed prose (q.v.), marked by abrupt phrases capturing cryptic meanings. He sought refuge from demonical whisperings (Q 114:1-6) and disclaimed being an angel (q.v.), possessing the treasures of God or knowing the unseen (Q 6:50; 11:31; see SECRETS; HIDDEN AND THE HIDDEN; KNOWLEDGE AND LEARNING). He felt inspired by a holy spirit (q.v.; Q 16:102; 26:192-4) and experienced God as speaking to him directly, by revelation (see REVELATION AND INSPIRATION) and from behind a veil (q.v.), or indirectly through the intermediary of an angel (Q 42:51), identified as Gabriel (q.v.; Q 2:97-8; cf. 66:4). He claimed to have received revelation as did the earth (q.v.; Q 99:5) and the bee (Q 16:68; see ANIMAL LIFE) or the prophets of old (Q 21:7; see PROPHETS AND PROPHETHOOD), such as Noah (q.v.; Q 23:27), Moses (q.v.; Q 20:13) and Joseph (q.v.; Q 12:15). He introduced qurʾānic passages by abstruse oaths (q.v.), following the old Arab custom of invoking idols (see IDOLS AND IMAGES) or natural forces as well as emulating the oracular style *(sajʿ)* of the pre-Islamic soothsayer in the wording of the qurʾānic proclamation (see also POETRY AND POETS).

Muḥammad swore by the name of God, e.g. "By God!" (*tallāhi*, Q 16:63), and, "But no! By your lord!" (*fa-lā wa-rabbika*, Q 4:65; see LORD), and solemnly uttered oaths by the setting of the stars, "But no! I swear *(fa-lā uqsimu)* by the setting of the stars" (Q 56:75; see PLANETS AND STARS). He swore by the powers of nature (see NATURE AS SIGNS), e.g. the heaven and its constellations (*wa-l-samāʾi dhāti l-burūj*, Q 85:1; see HEAVEN AND SKY), the star (*wa-l-najm*, Q 53:1), the sun (q.v.; *wa-l-shams*, Q 91:1) and the moon (q.v.; *wa-l-qamar*, Q 74:32), and invoked particular times of day by oaths, e.g. the daybreak (*wa-l-fajr*, Q 89:1), the night (*wa-l-layl*, Q 92:1), the forenoon (*wa-l-ḍuḥā*, Q 93:1) and the twilight (*wa-l-shafaq*, Q 84:16).

Raised unaware of revealed religion (cf. Q 42:52), he never read the Bible (Q 29:48; see SCRIPTURE AND THE QURʾĀN; GOSPEL; TORAH; PSALMS; BOOK; ILLITERACY; UMMĪ) but came into contact with Jews and Christians (Q 10:94). Through his wife Khadīja (q.v.), he was related to Waraqa b. Nawfal, a man known as a *ḥanīf* (q.v.) and one seeking a more satisfying religion than the old Arab polytheism (cf. Rubin, Ḥanīf, 402-3). Until the breakthrough to his prophetic call, identified by Muslim tradition with the divine command to "recite!" (*iqraʾ*, Q 96:1), received in an experience of retreat *(taḥannuth)* on Mount Ḥirāʾ outside Mecca, Muḥammad's prayer was a personal one (Ibn Hishām, *Sīra*, 151-2; cf. Kister, Al-taḥannuth, 223; Calder, Ḥinth, 213). After a short period of hesitation, however, he began to proclaim in Mecca the religious insights he had forged in the furnace of his personal prayer. Soon a small group of followers, most of them young and of little social standing, accepted his message and formed a nascent community which began to engage in communal prayer. This communal prayer eventually adopted characteristic elements that became constitutive for a prayer ritual, known as *al-ṣalāt*. The transition from Muḥammad's personal prayer practice and the communal prayer of his nascent community to a central and consistent ritual developed in two major stages, separated by the decisive change of the direction of prayer *(qibla)* in Medina (q.v.) in the year 2/624.

Ṣalāt, the common Arabic term for ritual prayer, does not occur in pre-qurʾānic poetry and clearly shows Aramaic influence in its particular qurʾānic orthography (cf. Spitaler, Schreibung, 217; see ARABIC SCRIPT; ORTHOGRAPHY OF THE QURʾĀN) and etymological derivation from the Syriac, *"ṣelotā,"* which in its basic meaning denotes the act of bowing (Nöldeke, *GQ*, i, 255; Jeffery, *For. vocab.*, 198-9; see FOREIGN VOCABULARY). In the Qurʾān, the noun *"ṣalāt"* occurs in the singular 78 times (65 times with the definite article, twice in a genitive construction, cf. Q 24:58, and 11 times with a pronoun affixed), while it occurs only 5 times in the plural. In addition, there are 16 occurrences of various forms of the verb *ṣallā* (second verbal form, with the meaning "to perform the *ṣalāt*"), which is derived from the noun, *ṣalāt*. A small number of derivatives of the verb *ṣallā* imply forms of prayer observed by pre-Islamic Arabs and hence suggest an Arab usage of both the verb (Q 108:2; 107:4) and the noun (Q 8:35; 9:99) for manifestations of prayers antedating Muḥammad's proclamation of the Qurʾān. These usages and the set way in which the definite noun, *al-ṣalāt*, is employed in the Qurʾān, indicate that the Arabic form of the word was already understood in Muḥammad's environment, and did not originate in the Qurʾān (see ARABIC LANGUAGE; LANGUAGE AND STYLE OF THE QURʾĀN).

In some instances the verb is constructed together with *ʿalā* (as in the extra-qurʾānic eulogy, *taṣliya*, commonly used after the Prophet's name) with reference to "blessing" (q.v.) bestowed by God and his angels (Q 33:43, 56). In this sense, "blessing" is understood as God's very own prayer upon his creatures rather than the calling down of God's blessing (cf. Goitein, Prayer, 78; pace Padwick, *Muslim devotions*, 155-7). By an analogous turn of phrase, Muḥammad is told in the Qurʾān, to bless those who have confessed their sins, "pray upon them *(ṣalli ʿalayhim)*, your prayers/blessings *(ṣalātaka)* are a comfort for them" (Q 9:103; cf. 2:157). He is, however, ordered, "do not pray over one of them *(lā tuṣalli ʿalā aḥadin minhum)* when he dies" (Q 9:84), with reference to the denial of the funeral prayer *(ṣalāt al-janāza)* for a deceased hypocrite (*munāfiq*, cf. Adang, Hypocrites, 468-72; see DEATH AND THE DEAD; BURIAL; HYPOCRITES AND HYPOCRISY). Finally, prayer received as a divine blessing may be meant in the case of the ancient Arab prophet Shuʿayb (q.v.; Q 11:87; cf. Paret, *Kommentar*, 241).

The Qurʾān makes a unique mention of *muṣallā*, "place of prayer" with reference to "Abraham's station," i.e. the central sanctuary of Mecca (Q 2:125; cf. Paret, *Kommentar*, 29; see PLACE OF ABRAHAM). This term *muṣallā* is applied in the Prophet's biography, however, to the large and open place of prayer in Medina (cf. Wensinck, Muṣallā, 659) where congregational prayers were performed on the two major Muslim festivals, the breaking of the fast (*ʿīd al-fiṭr;* see FASTING; RAMAḌĀN) and the feast of the sacrifice *(ʿīd al-aḍḥā)*. From the early centuries until today, the two public feast-day prayers *(ṣalāt al-ʿīdayn)* have been performed in the Muslim world in the forenoon, beginning after sunrise and ending before the sun reaches the zenith (see FESTIVALS AND COMMEMORATIVE DAYS). This practice, not cited in the Qurʾān, may nevertheless retain a trace of some of the oldest forms of the *ṣalāt* observed by Muḥammad and his early community (cf. Becker, Zur Geschichte, 374-5). The *muṣallā* is also cited in tradition, but not in the Qurʾān, as the place where, during a drought, Muḥammad would offer prayers for rain with his hands raised high to the sky *(ṣalāt al-istisqāʾ)*, echoing Noah's promise of plentiful rain (Q 71:10-11) and Moses' plea for water (q.v.; Q 2:60). Further, there is no qurʾānic reference to the particular prayer, also observed in the forenoon, in the case of an eclipse *(kusūf/khusūf)* of the sun or moon, termed *ṣalāt al-kusūf* ("prayer of the eclipse"), though it too appears to reflect some of the older forms of the *ṣalāt*.

Rather than in the Qurʾān itself, the earliest forms of Muḥammad's practice of the *ṣalāt* may be detected in accounts preserved in the traditional, historical and exegetical literature (cf. Rubin, Morning, 41; see ḤADĪTH AND THE QURʾĀN; EXEGESIS OF THE QURʾĀN: CLASSICAL AND MEDIEVAL; SĪRA AND THE QURʾĀN). If some of these fragmentary accounts can be trusted, Muḥammad used to go to the Kaʿba in the morning and, in daylight, performed the prayer of forenoon *(ṣalāt al-ḍuḥā)* some time after sunrise (cf. Q 91:1: "By the sun and its morning brightness," *wa-l-shamsi wa-ḍuḥāhā*). The Meccans did not object to this practice because they themselves were used to praying near the Kaʿba after sunrise. In addition, it was the custom of the Bedouins (see BEDOUIN), coming to town early in the morning to sell their wares, to extol God *(takbīr)* and bow in prayer *(sujūd)* at the Kaʿba after completing their business in the markets (q.v.). As the sun sank toward the horizon, however, Muḥammad and his companions had to scatter secretly in the ravines on the outskirts of Mecca to pray the afternoon prayer *(ṣalāt al-ʿaṣr)* before sunset (cf. Q 103:1 for the use of *ʿaṣr* in an oath). They were prevented from praying at the Kaʿba possibly because in the time from late afternoon until before sunset the Meccans would perform their rites of circumambulation *(ṭawāf)* at the sanctuary (cf. Muranyi, Zwischen, 101). Another explanation suggests that Muḥammad's performance of the *ʿaṣr* prayer was perceived by the Meccans as an alien practice modeled on the Jewish *minḥāh* (Goldziher, Bedeutung, 294; Rubin, Morning, 54).

The evolution of a communal prayer

Rather than chart the genesis of the *ṣalāt* in relation to the possible chronological sequence of Muḥammad's qurʾānic proclamation — a sketch of which was offered in the article on CHRONOLOGY AND THE QURʾĀN (Böwering, Chronology, 327-8) — the present article will assemble the characteristic elements of the two stages of development, i.e. those before and after the change of the *qibla*. In the first stage, which covers Muḥammad's prophetic career at Mecca as well as the earliest phase of his career in Medina until shortly after the battle of Badr (q.v.), the communal prayer practice of the nascent Muslim community evolves out of Muḥammad's personal prayer. At this stage the communal prayer practice is not yet organized as a full-fledged ritual, but nevertheless includes a number of characteristic liturgical features to which reference is made in scattered statements of the Qurʾān. The *ṣalāt* was performed in the standing position *(qiyām,* e.g. Q 2:238) and included acts of bowing *(rukūʿ,* e.g. Q 2:43) and prostration *(sujūd,* e.g. Q 4:102).

The physical postures of bowing and prostration are frequently mentioned in the Qurʾān (with *sujūd* and its cognates found much more frequently than those of *rukūʿ*). On occasion, they are used in tandem (Q 2:125; 3:43; 9:112; 22:26, 77; 48:29) as well as interchangeably (e.g. *rākiʿan,* Q 38:24, with the act of David's [q.v.] prostration in repentance identified as bowing; and *sujjadan,* Q 2:58 and 7:161, with bowing while entering a gate called a prostration). The faithful followers of Muḥammad are depicted in the Qurʾān as bearing a mark on their faces "from the effect of prostration" *(min athari l-sujūd,* Q 48:29). The precise ritual distinction between two gestures, namely (1) bowing as inclining the head and upper body with the palms of the hands placed at the level of the knees and (2) prostration as falling down on one's knees with the forehead touching the ground, found its specific technical definition only in post-qurʾānic times (cf. Tottoli, Traditions, 371-93). *Sujūd* was known among the peoples of the Middle East in pre-Islamic times as a gesture of respect at royal courts and as an act of adoration in Christian worship. Pre-Islamic poetry cites a few examples of prostration *(sujūd)* before a tribal chief in recognition of his superiority and as an expression of one's submission (cf. Tottoli, Muslim attitudes, 5-34).

The act of prostration hurt the pride (q.v.) of the Arabs (Q 25:60; 7:206; cf. 16:49; 32:15; 68:42-3) because it appeared to them as a humiliating gesture and an alien practice (cf. Kister, Some reports, 3-6).

Muḥammad, however, was uncompromising in commanding his early community to fall down before God in prayer, "O you who believe, bow down and prostrate yourselves *(arkaʿū wa-sjudū)* and worship your lord" (Q 22:77). In the Qurʾān, prostration was depicted as an act of adoration to be given only to God and not to any work of his creation (q.v.), such as the sun or the moon (Q 41:37). On account of this, the angels prostrating before Adam (cf. Schoeck, Adam, 22-6) upon the divine command and Iblīs' refusal to do so (Q 2:34; 7:11-2; 20:116; 17:61; 18:50; 38:71-6; 15:26-33; see ARROGANCE; DEVIL; ADAM AND EVE) created an exegetical dilemma for the commentators on the Qurʾān. It is difficult to establish the angelic adoration of God as a qurʾānic prototype for the human prostration in the *ṣalāt* because the Qurʾān does not make this linkage explicitly. The angels, however, are depicted in the Qurʾān as a heavenly host (Q 37:8; 38:69), "brought near to God" (*muqarrabūn,* Q 83:21, 28; 4:172; 56:11), who stand rank on rank around the divine throne (Q 39:75; 69:17; 89:22; see THRONE OF GOD; RANKS AND ORDERS), which some of them also carry (Q 69:17). They glorify and sanctify God (e.g. Q 2:32) and do not grow weary "glorifying *(yusabbiḥūna)* God night and day and never failing" (Q 21:20; cf. 42:5). It may be possible, however, to perceive in the postures of standing and bowing the physical analogue for the actual words of glorifying God, whether in case of the angelic adoration of God or in the human observance of extolling God's praise *(tasbīḥ, tamḥīd, takbīr).*

In fact, this exclamatory praise (*subḥāna,* mentioned 41 times in the Qurʾān) is pronounced by the qurʾānic, "Glory be to God!" (*subḥāna llāhi,* Q 12:108; 21:22; 23:91; 27:8; 28:68; 30:17; 52:43; 59:23), or with other designations for God by, "Glory be to my/your/our lord!" (*subḥāna rabbī,* Q 17:93; *subḥāna rabbika,* Q 37:180; *subḥāna rabbinā,* Q 17:108) or with pronouns, eg. Q 2:32 *(subḥānaka)* and Q 2:116 *(subḥānahu).* The qurʾānic glorification also introduces the verse (Q 17:1) interpreted in the commentary literature as referring to Muḥammad's night-journey and ascension (q.v.), which in the post-qurʾānic tradition serves as a backdrop for the divine institution of the *ṣalāt.* Employed together with, "High be he exalted!" (*taʿālā,* e.g. Q 10:18; 16:1; 30:40; 39:67), the exclamation, "Glory be to him!," stresses God's utter transcendence above creatures and complete dissociation with any partners, in particular when it is linked with the phrases, "above what they associate" (*ʿammā yushrikūna,* Q 52:43; 59:23; cf. Paret, *Kommentar,* 180) and "beyond what they describe" (*ʿammā yaṣifūna,* Q 6:100; 21:22; 23:91 37:159, 180; 43:82). On occasion, the qurʾānic glorification is paired with the laudatory exclamation *(tamḥīd),* "Praise belongs to God!" (*al-ḥamdu lillāhi,* mentioned 24 times in the Qurʾān, e.g. Q 1:2; cf. 15:98 and 39:75). The famous magnification of God *(takbīr)* by the exclamation, "God is great!" (*Allāhu akbar,* originally meaning greater than all demons), however, is not mentioned verbatim in the Qurʾān yet is signaled in Q 17:111 and 74:3. Another exclamation, "Blessed be God!" (*tabāraka llāhu,* Q 7:54; 23:14; 40:64), extols God as the creator and ruler (see KINGS AND RULERS) of the universe (Q 25:61; 43:85; 55:78; 67:1) as well as the benefactor of Muḥammad (Q 25:1, 10). Two qurʾānic glorifications (Q 36:36, 83) effectively illustrate the transition from Muḥammad's personal prayer to the communal prayer of the nascent community, as they express the summons addressed to Muḥammad, "Proclaim your lord's praise!" (*sabbiḥ bi-ḥamdi rabbika,* Q 15:98; 20:130; 40:55; 52:48; 50:39-40; cf. *sabbiḥhu,* Q 76:26), and then directed to his community, "O believers, remember God oft, and give him glory!" (*sabbiḥūhu,* Q 33:41-2; see also LAUDATION; GLORIFICATION OF GOD; PRAISE; GLORY).

In addition to the angelic glorification of God, two other powerful qurʾānic scenarios are actualized in the *ṣalāt.* The postures of standing and bowing in prayer are linked quite explicitly in the Qurʾān with the fear of judgment (q.v.) in the world to come (see ESCHATOLOGY; REWARD AND PUNISHMENT) and the hope in God's mercy (q.v.) and forgiveness (q.v.; Q 39:9; 25:64-5; 3:16-7). As such, both postures give a bodily expression in prayer to the ultimate account each human being must give before God on judgment day (see LAST JUDGMENT), i.e. standing to receive the final verdict in the presence of the divine majesty and bowing down to seek the divine pardon. It is as if the essential body movements of prayer capture and telescope the ultimate moment of a person's encounter with God. Another scenario calls to mind the natural adoration divinely invested in the creation of the universe. In the Qurʾān, bowing and prostrating in prayer mirror the rhythm of nature built into the cosmos, for "to God bow *(yasjudu)* all who are in the heavens and the earth, willingly or unwillingly, as do their shadows in the mornings and the evenings" (Q 13:15; cf. 16:48-9). The most powerful verse expressing this cosmic prayer is Q 22:18, "Have you not seen how to God bow *(yasjudu)* all who are in the heavens and on the earth, the sun and the moon, the stars and the mountains, the trees (see AGRICULTURE AND VEGETATION) and the beasts?" It is also tempting to see in references to God's face a qurʾānic imagery related to prayer, as for example, in Q 2:115, "wherever you turn, there is the face of God" (q.v.; *wajhu llāh,* cf. Q 55:27; 76:9; 92:20). Although Q 13:22 links those performing the *ṣalāt* with those "seeking the face of their lord" (*ibtighāʾa wajhi rabbihim;* cf. Q 2:272; 30:38-9), a phrase possibly comparable with the *biqqesh pene yhwh* of the Hebrew Bible (cf. Baljon, To seek, 261-5), the expression is employed predominantly with almsgiving *(zakāt)* for God's sake and without expectation of recompense (see GOD AND HIS ATTRIBUTES, esp. 323-4).

The inclusion of Qurʾān recitation as an essential element in the communal prayer (Q 35:29) provides another example of a prayer practice of the Prophet (cf. Q 29:45) to which his followers eventually joined themselves (see RECITATION OF THE QURʾĀN). In the form of the morning prayer, it came to be called "the recital of dawn" (*qurʾān al-fajr,* Q 17:78), "witnessed" (*mashhūdan,* Q 17:78) by the angels (?) in the early morning. Hence the Prophet is cautioned to begin each Qurʾān recitation by protecting himself against the forces of evil (see GOOD AND EVIL), "When you recite the Qurʾān, seek refuge in God against the accursed Satan" (Q 16:98; cf. 113:1-5; 3:36). According to Islamic tradition the Prophet is said to have used this formula frequently when beginning the *ṣalāt* (cf. Goldziher, *Abhandlungen,* i, 7-9). In all likelihood, the opening chapter of the Qurʾān (Sūrat al-Fātiḥa, Q 1:1-7; see FĀTIḤA) was deliberately composed to serve as a fixed and mandatory recitation for the communal prayer (cf. Goitein, Prayer, 82-4). Q 84:20-1 confirms that the Qurʾān recitation was accompanied by acts of prostration, "What ails them who do not believe (see BELIEF AND UNBELIEF), and when the Qurʾān is recited to them they do not bow *(lā yasjudūn)?*" When the Qurʾān is recited, people "fall down on their faces in prostration" (*sujjadan,* Q 17:107), just as the patriarchs "fell down prostrating and weeping" (q.v.; *sujjadan wa-bukiyyan,* Q 19:58) when the signs (q.v.) of the all-merciful (see GOD AND HIS ATTRIBUTES) were recited to them. Muḥammad is commanded, "do not raise your voice in your prayer *(lā tajhar bi-ṣalātika),* nor be hushed therein, but seek for a way between that" (Q 17:110), while his followers are told, "when the Qurʾān is recited, give ear and be silent" (Q 7:204). An explicit command for the mandatory communal performance of the prayer is stated by the direct summons to Muḥammad, "command your people to observe the *ṣalāt*" (Q 20:132) and "content yourself with those who invoke their lord" (Q 18:28). A group of his followers also join Muḥammad in prayer at night: "your lord knows that you keep vigil nearly two-thirds of the night or a half of it, or a third of it, and a party of those with you" (*ṭāʾifatun min alladhīna maʿaka,* Q 73:20; see VIGILS).

Such nocturnal prayers were a most distinctive mark of the early communal prayer at Mecca. These night vigils formed an essential part of Muḥammad's prayer practice and were adopted by his followers. When he labored to convey or chant a qurʾānic passage (Q 73:1-8), Muḥammad is commanded directly, "Keep vigil in the night!" (*qumi l-layla,* Q 73:2). The observance of prayer at night *(tahajjud),* cited only once in the Qurʾān by this term, is set in the context of the *ṣalāt* (Q 17:78), and explicitly enjoined on Muḥammad: "and as for the night, keep vigil a part of it" (*wa-mina l-layli fa-tahajjad bihi,* Q 17:79), and "bow down before him and glorify him through the long night" (Q 76:26). Reciting the Qurʾān during the night vigil is called "an extra" (*nāfilatan,* Q 17:79) of Muḥammad's prayer practice, a vocabulary later used in Islamic law to define supererogatory prayers (*ṣalāt al-nawāfil;* see LAW AND THE QURʾĀN). Muḥammad is commanded to "proclaim the praise of your lord… in the night and at the setting of the stars" (Q 52:48-9), to pray "nigh of the night" (*zulafan mina l-layl,* Q 11:114), to "proclaim your lord's praise in the watches of the night *(min ānāʾi l-layl),* and at the ends of the day" (*aṭrāfa l-nahār,* Q 20:130), and to "perform the prayer at the sinking of the sun to the darkening of the night" (*li-dulūki l-shamsi ilā ghasaqi l-layl,* Q 17:78). This nocturnal practice is observed by his godfearing followers (see FEAR; PIETY), "who pass the night *(yabītūna li-rabbihim)* prostrate to their lord and standing" (Q 25:64). Similarly, the dwellers of paradise (q.v.), while previously living on earth, kept night vigils: "little of the night would they slumber and into the last hours of the night *(wa-bi-l-asḥār)* would they seek forgiveness" (Q 51:17-8). Traditional accounts, included in the qurʾānic commentary literature, add that the zeal in observing these vigils caused Muḥammad's followers to suffer from swollen feet (cf. Wensinck, Tahadjdjud, 97).

It is possible that the practice of night vigils was adopted from Christian ascetic precedent (cf. Bell, *Origin,* 143; see ASCETICISM) because Q 3:113 states, "some of the People of the Book (q.v.) are a nation upstanding, that recite God's signs in the watches of the night *(ānāʾi l-layl),* bowing themselves." This practice appears to be meant also by Q 24:36-8, probably referring to Christian hermits, as "men whom neither commerce nor trafficking diverts from the remembrance of God" (Q 24:37). Night vigils may also have been intended by the "worship" *(qunūt)* adopted by Muḥammad's followers, "who worship in the watches of the night" *(a-man huwa qānitun ānāʾa l-layl),* bowing and standing (Q 39:9; cf. 20:130; 2:238). It has to be noted, however, that the language of *qunūt* is rooted in pre-Islamic imprecations (cf. Goldziher, Zauberelemente, 323) and interpreted by the traditional commentary literature in a great variety of ways (cf. Bashear, Qunūt, 36-65; see also OBEDIENCE). In the Qurʾān, the language of *qunūt* also expresses the cosmic scenario of prayer: "To him (God) belongs whosoever is in the heavens and the earth; all worship him" (*kullun lahu qānitūna,* Q 30:26; cf. 2:116; see COSMOLOGY). Furthermore, it is in line with the practice of two biblical characters cited in the Qurʾān, namely Mary (q.v.), "O Mary, worship your lord *(uqnutī li-rabbiki),* and prostrate and bow with those who bow" (Q 3:43), and Abraham (q.v.), "Abraham was a nation worshipping God" (*ummatan qānitan,* Q 16:120). The extra-qurʾānic *sūrat al-qunūt* in ʿUbayy's codex (cf. Nöldeke, *GQ*, ii, 35), however, lacks an explicit reference to both nocturnal prayer and *qunūt,* yet is replete with the vocabulary of prayer.

In the early phases of Muḥammad's prophetic career, the times of prayer are indicated by a rich variety of terms which stand in contrast to the standardized vocabulary for the five daily times of prayer *(mīqāt)* developed in post-qurʾānic Islamic law. In addition to the variable vocabulary for the prayer at night, the prayer times during the day reflect the general plethora of temporal vocabulary employed in the Qurʾān (see TIME). The Qurʾān states explicitly that the communal prayer was performed "at the two ends of the day" (*ṭarafayi l-nahār,* Q 11:114) or "at the ends of the day" (*aṭrāfa l-nahār,* Q 20:130), vaguely meaning morning and evening. But the Qurʾān does not explicitly specify whether these ends actually mean sunrise and sunset or dawn and dusk or possibly the morning just after sunrise and the evening just before sunset. The implication of "the ends of the day" seems to be before sunrise and after sunset, but Q 50:39 clearly says "before sunset" *(qabla l-ghurūb).* In addition, the two times, "in the morning and evening" (Q 6:52; 18:28; 7:205) are expressed by a varying vocabulary for "morning," *ghuduww* (Q 7:205), *ghadāt* (Q 6:52), *bukra* (Q 19:11), *ibkār* (Q 40:55), and for "evening," *ʿashiyy* (Q 40:55), *aṣīl* (Q 76:25), pl. *aṣāl* (Q 7:205). Q 20:130 explains these two "ends" as "before the rising of the sun and before its setting" (Q 20:130), which would mean at dawn and in the evening before sunset. These varying expressions clearly reflect a slowly evolving understanding of the two preferred prayer times at "the two ends of the day." There is no qurʾānic evidence to indicate whether "the two ends of the day" can be synchronized with the above-mentioned traditional accounts about Muḥammad's observance of the *ṣalāt al-ḍuḥā* and the *ṣalāt al-ʿaṣr.* Similarly, the question remains conjectural whether the insistent condemnation by Islamic tradition and law of a *ṣalāt* performed at the precise moments of sunset, sunrise or when the sun stands in the zenith as an ancient Arab cult of sun-worship actually preserves a trace of such an early prayer practice concealed in "the two ends of the day" (cf. Wensinck, Animismus, 232-5).

Much of his inspiration for the performance of prayer Muḥammad drew from the prophets of old, the qurʾānic models of prayer who, from Adam through Noah, Abraham and Israel (q.v.), "fell down prostrate [in prayer], weeping" (Q 19:58). They bade their people to pray, as did e.g. Ishmael (q.v.; Ismāʿīl, Q 19:55), Isaac (q.v.) and Jacob (q.v.; Q 21:73), or called out in the darkness (q.v.) invoking God, as did Jonah (q.v.; Q 21:87). Abraham offers a heart-wrenching prayer to his lord for a pure heart (q.v.), imploring his creator as the one who provides for him (see SUSTENANCE; GRACE), guides and heals him (see ERROR; ASTRAY; ILLNESS AND HEALTH), will make him to die, give him life, forgive his sin and offer him paradise (Q 26:83-9). Beseeching God, he asks that the privilege of performing the prayer be granted to him and his progeny (Q 14:40, cf. 14:37). Moses appeals to his lord to open his breast, unloose the knot upon his tongue and grant him Aaron (q.v.) as a helper to glorify God and remember him abundantly (Q 20:25-34), while God addresses him directly in solemn terms, "Verily I am God; there is no god but I; therefore serve me and perform the prayer of my remembrance" (*wa-aqimi l-ṣalāta li-dhikrī*, Q 20:14). Both Moses and his brother Aaron are bidden: "Take you, for your people, in Egypt (q.v.) certain houses; and make your houses a direction *(qiblatan)* for men to pray to; and perform the *ṣalāt;* and give good tidings to the believers" (Q 10:87; see GOOD NEWS). The feeble and gray-haired Zechariah (q.v.) begs his lord secretly to grant him a son (Q 19:3-6; 3:38-9), and Jesus (q.v.), God's servant (see SERVANTS) as yet in the cradle and made blessed by God, is enjoined to pray as long as he lives (Q 19:30-1).

The institution of the ritual prayer

In the few years before and after the emigration (q.v.; *hijra*) of Muḥammad and his followers to Medina, the ritual prayer *(ṣalāt)* developed into a central religious discipline of the Prophet's growing community and shows clear signs of becoming a consolidated ritual institution. This understanding may be derived from the direct statement that the *ṣalāt* is enjoined as "a timed prescription" (*kitāban mawqūtan,* Q 4:103), regulated in its performance and standardized in its choice of terms through the set phrases of *ṣalāt al-fajr* and *ṣalāt al-ʿishāʾ* for the morning and evening prayers respectively (Q 24:58), performed "at morn and eventide" (Q 7:204-6). A new time of "the middle prayer" (*al-ṣalāt al-wusṭā,* Q 2:238) is now added in Medina, a time also implied by the "midday heat" (*ẓahīra;* see NOON; HOT AND COLD), though not the midday prayer, in Q 24:58. That this prayer was actually performed at midday may be inferred from Q 30:17-8, which summons Muḥammad's community to give glory to God "when you come to evening and when you come to morning *(ḥīna tumsūna wa-ḥīna tuṣbiḥūna)*... and when you come to noon *(wa-ḥīna tuẓhirūna).*" On the other hand, the middle prayer may have been introduced in emulation of the *minḥāh,* observed by the Jews of Medina in the afternoon as one of their three prayer times (*shaḥarīth,* morning; *minḥāh,* afternoon; and *ʿarbīth,* evening, cf. Mittwoch, Zur Entstehungsgeschichte, 11-2). In general, Western scholarship (see POST-ENLIGHTENMENT ACADEMIC STUDY OF THE QURʾĀN) tends to interpret "the middle prayer" as referring to the noon prayer (*ṣalāt al-ẓuhr,* cf. Houtsma, Iets, 127-34; Paret, *Grenzen,* 31-5; pace Goitein, Prayer, 84-5, the plural *al-ṣalawāt* rather than the dual in Q 2:238 notwithstanding). Qurʾānic commentary, on the other hand, prefers to interpret "the middle prayer" as that of the afternoon *(ṣalāt al-ʿaṣr),* as it occupies the middle position in the eventual five prayer times, that were codified as a religious duty by Islamic law. In any event, the addition of the middle prayer appears to have been accompanied by a decrease in the nocturnal prayer, because a variety of reasons are now given as dispensations from the lengthy night vigils (Q 73:20).

Regularization of the prayer ritual is also presupposed by dispensations for altered ways of performing the prayer, known traditionally as "the prayer of fear" *(ṣalāt al-khawf),* when those facing hostilities from foes alternate bowing in prayer with those standing guard with weapons in hand (Q 4:102; see ENEMIES; FIGHTING; WAR; EXPEDITIONS AND BATTLES). Another feature of the regularization of prayer is the insistence on its punctual performance by "those who carefully observe their prayer" (*ʿalā ṣalātihim yuḥāfiẓūna,* Q 6:92; 70:34; 23:9; cf. 70:22-3) and the reprimand for those who are heedless in performing the *ṣalāt* (cf. Q 107:4-5). Furthermore, the Qurʾān now explicitly makes the *ṣalāt* mandatory also for women, commanding them,

"Perform the prayer!" (*aqimna l-ṣalāta,* Q 33:33), and addressing them, "Remember that which is recited in your houses!" (Q 33:34), and putting them on an equal footing with men in observing this obligation (cf. Q 33:35; see WOMEN AND THE QURʾĀN; GENDER; PATRIARCHY).

Early in the Medinan phase of the qurʾānic proclamation, the giving of the greeting of peace (q.v.; *taslīm*), cited in the second verbal form, "and give the salutation of peace" (*wa-sallimū taslīman,* Q 33:56; cf. 24:27, 61) became the liturgical salutation closing the *ṣalāt.* Already in the Meccan phase, *"salām"* (meaning "safety, salvation, peace, salutation") is mentioned frequently and employed in the greeting, "Peace be upon you!" (*salāmun ʿalaykum,* Q 13:24; 16:32; 39:73), given by the angels to the blessed of paradise (see GARDEN). Abraham exchanges "Peace!" (*salām,* Q 11:69; 51:25) with his guests and, threatened by his father (see ĀZAR), takes leave from him with, "Peace be upon you!" (*salāmun ʿalayka,* Q 19:47) while Moses dismisses Pharaoh (q.v.), "Peace be upon him who follows the right guidance!" (*wa-l-salāmu ʿalā mani ttabaʿa l-hudā,* Q 20:47). Now in Medina, however, Muḥammad follows the precedent of the Jewish *tefillā* (cf. Mittwoch, Zur Entstehungsgeschichte, 18) and includes the utterance of the salutation of peace as an essential feature of the prayer ritual. In addition, the observance of the *ṣalāt* is now frequently connected in consistent language with the giving of the *zakāt* ("alms-due"), a set phrase that occurs about two dozen times in the Medinan sūras (cf. Nanji, Almsgiving, 64-70). The qurʾānic command, addressed to Muḥammad's community, "perform the prayer and give the alms-due" (*wa-aqīmū l-ṣalāta wa-ātū l-zakāt,* Q 4:77, mentioned about two dozen times), clearly demonstrates by its in-tandem use the existence of two consolidated communal institutions, linked together and firmly established, the ritual prayer and the communal tax (see TAXATION).

The regularization of ritual prayer can also be inferred from the preparatory rites which were added during Muḥammad's qurʾānic proclamation at Medina. During this Medinan phase, the Qurʾān records specific instructions about ritual purification through ablutions to be observed in preparation of each ritual prayer (Q 4:43; 5:6) as well as dispensations for travelers (see JOURNEY) who may shorten the *ṣalāt* (Q 4:101) and use sand as a sign of purification in the absence of water (*tayammum,* Q 4:43; 5:6). There is no specific instruction to keep the head covered during prayer, most likely because this was commonly done and implicitly understood. The qurʾānic injunctions to wash the face (q.v.), the hands (q.v.) up to the elbows, the head and the feet (q.v.) up to the ankles, were based on the perception of ritual impurity (see also CONTAMINATION) resulting from sexual defilement (*junuban,* Q 4:43; 5:6; see SEX AND SEXUALITY) or intoxication (*sukārā,* Q 4:43; see INTOXICANTS; WINE). They laid the ground for the detailed rituals of *wuḍūʾ* (minor ablution) and *ghusl* (major ablution) developed in the post-qurʾānic legal literature of Islam (cf. Burton, Qurʾān, 21-58). Behind these stipulations lies the perception that water has the power to drive off demons (cf. Goldziher, Wasser als Dämonen, 27) as well as the solemn qurʾānic assertion that the Qurʾān is a sublime book only to be touched by "the purified" (*al-muṭahharūn,* Q 56:76-9; cf. Jeffery, *Qurʾān,* 13-7).

Another preparatory element of the *ṣalāt* is the public summons to prayer (Q 5:58), instituted by Muḥammad in Medina and expressed in the Qurʾān by derivatives of the verb *nādā* (third verbal form), "to call," foreshadowing the appearance of the word for the distinct muezzin's call *(adhān)* that came to be the widely-used term for the Muslim call to prayer (actually consisting of two calls, *adhān* from the minaret and *iqāma* in the mosque; see MOSQUE). According to Islamic tradition, the Prophet ordered that the believers be convoked by Bilāl, the first muezzin, and that the summons to prayer be called out rather than sounded by horns, announced by wooden clappers or signaled by lighting a fire. In Medina, the summons to prayer served in particular as an invitation to the prayer on "the day of assembly" (*yawm al-jumuʿati,* Q 62:9) on Friday (see FRIDAY PRAYER), the pre-Islamic market-day, mentioned only once in the Qurʾān (cf. Goitein, Muslim, 111-25; Brockelmann, Iqāmat aṣ-ṣalāt, 314-20). This public prayer is observed on Friday at midday in mosques throughout the Muslim world, although the Friday is not treated as a day of rest like the Sabbath (q.v.). In Muslim thought, God is always active conducting the affairs of the universe and never sits still, not even resting from his work of creation on the seventh day (Q 50:38; cf. Nagel, *Koran,* 172-84). The congregational prayer is preceded by a sermon *(khuṭba),* given in two parts, generally from a pulpit *(minbar/mimbar),* with the preacher standing upright and leaning on a staff or a lance (cf. Becker, Kanzel, 331; Goldziher, Chatib). The absence of any reference to *khuṭba* (and *minbar*) in the Qurʾān, however, does not preclude the possibility that it actually formed an essential part of the congregational prayer in Muḥammad's time, as did the sermon that followed the *ṣalāt* on the morning of the two big feast-days, as well as the special *ṣalāt* in the cases of a drought or an eclipse.

The most crucial institutional development of the *ṣalāt* at Medina, however, was the change of the prayer direction *(qibla)* toward the Kaʿba, the central sanctuary of Mecca, that can be traced to the year 2/624 after the *hijra*. This is the year the battle of Badr took place (Q 3:123), after which Muḥammad began to dissociate himself from the local Jewish tribes. The explicit qurʾānic directive (Q 2:142-50) must be understood against the background of Semitic prayer practices and their specific and particular orientations: the Jews offered their prayers in the direction of Jerusalem (q.v.), the Syriac Christians prayed eastward (see CHRISTIANS AND CHRISTIANITY) and the Essenes turned toward the rising sun. On account of extra-qurʾānic evidence, it is certain that, immediately after the *hijra,* Muḥammad prayed toward Jerusalem in accordance with Jewish custom, but then changed radically. This fact agrees with Q 2:142-3 which records his opponents' rebuke for his having turned in prayer in the opposite direction (Q 2:142; see OPPOSITION TO MUḤAMMAD). The radical change of the *qibla* required Muḥammad's followers in Medina to turn a half-circle and reorient their prayer toward the sanctuary of Mecca, "the holy mosque" *(al-masjid al-ḥarām,* Q 2:144, cf. 2:149, 150), generally identified with the Kaʿba (cf. Hawting, Kaʿba, 75-80). The significance for the institutional reorientation of Islam of changing the *qibla* cannot be underestimated: it visibly symbolizes the shift from a religion confirming the scriptures of the "People of the Book" (i.e. Jews and Christians) to an autonomous and newly directed religion, reconfirming the natural monotheistic religion of Abraham centered on the Kaʿba of Mecca, now both the new and the original focus of Islam.

In Medina, Muḥammad faced the task of uniting Meccan Emigrants *(muhājirūn)* and Medinan Helpers (*anṣār;* see EMIGRANTS AND HELPERS) into one community *(umma),* observing a common prayer ritual and facing in unison in the same direction of prayer. In the context of his fall-out with the Jews of Medina and his reorientation toward Mecca as the center of the old Arab religion of Abraham, the Meccan sanctuary (the foundations of which were laid by Abraham and Ishmael according to Q 2:127; cf. Firestone, Abraham, 6-11) supplants Jerusalem as the direction of prayer. The fact of this reorientation, however, does not solve the question of what the prayer direction might have been during the Meccan period of the qurʾānic proclamation before the *hijra* (for this complex question, cf. Wensinck, Ḳibla, 82-3). It may have been to the east in imitation of Christian prayer practice or to the Kaʿba itself as noted in the traditional account that Muḥammad did not dare turn his back to the sanctuary in his prayer. More likely, as also noted in the Islamic commentary literature, Jerusalem may have been Muḥammad's prayer direction in Mecca, a direction in agreement with the architectural orientation of the semicircular wall *(ḥaṭīm)*, enclosing the space of Ismāʿīl's tomb (lit. "womb," *ḥijr*), which at one time formed an integral part of the Kaʿba (see ARCHAEOLOGY AND THE QURʾĀN; ART AND ARCHITECTURE AND THE QURʾĀN). The institutional reorientation of the direction of prayer in Medina roughly coincides with the time when Muḥammad instituted the fast of the month of Ramaḍān (Q 2:183-5) that replaced the previously adopted Jewish custom of the ʿAshūrāʾ fast observed on the Day of Atonement (cf. Wagtendonk, Fasting, 180-5). It also occurs in the time frame of the battle of Badr, after which the Jewish tribe of the Banū Qaynuqāʿ (q.v.) was expelled from Medina. From this time on, the prayer direction toward the Kaʿba in Mecca has remained a cornerstone of the Muslim ritual performance of the *ṣalāt* and is architecturally indicated in every mosque by the "niche" *(miḥrāb)*. The latter term, however, does not appear in the Qurʾān in this architectural sense (cf. Q 3:37, 39; 19:11; 38:21; pl. *maḥārīb*, Q 34:13).

According to qurʾānic evidence, there is no certainty that Muḥammad and his community observed the duty of the *ṣalāt* five times a day as Muslims do today and have done over the centuries. Neither the number of the five daily prayers nor their exact times of performance had been fixed by the end of the qurʾānic proclamation. In all likelihood, while in Mecca, Muḥammad and his nascent community kept night vigils and performed prayers in the morning and evening. In Medina, a middle prayer was added, while the nocturnal prayers diminished. After a period of uncertainty in the decades after Muḥammad's death, the living tradition and then the literature of Islamic law codified a firm duty of the *ṣalāt* at five specific times of the day. These designated times, known by the technical term *mīqāt* ("appointed time," cf. Wensinck, Mīḳāt, 26-7), came to be specified as the prayer at daybreak *(ṣalāt al-fajr)*, at noon when the sun has left the zenith *(ṣalāt al-ẓuhr)*, in the afternoon when the shadows equal their objects *(ṣalāt al-ʿaṣr)*, at dusk after sunset *(ṣalāt al-maghrib)*, and at nightfall when the twilight has disappeared *(ṣalāt al-ʿishāʾ)*. The *ṣalāt al-witr*, not mentioned in the Qurʾān but frequently attested in Islamic tradition, presupposes the fixation of the five daily *ṣalāt*s and came to be observed as a voluntary prayer between the night prayer and that of daybreak (cf. Monnot, Ṣalāt, 930). The term *mīqāt*, taken from the Qurʾān, appears to indicate that the *ṣalāt* continued to be understood as an encounter with God, prefigured by Moses meeting and conversing with God at "an appointed time" (Q 7:142-3, 155; cf. Speyer, *Erzählungen*, 299-301; 310-11; 335-6; cf. 26:38, meeting with the sorcerers) and foreshadowing "the appointed time" of the ultimate encounter of each individual with God on judgment day (Q 56:50; 78:17; 44:40). Only once is the term used in the plural, *mawāqīt,* and that for the observation of the new moon (Q 2:189).

The answer to the establishment of five daily observances of the *ṣalāt,* which cannot be found in the Qurʾān, is given in Muslim tradition by two legendary scenarios depicting its divine institution: (1) during the Prophet's ascension to heaven *(al-miʿrāj),* God himself charged Muḥammad to impose five daily prayers on his community, or (2) the angel Gabriel, mentioned in the Qurʾān as the angel of revelation (Q 2:97), came down from heaven five times in one day and, by example, taught Muḥammad the performance of the five daily prayers. The recourse to such legends in Islamic tradition points to both the absence of clear stipulations with regard to the five daily prayers in the Qurʾān and the necessity of establishing an authoritative basis for the divine institution of the mandatory five daily prayers. Western scholarship, on the other hand, has suggested three principal explanations for the fixation of five daily prayers: (1) the five daily prayers are the result of duplications of the evening prayer (into *ṣalāt al-maghrib* and *ṣalāt al-ʿishāʾ*) and the midday prayer (into *ṣalāt al-ẓuhr* and *ṣalāt al-ʿaṣr,* cf. Houtsma, Iets, 127-34). This explanation is particularly reinforced by an Islamic tradition on the authority of ʿAbdallāh b. al-ʿAbbās (d. 68/687-8), arguing in the opposite direction, namely that the Prophet himself combined several *ṣalāt*s in Medina so as not to overburden his community (cf. Wensinck, Ṣalāt, 98); (2) the five daily *ṣalāt*s were patterned on the binding duty of five daily prayers observed in Zoroastrianism (Goldziher, Islamisme, 246; cf. Boyce, *Zoroastrians,* 32-3); (3) the five daily prayers were most likely chosen as a just median between the three services of the Jewish synagogue and the seven "hours" observed by Christian monks (cf. Goitein, Prayer, 84-6). For the post-qurʾānic developments, cf. Wensinck, Ṣalāt, 98; Monnot, Ṣalāt, 926-30.

The language of prayer in the Qurʾān

As stated above, it may be possible to trace two stages of development in the genesis of the *ṣalāt:* (1) from the Meccan phase of the qurʾānic proclamation until the change of the *qibla* in Medina, Muḥammad's personal prayer inspires an evolving communal prayer, which included group prayers in the morning and evening as well as during night vigils; and (2) with the change of the *qibla* in Medina, this communal prayer practice is transformed into a firmly instituted ritual, including three prayer times, morning, evening and a median prayer, as well as stipulations for preparatory and alternate rites. It is much more difficult, however, to coordinate the diverse Arabic terminology for various manifestations of prayer in the Qurʾān. Little research has been done on the semantic fields of *duʿāʾ, dhikr* and *ṣalāt* and their possible interrelatedness in the Qurʾān. It is obvious, however, that the derivatives of the roots for both *duʿāʾ* and *dhikr* are employed more than twice as frequently in the Qurʾān as those for *ṣalāt.* Among these three semantic fields, the vocabulary of *duʿāʾ* appears to represent the earliest layer of prayer language in Arabic as illustrated by the invocation of pre-Islamic deities (which has left more than a dozen traces in the Qurʾān, e.g. Q 4:117; 6:108; 7:194, 197; 10:66, 106; 13:14; 16:20; 19:48; 22:12, 62; 29:43; 31:30; 35:13; 39:38; 40:20, 66; 43:86; 46:5; see IDOLS AND IMAGES; RHETORIC AND THE QURʾĀN) as well as by the frequent occurrence of oaths in the Qurʾān that belong to the stock of Muḥammad's invocation of God (cf. Hawting, Oaths, 561-6).

In its pre-Islamic usage *duʿāʾ* could be employed both negatively and positively. A person could call upon an Arab deity with an invocation that could be directed either for or against someone, and hence could be turned into supplication for a blessing or imprecation for a curse. This double-edged signification is conveyed in the Qurʾān as in Q 17:11, "humanity prays for evil as he prays for good" *(yadʿu l-insānu bi l-sharri duʿāʾahu bi-l-khayr)*. The Qurʾān warns that the invocation of unbelievers, directed to their false gods, goes astray and receives no answer (Q 13:14; 35:13-4), contrary to the invocation of the true God, "who alone is truly called upon" (*lahu daʿwatu l-ḥaqq,* Q 13:14) and says, "I am near to answer the call of the caller, when he calls me" (*ujību daʿwata l-dāʿi idhā daʿānī,* Q 2:186). In the Qurʾān, the *duʿāʾ* becomes the invocation of the one true God to whom one directs both an appeal for divine succor in times of misfortune and a supplication for good fortune (Q 41:49-51). The classical example of this two-sided plea for divine assistance can be found in the first sūra of the Qurʾān (al-Fātiḥa, Q 1:1-7), which begins with the invocation of God's name and ends with the double-edged plea for guidance on the path of divine favor and protection against divine wrath (see PATH OR WAY; ANGER). God is the true hearer of prayer, literally, "the hearer of the invocation" (*samīʿu l-duʿāʾ,* Q 3:38; 14:39; see SEEING AND HEARING) and answers the pleas of the prophets, as in the cases of Abraham, who is granted progeny in his old age (Q 14:39-40; 19:48), and Zechariah, whose secret supplication for a son is answered (Q 19:3-6; 3:38-9).

The phrase for the hearer of prayer, which appears only in the context of these two qurʾānic passages, combines the language of *duʿāʾ* and *ṣalāt* (cf. Q 14:39-40 and 3:38-9): Abraham asks his lord, "make me a performer of the prayer" *(muqīma l-ṣalāt)* and "accept my plea" (*wa-taqabbal duʿāʾī,* Q 14:40), and Zechariah "invoked *(daʿā)* his lord" while he was "standing in prayer" (*qāʾimun yuṣallī,* Q 3:38-9). The intersection of these two semantic fields of prayer in prophetic narratives (q.v.) of the Qurʾān may illustrate the assimilation of *duʿāʾ*, an early Arab way of prayer, with that of *ṣalāt,* the prayer practice adopted by Muḥammad from a tradition rooted in the Aramaic background, despite the fact that *duʿāʾ* and its derivatives are rarely found in sūras (q.v.) judged as belonging to the first Meccan period.

A fusion of *duʿāʾ* and *ṣalāt* with the semantic field of *dhikr* could be reflected in the qurʾānic injunctions to pronounce the prayer in a moderate voice. With regard to *ṣalāt,* Muḥammad is commanded, "do not raise your voice in your prayer *(lā tajhar bi-ṣalātika),* nor be hushed therein, but seek you for a way between that" (Q 17:110). With regard to *duʿāʾ*, his followers are told, "invoke your lord *(udʿū rabbakum),* humbly and secretly" (*khufyatan,* Q 7:55). With regard to *dhikr,* Muḥammad is commanded, "remember your lord *(wa-dhkur rabbaka)* in your soul, humbly and fearfully, without raising the voice" (*dūna l-jahr,* Q 7:205). Another indicator for the blending of these three semantic fields for prayer in the Qurʾān may be detected in the linkage of the roots of *duʿāʾ* and *dhikr* with specific prayer times in the Qurʾān, not unlike in the case of *ṣalāt.* For example, with regard to *duʿāʾ*, Q 6:52 refers to "those who invoke their lord at morning and evening," while with regard to *dhikr,* Q 7:205 records the divine command to Muḥammad to remember God "at morn and eventide." Finally, the close relationship of *ṣalāt* to *dhikr* can be observed in Q 87:15 referring to the prosperous believer as one who "mentions the name of his lord and prays *(dhakara sma rabbihi fa-ṣallā)*"; in Q 20:14 when Moses is asked to "perform the prayer of my remembrance" *(wa-aqimi l-ṣalāta li-dhikrī);* in Q 5:91 which cautions against Satan desiring "to bar you from the remembrance of God *(dhikr Allāh)* and from the prayer *(al-ṣalāt)*"; and in Q 4:142 including the rebuke for standing lazily in the prayer *(al-ṣalāt)* while "not remembering God *(wa-lā yadhkurūna llāh)* save a little." The license given to those deluged by rain (see WEATHER) or suffering from sickness or prevented from observing the precise hours of prayer in times of war, however, appears to separate the *ṣalāt* from the *dhikr:* "when you have concluded the prayer *(al-ṣalāt),* then remember God *(fa-dhkurū llāh),* standing and sitting and on your sides" (Q 4:103).

In the Qurʾān, the term *dhikr* denotes primarily the act of "recalling God to mind," "reminding oneself of God," "mentioning God's name" or "remembering God" which imply both a vocal mention and a mental memory of the presence of God through recital by the tongue and commemoration in the heart (Q 13:28; 39:23; 57:16, cf. McAuliffe, Heart, 406-9). The recited word of the Qurʾān is linked directly with *dhikr* when the Qurʾān refers to itself as "remembrance, reminder" (*dhikr,* Q 7:63; cf. 3:58; 21: 50; 43:44; 68:52; *dhikrā,* e.g. Q 6:90; *tadhkira,* e.g. Q 20:3; 69:48; 74:49; see NAMES OF THE QURʾĀN), an identification most expressly encapsulated in the oath, "By the Qurʾān, containing the reminder" (*dhī l-dhikr,* Q 38:1). Furthermore, other revealed scriptures also are called *dhikr,* as shown by those possessing them being designated "People of the Remembrance" (*ahl al-dhikr,* Q 16:43; 21:7), in parallel to the standard phrase, *ahl al-kitāb* ("People of the Book"). Underlying the term *dhikr* in the Qurʾān, privileged by the divine promise of reciprocity, "remember me and I will remember you" (Q 2:152), there is the explicit exercise of mentioning or recalling God's name in prayer, vocally or mentally. This can be inferred from many qurʾānic passages, such as "and mention/remember the name of your lord" (Q 73:8; 76:25; cf. 2:114; 22:40; 24:36), "mention/remember your lord when you forget" (Q 18:24), "men and women who mention/remember God oft" (Q 33:35), "the hearts of those who believe are at rest in God's remembrance" (Q 13:28), "O believers, mention/remember God incessantly" (Q 33:41) or "let neither your possessions (see POSSESSION; WEALTH) nor your children (q.v.) divert you from God's remembrance" (Q 63:9).

In conclusion, it may be said that, in comparison to the sacred books of humanity, "there is perhaps no Scripture that is so totally a Book of Prayer as is the Qurʾān" (Roest Crollius, Prayer, 223). The Qurʾān is permeated by a powerful inner dynamic that makes this scripture in its entirety a book of prayer, not only because it contains various prescriptions and descriptions of prayer and includes a great number of prayers, hymns and invocations, but more importantly because it reflects a religious experience of prayer rooted in the heart of the Prophet and reiterated by the tongues of his followers throughout the ages as God's very own speech (q.v.) in matchless Arabic (see WORD OF GOD; INIMITABILITY). Only by listening again and again to the Qurʾān as a recited text, "honey begins to flow from the rock" (ibid., 223). In the experience of the Muslim, God speaks to human beings through the Qurʾān and human beings, reciting the Qurʾān, address themselves to God. Each in its own modality, *dhikr, duʿāʾ* and *ṣalāt,* return the word to God in the thought of recollection, the word of invocation and the action of ritual worship.

Gerhard Böwering

Bibliography
Primary: Ibn Hishām, *Sīra*.
Secondary: C. Adang, Hypocrites and hypocrisy, in *EQ*, ii, 468-72; A. d'Alverny, La prière selon le Coran, in *Proche-Orient Chrétien* 10 (1960), 214-226, 303-17; 11 (1961), 3-16; Arberry; J.M.S. Baljon, To seek the face of God in Koran and hadith, in *AO* 21 (1953), 254-66; S. Bashear, Qunūt in tafsīr and ḥadīth literatures, in *JSAI* 19 (1995), 36-65; C.H. Becker, Die Kanzel im Kultus des alten Islam, in C. Bezold (ed.), *Orientalische Studien Theodor Nöldeke zum siebzigsten Geburtstag*, Giessen 1906, 331-51; id., Zur Geschichte des islamischen Kultus, in *Der Islam* 3 (1912), 374-99; R. Bell, *The origin of Islam in its Christian environment*, London 1968; id., *Qurʾān;* G. Böwering, Chronology and the Qurʾān, in *EQ*, i, 327-8; M. Boyce, *Zoroastrians. Their religious beliefs and practices*, London 1979; C. Brockelmann, Iqāmat aṣ-ṣalāt, in G. Weil (ed.), *Festschrift Eduard Sachau*, Berlin 1915, 314-20; J. Burton, The Qurʾān and the Islamic practice of wuḍūʾ, in *BSOAS* 51 (1988), 21-58; N. Calder, Ḥinth, bir, taḥannuth. An inquiry into the Arabic vocabulary of vows, in *BSOAS* 51 (1988), 213-39; E.E. Calverly, *Worship in Islam*, Madras 1925; J. Corbon, Le sens du dhikr à travers la Bible et le Coran, in *MIDEO* 7 (1962-3), 81-108; R. Firestone, Abraham, in *EQ*, i, 6-11; S. Goitein, The Muslim Friday worship, in id., *Studies in Islamic history and institutions*, Leiden 1966, 111-25; id., Prayer in Islam, in id., *Studies in Islamic history and institutions*, Leiden 1966, 73-89; I. Goldziher, *Abhandlungen zur arabischen Philologie*, vol. i, Leiden 1896; id., Der Chatib bei den alten Arabern, in *WZKM* 6 (1982), 97-102; repr. in *Ignaz Goldziher Gesammelte Schriften* III, ed. J. Desomogyi, Hildesheim 1969, 27-32; id., Die Bedeutung der Nachmittagszeit im Islam, in *ARW* 9 (1906), 293-302; repr. in *Ignaz Goldziher Gesammelte Schriften* V, ed. J. Desomogyi, Hildesheim 1970, 23-31; id., Islamisme et Parsisme, in *RHR* 43 (1901), 119-47; repr. in *Ignaz Goldziher Gesammelte Schriften* IV, ed. J. Desomogyi, Hildesheim 1970, 232-60; id., Wasser als Dämonen abwehrendes Mittel, in *ARW* 13 (1910), 22-46; repr. in *Ignaz Goldziher Gesammelte Schriften* V, ed. J. Desomogyi, Hildesheim 1970, 170-96; id., Zauberelemente im islamischen Gebet, in C. Bezold (ed.), *Orientalische Studien Theodor Nöldeke zum siebzigsten Geburtstag*, Giessen 1906, 303-29; repr. in *Ignaz Goldziher Gesammelte Schriften* V, ed. J. Desomogyi, Hildesheim 1970, 32-58; G. Hawting, Kaʿba, in *EQ*, iii, 75-80; id., Oaths, in *EQ*, iii, 561-6; M.Th. Houtsma, Iets over den dagelijkschen çalat der Mohammedanen, in *Theologisch Tijdschrift* 24 (1890), 127-34; Jeffery, *For. vocab.;* id., *The Qurʾān as scripture*, New York 1952; M.J. Kister, Al-taḥannuth. An enquiry into the meaning of a term, in *BSOAS* 31 (1968), 223-36; id., Some reports concerning Ṭāʾif, in *JSAI* 1 (1979), 1-18; M.C.A. Macdonald and L. Nehmé, al-ʿUzzā, in *EI²*, x, 907-8; J.D. McAuliffe, Heart, in *EQ*, ii, 406-9; E. Mittwoch, Zur Entstehungsgeschichte des islamischen Gebets und Kultus, in *Abhandlungen der königlich preussischen Akademie der Wissenschaften* 2 (1913), 3-42; G. Monnot, Ṣalāt, in *EI²*, viii, 925-34; M. Muranyi, Zwischen ʿaṣr und maġrib in Mekka, in *WO* 23 (1992), 101-28; T. Nagel, *Der Koran*, München 1983; A. Nanji, Almsgiving, in *EQ*, i, 64-70; Nöldeke, *GQ;* C.E. Padwick, *Muslim devotions*, Oxford 1996; R. Paret, *Grenzen der Koranforschung*, Stuttgart 1950; id., *Kommentar;* A. A. Roest Crollius, The prayer of the Qurʾan, in *Studia missionalia* 24 (1975), 223-52; U. Rubin, Ḥanīf, in *EQ*, ii, 402-3; id., Morning and evening prayers in early Islam, in *JSAI* 10 (1987), 40-64; C. Schoeck, Adam and Eve, in *EQ*, i, 22-6; G. R. Smith, Oaths in the Qurʾān, in *Semitics* 1 (1970), 126-56; Speyer, *Erzählungen*, Hildesheim 1988; A. Spitaler, Die Schreibung des Typus *ṣlwt* im Ḳurʾān, in *WZKM* 56 (1960), 212-26; R. Tottoli, Muslim attitudes towards prostration, in *SI* 88 (1998), 5-34; id., Traditions and controversies concerning the suǧūd al-Qurʾān in ḥadīṯ literature, in *ZDMG* 147 (1997), 371-93; K. Wagtendonk, Fasting, in *EQ*, ii, 180-5; A.J. Wensinck, Animismus und Dämonenglaube im Untergrunde des jüdischen und islamischen rituellen Gebets, in *Der Islam* 4 (1913), 219-35; id., Ḳibla, in *EI²*, v, 82-3; id., Mīḳāt, in *EI²*, vii, 26-7; id., *Muhammad and the Jews of Medina*, ed. and trans. W. Behn, Freiburg im Breisgau 1975; id., Muṣallā, in *EI²*, vii, 658-9; id., Ṣalāt, in *EI*, iv, 96-105; id., Tahadjdjud, in *EI²*, x, 97-8.

Prayer Formulas

Invocations for every circumstance of life, both personal and social. There are numerous expressions of prayer in Islam, prayer being fundamentally one with the faith and the practice of Muslims (cf. Q 17:79-80, among numerous other verses). The life of the believer is immersed in a multitude of invocations, which operate as expressions of sincere faith as well as simple stereotyped formulaic phrases. The life of an observant Muslim can be compared to an extended liturgy, as expressed by the title of Ibn al-Sunnī's (d. 364/974) *ʿAmal al-yawm wa-l-layla,* "The work [or the liturgy?] of the day and the night," not only because of the five canonical prayers (see PRAYER), but because of the numerous invocations to God for every occasion. Even the ordinary sounds of daily life, such as the braying of a donkey, can prompt a prayer ("I take refuge in God from Satan the outcast," Ibn al-Sunnī, *ʿAmal,* 153). Other examples of the way in which the use of prayer formulas suffuses daily life are the invocation of the name of God (see BASMALA) before conjugal union, as well as in matters of personal hygiene (Ibn al-Sunnī, *ʿAmal,* 13).

A distinction can be made between "traditional," "common" or "canonical" expressions of praise and petition (including the codified, or ritual, formulas), and those which are left to the individual's own initiative. It should be noted that the former category encompasses all those formulas to be found in the Qurʾān, as well as those reported to have come from Muḥammad (or his Companions, etc.; see COMPANIONS OF THE PROPHET). To this category belong prayers (sing. *duʿa*) found in both the sunna (q.v.) and ḥadīth, i.e. the "Book of good manners" in Ibn Abī Shayba's (d. 235/849) *Muṣannaf* or the "Book of work of day and night" in al-Nasāʾī's (d. 303/915) *al-Sunan al-kubrā* (see ḤADĪTH AND THE QURʾĀN), as well as those contained in special collections such as Ibn Abī l-Dunyā's (d. 281/894) *al-Tahajjud wa-qiyām al-layl,* and especially Ibn al-Sunnī's *ʿAmal al-yawm wa-l-layla* (cf. also the Egyptian polymath al-Suyūṭī's [d. 911/1505] *Dāʿī l-falāḥ fī adhkār al-masāʾ wa-l-ṣabāḥ*).

The second grouping, those of the individually formulated *duʿa*s, may also contain material attributed to Muḥammad, but this material is integrated into longer prayers that are freely and spontaneously composed. When compared to Christianity, for example, Islam has relatively few "prayer" books (probably because of the importance of the five daily obligatory ritual prayers), yet some books of this type are well-known. Among them are the so-called "Psalms of Islam" (*al-Ṣaḥīfa al-kāmila al-sajjādiyya,* or *al-Ṣaḥīfa al-sajjādiyya al-ūlā;* Pers. *Zabur-i āl-i Muḥammad*), attributed to the fourth imām (q.v.), Zayn al-ʿĀbidīn ʿAlī b. al-Ḥusayn, also called al-Sajjād (d. bet. 92/710 and 99/717; cf. Sezgin, *GAS,* i, 826-8). These "Psalms" contain supplications such as "asking for the best" *(istikhāra),* the invocation on the beginning of Ramaḍān (q.v.), bidding farewell to Ramaḍān, etc. (see bibliography for details on translations of, and commentaries on, al-Sajjād's work, as well as other popular collections of prayers).

As freely expressed prayers are more common in Ṣūfism (cf. van Ess, Review, 185; see ṢŪFISM AND THE QURʾĀN), a third category of *duʿa* may be added: the Ṣūfī formulations (see below; cf. Gramlich, *Sendschreiben,* 364-71; Ghazālī, *Iḥyāʾ*).

Expressions of praise (q.v.) represent the true meaning of prayer (see also LAUDATION; GLORY; GLORIFICATION OF GOD). Mention can be made of the *ḥamdala,* "Praise be to God" *("al-ḥamdu lillāh"),* which expresses human gratitude for God's favors (see GRACE; BLESSING; GRATITUDE AND INGRATITUDE). This phrase opens the first chapter of the Qurʾān, Sūrat al-Fātiḥa (see FĀTIḤA), and is found about forty times within the Qurʾān. Similarly, the invocation of the name of God, the *basmala,* "In the name of God, the compassionate [forgiving??], the merciful" (*"bismi llāh,"* in its full form, *"bismi llāhi l-raḥmāni l-raḥīm"*), places all human activity under the divine will. This invocation is found at the beginning of each sūra (q.v.) except for one. Furthermore, there is the *takbīr:* "God is great," *("Allāhu akbar"),* which bears witness to the absolute transcendence of God (see

ANTHROPOMORPHISM). One could add mention of the profession of faith: "There is no god but God," (*lā ilāha illā llāh;* see WITNESS TO FAITH), contained particularly in the call to prayer, as well as the *talbiya,* spoken at the time of pilgrimage (q.v.): "Here I am! O God! Here I am! I come to you! There is none beside you! I come to you; to you be all glory, all grace and all power! There is none beside you" *(Labbayka allāhumma labbayka; labbayka lā sharīka laka; labbayka. Inna l-ḥamda wa-l-niʿmata [laka] wa-l-mulka laka, lā sharīka laka").*

Duʿāʾ as prayer of petition — not always considered of great importance by some theologians — is expressed in certain fixed forms, such as in the prayer asking for rain (*ṣalāt al-istisqāʾ,* cf. Q 71:11) or in the prayer for the dead, spoken before burial (q.v.; *ṣalāt ʿalā l-mayyit,* cf. Q 9:84), which adopts the invocation pronounced by the Prophet himself as reported by Abū Hurayra, or, finally, the prayer of fear (*ṣalāt al-khawf,* cf. Q 2:239 and 4:101-3), which was said in the past by Muslim armies as they went into battle against the enemy. Many prayers of petition, however, have different forms, which are left to the individual's own initiative.

In everyday life, there are numerous invocations for every occasion, such as those addressed to a sick person: "May God heal you" *(Allāh yashfīka);* to someone who is doing work: "May God give you strength" (*Allāh yaʿṭīka l-ʿāfiya,* or, in the Maghreb, *Allāh yaʿṭīka l-ṣaḥḥa*); about someone who has died: "May God have mercy upon him" *(Allāh yarḥamuhu);* to a father, about one of his children: "May God keep him for you" *(Allāh ikhallīlak iyyāhu),* etc.

The ritual expressions of prayer are primarily those of the canonical prayer, the *ṣalāt,* where the recitation of the first sūra of the Qurʾān, Sūrat al-Fātiḥa, is of tremendous importance. This constitutes the prayer *par excellence,* recited on all of life's occasions: it is used at events of personal importance, as well as communal ceremonies, like marriages and funerals, or circumcision (q.v.). It is also recited at the initiation of an individual into the Muslim community. Called *umm al-kitāb* ("the mother of the book" or "the standard of the book," depending on the interpretation), commentators have written much on the benefits of its recitation. During this prayer, particularly on Fridays (see FRIDAY PRAYER), numerous classic expressions are repeated, such as "God is great" *(Allāhu akbar)* or "Glory to God" *(subḥāna llāh).* This prayer is recited in accordance with a fixed ritual, which can be shortened when one is on a journey (q.v.; Q 4:101).

One should include here an elaborated form of the *tashahhud,* the profession of faith: "To God salutations, prayers, pious formulas. Peace be upon you, the Prophet, as well as the mercy (q.v.) of God and his blessings. May peace also be upon us and upon the righteous servants of God. I testify that there is no god but the one God, there is none beside him, and I testify that Muḥammed is his servant and his messenger" (*al-taḥiyyāt lillāh wa-l-ṣalawāt wa-l-ṭayyibāt; al-salāmu ʿalayka ayyuhā l-nabī wa-raḥmatu llāhi wa-barakātuhu; al-salāmu ʿalaynā wa-ʿalā ʿibādi llāhi l-ṣāliḥīn; ashhadu anna lā ilāha illā llāha, lā sharīka lahu wa-ashhadu anna Muḥammadan rasūluhu;* see WITNESSING AND TESTIFYING; PROPHETS AND PROPHET- HOOD; MESSENGER).

Like Sūrat al-Fātiḥa, which opens the Qurʾān, the two sūras which close the book, Sūrat al-Falaq ("The Dawn," Q 113) and Sūrat al-Nās ("People," Q 114) are frequently employed. They are called "the two that procure refuge" *(al-muʿawwidhatān)* because they employ the formulas *"aʿūdhu bi-rabbi l-falaq"* ("I seek protection from the lord of the dawn" — or, from the "lord of hell," according to the commentators; see HELL AND HELLFIRE) and *"aʿūdhu bi-rabbi l-nās*" ("I seek protection from the lord of humankind"). They have given birth to the very frequent formula, "I seek protection (q.v.) from God" *(aʿūdhu bi-llāh),* by which the believer places him- or herself in God's hands when faced with danger. "I entrust myself to God" (*tawwakaltu ʿalā llāh,* cf. Q 11:56) is another closely related formula.

Yet another type of invocation consists of the recitation of the divine names, or attributes, of God (see GOD AND HIS ATTRIBUTES) — some of which are qurʾānic: "the merciful," "the strong," "the powerful," etc. (see POWER AND IMPOTENCE). There are many lists of these names. According to tradition, there are ninety-nine names. The hundredth is said to be the "true name," which people cannot comprehend.

One qurʾānic verse, Q 2:255, has particular importance. Termed "the throne verse" *(āyat al-kursī),* it is very often recited (see THRONE OF GOD). Certain commentators say that it encompasses the name of God that cannot be spoken.

Finally, certain Ṣūfi formulations are used by mystics: *huwa* ("he") and *al-ʿishq* ("love"), to which are added the ceremonies (*dhikr* or *ḥaḍra*) of the litanies whose precise forms may vary among different brotherhoods. One of the most common customs is the continually repeated utterance of the divine name *Allāh,* "God" (see REMEMBRANCE).

Jean-Yves L'Hopital

Bibliography

Primary: Āghā Buzurg, Muḥammad Muḥsin b. ʿAlī, *al-Dharīʿa fī taṣānīf al-shīʿa,* 25 vols., Beirut 1983[2], xv, 18-21, on the five *al-Ṣaḥīfa al-sajjādiyya,* the post-Sajjād prayer collections, i.e. that of 1053/1642 by al-Ḥurr al-ʿĀmilī (d. 1104/1693); al-Ghazālī, Abū Ḥāmid Muḥammad, *Iḥyāʾ ʿulūm al-dīn,* 4 vols., Būlāq 1872, repr. Cairo 1933, i, 264-98 (Bk. 9); i, 299-328 (Bk. 10); Fr. trans. G.H. Bousquet, *Ih'ya ʿouloûm ed-dîn ou Vivification des sciences de la foi. Analyse et index,* Paris 1955, 95-9, 100-5; Eng. trans. (of Bk. 9) K. Nakamura, Al-Adhkar wa l-da'awat. *Invocations & supplications. Book IX of the Revival of the religious sciences,* Tokyo 1973, Cambridge, UK 1990[2] (rev. ed.); Ibn Abī l-Dunyā, *al-Tahajjud wa-qiyām al-layl,* ed. M.ʿA.M. al-Saʿdānī, Cairo 1994; Ibn Abī al-Shayba, Abū Bakr ʿAbdallāh b. Muḥammad b. Ibrāhīm, *al-Muṣannaf fī l-aḥādīth wa-l-āthār,* rev. ed. M.ʿA. Shāhīn, 9 vols., Beirut 1995, v, 210-343 (19. *K. al-Ādāb*); Ibn al-Sunnī, Abū Bakr Aḥmad b. Muḥammad al-Dīnawarī, *ʿAmal al-yawm wa-l-layla,* ed. B.M. ʿUyūn, Damascus 1987, 1994[3]; al-Jazūlī, Muḥammad b. Sulaymān al-Samlālī, *Dalāʾil al-khayrāt wa-shawāriq al-anwār fī dhikr al-ṣalāt ʿalā l-nabī al-mukhtār,* Cairo 1994 (a popular collection of prayers, which contains prayers not only for the Prophet, but also the description of his grave and a list of his names; see NAMES OF THE PROPHET); Nasāʾī, *Sunan,* vi, 3-281 (81. *K. ʿAmal al-yawm wa-layla*); Niʿmat Allāh al-Jazāʾirī, *Nūr al-anwār fī sharḥ al-Ṣaḥīfa al-sajjādiyya,* Beirut 2000 (a commentary on al-Sajjād's work); al-Sajjād, see below, under "Zayn al-ʿĀbidīn ʿAlī b. al-Ḥusayn"; Suyūṭī, *Dāʿī l-falāḥ fī adhkār al-masāʾ wa-l-ṣabāḥ,* ed. A.ʿA. Bājūr, Cairo 1994; Zayn al-ʿĀbidīn ʿAlī b. al-Ḥusayn, *al-Ṣaḥīfa al-sajjādiyya al-kāmila,* on http://www.al-islam.org/arabic/sahifa/, Eng. trans. W.C. Chittick, *The psalms of Islam,* Oxford 1988.

Secondary: M.A. Amir-Moezzi, *Le guide divin dans le shîʿisme original. Aux sources de l'ésotérisme en Islam,* Lagrasse 1992, 55; Eng. trans. E. Arnold, *Pearls of faith or Islam's rosary,* Boston 1883; M. Ben Cheneb, al-Djazūlī, in *EI*[2], ii, 527-8; W.C. Chittick (ed. and trans.), *A Shiʿite anthology,* Albany 1981, 9 (on *The scroll of al-Sajjād*), 113-22 (two prayers translated from *The Scroll*); K. Cragg, *Alive to God. Muslim and Christian prayer,* London 1970; id., Pilgrimage prayers, in *MW* 45 (1955), 269-80; P. Cuperly, *Ghazālī. Temps et prières,* Paris 1990 (extracts from *Kitāb al-Adhkār wa-l-daʿwāt* of the *Iḥyāʾ ʿulūm al-dīn*); J. van Ess, Review of W.C. Chittick, *The psalms of Islam.* Al-Ṣaḥīfa al-kāmila al-sajjadiyya. *By Imām Zayn al-ʿĀbidīn ʿAlī b. al-Ḥusayn,* Oxford 1988, in *Der Islam* 67 (1990), 184-7; id., *TG,* i, 274 (on *al-Ṣaḥīfa al-kāmila al-sajjāddiyya*); D. Gril, Prière et invocation dans le Coran, in G. Dporival and D. Pralon (eds. and comps.), *Prières méditerranéennes hier et aujourd'hui,* Provence 2000, 283-93; R. Gramlich, *Das Sendschreiben al-Qušayriš über das Sufitum,* Stuttgart 1989, chap. 99, Das Bittgebet *(duʿa),* 364-99 and passim; J. Jomier, Invocations pour les moments de la journée, in *MIDEO* 10 (1970), 271-90, repr. in id., *L'Islam vécu en Egypte,* Paris 1994, 221-40; id., *L'Islam vécu en Egypte,* Paris 1994; id., La place du Coran dans la vie quotidienne en Egypte, in *IBLA* 15 (1952), 131-65, repr. in id., *L'Islam vécu en Egypte*, Paris 1994, 185-219; M.J. Kister, Labbayka, Allāhumma, Labbayka... On a monotheistic aspect of Jāhiliyya practice, in *JSAI* 2 (1980), 33-57; L. Kohlberg, *A medieval Muslim scholar at work. Ibn Ṭāwūs and his library*, Leiden 1992 (see pp. 322-3, no. 522; 244-5, no. 346, for *"Majmūʿat Mawlānā Zayn al-ʿĀbidīn"*); Sezgin, *GAS*, i, 527 (on Niʿmat Allāh al-Jazāʾirī), 826-8 (on al-Sajjād); C. Padwick, The language of Muslim devotion, in *MW* 47 (1957), 5-21, 98-110, 194-209, 299-317; id., *Muslim devotions*, London 1961 (contains translations of some of the prayers found in al-Sajjād's works); S.M. Zwemer, The rosary in Islam, in *MW* 27 (1937), 329-43.

Pre-1800 Preoccupations of Qurʾānic Studies

Introduction

The Qurʾān refers in various ways to the teachings of the Christians and Jews, which it partially adopts, partially corrects or completely rejects (see CHRISTIANS AND CHRISTIANITY; JEWS AND JUDAISM; POLEMIC AND POLEMICAL LANGUAGE; DEBATE AND DISPUTATION). Thus it is not surprising that, from the beginning, the Qurʾān also became the object of Christian and Jewish interest. Furthermore, the fact that, for centuries, the polemical debate received the most attention, is not surprising. In the context of the times, this formed an understandable first stage for later attempts at a more scientific-objective treatment of the Qurʾān, attempts which only began in early modern times. Conditions for this later development were, on the one hand, easier access in the west to the original Arabic text of the Qurʾān, and, on the other hand, the development of Arabic philology to the standard of classical studies, which is inseparably linked with the names of Joseph Justus Scaliger (d. 1609) and Thomas Erpenius (d. 1624).

According to the so-called covenant of ʿUmar *(ʿahd ʿUmar)*, i.e. that of the second caliph (q.v.), ʿUmar b. al-Khaṭṭāb, non-Muslims were forbidden to teach their children the Qurʾān (cf. Bobzin, *Reformation*, 43 n. 35; see TEACHING AND PREACHING THE QURʾĀN). From this one can draw the conclusion that Muslims were not generally interested in allowing non-Muslims to participate in theological debates on the character of the holy book (see THEOLOGY AND THE QURʾĀN; INIMITABILITY). In any case, as "protected persons" (sing. *dhimmī*) living among Muslims, Christians and Jews must have possessed a certain basic knowledge of the most important teachings of the Qurʾān, not only through their constant contact with Muslims, but also because the Arabic language was deeply influenced by numerous qurʾānic words and idioms (see LITERATURE AND THE QURʾĀN; SLOGANS FROM THE QURʾĀN; EVERYDAY LIFE, THE QURʾĀN IN). Although there is a considerable amount of both Jewish and Christian polemical literature against Islam, it is nevertheless remarkable that the character of the Qurʾān as God's word and revelation (see WORD OF GOD; REVELATION AND INSPIRATION) did not stand at the forefront of theological debates. The questions of the unity of God (see GOD AND HIS ATTRIBUTES), the authenticity of the Jewish-Christian scriptures (see FORGERY; REVISION AND ALTERATION) and the proofs of Muḥammad's prophethood were debated much more frequently (see PROPHETS AND PROPHETHOOD; PROOF; SCRIPTURE AND THE QURʾĀN; PHILOSOPHY AND THE QURʾĀN). If Jews and Christians wrote in Arabic on subjects of central importance, such as the Qurʾān, they had to express themselves quite carefully in view of potential Muslim sensitivities. Hence, it is not surprising that the number of Arabic treatises by Jewish and Christian authors that deal exclusively with the Qurʾān is relatively low (cf. Steinschneider, *Polemische*, 313-6).

Christian-Arabic studies

Already in the third/ninth century the Nestorian scribe Abū Nūḥ al-Anbārī wrote a 'refutation of the Qurʾān' *(Tafnīd al-Qurʾān)*, which, however, is little known (cf. Graf, *GCAL*, ii, 118). Of greatest influence on the attitude of Christians to the Qurʾān was the polemical treatise in defense of Christianity published under the pseudonym ʿAbd al-Masīḥ b. Isḥāq al-Kindī (not to be confused with the famous philosopher Abū Yūsuf al-Kindī, d. after 252/865), which was conceived as a response to the invitation of the Muslim ʿAbdallāh b. Ismāʿīl al-Hāshimī. This so-called "Apology of al-Kindī" (*Risālat ʿAbd al-Masīḥ al-Kindī ilā ʿAbdallāh al-Hāshimī;* cf. Graf, *GCAL*, ii, 135-45) was in all likelihood written in the third/ninth century. It is a matter of debate whether the unknown author was a Jacobite (according to Massignon, al-Kindī; d'Alverny, Deux traductions, 91) or a Nestorian (Graf, ibid.; Troupeau, al-Kindī). Within the scope of his elaborate discussion of Islam the author also addresses the Qurʾān (al-Kindī, *Risāla*, ed. Tien, 128 f.; cf. ibid., ed. Tartar, *Dialogue*, 175 f.); the information about its origin and compilation deviates on some points from the orthodox Islamic view, however, and it does not always seem to be reliable (cf. Nöldeke, *GQ*, iii, 6 f. and 104). Above all, however, the author wants to prove the inauthentic and unoriginal nature of the Qurʾān, arguing that the contents of the Qurʾān were strongly influenced by a certain Christian monk named Sergius, alias Nestorius, who had wished to imitate the Gospels. After his death two Jews, ʿAbdallāh b. Salām and Kaʿb al-Aḥbār, had also added materials from Jewish sources. In any case, the argumentation of the *Risāla* reveals its author's own precise knowledge of the Qurʾān, from which he frequently makes exact quotations.

Al-Kindī's *Risāla* had a significant effect, particularly in the west. It belonged to the Arabic texts on Islam that, in Toledo during a visit to Spain in 1142-3 C.E., the Cluniac abbot Peter the Venerable (d. 1156 C.E.) arranged to be translated into Latin, along with the Qurʾān (cf. Kritzeck, *Peter the Venerable;* Bobzin, *Reformation*, 46 f.); thereby, the *Risāla*, under the title *"Epistula saraceni et rescriptum christiani,"* became a part of the so-called 'Corpus Toletanum.' This Corpus would, for centuries, prove to be for European scholars the most important basis for their knowledge of Islam. One century later, the *Rescriptum christiani* was integrated by Vincent of Beauvais (Vincentius Bellovacensis; d. ca. 1264) into his encyclopedic work *Speculum historiale* (written bet. 1247-59; first ed. Strasbourg 1473); from this source it reached Theodor Bibliander's 1543 edition of the Qurʾān (see below). As an original part of the 'Corpus Toletanum,' the *Risāla* was later used by authors like Dionysius Carthusianus (see below), Nicholas of Cusa (see below) and others.

Another important polemical work, which also deals in some detail with the Qurʾān, is the so-called 'Baḥīrā legend' (cf. Gottheil, Christian; Abel, Baḥīrā). It seems to follow in this respect al-Kindī's *Risāla*, when it recounts a similar tale about a Christian monk called Sergius, who was supposedly the teacher of Muḥammad and, thus, the real inspirer of the Qurʾān (cf. Graf, *GCAL*, ii, 145 f.; see MONASTICISM AND MONKS; INFORMANTS).

Of later authors the Coptic scholar al-Ṣāfī Abū l-Faḍāʾil b. al-ʿAssāl should be mentioned (d. bef. 1260 C.E.; Graf, *GCAL*, ii, 388). Within the scope of an apology for the New Testament scriptures, he also concerns himself with the Qurʾān, which he characterises as a source of revelation (Graf, ibid., 394). In the twelfth/eighteenth century, Ḥannā Maqār, in a polemical treatise against a Muslim scholar, proceeded with more precision against the Qurʾān (Graf, *GCAL*, iv, 165 f.). From among the Maronites, mention should be made of Yuḥannā al-Ḥawshabī (d. 1632; Graf, *GCAL*, iii, 304 and 345-7; Steinschneider, *Polemische*, 402), who wrote a book *Munāqaḍāt al-Qurʾān* ("On the contradictions of the Qurʾān"), and also Petrus b. Dūmīṭ Makhlūf (d. ca. 1707; Graf, *GCAL*, iii, 378-80), with his work *Miftāḥ al-bīʿa* ("The key of the church"). The Armenian-Catholic theologian Mkrtič al-Kasīḥ working in Aleppo (late seventeenth/early eighteenth century) wrote two treatises which dealt critically with the Qurʾān, namely *al-Nāsikh wa-l-mansūkh fī l-Qurʾān* ("On the abrogating and abrogated verses in the Qurʾān"; Graf, *GCAL*, iv, 83-6) as well as *Ṣidq al-Injīl wa-kidhb al-Qurʾān* ("On the truth of the Gospel and the falsehood of the Qurʾān").

Western theologians also availed themselves of the Arabic language from the seventeenth century onwards: the Franciscan Dominicus Germanus de Silesia (d. 1670; cf. Graf, *GCAL*, ii, 176 f.; Bobzin, Ein oberschlesischer Korangelehrter) in his work, *Antitheses fidei*, printed in Rome in 1638; the Jesuit Jean Amieu (d. 1653), who, from 1635, lived in Syria (Aleppo/Beirut) and wrote a refutation of the Qurʾān (Graf, *GCAL*, iv, 217); or the Capuchin Franciscus of Romontin (d. ca. 1700) who wrote an as yet unprinted refutation of the Qurʾān with the title *Īqān al-ṭarīq al-hādī ilā malakūt al-samawāt* (Graf, *GCAL*, iv, 201) at the request of Pope Innocent IV.

Eastern authors writing in Greek

The text written by the orthodox theologian John of Damascus (d. bef. 754 C.E.) in his *Liber de haeresibus* (although its authenticity is controversial) would become just as influential as al-Kindī's *Risāla*, with its hundredth (or 101st; cf. Sahas, *John of Damascus*, 57) chapter on the "heresy of the Ishmaelites" (*thrēskeia tōn Ismaēlitōn;* cf. Sahas, *John of Damascus*). In the text he also addresses the Qurʾān from which he knows the names of different sūras (like, for example, "The Young Cow" = Q 2, Sūrat al-Baqara; "The Women" = Q 4, Sūrat al-Nisāʾ; "The Table" = Q 5, Sūrat al-Māʾida). Included, however, are also names which are not traditional in Muslim sources: "The Camel (q.v.) of God" (but cf. Q 7:73; 54:27; 91:13). From some of these sūras he mentions certain regulations, e.g. the permission of polygamy with up to 4 wives (Q 4:3; see MARRIAGE AND DIVORCE; PATRIARCHY; WOMEN AND THE QURʾĀN) and the possibility of the dismissal of wives (Q 2:229 f.). Above all, however, John presents the marriage of Muḥammad to Zaynab bt. Jahsh, the wife of his own adoptive son Zayd b. Ḥāritha, in Q 33:37 f., as an example of his immorality. The reputation of John of Damascus and the wide distribution of his writings ensured that this episode became a steadfast constant of Christian polemical arguments against Islam, in the east (e.g. with al-Kindī), as in the west (e.g. Eulogius, see below), long before the appearance of the first complete Latin Qurʾān translation in the west (see TRANSLATIONS OF THE QURʾĀN).

The work of the Byzantine author Niketas of Byzantium became similarly influential (d. after 886 C.E.; but cf. Sahas, *John of Damascus*, 77 n. 1, where his dates are given as 842-912 C.E.). He wrote one of the oldest Byzantine polemical treatises against the Qurʾān (*Anatropē tēs para tou Arabos Mōamet plastographētheisēs biblou;* ed. J.-P. Migne, *PG*, cv, cols. 669-805; Ger. trans. Förstel, *Schriften zum Islam*). Not on account of his own knowledge of the original Arabic (Khoury, *Théologiens byzantins*, 119 f.), but rather on the basis of a Greek Qurʾān translation already available to him (Trapp, Gab es eine byzantinische Koranübersetzung?), in the second segment of his book he deals in detail with Q 2 to 18, from which he quotes numerous verses verbatim. The rest of the sūras are treated only summarily. The sūras, the first of which he does not consider to belong in the Qurʾān, he labels *logos, mythos* or *mytharion,* and calls them by their mostly translated, but now and then also simply transcribed, names. Most frequently cited are translated verses which refer to biblical figures, especially, of course, Jesus (q.v.). All together Niketas views the Qurʾān as an "unreasonable, unsystematically thrown together, shoddy piece of work, filled with lies, forgeries, fables and contradictions; his language is neither that of a Prophet, nor does it correspond with the dignity of a religious book or legal code" (Güterbock, *Der Islam,* 26 f.). Especially important is the misinterpretation of *al-ṣamad* (Q 112:2), one of the qurʾānic attributes of God, that Niketas, following the Greek translation of the Qurʾān at his disposal, reproduces as 'entirely compact' (*holosphyros,* variant: *holosphairos,* 'completely round'). He thereby provides the Qurʾān with a materialistic image of God, which is completely foreign to it in principle. This view was taken over by later theologians, as, for example, Euthymios Zigabenos (fl. twelfth century C.E.) in his *Panoplia dogmatikē* (*"Dogmatic panoply,"* Migne, *PG,* cxxx, 1348B), or in the so-called 'abjuration formula' for Muslim converts (Migne, *PG,* cxl, 124-36; cf. Montet, Rituel d'abjuration, 155).

From the time of the Palaiologues (fourteenth/fifteenth century), who deal with the Qurʾān in more detail, later Byzantine authors belong completely to the tradition of Latin authors (see below, Ricoldo).

Western authors writing in Latin

Use of the Qurʾān in Latin began on the Iberian peninsula, not surprisingly because of the strong presence there of Muslims. What is more surprising is that the Spanish Christian theologians in their polemic against the Qurʾān quite evidently fell back on arguments which had their origin in the tradition of eastern Christianity. Thus the author Eulogius of Cordoba (d. 859 C.E.) in his *Liber apologeticus martyrum* (Migne, *PL,* cxv, col. 860) quotes Q 33:37 to criticize Muḥammad's adulterous behaviour (see ADULTERY AND FORNICATION) — in exactly the same way as al-Kindī had already done in his *Risāla* and John of Damascus had done before him. The Jewish apostate Peter Alphonsi (Rabbi Moses Sephardi, d. after 1130 C.E.), who was one of the significant mediators of Arabic science to the occident, in his *Dialogi in quibus impiae Judaeorum opiniones… confutantur* also addressed the teachings of Islam, whose implausibility he tried to demonstrate with some correctly translated qurʾānic citations (Q 2:256; 4:157; 10:99 f., 108 f.; 11:118; 18:29; 29:46; 93:6-8; 109:1-4, 6; cf. Monnot, Citations coraniques).

The most important basic work for the qurʾānic knowledge and qurʾānic criticism of late-medieval authors was made, at the instigation of Peter the Venerable (1142-3 C.E.), by the English scholar Robert of Ketton (or Robert of Chester; more precise dates unknown). This was a quite inexact Latin paraphrase of the Qurʾān. Its influence, through the Basel printed editions of 1543 and 1550, and the translations based on it in Italian (1547), German (1616; 1623²) and Dutch (1641), however, extended far into the seventeenth century (cf. Bobzin, *Reformation,* 262 f.). Peter the Venerable himself wrote a shorter *Summa totius haeresis saracenorum,* a longer (now incomplete) treatise *Contra sectam saracenorum* and one *Epistula de translatione sua* addressed to Bernard of Clairvaux (d. 1153 C.E.), writings which, together with the paraphrase of the Qurʾān and the *Rescriptum christiani* from the *Risāla* of al-Kindī, became part of the so-called 'Corpus Toletanum.' Peter understood the Qurʾān as a 'law' *(lex)* or 'collection of regulations' *(collectaneum praeceptorum),* but held it to be inferior to the Bible, because it was compiled from 'Jewish fables and heretical gossip' *(tam ex fabulis Iudaicis quam ex haereticorum neniis confecta; Summa).* He maintained that, even if some words seem identical in the Bible and Qurʾān — as, for example, "word," "mind" or "envoy" — nevertheless, as he works out clearly, quite different concepts underlie them. In his argumentation he quotes only relatively rarely directly from the Qurʾān, and occasionally from the *Rescriptum christiani.* The *Annotationes* accompanying the qurʾānic paraphrase, which were only partly reproduced in Bibliander's edition of 1543 (i, 224-30; cf. d'Alverny, Deux traductions, 98 f.), have but recently come to be appreciated as informative pointers to the employment of the Qurʾān and Islamic commentaries by Mozarabic Christians (Burman, *Religious polemic,* 84 f.). They begin with a list of the so-called "beautiful names" of God *(al-asmāʾ al-ḥusnā)* and also contain a clue to the linguistic resemblance of Arabic with Hebrew. For example, the word 'Azoara' for the Arabic *al-sūra* is explained with reference to the Latin *vultus* 'face' (i.e. <Arabic *ṣūra!*) which points to the fact that the difference between the sibilants *s* and *ṣ* probably no longer existed.

Evidently, the anonymous treatise *Liber denudationis sive ostensionis aut patefaciens* (also known under the title of *Contrarietas alfolica;* cf. d'Alverny and Vajda, Marc de Tolède, 124 f.), which exists in a unique manuscript (Paris, BN Lat. 3394), and also follows an Arabic model, should be viewed in connection with the second complete qurʾānic translation by Mark of Toledo (d. after 1234 C.E.; cf. Bobzin, *Reformation,* 55 f.). It contains about 75 explicit Qurʾān citations, which, like the entire book, are translated in a very literal fashion. Furthermore, the sūras are usually designated by their titles and, in addition, different names are also used for the same sūra, as is familiar from the Islamic tradition. Regarding the origin of the Qurʾān, the familiar ḥadīth (cf. Nöldeke, *GQ,* i, 48 n. 3) is cited (see ḤADĪTH AND THE QURʾĀN), namely, that the Qurʾān would be "revealed" to Muḥammad "in seven *aḥruf,* of which every one would be good" (*descendit Alchoranus super me in septem litteris, et quicquid satis est sufficit; Liber denudationis,* chap. 6, par. 1, ed. Burman, *Religious polemic,* 274). The Latin text explains that these seven readings (see READINGS OF THE QURʾĀN) — this is what is meant here by *litterae* — are associated with the names Nafe (Nāfiʿ), Ebou Omar (Abū ʿAmr), Homra (Ḥamza), Elkessar (al-Kisāʾī), Asser (ʿĀṣim), filius Ketir (Ibn Kathīr) and filius Amer (Ibn ʿĀmir), who are also the founders of seven so-called "canonical" readings (see RECITERS OF THE QURʾĀN; RECITATION OF THE QURʾĀN). The text explains that they were not, however, contemporaries of Muḥammad, because during his lifetime only Abdalla filius Messoud (ʿAbdallāh b. Masʿūd), Zeid filius Thabet (Zayd b. Thābit), Othman filius Offan (ʿUthmān b. ʿAffān) and Ebi filius Chab (Ubayy b. Kaʿb) would have been familiar with the Qurʾān. Whether or not filius Abitaleb (ʿAlī b. Abī Ṭālib [q.v.]) was familiar with the Qurʾān, is controversial. Nevertheless, the Qurʾāns of the aforementioned people would have been different, which is why Mereban filius Elhekem (Marwān b. al-Ḥakam, i.e. the fourth Umayyad caliph, active 684-5) had them burned and a new text produced (see COLLECTION OF THE QURʾĀN; CODICES OF THE QURʾĀN; TEXTUAL HISTORY OF THE

QUR'ĀN). It was only after this that the abovementioned seven appeared as readers characterised as *praefecti*, who "contradicted each other so much in their grammar as in their use of idiom" (*contradixerunt sibi in gramatica et idiomatibus propriis, Liber denundationis*, chap. 6, par. 2, ed. Burman, *Religious polemic*, 276). Nevertheless, other accounts are mentioned which indicate that an official codex of the Qur'ān did not yet exist at Muḥammad's death. Only at the instigation of Abū Bakr was all the available material collected and assembled by him to become the Qur'ān that exists today (see MUṢḤAF). The purpose of these reports is to prove the unreliability or inauthenticity of the Qur'ān as a holy book. A chapter about the 'impure' things *(immundita)* also occupies a considerable amount of space, along with (the most extensive part) the chapter on the numerous contradictions to be observed in the Qur'ān. In the treatment of particular passages, the author relies upon a noteworthy knowledge of Islamic commentaries and traditional literature (see EXEGESIS OF THE QUR'ĀN: CLASSICAL AND MEDIEVAL). Although the work is extant in only a single manuscript, it had a notable effect and its use by some later authors can be demonstrated (see Ricoldo below).

The mendicant orders of the Dominicans and Franciscans, which arose as a consequence of the Crusades, counted among their tasks the resumption of attempts to convert the Muslims. For this purpose, at the instigation of Raymund of Pennaforte (d. 1275 C.E.), language academies for Arabic came into being in Spain and north Africa (cf. Altaner, Sprachstudien; id., Die fremdsprachliche). A graduate of one of these was Raymond Martin (Ramón Martí; Lat. Raymundus Martini; d. ca. 1284 C.E.; cf. Berthier, Maître), who, in his works *Pugio fidei aduersus Mauros et Iudaeos* and *Explanatio simboli apostolorum*, reveals a detailed knowledge of Arabic source texts including the Qur'ān, as well as the appropriate traditional literature (cf. Cortabarría Beitía, Connaissance; id., Sources arabes; see TRADITIONAL DISCIPLINES OF QUR'ĀNIC STUDY). Whether the so-called *Quadruplex reprobatio* can also be ascribed to him remains a matter of dispute (cf. Daniel, *Islam and the west*, 31; Burman, *Religious polemic*, 205 n. 44; Hernando y Delgado, De Seta Machometi, 356 f.). The so-called language canon of the Council of Vienna (1311/12 C.E.; cf. Altaner, Raymundus Lullus) goes back to the untiring activity of the Catalan Raymond Lull (Ramón Llull; Lat. Raymundus Lullus; d. ca. 1316 C.E.) to which later appeal was repeatedly made, above all for the study of the Arabic Qur'ān text. Lull himself possessed excellent knowledge of Arabic (cf. Brummer, Ramon Lull; Lohr, *Christianus arabicus*), which is revealed in many of his works; his qur'ānic knowledge comes to light especially in his *Disputatio Raymundi christiani et Hamar saraceni*, which was written in 1307 C.E. (cf. Daiber, Der Missionar). Belonging also to the Spanish context but known only in summary form, is the treatise *Sobre la seta Mahometana* by the archbishop of Jaen, Pedro Pascual (d. 1300 C.E.), who was, admittedly, later criticized by John of Segovia (see below) for not being faithful to the text. According to John of Segovia, Pedro reads teachings in the text of the Qur'ān which it does not contain (cf. Cabanelas Rodriguez, *Juan de Segovia*, 139).

To William of Tripoli (fl. second half of the thirteenth century C.E.), a Dominican from Syria, about whose life little is known, has, until now, been attributed the work *De statu sarracenorum* (see Prutz, *Kulturgeschichte* for the text edition), in which there are also reports on the content and creation of the Qur'ān. It has recently been proved that not this, but rather a similar work with the title *Notitia de Machometo et de libro legis qui dicitur Alcoran et de continentia eius et quid dicat de fide Domini nostri Iesu Christi* was written by him (cf. Engel's comments on his edition of William's work). The creation of the Qurʾān, according to William, occurred thus: 40 years after Muḥammad's death there were only seven of his Companions alive (see COMPANIONS OF THE PROPHET). These individuals then planned to produce a single "teaching" *(doctrina),* to be called the "law of Muḥammad" *(lex Machometi),* similar to the Jews' possessing the Torah of Moses and the Christians, the gospel of Christ. The composition of this work they delegated to 'Hesman filius Effran' (i.e. ʿUthmān b. ʿAffān) from Damascus, which he did "with hidden profundity" *(profunditate obscura).* Q 1, which is completely and correctly translated, is regarded by William as a "preface" *(prefatio)* and its content as an "expression of thanks and a prayer" (see FĀTIḤA). Q 2 counts as the first chapter, "concerning the cow" *(De vacca);* the shorthand *alif-lām-mīm* in verse 1 represents the word *alam* 'suffering' (see MYSTERIOUS LETTERS; ARABIC LANGUAGE). Special value is placed upon the qurʾānic references to Christ and the virgin Mary (q.v.), that were for the most part cited directly, above all from Q 3 and 19.

One of the most influential medieval works on the Qurʾān was written by the Florentine Dominican Ri(c)coldo da Monte Croce (d. ca. 1320 C.E.), who, between 1288 and 1300, worked as a preacher in the Middle East. His treatise *Contra legem sarracenorum* is based upon excellent knowledge of the Arabic qurʾānic text; nevertheless, he used passages from the *Liber denudationis,* as, for example, with respect to the creation of the qurʾānic text. Here, the above quoted ḥadīth on the seven readings is read as follows: *Descendit Alchoranus super me in VII uiris* [instead of: *litteris*]..., which admittedly fits better with the naming of the readings. Also with some of his almost 70 qurʾānic quotations, Ricoldo follows the text of the *Liber denudationis.* He calls the sūras always by their names, not by their numbers.

One can recognize Ricoldo's work both as a "classic" and as a very systematic summary of all Christian objections to the Qurʾān (cf. Bobzin, Treasury of heresies, 165 f.), which are, in brief: the Qurʾān is nothing but a mixture of older Christian heresies that had already been denounced by earlier church authorities. Because it is predicted by neither the Hebrew Bible nor the New Testament, the Qurʾān cannot be accepted as divine law; for the rest, the Qurʾān refers in some cases specifically to the Bible as an authority. Similarly, the theory of the textual falsification *(taḥrīf)* cannot be accepted (see REVISION AND ALTERATION). Regarding its style (see LANGUAGE AND STYLE OF THE QURʾĀN), the Qurʾān does not correspond with any "holy" writing; above all, its many fantastic stories make it impossible to accept a divine origin for the Qurʾān (see NARRATIVES; MYTHS AND LEGENDS IN THE QURʾĀN; LITERARY STRUCTURES OF THE QURʾĀN). Some ethical concepts would contradict basic philosophical convictions (see ETHICS AND THE QURʾĀN; PHILOSOPHY AND THE QURʾĀN). Above all, however, the Qurʾān contains numerous internal contradictions, apart from its entirely obvious lack of order (see FORM AND STRUCTURE OF THE QURʾĀN; CHRONOLOGY AND THE QURʾĀN). Furthermore, the Qurʾān was not witnessed by a miracle (q.v.). The Qurʾān goes against reason; this is apparent both in Muḥammad's life, which is branded as immoral, as well as in some blasphemous views on divine topics. The Qurʾān preaches force and allows injustice (see EXPEDITIONS AND BATTLES; WAR; FIGHTING; PATH OR WAY; JIHĀD; JUSTICE AND INJUSTICE; VIOLENCE). The history of the text of the Qurʾān ultimately proves the uncertainty of the text.

In the year 1385 C.E., Ricoldo's work was translated into Greek by the Byzantine scholar Demetrios Kydones (d. ca. 1398). This translation led to a late blooming of polemic literature against Islam, which is connected with the writings of two emperors (cf. Mazal, Zur geistigen Auseinandersetzung): John VI Kantakuzenos (r. 1347-54 C.E.) composed *Four arguments against the heresy of the Saracens* and *Four speeches against Muḥammad* (printed in Basel in 1543 in Bibliander's qurʾānic volume), and Manuel II Palaiologos (r. 1391-1425 C.E.) composed his *Dialogue with a Persian on the religion of the Christians* (cf. ed. Förstel; Trapp, *Manuel II. Palaiologos*). In both works, the traces of the work of Ricoldo-Kydones are clearly recognizable.

On the basis of the Greek text of Kydones, there followed a Latin retranslation by an otherwise unknown Bartholomaeus Picenus de Monte Arduo. The name of the author appears here, following the Greek model (here 'Ricoldo' became 'Rikardos'), as 'Richardus'. The first imprint of the Latin original appeared in 1500 in Seville under the title *Improbatio Alcorani* (with a Spanish translation *Reprobación del Alcorán* in 1501), again in Toledo in 1502, as well as in Venice in 1607 under the different title of *Propugnaculum fidei*. In many respects defective, the aforementioned Latin retranslation appeared for the first time in Rome in 1506 under the title *Confutatio Alcorani seu legis Saracenorum*. On the basis of this text, Martin Luther (d. 1546) composed his *Verlegung* [= refutation] *des Alcoran Bruder Richardi* (Wittenberg 1542); on the one hand, Luther shortened the text where it appeared too scholastic, on the other hand, he expanded it around some passages connected with the contemporary Turkish threat (cf. Bobzin, *Reformation*, 142 f.). Theodor Bibliander printed in his collection of 1543 (see below) both the Greek version of Kydones and its Latin retranslation: the latter, as it happens, was printed far more frequently than the original text!

The influence of the Turkish wars

The Turkish wars had a very great influence on European qurʾānic studies. The conquest of Constantinople in 1453 C.E. by the Ottoman sultan Mehmet II, which announced the final end of the Byzantine empire, caused, and was preceded by, a lively production of treatises on the "religion of the Turks." At the same time, a key roll fell to the German cardinal Nicholas of Cusa (Nikolaus of Kues; Lat. Nicolaus Cusanus, d. 1464). At the council of Basel (1431-49), he had become acquainted with the Spanish theologian, and later cardinal, John of Segovia (Juan de Segovia; d. ca. 1458), and through him he gained knowledge of the 'Corpus Toletanum.' During a trip to Constantinople on behalf of Pope Eugene IV (in 1437), he had certain passages from an Arabic qurʾānic text explained to him in a Franciscan monastery. He then came across the Latin Qurʾān translation from the 'Corpus Toletanum' in a Dominican convent. With the encouragement of Nicholas, the Carthusian monk Dionysius Rijkel, originally from the Netherlands, (Dionysius Carthusianus, d. 1471), who accompanied him on his trips from 1451 and after, wrote an extensive treatise against the Qurʾān: *Contra Alchoranum et sectam Machometicam* (printed in Cologne in 1533; German trans. Strasbourg 1540). It is based totally upon the writings of the 'Corpus Toletanum' and provides a refutation of various qurʾānic passages, quite schematically organized according to the sūras. Following the end of the Council of Basel (1449), John of Segovia withdrew from all church political activity, and busied himself with the study of Islam. In his treatise *De mittendo gladio divini spiritus in corda Saracenorum* ("On sending the sword of the divine spirit into the hearts of the Saracens"), he emphasized the importance of a thorough knowledge of the Qurʾān for fruitful disputation with the Muslims that could promote living together in peace. With his studies of the Qurʾān, the imperfection of the old Toledan translation became evident to him (as did that of other writings as, for example, those of Pedro de Pascual). After he moved in 1454 to the monastery of Aiton in Savoy, he succeeded in persuading the Muslim jurist ʿĪsā Dhā Jābir (alias Yça Gidelli) to undertake the journey from his home town Segovia to Aiton. There they worked for four months (winter 1455/56) on a new Qurʾān edition, one which contained a Castilian translation next to the Arabic text (cf. Cabanelas Rodriguez, Juan de Segovia; Wiegers, *Islamic literature*). Of this work, to which Juan added another Latin translation, only the prologue exists today. In it, a convincing criticism of the translation practice of Robert of Ketton is found.

In ca. 1460-1, Nicholas of Cusa himself composed his *Cribratio Alcorani* ("An examination of the Qurʾān"). It is dedicated to Pope Pius II (r. 1458-64), who imposed a crusading policy against the Turks. Nicholas' treatise is to be understood as a counter-programme: although he maintains the heretical nature of Islam, he is more willing to stress what Christianity and Islam have in common, as these clearly appear in the Qurʾān, the foundational document of Islam. For his understanding of the Qurʾān, he depends — along with the writings from the 'Corpus Toletanum' — above all, on the work of Ricoldo. As a consequence, he sticks to apologetic rather than philosophical arguments. Certainly the importance of the work is often overestimated for the 'dialogue' (cf. Flasch, *Nikolaus von Kues*, 544 f.).

The refutation of the Qurʾān by the Italian Petrus de Pennis (second half of the fifteenth century), *Tractatus contra Alcoranum et Mahometum* (Paris BN, Ms lat. 3646) — which relies above all on Ricoldo and Petrus Alphonsi — is still unpublished (cf. Daniel, *Islam and the west*, 76 f.).

A new and successful type of controversial literature was created by the Spanish Franciscan Alfonso de Spina (d. ca. 1491) with his work, *Fortalitium fidei in universos Christiane religionis hostes* ("A fortress of belief in view of all the enemies of the Christian religion"), printed in Strasbourg before 1471. As for Judaism, one chapter of the book is dedicated exclusively to Islam, with a section 'On the state of the teaching and the law of Mohammed' *(De qualitate doctrinae et legis Machometi)*. For his understanding of the Qurʾān, Alfonso, in addition to the work of Ricoldo, depends on Ramón Martís' *Pugio fidei* as well as the writings of John of Segovia. Alfonso's *Fortalitium* was reprinted with extraordinary frequency in the fifteenth century, and must be counted as an important source of qurʾānic knowledge in theological circles — Luther also demonstrably used this work (cf. Bobzin, *Reformation*, 77). In a very similar way to Alfonso de Spina, much later authors continue to explain Islam mainly on the basis of a brief representation of the teaching of the Qurʾān. Authors of works "On the truth of the Christian religion" *(De veritate religionis Christianae)*, as those of Juan Luis Vives (d. 1540) or Hugo Grotius (d. 1645), devote a separate book or chapter to the topic of Islam.

From the beginning of the sixteenth century comes the very influential writing of an Aragonese renegade by the name of Juan Andrés (latinised to Johannes Andreas Maurus) about whose life, except the year of his conversion to Christianity (1487), nothing is known. His work appeared in 1515 in Valencia under the title *Libro nueuamente imprimido que se llama confusion dela secta mahomatica y del alcoran* (Bobzin, Bemerkungen zu Juan Andrés) and was quickly translated into several other European languages (Italian, French, Latin, Dutch, English, German). Evidently, this writing was a kind of preparation for an intended complete Aragonese translation of the Qurʾān. Interlaced into the text are about 70 translated Qurʾān quotations; these were first of all provided in Latin transcription, and then translated. For his interpretation, Juan relies upon well-known authorities such as Azamahxeri (i.e. al-Zamakhsharī, d. 538/1144) and Buhatia (i.e. Ibn ʿAṭiyya al-Andalusī, d. 546/1151). In his view, the Qurʾān was divided into four books *(libros)* by the caliph ʿUthmān: Book 1 contains 5 chapters (*capitulos* or sūras, *cuar,* or *cura*) with Q 2 to 6; Book 2 contains 12 chapters (Q 7 to 18); Book 3 contains 19 chapters (Q 19 to 37). For the first three books Juan names each sūra by name, which deviate occasionally from their familiar titles (thus Q 9 is called *la espada* by Juan, Ar. *Sūrat al-Sayf,* that is, after Q 9:5, the so-called *āyat al-sayf;* cf. Bobzin, Bemerkungen zu Juan Andrés, 544 n. 58; see VERSES). The fourth part comprises 175 chapters, so that altogether there are 211 chapters — the number 175 probably occurred as a result of an old error, understandable from the Roman manner of writing the numbers for 75. Without that, not counting Q 1 as well as Q 113 and 114, the number 111 arises, which is thoroughly compatible with Islamic traditions (for example in Ibn Masʿūd). For the rest, Juan uses (next to the popular prophetic biography *Kitāb al-Shifāʾ fī taʿrīf ḥuqūq al-Muṣṭafā* of the Mālikī judge ʿIyāḍ b. Mūsā, d. 543/1149; see SĪRA AND THE QURʾĀN) a further unspecified *sīra* work *(acear),* quoting from it the first sūras (Q 96:1-5; 74:1-5 and 93:1-3) in a traditional chronology of revelation. Juan offers the oldest Latin attestation of a division of the Qurʾān into four *rubʿ,* used in Andalusian manuscripts and still today in Maghrebian editions, in which, certainly, a few differences are detectable, especially with regard to the end of the third and/or the beginning of the fourth section (today it is usually divided between Q 35 and 36; see MANUSCRIPTS OF THE QURʾĀN; ORNAMENTATION AND ILLUMINATION). Other anti-qurʾānic works printed in Spain do not appear to have had any effect outside Spain, as, for example, B. Bernardo Pérez de Chinchón, *Libro llamado Antialcorano: que quiere dezir contra el Alcoran de Mahoma,* (Valencia 1532), or Lope de Obregón, *Confutacion del Alcoran y secta Mahometana, sacado de sus propios libros, y de la vida del mesmo Mahoma* (Granada 1555; cf. Bunes Ibarra, Evolución).

Qurʾānic studies in the sixteenth century

Similar to the trend of the middle of the fifteenth century, the renewed strengthening of the Ottoman Turks from the time of the accession to government of Sultan Selīm (1512-20) had a more or less direct effect on the interest of scholars of the Orient in the Qurʾān as the "Bible of the Turks." Into this period falls the first Arabic imprint of the complete Qurʾān by the Venetian printer Alessandro de Paganini (ca. 1537/38; cf. Nuovo, Il Corano arabo ritrovato; Bobzin, Jean Bodin; Borrmans, Observations; see PRINTING OF THE QURʾĀN). This Qurʾān edition, which was most likely intended for export to the Ottoman empire, was so riddled with errors that it was unacceptable to Muslim users. That the Pope had it burned is a legend attested to since the start of the seventeenth century (cf. Nallino, Una cinquecentesca edizione). It has been proven, already through the works of older scholars like Johann Michael Lang (see below), Johann Buxtorf IV (d. 1732; *De Alcorani editione Arabica,* in Hase and Lampe, *Bibliotheca* [1722], 271 f.) and Giovanni Bernardo de Rossi (d. 1831; *De Corano ara-*

bico Venetiis Paganini typis impresso, Parma 1805) — that two European scholars possessed a copy of this Qurʾān: Teseo Ambrogio degli Albonesi (d. 1540), whose copy is still extant (Bobzin, *Reformation,* 184), and Guillaume Postel (d. 1581). Postel later dealt in detail with the Qurʾān in his extensive work *De orbis terrae concordia libri IV* (Basel 1544), from which — in a manner noteworthy for the time — remarkably he translated exactly an extensive section from Q 2, as well as numerous further extracts (survey in Bobzin, *Reformation,* 479 f.). In his *Grammatica arabica* (Paris ca. 1539), which had appeared a few years earlier, he had printed Q 1 in still quite clumsy Arabic characters and presented it along with a translation (Bobzin, *Reformation,* 470 f.; Secret, Guillaume Postel). In his polemical work *Alcorani seu legis Mahometi et Evangelistarum concordiae Liber* ("The book of the agreement between the Qurʾān and the law of Mohammed and the Protestant"; Paris 1543), Postel draws a parallel between the origin of Islam and the new "heresy" of the Lutherans.

The south German scholar and diplomat Johann Albrecht von Widmanstetter (Widmanstadius, d. 1557) possessed a small collection of mainly Andalusian Qurʾāns (today housed in Munich, at the Bayerische Staatsbibliothek); his work *Mahometis Abdallae filii theologia dialogo explicata,* which appeared in 1543, contained, next to the well-known text from the 'Corpus Toletanum,' the so-called *Doctrina Machometi* (called by him the *Theologia Mahometis*), also an abridged version of the Toledan Qurʾān translation and some *Notationes,* probably his own, in which, above all, connections were shown between qurʾānic and Jewish teachings (cf. Bobzin, *Reformation,* 349 f.).

A more enduring effect than the works of Postel and Widmanstetter was achieved by the collected volume of the Zurich theologian Theodor Bibliander (1504-64), the *Machumetis Saracenorum principis, eiusque successorum vitae, ac doctrina, ipseque Alcoran* (Basel 1543), published and produced by the Basel printer Johannes Oporinus. Next to the texts of the 'Corpus Toletanum,' this work also contained important polemical treatises *(Confutationes),* like, among others, the *Cribratio Alcorani* of Nicholas of Cusa, the *Confutatio Alcorani* of Ricoldo in the Greek version of Demetrios Kydones as well as in the Latin of Bartholomäus Picenus of Monte Arduo (cf. Bobzin, *Reformation,* 217 f.). Moreover, the book could only appear after violent discussions about whether such a "heretical" book might be printed in a "Christian" city like Basel. A letter that Martin Luther sent to the Council of the City of Basel in December 1542 contributed considerably to this debate (cf. on this dispute Bobzin, *Reformation,* 181-209). As far as the old Toledan translation of Robert of Ketton was concerned, Bibliander had only limited possibilities to correct this text, which he himself described as "very corrupted" (*depravatissimum;* Bibliander, *Machumetis...,* i, 230). Given his less than profound knowledge of Arabic, he was only able to add some marginal corrections or comments in his own *Annotationes* (Bibliander, *Machumetis...,* i, 230 f.); for example, he gave individual Arabic words, usually proper names, using Hebrew script (cf. Bobzin, *Reformation,* 237 f.). For his publishing activities, however, he used an Arabic qurʾānic manuscript, which revealed some marginal glosses and contained the abbreviation system fundamental to the study of editions of the didactic poem, the *Shāṭibiyya* (cf. Nöldeke, *GQ,* iii, 220; cf. Hottinger below).

Qurʾānic studies in the seventeenth century

The increasing professionalism of Arabic studies in the universities meant that increased attention was directed also to qurʾānic studies. In a letter to Etienne Hubert, the great philologist Joseph Justus

Scaliger had already clearly stated that one had to study the Qur'ān in order to learn the grammatical subtleties of Arabic (cf. Bobzin, *Reformation,* 192 n. 230; see GRAMMAR AND THE QUR'ĀN). Scaliger's most important student, the Orientalist Thomas Erpenius from Leiden (d. 1624), published accordingly in 1617 the Arabic text of Q 12 (Sūrat Yūsuf, "Joseph") together with two Latin translations — one very literal interlinear translation and one substantially freer (cf. Schnurrer, *Bibliotheca arabica,* no. 368). In the introduction, the old Toledan translation is vehemently criticized: "It is seldom that it expresses faithfully the true sense of the Arabic" *(veram Arabismi sententiam satis raro fideliter exprimens)*. On the other hand, the necessity of a serious study of the Qur'ān based exclusively on the Arabic text is emphasized. Accordingly, in the following period the exertions of a great number of scholars went into the publication, first of all of an Arabic text of the Qur'ān, accompanied where possible with a (mainly Latin) translation. The promise given by Erpenius in his *Historia Josephi patriarchae* to publish a complete Arabic Qur'ān with a newer Latin translation, was not, however, to be fulfilled. On the other hand, he printed in his second Arabic grammar, the *Rudimenta linguae arabicae* (Leiden 1620; cf. Schnurrer, *Bibliotheca arabica,* no. 55), for practice purposes, the text of Q 64 with a Latin translation and grammatical explanations; in a reprint of this grammar in 1656 (*Arabicae linguae tyrocinium;* cf. Schnurrer, *Bibliotheca arabica,* no. 81) Erpenius' successor, Jacob Golius (d. 1667), added two further sūras (Q 31 and 61). In the preface to his *Lexicon arabico-latinum,* which appeared in 1653, and which also draws on the vocabulary of the Qur'ān, Golius promised to publish an Arabic Qur'ān edition (cf. Juynboll, Zeventiende-eeuwsche Beoefenaars, 168 f.) just like his compatriot Ludovicus de Dieu (d. 1642), but neither did so. Rather, it was amateurs who repeatedly tried to produce their own Arabic types and to print at least a part of the Qur'ān. In this context should be mentioned the Breslau physician Petrus Kirsten (d. 1640) and the Zwickau pre-university teacher Johannes Zechendorff (d. 1662). The former printed the text of Q 1 in his *Tria specimina characterum arabicorum* (Breslau 1608; cf. Schnurrer, *Bibliotheca arabica,* no. 45); the latter presented Q 101 and 103, as well as Q 61 and 78 respectively, with literal translations, in two pamphlets (*Suratae unius atque alterius textum…* as well as *Specimen suratarum… ex Alcorani,* both Zwickau around 1638; cf. Schnurrer, *Bibliotheca arabica,* no. 369 f.). Also typical was the Arabic type developed in Altdorf in 1640 by the Orientalist Theodor Hackspan (1607-59) in his work *Fides et leges Mohammaedis exhibitae ex Alkorani manuscripto duplici, praemissis institutionibus arabicis* (Altdorf 1656; cf. Schnurrer, *Bibliotheca arabica,* no. 74); for the brief introduction to the Arabic language contained in this work he relied exclusively on qur'ānic material. Occasionally in the absence of suitable Arabic letter types the Arabic text was also printed in Hebrew characters. That is the case with the bilingual Qur'ān extract that Christian Ravius (d. 1677) brought out in the year 1646 in Amsterdam under the title *Prima tredecim partium Alcorani, Arabico-latini;* here the Arabic text (Q 1 to Q 2:80) is printed in the so-called Raschi-type, to which a transcription in Latin letters was added (cf. Schnurrer, *Bibliotheca arabica,* no. 371). On the other hand, Q 30 and 48 are presented in Hebrew block-writing with a Latin translation by the Augsburg scholar Matthias Friedrich Beck in his *Specimen arabicum* (Augsburg 1688; cf. Schnurrer, *Bibliotheca arabica,* no. 374). Taking up the efforts of Erpenius, Johann Georg Nissel (d. 1662), working in Leiden, published two sūras of the Qurʾān (Q 14 and 15), that treated biblical subjects: *Historia de Abrahamo et de Gomorra-Sodomitica e versione Alcorani* (Leiden 1658; cf. Schnurrer, *Bibliotheca arabica,* no. 372). The first attempt by Johann Andreas Danz (d. 1727) to publish a complete, bilingual Arabic-Latin Qurʾān, did not get further than Q 2:66 (cf. Schnurrer, *Bibliotheca arabica,* no. 375; Bojer, Einiges über die arabische Druckschriftensammlung, 87).

A temporary climax of early, philologically-oriented Qurʾān studies is represented by two Qurʾān editions, which appeared shortly after each other in Hamburg and Padua in the last decade of the century. The Hamburg head pastor Abraham Hinckelmann (1652-95), who had received an excellent education in Oriental studies in Wittenberg in 1668-72, had control over a remarkable collection of Qurʾān manuscripts that enabled him to publish a reliable text. This came out in 1694 under the title *Al-Coranus s. lex Islamitica Muhammedis, filii Abdallae pseudoprophetae* (cf. Schnurrer, *Bibliotheca arabica,* no. 376): the Arabic text cannot be assigned unambiguously to any specific reading tradition. The verse numbering also does not always agree with the well-known numbering systems. Hinckelmann offered no translation in his edition, but rather only the Arabic text; in his extensive Latin preface he not only explained, very generally, the value of the employment of Arabic literature, but also stressed that all Christian theologians should read the Qurʾān, as a fundamental work, in the original language, thus in Arabic. He justified his renunciation of a translation on the grounds that a large part of the Qurʾān can be understood simply, but that a smaller, difficult to understand part would make disproportionately large philological efforts necessary with, for example, recourse to commentaries and other special literature. The fact that the text beings with the invocation formula 'I.N.J.C.,' *'In Nomine Jesu Christi'* is a curiosity to be considered. An extensive errata-list at the end of the edition indicates that the text is not completely flawless. Above all, however, certain peculiarities of the qurʾānic orthography (q.v.) are not taken into consideration by Hinckelmann. In spite of all its imperfections as seen from our current point of view, herewith for the first time in the western scholarly world people had access to a printed Qurʾān text, which remained the essential basis for qurʾānic study until the appearance of Gustav Flügel's text edition (1834; cf. Braun, Hamburger Koran).

The extensive folio that the Italian priest Ludovico Marracci (d. 1700) brought out in 1698 in Padua, has a completely different character from Hinckelmann's edition. While Hinckelmann pursued primarily philological goals, Marracci's work belongs principally in the category of church polemics against Islam; it nevertheless, at the same time, is notable for its philological qualities. Already in 1691, Marracci had brought out a four volume refutation of the Qurʾān in Rome, under the title *Prodromus in refutationem Alcorani,* which contained numerous Qurʾān quotations in Arabic writing with very precise Latin translations. The four volumes follow in their subject matter the expected format of polemical theology: Muḥammad was not predicted by any prophecy (Book 1), his mission was not attested by any miracle at all (Book 2), the dogmas of the "Islamic sect" do not conform with the divine truth (Book 3), and a comparison of the laws of the Gospel and the Qurʾān proves the falsity of the beliefs of that "sect of the Hagarene" (Book 4). The comprehensive Qurʾān edition of 1698 (*Alcorani textus universus Ex correctioribus Arabum exemplaribus summa fide, atque pulcherrimis characteribus descriptus;* cf. Schnurrer, *Bibliotheca arabica,* no. 377) contained the complete Arabic qurʾānic text, along with the entire *Prodromus*, a description of the life of Muḥammad and an introduction to the Qurʾān — in addition to a very exact Latin translation. The Arabic text is indeed not printed consecutively, but rather divided into topical sections; the Latin translation also follows it. Then very extensive passages from special Islamic literature are provided in the original and partly in translation. Finally, a detailed refutation of the corresponding Qurʾān section from a Catholic perspective follows. Especially remarkable and indicative is the third section. For the information offered there, Marracci was able to fall back on the collection of Oriental manuscripts in the Vatican Library. The literature in this context used by Marracci is carefully put together by C.A. Nallino, in a detailed study (C.A. Nallino, Le fonte arabi); in addition to scholarly writings on the Qurʾān in the narrower sense, it also comprises theological, juridical and historic works. One can say therefore that Marracci was the first Christian scholar who actually composed a "commentary" to the text of the Qurʾān and to the establishment of its translation; certainly his work stood completely at the service of church polemics. Nevertheless, leaving the theological evaluation aside, it is still of inestimable value today because of the wealth of the information provided. The Arabic text is more exact than that of Hinckelmann's, but Marracci had just as little consideration for the peculiarity of qurʾānic orthography.

In 1721 the Protestant theologian Christian Reineccius (d. 1752) published in Leipzig the Latin text of Marracci in a handy Octavo edition *(Muhammedis filii Abdallae pseudo-prophetae fides islamitica, i.e. al-Coranus)*. He placed an introduction before Marracci's Latin text, in which he informs about the history of the Qurʾān and the system of Islamic belief, as well as its divergences from Christian doctrines. Above all, this edition helped Marracci's translation move beyond the borders of Italy and the Catholic scholarly world, and brought it to a larger audience. Marracci's *Prodromus* had in this respect a further effect, when a Maronite from Aleppo, Yaʿqūb Arūtīn (d. after 1738) translated it into Arabic (cf. Graf, *GCAL*, iii, 432). Beside the predominate effort to produce a text of the Qurʾān, there were also further, primarily theologically motivated, studies of the Qurʾān, which nevertheless profited considerably from the rise of Arabic philology. In this category belongs the work of a contemporary of Erpenius, the Englishman William Bedwell (d. 1632; cf. Hamilton, *William Bedwell*), with the extensive title of *Mohammedis imposturae: That is, a discovery of the manifold forgeries, falshoods, and horrible impieties of the blasphemous seducer Mohammed: With a demonstration of the insufficience of his law, contained in the cursed Alkoran...* (London 1615); one of two supplements to this work contained an *Index assuratarum Muhammedici Alkorani. That is a catalogue of the chapters of the Turkish Alkoran, as they are named in the Arabicke, and knowne to the Musslemans: Together with their severall interpretations.* The Lutheran dean from Marburg, Heinrich Leuchter, wrote an extremely polemical work, offering a pure systematization of the theological doctrines of the Qurʾān entirely on the basis of the Toledan translation published by Bibliander, *Alcoranus Mahometicus. Oder: Türckenglaub aufl defl Mahomets eygenem Buch genannt Alcoran... in ein kurtz Compendium zusammen gebracht* (Frankfurt am Main 1604). Of the Catholics, the work of the Jesuit Michel Nau (d. 1683) could be called exemplary. His work, *Religio Christiana contra Alcoranum per Alcoranum pacifice defensa et probata* (Paris 1680), is based on writings originally composed in Arabic, in which proofs of the truth of Christianity were drawn from the Qurʾān (*Ithbāt al-Qurʾān li-ṣiḥḥat al-dīn al-masīḥī;* cf. Graf, *GCAL*, iv, 219).

Of great influence on qurʾānic research was the work of the first Oxford Arabist Edward Pococke (d. 1691). In his book *Specimen historiae arabum* (Oxford 1650; repr. 1806) he provided important information on the basis of a textual fragment from the world history of Bar Hebraeus (d. 1286 C.E.), especially on the pre-Islamic history of the Arabs (q.v.; see also AGE OF IGNORANCE; PRE-ISLAMIC ARABIA AND THE QURʾĀN). He thereby cleared the way for an understanding of the Qurʾān based upon the history of religion (cf. Holt, Study). The first to profit from this was George Sale (d. 1736), who added a long *Preliminary discourse* to his 1734 English Qurʾān translation, which appeared in London. In it, Pococke is one of the most cited authors. Beside this, Sale had also intensively used the scholia of Marracci's Qurʾān edition. Much less successful than Pococke was his Arabist colleague at Cambridge, Abraham Wheelocke (d. 1653; cf. Arberry, *Cambridge school*, 9 f.). The printing of a translation and refutation of the Qurʾān prepared by him (ca. 1647/48) never occurred. From letters of Wheelocke to the theologian James Ussher (d. 1656) and to the Orientalist Christian Ravius (see above), it can be surmised 'that it consisted of parts of the Qurʾān translated into both Latin and Greek, together with a commentary consisting of virulent attacks on Islam and its prophet" (Toomer, *Eastern wisedome*, 89).

In 1658, the Zürich theologian and Orientalist Johann Heinrich Hottinger (d. 1667) published in Heidelberg his *Promtuarium; sive, Bibliotheca orientalis;* in this first, still very imperfect attempt at Oriental literary history he goes into great detail on the Qurʾān (pp. 105-62). He goes through it sūra by sūra, listing their names and briefly providing a summary of their contents. He also discusses different readings and addresses the Basel Arabic Qurʾān Codex once used by Bibliander, whose tabular survey of the Qurʾān readings he reproduces, although with many errors (cf. Bobzin, *Reformation*, 242). Then Hottinger provides an overview of Arabic Qurʾān commentators well-known at that time, as well as other special literature concerned with the Qurʾān.

Qurʾānic studies in the eighteenth century

For qurʾānic research, the eighteenth century was much less significant than the preceding one, for, apart from some new Qurʾān translations into different European languages, it made hardly any substantive progress. To be sure, the Dutch theologian and Orientalist Adrian Reland (d. 1718), in his important work *De religione Mohammedica* (Utrecht 1705; Eng.: 1712, Ger.: 1717, Fr.: 1721), had emphasized the importance of the use of the original sources, above all with the Qurʾān. If one studied the Qurʾān, however, this was usually done in translation: both of the extant printed Latin translations or, preferably, the French translation of André du Ryer (first ed., Paris 1647) or the English of George Sale (first ed., London 1734).

In 1701, a much-promising work appeared in Berlin, but it remained truncated: *Tetrapla Alcoranica, sive specimen Alcorani quadrilinguis, Arabici, Persici, Turcici, Latini.* Its author was the Breslau Orientalist Andreas Acoluthus (d. 1704; cf. Bobzin, Die Koranpolyglotte). His intention was, following the patterns of the great polylingual Bibles of Alcalá (1514-17), Antwerp (1569-72), Paris (1629-45) and London (1653-7), also to make the Qurʾān accessible in a polyglot edition. Acoluthus did not, however, get further than the first sūra. Next to the original Arabic text, he printed a Persian and Turkish version in addition to the Latin translation that belonged with each; this procedure was meaningful, because in this manner it could become clear to the non-linguist readers to what extent the Persian and/or Turkish textual paraphrases represented the original Arabic text. In an extensive treatise which follows the presentation of the text, Acoluthus provides precise details about the origin of the qurʾānic texts. It is noteworthy that the Turkish Qurʾān edition was in the possession of Franz von Mesgnien Meninski (d. 1698), the author of an important Persian-Turkish lexicon (Vienna 1680-7).

Clearly encouraged by the Qurʾān editions of Hinckelmann, Marracci and Acoluthus, the Altdorf Orientalist Johann Michael Lang (d. 1731) composed three texts that he allowed students to defend as disputations at his university. They addressed the problem of the first Qurʾān edition printed in Venice (*De Alcorani prima inter Europaeos editione Arabica;* Altdorf 1703), the various previous attempts to publish the Qurʾān or parts of it (*De speciminibus, conatibus variis atque novissimis successibus doctorum quorundam virorum in edendo Alcorano arabico,* Altdorf 1704) as well as, finally, the previous translations of the Qurʾān (*De Alcorani versionibus variis, tam orientalibus, quam occidentalibus, impressis et hactenus anekdotois,* Altdorf 1704). All three works contain much valuable information that otherwise is accessible today only with great difficulty — above all quotations out of the older literature. That applies also to the work of the Rostock theologian Zacharias Grapius, *Spicilegium Historico-Philologicum Historiam Literariam Alcorani sistens* (Rostock 1701). The *Histoire de l'Alcoran* that the Frenchman François Henri Turpin (d. 1799), author of numerous popular historical works, published in London in 1775 in two volumes, is without any value, as the Göttingen Orientalist Johann David Michaelis (d. 1791) in a contemporary review already correctly commented — it does not even really deserve its title.

As in the preceding century, further sections of the Qurʾān were published, usually in bilingual editions and with more or less detailed explanations. The Leipzig Orientalist Johann Christian Clodius (d. 1745) published Q 22 together with variants from a manuscript of the Qurʾān commentary of al-Bayḍāwī (d. prob. 716/1316-7), along with explanations (*Excerptum Alcoranicum de peregrinatione sacra;* Leipzig 1730; cf. Schnurrer, *Bibliotheca arabica,* no. 380); the Altdorf Orientalist Johann Michael Nagel (d. 1788) published Q 1 (*De prima Alcorani sura;* Altdorf 1743; cf. Schnurrer, *Bibliotheca arabica,* no. 382); the theologian and Orientalist Justus Friedrich Froriep (d. 1800) who, at that time, was working in Leipzig, also published Q 1 as well as Q 2:1-79 (*Corani caput primum et secundi versus priores, arabice et latine cum animadversionibus historicis et philologicis;* Leipzig 1768; cf. Schnurrer, *Bibliotheca arabica,* no. 383). A complete Arabic edition of the Qurʾān with Latin translation and enclosed lexicon was planned by the Helmstedt classical philologist and Orientalist Johann Gottfried Lakemacher (d. 1736). Lacking a publisher, however, it was not realised (cf. Koldewey, *Geschichte,* 114); only one specimen, comprising Q 2:1-14, appeared (cf. Schnurrer, *Bibliotheca arabica,* no. 379).

The fine Arabic Qurʾān edition that was published in 1787 in St. Petersburg is a special document. After the peace of Küçük Kaynarca, which concluded the Russian-Turkish war of 1768-74, numerous formerly Turkish zones fell to Russia. In the context of the religious politics that they owed to the Enlightenment, Empress Catherine II had for her numerous new Muslim subjects their holy book, the Qurʾān, printed in Arabic. In 1786/7, at imperial expense, a 'Tatar and Turkish Typography' was established in St. Petersburg; a domestic scholar, Mullah Osman Ismail, was responsible for the manufacture of the types. One of the first products of this printing house was the Qur'ān. Through the doctor and writer, Johann Georg v. Zimmermann (d. 1795), who was befriended by Catherine II, a copy of the publication arrived in the Göttingen University library. Its director, the philologist Christian Gottlob Heyne (d. 1812), presented the work immediately in the *Göttingische Anzeigen von gelehrten Sachen* (28 July 1788); therein he pointed especially to the beauty of the Arabic types. To the Arabic text marginal glosses have been added that consist predominantly of reading variants. The imprint was reproduced unchanged in 1790 and 1793 in St. Petersburg (cf. Schnurrer, *Bibliotheca arabica,* no. 384); later, after the transfer of the printing house to Kazan, editions appeared in different formats and with varying presentation (Dorn, Chronologisches Verzeichnis, 371). The original St. Petersburg edition is very rare; in an English book catalogue of 1827, it is stated that: "The whole impression, with the exception of about 20 copies, was sent for distribution into the interior; but owing to the Mahometan prejudices against printed books, could not be got into circulation. — About three years ago, 15 copies were all that were known to be in circulation, or in the Imperial library" (Dorn, Chronologisches Verzeichnis, 372). In any case this Qur'ān edition was the first authentic Muslim printed edition of the Qur'ān. See Figs. I-IV of PRINTING OF THE QUR'ĀN for examples from the Qur'ān printings of Hinckelmann, Marracci, St. Petersburg and Kazan.

Hartmut Bobzin

Bibliography

Primary: J. Andres, *Libro nueuamente imprimido que se llama Confusion dela secta Mahomatica y del Alcoran,* Valencia 1515; Anon., *Liber denudationis siue ostensionis aut patefaciens. ELFOLICA siue ALPHOLICA,* ed. T.E. Burman, in id., *Religious polemic and the intellectual history of the Mozarabs, c. 1050-1200,* Leiden 1994, 240-385; T. Bibliander (Buchmann), *Machumetis Sarracenorum principis, eiusque successorum vitae, ac doctrina, ipsque Alcoran...,* 3 vols., Basel 1543; H. Hinckelmann (ed.), *Al-Coranus s. lex islamitica Muhammedis, filii Abdallae pseudoprophetae. Ad optimorum codicum fidem edita,* Hamburg 1694; John of Damascus, *Ecrits sur l'islam* [Sources Chrétiennes, 383], ed. R. Le Coz, Paris 1992; id., *Liber de haeresibus,* in B. Kotter (ed.), *Die Schriften des Johannes von Damaskos,* Berlin/New York 1981, pt. 4; id., *Schriften zum Islam,* ed. R. Glei and A.T. Khoury, Würzburg 1995; John VI Kantakuzenos, *Contra Mahometem apologiae et orationes,* in J.-P. Migne, *PG,* cliv, 372-692; [al-Kindī], Apologia del Cristianismo, ed. M. Sendino, in *Miscelánea Comillas* 11/12 (1949), 337-460; [id.], *Dialogue islamo-chrétien sous le calife Al-Ma'mūn (813-834),* ed. G. Tartar, Paris 1985; [id.], *Risālat ʿAbdallāh al-Hāshimī ilā ʿAbd al-Masīḥ al-Kindī... wa-Risālat ʿAbd al-Masīḥ al-Kindī ilā ʿAbdallāh al-Hāshimī,* ed. A. Tien, London 1880; 1885²; 1912³; M. Luther, *Verlegung des Alcoran Bruder Richardi. Prediger Ordens. Anno* 1300, Wittenberg 1542, ed. in *D. Martin Luthers Werke (Kritische Gesamtausgabe)* 53 (1883), 261-396; Manuel II Palaiologos, *Dialoge mit einem Muslim* [Corpus islamo-christianum, Series graeca, 4/1-3], ed. K. Förstel, 3 vols., Würzburg 1993-6; L. Marracci (ed.), *Alcorani textus universus, ex correctioribus Arabum exemplaribus summa fide atque pulcherrimis characteribus descriptus, eadem fide ac diligentia pari ex Arabico idiomate in Latinum translatus, appositis unicuique capiti notis atque refutatione,* Padua 1698; J.-P. Migne (ed.), *PG = Patrologiae cursus completus. Series graeca,* 161 vols. in 166, Paris 1857-94; id. (ed.), *PL = Patrologiae cursus completus. Series latina,* 221 vols. in 222, Paris 1844-1902; Niketas of Byzantium, *Schriften zum Islam* [Corpus islamo-christianum, Series Graeca, 5], ed. and trans. K. Förstel, Würzburg 2000; G. Postel, *De orbis terrae concordia libri IV,* Basel 1544; Raymond Martin, *Explanatio simboli apostolorum,* ed. J. March, in *Anuari de l'Institut d'Estudis Catalans* [2] (1908), 450-96; id., *Pugio fidei adversus Mauros et Judaeos,* ed. J.B. Carpzov, Lipsiae [Leipzig] 1687, repr. Farnborough 1967; Ricoldo da Monte Croce, *Contra legem Sarracenorum,* see below, under "J.-M. Mérigoux"; William of Tripoli, *Notitia de Machometo. De statu Sarracenorum* [Corpus islamo-christianum, Series latina, 4], ed. P. Engels, Würzburg 1992.

Secondary: A. Abel, Baḥīrā, in *EI²*, i, 922-3; B. Altaner, Die fremdsprachliche Ausbildung der Dominikanermissionare während des 13. und 14. Jahrhunderts, in *Zeitschrift fur Missions- und Religionswissenschaft* 23 (1933), 233-41; id., Raymundus Lullus und der Sprachenkanon (can. 11) des Konzils von Vienne (1312), in *Historisches Jahrbuch* 53 (1933), 191-219; id., Sprachstudien und Sprachkenntnisse im Dienste der Mission des 13. und 14. Jahrhunderts, in *Zeitschrift fur Missions- und Religionswissenschaft* 21 (1931), 113-36; M.-Th. d'Alverny, Deux traductions latines du Coran au Moyen Age, in *Archives d'histoire doctrinale et littéraire du Moyen Age* 22/23 (1947/48), 69-131; id., *La connaissance de l'Islam dans l'Occident médiéval,* Aldershot 1994; id. and G. Vajda, Marc de Tolède, traducteur d'Ibn Tûmart, in *al-Andalus* 16 (1951), 100-40; 259-307; 17 (1952), 1-56; A.J. Arberry, *The Cambridge School of Arabic,* Cambridge 1948; A. Berthier, Un maître orientaliste du XIIIe siècle. Raymond Martin O.P., in *Archivum Fratrum Praedicatorum* 6 (1936), 267-311; H. Bobzin, "A treasury of heresies." Christian polemics against the Koran, in Wild, *Text,* 157-75; id., Bemerkungen zu Juan Andrés und zu seinem Buch Confusion dela secta mahomatica (Valencia 1515), in M. Forstner (ed.), *Festschrift für H.-R. Singer,* Frankfurt am Main 1991, 529-48; id., Die Koranpolyglotte des Andreas Acoluthus (1654-1704), in *Germano-Turcica. Zur Geschichte des Türkisch-Lernens in den deutschprachigen Ländern,* Bamberg 1987, 57-9; id., Ein oberschlesischer Korangelehrter: Dominicus Germanus de Silesia, O.F.M. (1588-1670), in G. Kosellek (ed.), *Die oberschlesische Literaturlandschaft im 17. Jahrhundert,* Bielefeld 2001, 221-31; id., From Venice to Cairo. On the history of Arabic editions of the Koran (16th — early 20th century), in E. Hanebutt-Benz et al. (eds.), *Middle Eastern languages and the print revolution. A cross cultural encounter,* Westhofen 2002, 151-76; id., Jean Bodin über den Venezianer Korandruck von 1537/38, in *WZKM* 81 (1991), 95-105; id., *Reformation;* H. Bojer, Einiges über die arabische Druckschriftensammlung der Bayerischen Staatsbibliothek, in H. Franke (ed.), *Orientalisches aus Münchener Bibliotheken und Sammlungen,* Wiesbaden 1957, 77-87; M. Borrmans, Observations à propos de la première édition imprimée du Coran à Venise, in *QSA* 8 (1990), 3-12; id., Présentation de la première édition du Coran impriée à Venise, in *QSA* 9 (1991), 93-126; H. Braun, Der Hamburger Koran von 1694, in C. Voigt and E. Zimmermann (eds.), *Libris et Litteris. Festschrift für H. Tiemann,* Hamburg 1959, 149-66; R. Brummer, Ramon Lull und das Studium des Arabischen, in *Zeitschrift für roman. Philologie* 85 (1969), 132-43; M.A. de Bunes Ibarra, La evolución de la polémica anti-islámica en los teólogos españoles del primer renacimiento, in H. Santiago-Otero (ed.), *Diálogo filosófico-religioso entre cristianismo, judaismo e islamismo durante la edad media en la península iberica,* Turnhout 1994, 399-418; T.E. Burman, *Religious polemic and the intellectual history of the Mozarabs, c.* 1050-1200 [Brill's Studies in Intellectual History, 52], Leiden 1994; id., Polemic, philology and ambivalence. Reading the Qur'ān in Latin Christendom, in *JIS* 15 (2004), 181-209; D. Cabanelas Rodriguez, Juan de Segovia y el primer Alcorán trilingue, in *al-Andalus* 14 (1949), 149-73; id., *Juan de Segovia y el problema islámico,* Madrid 1952; A. Cortabarría Beitía, La connaissance des textes arabes chez Raymond Martin O.P. et sa position... face de l'islam, in *Islam et chrétiens du Midi (XIIe-XIVe s.)* [Cahiers de Fanjeux, 18], Toulouse 1983, 279-300; id., Les sources arabes de l'"Explanatio simboli" du Dominicain catalan Raymond Martin, in *MIDEO* 16 (1983), 95-116; H. Daiber, Der Missionar Raimundus Lullus und seine Kritik am Islam, in *Estudios Lulianos* 25 (1981-83), 47-57; N. Daniel, *Islam and the west. The making of an image,* Edinburgh 1960; Oxford 1993²; B. Dorn, Chronologisches Verzeichnis der seit dem Jahre 1801 bis 1866 in Kasan gedruckten arabischen, türkischen, tatarischen und persischen Werke, in *Bulletin de l'Académie impériale des sciences de St.-Petersbourg* 11 (1867), 307-85; W. Eichner, Die Nachrichten über den Islam bei den Byzantinern, in *Der Islam* 32 (1936), 133-62; 197-244; K. Flasch, *Nikolaus von Kues. Geschichte einer Entwicklung. Vorlesungen zur Einführung in seine Philosophie,* Frankfurt am Main 1998; J. Fück, *Die arabischen Studien in Europa bis in den Anfang des 20. Jahrhunderts,* Leipzig 1955; R. Gottheil, A Christian Bahira legend, in *Zeitschrift für Assyriologie* 13 (1898), 189-242; 14 (1899/1900), 203-68; 15 (1900/01), 56-102; 17 (1903), 125-66; G. Graf, *GCAL = Geschichte der christlichen arabischen Literatur,* 5 vols., Vatican City 1947-53; C. Güterbock, *Der Islam im Lichte der byzantinischen Polemik,* Berlin 1912; L. Hagemann, *Der Ḳur'ān in Verständnis und Kritik bei Nikolaus von Kues* [Frankfurter Theologische Studien, 21], Frankfurt am Main 1976; A. Hamilton, *William Bedwell the Arabist* 1563-1632, Leiden 1985; T. Hase and F.A. Lampe, *Bibliotheca historico-philologico-theologica,* 8 vols., Bremen 1719-27; J. Hernando y Delgado, Le "De seta Machometi" du Cod. 46 d'Osma, oeuvre de Raymond Martin (Rámón Martí), in *Islam et chrétiens du Midi (XIIe-XIVe s.)* [Cahiers de Fanjeux, 18], Toulouse 1983, 351-71; P. M. Holt, The study of Arabic historians in seventeenth century England. The background and the work of Edward Pococke, in *BSOAS* 19 (1957), 444-55; W.M.C. Juynboll, *Zeventiende-eeuwsche Beoefenaars van het Arabisch in Nederland,* Diss., Utrecht 1931; A.T. Khoury, *Les théologiens byzantins et l'islam,* Louvain/Paris 1969²; id., *Polémique byzantine contre l'islam,* Paris 1972³; F. Koldewey, *Geschichte der klassischen Philologie auf der Universität Helmstedt,* Braunschweig 1895; repr. Amsterdam 1970; J. Kritzeck, *Peter the Venerable and Islam,* Princeton 1964; Ch. Lohr, Christianus arabicus, cuius nomen Raimundus Lullus, in *Freiburger Zeitschrift für Philosophie und Theologie* 31 (1984), 57-88; J. Martínez Gázquez, El Prólogo de Juan de Segobia al Corán *(Qur'ān)* trilinguë (1456), in *Mittellateinisches Jahrbuch* 38 (2003), 389-410; L. Massignon, al-Kindī, ʿAbd al-Masīḥ b. Isḥāḳ, in *EI¹*, iv, 1021; O. Mazal, Zur geistigen Auseinandersetzung zwischen Christentum und Islam in spätbyzantinischer Zeit, in *Orientalische Kultur und europäisches Mittelalter* [Miscellanea mediaevalia, 17], Berlin/New York 1985, 1-19; J.-M. Mérigoux, L'ouvrage d'un frère Prêcheur Florentin en orient à la fin du XIIIᵉ siècle. Le "Contra legem Sarracenorum" de Riccoldo da Monte Croce, in *Memorie Domenicane [NS]* 17 (1986), 1-144; G. Monnot, Les citations coraniques dans le "Dialogus" de Pierre Alphonse, in *Islam et chrétiens du Midi (XIIᵉ-XIVᵉ s.)* [Cahiers de Fanjeux, 18], Toulouse 1983, 261-77; E. Montet, Un rituel d'abjuration des Musulmans dans l'Eglise Grecque, in *RHR* 53 (1906), 145-63; C.A. Nallino, Le fonti arabe manoscritte dell'opera di Ludovico Marracci sul Corano, in id. (ed.), *Raccolta di scritti editi e inediti,* ed. M. Nallino, 6 vols., Rome 1940, ii, 90-134; M. Nallino, Una cinquecentesca edizione del Corano stampata a Venezia, in *Atti dell'Istituto Veneto di scienze, lettere ed arti, cl. di scienze morali, lettere ed arti* 124 (1965/66), 1-12; F. de Nave, *Philologia Arabica. Arabische studiën en drukken in de Nederlanden in de 16de en 17de eeuw,* Antwerp 1986 (museum catalogue); Nöldeke, *GQ;* A. Nuovo, Il Corano arabo ritrovato, in *La bibliofilia* 89 (1987), 237-71; id., A lost Koran rediscovered, in *The library,* 6th ser., 12/4 (Dec. 1990), 273-92; H. Prutz, *Kulturgeschichte der Kreuzzüge,* Berlin 1883; H. Röhling, Koranausgaben im russischen Buchdruck des 18. Jahrhunderts, in *Gutenberg-Jahrbuch* n.s. (1977), 205-10; D.J. Sahas, *John of Damascus on Islam. The "Heresy of the Ishmaelites,"* Leiden 1972; id., John of Damascus on Islam. Revisited, in *Abr Nahrain* 23 (1984/85), 104-18; C.F. de Schnurrer (ed.), *Bibliotheca Arabica,* Halle/Saale 1811, repr. Amsterdam 1968; F. Secret, Guillaume Postel et les études arabes à la Renaissance, in *Arabica* 9 (1962), 21-36; V. Segesvary, *L'Islam et la Réforme. Etude sur l'attitude des réformateurs Zurichois envers l'Islam (1510-1550),* Lausanne 1978; M. Steinschneider, *Polemische und apologetische Literatur in arabischer Sprachen zwischen Muslimen, Christen und Juden nebst Anhängen verwandten Inhalts,* Leipzig 1877, repr. Hildesheim 1966; G.J. Toomer, *Eastern wisedome and learning. The study of Arabic in seventeenth century England,* Oxford 1996; E. Trapp, Gab es eine byzantinische Koranübersetzung? in *Diptycha* 2 (1981/2), 7-17; id., *Manuel II. Palaiologos. Dialoge mit einem "Perser"* [Wiener byzantinistische Studien, 2], Vienna 1966; G. Troupeau, al-Kindī, ʿAbd al-Masīḥ, in *EI²,* v, 120-1; J. Vernet, Traducciones moriscos de El Coran, in W. Hoenerbach (ed.), *Der Orient in der Forschung. Festschrift für O. Spies,* Wiesbaden 1967, 686-705; G. Wiegers, *Islamic literature in Spanish and Aljamiado. Yça of Segovia (fl. 1450). His antecedents and successors* [Medieval Iberian peninsula, 8], Leiden 1994.

Predestination

see FREEDOM AND PREDESTINATION

Pregnancy

see BIOLOGY AS THE CREATION AND STAGES OF LIFE; BIRTH

Pre-Islamic Arabia and the Qurʾān

Definitions

The Qurʾān itself does not contain any concept equivalent to those designated in ancient and modern times by the term Arabia. That name is generally given today to a region understood to be the ancestral home of the Arabic speaking peoples (see ARABS). In the past the term has been applied to different geographical areas at different times, reflecting changing political and administrative divisions as well as changes of climate and settlement patterns. Currently it tends to be used predominantly with reference to the Arabian peninsula *(jazīrat al-ʿarab),* which, geographically, extends north into what is now usually called the Syrian desert. In classical and late antiquity, Arabia was a name given to one or more administrative divisions of the Roman empire situated east and south of Palestine.

The extent to which the Qurʾān has the concept of a pre-Islamic era depends on how the expression *al-jāhiliyya* (see AGE OF

IGNORANCE) is to be understood in it. Outside the Qurʾān the expression *al-jāhiliyya* is often used in Muslim tradition with reference to the way of life of the Arabs who lived in the northern and central Arabian peninsula before Islam (q.v.), a way of life from which they were delivered by the Prophet and the revelation (see REVELATION AND INSPIRATION; PROPHETS AND PROPHETHOOD). *Al-jāhiliyya* thus functions as the conceptual opposite of Islam *(al-islām)* and in many contexts within Muslim tradition it approximates to our usage of the expression, "pre-Islamic Arabia."

In the view of traditional and most modern scholars, the Qurʾān emerged in the first half of the seventh century C.E. in the western central region of the Arabian peninsula known as the Ḥijāz and the text is traditionally understood as containing many references and allusions to, or as presupposing, the practices and beliefs of the pre-Islamic inhabitants of the Ḥijāz and neighboring parts of Arabia such as Najd, Yamāma and Tihāma. To the extent that pre-Islamic Arabia is coterminous with the *jāhiliyya*, therefore, it is understood as the historical background to, and immediate point of reference for, the Qurʾān.

In contemporary usage, however, the expression pre-Islamic Arabia is used to refer to rather more than that covered by the traditional term *al-jāhiliyya*. It would include, for example, the development before Islam of the kingdoms and cultures of the southern, eastern and northern regions and extensions of the peninsula, and the interventions in Arabia by outside kingdoms and empires. Those aspects of pre-Islamic Arabian history are not usually included in traditional accounts of the *jāhiliyya* except for certain events (see below) understood as relating to the life of the Prophet and the rise of Islam.

The jāhiliyya *in Muslim tradition*

The view of the *jāhiliyya* that Muslim tradition presents is rather more complex than one might expect from the name itself, with its connotations of ignorance (q.v.) and barbarism. It is true that the salient features of the traditional reports about the way of life of the Arabs before Islam are their gross idolatry (see IDOLATRY AND IDOLATERS), their violent way of life (see FIGHTING; BLOOD MONEY; WAR), and their lack of sexual morality (see SEX AND SEXUALITY). The tradition is replete with details about the idols of the Arabs (see IDOLS AND IMAGES), their sanctuaries, the tribes who worshipped them, and the families who ministered to them. On the other hand, this idolatry is sometimes presented as not being taken seriously by the Arabs: for example, an idol made of dates and butter might be eaten in a time of famine (q.v.), or another would lose the allegiance of a devotee when he saw it urinated upon by foxes. The tradition also provides much information about the feuds and battles (*ayyām*, lit. "days") of the tribes before Islam and the chaotic and unregulated aspects of sexual relations, including prostitution, abuse of women, and lack of clarity in determining the paternity of children (q.v.). Unwanted female infants are said to have been disposed of by burial while still alive (see INFANTICIDE).

The negative image is, however, moderated by a number of things. The identification of the language of the Qurʾān as a language used in pre-Islamic Arabia (precisely which language is a question to which the tradition and modern scholarship offer variant answers) and the consequent high value put upon *jāhilī* poetry as a key to the understanding of the language is one such thing (see GRAMMAR AND THE QURʾĀN; POETS AND POETRY). Another is the admiration evident for some of the actions and qualities that represented the ideal of behavior among the pre-Islamic Arabs, summarized in the concept of *muruwwa,* "manliness, virtue": courage (q.v.), generosity, hospitality and support for the weaker members of one's tribe (see KINSHIP; HOSPITALITY AND COURTESY; TRIBES AND CLANS).

Equally important is the idea that Abraham (q.v.) had once introduced true monotheism to the Arabs and, although they had fallen away from it and had become immersed in the corruption of idolatry, remnants of that true monotheism still survived among them (see ḤANĪF). One such remnant was the Kaʿba (q.v.), built by Abraham and his son Ishmael (q.v.). Another was the religion of Abraham himself *(dīn ibrāhīm)* which still survived among certain individuals known in the tradition as *ḥanīf*s. These individuals are portrayed as rejecting the pagan religion into which their fellow Arabs had sunk and as holding on to a non-Christian and non-Jewish form of monotheism which Abraham himself had professed (see CHRISTIANS AND CHRISTIANITY; JEWS AND JUDAISM). This idea is related to Q 3:67, which refers to Abraham as neither a Christian nor a Jew but a *ḥanīf,* a *muslim* (see RELIGIOUS PLURALISM AND THE QURʾĀN).

The Qurʾān and the jāhiliyya

The most important function of pre-Islamic Arabia (in its more limited sense as the locus of the *jāhiliyya*), so far as the traditional understanding of the Qurʾān is concerned, is that it is viewed as the milieu in which the revelation was given. Thus it can be used as an explanatory device for making sense of details and passages in the Qurʾān. There is a certain tension between the idea that the Qurʾān is a revelation relevant for and applicable to all peoples and all times, and the view that at least some of it was revealed with reference to a specific society and time and to particular incidents in which the Prophet was involved (see OCCASIONS OF REVELATION).

In general the text is understood and analysed as composed in a form of the Arabic language existing in the *jāhiliyya:* its rhyming prose (*sajʿ;* see RHYMED PROSE) and certain types of oaths (q.v.) which it contains are said to be related to the language used by the soothsayers (q.v.; *kuhhān*) of the *jāhiliyya* to deliver their oracles (see FORETELLING; DIVINATION); and its vocabulary and grammar is explained by reference to the poetry of the *jāhiliyya,* originally transmitted orally and preserved in much later Islamic literary texts.

The way in which details of the Qurʾān are explained and understood as allusions to the life of the *jāhiliyya* can be illustrated with reference to a wide range of verses. Such material figures frequently in the form of commentary known as *asbāb al-nuzūl* (occasions of revelation), which seeks to explain passages of scripture by situating them in a historical context or by associating them with features of pre-Islamic Arabian life. Many of these "occasions of revelation" reports refer to events in which the Prophet and his Companions were involved (see COMPANIONS OF THE PROPHET).

Qurʾānic allusions to the practice of infanticide (Q 6:137, 140, 151; 16:57-9; 81:8-9) are understood as directed against the custom of the pre-Islamic Arabs of disposing of surplus female children by burying them alive *(waʾd).* Outside the Qurʾān this practice *(qatl al-mawʾūda)* figures prominently in descriptions of life in the *jāhiliyya.* The difficult verse Q 9:37 (see DIFFICULT PASSAGES), in which the *nasīʾ* is called "an excess of disbelief (*kufr;* see BELIEF AND UNBELIEF)" and which then goes on, apparently, to attack the practice of certain opponents who interfere with the number of months (q.v.) which God has made sacred (*ḥaram;* see PROFANE AND SACRED) is variously explained outside the Qurʾān as an attack on a custom of the pre-Islamic Arabs (or on the person responsible for putting the custom into practice). The practice involved prolonging certain years by intercalation in order to delay the onset of sacred months (see CALENDAR). The injunction not to approach "the houses from their backs" (Q 2:189) is again the subject of various explanations which have in common, however, the idea that it is an injunction against something which was a practice (religious or sexual) of the Arabs in the *jāhiliyya*.

Certain regulations in the area of marriage and divorce (q.v.), such as the insistence upon a "waiting period" (q.v.; *ʿidda*) before a woman whose sexual relationship with a man has been ended by divorce or death can begin another (Q 65:1 f.), are explained as attempts to reform the sexual immorality and licentiousness of the pre-Islamic Arabs. The limited polygamy which Islamic law allows men (see LAW AND THE QURʾĀN; PATRIARCHY) is understood to relate to Q 4:3, "marry of the women who please you two or three or four." That verse is generally understood as an intended amelioration of the pre-Islamic situation in which there were no limits on the number of women a man might marry, and more precisely as relating to the situation following the battle of Uḥud (see EXPEDITIONS AND BATTLES) in 3/625 when the Muslim community in Medina (q.v.) was faced with a surplus of women over men.

The polytheism and idolatry of the pre-Islamic Arabs is understood to be the referent for the attacks in the Qurʾān against those who practice *shirk*, the sin of associating other things and beings with God as an object of worship (q.v.; see POLYTHEISM AND ATHEISM). The names of the three "daughters of God" (Q 53:19-20) are explained as those of idols or goddesses worshipped in Mecca (q.v.) and elsewhere in the Ḥijāz before Islam, and the many qurʾānic passages that speak against those whom it accuses of practicing *shirk* are regularly understood to be directed against the Meccans or other Arab idolaters. Qurʾānic denigration of the prayer at the sanctuary of "those who disbelieve" as "mere whistling and hand clapping" (Q 8:35) is explained as referring to the way in which the pre-Islamic Arabs behaved when they came to Mecca to visit the Kaʿba (q.v.), and Q 7:31-2 in which people are commanded to "take care of your adornment" *(khudhū zīnatakum)* when at places of worship is explained (in different variants) as referring to a custom of the pre-Islamic association known as the Ḥums which controlled access to the Kaʿba. Various reports say that before Islam the Ḥums made some outsiders circumambulate the Kaʿba while naked. These are just examples of the many ways in which the traditional commentators relate the Qurʾān to the world of pre-Islamic Arabia.

Scholarship and the jāhiliyya

Most modern scholars have accepted the accounts of the *jāhiliyya* as reflections of a real historical situation and have agreed with the traditional scholars that the Qurʾān reflects in many places the society of pre-Islamic Arabia (see COMMUNITY AND SOCIETY IN THE QURʾĀN). Many modern scholars have tried to use some of the traditional information about the *jāhiliyya* to develop theories about the emergence of Islam in pre-Islamic Arabia.

The most influential such theory has been that an evolutionary process had led to the decline of traditional Arab paganism by the time of the Prophet, and that Islam was successful because it met the spiritual and moral needs of Arab, and especially Meccan, society around the beginning of the seventh century C.E. Reports about the lack of real respect for their idols by the pre-Islamic Arabs, and traditional material understood as evidence of monotheistic tendencies in the paganism of the *jāhiliyya* (such as the material on the *ḥanīf*s), have been interpreted according to evolutionary theories of religion. The moral injunctions of the Qurʾān towards charity (see ALMSGIVING), honesty and protection of the weak (see OPPRESSED ON EARTH, THE; OPPRESSION) are then often understood as reflecting the general and specific moral failings of the pre-Islamic Arabs.

Julius Wellhausen's *Reste arabischen Heidentums,* the first edition of which appeared in 1887, was influential in establishing this evolutionary interpretation, and elements of it have remained visible in works written late in the twentieth century. Sometimes the evolution of the pre-Islamic Arabs from idolatry and paganism to monotheism is presented as a natural development, one through which all societies pass in time; sometimes the influence on the Arabs of various types of monotheism from outside Arabia is mentioned as an explanatory factor; and sometimes the idea is postulated of a primitive Arab form of monotheism which had survived even though the Arabs generally had become polytheists.

The Qurʾān and pre-Islamic Arabia beyond the jāhiliyya

Like the traditional scholars, modern scholarship on the rise of Islam has concentrated on the regions of Arabia associated with the concept of the *jāhiliyya* — in general the central and northwestern parts of the peninsula in the two or three hundred years before the Prophet. That does not include important areas of pre-Islamic Arabian history such as the Nabatean and Palmyrene kingdoms that flourished in the north of Arabia some centuries before Islam (see SYRIA; GEOGRAPHY AND THE QURʾĀN), or the various states, richly attested by inscriptions and archaeological remains, in the south. Since the late nineteenth century knowledge of and scholarship on those areas of pre-Islamic Arabia have increased significantly, and some scholars have sought to relate them to the Qurʾān and emerging Islam.

Muslim tradition itself reports in some detail certain events connected with the Yemen (q.v.) in the century before the Prophet, and because certain passages of the Qurʾān are often understood as alluding to them, they are narrated also in works of qurʾānic commentary (*tafsīr;* see EXEGESIS OF THE QURʾĀN: CLASSICAL AND MEDIEVAL).

Prominent among these are accounts of the persecution of Christians by Dhū Nuwās, a Yemeni ruler who had accepted Judaism; the resulting conquest of the Yemen by the Christian state of Abyssinia (q.v.) and the governorship of the region by the Abyssinian general Abraha (q.v.); the collapse of the dam at Maʾrib in the Yemen, which is said to have triggered tribal migrations northwards; and the eventual conquest of the Yemen by the Sasanid Persians, with whom the Muslim conquerors of the region came into contact.

The "men of the elephant" of Q 105:1 are frequently understood as an allusion to an expedition reported in tradition as having been sent against Mecca by the Abyssinian Abraha, an expedition which involved one or more elephants and is recounted in some detail in Muslim literature outside the Qurʾān (see PEOPLE OF THE ELEPHANT). The "people of the ditch" (q.v.; Q 85:4) are often identified as the persecuted Christians of Najrān (q.v.), burned in a trench according to accounts found in Syriac and Arabic. The "violent flood" (*sayl al-ʿarim,* Q 34:16) is often understood to refer to the collapse of the dam at Maʾrib (see AL-ʿARIM), an event that may be attested in a pre-Islamic inscription from Maʾrib. The traditional interpretations of such passages are not, however, unanimous, and the names of Abraha, Dhū Nuwās and Maʾrib do not occur in the Qurʾān itself.

In addition, the Qurʾān refers to peoples, and the prophets whom God had sent to them, who are understood to have lived in parts of Arabia before Islam: Ṣāliḥ (q.v.) and Thamūd (q.v.), Shuʿayb (q.v.) and Madyan (see MIDIAN), Hūd (q.v.) and ʿĀd (q.v.). Thamūd is known from pre-Islamic sources as the name of a people of northern Arabia.

Modern scholars have used epigraphic and other evidence that may relate to the events reported in Muslim tradition in attempting to establish chronology and motivation (see CHRONOLOGY AND THE QURʾĀN; EPIGRAPHY AND THE QURʾĀN). Divine and personal names found in the inscriptions have been linked with names found in the Qurʾān and Muslim tradition. The best-known example is probably the divine name RḤMNN that has been seen by some scholars as the source of the qurʾānic and Islamic al-Raḥmān (see GOD AND HIS ATTRIBUTES). Since the inscriptions in which RḤMNN occurs are not easily identifiable as Jewish or Christian, some speculation about a "non-denominational form of monotheism" native to pre-Islamic Arabia arose which was linked with the reports about the *ḥanīf*s in the Muslim tradition (see also MUSAYLIMA).

Some of the names found in non-monotheistic inscriptions that have been identified as those of deities have been linked by scholars with the idols or gods whose names are given in the Qurʾān (such as those of the five "gods of the people of Noah [q.v.]" in Q 71:23), and knowledge of south Arabian polytheism has been used to put forward theories about the origins and nature of *jāhilī* polytheism (see SOUTH ARABIA, RELIGION IN PRE-ISLAMIC).

In general, scholars who connect the Qurʾān or Islam with evidence from pre-Islamic Arabia lying beyond the traditional scope of the *jāhiliyya* envisage that Muḥammad had contacts with and was influenced by the religious culture of those regions. For example, it has been suggested, on the basis of a small number of south Arabian inscriptions in which the root *sh-r-k* has been read, that both the qurʾānic word and the concept of *shirk* are derived from south Arabia. In the area of ritual, parallels have been drawn between some south Arabian practices regarding ritual purity (q.v.) and those of Islam. One problem with the attempts to explain qurʾānic and Islamic ideas, institutions and practices in this way is that south Arabia was itself part of the wider world of late antiquity and had contacts with the other Middle Eastern and Mediterranean regions.

How far does the Qurʾān reflect the background of pre-Islamic Arabia?

The relationship between the Qurʾān and pre-Islamic Arabia summarized above — the view that the text was formed in the Ḥijāz and constantly refers to or presupposes features of the life of the pre-Islamic inhabitants of northwestern and central Arabia — is one that depends mainly on Islamic traditional texts other than the Qurʾān itself. Works such as commentaries on the Qurʾān and biographies of the Prophet (see SĪRA AND THE QURʾĀN) provide the reports that are the basis of that view. The scripture itself, with its characteristically allusive style, does not explicitly inform us when or where it originated, nor does it closely specify its addressees or referents (see LANGUAGE AND STYLE OF THE QURʾĀN; FORM AND STRUCTURE OF THE QURʾĀN).

It is clear that the text contains a significant number of references to features of life associated especially with Arabs.

Sometimes that association is a common one as, for example, references to camels (see CAMEL). There are ten references in the text to tribal or nomadic Arabs (*aʿrāb;* see BEDOUIN) and the language of the Prophet and of the Qurʾān itself is called "Arabic" (*ʿarabī;* see ARABIC LANGUAGE; DIALECTS). Furthermore, the names of the "daughters of God" (Allāt, al-ʿUzzā and Manāt: Q 53:19-20), although widely attested in the ancient Middle East and around the Mediterranean, were especially associated with Arabia and the Arabs, and the list of the gods worshipped by the people of Noah (Q 71:23) also contains some names which are attested in inscriptions and graffiti found in various parts of Arabia.

Apart from the name, Muḥammad (q.v.), which occurs four times (Q 3:144; 33:40; 47:2; 48:29) and Aḥmad (Q 61:6; see NAMES OF THE PROPHET), the only Arab personal name (other than Arabic forms of biblical names; see SCRIPTURE AND THE QURʾĀN) is that of Abū Lahab (Q 111:1), whom tradition identifies as a leader of the pagan Meccans (see FAMILY OF THE PROPHET). The tribal name Quraysh (q.v.) is mentioned in Q 106:1 in a context that associates it with the sanctuary.

As for the names of places or institutions associated with Arabia, there are several in the Qurʾān; most of them are attested only once or twice, and several of them are only known outside Islam because they occur in Muslim tradition or are related to Muslim religious practice. Thus al-Ṣafā and al-Marwa (Q 2:158; see ṢAFĀ AND MARWA), ʿArafāt (q.v.; Q 2:198), and al-Kaʿba (Q 5:95, 97) are all associated with the Muslim sanctuary at Mecca *(makka)*. Much more common is *al-masjid al-ḥarām* (fifteen occurrences), the name given in Islam to the mosque (q.v.) at Mecca which contains the Kaʿba (see SACRED PRECINCTS). The name *makka* itself appears once (Q 48:24; *bakka* in Q 3:96 is identified in traditional commentary as an alternative name for it or a part of it). *Yathrib* (Q 33:13) is the only such place name in Arabia certainly attested in pre-Islamic sources (see MEDINA).

In other cases, the Qurʾān refers to features of Arab life known as such mainly from the traditional accounts of the *jāhiliyya*. In two passages (Q 52:29-30; 69:40-2) it is denied that the Prophet is a soothsayer *(kāhin)* or poet *(shāʿir),* two professions which figure large in traditional accounts of pre-Islamic Arabian life. The use of divining arrows *(azlām),* a practice associated in Muslim tradition with pre-Islamic Arabs, is condemned twice (Q 5:3, 90), and in the latter passage it is associated with other vices traditionally seen as characteristic of the *jāhiliyya* — drunkenness (see INTOXICANTS; WINE), gambling (q.v.; *al-maysir*) and idols *(al-anṣāb)*.

There is certainly material in the text of the Qurʾān itself, then, to indicate that it — or significant parts of it — reflects an environment which might indeed be called Arabian, although the elasticity of that term and the presence of Arabs in various parts of the Middle East outside the peninsula before Islam has to be borne in mind. The somewhat denigrating comments in the Qurʾān regarding the *aʿrāb* seem to show that the Bedouin at least were regarded as outsiders.

Some of those things, however, that the tradition shows as characteristically Arab — recourse to soothsayers, gambling and drinking, idolatry — could, of course, apply to many other social groups. Intercalation (connected with the *nasīʾ*) may have been a feature of Arab calendar (q.v.) calculations in the *jāhiliyya,* but if so it was a feature shared by other groups outside Arabia (such as rabbinical Jews). "Killing children," too, is an item of inter-religious polemic that need not refer to a specific practice of the *jāhilī* Arabs.

In one case in particular the information provided in the tradition about the pre-

Islamic Arabs and then used to explain the more allusive references in the Qurʾān actually seems to be at odds with the text. If one takes the material pertaining to idolatry and idolaters (*shirk* and the *mushrikūn*) in the Qurʾān and then compares it with what we are told about the idolatry of the pre-Islamic Arabs, there seems to be a significant disjunction. In the Qurʾān the idolaters appear to be people who would regard themselves as monotheists. From the perspective of the Qurʾān, that view of themselves is unjustified and their claimed monotheism is corrupt; it is thus justified to call them, polemically, idolaters (see POLEMIC AND POLEMICAL LANGUAGE). The imputation of idolatry is an item of inter-monotheist polemic widely attested outside the Qurʾān. In the traditional accounts of the *jāhiliyya,* on the other hand, the pre-Islamic Arabs are portrayed as immersed in a form of idolatry of the most literal and base kind, not simply an imperfect type of monotheism. The tradition seems to be attempting to impose an understanding of the religion of the *mushrikūn* that goes beyond the evidence of the Qurʾān itself, and it is possible to ask whether there is some distortion here and elsewhere in the traditional portrait of the *jāhiliyya.*

John Wansbrough suggested that the traditional focus on pre-Islamic Arabia in scholarship on the Qurʾān and early Islam should be understood as reflecting the ideas and preconceptions of the early Muslim scholars who wished to emphasize the connection of Islam with the Ḥijāz and the Arab prophet, Muḥammad (see ḤADĪTH AND THE QURʾĀN; POST-ENLIGHTENMENT ACADEMIC STUDY OF THE QURʾĀN). Wansbrough and others have understood Islam to be the result of more extensive historical developments than the Muslim tradition itself suggests. Many of those developments would have occurred outside Arabia in the century and more following the Arab conquest of the Middle East. In that perspective pre-Islamic Arabia, traditionally understood as the *jāhiliyya,* is of debatable importance for the end result.

Reaching a satisfactory evaluation is complicated by the fact that virtually all of our knowledge of the *jāhiliyya* (as distinct from pre-Islamic Arabia in the broader sense) depends on Muslim tradition found in texts the earliest of which date from more than a century after the death of the Prophet. Even the body of so-called *jāhilī* poetry is known only from those later texts and the question of its authenticity, therefore, has elicited a variety of responses. Furthermore, Wellhausen drew attention to the verbal and conceptual similarity of *jāhiliyya* in Islamic thought and the Greek word *agnoia* in Jewish and Christian usage. Both words have the basic connotation of ignorance in contrast with knowledge of the one, true God (see KNOWLEDGE AND LEARNING; ILLITERACY). Both can be applied generally, without any specific historical reference, or they can be applied to a variety of specific historical situations. In Islamic usage, for example, *jāhiliyya* has been applied to the pre-Islamic history of Iran and to modern secular western society.

Given the limited amount of evidence and its problematic nature, it is possible to continue to question the traditional understanding and presentation of pre-Islamic Arabia as the *jāhiliyya* and the strong connection which the tradition makes between it and the Qurʾān.

Gerald R. Hawting

Bibliography

Primary: al-Azraqī, Abū l-Walīd Muḥammad b. ʿAbdallāh, *Akhbār Makka,* ed. R. Malḥas, 2 vols., Beirut 1969; Ibn Isḥāq, *Sīra;* Ibn al-Kalbī, Abū l-Mundhir Hishām b. Muḥammad, *Kitāb al-Aṣnām* (text and German translation in R. Klinke-Rosenberger, *Das Götzenbuch,* Leipzig

1941; Eng. trans. N.A. Faris, *The book of idols,* Princeton 1952); Ibn Kathīr, *Tafsīr;* Muḥammad b. Ḥabīb, *Kitāb al-Muḥabbar,* ed. I. Lichtenstaedter, Hyderabad 1942; Qurṭubī, *Jāmiʿ; Répertoire chronologique d'épigraphie arabe,* Cairo 1931-; *Répertoire d'épigraphie sémitique, publié par la Commission du Corpus Inscriptionum Semiticarum,* Paris 1900-; al-Samhūdī, Abū l-Ḥasan ʿAlī b. ʿAbdallāh, *Wafāʾ al-wafāʾ,* 4 vols., Cairo 1955; Suyūṭī, *Lubāb al-nuqūl fī asbāb al-nuzūl,* Sidon 1999; Ṭabarī, *Tafsīr;* Wāḥidī, *Asbāb.*
Secondary: A. van den Branden, *Les inscriptions thamoudéennes,* Louvain-Heverlé 1950; C. Brockelmann, Allāh und die Götzen. Der Ursprung des islamischen Monotheismus, in *Archiv für Religionswissenschaft* 21 (1922), 99-121; J. Cantineau, *Le Nabatéen,* 2 vols., Paris 1932; C. Conti Rossini, *Chrestomathia arabica meridionalis epigraphica,* Rome 1931; J.A. Cooke, *A textbook of north Semitic inscriptions,* Oxford 1903; R. Dussaud and F. Macler, *Mission dans les régions desertiques de la Syrie moyenne,* Paris 1903; I. Ephʿal, "Ishmael" and "Arab(s)." A transformation of ethnological terms, in *JNES* 35 (1976), 225-35; U. Fabietti, The role played by the organization of the "Ḥums" in the evolution of political ideas in pre-Islamic Mecca, in *Proceedings of the Seminar for Arabian Studies* 18 (1988), 25-33; T. Fahd, *Le panthéon de l'Arabie centrale à la veille de l'héjire,* Paris 1968; J. Finkel, Jewish, Christian and Samaritan influences on Arabia, in *The Macdonald Presentation Volume,* Princeton 1933, 145-66; H.A.R. Gibb, Pre-Islamic monotheism in Arabia, in *Harvard theological review* 55 (1962), 269-80; Goldziher, *MS* (esp. i, 219-28; trans. i, 201-8, What is meant by "al-jāhiliyya"?); G.R. Hawting, *The idea of idolatry and the emergence of Islam,* Cambridge 1999; J.F. Healey, *The Nabataean tomb inscriptions of Madāʾin Ṣāliḥ,* Oxford 1993; J. Henninger, *Arabica sacra. Aufsätze zur Religionsgeschichte Arabiens und seiner Randgebiete,* Fribourg 1981; id., Pre-Islamic Bedouin religion (Eng. trans. in M.L. Swartz [ed.], *Studies on Islam,* New York 1981, 3-22); J.W. Hirschberg, *Jüdische und christliche Lehren im vor- und frühislamischen Arabien,* Cracow 1939; R.G. Hoyland, *Arabia and the Arabs from the Bronze Age to the coming of Islam,* London 2001; A. Jamme, Le panthéon sud-arabe préislamique d'après les sources épigraphiques, in *Muséon* 60 (1974), 54-147; ʿA. Jawād, *Taʾrīkh al-ʿarab qabla l-islām,* 8 vols., Baghdad 1951-60; M.J. Kister, *Concepts and ideas at the dawn of Islam,* Aldershot 1997; id., *Society and religion from Jāhiliyya to Islam,* Aldershot 1990; id., *Studies in Jāhiliyya and early Islam,* Aldershot 1980; H. Lammens, *L'Arabie occidentale avant l'héjire,* Beirut 1928; id., *Le berceau de l'islam,* Rome 1914; M. Lecker, Idol worship in pre-Islamic Medina (Yathrib), in *Muséon* 106 (1993), 331-46; E. Littman, *Thamūd und Ṣafā,* Leipzig 1940; D. Nielsen et al., *Handbuch der altarabischen Altertumskunde,* Copenhagen 1927; J. Obermann, Islamic origins. A study in background and formation, in N.A. Faris (ed.), *The Arab heritage,* Princeton 1944, 58-120; S. Pines, *Jāhiliyya* and *ʿilm,* in *JSAI* 13 (1990), 175-94; Ch. Rabin, The beginnings of classical Arabic, in *SI* 4 (1955), 19-37; A. Rippin, The function of the *asbāb al-nuzūl* in qurʾānic exegesis, in *BSOAS* 51 (1988), 1-20; id., RḤMNN and the *ḥanīfs,* in W.B. Hallaq and D.P. Little (eds.), *Islamic studies presented to Charles J. Adams,* Leiden 1991, 153-68; U. Rubin, *Ḥanīfiyya* and Kaʿba, in *JSAI* 13 (1990), 85-112; G. Ryckmans, *Les religions arabes préislamiques,* Leuven 1951²; J. Ryckmans, Les inscriptions anciennes de l'arabie du sud. Points de vue et problèmes actuels, in *Conférence prononcée à la societé "Oosters Genootschap in Nederland," le 15 mars 1973,* Leiden 1973, 79-110; J. Waardenburg, Un débat coranique contre les polythéistes, in *Ex orbe religionum. Studia Geo Widengren oblata,* Leiden 1972, 143-54; Wansbrough, *QS;* W.M. Watt, Belief in a "high god" in pre-Islamic Mecca, in *JSS* 16 (1971), 35-40; id., The Qurʾān and belief in a "high god," in *Der Islam* 56 (1979), 205-11; A.T. Welch, Allāh and other supernatural beings. The emergence of the qurʾānic doctrine of *tawḥīd,* in *Journal of the American Academy of Religion. Thematic issue: Studies in* Qurʾān *and tafsīr* (guest ed. A.T. Welch) 47 (1979), 733-53; J. Wellhausen, *Reste arabischen Heidentums,* Berlin 1897²; F.W. Winnett, *A study of the Lihyanite and Thamudic inscriptions,* Toronto 1937.

Preserved Tablet

According to Q 85:22, the location of the Qurʾān, traditionally understood to be in God's presence. The *lawḥ maḥfūẓ* is often identified with the heavenly book (q.v.) by association with other qurʾānic terms: "mother of the scripture" (*umm al-kitāb,* Q 13:39; 43:4; also 3:7), "hidden writing" (*kitāb maknūn,* Q 56:78). As *umm al-kitāb* it is the source *(aṣl)* not only of the Qurʾān but also of the other scriptures (*kutub;* see BOOK; SCRIPTURE AND THE QURʾĀN). As God's writing it contains all the divine decrees. These images and others associated with God's writing constitute a key element in qurʾānic thought (see INSTRUMENTS; WRITING AND WRITING

MATERIALS; ORALITY AND WRITING IN ARABIA). Taken literally, they are difficult to read as a coherent whole. Alternatively, they can be read, and often are in the Islamic tradition, as complementary, symbolic representations of God's knowledge and will (see KNOWLEDGE AND LEARNING; POWER AND IMPOTENCE; GOD AND HIS ATTRIBUTES). Traditional interpretation of this qurʾānic image owes much to ideas common in Semitic religions.

Although "preserved" is usually read as applying to the tablet, some authorities read the word as referring to the Qurʾān, which is thus simply "preserved on a tablet." Al-Ṭabarī (d. 310/923; *Tafsīr,* ad loc.) comments that there is little difference in meaning since either way the Qurʾān is preserved from alteration and change (see REVISION AND ALTERATION; CORRUPTION; FORGERY), perhaps against the demons (*al-shayāṭīn;* see DEVIL). The tablet is also associated with the isolated letter *"nūn"* of Q 68:1, said by some to be a tablet of light (q.v.). Apart from its importance in qurʾānic sciences (see TRADITIONAL DISCIPLINES OF QURʾĀNIC STUDY) as guarantor of the text's authenticity, the image of the Preserved Tablet plays a significant role in the discussions of theologians, philosophers, and mystics (see THEOLOGY AND THE QURʾĀN; PHILOSOPHY AND THE QURʾĀN; ṢŪFISM AND THE QURʾĀN).

The tablet figures in two major theological controversies: about predestination (see FREEDOM AND PREDESTINATION), and the createdness or otherwise of the Qurʾān (see CREATEDNESS OF THE QURʾĀN). Traditions found in exegetical works (*tafsīr;* see EXEGESIS OF THE QURʾĀN: CLASSICAL AND MEDIEVAL) focus particularly on predestination: God examines the tablet every day 360 (or 260) times, every time carrying out what he wills. It contains the characteristics of everything created, and everything about creatures (see CREATION; COSMOLOGY): the length of their lives (see FATE; DEATH AND THE DEAD); their allotted sustenance (q.v.); their actions; the verdict to be pronounced on them (see LAST JUDGMENT); the eventual punishment for their actions (see REWARD AND PUNISHMENT) — all this written by the pen (*al-qalam,* Q 68:1; 96:4), often said to be the first object created, but presumed by some to be pre-existent (see ETERNITY). In this context it becomes difficult to see whether the recording so often mentioned in the Qurʾān is describing human deeds and thoughts or rather determining them. A famous ḥadīth (see ḤADĪTH AND THE QURʾĀN) maintains that the pen is now dry; nothing determined can be changed. Q 13:39 raises a further difficulty: "God erases and confirms what he wills since with him is the *umm al-kitāb.*" Al-Ṭabarī (*Tafsīr,* ad loc.) quotes traditions to the effect that there must actually be two books: one God can change as he wills, the other unchanging. On "a blessed night" (Q 44:3) what is written on the tablet for the coming year is said to be transcribed and transmitted to the angels responsible (see ANGEL; DAY AND NIGHT).

The tablet is used in *kalām* principally to support belief in the uncreated Qurʾān. It cannot, however, resolve the issue of whether the heavenly prototype of the Qurʾān was created or is co-eternal with God. The tablet is by consensus above the seventh heaven (see HEAVEN AND SKY). Therefore Ibn Ḥanbal (fl. third/ninth cent.; al-Radd, 111-2) argued, defending the Qurʾān's uncreatedness, that the tablet containing it is not among the things scripture says were created: "the heavens, the earth and all they contain" (e.g. Q 44:38). Others could argue that, since according to some ḥadīth the tablet was created, the Qurʾān must be there by an act of creation (see also WORD OF GOD).

Among the philosophers the images of pen and tablet serve as useful support from the sacred text for the conclusions of reason (see INTELLECT), as well as points of departure for more esoteric speculations (see POLYSEMY). The pen is the first intellect, and the tablet the universal soul receiving impressions from it. For Ibn al-ʿArabī (d. 638/1240), the soul of Muḥammad is that universal soul, capable of receiving impressions directly from the intellect and passing them on.

In the Ṣūfī tradition, the images of pen and tablet are given great play by poets (see LITERATURE AND THE QUR'ĀN), though the sense of irrevocable predestination fits ill with those who encourage spiritual development. The tablet is more likely to be viewed as the believer's heart (q.v.) on which God impresses his image.

Daniel A. Madigan

Bibliography
Primary (in addition to the classical commentaries, esp. ad Q 13:39; 68:1; 85:22): al-Ghazālī, Abū Ḥāmid Muḥammad, *Tahāfut al-falāsifa,* ed. and trans. M.E. Marmura, Provo, UT 1997, 158-63; Ibn al-ʿArabī, Muḥyī l-Dīn, *al-Futūḥāt al-makkiyya,* 4 vols., Cairo [1911], i, 139 l. 35; ii, 282 l. 26; 439 l. 8; 675 l. 15; iii, 28 l. 32; Ibn Ḥanbal, al-Radd ʿalā l-zanādiqa wa-l-jahmiyya, in M. Seale (ed.), *Muslim theology,* London 1964, 96-125; Ibn Rushd, *Tahāfut al-tahāfut,* ed. M. Bouyges, Beirut 1930, 494-5; Suyūṭī, *Itqān* (*nawʿ* 16: *fī kayfiyyat inzālihi*); Zarkashī, *Burhān* (*nawʿ* 12: *fī kayfiyyat inzālihi*).
Secondary: E.R. Curtius, The book as symbol, in id., *European literature and the Latin Middle Ages,* trans. (from Ger.) W.R. Trask, New York 1953, 302-47; van Ess, *TG,* i, 186, 281; ii, 47, 283; iv, 617-30; v, 239, 437; L. Gardet, Kalām, in *EI²*, iv, 468-71; A. Schimmel, *Mystical dimensions of Islam,* Chapel Hill 1975, 194-7, 412-4; W.M. Watt, *The formative period of Islamic thought,* Edinburgh 1973, 82-116, 232-46; id., *Free will and predestination in early Islam,* London 1948; A.T. Welch, al-Ḳurʾān, in *EI²*, v, 400-32; A.J. Wensinck, *The Muslim creed,* London 1932; id./C.E. Bosworth, Lawḥ, in *EI²*, v, 698; G. Widengren, *The ascension of the apostle and the heavenly book,* Uppsala 1950; H.A. Wolfson, *The philosophy of the Kalam,* Cambridge 1976, chaps. 3, 8.

Pride

Inordinate self-esteem, conceit. Pride is very often denounced by the Qurʾān as a sin (see SIN, MAJOR AND MINOR) because of its similarity to a form of "partnership with God" (*shirk;* see POLYTHEISM AND ATHEISM): Do not the proud deem themselves or aspire to be like God in his greatness? Their *istikbār* looks to be a denial of their humble condition in their will to be equal to the one who alone is "the most high, the most great" (*al-ʿalī l-kabīr,* Q 22:62), "the supreme" (*al-mutakabbir,* Q 59:23). The verb *istakbara* is used forty times in the Qurʾān and its participle, *mustakbir,* six times. Although "pride" is the most common English rendition, there are a variety of translations of the concept. Pride is the sin of all those who refuse to surrender to God (*islām*). It was also Satan's (see DEVIL) first sin, when he was ordered to prostrate before Adam (see BOWING AND PROSTRATION; ADAM AND EVE): "[The angels] all prostrated except Iblīs (Satan), he refused (see DISOBEDIENCE) and was proud and was one of the disbelievers" (Q 2:34; 38:73-4; see BELIEF AND UNBELIEF; see also FALL OF MAN; INSOLENCE AND OBSTINACY).

Pride is also the sin of those who did not listen to the prophets' message in history (see PROPHETS AND PROPHETHOOD; MESSENGER; HISTORY AND THE QURʾĀN). This was the case of Noah's (q.v.) folk: "And they magnified themselves in pride" (Q 71:7); of Ṣāliḥ's (q.v.) people: "The leaders of those who were arrogant among his people" (Q 7:75) said "Verily, we are disbelievers in that which you believe" (Q 7:76; see BELIEF AND UNBELIEF); of Shuʿayb's (q.v.) relatives: "The chiefs of those who were arrogant" (Q 7:88); and of Hūd's (q.v.) kinsfolk: "As for ʿĀd (q.v.), they were arrogant" (Q 41:15). Pride was especially the sin of Pharaoh (q.v.) and his chiefs: "They were arrogant in the land" (Q 29:39; see ARROGANCE; OPPRESSION), they "behaved arrogantly and were criminals" (Q 10:75), and "were arrogant and they were people self-exalting" (Q 23:46). Consequently God says: "We sent on them the flood, the locusts, the lice, the frogs, and the blood…, yet they remained arrogant" (Q 7:133; see PLAGUES). Muḥammad himself faced the same difficulties from his adversaries (see OPPOSITION TO MUḤAMMAD): "Indeed they think too highly of themselves and are scornful with great pride" (*ʿataw ʿutuwwan kabīran,* Q 25:21), and even some of his followers were tempted to behave in the same manner (Q 34:31-3; 40:47-8). Pride makes people blind (see VISION AND BLINDNESS) and unable to recognize the signs (q.v.; *āyāt*) of God and to worship their lord (q.v.) righteously: "But as for those who refused his worship (q.v.) and were proud, he will punish them with a painful torment" (Q 4:173; see REWARD AND PUNISHMENT; CHASTISEMENT AND PUNISHMENT). In fact, "Those who reject our signs and treat them with arrogance, they are the dwellers of the fire" (q.v.; Q 7:36; cf. 6:93; 7:40; 40:60; see also HELL AND HELLFIRE).

Ultimately, though, "he [God] likes not the proud" (Q 16:23) and "seals up the heart (q.v.) of every arrogant *(mutakabbir)* tyrant *(jabbār)*" (Q 40:35). As for those who are not proud, God will welcome them with his satisfaction *(riḍwān)* and will accept their worship. All creatures "prostrate to God… and they are not proud" (Q 16:49), especially the angels (see ANGEL), who are always humble in God's presence (Q 7:206; 21:19), and the true believers who "glorify the praises of their lord, and they are not proud" (Q 32:15; see GLORIFICATION OF GOD; LAUDATION). Perhaps for this reason Christians are found to be "the nearest in love to the Muslims… because they are not proud" (Q 5:82; see CHRISTIANS AND CHRISTIANITY). Creatures have to be humble, and only God is "the greatest": He is "the compeller *(al-jabbār;* cf. Heb. *gibbōr;* see Ahrens, Christliches, 19), the supreme *(al-mutakabbir)*" (Q 59:23), "and his [alone] is the majesty *(al-kibriyāʾ;* cf. Ahrens, Christliches, 23, for discussion of this term as possibly derived from Ethiopic) in the heavens and the earth" (Q 45:37; see KINGS AND RULERS; POWER AND IMPOTENCE; GOD AND HIS ATTRIBUTES).

Maurice Borrmans

Bibliography
Primary: Rashīd Riḍā, *Manār;* Rāzī, *Tafsīr.*
Secondary: K. Ahrens, Christliches im Qoran. Eine Nachlese, in *ZDMG* 84 (1930), 15-68, 148-90; ʿA.Y. ʿAlī, *The glorious Qurʾān,* Riyadh 1973; Arberry; D. Masson, *Monothéisme coranique et monothéisme biblique,* Paris 1976, esp. 632-64; Pickthall, *Koran.*

Priests see CHRISTIANS AND CHRISTIANITY; MONASTICISM AND MONKS; ASCETICISM

Printing of the Qurʾān

The history of the printed Qurʾān has received little scholarly attention. Political and cultural historians, while often mentioning the introduction of the printing press into Islamic lands, tend to link printing with the modernizing efforts of sultans and shahs. Scholars who concentrate on printing history have followed the same path, albeit with greater depth and nuance. This article summarizes findings in the history of the printing of the complete Arabic Qurʾān produced by means of metal type or lithography. After an enumeration of the earliest imprints, the article discusses the background to printing the Qurʾān in the Muslim world and, within the limits of what is currently known, describes early printing efforts.

The article concludes with remarks on contemporary publishing. The focus is on the history of the printing of that qurʾānic text that is used by the majority of Sunnī Muslims, who are, in turn, the largest Muslim group.

Earliest printings of the Qurʾān

Although by 1543 there existed at least six different printings of the edition by Theodor Buchmann (Bibliander) of Robert of Ketton's Latin translation of the Qurʾān (Bobzin, *Der Koran,* 209 f.), the first complete Arabic Qurʾān said to have been printed by means of movable type appeared in Venice in 1537-8 (but cf. Nallino, Una cinquecentesca edizione, 10, where it is asserted that the printing was somewhere between 1530 and 1537). It was, however, destroyed — according to some accounts, at the order of the Pope (cf. Blachère, *Introduction,* 133; Bobzin, *Der Koran,* 182 f. argues against any ecclesiastical order to destroy this edition) or, according to Nuovo (Il Corano), because there was no market for it in the Middle East, for which it was intended. Others have suggested that the memory of this printing was based on a misunderstanding perpetuated in later sources. A copy of the printing, however, was discovered in Italy in the 1980s, displaying a very faulty text which is what likely led to its destruction (the opening pages of the text are illustrated in Bloom, *Paper before print,* 220; see PRE-1800 PREOCCUPATIONS OF QURʾĀNIC STUDIES).

The next printing was in Hamburg in 1694 by Abraham Hinckelmann, who provided an introduction in Latin (see Fig. I). This was followed four years later by the Arabic text with Latin translation and a refutation of Islam by Ludovico Marracci (see Fig. II). This is the well-known *Alcorani Textus Universus.* The most widely used Arabic edition, that of Gustav Flügel, first appeared in 1834, followed by printings of 1841, 1855, 1867, 1870, 1881, and 1893 (see Smitskamp, Flügel). This was the edition used by western scholars until the printed text became widely available in editions produced in the Islamic world after World War I.

Numerous early editions were printed in St. Petersburg under the patronage of Catherine II, with printings in 1787, 1789, 1790 (see Fig. III), 1793, 1796 and 1798 (see Rezvan, Qurʾān and its world, VIII/2). In the Volga city of Kazan, the Qurʾān was first printed, according to Sarkīs (*Muʿjam,* ii, 1501), in 1801, or, according to Schnurrer (*Bibliotheca,* 420), in 1803 (see Fig. IV for an example of a Kazan printing of the Qurʾān). The discrepancy may be the result of confusion over the date of the founding of the press by Tsar Pavel I (in 1801) and the actual date of the first imprint. Princeton University Library reports an 1820 imprint produced at Ṭabkhānah-yi Sayyidāt-i Kazān.

From 1842, it was reprinted annually at various presses, including Asiatic Typography and Rahīmjān Saʿīd Ugli. In 1905, a large-format Qurʾān was printed in St. Petersburg for presentation to dignitaries. Although not a typeset production — it was a photographic replication of a manuscript — this monumental work reproduced a large-format Kūfic Qurʾān similar to the one that is said to have belonged to the third caliph, ʿUthmān. In 1911-12, Qurʾāns in large and small format were printed in the Crimea. The Qurʾān was printed in London in 1833 and again in 1871 and 1875. Harvard University Library reports lithographed editions in 1845 and 1848 printed in London.

The Qurʾān was frequently printed in India. Bombay imprints include those of 1852, 1865, 1869, 1875, 1881, 1883, 1891 and 1897. The first Calcutta printings appeared in 1856 and 1857. The Bombay edition contained an introduction in

Persian by Muḥammad ʿAlī al-Qāshānī. The printings of Calcutta were produced by William Nassau Lees, ʿAbd al-Ḥayy and Khaddām Ḥusayn, and included the *tafsīr* of al-Zamakhsharī (d. 538/1144; see EXEGESIS OF THE QURʾĀN: CLASSICAL AND MEDIEVAL). Sarkīs lists a Lucknow printing of 1850, which would be the first Indian printed Qurʾān. Other Lucknow editions appeared annually from 1865 to 1869, then 1878, 1882, 1883, 1885 and 1890. There are Delhi imprints of 1863, 1876, 1889, and 1892. According to Sarkīs (*Muʿjam*, ii, 1500), other early printings included Talshīr [sic] (1882), the northern city of Bareilly (1886, 1876) and Kanpur (1878, 1882, 1884). An Arabic Qurʾān with English translation by Mirzā Abū Faḍl appeared in Allahabad in 1911. Sarkīs notes numerous printings of the text with the *Tafsīr al-Jalālayn* (ninth/fifteenth cent.). He also mentions that there were many translations into Persian and Bengali printed in cities throughout India including Lucknow, Lahore, Kanpur, Aligar, Sialkot, Bombay and Calcutta (see Sarkīs, *Muʿjam*, ii, 1500). Shcheglova *(Katalog)* mentions Bombay lithographs of 1862, 1886/89 and 1899/1902. These editions included Persian interlinear translations.

In Istanbul, the Qurʾān was printed from metal type in 1872 and lithographically by order of the Ministry of Education in 1873 and 1876 (Sarkīs, *Muʿjam*, ii, 1500). Other Istanbul editions cited by Sarkīs are those of the calligrapher Shakir Zāda (1881; see CALLIGRAPHY) and of the press of Muṣṭafā Efendi Qādirjī. There were Istanbul printings of 1886, 1889, and 1904 by the Baḥriyya and Ḥurriyat presses. The government press (Dār al-Ṭibāʿa al-Āmira) produced the Qurʾān from 1883-1906 (see Fig. v), and Harvard University Library reports an edition of 1888 printed at al-Maṭbaʿa al-ʿUthmāniyya.

Sarkīs (*Muʿjam*, ii, 1499-1500) lists numerous printings in Cairo, beginning with the Būlāq printings of 1864, 1866, 1881, and 1886. He cites other editions, e.g. those of Ḥasan Aḥmad al-Ṭūkhī of 1881 to 1883 and 1885, those of Muḥammad Abū Zayd of 1881 to 1883 and 1890, the press of Sayyid ʿAlī of 1883 and 1884, the imprints of Shaykh Sharaf of 1889 and 1890, and the press of Ḥasan al-Sharīf of 1887. He mentions a lithographed edition of Shaykh Muḥammad Raḍwān printed in 1890. He cites printings by the prolific ʿAbd al-Khāliq Ḥaqqī of 1892, 1895 and 1897 and annually from 1899 until 1904. From this time forward, Qurʾāns were continually printed by various publishers, including al-Bābī l-Ḥalabī (e.g. in two volumes, 1925) and the Ḥanafī Press (1936). The text was often accompanied by the popular *tafsīrs* of l-Bayḍāwī (d. prob. 716/1316) or al-Jalālayn. Reproduction of the text with these commentaries remains common through the beginning of the twenty-first century (see Sarkīs, *Muʿjam*, ii, 1499 f.).

There is disagreement over the first printing of the Qurʾān in Iran. Browne *(Press and poetry)* mentions an edition from a press supervised by Mirzā ʿAbd al-Wahhāb as early as 1816/17. He also mentions a lithographed edition printed in Tabrīz in the mid-1820s calligraphed by Mirzā Ḥusayn and printed by Mirzā Asad Allāh. Floor (Čāp) cites a Qurʾān from Shīrāz in 1829. Proudfoot (Lithography), perhaps following Browne, cites a Qurʾān printed in 1828. The Academy of Sciences in St. Petersburg mentions a Tehran printing of 1831 and a Tabrīz Qurʾān of 1833. Marzolph *(Narrative illustration)* states that the latter is a lithograph; it is, in fact, the first lithographed book known to have been produced in Iran. It was published in Tabrīz at the official press. Shūrbajī *(Qāʾima)* cites a Tabrīz imprint of 1843 printed by ʿAbbās Shafīʿ and an Arabic Qurʾān with Persian interlinear translation published in 1850.

Shcheglova *(Katalog)* lists an Arabic text with Persian translation of 1895 corrected and published by ʿAbd al-Bāqī Aḥmad Tafrīshī. The first Moroccan Qurʾān was lithographed in 1879 by al-Ṭayyib al-Azraq, the country's foremost printer of the period. In southeast Asia, a Qurʾān was lithographed in 1848 by Muḥammad Azharī of Palembang and reprinted in 1854.

One must be cautious in approaching any list of printing firsts. Early imprints are difficult to verify from library catalogues or enumerative bibliographies. Abdulrazak *(Kingdom)* demonstrates these difficulties in his examination of the Venice Qurʾān of the 1530s. He suggests that it is not a product of Gutenberg's invention at all, but rather a woodblock print. Likewise, bibliographer and antiquarian R. Smitskamp shows extreme caution in describing works in his catalogues of early Qurʾān imprints, such as the Qurʾān printed in Istanbul in 1850. He calls this edition, "The first Qurʾān to be printed in an Islamic country by way of lithography" (Smitskamp, *Het Oosters antiquarium,* cat. 602, item 547). The copy in hand was multicolored and gilt (see ORNAMENTATION AND ILLUMINATION) and "was executed in a way that can range this Qurʾān on the same level as a manuscript and represents a remarkable sample of early Ottoman lithography." Perhaps it was because of this resemblance to manuscripts that bibliographers have overlooked this edition. Further confusion attaches to this edition because, according to Smitskamp, the date of imprint (1246 A.H.) is incorrect.

Corrections to the record can be made only by close examination of the text. Smitskamp cites numerous other printings unknown to earlier bibliographers, such as the illuminated Qurʾān of 1887 ordered by Sultan ʿAbd al-Ḥamīd II "as gifts to the pious," a Bombay lithograph of 1880 calligraphed by al-Ḥājj Aḥmad b. al-Ḥājj Muḥammad (Smitskamp, *Het Oosters antiquarium,* cat. 591, item 804). He also cites a Teheran lithograph of 1856 (ibid., cat. 591, item 806 = 1273), and an Istanbul lithograph of 1877 (ibid., cat. 627, item 653), but cautions that this date may be mistaken.

The implication of the foregoing bibliographic lists is that the Qurʾān was more extensively printed than has been recognized. By the mid-nineteenth century there were locally printed Qurʾāns in nearly every Islamic region. It has been axiomatic among non-Muslims that there was an abiding aversion among Muslims to printing in general and to the printing of Islamic books and the Qurʾān in particular. Nuovo (Il Corano) puts it most directly, calling it the "well-known aversion *(avversione)* of Islam for the printing press." It is frequently held that the early attempts at printing the Qurʾān in Europe were aesthetically and editorially repugnant to Muslims. Indeed, Muslim authorities thwarted printing of Islamic texts until well into the nineteenth century. On the basis of his study of library holdings, Abdulrazak states, "... it seems that 1818 was a turning point in the history of printing in the Islamic world as increasing numbers of Islamic texts were being published from that date onwards" (Abdulrazak, *Kingdom*). Gdoura *(Le début)* places the date a good deal earlier and more precisely: 1803.

The debate over printing

Historians offer many explanations for the disinclination to use printed books or to adopt the means of producing them (for a recent discussion, see Bloom, *Paper before print*). The locus of the debate was Istanbul, capital of the Ottoman empire, where political and religious elites presented arguments for and against the importation of the press or printed books from Europe. Gdoura *(Le début)* recognizes that since the later part of the sixteenth century the decision about admitting the printing press into the empire was a political decision that rested with the sultan himself after consultation with secular and religious counselors. An economic reason often cited for the delay in adopting the press was the opposition of scribes and calligraphers, who feared the loss of their livelihood. Little by little, from the sixteenth through the eighteenth centuries, political opposition to the press relaxed. Bāyazīd II (r. 886-918/1481-1512) permitted Jews to print. Murād III (r. 982-1003/1574-95) permitted importation of European printed works in Arabic as long as they did not concern religion. Beginning in 1620, debate raged over the publication of Protestant books in Arabic, a move that was opposed by the Orthodox patriarch, who complained to the sultan, and the sultan intervened to close Greek and Arabic presses. It was nearly a hundred years later that the Hungarian-born convert to Islam, Ibrāhīm Mutafarriqa, finally convinced the sultan and the religious authorities that the printing press might help strengthen the empire vis-à-vis an increasingly threatening Europe. Mutafarriqa's arguments had their effect, and in 1726 the Shaykh al-Islām issued a *fatwā* declaring it legal to print (see MEDIA AND THE QUR'ĀN). The text of the decree read, in part:

If one is versed in the art of correctly printing with metal characters the above mentioned titles... [he] will furnish a means of reducing labor, multiplying copies, lowering costs and making acquisition [of books] easier and cheaper. I decide that this art... should be encouraged without delay, on the understanding that trained and intelligent men be chosen and that works from the press be corrected against the best originals.

The reference to the "above mentioned titles" points to the list of dictionaries, histories, military and geographical texts submitted to the authorities for approval. No religious works were included.

The strictures imposed by the Shaykh al-Islām applied to the Ottoman territories. By virtue of the primacy of the sultan in the Islamic world, the writ ran beyond Ottoman boundaries. When other countries of the region came to consider printing in the nineteenth century, their leaders were conscious of these strictures. As to the more distant Islamic populations, there was little — if any — printing from metal type. Iran, of course, lay beyond the influence of decisions taken in the capital of Sunnī Islam, but its early printing history bears many similarities to that of the Ottoman empire.

In addition to the political, cultural, and economic reasons for the slow introduction of printing, there were local reasons as well. Ṣābāt *(Tārīkh)* argues that the fundamental cause of the delay of printing in Egypt was the political chaos following the withdrawal of Napoleon's forces from Egypt in 1801. It took four years for Muḥammad ʿAlī to emerge above rival Mamlūk factions and to secure power. After consolidating his rule, he turned toward fashioning a modern administration, industrial base and military power. These ambitions led directly to the importation of the press and the recruitment of workers. Importation of machinery and supplies and training of pressmen took fifteen years. The first book was not published until 1822.

Lithographic printings of the Qur'ān in the Islamic world

Widespread printing of the Qur'ān in the Islamic world did not begin until well into the nineteenth century, or until the lithographic printing process became available to Muslims. At that point, there began a florescence of publishing that has continued to the present day. Lithographic printing is based on the repulsion of oil to water applied to a plane surface, such as a flat stone or metal plate. Ink adheres to the image and is repelled from the blank areas. Early Muslim lithographers used stones mined in various parts of Asia or imported from Europe. They copied their text on specially prepared paper from which it was transferred to the stone before being put through the press.

Invented in the late eighteenth century in Germany, lithography was soon employed by European publishers to print maps, drawings and other illustrative material. For Muslim publishers, lithography had three advantages over movable type in printing the Qur᾽ān. First, it is a much cheaper process, requiring importation of less complex machinery and materials. Second, it eliminated the need for complex type design for the Arabic script and large cases of type to accommodate the hundreds of Arabic letterforms. Finally, and perhaps most important of all, it permitted calligraphic preparation of the qur᾽ānic text to the point where a well designed and executed lithograph may be mistaken for a manuscript, thus prompting Proudfoot (Lithography) to characterize lithography as "the Islamic technology." Its principal disadvantage is that print runs had to be much smaller than books set in metal type. Yet, because the process was comparatively cheap, frequent new editions were possible, as we have seen in the case of Istanbul, Cairo, India and the Russian empire. And, Muslim printers, whether governmental or private, adopted improvements (developed in Europe), which included photographic and increasingly complex chemical and mechanical techniques. In terms of the quality of book design, it should be noted that — apart from sumptuous presentation copies prepared, for example, for the Ottoman sultan — the average lithographed Qur᾽ān was rather dull in appearance. Early printers did not use color for either the text or the ornamentation of the frontispiece. The objective of most printing, after all, was to make the scripture affordable, an Everyman's Qur᾽ān. It has been only recently, from perhaps the latter half of the twentieth century, that lavishly ornamental printed Qur᾽āns have entered the general book trade (see EVERYDAY LIFE, THE QUR᾽ĀN IN).

Earliest Egyptian printed Qur᾽āns

As was often the case wherever printing of the Qur᾽ān was contemplated, controversy arose. By 1822, planning and equipping the official press at Būlāq was complete and the first books were printed. Initially, these were technical manuals and linguistic aids aimed at furthering the ruler's plans for a modern army, industry and administration. The books were to be used as textbooks in the new curriculum. As need arose, the curriculum expanded to include such subjects as Turkish and Persian literature and European history.

None of the earliest Qur᾽āns printed in Egypt have survived. Raḍwān *(Tārīkh),* whose work in the Egyptian archives is the foundation of these remarks (except where noted), dates the first printing of portions of the Qur᾽ān *(ajzā᾽)* to April 1833. Because no copies of this printing have survived, Raḍwān's history and the brief mention of printing by A.A. Paton in his *A history of the Egyptian revolution* (1863) are the only indications that the edition ever existed. Unfortunately, without copies of this printing, no descriptive bibliography or textual analysis is possible. Certain aspects of the edition, however, are clear. It was printed in tablet or sheet form and is often referred to as *ajzā᾽ al-Qur᾽ān,* in distinction to a complete *muṣḥaf.* We do not know whether the text was typeset or lithographed. If the latter, we do not know the calligrapher: if the former, we do not know if specialized type was used for the printing. Most notable by its absence is any mention of a committee of scholars to consult on the preparation and correction of the text, a tradition that goes back to the seventh century recension of ʿUthmān.

In the early years of Egyptian printing, the *ʿulamā᾽* objected to printing religious books, questioning whether any part of the apparatus employed the skin of dogs. The director of the press was instructed to answer their questions; whether he did so, and how he answered, are not to be found in the sources. Before printing the 1833 edition, Muḥammad ʿAlī asked Shaykh al-Tamīmī, Muftī of Egypt, to put his seal on the printed copy, so that it could be sold or otherwise distributed. The shaykh agreed to this, according to Paton (quoted by Raḍwān, *Tārīkh*).

Muḥammad ʿAlī ignored the core works of the religious curriculum. His disdain for the religious establishment was reciprocated by the religious scholars (*ʿulamā᾽;* see SCHOLAR; KNOWLEDGE AND LEARNING; THEOLOGY AND THE QUR᾽ĀN). They viewed the press as an innovation *(bidʿa)*. To use metal letters or to apply heavy pressure in printing the name of God (see GOD AND HIS ATTRIBUTES) was reprehensible *(makrūh)*. They declared the use of the press for these purposes forbidden *(muḥarram)*. Further, use of printing equipment was inconsistent with the need for purity *(al-ṭahāra)* in preparing the text (see RITUAL PURITY). Ignoring opposition, Muḥammad ʿAlī authorized the first Egyptian printing of the Qur᾽ān. It is not clear whether the entire text or only portions of it were ready for distribution in 1833. Ṣābāt *(Tārīkh)* reports that the press operation at this stage did not have more than four correctors *(musaḥḥiḥūn)*. It is doubtful, therefore, whether this edition received the traditional attention of scholars and correctors before printing.

A year earlier (1832), an announcement appeared in the government's official news organ, *al-Waqā᾽iʿ al-miṣriyya,* announcing preparations to print sufficient copies of certain parts of the Qur᾽ān for pupils in the government schools. The exact portions of the text selected for printing were not specified. As a result of the solicitation, sixty sheets (*alwāḥ;* sing. *lūḥ*) were printed for distributi n to students, presumably students in the government's schools. Preceding the printing, the *ʿulamā᾽* were in contact with Muḥammad ʿAlī over the advantages of printing. Although they conceded some ground on this point, they declined to have books associated with religious instruction printed until the reforming Shaykh al-Azhar, Rifāʿa al-Ṭahṭāwī, petitioned the Egyptian ruler, Khedive Saʿīd (r. 1854-63), to print texts used at al-Azhar with government funding.

As was frequently the case with Būlāq imprints, there was a distribution beyond the schools for which they were printed and distributed, free of charge to students. The Qur᾽ān portions printed in 1833 were no doubt sold to the populace. Although we do not know the size of the print run or the price, we do know that 269 copies were collected in 1853 by order of Khedive ʿAbbās I (r. 1848-54). Acceding to the arguments of the *ʿulamā᾽* that the 1833 printing contained "some errors," ʿAbbās issued an order in May 1853 to confiscate the printing. The injunction did not have the intended effect, at least not immediately. Exactly one year later, in May 1854, the provincial government in Alexandria had to repeat the order against buying and selling the flawed edition. The copies were collected in a warehouse of the Ministry of the Interior *(dīwān al-dākhiliyya)*. The order legally to destroy them was difficult to carry out. Copies remained in storage until 1858 when Khedive Saʿīd inquired about providing some of them to students at the military school after they had been corrected. Fifty-two copies were thus distributed. It appears that sometime late in 1857 a project to correct the impounded *maṣāḥif* (see MUṢḤAF) was begun. The task of correcting them fell to a government scribe, Shaykh ʿAbd al-Bāqī l-Jarī (he was also a *ḥāfiz*, i.e. someone who had memorized the entire Qurʾān; see RECITERS OF THE QURʾĀN; RECITATION OF THE QURʾĀN), who had copied Ibn Khaldūn's (d. 784/1382) history.

From this time onward, the Būlāq Press proceeded to print the Qurʾān without objection from the *ʿulamāʾ* (for an example of a late nineteenth-century Būlāq printing, see Fig. VI). In order to ensure high standards of accuracy, a special department was established for matters pertaining to the Qurʾān *(maṭbaʿat al-muṣḥaf al-sharīf)*, the director of which would be independent of the overall administration of the Būlāq Press. Neither the press law of 1859 under Khedive Saʿīd nor the law of 1881 under Khedive Tawfīq made reference to the Qurʾān. One can infer that, by that time, the advantages of printing the Qurʾān were recognized by the entire society. Distribution of the 1833 *muṣḥaf* no doubt suffered from the general weakness of distribution of many of the titles from the government presses. To be sure, copies were distributed to appropriate schools, but beyond this there was no efficient way to get books to the public, even though there were attempts to open government bookshops. Private booksellers thus filled the gap. Such trade was to have stopped after the confiscation order of 1853, so by the 1860s private publishers like al-Bābī l-Ḥalabī began to fill the market with editions of their own.

Other early printings of the Qurʾān

The studies by Proudfoot (Lithography) and Abdulrazak *(Kingdom)* illustrate the importance of lithography in southeast Asia and Morocco respectively. According to Proudfoot, the first Qurʾān printed in southeast Asia was also the first book printed by a native of the region (see SOUTHEAST ASIAN LITERATURE AND THE QURʾĀN). In 1848, Muḥammad Azharī, a native of Sumatra, produced a lithographed Qurʾān that he reprinted in 1854. On his return home from a sojourn in Mecca, he stopped in Singapore to purchase the necessary equipment and supplies. He also hired an assistant, one Ibrāhīm b. Ḥusayn. Azharī himself copied the text. Inasmuch as there was no official body to vet his work, he established his bona fides in the colophon. He declares that the Qurʾān was printed on a stone press "in the handwriting of the man of God Almighty, Haji [sic] Muḥammad Azhari son of Kemas Haji Abdallah, resident of Pelambang, follower of the Shafiʿi school, of the Ashʿarite conviction...." (cited in Proudfoot, Lithography, 129) Both editions sold well (several hundred copies) and Proudfoot notes that Azharī quickly recovered the cost of his investment.

The case of Morocco adds other insights to the study of the Islamic press. The kingdom of Morocco, while not subject to the sultan in Istanbul, nor necessarily under the writ of the Ḥanafī Shaykh al-Islām in Istanbul, nevertheless followed the Ottomans in matters pertaining to printing. The lithographic press had been introduced in 1864 and was immediately used for religious books, although the Qurʾān was not printed until 1879. Abdulrazak *(Kingdom)* notes that the way was smoothed for printing because "those scribes who were also scholars were not prevented from copying books for printing. As a matter of fact, those scholars who were able to perform more than one aspect of printing were very attractive to printers and publishers."

Contemporary printings of the Qur'ān

Today, the Qur'ān is produced in a variety of shapes, sizes and degrees of production quality. The foremost printing centers are Cairo and Medina, but Qur'āns are produced in many Islamic countries and in the West. Since the 1920s, the Cairo edition, known as the King Fū'ad or "royal *(amīriyya)* edition," has become the standard edition in Egypt. Many Qur'āns printed elsewhere have been modeled on its calligraphic style, printing conventions and editorial notes contained at the end of the volume. ʿAbd al-Fattāḥ al-Qāḍī (Muṣḥaf) summarizes the history of this printing. He states that, because numerous non-standard editions were filling the market, the authorities at al-Azhar took the matter under consideration at this time. A committee was appointed, headed by Shaykh Muḥammad ʿAlī l-Ḥusaynī, the chief of the Egyptian Qur'ān reciters. Also on the committee were Ḥanafī Nāṣif, chief inspector of Arabic at the Ministry of Education, Muṣṭafā ʿAnānī, a teacher at Madrasat al-Muʿallimīn l-Nāṣiriyya, and Aḥmad al-Iskandarānī, also at the Nāṣiriyya school. These four persons determined to use the ʿUthmānic recension *(rasm)*, adopting the recitation conventions of Ḥafṣ *ʿan* ʿĀṣim, also noting whether the passages were Meccan or Medinan (see CHRONOLOGY AND THE QUR'ĀN). They decided on the markings for sūras (see SŪRA), *ajzā'*, and other guides to recitation. Al-Qāḍī remarks that, in spite of the editorial attentions of the committee and the officials who reviewed the work, there were "several shortcomings" *(baʿḍ al-hanāt)*.

When the first printing (i.e. that of 1924) was sold out, the National Library of Egypt determined to bring out another edition. The Library's director wrote to the Shaykh al-Azhar asking him to set up a committee for this purpose. ʿAbd al-Fattāḥ al-Qāḍī himself was appointed along with Shaykh Muḥammad ʿAlī l-Najjār, Shaykh ʿAlī Muḥammad al-Ḍibāʿ and Shaykh ʿAbd al-Ḥalīm al-Basyūnī. They reviewed the classical literature on all aspects of vocalization and recitation (see GRAMMAR AND THE QUR'ĀN; FORM AND STRUCTURE OF THE QUR'ĀN; LANGUAGE AND STYLE OF THE QUR'ĀN; TRADITIONAL DISCIPLINES OF QUR'ĀNIC STUDY). The result was what al-Qāḍī calls the second printing. The 1924 edition remained the basis of subsequent editions in Egypt.

A particularly well-made example is the printing of 1938 issued by ʿAbd al-Ḥamīd Salīm at al-Maṭbāʿat al-Shams al-Islāmiyya, a private firm. The original committee revised it. The government, too, issued an edition reviewed by the identical committee in 1936 called the Fārūq edition, after the Egyptian king, Fārūq (r. 1936-52). The version was corrected by Shaykh Naṣr al-ʿAdlī, chief corrector at the government *(amīriyya)* press. In addition to the signatures of the five persons involved, the work bears the seal of the Shaykh al-Azhar.

During the 1960s, the Qur'ān Review Section *(qism faḥṣ al-maṣāḥif)* of the al-Azhar administration controlled Qur'ān printing. Formerly, page proofs (Fr. *epreuves*, and thus Ar. *al-barūfāt*) of new editions would be reviewed only once before a permit was issued to print and distribute. Later, it was decided that a review was needed after printing and binding were complete. This change occurred after it was discovered that some copies had been misbound. During 1963, the Section re-

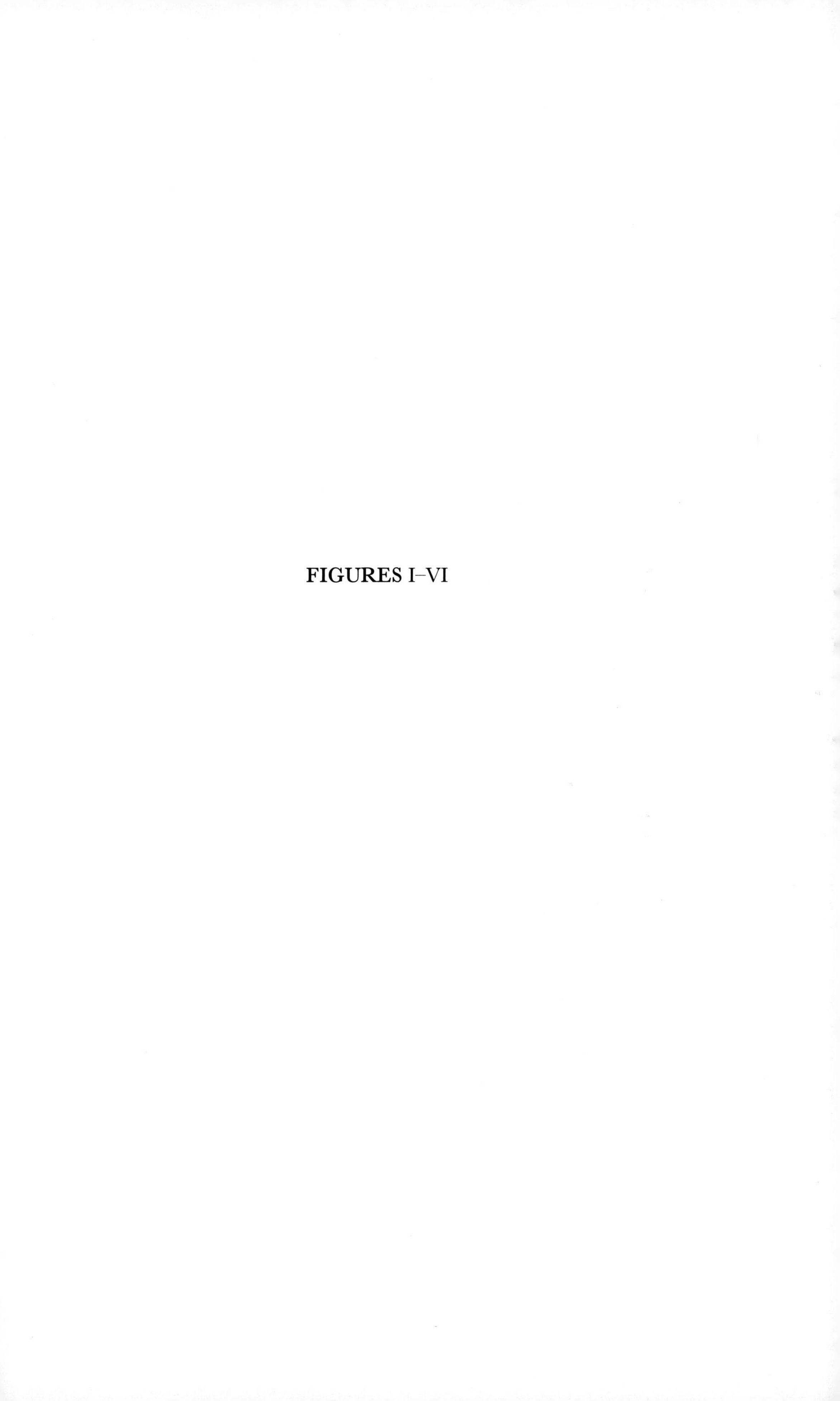

FIGURES I–VI

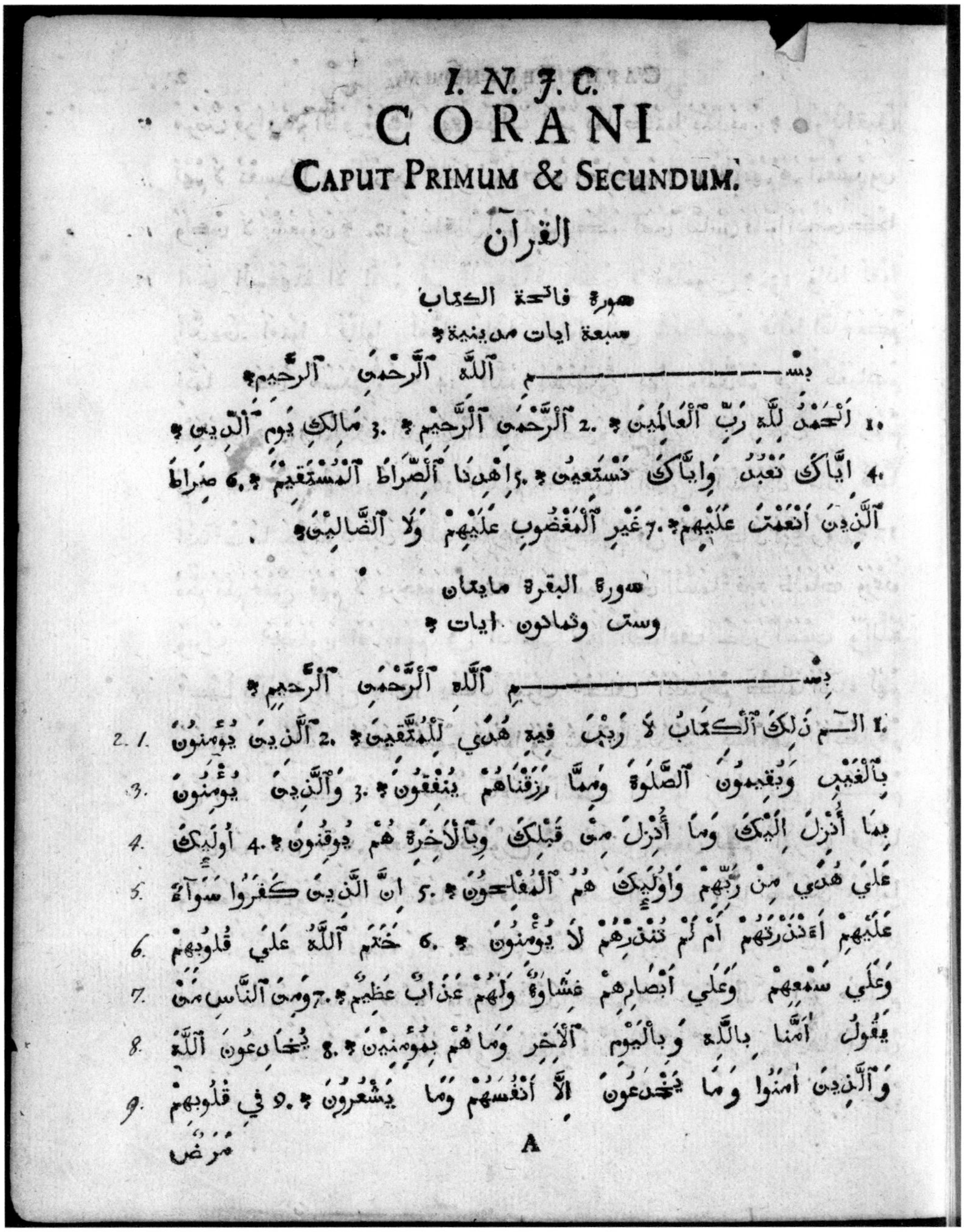

I. N. J. C.

CORANI

CAPUT PRIMUM & SECUNDUM.

القرآن

سورة فاتحة الكتاب

سبعة ايات من بنية

بسم الله الرحمن الرحيم

1. الحمد لله رب العالمين 2. الرحمن الرحيم 3. مالك يوم الدين

4. اياك نعبد واياك نستعين 5. اهدنا الصراط المستقيم 6. صراط

الذين انعمت عليهم 7. غير المغضوب عليهم ولا الضالين

سورة البقرة مايتان

وست وثمانون ايات

بسم الله الرحمن الرحيم

2. 1. 1. الم ذلك الكتاب لا ريب فيه هدي للمتقين 2. الذين يؤمنون

3. بالغيب ويقيمون الصلوة ومما رزقناهم ينفقون 3. والذين يؤمنون

4. بما انزل اليك وما انزل من قبلك وبالاخرة هم يوقنون 4. اولئك

5. علي هدي من ربهم واولئك هم المفلحون 5. ان الذين كفروا سواء

6. عليهم ءانذرتهم ام لم تنذرهم لا يؤمنون 6. ختم الله علي قلوبهم

7. وعلي سمعهم وعلي ابصارهم غشاوة ولهم عذاب عظيم 7. ومن الناس من

8. يقول امنا بالله وباليوم الاخر وما هم بمؤمنين 8. يخادعون الله

9. والذين امنوا وما يخدعون الا انفسهم وما يشعرون 9. في قلوبهم

مرض

A

[I] Hinckelmann's Qur'ān (Hamburg, 1694). Sūrat al-Fātiḥa (Q 1:1-7), and the beginning of Sūrat al-Baqara (Q 2:1f.), from this German printed Qur'ān are depicted here. Courtesy of Harvard University (OL 24152.2).

سورة الفاتحة مكية سبع ايات.

ALCORANI
SURA I.
APERIENS.

الجزو الاول
PARS I.

MECCANA COMMATUM VII.

1 بسم الله الرحمن الرحيم
2 الحمد لله رب العالمين 3 الرحمن الرحيم 4 مالك يوم الدين 5 اياك نعبد واياك
نستعين 6 اهدنا الصراط المستقيم 7 صراط الذين انعمت عليهم غير المغضوب
عليهم ولا الضالين

1. IN nomine Dei Miseratoris Misericordis. 2. Laus Deo, Domino
Mundorum: 3. Miseratori, Misericordi: 4. Regnanti diei Judi-
cii 5. Te colimus: & te in auxilium imploramus: 6. Dirige nos
in viam rectam: 7. Viam illorum, erga quos beneficus fuisti: non a-
ctum iracundè contra eos: & non Errantium.

NOTÆ.

PRæter Epigraphen huic Suræ jam appositam, nempè الفاتحة *Apriens*, seu فاتحة الكتاب *Aperiens Librum*, idest *Proœmialis*: aliis titulis à Mahumetanis inscribitur. Vocant enim illam ام الكتاب: *Matrem Libri*: سورة الكنز: *Suram thesauri*: سورة الحمد: *Suram Laudis*: سورة الصلاة: *Suram orationis*: سورة الشكر والدعاء *Suram gratiarum actionis*, *&* *precationis*: & (omissis aliis hujusmodi inanibus titulis) المبع الثانى: *Septem iterata*: quia septem illius versiculi sæpè à Mahumetanis repetuntur: vel quia illam Mahumetò bis à Gabriele traditam fuisse fabulantur: primò Meccæ; secundò Medinæ. Ab his duabus Urbibus Suræ omnes Alcorani, vel Meccanæ, vel Medinenses nominantur. Septem constat versibus, inter quos nonnulli primum non computantes, qui communis est etiam cæteris Suris; incipiunt septimum versum ab illis verbis: *non actum iracundè, &c.* sed non benè; nam sextus versus nullum haberet rhythmum seu cadentiam.

Quidam volunt Suram esse Meccanam, quidam Medinensem: quidam utramque. Hinc Beidavius: صح انها نزلت بمكة حين فرضت الصلاة وبالمدينة لما حولت

A

[II] Ludovico Marracci's *Alcorani Textus Universus* (Padua, 1698). This Italian printed Qur'ān contains Latin translation and notes, in addition to the Arabic text. Courtesy of Harvard University (OL 24155.1F).

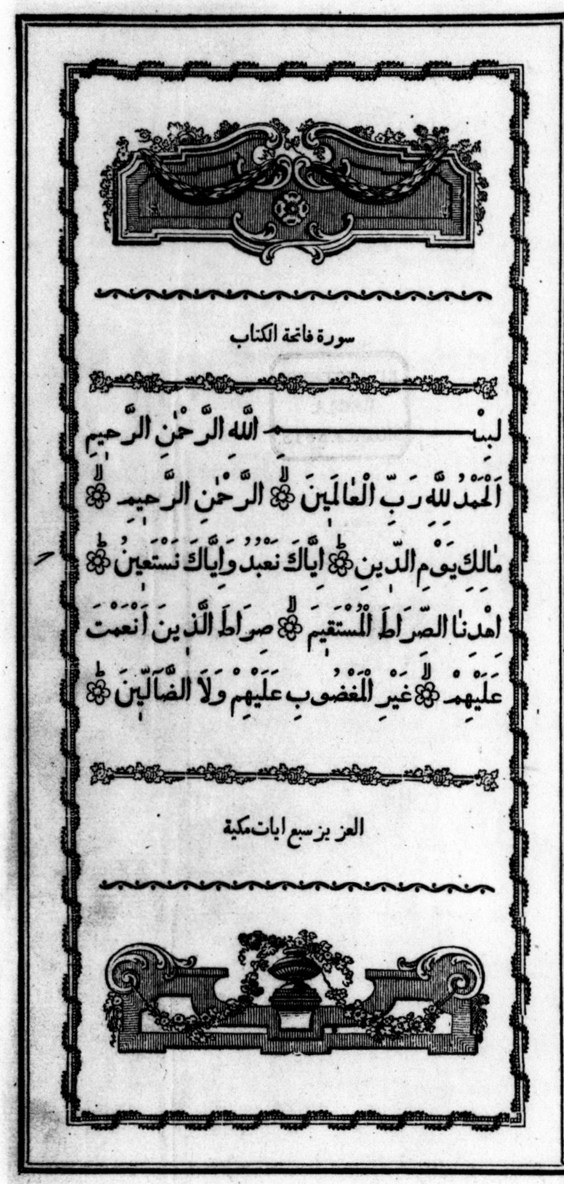

سورة فاتحة الكتاب

بسم الله الرحمن الرحيم
الحمد لله رب العالمين ۞ الرحمن الرحيم ۞
مالك يوم الدين ۞ اياك نعبد واياك نستعين ۞
اهدنا الصراط المستقيم ۞ صراط الذين انعمت
عليهم ۞ غير المغضوب عليهم ولا الضالين ۞

العز يز سبع ايات مكية

سورة فاتحة الكتاب العزيز
سبع ايات اختلف العلماء فی
نزولها علی قولين احدها
انها مكية و الثانی انها مدنية
وتسمی ام القران وام الكتاب
و السبع المثانی و البسملة عند
الامام الشافعی رحمه الله وكلا
مها مائة وعشرون كلمة وحرو
فها مائة وثلث وعشرون حرفا

قرا عاصم والكسای مالك يوم
الدين بالالف وقرا الباقون
بغير الف ملك يوم الدين

قرا قنبل السراط فی جميع
القران بالسين واخلف بالزا
ی الزراط و الاشمام وخلاد
انها هنا خاصة فی الاول والبا
قون بالصاد خالصة
قراءة عليهم بضم الهاء وابن
كثير وقالون بضم الميم التی
للجمع وبصلانها بواو مع الهمز
ة وغيرها و الباقون بكسر
الهاء عليهم

[III] St. Petersburg Qur'ān of 1790. The margins of this edition contain notes that primarily indicate variant readings. Courtesy of the Bayerische Staatsbibliothek, Munich (ESlg/2A.or.39).

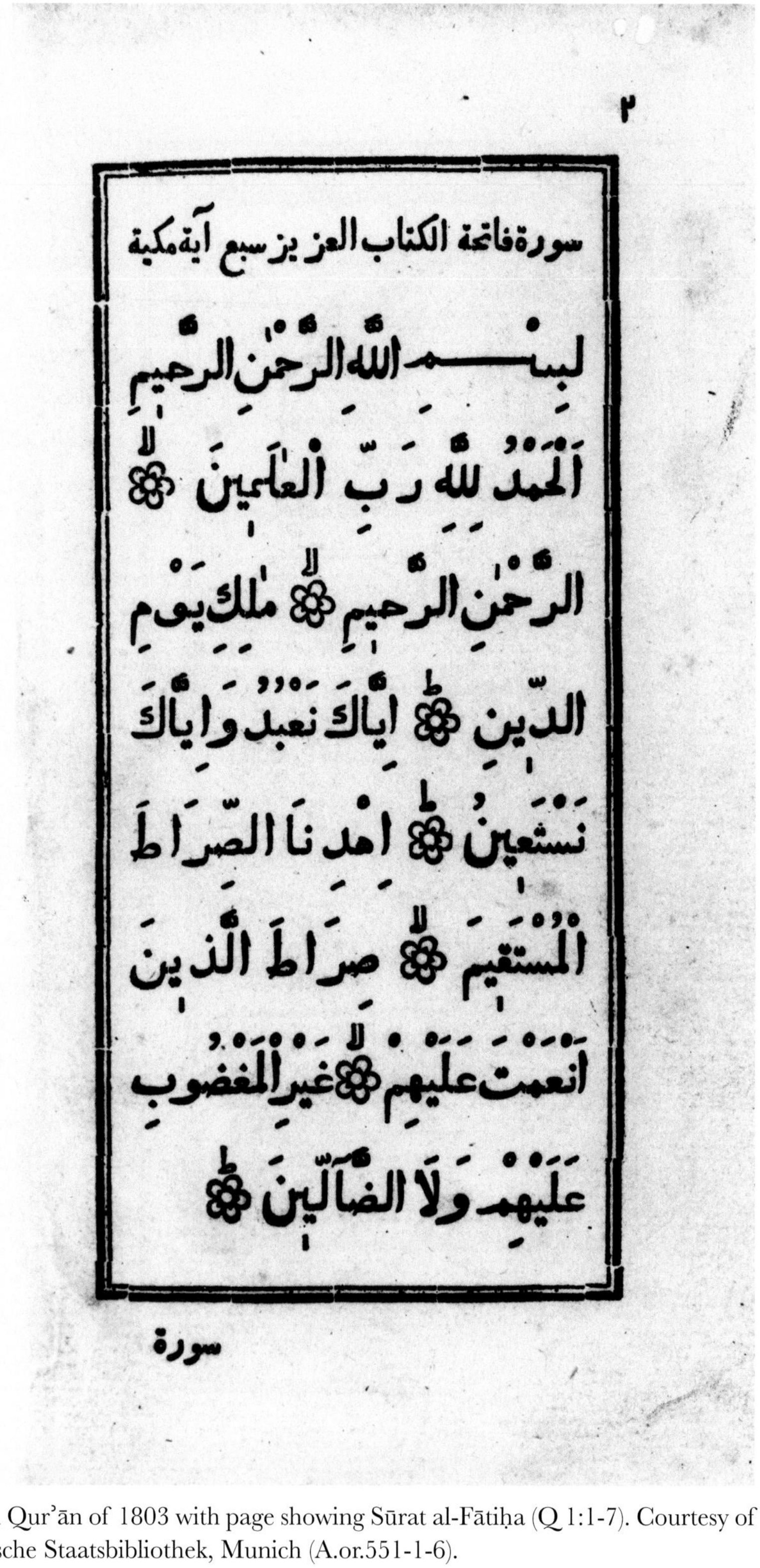

سورة فاتحة الكتاب العزيز سبع آية مكية

بِسْمِ اللهِ الرَّحْمٰنِ الرَّحِيمِ

الْحَمْدُ للهِ رَبِّ الْعَالَمِينَ ۞

الرَّحْمٰنِ الرَّحِيمِ ۞ مَلِكِ يَوْمِ

الدِّينِ ۞ اِيَّاكَ نَعْبُدُ وَاِيَّاكَ

نَسْتَعِينُ ۞ اهْدِنَا الصِّرَاطَ

الْمُسْتَقِيمَ ۞ صِرَاطَ الَّذِينَ

اَنْعَمْتَ عَلَيْهِمْ ۞ غَيْرِ الْمَغْضُوبِ

عَلَيْهِمْ وَلَا الضَّالِّينَ ۞

سورة

[IV] Kazan Qur'ān of 1803 with page showing Sūrat al-Fātiḥa (Q 1:1-7). Courtesy of the Bayerische Staatsbibliothek, Munich (A.or.551-1-6).

سورة فاتحة الكتاب

بسم الله الرحمن الرحيم
الحمد لله رب العالمين الرحمن الرحيم
مالك يوم الدين اياك نعبد واياك
نستعين اهدنا الصراط المستقيم
صراط الذين انعمت عليهم غير
المغضوب عليهم ولا الضالين

وهي سبع آيات

[v] Early Turkish printed Qur'ān (Istanbul, 1299/1881-2) with first sūra. Courtesy of the Library of Congress (Orien Arab BP100.A1).

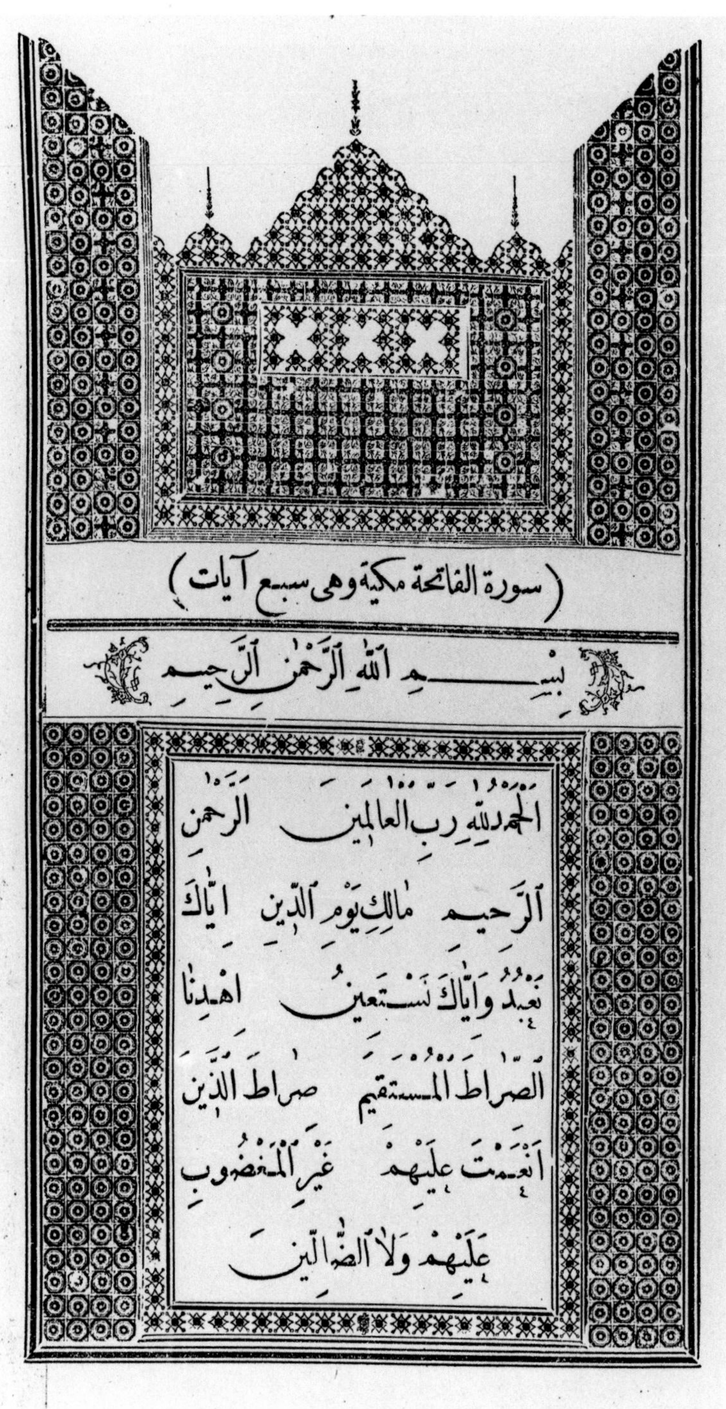

(سورة الفاتحة مكية وهى سبع آيات)

بسم الله الرحمن الرحيم

الحمد لله رب العالمين الرحمن
الرحيم مالك يوم الدين اياك
نعبد واياك نستعين اهدنا
الصراط المستقيم صراط الذين
انعمت عليهم غير المغضوب
عليهم ولا الضالين

[vi] al-Muṣḥaf al-Sharīf (Cairo: Būlāq, 1882), with the first sūra. Courtesy of Princeton University (Princeton, 2273.1882).

viewed forty-nine Qurʾān proofs written in the familiar Egyptian hand, eleven in Maghribī script (see ARABIC SCRIPT) and two from Brill. During the period from May 2, 1963 to November 20, 1963, the Section issued twenty-two licenses to print new *maṣāḥif* after review of page proofs by a committee appointed by the Section. In the same period, seventeen licenses were issued following review of the printed and bound copies. On the other hand, the Section withheld licenses in nine instances, most of them imported editions. The Section also had responsibility for examining imported *maṣāḥif* and those being exported. For the first eleven months of 1963 the Section reviewed 276,623 copies of the complete Qurʾān or parts of it exported to twenty-eight countries, an average of 25,158 copies per month. In 1967, al-Azhar, in cooperation with the government press, set out to reissue the Qurʾān in a printed rather than lithographed format. The first of these appeared in 1976 and was followed by printings in various sizes, with a total of 200,000 copies. The following year a special press was established specifically for printing the Qurʾān and other religious works. It began operation in 1985 (www.alazhar.org/english/about/quran/htm).

In Saudi Arabia, Qurʾān publishing is centered at the King Fahd Holy Qurʾān Printing Complex. Established in 1985 near Medina, the Complex may be one of the largest printing operations in the world. According to the website (www.quran.net/hadis/Madinah), the press employs 1,500 scholars, artists and technicians. Fourteen million copies of the Qurʾān in Arabic and six other languages have been printed since its founding. They are distributed free to pilgrims, as well as to mosques and other Islamic institutions worldwide. Another website (www.saudinf.com/main/y3694.htm), the information of which is dated February 4, 2002, puts the number of printed copies of the Arabic Qurʾān at 145 million since 1985. The Complex has a capacity of ten million copies per year. It is administered by the Ministry of Islamic Affairs, Endowments, Call, and Guidance. The government is not the only producer of Qurʾāns in Saudi Arabia. The publishing house Dār al-Salām is dedicated to printing the authentic Arabic text, translation and brief commentaries and marginal notes (www. dar-us-salam.com/about_us.htm). It was established in Riyadh in 1986 under the direction of ʿAbd al-Mālik Mujāhid. Besides offices in the United States and Britain, it has branches in Australia, Bangladesh, Malaysia, Pakistan, Qatar and Sri Lanka.

Over the last forty years the Qurʾān has been printed in many places, from Morocco to Indonesia. Iraq's first printing was in 1950. The Directorate of Endowments *(awqāf)* selected as its model a manuscript, which was then photographed at the Survey of Iraq. The original manuscript had been a gift of the mother of the Ottoman sultan ʿAbd al-Azīz to Shaykh Junayd al-Baghdādī in 1861. The manuscript had been copied in 1859 by Ḥāfiẓ Muḥammad Amīn Rushdī. The *awqāf* directorate formed an editorial committee of five to prepare the text for printing. Included in the group was the inspector of the Survey press, Ḥāshim Muḥammad al-Baghdādī. The press' calligrapher copied the text, adding headings for the sūras, "adjusting some of the *āyas*" (*taʿdīl baʿḍ al-āyāt;* see VERSES) and adding an index to the sūras, a common feature in printed Qurʾāns. The committee read the text to ensure conformity with Ḥafṣ and the *rasm* of ʿUthmān. The arrangement of *ajzāʾ*, *aḥzāb* and sūra titles was modeled on the Istanbul edition copied by Ḥāfiẓ ʿUthmān. The numbering of the sūras was taken from the official Cairo edition. The committee signed their names at the end of the text, as was customary with large projects. There is rich ornamentation on the first two pages of text. The second edition, based on the first, came out in 1966. It is beautifully printed and bound with the traditional Islamic flap cover. The colophon indicates that the work was directed by the Ministry of Endowments *(dīwān al-awqāf)* and contracted to Marār Trading Company of Baghdad for execution. The committee overseeing the edition was composed of Shaykh ʿAbdallāh al-Shaykhlī, Shaykh Kamāl al-Dīn al-Ṭaʿī, and Nūrī l-Qāḍī, director of Religious Charities at the *dīwān*. The work was printed in Germany by K.G. Lohse of Frankfurt.

The Qurʾāns of India and Pakistan are characteristically individual in appearance and are often the result of personal devotions rather than the product of corporate investment or organized outreach. The Qurʾān of 1964 published in Shillong, East Pakistan embodies these idiosyncrasies. It is an Arabic text with English translation and with running commentary by Khadim Rahmani. In his introduction he says, "This being the first edition and the process of printing being a difficult one, we had to engage a local press for doing the job, so as to maintain a constant vigil and guidance all along the printing. Yet in spite of our best efforts, some printing mistakes cropped up." The same difficulties are noted in *The divine Qurʾān* with Arabic text, translation into English and English commentary by S.M. Abdul Hamid published in Dacca in 1962. The English translation is typewritten and comments are typed footnotes. In his introduction Abdul Hamid laments the poor quality of the paper and printing: "Some of my friends desired better printing and paper. But those who are aware of the difficulties of publishing will admit that in Pakistan [sic] we are to depend on the paper supplied by the local mills, and printing cannot be controlled unless one has got his own press." Like Khadim Rahmani, Abdul Hamid calls on his readers to alert him to printing mistakes. Even the prestigious edition with English translation of Abdullah Yusuf Ali published serially in Lahore beginning in 1937 bears the translator's request for corrections.

Not all contemporary Indian or Pakistani editions are produced as small-scale projects. The *Alifī Qurʾān* printed in Bombay at al-Qurʾān Printers displays all the hallmarks of a well-financed project. The edition derives its name from the fact that each line of text begins with the letter *alif*, the first letter of the Arabic alphabet. It is also distinguished in that the *basmala* (q.v.), the invocation "In the name of God," at the head of each sūra "has been written in 113 different calligraphic styles which have evolved over the fourteen centuries of Islamic era [sic]." As with all major publishing projects, scholars reviewed the calligraphed copy for correctness. As is also customary with commercially printed Qurʾāns, the publisher claims copyright protection. Akber Khan, chairman of the company, is unusually explicit, threatening that "... any person or organization... [who]... attempts to reproduce the *Qurʾān alifī* in any size or form, its whole or part, runs the risk of legal prosecution."

As Lebanon is well-known for its large and sophisticated publishing industry, it is not surprising that the Qurʾān is frequently printed there. The Qurʾāns are handsomely printed and bound and available at modest prices. Editions are often accompanied by the commentaries of al-Bayḍāwī or al-Jalālayn, sometimes both. In the edition published by al-Maktab al-Islāmī (Beirut and Damascus 1984), Shaykh Muḥammad Aḥmad Kanʿān explained and corrected the commentaries as he saw fit. In the Dār al-Maʿārif edition (Beirut

1982), the qur'ānic text and the two commentaries were reviewed by the Qur'ān corrector *(mudaqqiq al-maṣāḥif)* of the Syrian Ministry of Endowments *(awqāf),* Marwān Suwār. In the edition of Dār al-ʿIlm lil-Malāyīn (Beirut 1984) the commentator and corrector, Muḥammad Aḥmad Kanʿān, whose edition appeared from al-Maktab al-Islāmī in the very same year, wrote a biography of al-Bayḍāwī and an explanation of his *Anwār al-tanzīl,* and describes why he chose to give a précis of the text, while assuring the reader that he has changed little of the original and did so only to "tie concepts together."

Despite the rigid requirements for Qur'ān publishing in the government context, experiments with the text continue in an attempt to make the scripture more universally comprehensible. One such effort appeared in Jakarta in 1973. This state-authorized experiment aligned the Arabic text with a romanized version for Muslims who wished to read the text in Arabic but who did not know the Arabic script or the complexities of the rules of recitation *(tajwīd).* The volume was produced by the Reading Institute of Religious Affairs in cooperation with the Committee on Publication of the Qur'ān and the publisher Bahrul Ulum. The introduction calls this the first attempt to romanize Arabic for Indonesians. The introduction says, "We hope that the Qur'ān in Latin can become a model for future improved romanization." In a memorandum from the Reading Institute to the printer, the firm of Sumatra in Bandung, the Institute asserts that the transcription is accurate and that the work may by printed for distribution.

Non-Ḥafṣ printings

In the foregoing discussion it is assumed that all the editions cited adhere to the Ḥafṣ reading *(riwāya).* Occasionally the Qur'ān is available in other readings. There is a 1964 *muṣḥaf* from Algeria in the Warsh *riwāya* and another version from Morocco. A Tunisian edition of the Qālūn *riwāya* was published by al-Dār al-Tūnisiyya lil-Nashr. In the Sudan the Dūrī reading was printed in 1989 by the Department of Religious Affairs and Endowments *(awqāf).*

Summary

A most thorough examination of the 400-year delay between Gutenberg's Bible and the first Qur'ān printed in Egypt is provided by Proudfoot and Robinson. Both take issue with the commonly held view of Orientalists that it was caused by an innate conservatism among the *ʿulamā'.* They adhere to a more complex and nuanced approach. Most importantly, they highlight the separate historical trajectories of the Ottoman lands and the eastern territories: Iran, India and southeast Asia. In the former, the press was expressly excluded from use until the early eighteenth century. In the latter, where political and religious controls were diffuse, i.e. where the clerical control was weakest, great preachers and teachers such as Sayyid Aḥmad Khān and the Deobandis (q.v.) were — while no less fervent than their coreligionists in western Asia and north Africa — without allegiance to a strong authority. Thus, they were able to exploit printing unhindered by government controls. Robinson points out that print was employed in India to promote Islam not only against the British but, more fundamentally, to strengthen the community in the face of the Hindu majority.

Proudfoot also emphasizes that printing religious texts was a lucrative business in south and southeast Asia and came to be viewed as such in the premier Islamic publishing center, Cairo. He speculates that one of the reasons for the failure of what he calls early experiments or false starts in printing in Istanbul and Cairo is that the works with the greatest potential for profit were forbidden. Nonetheless, in no case did the press, whether lithographic or typographic, lead to major improvements in the technology of printing. Doubtlessly, lithography ushered in a revolution in Islamic communications, education and self-definition in India, but it was not adapted to the same ends in the central Islamic lands (see TEACHING AND PREACHING THE QURʾĀN). Moreover, no technical innovations were developed in any Muslim region (see SCIENCE AND THE QURʾĀN). Every improvement in printing technique was developed in the West and eventually adopted by Muslims to often conservative religious ends. Thus, the basic point that the press was a late arrival in the Muslim world is correct and its use was entirely dependent on imported techniques.

Michael W. Albin

Bibliography
F. Abdulrazak, *The kingdom of the book*, Ph.D. diss., Ann Arbor 1990; id., *al-Maṭbuʿāt al-hajariyya fī l-Maghrib*, Rabat 1989; J. Bloom, *Paper before print. The history and impact of paper on the Islamic world*, New Haven 2001, 215-6; H. Bobzin, *Der Koran im Zeitalter der Reformation. Studien zur Frühgeschichte der Arabistik und Islamkunde in Europa*, Beirut/Stuttgart 1995; M. Borrmans, Observations à propos de la première edition imprimée du Coran à Venise, in *QSA* 7 (1990), 3-12; H. Braun, Der Hamburger Koran von 1694, in C. Voigt and E. Zimmermann (eds.), *Libris et litteris. Festschrift für H. Tiemann*, Stuttgart 1959, 149-66; E. Browne, *The press and poetry of modern Persia*, Los Angeles 1983; W. Floor, Čāp, in *Encyclopaedia Iranica*, iv, 760-4; W. Gdoura, *Le début de l'imprimerie arabe à Istanbul et en Syrie*, Tunis 1985; U. Marzolph, *Narrative illustration in Persian lithographed books*, Leiden 2001; M. Nallino, Una cinquecentesca edizione del Corano stampata a Venezia, in *Atti dell'Istituto Veneto di Scienzie, Lettere ed Arti. Classe di scienzie morali, lettere ed arti* 124 (1965/66), 1-12; Nöldeke, *GQ*, iii, 273-4; A. Nuovo, Il Corano arabo ritrovato, in *La bibliofilia* 89 (1987), 237-71; A. Paton, *A history of the Egyptian revolution*, London 1870[2]; I. Proudfoot, Lithography at the crossroads of the east, in *Journal of the Printing Historical Society* 27 (1998), 113-31; id., Mass producing Houri's moles, in P. Riddell and T. Street (eds.), *Islam. Essays on scripture, thought and society*, Leiden 1997; A. al-Qāḍī, Muṣḥaf fī dūr al-ṭibāʿa, in id., *al-Muṣḥaf al-sharīf. Abḥāth fī tarīkhihi*, Cairo 1968; A. Raḍwān, *Tārīkh maṭbaʿat Būlāq*, Cairo 1953; E. Rezvan, The Qurʾān and its world. VIII/1. *Contra Legen Saracenorum*. The Qurʾān in western Europe, in *Manuscripta orientalia* 4/4 (1998), 41-51; id., The Qurʾān and its world. VIII/2. *West-Östlichen Divans*. The Qurʾān in Russia, in *Manuscripta orientalia* 5/1 (1999), 32-62; F. Robinson, Technology and religious change. Islam and the impact of print, in *Modern Asian studies* 27 (1993), 229-51; Kh. Ṣābāt, *Tārīkh al-ṭibāʿa fī l-sharq al-ʿarabī*, Cairo 1966; Y. Sarkīs, *Muʿjam al-maṭbūʿāt al-ʿarabiyya wa-l-muʿarraba*, 11 pts. in 1 vol., Cairo 1928; O. Shcheglova, *Katalog litografirovannykh knig na persidskom iazyke v sobranii Vostochnogo otdele Nauchnoi biblioteki im A.M. Leningradskogo gosudarstvennogo universiteta*, Moscow 1989; C. Schnurrer, *Bibliotheca Arabica*, Amsterdam 1968; M. al-Shūrbajī, *Qāʾima bi-awāʾil al-maṭbuʿāt al-ʿarabiyya al-maḥfūẓa bi-Dār al-Kutūb*, Cairo 1963; R. Smitskamp, Flügel's Koran edition, in *ʿĀlam al-kutub* 15 (1410/1994), 533-5; [Smitskamp Oriental Antiquarium], *Het Oosters antiquarium*, Leiden 1992-, esp. cat. no. 602 (1995), item 547 [Istanbul 1850]; cat. no. 591 (1992), items 803 [Istanbul 1304/1887, 30 pts.], 804 [Bombay 1298] and 806 [Tehran 1273]; cat. no. 627 (2000), item 653 [Istanbul 1294/1877]; Wizārat al-Awqāf wa-Shuʾūn al-Azhar, *al-Azhar. Tārīkhuhū wa taṭawwuruhū*, Cairo 1964.

Prisoners

Persons physically detained by judicial authority in an institution for that purpose. The Qurʾān explicitly mentions prisoners *(al-masjūnūn)* only once, in Q 26:29, referring to Moses (q.v.). The noun "prison" *(al-sijn)* and its verbal forms are, however, found in the story of Joseph (q.v.) at Q 12:25 and in eight other places. Both of these narratives (q.v.) refer to the Pharaoh's (q.v.) prison in Egypt (q.v.), which some commentators described as "an underground place where a person was held without seeing or hearing anyone" (*Jalālayn*, 482, ad Q 26:29).

It seems unlikely that Mecca (q.v.) or Medina (q.v.) had any such dungeons during the time of Muḥammad, but some types of detention were known and rudimentary prisons in Medina and Baṣra are mentioned soon after Muḥammad's death. ʿUmar b. al-Khaṭṭāb reportedly had a house bought and turned into a prison in Mecca (Rosenthal, *Freedom*, 37-8; see CALIPH; COMPANIONS OF THE PROPHET); ʿAlī (see ʿALĪ B. ABĪ ṬĀLIB) likewise established a house prison in Baṣra (Schneider, *Imprisonment*, 167).

Generally, imprisonment is not counted as one of the qurʾānic punishments for crimes, even though Q 4:15 instructs that women who commit sexual indecency *(al-fāḥisha)* are to be held *(m-s-k)* in their homes (see ADULTERY AND FORNICATION; CHASTITY). There is a question as to whether such detention is equivalent to imprisonment, but the majority of scholars held that this verse was, in any case, abrogated (see ABROGATION) by Q 24:2, which decrees flogging (q.v.). Similarly, the Qurʾān refers to persons held in shackles *(riqāb, asīr)* but these are usually understood as referring either to slaves or captives (q.v.), not to prisoners (see also SLAVES AND SLAVERY).

The Prophet appears both to have detained someone on suspicion (*ḥabasa al-rajula fī tuhma*, Wensinck, *Concordance*, i, 411b) and also to have had someone bound *(rabaṭa)* to a pillar in the mosque (q.v.; Bukhārī, *Ṣaḥīḥ*, ii, 92 [44, Khusūmāt, 8]; Fr. trans. Houdas, *El-Bokhârî*, ii, 128), but there is no record of real imprisonment. The lack of clear qurʾānic and prophetic precedent has led to an occasional debate as to whether Islamic law sanctions imprisonment at all (Qurṭubī, *Jāmiʿ*, v, 85, ad Q 4:15; see LAW AND THE QURʾĀN; SUNNA).

Until the modern era, it seems that imprisonment was, in fact, little used by judges, usually restricted to a form of coercion (debtors' prisons) or conceived as an alternative or supplementary punishment. Political prisoners, however, appear to have been widely tolerated on the basis that the sultan has ultimate control over the freedom of his subjects (see KINGS AND RULERS; POLITICS AND THE QURʾĀN). The judicial reticence to enforce imprisonment may have its roots in a fundamental presumption of freedom as the natural state of humankind (see FREEDOM AND PREDESTINATION; OPPRESSION; OPPRESSED ON EARTH, THE). Along these lines, it is instructive to note that the Qurʾān describes Joseph's prison, in Q 12:25, with the same epithets usually reserved in the Qurʾān for hell: *ʿadhāb alīm*, a painful chastisement (see HELL AND HELLFIRE; REWARD AND PUNISHMENT). It also equates hell with prison directly in Q 17:8: "We have established hell for the unbelievers as a prison" *(wa-jaʿalnā jahannama lil-kāfirīna ḥaṣīran;* see BELIEF AND UNBELIEF). Al-Rāzī (d. 606/1210; *Tafsīr*, xx, 161, ad Q 17:8) distinguishes the two, emphasizing that while one will eventually be freed from an earthly prison, if only by death, hell "is a barrier *(ḥāṣir)* for people, surrounding them and offering no hope of release."

In contrast to judicial imprisonment, prisoners of war (q.v.) are discussed in Q 47:4, 8:67-9 and elsewhere. Such captives were sometimes pardoned or held for ransom but could also be enslaved or even killed. A minority argued that ransom or pardon were the only licit possibilities (Ibn Rushd, *Bidāya*, i, 382). Most modern interpreters embrace this minority opinion, thereby bringing rules on prisoners of war in line with international norms (Hashmi, Saving, 145).

Jonathan E. Brockopp

Bibliography
Primary: Bukhārī, *Ṣaḥīḥ* ed. Krehl; Fr. trans. O. Houdas, *El-Bokhârî. Les traditions islamiques,* 4 vols., Paris 1903; Ibn Rushd, Abū l-Walīd (al-Ḥafīd), *Bidāyat al-mujtahid wa-nihāyat al-muqtaṣid,* 2 vols., Beirut 1988 (repr.); *Jalālayn;* Qurṭubī, *Jāmiʿ;* Rāzī, *Tafsīr.*
Secondary: H. Abū Ghudda, *Aḥkām al-sijn wa-muʿāmalat al-sujanāʾ,* Kuwait 1987; A. Baghdādī, *Kitāb al-Sujūn fī Miṣr min al-fatḥ al-islāmī ilā l-ḥukm al-ʿuthmānī,* Cairo 1997; S. Hashmi, Saving and taking life in war. Three modern Muslim views, in J.E. Brockopp (ed.), *Islamic ethics of life. Abortion, war and euthanasia,* Columbia 2003, 129-54; M. al-Jaryawī, *al-Sajn wa-mūjibātuhu fī l-sharīʿa l-islāmiyya. Muqārana bi-niẓām al-sajn wa-l-tawqīf fī l-mamlaka l-ʿarabiyya l-saʿūdiyya,* 2 vols., Riyadh 1997 (repr.); F. Rosenthal, *The Muslim concept of freedom prior to the nineteenth century,* Leiden 1960; I. Schneider, Imprisonment in pre-classical and classical Islamic law, in *Islamic law and society* 2 (1995), 157-73; id., Sidjn, in *EI*[2], ix, 547-8; Wensinck, *Concordance.*

Profane and Sacred

What pertains to the non-divine realm and to the divine realm, respectively. The English word profane is derived from the Latin expression *pro fanum* describing the area in front of the shrine or persons who came to a temple without being initiated. The Latin *profanus* was used to denote the opposite of *sanctus,* "divine," and *sacer/sacratus,* "dedicated to God," both by Roman as well as Jewish and Christian authors. In everyday English language, "profane" can denote something of lesser value and is sometimes synonymous with temporal, non-religious, and secular. Since the second half of the nineteenth century and especially after Durkheim's 1912 study on the primary forms of religious life, profane has gained importance as a critical term in describing the origins and essential characteristics of religions. Indeed, Durkheim defined as a critical element of any religion the classification of all things as either profane or sacred. Despite the frequent occurrence of profane in modern studies of religion, however, no coherent concept of this term has been developed in scholarly discourse, and several studies on the topic have raised doubts as to whether profane may be viewed as an applicable operative concept of religious studies at all. Also, studies of the religion of Islam and Islamic culture frequently refer to the "profane" without providing a definition. Therefore, before reflecting on the relevance of profane in the context of the Qurʾān, a brief summary of various aspects of the profane as discussed in religious studies is necessary.

Problems of definition

In its original meaning, the word "profane" suggests a distinction between two different kinds of space. Profane, at this semantic level, denotes the space that is not sacred or holy and that encircles a sacred area that is set apart from the profane by a boundary. According to Eliade, a religious person perceives the non-homogeneity of space as the contrast between a well defined sacred place — either an edifice constructed for religious purposes (see SACRED PRECINCTS; HOUSE, DOMESTIC AND DIVINE; KAʿBA; MOSQUE; CHURCH) or a natural phenomenon that is religiously interpreted (see NATURE AS SIGNS; MARVELS; MIRACLES) — and the indefinite, amorphous space around it. Only particular, precious objects and privileged persons are permitted to remain in a sacred place. Outside or in front of the sacred enclosure extends the domain of ordinary objects and persons — the profane space. In some cases, however, one particular place may be regarded as sacred and non-sacred at the same time even by believers of one religion. In addition, religious communities, whose followers are spread over large territories, often believe a variety of places to be sacred (see MECCA; MEDINA; JERUSALEM; GEOGRAPHY). Consequently, the profane space outside a particular sacred enclosure may contain a number of other sacred places and is therefore not regarded as completely profane.

Although originating from a particular concept of space, the distinction between sacred and profane is not restricted to spatial categories (see SPATIAL RELATIONS). Reference to sacred objects, sacred time (q.v.), sacred states (see RITUAL PURITY), sacred acts (see PRAYER; FASTING; ALMSGIVING; PILGRIMAGE), and sacred personalities (see SAINT) in the context of various religions leads to the conclusion that there must be also profane objects, times, states, acts, and personalities (see EVERYDAY LIFE, THE QURʾĀN IN; MATERIAL CULTURE AND THE QURʾĀN; MEDIA AND THE QURʾĀN). Profane time may be described as the ordinary time of everyday life without the occurrence of any event of religious significance (see HISTORY AND THE QURʾĀN). Sacred periods are, for example, times of religious feasts during which critical events that occurred at an early point in a religion's history are celebrated and reenacted (see FESTIVALS AND COMMEMORATIVE DAYS). The believer changes from profane to sacred time by practicing particular rites. Also these rites contain elements of sacredness (see RITUAL AND THE QURʾĀN). They may therefore be regarded as sacred acts and the time of ritual practice can be viewed as sacred time.

Durkheim has pointed to another relationship between time and the profane. He observed that the passing of time may reduce the degree of profaneness and enlarge the degree of sacredness attributed to a religious phenomenon as, with time, the veneration of successive generations of believers in that particular phenomenon grows. Durkheim also mentioned the idea of various degrees of sacredness implicit in this observation in a number of other places in his study on the primary forms of religious life, *Les formes élémentaires de la vie religieuse*.

A profane person is described as someone who belongs to the world outside a sacred space, who illegitimately enters sacred space, or who transgresses the law that protects the sacred ideas and rites of a particular religion. There is a certain ambiguity in the establishment of the sacred in that, on the one hand, it is not arbitrary as when, for example, the significance of a sacred place is grounded in its unique character, a character that no purely human action can confer on it. In other cases, however, space obtains religious meaning precisely because it is chosen on an arbitrary basis. Furthermore, there is no intrinsic reason why a particular phenomenon should be more sacred than another, or even sacred at all. The manifestation of the sacred (hierophany) and the profane (prophanophany) is the result of an intellectual process and is, as such, always artificial and subjective. This leads to a situation where what is sacred to the faithful of one religious tradition may be conceived of as profane by the faithful professing another (see POLEMIC AND POLEMICAL LANGUAGE).

A precise circumscription of the profane in abstract terms is difficult because of its amorphous nature and the existence of various systems of belief and designations of sacredness (see BELIEF AND UNBELIEF; RELIGIOUS PLURALISM AND THE QURʾĀN). Therefore, the profane is often described in negative terms like non-religious or non-sacred. The sacred, however, is also defined in different ways based on various methodologies. This leads to uncertainty and inconsistency even when describing the profane as the opposite of the sacred. One occasion on which the border between the sacred and the profane becomes identifiable in a particular religion is the act of profanation. "To profane" means to take something away from the space of a sanctuary, to bring something from the world of the gods or the one God to the human world or, on a more practical level, to ignore sacred orders or laws. An example would be disregarding the observance of sacred periods of time by acting in a manner that is forbidden by the regulations of a particular religion during that sacred period (see MONTHS). This distorted or deviant approach to the sacred, that is, treating it with irreverence or contempt, is conveyed by the root letters *l-ḥ-d* — especially in Q 7:180 and 41:40 (see HERESY; ERROR; ASTRAY), and implies a violation of the sacred, as in blaspheming the names of God or his signs (q.v.; see also CURSE; BLASPHEMY; OATHS; BREAKING TRUSTS AND CONTRACTS). Profanation can be understood as one form of communication between the sacred and the profane.

Another form of communication between the sacred and the profane has been observed in sacrifice (q.v.) with the victim as a medium between the two spheres (see CONSECRATION OF ANIMALS). Interestingly, in Roman texts the Latin verb *profanare* described the act of selling or distributing the meat of the sacrifice to the populace in front of the temple. Inquiries into the nature of profane and sacred often attempt to answer two essential questions, namely what is defined as profane or sacred in a particular religion, and what believers are permitted or forbidden (q.v.) to do with or within the profane or the sacred. Various studies on the sacred have identified exclusiveness (being superior in dignity and power, being a means of communication with gods or the one God, or of access between the human world and divine realities), separateness, otherness, and remoteness from the ordinary as common traits of the "sacred." On the contrary, the "profane" is often characterized as the non-sacred, non-religious, secular, ordinary, and as being of no religious significance, or of lesser value than the "sacred."

The profane, the sacred and the Qurʾān

The existence of the profane as an autonomous phenomenon can only be acknowledged by someone who does not accept the idea of the absolute transcendence of the divine (see GOD AND HIS ATTRIBUTES; ANTHROPOMORPHISM). If divine creation (q.v.) of all things is presupposed, the profane can exist only if sacredness is not attributed to the whole of divine creation. The Qurʾān postulates the role of God as the creator of all things (Q 6:102; 13:16; 39:62; cf. 15:86; 36:81, etc.). Yet because the qurʾānic text may be interpreted as discussing phenomena of the profane on several occasions it can be argued that it does not support the view that everything that is created by God must only be regarded as sacred. Divine origin appears, however, as an important argument for the sacred character of the Qurʾān in the holy book (q.v.) itself (see CREATEDNESS OF THE QURʾĀN; INIMITABILITY). It is stated that the Qurʾān represents those parts of the heavenly book (q.v.) that were sent down to the prophet Muḥammad in the Arabic language (q.v.; cf. Q 12:2; 20:113; 41:3; 42:7; 43:3-4; see also REVELATION AND INSPIRATION). Q 10:37 implies that the character of the qurʾānic text proves its divine origin. Even if humans and jinn (q.v.) would combine their efforts they could not bring forth a text like the Qurʾān (Q 17:88). Those who claim to have received another version of the heavenly book present but a distorted version of it (Q 3:78). God warns those who have broken the Qurʾān into fragments, and thus distorted its meaning, about the consequences of such an act (cf. Q 15:90-2; see CORRUPTION; FORGERY). A person's attitude towards the Qurʾān is a clear indicator of the distinction between believers and unbelievers (see BELIEF AND

UNBELIEF). Also, any doubts regarding the unique character of the Qurʾān and its revelation to Muḥammad (cf. Q 25:4-6) are tantamount to profanation (see OPPOSITION TO MUḤAMMAD). Those who deny the divine origin of the Qurʾān are threatened with severe punishment on the day of resurrection (q.v.; Q 6:27; see also LAST JUDGMENT; REWARD AND PUNISHMENT). Whereas the true believers recite the Qurʾān and follow its commandments (q.v.), the unbelievers dispute the Qurʾān and are therefore hated by God and those who believe in God and Muḥammad as his messenger (cf. Q 29:46; 40:35). Reading the Qurʾān is described as an act of worship (q.v.) and, as such, represents a broader sense of communication with God (Q 3:79; 17:78; 73:20). These and other passages underscore the fact that the Qurʾān may not be regarded as part of, or comparable to, profane writing. It goes without saying that no other scripture is attributed with these exclusive qualities of the Qurʾān (see TORAH; PSALMS; GOSPEL; SCRIPTURE AND THE QURʾĀN; PEOPLE OF THE BOOK; ORALITY AND WRITING IN ARABIA).

The sacred character of the Qurʾān is confirmed by religious practice in the course of history. Reading and reciting the holy book, or parts thereof, is mentioned as a form of communication with God in historiographical sources (see RECITATION OF THE QURʾĀN). For example, we know that representatives of the military elite of the Mamlūk era paid great numbers of religious scholars to recite the Qurʾān in schools, Ṣūfī convents *(khānqāh)* and public places to secure for themselves the blessing (q.v.) of God (*baraka;* see also POPULAR AND TALISMANIC USES OF THE QURʾĀN). Until today, religious cultus in the private sphere includes recitation of qurʾānic passages on many occasions like, for example, during Ramaḍān (q.v.), wedding celebrations and funerals as a form of communication with God. For various reasons, however, the Qurʾān was never a critical element of official liturgical practice in Islam (outside of the ritual prayer; see also FORM AND STRUCTURE OF THE QURʾĀN).

Qurʾānic terminology of sacred and profane

As mentioned above, the word "profane" can be traced back to the linguistic context of classical Roman, Jewish and Christian writers including the Church Fathers. When using "profane" in the description of respective concepts in other religions, one has to take into consideration semantic differences between the terminology of the language of the scholar examining a particular system of belief (meta-language) and, if known, the language of the people whose religion is the object of study (object language). Terms of object language and meta-language usually do not represent identical concepts. Therefore, scholars seeking to develop definitions of the profane, must refer not only to the self-definition of the concept as provided in the language examined, but should also analyze concepts similar in content though without any terminological link, utilizing comparative methods of religious studies, sociology, history, psychology, and other disciplines.

Different forms of the Arabic root *ḥ-r-m* have been understood in western scholarship as conveying the meaning of sacred and, as a result, words of this root occurring in the Qurʾān are often translated as "sacred" in English renditions of the Qurʾān. According to later Islamic tradition, "the sacred mosque" of the Qurʾān (*al-masjid al-ḥarām,* Q 2:144, 149-50, 191, 196; 5:2; 8:34; 9:7, 19, 28; 48:25, 27) denotes the Prophet's mosque in Mecca (q.v.); "the sacred hill" (*al-mashʿar al-ḥarām,* Q 2:198), where, according to tradition, Muḥammad stood and prayed to God, is understood to refer to the hill of Quzaḥ in Muzdalifa;

and "the sacred house" (*al-bayt al-ḥarām,* Q 5:2, 97; cf. 14:37) is identified as the Kaʿba. Later tradition explains the "safe sanctuary" (*ḥaram āmin,* Q 28:57; 29:67) as the area surrounding Mecca, and the *ḥurumāt* are God's sacred ordinances (Q 22:30). English translations of the verb *ḥarrama* can be "to forbid" or "to hallow/to make sacred": in certain passages the latter meaning is regularly preferred (e.g. Q 27:91), although in other places the term is always translated as "to forbid" (Q 2:173, 275; 3:93; 5:72, etc.).

The various forms of the root *ḥ-r-m* highlight the exclusiveness of the sacred in the Qurʾān. The places denoted as *ḥarām* or *ḥaram* may be entered only by believers in a particular state of consecration, *iḥrām* (see RITUAL PURITY). The word *iḥrām* does not occur in the Qurʾān. The nominal form *ḥurum,* however, stands in some qurʾānic passages for a number of believers who have assumed the sacred state (Q 5:1, 95-6). This state of *iḥrām* permits the believer to enter the sacred area and prohibits certain activities that were allowable before he or she assumed the *iḥrām* (sexual intercourse, ointments or perfumes, the wearing of sewn garments, hunting, etc.; see HUNTING AND FISHING; CLOTHING; ODORS AND SMELLS; SEX AND SEXUALITY). Entrance into the sacred areas and places is forbidden to those who are not in a state of *iḥrām*. Consequently, the *iḥrām* has to be assumed by every believer when performing the minor or/and the major pilgrimage *(ʿumra, ḥajj)*.

The fourth form of *ḥ-r-m* is also used to describe the entrance into a sacred period, such as a sacred month, although, again, this usage does not occur in the Qurʾān itself. The phrase, *al-shahr al-ḥarām,* "the sacred month," is mentioned in Q 2:194, 217; 5:2, 97, but the particular month referred to in these verses has not been identified with any certainty. Q 2:5, however, suggests that the month of pilgrimage, Dhū l-Ḥijja, is meant. Q 9:5 speaks of sacred months *(al-ashhur al-ḥurum),* Q 9:36 more precisely of four sacred months. Again, sacredness, as denoted by the word *ḥarām,* is defined by what is forbidden during the exclusive period of the sacred month. Entering the time of prayer also requires the state of *iḥrām*. Ritual purity and a prescribed manner of dressing are necessary preconditions of *iḥrām*. The sacredness of *iḥrām* is also underscored in various commentaries (see EXEGESIS OF THE QURʾĀN: CLASSICAL AND MEDIEVAL) on Q 17:80, where it is said that angels are present during the *iḥrām* that must be assumed before prayer.

Another root used to denote the sacred in the Qurʾān is *q-d-s*. Words of this root may convey the meaning of being far removed from, or free of, evil, impurity, or imperfection (see CLEANLINESS AND ABLUTION; IMPECCABILITY; GOOD AND EVIL). The degree of perfection or purity described by words of the root *q-d-s* is extraordinary. This may have led to an interpretation of *q-d-s* as "sacred" in English translation. The Qurʾān characterizes various phenomena with words derived from this root. In Q 20:12 and 79:16 the valley of Ṭuwā (q.v.), where Moses (q.v.) was informed by God about his prophethood (see PROPHETS AND PROPHETHOOD), is denoted as *muqaddas*. In Q 59:23 and Q 62:1 the term *al-qudus* occurs as an epithet of God. The phrase *rūḥ al-qudus,* "holy spirit" (q.v.), identified in the commentaries as Gabriel (q.v.), mentioned in conjunction with Jesus (q.v.), occurs in Q 2:87, 253, 5:110 and Q 16:102. "The sacred area" *(al-arḍ al-muqaddasa)* in Q 5:21 is understood to signify the Dome of the Rock in Jerusalem and the area surrounding it.

The opposite of *ḥ-r-m* in the sense of to "be, or become forbidden, prohibited, or sacred," is expressed by words derived from the root *ḥ-l-l*. In some passages, words of the root *ḥ-l-l* denote what is, becomes or is declared permissible, lawful, or free from legal obligation (Q 2:228-30, 275; 3:50; 5:87, etc.; see LAWFUL AND UNLAWFUL). In other passages of the Qurʾān, words of this root may be understood as representing the meaning of profane. Q 5:2 commands the believers to avoid acts of profanation. The phrase used in this passage, *lā tuḥillū*, is often translated as "do not violate or render permissible something." Among that which shall not be profaned is the sacred month — *al-shahr al-ḥarām*. Attacking those who are on their way to the sacred house (understood as the Kaʿba) is also not permitted, and is tantamount to profanation. Leaving the state of *iḥrām* and returning to the profane state is expressed by the phrase *idhā ḥalaltum* in Q 5:2, where it is asserted that hunting is permissible for those who have returned to the profane state. In Q 9:37 the insertion of intercalary months (q.v.) is forbidden. The practice of declaring the month after Dhū l-Ḥijja sacred *(yuḥarrimūnahu)* during one year and, if the intercalary month is inserted, profane *(yuḥillūnahu)* during another year is rejected as a practice of unbelief *(kufr)*. In other Arabic sources, all months except those defined as sacred *(ḥarām, ḥurum)* are described as profane, using the word *ḥill*. Also, in certain cases the verb *aḥalla* may signify leaving the sacred state *(iḥrām)* or entering upon the profane months or the profane territories. When the believer finishes prayer he or she returns to the profane state *(ḥalāl)*. The tenth verbal form of *ḥ-l-l*, *istaḥalla*, means to deem permissible or lawful and, by extension, to profane or to desecrate something sacred. The term *muḥill* describes, among other things, a man who violates the sacred and commits an act of profanation.

The word *dunyā* (derived from the root *d-n-w*, "be, or become near"), sometimes rendered as "[profane] world" when encountered in modern texts, is found in many qurʾānic verses where it denotes the present world (the nearer dwelling place), as opposed to the hereafter, *al-ākhira* (the last dwelling place; see ESCHATOLOGY). *Dunyā* is often interpreted as signifying everything that befalls humans before death or every activity that is not aimed at the service of God. In both senses, *dunyā* may be taken to express aspects of the profane. When interpreted as the present world, however, *dunyā* may include such activities as rites and entrance into holy areas and sacred periods, all of which are part of a believer's life before the hereafter. *Dunyā*, then, cannot be understood as coterminus with the profane.

The word *ʿādī*, occasionally translated as profane when found in modern Arabic texts, does not occur in the Qurʾān in this sense.

Regulations of profane life in the Qurʾān

In the Qurʾān, phenomena of the sacred are not necessarily described by words derived from the roots *ḥ-r-m*, or *q-d-s*. For example, two places which were of religious significance before the advent of Islam (see PRE-ISLAMIC ARABIA AND THE QURʾĀN), al-Ṣafā and al-Marwa (Q 2:158; see ṢAFĀ AND MARWA), retained their sacred character in Islam but are not characterized as *ḥarām* or *muqaddas* in the Qurʾān. Moreover, if ritual practiced by believers at a particular place or directed towards it marks that place as "sacred," then not only the "sacred mosque," but also all mosques (Q 2:187; 9:17-8) and the *qibla* (q.v.), must be regarded as sacred.

Similarly, not all profane phenomena, as mentioned in the Qurʾān, are described by words derived from the roots *ḥ-l-l* or *d-n-w*. The Qurʾān contains rules that must be observed in profane, everyday life and that are not related to any ritual activity. Some of these rules, for example, the prohibition of usury (q.v.; Q 3:130) or the regulations of inheritance (q.v.; Q 4:11-2, 176) were later cited and explained in the chapters on worldly matters *(muʿāmalāt)* of the manuals of Islamic jurisprudence (see LAW AND THE QURʾĀN), whereas ritual and religious observances were discussed in the *ʿibādāt* chapters (see FAITH). The distinction between *ʿibādāt* and *muʿāmalāt* may, therefore, be interpreted as expressing the distinction between the sacred and the profane spheres of life in the Qurʾān.

Lutz Wiederhold

Bibliography
ʿAbd al-Bāqī; Arberry; C.C. Berg, Ṣawm, in *EI*[1], vii, 192-9; J. Berkey, *The transmission of knowledge in medieval Cairo. A social history of Islamic education,* Princeton 1992; Ph. Borgeaud, Le couple sacré/profane. Genèse et fortune d'un concept "opératoire" en histoire des religions, in *RHR* 211 (1994), 387-418; J.P. Brereton, Sacred space, in *ER,* xii, 526-35; E.C. Brewer, *Dictionary of phrase and fable,* Philadelphia 1898; F. Buhl, Koran, in *EI*[1], iv, 1063-76; id., Muzdalifa, in *EI*[1], vi, 800; J. Chelhod, La notion ambiguë du sacré chez les Arabes et dans l'Islam, in *RHR* 159 (1961), 67-79; id., *Les structures du sacré chez les Arabes,* Paris 1964; C. Colpe, Das Heilige, in H. Cancik, B. Gladigow, K.-H. Kohl (eds.), *Handbuch religionswissenschaftlicher Grundbegriffe,* 4 vols., Stuttgart 1988-98, iii, 80-99; id., The sacred and the profane, in *ER,* xii, 511-26; E. Durkheim, *Die elementaren Formen des religiösen Lebens,* Frankfurt 1994, trans. K.E. Fields, *The elementary forms of religious life,* New York 1995 (trans. of *Les élémentaires de la vie religieuse*); M.M. Dziekan, Miejsce Swiete w Islamie, in *Przeglad Orientalisticzny* 3-4 (2001), 185-93; M. Eliade, *Das Heilige und das Profane. Vom Wesen des Religiösen,* Hamburg 1957, Frankfurt 1985[2]; R. Friedland and R.D. Hecht, The politics of sacred space. Jerusalem's Temple Mount/al-haram al-sharif, in J. Scott and P. Simpson-Housley (eds.), *Sacred places and profane spaces. Essays in the geographics of Judaism, Christianity, and Islam,* New York 1991, 21-61; J. Horovitz, *Jewish proper names and derivatives in the Koran,* Hildesheim 1964 (repr.); id., *KU;* H. Hubert and M. Mauss, *Sacrifice, its nature and function,* London 1964; G. Krüger, *Religiöse und profane Welterfahrung,* Frankfurt 1973; Lane; G. van der Leeuw, *Phänomenologie der Religion,* Tübingen 1933; A. Neuwirth, Vom Rezitationstext über die Liturgie zum Kanon. Zu Entstehung und Wiederauflösung der Surenkomposition im Verlauf der Entwicklung eines islamischen Kultus, in Wild, *Text,* 69-106; M. Plessner, al-Muḥarram, in *EI*[1], vi, 698-9; id., Ramaḍān, in *EI*[1], vi, 1111; M. Radscheit, *Iʿǧāz al-Qurʾān* im Koran? in Wild, *Text,* 113-23; J. Sadan, A legal opinion of a Muslim jurist regarding the sanctity of Jerusalem, in *IOS* 13 (1993), 231-45; A. Schimmel, Sacred geography in Islam, in J. Scott and P. Simpson-Housley (eds.), *Sacred places and profane spaces. Essays in the geographics of Judaism, Christianity, and Islam,* New York 1991, 163-75; B.C. Sproul, Sacred time, in *ER,* xii, 535-44; W.S. Urquhart, Profanity, in *ERE,* x, 378-81; P. Veyne, Le sacré et le profane dans la religion gréco-romaine. Inviter les dieux, sacrifier, banqueter. Quelques nuances de la religiosité gréco-romaine, in *Annales: Histoire, sciences sociales* 55 (2000), 3-42; H. Vierling, *Die profane Alltagsreligion. Ein Beitrag zum integralen Religionsverständnis,* Frankfurt 1994; A.J. Wensinck, Iḥrām, in *EI*[1], iii, 455-7; id., Ḳibla, in *EI*[1], iv, 985-7.

Profanity see CURSE; BLASPHEMY

Progeny see CHILDREN

Prognostication see DIVINATION; FORETELLING; POPULAR AND TALISMANIC USES OF THE QURʾĀN

Prohibited Degrees

The various categories of persons a man may not marry. These are most completely laid out in Q 4:22-4, which read:

And marry not women whom your fathers married, except what is past... Prohibited to you are your mothers, daughters, sisters, father's sisters, mother's sisters, brother's daughters, sister's daughters, foster-mothers (see WET NURSING; LACTATION), foster-sisters, your wives' mothers, your step-daughters under your guardianship who are from women to whom you have gone in... wives of your natural sons, two sisters in wedlock at one and the same time... women already married except those whom your right hands possess. Except for these, all others are lawful...

The Muslim jurists point out four types of impediment to marriage in this passage (see MARRIAGE AND DIVORCE; LAW AND THE QURʾĀN): consanguinity (mother, daughters, sisters, paternal and maternal aunts, and nieces; see BLOOD AND BLOOD CLOT), fosterage (q.v.; foster-mother, foster-sisters), affinity by marriage (mothers-in-law, step-daughters under certain conditions) and sisterly conjunction (concurrent marriage to two women who are sisters to each other; see SISTERS). They also draw a distinction between temporary and permanent impediments. Also prohibited by this passage are free women married to other men — married female slaves are the exception (see SLAVES AND SLAVERY) — and widows (see WIDOW) of one's father (see also PARENTS; FAMILY; KINSHIP).

All women other than these *(mā warāʾa dhālikum)* are, this passage tells us if taken in its literal *(ẓāhir)* meaning, marriageable (see LAWFUL AND UNLAWFUL; FORBIDDEN). The key phrase *mā warāʾa dhālikum,* however, cannot, according to most jurists, be taken literally, since there are definitely other categories of unmarriageable women beyond those mentioned in Q 4:22-4. For example, Q 24:3 makes unchasteness *(zinā)* an impediment to marriage (see ADULTERY AND FORNICATION): the unchaste person may not marry a chaste person and a chaste person may not marry an unchaste person. An unchaste person who wishes to marry has only two options: he or she may only marry another unchaste person or an idolater (see POLYTHEISM AND ATHEISM; IDOLATRY AND IDOLATERS; COMMUNITY AND SOCIETY IN THE QURʾĀN). As Q 24:26 declares, the (morally) wicked are for their like to marry, and the morally (good) are for their like to marry (see GOOD AND EVIL; ETHICS AND THE QURʾĀN). In Q 5:5, however, the Qurʾān permits Muslim men to marry women from among those who were recipients of earlier scriptures (see PEOPLE OF THE BOOK; SCRIPTURE AND THE QURʾĀN). Other additional categories of unmarriageable women are: women who would through the contemplated marriage become fifth wives, women who are in the state of *ʿidda* (temporarily excluded from marriage following divorce; see WAITING PERIOD), women who are unmarriageable as a result of the prohibition of sexual intercourse during the pilgrimage (q.v.; see also RITUAL PURITY) and women who were previously divorced by the man with whom marriage is contemplated and have not married in the interval (see SEX AND SEXUALITY).

Finally, it should be noted that Muslim jurists in general have treated the terms *ummahāt,* "mothers," in Q 4:22-4 to be inclusive of all degrees *(darajāt)* of maternal ascent (mother, grandmother, etc.) and *banāt,* "daughters," to be inclusive of all degrees in the daughter line of descent (daughter, granddaughter, etc.). A quick glance at later commentaries of the Qurʾān — such as the mammoth and singularly comprehensive commentary of Fakhr al-Dīn al-Rāzī (d. 606/1210; see EXEGESIS OF THE QURʾĀN: CLASSICAL AND MEDIEVAL) — reveals a large variety of controversial issues pertaining to the subject of prohibited degrees. Al-Rāzī enumerates and discusses well over forty issues pertaining to Q 4:22-4 alone, quite apart from the other qurʾānic passages that have a bearing on this subject. In his treatment of each issue, he lays out the position of the different schools and then advances arguments for his own position in the manner typical of medieval Muslim legal scholasticism (see also THEOLOGY AND THE QURʾĀN).

Bernard Weiss

Bibliography
Primary: G.-H. Bousquet, *Ech-Chirâzî. Kitâb et-Tanbîh ou Le Livre de l'admonition,* annot. Fr. trans., 4 vols., Algiers [1951], iii, 10-3; Jaṣṣāṣ, *Aḥkām,* ed. Istanbul, ii, 112-39 (ad Q 4:22-4); Rāzī, *Tafsīr,* ed. Cairo, x, 23-51.
Secondary: ʿA. Ḥasab Allāh, *al-Zawāj fī l-sharīʿati l-islāmiyya,* Beirut 1971, 81-117; R. Roberts, *The social laws of the Qoran,* London 1990, 7-18; E. Zeys, *Traité élémentaire de droit musulman algérien (école malékite),* 2 vols., Algiers 1885-6, i, 16-21.

Promise see COVENANT

Proof

Clear evidence that brings about the conviction that something is true, as well as its ordered presentation. Several qurʾānic terms are used to refer to the divinely provided evidence for God's existence, unicity, power and guidance, and in particular for the truth (q.v.) of his messengers' claims (see MESSENGER). Among the most common is the adjective *bayyina* (pl. *bayyināt*), "clear, evident, manifest," usually used as a substantive, "clear evidence or proof." Occurring primarily in Meccan passages (cf. Suyūṭī, *Muʿtarak,* i, 460-3; see CHRONOLOGY AND THE QURʾĀN), its range of meanings may be illustrated from those cases where it occurs in conjunction with "sign" (*āya,* see SIGNS): "clear signs" include evidentiary miracles (q.v.; e.g. Q 2:211; 17:101; 28:36), visible reminders of God's guidance and wrath (Q 3:97; 29:35; see ASTRAY; FREEDOM AND PREDESTINATION; ANGER) and especially the verses (q.v.) of a revealed scripture (e.g. Q 24:1). A messenger comes with *bayyināt* (Q 2:87 is the first of many examples), may be said to be [relying] "upon a *bayyina*" (e.g. Q 6:57), or even himself be a *bayyina* (Q 98:1, 4).

It is the nature of *āyāt bayyināt* to be illuminating (Q 57:9) and convincing (cf. Q 2:99): Pharaoh's (q.v.) magicians were prepared to accept torment and martyrdom after the *bayyināt* brought by Moses (q.v.) constrained them to faith (q.v.; Q 20:72-3). While the qurʾānic hope, however, is that human beings may perhaps be reminded by the *āyāt bayyināt* (Q 24:1), the sad reality is that they are regularly met with divisiveness (e.g. Q 2:253), doubt (Q 40:34; see UNCERTAINTY), proud rejection (e.g. Q 29:39; 40:83; see PRIDE; ARROGANCE; LIE; BELIEF AND UNBELIEF), scorn (e.g. Q 5:110; 28:36; 61:6; see MOCKERY) and hostility (e.g. Q 22:72; see OPPOSITION TO MUḤAMMAD; ENEMIES). Some believe but then backslide (e.g. Q 2:209; 3:86). Because the unbelievers "deny the undeniable" (Mir, *Dictionary,* 128) they wrong themselves (e.g. Q 9:70) and will have no claim on God's mercy (q.v.) when cast into the fire (Q 40:49-50; see HELL AND HELLFIRE).

Yet more powerful than the clarity of the *bayyina* is the "brilliant manifestation" of the *burhān* (Gardet, Burhān), which, in Q 4:174, is set in parallel with "a clear light" (q.v.; cf. Ethiopic *berhān* for "light"). A *burhān* may be a vision (Q 12:24 according to many commentators and haggadic parallels; see VISIONS; DREAMS AND SLEEP) or an evidentiary miracle brought by a messenger (Q 28:32). *Mushrikūn,* i.e. those who associate other gods with God — or choose other gods instead (cf. Q 21:24; 27:64; 28:75) — as well as Jews and Christians (Q 2:111; see JEWS AND JUDAISM; CHRISTIANS AND CHRISTIANITY) are challenged to produce a *burhān* for their claims; but anyone who associates other gods with God emphatically has none (Q 23:117).

Other vocabulary covers some of the same ground. Those who claim knowledge of the unseen (see HIDDEN AND THE HIDDEN) are asked to bring a *sulṭān mubīn* (Q 52:38), here an "authoritative proof" (see AUTHORITY). Moses in particular is said to have been sent with "a clear warrant" (*sulṭān mubīn,* e.g. Q 11:96) while God has not sent down a *sulṭān* warranting idolatry (e.g. Q 3:151; see IDOLATRY AND IDOLATERS). God-given evidences viewed as proofs that ought to give insight to the mind (see INTELLECT) and heart (q.v.) may be called *baṣāʾir* (sing. *baṣīra*). They include the scriptures (Q 7:203; 28:43; see BOOK), signs in the creation (q.v.; Q 6:104; cf. 6:97-9; see NATURE AS SIGNS) and evidentiary miracles (Q 17:101-2).

Thus far this article has emphasized proof as manifest evidence rather than as demonstrative argument. The qurʾānic use of the word *ḥujja* includes the latter, twice referring to a *ḥujja* that comes from or belongs to God: in Q 6:(75-)83 it is the argument for God's unicity *(tawḥīd)* given to Abraham (q.v.; a passage highlighted in al-Ashʿarī's apology for *kalām* reasoning; see THEOLOGY AND THE QURʾĀN; PHILOSOPHY AND THE QURʾĀN); while in Q 6:148-9 God is said to have "the conclusive argument" over against human conjecture *(ẓann)*. Indeed, a human *ḥujja* may turn out to be null and void (Q 42:16). It should also be noted that, in addition to the qurʾānic lexemes connoting "proof," the Qurʾān contains arguments for its own veracity. For example, in his *Muqaddima* (285), Ibn Naqīb (d. 698/1298) deals with the *argumentum a fortiori* (i.e. Q 36:78-9, 81; 21:22). Perhaps the most comprehensive discussion of the diverse qurʾānic "proofs" or "arguments" is provided by Jalāl al-Dīn al-Suyūṭī (d. 911/1505), who lists the various types of rhetorical devices the Qurʾān employs to counter its detractors (cf. Suyūṭī, *Muʿtarak*, i, 456-63; id., *Itqān*, iv, 60-6; see also DEBATE AND DISPUTATION).

Finally, *falsafa* adopted the word *burhān* as the technical term for a methodologically rigorous demonstration leading to certain truth. Thus, in Arabic translation Aristotle's *Posterior analytics* became *Kitāb al-Burhān*. The same title is found in a number of Christian apologetic treatises in Arabic, beginning with that of the Nestorian *mutakallim* ʿAmmār al-Baṣrī (fl. third/ninth cent.) which may be seen as a response to the Qurʾān's challenge: *hātū burhānakum* (Q 2:111; see POLEMIC AND POLEMICAL LANGUAGE; CHRISTIANS AND CHRISTIANITY).

Mark N. Swanson

Bibliography

Primary: Ibn Abī l-Iṣba l-Miṣrī, *Badīʿ al-Qurʾān*, ed. Ḥ.M. Sharaf, Cairo 1957; Ibn Naqīb, *Muqaddima; Jalālayn;* Suyūṭī, *Itqān*, iv, 60-6 (chap. 38); id., *Muʿtarak al-aqrān fī iʿjāz al-Qurʾān*, ed. A.M. al-Bajāwī, 3 vols., Cairo 1969-72, i, 456-63 (chap. 30); Ṭabarī, *Tafsīr*.

Secondary: ʿAbd al-Bāqī; R. Brunschvig, Bayyina, in *EI²*, i, 1150-1; R.M. Frank, Al-Ashʿarī's *"al-Ḥathth ʿalā l-baḥth"*, in *MIDEO* 18 (1988), 83-152, esp. 137; L. Gardet, Burhān, in *EI²*, i, 1326-7; id. and M.G.S. Hodgson, Ḥudjdja, in *EI²*, iii, 543-4; A. Geiger, *Judaism and Islam*, Madras 1898, repr. New York 1970, 111; S.H. Griffith, ʿAmmār al-Baṣrī's *Kitāb al-burhān*. Christian *kalām* in the first Abbasid century, in *Muséon* 96 (1983), 145-81, esp. 155; Jeffery, *For. vocab.*, 77-8; Mir, *Dictionary*, 128-9; Paret, *Kommentar;* M.-Th. Urvoy, De quelques procédés de persuasion dans le Coran, in *Arabica* 49 (2002), 456-76.

Property

Wealth, goods, things owned. There is no formal, legal concept of property in the Qurʾān, nor is there a technical equivalent to the Latin *res* of Western tradition. There is, however, a general concern with property as is clearly indicated, for example, by the verses outlining the punishment for theft (q.v.; Q 5:38; see also BOUNDARIES AND PRECEPTS; CHASTISEMENT AND PUNISHMENT; LAW AND THE QURʾĀN). Roughly speaking, there are three contexts in which the Qurʾān addresses property: commercial, private and general.

In a commercial context, there are several terms used to designate property, the object generally being "goods," "commodities" or "possessions." In Sūrat Yūsuf (Q 12, "Joseph"), the term *biḍāʿa*, "goods," is used to refer to the property allegedly stolen by the brothers of Joseph (q.v.; Q 12:62, 65; see also BROTHERS AND BROTHERHOOD; BENJAMIN). In Sūrat al-Aʿrāf (Q 7, "The Heights"), the Madyanites (see MIDIAN) are warned "not to cheat people out of their property" (*lā tabkhasū l-nāsa ashyāʾahum*, Q 7:85; see CHEATING) — *ashyāʾ* (sing. *shayʾ*) meaning literally "things." The same admonishment is repeated in Q 26:183 (cf. Q 11:85). Also, the term *māl* (pl. *amwāl;* see below) is used in a commercial context in the sense of "counter-value."

In a private context, the verb *malaka*, "to own, possess," is used to denote property ownership (see POSSESSION AND POSSESSIONS). Several verses, for example, Q 4:3, 24, 25, 36, Q 16:71, Q 23:6 and passim, speak of "what your right hands possess" *(mā malakat aymānukum)*, the reference being to private ownership of (female) slaves (see SLAVES AND SLAVERY). In Q 24:61 private ownership of real estate is conveyed via the phrase "that whose keys you own/possess" *(mā malaktum mafātīḥahu)*.

In a general context, three terms are used to denote property or ownership. The first, *rabb*, "owner, lord," is used extensively to refer to God and his dominion or ownership over the universe (see LORD; KINGS AND RULERS; POWER AND IMPOTENCE). God is, *inter alia*, the "owner of the universe" (*rabb al-ʿālamīna*, Q 1:2; 2:131; 5:28; 6:45, and passim), the "owner of the heavens and the earth" (q.v.; *rabb al-samāwāti wa-l-arḍi*, Q 13:16; 17:102; 18:14; 19:65, and passim; see also HEAVEN AND SKY), "the owner of this [sacred] house" (*rabb hādhā l-bayti*, Q 106:3; see HOUSE, DOMESTIC AND DIVINE; PROFANE AND SACRED). While *rabb* in this sense refers almost exclusively to God, there is at least one instance where exegetes note its application to a human being, namely Potiphar (in Q 12:23; see EXEGESIS OF THE QURʾĀN: CLASSICAL AND MEDIEVAL).

Another term used for property in general is *khayr*. The basic meaning of *khayr* being "good," this term imputes an emphatically positive meaning to property and casts it in its most favorable light, i.e. "fortune." Speaking, for example, in the context of inheritance (q.v.), Q 2:180 refers to the property left by the deceased as *khayr*. Other verses mildly chide human beings, however, for over-indulging their (presumably natural) love of property. Q 100:8 refers to humans as "extremely severe in their love of property" *(li-ḥubbi l-khayri la-shadīdun)*. And Q 38:32 records the prophet Solomon's (q.v.) penitent self-criticism for having placed his love of property *(ḥubb al-khayr)* over the remembrance (q.v.) of his lord (see also REPENTANCE AND PENANCE).

The term used most extensively, however, for property in general is *māl* and its plural *amwāl*. While this term also carries the meaning of "money" or "cash" in the restricted sense, liquid currency was the exception rather than the norm in first/seventh century Arabia (see PRE-ISLAMIC ARABIA AND THE QURʾĀN; MONEY; NUMISMATICS; for further on this, see Foss, Coinage, for the review of a recent survey of the state of early Islamic coinage). As such, classical lexicographers and exegetes commonly define *māl* as "whatever men possess of *dirhams*, or *dīnārs*, or gold (q.v.), or silver (q.v.), or wheat, or barely or bread, or beasts, or garments or pieces of cloth, or weapons or other things," in short, "anything one possesses" (see ANIMAL LIFE; HIDES AND FLEECE; CLOTHING). On this understanding, *māl* is used in numerous, overlapping contexts, commercial, private and other. Q 2:177 praises those who "give of their property *(al-māl)*," while Q 18:46 informs us that, "property *(al-māl)* and progeny (see CHILDREN) are the adornments of life" (see GRACE; BLESSING). Q 2:155 affirms that God will "try humanity with... deficits in property *(naqṣ mina l-amwāli),*" while Q 64:15 declares property *(amwāl)* itself to be a "test" (*fitna;* see TRIAL; TRUST AND PATIENCE; POVERTY AND THE POOR; OPPRESSED ON EARTH, THE). Q 34:37 warns that neither property *(amwāl)* nor progeny bring closeness to God. And Q 69:28 records the lamentations of those who thought their property would avail them on the day of reckoning (see LAST JUDGMENT).

Again, these references to property are broad, flexible and grounded in Arabian custom and common usage. They do not constitute a formal doctrine, let alone a legal definition of property. The latter would have to await the legal acumen and jurisprudential imagination of the jurists and legal theorists of the formative period of Islamic law. See also WEALTH.

Sherman A. Jackson

Bibliography
Primary: ʿAbd al-Bāqī; Ibn Kathīr, *Tafsīr,* 4 vols., Cairo 2001; *Lisān al-ʿArab;* Shawkānī, *Tafsīr;* Ṭabarī, *Tafsīr.*
Secondary: C. Foss, The coinage of the first century of Islam. Review of Stephen Albume and Tony Goodwin, *Sylloge of Islamic coins in the Ashmolean Museum 1. The pre-reform coinage of the early Islamic period,* in *Journal of Roman archaeology* 16 (2003), 748-60; Lane.

Prophets

see PROPHETS AND PROPHETHOOD

Prophets and Prophethood

Those individuals who receive divine revelation and their collective vocation. In Arabic (as in Hebrew), the word for "prophet" is *nabī,* plural *nabiyyūn* and *anbiyāʾ*. These forms occur seventy-five times, apart from the term *nubuwwa,* "prophethood," which occurs five times. Much more prevalent, however, is the term *rasūl* (pl. *rusul*) which denotes a "messenger" (q.v.) or "apostle" (of God). Messengers are mentioned more than 300 times. A messenger is also referred to as *mursal,* which, together with its plural form *(mursalūn),* occurs more than thirty times. The form *risāla* (pl. *risālāt*) denotes a prophetic "message" and occurs ten times, mostly in the plural form.

Prophets and messengers

As in the New Testament, in which apostles seem to rank higher than prophets (e.g. 1 *Cor* 12:28-31; cf. *Eph* 3:5; 4:11), in the Qurʾān, too, *rasūl* seems to be somewhat more elevated than *nabī.* This is indicated, to begin with, by the fact that whenever both titles appear together, *rasūl* comes first, which may suggest that a messenger is more important than a prophet. Thus Q 22:52 describes Satan's (see DEVIL) attempts to lead astray (q.v.) any apostle *(rasūl)* or prophet *(nabī)* who was sent before Muḥammad. Muslim commentators say that in this verse *rasūl* stands for a prophet having a message, a book (q.v.), which must be delivered, whereas *nabī* has no such message or book. More specifically, al-Bayḍāwī (d. prob. 716/1316, according to van Ess; cf. Gilliot, Textes, 223-4) says that a *rasūl* is a prophet who establishes a new *sharīʿa* (religious law; see LAW AND THE QURʾĀN), whereas a *nabī* is one who continues an old one. This means, al-Bayḍāwī says, that *rasūl* is more distinguished than *nabī,* and therefore there were more *anbiyāʾ* ("prophets") than *rusul* ("messengers"). Or, he adds, a *rasūl* receives revelation from an angel, whereas a prophet experiences revelation only in dreams (Bayḍāwī, *Anwār,* ad Q 22:52).

The titles *rasūl* and *nabī* may also overlap and even refer to one and the same person, in which case *rasūl* again comes first. This applies to Moses (q.v.), about whom it is stated that he was "an apostle, a prophet" (*wa-kāna rasūlan nabiyyan,* Q 19:51). The same is stated about Ishmael (q.v.; Q 19:54) as well as about Muḥammad (Q 7:157). The combination of the two in one person is perhaps designed to indicate that this person belongs to the messengers among the prophets.

But not every messenger of God is also a prophet. God is said to have made the angels "messengers *(rusul)* flying (q.v.) on wings, two, and three, and four..." (Q 35:1; see ANGEL). As God's messengers, the angels bring good tidings to Abraham (q.v.) about the birth of Isaac (q.v.) and Jacob (q.v.), and they also destroy the people of Lot (q.v.; e.g. Q 11:69-81). God sends angels to guard people as well as to receive their souls (see SOUL) at the moment of death (cf. Q 6:61; 7:37). Their primary role as God's messengers is to inspect and write down the deeds of every human being (cf. Q 10:21; 43:80; see GOOD DEEDS; EVIL DEEDS).

The Qurʾān is careful to draw a clear line between God's celestial and human messengers. Prophets can only be mortals, because angels, the Qurʾān says (Q 17:95), do not walk about on earth (q.v.) as do its ordinary dwellers — for which reason people cannot grasp their physical presence. Therefore God does not send down angels as his prophets.

Angels do, however, bring down prophetic revelations in their capacity as God's messengers but they do not deliver them directly to the people, only to individual human prophets (see REVELATION AND INSPIRATION). The Qurʾān mentions the "word" *(qawl),* i.e. prophetic message, of one particular "honored messenger" (*rasūl karīm,* Q 69:40; 81:19). Some exegetes have identified this "messenger" with the angel Gabriel (q.v.) whose mission was to reveal the Qurʾān to Muḥammad. But Gabriel's task as God's messenger is not confined to prophetic revelations. He is also said to have been referred to in Q 19:19, in which God's messenger comes to Mary (q.v.) to give her a son (Jesus; q.v.). Even the *rasūl* mentioned in the story of the golden calf (Q 20:96; see CALF OF GOLD) was said to have been Gabriel. Most qurʾānic prophets/messengers are known from the Bible, but there are also some whose origin is somewhat obscure (for details about the individual prophets see Tottoli, *Biblical prophets;* see SCRIPTURE AND THE QURʾĀN).

The status of the prophets

Prophets (including the messengers among them) belong to the highest rank among various virtuous groups of human beings. These groups are listed in Q 4:69, in which their position in paradise (q.v.) is described: "And whoever obeys God and the messenger, these will be [in paradise] with the prophets and the truthful *(al-ṣiddīqūn)* and the martyrs (*al-shuhadāʾ;* see MARTYRS) and the righteous *(al-ṣāliḥīn),* upon whom God has bestowed favors (see GRACE; BLESSING)." As for the prophets, their presence among their respective peoples — for example, among the Children of Israel (q.v.) — is perceived as a sign of God's benefaction *(niʿma)* unto these peoples (Q 5:20).

God started sending prophets after humankind became separated, when the initial state of righteousness was replaced by moral corruption (q.v.; see also FALL OF MAN; GOOD AND EVIL; VIRTUES AND VICES, COMMANDING AND FORBIDDING). This, at least, is how the exegetes explain Q 2:213 in which it is stated: "The people were [united in] one nation *(umma wāḥida),* then [they became divided, and] God sent the prophets to bear good tidings (see GOOD NEWS) and to warn (see WARNER)..." (see PARTIES AND FACTIONS).

The prophets emerge in succession. The Qurʾān says that they were sent "one after another" (*qaffaynā*, Q 2:87), or "one by one" (*tatrā*, Q 23:44). Moreover, the prophets belong to the same genealogical descent. Thus Q 19:58 reads: "These are the prophets on whom God bestowed favors, of the seed *(dhurriyya)* of Adam (see ADAM AND EVE), and of those whom we carried with Noah (q.v.), and of the seed of Abraham and Israel (q.v.)...." The same idea is conveyed in Q 6:84, in which it is stated about Abraham: "And we gave to him Isaac and Jacob; each did we guide, and Noah we guided before, and of his descendants *(dhurriyyatihi)* David (q.v.) and Solomon (q.v.) and Job (q.v.) and Joseph (q.v.) and Moses and Aaron (q.v.)...."

The fact that the prophets are said to have been "guided" by God means that they represent a divinely chosen pedigree, as is indicated, for example, in Q 3:33-4: "Surely God chose *(iṣṭafā)* Adam and Noah and the house *(āl)* of Abraham and the house *(āl)* of ʿImrān (q.v.) above all beings. [They are] the offspring *(dhurriyyatan)* one of the other...." The chosen prophetic lineage begins here with Adam, which indicates that he, too, is considered a prophet. The house of ʿImrān stands for Moses (the son of the biblical Amram), but can also refer to Jesus, whose mother Mary is considered a member of that house.

The verb *iṣṭafā*, which signifies here divine election (q.v.), recurs in more verses dealing with prophets, as well as with angels. Thus in Q 22:75 it is stated that God chooses *(yaṣṭafī)* messengers *(rusul)* from among the angels and from among the people. The same verb is used to describe election of individual prophets, such as Abraham (Q 2:130), Moses (Q 7:144) and Mary (Q 3:42), as well as of kings (see KINGS AND RULERS), namely Saul (q.v.; Ṭālūt, Q 2:247).

Another verb, *ijtabā*, also denotes divine election of prophets, such as Adam (Q 20:122), Abraham (Q 16:121), Joseph (Q 12:6) and Jonah (q.v.; Q 68:50). Less frequent is the verb *ikhtāra* that denotes the same type of divine election (Q 44:32) and describes the election of Moses (Q 20:13). The latter's election is also conveyed by the verb *iṣṭanaʿa* (Q 20:41).

The divine election of the prophets provides them with abilities not shared by ordinary humans. This pertains mainly to knowledge of the unseen (*ghayb;* see HIDDEN AND THE HIDDEN). Thus in Q 72:26-7 it is stated that God knows the unseen and he does not reveal his secrets to anyone, except to an apostle with whom he is well pleased *(irtaḍā)*. In Q 3:179 we are told again that God does not make people acquainted with the unseen, but he "chooses *(yajtabī)* of his apostles whom he pleases."

The guided and divinely chosen prophets possess moral virtues that render them immune to sin and misbehavior (see IMPECCABILITY). Thus, in Q 3:161 it is stated that it is not attributable to a prophet that he should act unfaithfully *(yaghulla)*. The election of the prophets has made them belong to the righteous *(mina l-ṣāliḥīn)*, a fact stated regarding several of them, e.g. Zechariah (q.v.), John (see JOHN THE BAPTIST), Jesus, Elijah (q.v.; Q 6:85) and others. John is described in Q 3:39 as honorable *(sayyid)* and chaste (*ḥaṣūr;* see CHASTITY) and a prophet from among the righteous *(mina l-ṣāliḥīn)*. Some of them are also described as truthful *(ṣiddīq)*, as is Abraham (Q 19:41) and Idrīs (q.v.; Q 19:56). Ishmael is described in Q 19:54 as "truthful in his promise" *(ṣādiq al-waʿd)*.

Some prophets possess unique traits that mark their singular status among the rest of the prophets. Abraham is described in Q 4:125 as one whom God took as a friend (*khalīl;* see FRIENDS AND FRIENDSHIP). Moses is described as pure (*mukhlaṣ*,

Q 19:51) and as one whom God brought near in communion (*wa-qarrabnāhu najiyyan,* Q 19:52) and with whom God spoke (*kallama,* Q 4:164). This is the origin of Moses' title, *kalīmu llāh,* by which he is known in Islamic tradition. Tradition also elaborates on Moses' communion *(munājāt)* with God.

Later tradition has provided Muḥammad with a title of his own, namely, *ḥabību llāh* "God's beloved," which together with the previous prophets, completes the unique group of prophets having an intimate relationship with God. In fact, Muslim tradition has elaborated on Muḥammad's honorific titles and produced long lists of them (see NAMES OF THE PROPHET).

The existence of distinguished groups among the prophets is a fact that the Qur'ān declares openly. Q 17:55 states that God has made some of the prophets to excel others and in Q 2:253 the same statement is repeated, alongside names of some of the excelling prophets:

We have made some of these apostles to excel the others, among them are they to whom God spoke *(kallama),* and some of them he exalted by [many degrees of] rank; and we gave clear arguments (*bayyināt;* see PROOF) to Jesus son of Mary, and strengthened him with the Holy Spirit (q.v.)....

In Q 33:7 some prophets are singled out as those with whom God made a special covenant (q.v.; *mīthāq*): "And when we made a covenant with the prophets and with you [Muḥammad], and with Noah and Abraham and Moses and Jesus son of Mary, and we made with them a firm covenant."

A special group of God's messengers is mentioned in Q 46:35, being called "those endowed with constancy *(ūlū l-ʿazm).*" The Qur'ān says that they have borne patiently (the hardships of their mission; see TRIAL) and Muslim exegetes are not unanimous as to who they were. Some say that they were those who established a law *(sharīʿa)* among their nations, like Noah, Abraham, Moses, and Jesus, as well as Muḥammad. Others hold that they were those who suffered the hardest trials or the deepest remorse (see REPENTANCE AND PENANCE). In the latter case, they include Jacob, Joseph, Job and David, in addition to the five prophets already mentioned. But in spite of divine election, the prophets always remain God's servants (*ʿibād;* e.g. Q 37:171; see SERVANTS), for which reason people are not servants to them but to God (Q 3:79).

Modes of prophetic revelation

Various verbs convey the idea of prophetic revelation, the most frequent being those derived from the root *n-z-l,* namely, *nazzala* and *anzala.* They denote an act of bringing down, which means that the prophetic revelation is perceived as being sent down from heaven (see HEAVEN AND SKY). Occasionally, the revelation itself is described as descending *(nazala, tanazzala),* without specifying the agent that causes it to come down. A common name of the qur'ānic revelation is *tanzīl* (e.g. Q 20:4; 26:192; 32:2, etc.), i.e. a "bringing down." A less common name is *amr,* "affair," which in Q 65:12 is said to have been descending *(yatanazzalu)* through the seven heavens (see NAMES OF THE QUR'ĀN). Muslim exegetes explain that the "affair" stands here for divine revelation that is being brought down from heaven to earth.

Revelation originates in God, as is indicated in verses in which God speaks in the first person: "I have sent down [the Qur'ān]" (Q 2:41), and more often: "We have sent down [the Qur'ān]" (e.g. Q 44:3; 76:23; 97:1). But revelation does not come down directly to the prophets. The intermediate agents are the angels. God sends them down with the revelations, as is implied in Q 16:2 : "He sends down *(yunazzilu)* the angels with the spirit (q.v.; *al-rūḥ*) by his commandment on whom he pleases of his servants...." Muslim exegetes hold, however, that only Gabriel is meant here, the angel who was commissioned to bring down prophetic revelations, or the "spirit," to Muḥammad. In Q 16:102 the agent bringing down *(nazzalahu)* the qurʾānic revelation is himself called "the Holy Spirit" *(rūḥu l-qudus)*, which is again interpreted as an epithet of Gabriel. The same applies to Q 26:193, in which the revelation is brought down *(nazala bihi)* by the "faithful spirit" *(al-rūḥ al-amīn)*. Similarly, the exegetes say that it is Gabriel who says to the Prophet in Q 19:64: "We do not descend [with revelations] but by the command of your lord (q.v.)."

As far as Muḥammad's own prophetic experience is concerned, the process of sending down revelations ends at the Prophet's heart (q.v.; *ʿalā qalbika*) and Gabriel is mentioned explicitly as the one who brings it down to him (Q 2:97; see MUḤAMMAD). The Qurʾān provides specific, though not entirely coherent, details of the time when the revelation began coming down to Muḥammad. This took place either on a "blessed night" (Q 44:3) or on *laylat al-qadr* (Q 97:1; see NIGHT OF POWER) or during the month of Ramaḍān (q.v.; Q 2:185). The exegetes explain that all passages refer to one and the same night, namely *laylat al-qadr* that falls in Ramaḍān.

There are various terms denoting the actual revelation that is being brought down. Most often it is called "signs" (q.v.; *āyāt*), which commentators on the Qurʾān have identified with the qurʾānic verses (q.v.; e.g. Q 57:9, etc.). Elsewhere, what God sends down is called *sūra* (q.v.; Q 9:86, etc.), a term that came to be identified with the qurʾānic chapters and, most obviously, the term *qurʾān*, too, stands for something which God sends down (Q 76:23). Another locution standing for a whole unit of revelations being sent down is *kitāb*, a "book, scripture" (e.g. Q 7:2; see BOOK). Specific scriptures, namely the Torah (q.v.) and the Gospel (q.v.), are also described as being sent down by God (Q 3:3-4), which implies that all monotheistic scriptures represent the same divine revelation. Metaphorical terms are also used to describe a descending revelation, one of which being the somewhat obscure title *furqān* (Q 3:4; see CRITERION). Some exegetes have explained it in the sense of a scripture distinguishing between truth and falsehood. Light (q.v.; *nūr*) is also a name for the guiding revelation that God has sent down (Q 64:8).

Another widely used verb denoting the act of providing revelation is *awḥā*, with *waḥy* as the noun denoting the revelation itself. The verb means to "prompt, inspire, suggest" but it is not confined to prophetic revelations. Occasionally it simply means to "instruct," or "command," as in Q 8:12 in which God instructs *(yūḥī)* the angels to support the believers. In Q 99:4-5 God instructs *(awḥā)* the earth to tell its story on the day of resurrection (q.v.), and in Q 16:68 he instructs *(awḥā)* the bee to make hives in the mountains (see ANIMAL LIFE; HONEY), etc. Even when prophets are addressed, the verb *awḥā* can be a request to act rather than imparting a text for recitation (see RECITATION OF THE QURʾĀN). Thus in Q 23:27 God instructs *(awḥaynā)* Noah to make the ark (q.v.) and in Q 7:117 God prompts *(awḥaynā)* Moses to cast his rod (q.v.). An act designated as *awḥā* can also be performed by humans. In Q 19:11, for example, Zechariah signals *(awḥā)* to his people that they should glorify God in the morning (q.v.) and evening (q.v.; see also GLORIFICATION OF GOD; DAY, TIMES OF). In most cases, however, *awḥā* stands for an act performed by God himself, as in Q 41:12. Here God reveals *(awḥā)* the "affair" *(amr)* of the seven heavens, i.e.

enjoins his commandment on the heavens. But what God reveals mostly as *waḥy* is the prophetic inspiration itself. This is the case in Q 42:52 in which God reveals *(awḥaynā)* a "spirit" *(rūḥan)* to his prophet. The spirit is interpreted here as standing for the qurʾānic revelation. This accords with Q 53:4-5, in which the Qurʾān is explicitly described as a revelation *(waḥyun)* that is revealed *(yūḥā)*. In Q 35:31 it is the "book" that has been revealed as *waḥy*.

The revelation *(waḥy)* can be a prolonged process, as is the case with the revelation to Muḥammad. He is advised not to make haste before the process is completed (Q 20:114). When the reception of the *waḥy* is completed the Prophet is supposed to recite it in public (Q 29:45). The same process of *waḥy* was experienced also by previous prophets, as stated in Q 4:163: "Surely we have revealed *(awḥaynā)* to you as we revealed to Noah, and the prophets after him, and we revealed to Abraham and Ishmael and Isaac and Jacob and the tribes (see TRIBES AND CLANS), and Jesus and Job and Jonah and Aaron and Solomon…."

The *waḥy* does not always come directly from God to the prophets. An angel acting as God's messenger may deliver the divine *waḥy* to them. This comes out in Q 42:51, in which it is stated: "It is not for any mortal that God should speak to them, except by inspiration *(waḥyan)* or from behind a veil (q.v.; *ḥijāb*), or by sending a messenger *(rasūl)*, to reveal *(fa-yūḥiya)* by his permission what he will." As was mentioned above, the exegetes say that the messenger delivering the *waḥy* is Gabriel.

As for the contents of what is being revealed as *waḥy*, in some cases it consists of the sheer idea of monotheism (see GOD AND HIS ATTRIBUTES; POLYTHEISM AND ATHEISM). Thus in Q 21:108 it is stated: "Say: It is only revealed *(yūḥā)* to me that your God is one God." In other cases the *waḥy* revolves around specific legal obligations (see BOUNDARIES AND PRECEPTS). God reveals *(awḥaynā)* to the previous prophets "the doing of good and the keeping up of prayer (q.v.) and the giving of alms" (Q 21:73; see ALMSGIVING). The Qurʾān repeats several times the injunction given to the Prophet to follow *(ittabiʿ)* what has been revealed *(yūḥā)* to him (e.g. Q 10:109; 33:2, etc.).

In Q 17:39 the content of the *waḥy* is defined as "wisdom" (q.v.; *ḥikma*), which seems to refer to moral lessons which must be derived from the history of past generations (q.v.). This is confirmed by the fact that in Q 11:49 the *waḥy* consists of "accounts of the unseen" *(anbāʾ al-ghayb)*, i.e. stories of the history of past generations which are now being revealed to the Prophet. The stories deal with sinful nations that God punished and destroyed because they had rejected their prophets (see PUNISHMENT STORIES).

There are also other, less frequent, terms of prophetic revelation, one of which being to "cast" *(alqā)*, as in Q 40:15. Here God is said to have cast *(yulqi)* "the inspiration *(rūḥ)* by his command upon whom he pleases of his servants." In Q 28:86 it is the book that has been cast unto the Prophet, while in Q 77:5 some unspecified persons are mentioned who are described as "casting the reminder" *(fa-l-mulqiyāti dhikran)*. The exegetes say that the "reminder" signifies the prophetic inspiration and that those who cast it are the angels who deliver it to God's prophets and messengers.

"To give" *(ātā)* may also signal prophetic revelation, as is the case in Q 2:87, in which God "gives" Moses "the book."

Another verb, *alhama* (from *l-h-m*), also denotes divine inspiration but not specifically prophetic. Thus in Q 91:8 it is indicated that God has inspired *(fa-alhamahā)* the human soul to understand what is right and wrong for it.

Dreams *(ruʾyā)* may also function as prophetic visions (q.v.; see also DREAMS AND SLEEP). Abraham found out by such a dream that he had to sacrifice (q.v.) his son (Q 37:105) and Muḥammad knew from his own dream that he was about to enter Mecca (q.v.) safely (cf. Q 48:27). Another vision of the Prophet, which is mentioned in Q 17:60, was interpreted as referring to his nocturnal journey and ascension (q.v.; *isrāʾ/miʿrāj*).

The Qurʾān is also aware of false revelations that seem prophetic but come from Satan, which means that only a thin line separates genuine divine inspiration from satanic temptation. This is demonstrated in the common vocabulary that the Qurʾān uses for the divine as well as the satanic spheres. Thus satans *(shayāṭīn),* like God, can deliver *waḥy* (Q 6:112, 121) which is deceiving in its varnished outward appearance. But the more common verb denoting satanic inspiration is *waswasa,* to "whisper" (e.g. Q 7:20; 20:120). Satan also casts *(alqā)* his own verses into genuine revelations received by every prophet "but God annuls that which Satan casts" (Q 22:52). Moreover, the satans can be God's messengers but he sends *(arsalnā)* them against the unbelievers (Q 19:83).

The distinction between a true prophet and other persons endowed with unique spiritual powers is also stated very clearly, in passages stressing that Muḥammad's prophetic message is not the words of a "soothsayer" (*kāhin*), nor of a poet (see POETRY AND POETS; SOOTHSAYERS) nor a *majnūm,* i.e. a madman possessed by demons (cf. Q 52:29; 69:41-2; 81:22; see INSANITY).

Imposters are severely denounced. Q 6:93 states: "And who is more unjust than he who forges a lie (q.v.) against God, or says: It has been revealed *(ūḥiya)* to me; while nothing has been revealed to him, and he who says: I can bring down *(sa-unzilu)* the like of what God has brought down *(anzala)*?" The exegetes say that this passage refers to persons like Musaylima (q.v.) and others who pretended to receive revelations similar to those of Muḥammad.

Signs and miracles

God not only provides his messengers with the prophetic inspiration but he also stays with them when they deliver his message, as is formulated in Q 72:27-8: "For surely he makes a guard to march before [his messenger] and after him, so that he may know that they have truly delivered the messages of their lord...." The "guards" accompanying the prophets are said to be the angels and elsewhere it is asserted that God is always aware of what his apostles are doing (Q 23:51). God's presence renders his apostles immune to dangers (Q 27:10) and his help *(naṣr)* is always ensured for them (Q 12:110; cf. 40:51; see PROTECTION; VICTORY).

God also provides his prophets with concrete means designed to increase their power of persuasion. These are called *bayyināt,* i.e. clear "proofs" or "arguments." Occasionally the exegetes interpret this term as "miracles" (see MIRACLES; MARVELS). For example, in Q 2:87 (see also Q 2:253), God provides Jesus with the *bayyināt* and strengthens him with the Holy Spirit. The exegetes say that the latter stands for Gabriel and that the *bayyināt* are miracles which Jesus performed. Such miracles are described in Q 3:49, where Jesus says to the Children of Israel:

I have come to you with a sign *(āya)* from your lord, that I create *(akhluqa)* for you out of dust like the form of a bird, then I breathe into it and it becomes a bird with God's permission, and I heal the blind and the leprous, and bring the dead (see DEATH AND THE DEAD) to life with God's permission, and I shall inform you of what you eat and what you have stored in your houses....

But miracles do not render the prophets divine, as is stressed especially with respect to Jesus. The Qurʾān insists that he is "only an apostle *(rasūl)* of God and his word *(kalimatuhu)* which he cast *(alqāhā)* unto Mary, and a spirit *(rūḥ)* from him. Believe therefore in God and his apostles, and say not: Three" (Q 4:171; see TRINITY; WORD OF GOD; SPEECH).

Other prophets also brought such *bayyināt* to their own nations, alongside of revealed scriptures, but they were rejected (Q 3:184; 35:25). Muḥammad, too, has brought (unspecified) *bayyināt* to his people but they have discarded them as sheer magic (q.v.; Q 61:6). The term *burhān*, "proof," is also used to signal what Muḥammad has brought to his audience (Q 4:174).

The listeners, however, not only reject the *bayyināt* but demand to receive a "sign" *(āya)* of their own choice (Q 2:118; 21:5, etc.). Often they request, for instance, to see an angel being sent down with Muḥammad (Q 23:24; 25:7, etc.), or a treasure descending upon him (Q 11:12), or a fountain being made to gush forth from the earth for them (Q 17:90). The Qurʾān responds to such demands by asserting that God's messengers can only produce signs with God's permission (Q 40:78) and that they are just mortals (Q 14:11). They may even have wives and children (Q 13:38; see WIVES OF THE PROPHET; FAMILY OF THE PROPHET; PEOPLE OF THE HOUSE). Elsewhere it is stressed that they are merely humans *(rijāl)* receiving revelation (e.g. Q 12:109; 16:43, etc.), and that they eat food and go about in the markets (q.v.; Q 25:20).

But God may at times send a sign *(āya)* in response to a specific request. This was the case with the prophet Ṣāliḥ (q.v.) who was sent as a warner to Thamūd (q.v.). They asked him for a sign, and he produced a she-camel *(nāqa)*. They were ordered to share their water with her at appointed intervals (Q 26:154-5) or, according to another version (Q 11:64), to leave her to pasture on God's earth and not harm her. But Thamūd slaughtered the she-camel (Q 11:65), for which reason God no longer sends signs on demand (Q 17:59).

Nevertheless, Moses, too, brought a sign *(āya)* in response to the demand of Pharaoh (q.v.; Q 7:106; 26:31). The sign was that the rod of Moses was turned into a serpent and his hand became "white to the beholders." The audience denied the double sign as evident magic (Q 7:107-9; 26:31-4). But these two signs were given to Moses in advance, upon his first encounter with God (Q 20:17-23; 27:10-2; 28:31-2). They formed part of nine (not ten, as in the Hebrew Bible) signs which God gave to Moses and they are therefore not just *āyāt* but rather *āyāt bayyināt* (Q 17:101; cf. 28:36) as well as *burhān*, "proof" (Q 28:32). Elsewhere a list of all the signs, i.e. the calamities, is provided (Q 7:130-5; see PLAGUES).

Prophets and scriptures

The core of the prophetic revelation consists in revealed scriptures that are sometimes (e.g. Q 3:184) referred to as *zubur* (sing. *zabūr*) or *ṣuḥuf* (sing. *ṣaḥīfa*). The latter term signifies "scrolls" (q.v.), as, for example, in Q 87:19, in which the scrolls *(ṣuḥuf)* of Abraham and Moses are mentioned.

The most frequent name for a revealed scripture is *kitāb*, namely, something written down, or simply a "book." A *kitāb* is always of high solemnity. It may stand for the written list of deeds which determines the destiny of all people on the day of resurrection (e.g. Q 39:69) or the pre-existent divine book (see HEAVENLY BOOK) in which the pre-ordained law of God has been recorded. This is, at least, how Muslim exegetes explain the locution "book of God" in Q 33:6 (also Q 30:56), which, so they hold, is identical with the "guarded tablet" (*lawḥ maḥfūẓ*; see PRESERVED TABLET) mentioned in Q 85:22. The Qurʾān is said to have formed part of this tablet (Q 85:21), so that this revealed book is actually a reflection of a celestial text. Another locution which is taken to refer to the original celestial version of the universal book is *umm al-kitāb* mentioned in Q 43:4. Here it is stated that the Qurʾān is in the *umm al-kitāb* "with us, truly elevated, full of wisdom." The exegetes maintain that it is another name for the tablet, the origin of all revealed books.

The divine origin of the qurʾānic revelation comes out in the idea that no one can alter God's words as revealed to Muḥammad: "Recite *(utlu)* what has been revealed *(ūḥiya)* to you of the book of your lord; there is none who can alter his words..." (Q 18:27). God sent down the book to Muḥammad without any "crookedness" (*ʿiwaj*, Q 18:1), so that the revealed Qurʾān has remained faithful to the original message of the divine book (see CORRUPTION; FORGERY; REVISION AND ALTERATION). In other words, the book was sent down to Muḥammad "with the truth *(bi-l-ḥaqq)*" (e.g. Q 39:2). It has also been sent down as a "blessed" *(mubārak)* book (e.g. Q 6:155; 38:29) and as a book "conformable" *(mutashābih)* in its various parts (Q 39:23). Not just the Qurʾān but any other revealed book is of the same divine origin, for which reason the Qurʾān recognizes the authenticity of previous revelations, saying that previous messengers *(rusul)*, too, brought their peoples "clear arguments *(bayyināt)*, scriptures *(zubur)* and the illuminating book" (*al-kitāb al-munīr*, Q 35:25; see also Q 3:184; 57:25).

Being an essential component of the prophetic message, the term *kitāb* often appears side by side with the term *nubuwwa*, "prophethood," and both are perceived as components of a divine legacy that runs in a genealogical line of a chosen pedigree. Thus in Q 29:27, the prophethood *(nubuwwa)* and the book are said to have remained in the seed *(dhurriyya)* of Abraham, Isaac and Jacob. The same is said of the offspring of Noah and Abraham (Q 57:26). The book is therefore a divine legacy that God has bequeathed *(awrathnā)* to whom he chose of his servants (Q 35:32). Of the previous prophets, Moses in particular is mentioned as one to whom God gave the book (Q 2:87). His book is described as "a light and a guidance to the people" (Q 6:91).

Apart from the term *kitāb*, previous scriptures are also mentioned by their individual titles, such as the Torah *(tawrāt)* of the Israelite prophets (Q 5:44), David's Psalms (q.v.; *zabūr*, Q 4:163; 17:55) and Jesus' Gospel *(injīl)*. About the latter it is stated that it was full of guidance and light (Q 5:46).

The prophets and Muḥammad

The revelation of the book was a new experience for Muḥammad (Q 42:52) and the Arabs (q.v.), too, never had messengers sent to them before him, nor had they any revealed books (cf. Q 34:44). This means that as an Arab, Muḥammad did not have any genealogical relationship to the previous prophets. The gap between him and them was also a chronological one, as is indicated in Q 5:19, in which it is stated that the qurʾānic Prophet emerged "after a cessation *(fatra)* of the [mission of the] apostles *(rusul)*...."

Nevertheless, the Qurʾān quite easily includes Muḥammad in the honorable group of prophets. The most straightforward way to achieve this is simply to declare Muḥammad to be "one of the apostles" (*mina l-mursalīna*, e.g. Q 2:252). This universalized perception of Muḥammad's mission leads to the conclusion that he is actually not the first of the messengers *(rusul)* on earth (Q 46:9) and that apostles already passed away before him (Q 3:144). This means that Muḥammad is a link in the same chain of prophets to which prophets like Jesus also belong. Before the latter other messengers had already passed away (Q 5:75).

As for Muḥammad's own revealed book, the Qurʾān, it is indeed an Arabic scripture (Q 12:2; 13:37) but is nevertheless perceived as closely related to previous scriptures. Time and again the Qurʾān stresses that Muḥammad's book confirms, or verifies *(muṣaddiq)*, what was revealed before it. For example, in Q 3:3-4 we read: "He has sent down to you the book with truth, verifying that which is before it, and he brought down the Torah and the Gospel aforetime...." This means that all scriptures represent identical links in the same successive chain of revelations. This idea recurs in the qurʾānic description of Jesus who is said to have verified the Torah that was revealed before him (Q 5:46). Since the Qurʾān itself verifies the Torah as well as the Gospels, the Jews and the Christians alike, whom the Qurʾān addresses as the "People of the Book" (q.v.), are commanded on their part to believe in the Qurʾān (Q 4:47; see also Q 2:41).

The equality of all scriptures as links in the same successive chain of revelations entails that true believers are only those who believe in all the revealed books, without exception (see BELIEF AND UNBELIEF). This idea, which is encountered already in the New Testament (in *Acts* 24:14 Paul believes in all things which are written in the Torah and in the books of the prophets), is stated explicitly several times. For example, Q 2:136 says:

Say: We believe in God and [in] that which had been sent down to us, and [in] that which was revealed to Abraham and Ishmael and Isaac and Jacob and the tribes, and [in] that which was given to Moses and Jesus, and [in] that which was given to the prophets from their lord, we do not make any distinction between any of them, and to him do we submit.

The same is repeated in several other places in which it is stressed that true righteousness is based on belief in the previous prophets and in their books as well as in the angels and in the last day (e.g. Q 2:177, 285; 4:136; see ESCHATOLOGY; FAITH). At the last judgment (q.v.) people will be asked about their belief in the messengers who had come to them (Q 28:65; 39:71). The previous revelations have remained relevant to the Muslims, as is implied in Q 3:194. Here an Islamic prayer is addressed to God, imploring him to "grant us what you have promised us by your apostles."

The conviction that one should believe in all the revealed books means that one should also believe in Muḥammad's Qurʾān. Therefore those who only believe in some books, like the Jews who denied the Qurʾān, are not true believers and they are denounced in Q 2:85 as it is commonly understood. Moreover, the duty to believe in Muḥammad's own revelation has become the core of the religion of all prophets. This finds expression in the notion that God already commanded all the previous prophets to believe in Muḥammad. In Q 3:81 we read:

And when God made a covenant *(mīthāq)* with the prophets: Surely, the book and the wisdom that I have given you — then an apostle comes to you verifying that which is with you, you must believe in him, and you must aid him. [God] said: "Do you affirm and accept my compact in this [matter]?" The [prophets] said: "We do affirm."

[God] said: "Then bear witness, and I [too] am of the bearers of witness with you."

The exegetes explain that the apostle in whom the prophets are commanded to believe is Muḥammad. The Arabian messenger of God has thus become the peak of the prophetic chain of revelations and this is also demonstrated in his title: "Seal *(khātam)* of the prophets" (Q 33:40).

The prophets were not only required to believe in Muḥammad, but some were also familiar with his titles, which were included in their own revealed scriptures. Thus in Q 7:157 it is stated that Muḥammad was mentioned as a "gentile" (*ummī* [q.v.]; see also ILLITERACY) in the Torah and the Gospel. Jesus, it is said in Q 61:6, announced the appearance of an apostle who would come after him, his name being Aḥmad. This quest for universal legitimacy is found already in the New Testament (*Matt* 2:23), where prophets predict that Jesus will be called the Nazarene.

Since belief in Muḥammad has always been at the core of the religion of the previous prophets, it comes as no surprise that the Israelite prophets to whom the Torah was revealed are described as "those who were Muslims" (*alladhīna aslamū*, Q 5:44). Furthermore, the religion that was enjoined upon the prophets was the same as the one given to the Muslims, a fact stated in Q 42:13: "He has enjoined upon you *(sharaʿa)* for religion what he prescribed to Noah and that which we have revealed to you and that which we enjoined upon Abraham and Moses and Jesus…."

The uniformity of the religion of the prophets, however, is abandoned in several passages in which Abraham's religion is set apart from the rest of the prophets and a direct line is drawn between him and Muḥammad. Such passages seem to have been designed to highlight the Arabian identity of the qurʾānic revelation and to dissociate its message from that of the Jewish and the Christian scriptures. The dissociation is achieved by insisting that Abraham was neither Jew nor Christian but rather a *ḥanīf* (q.v.). As a *ḥanīf* he has become a model for Muḥammad, whom God commands to follow Abraham's religion (Q 2:135; 4:125; 16:123, etc.; see also RELIGIOUS PLURALISM AND THE QURʾĀN).

The scope of the prophetic mission

The prophets are sent each to his own nation *(umma)* or people *(qawm)*. This notion is expressed in verses asserting that each nation has its own prophets sent to it (Q 10:47; 16:36) and that every apostle was only sent "with the language *(lisān)* of his people" (*qawmihi*, Q 14:4; see ARABIC LANGUAGE). Thus Moses, for example, says to his people *(li-qawmihi)* that he is God's messenger to them (Q 61:5). Moreover, some prophets are described as the "brothers" of the peoples to whom they were sent (Q 26:106, 161, etc.; see BROTHER AND BROTHERHOOD). This is again an appropriate precedent for Muḥammad, the Arabian prophet who has brought to his nation an Arabic Qurʾān (e.g. Q 12:2). His Arabic Qurʾān was revealed to him that he may warn "the mother of cities" (*umm al-qurā*, Q 42:7; see also Q 6:92), which is Mecca, according to the exegetes.

But unlike the previous prophets, Muḥammad appears in some other passages as a universal prophet whose mission goes beyond ethnic boundaries. In Q 4:79 he is said to have been sent "to mankind *(lil-nās)* as an apostle," and in Q 21:107 he is sent with mercy "to the worlds *(lil-ʿālamīn)*." His audience includes the jinn (q.v.; Q 46:30), to whom messengers of their own kind were also sent (Q 6:130).

The aims of the prophetic mission

The purpose for which the qur'ānic prophet has been sent is to make God's religion, i.e. Islam, prevail over all religions (Q 9:33; 48:28; 61:9). This may involve waging war (q.v.) on the infidels, as is stated about the preceding prophets in Q 3:146: "And how many a prophet has fought *(qātala),* and with them were many worshippers of the lord; so the [prophets] did not become weak-hearted on account of what befell them in God's way (see PATH OR WAY), nor did they weaken, nor did they abase themselves; and God loves the patient." But in other qur'ānic passages the religious campaign is based on preaching and is focused on the mere idea of monotheism and on the refutation of polytheism *(shirk).* Several times the previous prophets are described as imploring their respective peoples to "serve nothing *(allā ta'budū)* but God..." (e.g. Q 41:14). God also tells Muḥammad himself that this was the main mission of the prophets who were sent before him (Q 21:25, etc.), and he himself says to his audience: "I am only a mortal like you; it is revealed to me that your God is one God, therefore follow the right way to him and ask his forgiveness; and woe to the polytheists" (*waylun lil-mushrikīna,* Q 41:6; see also Q 18:110).

On the other hand, the mission of the prophets has also a grimmer aspect, namely, to warn stubborn unbelievers of their fate in hell (see HELL AND HELLFIRE), in case they do not repent (see REPENTANCE AND PENANCE). But the warning usually goes hand in hand with good tidings of paradise for those who believe. Thus Q 6:48, for example, asserts that God's messengers were sent as "announcers of good news and givers of warning *(mubashshirīna wa-mundhirīna),* then whoever believes and acts aright, they shall have no fear (q.v.), nor shall they grieve" (see JOY AND MISERY; see also Q 4:165; 18:56, etc.). The same twofold message was entrusted to Muḥammad (Q 33:45, 48:8).

The messengers are not responsible for the success or failure of their message and the Qur'ān repeatedly asserts that nothing is incumbent upon the apostles except a "plain delivery" (*al-balāgh al-mubīn,* e.g. Q 16:35). Furthermore, the apostles are not even capable of changing the fate awaiting the unbelievers: "It is not [fit] for the Prophet and those who believe that they should ask forgiveness (q.v.) for the polytheists, even though they should be near relatives (see KINSHIP), after it has become clear to them that they are inmates of the flaming fire" (Q 9:113; cf. 9:80, 84; see INTERCESSION).

On the last judgment, believers and unbelievers will realize that the apostles had spoken the truth about their respective fate in paradise or hell (Q 7:43, 53; 36:52). The prophets themselves will be present on the scene of judgment and will act as witnesses (*shuhadā',* sing. *shahīd*) as to who is righteous and who is a sinner (e.g. Q 4:41; 7:6; 16:84, 89; see WITNESSING AND TESTIFYING; SIN, MAJOR AND MINOR). But according to Q 5:109, the messengers will not dare testify and God himself will know what the people were doing.

But mercy (q.v.; *raḥma*) is also a significant component of the prophetic message and emanates mainly from the guidance that is inherent in the revealed book. This is stated in Q 16:89: "We have revealed the book to you explaining clearly everything, and a guidance *(hudan)* and mercy and good news for those who are Muslims." Being the ultimate source of guidance, some prophets are occasionally described as imāms (see IMĀM) who guide the people by God's command (Q 21:73) and their revealed book, too, is called "*imām* and mercy" (Q 11:17; 46:12). Guidance is achieved by the actual teaching of the book and therefore Muḥammad is often described as a messenger teaching "the book and the wisdom" (e.g. Q 2:129, 151; 3:164).

A prophet is not only a spiritual guide but a judge as well, whose adjudication is based on the revealed book. This was the case among the Jews for whom the prophets judged according to the revealed Torah (Q 5:44; 2:213) and the same is said about Muḥammad to whom God revealed the book "that you may judge between people by means of that which God has taught you" (Q 4:105; see JUDGMENT).

The reception of the prophets

The nations to whom prophets have been sent are expected to receive them with consent and obedience (q.v.). As Q 4:64 puts it: "And we did not send any apostle but that he should be obeyed *(li-yuṭāʿa)* by God's permission...." But the prophets were received with anything but obedience. They were mocked (e.g. Q 15:11; see MOCKERY) and called liars (e.g. Q 3:184; 22:42; 23:44; 35:25), and their message was denied (Q 11:59), and denounced as "medleys of dreams" (*aḍghāthu aḥlām*, Q 21:5). The prophets were rejected mainly on account of their being ordinary human beings (sing. *bashar*, e.g. Q 14:10; 17:94; 36:15; 64:6), and were accused of being mere poets (sing. *shāʿir*), magicians (sing. *sāḥir*) and madmen (sing. *majnūn;* e.g. Q 21:5; 51:52). Some of them were received with skeptical questions (Q 2:108), and above all, their audience expressed devotion to the tradition of the ancestors (Q 43:23).

Prophets have also suffered actual persecution, such as the threat of expulsion (e.g. Q 14:13), and also death at the hands of their own peoples, as was the fate of the Israelite prophets (e.g. Q 2:61, 91). The sufferings of the previous prophets are recounted to reassure Muḥammad that his own distress resembles that of his precursors (see OPPOSITION TO MUḤAMMAD). As stated in Q 41:43: "Nothing is said to you but what was said indeed to the apostles before you...." Not only humankind but also the satans rose as enemies to the prophets. In Q 6:112, God says: "And thus did we make for every prophet an enemy (see ENEMIES), the satans from among humans and jinn...." Satan's enmity is seen in this that he makes rebellion (q.v.) look attractive to nations to whom apostles were sent (Q 16:63). Rejection is met with retribution (see RETALIATION; VENGEANCE). Time and again the Qurʾān describes how nations that disobeyed (see DISOBEDIENCE) their prophets were punished by severe calamities, a motif recurrent mainly in the "punishment stories" (q.v.). Rejection of messengers renders retribution inevitable, as stated in Q 7:94: "And we did not send a prophet in a town but we overtook its people with distress and affliction in order that they might humble themselves." The divine logic that comes out here is that God is enemy to anyone who is "the enemy of God and his angels and his apostles and Gabriel and Michael" (cf. Q 2:98). Retribution is the direct result of the fact that God has promised to protect the prophets (cf. Q 14:47), and is defined as God's way (*sunna*, q.v.) with respect to those who persecute the prophets (Q 17:76-7). Destruction is never arbitrary or unjust, and is only inflicted on towns that have been warned in advance by their prophets (Q 17:15; 28:59). The prophets and their close entourage are always saved from the collective disaster (Q 10:103, etc.).

Stories of prophets

Apart from general declarations about the prophets, the Qurʾān provides stories about individual ones (see NARRATIVES). These stories always form part of the discourse between God and Muḥammad. God tells Muḥammad about them or requests Muḥammad to tell his audience about them. This literary structure (see LITERARY STRUCTURES OF THE QURʾĀN) stems from the idea that the prophetic revelation experienced by the previous prophets is the same as that of Muḥammad and that all of them are sent to fulfil the same mission among humankind. Therefore, the allusions to the previous prophets are essentially designed to provide a legitimizing as well as an encouraging precedent for Muḥammad's own prophetic challenge. Many of the stories draw on biblical themes. Some appear in a condensed form, while others, such as those of Abraham, Moses, and Jesus, are given in elaborate detail and even with subtle revisions of the biblical accounts. Elements not known from the Bible appear mainly in the punishment stories.

The Qurʾān itself is aware of the affinity between the stories about the prophets and the biblical literature, for which reason the Jews and the Christians are called upon to confirm the truth of the qurʾānic allusions to the previous prophets. This is at least how Muslim exegetes explain the meaning of Q 16:43 (see also Q 21:7) which says: "And we did not send before you any but humans to whom we sent revelation, so ask the people of the reminder if you do not know." The exegetes say that the "people of the reminder" *(ahl al-dhikr)* are scholars (see SCHOLAR) well versed in the Torah and the Gospel, which means that they know best about the history of the prophets from their own scriptures.

"Reminder" is also the label used for the qurʾānic stories about the prophets which Muḥammad recites to his audience, as with the story of Dhū l-Qarnayn (Q 18:83; see ALEXANDER). Nevertheless, the term is also the name of the entire revelation (Q 16:44, etc.), probably because it alludes quite frequently to stories of past generations. In fact, the injunction *udhkur fī l-kitāb*, "mention in the book," is frequently used in passages prompting the qurʾānic Prophet to remind the audience of stories about previous prophets (Q 19:16, 41, etc.).

Narrative units about prophets, which Muḥammad is expected to recite, are also called *nabaʾ* (pl. *anbāʾ*), "report, tidings" (see NEWS). For example, the Prophet is instructed to recite *(utlu)* the *nabaʾ* of the two sons of Adam (Q 5:27; see CAIN AND ABEL), the *nabaʾ* of Noah (Q 10:71) and of Abraham (Q 26:69). These units are also being "related" *(naquṣṣu)* to him upon being revealed (Q 7:101; 11:100, 120; 18:13; 20:99). They are also referred to as *anbāʾ al-ghayb*, "stories of the unseen" because they happened long ago and the Prophet did not witness them in person (Q 3:44, of Mary; Q 11:49, of Noah; Q 12:102, of Joseph). The information labeled as *nabaʾ/anbāʾ* is imparted to Muḥammad "to strengthen your heart therewith" (Q 11:120) as well as to teach the audience the bitter lesson of disbelief and disobedience which already led ancient towns to destruction (Q 7:101; 9:70; see GEOGRAPHY). But the listeners are not responsive, and they discard the qurʾānic message as "tales *(asāṭīr)* of the ancients" (*al-awwalīna*, Q 16:24).

The list of prophets mentioned in the Qurʾān is not complete, in the sense that some of them were left out on purpose. This is stated in Q 40:78 (see also Q 4:164): "And certainly we sent apostles before you: there are some of them of whom we related *(qaṣaṣnā)* to you and there are others of whom we have not related *(lam naqṣuṣ)* to you...." The exegetes explain that the prophets were too numerous to mention, and according to some, God sent 8,000 prophets, 4,000 of whom were Israelites.

Prophets in extra-qurʾānic sources

The prophets form an essential element in the Islamic perception of the past and they are treated not only in the Qurʾān but also in ḥadīth collections (see ḤADĪTH AND THE

QUR'ĀN) as well as in historiographical works (see HISTORY AND THE QUR'ĀN). Compilers of ḥadīth dedicated special sections (*kitābs*) to traditions about them, one of the earliest examples being al-Bukhārī's (d. 256/870) *Ṣaḥīḥ*, in which the *kitāb* no. 60 is called: *aḥādīth al-anbiyā'*, "Traditions about the prophets." There are also independent collections of traditions about the prophets; perhaps the best known is al-Thaʿlabī's (d. 427/1035) *ʿArāʾis al-majālis* or *Qiṣaṣ al-anbiyā'*.

The interest in the prophets taken by Muslims was focused on the need to define the relationship between Muḥammad and the previous prophets, which signaled the relationship between the Islamic *umma* and the non-Muslim communities (see COMMUNITY AND SOCIETY IN THE QUR'ĀN). Many of the traditions place Muḥammad over and above the rest of the prophets. For example, one tradition states that the lords of the prophets are five and Muḥammad is the lord of the five: Noah, Abraham, Moses, Jesus and Muḥammad. This statement was circulated as a tradition of the Companion Abū Hurayra (Ḥākim, *Mustadrak*, ii, 546; see COMPANIONS OF THE PROPHET). On the other hand, there are also traditions in which the status of the prophets is in no way inferior to that of Muḥammad (cf. Andrae, *Person*, 245 f.; Wensinck, *Muslim creed*, 113 f.). In one of these traditions, Muḥammad prohibits the believers to say that he was better than Moses (Bukhārī, *Ṣaḥīḥ*, iii, 158 [44:1]). Even a less prominent prophet like Jonah was not inferior to Muḥammad, as is indicated in Muḥammad's reported utterance: "No prophet is allowed to say: 'I am better than Jonah the son of Amittai'" (Abū Dāwūd, ii, 521 [39.13]). Such traditions seem to have been designed to retain the qur'ānic idea that one should not make any distinction among God's prophets and messengers.

The historiographical sources also retain the qur'ānic idea that all the prophets represent links in a universal chain of successive revelations. But there is no agreement about where this chain begins. In some traditions, the first person ever to be sent by God to warn his people is Noah (Ṭabarī, *Ta'rīkh*, i, 183-4). Enoch, too, is described as a prophet in traditions identifying him with Idrīs, who is said to have been the first man to whom prophecy was given (Ibn Hishām, i, 3.). Alternately, Enoch/Idrīs is said to have been the first to be sent as a prophet after Adam (Ibn Saʿd, *Ṭabaqāt*, i, 40, 54). In another tradition, Seth is the first prophet after Adam (Ibn Qutayba, *Maʿārif*, 26) and Adam himself, so a tradition tells us on the authority of no other than Muḥammad, was the first prophet God sent (Ibn Saʿd, *Ṭabaqāt*, i, 32, 54). Thus, Adam and Muḥammad became the two ends of the universal chain of prophets. This correlation between them has been noted in a tradition of the Yemenite scholar Wahb b. Munabbih (d. 110/728) on the authority of Ibn ʿAbbās (d. ca. 68/686). Wahb declares that Adam was the first of God's messengers and Muḥammad the last (Ibn Qutayba, *Maʿārif*, 26).

Islamic historiography has understood the prophets as bearers of a successive religious legacy that is being passed on from generation to generation in a hereditary line. The earliest description of the transmission of the prophetic legacy from generation to generation is found in passages quoted by al-Ṭabarī (d. 310/923) in his famous *History (Ta'rīkh al-rusul wa-l-mulūk)* from Ibn Isḥāq (d. 150/768). The latter was one of the first systematic biographers of Muḥammad (see SĪRA AND THE QUR'ĀN). Most of Ibn Isḥāq's material about the prophets is derived from Jewish sources whom Ibn Isḥāq often calls "people of the first book" *(ahl al-kitāb al-awwal)*, i.e. the Torah (e.g. Ṭabarī, *Taʾrīkh,* i, 139-40). Ibn Isḥāq describes how the various prophets, beginning with Adam, bequeathed their religious legacy and administrative authority (q.v.) to their descendants. They appointed them to be their heirs *(waṣī)* and put them in charge of their subjects. The legacy included revealed scriptures *(ṣaḥīfa),* which were handed down from generation to generation. Each bearer was considered as God's chosen leader upon earth, and defended the sacred legacy against change and corruption. Such perception of the role of the antediluvian ancestors is discernible already in Flavius' *Antiquities* (for details see Rubin, Prophets and progenitors).

Ibn Isḥāq describes the course of the legacy till Noah, but does not delineate an uninterrupted hereditary legacy during the generations between Noah and Abraham. The reason seems to be that Abraham is regarded as opening a new era, being a believer born to pagan ancestors who could not act as bearers of any legacy of righteousness. Al-Ṭabarī himself has recorded traditions from other sources that mention the transmission of the legacy through later generations of Israelite prophets. They describe, for example, the transition of the *waṣiyya* from Jacob to Joseph and from Joseph to Judah his brother (Ṭabarī, *Taʾrīkh,* i, 413). A detailed description of a successive authority running along the generations since Adam, and continued through the Israelites, is provided by the Shīʿī author al-Yaʿqūbī (d. 283/897; see SHĪʿISM AND THE QURʾĀN). His *Taʾrīkh* abounds with quotations from the Bible and other Jewish and Christian sources, and they form the axis around which his account of pre-Islamic history revolves. Some further traditions focus on individual links in the universal chain, for example, David and Solomon, who constituted the first links in the house of David. A tradition recorded in the *Mustadrak* by al-Ḥākim al-Naysābūrī (d. 405/1014) relates that God chose David to be his prophet and messenger and he gathered for him light and wisdom and revealed to him the *zabūr* (the Psalms), adding it to the scriptures already revealed to previous prophets. When David was about to die, God commanded him to bequeath the light of God *(nūr Allāh),* as well as the hidden and the revealed knowledge (see KNOWLEDGE AND LEARNING), to his son Solomon, and so he did (Ḥākim, *Mustadrak,* ii, 587).

Muslims paid special attention to the relationship between the last Israelite prophet, namely Jesus, and Muḥammad. Chronologically speaking, Jesus was the closest Israelite prophet to Muḥammad and this temporal closeness was understood in Islam as a blood relationship. This is the intent of a tradition transmitted by one of the Prophet's Companions, Abū Hurayra (d. 57/677), in which Muḥammad declares: "I am the closest person *(awlā l-nās)* to Jesus the son of Mary in this world and in the world to come." When asked how this could be, the Prophet went on, explaining: "The prophets are brothers born to fellow-wives *(ʿallāt),* i.e. their mothers are various and their religion is the same. There is no prophet between me and him" (Ibn Ḥibbān, *Ṣaḥīḥ,* xiv, no. 6194). The prophets are likened here to sons of the same father by various mothers. The father stands for the one unchanging religion of God that unites them all and this makes them brothers in the same religion. Among them Jesus and Muḥammad are the closest pair. Their various mothers, so it was explained by some Muslim scholars, represent their various types of *sharīʿa,* i.e. the distinctive religious laws which differ from one monotheistic community to the other (Ibn Ḥajar, *Fatḥ al-bārī,* vi, 354).

Just as Muḥammad was said to have been the closest person to Jesus, he was also presented as the closest one to Moses. This comes out in traditions recounting the history of the ʿĀshūrāʾ day (see FASTING; ATONEMENT). In some of these traditions a relationship between this day and the Jewish Day of Atonement is implied. It is related that when Muḥammad came to Medina after his emigration *(hijra)* from Mecca, he found out that the Jews of that city used to fast on the day of ʿĀshūrāʾ. He asked them to tell him the reason for that and they told him that this day was a holiday because on it God delivered the Children of Israel from their enemies and therefore Moses had fasted on this day. Then Muḥammad said to the Jews: "I am more worthy of Moses than you are" *(anā aḥaqqu bi-Mūsā minkum)* and thereupon he started to fast on the day of ʿĀshūrāʾ and ordered the Muslims to follow suit (e.g. Bukhārī, *Ṣaḥīḥ*, iii, 57 [30.69]). This means that the Islamic *umma* rather than the Jews are the most authentic bearers of the legacy of Moses.

In further traditions the concept of the unchanging divine legacy that transmigrates through the generations from Adam to Muḥammad has been combined with the idea of Muḥammad's pre-existence (for which see Rubin, Pre-existence). The successive legacy has been identified with Muḥammad's own pre-existent entity. The prophets have thus become mere vessels carrying the pre-existent Muḥammad. Traditions reflecting this notion can easily be identified by recourse to the commentaries on Q 26:219. This verse deals with the Prophet's movement *(taqallub)* among those who prostrate themselves (*al-sājidīn*, see BOWING AND PROSTRATION). A tradition of Ibn ʿAbbās as recorded by Ibn Saʿd (d. 230/845) says that the Qurʾān speaks here about the transmigration of Muḥammad "from prophet to prophet and from prophet to prophet, till God brought him forth as a prophet" (Ibn Saʿd, *Ṭabaqāt*, i, 25; cf. Rubin, Pre-existence, 80 with note 78).

Shīʿīs, Umayyads and prophets

The notion of a universal chain of prophets bearing a successive divine legacy was adapted to the specific needs of various groups who vied for predominance in Islamic society (see POLITICS AND THE QURʾĀN). Each group tried to gain for its leaders recognition as Muḥammad's exclusive heirs, from whom they inherited the universal legacy that had reached him from the previous prophets. Among these groups the best known are the Shīʿīs. They have developed the doctrine according to which the line of transmission was continued after Muḥammad through their own imāms. The latter were described as legatees of the prophets and as bearers of a divine light that they had inherited from the prophets. This doctrine was designed to establish the status of the Shīʿī imāms as agents of divine inspiration and guidance (for details see Rubin, Prophets and progenitors).

The Umayyad caliphs (see CALIPH), too, considered themselves links in a chosen pedigree originating in the biblical prophets. Their views on this claim are revealed in a letter sent to the garrison cities on behalf of the Umayyad caliph Walīd II (r. bet. 125-6/743-4) concerning the designation of his successors (for details see Crone and Hinds, *God's caliph*, 26-8; Rubin, Prophets and caliphs).

Qurʾānic prophets and modern scholarship

Modern scholars have tried to detect an evolution in the qurʾānic prophetology, which they reconstructed according to the assumed chronology of revelation (see CHRONOLOGY AND THE QURʾĀN; OCCASIONS OF REVELATION; POST-ENLIGHTENMENT

ACADEMIC STUDY OF THE QUR'ĀN). The "punishment stories," for example, have been explained as reflecting Muḥammad's situation in Mecca, before the *hijra*, the emigration (q.v.) to Medina (q.v.), when he suffered rejection. The description in these stories of the rejection of previous prophets was interpreted as designed to encourage Muḥammad during this difficult period (Tottoli, *Biblical prophets*, 7). The idea of one religion common to all prophets as well as the notion of the religion of Abraham, was explained as stemming from the polemical encounter with the Jews of Medina (Tottoli, *Biblical prophets*, 8-9; see JEWS AND JUDAISM). The usage of the terms *rasūl* and *nabī* was also connected with Muḥammad's life and it was argued that Muḥammad began to use *nabī* as his own epithet only during the later Medinan period (Tottoli, *Biblical prophets*, 74-5). In view, however, of doubts expressed by some scholars who have been of the opinion that not all parts of the scripture stem from Muḥammad's own time, the history of the link between the qur'ānic prophetology and Muḥammad's personal experience is no longer clear.

Uri Rubin

Bibliography
Primary (including post-qur'ānic "proofs of prophecy" literature): ʿAbd al-Jabbār, *Tathbīt dalāʾil al-nubuwwa*, ed. ʿA.al-K. ʿUthmān, Beirut 1966 (a "proofs of prophecy" work); Abū Dāwūd, 2 vols, Cairo 1952; Abū Ḥātim al-Rāzī, Aḥmad b. Ḥamdān, *Aʿlām al-nubuwwa*, ed. Ṣ. Ṣāwī and Gh.R. Aʿwānī, Tehran 1977 (on the "peaks of prophecy"); Bayḍāwī, *Anwār;* al-Bayhaqī, Aḥmad b. al-Ḥusayn, *Dalāʾil al-nubuwwa*, ed. ʿA.M. ʿUthmān, 2 vols., Medina 1969 (on "proofs of prophecy"); Bukhārī, *Ṣaḥīḥ*, 9 vols., Cairo 1958; al-Ḥākim al-Naysābūrī, Muḥammad b. ʿAbdallāh, *al-Mustadrak ʿalā l-Ṣaḥīḥayn*, 4 vols., Hyderabad 1923; Ibn Ḥabīb al-Ḥalabī, Badr al-Dīn al-Ḥasan b. ʿUmar, *al-Najm al-thāqib fī ashraf al-manāqib*, ed. M. al-Dhahabī, Cairo 1996 (on "proofs of prophecy"); Ibn Ḥajar, *Fatḥ al-bārī. Sharḥ Ṣaḥīḥ al-Bukhārī*, 13 vols., Cairo 1892, repr. Beirut n.d.; Ibn Ḥibbān, Muḥammad b. Aḥmad al-Bustī, *al-Iḥsān fī taqrīb Ṣaḥīḥ Ibn Ḥibbān*, ed. Shuʿayb al-Arnaʾūṭ, 16 vols., Beirut 1988; Ibn Isḥāq, *Sīra*, ed. al-Saqqā, repr. Beirut 1971; Ibn Qutayba, *Kitāb al-Maʿārif*, ed. M.I. al-Ṣāwī, Beirut 1970; Ibn Saʿd, *Ṭabaqāt*, ed. I. ʿAbbās, 8 vols., Beirut 1960; Ṭabarī, *Taʾrīkh*, ed. De Goeje; Yaʿqūbī, *Taʾrīkh*, 2 vols., Beirut 1960.
Secondary: P.S. Alexander, Jewish tradition in early Islam. The case of Enoch/Idrīs, in G.R. Hawting, J.A. Mojaddedi and A. Samely (eds.), *Studies in Islamic and Middle Eastern texts and traditions in memory of Norman Calder* [JSS, supp. 12], Oxford 2000, 11-29; T. Andræ, *Die Person Muhammeds in Lehre und Glauben seiner Gemeinde*, Uppsala 1917; R. Bell, Muhammad and previous messengers, in *MW* 24 (1934), 330-40; W.A. Bijlefeld, A prophet and more than a prophet? Some observations on the qur'anic use of the terms 'prophet' and 'apostle,' in *MW* 59 (1969), 1-28 (with references to earlier scholarship); P. Crone and M. Hinds, *God's caliph. Religious authority in the first centuries of Islam*, Cambridge 1986; T. Fahd, *La divination arabe*, Leiden 1966; C. Gilliot, Textes, in *MIDEO* 24 (2000), no. 98; T. Khalidi (ed. and trans.), *The Muslim Jesus. Sayings and stories in Islamic literature*, London 2001, 9-17; D.A. Madigan, *The Qurʾān's self-image. Writing and authority in Islam's scripture*, Princeton 2001; D. Marshall, *God, Muhammad and the unbelievers*, Richmond, Surrey 1999; F. Rosenthal, The influence of the biblical tradition on Muslim historiography, in B. Lewis et al. (eds.), *Historians of the Middle East*, London 1962, 35-45; U. Rubin, Pre-existence and light. Aspects of the concept of Nūr Muḥammad, in *IOS* 5 (1975), 62-119; id., Prophets and caliphs. The biblical foundations of the Umayyad authority, in H. Berg (ed.), *Method and theology in the study of Islamic origins*, Leiden 2003, 73-99; id., Prophets and progenitors in the early Shīʿa tradition, in *JSAI* 1 (1979), 41-65; G.G. Stroumsa, Seal of the prophets. The nature of a Manichaean metaphor, in *JSAI* 7 (1986), 61-74; id., The signs of prophecy. The emergence and early development of a theme in Arabic theological literature, in *Harvard theological review* 78/1-2 (1985), 101-14; R. Tottoli, *Biblical prophets in the Qurʾān and Muslim literature*, Richmond, Surrey 2002; Watt-Bell, *Introduction;* A.J. Wensinck, Muhammed und die Propheten, in *AO* 2 (1924), 168-98, trans. M. Richter-Bernburg, Muḥammad and the Prophets, in U. Rubin (ed.), *The life of Muḥammad*, Ashgate 1998, 319-43; id., *The Muslim creed*, Cambridge 1932; S. Wild, "We have sent down to thee the book with truth...'. Spatial and

temporal implications of the qur'ānic concepts of *nuzūl, tanzīl* and *'inzāl*, in Wild, *Text,* 137-56.

Prosperity see WEALTH

Prostitution see ADULTERY AND FORNICATION; SLAVES AND SLAVERY; SEX AND SEXUALITY

Prostration see BOWING AND PROSTRATION

Protection

Shielding from injury or destruction. The Qur'ān uses a variety of different Arabic words for "protection," with meanings that can shade into "defense," "security," "guarding," or "preservation." Numerous verses refer to God protecting the faithful (see BELIEF AND UNBELIEF), to the absence of protection for evil-doers (see EVIL DEEDS) against God's wrath (see ANGER), or to people protecting themselves or others from a variety of evils (see GOOD AND EVIL). The Arabic roots under consideration here are *'-w-dh, ḥ-f-ẓ, '-ṣ-m, w-q-y, w-l-y* (see CLIENTS AND CLIENTAGE), *m-n-'*, *j-w-r, '-m-n* and *h-y-m-n*.

Five of the ninety-nine beautiful names of God (see GOD AND HIS ATTRIBUTES) come under the broad meaning of "protector": *al-mu'min,* "author of safety and security" (Q 59:23; cf. Ṭabarī, *Tafsīr;* Ṭūsī, *Tibyān;* Bayḍāwī, *Anwār;* Zamakhsharī, *Kashshāf,* ad loc.; Rāzī, *Lawāmi',* 189; see also Gimaret, *Noms,* 359-61 for further glosses of this name); *al-muhaymin,* "protector and guardian" (Q 59:23; cf. 5:48, where the same word is applied to the book revealed to Muḥammad; see Gimaret, *Noms,* 361-3); *ḥafīẓ,* "preserver" (Q 11:57; 34:21; 42:6; see Gimaret, *Noms,* 270-1); *al-walī,* "patron" (Q 42:28; cf. Gimaret, *Noms,* 323-6; Nwyia, *Exégèse,* 114-5); and *māni',* "he who repels those things detrimental to his creation" (q.v.; cf. Gimaret, *Noms,* 335-6). This last-mentioned is one of the ninety-nine names that are not explicitly recorded in the Qur'ān itself (all English renderings are per Stade's translations of al-Ghazālī).

God is the only protector and protects everything (cf. Q 2:286; 3:150; 6:51, 62; 8:40; 11:57; 13:11; 18:44, and many more), while he himself has no need of a protector (Q 23:88). God protects the heavens from every satan (Q 15:17; 37:7; cf. 21:32; see DEVIL) and protects the believers (Q 46:31-2; 47:11), while the righteous will be in a position of security, protected from hell (Q 44:51, among others; see HELL AND HELLFIRE). God has protected the Qur'ān from corruption (Q 15:9); the Qur'ān is in a guarded tablet (Q 85:22; see PRESERVED TABLET) and itself guards earlier revelations (Q 5:48; see REVELATION AND INSPIRATION). God set guardians over people or souls (Q 6:61; 82:10; 86:4; see GUARDIANSHIP), protected Moses (q.v.) from the people of Pharoah (q.v.; Q 40:45), guarded the devils who worked for Solomon (q.v.; Q 21:82), and will protect Muḥammad against unbelievers (Q 5:67; see OPPOSITION TO MUḤAMMAD). God also provided humankind with shirts to protect them from the heat (see HOT AND COLD; CLOTHING) and coats of mail to protect them in battle (Q 16:81; see INSTRUMENTS; FIGHTING).

While God protects the believers, for the unbelievers there is no protector from God and his wrath, both in this world and on the day of judgment (Q 13:34, 37; 21:43; 40:21, 33; 67:28; 72:22, among others; see LAST JUDGMENT; REWARD AND PUNISHMENT). Noah's (q.v.) rebellious son sought protection in vain from the flood on a mountain (Q 11:43), while fortresses did not protect the Jewish tribe (see JEWS AND JUDAISM) of Banū l-Naḍīr (see NAḌĪR, BANŪ AL-) after the battle of Uḥud (q.v.; cf.

Q 59:2). The Qurʾān tells of people who erroneously sought protection in jinn (q.v.; Q 72:6) and people of the towns who rejected the prophets but who nonetheless mistakenly believed themselves secure from God's wrath (Q 7:98-9; see PUNISHMENT STORIES; PROPHETS AND PROPHETHOOD).

People need protection against their own inner weaknesses as well as against others. People who sought protection against their own weaknesses include Noah, who sought protection from asking God for something of which he had no knowledge (Q 11:47; see KNOWLEDGE AND LEARNING), Joseph (q.v.), who sought protection from being unjust (Q 12:79; see JUSTICE AND INJUSTICE) and Moses (q.v.), who sought protection from being ignorant (Q 2:67; see IGNORANCE). People can also be protected from their own avarice (q.v.; Q 59:9; 64:16). People who sought protection from God against Satan and others include Joseph, who sought protection from the sexual temptations of the Egyptian's wife (Q 12:23) and Moses, who sought protection from the arrogant people (Q 40:27; see ARROGANCE; PRIDE). Mary's (q.v.) mother sought protection for Mary and her offspring (Q 3:36), while Mary sought protection from sexual defilement (cf. Q 19:18; see SEX AND SEXUALITY). The Qurʾān enjoins Muḥammad to seek protection from the suggestions of Satan (cf. Q 7:200; 23:97-8; 41:36) and a variety of evils (Q 113:1-2; 114:1-4) and to seek protection with God from the accursed Satan when beginning to recite the Qurʾān (Q 16:98), a practice that, in general, Muslims to this day have followed (see RECITATION OF THE QURʾĀN; RITUAL AND THE QURʾĀN).

The Qurʾān also provides examples of how people are responsible for protecting themselves. The faithful are to guard their prayers (Q 2:238; see PRAYER) and oaths (q.v.; Q 5:89), while women are to protect their modesty (q.v.; Q 4:34). People also can guard others in the course of ordinary social relations, as when Joseph's brothers pledged to protect Joseph and Benjamin (q.v.; Q 12:11-2, 63, 65; see BROTHER AND BROTHERHOOD). At a time when Muḥammad may be defeated by his opponents, hypocrites (see HYPOCRITES AND HYPOCRISY) may claim to have protected the unbelievers from the believers (Q 4:141), while Muḥammad can grant protection to idolators who seek it from him (Q 9:6; see IDOLATRY AND IDOLATERS; COMMUNITY AND SOCIETY IN THE QURʾĀN). The Qurʾān also emphasizes that Muḥammad was sent as a messenger, not as a guardian (Q 4:80, among others). Nor are sinners guardians of the righteous (Q 83:33; see SIN, MAJOR AND MINOR).

Robert Schick

Bibliography
Primary: Bayḍāwī, *Anwār;* Fakhr al-Dīn al-Rāzī, *Lawāmiʿ al-bayyināt fī l-asmāʾ wa-l-ṣifāt,* ed. Ṭ. Saʿd, Cairo 1976; Ṭabarī, *Tafsīr,* ed. Shākir (for Q 1 to Q 14:27); ed. A.S. ʿAlī (for Q 14:27 to the end); Ṭūsī, *Tibyān;* Zamakhsharī, *Kashshāf.*
Secondary: D. Gimaret, *Les noms divins en Islam,* Paris 1988; H. Kassis, *A concordance of the Qurʾān,* Berkeley 1983; Nwyia, *Exégèse;* R. Stade, *Ninety-nine names of God in Islam,* Ibadan 1970 (trans. of al-Ghazālī, *al-Maqṣad al-asnā*).

Provision see SUSTENANCE

Provocation

An arousal of anger by words or deeds. Provocation consists of manifesting disdain for individuals or their values and is always characterized by a certain degree of unfairness. Instead of attempting to come to terms with a contentious issue between conflicting parties, an act of provocation aims at stirring up the opponents' emotions and leading them to an ill-considered reaction. In order for an action to qualify as a provocation, at least one of two conditions must be met: an underlying intention to provoke and a consequent feeling of anger. If both conditions are fulfilled, the provocation is successful; if only the first, it is a failure; if only the second, the provocation is unintentional. It follows, then, that merely describing a particular behavior or citing a potentially provocative statement does not suffice to identify an act as a provocation. Additional information about the thoughts and emotions of the parties involved is needed. It is necessary to keep these initial considerations in mind, as we turn to the question of provocation in the Qurʾān.

Provoking opponents

Many qurʾānic passages evoke an atmosphere of polemics (see POLEMIC AND POLEMICAL LANGUAGE) with reference to both the behavior and the utterances of the adversaries of God's messengers (see MESSENGER; OPPOSITION TO MUḤAMMAD) and of the believers (see BELIEF AND UNBELIEF). Except in the case of Pharaoh (q.v.) and the enigmatic Abū Lahab (q.v.) in Q 111, these adversaries are not identified by proper names (see ENEMIES; OPPOSITION TO MUḤAMMAD). Rather, there are several general designations for oppositional groups. The opponents of the pre-Islamic prophets are mostly referred to with ethnic names like ʿĀd (q.v.), Thamūd (q.v.), "Children of Israel" (q.v.), or "people of Noah (q.v.)." The adversaries of the actual qurʾānic preaching, however, are mainly labeled in terms of religion, as the "People of the Book" (q.v.; *ahl al-kitāb*), Jews and Christians (see JEWS AND JUDAISM; CHRISTIANS AND CHRISTIANITY), hypocrites (*munāfiqūn;* see HYPOCRITES AND HYPOCRISY), disbelievers (*kāfirūn*) and idolaters (*mushrikūn;* see IDOLATRY AND IDOLATERS; POLYTHEISM AND ATHEISM). But for the most part, the adversaries' identities are veiled in anonymity. Nevertheless, they are vividly present in the text in the rich vocabulary used to describe their words and deeds. They "dispute" (*jādala,* e.g. Q 6:25; 22:68; see DEBATE AND DISPUTATION), "oppose" (*ḥādda,* e.g. Q 9:63; 58:5), "make a breach" (*shāqqa,* e.g. Q 4:115; 8:13), "transgress" (*iʿtadā,* e.g. Q 3:112; 5:78), "turn away" (*aʿraḍa,* e.g. Q 18:57; 54:2), "revile" (*sabba,* Q 6:108), "defame" (*lamaza,* e.g. Q 9:58, 79), "contrive" (*kāda,* e.g. Q 7:195; 77:39), "plot" (*makara,* e.g. Q 6:123; 35:10), "forge a lie [against God]" (*iftarā l-kadhiba,* e.g. Q 29:68; 61:7), "lie" (*kadhaba,* e.g. Q 2:10; 39:32); "cry lies" (*kadhdhaba,* e.g. Q 35:25; 83:12), "grow arrogant" (*istakbara,* e.g. Q 6:93; 37:35), "mock" (*istahzaʾa,* e.g. Q 9:65; 2:14), "deride" (*sakhira,* e.g. Q 6:10; 9:79), "laugh" (*ḍaḥika,* e.g. Q 23:110; 83:29), "chatter" (*khāḍa,* e.g. Q 6:68; 9:69), "play" (*laʿiba,* e.g. Q 9:65; 43:83), etc. It is further asserted in the Qurʾān that both the earlier and the contemporary adversaries share the same hostile attitude, as can be seen in verses like Q 6:10: "Messengers indeed were mocked at before you" (cf. Q 6:34, 148; 10:39; 13:32; 22:42; 34:34; 35:4, 25; 2:108, etc.; see MOCKERY).

As strife is considered to be demon-inspired (e.g. Q 6:121; 7:200; 17:53; see DEVIL; CORRUPTION), the Prophet and the believers are repeatedly exhorted not to get involved in polemical disputes with their opponents. Instead, they are ordered to turn away from their enemies (e.g. Q 6:68; 28:55), to "repel with that which is fairer" (Q 41:34; cf. 13:22; 28:54; 17:53) and to "dispute with them in the better way" (Q 16:125; cf. 29:46). The adversaries, however, must bear the consequences of their behavior. This holds true in the case of the divine punishment of wicked peoples in former times (e.g. Q 36:30-1; 40:4-5; see PUNISHMENT STORIES; GENERATIONS), as well as of the condemnation of the sinners at the end of days (e.g. Q 45:34-5; 70:42-4;

see SIN, MAJOR AND MINOR; REWARD AND PUNISHMENT).

Two concepts describe the relation between behavior and consequences. On the one hand, there seems to be a *talio*-like automatism installed by God (see RETALIATION). This is indicated by formulations like: "They shall be encompassed *(ḥāqa)* by that at which they mocked" (Q 11:8; cf. 6:10; 16:34, etc.; see also Q 2:81; 3:117; 30:9; 83:14), and by passages assuring that just as the adversaries deride, plot, contrive and mock, so does God (e.g. Q 2:14-5; 9:79; 27:50-1; 52:42). On the other hand, since their behavior is said to arouse God's "wrath" (*ghaḍab,* e.g. Q 16:106; 42:16; see ANGER) and "hate" (*maqt,* e.g. Q 35:39; 40:35), this behavior is, in the first place, clearly understood as a provocation of God (cf. Q 6:33: "It is not you they cry lies to, but the evildoers — it is the signs of God that they deny"). Thus, the punishments inflicted upon the opponents appear as God's reaction to this provocation, as his "revenge" (*intiqām,* e.g. Q 3:4; 14:47; see VENGEANCE). The integration of the notion of God's wrath into a pattern of disobedience (q.v.) and retribution is familiar in the biblical tradition, too (e.g. *Num* 11:1; *Deut* 1:34; *Rom* 2:5; *Rev* 16:1). R. Otto (*Das Heilige,* 21 f.) explained it as a rationalization of the *mysterium tremendum,* the basic experience of the awe-inspiring god (cf. Q 8:12; 33:26; 39:23). Nevertheless, the anthropopathism inherent in this notion was to become a challenge for later Muslim scholars, who debated particularly about the nature of God's wrath and its compatibility with his mercy (q.v.; cf. the qurʾānic commentaries ad Q 1:7).

The polemic passages

The opponents are not only characterized by the above-mentioned vocabulary, they are also described as uttering criticism, challenges, invectives and the like, directed against the messenger and his message. These citations appear in direct discourse, introduced by the verb "to say" *(qāla)*. The opponents' utterances are then followed by or imbedded in statements that contain the appropriate answers, retorts, warnings (see WARNER), etc. If the opponents cited belong to the past, it is usually the messengers who were sent to them at the time who reply (e.g. Noah at Q 7:59 f.; Hūd [q.v.] at Q 7:65 f.). For the polemics directed at Muḥammad, however, the answering statements either have no introduction, in which case the heavenly voice speaks directly without a mediator (e.g. Q 44:14; 51:52; 68:15-6), or they are introduced by the imperative "say" *(qul)*.

This imperative, which occurs more than 300 times, is one of the most puzzling features of the qurʾānic style (see LANGUAGE AND STYLE OF THE QURʾĀN; RHETORIC AND THE QURʾĀN; LITERARY STRUCTURES OF THE QURʾĀN). It can be argued, however, that its main function is to introduce the figure of a prophet into a text whose fundamental literary character seems rather to preclude this (see NARRATIVES). That is to say, the Qurʾān basically belongs to the genre of anonymous religious literature. It is not an historical account of the life and times of a prophet; there is no biographical framework providing information about the circumstances of the revelation (see OCCASIONS OF REVELATION). Not even the title of the scripture, namely *al-qurʾān al-karīm* or *qurʾān karīm,* bears any attribution to its recipient (see NAMES OF THE QURʾĀN). Furthermore, aside from the polemical passages, God is referred to throughout in either the first person (mostly plural, sometimes singular, e.g. Q 2:40-1; 13:32; 22:48; 32:13) or in the third person. This implies that it is either he, or some angelic messenger (see ANGEL), speaking (the latter is the case even in the first person plural at Q 19:64; perhaps also

Q 30:35; 37:164-6). This literary form carries a strong claim of authority, as it suggests simultaneously a divine origin and a genuine transmission of the text. Any human recipient is reduced thereby to a mere mouthpiece who remains hidden behind the message — an effect which finds its precise expression in the Islamic dogma of revelation (see CREEDS; THEOLOGY AND THE QURʾĀN). Seen against this background, the imperative "say" can be considered a literary device used to root the idea of a divinely-inspired prophet in a document that is otherwise characterized as an unmediated revelation.

The formal nucleus of the polemic passages is the pattern "(they) say: … say (you): …" (*qālū/yaqūlūna … qul*, e.g. Q 2:80; 10:20; 17:49-51). This pattern is frequently modified by adding further answers and comments (e.g. Q 3:73-4; 6:148-51; 34:22), as well as by rearranging its elements into *qul … yaqūlūna* (e.g. Q 23:84 f; cf. 29:63). The polemical passages thus formed deal mainly with two issues: questions of belief on the one hand, and the legitimacy of the prophet on the other (see LIE; INFORMANTS; IMPECCABILITY). Doctrinal issues that are defended against the adversaries' contentions and denials include such themes as the notion of true monotheism, God's omnipotence and omniscience (see POWER AND IMPOTENCE) and the truth of eschatological events (see ESCHATOLOGY) — the bodily resurrection (q.v.), the last judgment (q.v.) and the eternal punishment in hell (see HELL AND HELLFIRE) or the reward in paradise (q.v.; e.g. Q 2:80; 4:78; 5:17; 10:18, 48-51; 11:7-8; 13:5; 17:49-52; 21:3-4; 27:67-72; 34:3; 36:78-9; 39:38). Refutation of the teachings of the Jews and Christians, the "People of the Book" (cf. i.e. Q 2:80, 94, 111; 5:18-9; 10:68-9, etc.), belongs to this category as well.

In respect to the legitimacy of the Prophet, the polemical passages discuss criteria of credibility and conceptions of pseudo-prophecy (see MUSAYLIMA). Most prominent is the opponents' call for signs (q.v.; *āyāt*, sing. *āya*): "The unbelievers say, 'Why has a sign not been sent down upon him from his lord?'" (Q 13:7; cf. 2:118; 6:37, 109; 10:20; 13:27, etc.). Verses like Q 6:124 ("They said, 'We will not believe until we are given the like of what God's messengers were given'"; cf. Q 21:5) or the short list in Q 17:90-3 show that "signs" can be understood to mean miracles (q.v.). The unbelievers demand that revelation (see REVELATION AND INSPIRATION), too, should be accompanied by miracles like theophany (q.v.; Q 2:118; 17:92), the appearance of angels (e.g. Q 23:24; 25:21), the Prophet's ascension (q.v.) to heaven (Q 17:93; cf. 6:35; 52:38) or the sending down of "a book (q.v.) on parchment" (Q 6:7; cf. 74:52). In addition, they accuse the Prophet of forging his message (*iftarā[hu]*; e.g. Q 10:38; 11:13; 34:8; 42:24; cf. 52:33; see FORGERY) and call him "a man possessed" (*majnūn*, e.g. Q 15:6; 37:36; 44:14; see INSANITY; JINN), "a soothsayer" (*kāhin*, cf. Q 69:42; see SOOTHSAYERS), "a sorcerer" (*sāḥir*, Q 10:2; 38:4; cf. 6:7; 11:7; see MAGIC) or "a poet" (*shāʿir*, e.g. Q 21:5; 37:36; 52:30; see POETRY AND POETS) — all of these being prominent characterizations of pseudo-prophecy and unreliable inspiration.

It is through answering these false conceptions and demands that the qurʾānic prophetology is formulated. It is asserted in the Qurʾān that God's messengers and prophets are human beings (Q 17:93; 18:110; 41:6; cf. 6:50; 11:12, 31; see PROPHETS AND PROPHETHOOD) who all along have been mocked (see above; this is also demonstrated overtly by the literary form of the polemical passages themselves). They receive revelation by means of *waḥy* — a kind of non-verbal communication that they then have to translate into human language (e.g. Q 18:110; 21:45; the only exception is Moses [q.v.], to whom God spoke directly: Q 4:164; cf. 42:51; see also WORD OF GOD). They do not need miracles to justify their message (cf. Q 13:27; 29:50). It suffices to point to God's signs *(āyāt)* in nature and history, which can be interpreted as proofs for God's sole power, his care for humankind, the resurrection and the reality of the divine judgment (e.g. Q 10:31 f.; 27:59-60, 65 f.; 29:20; 30:42).

From a literary viewpoint, the polemical passages are not the prophetic message proper. They appear instead as meta-level reflections upon such a message and its reception. Yet, they hardly represent reports of historical disputes. Inasmuch as their actors are veiled by anonymity and since most of the topics dealt with can be traced back to the tradition of religious polemical literature, they should rather be considered constructed dialogues. One of their purposes seems to be, then, that they characterize the qurʾānic Prophet and establish the relation between him and his prophetic predecessors and the other, that they contribute to the formulation of a Muslim identity as distinct from rival religions (see RELIGIOUS PLURALISM AND THE QURʾĀN; ISLAM).

The qurʾānic challenge

Among the passages of provocation and polemic are several verses where the heavenly voice — either directly (e.g. Q 10:68; 28:75; 37:156-7; 68:37) or via the Prophet (e.g. Q 27:64; 34:27; 35:40; 46:4) — challenges the adversaries to justify their beliefs and practices, e.g. the Jewish rules concerning food (Q 3:93; see FOOD AND DRINK; BOUNDARIES AND PRECEPTS; LAWFUL AND UNLAWFUL) or the Jewish and Christian claim of entering paradise exclusively (Q 2:111; cf. 2:94). More often, however, a justification for idolatry *(shirk)* is demanded (e.g. Q 6:148 f.; 7:194-5; 10:68; 21:24; 27:64). The opponents are exhorted to present those venerated beside God ("Say: 'Show me those you have joined to him as associates *[shurakāʾ]!*'," Q 34:27; cf. 7:195; 68:41) or to bring their "witnesses" (*shuhadāʾ*, Q 2:23; see WITNESSING AND TESTIFYING), "proof" (q.v.; *burhān*, Q 2:111; 21:24; 27:64; 28:75), "authority" (q.v.; *sulṭān*, Q 10:68; 37:156), "knowledge" (*ʿilm*, Q 6:148) or "oaths" (q.v.) from God (*aymān*, Q 68:39). But the demand most revealing of the qurʾānic notion of authority and legitimacy is the challenge to the adversaries to prove their contentions with a "book" *(kitāb):* "Bring your book, if you are truthful!" (Q 37:157; cf. 46:4; 35:40; 68:37). And in Q 3:93, the Children of Israel (q.v.) are called upon to bring the Torah (q.v.) and to recite from it, in order to justify their restrictions on food.

Still another group of verses falls under this same heading, the so-called "challenge" *(taḥaddī)* verses. These verses issue a challenge *(taḥaddin)* to the opponents who reject the prophetic message to bring — as counterevidence, so to speak — "a sūra like it" (*fa-ʾtū bi-sūratin mithlihi*, Q 10:38; cf. 2:23; see SŪRAS), "ten sūras the like of it" (*bi-ʿashri suwarin mithlihi*, Q 11:13) or "a discourse like it" (*bi-ḥadīthin mithlihi*, Q 52:34), and they are exhorted to call their "witnesses apart from God" (*wa-dʿū shuhadāʾakum min dūni llāhi*, Q 2:23; cf. 10:38; 11:13). Furthermore, in Q 17:88 it is assured: "Say: 'If men and jinn banded together to produce the like of this *qurʾān (bi-mithli hādhā l-qurʾāni)*, they would never produce its like, not though they backed one another.'" These passages are reminiscent of Isaiah 43:9: "Let all the nations be gathered together, and let the people be assembled: who among them can declare this, and show us former things? Let them bring forth their witnesses, that they may be justified: or let them hear, and say: It is truth" (cf. *Isa* 41:21 f.; 44:6 f.). In both the Qur'ān and (Deutero-) Isaiah, the foreign gods have no reality; they are mere names and handmade idols (*Isa* 44:9 f.; Q 7:71; 12:40; 16:20-1, etc.). Underscoring the basic metaphysical difference between God and the rival gods, however, both passages highlight God's well-attested activity, past and present. Now, from the qur'ānic point of view, this activity is demonstrated first of all in God's signs *(āyāt)* in nature and history (see NATURE AS SIGNS; HISTORY AND THE QUR'ĀN). And since the terms *ḥadīth* (see ḤADĪTH AND THE QUR'ĀN), *sūra* and *qur'ān* should be understood here as revelation texts referring to these signs (cf. Radscheit, *Koranische Herausforderung*, 94 f.), it becomes clear why the idolaters cannot meet the qur'ānic challenge: it is not possible to bring a revelation that argues by means of the *āyāt* for the existence of gods beside God.

It is well known that Muslim exegetes (see EXEGESIS OF THE QUR'ĀN: CLASSICAL AND MEDIEVAL) interpret the *taḥaddī*-verses primarily in the light of the doctrine of the inimitability (q.v.; *iʿjāz*) of the Qur'ān. The beginnings of this doctrine can hardly be dated before the third/ninth century and presuppose several stages of theological and cultural development. The prerequisite developments include the final codification of the qur'ānic texts (see CODICES OF THE QUR'ĀN; COLLECTION OF THE QUR'ĀN), the sharpening and polishing of a unique Islamic prophetology vis-à-vis Judaism and Christianity, and the emergence of the *shuʿūbiyya*, the cultural conflict between Arabs (q.v.) and non-Arabs, especially Persians. According to the *iʿjāz*-doctrine, the Qur'ān in itself — by virtue of its inimitability — is the miracle that legitimizes the prophetic mission of Muḥammad and corresponds in this regard to the miracles that were given to Moses and to Jesus (q.v.). The question about how the Qur'ān must be considered a miracle — because of its contents or because of style — has remained controversial, and therefore productive of a profusion of interpretations, up to this day (see EXEGESIS OF THE QUR'ĀN: EARLY MODERN AND CONTEMPORARY). Yet there has always been a broad consensus as to how to prove the miraculous nature of the Qur'ān.

The core argument is that an imitation *(muʿāraḍa)* of the Qur'ān has never actually appeared, although every good reason existed to create one (see PARODY OF THE QUR'ĀN). In this respect the *taḥaddī*-verses are of paramount importance. The heathen Arabs were a people described as defining themselves by their eloquence and rhetorical ability on the one hand, and by their pride and belligerent character on the other. It is inconceivable that such a people never tried to imitate the Qur'ān, although Muḥammad provoked them time and again with the *taḥaddī*-verses, goading them to the utmost degree, foretelling their inability to meet the challenge and threatening them with physical annihilation. It was the ingenious Iraqi scholar Abū ʿUthmān al-Jāḥiẓ (d. 255/869) of the Muʿtazila (see MUʿTAZILĪS), who, in his treatise *Ḥujaj al-nubuwwa*, "Arguments for the prophecy [of Muḥammad]," expressed this idea so convincingly that most subsequent theologians have followed him. And since — according to al-Jāḥiẓ — Muḥammad intended to provoke the Arabs and since they, as a result, became angry, the qur'ānic challenge must be considered a successful provocation.

Matthias Radscheit

Bibliography

Primary: al-Jāḥiẓ, Abū Uthmān ʿAmr b. Baḥr, *Ḥujaj al-nubuwwa*, in ʿAbd al-Salām Hārūn (ed.), *Rasāʾil al-Jāḥiẓ*, 4 vols., Cairo 1979, iii, 223-81, 273 f.

Secondary: K. Aland, The problem of anonymity and pseudonymity in Christian literature of the first two centuries, in *Journal of theological studies* [N.S.]12 (1961), 39-49; H. Bandt et al., Zorn Gottes, in K. Galling (ed.), *Die Religion in Geschichte und Gegenwart. Handwörterbuch für Theologie und Religionswissenschaft,* 6 vols., 1957-62[3], vi, cols. 1929-33; R. Ettinghausen, *Antiheidnische Polemik im Koran,* Gelnhausen 1934; R. Otto, *Das Heilige,* München 1979, 14-22; M. Radscheit, *Die koranische Herausforderung. Die* taḥaddī-*Verse im Rahmen der Polemikpassagen des Korans,* Berlin 1996; id., Word of God or prophetic speech? Reflections on the qurʾānic *qul*-statements, in L. Edzard and Chr. Szyska (eds.), *Encounters of words and texts. Intercultural studies in honor of Stefan Wild,* Hildesheim 1997, 33-42; G. Richter, *Der Sprachstil des Koran,* Leipzig 1940; H. Strathmann, Martus, in *Theologisches Wörterbuch zum Neuen Testament* 4 (1942), 486-7.

Psalms

The title of a book of religious songs and poems of praise and prayer poems in the Hebrew Bible to which, according to most interpretations, reference is made in the Qurʾān. It is called *Tehillim* in rabbinical Hebrew (lit. "songs of praise") with the connotation in post-exilitic Bible books of "songs of Temple worship"; *psalmos* is Greek for "a song sung to a harp." One of the common words for this kind of composition found in the book of Psalms itself is *mizmōr,* which is related to the Arabic *mizmār,* "single-pipe woodwind instrument resembling the oboe," and *mazmūr,* "psalm." The Hebrew psalms were not all composed at the same time but — because they exist in Greek translation — they must date back to at least the second half of the second century B.C.E. The so-called Davidic psalms constituted the very first stage in the compilation of the Hebrew book of Psalms.

Although the various versions of the book of Psalms consist of 149, 150 or 151 psalms, 150 seems to be the ideal number because the Greek version contains an additional psalm which is considered supernumerary, that is, Psalm 151 which is also marked as apocryphal. The book of Psalms is divided into five chapters or books, each comprising a number of psalms. Each of the first four books is marked off by a doxology or formulaic expression of praise to God, for instance, "Blessed is the Lord, from eternity to eternity," "Blessed be the Lord into eternity," or "Amen and amen."

There are several genres to be distinguished in the Psalms: the leading one is the hymn. Some psalms specifically extol God's royal role in the universe, his city, and his Torah (q.v.). About one third of the Psalter is devoted to laments in which the speaker may be either the individual or the community (faced with national oppression or misfortune) making a strong plea for divine help. Those songs in which one is sure of God's help are called "psalms of confidence." There is also the genre of thanksgiving. The "royal psalms," in which the center of attention is the anointed one (Messiah) of God, the earthly king of Israel, and which contain no direct reference to a reigning monarch, constitute a separate class. Another genre derives from wisdom literature; psalms of this type may be reflective or sententious. The contents are often linked to particular situations such as repentance for the sins of the poet, or thanksgiving to the lord for liberating the poet from his enemies (see GRATITUDE AND INGRATITUDE).

The mixing of genres to be found in the Psalms is paralleled in the Qurʾān, which is not a homogeneous collection but a combination of many genres whose sūras (q.v.) are often mixed compositions (see FORM AND STRUCTURE OF THE QURʾĀN). A comparison of the two holy books — the Hebrew Psalms and the Arabic Qurʾān — makes us aware of the complex composition of these sacred scriptures: individual genres such as hymns, wisdom sentences, prophecies and poetry are combined, each genre having its own style, vocabulary and formal language (see LANGUAGE AND STYLE OF THE QUR᾿ĀN). Some sense of this similarity is captured in the Qur᾿ān, where the *zabūr,* "the book of Psalms granted by God to David" (Q 4:163; 17:55), is recognized as a holy scripture preceding the Qur᾿ān (see SCRIPTURE AND THE QUR᾿ĀN).

Legendary authors of psalms were the kings David (q.v.) and, to a lesser extent, Solomon (q.v.), and sometimes the situation of the poet in the psalms can be linked to events that took place during David's lifetime. The book of Psalms was considered as "the writings of David." Musical-recitative accompaniment is attributed to Davidic innovation (2 *Chron* 23:18). According to the Talmud, the Psalms were inspired (Pes. 117a) and music helped to supply the inspiration: "A harp was suspended above the bed of David. When midnight came the north wind blew on it and it produced music of its own accord. Immediately David arose and occupied himself with the Torah.... Until midnight he occupied himself with the Torah; and from then with songs and praises." In Islamic literature, the tradition that David devoted himself to the Torah is also mentioned by al-Ṭabarī (d. 310/923; *Ta᾿rīkh,* i, 567; Eng. trans. *History,* iii, 147).

In the Qur᾿ān, the ḥadīth (see ḤADĪTH AND THE QUR᾿ĀN), the "tales of the prophets" (*qiṣaṣ al-anbiyā᾿;* see PROPHETS AND PROPHETHOOD; NARRATIVES) and Arabic historical writings, the prophet David is considered a famous musician. He is mentioned in several places in the Qur᾿ān. In Q 21:105 the word *zabūr* is used again by God: "We have written in the *zabūr*... that my righteous servants shall inherit the earth," which verse is reminiscent of a Hebrew psalm (*Ps* 37:9, 11, 29: "they who shall inherit the earth"). God gave David the rule of the kingdom (see KINGS AND RULERS), knowledge (*ʿilm;* see KNOWLEDGE AND LEARNING) and wisdom (q.v.; *ḥikma*), and the ability to do justice (*ḥukm,* esp. Q 21:78 f.; cf. 38:20-4, 26; see JUSTICE AND INJUSTICE). God made the birds and mountains his servants, so that they unite in his praise (Q 21:79; 34:10; 38:18 f.). There is no mention of the wrong David did to Uriah in order to win Bathsheba's affection, but some qur᾿ānic verses show that the king feels himself to be guilty. His prayer for forgiveness (q.v.) is heard (Q 38:24 f.).

The ḥadīth (accounts of Muḥammad's deeds and sayings) stress David's zeal in prayer (q.v.) and especially in fasting (q.v.) and his readiness to do penance (see REPENTANCE AND PENANCE). Another favorite theme is David's gift in singing psalms. His voice has magical power over not only humans but also over wild beasts and inanimate nature (see MAGIC). In other Islamic literature, such as that of Qur᾿ān commentators, historians and compilers of the "tales of the prophets," the works of the two historians al-Yaʿqūbī (d. ca. 292/905) and al-Ṭabarī are especially important. Even though both probably based their works upon texts derived from the same sources (cf. Thaʿlabī-Brinner, *Lives,* 462-81), the works of these two men are strikingly independent of each other.

Al-Yaʿqūbī has a long passage about David (cf. Ebied and Wickham, Al-Yaʿḳūbī's account, 87-91 for an Eng. trans. of al-Yaʿqūbī's text on David). He is portrayed as the successor to Saul (q.v.) and as subduing the Philistines. The affair with Bathsheba and the prophet Nathan's words of reproach to David are mentioned, the child he had with Bathsheba being the later king, Solomon. The family affairs with his brothers are described more or less according to the Bible, such as the revolt by his son Absalom, who is killed by Yoab. Contrary to the biblical version, in al-Yaʿqūbī's text Barzillay marched against David and when God saved David from his hands, David recited a psalm. This psalm is reported in Arabic and is very similar to Psalm 18, in which he thanks God for having saved him from his enemies. There then follows an Arabic rendition of Psalm 1, which begins "Blessed are the ones who do not follow the path of the sinners." Other laudatory psalms are quoted in Arabic, reflecting, respectively, Psalms 148, 149 and 150. Then the apocryphal Psalm 151 is also quoted in Arabic. This psalm is conceived as highly autobiographical: in it David tells us that he was the youngest among his brethren, herded the sheep of his father and cut flutes from reed. But God sent his angels and took him away from his sheep and from his brethren and destined him to fight Goliath (q.v.). David killed this worshipper of idols (see IDOLATRY AND IDOLATERS) by cutting off his head with his own sword. After this passage, al-Yaʿqūbī deals with David's old age and Solomon, David's successor.

Al-Ṭabarī collects the comments of early qurʾānic exegetes (see EXEGESIS OF THE QURʾĀN: CLASSICAL AND MEDIEVAL) in his *Tafsīr* (his exegetical work), including definitions of terms such as *zabūr* (with the plural *zubur*), which vary depending on the verse. In his commentary on Q 21:105, he records a variety of meanings for *zabūr:* "all the books of the prophets that God brought down to them" (Saʿīd b. Jubayr, Ibn Zayd; see BOOK), "the books revealed to the prophets after Moses" (q.v.; Ibn ʿAbbās, al-Ḍaḥḥāk) and "a specific book revealed to David" (ʿĀmir, al-Shaʿbī). In his commentary on Q 3:184, *al-zubur* is a generic term for a book based on pre-Islamic poetic evidence (see POETRY AND POETS; PRE-ISLAMIC ARABIA AND THE QURʾĀN). Commenting on Q 4:163, he writes "the Arabs (q.v.) say *zabūr dāwūd* (David), and because of that the rest of the peoples know his book."

Al-Ṭabarī includes a section on Saul, David and Solomon in his *Taʾrīkh,* i.e. his history of the world. In this work, he explains David's connection with the Psalms thus:

When the Israelites gathered around David, God revealed the Psalms to him, and taught him ironworking, making it supple for him. He also ordered the mountains and the birds to sing praise with him when he sang. According to what they have mentioned, God did not give anyone in his creation a voice like his. So when David recited the Psalms, wild beasts would gaze at him with delight, until they were lined up, intently listening upon hearing his voice. The demons invented flutes, lutes and cymbals with only his voice as a model. David was extremely diligent, constant in worship (q.v.) and wept much (*Taʾrīkh,* i, 562; Eng. trans. *History,* iii, 143; see WEEPING).

Al-Ṭabarī incorporates Qurʾān as well as ḥadīth passages into his *Taʾrīkh;* among them is Q 38:17-8, in which God describes David to Muḥammad, saying: "And remember our servant David, possessor of might. Lo! We subdued the hills to sing the praises with him at nightfall and sunrise." Al-Ṭabarī adds, "It has also been mentioned to us that David would stay up at night and fast half of the time. And according to what has been mentioned, four thousand men guarded him every day and night." Just as Abraham (q.v.) was put to the test with the sacrifice (q.v.) of his son, and Jacob (q.v.) was tested with his grief over his son Joseph (q.v.), David wanted to be tested. But he did not withstand the temptation when confronted with the seductive beauty of Bathsheba, who was married to Uriah (Ahriya). Although in the Qurʾān there is no mention of the Bathsheba story, al-Ṭabarī quotes Q 38:24 when speaking about David's repentance for marrying Bathsheba and getting rid of her husband Uriah: "He fell down prostrate (see BOWING AND PROSTRATION) and he repented." All these items of course refer to David as the singer of psalms in praise of God as well as of penitential ones. (See also Hasson, David; according to other Muslim traditions Bathseba was only engaged to Uriah, not married to him.)

At an early stage, the book of Psalms was available in Arabic translation, as we have learned from the translations of al-Yaʿqūbī. A fragment of a Christian Arabic translation of the Psalms (containing *Ps* 78: 20-31, 51-61 in Greek majuscule writing from the second/eighth century) was identified in Damascus by B. Violet (Ein zweisprachiges Psalmfragment).

In Jewish and Christian circles, the *Tafsīr* (= translation into Arabic with commentary) by Saʿadyā Gaon alias Saʿd b. Yūsuf al-Fayyūmī (d. 331/942) was especially famous, but members of the Karaite sect such as Japheth b. Eli (Abū ʿAlī Ḥasan b. ʿAlī al-Baṣrī; fourth/tenth century) are also worth mentioning. In Spain, interest in the Psalms reached its apogee with Ibn Ḥazm's (384-456/994-1064) "Book on religions" *(al-Fiṣal fī l-milal)*. Already in third/ninth century Muslim Spain, Ḥafṣ al-Qūṭī translated the Psalter into Arabic *rajaz* verse, probably not directly from Arabic but from a Latin version of Jerome (347-420 C.E.). By that time there were already two prose translations of the Psalms in al-Andalus. Ibn Ḥazm in his *Fiṣal* criticized very much the contents of a number of psalms, such as Psalm 2:7, which has a statement about God's son (see EZRA; JESUS; POLEMIC AND POLEMICAL LANGUAGE). He also dealt with about ten other psalms, e.g. *Ps* 81:6 and 44:7 (cf. Ljamai, *Ibn Ḥazm,* 115-8). This is a sign of the immense popularity of the Psalms, which is also reflected in the style of some poems by poets from the east as well as the west of the Islamic world, such as Abū l-ʿAtāhiya (130-211/748-826) and Ibn Khafāja (450-533/1058-1139). The Andalusian poet Ibn Khafāja says in one of his poems (*Dīwān,* no. 162): "Happy is the one who stands in the fear of the lord (q.v.) while darkness (q.v.) sets up its cupola of darkness," which clearly echoes Psalm 1:1. In modern times the Urdu poet Iqbāl (1877-1938) has composed a Psalter, but the poems are not really reminiscent of Davidic psalms (see also LITERATURE AND THE QURʾĀN; see esp. NATURE AS SIGNS; PRAISE for discussion of "psalmodic" qurʾānic passages).

Arie Schippers

Bibliography

Primary: Ibn al-Athīr, *Kāmil,* i, 153-9; Ibn Ḥazm, *Milal,* ch. 15 (end: criticisms of the Psalms of David); Sp. trans. M. Asín Palacios, *Abenházam de Córdoba y su Historia crítica de las ideas religiosas,* Madrid 1928, ii, 363-6; Ibn Khafāja, *Dīwān,* ed. M. Ghāzī, Alexandria 1960; M. Iqbal, *Persian psalms (Zabūr-i ʿajam),* trans. A.J. Arberry, Lahore 1948; Japheth b. Eli, *In librum psalmorum commentarii Arabici,* ed. L. Bargès, Paris 1846; Kisāʾī, *Qiṣaṣ,* 252-78; Masʿūdī, *Murūj,* i, 106-10; Saʿadyah Gaon, *Psalms with translation into Arabic and commentary,* ed. Y. Kapakh, Jerusalem 1966 [5726]; Suyūṭī, *Durr,* vii, 148-76; Ṭabarī, *Tafsīr,* ed. Shākir, v, 354-71; ix, 401-2; xi, 507-8; xvii [ed. M.M. al-Ḥalabī, 30 vols, Cairo 1968], 50-4; id., *Taʾrīkh,* ed. M.J. de Goeje, i, 554-72; Eng. trans. W. Brinner, *The history of al-Ṭabarī. iii. The Children of Israel,* New York 1991, 135-51; Thaʿlabī-Brinner, *Lives* = Thaʿlabī, *Qiṣaṣ,* trans. W.M. Brinner, *Lives of the prophets,* Leiden 2002; M.-T. Urvoy, *Le Psautier mozarabe de Hafs le Goth,* Toulouse 1984; Yaʿqūbī, *Taʾrīkh,* i, 53-64; Dutch trans. G. Juynboll, in A. Vrolijk, *Taal der engelen,* Amsterdam 2002, 69-77.

Secondary: C. Adang, *Muslim writers on Judaism and the Hebrew Bible. From Ibn Rabban to Ibn Hazm,* Leiden 1996, 119 f.; B. Carra de Vaux, Dāʾūd, in *EI*[1], i, 927-8; R.Y. Ebied and L.R. Wickham, Al-Yaʿḳūbī's account of the Israelite prophets and kings, in *JNES* 29 (1970), 80-98; F. Eifller, *Königspsalmen und karäische Messiaserwartung,* Tübingen 2002; *Encyclopaedia judaica,* Jerusalem 1971, s.v. "Psalms" and "David"; I. Hasson, David, in *EQ*, i, 495-7; J. Horovitz/R. Firestone, Zābūr, in *EI²*, xi, 372-3; A. Ljamai, *Ibn Ḥazm et la polémique islamo-chrétienne dans l'histoire de l'islam,* Leiden 2003; D. Masson, *Le Coran et la révélation judéo-chrétienne,* Paris 1958, 21-3; 40-4; 245; Neuwirth, *Studien,* 9; R. Paret, Dāwūd, in *EI²*, ii, 182; J. Sadan, Some literary problems concerning Judaism and Jewry in medieval Arabic sources, in M. Sharon *Studies in Islamic history and civilization in honour of Professor David Ayalon,* Jerusalem/Leiden 1989, 396-7 (on the apocryphal psalms known as the *Zabūr*); A. Schippers, Ḥafṣ al-Qūṭī's Psalms in Arabic *rajaz* metre (9th century). A discussion of translations from three psalms (Ps. 50, 1 and 2), in U. Vermeulen et al. (eds.), *Law, Christianity, and modernism in Islamic society,* Leuven 1998, 133-46; B. Violet, Ein zweisprachiges Psalmfragment aus Damascus, in *OLZ* 4 (1901), 384-403, 425-41, 475-88; Wild, *Text,* 95.

Psychology

see SOCIAL SCIENCES AND THE QUR'ĀN

Puberty

see MATURITY; BIOLOGY AS THE CREATION AND STAGES OF LIFE

Punishment

see CHASTISEMENT AND PUNISHMENT; REWARD AND PUNISHMENT; PUNISHMENT STORIES; RETALIATION; VENGEANCE

Punishment Stories

The Qur'ān contains many stories, overwhelmingly from the Meccan period (see CHRONOLOGY AND THE QUR'ĀN), which describe God's destruction of unbelieving communities in the generations before Muḥammad (see BELIEF AND UNBELIEF). A key feature of these stories, at least in their more developed forms, is the encounter between a messenger (q.v.) and the particular community to which he is sent to preach God's message. The messenger typically encounters opposition and ridicule but finally God intervenes to destroy the unbelievers. It is to be noted that these stories depict a punishment inflicted by God in this world rather than in the afterlife (see CHASTISEMENT AND PUNISHMENT; REWARD AND PUNISHMENT). This article gives a survey of the relevant qur'ānic material and also suggests how these stories illuminate the context in which Muḥammad was preaching (see OCCASIONS OF REVELATION).

Early Meccan period

From this period there are a number of passages which are so brief that they can scarcely be described as punishment stories, but which nevertheless point ahead to the more developed narratives (q.v.) to be considered below (see FORM AND STRUCTURE OF THE QUR'ĀN). These early Meccan passages give short, allusive accounts of the destruction by God of unbelieving communities of the past, along with occasional references to messengers sent by God. The relevant passages, in chronological order, are: 105; 91:11-5; 85:17-20; 73:15-6; 79:15-26; 89:6-14; 53:50-4; 69:4-12; 51:24-46. (See for an analysis of these passages Marshall, *God,* 39-52.)

Middle and late Meccan periods

Many of the typical features of the punishment stories from these periods are present in the following account of the preaching of the messenger Shu'ayb (q.v.) to the "men of the thicket" (see PEOPLE OF THE THICKET), their rejection of his message and their consequent punishment by God.

The men of the thicket cried lies to the envoys when Shu'ayb said to them: "Will you not be godfearing? I am for you a faithful messenger, so fear God and obey me (see FEAR; OBEDIENCE). I ask of you no wage for this; my wage falls only upon the lord (q.v.) of all being. Fill up the measure, and be not cheaters, and weigh with the straight balance, and diminish not the goods of the people (see ECONOMICS; WEIGHTS AND MEASURES; MEASUREMENT; JUSTICE AND INJUSTICE), and do not mischief in the earth, working corruption (q.v.). Fear him who created you (see CREATION), and the generations (q.v.) of the ancients." They said: "You are merely one of those that are bewitched (see INSANITY); you are nothing but a mortal, like us; indeed, we think that you are one of the liars (see LIE). Then drop down on us lumps from heaven, if you are one of the truthful." He said, "My lord knows very well what you are doing." But they cried him lies; then there seized them the punishment of the day of shadow; assuredly it was the punishment of a dreadful day. Surely in that is a sign, yet most of them are not believers. Surely your lord, he is the all-mighty, the all-compassionate (Q 26:176-91).

This is the last of seven stories, which together form a long narrative chain constituting virtually the whole of sūra 26. Of these seven, the final five, focusing in turn on the messengers Noah (q.v.), Hūd (q.v.), Ṣāliḥ (q.v.), Lot (q.v.) and Shuʿayb, have many similarities in both form and content and are linked by a number of repeated phrases.

These five stories begin with a brief statement of the unbelieving response of a particular people to God's messenger, who is typically one of their kin. The first word of each story is the verb *kadhdhabat,* denoting the unbelievers' denial of the truth (q.v.) of the messengers' words. This repetition emphatically introduces the phenomenon of unbelief as the burden of these stories. The opening is followed by an account of the messenger's preaching, which calls his people to be god-fearing and to acknowledge his own authority (q.v.) and trustworthiness. In most cases the messenger also criticizes forms of immorality or social injustice displayed by the community in question (see VIRTUES AND VICES, COMMANDING AND FORBIDDING; ETHICS AND THE QURʾĀN). This prompts a scornful, unbelieving response that might also include a threat of violence towards the messenger who, in some cases, now prays for God to deliver him and his followers or household. Then, in a variety of ways, God intervenes to destroy the unbelievers. Each passage concludes with a reminder to the Meccan listeners that this story is a "sign" *(āya),* a call to respond in humility to the mighty but merciful God; there is also, however, a note of resigned recognition that "most of them are not believers."

God sends a messenger; the messenger is rejected; the unbelievers are punished. This basic narrative pattern underlies the great majority of the many punishment stories that occur in the middle and late Meccan periods, although there is also significant variety among them. The same essential story about the five messengers mentioned above occurs especially frequently, but there are also many stories involving other messengers, particularly Abraham (q.v.) and Moses (q.v.; the latter occasionally linked to Aaron [q.v.]). The stories about Abraham are not punishment stories in the full sense, as they contain no reference to his people being destroyed, but Abraham sometimes features in the stories of the punishment of Lot's people, as at Q 11:69-83. Some punishment stories refer to unnamed messengers (e.g. Q 23:31-41). Mention should also be made of Jonah (q.v.), the only messenger whose people repent (see REPENTANCE AND PENANCE) in response to his preaching and who therefore escape punishment (Q 37:139-48; 10:98). In addition to the peoples of the messengers already mentioned, the Qurʾān also refers to other punished peoples, such as al-Rass (q.v.) and Tubbaʿ (q.v.; Q 50:12, 14), about whom nothing further is said. There is also a story about the punishment of the people of Sheba (q.v.; 34:15-21), which is unusual in not including any mention of a messenger. The nature of the punishment inflicted by God is in some cases made explicit (e.g. the flood which destroyed Noah's [q.v.] people; the drowning of Pharaoh's [q.v.] army; stones being rained from heaven on Lot's people); but in many cases it is left unspecific (e.g. Q 26:189, in the story quoted above, refers to "the punishment of the day of shadow").

It is difficult to overstate the significance of the punishment stories in the middle and late Meccan periods, where they constitute a very considerable proportion of the qurʾānic text. The following list includes a number of passages (e.g. especially Q 11:25-99 and Q 7:59-137, as well as Q 26:8-191, mentioned above) in which several narratives are linked to form a chain of punishment stories, suggesting that human history has been a sequence of such encounters between God's messengers and unbelievers (see HISTORY AND THE QURʾĀN): Q 54:9-42; 37:71-148; 71; 44:17-33; 50:12-4; 20:9-99; 26:8-191; 15:51-84; 38:12-5; 36:13-32; 43:46-56; 23:23-49; 27:7-58; 25:35-40; 17:101-3; 18:32-43; 41:13-8; 11:25-99; 14:5-14; 40:5-6; 40:23-46; 28:3-43; 28:76-82; 29:14-40; 10:71-92; 34:15-21; 7:59-137; 46:21-7 (a brief summary of the contents of each of these passages is provided at Marshall, *God*, 71-3).

In addition to this list of narrative passages there are also many brief and generalized references to God's acts of punishment in the world. Typical in this regard are the refrain "How many a generation we destroyed..." (e.g. Q 6:6; 10:13-4; 17:17; 19:74; 50:36) and variants on "Have they not journeyed in the land and beheld how was the end of those that were before them?" (Q 35:44; cf. 6:11; 12:109; 30:42; 40:21-2, 82-4; see GEOGRAPHY). Similar passages occur at Q 43:23-5; 67:18; 21:6-15; 18:55-9; 32:26; 39:25; 7:4-5; 6:42-5. The combination of extended punishment stories and these widely scattered brief references to God's acts of punishment in this world ensure that this theme thoroughly pervades the qurʾānic material of these periods.

The Medinan period

It is therefore very striking, and a point little commented on, that in Medinan passages there are no developed punishment stories and only very few brief references to God's past acts of punishment. Q 22:42-9 and 64:5-6 are examples of early Medinan passages which echo the themes and threats of the Meccan punishment stories (on the dating and significance of Q 22:39-49 see Marshall, *God*, 119-24); isolated later Medinan examples can be found at passages such as Q 3:10-1, Q 9:70, and Q 47:10. Comment will be offered below on the absence of punishment stories in Medinan passages after the abundance of them in Meccan passages.

The significance of the punishment stories

The point is widely recognized that the punishment stories provide a window onto the situation of Muḥammad at Mecca (q.v.). These stories reflect both the wider context in which Muḥammad was preaching and also something of his own experience of being rejected by the unbelievers in Mecca (Marshall, *God*, x, 29-30 and 36-7; see OPPOSITION TO MUḤAMMAD).

Working from this assumption, it is possible to explore the functions these stories served. Their primary purpose was to warn of a punishment from God that would fall upon the Meccan unbelievers if they did not repent and accept Muḥammad's message. Thus, if the unbelievers reject his message, Muḥammad is bidden to tell them: "I warn you of a thunderbolt like to the thunderbolt of ʿĀd (q.v.) and Thamūd" (q.v.; Q 41:13). What had happened to unbelieving communities in the past could happen to the Meccans in the present if they persisted in their rejection of Muḥammad's message (Marshall, *God,* 54-7).

In addition to exercising this warning function, the punishment stories also served to encourage Muḥammad and his followers to persevere in the face of hostile unbelief. This is implicit throughout the stories as they depict the final vindication of God's messengers and their followers (e.g. especially the sequence of stories at Q 37:71-148) and is made explicit in the qurʾānic comment on the stories in sūra 11: "And all that we relate to you [Muḥammad] of the tidings of the messengers is that whereby we strengthen your heart" (q.v.; Q 11:120; see NEWS).

There is further interest in the punishment stories, however, in that they also give some fascinating insights into Muḥammad's experience in Mecca. The observation of Horovitz (*KU,* 18) that "Muḥammad's feelings and experiences repeatedly come to expression in the speeches of the earlier messengers of God and their opponents" is perhaps best illustrated in the story of Noah at Q 11:25-49, with its memorable account of Noah's anguish over his unbelieving son (Marshall, *God,* 97-105; note the striking comments of Quṭb, *Taṣwīr,* 58). On this passage Newby (Drowned son, 29) comments: "the compassion of Noah tells us of Muḥammad's concern for those who would not heed his message."

This approach to the punishment stories, emphasizing their relevance to and reflection of Muḥammad's actual context in Mecca, can also be extended to offer a possible explanation for their disappearance after the emigration (q.v.; *hijra*) from Mecca to Medina (q.v.). In the Medinan passages the theme of the punishment of unbelievers in this world by God undergoes significant developments. With the onset of military conflict between Muḥammad's community and the Meccan unbelievers, as well as other opponents, the Qurʾān gradually unfolds a new paradigm (see FIGHTING; WAR; EXPEDITIONS AND BATTLES). In the Meccan period the punishment stories had reflected the expectation that God would intervene suddenly to destroy the unbelievers directly, without human mediation (Marshall, *God,* 66-8). In Medina, however, it is recognized that it is through the believers and in the course of a military campaign that the divine punishment will be inflicted on the unbelievers (key Medinan passages articulating this transition are Q 8, Q 47:4 and Q 9:14; see Marshall, *God,* 134-44, 153-7). Therefore, whereas in Mecca the punishment stories functioned with purposes specific to that context, after the *hijra* — and particularly after the battle of Badr (q.v.) — the changed context of Muḥammad and his community mean that these stories had in a sense been outgrown. The messengers who had so regularly been invoked as forerunners of Muḥammad in the Meccan context were not so relevant in the very different circumstances of Medina (Marshall, *God,* 158-60).

It should also be noted that narrative as a whole — not just the particular case of the punishment stories — is a rare phenomenon in Medinan passages in comparison with Meccan passages. It can be argued that this is another reflection of the difference between the two contexts. In Mecca the abundant use of narrative, with its indirect way of commenting on Muḥammad's circumstances, seems to reflect, at least in part, a situation of weakness and lack of authority. Medina, in contrast, is a context of growing power and authority for Muḥammad and his community (see POLITICS AND THE QURʾĀN), and there is here a tendency to comment much more directly on events, without recourse to the medium of narrative (Marshall, *God,* 161-4). This interpretation sheds further interesting light on the way in which the Meccan punishment stories functioned in context within the life of a struggling and vulnerable community.

David Marshall

Bibliography
Primary: Kisāʾī, *Qiṣaṣ,* trans. W.M. Thackston, *The tales of the prophets of al-Kisa'i,* Boston 1978; Thaʿlabī, *Qiṣaṣ,* trans. W.M. Brinner, *Lives of the prophets,* Leiden 2002.
Secondary: R. Bell, *The origin of Islam in its Christian environment,* London 1926 (Lecture IV); Horovitz, *KU;* D. Marshall, *God, Muḥammad and the unbelievers,* Richmond 1999; G. Newby, The drowned son. Midrash and Midrash making in the Qurʾān and tafsīr, in W.M. Brinner and S.D. Ricks (eds.), *Studies in Islamic and Judaic traditions,* Atlanta 1986, 19-32; R. Paret, Der Koran als Geschichtsquelle, in *Der Islam* 37 (1961), 24-42; repr. in R. Paret (ed.), *Der Koran,* Darmstadt 1975, 137-58; S. Quṭb, *al-Taṣwīr al-fannī fī l-Qurʾān,* Cairo 1993; U. Rubin, Exegesis and *ḥadīth.* The case of the seven *mathānī,* in Hawting and Shareef, *Approaches,* 141-56; Speyer, *Erzählungen;* R. Tottoli, *Biblical prophets in the Qurʾān and Muslim literature,* Richmond 2002; W.M. Watt, *Muhammad's Mecca. History in the Qurʾān,* Edinburgh 1988; Watt-Bell, *Introduction,* 127-35; A. Welch, Formulaic features of the punishment-stories, in I.J. Boullata (ed.), *Literary structures of religious meaning in the Qurʾān,* Richmond 2000, 77-116; M. Zwettler, A mantic manifesto. The sūra of "The Poets" and the qurʾānic foundations of prophetic authority, in J.L. Kugel (ed.), *Poetry and prophecy. The beginnings of a literary tradition,* Ithaca 1990, 75-119.

Purgatory

see DEATH AND THE DEAD; PARADISE; HELL AND HELLFIRE; BARZAKH

Purification

see CLEANLINESS AND ABLUTION; RITUAL PURITY; CONTAMINATION

Purity and Impurity

see RITUAL PURITY; CLEANLINESS AND ABLUTION; CONTAMINATION

Q

Qarnayn, Dhū l- see ALEXANDER

Qārūn see KORAH

Qaynuqāʿ (Banū)

One of the Jewish tribes of Medina (q.v.), generally considered part of the triad that also includes the Banū l-Naḍīr (see NAḌĪR [BANŪ AL-]) and the Banū Qurayẓa (q.v.). A so-called "market of the Banū Qaynuqāʿ" in Medina was known in pre-Islamic times, and various sources state that the Qaynuqāʿ were famous as goldsmiths but — in contrast to the other Jewish tribes — they possessed no arable land. Their quarter, al-Quff, close to the center of Medina, housed a Jewish assembly-place (see JEWS AND JUDAISM; PRE-ISLAMIC ARABIA AND THE QURʾĀN; SOUTH ARABIA, RELIGION IN PRE-ISLAMIC). The most prominent members of the Qaynuqāʿ were Finḥāṣ al-Yahūdī, Shaʾs b. Qays and, above all, ʿAbdallāh b. Salām; several of ʿAbdallāh's descendants are quoted in later chains of transmission in ḥadīth (see ḤADĪTH AND THE QURʾĀN). In early *sīra* accounts (accounts that belong to the biography of the Prophet; see SĪRA AND THE QURʾĀN) most of the Medinan Jews known by name are ascribed to the Qaynuqāʿ, although this tribe was, if compared with those of al-Naḍīr and Qurayẓa, of minor importance, and allegedly left Medina only two or three years after the Prophet's arrival. In Islamic legal sources (see LAW AND THE QURʾĀN) the Qaynuqāʿ are said, on the authority of al-Shāfiʿī (d. 204/820) and al-Awzāʿī (d. 157/774), to have participated in Muslim raids (see EXPEDITIONS AND BATTLES) and even to have received a share in the booty (q.v.). The most important event concerning the Qaynuqāʿ in mainstream Islamic tradition is, however, their siege and ensuing expulsion from Medina by the Muslims.

According to Islamic tradition, this conflict was either the result of the refusal of the Qaynuqāʿ to accept Islam or the breaking of a non-aggression treaty which they had concluded with the Prophet (see BREAKING TRUSTS AND CONTRACTS; CONTRACTS AND ALLIANCES); according to reports told by Ibn Hishām (d. 218/834) and al-Wāqidī (d. 207/822), however, and ultimately adopted in most later sources, a member of the Qaynuqāʿ had mocked a Muslim woman in their market (see MARKETS), and that led eventually to the siege of their quarter after the battle of

Badr (q.v.). For a fortnight in 2/624 — or in year 3, according to al-Ṭabarī (d. 310/923) — the Qaynuqāʿ were besieged by the Muslims, and after their surrender they were expelled to the Syrian town of Adhriʿāt. The Prophet is believed to have intended a harsher fate for them but the hypocrite (see HYPOCRITES AND HYPOCRISY) ʿAbdallāh b. Ubayy successfully interceded with him on their behalf. The Jews were allowed to leave Medina but their weapons were taken by the Muslims and a part thereof was distributed among the Prophet's Companions (see COMPANIONS OF THE PROPHET).

In the case of the Qaynuqāʿ it is very difficult to assess the reliability of the Islamic tradition. Ibn Isḥāq's (d. 150/767) account is mainly constructed from exegetical material concerning verses Q 3:12 f. and Q 5:51-6 and does not mention the expulsion of the Qaynuqāʿ, let alone an exact date for this event. In addition, a number of exegetical authorities state that the later expulsion of the Jewish al-Naḍīr was "the first expulsion of Jews from Medina," a claim which obviously belies the Qaynuqāʿ episode as found in the later "orthodox" version. This "orthodox" version largely depends on the account by al-Wāqidī, whose conflation of reports and sources seems in this case to be more extensive than usual. Apart from the incident in the market of the Qaynuqāʿ, he stresses the treachery of the Qaynuqāʿ and repeatedly refers to Q 8:58 in this context: "And if you fear treachery any way at the hands of a people, dissolve it with them equally; surely God loves not the treacherous" — a verse generally applied to the Jewish Banū Qurayẓa. Modern research suggests, thus, that the episode of the conflict with the Qaynuqāʿ is somewhat intrusive in the *sīra* tradition and probably a result of the conversion of exegetical material into history, backed by an interest in its legal and chronological implications (see CHRONOLOGY AND THE QURʾĀN; HISTORY AND THE QURʾĀN). In any case, important early *sīra* authorities such as Ibn Shihāb al-Zuhrī (d. 124/742) and Mūsā b. ʿUqba (d. 141/758) do not seem to have known of the expulsion of the Qaynuqāʿ, and the account of Ibn Isḥāq remains inconclusive. The qurʾānic verses adduced in support of the Qaynuqāʿ episode are too vague to allow for firmer conclusions.

Marco Schöller

Bibliography

Primary (in addition to the Qurʾān commentaries, esp. ad Q 2:84 f.; 3:12 f., 181; 5:51 f.; 8:58; 59:15, the legal compendia and anthologies of traditions — including those dealing with the "proofs of prophethood" — and virtually all *sīra* writings, which provide information about the Qaynuqāʿ): al-Samhūdī, Abū l-Ḥasan ʿAlī b. ʿAbdallāh, *Wafāʾ al-wafāʾ*, ed. M. Muḥyī l-Dīn ʿAbd al-Ḥamīd, 2 vols., Cairo 1955, repr. Beirut 1973 (part. trans. J. Wellhausen, *Geschichte der Stadt Medina*, Göttingen 1860; this work remains of paramount importance for topographical details); al-Wāqidī, *Maghāzī* (the most influential and detailed "orthodox" version of events).
Secondary: J. Bouman, *Der Koran und die Juden. Die Geschichte einer Tragödie*, Darmstadt 1990, 73 f.; R.S. Faizer, Muḥammad and the Medinan Jews. A comparison of the texts of Ibn Isḥāq's *Kitāb sīrat rasūl Allāh* with al-Wāqidī's *Kitāb al-maghāzī*, in *IJMES* 28 (1996), 463-89; M. Gil, The origin of the Jews of Yathrib, in *JSAI* 4 (1984), 203-24; M. Lecker, The conversion of Ḥimyar to Judaism and the Jewish Banū Hadl of Medina, in *WO* 26 (1995), 129-36; id., Did Muḥammad conclude treaties with the Jewish tribes Naḍīr, Qurayẓa and Qaynuqāʿ? in *IOS* 17 (1997), 29-36; id., *Jews and Arabs in pre- and early Islamic Arabia*, Aldershot 1998; id., *Muslims, Jews and pagans. Studies on early Islamic Medina*, Leiden 1995; id., On the markets of Medina (Yathrib) in pre-Islamic and early Islamic times, in *JSAI* 8 (1986), 133-47; G.D. Newby, *A history of the Jews of Arabia*, Columbia 1988, 85 f.; M. Schöller, *Exegetisches Denken und Prophetenbiographie. Eine quellenkritische Analyse der Sīra-Überlieferung zu Muḥammads Konflikt mit den Juden*, Wiesbaden 1998 (esp. chaps. 6 and 7); id., In welchem Jahr wurden die Banū l-Naḍīr aus Medina vertrieben? in *Der Islam* 73 (1996),

1-39; id., *Sīra* and *tafsīr*. Muḥammad al-Kalbī on the Jews of Medina, in H. Motzki (ed.), *The biography of Muḥammad. The issue of the sources*, Leiden 2000, 18-48; A.J. Wensinck, *Muḥammad and the Jews of Medina*, trans. W.H. Behn, Berlin 1982[2].

Qibla

A direction one faces in order to pray (see PRAYER). Q 2:142-50 is concerned with the Muslims' *qibla* and appears to say the following: There is about to be a change of *qibla*. Foolish people will make an issue of the change and they should be answered with an affirmation of God's absolute sovereignty (q.v.; see also POWER AND IMPOTENCE). God has made the believers neither Jews nor Christians (see BELIEF AND UNBELIEF; JEWS AND JUDAISM; CHRISTIANS AND CHRISTIANITY) but an example to all, just as the messenger (q.v.) is an example to the believers. The former *qibla* was instituted only as a test, to see who would follow the messenger's example and who would turn away. It was a hard test but not for those whom God guided (see ASTRAY; ERROR; FREEDOM AND PREDESTINATION). To reward their faith (q.v.) and in response to the messenger's own silent appeal, God will now institute a *qibla* to the messenger's liking. He and the faithful, wherever they may be, should now turn their faces toward 'the sacred place of worship' *(al-masjid al-ḥarām)*. Both Jews and Christians know that this is the true *qibla* but no matter what proof of this the messenger might bring them they will never follow his *qibla*. They cannot even agree on a *qibla* between themselves. They do as they please but the messenger knows better. In fact they know better, too, but one group of them deliberately conceals the truth. The faithful should turn their faces toward the sacred place of worship so that none but the perverse will have any argument against them. They should not fear such people but only God who has chosen to bestow on them his favor.

The change of qibla *in Muslim tradition*

Traditional Muslim exegesis (see EXEGESIS OF THE QURʾĀN: CLASSICAL AND MEDIEVAL) has provided this passage with a quasi-historical setting in Medina (q.v.). It is commonly reported that when he first arrived in Medina the prophet Muḥammad prayed towards Jerusalem (q.v.) or at least towards Syria (q.v.). This is usually simply stated without any explanation. Occasionally it is noted that Jerusalem was the *qibla* of the Jews and one report implies that Muḥammad himself chose this direction in order that the Jews might believe in him and follow him (Ṭabarī, *Tafsīr*, iii, 138). This should not be taken at face value. The purpose of the report is to claim the change of *qibla* as evidence for the theory of abrogation (q.v.; *naskh*), which proposes that qurʾānic rulings were sometimes abrogated by later rulings. The report faces the difficulty that whereas the Qurʾān provides an abrogating ruling — the new *qibla* — it does not easily yield an abrogated ruling, as the theory requires. There is no instruction anywhere in the Qurʾān to pray towards either Jerusalem or Syria. The problem is solved with Q 2:115, "To God belong the east and the west. Wherever you turn, there is the face of God (q.v.)." It was evidently on the basis of this permissive ruling that Muḥammad himself chose to pray towards Jerusalem and appealing to the Jews provides a plausible motive for him to do so. A superficially similar report says contrarily that God ordered Muḥammad to pray towards Jerusalem. This pleased the Jews of Medina, though the report does not presume to know that this was God's motive. Muḥammad, we now learn, would have preferred what is here referred to as the *qibla* of Abraham (q.v.), with the obvious implication that Mecca (q.v.) — and not Jerusalem — was the true focus of the Abrahamic cult. The Jews' initial pleasure is mentioned only to prepare for their subsequent displeasure when the change is made. The point of this report is not now *naskh* but a simple appropriation of the Abrahamic legacy (Ṭabarī, *Tafsīr,* iii, 138-9; this and the preceding report are conflated at ibid., ii, 527; see also ḤANĪF). In both reports the circumstantial detail is plainly subordinate to the main point, but on such slight foundations rests the well-established notion that Muḥammad tried to reconcile the Jews of Medina before their perverse ingratitude for his prophetic attentions compelled him to take stronger measures (see PROPHETS AND PROPHETHOOD; GRATITUDE AND INGRATITUDE; OPPOSITION TO MUḤAMMAD).

It is variously reported that the change of *qibla* came when Muḥammad had been in Medina for two, nine, ten, thirteen, sixteen or seventeen months (Ibn Isḥāq, *Sīra,* i, 550, 606; Mālik, *Muwaṭṭa',* i, 196; Ibn Māja, *Sunan,* i, 322; Ṭabarī, *Tafsīr,* iii, 132-7; id., *Ta'rīkh,* i, 1279-81). Most reports of the actual occurrence turn out to be stereotyped vehicles for another theoretical point. The change of *qibla* by the Prophet himself is not observed directly but reported by a single individual, usually anonymously, who happens to pass by a group of other Muslims in the middle of their prayer. He tells them that the Prophet has now been told to pray towards the Kaʿba (q.v.) or that he has seen him do so, and they immediately turn around and do the same (Mālik, *Muwaṭṭa',* i, 195; Shāfiʿī, *Risāla,* 406-8; Bukhārī, *Ṣaḥīḥ,* i, 110-1, vi, 25; Muslim, *Ṣaḥīḥ,* i, 374-5; Ṭabarī, *Tafsīr,* iii, 133-4). The point is to prove for later generations the reliability of *khabar al-wāḥid,* a report of the Prophet's sunna (q.v.) attributed to only one of his Companions (see COMPANIONS OF THE PROPHET). It quite deliberately shows the Prophet's own Companions unhesitatingly changing their practice in the most important religious duty for all Muslims on the evidence of just one of their number. His anonymity supports the point, as it cannot now be argued that a particular Companion was regarded as exceptionally trustworthy. Any Companion would have done and so, we must conclude, does any one Companion whom later generations know through chains of transmitters of ḥadīth (*isnāds*) as the sole witness to a particular ruling of the Prophet (see LAW AND THE QUR'ĀN; ḤADĪTH AND THE QUR'ĀN). There is a report in which Muḥammad himself is observed praying two prostrations (*rakʿas*; see BOWING AND PROSTRATION) of the midday prayer (see NOON) towards Jerusalem and then suddenly turning around towards the Kaʿba before completing the prayer (Ṭabarī, *Tafsīr,* iii, 135). This seems more likely to derive from the forgoing reports than vice versa.

That "the sacred place of worship" is indeed the Kaʿba in Mecca is unquestioned and frequently stated. The foolish people who will question the change are identified as the Jews (several of whom are named in one report) or as the People of the Book (q.v.) or as the hypocrites (see HYPOCRITES AND HYPOCRISY). The Jews are said to have wanted to seduce Muḥammad away from his religion or were disappointed at losing the satisfaction of seeing him follow their own practice and the hope that he might turn out to be a Jewish prophet after all. The hypocrites just wanted to scoff (Ibn Isḥāq, *Sīra* i, 550; Ṭabarī, *Tafsīr,* iii, 132, 134, 138-40, 157-8; see MOCKERY).

As John Burton has pointed out, there is nothing in the Qur'ān either to prove or to disprove that the former *qibla* referred to in Q 2:142-3 was Jerusalem (Burton, *Sources,* 179). He might have added, though he does not, that there is nothing in it either to prove or disprove that the latter *qibla,* the "sacred place of worship" referred to in Q 2:144, was the Kaʿba in Mecca. The historical and geographical referents of Q 2:142-50 are known only from Muslim exegesis and it is clear that the exegetes' purpose in examining this passage was not the disinterested satisfaction of historical curiosity (see HISTORY AND THE QURʾĀN). The preoccupation with abrogation is pervasive. Al-Ṭabarī (d. 310/923) coolly twists the meaning of Q 2:143 so that not the former *qibla* itself but the change of *qibla,* the apparently arbitrary phenomenon of abrogation, becomes the test of faith for the believers. This enables him to consider an issue that, for those who assert the reality of the phenomenon of *naskh,* is theoretically interesting: namely, whether those believers who lived and died under the abrogated ruling will be rewarded in the same way as those who survived to obey the new one (Ṭabarī, *Tafsīr,* iii, 163-70). Why some should have found it hard to pray towards Jerusalem, if that was indeed the former *qibla,* is not a question he raises.

For all that, it seems clear from the text that Q 2:142-50 is a residue of the process by which Islam asserted its independence as the one true religion (q.v.) from its Jewish and Christian antecedents (see RELIGIOUS PLURALISM AND THE QURʾĀN). This becomes clearer still when the passage is examined, as Burton (*Sources,* 171-3, 179-83) has shown, in its larger context. Q 2 as a whole is intensely polemical, with sustained attacks on the authenticity of the Jewish religion and in particular the Jewish claim of continuing adherence to God's covenant (q.v.) with Abraham. It stakes Islam's own claim to the covenant through Ishmael (q.v.) and prepares the ground for Q 2:142-50 with an account of Abraham's foundation, with Ishmael's help, of a sanctuary as a place of prayer and ritual (Q 2:125-8; see RITUAL AND THE QURʾĀN). This Abrahamic sanctuary is referred to only as "the house" or "my (God's) house" but is easily identified with "the sacred place of worship" *(al-masjid al-ḥarām)* of Q 2:142-50 or the *qibla* of Abraham as the exegetes call it (see HOUSE, DOMESTIC AND DIVINE). At Q 3:96 this sanctuary is said to have been at Bakka, which everyone has been taught is an old name for Mecca. Even if that might be doubted, the polemical context at both Q 3:96 and Q 2:125-8 makes almost inescapable the implication that, wherever it was, the Qurʾān's Abrahamic sanctuary was definitely not in Jerusalem. To that extent the exegetes' identification of the abrogated *qibla* with Jerusalem makes obvious sense of the text.

The fundamental issue behind the polemic of Q 2 is the problem of changing the law within a monotheistic intellectual tradition which insists that the law is God's law and that God's law is immutable. The problem and some of its solutions are older than the Qurʾān but the solution seen in Q 2:142-50 is the most typically qurʾānic one. The new *qibla* is not an innovation (q.v.) but a restoration. If it differs from the practice of Jews and Christians, it is the latter who have arbitrarily departed from what they themselves know, but will never admit, is the truth. The heat of qurʾānic polemic against the Jews in Q 2 is a smokescreen for this sleight of hand (see POLEMIC AND POLEMICAL LANGUAGE). Whereas for early Christianity the crux issue with Judaism was the Sabbath (q.v.), for early Islam it was evidently the *qibla.* Once the crux is overcome (in Q 2:142-50), the way is open for the rush of new legislation that follows in the remainder of the sūra.

The early qibla *in history*

Whether the early Muslims ever did pray towards Jerusalem we shall probably never know. In 1977 Patricia Crone and Michael Cook proposed that they did once pray towards a sanctuary somewhere in north-western Arabia. Their evidence, reviewed in detail by Robert Hoyland in 1997, is firstly that two Umayyad mosques in Iraq, one at Wāsiṭ and one at Iskāf Banī Junayd, are known from modern archeological investigation to have been oriented in a westerly direction much further north than that of Mecca. Secondly, there are reports in Muslim literary sources that the first mosque built in Egypt was oriented in an easterly direction that was also further north than that of Mecca. In addition, Jacob of Edessa, a seventh century C.E. Syrian Christian writer, says that Jews and Muslims in Egypt prayed to the east and in Babylonia to the west (Crone and Cook, *Hagarism,* 23-4; Hoyland, *Seeing Islam,* 560-73; see MOSQUE).

Put together, these fragments of evidence are suggestive — but if each fragment is considered separately none is very persuasive. The archeological evidence tells us nothing of the early mosque builders' intentions unless we know how accurate their technical means of putting their intentions into effect were. As David King (Ḳibla, 87-8) has argued, it is likely that the earliest mosque builders adopted a local convention rather than a scientifically exact direction for the Kaʿba. In the case of the mosque of Iskāf Banī Junayd, the archeological report of its misorientation observes, "the error seems to have been aggravated by the fact that the line of the Nahrawan (Canal) clearly influenced and dictated that of the mosque in large degree" (Creswell, *Short account,* 268). Muslim literary reports that the first mosque in Egypt was orientated too far to the north put it down to a personal idiosyncrasy of the Muslim commander and conqueror of Egypt ʿAmr b. al-ʿĀṣ, who oversaw its construction. They note that other worshippers in the mosque used to turn themselves off to the south until the mosque itself was finally rebuilt and realigned (see also SCIENCE AND THE QURʾĀN).

Literary evidence also needs to be judged against the possibility that the writer is working with a simplified and schematic mental map. Jacob of Edessa's point about Muslims is that they do not pray everywhere in the same geographical direction. They pray towards the Kaʿba, so that in Egypt they pray to the east, in Babylonia to the west, from south of the Kaʿba to the north, and in Syria to the south. Does this really help us to locate the Kaʿba? It is equally likely that Jacob himself, for the sake of simplicity, reported only approximately what he had actually observed or that Muslims in all those parts of the world prayed in any case only approximately in the direction of Mecca. In the end, it may not be significant where exactly their approximate direction happened to lie.

Richard Kimber

Bibliography

Primary: Bukhārī, *Ṣaḥīḥ,* Cairo 1958; Ibn Isḥāq, *Sīra,* Cairo 1955, 550-1; Ibn Isḥāq-Guillaume, 258-9 and index; Ibn Māja; Mālik, *Muwaṭṭaʾ,* Cairo 1952-3; Muslim, *Ṣaḥīḥ,* Cairo 1955-6; Shāfiʿī, Muḥammad b. Idrīs, *al-Risāla,* ed. A.M. Shākir, Cairo 1940; Ṭabarī, *Tafsīr,* Cairo 1954-68, ii, 526-36; iii, 129-208; id., *Taʾrīkh,* Leiden 1879-1901, i, 1279-81; W.M. Watt and M.V. McDonald (trans.), *The history of al-Ṭabarī.* vii. *The foundation of the community,* Albany 1987, 24-5.
Secondary: J. Burton, *The sources of Islamic law. Islamic theories of abrogation,* Edinburgh 1990; K.A.C. Creswell, *A short account of early Muslim architecture,* Aldershot 1989; P. Crone and M. Cook, *Hagarism. The making of the Islamic world,* Cambridge 1977; R.G. Hoyland, *Seeing Islam as others saw it. A survey and evaluation of Christian, Jewish and Zoroastrian writings on early Islam,* Princeton 1997; W.M. Watt, *Muhammad at Medina,* Oxford 1956, 198-202; A.J. Wensinck/D.A. King, Ḳibla, in *EI²,* v, 82-8.

Qirāʾa see READINGS OF THE QURʾĀN

Quails see ANIMAL LIFE

Queen of Sheba see BILQĪS; SHEBA; SOLOMON

Quraysh

Name of a tribe in Mecca (q.v.) to which Muḥammad belonged (for the meaning of the name, see Watt, Ḳuraysh). It is mentioned only once in the Qurʾān (Q 106:1), in a chapter dealing with their winter and summer caravans (see CARAVAN). The exegetes quote detailed traditions about their pre-Islamic commercial system which acquired international dimensions, their trade caravans being said to have reached as far as Byzantium in the north (see BYZANTINES), Persia in the east, Abyssinia (q.v.) in the west and Yemen (q.v.) in the south. The qurʾānic chapter itself requests the Quraysh to remember that their prosperity and security (see WEALTH) comes from God; therefore they must worship him alone (see ILĀF).

Blessed by God

Sūra 105, "The Elephant," is also closely associated with the Quraysh (see PEOPLE OF THE ELEPHANT), and mainly with the origin of their elevated status among the Arabs (q.v.). The exegetes adduce traditions relating that the sūra (q.v.) describes the defeat of an Abyssinian army under the command of Abraha (q.v.), that came from the Yemen to destroy the Kaʿba (q.v.). God sent upon them birds in flocks that smote them with stones of baked clay, and caused them to become like straw eaten up. Tradition has it that "When God turned back the Abyssinians from Mecca and executed his vengeance (q.v.) upon them, the Arabs held the Quraysh in great honor, saying, 'They are the people of God: God fought for them and thwarted the attack of their enemies'" (Ibn Isḥāq-Guillaume, 28). The key figure in these traditions on the Meccan side is ʿAbd al-Muṭṭalib, Muḥammad's grandfather, who is said to have negotiated with Abraha on behalf of the Quraysh.

Reference to God's bounty, which was the origin of the security and prosperity enjoyed by the Quraysh in their sacred territory (*ḥaram;* see SACRED PRECINCTS; PROFANE AND SACRED), is made in some further verses, which urge the Meccans to be aware that God is their only benefactor and not to reject the message of the Qurʾān (cf. Q 28:57; 29:67; see BELIEF AND UNBELIEF). In Q 14:37 the prosperity bestowed on the people of Mecca originates in their being offspring of Abraham (q.v.). Here this patriarch asks God to bless his offspring who dwell near God's sacred "house" (see HOUSE, DOMESTIC AND DIVINE), the Kaʿba, to "make the hearts of [some] people yearn towards them and provide them with fruits." This is supposed to make them grateful to God (see GRATITUDE AND INGRATITUDE).

Their genealogical descent goes back to Abraham as well as to Ishmael (q.v.), which is implied in the fact that, in Q 2:127-8, both patriarchs are engaged in the building of the "house" while asking God to raise from their offspring a nation submitting to him *(umma muslima)*.

Their noble descent from Ishmael who is regarded the ancestor of the northern Arabs implies pride in their Arabian origin. This is reflected also in the exegesis on Q 14:4 which says that "God did not send any apostle (see MESSENGER) but with the language of his people" (see ARABIC LANGUAGE; LANGUAGE AND STYLE OF THE QURʾĀN). Traditions adduced by the exegetes for this verse assert that the Qurʾān was revealed in the language of the Quraysh (see DIALECTS).

Muḥammad's opponents
But in most verses interpreted as referring to the Quraysh, they act as Muḥammad's opponents (see OPPOSITION TO MUḤAMMAD). Their enmity to Muḥammad has been read by Muslim exegetes into endless passages which cannot be fully detailed here. Only some characteristic examples will be mentioned.

To begin with, their religious tenets are ridiculed in passages blaming them for believing that God has daughters who function as goddesses (see GOD AND HIS ATTRIBUTES; POLYTHEISM AND ATHEISM; PRE-ISLAMIC ARABIA AND THE QURʾĀN; SOUTH ARABIA, RELIGION IN PRE-ISLAMIC). The Qurʾān asserts the absurdity of this tenet by pointing out that no man wishes daughters for himself (see CHILDREN; GENDER; INFANTICIDE), so how can they attribute daughters to God? This idea is clearly stated in Q 53:19-23, in which the names of the goddesses are also provided. One of these goddesses is al-ʿUzzā, and Muslim exegetes have associated with her worship a prominent leader of the Quraysh, namely Abū Lahab (q.v.), Muḥammad's own uncle. Some traditions say that he was especially devoted to this deity, for which reason God has cursed him as well as his wife in Q 111 (see CURSE).

The ritual practices of the Meccans, as performed in the vicinity of the Kaʿba, are deplored in Q 8:35: "And their prayer before the house is nothing but whistling and clapping of hands...." Even the fact that the Quraysh were guardians of the sacred mosque, i.e. the Kaʿba and its surroundings, was no excuse for them in the eyes of God. On the contrary: in Q 9:19 God asserts that the providing of drink to the pilgrims and the guarding of the sacred mosque cannot substitute for believing in God.

Muslim traditions relate that the Quraysh belonged to a confederation of tribes who called themselves the Ḥums, i.e. "religiously zealous"; they reportedly adopted certain ritual rules which distinguished them from the rest of the Arab tribes (Kister, Mecca and Tamīm). Muslim exegetes have pointed out some verses in which the Quraysh and their confederates of the Ḥums are supposedly urged to give up their particular principles. For example, in Q 2:199, God requests that the rite of the *ifāḍa* (going in crowds from one place to another) be performed from where "the people" use to perform it. The exegetes say that here the Quraysh are requested to act like all the rest of the people during pilgrimage (q.v.), and come to ʿArafāt (q.v.) — a station of the pilgrimage which the Quraysh reportedly did not recognize as a sacred precinct — and start the *ifāḍa* from there.

In Q 2:189 the believers are requested to abandon the habit of entering the houses from behind them, rather than through their front doors. This, too, according to some exegetes, is designed to make the Quraysh abandon a special ritual act observed by the Ḥums during the time of pilgrimage. They reportedly considered it of great piety (q.v.) to remain under the open sky and not to enter the doors of their houses during the days of the pilgrimage.

Unsuccessful attempts at conversion
The leaders of the Quraysh are said to have refused to abandon their old religious tradition, and their reaction is provided most clearly in Q 38:4-7. Here they accuse the Prophet of being a conjurer and an impostor (see SOOTHSAYERS; MAGIC; LIE), and say to each other that they should cling to their deities and reject Muḥammad's monotheistic ideas. They point out

that such ideas were never heard of in their own old religion. Various other passages were explained as representing the reaction of the leaders of the Quraysh to Muḥammad's message (cf. Rubin, *The eye*, 151). In some of them they accuse him of plagiarism, assert their refusal to accept his message, and challenge him to prove his case through miracles (e.g. Q 16:103; 17:90-3; 25:7-8; 41:5; see MIRACLES; PROOF).

Nevertheless, Muḥammad is said to have tried to convert some of his closest relatives among the leaders of the Quraysh, and especially his uncle Abū Ṭālib, father of ʿAlī (see FAMILY OF THE PROPHET; ʿALĪ B. ABĪ ṬĀLIB). Such attempts were read by the exegetes into several qurʾānic passages. For example, some traditions say that the Prophet asked Abū Ṭālib, who was on his deathbed, to utter the *shahāda* (see WITNESS TO FAITH) but the latter refused, saying that he adhered to the religion of the old ancestors. Some versions relate that at this point Q 28:56 was revealed, which says that the qurʾānic Prophet cannot guide whom he likes (see GUIDANCE; FREEDOM AND PREDESTINATION). Q 9:113 is also said to have been revealed on the same occasion. It says that it is not for the qurʾānic Prophet and the believers to ask pardon for the polytheists (Rubin, *The eye*, 153; see FORGIVENESS; INTERCESSION). Moreover, in Q 6:108 the believers are requested not to abuse the idols worshipped by the polytheists (see IDOLS AND IMAGES), lest the latter should abuse God in return. The exegetes say that this verse was revealed as a result of the stubborn reaction of the leaders of the Quraysh, and their threat to abuse Muḥammad's God, in case he did not stop harassing them (ibid., 154; see also SATANIC VERSES).

Opposition and persecution

The Qurʾān also accuses the unbelievers of active persecution of the Prophet, and the exegetes explain that these accusations pertain to the hostile actions of the Quraysh that were carried out against Muḥammad in Mecca itself, before the emigration (q.v.; *hijra*), as well as in Medina (q.v.), after the *hijra*.

Persecution in Mecca, according to the exegetes, began as soon as Muḥammad started preaching in public. This he reportedly was requested to do in Q 26:214, in which God tells him to warn his nearest relations. The exegetes adduce for this verse traditions describing how Muḥammad summoned the clan of Hāshim of the Quraysh, and how they rejected his message. Their opposition was led by Muḥammad's uncle Abū Lahab (see Rubin, *The eye*, 127-38). Another prominent opponent in Mecca was Abū Jahl of the clan of Makhzūm, and his persecution of the Prophet was read into Q 96:9-19. Here a scene is described in which an unbeliever prevents a "servant" from praying. Most traditions maintain that the servant is Muḥammad, and the unbeliever is Abū Jahl who threatened to tread on the Prophet if he performed prostration (see BOWING AND PROSTRATION; PRAYER; RITUAL AND THE QURʾĀN). God instructs his servant not to obey him and to prostrate himself before God. A plan to assassinate the Prophet is pointed out by the exegetes in the commentary on Q 8:30: "And when those who disbelieved devised plans against you that they might confine you or slay you or drive you away...." This was taken to refer to a council held by Quraysh in which they discussed various options in order to eliminate the Prophet, and finally they agreed upon killing him while he was asleep in his bed. Muḥammad found out about it, and this was the immediate reason for his *hijra* to Medina.

The exegetes also point out verses in which reference is made to God's vengeance upon Muḥammad's adversaries from among the Quraysh. For example, in Q 15:95 God, speaking to the Prophet, promises to eliminate "those who scoff." The exegetes hold that this refers to a group of leaders from the Quraysh, on each of whom God brought death through a certain misfortune.

Collective punishment of the Quraysh is referred to, according to the exegetes, in Q 16:112 in which God sets forth a parable about a town safe and secure, a town whose means of subsistence came in abundance from every quarter; but it became ungrateful to God's favors, and therefore God made it taste the utmost degree of hunger and fear (see PARABLES). This has been taken as referring to a seven-year drought that God inflicted upon the Quraysh at the behest of the persecuted Prophet. The exegetes have associated this hunger with some further qurʾānic passages (Q 23:64, 75-7; 44:10-6).

Among the verses interpreted as referring to the acts of the Quraysh against Muḥammad after the *hijra*, are those in which the unbelievers are accused of preventing the believers from entering Mecca and the sacred mosque (Q 2:217; 8:34; 22:25; 48:25). In the traditions, this conduct is associated especially with the events of the year 6/628, when the Prophet left Medina with the believers and approached Mecca with a view of performing the lesser pilgrimage. The Quraysh stopped him at the outskirts of the town, near Ḥudaybiya, and the negotiations that followed reportedly ended up with the well-known pact of Ḥudaybiya (q.v.).

Also noteworthy are the verses to which the exegetes linked the military clashes between the Quraysh and the Prophet (see EXPEDITIONS AND BATTLES; FIGHTING; WAR). In some cases the link is obvious, as with the battle of Badr (q.v.; 2/624), which is mentioned in a passage describing angels assisting the fighting believers (Q 3:123-8; see ANGEL). Additional passages were linked to Badr by means of commentary, mainly Q 8:1-19 in which the division of spoils (see BOOTY) is discussed, and the help of angels smiting the unbelievers is described yet again. Various passages predicating divine punishment for the unbelievers (as in Q 18:55; 44:16, etc.) were also interpreted as referring to the defeat of the Quraysh at Badr (see CHASTISEMENT AND PUNISHMENT; PUNISHMENT STORIES).

The Battle of the Ditch (5/626-7), in which Medina was besieged by the Quraysh and their allies, is alluded to, according to the exegetes, in Q 33:9-27. Here the Qurʾān describes hosts of confederates *(aḥzāb)* coming against the believers, whom God defeats by means of winds (see AIR AND WIND) and unseen legions (of angels; see RANKS AND ORDERS).

The conquest of Mecca (8/630) which marked Muḥammad's final victory over the Quraysh is celebrated, according to the exegetes, in Q 110:1-3. Some have also associated Q 48:1 with this event: "Surely we have given you a clear victory (q.v.; *fatḥ*)," but others maintain that the latter passage refers to the affair of Ḥudaybiya.

Believers

The Qurʾān also refers to groups among the Quraysh who eventually became believers by embracing Islam, and some exegetes say that those who were first to do so are mentioned in Q 56:10, which speaks about those who were "foremost" (*al-sābiqūn;* cf. also Q 9:100; 59:10).

Another group is referred to as *al-mustaḍʿafūn,* "the weak" (see OPPRESSION; OPPRESSED ON EARTH, THE). They are mentioned in Q 4:75, in which the believers are requested to fight for the sake of the weak among the men and women and children. These weak say: "Our lord! Let us go out of this town, whose people are oppressors, and give us from you a guardian and give us from you a helper." The exegetes explain that these are some oppressed Muslims, converts from the Quraysh, who could not get out of Mecca and perform the *hijra* to Medina.

The most prominent group of Muslims among the Quraysh is the *muhājirūn,* the "emigrants" (see EMIGRANTS AND HELPERS). They are mentioned in numerous passages, for example in Q 59:8, in which the "poor emigrants who were driven out of their homes and their possessions" are promised a share in the spoils.

Outside the Qurʾān, one finds numerous traditions praising the Quraysh, and their circulation was no doubt triggered by the fact that the caliphs of the Islamic state were all from the Quraysh (the four "righteous" caliphs, the Umayyads and the ʿAbbāsids; see CALIPH). Therefore these traditions were designed to provide the legitimate basis for the authority of the Qurashī caliphs, as well as to defy claims of other ambitious groups from within the Quraysh themselves (e.g. Shīʿīs), or of south Arabian descent, not to speak of the aspirations of non-Arab members of Islamic society (see COMMUNITY AND SOCIETY IN THE QURʾĀN; POLITICS AND THE QURʾĀN).

Uri Rubin

Bibliography

Primary: al-Balādhurī, Aḥmad b. Yaḥyā, *Jumal min ansāb al-ashrāf,* ed. S. Zakkār and R. Ziriklī, 13 vols., Beirut 1996; Ibn Isḥāq, *Sīra;* Muḥammad b. Ḥabīb, *Kitāb al-Muḥabbar,* ed. I. Lichtenstaedter, Hyderabad 1942; Suyūṭī, *Durr;* Ṭabarī, *Tafsīr;* al-Zubayrī, al-Muṣʿab b. ʿAbdallāh, *Nasab Quraysh,* ed. E. Levi-Provençal, Cairo 1953.

Secondary: P. Crone, *Meccan trade and the rise of Islam,* Princeton 1987; id. and M. Hinds, *God's caliph. Religious authority in the first centuries of Islam,* Cambridge 1986; F. Donner, Muḥammad's political consolidation in Arabia up to the conquest of Mecca, in *MW* 69 (1979), 229-47; G.R. Hawting, Al-Ḥudaybiyya and the conquest of Mecca. A reconsideration of the tradition about the Muslim takeover of the sanctuary, in *JSAI* 8 (1986), 1-23; M.J. Kister, Mecca and Tamīm, in *JESHO* 8 (1965), 113-63; id., Social and religious concepts of authority in Islam, in *JSAI* 18 (1994), 84-127; M. Muranyi, Die ersten Muslime von Mekka — soziale Basis einer neuen Religion? in *JSAI* 8 (1986), 25-36 (trans. The first Muslims in Mecca. A social basis for a new religion? in U. Rubin [ed.], *The life of Muḥammad,* Ashgate 1998, 95-104); T. Nagel, Some considerations concerning the pre-Islamic and the Islamic foundations of the authority of the caliphs, in G.H.A. Juynboll (ed.), *Studies on the first century of Islamic society,* Carbondale 1982, 177-97; F.E. Peters, The commerce of Mecca before Islam, in F. Kazemi and R.D. McChesney (eds.), *A way prepared. Essays on Islamic culture in honor of Richard Bayly Winder,* New York 1988, 3-26; U. Rubin, Abū Lahab and sūra CXI, in *BSOAS* 42 (1979), 13-28; id., Apocalypse and authority in Islamic tradition. The emergence of the Twelve Leaders, in *al-Qanṭara* 18 (1997), 11-42; id., *The eye of the beholder. The life of Muḥammad as viewed by the early Muslims,* Princeton 1995; id., Muḥammad's curse of Muḍar and the blockade of Mecca, in *JESHO* 31 (1988), 249-64; W.M. Watt, Ḳuraysh, in *EI²*, v, 434-5.

Qurayẓa (Banū al-)

One of the Jewish tribes of Medina and traditionally part of the triad that also includes the Banū Qaynuqāʿ (q.v.) and the Banū l-Naḍīr (see NAḌĪR [BANŪ AL-]). Although the origin of the Qurayẓa, like that of the other Medinan Jews, and their coming to Medina (q.v.) are not known with certainty, the sources provide some information concerning their role in pre-Islamic times. Thus, members of the Qurayẓa allegedly persuaded the Yemenite ruler Asʿad Abū Qarib not to attack Medina and caused him to convert to Judaism (see JEWS AND JUDAISM; YEMEN; PRE-ISLAMIC ARABIA AND THE QURʾĀN; SOUTH ARABIA, RELIGION IN PRE-ISLAMIC). Other reports state that in pre-Islamic Medina, the Qurayẓa were in constant conflict with their fellow tribe of the Banū l-Naḍīr (cf. Q 2:84 f.), yet both are often called "brothers" and commonly referred to as the "two Israelite tribes" *(al-sibṭān)* or the "two priest clans" *(al-kāhinān)*. In pre-Islamic poetry (see POETRY AND POETS), the Qurayẓa are variously mentioned, and the poems of their own members were, as it seems, collected in a (now lost) *Kitāb Banī Qurayẓa* (see Āmidī, *Muʾtalif*, 211). The area inhabitated by the Qurayẓa — and their sub-clans such as the Banū Kaʿb b. Qurayẓa and the Banū ʿAmr b. Qurayẓa — on the outer fringes of Medina, most notably the Wādī Mahzūr, can be assessed from geographical accounts, and a Medinan cemetery as well as a later mosque, built upon their land, were known by their name. Some details in the story of Salmān al-Fārisī suggest that the Qurayẓa had parental ties with the Jews of Wādī l-Qurā in the northern Ḥijāz.

The conflict of the Muslims with the Qurayẓa after the "Battle of the Ditch" in 5/627 is the most conspicuous story of the Prophet's dealing with the Medinan Jews in the prophetic biography tradition (*sīra;* see SĪRA AND THE QURʾĀN). The Muslim attack and siege of the Qurayẓa was a response to their open, probably active support of the Meccan pagans and their allies during that battle (see MECCA; POLYTHEISM AND ATHEISM; HYPOCRITES AND HYPOCRISY). After bloody fighting the Jews surrendered and the male members of the Qurayẓa were executed, the women and children taken captive and sold into slavery (see CAPTIVES; SLAVES AND SLAVERY); and the booty (q.v.) gained — money, weapons and land — were distributed among the Muslim fighters, according to most sources. The execution itself, during which between 400 and 900 men were killed, is largely undisputed in the Islamic sources and has aroused much dismay in the western perception of early Islam. It is not the Prophet himself, however, who is portrayed as having pronounced the condemnation but rather his Companion, Saʿd b. Muʿādh (see COMPANIONS OF THE PROPHET), who was fatally wounded by an arrow in the battle before this event took place. The qurʾānic passage commonly associated with these events is Q 33:26 f. (see EXPEDITIONS AND BATTLES; FIGHTING; BLOODSHED):

> And he brought down those of the People of the Book (q.v.) who supported them from their fortresses and cast terror in their hearts; some you slew, some you made captive. And he bequeathed upon you their lands, their habitations, and their possessions, and a land that you never trod; God is powerful over everything.

Rayḥāna l-Quraẓiyya, of uncertain parentage but most probably belonging to the Banū ʿAmr b. Qurayẓa, was captured after the Banū Qurayẓa episode. She then either became the Prophet's concubine or, according to many reports, was married to him and later divorced; she eventually died before the Prophet (see WIVES OF THE PROPHET; CONCUBINES). The Islamic tradition knows a number of descendants from the Qurayẓa by name, most famous among them being the traditionist Muḥammad b. Kaʿb al-Quraẓī, who was born a Muslim and died in Medina in 120/738 or some years before (see ḤADĪTH AND THE QURʾĀN). Others include his father Kaʿb b. Asad b. Sulaym and his brother Isḥāq, as well as ʿAṭiyya al-Quraẓī, al-Zubayr (?) b. ʿAbd al-Raḥmān b. al-Zabīr, ʿAlī b. Rifāʿa and the progeny of Abū Malik al-Quraẓī. This suggests that, in contrast to what is reported in the Islamic tradition, several male persons of the Qurayẓa did survive the conflict in Medina, probably because of their young age at the time.

Marco Schöller

Bibliography
Primary (All *sīra* writings provide information about the Qurayẓa; the "orthodox" version of events, adopted in most later sources, is that by Ibn Isḥāq. Much material contains works about the so-called "occasions of revelation" *[asbāb al-nuzūl]*, and further information is found in many Qurʾān commentaries: see in particular the classical works of *tafsīr* at Q 2:84 f., 214; 3:124 f.; 5:42, 51 f.; 8:27 f., 56 f.; 33:26 f. and 59:2 f. Additional notices are found in legal compendia, especially in the "war chapters," and ḥadīth collections. Even dictionaries [s.v. *q-r-ẓ*] and geographical writings yield interesting notices. On Rayḥāna al-Quraẓiyya see also writings on the Prophet's wives and concubines. The following is only a partial list of these works.): al-Āmidī, Abū l-Qāsim al-Ḥasan b. Bishr, *al-Muʾtalif wa-l-mukhtalif,* Cairo 1961, 211 (for the abovementioned *Kitāb Banī Qurayẓa*); al-Dimyāṭī, ʿAbd al-Muʾmin b. Khalaf, *Kitāb Nisāʾ rasūl Allāh,* ed. F. Saʿd, Beirut 1989 (on Rayḥāna al-Quraẓiyya); Ibn Durayd, *Kitāb Jamharat al-lugha,* 3 vols., Beirut 1987-8 (a dictionary); Ibn Isḥāq, *Sīra;* Ibn Isḥāq-Guillaume; Muḥibb al-Dīn al-Ṭabarī, *al-Simṭ al-thamīn fī manāqib ummahāt al-muʾminīn,* var. eds., e.g. Cairo 1996 (on Rayḥāna al-Quraẓiyya).
Secondary: W. Arafat, New light on the story of Banū Qurayẓa and the Jews of Medina, in *JRAS* n.s. (1976), 100-7; J. Bouman, *Der Koran und die Juden. Die Geschichte einer Tragödie,* Darmstadt 1990, 73 f.; M. Kister, The massacre of the Banū Qurayẓa. A reexamination of a tradition, in *JSAI* 8 (1986), 61-96; M. Lecker, *Jews and Arabs in pre- and early Islamic Arabia,* Aldershot 1998; id., *Muslims, Jews and pagans. Studies on early Islamic Medina,* Leiden 1995; id., Did Muḥammad conclude treaties with the Jewish tribes Naḍīr, Qurayẓa and Qaynuqāʿ? in *IOS* 17 (1997), 29-36; M. Schöller, *Exegetisches Denken und Prophetenbiographie. Eine quellenkritische Analyse der Sīra-Überlieferung zu Muḥammads Konflikt mit den Juden,* Wiesbaden 1998; W.M. Watt, The condemnation of the Jews of Banū Qurayẓah, in *MW* 42 (1952), 160-71; A.J. Wensinck, *Muhammad and the Jews of Medina,* trans. W.H. Behn, Berlin 1982[2].

R

Rabbi

see JEWS AND JUDAISM; SCHOLAR

Races

Persons or animals or plants connected by common descent. This concept emerges in the Qurʾān mainly in relationship with the glory (q.v.) of God who in his might was able to create a multitude of species upon earth (see CREATION; POWER AND IMPOTENCE). Thus in Q 36:36: "Glory be to him who created pairs of all things, of what the earth grows, and of their own kind and of what they do not know" (see GLORIFICATION OF GOD). The phrase "of what they do not know" is taken to refer to species unknown to humans. Similarly, in Q 20:53 God is praised (see PRAISE) for producing from the earth many species of various plants (see AGRICULTURE AND VEGETATION; GRASSES). Especially clear is Q 35:27-8, in which all colors of fruits and of men and beasts and cattle are adduced as signaling God's creative powers (see ANIMAL LIFE; NATURE AS SIGNS). In Q 30:22, the signs of God are manifest not only in the creation of humankind in many colors but also in the various languages that were given to them (see FOREIGN VOCABULARY; DIALECTS; PRE-ISLAMIC ARABIA AND THE QURʾĀN).

Apart from humans, the Qurʾān is also familiar with another species of intelligent creatures, namely the jinn (q.v.), i.e. demons (see DEVIL). God has created them of a flame of fire (q.v.; Q 15:27; 55:15) and they, like humans, are considered a "nation" (*umma,* as is the case in Q 7:38; 41:25; 46:18). Fire was also the origin of the creation of Iblīs (Q 38:74-6), who in Q 18:50 is considered one of the jinn, and has offspring. Some exegetes, however, take the allusion to his offspring in a metaphorical sense (see METAPHOR; EXEGESIS OF THE QURʾĀN: CLASSICAL AND MEDIEVAL).

In the celestial sphere, God has created the angelic species and in Q 35:1 God is praised for having made the angels "messengers [flying] on wings, two, and three, and four" (see ANGEL; FLYING). As for humans, God has subdivided them into peoples *(shuʿūb)* and tribes *(qabāʾil),* but their ethnic affiliation has no bearing on their moral status before God (see KINSHIP; TRIBES AND CLANS; ETHICS AND THE QURʾĀN; COMMUNITY AND SOCIETY IN THE QURʾĀN). They were thus divided only for the sake of identification, while the most honorable of them with God is the one most pious among them (Q 49:13; see PIETY). This particular statement was later adduced by the *shuʿūbiyya* in support of their struggle for equality between Arab and non-Arab races within Islamic society (see Enderwitz, Shuʿūbiyya).

Therefore, from the viewpoint of faith (q.v.), the Qurʾān considers all peoples as "one nation" *(umma wāḥida)*. This was the initial state of humankind till they began to differ and thereupon God sent prophets to guide them (Q 2:213; 10:19; see PROPHETS AND PROPHETHOOD; ASTRAY; ERROR). If God had pleased, he would have left all people in the state of "one nation" but he decided to try them and to guide only whomever he chose to (Q 5:48; 11:118; 16:93; 42:8; see TRIAL; FREEDOM AND PREDESTINATION). For this reason, Muḥammad's own scope of mission is not confined to one ethnic group but rather encompasses all humankind (Q 34:28) as well as the jinn (Q 46:29). Muslim tradition has elaborated on this idea, stating that Muḥammad was the only prophet who was not sent just to his own people but rather "to all red and black." The latter expression was explained as referring to the jinn and the humans, respectively (cf. Goldziher, *Introduction*, 28, with note 34).

On the other hand, the Qurʾān does acknowledge genealogical descent as indicating excellence but this is confined mainly to prophets. The Qurʾān sees in them a chosen pedigree as indicated in Q 3:33-4. Here God is said to have chosen Adam (see ADAM AND EVE) and Noah (q.v.) and the descendants of Abraham (q.v.) and the descendants of ʿImrān (q.v.) above the nations, they being offspring one of the other (see ELECTION; CHILDREN OF ISRAEL).

As for the offspring of Abraham, the Qurʾān identifies them as the inhabitants of Mecca (q.v.) — i.e. the Quraysh (q.v.) — which is implied, for example, in Q 2:127-8: Here Abraham as well as Ishmael (q.v.) are engaged in the building of the "house," the Kaʿba (q.v.; see also HOUSE, DOMESTIC AND DIVINE), and ask God to raise from their offspring a nation submitting to him (*umma muslima;* see BELIEF AND UNBELIEF; OBEDIENCE; ISLAM). The presence of Ishmael was taken as indicating that by *umma muslima* only Arabs (q.v.) were meant (see Suyūṭī, *Durr,* ad Q 2:128). More accurately, Ishmael is regarded mainly as the ancestor of the northern Arabs, including the Quraysh.

In fact, Arabian consciousness is manifest also in verses noting that the Qurʾān was revealed in Arabic (see ARABIC LANGUAGE). This is stated with evident pride, while stressing that it is not *aʿjamī,* i.e. "non-Arab" or "foreign" (e.g. Q 16:103). This is part of the general idea that "God did not send any apostle but with the language of his people" (Q 14:4). Traditions adduced by the exegetes for this verse assert that the Qurʾān was revealed in the language of Quraysh.

Uri Rubin

Bibliography
Primary: Ibn Ḥazm, *Jamharat ansāb al-ʿarab,* ed. ʿA. Hārūn, Cairo 1962; Suyūṭī, *Durr;* Ṭabarī, *Tafsīr.*
Secondary: F. Buhl, Fasste Muḥammed seine Verkündigung als eine universelle, auch für Nichtaraber bestimmte Religion auf? in *Islamica* 2 (1926/27), 135-49; S. Enderwitz, al-Shuʿūbiyya, in *EI²*, ix, 513-6; I. Goldziher, *Introduction to Islamic theology and law,* trans. A. and R. Hamori, Princeton 1981 (trans. of *Vorlesungen über den Islam*); B. Lewis, *Race and color in Islam,* New York 1971.

Raḥmān see GOD AND HIS ATTRIBUTES

Raid(s) see WAR; EXPEDITIONS AND BATTLES

Rain see WEATHER; WATER; SUSTENANCE; AGRICULTURE AND VEGETATION; NATURE AS SIGNS; GRACE; BLESSING

Ramaḍān

The ninth month of the Islamic calendar, during which Muslims fast from sunrise to sunset and commemorate the revelation of the Qurʾān to Muḥammad. To understand Ramaḍān as a crucial scriptural and ritual issue in a major world religion, it is useful to look at its emergence and liturgical enactments from a comparative perspective (see SCRIPTURE AND THE QURʾĀN; RITUAL AND THE QURʾĀN). It is obvious that, in phenomenological terms, three historically interrelated festivals — Pesach (Passover), Easter and Ramaḍān — display a close relation to acts of violence (q.v.) in that each celebrates a community's salvation from a threat of annihilation (see JEWS AND JUDAISM; CHRISTIANS AND CHRISTIANITY; CHILDREN OF ISRAEL; PEOPLE OF THE BOOK). Although this experience of violence played a foundational role in the identity formation of the respective communities, the feasts that commemorate the events are enacted in all three communities by rites of fulfillment: communal meals preceded by ascetic practices (see ASCETICISM) or fasting, performances that contribute substantially to affirming the coherence of the community (Neuwirth, Three religious feasts). To elucidate the interrelation between the celebrations, a brief historical survey of the three feasts and their etiologies will be given, followed by an evaluation of the qurʾānic evidence about fasting (i.e. prior to the establishment of the fast of Ramaḍān), its rulings and successive stages of development, as well as the role played by earlier religious structures in shaping it. In order to shed light on the religious meaning of Ramaḍān that emerged in the early community, we will then look into the complex etiology of that institution, focusing on its commemorative character (see FESTIVALS AND COMMEMORATIVE DAYS). The final section of this article presents some reflections on the impact of Ramaḍān on the perception of salvation history (see HISTORY AND THE QURʾĀN).

Predecessors, interrelations

Passover (Heb. *pesaḥ*), a spring festival corresponding to the pre-Islamic *ʿumra* (see PILGRIMAGE), constitutes a merger of two originally independent feasts (cf. *Encyclopaedia Judaica*, xiii, 169 f.). One was *pesaḥ*, originally not a pilgrimage feast but a domestic ceremony celebrated by transient breeders of sheep or goats (and, later, by the Israelites) to secure protection for the flocks before leaving the desert winter pasture for cultivated regions. This consisted of the slaughtering and eating of the paschal animal on the fourteenth day of the first month of the year, and the rite of touching the lintel and the doorposts of the house — or formerly the tent — with blood from the paschal animal. The oldest literary record of this domestic ceremony, which appears in the context of the last plague, the killing of the Egyptian firstborn (Exodus 12:21), already presupposes the Passover, i.e. the notion of the divine "overleaping" (Heb. *pesaḥ*) of the houses marked by the apotropaeic staining with blood. This historicization has determined the character of the Passover: it became the feast commemorating the exodus of the Israelites from Egypt. The other feast that was incorporated into the Jewish Passover is the seven-day "feast of unleavened bread" *(ḥagg ha-maṣṣōt),* which was celebrated in the same month as the slaughter and eating of the paschal animal and was, unlike the Passover, probably taken over from the Canaanites. It was a seasonal festival connected with a pilgrimage, and celebrated to consecrate the first parts of the harvest. Unleavened bread has been identified as a symbol of the interruption between two cycles of harvest — leavens from the grain of the old harvest not being allowed to enter into the first bread made from the new harvest (Rendtorff, Entwicklung). It was integrated into the feast of deliverance from Egyptian bondage by re-interpreting the motive for the preparation of unleavened bread as the hastened exodus of the people who had no time left for them to prepare proper bread.

Violence, divinely inflicted "in history" on the enemy (for the interpretation of similar themes in the qur'ānic milieu, see JIHĀD; FIGHTING; ENEMIES; PUNISHMENT STORIES; CHASTISEMENT AND PUNISHMENT), is thus, through the ritual act of spilling blood, connected with the primordial custom of sacrificing in a seasonal framework. Though etiologically justified as a measure to induce a stubborn enemy of the Israelites to allow them to leave the land, it retains its cosmic imagery serving to mark the renewal of a particular time of the year. *Pesaḥ* thus developed from its ritual beginnings as part of the seasonal cycle and became a feast commemorating an event significant for salvation history.

Easter is already closely linked to Passover externally in terms of timing, being the commemoration of an event that took place in the Passover week. Insofar as Easter claims Passover as its temporal and ceremonial backdrop, the Jewish festival confers on the later feast important traits bearing ritual and symbolic significance: a vicarious sacrifice, a commemorative meal and the remembrance of an event of deliverance. But Easter — which was celebrated in the early church on the date of Passover — also raises the additional claim of being the new Passover. Through a mythic re-interpretation, it has become the Passover par excellence: Deliverance from servitude in history is eclipsed by deliverance from the servitude of the fear of death; the sacrificial lamb to be slaughtered is replaced by the Son of God who was sacrificed, a connection established early in Christian sources like the Gospel of John and a large corpus of hymns. The notion of the sacrificial lamb's vicarious suffering of death merges with the idea of a father sacrificing his beloved son — prefigured in Abraham's (q.v.) sacrifice (q.v.).

The relation between Passover and Ramaḍān is less obvious. No line of genetic relationship can be drawn with certainty, nor has a mythicization of the earlier feast taken place in the later; the relation is rather one of analogy. Both feasts share a number of basic notions leading back into the earliest historical layers of the festivals. Ramaḍān, the Muslim month of fasting commemorating the revelation of the Qur'ān (see REVELATION AND INSPIRATION), is, like Passover, grafted on a seasonal festival, the *jāhilī* (see AGE OF IGNORANCE; PRE-ISLAMIC ARABIA AND THE QUR'ĀN) pilgrimage of the *ʿumra,* which, prior to Islam, took place in the month of Rajab (Wellhausen, *Reste,* revised by Wagtendonk, *Fasting in the Koran;* see also FASTING; MONTHS; SEASONS). The *ʿumra* was a festival of spring thanksgiving, the time of slaughtering sacrificial animals (*atāʾir;* see SACRIFICE; CONSECRATION OF ANIMALS) and the first born of the flocks and herds, somewhat like *pesaḥ;* still it is difficult to determine any genetic link between the festivals. The ritual practices of the *ʿumra* survived into early Islam, but — being perceived as obsolete — were abolished by the caliphs Abū Bakr and ʿUmar (Kister, Rajab; see CALIPH), the *ʿumra* as such having been integrated into the *ḥajj* already by the Prophet. Also like *pesaḥ* — which culminates in a particular night of the seven-day festival — the climax of the month of the *ʿumra* was a particular night, presumably that which the Qurʾān calls *laylat al-qadr*, the "night of decision" (see NIGHT OF POWER). Prepared for by a period of abstention and devotion (*ʿukūf* and *wuqūf*; see ABSTINENCE; PIETY; PRAYER; VIGILS), this night appears to have marked a kind of New Year, the opening of a new cycle of events, similar to the notion underlying the *ḥagg ha-maṣṣōt* which opened a new harvest cycle, and like the New Year, was associated with the sacrifice of a *pesaḥ* lamb (*Exod* 12:3; see below for the connection between qurʾānic [pre-Ramaḍān] fasting and Yom Kippur, the Jewish "day of atonement"; see also ATONEMENT). It may likewise be compared with the Easter vigil which, since the early days of the church, has presented itself as a cosmic and spiritual New Year, declaring the spiritual renewal of creation and the moral new beginning of humankind. The *laylat al-qadr* as well as the fasting period that preceded it were transferred from Rajab into Ramaḍān, once Ramaḍān was identified as the month in which a religiously momentous experience of the community took place. Thus, the pre-Islamic seasonal festival with its ascetic preparations preceding sacrifice was reshaped to become a new salvation-historical scriptural festival with diverse procedures of commemoration. The development re-enacts the emergence of Passover, a feast of scriptural memory, out of a previous seasonal feast involving sacrifice. It mirrors at the same time Christianity's sublimation of sacrifice through its substitution by a commemorative rite.

The qurʾānic evidence: Rulings and developments of pre-Ramaḍān fasting (Q 2:183-6)

It was the precedent of the fast practiced by the Jews in Medina (q.v.) that triggered the process of the introduction of fasting into the ritual rulings of the early Muslim community. Though fasting had been ranked prominently in Rajab before Islam, this had not been sanctioned by a qurʾānic ruling. We know nothing certain about the ascetic rites upheld by the adherents of Muḥammad in Mecca (q.v.). The particular rhetorical style and the explicit reference to the monotheistic forebears in Q 2:183 mark the verse about the first Islamic fast as a text belonging to the Medinan period (see CHRONOLOGY AND THE QURʾĀN; FORM AND STRUCTURE OF THE QURʾĀN). Fasting was raised to the rank of a monotheistic duty: "Oh believers, fasting is prescribed for you as it was for those before you; perchance you will guard yourselves [against evil]" (Q 2:183).

It is not known whether this ruling was implemented immediately with the emigration (q.v.; *hijra*) of Muḥammad from Mecca to Medina, whose cardinal event — the arrival of the Prophet and his Companions (see COMPANIONS OF THE PROPHET) in Medina — is reported to have coincided with the Jewish Yom Kippur, a day of fasting which falls on the tenth of the first month of the Jewish calendar, Tishri (*Lev* 16:29). A well-known tradition going back to Ibn ʿAbbās (d. 68/686-8; see ḤADĪTH AND THE QURʾĀN) presents the earliest Islamic fast as a Yom Kippur fast: At the arrival of the Prophet in Medina, the Medinan Jews, who were celebrating the Day of Atonement, Yom Kippur (Aramaic *ʿāsōrā*, Arabic *ʿāshūrāʾ*), with their strict observation of the highly demanding rites — fasting over a twenty-four hour period, liturgical recitations (Elbogen, *Jewish liturgy*, 124 f.) — attracted the attention of the newly arrived Muslims. Asked about the meaning of their celebration, they mentioned the Israelites' deliverance from Pharaoh (q.v.). This Mosaic etiology must have been significant to the Muslim newcomers, who perceived themselves as continuing the Mosaic tradition (see Neuwirth, Erzählen). Muḥammad is reported to have said: "We have a better right to Moses (q.v.) than they have" (Ṭabarī, *Taʾrikh*, iii, 1281; id., *History*, vii, 26; Muslim, *Ṣaḥīḥ*, ii, 1330, 149-50; but not found in Ṭabarī's *Tafsīr*) and to have imposed the fast on his community. The fasting of ʿĀshūrāʾ is, however, not always identified in Islamic tradition with the one imposed in Q 2:183, but is in some ḥadīths rather remembered as one "ordered" by the Prophet *(yaʾmurunā bi-ṣiyāmihi)* because the Jews — in general, or of Khaybar, or the Jews and the Christians — were keeping it. There is even a tradition stressing Muḥammad's view that "God had not prescribed it" for the Muslims (*lam yaktubi llāhu ʿalaykum ṣiyāmahu;* Muslim, *Ṣaḥīḥ*, ii, 153). The fasting of ʿĀshūrāʾ, thus, was one of the diverse Jewish rites that were introduced during the emergence of the community, but were given up during the later Medinan period. Indeed, it became the object of polemics once the community wished to distance itself from its monotheistic counterparts (see POLEMIC AND POLEMICAL LANGUAGE; RELIGIOUS PLURALISM AND THE QURʾĀN).

The Mosaic reference that is said to have so immediately appealed to the Muslim newcomers' religious consciousness is not without implications. It is true that the etiology for the Jewish fast is not exactly the historical one. But, as Wagtendonk *(Fasting)* has emphasized, Mosaic memories do play a role in the service of the feast, particularly the second giving of the tablets of the law to Moses. Goitein (Ramadan) has also drawn attention to the striking fact that the qurʾānic section on the Ramaḍān rulings (Q 2:183-7) includes an unambiguous reference to one of the most prominent liturgical elements of the Yom Kippur penitential litanies (*selīḥōt;* Elbogen, *Jewish liturgy*, 180-2), particular prayers that frequently end in the plea, *anēnū*, "answer us" (cf. Psalm 20:10). The qurʾānic version reads: "When my servants question you about me, [tell them that] I am near. I answer the prayer of the suppliant when he calls to me; therefore let them answer my call and put their trust in me, that they may be rightly guided" (Q 2:186; see ASTRAY; ERROR). This verse does not smoothly connect with its immediate halakhic context but it strikingly switches from the section's prevalent addressee — a group of receivers or listeners *(antum)* — to addressing the Prophet. The Prophet is instructed to remind his followers *(ʿibād)* of the closeness and faithfulness of the divine sender, which sounds like an indirect exhortation to utter prayers, perhaps like those of the Jewish service, where penitential litanies *(selīḥōt)* are recited. These litanies are built on the so-called "thirteen attributes" (i.e. divine attributes, like "lord, merciful, compassionate," etc.) that were revealed to Moses when he received the second set of tablets (cf. *Exod* 34:6-7): "The lord, the lord, God, merciful and gracious, long-suffering and abundant in goodness and truth, keeping mercy for thousands, forgiving sin and transgression, seeking the iniquity of the fathers on the children and upon the children's children until the third and fourth generation." Early on, Jewish tradition interpreted that event in terms of a divine instruction to Moses on how to perform the penitential prayer: "God showed Moses the order of prayer. He said to him, 'Whenever Israel sins, let them perform this rite before me and I shall forgive them'; 'There is a covenant that the Thirteen Attributes do not return unanswered'" (*Babylonian Talmud*, Rosh Hashana 17b). This Talmudic conception explains how the "thirteen attributes" became the nucleus of all prayers for atonement; to this day, they serve as a refrain constantly repeated in all the *selīḥōt* (cf. Elbogen, *Jewish liturgy*, 177 f.). When viewed from this intertextual perspective, the qurʾānic verse about the attitude to be adopted during the fast and which paraphrases two of the "thirteen attributes" (Q 2:186), refers to the very heart of the Yom Kippur liturgy (cf. Neuwirth, Meccan texts). It is noteworthy that Ṣūfī exegesis of Q 2:186 further elaborates the aspect of the divine attributes in the verse (see e.g. Sulamī, *Ziyādāt,* 16; see GOD AND HIS ATTRIBUTES; ṢŪFISM AND THE QURʾĀN; EXEGESIS OF THE QURʾĀN: CLASSICAL AND MEDIEVAL).

Thus, the first form of religiously imposed fasting in Islam was originally a custom shared with the Jews. The Islamic assimilation of the Jewish ritual remained, however, limited. The central performance in the Jewish service of the fast, the communal confession of sins, seems not to have been introduced into the Islamic sphere with the acceptance of the ʿĀshūrāʾ fast (see SIN, MAJOR AND MINOR; VIRTUES AND VICES, COMMANDING AND FORBIDDING). A genuine ceremony devoted principally to communal confession has never developed in Sunnī Islam nor is there a fixed form of individual confession such as Christianity has cherished over the ages and which in modern time has translated into new kinds of secular self-inquiring (see Hahn, Zur Soziologie). The fast of ʿĀshūrāʾ, however, was never completely abolished: the tenth of Muḥarram, which corresponds to the date of the Jewish Yom Kippur, was retained as a voluntary fast day in Sunnī Islam (Muslim, *Ṣaḥīḥ,* ii, 147-9). It was only in the Shīʿī tradition, however, that ʿĀshūrāʾ recovered, in the course of time, its original character as a ceremony of repentance (see REPENTANCE AND PENANCE) and atonement. The tenth of Muḥarram became a festival commemorating the martyrdom that the grandson of the Prophet, al-Ḥusayn b. ʿAlī, suffered at Karbalāʾ in 61/680 (see MARTYRS; SHĪʿISM AND THE QURʾĀN; ʿALĪ B. ABĪ ṬĀLIB; FAMILY OF THE PROPHET; PEOPLE OF THE HOUSE). As Gerald Hawting (The tawwābūn) has shown, the proto-Shīʿī group of the *tawwābūn,* "penitents" — in whose thinking atonement and expiation were prominent, and who in 65/685 revolted against the Umayyads in order to expunge their guilt for forsaking Ḥusayn — may, when they sacrificed themselves, have been under the spell of the solemn atmosphere of the prominent day in the Jewish calendar.

The earliest qurʾānic injunction maintains that fasting was to be observed for several — probably ten — days (*ayyām maʿdūdāt,* Q 2:184) but the month is not made explicit. The concept of "counted days" *(ayyām maʿdūdāt)* appears Arabian. A reference to a sacred time-period, again presumably "ten," is found in a very early qurʾānic text (Q 89:2 *wa-layālin ʿashrin,* "By the ten nights"), which is usually understood as referring to the first ten days of the *ḥajj* (see PILGRIMAGE). It is thus likely that in Q 2:184 an existing Arabian religious period was revived. Wagtendonk *(Fasting)* argues that the *iʿtikāf* period in Rajab "was chosen for the fast of the 'counted days' because the Night of Destiny *(laylat al-qadr)* with which the revelation of the Qurʾān was connected, occurred during it." That night, originally falling on the twenty-seventh of Rajab, had been celebrated in an early sūra (Q 97) as a unique night excelling over other time periods (see DAY AND NIGHT; DAY, TIMES OF), a night when communication between heaven (see HEAVEN AND SKY) and earth (q.v.) moves easily; it is presented as the night of revelation par excellence:

Behold we sent it down in the night of decision
And what shall teach you what is the night of decision?

The night of decision is better than a thousand months,
In it the angels (see ANGEL) and the spirit (q.v.; see also HOLY SPIRIT) descend
By the leave of their lord (q.v.), upon every command
Peace it is, till the rising of dawn (q.v.; Q 97:1-5)

This particular night, characterized as a "blessed night" *(layla mubāraka),* is further referred to in a later Meccan sūra (Q 44:3-6), where it is described as a time in which "every wise precept is made plain, distinct" (*fīhā yufraqu kullu amrin ḥakīm,* Q 44:4). The two texts are the exclusive qurʾānic testimonies for the temporal setting of revelation within the calendar (q.v.) of the year. The Qurʾān alludes to the affinity between sacred time (q.v.) and revelation; the particular night is a time when the borderlines between the heavenly and earthly domains are permeable (Q 97:4; cf. al-Miṣrī, *Ramaḍān;* Ṭūqān, *Riḥla,* 18-9; id., *Mountainous journey,* 16-21). It is also a time of divine separating or distinguishing *(yufraqu)* between good and evil (q.v.), and is thus closely related to Yom Kippur, when the divine decision is made concerning the fate (q.v.; see also DESTINY) of individuals for the following year (Q 44:4). The Qurʾān itself can, as such, be regarded as a divine intervention (*furqān,* Q 17:106; see CRITERION; NAMES OF THE QURʾĀN), although it is not explicitly labeled *furqān* before the Medinan period (Q 25:1; 3:4). The noun *furqān,* etymologically an Aramaic loan word from *purqānā,* "salvation" (see FOREIGN VOCABULARY), is not yet a synonym for revelation in the Meccan sūras; rather, it is used in one Meccan sūra (Q 21:48) to denote an historical event, the salvation of the Children of Israel by the separation of the Red Sea (cf. Q 2:50).

If Rajab was the month in which the initial Islamic practice of fasting took place, then the etiology of this fast has to be related to both the momentous aura of the *laylat al-qadr* as a time of divine decrees and to the event of the qurʾānic revelation (Q 97:1; cf. 44:3). This complex etiology was to be transferred to the fasting of Ramaḍān in due time.

The imposition of the "counted days" fast is followed immediately by an alleviating amendment:

Fast a certain number of days,
But if any one of you is ill or on a journey let him fast a similar number of days
And for those that can afford it there is a ransom
The feeding of a poor man (see POVERTY AND THE POOR).
He that does good of his own accord shall be well rewarded (see REWARD AND PUNISHMENT)
But to fast is better for you,
If you but knew it (Q 2:184).

The ruling is made easy: not only are sick persons and travelers (see ILLNESS AND HEALTH; JOURNEY) exempted from keeping the fast but those unable to sustain the fast may ransom themselves with a charitable deed *(fidya).* In Wagtendonk's (Fasting, 182) view, the text betrays "the same uncertainty as that which accompanied the change of *qibla* (q.v.)."

Rulings and developments concerning Ramaḍān

The text then switches abruptly to the introduction of Ramaḍān (Q 2:185) as a full month of fasting. The verse that replaces the earlier, less demanding ruling of the "counted days" has been understood in the Muslim tradition (Ṭabarī, *Tafsīr,* iii, 420) as an abrogation (q.v.) of the previous institution (see for the problematics, Radtke, *Offenbarung*). The text also puts forward a new etiology for the fast, alluding to both the sending down of the Qurʾān (as in

Q 97:1; here, however, designated *furqān;* cf. its indirect classification as such in Q 17:106) and an experience of deliverance (a notion equally conveyed by the term *furqān*), although the Qurʾān does not explicitly name the particular historical event: "The month of Ramaḍān in which the *qurʾān* was sent down as a guidance for humankind and proofs of the guidance and of the *furqān*" (Q 2:185).

Although some commentators (Ṭabarī, *Tafsīr,* iii, 415-7), followed by Goitein (Ramadan), hold that the implementation of a whole month of fasting is no more than the extension of the already prescribed fasting, Wagtendonk seems right in considering that the emphatic mention of Ramaḍān in the verse suggests an innovation. Moreover, the double excellence attributed to the month is new, consisting of the event of the revelation, *furqān,* and simultaneously of the occurrence of the guidance and the salvation (again, *furqān*). The homonymous use of that word is striking; as Wagtendonk has realized, "we see here the subordination of the *furqān* to the Qurʾān instead of the juxtaposition of book and *furqān* or the identification of both found elsewhere. It is as if the notion of *furqān* was essential but, at the same time, the priority of the sending down of the revelation had to be maintained by all means" (Fasting, 183). The complex use made of the word *furqān* presents an enigma that is not solvable based on the section that deals with fasting alone.

Again, instructions are given about the performance of the fast, which no longer permit the *fidya:*

Whosoever of you is present in that month, let him fast.
But he who is ill or on a journey shall fast a similar number of days.
God desires your well being, not your discomfort.
He desires you to fast the whole month so that you may magnify him for giving you his guidance
and render thanks to him (Q 2:185; see GLORIFICATION OF GOD; LAUDATION; GRATITUDE AND INGRATITUDE).

The extended length of the new commandment of fasting is counter-balanced by alleviation:

It is lawful for you (see LAWFUL AND UNLAWFUL) to go to your wives on the night of the fast;
they are a comfort to you as you are to them.
God knew that you were deceiving yourselves
and he has turned in mercy (q.v.) towards you and relieved you.
Therefore you may now go to them
and seek what God has ordained for you (see CHASTITY; SEX AND SEXUALITY).
Eat and drink until you can tell the white thread
from the black one in the light of dawn.
Then resume the fast till nightfall
and do not approach them,
when you stay at your prayers in the mosques (see MOSQUE).
These are the bounds set by God (see BOUNDARIES AND PRECEPTS).
Do not come near them.
Thus he makes known his revelations to humankind
that they may guard themselves against evil (Q 2:187).

The amendment in Q 2:187 clearly comes to rectify the first fasting rulings which must have been extremely severe, extending over full day and night periods and imposing strict sexual abstention. They must have proved difficult to observe and thus had to be alleviated. Strikingly, the ruling to start the fast at daybreak (Q 2:187) clearly reveals its Jewish origin. Its demand that believers start to fast once they can distinguish the white thread from the black thread reflects a Jewish practice in determining the time of the beginning of the fast: by using the black and white threads of the prayer shawl of the male worshiper as a criterion. The reference to the prayer shawl, a characteristic liturgical requisite of Jewish worship, which has no reasonable place in non-Jewish imagination and remains unmentioned in qurʾānic commentary, can only be understood as reflecting information provided by Jews on the matter of when exactly fasting should begin.

Ramaḍān — the month of an event of salvation in history

In order to solve the enigma of the etiology for the Ramaḍān fast, Wagtendonk *(Fasting)* has proposed drawing on Q 8:41 f., where the word *furqān* is used to refer to the victory in the battle of Badr (q.v.) on 17 Ramaḍān 2/623. The qurʾānic text that commemorates this battle (Q 8:41-4; see EXPEDITIONS AND BATTLES) is prefaced by a recapitulation of the history preceding the decisive new development and an exhortation to remember it (see EXHORTATIONS). It is at once a reckoning with the Meccan foes, whose persecution of the community that could have led to its annihilation is recorded. Against that, the believers (see BELIEF AND UNBELIEF) are reassured of the long expected "deliverance" *(furqān)* that has been finally granted. This text is strongly text-referential and summarizes the predicament described in the sūras of the Meccan period, while also recalling biblical records. Q 8:29, moreover, paraphrases, as Wagtendonk *(Fasting)* has observed, a particular biblical text related to Passover: "Have no fear, stand firm and you will see what YHWH will do to save you today" (*Exod* 14:13; the Hebrew *yeshūʿah* corresponds to Aramaic *purqānā;* Arabic *furqān*). The section as a whole reminds one strongly of a similarly retrospective summary of divine support granted to the Israelites, particularly their salvation through their exodus (*Deut* 26:5-9, a text which is part of the Pesach Haggada and thus is recited in the framework of the Passover celebration). Although it is impossible to ascertain that *Deut* 26:5-9 was part of the Passover ceremony at the time and place of the emergence of the Qurʾān, it should be adduced here since it conveys, typologically, a recollection of salvation from tribulation strikingly similar to that of Q 8:26-46:

A wandering Aramaean was my father, and he went down into Egypt, and sojourned there few in number. And he became there a nation, great, mighty and populous. And the Egyptians dealt ill with us and afflicted us and laid upon us hard bondage. And we cried unto the lord, the God of our fathers and the lord heard our voice, and saw our afflictions and our toil and our oppression. And the lord brought us forth out of Egypt with a mighty hand and with an outstretched arm and with great terribleness, and with signs and with wonders.

The idea that a divine act of salvation has to be remembered is the dominant idea of the biblical story of the Israelite exodus; its liturgical re-enactments have woven a dense meta-text of memory recalling the divine salvation of the Israelites throughout their entire history (see Yerushalmi, *Zakhor*). The notion of a miraculous deliverance, which is central to the Jewish Passover story, also prevails in the qurʾānic story of the victory at Badr that brought about a divine decision *(f-r-q)*. The term *furqān* has thus, in this context, acquired new meaning. Used in earlier qurʾānic texts to denote divine revelation — received by Muḥammad (paraphrased in Q 17:106) — as well as divine salvation from threatening foes in history — as experienced by Moses during the Exodus (Q 2:53), it has now come to denote the deliverance of the Muslim community in their contemporary history (see OPPOSITION TO MUḤAMMAD). Q 8:44 conveys this understanding: the event of Badr is perceived as a grave worldly trial, displaying a strong eschatological awareness. The remembrance of the *furqān*, the deliverance or salvation, has become an article of faith (q.v.; Q 8:41). It is the miraculous deliverance from the fear inflicted by overwhelming enemies understood as achieved not by a victorious army but by divine intervention that is a reminder of the equally miraculous escape of the people of Moses during their exodus from Egypt (q.v.).

Liturgical enactments

Jan Assmann (Der zweidimensionale Mensch) has emphasized that people are "destined to live in two worlds. Life cannot be limited to everyday life. Feasts are needed to counterbalance daily routine. They have to provide spaces where the other that is excluded from the daily routine can occur. The other, however, does not occur by itself, but has to be staged, it has to be enacted." The enactments of Passover — synagogue services and a ritual meal, the *seder* ceremony — and Easter — church services and the mystical meal of the Eucharist — rely on scriptural texts that have been preserved in a mythicized form, and those events are commemorated at the feast. The scriptural readings not only form a sequence of accounts communicated roughly in the chronological order of the events they relate, but are also bound to particular times held sacred by the listeners. Yerushalmi (*Zakhor*, 42) has stressed that two temporalities are involved: "The historical events… remain unique and irreversible. Psychologically, however, those events are experienced cyclically, repetitively, and to that extent at least, atemporally." The events thus "occur" each time the congregation assembles, history being dramatized. There is "a synchronic reading and experiencing in the cult which is yielded by a metaphorization or symbolization of the events of history, so that they never lose their actuality for all generations" (Lacocque, Apocalyptic symbolism, 6-15).

In Islam, in contrast, there is no special qurʾānic reading for Ramaḍān to be recited in the service of the *ʿīd al-fiṭr* (the feast that concludes the month of fasting), or in the *laylat al-qadr* (celebrated on the twenty-seventh of Ramaḍān), or during the many religious gatherings in the mosque or at home (that take place particularly during the last ten days of the month, the *iʿtikāf* period). This striking fact is not a historical coincidence and can be explained by a tendency inherent in the texts themselves: a strong, generally-held reservation about a mythic reading of biblical or contemporary events (see Neuwirth, Qurʾān, crisis and memory). Neither the rulings about fasting (Q 2:183-7) nor the story of the battle of Badr (Q 8:41-4) presents a mythopoeic version of the events, shaped dramatically enough to turn the event into a cosmic turning point (see MYTHS AND LEGENDS IN THE QURʾĀN) — save perhaps the short qurʾānic text about *laylat al-qadr* (Q 97:1-5), which dwells on an already given cosmic event. The historical events are overshadowed by the single fact of election (q.v.), manifest in revelation itself. Thus, the Qurʾān in its entirety *(khātima)* is supposed to be recited during Ramaḍān — according to tradition, it is for this very reason that the corpus has been divided into thirty equally long parts (*juzʾ*, pl. *ajzāʾ*) and seven portions (*manzila*, pl. *manāzil*), permitting it to be recited on a daily or a weekly basis (see MANUSCRIPTS OF THE QURʾĀN; CODICES OF THE QURʾĀN). This Islamic option implies that the function of salvation history is viewed differently: Whereas the two older religions review the process of their salvation history as a narrative running parallel to their real experienced history, Islam does not focus on the narrative of its emergence but commemorates exclusively one event: the revelation of the Qurʾān to Muḥammad. The fact that the Qurʾān is recited by the individual believer, who thus passes God's "personal" words over his lips and reproduces them through his voice, is in itself a "representation" of Muḥammad's receiving the words. The presence of the divine speaker, or the transcendent "author," of the text could hardly be imagined as ever being closer to the senses than during this kind of commemoration. One might duly speak of a re-enactment of the "first divine communication," a text perceived as superhuman being recited in a "supernatural" performance. Qurʾān recitation and frequent prayer, particularly the *tarāwīḥ* practice — forty continuously performed sequences of *ṣalāt* — translate the pious feeling of the gates of heaven being opened during Ramāḍan into practice. Communication is sought not only with the living but also with the dead (for *ziyārat al-maqābir*, see Nabhan, *Das Fest;* for the *ruʾyat al-hilāl* and other cosmic determinations of time, see Lech, *Geschichte des islamischen Kultus;* see DEATH AND THE DEAD; BURIAL). The alternating of fasting and feasting, the particular prominence given to the family meal in which the single days of fasting culminate, strongly enhances social coherence. Like the *seder* meal held on Passover and the Eucharist given after the Easter vigil, the *ifṭār* meal concluding the day of fasting affirms the overcoming of crisis and turns the memory of suffering (q.v.) into fulfillment.

Angelika Neuwirth

Bibliography

Primary: Muslim, *Ṣaḥīḥ;* Sulamī, *Ziyādāt;* Ṭabarī, *Tafsīr,* ed. Shākir; id., *Taʾrīkh,* ed. de Goeje; trans. M.V. McDonald, *The history of al-Ṭabarī.* vii. *The foundation of the community,* Albany 1987.

Secondary: J. Assmann (ed.), *Religiöse Kontrapunkte zur Alltagswelt. Das Fest und das Heilige. Studien zum Verstehen fremder Religionen,* Gütersloh 1991 (esp. Assmann's "Der zweidimensionale Mensch. Das Fest als Medium des kollektiven Gedächtnisses"); I. Elbogen, *Der jüdische Gottesdienst in seiner geschichtlichen Entwicklung,* Frankfurt am Main 1931; trans. R.P. Scheindlin, *Jewish liturgy. A comprehensive history,* New York/Jerusalem 1993; *Encyclopaedia Judaica,* Jerusalem 1973; S.D. Goitein, Ramadan. The Muslim month of fasting, in id., *Studies in Islamic history and institutions,* Leiden 1966, 90-100; Graham, *Beyond;* G.E. von Grunebaum, *Muhammedan festivals,* New York 1951; A. Hahn, Zur Soziologie der Beichte und anderer Formen institutionalisierter Bekenntnisse. Selbstthematisierung und Zivilisationsprozess, in *Kölner Zeitschrift für Soziologie und Sozialpsychologie* 3 (1982), 407-34; G.R. Hawting, The tawwābūn, atonement and ʿĀshūrāʾ, in *JSAI* 17 (1995), 166-81; M.J. Kister, Rajab is the month of God, in *IOS* 1 (1971), 191-223; A. Lacocque, Apocalyptic symbolism. A Ricoeurian hermeneutical approach, in *Biblical research* 26 (1981), 6-15; E.W. Lane, *Manners and customs of the modern Egyptians,* London 1836, repr. The Hague/London/Cairo 1985; K. Lech, *Geschichte des islamischen Kultus.* i. *Das ramaḍān-Fasten,* Wiesbaden 1979; Ph. Marcais, ʿĀshūrāʾ, in *EI²*, i, 705; H. Maṣrī, *Ramaḍān fī l-shiʿr al-ʿarabī wa-l-fārisī wa-l-turkī,* Cairo n.d.; L. Nabhan, *Das Fest des Fastenbrechens* (ʿīd al-fiṭr) *in Ägypten. Untersuchung zu den theologischen Grundlagen und der praktischen Gestaltung,* Berlin 1991; A. Neuwirth, Erzählen als kanonischer Prozeß. Die Mose-Erzählung im Wandel der koranischen Geschichte, in U. Rebstock et al. (eds.), *Islamstudien ohne Ende,* Würzburg 2002, 323-44; id., Meccan texts — Medinan additions? Politics and the re-reading of liturgical communications, in R. Arnzen and J. Thielmann (eds.), *Festschrift für Gerhard Endress,* (forthcoming); id., Qurʾān, crisis and memory. The qurʾānic path towards canonization as reflected in the anthropogonic accounts, in A. Neuwirth, *A Pflitsch. Crisis and memory in Islamic societies,* Beirut/Würzburg 2001, 113-52; id., Three religious feasts between narratives of violence and liturgies of reconciliation, in Th. Scheffler (ed.), *Religion between violence and reconciliation,* Beirut/Würzburg 2002, 49-82; R. Paret, Furḳān, in *EI*[2], ii, 949-50; A. Radtke, *Offenbarung zwischen Gesetz und Geschichte. Quellenstudien zu den Bedingungsfaktoren frühislamischen Rechtsdenkens,* Wiesbaden 2003; R. Rendtorff, Die Entwicklung des altisraelitischen Festkalenders, in J. Assmann (ed.), *Das Fest und das Heilige. Religiöse Kontrapunkte zur Alltagswelt,* Gütersloh 1991, 185-205; F. Ṭūqān, *Riḥla ṣaʿba, riḥla jabaliyya,* Amman 1988; trans. O. Kenny, *A mountainous journey. The life of Palestine's outstanding woman poet,* London 1996; K. Wagtendonk, Fasting, in *EQ,* ii, 180-5; id., *Fasting in the Qurʾān,* Leiden 1968; J. Wellhausen, *Reste Arabischen Heidentums,* Berlin 1927[2]; Y.H. Yerushalmi, *Zakhor. Jewish history and Jewish memory,* Seattle 1982; M. Zobel, *Das Jahr des Juden in Brauch und Liturgie,* Berlin 1936.

Ramparts see PEOPLE OF THE HEIGHTS

Rank(s) see RANKS AND ORDERS

Ranks and Orders

Arrangement of heavenly or earthly beings in military or other formation. *Ṣaff,* plural *ṣufūf,* literally "rank, row or line, company of men standing in a rank, row or line" (Lane, 1693, col. 3), is a term used in several different contexts and with various significations. The purely literal meaning, a very early understanding, referred to "straight lines and rows" of Muslim believers when offering obligatory prayers (see PRAYER; RITUAL AND THE QURʾĀN; COMMUNITY AND SOCIETY IN THE QURʾĀN). Over time, the additional meaning of "ranks and orders" acquired a certain sense of hierarchy, be it material (military) or spiritual, individual or communal, male or female (see GENDER). In this meaning, a sense of superiority and preferential treatment accorded by God to certain individuals or communities became a common understanding (see ELECTION; FREEDOM AND PREDESTINATION).

The Qurʾān mentions *ṣaff* six times. The predominant context in which the term is used (four out of the six occurrences) is apocalyptic in nature (see APOCALYPSE). In this context, human beings will be marshaled before their lord in "rows" to settle accounts when angels (see ANGEL), the spirit (q.v.; see also HOLY SPIRIT; GABRIEL) and other celestial beings will also be standing in "rows," obediently (see OBEDIENCE), in the presence of God on that last day (see LAST JUDGMENT). One sūra, however, Q 61 (Sūrat al-Ṣaff, which takes its name from Q 61:4, "God loves those who fight in his way in ranks [rows], as though they were a building well-compacted"), is generally translated into English as "The Battle Array." The last reference to *ṣaff* occurs as a challenge posed by Moses (q.v.) when he challenges Pharaoh's (q.v.) magicians (Q 20:64; see MAGIC) to muster all their (magic) forces together and act in a "concerted" *(ṣaff)* manner.

Based on the above contexts, *ṣaff* historically came to acquire three, perhaps four, distinct meanings: religious, military, social (particularly in the north African context) and spiritual. Religious: *ṣaff* as rows meant the lines of worshippers assembled in the mosque (q.v.) or elsewhere for the prescribed worship (q.v.; *ṣalāt*). The two related terms strengthening this religious connotation are *ṣāffāt* and its masculine plural *ṣāffūna.* Both these terms appear in Sūrat al-Ṣāffāt (Q 37, "Those Ranged in Ranks") where the former is interpreted as angels and the latter as "those beings who declare the glory of their lord (q.v.)," i.e. "angels" (see GLORIFICATION OF GOD). *Ṣāffāt* occurs three times in the Qurʾān and *ṣāffūna* once (Rippin, Ṣāffāt). Military: history records that in the engagements of the

Arabs (q.v.) with the imperial Sāsānid army in Iraq (q.v.) in the 630s C.E., the Arabs drew themselves into *ṣufūf* or ranks. "The Prophet is said to have straightened, with an arrow held in his hand, the *ṣufūf* of the Muslims before the battle of Badr (q.v.) in 2/624" (Bosworth, Ṣaff, 794). Thus, Q 61:4 was interpreted to mean the rank formation, *ṣaff,* in battle. Social organization in north Africa: *ṣaff* denotes in certain parts of the Maghrib, chiefly Algeria, southern Tunisia and Libya, a league, alliance, faction or party (Bosworth, Ṣaff). Spiritual: many mystics (Ṣūfīs) and some Shīʿī groups believe that, with immense spiritual discipline and meditation, one would be accorded the status of *al-ṣāffūna* (Q 37:165), those of a (higher) rank and order or those beings who declare the glory of God, i.e. the angels (Ibn al-ʿArabī, *Tafsīr,* ii, 335; see SHĪʿISM AND THE QURʾĀN; ṢŪFISM AND THE QURʾĀN). Jalāl al-Dīn Rūmī (d. 672/1273) furnishes one such example, claiming a high status for the deserving Ṣūfī by quoting this particular verse in one of his poems (Rūmī, *Dīwān,* poem no. 1948).

Ṣaff *in the commentary and ḥadīth literature*

Liturgical and eschatological contexts

A sample of this literature reveals several traditions emphasizing the need to form straight rows when performing obligatory prayers. The manner in which the prophetic traditions are organized in the various commentaries on the Qurʾān (*tafāsīr,* sing. *tafsīr;* see EXEGESIS OF THE QURʾĀN: CLASSICAL AND MEDIEVAL) points to an attempt to link the mode of worship of the angels in the heavens with the Muslim worshippers on earth. Angels worship God standing in "rows" (in obedience and discipline) and Muslims should do the same. Several prophetic traditions (especially those that describe Muḥammad's "heavenly ascent," the *miʿrāj;* see ASCENSION) exhort believers to emulate or mirror this mode of worship. It is worth noting here that Muslim tradition attributes the divine command to offer "five" obligatory prayers daily as having been received by Muḥammad during his "heavenly ascent" where he also witnessed angels offering prayers continually. In addition, there is an attempt to synchronize the times of the believers' worship with that of the angels based on another prophetic tradition: "If anyone of you says *āmīn* [during the prayer at the end of the recitation of Sūrat al-Fātiḥa; see FĀTIḤA] and the angels in heaven say the same, and the sayings of the two coincide, all his past sins will be forgiven" (Ḥilālī and Khān, *Qurʾān,* vi, 479; see FORGIVENESS; SIN, MAJOR AND MINOR).

Ibn Kathīr (d. 774/1373; *Tafsīr,* 807, col. 1) links three instances of the word *ṣaff* (those of Q 18:48, Q 78:38 and Q 89:22) in his explanation of the word in an eschatological context. He says, "it seems that the intention here is that all created beings will stand in the presence of God in 'one row' as he says in Q 78:38 and he speaks the truth. It is possible that they would stand in rows after rows as he says in Q 89:22." The commentary ordinarily published under the name of Ibn al-ʿArabī (d. 543/1148; *Tafsīr,* i, 765; actual author is ʿAbd al-Razzāq al-Qāshānī [d. 731/1330]) and the works of several other commentators add to this explanation by clarifying that the rows will be formed such that none will be able to "hide" or "veil" another during this time of resurrection (q.v.) when facing the lord (see INTERCESSION; FACE OF GOD). The emphases on personal responsibility and accountability are a clear objective here.

Hierarchy and egalitarianism

Several modern Muslim thinkers and commentators (see EXEGESIS OF THE QURʾĀN: EARLY MODERN AND CONTEMPORARY) offer the *ṣaff* formation in prayer as proof of

Islam's egalitarianism (see JUSTICE AND INJUSTICE; OPPRESSION). It is clearly evident that the prince or the ruler of the land prays in the same row with his humble subjects, together acknowledging the "createdness" of all beings (see CREATION; KINGS AND RULERS). Non-Muslim observers have often singled out the *ṣaff* formation of Muslims in prayers as one of the most remarkable and poignant aspects of the Islamic prayer ritual. Early and classical commentators do not, however, connect the *ṣaff* formation with any notions of egalitarianism. Ironically, in these works, *ṣaff* seems to have been used to draw distinctions as opposed to emphasizing egalitarianism.

Ibn Kathīr (*Tafsīr,* 1129, col. 1) records a sound tradition (see ḤADĪTH AND THE QURʾĀN) attesting to the fact that "men and women used to pray together until Q 37:164-5 were revealed, 'There is not one of us but has his known position, we are those who glorify God." Most commentators agree that the speaker in Q 37:164 is the angel, especially based on the following three verses (Q 37:165-7), which are commonly understood as having been spoken by angels. Nevertheless, this verse was interpreted as a divine command to segregate genders during obligatory prayers (*maqām maʿlūm,* "known position," interpreted by most commentators as *maqāmahu wa-martabatahu,* "his place and status/rank," except al-Kāshānī [*Tafsīr,* ii, 1208] who interprets it as "limits set by God not to be transgressed"; see BOUNDARIES AND PRECEPTS). Therefore, "at the time of its revelation," Ibn Kathīr informs us, "men came forward and women moved behind. Hence, Q 37:165, "We are those who declare the glory of God," means that we stand in rows (in accordance with our special status, rank, or place) in obedience, as was said in Q 37:1, "Those [angels] standing in rows."

Another tradition records how orderly rows were commissioned and institutionalized. Abū Nadra said, "'Umar used to approach people facing them, when *ṣalāt* was established, saying, 'Stand in rows, straighten your lines out, God the exalted wishes from you the manner of the angels,' quoting Q 37:165, and continued, 'so and so, you go back, so and so, you come forward.' Only then would he give the *takbīr*" (i.e. say *Allāhu akbar* to start the prayer; Ibn Kathīr, *Tafsīr,* 1129, col. 2).

Thus, in classical times *ṣaff* came to be understood as a hierarchical term whence superiority and preference. The meaning moved to a metaphorical and symbolic plane, whether to connote physically imitating the angelic "mode of worship" or to claim higher rank based on superior spiritual achievements. The following prophetic tradition is often cited for justification: "We [members of my community] have been bestowed superiority over others in three ways: our ranks and rows are made like the ranks and rows of the angels, earth is made a *masjid* (place of worship; see BOWING AND PROSTRATION) for us (i.e. a Muslim can pray anywhere on earth), and finally, its soil is made pure, in case of non-availability of water" (to be used for ablutions before prayer instead of water; Ibn Kathīr, *Tafsīr,* 1129, col. 2; see CLEANLINESS AND ABLUTION).

Nargis Virani

Bibliography

Primary: Ibn al-ʿArabī, *Tafsīr,* ed. M. Ghālib, 2 vols., Beirut 1978; Ibn Kathīr, *Tafsīr,* abr. ed. M.A. Muṣṭafā al-Khinn, 1 vol., Beirut 2000; Jalāl al-Dīn Rūmī, *Kulliyyāt-i shams, yā dīwān-i kabīr,* ed. B. Furūzānfar, 10 vols., Tehran 1336-46 [1957-67]; al-Kāshānī, Mawlā Nūr al-Dīn Muḥammad b. Murtaḍā, *Tafsīr al-muʿīn,* 4 vols., Qom n.d.; Suyūṭī, *Durr,* 8 vols., Beirut 1983.
Secondary: C.E. Bosworth, Ṣaff, in *EI*², viii, 793-4; M.T. al-Hilālī and M.M. Khān, *The noble Qurʾān,* 9 vols., New York 2000; Quṭb, *Ẓilāl;* A. Rippin, al-Ṣāffāt, in *EI*² viii, 798.

Ransom see CAPTIVES

Raqīm

Name mentioned at the beginning of the qurʾānic version of the story of the Seven Sleepers (see MEN OF THE CAVE), where the Qurʾān states: "Or do you think the Men of the Cave and al-Raqīm were among our signs (q.v.) a wonder?" (Q 18:9).

The isolated mention in this passage with no other specification or occurrences of the term prompted an abundance of exegetical explanations and interpretations. One tradition mentioned in some commentaries attests that al-Raqīm was one of the four words in the Qurʾān that Ibn ʿAbbās (d. ca. 68/688; see COMPANIONS OF THE PROPHET; ḤADĪTH AND THE QURʾĀN) could not satisfactorily explain and had thus to rely upon the explanation of Kaʿb al-Aḥbār. Following the meaning of the root *r-q-m,* i.e. "to write," commentaries suggest that the word could mean "a writing," a written tablet. Thus, al-Raqīm was a tablet, i.e. a stone, iron or lead tablet (Farrāʾ, *Maʿānī,* ii, 134) hanging at the entrance of the cave (q.v.) where the sleepers stayed and in which their story, names or genealogies were written. According to a report quoted by Muqātil b. Sulaymān (d. 150/767; *Tafsīr,* ii, 574), al-Raqīm was a writing *(kitāb)* inscribed on a tablet by two men named Mātūs and Asṭūs, two who were secretly believers in God at the time of Decius. The major commentaries also include other interpretations, such as al-Raqīm as the name of a village, a mountain or a valley. One further explanation states that al-Raqīm could have been the name of the dog (q.v.) of the sleepers. This is also suggested by a verse of the pre-Islamic poet Umayya b. Abī l-Ṣalt, cited, for instance, by Abū Ḥayyān in his commentary (*Baḥr,* vii, 142). The presence of the dog is, in fact, mentioned in the qurʾānic text — "And their dog stretching its paws on the threshold" (Q 18:18) and "And their dog" (Q 18:22) — though the commentaries on these passages usually state that its name was Qiṭmīr (see as early as Muqātil, *Tafsīr,* ii, 578). According to a report going back to the Prophet, such as in al-Thaʿlabī's (d. 427/1035) *tafsīr* (*Kashf,* vi, 145-6; but see an earlier reference in Ibn Abī Ḥātim al-Rāzī, *Tafsīr,* vii, 2347), al-Raqīm is a reference to the vicissitudes of three men who escaped and found refuge in a cave. This story had already been recorded in early *ḥadīth* collections such as Ibn Ḥanbal's (d. 241/845) *Musnad* (no. 18445; other references in Suyūṭī, *Durr,* 363-5) and its identification with al-Raqīm is suggested in later sources (see Hérnandez Juberías, *La península,* 139 f.) and, above all, the commentaries on Q 18 (see for example Bayḍāwī, *Tafsīr,* ii, 5: *aṣḥāb al-raqīm*).

The meaning of the word has attracted the attention of western scholars. Horovitz (*KU,* 95) — who reviewed the various interpretations of al-Raqīm — was among those to underline the difficulties in arriving at a satisfactory understanding of the term. Torrey (Three difficult passages), whose understanding Horovitz rejected, had in fact maintained that al-Raqīm could have been a misreading of the name Decius in Hebrew. This interpretation was further dismissed by Jeffery, who added the observation that, although this misreading looks easy in Hebrew characters, it is not so obvious in Syriac and that, following Horovitz, it does not explain the article of the Arabic term. According to Jeffery, "the probabilities are that it is a place-name" (Jeffery, *For. vocab.,* 144). A more recent explanation by Bellamy (Raqīm or ruqūd) suggests that at this point the qurʾānic text must be corrupt: he maintained that the qurʾānic lexeme is a corruption of *al-ruqūd,* "sleepers," quoted in Q 18:18. Western translations of the Qur'ān mention the term as a name or, in some cases, translate it as "inscription" (cf. Paret, *Der Koran*).

Roberto Tottoli

Bibliography
Primary: ʿAbd al-Razzāq, *Tafsīr*, ed. M.M. Muḥammad, 3 vols., Riyadh 1989, i, 397; Abū Ḥayyān, *Baḥr*, Beirut 1992, vii, 142; Abū l-Layth al-Samarqandī, *Tafsīr*, ed. ʿA.M. Muʿawwaḍ and ʿĀ.A. ʿAbd al-Mawjūd, 3 vols., Beirut 1993, ii, 289-90; Abū ʿUbayda, *Majāz*, i, 394; Bayḍāwī, *Anwār*, Cairo 1968, ii, 4-5; Farrāʾ, *Maʿānī*, ii, 134; Hūd b. Muḥakkam, *Tafsīr*, ii, 451; Ibn Abī Ḥātim al-Rāzī, Abū Muḥammad, *Tafsīr*, ed. A.M. al-Ṭayyib, 10 vols., Mecca 1997, repr. Beirut 1999, vii, 2346-7; Ibn Ḥanbal, *Musnad*, 10 vols., Beirut 1991, vi, 387-8 no. 18445; Ibn Kathīr, *Tafsīr*, 4 vols., Beirut n.d., iii, 119-20; Ibn Qutayba, *Gharīb*, 263; Māwardī, *Nukat*, iii, 286-7; Muqātil, *Tafsīr*, ii, 574; Rāzī, *Tafsīr*, Beirut 1990, xxi, 70; Suyūṭī, *Durr*, 8 vols., Cairo 1983, v, 362-5; Ṭabarī, *Tafsīr*, Cairo 1968, xv, 197-9; Thaʿlabī, *al-Kashf wa-l-bayān ʿan tafsīr al-Qurʾān*, ed. Abū Muḥammad b. ʿĀshūr, 10 vols., Beirut 2002, vi, 145-7; id., *Qiṣaṣ*, 370-1.
Secondary: J.A. Bellamy, Al-raqīm or al-ruqūd? A note on sūrah 18:9, in *JAOS* 111 (1991), 115-7; J. Hérnandez Juberías, *La península imaginaria. Mitos y leyendas sobre al-Andalus*, Madrid 1996, 139-61; Horovitz, *KU*, 95; Jeffery, *For. vocab.*, 144; F. Jordan, *La tradition des sept dormants. Une rencontre entre chrétiens et musulmans*, Paris 2001; H. Kandler, *Die Bedeutung der Siebenschläfer* (Aṣḥāb al-kahf) *im Islam*, Bochum 1994, 19-23; C. Luxenberg, *Die Syro-aramäische Lesart des Koran*, Berlin 2000, 65-7; R. Paret, Aṣḥāb al-kahf, in *EI²*, i, 691; id., *Koran*; C.C. Torrey, Three difficult passages in the Koran, in T.W. Arnold and R.A. Nicholson (eds.), *A volume of oriental studies presented to Edward G. Browne (...) on his 60th birthday*, Cambridge 1922, 457-9.

Rass

Term mentioned twice in the Qurʾān in connection with the expression *aṣḥāb al-rass*, "the people of al-Rass": "We have prepared for the evildoers a painful chastisement. And ʿĀd (q.v.), Thamūd (q.v.) and the people of al-Rass, and between that, many generations" (Q 25:37-8); "The people of Noah (q.v.) and the people of al-Rass, and Thamūd and Pharaoh (q.v.), and ʿĀd and the brothers of Lot (q.v.) cried lies before them..." (Q 50:12). Although there are no other elements that help clarify who the people of al-Rass were, the fact that they are mentioned alongside other ancient peoples who were punished suggests that they, too, could have been one of these peoples (see PUNISHMENT STORIES).

Commentators (see EXEGESIS OF THE QURʾĀN: CLASSICAL AND MEDIEVAL) as well as later traditions (see ḤADĪTH AND THE QURʾĀN) are at a loss when attempting to identify this people and the location of the place referred to as al-Rass. According to some interpretations, al-Rass is the proper name of a village, or a region between Najrān (q.v.), Yemen (q.v.) and Ḥaḍramawt, or a town of the Yamāma or the name of a river (see PRE-ISLAMIC ARABIA AND THE QURʾĀN; GEOGRAPHY AND THE QURʾĀN). Some other explanations rely upon the meaning of the term *rass* as anything having been excavated, such as a pit, a well or a tomb (Ṭabarī, *Tafsīr*, xix, 14). The explanation of *al-rass* as meaning "the well" is by far the favorite of the exegetes, and so these people are very frequently identified as "the people of the well" (Farrāʾ, *Maʿānī*, ii, 268 makes this connection already in the early Islamic period). Additional (sometimes contradictory) reports attempt to elucidate whether the well was near Madyan (see MIDIAN), in Antioch or in Azerbaijan, and provide narratives that furnish the background setting of the story. So it is said that these people of al-Rass were one of the two peoples to whom Shuʿayb (q.v.) was sent (see PEOPLE OF THE THICKET), but, since they refused him, were then punished. It is also thought they may have been people to whom a prophet descending from Jacob (q.v.) was sent (see PROPHETS AND PROPHETHOOD; WARNING).

An alternative account is that they were people who received the mission of two different prophets and killed both of them. Their description as "the people of the well" is explained by recounting that it was into this well that they threw a prophet, killing him. Some reports identify the prophet who unsuccessfully tried to summon them as Ḥanẓala b. Ṣafwān and specify that their evil behavior led to their destruction (see GOOD AND EVIL; VIRTUES AND VICES, COMMANDING AND FORBIDDING; EVIL DEEDS). Following a saying of the Prophet (not mentioned in the major collections) according to which the first to enter paradise will be a black servant (see SLAVES AND SLAVERY; SERVANT), another exegetical explanation identifies this servant as a pious man who tried to save a prophet who had been thrown into a well by his people, who were thereafter known as "the people of the well." Other reports state that the "people of the well" were indeed the people of Yā-Sīn, i.e. Antioch, whose story is mentioned in Q 36:13-29 (see the early account in Muqātil, *Tafsīr,* iii, 235) and that the prophet thrown into the well was Ḥabīb al-Najjār. Further interpretations are added in most of the later sources: they were of the remnants of the Thamūd, or they were indeed the People of the Ditch (q.v.; Q 85:4), or they were idolatrous people who used to worship the stone pine (*ṣanawbar,* see Thaʿlabī, *Tafsīr,* viii, 135-8) or they were punished through the prodigious bird called *ʿanqāʾ.*

Among recent western interpretations of the meaning of *"al-rass,"* Bellamy has proposed that the written form *"al-rass"* could simply be a misspelling of the name Idrīs (q.v.; see also ORTHOGRAPHY; ARABIC SCRIPT). The few qurʾānic passages, however, do not contain any narrative setting or other elements that might help clarify the exact identification of *"al-rass."* Though the context suggests that reference is made to a people who, in the qurʾānic vision of history (see HISTORY AND THE QURʾĀN), had received a prophet and then were punished for rejecting his teachings, these people cannot be identified.

Roberto Tottoli

Bibliography
Primary: Farrāʾ, *Maʿānī,* ii, 268; Ibn Kathīr, *Tafsīr,* 4 vols., iii, 509-10; Ibn Qutayba, *Gharīb,* 313; al-Majlisī, Muḥammad Bāqir, *Biḥār al-anwār,* 110 vols., Tehran 1956-72, Beirut 1983², xiv, 148-60; Māwardī, *Nukat,* iv, 145-6; Muqātil, *Tafsīr,* iii, 235; Qurṭubī, *Jāmiʿ,* xiii, 31-3 (ad Q 25:37-8); xvii, 8 (ad Q 50:12); Rāzī, *Tafsīr,* Beirut 1990, xxiv, 72-3; Suyūṭī, *Durr,* 8 vols., Cairo 1983, vi, 256-8; Ṭabarī, *Tafsīr,* Cairo 1968, xix, 13-5; Thaʿlabī, *al-Kashf wa-l-bayān ʿan tafsīr al-Qurʾān,* ed. A.M. b. ʿĀshūr, 10 vols., Beirut 2002, viii, 133-9; id., *Qiṣaṣ,* 131-5.
Secondary: Bell, *Commentary,* ii, 8; J.A. Bellamy, Textual criticism of the Koran, in *JAOS* 121 (2001), 5-6; H. Busse, Antioch and its prophet Ḥabīb al-Najjār, in *JSAI* 24 (2000), 155-79; Horovitz, *KU,* 94-5; D. Marshall, *God, Muhammad and the unbelievers,* Richmond, Surrey 1999; B. Scarcia Amoretti, Un'interpretazione iranistica di *Cor.* XXV, 38 e L, 12, in *RSO* 43 (1968), 27-52; R. Tottoli (ed.), *The stories of the prophets of Ibn Muṭarrif al-Ṭarafī,* Berlin 2003, 108-9.

Rasūl see MESSENGER; PROPHETS AND PROPHETHOOD

Read, Reading see RECITATION OF THE QURʾĀN

Readers of the Qurʾān see RECITERS OF THE QURʾĀN; READINGS OF THE QURʾĀN; RECITATION OF THE QURʾĀN

Readings of the Qurʾān

A term generally used to denote the *qirāʾāt,* the different ways of reciting the Qurʾān. Variant readings are an important aspect of Qurʾān recitation (see RECITATION OF THE QURʾĀN; RECITERS OF THE QURʾĀN), but *qirāʾāt* refer to more than that. Other elements — such as differences concerning length of syllables, when to assimilate consonants to following ones, and where to pause or insert verse endings — form an integral part of the different *qirāʾāt* systems.

Reports about different ways of reciting or reading the Qurʾān were transmitted from the beginning of Islam. Traditions from the time of the Prophet (see HADĪTH AND THE QURʾĀN) mention that differences in recitation occurred and that they were permitted by him, but there is no specification of the nature of these differences. In the canonical traditions that go back to Muḥammad these differences in recitation are linked to the seven *aḥruf* (sing. *ḥarf*) according to which Gabriel (q.v.; Jibrīl) recited the Qurʾān to Muḥammad. The contexts of these traditions suggest that with *ḥarf* either a mode of recitation or a manner of pronunciation is meant (see ORALITY; ARABIC LANGUAGE). From early works, however, it is clear that in the second/eighth century *ḥarf* was taken to mean the same thing as *qirāʾa* in its narrow sense of "variant reading." Early commentaries on the Qurʾān, such as those of Mujāhid (d. 104/722), Sufyān al-Thawrī (d. 162/778), ʿAbdallāh b. Wahb (d. 197/812), ʿAbd al-Razzāq al-Ṣanʿānī (d. 211/827), al-Akhfash al-Awsaṭ (d. bet. 210/825 and 221/835) and al-Farrāʾ (d. 207/822), demonstrate that these variant readings did indeed occur across the whole range of lexical issues: from simple pronunciation variants through different case endings or verbal forms, synonyms or near synonyms, to interpolations of whole phrases (see EXEGESIS OF THE QURʾĀN: CLASSICAL AND MEDIEVAL; GRAMMAR AND THE QURʾĀN).

Readings before the general acceptance of the ʿUthmānic muṣḥaf

The introduction of the ʿUthmānic *rasm* (unmarked consonantal structure of an Arabic document; see ARABIC SCRIPT; CODICES OF THE QURʾĀN; COLLECTION OF THE QURʾĀN) does not seem to have had an immediate, decisive effect on the limitation of variant readings with a different *rasm*. In Sufyān al-Thawrī's relatively short *Tafsīr*, for instance, 67 variant readings — all introduced with *fī qirāʾat...* ("in the reading of...") or *kāna... yaqraʾūnahā...* ("... they used to read it as...") — are mentioned, 24 of which have a different *rasm*. Most of these are synonyms that are attributed to Ibn Masʿūd (d. 32/652-3). On the whole, it appears that in the second Islamic century variant readings with a different *rasm*, especially from Ibn Masʿūd's codex, were still freely discussed and were called either *qirāʾāt* or, less commonly, *ḥurūf*. The reading *wa-amdadnāhum bi-ʿīsin ʿīnin* ("and we shall support them with grayish white ones, with beautiful eyes") instead of *wa-zawwajnāhum bi-ḥūrin ʿīnin* ("and we shall pair them off with white ones, with beautiful eyes"; Q 44:54) is mentioned by al-Farrāʾ (*Maʿānī*, iii, 44) as the *qirāʾa* of Ibn Masʿūd (see HOURIS). In his commentary on Q 44:54, ʿAbd al-Razzāq al-Ṣanʿānī (*Tafsīr*, iii, 210) simply mentions *bi-ʿīsin ʿīnin* as the *ḥarf* of Ibn Masʿūd, whereas Sufyān al-Thawrī (*Tafsīr*, ad Q 52:20) notes it as Ibn Masʿūd's *qirāʾa*, and al-Ṭabarī (d. 310/923; *Tafsīr*, ad Q 44:54) records a tradition which calls this reading a *qirāʾa* and another which calls it a *ḥarf*. ʿAbd al-Razzāq (*Tafsīr*, i, 390) shows a corresponding use of the terms. Even though there seems to be a preference for the term *ḥarf*, especially in connection with Ibn Masʿūd's readings, both terms, *ḥarf* and *qirāʾa*, are apparently used interchangeably, both for ʿUthmānic and non-ʿUthmānic readings. In connection with Q 17:93, ʿAbd al-Razzāq mentions a tradition from Mujāhid: "We did not know what 'a house of ornament *(zukhruf)*' was until we saw in the *qirāʾa* of Ibn Masʿūd 'a house of gold *(dhahab)*'." Thus, the possibility that *ḥarf* could refer to a written variant and *qirāʾa* to an oral one is not borne out by early texts.

Examination of the discussions treating variant readings in the second/eighth and third/ninth centuries indicates that the readings of Ibn Masʿūd gained increasing prominence as the possible or plausible variants of an apparently widely received, more or less standard text which largely agreed with the ʿUthmānic *rasm*. Al-Farrāʾ *(Maʿānī)* is particularly noteworthy for his discussion of a wealth of variant readings, especially from Ibn Masʿūd, many of which have a *rasm* different from that of the ʿUthmānic codex.

The treatment by al-Farrāʾ of these variants shows that in his time they could still be discussed on equal terms with the ʿUthmānic text. And in Sufyān al-Thawrī's and ʿAbd al-Razzāq's *Tafsīrs* there is no mention of their being unacceptable. The guiding principle for acceptance of a reading appears to have been that it should be well known, either from a codex or from a well-established tradition. For al-Farrāʾ — but probably also for others — another criterion was clearly in place, namely that an acceptable variant reading should be in accordance with the rules of the Arabic language (Leemhuis, Ursprünge).

Of course, the ʿUthmānic text itself still left room for different readings. The codices of Medina, Mecca, Damascus, Kūfa and Baṣra are said to have presented some slight differences in a number of places, mainly concerning an extra *wāw* or *alif*, or a *dhī* instead of *dhū* or *dhā*. The chapter about the differences among these codices in Ibn Abī Dāwūd al-Sijistānī's (d. 316/929) book on the ancient codices (Jeffery, *Materials*, 39-49 of the Arabic text) sums them up in lists that appear to have been well established by then.

The discussion, however, of which was the primary text, the codified text or the recited text, also played an important part in the history of the gradual acceptance of the ʿUthmānic codex as exclusively authoritative. This is clear from the different treatment of variant readings in the *Maʿānī l-Qurʾān* by al-Akhfash al-Awsaṭ (d. 215/830) and in al-Farrāʾ's work with the same title. Both books serve the same general purpose: to establish a correct reading of the Qurʾān and, where necessary, to advance arguments for their choices of correct readings. Many — but by no means all — of the discussed *qirāʾāt* are common to both authors. Al-Farrāʾ treats variant readings that presuppose a different *rasm* much more often than does al-Akhfash. And, unlike al-Farrāʾ, al-Akhfash's prime criterion for not admitting such readings is that, although they may be good Arabic, they do not agree with the writing of the *"muṣḥaf"* (q.v.) — by which is quite clearly meant the ʿUthmānic text. This argument is of overriding importance for al-Akhfash and appears to be his guiding principle (Leemhuis, Ursprünge).

The difference in opinion between al-Akhfash and al-Farrāʾ on this issue shows that by the end of the second Islamic century this controversy had not yet been resolved. It also appears from their works that certainly at the same time, but arguably already a generation or two earlier, a generally received text existed which had *de facto* been accepted as the standard text. The weight of this standard text, however, does not yet appear to have been such that specialists would necessarily have considered variant readings with a different *rasm* to be invalid on the basis of that fact alone.

Readings accepted after the general authorization of the ʿUthmānic muṣḥaf *and those that were not*

Two generations later, Ibn Qutayba (213-76/822-89) expressed the view that all ways of reciting the Qurʾān which are in accordance with the *rasm* of "our *muṣḥaf*" (*Mushkil*, 42) were allowed. He quotes ʿUthmān's opinion that the difference between *qirāʾa* and *kitāb* was a matter of the accent *(laḥn)* of the Arabs (q.v.; see also DIALECTS) and that the *rasm* should be left as it was (ibid., 51). In al-Ṭabarī's commentary, which was written near the end of the third/ninth century, the criterion for not accepting a reading was its not being in accordance with the codices of the five cities to which the ʿUthmānic text was sent. Al-Ṭabarī formulated this principle quite explicitly, e.g. in connection with the reading of Abū ʿAmr of *li-yahaba laki*, "in order that he will give you," instead of *li-ahaba laki*, "in order that I shall give you," in Q 19:19. For al-Ṭabarī the correct reading is the latter, because "that is how it is in the codices of the Muslims and this is the reading which the ancient and the recent [authorities] follow, except Abū ʿAmr. It is not permissible to differ from them in what they agree upon. And no one is allowed to disagree with their codices."

It is in this period that, in liturgical use, readings based on the ʿUthmānic *rasm* finally eclipsed those presupposing another *rasm*, notably that of Ibn Masʿūd. This was largely due to the activities of Ibn Mujāhid (d. 324/936), whose view on the admissibility of variant readings was enforced by the vizier Ibn Muqla in 323/935. Ibn Shannabūdh (d. 328/939), who had, in public worship, confidently recited readings of Ibn Masʿūd and other older readings which were not in accordance with the ʿUthmānic codex, was brought to trial and flogged, whereupon he recanted his defense of the non-ʿUthmānic readings (Baghdādī, *Taʾrīkh Baghdād*, i, 280-1). It can be said that, from then on, the codified text in the form of the ʿUthmānic codex was considered to be *the* primary text and the only one admissible for reciting the Qurʾān. The meaning of the term *qirāʾa* shifted from "manner of reciting the Qurʾān" to "manner of reciting the established written text of the Qurʾān."

In the introduction to his book on the seven readings, Ibn Mujāhid does not specifically defend his choice for presenting the seven readings. But his choice is clearly motivated by three hierarchical criteria: (1) the reading should be in accordance with one of the ʿUthmānic codices of the five cities that had received it; (2) it should be authoritatively transmitted and broadly authenticated, i.e. agreed upon by the majority of scholars; and (3) it should conform to the rules of Arabic grammar.

The first criterion still provided some leeway since it was accepted that there were some slight differences in the *rasm* of the ʿUthmānic codices of the five cities. Ibn Mujāhid apparently accepted the divergences between the ʿUthmānic codices as they were known in his time. Of the fifty cases mentioned in the lists that Ibn Abī Dāwūd al-Sijistānī (d. 316/929) gives in his *Kitāb al-Maṣāḥif* (39-49), only four are not accepted by Ibn Mujāhid in his *Kitāb al-Sabʿa fī l-qirāʾāt*. Even so, some adaptation could occasionally be devised in order to accommodate a well-known reading to the *rasm*. The reading of Abū ʿAmr of *li-yahaba laki* in Q 19:19, which was rejected by al-Ṭabarī, is retained by the statement that Abū ʿAmr and Nāfiʿ (according to the transmissions of Warsh and al-Ḥalawānī of Qālūn) read it — according to the *rasm*, but without the *hamza* of the *alif* — as *līhaba*. But recitation according to another *rasm* was clearly ruled out, as the example of Ibn Shannabūdh was meant to show. Ibn Mujāhid recognized that, in the past, the majority of Kūfans had recited the Qurʾān according to Ibn Masʿūd; but he had a simple reason for rejecting this *qirāʾa:* it predated the *ḥarf* on which ʿUthmān united the people.

That, for Ibn Mujāhid, the second criterion had precedence over the third is shown by the story of Ibn Miqsam (fl. fourth/tenth cent.; Baghdādī, *Taʾrīkh Baghdād,* ii, 206-8), an expert on *qirāʾāt* who is said to have held as acceptable all readings that the *rasm* allowed as long as they conformed to good Arabic. Like Ibn Shannabūdh a year later, he was brought to trial, but he recanted before being punished.

In applying these criteria, Ibn Mujāhid selected and presented the readings of authoritative readers from the places that were associated with the presentation of the first five copies of the ʿUthmānic codex: from Medina, Nāfiʿ b. ʿAbd al-Raḥmān (d. 169/785); from Mecca, ʿAbdallāh b. Kathīr (d. 120/738); from Kūfa, ʿĀṣim b. Abī l-Najūd (d. 127/745), Ḥamza b. Ḥabīb al-Zayyāt (d. 156/773) and ʿAlī b. Ḥamza al-Kisāʾī (d. 189/804); from Baṣra, Abū ʿAmr b. al-ʿAlāʾ (d. 154/770); and from Damascus, ʿAbdallāh b. ʿĀmir (d. 118/736).

Ibn Mujāhid not only presented permissible variant readings, he also preserved more or less coherent pronunciation systems. This is also shown by the exposition of more general characteristics of the respective readings. Thus Ibn Mujāhid discusses, for instance, the positions of the different readers about the vowel of the personal suffix *-hum* (whether it had to become */i/* if the vowel before the */h/* was an */i/*, or should remain */u/*), and whether the */m/* should be without a vowel or with an added long or short */u/*. Likewise, he notes their positions on the assimilation of vowel-less consonants to a similar first consonant of a following word, e.g. whether *bal rafaʿahu llāhu ilayhi,* "God raised him up to him" (Q 4:158) should be pronounced *bar rafaʿahu llāhu ilayhi.* These peculiarities represent quite different styles of recitation and they most probably reflect original dialectal differences in the pronunciation of Arabic; but a systematic evaluation of these data remains elusive. At least one phenomenon, however, seems to be significant in this respect. The treatment of the glottal stop in the different readings appears to reflect the variance between ancient east and west Arabian dialects. According to Warsh's transmission of Nāfiʿ's reading, the *hamza,* or glottal stop, is not pronounced when it is without a vowel. The same is mentioned of Abū ʿAmr for the recitation of the Qurʾān in the *ṣalāt.* According to this pronunciation, e.g. *alladhīna yuʾminūna,* "those who believe" (Q 2:3 and passim), is read *alladhīna yūminūna,* and *biʾr,* "well, spring" (Q 22:45), is read *bīr.* This is in accordance with what is known of the west Arabian pronunciation and is, moreover, in accordance with the pronunciation that the *rasm* suggests. Ibn Mujāhid discusses all these general rules in excursuses, mostly in connection with the passages where these general differences first appear.

Ibn Mujāhid's work had an enormous influence on the recitation of the Qurʾān, especially because he enjoyed the clear support of the ʿAbbāsid authorities (see POLITICS AND THE QURʾĀN). From then on, the non-ʿUthmānic readings disappeared, and there were only two kinds of readings based on the ʿUthmānic *rasm:* those that were allowed in recitation because they were authoritatively transmitted and broadly authenticated, and those that were not. Only the first of these, which later were indicated as *mutawātira* — Ibn Mujāhid did not use the term — were allowed in recitation. The other readings became known as *shādhdha,* "solitary, isolated," i.e. lacking a sufficient number of authoritative chains of transmission. Ibn Mujāhid wrote a large book on these readings, but it is not extant. Indeed, many of these readings and also readings that presuppose a different *rasm* remained in circulation in specialized works in order to support or discuss the meaning of words or expressions. For instance, the above-mentioned reading of Ibn Masʿūd in Q 44:54 is still noted in connection with that passage in the *Tafsīr*s of al-Zamakhsharī (d. 538/1144) and Fakhr al-Dīn al-Rāzī (d. 606/1210).

The combination of the power of the ʿAbbāsid state and Ibn Mujāhid's authority and reputation in the field of qurʾānic readings proved to be quite effective, and in probably less than half a century his system of the seven canonical readings was largely accepted. It was also further systematized. In some cases, as in the case of Nāfiʿ, Ibn Mujāhid had mentioned quite a number of transmitters and, in other cases, as in the case of ʿĀṣim, only one. In the *Taysīr* of the Andalusian Abū ʿAmr al-Dānī (371-444/912-1053), there are for each reader only two *rāwī*s, "transmitters." Some of these, however, do not figure in Ibn Mujāhid's list, although this format of dual transmission eventually became the fixed system.

There were other problems that were addressed. Ibn Mujāhid had limited his choice of readers to seven, apparently because these seven met the criterion of broad authentication. At the same time, this choice of seven suggested that these were in fact the seven *aḥruf* of the prophetic traditions, although this equivalency was not universally accepted. On the basis of the criterion of broad authentication, which was somewhat fluid anyhow, readings of other famous readers were advanced as meeting the same criterion. Already Abū l-Ḥasan Ṭāhir b. ʿAbd al-Munʿim b. Ghalbūn (d. 399/1008) had included a second Baṣran reader in his *al-Tadhkira fī l-qirāʾāt* who became accepted as an eighth reader, namely Abū Muḥammad Yaʿqūb b. Isḥāq al-Ḥaḍramī (d. 205/821). It could also be argued that Abū Jaʿfar Yazīd b. al-Qaʿqāʿ (d. 130/747), one of the teachers of Nāfiʿ who was so eulogized by Ibn Mujāhid, should have his rightful place in the system — especially as both Ḥamza and al-Kisāʾī, who were teacher and pupil, had been included in the list. Khalaf b. Hishām al-Bazzār (d. 229/843), who was one of the transmitters of Ḥamza but who had selected some 120 readings of his own which differed from Ḥamza, had also gained the reputation of an independent reader. This soon led to the general acceptance of these three readers, each again according to two main transmitters. These became known as the "three after the seven." The question whether these readings were also *mutawātira*, "broadly authenticated," or just *mashhūra*, "well known," proved in the end to be merely academic. Together with the seven of Ibn Mujāhid, these three became known as the system of the ten and, at least in later times, these ten readings were all considered *mutawātira*.

But things did not stop there. The idea that the valid transmission of a reading was enough to make it fit for recitation, if the other two criteria were met, continued to attract some followers. Abū Muḥammad Makkī b. Abī Ṭālib al-Qurṭubī (d. 437/1045) was probably the first to advocate this view. Ibn al-Jazarī (d. 833/1429) quotes with approval in his *Nashr* (13-4) Makkī's opinion that there are three kinds of readings. The first is "what is recited nowadays and in which three characteristics are united." These characteristics are: (1) transmission from the Prophet on the authority of reliable authorities *(thiqāt)*; (2) accordance with the Arabic in which the Qurʾān was revealed; and (3) conformity with the writing of the *muṣḥaf*. It is this last criterion that decides whether or not a reading is considered to be based on general agreement. Readings that meet these three criteria are accepted and can be recited, and whoever rejects them is an unbeliever (see BELIEF AND UNBELIEF). The second kind of readings consists of those that meet the first two criteria but not the third. This kind of reading is acceptable but cannot be used in recitation, but whoever rejects it is not an unbeliever — a point, however, on which, Ibn al-Jazarī adds, the scholars do not agree. A minority of them held the view that it was permissible to recite such readings — among others, the reading of Ibn Masʿūd is meant — in the prayer (q.v.; *ṣalāt*) on the basis that the Companions of the Prophet (q.v.) and the successors of his Companions did so. The third kind consists of readings that do not meet either or both of the two first criteria. These are unacceptable even when they are in accordance with the writing of the *muṣḥaf*, and whoever rejects them is not an unbeliever.

Whether or not this reformulation of Ibn Mujāhid's three criteria had made its appearance already in the time of Makkī, is not entirely clear — but the argument that conformity with the ʿUthmānic text in itself constituted *ijmāʿ*, or general agreement, made room for the addition of another four readers to the list: "the four after the ten." The adherents of the system of the fourteen readers generally based their opinion on Makkī and Ibn al-Jazarī and gained some, but certainly not general, acceptance. They continued to be regarded as *shādhdha* — like all the others outside the system of the ten — by most authorities. Nevertheless, the boundary between acceptable and unacceptable readings remained somewhat blurred. Abū l-Qāsim Muḥammad b. Juzayy al-Gharnāṭī (d. 741/1340), who, in his *Tafsīr*, followed Warsh *ʿan* Nāfiʿ's reading because "it is the reading that is used in al-Andalus and the other countries of the Maghrib," gave the following short definition: "The *qirāʾāt* fall into two classes — the well known, established *(mashhūra)*, and the isolated, deviant *(shādhdha)* ones. The *mashhūra* are the seven readings and those which are similar to them, like the reading of Yaʿqūb and Ibn Muḥayṣin. *Shādhdha* is what is unlike that" (*Tashīl*, 7).

In the full system of the fourteen readings, each reader is represented by two *riwāya*s, or transmissions, and a reading is generally referred to by both the reader and one of the *rāwī*s in the following form: *qirāʾat Warsh ʿan Nāfiʿ, Ḥafṣ ʿan ʿĀṣim, al-Dūrī ʿan Abī ʿAmr* ("the reading of Warsh from Nāfiʿ," or "Ḥafṣ from ʿĀsim," or "al-Dūrī from Abū ʿAmr"), etc.

The system of the fourteen readings

1. Nāfiʿ b. ʿAbd al-Raḥman (d. 169/785)
   a. Warsh, ʿUthmān b. Saʿīd b. ʿAbdallāh al-Quṭbī (d. 197/812)
   b. Qālūn, Abū Mūsā ʿĪsā b. Mīnā l-Zarqī (d. 220/835)
2. ʿAbdallāh b. Kathīr (d. 120/738)
   a. Abū l-Ḥasan Aḥmad b. Muḥammad al-Bazzī (d. 240/845 or 250/864)
   b. Qunbul, Abū ʿAmr Muḥammad b. ʿAbd al-Raḥmān (d. 280/893 or 291/904)
3. Abū ʿAmr b. al-ʿAlāʾ (d. 154/770)
   a. al-Dūrī, Abū ʿAmr Ḥafṣ b. ʿUmar b. ʿAbd al-ʿAzīz (d. ca. 246/291)
   b. al-Sūsī: Abū Shuʿayb, Ṣāliḥ b. Ziyād al-Riqqī (d. 261/874)
4. ʿAbdallāh b. ʿĀmir (d. 118/736)
   a. Abū l-Walīd Hishām b. ʿAmmār al-Sulamī l-Dimashqī (d. 245/859)
   b. Abū ʿAmr ʿAbdallāh b. Aḥmad b. Bishr b. Dhakwān (d. 242/856)
5. ʿĀṣim b. Abī l-Najūd (d. 127/745)
   a. Abū Bakr Shuʿba b. ʿAyyāsh b. Sālim (d. 193/809)
   b. Abū ʿAmr Ḥafṣ b. Sulaymān b. al-Mughīra (d. 180/796)
6. Ḥamza b. Ḥabīb al-Zayyāt (d. 156/773)
   a. Khalaf Abū Muḥammad al-Asadī al-Bazzār al-Baghdādī (d. 229/844)

b. Abū ʿIsā Khallād Ibn Khālid al-Baghdādī (d. 220/835)

7. ʿAlī b. Ḥamza al-Kisāʾī (d. 189/804)
   a. Abū l-Ḥārith al-Layth Ibn Khālid al-Baghdādī (d. 240/854)
   b. al-Dūrī, the same as Abūʿ Amr's first *rāwī*
8. Abū Jaʿfar Yazīd b. al-Qaʿqāʿ (d. 130/747)
   a. Abū l-Ḥārith ʿĪsā b. Wirdān al-Madanī (d. ca. 160/777)
   b. Abū l-Rabīʿ Sulaymān b. Muslim b. Jummāz al-Madanī (d. 170/786)
9. Abū Muḥammad Yaʿqūb b. Isḥāq al-Ḥaḍramī (d. 205/821)
   a. Ruways Abū ʿAbdallāh Muḥammad b. al-Mutawakkil al-Baṣrī (d. 238/852)
   b. Abū l-Ḥasan Rawḥ b. ʿAbd al-Muʾmin al-Baṣrī (d. 234/848)
10. Khalaf, the same as Ḥamza's first *rāwī*
   a. Abū Yaʿqūb Isḥāq b. Ibrāhīm al-Warrāq al-Marwazī al-Baghdādī (d. 286/899)
   b. Abū l-Ḥasan Idrīs b. ʿAbd al-Karīm al-Ḥaddād al-Baghdādī (d. 295/908)
11. Muḥammad b. ʿAbd al-Raḥmān b. Muḥayṣin (123/740)
   a. al-Bazzī, the same as Ibn Kathīr's first *rāwī*
   b. Abū l-Ḥasan Muḥammad b. Aḥmad b. Ayyūb b. Shannabūdh (d. 328/939)
12. al-Yazīdī, Abū Muḥammad Yaḥyā b. al-Mubārak b. al-Mughīra al-Baṣrī (d. 202/817)
   a. Abū Ayyūb Sulaymān b. Ayyūb b. al-Ḥakam al-Baghdādī (d. 235/849)
   b. Abū Jaʿfar Aḥmad b. Faraḥ b. Jibrīl al-Baghdādī (d. 303/915)
13. al-Ḥasan al-Baṣrī (d. 110/728)
   a. Abū Nuʿaym Shujāʿ b. Abī Naṣr al-Balkhī l-Baghdādī (d. 190/806)
   b. al-Dūrī, the same as Abū ʿAmr's first *rāwī*
14. Abū Muḥammad Sulaymān b. Mahrān al-Aʿmash al-Kūfī (d. 148/765)
   a. Abū l-ʿAbbās al-Ḥasan b. Saʿīd b. Jaʿfar al-Muṭawwiʿa al-Baṣrī (d. 371/981)
   b. Abū l-Faraj Muḥammad b. Aḥmad b. Ibrāhīm al-Shannabūdhī l-Baghdādī (d. 388/998)

Spread and occurrence of the accepted readings

Not much can be said with certainty about the actual occurrence of the different readings, or whether most of them had anything more than theoretical significance. The analysis of the numerous preserved historical Qurʾān manuscripts should be of great help in establishing a clearer picture, but these data have only begun to be analyzed (Dutton, Early muṣḥaf; see MANUSCRIPTS OF THE QURʾĀN).

At first, most readings appear to have been favored by the regions in which they originated. It is conceivable that some readings predate the reader with whom they were associated by Ibn Mujāhid (Dutton, Early muṣḥaf). About the subsequent history in some regions a little bit more is known. In the Maghrib, Ḥamza's reading was supplanted by Nāfiʿ's, which also became the favored reading in al-Andalus. Nowadays, the most widespread reading in west and north Africa, except Egypt, is Warsh *ʿan* Nāfiʿ. In Libya and in parts of Tunisia and Algeria Qālūn *ʿan* Nāfiʿ also has some following. In Egypt, the reading of Warsh *ʿan* Nāfiʿ was equally well spread until about the tenth/sixteenth century, but the reading of Abū ʿAmr was also not unknown. The commentary known as *al-Jalālayn,* for instance, follows this reading. The reading of Abū ʿAmr is said to have been dominant in the Ḥijāz, Syria and the Yemen from the fifth/eleventh century, when it superseded Ibn ʿĀmir's. This latter nevertheless is reported to be in use in some parts of the Yemen. Nowadays, the reading of al-Dūrī *ʿan* Abī ʿAmr appears still to be used in parts of west Africa, the Sudan, Somalia and Ḥaḍramawt. Some (as yet unpublished) leaves of a qurʾānic manuscript that were found during emergency excavations in the town of al-Qaṣr in the Dakhla oasis in the western desert of Egypt show what is an interesting, and apparently eclectic, reading (for material from this excavation, see Figs. III and IV of SHEETS). For, in a number of cases, this manuscript — which generally follows Abū ʿAmr — adopts a Meccan reading concerning the pronunciation of the *hamza* (pace Ibn Kathīr and Ibn Muḥayṣin). This *muṣḥaf* probably was in use before or in the nineteenth century C.E.

The great unifying change came in the tenth/sixteenth century, as the Ottoman empire adopted the Ḥafṣ *ʿan* ʿĀṣim reading. In the course of time this reading became and remained by far the most widespread. Only on the fringes of the Ottoman empire or outside of it, as in northwest Africa, did other readings remain in use. The printing of the Egyptian government edition of the Qurʾān, which appeared in 1342/1923 and which followed the Ḥafṣ *ʿan* ʿĀṣim reading, although with a *rasm* with far fewer *alif*s, immensely advanced the spread of this reading, albeit after the fall of the Ottoman empire (see PRINTING OF THE QURʾĀN). Apart from this reading, only the Nāfiʿ reading in both *riwāya*s seems to be available in printed form.

Registration of the readings

In modern times it became possible to register the readings on gramophone records (see MEDIA AND THE QURʾĀN). The earliest recordings appear to date from the 1920s. The first complete recording of the whole Qurʾān in the *murattal* style according to both the Ḥafṣ *ʿan* ʿĀṣim and the Warsh *ʿan* Nāfiʿ was done in the 1960s by the Egyptian *shaykh al-maqāriʾ* Maḥmūd Khalīl al-Ḥuṣarī (d. 1980). Since then, numerous recitations of the Qurʾān have become available, especially on audiocassettes, CDs and websites. The vast majority of these recordings follow the reading of Ḥafṣ *ʿan* ʿĀṣim, but recitations according to the readings of Warsh *ʿan* Nāfiʿ, Qālūn *ʿan* Nāfiʿ and al-Sūsī *ʿan* Abī ʿAmr and al-Dūrī *ʿan* Abī ʿAmr also exist. Recitations are broadcast not only by radio stations (like the Egyptian *Idhāʿat al-Qurʾān al-karīm*), but also by several sites on the Internet (see COMPUTERS AND THE QURʾĀN). With this modern development the diversity of what is essentially an oral tradition is being revived.

Before modern times the differences among the readings were, of course, transmitted orally, but there were also specialized books that described them. At an early stage, graphical signs were devised which were added to the *rasm* of manuscripts of the Qurʾān in order to establish the correct pronunciation. First, a system of little dashes was introduced to differentiate between characters with similar forms. Later, these dashes were changed to dots (see ARABIC SCRIPT). Two slightly different systems evolved. What is now considered the western system, which was and is still used in the Iberian peninsula and north Africa, differentiates between the letters *fāʾ* and *qāf*, by the placement of one dot under the former and one dot above the latter. The eastern system uses one dot above the *fāʾ* and two dots above the *qāf*. Nearly the same system is already in place in the inscriptions of the Dome of the Rock in Jerusalem, with the exception that there the *fāʾ* and *qāf* are distinguished by one dash above the first and one dash under the latter (see EPIGRAPHY AND THE QURʾĀN; ART AND ARCHITECTURE AND THE QURʾĀN). Interestingly, the same divergence is found in some early Qurʾān manuscripts, e.g. an early Ḥijāzī *muṣḥaf* in the Austrian National Library in Vienna (cod. mixt. 917), an early, probably Yemeni one (Ṣanʿāʾ, Dār al-Makhṭūṭāt, inv. no. 01-29.2), and an early Ḥijāzī *muṣḥaf* in St. Petersburg (inv. no. E-20). In some instances in this last mentioned example, however, the double dots above the *qāf* were added (see also CALLIGRAPHY; ORNAMENTATION AND ILLUMINATION).

Probably at a later stage, colored, usually red, dots were added in order to distinguish vowels and the *hamza,* or glottal stop. Sometimes the *hamza* is also represented by a dot of a different color, usually green. It is not known when this system was devised, but it may be noted that it is already used in what is claimed to be a very early *muṣḥaf* among the Qur'ān manuscripts that were found in the Great Mosque of Ṣan'ā' (Ṣan'ā', Dār al-Makhṭūṭāt, inv. no. 20-33.1). As with other early manuscripts of the Qur'ān, it is possible that these colored dots were added later, but in the time of Ibn Abī Dāwūd al-Sijistānī (d. 316/929) this was apparently common practice. He devoted a chapter to it in his *Kitāb al-Maṣāḥif* (Jeffery, *Materials,* 144-7 of the Arabic text). Some early manuscripts of the Qur'ān, now housed mainly in the Bodleian Library, mark alternative readings, from the "seven" or the "ten" and also *shādhdh* readings, by dots of a different color (Dutton, Red dots). The problem with early qur'ānic manuscripts is that no consensus about their dating exists. Most of these are assigned to the third/ninth and fourth/tenth centuries, although some are probably earlier.

Apart from signs for vowels, *alif*s were also added, usually in red, to make up for an orthography which did not denote a long /*a*/. In the course of time more signs came into existence to denote further niceties of recitation, like signs for nasalization and signs to indicate where a *waqf,* or pause, must, could or must not be inserted. In imitation of the Egyptian government edition of the Qur'ān, modern printed editions of the Qur'ān usually include a list that explains the meaning of these signs. Some remnants of older systems have survived in the western tradition where *hamza*s are written above, below or in the middle of an *alif* to denote whether it is to be pronounced with an /*a*/, an /*i*/ or a /*u*/, respectively. An interesting new development is an edition of the Qur'ān (Damascus 1414/1993) according to the reading of Ḥafṣ *'an* 'Āṣim in which different colors are used to denote the varying lengths of syllables; gray is used for letters that should not be pronounced.

The knowledge of the readings is nowadays greatly advanced by the publication of Qur'ān editions that give in the margins the differences between the accepted readings according to the system of the "ten" or the "fourteen."

Frederik Leemhuis

Bibliography

Primary: 'Abd al-Razzāq, *Tafsīr,* Riyadh 1410/1989; Abū l-Ṭayyib 'Abd al-Mun'im b. 'Abdallāh b. Ghalbūn, *Kitāb al-Istikmāl,* ed. 'A. Buḥayrī Ibrāhīm, Cairo 1991; id., *Kitāb al-Tadhkira fī l-qirā'āt,* ed. 'A. Buḥayrī Ibrāhām, 2 vols, Cairo 1990; Akhfash, *Ma'ānī;* al-Azharī, Abū Manṣūr Muḥammad b. Aḥmad, *Kitāb Ma'ānī l-qirā'āt,* ed. 'Ī.M. Ruwaysh and 'A. al-Qawzī, 3 vols., Cairo 1991-3; Dānī, *Muqni';* id., *Taysīr;* Dhahabī, *Qurrā';* Fārisī, *Ḥujja;* Farrā', *Ma'ānī;* Ibn Abī Dāwūd al-Sijistānī, *Kitāb al-Maṣāḥif,* in Jeffery, *Materials,* 39-49, 144-7; Ibn al-Jazarī, *Ghāya;* id., *Munjid;* id., *Nashr;* Ibn Jinnī, *Muḥtasab;* Ibn Juzayy al-Gharnāṭī, Abū l-Qāsim Muḥammad b. Aḥmad *al-Tashīl li-'ulūm al-tanzīl,* Beirut 1983; Ibn Mujāhid, *Sab'a;* Ibn Qutayba, *Ta'wīl;* Ibn Wahb, *al-Jāmi';* Makkī, *Ibāna;* id., *Kashf;* Mujāhid, *Tafsīr;* Sufyān al-Thawrī, *Tafsīr;* Ṭabarī, *Tafsīr.*

Secondary: A. Brocket, The value of the Ḥafṣ and Warsh transmissions for the textual history of the Qur'ān, in Rippin, *Approaches,* 31-45; Kh. Aḥmad Muftī, *Naḥw al-qurrā' al-kūfiyyīn,* Mecca 1985; A. al-Baylī, *al-Ikhtilāf bayna l-qirā'āt,* Beirut 1988 (especially 63-91); E. Beck, 'Arabiyya, Sunna und 'Āmm in der Koranlesung des zweiten Jahrhundert, in *Orientalia* 15 (1946), 180-224; id., Die b. Mas'ūdvarianten bei al-Farrā', in *Orientalia* 25 (1956), 353-83; 28 (1959), 186-205, 230-56; id., Die dogmatisch religiöse

Einstellung des Grammatikers Yaḥyā b. Ziyād al-Farrā', in *Muséon* 54 (1951), 187-202; id., Die Kodizesvarianten der Amṣār, in *Orientalia* 16 (1947), 353-76; id., Studien zur Geschichte der Kufischen Koranlesung in den beiden ersten Jahrhunderten, in *Orientalia* 17 (1948), 326-55; 19 (1950), 328-50; 20 (1951), 316-28; 22 (1953), 59-78; id., Der ʿuṯmānischen Kodex in der Koranlesung des zweiten Jahrhunderts, in *Orientalia* 14 (1954), 355-73; id., Die Zuverlässigkeit der Überlieferung von ausser ʿuṯmānischen Varianten bei al-Farrā', in *Orientalia* 23 (1954), 412-35; G. Bergsträsser, Nichtkanonische Koranlesarten im Muḥtasab des Ibn Ǧinnī, in *Sitzungsberichte der Bayerischen Akademie der Wissenschaften* 2 (1933), 5-92; id., Plan eines Apparatus Criticus zum Koran, in *Sitzungsberichte der Bayerischen Akademie der Wissenschaften* 7 (1930), 3-11, repr. in Paret (ed.), *Koran,* 389-97; H.-C. Graf von Bothmer, Vroege koranmanuscripten, aangetroffen in de Grote Moskee van Sana'a, Jemen, in M.B. Piotrovski and J. Vrieze (eds.), *Aardse schoonheid, hemelse kunst. Kunst van de islam,* Amsterdam 1999, 98-105; J. Burton, Muṣḥaf, in *EI²*, vii, 668-9; S. Carboni, Die arabischen Handschriften, in J.A. Petrosjan et al. (eds.), *Von Bagdad bis Isfahan. Buchmalerei und Schriftkunst des Vorderen Orients (8.-18. Jh) aus dem Institut für Orientalistik, St. Petersburg,* Lugano 1995, 85-100; F. Déroche, *Catalogue des manuscrits arabes,* 2ᵉ partie, I/1. *Les manuscrits du Coran. Aux origines de la calligraphie coranique,* Paris 1983; Y. Dutton, An early muṣḥaf according to the reading of Ibn ʿĀmir, in *Journal of qur'anic studies* 3 (2001), 71-89; id., Red dots, green dots, yellow dots & blue. Some reflections on the vocalisation of early qur'ānic manuscripts, in *Journal of qur'anic studies* 1 (1999), 115-140; 2 (2000), 1-24; Jeffery, *Materials;* id., Progress in the study of the Qur'ān text, in *MW* 25 (1935), 4-16; G.H.A. Juynboll, *Ibn Miḳsam,* in *EI²* [sup.], 393; Muḥammad Fahd Khārūf, *al-Muyassar fī l-qirā'āt al-arbaʿa ʿashara,* Damascus 1995; ʿAbd al-Laṭīf al-Khaṭīb, *Muʿjam al-qirā'āt,* 11 vols., Damascus 2002; F. Leemhuis, Ursprünge des Koran als Textus Receptus, in S. Wild and H. Schild (eds.), *Akten des 27. Deutschen Orientalistentages (Bonn — 28. September bis 2. oktober 1998). Norm und Abweichung,* Würzburg 2001, 301-8; Muḥammad Sālim Muḥaysin, *al-Irshādāt al-jaliyya fī l-qirā'āt al-sabʿ min Ṭarīq al-Shāṭibiyya,* Beirut 1997; M. Muranyi, Neue Materialien zur *Tafsīr*-Forschung in der Moscheebibliothek von Qairawan, in Wild, *Text,* 225-55; K. Nelson, *The art of reciting the Qur'ān,* Austin, TX 1985; A. Neuwirth, Koran. Textgeschichte, in *GAP,* ii, 106-13 (with detailed bibliography); Nöldeke, *GQ,* iii; R. Paret, Ḳirā'a, in *EI²*, v, 127-9; G-R. Puin, Observations on early Qur'ān manuscripts in Ṣanʿā', in Wild, *Text,* 107-11; ʿAbd al-Fattāh al-Qāḍī, *al-Qirā'āt al-shādhdha wa-tawjīhuhā min lughat al-ʿArab,* Cairo 1975; Muḥammad Aḥmad Mufliḥ al-Quḍāh, Aḥmad Khālid Shukrī and Muḥammad Khālid Manṣūr, *Muqaddimāt fī ʿilm al-qirā'āt,* Amman 2001; Muḥammad Karīm Rājiḥ and Muḥammad Fahd Khārūf, *al-Qirā'āt al-ʿāshr al-mutawātira min ṭarīqay al-Shāṭibiyya wa-l-Durra bi-hāmish al-Qur'ān al-karīm bi-l-rasm al-ʿUthmānī,* Damascus 1994²; E.A. Rezwan, Frühe Abschriften des Korans, in J.A. Petrosjan et al. (eds.), *Von Bagdad bis Isfahan. Buchmalerei und Schriftkunst des Vorderen Orients (8.-18. Jh) aus dem Institut für Orientalistik, St. Petersburg,* Lugano 1995, 117-25; S. de Sacy, Du manuscrit arabe no 239 de la Bibliothèque Impériale..., in *Notices et extraits des manuscrits de la Bibliothèque Impériale* 8 (1810), 290-332 (a seminal contribution to the field); Tarif al-Samman and Otto Mazal, *Die arabische Welt und Europa. Ausstellung der Handschriften- und Inkunabelsammlung der Österreichischen Nationalbibliothek,* Graz 1988, 76 and Table 1a; Sezgin, *GAS,* i, 3-18; A. Spitaler, Die nicht-kanonischen Koranlesarten und ihre Bedeutung für die arabische Sprachwissenschaft, in Paret (ed.), *Koran,* 413-4; J.C. Vadet, Ibn Masʿūd, in *EI²*, iii, 873-5; A.T. Welch, al-Ḳur'ān. History of the Ḳur'ān after 632, in *EI²*, v, 404-9; E. Whelan, Forgotten witness. Evidence for the early codification of the Qur'ān, in *JAOS* 118 (1998), 1-14; id., Writing the word of God. Some early Qur'ān manuscripts and their milieux, in *Ars orientalis* 20 (1990), 113-47.

Rebellion

Opposition to authority. Whether the Qur'ān has anything to say on the subject of rebellion and political violence (q.v.; see also POLITICS AND THE QUR'ĀN) is not an issue that can easily be resolved by reference to the text of the Qur'ān alone. Although the Qur'ān does not seem to address the issue explicitly, classical Muslim jurists (see LAW AND THE QUR'ĀN) argued that particular verses in the Qur'ān were intended to guide legal determinations regarding rebellion, or what is known as the problem of *al-khurūj ʿalā l-ḥākim,* "disobeying and rebelling against the ruler" (see DISOBEDIENCE; KINGS AND RULERS). Within the first centuries of Islam, the political and legal debate focused on three qur'ānic pronouncements, all three of which do not appear to address directly the issue of rebellion. The first pronouncement commanded Muslims to obey God, the Prophet and those who are in charge of the Muslim community (Q 4:59; see OBEDIENCE; AUTHORITY). Not surprisingly, the Umayyad caliphs (see CALIPH) and later on the ʿAbbāsids, confronted by multiple rebellions, argued that this qurʾānic verse mandated strict obedience to rulers and forbade all forms of rebellion. In support of this position, a large number of traditions attributed to the Prophet were circulated in the first two centuries of Islam banning rebellion even against an unjust ruler (e.g. Shaybānī, *Sunna,* 29, 445, 491, 492-4; see OPPRESSION).

The second is an ambiguous qurʾānic pronouncement which strongly condemns people who fight God and his Prophet and spread corruption (q.v.) on the earth *(mufsidūn fī l-arḍ)* by destroying property (q.v.) and life (*wa-yasʿawna fī l-arḍi fasādan,* Q 5:33). The verse (known as *āyat al-ḥirāba*) sets out severe punishments, including banishment and death, for those who commit such a hideous deed (see FIGHTING; CHASTISEMENT AND PUNISHMENT). Various historical accounts report that this verse was revealed when a group from the tribe of ʿUrayna pretended to convert to Islam, only to turn around, steal the properties entrusted to them by Muslims and then torture to death a poor shepherd boy who was sent to instruct them in Islam (cf. Rāzī, *Tafsīr;* Ibn Kathīr, *Tafsīr;* Ibn al-Jawzī, *Zād;* Zamakhsharī, *Kashhāf;* Ṭabarsī, *Majmaʿ,* ad Q 5:33; see OCCASIONS OF REVELATION). But because of the verse's broad and strong condemnatory language and its mandate of severe punishments for those who cause corruption on earth, various state functionaries and rulers, commencing with the period of the Umayyads, and continuing even at times to the present age, have asserted that this verse was intended to apply to rebels. Accordingly, various rulers, especially in the first three centuries of Islam, contended that rebellion was strictly prohibited and that rebels are corrupters of the earth *(mufsidūn fī l-arḍ)* and therefore, ought to be treated according to the harsh penalties set out in the qurʾānic verse (e.g. Ṭabarī, *Taʾrīkh,* v, 141-2, 159, 202-37; Ibn al-Athīr, *Kāmil,* iii, 336, 343-4, 455; Ibn al-Aʿtham, *Futūḥ,* iii, 114-52; Ibn al-Jawzī, *Muntaẓam,* vii, 211-12).

The third qurʾānic verse (Q 49:9; known as *āyat al-baghy*) was the one most central to the early Islamic debates on rebellion and it is also the one after which the law of rebels and rebellion *(aḥkām al-bughāt)* was named. This verse instructs Muslims to seek a peaceful solution to any dispute or conflict that occurs between them and further instructs that if one of the disputing parties refuses to accept a peaceful resolution, then such a party has become a transgressor and Muslims should fight against such a transgressor until he concedes to a peaceful resolution (see CONTRACTS AND ALLIANCES; BREAKINGS TRUSTS AND CONTRACTS). Interestingly enough, this is the qurʾānic commandment that the classical jurists argued is the most relevant to the issue of rebellion. Contrary to the claims of the Umayyads and early ʿAbbāsids, Muslim jurists argued that the qurʾānic verse regarding corruption of the earth was intended to apply to highway robbers and bandits (*quṭṭāʿ al-ṭuruq;* see THEFT), and not to rebels (Jaṣṣāṣ, *Aḥkām,* ii, 409-11, 413-4; Ibn Abī Zayd, *Nawādir,* xiv, 474). This was significant because, in effect, it meant that rulers cannot claim that the harsh treatment of rebels is mandated or sanctioned by the Qurʾān. According to the jurists, the Qurʾān mandated reconciliation and the reaching of peaceful resolutions for all inter-Muslim conflicts, including conflicts with rebels (cf. e.g. Māwardī, *Kitāb al-Qitāl*, 70-3, 75).

Muslim jurists agreed that obedience to a ruler is mandatory unless such a ruler commands something unlawful (*al-ṭāʿa wājiba li-kulli ḥākim mā lam yaʾmur bi-maʿṣiya;* cf. Abū Dāwūd, *Sunan,* iv, 94; see LAWFUL AND UNLAWFUL; VIRTUES AND VICES, COMMANDING AND FORBIDDING). There was quite a bit of disagreement, however, as to what ought to happen if a ruler does command an unlawful act, with jurists venturing responses ranging from passive resistance to armed rebellion. In general, Muʿtazilī (see MUʿTAZILĪS), Shīʿī (see SHĪʿISM AND THE QURʾĀN) and a significant number of Sunnī jurists argued that armed rebellion against an unjust and illegitimate ruler is mandatory (Ibn Karrāma, *Risāla,* 97). After the fourth/tenth century, with the disintegration of the ʿAbbāsid caliphate and increasing incidents of political and social turmoil (*fitna,* pl. *fitan*), the Muʿtazilī, Shīʿī and the Sunnī Ashʿarī responses (see THEOLOGY AND THE QURʾĀN) became increasingly pragmatic, and less idealistic, in nature and they also became substantially similar to one another. They argued that rebellion against an unjust ruler is justified only if there is a real possibility that such a ruler can be removed through rebellion and the rebellion will not result in more social turmoil and suffering than that experienced because of the injustice of the ruler. In effect, Muslim jurists advocated a type of balancing test according to which rebellion is justified only if the total good outweighs the total anticipated evil (e.g. Ibn ʿĀbidīn, *Radd,* vi, 415; Ibn Mufliḥ, *Furūʿ,* vi, 160; Juwaynī, *Ghiyāth,* 115). In all cases, however, most Sunnī and Shīʿī jurists maintained that it is unlawful to participate or actively to support an unjust ruler in carrying out his unlawful commands (e.g. Ibn Taymiyya, *Siyāsa,* 77; Ibn Fahd al-Ḥillī, *Muhadhdhab,* ii, 327).

Interestingly, the main focus of Sunnī and Shīʿī jurists writing after the fourth/tenth century was not on the justifiability or permissibility of rebellion but on the treatment that ought to be afforded rebels. Basing themselves on *āyat al-baghy* and the precedent of ʿAlī b. Abī Ṭālib's (q.v.) conduct in fighting those who rebelled against him in the battles of the Camel and Ṣiffīn (see ṢIFFĪN, BATTLE OF), Muslim jurists developed an intricate field of law known as *aḥkām al-bughāt,* which is concerned with the lawfulness of rebellion and the treatment that should be afforded rebels. According to the provisions of *aḥkām al-bughāt,* special rules apply to rebels who fight while relying on a plausible interpretation *(taʾwīl muḥtamal)* or just cause *(dhikr maẓlama)*. Muslims who rely on a plausible religious interpretation or a plausible just cause are designated as *bughāt* and are treated with a certain degree of benevolence. Conversely, Muslims who fight because of tribal reasons *(ʿaṣabiyya)* or out of mere greed are not considered *bughāt* and are not entitled to benevolent treatment. According to classical jurists, those who do not rely on a plausible interpretation or just cause are treated as bandits or highway robbers and are to be killed or executed, and in certain circumstances amputated or banished (cf. e.g. Ibn al-Muqriʾ, *Ikhlāṣ,* iv, 128; Ibn ʿĀbidīn, *Radd,* vii, 188; Nawawī, *Rawḍa,* vii, 364-5; see BOUNDARIES AND PRECEPTS). In other words, *āyat al-ḥirāba* only applies to either regular highway robbers or to rebels who lack a plausible interpretation or just cause and thus do not qualify as *bughāt.* If rebels do qualify, however, as *bughāt,* their fugitive and wounded may not be dispatched. Rebel prisoners may not be executed or enslaved and the children and women of the rebels may not be intentionally killed, imprisoned or enslaved. Imprisoned male rebels must be released once the fighting or the danger of continued fighting ends.

Furthermore, the property of the rebels may not be taken as spoils and any property taken must be returned after the cessation of fighting. Furthermore, means of mass destruction such as mangonels, flamethrowers or flooding may not be used unless absolutely necessary, and rebels may not be mutilated or tortured under any circumstance, nor may they be denied a proper Muslim burial (q.v.; see also DEATH AND THE DEAD). Additionally, rebels may not be punished or held liable for acts committed during the fighting. Most significantly, the *bughāt,* according to the majority of the schools, are not sinners or criminals (see SIN, MAJOR AND MINOR). Furthermore, according to Muslim jurists, the term *bughāt* does not connote censure or blame (*laysa bi-ism dhamm;* cf. e.g. Māwardī, *Kitāb al-Qitāl,* 164-5; Ibn Qudāma, *Mughnī,* x, 61). The notable exception to this determination were the Ḥanafī jurists, who held that the *bughāt* are sinners but agreed that they should not be treated as common criminals (e.g. Jaṣṣāṣ, *Aḥkām,* iii, 402-4).

The requirement of a *taʾwīl,* "interpretation or cause," which qualifies rebels to be treated as *bughāt,* is somewhat vague. In essence, it appears to mean that the rebels rely on a religious interpretation that, in the view of the jurists, is not heretical (see HERESY). As noted above, this is correlative to the alternative justification, i.e. a grievance from a perceived injustice (*dhikr maẓlama;* see OPPRESSION; JUSTICE AND INJUSTICE). In principle, Muslim jurists were not willing to equate Muslims who fight or rebel because of "higher motives" or unselfish reasons to those who resort to violence out of the desire for prurient gain or out of blind allegiance to a tribe or family (q.v.; see also TRIBES AND CLANS; KINSHIP). Regardless of the nature of the *taʾwīl,* Muslim jurists held that in order for the *bughāt* to qualify for preferential treatment, they must have a degree of strength, or *shawka*. Strength, in this context, means that the *bughāt* must be of a certain number so that they are not easily overcome or defeated. Muslim jurists do not specify how many individuals are needed for *shawka* to exist, but simply state that one or two people is not sufficient. They justify this numerical requirement by arguing that since the *bughāt* are not held liable for life and property destroyed during the course of fighting, if the status of *bughāt* is given to individuals, regardless of the degree of support that they might enjoy, suffering will increase. As the jurists put it, without the requirement of *shawka,* anarchy and lawlessness will spread *(ḥattā la tafsad al-siyāsāt)*. They contended that without the requirement of *shawka,* every corrupt person will invent or fabricate a *taʾwīl* and claim to be a *bāghī* (singular of *bughāt;* cf. e.g. Ghazālī, *Wajīz,* 164; Ṭūsī, *Mabsūṭ,* vii, 264, 268). Hence, if a person resorts to force while relying on a plausible *taʾwīl* but does not have a *shawka,* he or she will be treated as a common criminal and will be held liable for any life or property destroyed.

Sunnī and Shīʿī jurists writing after the Mongol invasions in the seventh/thirteenth century started emphasizing an issue that perhaps is particularly pertinent to the modern age. A large number of jurists argued that certain methods of armed rebellion are so reprehensible and immoral that rebels who choose to utilize such methods are to be treated according to *āyat al-ḥirāba,* as corrupters of the earth, and not according to *āyat al-baghy,* as *bughāt*. These jurists argued that rebels who attack by stealth and indiscriminately slaughter innocent civilians (see MURDER; BLOODSHED) should not be afforded the status of *bughāt,* even if they adhere to a *taʾwīl* and enjoy a *shawka*. Rather, because of their indiscriminate and terror-inducing methods, such rebels ought to be treated as *muḥāribūn* under *āyat al-ḥirāba* and, therefore, may be held liable for their crimes and even executed. Despite their reliance on a religious interpretation or legitimate grievance, such *muḥāribūn* are committing a grievous sin that ought to be punished on this earth and that will be punished by God in the hereafter (e.g. Ibn al-Muqriʾ, *Ikhlāṣ*, iv, 128; Ibn ʿĀbidīn, *Radd*, vii, 188). Not surprisingly, several modern scholars have noted the similarity between what premodern jurists condemned as *muḥāribūn* and the actions of terrorists today. See also DISSENSION; APOSTASY; KHĀRIJĪS.

Khaled Abou El Fadl

Bibliography

Abū Dawūd, *Sunan,* Cairo 1988; al-Ghazālī, Abū Ḥāmid Muḥammad, *al-Wajīz fī fiqh madhhab al-Imām al-Shāfiʿī,* Cairo 1317/1899; Ibn ʿĀbidīn, Muḥammad Amīn b. ʿUmar al-Dimashqī, *Ḥāshiyat Radd al-muḥtār ʿalā l-Durr al-mukhtār,* ed. ʿĀ.A. Muʿawwaḍ, 8 vols., Beirut 1994; Ibn Abī Zayd al-Qayrawānī, *al-Nawādir wa-l-ziyādāt ʿalā mā fī l-Mudawwana min ghayrihā min al-ummahāt,* ed. ʿA.M. al-Ḥulw/M. Ḥajjī, 15 vols., Beirut 1999; Ibn al-Aʿtham al-Kūfī, *al-Futūḥ,* 8 vols. in 4, Beirut 1986; Ibn al-Athīr, ʿIzz al-Dīn, *al-Kāmil fī l-tārīkh,* ed. A.ʿA. al-Qāḍī, 10 vols., Beirut 1987; Ibn Fahd al-Ḥillī, Jamāl al-Dīn Abū l-ʿAbbās Aḥmad b. Muḥammad, *al-Muhadhdhab al-bāriʿ fī Sharḥ al-Mukhtaṣar al-Nāfiʿ,* ed. M. al-ʿIrāqī, 5 vols., Qom 1987-92; Ibn al-Jawzī, *Muntaẓam,* ed. ʿAbd al-Qādir; id., *Zād;* Ibn Karrāma, al-Ḥākim Abū Saʿd al-Muḥassin b. Muḥammad al-Bayhaqī al-Jishumī, *Risālat Iblīs ilā ikhwānihi al-manāḥīs,* ed. Ḥ. Mudarrisī Ṭabāṭabāʾī, Qom 1986; Ibn Kathīr, *Tafsīr;* Ibn Mufliḥ, Shams al-Dīn Muḥammad al-Maqdisī, *Kitāb al-Furūʿ,* 6 vols., Beirut 1985; Ibn al-Muqriʾ, Sharaf al-Dīn Ismāʿīl b. Abī Bakr, *Ikhlāṣ al-nāwī,* ed. ʿA. ʿAṭiyya Zalaṭ, 4 vols., Cairo 1989; Ibn Qudāma al-Maqdisī, *al-Mughnī,* 12 vols., Beirut n.d.; Ibn Taymiyya, *al-Siyāsa al-sharʿiyya fī iṣlāḥ al-raʿy wa-l-raʿiyya,* Beirut 1983; Jaṣṣāṣ, *Aḥkām,* 3 vols., Beirut 1986; al-Juwaynī, ʿAbd al-Malik, *Ghiyāth al-umam fī ltiyāth al-ẓulam,* ed. ʿA. al-Dīb, Qatar 1980; Māwardī, *Kitāb Qitāl ahl al-baghy min al-Ḥāwī al-kabīr,* ed. I. Ṣandūqjī, Cairo 1987; Nawawī, *Rawḍat al-ṭālibīn,* ed. ʿĀ.A. ʿAbd al-Mawjūd and ʿA.M. Muʿawwaḍ, 8 vols., Beirut 1992; Rāzī, *Tafsīr;* al-Shaybānī, Abū Bakr al-Ḍaḥḥāk b. Makhlad, *Kitāb al-Sunna,* ed. M.N. al-Albānī, Beirut 1993; Ṭabarī, *Taʾrīkh,* 13 vols., Beirut 1987; Ṭabarsī, *Majmaʿ;* Ṭūsī, *al-Mabsūṭ fī fiqh al-imāmiyya,* ed. M. Taqī l-Kashafī, 8 vols. in 4, Tehran 1967-73[2]; Zamakhsharī, *Kashshāf.*

Recitation of the Qurʾān

The vocal rendition of the Qurʾān. *Tilāwat al-Qurʾān* is to render the Arabic Qurʾān in voice. It is a branch of the sciences of the "readings" *(qirāʾāt)* of the Qurʾān (see READINGS OF THE QURʾĀN). In the Qurʾān, the term *tilāwa* (which appears in both nominal and verbal forms) often refers to the signs (q.v.) of God that are "rehearsed" therein, i.e. the narration of accounts of previous messengers and communities in sacred history (see NARRATIVES; MESSENGER; GENERATIONS; PUNISHMENT STORIES), as well as the actual act of the recitation of the Qurʾān itself. In general, when the word *tilāwa* refers to the practice of reading the Qurʾān aloud, it conveys a sense of "following" the qurʾānic message as it is rendered in human voice.

The practice of reciting the Qurʾān is performed according to a set of guidelines known as *tajwīd. Tajwīd,* although not a qurʾānic term, is the fundamental system of rules for the correct pronunciation of the Qurʾān as it was understood to have been revealed to the prophet Muḥammad (see REVELATION AND INSPIRATION). Recitation of the Qurʾān according to *tajwīd* has many names across the Muslim-majority and Muslim-minority worlds. Some of these terms are variants of the qurʾānic expression *tartīl,* which conveys a sense of "measuring" out the speech of the Qurʾān in a careful and deliberate manner.

Some recitation of the Qurʾān is always required of Muslims for the performance of one of the canonical acts of Islamic worship (q.v.), prayer (q.v.; *ṣalāt*); reading the Qurʾān aloud is also a key observance of supererogatory Islamic piety. In Muslim traditions of learning and education, the oral/aural recitation of the memorized Qurʾān is the most authoritative mode of its transmission (see TEACHING AND PREACHING THE QURʾĀN). In some contemporary societies, promoting engagement with the recited Qurʾān is the basis of popular Muslim revitalization movements (see ORALITY; TRADITIONAL DISCIPLINES OF QURʾĀNIC STUDY).

Reference to recitation

The Qurʾān on its recitation

The word "Qurʾān" is often said to be a form of the root *q-r-ʾ* meaning "to read, to recite." When understood in this sense, "Qurʾān" could be said to be as much an action as an object. Besides the actual word, the Qurʾān includes other names for itself that also emphasize the active components of engaging the Qurʾān in voice, such as *dhikr,* "reminder" (see MEMORY; REMEMBRANCE; NAMES OF THE QURʾĀN). Characteristic of the self-referentiality of qurʾānic content, the Qurʾān also contains many descriptions of its own recitation. Because of the Qurʾān's unmatched authority as a guide to thought and action in Islamic systems, the Qurʾān's own descriptions of the recited Qurʾān are also directives for believers.

The Qurʾān conveys instructions about its proper recitation in general terms, although not in specific or technical ones. The verses of the Qurʾān that are said to have been among the very first to have been revealed to the Prophet, those that open Q 96, are interpreted as a command to voice the Qurʾān: "Recite! In the name of your lord (q.v.) who created, created humanity from a clot" (see CREATION). The Qurʾān provides some instruction about how to perform its own recitation, in the form of *tartīl,* as in Q 73:4: "Recite/read the Qurʾān with *tartīl*" *(wa-rattili l-Qurʾān tartīlan).* The verbal form *tilāwa* appears in Q 25:32, where it refers to the reading of the Qurʾān as an act of chanting distinctly. There is also qurʾānic instruction on reading the Qurʾān, e.g. Q 75:16-8: "Do not move your tongue concerning it in order to make haste with it; it is for us to collect it and to read it *(qurʾānahu);* when we recite it *(qaraʾnāhu),* follow then its recitation *(qurʾānahu).*" Believers are also told in the Qurʾān to "remember" (i.e. *udhkur*), "preserve," (i.e. *taḥfīẓ*) and "read [aloud]" (i.e. *qurʾān; tartīl; tilāwa*) when reciting. The ideal reading of the Qurʾān is described as occupying the full concentration of the reciter; this activity is said to be one of which God, who is omniscient, is aware (Q 10:61). The Qurʾān also recommends its reading at night as an act of supererogatory piety (q.v.; Q 3:113-4; see VIGILS).

The Qurʾān contains many descriptions of its effects on listeners even as it is being recited; these, naturally, also function prescriptively in a qurʾānic context (see RITUAL AND THE QURʾĀN). The Qurʾān provides numerous depictions of embodied, emotive responses to itself when it describes the normative response among believers to hearing its message recited to them. For instance, the recitation of the Qurʾān causes the senses of the faithful to react with "shivering" skin, "trembling" heart (q.v.), and weeping (q.v.; e.g. Q 19:58 and 39:23). Descriptions of such embodied responses to the recited Qurʾān's message are often immediately followed with an affirmation of a corresponding change in the listeners' moral state, such as the following: "When it is recited to them, they fall down upon their faces, prostrating (see BOWING AND PROSTRATION), and say: 'Glory be to our lord (see GLORIFICATION OF GOD; LAUDATION)! Our lord's promise is fulfilled.' And they fall down upon their faces, weeping; and it increases them in humility" (Q 17:107-9); and, "And when they hear what has been sent down to the messenger, you see their eyes overflow with tears because of what they have recognized of truth (q.v.). They shout: 'Our lord! We believe'; so you will write us down among the witnesses [to the truth]" (Q 5:83; see WITNESSING AND TESTIFYING).

Traditions on recitation

Throughout the formative history of the development of the sciences of qurʾānic "readings" *(qirāʾāt)* and *tajwīd* up to the present day, Muslims have based the theory and practice of the recited Qurʾān upon the most authoritative of sources: first, the Qurʾān and accounts relating the practice of the prophet Muḥammad (ḥadīth; see ḤADĪTH AND THE QURʾĀN); and, second, accounts about the Companions of the Prophet (q.v.) and those who followed them. Within this material, it is ḥadīth reports that convey the ideal intensity of qurʾānic engagement through the ethico-legal injunction to follow the model of the Prophet (*sunna* [q.v.]; see also LAW AND THE QURʾĀN; ETHICS AND THE QURʾĀN).

Ḥadīth collections include many separate accounts indicating that Muḥammad valued beautiful voices among readers of the Qurʾān, such as the following reports of statements ascribed to the Prophet as collected by al-Bukhārī (d. 256/870) and others: "He is not one of us who does not sing *(yataghannā)* the Qurʾān," and, "God has not heard anything more pleasing than listening to a prophet reciting the Qurʾān in a sweet, loud voice." Also transmitted in al-Bukhārī and other collections, on the authority of Abū Mūsā l-Ashʿarī, there is the report that the Prophet said, "O Abū Mūsā! You have been given one of the musical instruments [voice] of the family of David (q.v.)!" Compilers of traditions also relate accounts about the Prophet's reaction to hearing the Qurʾān, such as his shedding tears.

Ḥadīth accounts also preserve information about the prophet Muḥammad's own recitation of the Qurʾān. Ḥadīth material includes detailed information about particular sūras (q.v.) recited by Muḥammad; they report, for example, which sūras the Prophet preferred to recite at particular times of day (see DAY, TIMES OF), as well as which parts of the Qurʾān the Prophet would repeat in his recitation (related to this is the abundant ḥadīth material on the merits of the recitation of particular sūras of the Qurʾān). Ḥadīth accounts provide some detail about the Prophet's comportment in recitation, such as the following report in al-Bukhārī: "'ʿĀʾisha (see ʿĀʾISHA BINT ABĪ BAKR) narrated: 'Whenever the Prophet went to bed every night, he used to cup his hands together and blow over them after reciting Sūrat al-Ikhlāṣ (Q 112, "Unity"; also termed al-Tawḥīd), Sūrat al-Falaq (Q 113, "The Dawn") and Sūrat al-Nās (Q 114, "People"), and then rub his hands over whatever parts of his body he was able to rub, starting with his head, face and front of his body. He used to do that three times.'" (*Ṣaḥīḥ*, viii, 110, no. 4372). The Prophet also enjoyed listening to the recitation of others, and there are many reports about weeping when hearing the Qurʾān recited (e.g. Bukhārī, *Ṣaḥīḥ*, viii, 122-3, nos. 4411-3), based on his practice.

In general, accepted ḥadīth accounts and other authoritative material from the earliest period of Islam emphasize the occasions and merits of recitation rather than practical technique. Later authorities continued the precedent of collecting reports about the recitation practice of the prophet Muḥammad, also compiling further information about the recitation habits of other pious people. This material on the proper comportment *(adab)* of recitation documents the recitation practices of famous religious figures, such as the first four caliphs in Sunnī tradition (see CALIPH). These reports provide information on matters such as the desirability of completing the recitation of the entire Qurʾān at nightfall, daybreak, and just before prayer times (see DAWN; EVENING); they also treat common challenges that reciters face, like confusing pauses and starts in sectioning. Issues that recur in this recitation literature include, for example, questions of how rapidly to recite and what is the proper portion of the book to complete in a given amount of time. One report transmitted by Abū Dāwūd (d. 275/889) and al-Tirmidhī (d. 279/892), for example, states, "Whoever recites the Qurʾān in less than three days does not understand it" (Nawawī, *Tibyān*, 103). Al-Ghazālī (d. 505/1111) sums up many such reports that were in circulation about the reading of the Qurʾān, from canonical ḥadīth collections and elsewhere, in his *Iḥyāʾ ʿulūm al-dīn* (Book 8).

Much of the authoritative material on the *adab* (comportment) of recitation addresses the intents behind recitation, such as that of seeking a worldly reward or payment for teaching or performance (see RECITERS OF THE QURʾĀN). It also includes strong prohibitions against reciting the Qurʾān ostentatiously or for show, a matter addressed in accepted ḥadīth traditions. For example, al-Bukhārī reports (*Ṣaḥīḥ*, viii, 123, no. 4415): "Abū Saʿīd al-Khudrī narrated: I heard God's messenger saying: 'There will appear some among you whose prayers will make you look down on yours, and whose fasting will make you look down on yours, and whose (good) deeds will make you look down on yours; but they will recite the Qurʾān and it will not exceed their throats.'" Another well-known report in most collections compares the piety of Qurʾān readers with the sweet and bitter smells and tastes of different plants and fruits. In this literature, the danger of such hypocrisy is balanced by the instruction to focus on the voicing of the speech (q.v.) of God (see also WORD OF GOD). There is a ḥadīth, for example, that the Prophet said: "Read the Qurʾān as long as your hearts are in harmony with it. When they are not in harmony, get up and stop reading it" (Bukhārī, *Ṣaḥīḥ*, viii, 124, no. 4417; also reported in Muslim's *Ṣaḥīḥ*).

Within the material known as *Adab tilawāt al-Qurʾān*, "Comportment of reciting the Qurʾān," and *Faḍāʾil al-Qurʾān*, "Excellences of the Qurʾān," there is strong emphasis on the idea that the recitation of the Qurʾān brings both individual and collective rewards. This is, for example, expressed in the following statement of Abū Hurayra (d. ca. 58/678), cited in sources such as al-Ghazālī's *Iḥyāʾ ʿulūm al-dīn* (Book 8): "Surely the house in which the Qurʾān is recited provides easy circumstances for its people, its good increases, angels come to it [in order to listen to the Qurʾān] and satans leave it. The house in which the Book of God is not recited provides difficult circumstances for its people, its good decreases, angels leave it, and satans come to it" (Ghazālī, *Recitation*, 25; there are many versions of this report). In addition to describing the immediate peace and tranquility (*sakīna;* see SHEKHINAH) that descends when the Qurʾān is read by the pious in this world, the results of the act of recitation, including knowing the Qurʾān by heart and not forgetting it, as well as "learning and teaching" the Qurʾān, are emphasized many times in numerous accounts found in the major ḥadīth collections. Such consequences of piety and committed action are not only described in terms of this world, but also with respect to the accounting of the day of judgment and future existence in the world to come (see LAST JUDGMENT; REWARD AND PUNISHMENT).

In an eschatological mode (see ESCHATOLOGY) of devotional piety, it is said that the Qur'ān itself will testify to the pious practice of the reader in his or her lifetime. In many ḥadīth and other pious literature such as al-Ghazālī's *Iḥyā' ʿulūm al-dīn* (Book 8), rewards for reciting the Qur'ān that will be credited on the day of judgment are calculated sūra by sūra and even *āya* by *āya*, based on reports in collections such as Abū Dāwūd, Aḥmad b. Ḥanbal, Muslim, al-Nasāʾī and al-Tirmidhī (see Wensinck, *Handbook*, 131). Not only sūra by sūra, or *āya* by *āya*, but there are even claims that rewards may be achieved letter by letter (see ARABIC SCRIPT; NUMEROLOGY; MAGIC; POPULAR AND TALISMANIC USES OF THE QUR'ĀN), such as the report transmitted by al-Tirmidhī: "For every letter that you read you will get tenfold reward," and the report that Ibn Masʿūd (d. 32/652-3) said: "[The Prophet] said 'Read the Qur'ān for you will be rewarded at the rate of [the recompense of] ten good deeds (q.v.) for reading every letter of the Qur'ān. Take notice, I do not say that *alif lām mīm* [a combination of three letters that opens Q 2; see MYSTERIOUS LETTERS] constitute one letter. Rather, I should say that *alif* is one letter, *lām* is another, and *mīm* is [still] another'" (Ghazālī, *Recitation*, 24).

The development of early traditions of ascetic piety lent heightened emphasis to such material within Islamic tradition (see ASCETICISM). Among the heirs to this early qur'ānic tradition of piety, Ṣūfīs especially developed the soteriological and interiorized qur'ānic traditions (see POLYSEMY; ṢŪFISM AND THE QUR'ĀN). Statements of well-known Ṣūfīs represent the Qur'ān as having a palpable presence for practitioners in their dreams as well as in waking states (see DREAMS AND SLEEP). This presence is depicted as an ongoing intimacy, at times framed in terms of the key concept of "friendship" (*wilāya;* see FRIENDS AND FRIENDSHIP; CLIENTS AND CLIENTAGE). This is indicated by personal accounts, as well as in prophetic narrations, such as: "Those who are concerned with the Qur'ān *(ahl al-Qur'ān)* are friends of God *(awliyā' Allāh)* and are special to him," which al-Ghazālī, for example, relates on the authority of Aḥmad b. Ḥanbal (d. 241/845). Ideally, engaging the Qur'ān in practice should conform to the reciter's close and immediate experience of the reading in his or her "heart." This ideal is central to the tradition of the recitation of the Qur'ān in pietistic circles.

Tajwīd *and systems of recitation*

History and development of qirā'āt

Early readers and transmitters of the Qur'ān were known for their knowledge as well as their piety (see SCHOLAR; KNOWLEDGE AND LEARNING). There are reports that the prophet Muḥammad dispatched "readers" *(qurrā')* in order to teach the Qur'ān to others. Such figures held an important position throughout the earliest period of Islam and some readers were also known for their religiously-inspired political leanings (see POLITICS AND THE QUR'ĀN). Those in the category of readers are listed in biographical dictionaries. According to some Muslim historical narratives, the deaths of many of Muḥammad's Companions in the wars of "apostasy" (q.v.), along with the spread of Islam to non-Arab areas, precipitated the standardization of the text of the Qur'ān (see COLLECTION OF THE QUR'ĀN; CODICES OF THE QUR'ĀN; ORTHOGRAPHY), as well as the beginning of the development of the qur'ānic sciences (see GRAMMAR AND THE QUR'ĀN; EXEGESIS OF THE QUR'ĀN: CLASSICAL AND MEDIEVAL). As Frederick Denny (Exegesis) has shown, the qur'ānic sciences of grammar, exegesis and recitation (including *qirā'a,* the study of variant readings or vocalizations of the standard text) developed simultaneously and all in response to similar circumstances and conditions. Like the standardization of the 'Uthmānic text, the technical guidelines for *tilāwa* and readings of the Qur'ān were systematized as a reaction to the potential variability of Muslim practices of recitation.

In technical and restricted usage, the term *qirā'āt* usually denotes the accepted variant readings of the Qur'ān. These readings do not relate to pitch variation or to alternate texts. Rather, they are minor differences in the vocalization of the same 'Uthmānic text, and all deploy the same system of guidelines for recitation, *tajwīd.* In a straightforward example of "variation" among the readings, a word in the fourth verse from the opening chapter, Sūrat al-Fātiḥa (Q 1:4), may be rendered either as *māliki* or *maliki* but both convey the same sense, which is God's dominion over the day of judgment. In another example, Q 5:6, which has generated differences of legal opinion on the ritual law for ablution (see CLEANLINESS AND ABLUTION; RITUAL PURITY), may carry two meanings depending on its vocalization. The vocalization and the nuances in the meaning depend on the decision to read a verb with or without a related preposition. If the phrase "your legs" *(arjulakum)* is read in the accusative, as according to Nāfi' and Ḥafṣ, it is understood as the object of the verbal imperative *"amsaḥū"* (yielding the meaning "wash your legs"). If it is read in the genitive *(arjulikum),* as according to Ibn Kathīr and Abū 'Amr, "your legs" are like the preceding *"ru'ūsikum"* ("your heads"), the object of the verb *(amsaḥū)* with the preposition *bi-* and the phrase is glossed as "wipe your legs." Some scholars, including those in the European tradition of textual analysis (see TEXTUAL CRITICISM OF THE QUR'ĀN), have considered the technical differences among the standard readings to be an important source of information about qur'ānic language and its historical parameters (see ARABIC LANGUAGE; DIALECTS).

There are seven accepted readings in the system of *qirā'āt.* The number seven is based on a well known ḥadīth of several variants, in which the Prophet is reported to have said: "This Qur'ān has been revealed to be recited in seven different modes *(aḥruf),* so recite of it whichever is easiest for you" (but cf. Melchert, Ibn Mujāhid). Some versions of this report narrate that the occasion of the revelation of the verse was a dispute over the proper reading of Q 25 (see OCCASIONS OF REVELATION). Another report, preserved by al-Bukhārī, relates that the Prophet stated that the angel Gabriel (q.v.) would recite the Qur'ān in different ways for him. These reports have been open to a variety of interpretations in Islamic tradition, including the ideas that the *aḥruf* may refer to differing dialects among the Arabs at the time of the revelation of the Qur'ān, or to the technical rules of *tajwīd.* The dominant interpretation, however, is that the *aḥruf* refer to what became known as the "seven readings" in tradition. Various reasons are given for the diversity of these accepted readings. Among them is the claim that they make the reception of the Qur'ān easier for those who are learning it. Another justification for their existence is that they enhance the multifaceted layers of qur'ānic meanings, including the proscriptive or legal (for elaboration of this last reason, see Burton, *Collection;* see LAWFUL AND UNLAWFUL; BOUNDARIES AND PRECEPTS; FORBIDDEN).

Abū Bakr b. Mujāhid (d. 324/936) is credited with the establishment of the accepted range of variations in the readings of the text, although additional readings are recorded and historically the content of actual enumerated lists has varied. The seven readings that were standardized in Ibn Mujāhid's time as the accepted *qirāʾāt* represented prominent schools of recitation in five centers of Muslim learning in the early Islamic period: Mecca, Medina, Damascus, Baṣra, and Kūfa. Ibn Mujāhid's selection includes the following seven readers: Ibn Kathīr (Mecca, d. 120/738), Nāfiʿ (Medina, d. 169/785), Ibn ʿĀmir (Damascus, d. 118/736), Abū ʿAmr (Baṣra, d. 154/770), ʿĀṣim (Kūfa, d. 127/745), Ḥamza (Kūfa, d. 156/773), and al-Kisāʾī (Kūfa, d. 189/804). This selection was justified by taking independent lines of transmission from scholars who were spread over a large geographic area. There was some controversy over the authority of this selection during Ibn Mujāhid's lifetime. It is also clear that there was continued development in the enumeration of "variant readings" after the time of Ibn Mujāhid since the later, influential scholar Ibn al-Jazarī (d. 833/1429) describes ten readings, while other scholars have cited fourteen. Despite this variation, Ibn Mujāhid's system of seven readings has continued to prevail and is considered standard. Today, the most popular readings (of those listed above) are those transmitted by Ḥafṣ (d. 180/796) on the authority of ʿĀṣim and Warsh (d. 197/812) on the authority of Nāfiʿ.

The system of tajwīd

Technical components of *tilāwa* convey theory and practice for the proper recitation of the Qurʾān. While not easily translated, there are two key terms for the applied aspects of the recited Qurʾān: *tartīl* and *tajwīd.* The terms are closely related; for example, the Qurʾān's instruction, "Recite the Qurʾān with *tartīl*" (Q 73:4) has been taken to mean, "Recite the Qurʾān according to the rules of *tajwīd.*" The term *tajwīd* refers to a rigorous system of rules that establish the proper vocalization of the Qurʾān, thereby determining its actual rhythm and sound (although not pitch variation, which is always improvised). The root of the word *tajwīd (j-w-d)* connotes "to be correct" and "to improve." For the reciter, the system of *tajwīd* includes instructions on the correct articulation of phonetic sounds, the assimilation of juxtaposed vowels or consonants, and the proper rhythmic duration of vowel sounds. *Tajwīd* also determines the parameters for non-melodic improvisational flexibility. These include, for example, pauses and starts in reading, which allow the reciter to stress specific words, phrases, or sections. *Tajwīd* structures the unique sound of qurʾānic recitation and thereby distinguishes it from ordinary Arabic speech and singing. Overall, *tajwīd* shapes the rhythm and cadences of Qurʾān recitation and gives it a musical quality, although Muslims do not consider the recited Qurʾān to be the equivalent of a human product such as music.

Tajwīd is a classic qurʾānic science, part of the science of readings. It is treated in detail in writings such as al-Suyūṭī's (d. 911/1505) *Itqān fī ʿulūm al-Qurʾān. Tajwīd* is often defined in the sources by some variant of the phrase, "giving each sound its correct weight and measure." Formalization of the rules of *tajwīd* may be seen as a solution to the historical problem of standardizing style and sound in recitation with respect to the great linguistic and geographical diversity of the Islamic world. The rules of *tajwīd* expressly provide clear guidelines, assuring a uniformity and consistency of pronunciation of the divine speech. Being a native speaker of Arabic of any register or dialect does not guarantee proficiency in the practice of *tajwīd*. Even if the pronunciation renders the word intelligible and grammatically correct, the rules of *tajwīd* stipulate further scrupulous attention to the technicalities of sound production. *Tajwīd* is learned implicitly when children repeat what they hear but is also taught as a formal course of study. For the four-fifths of today's Muslims who are not native speakers of Arabic, *tajwīd* and the Arabic Qurʾān are learned together. Handbooks for elementary *tajwīd* instruction open by introducing students to the points of articulation *(makhārij al-ṣawt)*, i.e. the proper methods for the articulation of the letters of the Arabic alphabet (see Fig. 1 for one such diagram).

Although, as mentioned above, the term *tajwīd* does not appear in the Qurʾān, the practice of recitation according to such guidelines is understood to have been a central dimension of Islamic piety since the time of the Prophet. And, according to Muslim tradition, the prophet Muḥammad learned the recitation of the Qurʾān, as well as the rules for its vocalization, directly from the angel Gabriel, who delivered it from the divine source (see HEAVENLY BOOK; PRESERVED TABLET). Recitation manuals consolidated what had certainly been long-accepted techniques and definitions, and systematic treatises on *tajwīd*, such as those of Ibn Mujāhid and al-Dānī (d. 444/1052), appeared in the fourth/eleventh century and were circulated widely after that time. In later centuries, *tajwīd* was fully developed and qualified as both a term and a practice, particularly with the work of Ibn al-Jazarī. Most manuals and discussions after the time of Ibn al-Jazarī follow his systematization. The formal system of *tajwīd* has two branches. These are, first, the correct vocalization of letters, especially the letter *nūn*, and, second, the proper relative duration of vowels. In addition, the field covers the mandatory and recommended points in the text where the reciter may pause and those where the recitation must continue without interruption. The manuals of *tajwīd* also discuss matters which deal with the proper etiquette or comportment surrounding the Qurʾān *(adab al-Qurʾān)*, such as ritual ablutions and respectful attention during recitation sessions.

In learning to read the Qurʾān aloud the student first studies the *makhārij*, or "points of articulation" of letters. These are identified in classical terminology in relation to the parts of the mouth in which they originate, such as *lisānī*, "tongue" letters (i.e. *qāf, kāf, jīm, shīn, yāʾ, lām, nūn, rāʾ, fāʾ*) and *shafawī*, "lip" letters *(bāʾ, mīm, wāw)*, as opposed to *ḥalq*, "throat," or guttural letters (*ʿayn, ḥāʾ, ghayn, khāʾ* and the *hamza*, the glottal stop), which are articulated back in the throat. The systemization of phonemes in *tajwīd* contains far more information about the Arabic letters than is included in this basic typology, however. For example, the alphabet is also grouped according to classes of "attributes" *(ṣifāt)*, which determine degrees of sound assimilation. These include qualities such as elevation *(istiʿlāʾ)*, depression *(istisfāl)*, softness *(tarqīq)* and heaviness *(tafkhīm)*. These attributes may be classified as necessary or conditional, depending on whether they are influenced by a given vowel *(ḥaraka)* combination. An individual letter has at least five essential *(lāzim)* or basic *(aṣlī)* attributes, each of which is expressed as one of a pair of opposites (such as *shadīda*, "strong," or *rikhwa*, "soft"). In addition, there are also ten (sometimes said to be seven) secondary but essential attributes which are not arranged in pairs of opposites, and a letter may have one or two of these ten attributes (such as the *ṣāfira,* sibilant or "whistling" letters, which are *ṣād, sīn,* and *zāʾ;* there is also another important classification known as *qalqala* letters).

A first principle of *tajwīd* is that consonants with the same point of articulation assimilate or blend together. All letters are classified in terms of a basic type of this process; the alphabet contains fourteen *shamsī,* "solar, or sun" letters and fourteen remaining *qamarī,* "moon" letters. Sun-letters are those that blend. For example, as in spoken Arabic, *al-rasūl,* "the Prophet," is pronounced as *ar-rasūl* because *rāʾ* is a blending sun-letter. In *tajwīd,* other kinds of consonantal assimilations (and partial assimilations), which are not heard in ordinary spoken Arabic, also occur.

Unique to qurʾānic pronunciation are rules for particular letters, such as *mīm* and especially *nūn.* There are special conventions for nasalized pronunciation *(ghunna)* of the letters *mīm* and *nūn* when they are doubled in a word or if their doubling happens between two words. There is also a class of rules related to changes that these letters undergo based on adjacent consonants. For example *mīm* and *nūn* do not get clear pronunciation *(iẓhār)* when they have been modified in the following ways: full assimilation (*idghām,* when they are voiced as the adjacent consonant), suppressed pronunciation (*ikhfāʾ,* when the sound is influenced by letters with similar points of articulation), and change or conversion (*qalb* or *iqlāb,* which applies to *nūn* only when it is pronounced as a *mīm*). As an example of the latter case, *a<u>n</u>biyāʾ,* "prophets," is pronounced as *a<u>m</u>biyāʾ* in the Qurʾān, since according to the rule of *iqlāb* the *nūn* is changed to a *mīm* by the following *bā*. (*Iqlāb* is marked in the text with a *mīm* symbol and some other types of assimilations are also marked; see MANUSCRIPTS OF THE QURʾĀN; ORNAMENTATION AND ILLUMINATION.)

Consonantal assimilation (*idghām,* occurring with the letter *nūn*), the first case given above, receives a great deal of attention from the beginning student, in part because it appears so frequently. (Indefinite case endings on nouns usually carry a terminal *nūn* sound, *tanwīn,* which is not written as an explicit letter in the text.) An example of this type of assimilation is the pronunciation of *<u>an-lā</u>,* "that no," which is voiced as *<u>al-lā</u>,* as in the testimony of faith — the *shahāda,* the first pillar of Islam (see WITNESS TO FAITH; FAITH) — and heard, with the application of *tajwīd,* in the *ādhān,* the "call to prayer": *ashhadu <u>an lā</u>* — pronounced *<u>al-lā</u>* — *ilāha illā āllāh,* "I testify that there is no god except God." In another example from the *shahāda,* the final nasal *nūn* of the indefinite accusative case ending on the name of the Prophet is also assimilated: *wa-anna Muḥammadan <u>rasūl</u>* — pronounced *Muḥammada<u>rr</u>asūl* — *-ullāh,* "and that Muḥammad is the messenger of God." In addition, the *nūn* may assimilate in ways that are not heard in spoken Arabic and vowels may adapt according to the preceding sounds (such as the long /*ā*/ in the name of God, *Allāh*).

A second major area of elementary *tajwīd* study pertains to the articulation of vowels. There are three vowel sounds in Arabic: /*a*/, /*i*/, and /*u*/ in long and short forms. Adjacent consonants affect not only their sound shape (as occurs in standard spoken Arabic) but, in Qurʾān recitation, also their duration. In the system of *tajwīd,* vowels are classified according to their duration or elongation, which is called *madd. Madd* is measured in terms of a basic unit or weight — called *madd aṣlī* or *madd farʿī* — of one short vowel (a long vowel counts as two basic units, "movements," or beats, called *ḥarakāt*). The relative weight of a vowel may be extended through the rules of *madd* or shortened through *qaṣr*. For example, vowels before doubled consonants (two consonants together) are shortened, as in the following: *ashhadu an-lā illāha illā Allāh* — pronounced *"illallāh"* —, "I testify that there is no god except God." *Madd*, or elongation of vowels, occurs when a long vowel (*madda* letter) and a "condition of *madd*," such as a glottal stop *(hamza)* appear together. For example, when a long vowel is followed by the glottal stop it is subsequently lengthened, usually by a degree of 3-1 or 2-1. An instance of this is the word *al-malāʾikatu*, "the angels," which is pronounced with an extended /ā/ counted with three beats of measure: *al-ma-la*[1]*-a*[2]*-a*[3]*-i-ka-tu*. There are four kinds of extended *madd (madd farʿī)*. These are: *wājib* or *muttaṣil*, "compulsory or joint" *madd* (occurring within a single word); *jāʾiz* or *munfaṣil*, "permissible or separating" *madd* (occurring between two adjacent words); *ṣila* or *talaffuẓī*, "temporary" *madd;* and *lāzim*, "permanent or essential" *madd*, of which there are four additional sub-types. A further rule is that a long vowel before a certain rare class of modified doubled consonants is lengthened, such as in the word *ḍāllīn*, the last word of Sūrat al-Fātiḥa (Q 1). In this case, the /ā/ of *ḍāllīn*, "those who have gone astray," with *lām*s doubled from an original form *ḍālilīn*, "astray," is pronounced drawn out with five "original" or fundamental *(aṣlī)* weights of measure *(ḥarakāt): ḍa*[1]*-a*[2]*-a*[3]*-a*[4]*-a*[5]*-ll-i*[1]-i[2]*-n*.

Another rule relating to vowel durations is pausal abbreviations occurring on words at the end of sectioned phrasings. These may occur at the marked ends of *āya*s but this is not always the case, as in *āya*s which are too long to recite in one breath. In pausal form, the final element is left unvoiced *(sākin)* whether it be a case of *tanwīn* (a nasalized ending on indefinite nouns, as in *Muḥammadan* above, which would be pronounced as *Muḥammada*), a declensional or conjugational vowel (*iʿrāb*, which could also include final short vowels on pronoun suffixes), or a *tāʾ marbūṭa*, pronounced /t/ (as in *al-malāʾikatu*, which would be pronounced as *al-malāʾika*). Because pausal abbreviation may leave out grammatical cues to meaning, it is advised that after such abbreviation, the reciter resume by repeating the final word of the previous phrase (which, now being the first and not the last word to be voiced, would not be in pausal form). There are also rules that pertain to giving a dropped terminal vowel *(ḥaraka)* some indication by a subtle prolongation or by making the shape of the vowel with the lips but without voicing it.

A final class of rules in the system of *tajwīd* pertains to stops and starts in sectioning or phrasing *(al-waqf wa-l-ibtidāʾ)*, which may only occur at the end of a complete word. Stops are classified according to the reasons for the stop: "forced" *(iḍṭirārī)*, which is an unplanned stop, like coughing; "informative" *(ikhtibārī)*, which would be a stop made in order to teach or to explain meaning; and "voluntary" *(ikhtiyārī)*, such as taking a breath. Stops are classified in terms of their desirability and appropriateness with respect to the meaning at that particular place within the text: there are "perfect" stops *(al-waqf al-tāmm)*, such as at the end of an *āya* when there is no connection in meaning to the one that follows; "sufficient" stops *(al-waqf al-kāfī)*, which occur at the end of a verse in which the sense of meaning continues in the following verse; "good" stops *(al-waqf al-ḥasan)*, which occur in the middle of an *āya* when a phrase is complete but when there is still a meaningful relation to the remainder of the verse; and, there are also bad or "ugly" stops *(al-waqf al-qabīḥ)*. An example of the last is Q 4:43, which is the place of an impermissible stop. This is because reciting only the beginning part of the *āya*, "Do not approach prayer," and stopping there without completing the phrase with

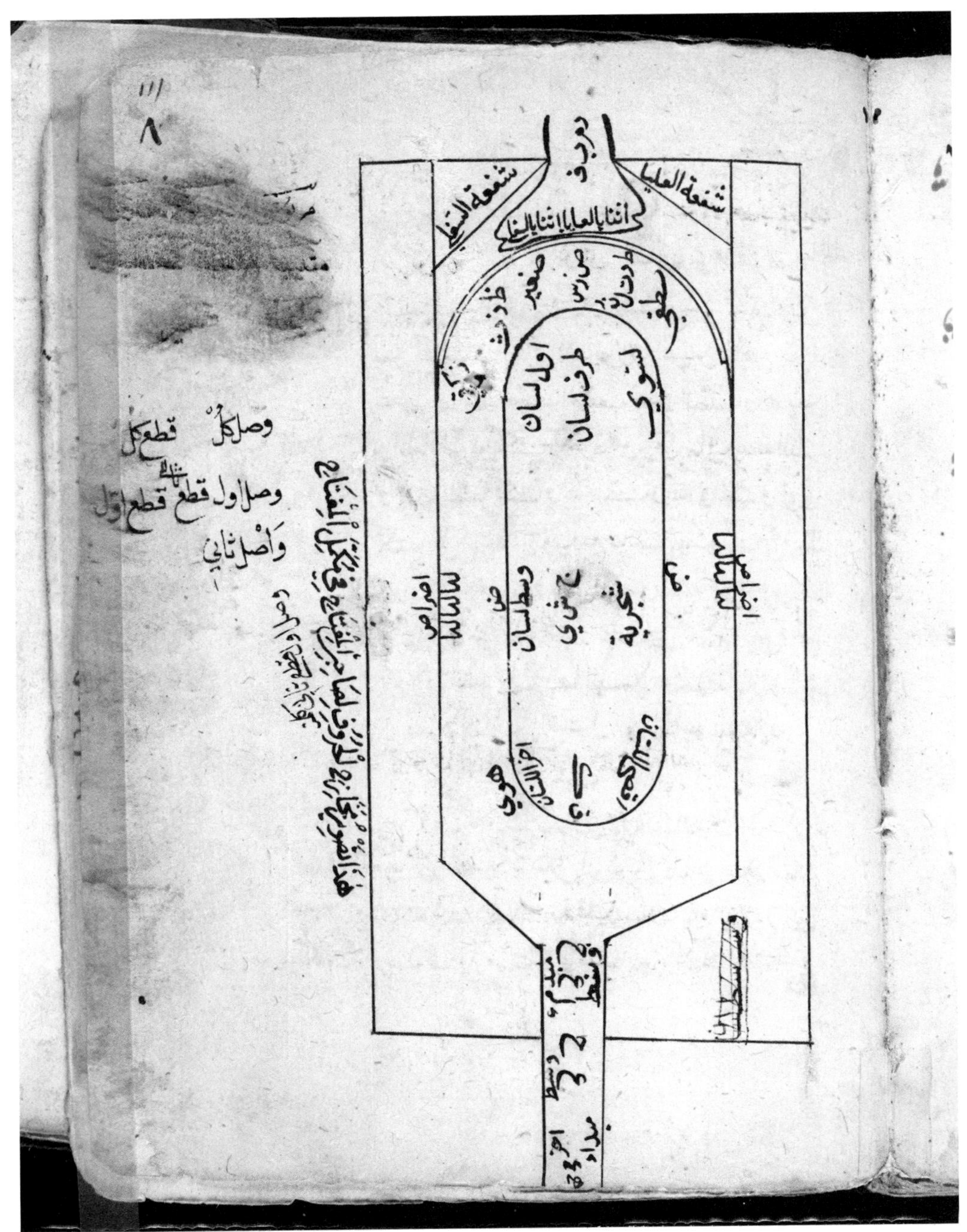

[1] Diagram of the "points of articulation" (*makhārij al-ḥurūf*) for the Arabic language, illustrating Yūsuf b. Abī Bakr al-Sakkākī's (d. 625/1228) compendious *Miftāḥ al-ʿulūm* (taken from an early twelfth/eighteenth century manuscript, *Taṣwīr makhārij al-ḥurūf li-ṣāḥib al-Miftaḥ*). Courtesy of Beinecke Rare Book and Manuscript Library, Yale University (Arabic MSS suppl. 143).

[II] Judging the Qur'ān memorization event, National Recitation Contest, Indonesia, 1997. Courtesy of Anna Gade, Oberlin College.

what follows ("when your mind is not clear"), would render the meaning nonsensical.

At certain points in the text of the Qur'ān, a range of permissible and impermissible stops are marked, according to the classification of their desirability. There are seven most general forms of stop, such as the *lāzim* stop (marked *mīm*), where a stop must be made or else the meaning would be distorted. There are also places, as in the example of Q 4:43 above, at which it is impermissible to stop (marked *lā*, meaning "no," i.e. no stop). In between these classifications there are at least five levels of preference, such as "permissible to continue, but stopping is better" (*jīm*, symbol for *jā'iz*), or "permissible to stop but it would be better to continue" (*ṣād*, symbol for *murakhkhaṣ*). Other passages are designated as "embracing," in which there is one meaning if a stop is made but another if reading is continuous and both are allowed. In some manuscripts of the Qur'ān, these are designated by the letters *mīm* and *ʿayn*, which stand for the term *muʿāniqa*, meaning that the phrase or the word may be understood to "embrace" either the passage that precedes or follows it. They are sometimes also marked by three dots. One example is in Q 2:2. In addition, some scholars have also added approximately eight more marks in common use, such as one that indicates that some authorities have said that there is to be a stop while others have not *(q-l-ā)*, marks for weak preferences, and places in which it is permitted to pause but it is not permitted to take a breath (marked *w-q-f-h*). Finally, there is a further stop, called "waiting" *(intiẓārī)*, which covers a switch between one of the seven standard *qirā'āt*.

Norms of qur'ānic recitation and preservation

Differing styles of recitation are usually identified by their relative rapidity, although terms for this vary across the Muslim-majority and Muslim-minority worlds. Usually, *ḥadr* is the expression for quick recitation, performed from memory or for the purpose of reading large portions of the text aloud; recitation of the Qur'ān in canonical worship *(ṣalāt)* tends to be fairly fast as well. *Tartīl (murattal)* is at a slower pace, used for study and practice (sometimes called *tadarrus*). In many places, the term *tajwīd* has a non-technical meaning of cantillated recitation. The term *mujawwad* refers to a slow recitation that deploys heightened technical artistry and melodic modulation.

Reciting the Qur'ān is dictated by norms of practice known as *adab*. These include respectful silence when listening, sitting facing the *qibla* (q.v.; the direction of prayer) if possible, observing norms of ritual purity, repeating verses (q.v.), and reciting the standard opening and closing formulae. These latter formula are, first, the opening statement, the *taʿawwudh: aʿūdhu bi-llāhi mina l-shayṭāni l-rajīm*, "I take refuge in God from the accursed Satan (see DEVIL)," which is always followed by the *basmala* (q.v.): *bi-smi llāhi l-raḥmāni l-raḥīm*, "In the name of God, the merciful, the compassionate," no matter where in the Qur'ān the reader begins (the *basmala* also opens every sūra except the ninth, Sūrat al-Tawba, "Repentance," with the contested case of its placement as the first *āya* of Sūrat al-Fātiḥa). Second, the reciter always closes a reading with the formula: *ṣadaqa allāhu l-ʿaẓīm*, "Thus almighty God has spoken truly." If the reciter is interrupted by a greeting *(salām)* when reading, he or she is to stop to return the greeting; he or she is also to stop when hearing the *adhān*, the call to prayer. While in some parts of the Muslim world there is concern over men listening to the voices of women reciting the Qur'ān, in other places, such as Indonesia, women reciters are very popular.

Reciters and listeners may observe *sajdat*

al-tilāwa, which is a prostration that, on the basis of a ḥadīth, is to be performed at fourteen or fifteen *āyāt* in the Qurʾān. These are *āyāt* that refer to created beings who bow before their creator (Q 7:206; 13:15; 16:49-50; 17:107; 19:58; 22:18; [22:27]; 25:60; 27:25-6; 32:15; 38:24-5; 41:38; 53:62; 84:20-1; 96:19). *Sajda* is performed by forming *niyya,* "intention," for the act, saying the *takbīr (allāhu akbar)* while facing the *qibla,* touching the ground while saying a formula to glorify God and then rising with another statement of the *takbīr*. After this, the reading continues.

Memorization of the Qurʾān, which is known as its "preservation" *(taḥfīẓ),* was encouraged from the earliest time of Islam. The wives of the Prophet (q.v.), for example, were among those known especially for the memorization and preservation of the Qurʾān. There are many ḥadīth reports that encourage Muslims to read and know the Qurʾān by heart. According to traditions of Islamic law, memorization is a recommended act of piety (see LAWFUL AND UNLAWFUL); it is classified as *farḍ kifāya,* which means an obligation always to be observed at least by some members of a community on behalf of the whole community. This renders Qurʾān memorizers *(ḥuffāẓ)* a special class of Qurʾān readers and they command a special respect within their communities. Traditionally, formal education begins with the memorization of the Qurʾān at an early age and then continues with other subjects; this practice is still observed in many Islamic societies. Morocco, for example, is especially well known for traditions of Qurʾān memorization. For educated Muslims who do not memorize the Qurʾān, it is still is a basic goal to have memorized the final, thirtieth part *(juzʾ)* of the Qurʾān, as well as to have read the entire Qurʾān through with a teacher; the latter, known as *khatm al-Qurʾān,* is marked by life-cycle celebrations in some parts of the Muslim world.

There are life-long challenges that come with the responsibility of memorizing the Qurʾān. First, there is the requirement not to forget any part of the Qurʾān already memorized, which represents an ongoing task due to the uniquely nonlinear structure and style of Qurʾān (see FORM AND STRUCTURE OF THE QURʾĀN; LANGUAGE AND STYLE OF THE QURʾĀN), continually demanding rehearsal. Memorizers often cite a ḥadīth of several variants on this challenge, to the effect that the Prophet said that memorizing the Qurʾān is more difficult than trying to tie up a camel (q.v.) that is always trying to run away. Memorizers who have committed the entire Qurʾān to memory often repeat one-seventh of the Qurʾān each day of the week for continual rehearsal. In addition, handbooks circulate among students committing the text to memory for the first time, allowing them to study particularly difficult aspects of the Qurʾān, such as certain verses that closely resemble one another.

Memorizers and readers of the Qurʾān are said to be held to higher moral standards in this world and the next by virtue of "holding" the entire Qurʾān in memory. More specifically, literature on the norms of earning a livelihood by teaching or reading the recited Qurʾān addresses the problem of receiving remuneration for this practice. Ḥadīth reports on this point cited by the pious in the formative period underscore that the Qurʾān is to be cherished for its own sake and should not be deployed for worldly gain. As "preservers," those who carry the Qurʾān have a responsibility to contribute to the overall ethical order of society. Moral responsibility to the community is often illustrated in the classical literature through representations of the memorizer's or reciter's unending commitment, portrayed as a practice continuing both night and day: Qurʾān reading by night and constructive moral action by day. For example, there are many variants of the ḥadīth which states, "The best of believers are those who arise at night," found in the collections of Abū Dāwūd and others. In addition to maintaining a direct relationship with the Qurʾān, accomplished readers have special responsibilities to the community that involve social interaction, as indicated in the well-known statement repeated by many transmitters, including al-Fuḍayl b. ʿIyāḍ (d. 187/803), a figure famous for his piety, stating, "A man bearing the Qurʾān is [in effect] bearing the standard of Islam," and thus should be scrupulous in behavior in every situation.

Practice, piety and the recited Qurʾān

Doctrine, worship and piety

The Qurʾān is the speech of God, according to Islamic tradition, and its recitation is thus the actual voicing of divine speech. In the early period, philosophical controversies arose regarding questions of temporality and agency in "following" divine speech in voice; these disputes related to foundational controversies over the issue of the "createdness of the Qurʾān" (q.v.) in time (see also PHILOSOPHY AND THE QURʾĀN; THEOLOGY AND THE QURʾĀN; INIMITABILITY). Similar questions have arisen as practical issues throughout the history of qurʾānic tradition, such as the problem of the reciter's technical artistry potentially being confused with the transcendent power of the Qurʾān. Al-Ghazālī's "rules" for recitation in the eighth book of the *Iḥyāʾ ʿulūm al-dīn* resolve such an apparent tension by positing both an "external" and an "internal" dimension to the act of voicing God's speech. In his scheme, the intents, consciousness, and sensibilities of the reciter are subordinated to the divine presence through purposive effort. The reciter is thus to strive to diminish the aspects of performance that are not pure amplifications of the manifestation of an idealized presence. Well-defined and specific techniques of presentation and performance may be applied in order to achieve this ideal.

Many such theoretical and practical issues relating to the recited Qurʾān are connected to the doctrine of *iʿjāz*, which is the idea of the "inimitable" nature of God's speech. This is linked to the ontology of the Arabic text as a "miraculous" revelation and to the speech of the Qurʾān as being a unique class of discourse (see MIRACLES; REVELATION AND INSPIRATION).

The practice of reciting the Qurʾān according to the rules of *tajwīd* is a foundational element of Islamic education, practice and piety. During the fasting (q.v.) month of Ramaḍān (q.v.), the entire Qurʾān is read over the course of the month in night prayers called *tarāwīḥ*. One of the standard divisions of the Qurʾān is its partition into thirty equal, consecutive parts, or *juzʾ* (pl. *ajzāʾ*); this sectioning facilitates complete recitation over the course of a month. In addition, during Ramaḍān or during the days of the pilgrimage (q.v.; *ḥajj*), pious Muslims may recite the entire Qurʾān in one night. Muslims read the Qurʾān frequently as an act of supererogatory piety, and recitation — especially at night — is performed by committed Muslims.

Reciting the Qurʾān is a required component of one of the fundamental acts of worship in Islam, *ṣalāt*, canonical prayer. Observant Muslims recite the opening sūra, Sūrat al-Fātiḥa, seventeen times because of its liturgical use as a component of *ṣalāt*. This chapter of the Qurʾān is also used in other contexts, such as blessings and the sealing of contractual agreements (see FĀTIḤA; CONTRACTS AND ALLIANCES;

BLESSING). During obligatory prayer, it is required to recite another, unspecified part of the Qurʾān besides Sūrat al-Fātiḥa. When the prayer is conducted in private, usually this is one of the short Meccan sūras that are the thirtieth *juzʾ* of the Qurʾān; if the prayer is led by an imām (q.v.), this reading will be his choice. In addition, it is common in worship and other practices of Muslim piety to hear the well known Light Verse (Q 24:35; see LIGHT) or Throne Verse (Q 2:255; see THRONE OF GOD). The final *juzʾ* of the Qurʾān as well as these other passages are commonly memorized by Muslims. Sūrat al-Mulk ("Kingship," Q 67) and Sūrat al-Ḥujurāt ("Private Apartments," Q 49) are also commonly memorized. Other parts of the Qurʾān that are particularly well known and read on certain occasions include Sūrat Yā Sīn (Q 36), read for the deceased or dying (see DEATH AND THE DEAD; FESTIVALS AND COMMEMORATIVE DAYS) in a sometimes controversial practice, and Sūrat Yūsuf ("Joseph," Q 12; see JOSEPH) and Sūrat al-Kahf ("The Cave," Q 18; see MEN OF THE CAVE) are also often read communally.

The recitation of the Qurʾān is a prototype for the practice of *dhikr,* a qurʾānic word for "reminder" and a practice associated with Ṣūfī piety. The Qurʾān is the basis of the formulae used for such recitational piety, as well as the recitation of the ninety-nine names of God (*al-asmāʾ al-ḥusnā;* see GOD AND HIS ATTRIBUTES). These "beautiful" names are referred to in Q 17:110, part of which reads: "Say, 'Call on Allāh or call on al-Raḥmān. By whatever name you call [God], his are the most beautiful names *(al-asmāʾ al-ḥusnā).*" The Qurʾān provides a brief listing of some of the names in Q 59:22-4. Not all of the names are given directly in the Qurʾān, however.

Throughout Islamic tradition, the appreciation of the vocal artistry of trained reciters has been part of Muslim religious and social life. Much of the theorization and practice related to the aesthetics of Qurʾān recitation is connected to the key idea of "spiritual audition." This term, *samāʿ,* is usually associated with Ṣūfī traditions but in the case of the recited Qurʾān multiple styles of classical piety overlap. In Islamic tradition normative questions relating to musical practice and its application and acceptability are tied to the issue of *samāʿ*. These legal debates usually center on the intents and contexts of practice. For Qurʾān recitation, the most authoritative sources on what Kristina Nelson has termed the "*samāʿ* polemic" highlight a tension between the cultivation of experiential perceptions related to "listening" *(samāʿ)* on the one hand and the ideal of the absolute separation of transcendent revelation and human components on the other.

Aesthetics and artistry

According to Islamic tradition, the "melodic" aspects of Qurʾān recitation may not be fixed in any one performance or in an overall system. This is in order that God's speech in the form of the revealed Qurʾān will not be associated with human technical artistry. It is not known what melodic structures were used in the recitation of the Qurʾān in the earliest period. It is documented, however, that practices of Qurʾān recitation developed into something resembling the *mujawwad* style in the ʿAbbāsid period, when reciters began to deploy the emerging modal system of music (*maqām,* pl. *maqāmāt*). It is in this period that the issue of "recitation with melody" *(qirāʾa bi-l-alḥān)* appears in the literature, and the melodic structures deployed in this time were apparently those of Arab art music. Today, the highly proficient style of recitation known as *mujawwad* also uses melodic structures found in Arab art music.

Maqām (pl. *maqāmāt*) denotes a musical "mode," both scalar pitch class and melody type. This system of "qurʾānic" *maqāmāt* that became globally widespread in the latter part of the twentieth century had developed over centuries from multiple and converging branches of influence. It is difficult to prove that any of these branches is a continuous line extending from the early Muslim community since little historical data on the musical practices of the Arabs before the third/ninth century are available. The important source, *Kitāb al-Aghānī*, "Book of songs," by Abū l-Faraj al-Iṣfahānī (d. 356/967), dates to the fourth/tenth century and it is in this period that *maqām* developed as a theory and a practice of art music by way of a synthesis of Arabic and Persian forms. Also in this period, intellectuals analyzed the system, such as in the writings of the great philosophers al-Fārābī (d. 338/949), Ibn Sīnā (d. 428/1037) and especially al-Kindī (d. ca. 252/866), whose treatise on music was foundational. The system also received more esoteric formulations within cosmological frameworks (such as in the thought of the esoteric group, the "Brethren of Purity," the Ikhwān al-Ṣafāʾ), developing concepts like the Greek idea of scale, analyzed along with rhythmic cycles, with reference to mode being made in terms of the fretting board of the lute instrument, the *ʿūd*.

Diversity and flexibility characterizes the modal system both diachronically and synchronically. The treatises of the renowned musician and writer on the history of music, ʿAbd al-Muʾmin Ṣafī l-Dīn al-Urmawī (d. 693/1294) formulated an analytical framework for the system that was followed for centuries, deploying musical characteristics in the identification of mode, such as initial and final pitch as well as, in some cases, melody types. Not only are modes applied flexibly in practice, but also the overall musical system itself is historically and geographically fluid and thus difficult to formalize or classify. In the early nineteenth century, a system for analyzing scale (based on quarter-tones) became widespread in the Middle East. An attempt was also made to codify all of the *maqāmāt* used in Arab countries at the historic Cairo Congress on Arab Music in 1932. This effort, however, along with subsequent ones, faced the challenge of systematizing the diversity of the entire musical system as well as the problems of notation and standardization.

Contemporary performers of the recited Qurʾān in the style called *mujawwad* have been increasingly popular in recent decades due to broadcast and recording technologies and other trends (see MEDIA AND THE QURʾĀN). The development of the first recorded version of the recited Qurʾān in Egypt is documented by Labīb al-Saʿīd. In *The art of reciting the Qurʾān*, Kristina Nelson examines the practices of Egyptian reciters, the same figures who have become influential the world over because of the dissemination of their recordings. The singing of the great women vocalists from the Arab world, such as Fayrūz, Warda, and, above all, Umm Kulthūm (as well as men like ʿAbd al-Wahhāb) have influenced the improvisational styles of these performers. Across the Muslim-majority and Muslim-minority worlds of Islam in the later twentieth century, the recitation recordings of a few Egyptian reciters (many of whom were trained in classical Arabic music: e.g. ʿAbd al-Bāsiṭ ʿAbd al-Ṣamad) were the most influential models for aspiring reciters.

Qurʾānic revitalization and contemporary daʿwa

Since the late twentieth century, changes in technology have combined with the so-called global "Islamic awakening," to encourage a widespread revitalization of the practice of the popular recitation of the Qurʾān. Evidence of this is the worldwide women's mosque movement that focuses on reciting the Qurʾān and improving recitation technique. Transnational connections support curricula for teaching recitation. For example, in the 1960s and 1970s, the Egyptian government, with official Indonesian support, brought many of the most renowned Egyptian reciters to southeast Asia, a region of the world with as many Muslims as the population of the entire Arabic-speaking world, in order to teach and to perform.

Daʿwa is a qurʾānic term interpreted and applied in different ways in different global contexts (see INVITATION). Most basically, the term means a "call" to deepen one's own or encourage others' Islamic piety. As such, it has been a crucial concept in the historical propagation of the Islamic religious tradition. *Daʿwa* is key to understanding how the Qurʾān functions as a basis of contemporary Islamic revitalization movements. Qurʾānic *daʿwa* promotes recitational aesthetics and schooling as the basis for programs among Muslims of diverse orientations.

In the most populous Muslim-majority nation in the world, Indonesia, the recitation of the Qurʾān was the focus of an energetic movement in Islamic revitalization in the late twentieth century. Southeast Asia is well known for world-class recitation, evidenced in the popularity of the woman reciter from Jakarta, Hajja Maria Ulfah. Southeast Asia also has traditionally been known for the production of exceedingly clear and precise methods and materials. In Indonesia in the 1990s, mainstream *daʿwa* was viewed as an "invitation" to voluntary Islamic piety issued to Muslims, and much *daʿwa* highlighted engagement with the recited Qurʾān. Examples of the energy of this movement are the massive "Baitul Qurʾan" exhibit near Jakarta, as well as the promotion of a wide array of qurʾānic arts like recitation and calligraphy (q.v.).

As the Qurʾān increasingly became the focus of programs to promote Islamic engagement, learning to read the Qurʾān became the basis of a widespread revitalization movement in Indonesia, and new pedagogies blended with traditional methods of teaching and learning recitation. Popular activities ranged from basic study of *tajwīd* to performance in the highly proficient *mujawwad* style of recitation. The phenomenon of qurʾānic learning and engagement was not limited to young people; it also included mature Muslims who labeled themselves as "learners." As part of a resurgent movement in the "fundamentals" of religious practice in Indonesia during the 1990s, religiously oriented individuals actively adopted and promoted projects such as local and national Qurʾān recitation competitions (see Fig. II), a widespread movement in "Qurʾān kindergartens," revitalized efforts to memorize the Qurʾān, and lively women's mosque groups trained in the development of reading skills. At this time, virtuoso readings in the *mujawwad* style were not considered the most effective means of inducing heightened experiential states. Rather, the emphasis was on the listeners' own efforts to emulate actively such a performance. Expert performances from the Arab world and by Indonesians doubled as pedagogy for ordinary practitioners, a pedagogy that was disseminated and mediated by competition frameworks and other programs and interests. Under these educationally oriented influences, a great variety of material — including the recordings of great Egyptian reciters — became educational curriculum in Indonesia; reciters at all levels were instructed to listen avidly to these performances in order to improve their *mujawwad* Qur᾿ān recitation and especially to master the modal system.

The Indonesian term *lagu,* also denoting "song," is used for musical qualities of recitation, doubly conveying the ideas of scalar pitch class and melody type. Contemporary Indonesian and Malaysian sources on recitation group the Arab-derived *maqāmāt (lagu)* used in Qur᾿ān recitation into two principal types: *misri* and *makawi*. *Misri lagu* are the *maqāmāt* that were introduced in the 1960s and after, denoting modes that were known and used in Egypt (hence *misri* = Ar. *miṣrī*). *Makawi lagu* are understood to comprise an older system from the Middle East, reportedly deriving from the recitational practices of Indonesian pilgrims and students who traveled to the Arabian peninsula (and Mecca, hence the term *makawi*) earlier in the century and before. There are also indigenous southeast Asian *lagu daerah,* "local *lagu*." In Indonesia, the system of *mujawwad* style Qur᾿ān recitation that developed in the 1990s was based on styles from Egypt. Competition *lagu* were based on seven *maqāmāt* prototypes: *bayati, rast, hijaz, soba, sika, jiharka,* and *nahawand*. Performances and pedagogies increasingly accepted this style as normative for all readers, especially under the influence of competitional readings and regimens.

Apart from the influence of the competition system, the adoption of Arabic, and more specifically Egyptian *(misri)* modes, were supported in Indonesia by the perception that they are more normatively qur᾿ānic. New kinds of theorization accompanied the reception of the Arabic *lagu,* which became increasingly an aspect of the recited Qur᾿ān in Indonesia in the 1990s. Partially because of the popularity of contests and in part also due to the acceptance of the Egyptian-inspired model as the ideal, competence in these seven modes has become the goal of intermediate and advanced-level recitational training in modern Indonesia. A competition system had a great deal to do with the standardization and popularization of these structures.

Recitation contests in Indonesia were interpreted as a form of *daʿwa*. The increasing popularity of Qur᾿ān reciting and recitation contests and, since 1997, their promotion by the *Lembaga Pengembangan Tilawatil Quran,* the Institute for the Development of the Recitation of the Qur᾿ān (LPTQ), and other organizations, contributed to an explosion of interest and the creation of new media and techniques for the study and appreciation of the recited Qur᾿ān. Possible controversy over the voicing of the speech of God as a competition was overcome in Indonesia by recognizing the positive effects of the events for Islamic youth. Recitation tournaments, especially the *Musabaqah tilawatil Qur᾿ān,* the National Contest for the Recitation of the Qur᾿ān (MTQ), have come to be viewed by many in Indonesia as an avenue for *syiʿar Islam,* or the propagation and deepening of Islamic practice through an appreciation of qur᾿ānic knowledge and ability, as well as an avenue for the expression of distinctive aspects of Indonesian Islamic piety within the context of the global Muslim community. Competitions as *syiʿar Islam* were understood to be simultaneously a form of education and an invitation to Muslim practice.

Conclusion

The recitation of the Qur᾿ān is foundational to the history of Islamic worship and piety. As such, it has served as the paradigm for the category of "scripture" in the academic study of religion as developed by comparativists and Islamicists such as Mahmoud Ayoub, Frederick Denny, Michael Sells, Wilfred Cantwell Smith, Marilyn Waldman, and especially William

Graham (see SCRIPTURE AND THE QUR'ĀN; POST-ENLIGHTENMENT ACADEMIC STUDY OF THE QUR'ĀN). These scholars have recognized not only the aural/oral nature of religious texts based on the unique qur'ānic case, but they have also highlighted the communal lifeworlds of the recited Qur'ān. This theme of the inherently social nature of the recitation of the Qur'ān echoes throughout the classical literature, even in interiorized systems such as al-Ghazālī's. Al-Bukhārī's *Ṣaḥīḥ* and other major collections of ḥadīth, for example, relate the tradition in which the Prophet reportedly said, "The best among you are those who learn the Qur'ān and teach it to others" (on the authority of ʿUthmān b. ʿAffān). In the contemporary world, teaching, learning, and practicing the Qur'ān are voluntary open-ended projects, drawing inspiration from the models of others' piety. Al-Bukhārī relates, on the authority of Abū Hurayra, that the Prophet said, "There is no envy (q.v.) except of two kinds: First, a person whom God has taught the Qur'ān and who recites it during the hours of the night and during the hours of the day and his neighbor who listens to him and says, 'I wish I had been given what has been given to so-and-so, so that I might do what he does'; and, secondly, a person to whom God has given wealth (q.v.) and he spends it on what is just and right whereupon another person may say, 'I wish I had been given what so-and-so has been given for then I would do as he does'" (Bukhārī, *Ṣaḥīḥ*, viii, 113, nos. 4389-90). In reading the Qur'ān aloud, the Qur'ān states that Muslims may affect others' religiosity and thereby build the religious community (see COMMUNITY AND SOCIETY IN THE QUR'ĀN): "The believers are only they whose hearts tremble when God is mentioned; and, when his signs [or verses of the Qur'ān] are recited to them, they multiply in faith (q.v.) and put their trust (see TRUST AND PATIENCE) in their lord" (Q 8:2).

Anna M. Gade

Bibliography

Primary: Bukhārī, *Ṣaḥīḥ*, 8 vols., Cairo 1983; Dānī, *Taysīr;* al-Ghazālī, Abū Ḥāmid Muḥammad b. Muḥammad, *The jewels of the Qur'ān. Al-Ghazālī's theory*, annot. trans. M. Abul Quasem of *Kitāb Jawāhir al-Qur'ān*, London 1977; id., *The recitation and interpretation of the Qur'ān. Al-Ghazālī's theory*, trans. M. Abul Quasem of bk. 8 of *Iḥyā' ʿulūm al-dīn*, London 1982; Ibn al-Jazarī, *Nashr*, 2 vols., Damascus 1926; id., *al-Tamhīd fī ʿilm al-tajwīd*, ed. ʿA.Ḥ. al-Farrā', Cairo 1908; Muslim, *Ṣaḥīḥ;* al-Nawawī, Abū Zakariyyā' Yaḥyā b. Sharaf al-Dīn, *al-Tibyān fī adab ḥamalat al-Qur'ān*, excerpt translated into English in A. Rippin and J. Knappert (eds.), *Textual sources for the study of Islam*, Chicago 1986, 100-5; Qurṭubī, *Jāmiʿ*, 20 vols. in 10, Cairo 1968, i; Suyūṭī, *Itqān*.

Secondary: Anon., The contest of recitation of the Qur'ān in Indonesia. History of a quarter century, in *Studia islamika* 1/2 (1994), 1-6 (special issue); V. Danielson, *The voice of Egypt. Umm Kulthūm. Arabic song and Egyptian society in the twentieth century*, Chicago 1997; A. von Denffer, *ʿUlūm al-Qur'ān. An introduction to the sciences of the Qur'ān*, London 1983; F.M. Denny, The *adab* of Qur'ān recitation. Text and context, in A.H. Johns (ed.), *International Congress for the Study of the Qur'ān*, Canberra 1981, 143-60; id., Exegesis and recitation. Their development as classical forms of qur'ānic piety, in F.E. Reynolds and Th.M. Ludwig (eds.), *Transitions and transformations in the history of religions. Essays in honor of Joseph M. Kitagawa*, Leiden 1980, 91-123; id., The great Indonesian Qur'ān chanting tournament, in *The world and I. A chronicle of our changing era* 6 (1986), 216-23; id., Qur'ān recitation. A tradition of oral performance and transmission, in *Oral tradition* 4/1-2 (1989), 5-26; id., Qur'ān recitation training in Indonesia. A survey of contexts and handbooks, in Rippin, *Approaches*, 288-306; id., Tadjwīd, in *EI*², x, 72-5; D.F. Eickelman, The art of memory. Islamic education and its social reproduction, in *Comparative studies in society and history* 20/4 (1978), 485-516; L.I. al-Faruqi, Accentuation in qur'ānic chant. A study in musical *tawāzun*, in *Yearbook for traditional music* 10 (1978), 53-68; id., *An annotated glossary of Arabic musical terms*, Westport, CT 1981; id., The cantillation of the Qur'ān, in *Asian music* 19/1 (1987),

2-25; id., Music, musicians and Muslim law, in *Asian music* 17/1 (1985), 13-36; id., Qur'ān reciters in competition in Kuala Lumpur, in *Ethnomusicology* 31/2 (1987), 221-8; A.M. Gade, *Perfection makes practice. Learning, emotion, and the recited Qur'ān in Indonesia,* Honolulu 2004; C. Glassé (ed.), *The concise encyclopedia of Islam,* New York 1989, 232-41 ("Koran Chanting"); Graham, *Beyond;* id., Qur'ān as spoken word. An Islamic contribution to the understanding of scripture, in R. Martin (ed.), *Approaches to Islam in religious studies,* Tucson 1985, 23-40; id., Scripture as spoken word, in M. Levering (ed.), *Rethinking scripture. Essays from a comparative perspective,* Albany 1989, 129-69; id., Those who study and teach the Qur'ān, in A.H. Johns (ed.), *International Congress for the Study of the Qur'ān,* Canberra 1981, 9-28; J. Houtsonen, Traditional qur'ānic education in a southern Moroccan village, in *IJMES* 26 (1994), 489-500; S.K. Husaini, *Easy tajwīd. A text book on phonetics and rules of pronunciation and intonation of the glorious Qur'ān,* trans. S.N. Khadri and Q.H. Khan, Chicago 1990; Jeffery, *Materials;* A.H. Johns, The Qur'ān on the Qur'ān, in A.H. Johns (ed.), *International Congress for the Study of the Qur'ān,* Canberra 1981, 1-8; G.H.A. Juynboll, The position of Qur'ān recitation in early Islam, in *JSS* 19 (1974), 240-51; id., The *qurrā'* in early Islamic history, in *JESHO* 16 (1973), 113-29; P. Kahle, The Arabic readers of the Koran, in *JNES* 8 (1949), 65-71; S. Marcus, Modulation in Arabic music. Documenting oral concepts, performances, rules, and strategies, in *Ethnomusicology* 36/2 (1992), 171-95; id., The periodization of modern Arab music theory. Continuity and change in the definition of maqāmāt, in Pacific review of ethnomusicology 5 (1989), 33-48; R.C. Martin, Tilāwah, in *ER,* x, 526-30; id., Understanding the Qur'ān in text and context, in *History of religions* 21/4 (1982), 361-84; Ch. Melchert, Ibn Mujāhid and the establishment of seven qur'ānic readings, in *SI* 91 (2000), 5-22; D. Mulder, The ritual of the recitation of the Quran, in *Nederlands Theologisch Tijschrift* 37 (1983), 247-52; S.H. Nasr, Islam and music. The legal and spiritual dimensions, in L.E. Sullivan (ed.), *Enchanting powers. Music in the world's religions,* Cambridge, MA 1997, 219-36; K. Nelson, *The art of reciting the Qur'ān,* Austin 1985; id., Reciter and listener. Some factors shaping the *mujawwad* style of qur'ānic reciting, in *Ethnomusicology* 26/1 (1982), 41-8; R. Paret, Ḳirā'a, in *EI²,* v, 127-9; J.R.T.M. Peters, *God's created speech. A study in the speculative theology of the Mu'tazilī Wadī l-Quḍāt Abū l-Ḥasan 'Abd al-Jabbār b. Aḥmad al-Ḥamdānī,* Leiden 1976; H.S. Powers, Mode, in S.S. Sadie (ed.), *The new Grove dictionary of music and musicians,* 29 vols., New York 2001, xvi, 775-860; R.B. Qureshi, Sounding the word. Music in the life of Islam, in L.E. Sullivan (ed.), *Enchanting powers. Music in the world's religions,* Cambridge, MA 1997, 263-98; A.J. Racy, Arabian music and the effects of commercial recording, in *World of music* 20/1 (1978), 47-57; id., Creativity and ambience. An ecstatic feedback model from Arabic music, in *World of music* 33/3 (1991), 7-28; A. Rasmussen, The Qur'ān in Indonesian daily life. The public project of musical oratory, in *Ethnomusicology* 45/1 (2001), 30-57; L. al-Sa'īd, *al-Jam' al-ṣawtī l-awwal lil-Qur'ān al-karīm aw al-muṣḥaf al-murattal,* Cairo 1967; trans. B. Weiss, M.A. Rauf and M. Berger, *The recited Koran,* Princeton 1975; Kh. Seeman, *Tajwīd* as a source in phonetic research, in *WZKM* 58 (1962), 112-20; M. Sells, *Approaching the Qur'ān. The early revelations,* Ashland, OR 1999 (book and sound recording); id., Sound and meaning in *Sūrat al-qāri'a,* in *Arabica* 40 (1993), 403-40; id., Sound, spirit, and gender in *Sūrat al-qadr,* in *JAOS* 111/2 (1991), 239-59; Kh. Shalihah, *Perkembangan seni baca al Quran dan qiraat tujuh di Indonesia* ("The development of the art of reciting the Qur'ān and the seven readings in Indonesia"), Jakarta 1983; A. Shiloah, The Arabic concept of mode, in *Journal of the American Musicological Society* 34 (1981), 19-42; id., *Music in the world of Islam. A socio-cultural study,* Detroit 1996; id., *The theory of music in Arabic writings, c. 900-1900,* Munich 1979; W. Cantwell Smith, *What is scripture? A comparative approach,* Minneapolis 1993; B. Stowasser, *Women in the Qur'ān, traditions and interpretation,* New York 1994; 25 *Tahun musabaqah tilawatil Quran dan 17 Tahun Lembaga Pengembangan Tilawatil Quran,* Jakarta 1994; M. Talbi, La Qirā'a bi-l-alḥān, in *Arabica* 5 (1958), 183-90; A.L. Tibawi, Is the Qur'ān translatable? Early Muslim opinion, in *MW* 52 (1962), 4-16; H.H. Touma, The *maqam* phenomenon. An improvisation technique in the music of the Middle East, in *Ethnomusicology* 15 (1971), 34-48; id., *The music of the Arabs,* Portland, OR 1996; D.A. Wagner and A. Lotfi, Learning to read by 'rote', in *International journal of the sociology of language* 42 (1983), 111-21; D.A. Wagner and J.E. Spratt, Cognitive consequences of contrasting pedagogies. The effects of quranic preschooling in Morocco, in *Child development* 58 (1987), 1207-19; U. Wegner, Transmitting the divine revelation. Some aspects of textualism and textual variability in qur'ānic recitation, in *World of music* 26/3 (1986), 57-78; Wensinck, *Concordance;* id., *Handbook;* O. Wright, *The modal system of Arab and Persian music.* A.D. 1250-1300, London 1978; H.A. Muhaimin Zen, *Tata Cara/Problematika menghafal al Qur'ān dan petunjuk-petunjuknya,* Jakarta 1985.

Reciters of the Qur'ān

Those entrusted with the oral recitation of qur'ānic passages, or the entire text. The term "reciter" (Ar. sing. *qāri'* and *muqri'*) in its basic, general signification refers to one who reads or recites. With reference to reciters of the Qur'ān, the plural *qurrā'* is much more common than *muqri'ūn*. In a broad sense, the term *qurrā'* is used in various sources to refer both to professional reciters, namely those who accepted payment for their recitation and were often employed by the state, and to pious, non-professional ones who did not seek to make a living from their recitation. Other names less frequently used for Qur'ān reciters are *ḥamalat al-Qur'ān* (literally "bearers of the Qur'ān") and *ahl al-Qur'ān* ("people of the Qur'ān"). *Tilāwa* is a synonym of *qirā'a* in the sense of "recitation" but the active participle *tālī* is seldom seen in place of *qāri'*. *Ḥāfiẓ* commonly denotes one who has memorized the Qur'ān (it is also used to denote one who has memorized unusual quantities of ḥadīth; hence, for example, al-Dhahabī's *Ṭabaqāt al-ḥuffāẓ* is a biographical dictionary of traditionists, not Qur'ān reciters; see ḤADĪTH AND THE QUR'ĀN).

Politics

There was a distinctive party called *qurrā'* in earliest Islamic Iraqi politics (see IRAQ), who took part on all sides in the first two civil wars (see POLITICS AND THE QUR'ĀN). In particular, a significant number of the *qurrā'* broke away from 'Alī's army (see 'ALĪ B. ABĪ ṬĀLIB) to join the Khawārij (see KHĀRIJĪS) in 37/657 (see Sayed, *Die Revolte*). The obvious — and widespread — interpretation is that they were the ultra-pious party, marked by their devotional recitation of the Qur'ān (q.v.). Norman Calder, however, has suggested alternatively that *qāri'* originally referred to temporary or seasonal troops, serving for a *qar'* or *qur'* (period). M.A. Shaban's (*Islamic history*, 50-1) identification of *qurrā'* as people of villages *(qurā)* is fanciful.

Early Muslim rulers were highly interested in the Qur'ān. Some sources ascribe the earliest official appointment of Qur'ān reciters to the second caliph (q.v.), 'Umar b. al-Khaṭṭāb, who, in 14/635-6, appointed two reciters, one each to lead men and women in prayer (q.v.; Ṭabarī, *Ta'rīkh*, i, 2749; Ibn Sa'd, *Ṭabaqāt*, iii, 202). Al-Ḥajjāj, governor of Iraq (75-95/694-714), is credited in the Sunnī tradition with introducing vowel signs into the written text of the Qur'ān (see ORTHOGRAPHY; MANUSCRIPTS OF THE QUR'ĀN; ARABIC SCRIPT; ARABIC LANGUAGE); by some revisionist historians, even with formally fixing the qur'ānic canon (see Mingana, Transmission; see COLLECTION OF THE QUR'ĀN; CODICES OF THE QUR'ĀN). Public recitation ideally entailed simultaneous exegesis (Arabic *tafsīr* or *ta'wīl;* see Versteegh, *Grammar and exegesis*, 185; see EXEGESIS OF THE QUR'ĀN: CLASSICAL AND MEDIEVAL). Early judges *(qāḍīs)* were often responsible for preaching *(qaṣaṣ)* and public recitation of the Qur'ān, as well as deciding lawsuits and other matters (see LAW AND THE QUR'ĀN; see, for example, a sermon by the Baṣran *qāḍī* Ṣāliḥ al-Murrī [d. 172/788-9?], which includes qur'ānic recitation, prayers and weeping by preacher and audience alike; Abū Nu'aym, *Ḥilya*, vii, 165-7). One of the complaints against the caliph 'Uthmān in the Khārijī Ibn Ibāḍ's letter to the caliph 'Abd al-Malik (r. 65-86/685-705) is that he prevented *qaṣaṣ* in the mosques (*an yuqaṣṣa fīhā bi-kitāb Allāh;* see MOSQUE). The *qurrā'* of Marwānid times were subject alternately to repression and bribery. Al-Ḥasan al-Baṣrī (d. 110/728), for example, complained of *qurrā'* standing at the governor's gate (Abū Nu'aym, *Ḥilya*, ii, 151), while Ḥammād b.

Salama (d. 167/783-4) warned against going to the governor *(amīr)* even if he should ask for so little as to recite *qul huwa llāhu aḥad* (Q 112; ibid., vi, 251; a similar report is attributed to Sufyān al-Thawrī [d. 161/778?], cf. Abū Nu'aym, *Ḥilya*, vi, 387).

Devotional recitation

From an early period, excellence in qur'ānic recitation seems to have been regarded as conferring a higher religious and social, even political, status on the individual. A well known prophetic ḥadīth states, "The best of them at reciting the book (q.v.) of God will lead the people" (see KINGS AND RULERS). This ḥadīth is frequently cited in the literature on the excellences of the Companions (see COMPANIONS OF THE PROPHET) and invoked in the debates between the Sunnīs and the Shī'īs (see SHĪ'ISM AND THE QUR'ĀN; SHĪ'A) to affirm the greater right of Abū Bakr or 'Alī, respectively, to assume the caliphate on account of each candidate's superior proficiency in qur'ānic recitation. This ḥadīth is cited in various other contexts as well, particularly to underscore the equality of Muslims regardless of social and ethnic background, and to recognize differences only in religious piety (Afsaruddin, Excellences, 18).

Fasting (q.v.) by day and staying awake by night (see VIGILS; DAY AND NIGHT) seem to have been the most usual components of the devotions of Muslim ascetics (*zuhhād, nussāk;* see ASCETICISM) in the second/eighth century. Ritual prayer was commonly the main occupation of night vigils, but it might be supplemented by qur'ānic recitation or integrated with it. We are told, for example, that the blind Baṣran jurisprudent and traditionist Qatāda (d. ca. 115/735) normally recited the whole Qur'ān weekly, over three days during the first two-thirds of Ramaḍān (q.v.), and daily during the last ten days (Abū Nu'aym, *Ḥilya*, ii, 338-9). The Kūfan jurisprudent al-Ḥasan b. Ṣāliḥ b. Ḥayy (d. 199/814-5), his brother 'Alī (d. 151/768-9?) and their mother used to recite the Qur'ān nightly in shifts; then the two brothers in shifts after their mother died; finally al-Ḥasan alone after his brother died ('Ijlī, *Tārīkh*, 114, 347). Sometimes, however, an ascetic would meditate for a very long time on just one verse; as did, as is reported below, the Baṣran Sulaymān al-Taymī (d. 143/760-1; Abu Nu'aym, *Ḥilya*, iii, 29). Qur'ānic recitation was so strongly associated with renunciation of the world that *qāri'* itself became a regular term for "renunciant" or "ascetic."

Disquiet with renunciant practice is evident in the ḥadīth extolling the merits of contemplating the meaning of the verses as one recites them (e.g. Abū 'Ubayd, *Faḍā'il*, 156-8). Completion of qur'ānic recitation in an exceptionally short time, particularly to attract public acclaim or alms, was looked at askance (e.g. Nawawī, *Tibyān*, 50). Several of the six canonical collections of ḥadīth include a warning from the Prophet, "One who has recited the [entire] Qur'ān in less than three days has not comprehended [it]" (Abū Dāwūd, *Sunan, Shahr Ramaḍān*, 8; Tirmidhī, *Ṣaḥīḥ, al-Qirā'āt*, 11; Ibn Māja, *Sunan, Iqāmat al-ṣalāt*, 178). Public rituals to mark an individual's completion of recitation of the sacred text *(khatma)* were likewise controversial, although they were usual from as early as the second/eighth century (Ibn al-Jawzī, *Talbīs*, 176).

There is evidence that early recitation conventions did not observe full declensional endings as later became customary. Hortatory reports were circulated to exhort the faithful to recite the qur'ānic text with *i'rāb* (desinential inflection; see GRAMMAR AND THE QUR'ĀN). One such report quotes the Prophet as saying, "Whoever recites the Qur'ān without full inflection, the attending angel records for him 'as revealed' with ten merits for each letter; whoever inflects only part of the Qur'ān, two angels are assigned to him who write down for him twenty merits; and whoever inflects the [entire] Qur'ān, four angels are assigned to him who record seventy merits for each letter" (see Qurṭubī, *Tadhkār,* 84-5; also Kahle, Qur'ān and 'Arabīya). The rise of schools of grammar by the second/eighth century, particularly at Kūfa and Baṣra, and the rapidly growing influence of the grammarians, who concerned themselves to a considerable extent with the correct reading of the qur'ānic text, played a key role in the final development of the *scriptio plena.* This and similar reports very likely also encode rivalry between the pious, non-professional *qurrā'* and the professional grammarians. These pious reciters were inclined to view the grammarians as excessively concerned with the mechanics of language and thus with primarily humanistic perspectives (see LANGUAGE AND STYLE OF THE QUR'ĀN; CREATEDNESS OF THE QUR'ĀN; INIMITABILITY), while the grammarians viewed the pious reciters as amateurs lacking in linguistic competence and thus in scholarly authority (see Afsaruddin, Excellences, 7-8; Versteegh, *Grammar and exegesis,* 178). Some of the *qurrā'* were regarded by the scholarly establishment as unreliable transmitters of ḥadīth; in classical biographical *(rijāl)* works they are likely to be praised for their personal piety but denounced for their dubious status as ḥadīth narrators (see Afsaruddin, Excellences, 21-2).

Al-Ghazālī (d. 505/1111) devoted the eighth book of *Iḥyā' 'ulūm al-dīn* to the etiquette of reciting the Qur'ān. Among other things, he proposes ten outward rules of proper recitation: for the reciter to be in a state of ritual purity (q.v.); to recite no more at one session than one can properly contemplate; to recite by recognized units such as sevenths *(aḥzāb);* to write the Qur'ān properly; to recite at a pace conducive to contemplation; to weep as one recites (see WEEPING); to prostrate oneself at the appropriate verses (as a Shāfi'ī, al-Ghazālī names fourteen; in printed Qur'āns, these verses are commonly indicated by lines in the text and the word *sajda* in the margin; see BOWING AND PROSTRATION; PRINTING OF THE QUR'ĀN; ORNAMENTATION AND ILLUMINATION); to preface one's recitation with certain formulas, e.g. *a'ūdhu bi-llāhi l-samī',* etc., and to conclude it with others, e.g. *ṣadaqa llāhu ta'ālā,* etc.; to recite aloud, unless one finds oneself taking excessive pride in it; and to recite in a comely voice. These ten are complemented by ten inward dispositions (see also Nelson, *Art of reciting,* ch. 4.; see RECITATION OF THE QUR'ĀN).

Famous reciters

Particular versions or "readings" *(qirā'āt)* of the qur'ānic text are sometimes associated with Companions, above all Ibn Mas'ūd and Ubayy b. Ka'b, but more usually with regions (e.g. "the people of Medina [q.v.] recited thus") and, increasingly over time, with various experts of the second/eighth century (Nöldeke, *GQ,* 2-3 is basic; see also Brockett, Qur'ān readings; see READINGS OF THE QUR'ĀN). Ibn Mujāhid (d. 324/936) is famous for identifying the seven most respected readings (see Ibn Mujāhid, *Sab'a*). He was involved in the trials of two famous reciters before Baghdādī *qāḍīs* for reciting unacceptable readings: Muḥammad b. al-Ḥasan b. Miqsam in 322/934 and Muḥammad b. Aḥmad b. Shannabūdh (alternatively Shanbūdh and Shanabūdh) in 323/935. Their offences, however, were not that they recited variants not included among Ibn Mujāhid's seven but that they recited variants based only on philological possibility (in the case of Ibn Miqsam), or only on traditions going back to Companions but not endorsed by the caliph ʿUthmān (in the case of Ibn Shanabūdh; see Jeffery, *Materials;* Melchert, Ibn Mujāhid).

Partly through the influence of his disciples, Ibn Mujāhid's choice of the seven most acceptable readings seems to have commanded general assent from late in the fourth/tenth century, especially in Syria and points west. Three more readings were recognized at that time as the next most highly respected, especially in Iraq and the east (see Nöldeke, GQ, iii, 225). Finally, four more readings were identified as having unusually great historical interest without retaining their one-time liturgical use (see FORM AND STRUCTURE OF THE QURʾĀN); that is, one could no longer recite them as part of a valid ritual prayer *(ṣalāt).* Medieval scholarly interest in different sets of readings may be estimated from titles in Ḥājjī Khalīfa, *Kashf al-ẓunūn:* of 155 books having to do with an identifiable number of readings, seventy-four treat the seven, forty-four treat the ten, seven treat the eight, while the remaining twenty-nine treat other numbers of readings, of which just one is devoted to the whole fourteen.

The fourteen are listed here in order after al-Dimyāṭī, *Itḥāf fuḍalāʾ al-bashar,* but it is not hard to find other orderings. Italics indicate the most common designation for each:

(1) *Nāfiʿ* b. ʿAbd al-Raḥmān (d. ca. 169/785-6), Medinese;
(2) ʿAbdallāh *b. Kathīr* al-Dārī (d. 120/737-8), Meccan;
(3) *Abū ʿAmr* Zabbān *b. al-ʿAlāʾ* (d. ca. 154/770-1), Baṣran;
(4) ʿAbdallāh *b. ʿĀmir* (d. 118/736), Damascene;
(5) *ʿĀṣim* b. Abī l-Najūd Bahdala (d. ca. 127/744-5), Kūfan;
(6) *Ḥamza* b. Ḥabīb (d. ca. 156/772-3), Kūfan;
(7) ʿAlī b. Ḥamza *al-Kisāʾī* (d. ca. 189/804-5), Kūfan, lived in Baghdād;
(8) *Abū Jaʿfar* Yazīd b. al-Qaʿqāʿ al-Makhzūmī (d. ca. 130/747-8), Medinese;
(9) *Yaʿqūb* b. Isḥāq *al-Ḥaḍramī* (d. 205/820-1), Baṣran;
(10) *Khalaf* b. Hishām (d. 229/844), Baghdādī;
(11) Muḥammad b. ʿAbd al-Raḥmān *b. Muḥayṣin* (d. ca. 123/740-1), Meccan;
(12) *al-Ḥasan al-Baṣrī* (d. 110/728), Baṣran;
(13) Sulaymān b. Mihrān *al-Aʿmash* (d. ca. 148/765), Kūfan;
(14) Yaḥyā b. al-Mubārak *al-Yazīdī* (d. 202/817-8), Baṣran, lived in Baghdād.

All of these but numbers 3 and 4 were clients *(mawālī),* not ancestral Arabs (q.v.; see also CLIENTS AND CLIENTAGE). Only a few were major figures outside the field of qurʾānic recitation: al-Kisāʾī in grammar; al-Ḥasan al-Baṣrī in preaching, ḥadīth, law, and piety; al-Aʿmash in ḥadīth, law, and piety. Particular readings tended to prevail in particular regions. For example, in the late fourth/tenth century, it was reported that most Baṣrans preferred the reading of Abū ʿAmr but the imām (q.v.) of the chief mosque refused to recite any but that of Yaʿqūb (Ibn al-Jazarī, *Ghāya,* ii, 387), while the reading of Ibn ʿĀmir is said to have prevailed in Syria until the beginning of the sixth/twelfth century, thereafter the reading of Abū ʿAmr (ibid., i, 292). Manuscripts of the *Muwaṭṭaʾ* of Mālik (d. 179/795) normally quote the Qurʾān after the reading of Nāfiʿ, which has usually been favored in north Africa (see Dutton, *The origins,* ch. 4; also Cook, A koranic codex).

From the fifth/eleventh century the two most important transmitters (sing. *rāwī,* pl. *ruwāt*) from each of the first seven were identified, later from all of the first ten (the following list is based chiefly on Ibn al-Jazarī, *Taḥbīr al-taysīr;* cf. as-Said, *Recited Koran,* 127-30):

(1) ʿĪsā b. Mīnā *Qālūn* (d. ca. 220/835), Medinese, and ʿUthmān (Saʿīd?) b. Saʿīd *Warsh* (d. 197/812-3), Egyptian;
(2) Muḥammad b. ʿAbd al-Raḥmān *Qunbul* (d. ca. 291/903-4), Meccan, and Aḥmad b. Muḥammad *al-Bazzī* (d. ca. 250/864-5), Meccan;
(3) *Abū ʿUmar* Ḥafṣ b. ʿUmar *al-Dūrī* (d. ca. 246/860-1), Baghdādī, and *Abū Shuʿayb* Ṣāliḥ b. Ziyād *al-Sūsī* (d. ca. 261/874), Mesopotamian;
(4) ʿAbdallāh b. Aḥmad *b. Dhakwān* (d. 242/857), Damascene, and *Hishām* b. ʿAmmār al-Sulamī (d. 245/859-60?), Damascene;
(5) *Abū Bakr* Shuʿbah (Sālim?) b. ʿAyyāsh (d. ca. 193/809), Kūfan, and *Ḥafṣ* b. Sulaymān, also called Ḥufayṣ (d. ca. 180/796-7), Kūfan;
(6) *Khalaf* (no. 10 among the chief reciters) and Abū ʿĪsā *Khallād* b. Khālid (Khulayd? ʿĪsā? d. 220/835), Kūfan;
(7) *Abū ʿUmar al-Dūrī* (as from no. 3) and *Abū l-Ḥarith* al-Layth b. Khālid (d. 240/854-5), Baghdādī;
(8) Abū l-Ḥārith ʿĪsā *b. al-Wardān* (d. ca. 160/776-7), Medinese, and Sulaymān b. Muslim *b. Jammāz* (d. after 170/786-7), Medinese;
(9) Muḥammad b. al-Mutawakkil *Ruways* (d. 238/852-3), Baṣran, and *Rawḥ* b. ʿAbd al-Muʾmin (d. ca. 235/849-50), Baṣran;
(10) Isḥāq b. Ibrāhīm *al-Warrāq* (d. 286/899-900), Baghdādī, and *Idrīs* b. ʿAbd al-Karīm al-Ḥaddād (d. ca. 292/905), Baghdādī.

In time, of course, specialists worked out the most important means of transmission (*ṭarīq,* pl. *ṭuruq*) from each of the *ruwāt.*

Modern scholars have often associated the seven most highly respected readings with the seven *aḥruf* in which, according to a prophetic ḥadīth report, the Qurʾān was originally revealed; most medieval scholars, however, denied any such association (see Melchert, Ibn Mujāhid, 19). Similarly, modern Muslims have often discerned a close connection between the different readings and dialectal differences (e.g. as-Said, *Recited Koran,* 84; see DIALECTS); this, however, also departs from the medieval tradition, which generally recognizes that the leading reciters themselves derived their readings by choosing *(ikhtiyār),* usually among transmitted variants. Commentaries on the readings justify them in terms of grammar and meaning, not transmission history — and only sometimes dialectal usage (e.g. Ibn Khālawayh, *Ḥujja,* and Makkī, *Kashf*). Medieval sources also sometimes use the term *ḥurūf* in connection with the transmission of textual variants; e.g. the Meccan traditionist Sufyān b. ʿUyayna (d. 198/814) is commended for unusual accuracy in transmitting the *ḥurūf* (Ibn al-Jazarī, *Ghāya,* i, 308). The distinctions and connections among *aḥruf, ḥurūf,* and *qirāʾa,* necessary for a sound understanding of the early history of qurʾānic recitational modes, await a thorough study.

It is difficult to name the most important reciters of later centuries since the main creative work of fixing the text had already been done. On the side of performance, there were doubtless reciters of outstanding originality and skill. Their work is mostly undocumented. For the long controversy over musical recitation, see Talbi (La qirāʾa) and Nelson *(Art of reciting).* The latter gives examples of changes in style across the twentieth century, which are observable, at last, in recordings (see RECITATION OF THE QURʾĀN).

There is a substantial literature on some further aspects of recitation. One example of the results of such attention over the centuries is visible in many copies of the

Qurʾān, where certain symbols indicate the editors' preferences in recitation; notably, *q-l-y* to indicate *al-waqf awlā* (better to stop but permissible to continue), *ṣ-l-y* to indicate *al-waṣl awlā* (better to continue but permissible to stop), *j* to indicate *jāʾiz* (equally permissible to stop or go on), *lā* (to indicate that one must not stop), and three dots forming a pyramid to indicate parentheses, the words of which must go either with what follows or with what has preceded; e.g. at Q 2:2, where *fīhi* may be read with either the preceding *lā rayba* ("there is no doubt in it") or the following *hudan lil-muttaqīna* ("in it is guidance for the godfearing"). These preferences are closely related to a long tradition, but naturally the tradition includes many alternatives, as described in the literature of *al-waqf wa-l-ibtidāʾ* (e.g. al-Dānī, *al-Muktafā*). Tiny *alif, wāw* and *yāʾ* indicate the prolongation of a vowel sound; e.g. at Q 2:7, where the *alif maqṣūra* of the third *ʿalā* is prolonged compared with the *alifs* of the first two. Tiny *mīm* indicates that an /*n*/ sound (usually of the *tanwīn*) is to be pronounced as /*m*/ before a /*b*/; e.g. at Q 2:18, where *ṣummun* becomes *ṣummum*. But some subtleties of correct recitation have escaped representation in writing; e.g. *imāla*, the pronunciation of /*ā*/as though it were /*ay*/, and the peculiar shaking *(qalqala)* of some consonants *(q, d, ṭ, b, j)* immediately before another consonant.

Technique of Qurʾān transmission

Muslim children have normally learnt the Qurʾān from around seven years of age but naturally there is much variation; for example, Khalaf, no. 10 on the list of reciters, memorized the Qurʾān at ten (Ibn al-Jazarī, *Ghāya*, i, 273), while the biographer Ibn al-Jazarī (d. 833/1429) memorized the Qurʾān at thirteen (ibid., ii, 247). Learning additional readings would of course come later. *Samāʿ* describes the student's listening to the teacher's dictation, while *qirāʾa* and *ʿarḍ* describe the opposite procedure, of the student's reciting for the teacher, subject to correction as necessary. Teaching by *samāʿ* might involve very large groups, *qirāʾa* normally no more than three students at a time. Traditionists who dictated ḥadīth for payment were generally scorned in the early centuries, but payment to teachers of the Qurʾān, although controversial, seems to have been better accepted, as in literary studies generally.

Transmission of the Qurʾān has usually depended on a combination of writing and audition. Writing was not necessary, hence the fairly large number of blind Qurʾān reciters (perhaps 10% in the Middle Ages — there had to be far fewer deaf qurʾānic reciters, such as Qālūn, the transmitter from Nāfiʿ, who corrected students on the basis of lip-reading). Differences among the accepted readings, however, often turn on the interpretation of the consonantal outline *(rasm)*; for example, whether diacritics go above or below the line, so making a verb masculine or feminine. Therefore, transmission by writing must have been crucial to transmission of variant readings and, indeed, their very generation in the first place. Ibn Mujāhid (d. 324/936) called for reciters to master Arabic grammar as an aid to remembering case endings, although he observed that Ibn Muḥayṣin (no. 11 on the list of reciters) went too far in allowing Arabic grammar to dictate his reading, instead of restricting his choice to transmitted variants, hence his loss of popularity in Mecca to Ibn Kathīr (d. 120/738; Ibn Mujāhid, *Sabʿa*, 45-6; Ibn al-Jazarī, *Ghāya*, i, 167). Ḥadīth recommends reading with the written *muṣḥaf* (q.v.) open before one, even if one has memorized the text.

The mosque was originally the main locus of transmission for all the Islamic sciences (see TRADITIONAL DISCIPLINES OF

QUR'ĀNIC STUDY). From the fifth/eleventh century, the *madrasa* (pl. *madāris*) became the premier institution of Islamic higher education. The chief teacher at any particular *madrasa* was normally the specialist in Islamic law, but qur'ānic recitation was often taught at the *madrasa* as an ancillary science. The Baghdādī Niẓāmiyya *madrasa*, for example, included a position for a *muqri'* (Ibn al-Jawzī, *Muntaẓam*, s.a. 485). In the Mamlūk period, there also appeared an institution dedicated entirely to teaching the Qur'ān *(dār al-Qur'ān)*. Despite that, the majority of Qur'ān teachers of whom we have any information continued to be associated with ordinary mosques.

Today, mosques continue to offer training in reciting the Qur'ān. Governments, however, are much more involved in religious instruction than ever before and not only provide qur'ānic instruction in state institutions of learning but often appoint, supervise, pay, and dismiss mosque personnel (see TEACHING AND PREACHING THE QUR'ĀN). It is nowadays quite common for Islamic countries to host international competitions in recitation of the Qur'ān. Regional mosques and religious organizations often organize similar events on a smaller, local scale.

Qur'ānic recitation is now heard by radio and television broadcasting, also by means of tape and digital recordings (see MEDIA AND THE QUR'ĀN). Gifted reciters may achieve considerable popular followings. Two of the best known reciters in recent times are Maḥmūd al-Ḥuṣrī and ʿAbd al-Bāsiṭ ʿAbd al-Ṣamad, both from Egypt, whose taped recitations remain widely available in the Islamic world even after their deaths. The different readings continue to be cultivated by specialists. Recordings of all but Ḥafṣ *ʿan* ʿĀṣim are difficult to find, and printed versions almost impossible (except for that of Nāfiʿ in the Maghrib). There are, however, signs that alternative readings will become ever more easily available.

Modern research

Gotthelf Bergsträsser and Otto Pretzl edited a large proportion of the most useful medieval scholarship on the readings of the Qur'ān. Nelson *(Art of reciting)*, Graham *(Beyond)*, Denny (The *adab*), and others have laid new stress on the Qur'ān as liturgy, principally experienced by aural recitation rather than silent reading (see ORALITY; ORALITY AND WRITING IN ARABIA). A number of studies have appeared concerning the readings and recitation practice of particular regions, of which Shalabī *(al-Qirā'āt)* is an outstanding example. There is still much work to do on the origins of the variant readings. See Puin (Observations) for exciting new manuscript evidence. The authors of this article see special promise in the investigation of the social setting of recitation.

Christopher Melchert and
Asma Afsaruddin

Bibliography

Primary: Abū Nuʿaym, Aḥmad b. ʿAbdallah al-Iṣfahānī, *Ḥilyat al-awliyā'*, 10 vols., Cairo 1932-8; Abū ʿUbayd, *Faḍā'il;* Dānī, *al-Muktafā fī l-waqf wa-l-ibtidā'*, ed. Y.ʿA.R. al-Marʿashlī, Beirut 1987; id., *Taysīr* (earliest identification of the most authoritative transmitters from each of the seven); Ḥājjī Khalīfa, *Kashf* (for literature on qur'ānic science to the mid-eleventh/seventeenth century); Ibn al-Jawzī, *Muntaẓam;* id., *Talbīs Iblīs*, ed. S. al-Jumaylī, Beirut 1985 (no standard edition); Ibn al-Jazarī, *Ghāya* (the most comprehensive medieval biographical dictionary of reciters); id., *Taḥbīr al-taysīr*, Amman 2000; Ibn Khālawayh, *Ḥujja;* Ibn Mujāhid, *Sabʿa;* Ibn al-Nadīm, *Fihrist* (numerous editions; for literature on qur'ānic science to 377/987); Ibn Saʿd, *Ṭabaqāt*, ed. Leiden; al-ʿIjlī, Abū l-Ḥasan Aḥmad b. ʿAbdallāh, *Tārīkh al-thiqāt*, ed. ʿA. Qalʿajī, Beirut 1984; Makkī, *Kashf;* Muḥammad b. Saḥnūn, Abū ʿAbdallāh al-Tanūkhī, *Kitāb Ādāb al-muʿallimīn*, ed. M. ʿAbd al-Mawlā, Algiers n.d. (on elementary education, stressing the Qurʾān); Mālik, *Muwaṭṭaʾ*; Nawawī, *al-Tibyān fī ādāb ḥamalat al-Qurʾān*, ed. J.ʿA. al-Khūlī, Cairo 1976 (no standard edition); Qurṭubī, *al-Tadhkār fī afḍal al-adhkār*, ed. Th.M. Nāfiʿ, n.p. 1979; Ṭabarī, *Taʾrīkh*. Secondary: A. Afsaruddin, The excellences of the Qurʾān, in *JAOS* 122 (2002), 1-24; A. Brockett, Qurʾān readings in *Kitāb Sībawayhi*, in *Occasional papers of the School of ʿAbbāsid Studies* 2 (1988), 129-206; N. Calder, The qurrāʾ and the Arabic lexicographical tradition, in *JSS* 36 (1991), 297-307; M. Cook, A koranic codex inherited by Mālik from his grandfather, in *Graeco-arabica* 7-8 (1999-2000), 93-105; F.M. Denny, The *adab* of Qurʾān recitation. Text and context, in A.H. Johns and S.H.M. Jafri (eds.), *International Congress for the Study of the Qurʾān*, Canberra 1980, 143-60; Y. Dutton, *The origins of Islamic law. The Qurʾān, the* Muwaṭṭaʾ *and Madinan* ʿAmal, Richmond, Surrey 1999; Graham, *Beyond*; Jeffery, *Materials*; id., The Qurʾān readings of Ibn Miqsam, in S. Löwinger and J. Somogyi (eds.), *Ignace Goldziher memorial volume. Part* 1, Budapest 1948, 1-38; G.H.A. Juynboll, The position of Qurʾān recitation in early Islam, in *JSS* 20 (1974), 240-51; P. Kahle, The Qurʾān and the ʿArabīya, in S. Löwinger and J. Somogyi (eds.), *Ignace Goldziher memorial volume. Part* 1, Budapest 1948, 163-82; Ch. Melchert, Ibn Mujāhid and the establishment of seven qurʾānic readings, in *SI* 91 (2000), 5-22; A. Mingana, The transmission of the Ḳurʾān, in *Journal of the Manchester Egyptian and Oriental Society* 5 (1916), 25-47; K. Nelson, *The art of reciting the Qurʾān*, Austin 1985; G.R. Puin, Observations on early Qurʾān manuscripts in Ṣanʿāʾ, in Wild, *Text*, 107-11; L. as-Said, *The recited Koran*, trans. B. Weiss et al., Princeton 1975; R. Sayed, *Die Revolte des Ibn al-Ašʿaṯ und die Koranleser*, Freiburg 1977; M.A. Shaban, *Islamic history*, Cambridge 1971; H. Shalabī, *al-Qirāʾāt bi-Ifrīqiyya min al-fatḥ ilā muntaṣaf al-qarn al-khāmis al-hijrī*, Tunis 1983; A. Spitaler, *Die Verzählung des Koran*, Munich 1935 (on the leading divisions of the Qurʾān into verses); M. Talbi, La qirāʾa bi-l-alḥān, in *Arabica* 5 (1958), 183-90; C.H.M. Versteegh, *Arabic grammar and qurʾānic exegesis in early Islam*, Leiden 1993.

Recompense

see REWARD AND PUNISHMENT

Reconciliation

see PEACE

Record of Human Actions

see BOOK; HEAVENLY BOOK; LAST JUDGMENT; GOOD DEEDS; EVIL DEEDS

Reeds

see AGRICULTURE AND VEGETATION; GRASSES

Reflection and Deliberation

Thinking about, and deciding a course of action based upon perceptions or observed events. To convey this concept, the Qurʾān most frequently employs the triliteral Arabic root *f-k-r*. Second and fifth forms of the root *f-k-r* are attested eighteen times in the Qurʾān. In contrast to certain conceptions in later mystic circles (see ṢŪFISM AND THE QURʾĀN), the Qurʾān itself does not consider the notion of reflection *(tafakkur)* as inferior to remembrance (q.v.) of God *(dhikr)*. But unlike *dhikr*, the Qurʾān never uses *tafakkur* with regard to God.

Rather, the Qurʾān mentions the creation (q.v.) of the heavens (see HEAVEN AND SKY) and earth (q.v.) and everything between, to request humans to reflect on and to realize divine omnipotence (see POWER AND IMPOTENCE) and the reality of resurrection (q.v.): "Do they not reflect in their own minds? But not in truth and for a term appointed, did God create the heavens and the earth, and what is between them: yet are there truly many among the people who deny the meeting with their lord [q.v.; at the resurrection]!" (Q 30:8; see also Q 45:13). Natural phenomena are interpreted in a similar way (see NATURE AS SIGNS; PSALMS): "The likeness of the life (q.v.) of the present is as the rain which we send down from the skies: by its mingling arises the produce of the earth from which people and animals eat (see SUSTENANCE): [It grows] till the earth is clad with its golden ornaments and is decked out [in beauty]: the people to whom it belongs think they have all powers of disposal over it: There reaches it our command by night or by day, and we make it like a harvest [clean-mown], as if it had not flourished only the day before! Thus do we explain the signs (q.v.) in detail for those who reflect" (Q 10:24). The singular status of the Prophet is another fact perceptible by means of reflection, as the Qurʾān points out: "Say: 'I do admonish you on one [point]: that you do stand up before God — [It may be] in pairs, or [it may be] singly — and reflect (within yourselves): your companion is not possessed (see INSANITY; JINN): he is no less than a warner (q.v.) to you, in face of a terrible chastisement'" (Q 34:46; see CHASTISEMENT AND PUNISHMENT). Even human relations in general are read as a sign of divine truth (Q 30:21). This refers also to the recall of souls (q.v.) by God during sleep (q.v.) or at death (see also DREAMS AND SLEEP; DEATH AND THE DEAD): "[It is] God [that] takes the souls (of men) at death; and those that die not [he takes] during their sleep: those on whom he has passed the decree of death, he keeps back [from returning to life], but the rest he sends [to their bodies] for a term appointed. Verily in this are signs for those who reflect" (Q 39:42). These verses, among others, aim at divine omnipotence that comprises everything in creation. By reflecting upon these signs, people, as the Qurʾān explains, should be able to recognize this divine power.

In addition to *f-k-r*, mention should be made of three other qurʾānic exhortations to reflection and deliberation on the "signs" of God and his power. Through its frequent employment of the refrain, "Which of the favors of your lord (q.v.) do you deny (see LIE)," an entire sūra (Q 55, Sūrat al-Raḥmān, "The Merciful") reminds the qurʾānic audience of God's beneficence (see GRACE; BLESSING; EXHORTATIONS; FORM AND STRUCTURE OF THE QURʾĀN; SŪRAS; RHETORIC AND THE QURʾĀN) — albeit without a lexeme connoting "deliberation" or "reflection."

Another qurʾānic term for "reflection" appears in Q 59:2: at the end of a passage relating God's punishment of the "unbelievers (see BELIEF AND UNBELIEF) from the People of the Book (q.v.)," "those who can see" (see SEEING AND HEARING; VISION AND BLINDNESS) are told to "take heed" (*fa-ʿtabirū yā ūlī l-abṣār;* see PUNISHMENT STORIES; NAḌĪR [BANŪ AL-]; OPPOSITION TO MUḤAMMAD). In this case, not *f-k-r*, but the eighth verbal form of the root letters *ʿ-b-r* are used to connote reflection and deliberation on a warning. Finally, mention should be made of Q 4:82 and 47:24 (see also Q 23:68; 38:29 for the eighth rather than the fifth form of *d-b-r*) which call for careful pondering of the qurʾānic message.

In tradition, reflection upon the holy scripture is especially emphasized. It is told, for instance, that Zayd b. Thābit discouraged rapid recitation of the Qurʾān (q.v.). Rather, he preferred to recite it over a longer period, "So that I can reflect on it and pause in it" (see Mālik, *Muwaṭṭaʾ*, no 15.3.4.).

As mentioned above, the attitude of mystics towards the intellectual act of reflection *(fikr/tafakkur)* was rather ambiguous. While (mystic) *dhikr* aims at an entire dissolution of self-consciousness before the object of recollection, i.e. God, reflection rather refers to the meditative grasping of an object. Both ways, however, aim at the same result, that is, the deep awareness of divine presence and omnipotence in contrast to the limitation of human contingency. See also KNOWLEDGE AND LEARNING; INTELLECT; MEMORY.

Angelika Brodersen

Bibliography
Primary: Ibn al-ʿArabī, Muḥyī l-Dīn, *al-Futūḥāt al-makkiyya*, 14 vols., Cairo 1972-83, chap. 144; Mālik, *Muwaṭṭaʾ*.
Secondary: L. Gardet, Fikr, in *EI*[2], ii, 891-2.

Refrains see LANGUAGE AND STYLE OF THE QUR'ĀN; FORM AND STRUCTURE OF THE QUR'ĀN; RHETORIC AND THE QUR'ĀN

Relatives see FAMILY; KINSHIP; PARENTS; CHILDREN

Religion

Prior to the twentieth century, the English word "religion" had no direct equivalent in Arabic nor had the Arabic word *dīn* in English. They became partially synonymous only in the course of the twentieth century as a result of increased English-Arabic encounters and the need for consistency in translation (see TRANSLATIONS OF THE QUR'ĀN). In the same way the English word "religion" carries a genealogy of meanings, as revealed in W.C. Smith's groundbreaking book *The meaning and end of religion,* so does the Arabic word *dīn.* This co-existence of diverse meanings makes the interpretation of both words fluid in terms of their current and past usages as well as their contemporary interrelationship.

The present examination of the concept of *dīn* in the Qur'ān therefore requires a dual approach: first, reconstructing its meanings within the linguistic context of the period during which the Qur'ān was revealed (cf. e.g. Bravmann, *Spiritual background,* 1-7, for discussion of the relationship between *dīn* and the pre-Islamic Arab concept of *muruwwa;* see also REVELATION AND INSPIRATION; ARABIC LANGUAGE; DIALECTS; PRE-ISLAMIC ARABIA AND THE QUR'ĀN), using both intra- and inter-textual approaches to processes of interpretation (hermeneutics); second, writing those reconstructed meanings in English, using words with contemporary meanings that can only approximate their Arabic equivalents. In the face of this double challenge, the primary danger to avoid is the simplistic reduction of the Arabic word *dīn* to that of the English "religion." A rich history of distinct past and interrelated current meanings emerges through an analysis of intra- and inter-textual qur'ānic hermeneutics.

Intra-textual hermeneutics

The word *dīn* occurs ninety-two times in the Qur'ān: forty-seven times in the Meccan sūras and forty-five times in the Medinan sūras (see CHRONOLOGY AND THE QUR'ĀN). It is possible to distinguish further between three Meccan sub-periods, although such detailed chronological taxonomy is subject to scholarly debate. Using René Blachère's chronological subdivisions as her primary taxonomic framework of analysis, Yvonne Yazbeck Haddad (The conception) suggested that the diversity of meanings attached to the word *dīn* in the Qur'ān can be divided into three chronological stages, which overlay the French scholar's Meccan periods and one later Medinan period.

In the first stage, corresponding to the first and second Meccan periods, the word *dīn* means "judgment" (q.v.) or "retribution" (see RETALIATION; CHASTISEMENT AND PUNISHMENT) when used in the expression *yawm al-dīn,* which accounts for almost half of the occurrences. The expression as a whole, often translated as "day of judgment," refers to a particular moment or time in the future rather than a specific day when God will act in history and human beings will be accountable for their actions (see LAST JUDGMENT). Human beings either heed this *yawm al-dīn* or not, according to their personal response to God's signs (q.v.; *āyāt;* see also BELIEF AND UNBELIEF; NATURE AS SIGNS; GRATITUDE AND INGRATITUDE; REFLECTION AND DELIBERATION). The implication of taking *yawm al-dīn* seriously leads to a life of devotion to God and responsibility (q.v.) towards others. Its denial reflects a lack of awareness of God's involvement in the world (see LIE). In both cases, *yawm al-dīn* implies personal accountability before God, whether individually acknowledged or not. By validating the existence of *yawm al-dīn,* human beings are called to live a life of integrity in the image of God's integrity towards human beings (see JUSTICE AND INJUSTICE).

The second stage corresponds to almost thirty occurrences found in the third Meccan period, with nine sub-categories of meaning that focus primarily on commitment and God's unity (*tawḥīd;* see POLYTHEISM AND ATHEISM; GOD AND HIS ATTRIBUTES). The word *dīn* is now no longer only about accountability for a future day of judgment: *dīn* is God's right path for human beings on earth at all times (see ASTRAY; ERROR; PATH OR WAY). Human beings become accountable by following the *dīn* of God, which requires total obedience (q.v.) and personal commitment to God's integrity and unity.

By contrast, a third stage of meaning emerges in the final part of the third Meccan period. In Q 6:161, *dīn* is associated with the Abrahamic community *(millat Ibrāhīm)* and the "straight path of right guidance" *(ṣirāṭin mustaqīmin).* The former identification adds a layer of meaning to the initial personal commitment. This verse introduces a new emphasis that becomes central during the Medinan period: with God's unity is associated the unity of the nascent Muslim community (*umma;* see COMMUNITY AND SOCIETY IN THE QURʾĀN). *Dīn* is now about collective commitment to live up to God's "straight path." *Dīn* then means "religion" both in the sense of a prescribed set of behaviors (see ETHICS AND THE QURʾĀN; VIRTUES AND VICES, COMMANDING AND FORBIDDING) as well as a specific community of Muslims. There is only one *dīn,* God's unchanging *dīn.* It exists on earth with different degrees of purity (i.e. Jews and Christians only partake in parts of this *dīn* because they have corrupted it over the centuries; see CORRUPTION; JEWS AND JUDAISM; CHRISTIANS AND CHRISTIANITY). It is also during the Medinan period that there emerged the concept of fighting (q.v.) for the *dīn* of God to preserve the unity of the *umma.* Both Q 3:19 and Q 3:85 make the Islamic *umma* co-extensive with *dīn.* The integration of all three meanings, the *dīn* of God, God's community of Muslims and Islam as a religion is achieved by the end of the Medinan period. This final, third stage in the qurʾānic meaning of *dīn* is then carried down over the centuries as the principal meaning of *dīn* through a complex process of inter-textual hermeneutics.

Inter-textual hermeneutics

The first level of inter-textual hermeneutics requires an etymological examination that rests on comparative linguistics, itself the result of a comparison between various texts preceding or synchronic to the formation, in the present case, of the qurʾānic literary corpus. Although some of the earlier studies on the language of the Qurʾān may have understood it as an Arabic word, derived from the root *d-y-n,* later scholars such as al-Khafājī (d. 1069/1659; cf. Brockelmann, *GAL* S, ii, 396) and al-Thaʿālibī (d. 429/1038; cf. Brockelmann, *GAL,* i, 284) considered it a foreign word on the basis that it had no Arabic verbal roots (Jeffery, *For. vocab.,* 132; see FOREIGN VOCABULARY; GRAMMAR AND THE QURʾĀN; INIMITABILITY; LANGUAGE AND STYLE OF THE QURʾĀN). Like its Syriac cognate, the Arabic *dīn* has a polysemous sense: "code of law" (as with the Persian *dēn*) and "judgment" (as in the Aramaic *dīnā*). This dual meaning (attested in pre-Islamic Arabic poetry; see POETRY AND POETS) has led to the supposition that the term entered

Arabic through Syriac, a northern Aramaic dialect, in which language both meanings are attested in the early Christian period (even though a Jewish use of Aramaic in the oasis of Yathrib could have introduced *dīn* in the sense of "judgment" into the Arabic language, this would not explain its second sense in Arabic of "code of law"; see also MEDINA; cf. Ahrens, Christliches, 34-5, in which it is posited that the Arabic term was borrowed from Persian, directly or through Syriac).

Unlike the first level of inter-textual hermeneutics which remains largely synchronic with the period of qurʾānic textual production (see COLLECTION OF THE QURʾĀN), the second level is diachronic, that is, it spans a fourteen-century history of qurʾānic hermeneutics as found in *ʿulūm al-Qurʾān,* "the qurʾānic sciences" (see TRADITIONAL DISCIPLINES OF QURʾĀNIC STUDY). In this long and rich Islamic tradition of interpreting the Qurʾān, the dominant meaning of *dīn* reflects the later qurʾānic meaning associated with the Medinan period. For example, in his famous commentary, al-Ṭabarī (d. 310/923) interpreted the word *dīn* in Q 3:85 as synonymous with *islām*. In the commentary of Ibn Kathīr (d. 774/1373), this verse is juxtaposed with Q 3:19 in which *dīn* is glossed as *islām*. In the early twentieth century, however, a plurality of meanings re-emerges as more explanations of the qurʾānic word *dīn* are needed in response to the dominant western Orientalist interpretation of Islam as one religion among many, rather than the Muslim belief of its being the one religion of God (see RELIGIOUS PLURALISM AND THE QURʾĀN). In the first volume of *Tafhīm al-Qurʾān,* as well as in a separate book entitled *Four basic qurʾānic terms,* Sayyid Abū l-Aʿlā Mawdūdī (1903-1979) explicitly defines *dīn* as found in Q 2:132 as "a qurʾānic technical term, signifying the way of life, the system of conduct, and the code on which man bases his entire mode of thought and action" (cf. id., *Towards understanding,* ii, 114 for Eng. trans.; see POLITICS AND THE QURʾĀN). The first two expressions, "way of life" and "system of conduct," on the one hand, and the third expression, "code," on the other, respectively reflect modern English as opposed to pre-modern qurʾānic semantic resonances, thereby demonstrating Mawdūdī's extensive interaction with western thought. This link is even clearer in the fourth volume of his commentary, when he considers the expression *dīn Allāh* as opposed to *dīn al-malik* (*dīn* of the king), translating *dīn* as "law" in both cases (see LAW AND THE QURʾĀN; KINGS AND RULERS). Building again on both Q 3:19 and Q 3:85, he concludes that "These [three] verses require that believers should totally submit themselves to din. And din, apart from prescribing Prayer (q.v.) and Fasting (q.v.), also lays down laws relevant for operating the social system and the administration of a country" (Eng. trans. in id., *Towards understanding,* iv, 197). Here, Mawdūdī integrates both the western (heavily Christian) understanding of religion as a set of beliefs and rituals (see RITUAL AND THE QURʾĀN) with an older legal qurʾānic meaning for *dīn* reflected in the use of English words such as "code" and "law."

In this modern exegesis (see EXEGESIS OF THE QURʾĀN: EARLY MODERN AND CONTEMPORARY), both older and newer meanings of the word *dīn* are given. These meanings are further affected by their translation into expressions that dovetail with popular definitions of "religion" in the English language of the later twentieth and early twenty-first centuries. For example, in the sixth section of the chapter "Basic concepts of Islam" in the book *Islam in focus,* easily available through the internet, Dr. Ḥammūdah ʿAbd al-ʿĀṭī writes that "genuine religion must come from God for the right guidance of man." This implicit definition of "religion" is prescriptive and overlaps in part with a more popular western understanding of the word "religion" as both linked to God and to a divine revelation whose purpose is to guide humankind. Yet, on the basis of Q 3:19 and 3:85, ʿAbd al-ʿĀṭī argues that the only genuine religion is Islam. This emphasis on the degree of quality of religion — that there may be different religions but only one is genuinely true — reflects the old third stage, Medinan qurʾānic meaning of *dīn,* which only appears in the singular form, to refer to a personal commitment to a transcendent God *(tawḥīd)* by way of submission *(islām)* as part of a community of Muslim persons *(umma).*

In short, the equivalent in contemporary English would be the emphasis of Religion with a capital R over either "religion" or "religions" in the plural. But what happens when such a distinction between upper- and lower-case letters does not exist in the Arabic language? The constant contemporary usage of both "religion" (sing.) and "religions" (pl.) in western languages has required the development of an Arabic plural form for *dīn.* In fact, two different forms have emerged: *adyān* and *diyānāt.* How these new variants of *dīn,* currently synonymous, might be distinguished in the future is unclear, as is how they might affect, in turn, the interpretation of the singular form *dīn.* What is certain, however, is that these linguistic changes in contemporary Arabic reflect the unavoidable influence of the current global power dynamics that affect almost unilaterally the direction of change: the meanings traditionally associated with the Arabic word *dīn* are gradually merging into those associated with the English words "religion" and "religions" as well as the use of cognate terms in other Western languages.

The very name of this entry within an English language *Encyclopaedia of the Qurʾān* reinforces such power dynamics, affecting our efforts at reconstructing a qurʾānic understanding of the concept *dīn.* Yet, as the title of this entry uses a capital R, it may reflect a very subtle possibility of meaning more closely akin to the singular, solely qurʾānic use of *dīn.* In this respect, both this encyclopedia entry and ʿAbd al-ʿĀṭī's juxtaposition of *dīn* and "religion" demonstrate how meanings are constantly created and re-created within both culturally received yet continually changing hermeneutical processes.

Patrice C. Brodeur

Bibliography

Primary: Ibn Kathīr, *Tafsīr,* Gizah 2000; Ṭabarī, *Tafsīr,* Damascus 1997; abr. trans. W.F. Madelung and A. Jones (eds.), *The commentary on the Qurʾān,* Oxford 1987.

Secondary: Ḥ. ʿAbd al-ʿĀṭī, *Islam in focus,* Singapore 1980; K. Ahrens, Christliches im Qoran. Eine Nachlese, in *ZDMG* 84 (1930), 15-68, 148-90; M. Bravmann, *The spiritual background of early Islam. Studies in ancient Arab concepts,* Leiden 1972, 1-7 (on the relationship between *muruwwa* and *dīn*); Brockelmann, *GAL;* L. Gardet, Dīn, in *EI*[2], ii, 293-6; Goldziher, *MS,* i, 1-46; Y.Y. Haddad, The conception of the term *dīn* in the Qurʾān, in *MW* 64 (1974), 114-23; Izutsu, *God,* 219-29; Jeffery, *For. vocab.,* 131-2; D.B. Macdonald, Dīn, in *EI*[1], i, 975; Sayyid Abū l-Aʿlā Mawdūdī, *Four basic qurʾānic terms,* Eng. trans. Abu Asad, Lahore 1979, 93-103; id., *Tafhīm al-Qurʾān,* trans. Z.I. Ansari, *Towards understanding the Qurʾān,* 7 vols. to date, Leicester 1988-; J.D. McAuliffe, Text and textuality. Q 3:7 as a point of intersection, in I.J. Boullata (ed.), *Literary structures of religious meaning in the Qurʾān,* Richmond, UK 2000, 56-76; H. Ringgren, The pure religion, in *Oriens* 15 (1962), 93-6; W.C. Smith, *The meaning and end of religion,* New York 1963, repr. 1991, 90-100, 287-90.

Religious Pluralism and the Qurʾān

In traditional Muslim thought, Muḥammad is the "seal of the prophets," and his message, contained in the Qurʾān, continues, confirms — and abrogates — all previous prophetic messages. The Qurʾān demonstrates an awareness of those previous messages, at least some of them, and evidences knowledge of a variety of religious groups in its milieu. The earliest commentators on the Qurʾān were alert to these allusions and their efforts at identification became a traditional topic in classical exegetical works (McAuliffe, *Qurʾānic,* 16-31). Such efforts formed part of a larger agenda, that of providing historical specificity to certain segments of the text. The desire to do so was motivated less by an embracive and encyclopedic scholarly attitude than by the desire to determine both the chronological parameters of qurʾānic directives and the precise groups to whom they applied. Among the qurʾānic "sciences" the subfield known as "occasions of revelation" (q.v.; *asbāb al-nuzūl*) accumulated the results of these narrative elaborations of the qurʾānic text.

Numerous qurʾānic passages allude to individuals, or to groups, who did not accept Muḥammad as a prophet, but are nevertheless identified with one or another "religious" category about which the Qurʾān has a variety of not necessarily uniform opinions. Explicit in its condemnation of polytheists/idolaters (*mushrikūn,* i.e. Q 4:48, 116; 30:31; 39:65; but cf. Hawting, *Idea of idolatry,* for the argument that the qurʾānic polemic against these *mushrikūn* reflects "disputes among monotheists rather than pagans and that Muslim tradition does not display much substantial knowledge of Arab pagan religion" [16]), as well as the so-called "hypocrites" (*munāfiqūn,* also glossed as "cowards" or those who shirked their military responsibilities; cf. Q 4:138, 145; 9:68; 33:73), the Qurʾān does not deny the continued existence of Judaism and Christianity in its own milieu (i.e. seventh century Arabia; for two revisionist arguments that place the origins of the Qurʾān elsewhere, see Crone and Cook, *Hagarism,* and Wansbrough, *Sectarian milieu;* but cf. Donner, *Narratives,* 35-61) and also alludes to other religious groups who are not directly connected to the qurʾānic message (i.e. the enigmatic Sabians and Magians).

For at least the last century and a half, western scholarship has discussed the "monotheistic influence" on Muḥammad and the Qurʾān (see POST-ENLIGHTENMENT ACADEMIC STUDY OF THE QURʾĀN). Examples include A. Geiger's nineteenth century doctoral thesis at the University of Marburg, *Was hat Mohammed aus dem Judenthume aufgenommen?* (Eng. trans. *Judaism and Islam* 1898, repr. New York 1970), R. Dozy's *Die Israeliten zu Mekka* (Leiden 1864); H. Lammens' Les Chrétiens à la Mecque à la veille de l'hégire, in *BIFAO* 14 (1918), 191-230; T. Andrae's Der Ursprung des Islams und das Christentum, in *Kyrkohistorisk Arsskrift* (1923-5), with a French translation, *Les origins de l'Islam et le Christianisme* (Paris 1955); R. Bell's *The origin of Islam in its Christian environment* (Edinburgh 1926); and C.C. Torrey's *The Jewish foundations of Islam* (New York 1933). Other studies have focused on the possible presence of Christian, Jewish or Judeo-Christian sectarian groups in the qurʾānic milieu, and there has been abundant speculation about the identity of the *zindīq*s of Mecca (Manichaeans and Mazdakites have been suggested; cf. Hawting, *Idea of idolatry,* 15, for bibliography; see also HERESY). Further, it has long been acknowledged that much of the qurʾānic message exhibits knowledge of, and similarity to, aspects of Judaism and Christianity, particularly as regards the narrative accounts of the prophets and several of the religious practices of the nascent community (see NARRATIVES; PROPHETS AND PROPHETHOOD; RITUAL AND THE QURʾĀN). Recent work on, for example, inter-communal similarities continues this long line of scholarship (cf. Donner, *Narratives*, 64-75 for a discussion of qurʾānic piety in this context).

The Qurʾān categorizes and alludes to the various religious groups that appear to have inhabited its milieu (cf. Rubin, *Eye*, 45-53, for an overview of the religious communities present in pre-Islamic south Arabia: namely Jews, Christians, polytheists and *ḥunafāʾ*) in a variety of ways. Additionally, the qurʾānic vocabulary for "religion" (q.v.) is itself multivalent and distinct from the terminology for "faith" (q.v.) or belief (see BELIEF AND UNBELIEF; GRATITUDE AND INGRATITUDE). This article will discuss the development of the qurʾānic attitude towards religious pluralism by looking first at the vocabulary employed by the Qurʾān to designate either "religion" or the various religious groups with which it expresses familiarity. It will then focus upon the instances of "interreligious" encounter between Muḥammad and his followers and non-Muslims, primarily Christians, recognizing the fluidity of these categories. The final section will examine the qurʾānic passages which have formed Muslim attitudes toward the present plurality of religions.

Qurʾānic vocabulary

In addition to the explicit mentions of various religious groups, Jews, Christians, Sabians and Magians — the so-called "People of the Book" (q.v.) — as well as of polytheists/idolaters and the enigmatic *ḥunafāʾ* (sing. *ḥanīf*), the Qurʾān uses a range of words, both Arabic and Arabized non-Arabic (see FOREIGN VOCABULARY), to signify what contemporary readers understand as "religion."

General terms: *dīn, milla, ʿibāda*

Traditional Muslim writings on the religious teachings contained in the Qurʾān often maintain that there is a sharp distinction between the polytheism that dominated pre-Islamic Arabian religious life and the monotheism preached by Muḥammad. In the late nineteenth century, Goldziher *(Muhammedanische Studien)* and others took up this theme of the asserted difference and attempted to contrast a pre-Islamic communal, tribal "materialistic" virtue *(muruwwa)* with the Islamic and qurʾānic concept of religion as individual affiliation (*dīn;* cf. Bravmann, *Spiritual background*, 2, and more generally, 1-7, for a counterargument that maintains that *muruwwa* — like *dīn* — had a moral-spiritual significance, and that "virtus and the virile ethics of the heathen period were appreciated even in the Islamic period, only that in the course of time other qualities, of purely religious character, were added to them"). The most common term for "religion" is *dīn* (over 90 occurrences), an Arabized word with a diglossic background: the Persian *dēn* meaning "religion" or "cult" and the Akkadian *dānu* meaning "judgment" (q.v.; Jeffery, *For. vocab.*, 131-3; cf. *Lisān al-ʿArab* for other glosses, namely "custom, usage" and also "punishment, reward"). In the Qurʾān the Arabic *dīn* has both these senses (as, incidentally, in Christian writings does its Syriac cognate, *dīnâ/dīn;* cf. Jeffery, op. cit., 132-3 for an overview of the complex background of the Syriac term; for additional discussion of the qurʾānic *dīn* — particularly its eschatological usage — see LAST JUDGMENT). Gardet (Dīn) distinguishes between the usage in the Meccan and Medinan periods: in the former, the sense of "judgment" predominates, whereas the latter emphasizes the sense of "religion," with echoes of the "practical" or cultic aspect of the Persian *dēn*. As seen in the exegesis of Q 109:6 ("to you your *dīn*, and to me my *dīn*"), *dīn* is a term that can be applied to believers and unbelievers (cf. e.g. Ṭabarī, *Tafsīr*, ad loc., where the enduring quality of religious affiliation is asserted). But it must be emphasized that when *dīn* is used with the sense of "religion" it involves the "act of worship," derived from the Arabic sense of debt, i.e. rendering to God what is his due — that is, the obligations and prescriptions set out in the Qurʾān.

Another term for religion is *milla,* unattested in Arabic prior to its qurʾānic usage (cf. Bosworth, Milla). Likely of Syriac origin, in which *meltâ* may signify "word" (Gk. *logos*) and is used as a technical term for religion (Jeffery, *For. vocab.,* 268-9), in the Qurʾān *milla* denotes "religion" or "sect," and is frequently employed to designate the creed of Abraham (q.v.; 8 out of the 15 occurrences: Q 2:130, 135; 3:95; 4:125, in which the *milla* of Abraham is identified with "submission" to God; 6:161; 12:38; 16:123; 22:78). But again, and also like the qurʾānic *umma,* which is used for the Muslim community as well as for the communities of non-Muslims (even the animals and birds are said to constitute *umma*s, cf. Q 6:38), *milla* is not the exclusive provenance of "believers" or Muslims: it is used for the religion of prophets prior to Muḥammad (i.e. Q 12:38), Christians and Jews (Q 2:120) and polytheists or unbelievers (Q 7:88-9, the religion of the people of Shuʿayb [q.v.]; 12:37; 14:13; 18:20; 38:7). Q 12:37 and 38 exemplify most clearly the range of uses: in Q 12:37, Joseph (q.v.) says, "I have abandoned the *milla* of a people who do not believe in God and deny the hereafter (see ESCHATOLOGY)," and in the following verse he says, "I followed the *milla* of my fathers Abraham and Isaac (q.v.) and Jacob (q.v.); we do not associate anything with God."

Closely related to the semantic range of *dīn,* a third general term for "religion" or religious praxis is *ʿibāda,* "worship" (the nominal form occurs 9 times; various verbal forms of the root *ʿ-b-d* are much more frequent). The root meaning, however, is "to make, to do, to work" — from which the sense of "to serve" is derived (see Jeffery, *For. vocab.,* 209-10; see SERVANT). As with *dīn* and *milla, ʿ-b-d* is used both in reference to the service of the one, true God and the (albeit vain) service of that which is not God (i.e. Q 5:60, 76; 10:104). In later Islamic thought, the "service" to the one God is explained as essentially involving the five "pillars" of Islamic faith, although sometimes other duties, such as marriage (see MARRIAGE AND DIVORCE) and circumcision (q.v.), are included in the books of law (cf. Bousquet, ʿIbādāt).

Terms conveying qurʾānic approval: *islām, ḥanīf, sharīʿa*

Literally "surrender, submission," *islām* (q.v.) occurs 8 times, most notably at Q 5:3, wherein God says to Muḥammad: "I have completed my blessing upon you and I have approved *al-islām* as [your] religion" (cf. Q 3:19: "the [true] religion with God is *al-islām*"). It is not clear from the Qurʾān what, exactly, is meant by *islām:* most notably, there is no clear differentiation between "faith" *(īmān)* and "submission to God" (*islām,* although cf. Q 49:14; for a clear presentation of the relation of these two terms and *dīn* throughout the history of qurʾānic exegesis see Smith, *Historical*). Some later ḥadīth (cf. Eng. trans. of one such account in Bukhārī, *Ṣaḥīḥ,* i, 42-3, related on the authority of Abū Hurayra), however, associate *islām* with the public marks of a Muslim believer, i.e. the five "pillars" of Islam, and *īmān* with belief in God, his messengers and books, the angels (see ANGEL), and the last day (see Smith, *Historical,* 12-3, for the various renditions of this tradition; for a rather different understanding of *islām* and *īmān,* see Bravmann, *Spiritual background,* 7-31, and his theory that the former is a pre-Islamic concept implying defiance of death in the face of struggle with an enemy, while the latter connotes the sense of security associated with the triliteral Arabic root *ʾ-m-n*, particularly in the context of protection against "fate"; see FATE). In light of the ambiguity of qurʾānic language, subsequent theological debates raised the question of whether non-Muslims, especially Jews and Christians, could be considered "believers" (see Donner, Believers, for a recent discussion). Eventually, however, *islām* was used for both the "personal relationship between man and God and the community of those acknowledging this relationship" (Smith, *Historical*, 2). It also must be noted that, although certain people prior to Muḥammad (notably Abraham) are said to have been *"muslims"* (the active participle of *islām*), the Qurʾān is explicit in its insistence that obedience (q.v.) to God involves obedience to his messenger (q.v.), namely Muḥammad (cf. Q 4:65; 33:36), an obedience that includes following the prescriptions and proscriptions that the Qurʾān exhorts.

Although *ḥanīf* (q.v.; 12 occurrences, nearly all of which are explicitly linked to Abraham) is used in the Qurʾān with the sense of a "true monotheistic believer," a Syriac cognate *(ḥanpâ)* has the connotations of "pagan" (but see Rubin, Ḥanīf, 402, who emphasizes the significance of the Arabic root meaning "to incline," as in having abandoned the prevailing religion and 'inclined' to a religion of one's own). The tension between the apparent qurʾānic meaning and the close Syriac cognate, which is not always mentioned in contemporary discussions of the topic (i.e. Hawting, *Idea of idolatry*), has yet to be explained satisfactorily, particularly with regards to its usage in a Muslim framework (see Watt, Ḥanīf; Jeffery, *For. vocab.*, 113-5). Here it should be noted that Crone and Cook's discussion of the term (*Hagarism*, 13-14) focuses on Syriac Christian accounts of the seventh century Arab conquests, in which there is an apparent conflation of *ḥanpē* and *mahgrayē* (which latter term, in Cook and Crone's reading, designates the "Hagarenes," a Judeo-Arab group who migrated from Arabia) as terms identifying the conquerors. They maintain that the qurʾānic concept of *ḥanīf* was an intentional borrowing of the Syriac cognate by the 'Hagarenes,' but was used instead to "designate an adherent of an unsophisticated Abrahamic monotheism" in a contrivance "to make a religious virtue of the stigma of their pagan past" (*Hagarism*, 14; cf. also Watt, Ḥanīf). There is also a lack of scholarly consensus about whether the qurʾānic employment of *ḥanīf* connotes an actual pre-Islamic religious grouping (see, for example, Rubin, *Eye*, and Hawting, *Idea of idolatry*, s.v., for two different viewpoints in contemporary scholarship). According to the semantic analysis of T. Izutsu, the qurʾānic *ḥanīf* encompasses "(1) the true religion deep-rooted in the natural disposition in every human soul to believe in the One God, (2) absolute submission to this One God, and (3) [...] the antithesis to idol-worshipping" (Izutsu, *Ethico-religious concepts*, 191). See further discussion of this term below, under *Religious communities*.

Perhaps parallel to the Christian designation of their religion as the "way," *sharīʿa* (later used as the comprehensive designation of the Islamic law), with one occurrence at Q 45:18, has been understood with the sense of God's having set Muḥammad on the "open way, clear way, right way."

Terms denoting qurʾānic toleration or ambivalence

Ahl al-kitāb, dhimma

A more comprehensive designation are the so-called "People of the Book" (or "those who have been given the book," cf. Q 2:121; also "people of the Gospel," Q 5:47), which appears over 30 times, with multiple connotations. Although Jews and Christians (the Children of Israel [q.v.]) are considered the prime designates of this terminology and were, subsequently, accorded a "protected" — albeit subordinate — status in later Islamic societies, the Magians and Sabians also appear in the Qurʾān in conjunction with these "scriptured" peoples (cf. Q 22:17), leading to their inclusion among the protected minorities in developed Islamic thought (see below, under *Religious groups*). While in post-qurʾānic times, *ahl al-kitāb* became nearly synonymous with *dhimmī* (or *ahl al-dhimma*, the "protected" persons living in the Islamic state, i.e. religious minorities), the qurʾānic *dhimma* (Q 9:8, 10), from which these latter terms derive, indicates merely "pact, treaty," without any specification of the terms thereof, or of the persons to whom it applies. Later Islamic tradition developed these conditions (as exemplified in the so-called "covenant of ʿUmar"; cf. Tritton, *Caliphs*), and those non-Muslim groups living in Islamic lands to whom they were extended were subsequently termed *dhimmīs/ahl al-dhimma* (cf. Cahen, Dhimma). The designation of a specific group of people with a (revealed) "book" suggests that written scriptures were accorded respect, and those communities that claimed a written revealed text were set apart from others (see ORALITY AND WRITING IN ARABIA). The People of the Book are to be consulted for the meaning of scripture (cf. Q 10:94: "If you [Muḥammad] are in doubt about what we have revealed to you, ask those who recite/read *[yaqraʾūna]* the book before you"), but are also presented in the Qurʾān as people who are in disagreement over the scriptures (cf. Q 3:64, 65, wherein the People of the Book are said to be disputing concerning Abraham; see GOSPEL; TORAH; PSALMS; BOOK).

Parties/factions

In addition to the indicators of religious adherence — generally positive *(ahl al-kitāb, ḥanīf, muslim, muʾmin)*, negative *(mushrik)* and neutral *(dhimma, milla)*, as well as the religious groups whose adherents are named in the Qurʾān (Jews, Christians, Magians, Sabians) — there are a few terms that indicate divisions among the adherents of a religion, terms that may also be used for secular divisions. These qurʾānic lexemes include *ḥizb* (pl. *aḥzāb*), *ṭāʾifa* and *farīq* (the second verbal form of the root *f-r-q* is also used in this sense; cf. Q 6:159 and 30:32, as well as Q 20:94 and 9:107), *shīʿa* (q.v.; pl. *shiyaʿ*, *ashyāʿ*, e.g. Q 6:159; 15:10, but also Q 28:15), *zubur* (Q 23:53), *ṭaraf* (e.g. Q 3:127), *ṭarīqa* (pl. *ṭarāʾiq*, e.g. Q 72:11), etc. All of this vocabulary has been variously translated as group, party, sect or division, among other renderings, with the terms generally carrying a negative value. Charges of sectarian division are not infrequent in the Qurʾān and although primarily aimed at the Children of Israel, they are also made against Muslims — as in the designation of those who shirked their military duties as "hypocrites" (see HYPOCRITES AND HYPOCRISY; cf. Rubin, *Between*, esp. 117-46). Such accusations became a prominent theme in Muslim polemics against Christians, who were excoriated for multiple and visible divisions (see below, under "Jews and Christians").

This review of qurʾānic vocabulary demonstrates the complexity of the qurʾānic notion of religion which does not easily map to contemporary Western understandings of religious pluralism. Adherence to the divinely revealed message encompasses more than a profession of faith (i.e. *īmān*); it entails an entire way of life (namely the behavior implied by *sharīʿa*, *islām*, *ʿibāda*) — both public and private — a communal concept closer to the qurʾānic concept of *umma* than the juridical/canonical/liturgical notion more familiar to today's Euro-American societies. Even though the Qurʾān acknowledges the fact of the diversity of religions, it asserts that, had God so willed, he could have made them all one nation (*umma*, see Q 42:6-9; see PARTIES AND FACTIONS).

Religious communities

In addition to the terms that connote religion as a collective category, the Qurʾān names adherents of several religious communities. Most mentions, whether of Islam (i.e. those who adhered to the qurʾānic message) or of other religious groupings, point to people and physical structures rather than conceptual abstractions (note the reference in Q 5:44 to Jewish "rabbis" *[al-rabbāniyyūn]* and "religious scholars" [*al-aḥbār:* also understood to refer to Christian religious authorities in Q 9:31, 34]; Christian "priests" *[qissīsīn]* and "monks" *[ruhbān]* of Q 5:82; the mention in Q 22:40 of God's prevention of the destruction of four different places identified with religious institutions: *ṣawāmiʿ*, identified as monasteries, *biyaʿ* — churches, *ṣalawāt* — synagogues, and *masājid* — mosques, lit. places of "prostration"; see CHURCH; MONASTICISM AND MONKS). For example, the Qurʾān mentions Christians but has no term for Christianity (but cf. i.e. Q 2:62 for a possible attestation of "Judaism"). Here it should be noted that the Qurʾān does not always link *islām* with "religion" (but see Q 3:19, 85; 5:3), although most of the qurʾānic attestations of *islām* denote the relationship of a human being to God: e.g. Q 9:74; 49:17; 61:7. The concept of Islam as distinct from *islām* emerged over time, and received differing nuances in different settings (Smith, *Historical*). Since, as recent scholarship has shown, Christianity and Judaism in the world of late antiquity were not as well-defined as their contemporary apologists have portrayed them (e.g. Boyarin, *Radical Jew;* id., *Sparks of the logos;* cf. also Cameron, *Mediterranean world*), our inability to designate precisely the referents of these qurʾānic mentions is not surprising. Some of these religious groupings appear a number of times (Jews, Christians and polytheists), while others are mentioned only rarely (Sabians, Q 2:62; 5:69 and 22:17 and Magians, Q 22:17). Often, it is not clear if the qurʾānic concept indicates an actual, contemporary religious group identifiable as such to the qurʾānic audience, a pre-Islamic group or a theological concept (i.e. the enigmatic *ḥanīf*).

Further, despite the apparent distinction of these groups from one another and from the emergent community that heeded Muḥammad and his message, the specific nature of the various groups to which these people belonged is by no means clear. There is also a range of qurʾānic judgment on some of them, particularly the Jews and the Christians. Indeed, the Qurʾān has many scriptural figures and concepts familiar to Jews and Christians, making analysis of the degree of real separation and distinction among the communities in the qurʾānic milieu difficult. The prevalence of the qurʾānic attestations of "believers" is a case in point: in passages such as Q 33:35, believers and Muslims are both mentioned — and it is not clear whether one modifies the other, or if they are separate categories. Might Jews and Christians, particularly those not hostile to Muslims, be considered "believers" (as was the claim of Christian apologists such as Theodore Abū Qurra [d. ca. 214/830]; cf. id., *Discussion,* 75-6; see also Donner, Believers)? Despite such irenic arguments, the fact that there are different terms for Jews, Christians and Muslims does indicate a significant qurʾānic distinction among these groups. Finally, the long history of qurʾānic commentary has complicated the identification of, and attitude towards, the following groups and, consequently, their relationship to contemporary religious groups and the resultant behavior towards them demanded of Muslims. A brief sketch of those communities to which the Qurʾān alludes in various ways and in varying detail, follows. See, however, the articles JEWS AND JUDAISM; CHRISTIANS AND CHRISTIANITY; SABIANS; ḤANĪF; MAGIANS; POLYTHEISM AND ATHEISM for a fuller discussion of each.

Jews and Christians

As mentioned above, the Qurʾān uses the designation People of the Book and Children of Israel to include both Jews and Christians — with the latter phrase, however, carrying a less obviously Christian valence. But reference to Jews and Christians as separate entities is also made. Often with a negative connotation, "Jews" *(yahūd)* are explicitly mentioned multiple times in the Qurʾān (Q 2:113, 120; 5:18, 51, 64, 82; 9:30; cf. also 22:17, etc.), and once the singular appears — in an assertion that Abraham was *not* a Jew (Q 3:67). Although the origins and the rituals of the Jewish groups in Muḥammad's milieu are not well attested, the qurʾānic evidence, as well as other sources (such as ḥadīth and the *sīra;* see ḤADĪTH AND THE QURʾĀN; SĪRA AND THE QURʾĀN), point to the presence of Jewish communities in seventh century Arabia. (The qurʾānic identification of the individual who, in Q 20:85-95, prompts the Israelites to create the calf of gold [q.v.] as al-Sāmirī may also indicate some familiarity with Samaritans [q.v.]). "Christians" (*al-naṣārā* and other phrases; cf. McAuliffe, *Qurʾānic,* esp. 1-5 and 94-128) also appear a number of times in the Qurʾān (Q 2:62, 111, 113, 120, 135, 140; 5:14, 18, 51, 69, 82; 9:30; 22:17) — with only one occurrence in the singular *(naṣrāniyyan),* again in a denial of Abraham's being one (Q 3:67). But, unlike the frequent qurʾānic condemnation of "Jews," "Christians" are sometimes commended (Q 5:82: "The nearest of them in love to the believers are those who say, 'We are Christians'"; see also Q 24:37-8). As is the case with the Jews, there is more speculation than knowledge about the exact nature of the Christianity present in seventh century Arabia, but the Qurʾān and other, contemporary sources attest to a Christian presence in the peninsula — although the depth of their penetration is not known (cf. Shahid *[Byzantium and the Arabs]* and Griffith [Gospel] for varying opinions on the extent of the "Arabic" nature of pre-Islamic Christianity in the Arabian peninsula; Hoyland maintains that although "in the fourth to sixth centuries Christianity made major inroads into Arabia... it was particularly the inhabitants of north Arabia who were won over to Christianity in large numbers"; cf. Hoyland, *Arabia,* 146-59, esp. 147). Unfortunately — reflecting the paucity of information available for pre-Islamic Arabia — many recent works on Arabia or the Arabs do not explore the religious situation of the inhabitants of the peninsula in depth (cf. Retsö, *The Arabs*). Apart from epigraphic sources, which are currently inaccessible to many western researchers, there is little historical attestation of the Arabian peninsula other than the Islamic annals — which were composed, at the earliest, in the second or third Islamic century. The following is an outline of the state of current knowledge on the subject (see also EPIGRAPHY AND THE QURʾĀN; PRE-ISLAMIC ARABIA AND THE QURʾĀN; SOUTH ARABIA, RELIGION IN PRE-ISLAMIC).

There appears to have been a Jewish presence in the Arabian peninsula since the first century C.E. In the sixth century there was even a south Arabian Jewish "kingdom" of Ḥimyar that flourished for a brief period of time (for details see

Hoyland, *Arabia*, 49-57; 146-7; Lecker, Conversion, 129-36). Thus, it is not surprising to learn that there were a number of presumably Arabic-speaking Jewish tribes in Medina (q.v.) and its surroundings during Muḥammad's lifetime. These Jewish tribes figure prominently in Muḥammad's struggle for the establishment of a political entity in Medina after his emigration (q.v.; *hijra*) from Mecca (q.v.), and various qurʾānic verses are traditionally associated with the different stages of this early "Muslim-Jewish" conflict (see Schöller, *Exegetisches*). For example, the biographers of Muḥammad associate the revelation of Q 3:12 f., which alludes to the Muslim victory at Badr (q.v.) as a warning for the disbelievers, and Q 5:51-6, which urges the believers not to take Jews and Christians as friends (cf. Ibn Isḥāq, *Sīra*, 388, 545-6; Eng. trans. Ibn Isḥāq-Guillaume, 260, 363; see FRIENDS AND FRIENDSHIP), with the confrontation and expulsion of the tribe of Qaynuqāʿ (see OCCASIONS OF REVELATION). Also, Q 59:2-15 (cf. Ibn Isḥāq, *Sīra*, 654; Eng. trans. Ibn Isḥāq-Guillaume, 438) has been connected to the expulsion of the tribe of Naḍīr; and Q 33:26 f. (cf. Ibn Isḥāq, *Sīra*, 693; Eng. trans. Ibn Isḥāq-Guillaume, 468) to the extermination of the males [who participated in battle against the Muslims] from the tribe of Qurayẓa (see NAḌĪR; QURAYẒA; QAYNUQĀʿ for further discussion of the classical Islamic interpretation of these verses).

Although the Christian presence was less localized and less cohesive than the Jewish one, there is ample attestation of Christian communities in pre-Islamic south Arabia. The precise nature, however, of their liturgy, or even their beliefs, is not known (for two different perspectives in modern scholarship on the nature and extent of the spread of Christianity in pre-Islamic Arabia, see the above-mentioned works of Shahid and Griffith on this topic). After the Christological controversies in the early/middle fifth century C.E., the eastern Christians were divided into three groups: those who adhered to the pronouncements of the Council of Chalcedon (451 C.E.; i.e. that in the one person and hypostasis of Christ was a fully human nature and a fully divine one); and two non-Chalcedonian groups, ordinarily known as the Nestorians and Monophysites. Each of these groups existed in south Arabia prior to Muḥammad's lifetime, but the Monophysites, with their connection to Abyssinia, were the politically dominant (cf. the story of the Christian city of Najrān and its famous martyrs). The Persian Nestorians also had a fairly visible role (see below, under "Najrān" in *Episodes*). In addition to the explicit mentions of "Christians" or Christian doctrines that appear in the Qurʾān, certain verses are understood to be allusions to Muḥammad's (or his followers') encounters with specific Christian groups (see below under *Episodes*).

Like the Jews, the Christians are included in such categories as "Children of Israel" and "People of the Book." But, rather than a literal translation of the Greek term "Christian" (i.e. the Ar. *masīḥiyya*), the qurʾānic Christians are termed *al-naṣāra*, most likely in reference to the *nisba* of Jesus (q.v.), i.e. the "Nazarene" (for discussion of the possible significations of this term, see McAuliffe, *Qurʾānic*, 93-128). This term, one that appears to be unique to the Qurʾān, as well as the qurʾānic descriptions of their beliefs, has led to some speculation about the exact nature of the Christians in the qurʾānic milieu: were they (an otherwise-unattested) Jewish-Christian sect (i.e. pace S. Pines, Notes; cf. id., *Jewish Christians;* id., Gospel quotations; but, for an argument against any Muslim awareness of "Jewish-Christians," cf. S.M. Stern, New light; cf. also id., Quotations)? Besides the lack of external evidence for the presence of

"Jewish Christians" in the qurʾānic milieu, the polemical intent of the Qurʾān must be considered when reading the passages that allude to other monotheists. If the Prophet's qurʾānic preaching assumes a knowledge on the part of its audience of the phenomena of which it speaks, it would have the liberty to exaggerate and distort — even "name-call" — in its efforts to persuade its own listeners (i.e. once it became clear that the Jews and Christians would refuse to accept Muḥammad as a prophet in the path of Abraham, Moses [q.v.] and Jesus). In this context, the change of both the *qibla* (q.v.), or direction of prayer, as well as the parameters for fasting (q.v.) have been cited as evidence of the concrete measures that were taken to distance the qurʾānic adherents from the "People of the Book" (cf. Katz, *Body of text,* for discussion of the historical arguments for permissible mingling, or mandatory separation, of the communities due to arguments of ritual cleanliness; see CLEANLINESS AND ABLUTION; RITUAL PURITY). Thus, the abbreviated references to "Christian" or "Jewish" doctrines need not be taken as unambiguous and accurate attestation of the specific tenets (or practices) of these communities, although the qurʾānic indications of Jewish and Christian arguments over Abraham and the Sabbath (q.v.) may well be reflective of such disputes in Muḥammad's milieu.

A further indication of the close contact of the first Muslim community with Jews and Christians is found in the early ḥadīth and *sīra* accounts. The format of the argumentation for Muḥammad's prophethood closely parallels that present in Talmudic and Christian prophetology. Additionally, such discussions often cite Christian and/or Jewish texts as supporting Muḥammad's prophethood (in this regard one may note, respectively, the discussions of Muḥammad as "Aḥmad," understood by Muslim commentators to be the Johannine Paraclete and as the *"ummī"* [q.v.] — or gentile [i.e. *goy*] — prophet; see McAuliffe, Qurʾānic context; see also ILLITERACY). The commentaries on the Qurʾān (which probably emerge as separate works at a slightly later date than the *sīra* and ḥadīth) incorporate these arguments, continuing the trend of inter-communal dependence (for further discussion of the chronology of the early Islamic literature, see Rubin, *Eye,* chaps. 1 and 14).

Magians, Sabians and *ḥunafāʾ*

A *hapax legomenon,* the "Majūs" (commonly understood to be Zoroastrians) are added to the list of qurʾānic "Peoples of the Book" in the late Medinan Q 22:17. The commentators, however, ordinarily stress the distinctions among all of the groups mentioned in this verse. Al-Ṭabarī (d. 310/923), for example, cites Qatāda in glossing *al-majūs* as those who worship the sun, the moon and fire (*Jāmiʿ,* ad loc.).

Whether they are to be considered as "People of the Book" was a debated issue in Islamic law, but, traditionally, the Zoroastrians have been accorded the status of *dhimma* (protected religious minority) in Islamic states. Originally an ancient Iranian priestly class (closely associated with the ruling elite in Sasanid Persia), in the Qurʾān and later Arabic sources, the term *majūs* primarily connotes Zoroastrians, the public cult of which involved fire ceremonies, animal sacrifices and liturgical recitations. Manichaeism, Buddhism and conversion to Christianity all contributed to the erosion of the position of the Zoroastrians within Persian areas during Sasanian times; during Muḥammad's lifetime, descendants of Persian soldiers in the Yemen were converted to Islam; in Iraq, units of the Sasanian army converted to Islam; and, by 101/720, the Majūs in al-Ḥīra were

Muslims (Morony, Madjūs, 1111). At the fall of Sasanian Persia to the Muslims in 30/651, the Magians were accorded the status of *dhimma* so long as they paid the poll tax or *jizya* (for further discussion, see Morony, Madjūs).

The Sabians appear in three qurʾānic verses (Q 2:62; 5:69; 22:17), always in conjunction with "believers" (*alladhīna āmanū,* frequently glossed by Muslim commentators as those who believe 'in the Qurʾān'), Jews and Christians, and once with Magians, as well. Not to be confused with the Sabaeans (i.e. the inhabitants of Sheba [q.v.]), it is not clear exactly which group the Qurʾān intends by this designation (see the *EI²* articles Ṣābiʾ and Ṣābiʾa for the differing opinions of DeBlois and Bosworth as to their identity). Mandaeans and Elchasaites (an ancient Jewish Christian sect that persisted in southern Iraq), as well as Manichaeans, have been proposed (see DeBlois, Ṣābiʾ). It is apparent, however, that they are considered a group separate from the Jews, Christians, polytheists and Zoroastrians (i.e. Magians) and that they were distinct or visible enough to warrant qurʾānic mention. In any event, the qurʾānic Sabians should not be equated with the polytheists in Ḥarrān who adopted the term "Sabian" to designate themselves in the third/ninth century in order to obtain the status of *dhimma* within the Islamic state (DeBlois, Ṣābiʾ; see also Watt, Ḥanīf, for a discussion of the claims of these Harranian Hellenized pagans to the qurʾānic monotheistic designation of *ḥanīf;* for further discussion of the exegetical identification of the qurʾānic Sabians, see McAuliffe, Exegetical identification).

As mentioned above, for the Qurʾān Abraham is the prime example of a *ḥanīf,* or true monotheistic believer — and neither a Jew nor a Christian. Never mentioned in the qurʾānic listings of religious groups (e.g. Q 5:69; 22:17), it has been suggested that *ḥanīf* is a term used specifically by Arabian monotheists who had rejected the idolatrous religion of their families, although it was also used by polytheists who only observed some rites of their religion. Muslim sources indicate that there was a pre-Islamic monotheistic cult or religion of Abraham in Arabia, members of which appeared even to inhabit Muḥammad's milieu (i.e. his wife Khadīja's [q.v.] relative Waraqa b. Nawfal; cf. Ibn Isḥāq, *Sīra,* 143-9; Eng. trans. Ibn Isḥāq-Guillaume, 98-103; see INFORMANTS for a critique of the traditional Muslim account of the monotheists in Muḥammad's milieu). The *Sīra* of Ibn Isḥāq (d. ca. 150/767), for example, describes the *ḥanīf* as turning away from the idolatry of their parents, adopting the religion of Abraham, but not necessarily becoming Muslims (i.e. Zayd b. ʿAmr: Ibn Isḥāq, *Sīra,* 144-7; Eng. trans. Ibn Isḥāq-Guillaume, 99-101; cf. Wansbrough, *Sectarian milieu,* 4-7; Rubin, *Eye,* 47-8). Regardless of the status of the *ḥanīf* in pre-Islamic times, the qurʾānic identification of *ḥanīf*s with true believers, but not necessarily Muslims, is continued in later Islamic history (although, unlike Jews, Christians, Sabians and Magians, the Qurʾān does indicate that a *ḥanīf* can be identical with a Muslim — in connection with Abraham, cf. Q 3:67). While the qurʾānic Magians and Sabians are not *ḥanīf*s, in the post-qurʾānic period a group who termed themselves Sabians also appears to have claimed the designation of *ḥanīf* (see Watt, Ḥanīf). In short, it is not obvious whether — or if ever — the *ḥunafāʾ* were considered by their contemporaries to be an identifiable religious group.

Polytheists and idolaters

Traditional discussions of the Meccan milieu in which Muḥammad was born identify the majority of Meccans as neither Jews nor Christians, but as practitioners of traditional tribal cultic practices. In the Qurʾān, these individuals are termed *mushrikūn* (lit. "associators"), and there are also allusions to people who worship idols (*aṣnām;* see IDOLS AND IMAGES; IDOLATRY AND IDOLATERS). Whatever their religious orientation, the *mushrikūn* are the Meccans who did not acknowledge Muḥammad as a prophet sent from God, or accept his claim that there is only one true God. As presented in traditional Muslim sources, the reasons for their denial of Muḥammad's prophethood fluctuate between their desire to maintain control of the polytheistic sanctuary at Mecca and their jealous protection of the social status that they had attained through the lucrative caravan (q.v.) trade. In one reading of the reasons for the rise of Islam, Muḥammad preached a message that appealed to people who were becoming marginalized within a society of increasing wealth and of sharp disparities between the rich and the poor. Further, the wealthy Meccans feared that the "radical" social component of Muḥammad's message would weaken their hold on the economy of the city, and that his deposing of the gods would disrupt the profitable pilgrimage (q.v.) to the Kaʿba (q.v.). In this version of early Islamic history, Muḥammad eventually appropriated the mechanism established by the Meccan traders, facilitating the spread of Islam (cf. Watt, *Muhammad at Mecca;* for a revisionist reading of the rise of Islam, see Crone, *Meccan trade,* where it is argued that rather than Meccan trading interests, local Arab tribal concerns prompted the rise and spread of Islam).

Although it is not clear to what extent, in the qurʾānic purview, Jews, and particularly Christians, might fall in the category of "associators," later Muslim exegetes have often placed Christians and Jews, despite their status as "People of the Book," in this category. The polemical writings of John of Damascus (d. 135/753) attest that within the first Islamic century, Christians were termed "associators" by the Muslims (although John's Greek text uses the term Saracenes, and not Muslims; cf. his *De haeresibus,* chap. 100-1 in Sahas, *John of Damascus;* for further and more recent discussion of early non-Muslim perceptions of Islam, the Qurʾān and Muḥammad see Hoyland, Earliest Christian writings on Muḥammad).

In general, it may be said that, despite the qurʾānic distinction between "Peoples of the Book" and those who have no book — the Arabian "idolaters" or "polytheists" — as well as the distinctions made between the Jews and Christians, in both the Qurʾān and later exegesis, those who would deny Muḥammad and the Qurʾān — be they associators, Christians or Jews — are viewed as falling within the general rubric of "disbelief" or "ingratitude," i.e. *kufr.* Q 2:105 and 98:1 are often cited in this context, as well as Q 9:31, which accuses Christians of taking their religious leaders and Jesus as "lords" — in place of the one, true lord: i.e. God (cf. Hawting, *Idea of idolatry,* 49-50 for a fuller discussion of this concept). That being said, however, there is no one formula for the ways in which Muslims interacted with, or categorized, non-Muslims — either in the Qurʾān or later in Islamic history. Pragmatic, as well as doctrinal, concerns affected the treatment of those who were not Muslims. For example, despite the traditional understanding of the so-called Sword Verses (Q 9:5 and 9:29), which exhort the conversion to Islam of "associators" and the "tolerance" of People of the Book, in India, Hindus — not one of the qurʾānic Peoples of the Book — were allowed to practice their religion as long as they paid the poll tax (*jizya;* for more on this topic, see below under "Guidance for Muslim behavior"; see also TOLERANCE

AND COMPULSION; POLITICS AND THE QUR'ĀN).

Qur'ānic indications of interreligious interactions

Episodes

In addition to the above-mentioned political conflicts with the Jewish tribes of Medina, there are a number of qur'ānic indications of early interactions with non-Muslims of a specifically religious nature. All of these interactions occur with Christians, specifically with Monophysite Christians. In addition to the allusions to the "Byzantines" (q.v.; *al-Rūm*, i.e. Q 30:2 — albeit in a military context), Muslim commentators have traditionally understood certain qur'ānic passages to refer to two particular Christian polities: Abyssinia (q.v.) and Najrān (q.v.). According to the traditional Muslim sources, Muḥammad and the nascent Muslim community had political and theological exchanges with both, as will be seen below. But first a discussion of Muslim claims that individual Christians attested to the truth of Islam is in order.

Although not mentioned in the Qur'ān, later Islamic sources claim that Muḥammad had personal encounters with Christian monks who, in the Muslim reports, recognized the "signs of prophecy" on the Prophet (cf. Rubin, *Eye*, 48, for some instances of Companions meeting Christian scholars and hermits in pre-Islamic times, who knew of Muḥammad's impending mission through their own knowledge of their scriptures; see COMPANIONS OF THE PROPHET). Christian sources also describe encounters with Christian monks but in these accounts, the Christian acts as Muḥammad's informant about divine revelation. Interestingly, although frequently this monastic informant is termed a 'Nestorian,' the denomination of the informant does vary, depending upon the community in which the account is relayed. For example, it is likely that the accounts of the Nestorian Sargis-Baḥīrā circulated in a Syrian Jacobite (i.e. "monophysite") milieu (cf. Griffith, Syriac writers, 48; see also Abel, Baḥīrā, for instances of Jacobite, Arian and iconoclast informants; see also ICONOCLASM). The most common figure in both the Christian and Muslim accounts is the monk Baḥīrā (for discussion of this figure see Roggema, Christian reading; id., Legend). There are also accounts of a Jewish scribe of Muḥammad who, again, depending on the vantage point of the relater, either instructs Muḥammad in the Jewish faith, or confirms Muḥammad's prophethood (for details, see Gilliot, Informants). Finally, members of the family of Muḥammad's first wife, Khadīja, appear to have been Christian (or at least monotheists in the tradition of Abraham), and to have confirmed his claims to prophesy.

In addition to these non-qur'ānic assertions of independent (primarily Christian) attestation to the truth of Muḥammad's mission, there are traditions about two face-to-face encounters between the nascent Muslim community and Christians and consequent discussions concerning the nature of Jesus, the son of Mary (q.v.), traditions that invoke qur'ānic verses in support of the 'historicity' of these meetings.

Abyssinia

An ancient Monophysite Christian kingdom that had ruled part of southern Arabia in the sixth century (see ABRAHA), Abyssinia was also the destination of the first emigration (q.v.) out of Mecca (ca. 615 C.E.) of a small group of Muḥammad's followers. Due to the persecution by the Meccan pagans, Muḥammad encouraged some of the Muslims to leave and to go to Abyssinia (Ibn Isḥāq, *Sīra*, 208; Eng. trans. Ibn Isḥāq-Guillaume, 146; cf. Watt,

Muhammad at Mecca, 112-7). The Negus (*al-najāshī,* i.e. the Abyssinian ruler) is said to have granted them refuge, after asking about their knowledge of Jesus, the son of Mary (cf. Wansbrough, *QS,* 38-43, for one interpretation of the later Islamic tradition on the welcome accorded the Muslims refugees). Q 19:16-21 was revealed just prior to this emigration, and it is this passage that is traditionally considered to have constituted the emigrants' response to the Negus' questioning: "Mention in the book Mary when she withdrew from her family to an eastern place. She placed a *ḥijāb* [to screen herself; see VEIL] from them, and we sent her our spirit (q.v.) who appeared to her as a man, complete. She said: 'I seek refuge in the merciful from you — if you fear God.' He said: 'I am only a messenger of your lord [to tell] you of the gift of a holy son.' She said: 'How can I have a son since no man has touched me and I am not unchaste (see CHASTITY)?' He said: 'Like this. Your lord says...'" Although most of these first emigrants did not stay in Abyssinia, but returned to Mecca or left for Medina, this memory of Abyssinia and its Christians remained enshrined in later Muslim consciousness.

Najrān

Another early Muslim-Christian encounter, but one of a slightly different nature, concerns a delegation from the Christian martyropolis of Najrān (q.v.; not named in the Qurʾān, but probably alluded to in Q 34:18, 85:10 and also possibly in Q 85:4-9, although Shahid disputes this last claim; see NAJRĀN) sent to Muḥammad in Medina, after the Muslim conquest of south Arabia. Although some sources indicate that this mission had a theological purpose, namely to understand the Muslim position on the nature of Jesus (i.e. Ṭabarī, *Tafsīr;* Ibn Kathīr, *Tafsīr,* ad Q 3:61), the delegation to Muḥammad seems to have been prompted by the political exigency of determining the conditions of Christian life under the new Muslim rulers. Q 3:61 is believed to have been revealed in response to the challenge posed by the Christians, a challenge in which the parties of the dispute would present their case, pray and invoke the curse (q.v.) of God upon the liars. The delegation from Najrān, however, withdrew from the contest, averting the mutual adjuration (*mubāhala;* see OATHS). Muḥammad did, however, conclude a treaty with them (the first between the Muslim state and an independent Christian entity), in which they were assured of their freedom of worship in exchange for the payment of the annual tribute (see POLL TAX; TAXATION).

The theological orientation of these Najrān Christians is not clear; although traditionally a center of Monophysite Christianity (Shahid, Nadjrān), some of the Nestorian missionaries who followed the trade routes to India settled in the area of the Persian Gulf and south Arabia (Holmberg, Nasṭūriyyūn, 1030). Additionally, the Persian conquest of south Arabia in 597 C.E. may have witnessed an increased Nestorian presence in the area (further to this see Shahid, Nadjrān; Pellat, Ḳuss b. Sāʿida al-Iyādī; Holmberg, Nasṭūriyyūn).

Although contact with Jews appears to have been of a shorter duration (i.e. concentrated in the late Meccan and early Medinan periods), it was much more problematic for the early Muslim community, as it had negative political ramifications when the Jewish tribes of Medina allied themselves with Muḥammad's Meccan opponents in an attempt to undermine his leadership in Medina. The increasingly harsh measures taken against these Jewish tribes — successive expulsions of two of the major tribes in 624 and 625 C.E., culminating in the massacre of the men and enslavement of the women and children of Banū Qurayẓa in 627 C.E. — appears to have precluded any conciliatory contact (along the lines of that with the Christians) between the early Muslims and Jews. Nevertheless, the picture of early Jewish-Muslim contacts is not entirely bleak: there are accounts, for example, of Jewish converts to Islam — at least one of Muḥammad's Companions, and probably one of his wives, were Jews (see QURAYẒA). Finally, it should be noted that there are no attestations of Muḥammad's coming into contact himself with either the "Majūs" or the "Ṣābiʾūn."

But the qurʾānic discourse concerning non-Muslims is not limited to those incidents in which, according to the traditional interpretations, Muḥammad or the Muslims actually had political and theological discussions with individuals who did not accept the qurʾānic message. In fact, the majority of allusions to the People of the Book or Children of Israel (which references are more numerous than those to Jews or Christians) are understood to be assertions about what these people believe — or how they have gone astray (q.v.) from God's divinely revealed message (see REVELATION AND INSPIRATION) — independent of any precipitating interaction with a Jew or Christian. And this rhetoric has generated a great deal of commentary on the part of Muslim exegetes and, later, spurred the composition of many apologetic treatises by those Christians and Jews living in Islamic lands.

Rhetoric: polemic and apologetic

Besides the Arabian "associators," the Jews and the Christians are clearly the two religious communities with whom Muḥammad and the Qurʾān had the most experience (although it should be emphasized that, aside from the Jewish tribes of Medina and the Christian delegation from Najrān, Muḥammad seems not to have had contact with any Jewish or Christian community per se, but rather only with individual Jews and Christians). Once the qurʾānic proclamation of an exclusively monotheistic religion is put forth, the *mushrikūn* are seen as unbelievers who need to be brought to the true faith. Concerning the Jews and Christians, with whom the Qurʾān shares a common scriptural heritage, there is a much more ambivalent depiction. In short, it appears that the qurʾānic attitudes towards these groups fluctuate in accordance with the political situation of Muḥammad and the Muslim community, as well as with regard to these groups' acceptance or rejection of the message that Muḥammad proclaimed. The following provides just a few examples of the qurʾānic rhetoric about, and in response to, Jews and Christians (see also POLEMIC AND POLEMICAL LANGUAGE).

Polemic

Although the initial and most virulent thrust appears aimed at the Jews, the boundary between anti-Jewish and anti-Christian polemic is quickly blurred. Aside from a few positive statements about Christians that are in marked contrast to those about Jews (i.e. Q 5:82), what seems to be a defense of Jesus against Jewish slander (their non-acceptance of his prophetic status; his crucifixion; and the calumny against Mary) is also a chastisement of Christians for "exaggerating" in their religion, particularly as regards the Incarnation and the Trinity. In a passage whose exact meaning varies depending upon its grammatical analysis, Christians are also accused of "inventing monasticism" (Q 57:27). Additionally, there is the rather enigmatic polemical accusation that Jews have taken Ezra (q.v.) as a son of God (Q 9:30). Although the polemic against the

Christians is less pervasive and somewhat less virulent than that against the Jews, in the final analysis, Jews and Christians are considered allies of one another — and are not to be taken as friends by the believers (Q 5:51).

Apologetic

In addition to the negative remarks about Judaism and Christianity mentioned above, the Qurʾān also contains positive assertions about its own message and the prophethood of Muḥammad, assertions that seem to be a clear response to Jewish or Christian challenges (for this theme, see Gaudeul, *Encounters*, i, 12-19). To the Jewish challenge that racially Muḥammad could not be a prophet (there are no prophets outside of Israel), the Qurʾān responds that Abraham was not a Jew, but was a believer, a Muslim, a *ḥanīf* (Q 3:67). The argument that Muḥammad's teachings do not conform to the Bible (see SCRIPTURE AND THE QURʾĀN) is also turned against the Jews, for they have broken God's covenant (q.v.; cf. e.g. Q 2:27, 63-4), falsified their scriptures (cf. e.g. Q 2:77-9; see REVISION AND ALTERATION), and rejected his prophets, among them Moses and Jesus (e.g. Q 2:67 f., 87 f.; see also DISOBEDIENCE; cf. Q 2:65). There are also self-conscious rejections of Jewish practices: i.e. the change of the *qibla* from Jerusalem (q.v.) towards Mecca (Q 2:142), as well as the reduction of the fasting of ʿĀshūrāʾ (cf. Q 2:183-5; see Goitein, Ramadan; see also RAMAḌĀN). The response to the Christians focuses mainly on Trinitarian or Christological themes (i.e. Q 5:73, do not say God is a third of three, *thālithu thalāthatin;* cf. Griffith, Syriacisms, for an argument that this is an Arabicized rendition of a Syriac word that, in the new linguistic medium, loses its original sense — i.e. the Syriac epithet *thlīthāyâ,* a title of Christ), but there are some assertions of what could be read as Christian-Muslim collaboration or complicity (i.e. Q 61:6, wherein Jesus foretells a prophet called 'Aḥmad'). See also APOLOGETICS.

Responses

The early ʿAbbāsid period (i.e. 132-441/750-1050) saw a particularly rich production of Muslim and Christian polemic. Intent on disabusing Muslims of the image conveyed in the Qurʾān, and encouraged by an atmosphere of perhaps unparalleled interreligious communication, Christians (and Jews) wrote a number of treatises in defense of their faith. For their part, Muslims went beyond the qurʾānic claims and demonstrated an intimate knowledge of the various religious communities of their own day — even down to the confessional divisions among the Christians (e.g. ʿAbd al-Jabbār's *Tathbīt dalāʾil al-nubuwwa;* for a survey of the Islamic sources, see Thomas, *Anti-Christian polemic*, 31-50; Griffith, The monk in the emir's *majlis*, presents an overview of the earliest such Christian apologetics; see also Ibn Kammūna [d. 683/1284-5], *Tanqīḥ al-abḥāth lil-milal al-thalāth,* for an example of early Jewish apologetics).

Additional attestation of interest in, and intimate knowledge of, Jewish and Christian literature is demonstrated by the familiarity of Muslim authors with extra-canonical Jewish and Christian lore that is evidenced in the genre of Islamic literature known as *Isrāʾīliyyāt,* much of which is incorporated in the post-qurʾānic "stories of the prophets" (see McAuliffe, Assessing). The development of both Islamic dialectical theology *(kalām)* and Islamic mysticism, which flourished in the early ʿAbbāsid period, may also trace its roots to the interactions with the Christians in the conquered lands, especially those living on the frontier between Byzantium and Persia (see ṢŪFISM AND THE QURʾĀN; THEOLOGY AND THE QURʾĀN).

Although the early debates over the createdness of the Qurʾān (q.v.; see also INIMITABILITY) and the Muslim literature on "proofs of prophethood" (e.g. ʿAbd al-Jabbār's *Tathbīt*) may plausibly have arisen in a religiously pluralistic environment in which Christians, in particular, took part (cf. e.g. Thomas, *Christians at the heart of Islamic rule;* id., *Anti-Christian polemic in early Islam;* id., *Early Muslim polemic against Christianity*), the classical Islamic response to religious pluralism is perhaps best seen in the development of the sectarian and heresiographical genre (*ʿilm al-firaq* and *al-milal wa-l-niḥal*). Representative works of this genre include ʿAbd al-Qāhir al-Baghdādī's (d. 429/1037) *al-Farq bayna l-firaq,* Ibn Ḥazm's (456/1064) *al-Fiṣal fī l-milal wa-l-ahwāʾ wa-l-niḥal* and al-Shahrastānī's (d. 548/1153) *Kitāb al-Milal wa-l-niḥal.* Such works catalogue and discuss, variously, heterodox versions of Islam, non-Muslim religions and forms of philosophical speculation. Further reflection on Jewish and Christian material is provided by works that consider the relation of earlier scriptures and the qurʾānic revelation. There is a long tradition of Muslim biblical scholarship that spans works of history, exegesis, and heresiography (McAuliffe, Qurʾānic context).

Inferring a qurʾānic attitude toward religious pluralism?

As already indicated, there is no single qurʾānic attitude towards members of other religions. An uninitiated reader of the Qurʾān might have difficulty in discerning the Qurʾān's opinion of a plurality of religions. Commentators found it helpful, therefore, to see the various — even, at times, conflicting — passages dealing with members of other religions as coming in response to certain incidents in Muḥammad's life. But it is equally important to understand how the passages have been utilized by later interpreters of the Qurʾān as either supporting or condemning the beliefs, practices — even existence — of non-Muslims within the domain of Islam. The following is a brief overview of a selection of modern Muslim attitudes towards the subject, as well as certain qurʾānic passages that have frequently been used by Muslims in discussions about members of other faith communities, followed by a presentation of some possible qurʾānic "guidelines" for Muslim behavior towards non-Muslims in the face of a plurality of religions.

Approbation and denigration

There is no one qurʾānic judgment about religious plurality. On the one hand, there are statements, frequently cited today by prominent religious spokespersons like Yūsuf al-Qaraḍāwī and other advocates of the virtues of the Islamic state (cf. e.g. Qaraḍāwī, al-Aqaliyyāt wa-taṭbīq al-sharīʿa al-islāmiyya), that may be read as an exhortation to tolerance of other religions (cf. Mottahedeh, Toward an Islamic theology of toleration). In this reading, religious plurality is permissible (at least as far as monotheists/People of the Book are concerned), as long as Muslims dominate the political sphere and the minorities adhere to the rules put forth in the *sharīʿa* for the proper comportment of non-Muslims. Behind the qurʾānic statements that allow for the existence of other religions is an implicit acknowledgment of the virtues of adherents of other religions, e.g. references to the notion that Christians have helped Muslims, and Jews and Christians have some knowledge of scripture. On the other hand, contemporary extremists such as Usāma b. Lādin, in the tradition of exegetes like Ibn Taymiyya (d. 728/1328) and Sayyid Quṭb (d. 1966), may cite certain verses (e.g. Q 9:5) in support of a rejection of the plurality of religions, and a negative judgment on non-Muslims. In this reading, there can be no legitimate compromise or collaboration with non-Muslims, or, for that matter, with bad Muslims. Qurʾānic themes such as the eschatological punishment of non-Muslims, their opposition to Muḥammad (q.v.), Islam as the only true religion in God's eyes, Jews and Christians having gone beyond the bounds of their religion — form part of this reading of the qurʾānic denigration of other religions, and a resultant denial of the legitimacy of religious plurality. In the light of these conflicting qurʾānic themes, the question remains: What does the Qurʾān exhort Muslims to do in the face of a plurality of religions?

Guidance for Muslim behavior

While verses such as Q 109:6 have been understood to acknowledge the existence of a plurality of religions ("to you your *dīn* and to me mine"), there have been various interpretations of what this means: it was directed to those of the Quraysh (q.v.) who mocked *(al-mustahziʾūn)* Muḥammad's monotheism (Muqātil, *Tafsīr,* iv, 887-8; see SATANIC VERSES); it is an affirmation of the distinction between the religion of the Muslim and the *mushrik* (and not "true" Jews, for Jews worship God; ibid.), it is a disavowal of everything in which the idolaters are involved (Ibn Kathīr, *Tafsīr,* ad loc.). Likewise, Q 2:256, "there is no compulsion in religion," thought to have been revealed after the submission of the Arabs (cf. Muqātil, *Tafsīr,* ad loc., for a discussion of the distinction between the terms of submission for the People of the Book and those who were not such; also Ibn Kathīr, *Tafsīr,* ad loc., where reference is to the situation of children of the Helpers who were being raised among the Banū l-Naḍīr at the time of their expulsion; see EMIGRANTS AND HELPERS), indicates a qurʾānic acknowledgment that not everyone will accept the truth of the Qurʾān's message. But this, too, has received a variety of interpretations: Muḥammad did not compel any of the Meccans to accept Islam; the people of the two books and the Magians may pay the *jizya* and live peaceably in an Islamic state; there is never force against anyone who has paid the *jizya* (Ṭabarī, *Tafsīr,* ad loc.) A survey of Muslim exegesis, however, reveals that there is certainly no glorification of the diversity of religious belief. Rather, it is accepted as an inevitable aspect of human existence. Generally, the exegetes do not interpret the Qurʾān as exhorting a forcible conversion to Islam. But there is also no false irenicism: those who do not heed the qurʾānic message are promised punishment in the afterlife (see REWARD AND PUNISHMENT). The passages that extol the virtues of peoples of other faith communities are almost universally interpreted with a limited sense, i.e. those commendable individuals are people who did not go beyond the bounds of their religion, or who in some way assisted the Muslims or at least did not harm them. They know their proper place and do not put themselves above Muslims.

Although qurʾānic passages such as Q 2:256 ("there is no compulsion in *dīn*") or Q 109:6 ("to you your *dīn* and to me mine") are often cited as prooftexts for an Islamic tolerance of non-Muslims, as noted above, they have been variously interpreted over the course of Islamic history. Further, historical examples like the contrast between medieval Spain's expulsion of Jews and Istanbul's welcoming of them are frequently offered to argue for the benefits to non-Muslims of living in an Islamic polity, past or present (cf. Qaraḍāwī, al-ʿAqaliyyāt). But there are other passages that are not at all ambiguous in their exhortations of Islam as the true religion and their warnings to maintain a distance from (adherents of) other religions.

Q 9:5 and 9:29 are perhaps the most famous or infamous of the qurʾānic verses that prescribe 'proper' behavior towards non-Muslims (see McAuliffe, Fakhr al-Dīn). But there are other, less frequently cited, verses that shed light on what may be called the "qurʾānic attitude to non-Muslims." The following is a sampling of these verses: Q 5:3, "I have approved Islam for your religion"; Q 30:30, "That is the right religion" (cf. Q 30:43; 39:3; 61:9; 98:5); Q 30:32, "those who have divided up their religion and become sects"; Q 2:193, "fight them until there is no persecution and the religion in God's"; Q 24:2, "let no tenderness for them seize you in the matter of God's religion"; Q 4:171, "People of the Book, go not beyond the bounds in your religion" (cf. Q 5:77); Q 40:26, "I fear that he may change your religion."

Taken as a whole, the Qurʾān does evince a negative judgment on the People of the Book, claiming that they have exaggerated in their religion and even altered their scriptures (see also DISTORTION; FORGERY; PROVOCATION). The Muslims, therefore, should keep their distance and, when necessary, fight them — as well as other non-Muslims. It is the later exegetical literature, however, and the doctrine of abrogation (q.v.), that have formed the lenses through which the Qurʾān is viewed, and which have informed the traditional Muslim attitude towards non-Muslims. For despite the preponderance of qurʾānic passages that allude to the eschatological punishment of non-believers, it is the tendency of later exegetes to place all non-Muslims, even People of the Book, in that category that has encouraged a reading of the Qurʾān that can support an antagonistic attitude towards non-Muslims, and even towards Muslims who are considered not to be 'true' Muslims (cf. McAuliffe, Christians in the Qurʾān, for further discussion of the distinction between qurʾānic pronouncements and the later exegesis thereof).

Conclusion

It is generally established that by the end of the Umayyad period (ca. 132/750) Islam had come to be seen as the "religion of the Arabs." Emblematic of this association is the famous ḥadīth in which Jews and Christians are banned from the Arabian peninsula (based on the ritual impurity of "associators," mentioned in Q 9:28; cf. Rubin, Jews; cf. Katz, *Body of text,* for discussion of the "impurity" of the People of the Book), a situation still in evidence today (signs outside of Mecca and Medina prevent non-Muslims from entering the city limits). But whether Muḥammad intended such a situation is difficult to determine. In any event, Christian Arabs after the advent of Islam have experienced an inevitable crisis of identity (as "Arab" came to be all but synonymous with "Muslim," an identification that appears to have occurred at an early date; cf. the legal ruling in al-Shāfiʿī's *Kitāb al-Umm* that Christian Arabs are not "People of the Book," cited in Tritton, *Caliphs,* 92, and the Christian Arab refusal to pay the *jizya* on the basis of their being Arabs, cited in ibid, 89) and since the classical period Jewish tribes in Arabia have been all but unknown. In keeping with the qurʾānic injunction found in Q 9:29, Christians (and Jews, and, to a lesser extent, Mandaeans and Zoroastrians) have lived in Arabic-speaking areas of the Muslim world as protected (religious) minorities *(dhimma),* subject to their own religious authorities in legal cases, at least those that do not involve Muslims. As for their situation in non-Arab lands, there has been a relaxation of the traditional exclusion of polytheists from the status of protected religious minority. For example, in India,

Hindus were extended the protection of the Islamic state in exchange for a payment of the requisite tax, as was noted above. In keeping with the qurʾānic differentiation between Muslims and non-Muslims, and also with the qurʾānic injunctions of tolerance for non-Muslims, these non-Muslims have been allowed to live in Islamic lands, albeit as "second-class" citizens (and, it should be remarked, often subject to Islamic law).

History, however, continues to shape the reception of the Qurʾān and its interpretation. Considering the Crusades, the era of capitulations, colonialism and the more recent establishment of the state of Israel, a long sequence of events which is associated with the aggression of western imperialism, contemporary Muslim exegetes have tended to consider the qurʾānic verses that exhibit a more welcoming or tolerant attitude towards non-Muslims as abrogated by those that contain a harsher judgment of people who will not accept the truth of Islam, particularly when they are living in an Islamic polity.

Clare Wilde and
Jane Dammen McAuliffe

Bibliography

Primary: ʿAbd al-Jabbār b. Aḥmad al-Hamdhānī, *Tathbīt dalāʾil al-nubuwwa*, ed. ʿA. ʿUthmān, Beirut 1966; Theodore Abū Qurra, *La discussion d'Abū Qurra avec les ulémas musulmans devant le calife al-Maʾmūn*, [in Arabic] ed. I. Dick, Aleppo 1999; Bukhārī, *Ṣaḥīḥ*, Eng. trans. M.M. Khan, *The translation of the meanings of Sahih Al-Bukhari* (Arabic — English), 9 vols., New Delhi [1985][5]; Ibn Isḥāq, *Sīra*, ed. Wüstenfeld; Eng. trans. Ibn Isḥāq-Guillaume; Ibn al-Kalbī, Hishām b. Muḥammad, *The book of idols*, trans. (of *Kitāb al-Aṣnām*) N.A. Faris, Princeton 1952; Ibn Kammūna, *Tanqīḥ al-abḥāth lil-milal al-thalāth*, Berkeley 1967; trans. M. Perlmann, *Ibn Kammūna's examination of the three faiths*, Berkeley 1971; Ibn Kathīr, *Tafsīr;* Ibn Qayyim al-Jawziyya, *Aḥkām ahl al-dhimma*, ed. Y. al-Bakrī and Sh. al-ʿĀrūrī, Riyadh 1997; Muqātil, *Tafsīr;* Rāzī, *Tafsīr;* D.J. Sahas, *John of Damascus on Islam. The "heresy of the Ishmaelites,"* Leiden 1972; Ṭabarī, *Tafsīr*.

Secondary: I. ʿAbbās, Two hitherto unpublished texts on pre-Islamic religion, in *La signification du bas moyen âge dans l'histoire et la culture du monde musulman*, Aix-en-Provence 1976, 7-16; A. Abel, Baḥīrā, in *EI²*, i, 922-3; M. Accad, The Gospels in the Muslim discourse of the ninth to the fourteenth centuries. An exegetical inventorial table (parts 1-4), in *Islam and Christian-Muslim relations* 14/1-4 (2003), 67-92; 205-20; 337-52; T. Andrae, *Les origins de l'Islam et le Christianisme*, Paris 1955 (Fr. trans. of his *Der Ursprung des Islams und das Christientum*, Uppsala 1926); J. Beaucamp, F. Briquel-Chatonnet and C. Robin, La persécution des chrétiens de Nagrān et la chronologie himyarite, in *ARAM* 11-12 (1999-2000), 15-83; R. Bell, Muhammad and previous messengers, in *MW* 24 (1934), 330-40; id., *The origin of Islam in its Christian environment*, Edinburgh 1926; H. Birkeland, *The Lord guideth. Studies on primitive Islam*, Oslo 1956; C.E. Bosworth, Ṣābiʾa, in *EI²*, viii, 675-9; id./F. Buhl, Milla, in *EI²*, vii, 61; G.-H. Bousquet, ʿIbādāt, in *EI²*, iii, 647-8; id., *Les grandes pratiques rituelles de l'Islam*, Paris 1949; D. Boyarin, *A radical Jew. Paul and the politics of identity*, Berkeley 1994; id., *Sparks of the logos. Essays in rabbinic hermeneutics*, Leiden 2003; M.M. Bravmann, *The spiritual background of early Islam*, Leiden 1972; C. Buck, The identity of the Ṣābiʾūn. An historical quest, in *MW* 74 (1984), 172-86; H. Busse, Der Islam und die biblischen Kultstätten, in *Der Islam* 42 (1966), 113-47; id., Monotheismus und islamische Christologie in der Bauinschrift des Felsendoms in Jerusalem, in *Theologische Quartalschrift* 161 (1981), 168-78; C. Cahen, Dhimma, in *EI²*, ii, 227-31; N. Calder, From midrash to scripture. The sacrifice of Abraham in early Islamic tradition, in *Muséon* 101 (1988), 375-402; A. Cameron, *The Mediterranean world in late antiquity. A.D. 395-600*, London 1993; id. and L.I. Conrad (eds.), *The Byzantine and early Islamic Near East. i. Problems in literary source material*, Princeton 1993; J. Choksy, *Purity and pollution in Zoroastrianism. Triumph over evil*, Austin 1989; L. Conrad, Abraha and Muḥammad. Some observations apropos of chronology and literary *topoi* in early Arabic historical tradition, in *BSOAS* 50 (1987), 225-40; P. Crone, *Meccan trade and the rise of Islam*, Princeton 1987; id. and M. Cook, *Hagarism. The making of the Islamic world*, Cambridge 1977; P. Crone and M. Hinds, *God's caliph. Religious authority in the first centuries of Islam*, Cambridge 1986; F.C. DeBlois, Ṣābiʾ, in *EI²*, viii, 672-5; D.C. Dennett, *Conversion and the poll-tax in early Islam*, Cambridge 1950; F. Donner, From believers to Muslims. Confessional self-identity in the early Islamic community, in *al-Abhath* 50-51 (2002-3), 9-53; repr. in L.I. Conrad (ed.), *The Byzantine and early Islamic Near East. iv. Patterns of communal identity*, Princeton (forthcoming); id.,

Narratives of Islamic origins. The beginnings of Islamic historical writing, Princeton 1998; R. Drory, The Abbasid construction of the Jahiliyya. Cultural authority in the making, in *SI* 83 (1996), 33-49; T. Fahd, *La vie du prohète Mahomet,* Paris 1983; id., *Le panthéon de l'Arabie centrale à la veille de l'héjire,* Paris 1968; N.A. Faris and H.W. Glidden, The development of the meaning of the koranic ḥanīf, in *Journal of the Palestine Oriental Society* 19 (1939), 1-13, esp. 6-9 for pre-Islamic material; A. Fattal, *Le statut legal des non-musulmans en pays de l'Islam,* Beirut 1958; J. Finkel, Jewish, Christian and Samaritan influences on Arabia, in *The Macdonald presentation volume,* Princeton 1933, 145-66; R. Firestone, *Journeys in holy lands. The evolution of the Abraham-Ishmael legends in Islamic exegesis,* Albany 1990; id., The Qurʾān and the Bible. Some modern studies of their relationship, in J.C. Reeves (ed.), *Bible and Qurʾān. Essays in scriptural intertextuality,* Atlanta, GA 2003, 1-22; Y. Friedmann, *Tolerance and coercion in Islam,* Cambridge 2003; L. Gardet, Dīn, in *EI*[2], ii, 293-6; J.M. Gaudeul, *Encounters and clashes. Islam and Christianity in history,* 2 vols., Rome 2000; A. Geiger, *Judaism and Islam,* repr. New York 1970 (Eng. trans. of *Was hat Mohammed aus dem Judenthume aufgenommen?*); H.A.R. Gibb, Pre-Islamic monotheism in Arabia, in *Harvard theological review* 55 (1962), 269-80; M. Gil, The origin of the Jews of Yathrib, in *JSAI* 4 (1984), 203-24; C. Gilliot, Informants, in *EQ*, ii, 512-18; S. Goitein, Ramadan. The Muslim month of fasting, in id., *Studies in Islamic history and institutions,* Leiden 1966, 90-110; Goldziher, *Muhammedanische Studien,* esp. i, 1-39; S.H. Griffith, The Gospel in Arabic. An inquiry into its appearance in the first ʿAbbāsid century, in *Oriens christianus* 69 (1985), 126-67; id., The monk in the emir's *majlis*. Reflections on a popular genre of Christian literary apologetics in Arabic in the early Islamic period, in H. Lazarus-Yafeh et al. (eds.), *The majlis. Interreligious encounters in medieval Islam,* Wiesbaden 1999, 13-65; id., Syriac writers on Muslims and the religious challenge of Islam, *Mōrān ʿEthō* Series 7 (1995), 1-52; id., Syriacisms in the Qurʾān's Arabic diction. Reflections on the Aramean context of early Islam: Who said 'Allāh is Third of Three?' (paper delivered in Budapest, May 2003; forthcoming); S. Gündüz, *The knowledge of life. The origins and early history of the Mandaeans and their relation to the Sabians of the Qurʾān and to the Harranians,* Oxford 1994; G. Hawting, *The idea of idolatry and the emergence of Islam,* Cambridge 1999; id., The significance of the slogan *lā ḥukma illā li'llāh...,* in *BSOAS* 41 (1978), 453-63; id. and Shareef (eds.), *Approaches;* B. Heller, The relation of the Aggada to Islamic legends, in *MW* 24 (1934), 281-6; J.W. Hirschberg, *Jüdische und christliche Lehren im vor- und frühislamischen Arabien. Ein Beitrag zur Entstehungsgeschichte des Islams,* Krakow 1939; J. Hjärpe, *Analyse critique des traditions arabes sur les Sabéens Ḥarraniens,* Uppsala 1972; B. Holmberg, Nasṭūriyyūn, in *EI*[2], vii, 1030-3; R. Hoyland, *Arabia and the Arabs. From the Bronze Age to the coming of Islam,* London 2001; id., Earliest Christian writings on Muḥammad, in H. Motzki (ed.), *The biography of Muḥammad. The issue of the sources,* Leiden 2000; id. (ed.), *Muslims and others in early Islamic society,* Burlington, VT 2002; id., Sebeos, the Jews and the rise of Islam, in *Studies in Muslim-Jewish relations* 2 (1996), 89-102; id., *Seeing Islam as others saw it,* Princeton 1997; T. Izutsu, *God and man in the Koran,* Tokyo 1964; id., *The structure of the ethical terms in the Qurʾān,* Tokyo 1959; repr. as *Ethico-religious concepts in the Qurʾān,* Montreal 2002; Jeffery, *For. vocab.;* id., *Materials;* M. Katz, *Body of text. The emergence of the Sunni law of ritual purity,* Albany 2002; M.J. Kister, Ḥaddithū ʿan banī isrāʾīla wa-lā ḥaraja. A study of an early tradition, in *Israel Oriental studies* 2 (1972), 215-39; id., Social and religious concepts of authority in Islam, in *JSAI* 18 (1994), 84-127; id., *Studies in jāhiliyya and early Islam,* London 1980; M. Lecker, The conversion of Ḥimyar to Judaism and the Jewish Banū Hadl of Medina, in id., *Jews and Arabs in pre- and early Islamic Arabia,* Aldershot 1998, no. XIII: 129-36; id., *Muslims, Jews and pagans. Studies on early Islamic Medina,* Leiden 1995; id., Wāqidī's account of the status of the Jews of Medina. A study of a combined report, in *JNES* 54 (1995), 15-32; D.A. Madigan, Reflections on some current directions in qurʾanic studies, in *MW* 85 (1995), 345-62; J.D. McAuliffe, Assessing the *Isrāʾīliyyāt*. An exegetical conundrum, in S. Leder (ed.), *Story-telling in the framework of non-fictional Arabic literature,* Wiesbaden 1998, 345-69; id., Christians in the Qurʾān and tafsīr, in J. Waardenburg (ed.), *Muslim perceptions of other religions. A historical survey,* New York 1999, 105-21; id., Exegetical identification of the Sabiʾun, in *MW* 72 (1982), 95-106; id., Fakhr al-Dīn al-Rāzī on āyat al-jizyah and āyat al-sayf, in M. Gervers and R.J. Gikhazi (eds.), *Conversion and continuity. Indigenous Christian communities in Islamic lands, eighth to eighteenth centuries,* Toronto 1990, 104-19; id., Persian exegetical evaluation of the ahl al-kitab, in *MW* 73 (1983), 87-105; id., *Qurʾānic;* id., The qurʾānic context of Muslim biblical scholarship, in *Islam and Christian-Muslim relations* 7 (1996), 141-58; F. Millar, Hagar, Ishmael, Josephus and the origins of Islam, in *Journal of Jewish studies* 44 (1993), 23-45; A. Moberg (ed. and trans.), *Book of the Himyarites,* Lund 1924; G. Monnot, *Islam et religions,* Paris 1986; id., L'histoire des religions en Islam. Ibn al-Kalbī et Rāzī, in *RHR* 188 (1975), 23-34;

M. Morony, Madjūs, in *EI*[2], v, 1110-8; R. Mottahedeh, Toward an Islamic theology of toleration, in T. Lindholm and K. Vogt (eds.), *Proceedings of the Seminar on Human Rights and the Modern Application of Islamic Law, Oslo* 14-15 *February* 1992, Copenhagen 1993, 25-36; Y. Nevo, Towards a prehistory of Islam, in *JSAI* 17 (1994), 108-41; J. Nielsen, Contemporary discussions on religious minorities in Muslim countries, in *Islam and Christian-Muslim relations* 14 (2003), 325-35; H.S. Nyberg, Sassanid Mazdaism according to Muslim sources, in *Journal of the Krlama Oriental Institute* 39 (1958), 1-63; Ch. Pellat, Ḳuss b. Sāʿida al-Iyādī, in *EI*[2], v, 528-9; S. Pines, Gospel quotations and cognate topics in ʿAbd al-Jabbār's *Tathbīt* in relation to early Christian and Judaeo-Christian readings and traditions, in *JSAI* 9 (1987), 195-278; id., *The Jewish Christians of the early centuries of Christianity according to a new source (Proceedings of the Israel Academy of Sciences and Humanities.* vol. ii. no. 13), Jerusalem 1967; id., Notes on Islam and on Arabic Christianity and Judaeo-Christianity, in *JSAI* 4 (1984), 135-52; id., Studies in Christianity and Judaeo-Christianity based on Arabic sources, in *JSAI* 6 (1985), 107-61; Y. al-Qaraḍāwī, al-ʿAqaliyyāt wa-taṭbīq al-sharīʿa al-islāmiyya, in *al-Muʾtamar al-thāmin li-Majmaʿ al-Buḥūth al-Islāmiyya,* 2 vols., Cairo 1977, i, 210-31; J. Retsö, *The Arabs in antiquity. Their history from the Assyrians to the Umayyads,* London 2003; A. Rippin, RḤMNN and the ḥanīfs, in W.B. Hallaq and D.P. Little (eds.), *Islamic studies presented to Charles J. Adams,* Leiden 1991, 153-68; B. Roggema, A Christian reading of the Qurʾān. The legend of Sergius-Baḥīrā and its use of Qurʾān and sīra, in D. Thomas (ed.), *Syrian Christians under Islam. The first thousand years,* Leiden 2001, 57-73; id., The legend of Sergius-Baḥīrā. Some remarks on its origin in the east and its traces in the west, in K. Ciggaar and H. Teule (eds.), *East and west in the crusader states. Context — contacts — confrontations. ii. Acta of the Congress held at Hernen castle in May* 1997 [Orientalia Lovaniensa Periodica, 92], Leuven 1999, 107-23; U. Rubin, *Between Bible and Qurʾān. The Children of Israel and the Islamic self-image,* Princeton 1999; id., *Eye;* id., Ḥanīf, in *EQ*, ii, 402-4; id., Jews and Judaism, in *EQ*, iii, 21-34; A.A. Said and M. Sharify-Funk (eds.), *Cultural diversity in Islam,* New York 2003; R.M. Savory, Relations between the Safavid state and its non-Muslim minorities, in *Islam and Christian-Muslim relations* 14 (2003), 435-58; M. Schöller, *Exegetisches Denken und Prophetenbiographie. Eine quellenkritische Analyse der Sīra-Überlieferung zu Muḥammads Konflikt mit den Juden,* Wiesbaden 1998; I. Shahid *Byzantium and the Arabs in the fifth century,* Washington, DC 1989; id., *Byzantium and the Arabs in the fourth century,* Washington, DC 1984; id., *Byzantium and the Arabs in the sixth century,* Washington, DC 1995-; id., *The martyrs of Najrān,* Leuven 1971; id., Nadjrān, in *EI*[2], vii, 871-2; M. Sharon, The birth of Islam in the holy land, in id. (ed.), *Pillars of smoke and fire. The holy land in history and thought,* Johannesburg 1988, 225-35; J. Smith, *An historical and semantic study of the term 'islām' as seen in a sequence of Qurʾān commentaries,* Missoula, MT 1975; W.R. Smith, *The religion of the Semites,* New York 1972 (repr.); M. Steinschneider, *Polemische und apologetische Literatur in arabishcer Sprache zwischen Muslimen, Christen and Juden,* Leipzig 1877; S.M. Stern, New light on Judaeo-Christianity? in *Encounter* 28/5 (May 1967), 53-7; id., Quotations from apocryphal gospels in ʿAbd al-Jabbār, in *Journal of theological studies* [N.S.] 18 (April 1967), 34-57; D. Thomas, *Anti-Christian polemics in early Islam. Abū ʿĪsā al-Warrāq's 'Against the Trinity',* Cambridge, UK 1992; id. (ed.), *Christians at the heart of Islamic rule. Church life and scholarship in ʿAbbasid Iraq,* Leiden 2003; id. (ed. and trans.), *Early Muslim polemic against Christianity. Abū ʿĪsā al-Warrāq's "Against the Incarnation,"* Cambridge 2002; A.S. Tritton, *The caliphs and their non-Muslim subjects. A critical study of the Covenant of ʿUmar,* London 1970; J. Waardenburg, Towards a periodization of earliest Islam according to its relations with other religions, in R. Peters (ed.), *Proceedings of the Ninth Congress of the Union Europeene des Arabisants et Islamisants, Amsterdam* 1978, Leiden 1981, 304-26; id., Un débat coranique contre les polytheists, in *Ex orbe religionum. Studia Geo Widengren oblata,* 2 vols., Leiden 1972, 143-54; Wansbrough, *QS;* id., *The sectarian milieu,* London 1978; S. Wasserstrom, *Between Muslim and Jew. The problem of symbiosis under early Islam,* Princeton 1995; W.M. Watt, Ḥanīf, in *EI*[2], iii, 165-6; id., *Muhammad at Mecca,* Oxford 1953; id., The Qurʾān and belief in a high God, in *Der Islam* 55 (1979), 205-11; A. Welch, Allah and other supernatural beings. The emergence of the qurʾanic doctrine of tawhid, in *JAAR* 47 (Dec. 1979: Thematic issue, *Studies in Qurʾan and tafsir*), no. 4 S 733-53.

Remembrance

Recollection; state of being held in mind. Verbal and substantive expressions *(dhikr, dhikrā, tadhkira)* derived from the radical *dh-k-r* appear in 274 verses of the Qurʾān (excluding passages rendering the meaning of "male") and these have different connotations depending on context (see Ahrens, Christliches, 39 for discussion of the etymology). In addition to the basic meaning of "remembrance" this vocabulary can be employed in the sense of "thinking of, speaking about, mentioning, reporting on, relating" as well as "admonition, warning."

Remembrance of God

The most important signification of the first form of the verb is "thinking about" or "calling to mind," with the remembrance of God being the primary focus (see MEMORY; PRAYER). In Q 29:45, "Recite what is sent of the book (q.v.) to you by inspiration (see REVELATION AND INSPIRATION; RECITATION OF THE QURʾĀN), and establish regular prayer, for prayer restrains from shameful and evil deeds (q.v.), and remembrance of God is the greatest [thing in life] without doubt." Remembrance of God is even deemed superior to the religiously-mandated duties (e.g. the obligatory duty of prayer; see WORSHIP; RITUAL AND THE QURʾĀN). Some further examples of qurʾānic descriptions of the remembrance of God are: Q 13:28, "Those who believe, and whose hearts find satisfaction in the remembrance of God; for without doubt in the remembrance of God do hearts find satisfaction" (see HEART; BELIEF AND UNBELIEF); Q 18:101, "[Unbelievers] whose eyes had been under a veil (q.v.) from remembrance of me, and who were unable to hear" (see SEEING AND HEARING; VISION AND BLINDNESS; HEARING AND DEAFNESS); and Q 20:14, "Verily, I am God. There is no god but I, so serve me [only], and establish regular prayer for my remembrance" (see WITNESS TO FAITH).

The Qurʾān sometimes specifies that the "name of God" should be remembered, as in Q 87:14-5: "But he will prosper who purifies himself, and remembers the name of his lord (q.v.), and prays" (see CLEANLINESS AND ABLUTION; RITUAL PURITY); and Q 22:40: "If God had not checked one set of people by means of another, monasteries, churches, synagogues, and mosques (see SACRED PRECINCTS; MONASTICISM AND MONKS; CHURCH; MOSQUE), in which the name of God is commemorated in abundant measure, would surely have been pulled down." This exhortation includes the proclamation of the divine name over slaughtered animals (see CONSECRATION OF ANIMALS; SLAUGHTER), e.g. Q 22:28: "That they may witness the benefits [provided for them], and celebrate the name of God, through the days appointed, over the cattle which he has provided for them [for sacrifice]: then eat thereof and feed the distressed ones in want" (see ALMSGIVING; POVERTY AND THE POOR; cf. Q 22:34 and 36 regarding the eating of sacrificial animals); and concerning the eating of animals in general, Q 5:4: "They ask you what is lawful (see LAWFUL AND UNLAWFUL) to them [as food]. Say: Lawful unto you are [all things] good and pure: and what you have taught your trained hunting animals [to catch] in the manner directed to you by God: eat what they catch for you, but pronounce the name of God over it (see BASMALA): and fear God; for God is swift in taking account" (see also Q 6:119, 121; see HUNTING AND FISHING; FOOD AND DRINK).

Also, individual acts attributed to God, like his favor (*niʿma;* see GRACE; BLESSING), can occur as an object of remembrance, e.g. Q 5:7: "And call in remembrance the favor of God to you, and his covenant (q.v.), which he ratified with you, when you said: 'We hear and obey.' And fear God, for God knows well the secrets (q.v.) of your hearts" (see OBEDIENCE; HIDDEN AND THE HIDDEN; REFLECTION AND DELIBERATION); Q 5:11, "O you who believe! Call in remembrance the favor of God to you when certain men formed the design to stretch out their hands towards you, and he stopped their hands from you: so fear God. And on God let believers put [all] their trust"; or Q 5:20, when Moses (q.v.) says, "O my people! Call in remembrance the favor of God to you, when he produced prophets (see PROPHETS AND PROPHETHOOD) among you, made you kings (see KINGS AND RULERS), and gave you what he had not given to anyone in the world."

Sometimes *ālāʾ*, "benefits," is used instead of *niʿma*, particularly to recall a legendary occurrence in the past (see GENERATIONS; MYTHS AND LEGENDS IN THE QURʾĀN), e.g. Q 7:69: "Do you wonder that there has come to you a message from your lord through a man from among you, to warn you (see WARNER; MESSENGER)? Call in remembrance that he made you inheritors after the people of Noah (q.v.), and gave you a stature tall among the nations. Call in remembrance the benefits [you have received] from God. That you may prosper"; also Q 7:74: "And remember how he made you inheritors after the ʿĀd (q.v.) and gave you habitations in the land: you build for yourselves palaces and castles in [open] plains, and carve out homes in the mountains; so bring to remembrance the benefits (you have received) from God, and refrain from evil and mischief (see CORRUPTION) on the earth." God's behavior towards humankind is sometimes specified more precisely. For instance, people are reminded that they are created by God (e.g. Q 19:67: "Does not man recall [*yadhkuru*] that we created him before from nothing?"; see COSMOLOGY; CREATION), or that God instructs them (e.g. Q 2:239: "... But when you are secure, remember God [*udhkurū llāha*] in the manner he has taught you, which you knew not [before]"), and leads them the right way (e.g. Q 2:198, "... Remember him [*udhkurūhu*] as he has directed you, even though, before this, you went astray [q.v.]").

But the Qurʾān also recalls God or his benefits by recounting past events without the explicit use of the terminology for remembrance. Examples occur particularly in the long late Medinan sūras (q.v.; see also MEDINA; CHRONOLOGY AND THE QURʾĀN) when the Israelites (see CHILDREN OF ISRAEL), for instance, are called to remember God's mercy (q.v.) and his benefits. While Q 2:47 uses the imperative *udhkurū* to exhort the Israelites to recall God's blessings upon them ("Children of Israel! Remember my favor wherewith I favored you and how I preferred you to (all) creatures"), the individual benefits of God are mentioned by means of a narrative (see NARRATIVES) about Moses (Q 2:49-73; e.g. Q 2:49: "And [remember], we delivered you from the people of Pharaoh [q.v.]: They set you hard tasks and punishments, slaughtered your sons and let your women-folk live; therein was a tremendous trial from your lord"). In this fashion, the Israelites are urged to recall these events and to acknowledge God as their author. Similarly, later in the same sūra, the Israelites are requested to recall the divine mercy (Q 2:122) and then their attention is called to a tale about Abraham (q.v.; Q 2:124-34).

The aim of these different demands for the remembrance of God can be summarized as follows. God must be remembered as creator and preserver of both humankind and the whole creation, but the request for this recollection can be either explicit or implicit (e.g. by the qurʾānic citation of past events as examples of God's mercy and his benefits).

Thus, the Qurʾān points again and again to human forgetfulness of God (see GRATITUDE AND INGRATITUDE), one of humanity's enduring characteristics. Q 5:12-4 presents the consequences of this forgetfulness, using the Israelites and Christians as a warning (see JEWS AND JUDAISM;

CHRISTIANS AND CHRISTIANITY). The peaceful communities dissolve while hatred and hostility take their place, a negative elucidation of the fact that people profit by constant remembrance of God and his deeds. For not only the community, but also the individual, can find peace and satisfaction by remembering God: "Those who believe, and whose hearts find satisfaction in the remembrance of God; for without doubt in the remembrance of God do hearts find satisfaction" (Q 13:28; see COMMUNITY AND SOCIETY IN THE QURʾĀN; BELIEF AND UNBELIEF).

Means of remembering God

Although the Qurʾān does not always directly invite people to remember God, it does refer to itself as a revelation which conveys the divine word and thus commands actions approved by God. And, although the Qurʾān acknowledges the existence of other "scriptures" (e.g. the Torah [q.v.] and the Gospels [q.v.]; see also SCRIPTURE AND THE QURʾĀN; cf. Q 2:63, which is in reference to Moses and the Children of Israel: "And remember we took your covenant and we raised above you the mount [saying:] 'Hold firmly to what we have given you and bring [ever] to remembrance what is therein: Perchance you may fear God'."), the Qurʾān itself is sometimes designated as "remembrance" or "reminder" (*tadhkira;* see NAMES OF THE QURʾĀN) — as in Q 43:5, "Shall we then turn away the reminder from you altogether, for that you are a people transgressing beyond bounds (see BOUNDARIES AND PRECEPTS)?" — or as an admonition, as in Q 74:54-5: "Nay, this surely is an admonition: Let any who will, keep it in remembrance!" Q 38:1 indicates an exceptional case, in which the Qurʾān and the admonition appear together as a so-called oath formula (see OATHS; LANGUAGE AND STYLE OF THE QURʾĀN): "By the Qurʾān, full of admonition: [this is the truth]." Q 11:120 refers in particular to the individual narratives (q.v.) concerning the former messengers: "All we relate to you of the stories of the messengers — with it we make firm your heart: in them there comes to you the truth, as well as an exhortation (q.v.) and a message of remembrance *(dhikrā)* to those who believe."

In this context, the meaning of the second form of *dh-k-r* — "remind of, call attention to" in the sense of "warn, admonish" — especially stands out. For the Qurʾān is singled out as a means of warning humankind against the consequences of overlooking God: "Leave alone those who take their religion to be mere play and amusement (see HUMOR; MOCKERY), the life of this world deceives them. But continue to admonish with it [the Qurʾān] lest a soul is caught in its own ruin by its own actions" (Q 6:70; see also e.g. Q 87:9). Likewise, the signs (q.v.; or verses [q.v.], *āyāt*) of God which do the admonishing, are mentioned, e.g. Q 18:57: "And who does more wrong than one who is reminded of the signs of his lord, but turns away from them, forgetting the [deeds] which his hand has sent forth?" (see also Q 25:73; 32:22). Sometimes divine activity within nature is specifically referenced (see NATURE AS SIGNS): "Do you not see that God sends down rain from the sky, and leads it through springs in the earth (see WELLS AND SPRINGS)? Then he causes to grow, therewith produce of various colors: then it withers; you will see it grow yellow; then he makes it dry up and crumble away. Truly, in that is a message of remembrance to people of understanding" (Q 39:21; see also Q 16:10-3; 25:45; for discussion of the *idhā-* phrases that contain an implicit exhortation to be mindful of God and the afterlife, see FORM AND STRUCTURE OF THE QURʾĀN).

Remembrance in tradition (ḥadīth)

Numerous traditions deal with the remembrance of God (see ḤADĪTH AND THE QURʾĀN) and, in general, address the qurʾānic themes on the subject. As an example, Muslim (d. ca. 261/875; *Ṣaḥīḥ*, bk. 37, *K. al-Tawba*, chap. 1, *Faḍl dawām al-dhikr wa-l-fikr fī umūr al-ākhira wa-l-murāqaba*, no. 4937) relates that Ḥanẓala Usayyidī, reportedly one of the Prophet's scribes, was tortured with doubts about the sincerity of his belief. As long as he was within the circle of Muḥammad's adherents, he was able to consider the things concerning the other world (see ESCHATOLOGY). As soon as he returned to everyday life, to his wife, his children or his business, however, he seemed to forget everything else. The Prophet would reassure him: "By him in whose hand is my life, if your state of mind remains the same as it is in my presence and you are always busy in remembrance (of God), the angels will shake hands with you in your beds and in your paths but, Ḥanẓala, time should be devoted (to the worldly affairs) and time (should be devoted to prayer and meditation)." Thus this ḥadīth expresses the conviction that remembrance of God is an important virtue that can compensate for other negligence. Abū Dāwūd (d. 275/889; *Sunan*, bk. 41, *K. al-Adab. Bāb fī kaffāra al-majlis*, no. 4216) relates an account of assemblies which serve a noble cause or are held for the remembrance of God: "There are some expressions which, if a man utters [them] three times when he gets up from an assembly, he will be forgiven for what happened in the assembly; and no one utters them in an assembly held for a noble cause or for remembrance of God but that [it] is stamped with them just as a document is stamped with a signet-ring. These expressions are: Glory be to you, oh God, and I begin with praise of you, there is no God but you; I ask your pardon, and return to you in repentance" (see REPENTANCE AND PENANCE; FORGIVENESS; LAUDATION; GLORIFICATION OF GOD). Again, in al-Bukhārī's (d. 256/870) *Ṣaḥīḥ* (bk. 10, *K. Mawāqīt al-ṣalāt*, chap. 37, *Man nasiya ṣalāt fa-l-yasilidha dhakara wa-lā yuʿīdu illā tilka l-ṣalāt*, no. 562; Eng. trans. i, 328), there is a report about the Prophet's declaration concerning the relationship between prayer and remembrance of God, in which he cites Q 20:14: "The Prophet said, 'If anyone forgets a prayer he should pray that prayer when he remembers it. There is no expiation except to pray the same.' Then he recited: 'Establish prayer for my remembrance'." Another combination of remembrance of God with ritual duties is found in Abū Dāwūd (*Sunan*, bk. 10, *K. al-Manāsik wa-l-ḥajj. Bāb fī l-raml*, no. 1612): "The apostle of God (peace be upon him) said: Going round the house (the Kaʿba), running between al-Ṣafā and stoning of the pillars are meant for the remembrance of God" (see also Q 2:197-200; see KAʿBA; ṢAFĀ AND MARWA; PILGRIMAGE; PRE-ISLAMIC ARABIA AND THE QURʾĀN).

As these few examples illustrate, the remembrance of God is not simply a theological postulate but is also important in the everyday life of the believing community (see EVERYDAY LIFE, THE QURʾĀN IN).

Remembrance in theology

Muslim theologians have also addressed aspects of the concept and the function of remembrance. In his explanation of Q 21:2 the Ashʿarī writer al-Bāqillānī (d. 403/1013) interprets remembrance *(dhikr)* as *waʿẓ*, admonition by the Prophet, and, at the same time, promise *(waʿd)* and intimidation *(takhwīf)*. Based on the qurʾānic characterization of this prophetic "admonition" as originated *(muḥdath),* he draws the conclusion that there must also exist an eternal kind of *dhikr.* Al-Bāqillānī considers another meaning of *dhikr* as underlying Q 65:10-1, in which the messenger of God himself is called *dhikr,* that is to say, divine admonition for humankind, by his recitation of the verses of God (see NAMES OF THE PROPHET).

In contrast, the Māturīdī theologian al-Ṣaffār al-Bukhārī (d. 534/1139) refers to remembrance in the sense of "pointing out" or "informing" *(tanabbuh),* with reflection *(fikr)* on the subject being possibly but not absolutely demanded. Further, the author reads *dhikr* as remembrance of God by speaking of the Qurʾān as containing the details of the true religion (see RELIGIOUS PLURALISM AND THE QURʾĀN).

A transition towards Ṣūfism can be found in the theosophy of Ibn al-ʿArabī (d. 638/1240). In *al-Futūḥāt al-makkiyya* (chap. 142, *Fī maʿrifat maqām al-dhikr wa-asrārihi:* ii, 228-9) the author describes *dhikr* as a divine attribute (see GOD AND HIS ATTRIBUTES) and Q 2:152 as the answer to the *dhikr* of creatures. According to Ibn al-ʿArabī, mentioning or remembering the name of God refers to his essence *(ʿayn).* For this reason, *dhikr* should not be restricted to certain forms, but should be expressed by calling the divine name (see also THEOLOGY AND THE QURʾĀN).

Remembrance in Islamic mysticism

The admonition to remember God that is constantly expressed by the Qurʾān, together with a recognition of the divine activity of creation and of God's signs within the world finally led to the special connotation of *dhikr* in Ṣūfism (see ṢŪFISM AND THE QURʾĀN). In this connection, *dhikr* means, first of all, the act of remembrance itself, but also the oral expression of this act and, finally, the special form of that orality. As mentioned above, in Q 29:45 remembrance of God is equated with ritual prayer, if not esteemed more highly. Nevertheless, mystics were often reproached for choosing *dhikr* above ritual prayer *(ṣalāt).*

In general, remembrance of God in Ṣūfism can be performed in silence (individual *dhikr*) or aloud (individual or collective *dhikr*). Likewise, the threefold classification that comprises *dhikr* of the tongue, *dhikr* of the heart, and *dhikr* of the inner self *(sirr)* became a characteristic of Ṣūfism. This special kind of divine service distinguishes Ṣūfīs from other believers, and the different Ṣūfī brotherhoods have developed different forms of these rituals. Through constant repetition of the divine name or of certain formulas like the profession of faith *(shahāda)* the whole being of the Ṣūfī is consumed by remembrance of God. All else is effaced and states of ecstasy are experienced during voiced and collective *dhikr.*

Angelika Brodersen

Bibliography

Primary: Abū Dāwūd, *Sunan,* on CD-Rom: *Mawsūʿat al-ḥadīth al-sharīf,* Cairo 1997²; al-Bāqillānī, *Kitāb al-Tamhīd,* Beirut 1957, 248; Bukhārī, *Ṣaḥīḥ,* on CD-Rom: *Mawsūʿat al-ḥadīth al-sharīf,* Cairo 1997²; Eng. trans. M.M. Khan, *The translation of the meanings of Ṣaḥīḥ al-Bukhārī,* 9 vols., Medina 1973-6² (rev. ed.); Ibn al-ʿArabī, Muḥyī l-Dīn, *al-Futūḥāt al-makkiyya,* 4 vols., Būlāq 1327/1909, repr. Beirut n.d.; Muslim, *Ṣaḥīḥ,* on CD-Rom: *Mawsūʿat al-ḥadīth al-sharīf,* Cairo 1997²; al-Ṣaffār al-Bukhārī, Abū Isḥāq Ibrāhīm, *Talkhīṣ al-adilla li-qawāʿid al-tawḥīd,* British Museum ms. no. mdlxxvii, fol. 74ʳ.

Secondary: K. Ahrens, Christliches im Qoran. Eine Nachlese, in *ZDMG* 84 (1930), 15-68, 148-90 (see esp. p. 39 for the etymology of *dhikr*); L. Gardet, Dhikr, in *EI²,* ii, 223-7; id., La mention du nom divin, in *Revue thomiste* 6 (1952-3), 197-216; Nagel, *Koran,* 248-9; A. Schimmel, *Mystical dimensions of Islam,* Chapel Hill, NC 1975, 167-78.

Remnant

The remains of a destroyed abode of sinful people. The total destruction of former generations (q.v.) is a historical lesson for contemporary sinners (see SIN, MAJOR AND MINOR), as stated, for example, in Q 19:98: "And how many a generation *(qarn)* have we destroyed before them! Do you see any one of them or hear a sound of them?" (see GEOGRAPHY; HISTORY AND THE QURʾĀN). Among these extinct sinners there were the peoples of ʿĀd (q.v.) and Thamūd (q.v.) about whom it is declared in Q 69:8 that one cannot see any remnant *(bāqiya)* of them. The Qurʾān emphasizes that God has cut off the last of them *(quṭiʿa dābiru l-qawmi;* see Q 6:45; 7:72), as was the case with the people of Lot (q.v.; Q 15:66).

Although the sinners of old were totally wiped out, God left remnants of their abodes to serve as a lesson for posterity. The lesson is called "a sign" (*āya;* see SIGNS), as is the case in Q 27:52, which deals with the sinners of Thamūd: "So those are their houses fallen down because they were unjust (see JUSTICE AND INJUSTICE). Most surely there is a sign in this for people who know." The desolate abodes *(masākin)* of Thamūd as well as of ʿĀd, which remained after their inhabitants had been destroyed, are mentioned also in Q 29:38 and Q 46:25 (cf. Q 14:45; 28:58). Muḥammad's unbelieving contemporaries actually used to go about among these dwellings (Q 20:128). In further passages, the unbelievers are requested to travel in the land and see what was the end *(ʿāqiba)* of the sinners of old, who, however, are not specifically identified (Q 3:137; 6:11; 12:109; 16:36; 27:69; 30:9; 35:44; 40:21, 82; 47:10; see LIE; GRATITUDE AND INGRATITUDE).

Remnants of the town of Lot (Sodom) also survived and God declares that he has left a clear sign of this town for people who understand (Q 29:35; also Q 32:26; 51:37; see KNOWLEDGE AND LEARNING). The Qurʾān stresses that the remnants of Lot's town can be seen by Muḥammad's unbelieving contemporaries who pass by when they go about their business in the land (Q 25:40; 37:137). They can see these remnants because they overlook the main road (Q 15:76). This applies also to the remains of the city of al-Ayka (Q 15:79; see PEOPLE OF THE THICKET). Remnants of Noah's (q.v.) ark (q.v.) could also be seen, as is implied in Q 54:15. This passage asserts that God left it as a sign.

A different type of remnant is called *baqiyya* (from *b-q-y,* "to remain"), which stands for a divine religious or moral relic that has an everlasting value. Hence in Q 11:116, the phrase *ūlū baqiyya* signifies people possessing such a relic or possessing qualities of religious and moral excellence (see ETHICS AND THE QURʾĀN). In Q 11:86 the *baqiyya* explicitly belongs to God and emanates from him to his obedient servants (see OBEDIENCE; SERVANT). In Q 2:248 it is evidently material, as it stands for the relics left by the Children of Israel (q.v.) within the ark of the covenant (q.v.; *tābūt*). Muslim exegetes (see EXEGESIS OF THE QURʾĀN: CLASSICAL AND MEDIEVAL) maintain that these relics included the Tablets, the rod (q.v.) of Moses (q.v.) and the turban of Aaron (q.v.).

Uri Rubin

Bibliography
Primary: Suyūṭī, *Durr;* Ṭabarī, *Tafsīr.*
Secondary: R. Sellheim, Noch einmal. *Baqīya* im Koran, in J. Cobet et al. (eds.), *Dialogos. Für Harald Patzer zum 65. Geburtstag von seinen Freunden und Schülern,* Wiesbaden n.d., 301-5.

Repentance and Penance

Contrition or regret and self-mortification, with the intention of obtaining God's pardon (see FORGIVENESS). Repentance is generally designated in the Qurʾān as *tawba* which basically means "return" (from sin; see SIN, MAJOR AND MINOR). For example, in Q 66:8 God demands of the believers a "sincere return" *(tawbatan naṣūḥan)* and he in turn will make them enter paradise (q.v.). God himself is described as "the accepter of *tawba*" (Q 9:104; 42:25; also Q 40:3: accepter of *tawb*), and this represents a crucial aspect of his compassion for the believers (see MERCY). Repentance can, however, only be accepted as long as one remains a believer (see BELIEF AND UNBELIEF; FAITH). Q 3:90 asserts that "those who disbelieve after their believing then increase in disbelief, their repentance *(tawbatuhum)* shall not be accepted and these are they who go astray (q.v.; see also ERROR)." Similarly, the repentance of unbelievers that has been postponed till the last moment of life is doomed to rejection (Q 4:18; see DEATH AND THE DEAD).

But the term *tawba* may denote not just human "return" from sin but also God's "return" (from wrath; see ANGER). This is the case in Q 4:92, in which a Muslim guilty of unintentional murder (q.v.; see also BLOODSHED) is demanded to fulfill some duties, including the payment of blood money (q.v.), which are imposed on him in order to gain God's *tawba* (see RETALIATION). The blood money forms part of the sinner's penance and, as will be shown below, there are other references to penance in the Qurʾān although repentance is mostly answered with forgiveness, without any allusion to specific penance.

Another key term is *tawwāb*, which, like *tawba*, has a two-fold function. On the one hand, it describes humans who repent repeatedly (cf. Q 2:222) but in most cases it stands for God who is willing to accept a human being's repentance. In the verses applying this epithet to God (see GOD AND HIS ATTRIBUTES), his merciful response is promised to the Prophet himself (Q 110:3) as well as to Muslims who have acted unjustly towards other Muslims (see JUSTICE AND INJUSTICE), mainly through slander and spying (Q 24:11; 49:12; see GOSSIP) or disobedience (q.v.) to the Prophet on legal matters (Q 4:64 f.; see OBEDIENCE; LAW AND THE QURʾĀN; AUTHORITY) or stayed behind the fighting (q.v.) ranks (Q 9:118; see RANKS AND ORDERS; WAR; EXPEDITIONS AND BATTLES), etc.

Another form connected with repentance is *tāʾibūn*, which designates persons who repent, as is the case in Q 9:112. This verse provides a list of basic characteristics of the ideal Muslim and the fact that repentance is included in the list means that a believer must always be on guard with respect to his or her unblemished virtues (see VIRTUES AND VICES, COMMANDING AND FORBIDDING). This applies also to Muḥammad's wives, as indicated in Q 66:5 (*tāʾibāt;* see WIVES OF THE PROPHET).

In many other passages the idea of repentance is conveyed by the verb *tāba*, with its various tenses. Here again, a two-fold function is discernible. On the one hand, *tāba* (with *ilā*) denotes returning from sin to God and, on the other (with *ʿalā*), it signifies God's returning from wrath to forgiveness. When denoting human repentance, *tāba* is not necessarily confined to believers and may also allude to unbelievers acting against the Muslims. In their case, returning to God means simply embracing Islam (q.v.; Q 19:60; 25:70-1). This is the only option open to them, other than death (Q 5:34; 9:3, 5, 11) or being punished on the day of judgment (Q 11:3; 28:67; 85:10; see LAST JUDGMENT; REWARD AND PUNISHMENT; CHASTISEMENT AND PUNISHMENT). The fact that repentance may mean embracing Islam comes out most clearly in the fact that those who have followed the Prophet are called in Q 11:112 "those who have returned *(man tāba)*." Similarly, in Q 40:7, the angels beseech God to pardon those who have returned (*tābū*, i.e. to him) and followed his way and to save them from the punishment of hell (see HELL AND HELLFIRE; ANGEL; INTERCESSION). Repentance is also offered to the hypocrites (*munāfiqūn;* see HYPOCRITES AND HYPOCRISY), in which case it means restoring their faith (q.v.) to its proper sincerity. Otherwise they, too, are condemned to hell (Q 4:145-6; 9:74). The same fate awaits apostates if they do not repent (Q 3:86-9; see APOSTASY; BOUNDARIES AND PRECEPTS). When referring to the believers, the verb *tāba* means mainly desisting from all kinds of sins against other believers, such as slander (Q 24:4-5; 66:3-4) or finding fault with each other (Q 49:11) or accepting usury (q.v.; Q 2:278-9). The repentance of the believers is also accepted in cases of unintentional crimes (Q 4:17; 6:54; 16:119).

Generally speaking, the believer's repentance is considered a constant state of self-trial and improvement, therefore the need to repent is relevant at all stages of life. For example, in Q 46:15, one is requested to "return" to God when one is forty years old, i.e. has reached the peak of one's abilities (see MATURITY). In the same vein, in Q 24:31 God addresses all believers, saying: "return *(tūbū)* to God all of you, O believers, so that you may be successful" (see VICTORY). As noted above, the verb *tāba* (with *ʿalā*) also signifies God's returning from wrath to forgiveness (e.g. Q 3:128; 33:24), and his mercy is reserved mainly for believers. For this reason *tāba* may occur in contradistinction to the punishment awaiting the hypocrites and the unbelievers (Q 33:73; see also Q 9:14-5, 27, 101-2, 106).

It should be observed that there is a mutual dependence between God's mercy, as conveyed by the verb *tāba*, and the believer's repentance, which is conveyed by the same verb. This comes out explicitly in Q 5:39: "Whoever returns *(tāba)* after his iniquity and reforms [himself], then surely God will return to him" (*yatūbu ʿalayhi;* see also Q 2:160). God's mercy is sometimes the first cause that generates repentance, as appears to be the case in Q 4:26-7: "God desires to explain to you, and to guide you into the ways of those before you, and to return unto you *(wa-yatūba ʿalaykum)*." Some exegetes explain that God guides and "returns" to the believer so that the latter may see the way leading to repentance (Ibn al-Jawzī, *Zād*, ii, 59, from al-Zajjāj: *yurīdu an yadullakum ʿalā mā yakūnu sababan li-tawbatikum;* see also PATH OR WAY; FREEDOM AND PREDESTINATION). This correlation between divine mercy and human repentance is even more explicit in Q 9:118, in which God "returns" to some persons *(tāba ʿalayhim)*, so that they might also return (to him; *li-yatūbū*). The verse concludes with the statement that God is *tawwāb*, i.e. willing to accept the believer's repentance (and see also Q 4:16).

The idea of repentance comes out in further passages employing roots synonymous to *t-w-b*, such as *n-w-b*, which always occurs in the fourth form *(anāba)*, and denotes "return" (from sin to God). It is usually employed to describe one's desisting from idolatry (see IDOLATRY AND IDOLATERS) and returning to God, so that *anāba* actually means embracing Islam (i.e. Q 39:54; see also Q 30:31, 33; 31:15; 34:9; 39:8, 17; 40:13; 50:8, 33; 60:4). Some verses employing this form bring out yet again the mutual dependence between human repentance and divine mercy and guidance. In Q 13:27 it is stated that God guides towards himself those who return (*anāba;* i.e. to him), which means that return to God is the result of God's willing. The same idea recurs in Q 42:13, which states: "God chooses for himself whom he pleases, and guides him who returns *(yunību)* towards himself."

The root *a-w-b,* which also means "return," features in the sense of repentance in the form *awwābīn* (Q 17:25). The exegetes usually say that *awwābīn* is identical with *tawwābīn* (for further explanations see Ibn al-Jawzī, *Zād,* v, 26; see EXEGESIS OF THE QUR'ĀN: CLASSICAL AND MEDIEVAL). This is also how they tend to perceive the form *awwāb* that occurs in Q 50:32. The verb *raja'a,* "return," may also occur in the sense of repentance, in verses dealing with God's "signs" (q.v.; *āyāt*), which are said to have been presented to the people in order that they may "return" (from their sins; Q 7:174), or ones dealing with God's punishment, which is inflicted on sinners for the same purpose (Q 30:41; see REFLECTION AND DELIBERATION; NATURE AS SIGNS; PUNISHMENT STORIES).

Closely associated with the idea of repentance is the idea of desisting from sin, as conveyed by the verb *intahā* (with *'an*). Desisting from sin is demanded in many passages that promise a reward for those who desist and a punishment for those who do not. Some of these passages address the Christians in particular (see CHRISTIANS AND CHRISTIANITY). The latter are entreated to desist from believing in the divinity of Jesus (q.v.): if they do so, this would be better for them (Q 4:171), but if they do not, punishment awaits them (Q 5:73; see POLEMIC AND POLEMICAL LANGUAGE). Other passages demand that the idolaters desist from disbelief and from persecuting the believers, which will assure them God's forgiveness (Q 2:192-3; 8:19, 38-9; see OPPOSITION TO MUḤAMMAD).

The Qur'ān allots a significant place to historical precedents of repentance, with a view to edifying Muḥammad's contemporaries (see HISTORY AND THE QUR'ĀN; OCCASIONS OF REVELATION; REVELATION AND INSPIRATION). Such a precedent appears, to begin with, in the story of Cain and Abel (q.v.), which is recounted in the Qur'ān without mentioning the names of the two. In Q 5:31 Cain is said to have become "of those who regret" *(mina l-nādimīn),* and the exegetes maintain that regret is usually a sign of repentance *(tawba).* They wonder, however, why Cain's regret was not accepted, and provide various answers, one of which is that regret is considered repentance only with Muslims, but not with sinners of earlier generations (q.v.; Ibn al-Jawzī, *Zād,* ii, 339). Further precedents emerge in passages recounting the history of the Children of Israel (q.v.). The passages relating to the Israelites employ the root *t-w-b,* as is the case in Q 20:81-2, where God warns the Israelites against sin and promises to forgive those who "return" *(tāba).* As indicated in Q 7:152-3, the sin of the Israelites, from which they must "return," is the making of the golden calf (see CALF OF GOLD). The demand for them to repent following this sin, as formulated in Q 2:54, brings out clearly the mutual dependence of divine mercy and repentance: "return *(tūbū)* to your creator and kill each other, that is best for you with your creator: then [God] returned unto you *(fa-tāba 'alaykum),* for surely he is the *tawwāb,* the merciful." The command "kill each other" represents the penance imposed by God, and he has responded to it with mercy, as indicated in the fact that he is described as *tawwāb.* In another version of the affair of the golden calf, the Children of Israel repent on their own accord after having made the image (see IDOLS AND IMAGES). Their regret is conveyed by a special idiomatic phrase: *suqiṭa fī aydīhim* (Q 7:149), i.e. "[remorse] was made to fall upon their hands." Another precedent is provided in Q 2:58-9 and reiterated in Q 7:161-2. Before entering the holy land (see SYRIA; JERUSALEM; PROFANE AND SACRED), the Israelites are requested to enter the gate (of a city there) while prostrating themselves and are commanded to say *ḥiṭṭa* (See Rubin, *Between Bible*, 83-99), so that God may forgive them their sins. This is the penance that God imposes on them but they say another word instead and are therefore destroyed by a pestilence from heaven. Another community which has repented is the people of Jonah (q.v.). They are mentioned in Q 10:98, where it is stated that they were the only (sinful) people whose (return to) belief helped them gain God's mercy.

The Qurʾān gleans precedents of repentance not only from the history of sinful nations but also from the history of some prophets (see PROPHETS AND PROPHETHOOD). In their case, repentance serves as a model that every pious believer should follow. To begin with, in Q 2:37 Adam is said to have received (some) words from his lord, so God "returned" unto him *(tāba ʿalayhi),* because God is *tawwāb* and merciful (see ADAM AND EVE; FALL OF MAN). The words given to Adam appear to represent the penance imposed on him, i.e. words of repentance, to which God, the *tawwāb*, has responded with mercy. The mutual aspect of the "return" in the case of Adam reappears in Q 20:122, where it is stated that God chose Adam, turned unto him *(tāba)* and guided (him). The exegetes explain that God guided Adam by showing him how to return (Ibn al-Jawzī, *Zād*, v, 330). In the case of Abraham (q.v.) and Ishmael (q.v.), no sin is mentioned in the Qurʾān for which God had to forgive them; nevertheless they pray to God in Q 2:128 that he may return to them (*wa-tub ʿalaynā;* see PRAYER). Some exegetes explain that they had committed some unintentional misdeeds, or that they were asking merely out of modesty and as a lesson to their posterity (Bayḍāwī, *Anwār*, ad loc.). Indeed, in Q 43:28, Abraham's words in which he renounces his father's idolatry are said to have been preserved as an example for his posterity, that they may return *(yarjiʿūna)* from their sins. As for Abraham himself, his penitent "return" is mentioned in Q 11:75, where he is said to have been a *munīb*, which again does not refer to any specific sin, but merely indicates his constant self-reforming. Moses (q.v.), however, has a specific reason for repentance, which is spelled out in Q 7:143. He was bold enough to ask God to reveal himself to him. After having fallen down in a swoon, Moses recovers and states his penitent "return" *(tubtu)* to God. Shuʿayb (q.v.) states in Q 11:88 that he "returns" *(unīb)* to God, which seems to mean that he too is in a state of constant self-reforming. The same applies to David (q.v.) who is described in Q 38:17 as *awwāb*. Elsewhere (Q 38:24), David is said to have sought his lord's forgiveness and to have fallen down in prostration (see BOWING AND PROSTRATION) and to have returned *(anāba)*. Here, the exegetes explain, David repents his sin with Uriah's wife, and the Qurʾān itself says that God has finally forgiven him (Q 38:25). Solomon (q.v.) is described in Q 38:30 as *awwāb* and the exegetes note that here the term refers to "return" from minor unintentional misdeeds (Ibn al-Jawzī, *Zād*, vii, 127). A few verses later (Q 38:34) Solomon is said to have "returned" *(anāba),* and some exegetes say that his sin here was that he preferred the good things to prayer, as stated in Q 38:32 (ibid., vii, 133). Job (q.v.), too, is described in Q 38:44 as repenting, being referred to as *awwāb*. The exegetes explain that his "return" meant that in spite of his terrible sufferings (see TRIAL; TRUST AND PATIENCE; SUFFERING) he continued to obey his lord (Bayḍāwī, *Anwār*, ad loc.). Dhū l-Nūn, i.e. Jonah, repents after having tried to avoid his prophetic mission. Although it is never stated explicitly that he repented, he nevertheless utters words of remorse when saying to God in Q 21:87: "There is no god but you, glory be to you (see GLORIFICATION OF GOD); surely I am of those who have been of the evil-doers (*ẓālimīn;* see EVIL DEEDS; GOOD AND EVIL)." God responds to his repentance with mercy and delivers him from his grief (Q 21:88; see JOY AND MISERY).

The prophet Muḥammad himself is associated in the Qurʾān with the theme of repentance. Q 9:117 states that God has "returned" *(tāba)* to the Prophet as well as to his Companions (see COMPANIONS OF THE PROPHET), after "the hearts of some of them were about to deviate" (see HEART). The exegetes explain that God only "returned" from his anger with the Companions, and that Muḥammad is mentioned with them only because he was the reason for their repentance (Ibn al-Jawzī, *Zād,* iii, 511). Here, too, the exegetes assume a mutual dependence between divine mercy and repentance, Muḥammad being regarded as an agent of the divine mercy that generates repentance. In Q 42:10, the Prophet states that he relies on God and returns *(unību)* to him. The exegetes explain that returning unto God means here turning to him at times of distress. Hence repentance is mentioned here in the sense of seeking God's help.

The theme of repentance emerges also in the eschatological sphere (see ESCHATOLOGY), where it is always futile. In some of the relevant passages the sinners ask God for a respite before being punished in hell, so that they can amend their ways and become believers (Q 14:44; 63:10). But, as asserted in Q 44:15, even if given a respite, they will surely return (to evil). In other passages, the repenting sinners who have already been resurrected for the final judgment, ask in vain to be returned to this world to become believers (Q 6:27; 7:53; 26:102; 32:12; 35:37; 39:58; 42:44; 23:99; see RESURRECTION). Some of the passages use the term *ḥasra* (pl. *ḥasarāt*), "regret," to convey the remorse of the hopeless sinners for failing to repent while they were still living their first life (Q 2:167). Accordingly, the day of resurrection is called "the day of regret" (Q 19:39). Their (hopeless) regret on that day is also referred to as *nadāma* (Q 10:54; 34:33).

As for repentance in post-qurʾānic literature, a good overview can be gained from Ibn Qudāma's (d. 690/1291) *Kitāb al-Tawwābīn.* Apart from chapters revolving around the qurʾānic instances of repentance, there are also numerous chapters containing edifying folk tales praising the pious repentance of figures from among the Children of Israel, as well as from the pre-Islamic Arabs (see PRE-ISLAMIC ARABIA AND THE QURʾĀN; SOUTH ARABIA, RELIGION IN PRE-ISLAMIC). Further, there are also traditions about Companions of the Prophet and other ascetics of the first Islamic eras (see ASCETICISM). For repentance among the Ṣūfīs and the Shīʿīs (see ṢŪFISM AND THE QURʾĀN; SHĪʿISM AND THE QURʾĀN), see Ayoub, Repentance.

Uri Rubin

Bibliography
Primary: Bayḍāwī, *Anwār;* Ibn al-Jawzī, *Zād;* Ibn Qudāma, ʿAbdallāh b. Aḥmad, *Kitāb al-Tawwābīn,* ed. ʿA. al-Arnāʾūṭ, Beirut 1974.
Secondary: M. Ayoub, Repentance in the Islamic tradition, in A. Etzioni and D.E. Carney (eds.), *Repentance. A comparative perspective,* Lanham, MD 1997, 96-121; F.M. Denny, Tawba, in *EI²,* x, 385; G.R. Hawting, The tawwābūn, atonement and ʿĀshūrāʾ, in *JSAI* 17 (1994), 166-81; U. Rubin, *Between Bible and Qurʾān,* Princeton 1989.

Repetition see RHETORIC AND THE QURʾĀN

Repudiate see MARRIAGE AND DIVORCE

Responsibility

The relation of an agent to a norm-giving and evaluative instance. It consists of the imposition of a set of norms, action in regards to these norms, and the assessment of the committed acts according to these norms with any consequences that might ensue. The idea of responsibility is a central feature of social activities, law, ethics and religion (q.v.; see also LAW AND THE QURʾĀN; ETHICS AND THE QURʾĀN; SOCIAL INTERACTIONS).

As a result of the complexity of the concept of responsibility, there are several Arabic terms relating to different aspects of it. The common Arabic term for "responsibility," *masʾūliyya*, is an abstract noun derived from the passive participle of *saʾala*, "to ask." Although the Qurʾān uses forms of *saʾala* or the passive *suʾila* in the sense of "to hold responsible" and "to be made responsible," respectively (e.g. Q 7:6; 15:92; 16:93; 21:23; 29:13; 37:24), the term *masʾūliyya* itself is not classical; lexicographical references probably cannot be found before the nineteenth century (cf. Fleischer, *Kleinere Schriften*, ii, 549; see ARABIC LANGUAGE). In Islamic law *ḍamān* or *kafāla* denote civic responsibility in general, and the responsibility of surety in the law of obligations in particular. The terms with which the notion of responsibility is usually discussed in the field of Islamic theology (see THEOLOGY AND THE QURʾĀN) are *taklīf*, "imposition," on the part of God, and *kasb*, "acquisition," on the part of man (see REWARD AND PUNISHMENT; CHASTISEMENT AND PUNISHMENT). The verb *kallafa*, "to impose" (of which *taklīf* is the verbal noun), is used in a nearly stereotyped wording in seven qurʾānic verses (see below). And though the word *taklīf* does not occur in the Qurʾān, it was used as early as the time of Abū Ḥanīfa (d. 150/767) as a technical term for the religious obligation that is incumbent upon humans (cf. van Ess, *TG*, i, 207). On the other hand, *kasb* is the verbal noun of *kasaba*, "to acquire," which often appears in the Qurʾān (see below). In theology, *kasb* was first used by Ḍirār b. ʿAmr (d. 200/815) to denote the role the individual plays in his or her actions (see Ashʿarī, *Maqālāt*, 408; see FREEDOM AND PREDESTINATION).

The structure of responsibility in the Qurʾān

In the Qurʾān, the idea of responsibility is the core of the relationship between humans and God. Time and again, the Qurʾān promises abundant reward to those who believe in God (see BELIEF AND UNBELIEF) and do the deeds of righteousness (*alladhīna āmanū wa-ʿamilū l-ṣāliḥāt*, e.g. Q 2:25; 5:9; 10:9; 18:107 f.; 24:55; 98:7 f.; see GOOD DEEDS). That this differentiation between belief and deeds (see FAITH) is more than mere rhetoric (see RHETORIC AND THE QURʾĀN) is evident from the different valences which are thereby established: Those who believe, but do not comply with specific divine commands, can still hope to be saved, provided that they repent honestly (e.g. Q 4:31; 20:82; 25:70; 29:7; 42:25; 47:2; see REPENTANCE AND PENANCE), while those who do not believe are definitely condemned to hell (see HELL AND HELLFIRE), no matter what they do (e.g. Q 3:21-2; 5:5; 6:88; 14:18; 18:105; 47:1; see FORGIVENESS). Responsibility, therefore, comprises two distinct levels. The basis is God's demand for belief. Given divine omnipotence (see POWER AND IMPOTENCE), this demand tolerates no refusal. There is no neutral position for the human being in the face of it, but only the choice between "the way of God" (*sabīl Allāh*, a metaphor that occurs more than a hundred times, cf. also Q 1:6; 2:142, etc. for similar metaphors; see PATH OR WAY) and "the way of error" (q.v; *sabīl al-ghayy*, Q 7:146; cf. 4:76; 6:55; 7:142; 10:89, etc. for variants: i.e. "the way of sinners," etc.; see also ASTRAY; SIN, MAJOR AND MINOR; DEVIL). But while the decision to reject belief will inevitably lead the individual to eternal torture (see

ETERNITY), the decision to believe does not automatically result in heavenly reward (see PARADISE). It only opens a second level of human responsibility before God. Belief, in this context, is the individual's recognition of God's authority (q.v.), i.e. the willingness to act according to God's norms and to accept his judgment regarding one's conduct (see LAST JUDGMENT; HEAVENLY BOOK). This two-fold nature of responsibility in the Qurʾān gave rise to the controversial discussions of later Islamic theologians about the concepts of "faith" *(īmān)* and "works" *(aʿmāl)*.

Responsibility and free will

The Qurʾān repeatedly emphasizes that on the day of judgment each person will be responsible exclusively for his or her own deeds (e.g. Q 6:164; 17:15; 34:25; 39:7; see INTERCESSION). The attribution of an act to a person, however, presupposes freedom of will. It is well known that there are verses in the Qurʾān that support the assumption that humans are endowed with free will (e.g. Q 18:28; 73:19; 79:37 f.; 88:23 f.), while others suggest determinism and thus seem to exclude the possibility of human responsibility (e.g. Q 13:27; 14:14; 35:8; 42:46). Certainly, the tension between human freedom and God's omnipotence can be understood as a fundamental characteristic of monotheism. The Qurʾān, however, largely associates these opposite notions with an idea that was already held in rabbinic Judaism: God guides the believers and leads the unbelievers astray, meaning that he merely reinforces already existing tendencies (e.g. Q 14:27; 18:57; 19:75 f.; 36:7 f.; 59:19; 92:4 f.; cf. Q 2:81 and 83:14, where sin is described as enclosing man and lying like rust on his heart [q.v.], respectively). Yet, there is no definitive orientation since a believer may apostatize and God may grant undeserved grace (q.v.; see also BLESSING; APOSTASY). Within the scope of this idea, the verbs *kasaba* (forty-nine times) and *iktasaba* (three times, at Q 2:286; 24:11; 33:58), literally "to acquire," metaphorically express the idea that individuals incur the moral responsibility for their own acts — good or bad — and that they will be rewarded or punished for them, as in, for instance, Q 2:281: "And fear (q.v.) a day wherein you shall be returned to God, then every soul shall be paid in full what it has earned *(mā kasabat);* and they shall not be wronged."

The notion of responsibility in Islamic theology

Islamic theologians ordinarily dealt with the question of responsibility in the context of their teachings concerning either God's justice (see JUSTICE AND INJUSTICE) or his omnipotence. Thus, the Muʿtazila (see MUʿTAZILĪS) deduced from their basic doctrine of God's justice *(ʿadl)* that the determinant motive for God's action towards humanity is the latter's benefit or even highest benefit (*ṣalāḥ* or *aṣlaḥ*). And, since God's imposition of his law *(taklīf)* is a means to a supreme good, i.e. heavenly reward, it is in itself a benefit and therefore necessary. Further, it is incompatible with God's justice that he should impose upon people that which is impracticable *(taklīf mā lā yuṭāq)*. In this respect, the Muʿtazila referred to Q 2:286: "God does not charge *(lā yukallifu)* any soul save to its capacity" *(wusʿahā;* cf. Q 2:233; 6:152; 7:42; 23:62; 65:7; also Q 4:84). Therefore, according to the Muʿtazila, for *taklīf* to be in force, three conditions must be met: People need knowledge *(maʿrifa)* about the obligation that is incumbent upon them; they must have freedom of choice *(ikhtiyār)* whether to obey or to disobey (see OBEDIENCE; DISOBEDIENCE); and, finally, they have to possess the capacity to act *(istiṭāʿa)* to implement their decisions. Since *taklīf* is a benefit, however, it must be possible for everyone to meet each of these conditions. Thus, the central problem for the Muʿtazila concerning the notion of responsibility was "the obligation to something unknown" *(al-taklīf bi-mā lā yuʿlam),* i.e. how can someone, who has not even heard about God, acquire the knowledge about his or her obligation? Most Muʿtazilīs found the solution in the idea that such a person, startled by a sudden suspicion *(khāṭir)* that there might be a God who will punish him or her if no gratitude is shown, begins to reflect upon the contingency of the world. The individual then realizes the existence of the world's creator and the possibility that he imposes commands upon humans (see CREATION; VIRTUES AND VICES, COMMANDING AND FORBIDDING). By further reflection, people will discern that there are obligations which can be deduced by reason alone *(taklīf ʿaqlī)* — especially the principles of ethics — and that there might be others which can only be known through revelation (*taklīf samʿī* or *sharʿī*, see REVELATION AND INSPIRATION) and about which they have to make additional inquiries — as about regulations of cult (see RITUAL AND THE QURʾĀN; RELIGIOUS PLURALISM AND THE QURʾĀN).

By contrast, the Ashʿarīs treated the idea of responsibility from the perspective of God's omnipotence. This becomes clear in their definition of the just act *(ʿadl)* as an act that one is entitled to do *(fiʿl mā lil-fāʿil an yafʿalahu):* Inasmuch as God is unrestricted in his omnipotence, everything he does is just. He may pardon the unbeliever and he does not have to reward the believer. Therefore, *taklīf* establishes no causal connection between belief and reward or unbelief and punishment, as it does in Muʿtazilī theology. It is not even necessary that everybody should know about *taklīf*. Certainly, knowledge about God can be acquired by reason but there is no obligation to reflect. *Taklīf* is valid only if one hears about it and, so, the paradox of an "obligation to something unknown" is not a major problem for the Ashʿarīs. Their understanding of God's omnipotence implies that, since there is no creator save him, he also creates human acts *(khāliq afʿāl al-ʿibād)*. Thus, to secure the possibility of attributing acts to humans, the Ashʿarīs developed the concept of "acquisition" *(kasb):* Together with the act, God creates in each person a "temporary ability" *(qudra muḥdatha),* on the basis of which the individual "acquires" *(kasaba)* the act and is made responsible for it. Al-Baghdādī (d. 429/1037; *Farq,* 328) condensed this concept into the formula: "[The person] acquires his act *(muktasib li-ʿamalihi)* and God creates his acquisition *(khāliq li-kasbihi)*." The question whether the existence of this "temporary ability" is the only condition for the attribution of an act to an individual or whether further elements are required, too — like the person's knowledge of the act *(ʿilm)* and the will to act *(irāda)* which are, however, equally created by God — remained a debatable issue for the Ashʿarīs. Because the *kasb* concept implies that God can impose an act upon someone while not creating in that person the necessary ability to carry it out, the Ashʿarīs defended the reality of the "imposition of something that cannot be done" *(taklīf mā lā yuṭāq)*. Yet, although they would not regard God's hypothetical imposition of something that is humanly unfeasible as nonsensical *(ʿabath; safah),* they nevertheless asserted that it does not happen.

Matthias Radscheit

Bibliography

Primary: ʿAbd al-Jabbār (attr.; actual author is Mānkdīm Shashdīw, d. 485/1034), *Sharḥ al-uṣūl al-khamsa,* ed. ʿA. ʿUthmān, Cairo 1965, 509 f., 609 f.; al-Ashʿarī, Abū l-Ḥasan ʿAlī b. Ismāʿīl, *Maqālāt al-islāmiyyīn,* ed. H. Ritter, Wiesbaden 1963²; al-Baghdādī, ʿAbd al-Qāhir b. Ṭāhir, *Farq,* Cairo 1910; id., *Uṣūl al-dīn,* Istanbul 1928, 206 f.; Ibn Fūrak, Abū Bakr Muḥammad b. al-Ḥasan, *Mujarrad maqālāt al-Ashʿarī,* ed. D. Gimaret, Beirut 1987, index.

Secondary: P. Boneschi, *Kasaba* et *iktasaba*. Leur acception figurée dans le Qurʾān, in *RSO* 30 (1955), 17-53; Cl. Cahen and L. Gardet, Kasb, in *EI²*, iv, 690-4; van Ess, *TG*, i; H.L. Fleischer, *Kleinere Schriften*, 3 vols., Leipzig 1888, ii; L. Gardet, Īmān, in *EI²*, iii, 1170-4; D. Gimaret, Taklīf, in *EI²*, x, 138-9; id. *Théories de l'acte humain en théologie musulmane*, Paris 1980; J. Jomier, *Dieu et l'homme dans le Coran*, Paris 1996, 117-60; Y. Linant de Bellefonds, Kafāla, in *EI²*, iv, 404-5; H. Räisänen, *The idea of divine hardening*, Helsinki 1976, 13-44; J. Schacht, *An introduction to Islamic law*, Oxford 1964, index; E. Stiegman, Rabbinic anthropology, in *Aufstieg und Niedergang der römischen Welt [ANRW]* Principat 19/2 (1979), 487-579, 523 f.; W. Weischedel, *Das Wesen der Verantwortung*, Frankfurt-am-Main 1933; H. Zirker, *Der Koran. Zugänge und Lesarten*, Darmstadt 1999, 128 f., 148 f.

Rest(ing) see SLEEP; SABBATH

Resurrection

The "rising again" of all the human dead before the final judgment. The expression "day of resurrection" *(yawm al-qiyāma)* occurs seventy times in the Qurʾān (although the concept of "rising" — from the triliteral root *q-w-m* — is not limited to this eschatological sense; it is also employed in other instances, with a wider range of meanings). The resurrection of dead human bodies (see DEATH AND THE DEAD; BURIAL) follows the annihilation of all creatures *(al-fanāʾ al-muṭlaq)* and precedes the "day of judgment" (*yawm al-dīn*, thirteen attestations in the Qurʾān; see LAST JUDGMENT) or the "day of reckoning" (*yawm al-ḥisāb*, with four mentions: Q 38:16, 26, 53; 40:27; see ESCHATOLOGY; WEIGHTS AND MEASURES). There will be the last "hour" *(al-sāʿa)* and people will be "gathered." "On the day when the earth shall be cleft off from them, [they will come out] hastening forth. That will be a gathering" (*ḥashr*, Q 50:44). "As such (will be) the resurrection" (*al-nushūr*, Q 35:9).

The "last hour" (forty-eight occurrences) is frequently announced in the Qurʾān, and its establishment is assured (Q 30:55). "The hour is their appointed time, and the hour will be more grievous and more bitter" (Q 54:46). Only God knows its actual "appointed time": "Say: The knowledge thereof is with my lord (q.v.). None can reveal its time but he" (Q 7:187; cf. 31:34), but "It may be that the hour is near!" (Q 33:63). As for the signs (q.v.) of the hour — "Some of the signs of your lord should come" (Q 6:158) — the Islamic tradition, in its apocalyptic literature, has always proposed a list of ten signs (see APOCALYPSE): the coming of the smoke (q.v.; *dukhān*), of the deceiver (*dajjāl;* see ANTICHRIST), and of the beast *(dābba)*, the rising of the sun (q.v.) from the west, the return of Jesus (q.v.), the "great mischief" of Gog and Magog (q.v.) in the land, the earthquakes in the east, in the west, and in Arabia, and finally the fire (q.v.). Three of these signs occur in the Qurʾān and the others are often described in the sunna (q.v.) and in eschatological traditions. As for the smoke, the Qurʾān says: "Then wait you for the day when the sky will bring forth a visible smoke, covering the people.... On the day when we shall seize you with the greatest seizure. Verily, we will exact retribution" (Q 44:10-6). The beast is announced in Q 27:82: "When the word [of torment; see CHASTISEMENT AND PUNISHMENT; REWARD AND PUNISHMENT] is fulfilled against them, we shall bring out from the earth a beast for them, to speak to them because humankind believed not with certainty in our signs." Finally, Gog and Magog are the third of these three apocalyptic signs mentioned in the Qurʾān: When Gog and Magog, the apocalyptic people, "are let loose [from their barrier], and they swoop down from every mound" (Q 21:96), "on that day, we shall leave them to surge like waves on one another, and the trumpet *(al-ṣūr)* will be blown, and we shall collect them [the creatures] all together" (Q 18:99).

Sūra 99, "The Earthquake," describes very well the last events of history: "When the earth is shaken with its [final] earthquake, and when the earth throws out its burdens, and humankind will say: 'What is the matter with it?' That day it will declare its information, because your lord will inspire it. That day people will proceed in scattered groups that they may be shown their deeds (see GOOD DEEDS; EVIL DEEDS; HEAVENLY BOOK). So whoever does good equal to the weight of an atom shall see it, and whoever does evil equal to the weight of an atom shall see it" (Q 99:1-8; see GOOD AND EVIL). Then, it is said, "listen on the day when the caller will call from a near place, the day when they will hear the shout *(al-ṣayḥa)* in truth: that will be the day of coming out [from the graves]" (Q 50:41-2). God will gather people (Q 50:44) together (Q 10:45), the believers and the disbelievers alike (Q 19:85; 20:102; see BELIEF AND UNBELIEF), the jinn (q.v.) and the angels (see ANGEL), for a universal gathering. And it is only on "that day" that "some faces shall be shining and radiant *(nāḍira)* looking *(nāẓira)* at their lord" (Q 75:22-3; see FACE OF GOD).

The qurʾānic arguments in support of the resurrection of the body, and not only the "return" of spiritual souls (*maʿād,* Q 28:85), could be described as follows: the resurrection represents a new creation (q.v.) on the part of the all-powerful God (Q 17:49; 18:48; 21:104; 27:64; 53:47; 29:19; 30:27; 75:40; 86:5-8; see POWER AND IMPOTENCE), a revivification of the soil and its production of vegetables and fruits (Q 6:95; 7:57; 10:31; 30:19; 35:9; 50:11; see AGRICULTURE AND VEGETATION), and includes the reviving of dead people by God, as in the case of the "seven sleepers" (Q 18:9-25; see MEN OF THE CAVE). But two other terms are also important in the Qurʾān. Resurrection is also called the "raising up" (*baʿth,* which occurs fourteen times) of people by God. People are in doubt about "the day of resurrection" (*yawm al-baʿth,* Q 30:56; cf. 16:21; 22:5; 31:28), but "God will raise them up, then to him they will be returned" (Q 6:36; cf. 58:6, 18). Twice in the Qurʾān human life is depicted in three stages (see BIOLOGY AS THE CREATION AND STAGES OF LIFE): "Peace be on him (i.e. John [Yaḥyā]; see JOHN THE BAPTIST) the day he was born, and the day he dies, and the day he will be raised up alive" (Q 19:15) and "Peace be on me (i.e. Jesus) the day I was born, and the day I die, and the day I shall be raised alive" (Q 19:33). And Jesus himself states that "I bring the dead to life by God's leave" (Q 3:49; cf. 5:110; see MIRACLES; MARVELS). So resurrection is also the gift of life (q.v.; *ḥayāt*) because God himself is "the living one, the ever subsistent" (Q 2:255; see GOD AND HIS ATTRIBUTES): "You were dead and he gave you life. Then he will give you death, then again will bring you to life [on the day of resurrection] and then unto him you will return" (Q 2:28; cf. 22:66; 30:40). Many times God is qualified in the Islamic tradition as the "giver of life" *(muḥyī)* and the "giver of death" *(mumīt)* because in the Qurʾān one reads "God makes people live and die" (*Allāhu yuḥyī wa-yumītu,* e.g. Q 3:156; cf. 41:39).

Maurice Borrmans

Bibliography

Primary: Rashīd Riḍā, *Manār;* Rāzī, *Tafsīr.*
Secondary: ʿA.Y. ʿAlī, *The glorious Qurʾān,* Riyadh 1973; Arberry; Arkoun, *Lectures;* R. Eklund, *Life between death and resurrection according to Islam,* Uppsala 1941; D. Galloway, The resurrection and judgement in the Koran, in *MW* 12 (1922), 348-72; L. Gardet, *Dieu et la destinée de l'homme,* Paris 1967, esp. 259-90; D. Masson, *Monothéisme coranique et monothéisme biblique,* Paris 1976, esp. 687-703; T. O'Shaughnessy, *Muhammad's thoughts on death. A thematic study of the qur'anic data,* Leiden 1969; Pickthall, *Koran;* J.I. Smith, *The Islamic understanding of death and resurrection,* Albany 1981.

Retaliation

Act of returning like for like. The Arabic term usually rendered as "retaliation" is *qiṣāṣ*, although *qiṣāṣ* also means punishment for a wrongful act (see CHASTISEMENT AND PUNISHMENT; EVIL DEEDS). The Qurʾān mentions *qiṣāṣ* on several occasions, mostly in the sense of punishment for murder (q.v.) or physical injury and once in the sense of retaliation or reprisal for a wrongful act. In Sūrat al-Baqara (Q 2, "The Cow") the Qurʾān affirms the pre-Islamic practice of considering certain months (q.v.) in the year to be sanctified (see PROFANE AND SACRED) and, therefore, of prohibiting warfare (see WAR; FIGHTING) and the shedding of blood for the duration of these months (see BLOODSHED). The Qurʾān, however, states that *qiṣāṣ*, in the sense of retaliation or reprisal, is permitted during these months if the Muslims are attacked first. Although, according to the Qurʾān, these months are sanctified, Muslims may respond in kind if attacked (Q 2:194). Earlier in the same sūra, the Qurʾān uses the word *qiṣāṣ* in the sense of punishment or retaliation, but in a very different context. Addressing the case of murder, the Qurʾān prescribes proportionality between the crime and the punishment (Q 2:178). Muslim scholars took this to mean that the pre-Islamic practice of tribal feuding and disproportionate retaliation for the killing of noblemen or tribal chiefs was abrogated (Jaṣṣāṣ, *Aḥkām*, i, 164; Ibn al-ʿArabī, *Aḥkām*, i, 89-100; ii, 128). The Qurʾān mandates that no more than a single life be taken for another, but it also urges the next of kin (see KINSHIP) to show forgiveness (q.v.) towards the offender by dropping the demand for retaliation. Instead, the next of kin may accept compensation, which according to the Qurʾān must be paid promptly and with gratitude (see BLOOD MONEY; GRATITUDE AND INGRATITUDE). The Qurʾān also asserts a general principle, namely that the implementation of the rule of *qiṣāṣ* would preserve and protect life (Q 2:179). The meaning and import of this assertion has been the subject of a wide debate among Qurʾān commentators. Some argued that the Qurʾān meant to affirm the importance of proportionality between the crime and punishment (see JUSTICE AND INJUSTICE), while others, especially modern commentators, argued that the Qurʾān meant to emphasize that a strict penal law helps emphasize the value of life and protect the interests of society (Quṭb, *Ẓilāl*, ii, 162-77; Ṭabarī, *Tafsīr*, ii, 102-15; see LAW AND THE QURʾĀN; EXEGESIS OF THE QURʾĀN: EARLY MODERN AND CONTEMPORARY). In a different sūra, the Qurʾān references *qiṣāṣ* as punishment for intentional physical injuries. The Qurʾān states that God had prescribed for the Israelites that a life is for a life, an eye is for an eye and a tooth is for a tooth and that there should be an equal punishment for all injuries (see LIFE; EYES; TEETH). The Qurʾān goes on to say that whoever forgives and does not demand an exact punishment will be rewarded by God (Q 5:45; see REWARD AND PUNISHMENT).

Relying, in part, on these qurʾānic verses, pre-modern jurists developed a law of talion that, in significant respects, was similar to the rules of *lex talionis* in Roman law and the rules prevalent in Germanic and Anglo-Saxon law as well as other ancient legal systems. According to the rules developed by pre-modern Muslim jurists, there were three possible responses to physical injuries: *qiṣāṣ* (punishment or talion), *diya* (a prescribed blood money amount or wergild paid in compensation for a wrongful death or certain other physical injuries), or forgiveness. *Qiṣāṣ* was possible only in intentional and quasi-intentional killings and physical injuries (quasi-intentional killings would be akin today to manslaughter and other recklessly induced offenses). The Ḥanafī, Mālikī, and Shāfiʿī schools of law held that in the case of intentional homicide or injury the remedy is *qiṣāṣ* — *diya* is not a co-equal alternative. Consequently, if the heirs of a victim forgive the offender, an automatic right to *diya* does not arise. Nevertheless, *diya* could be payable through a settlement *(ṣulḥ)* pursuant to which the offender agrees to pay an amount that may be more or less than the specified *diya*. Schools that considered *diya* to be a co-equal alternative to *qiṣāṣ* did not require the offender's consent to paying the *diya;* the choice was entirely that of the victim or the heirs. In effect, according to the first approach, if an intentional or quasi-intentional offense takes place, the victim or his family have one of three choices: (1) demand exaction; (2) reach an agreement with the offender on the amount to be paid, which could be more or less than the legal *diya;* or (3) forgiveness. According to the second school, the victim or relative can demand exaction, the specified amount of the *diya* or forgive. In deliberate injuries, however, a particularly heavy *diya* is prescribed *(diya mughallaẓa)*. *Qiṣāṣ* being applicable only in intentional and quasi-intentional offenses, in the case of accidental injuries, *diya* is the only legal remedy. Even in intentional offenses, however, *diya* might become the only legal recourse if certain legal deficiencies preclude the application of talion. For example, if talion cannot be enforced because strict equality is not achievable, the only option other than an outright pardon is the right to full or partial *diya*. Accordingly, no talion is admitted in the case of fractured bones or if experts testify, in a case not involving murder, that talion is likely to endanger the life of the offender. Furthermore, a right to *diya* is the only recourse if talion is not possible because of certain evidentiary deficiencies. Whether a rule of strict liability or negligence applies to accidental torts is a debated issue. Furthermore, Muslim jurists disagreed on whether in the case of dangerous crimes the state possesses a separate right to punish the offender, regardless of what the victim or heirs decide to do (Ibn Rushd, *Distinguished,* ii, 479-514; Bājī, *Muntaqā,* ix, 3-128; ʿĀmilī, *Lumʿa,* x, 11-320; Shirbīnī, *Mughnī,* iv, 20-138; Kāsānī, *Badāʾiʿ,* vi, 272-414).

Khaled Abou El Fadl

Bibliography
al-ʿĀmilī, Muḥammad Jamāl al-Dīn Makkī, *al-Lumʿa al-dimashqiyya,* Qom n.d.; al-Bājī, Abū l-Walīd Sulaymān b. Khalaf b. Saʿd b. Ayyūb, *Muntaqā sharḥ Muwaṭṭaʾ Mālik,* 9 vols., Beirut 1999; Ibn al-ʿArabī, *Aḥkām,* 4 vols., Beirut n.d.; Ibn Rushd, Abū l-Walīd b. Aḥmad, *The distinguished jurist's primer: Bidāyat al-mujtahid,* trans. I.A. Khan Nyazee, 2 vols., Doha 1994-6, Reading, UK 1996; Jaṣṣāṣ, *Aḥkām,* 4 vols., Beirut n.d.; al-Kāsānī, ʿAlāʾ al-Dīn Abū Bakr b. Masʿūd, *Badāʾiʿ al-ṣanāʾiʿ fī tartīb al-sharāʾiʿ,* 6 vols., Beirut 1998; Quṭb, *Ẓilāl,* Beirut 1977; al-Shirbīnī, Shams al-Dīn Muḥammad b. al-Khaṭīb, *Mughnī l-muḥtāj ilā maʿrifat maʿānī alfāẓ al-Minhāj,* Beirut 1997; Ṭabarī, *Tafsīr.*

Retribution see REWARD AND PUNISHMENT; RETALIATION

Revelation and Inspiration

The communication of God's knowledge (see KNOWLEDGE AND LEARNING) and will (see POWER AND IMPOTENCE), warning (q.v.) and promise to humanity. The English word "revelation" covers a range of qurʾānic terms, principal among them *waḥy,* "communication" and *tanzīl,* "sending down," with their cognate verbal forms. In the Qurʾān revelation is always mediated, rather than being direct: first, in the sense that it consists in the transmission of a message rather than the "unveiling" of God himself implied by the English word with its Christian origins and, secondly, because even that message is considered to have been delivered by an intermediary, generally identified as Gabriel (q.v.; Jibrīl). The concept of revelation is central to the nature of the Qurʾān. The Qurʾān itself, however, recognizes the phenomenon as extending beyond prophecy (see PROPHETS AND PROPHETHOOD) and scripture (see BOOK).

Revelation before and beyond scripture

One of the Qurʾān's most insistent claims is that God is constantly offering "signs" (q.v.; *āya,* pl. *āyāt*) that manifest all we need to know. The *āyāt* that constitute God's revelation exist in nature (see NATURE AS SIGNS) and in time (q.v.) before they come to the people as verses (q.v.; also *āyāt*) of scripture. Indeed, the role of the prophetic scriptures is to call people back to the acknowledgment of a truth (q.v.) already expressed in the signs of nature and in the history of God's dealings with humanity (see HISTORY AND THE QURʾĀN). It could be said that there is no essential difference between the verses and the natural or historical signs: all are there to be comprehended by anyone who has the intelligence (q.v.; *ʿaql*) to reflect on them, to acknowledge their truth *(taṣdīq)* and to respond with faithful submission (*īmān, islām;* see FAITH; BELIEF AND UNBELIEF; ISLAM). Many such passages in the Qurʾān cite natural phenomena as symbols pointing to the creator (see CREATION; AGRICULTURE AND VEGETATION). Among the more important are Q 2:164; 3:190-1; 6:95-9; 10:5-7; 13:2-4; 16:10-6, 78-81; 23:21-2; 26:7-8; 27:86, 93; 29:44; 30:20-8, 46; 32:27; 34:9; 36:33-47, 39:21; 41:37, 39, 53; 42:29-34; 45:1-6, 12-13; 50:6-11; 51:20.

Historical events, too, are among the "signs" of God. The fate of nations that have passed away (*umam qad khalat,* Q 7:38; 46:18; cf. 13:30; 41:25; see GEOGRAPHY; PUNISHMENT STORIES; GENERATIONS) is a warning to people that they should take seriously the message of the Prophet (Q 12:109; 14:13; 23:23-30; 31:31-2; 32:26; 36:13-31; 46:27). In these cases the Qurʾān is not revealing something not already known to everybody; rather, it is pointing to these facts of history as revealing the ways of God and the reality of God's threatened judgment (see LAST JUDGMENT; JUSTICE AND INJUSTICE). On other occasions the revelation consists in God's communicating "tidings of the unseen" (*anbāʾ al-ghayb,* Q 3:44; 11:49; 12:102; see HIDDEN AND THE HIDDEN), details of prophetic history that neither Muḥammad nor his people would otherwise have known.

Scriptural revelation prior to the Qurʾān

In the Qurʾān it is axiomatic that the present revelation contains fundamentally the same message as that given to earlier messengers (see MESSENGER). The believers are expected to accept the revelations given before Muḥammad (Q 2:4, 136; 4:60, 162) since God communicated with those messengers as he has done with Muḥammad: "We revealed to you *(awḥaynā ilayka)* as we revealed to Noah (q.v.) and the prophets after him, and as we revealed to Abraham (q.v.) and Ishmael (q.v.) and Isaac (q.v.) and Jacob (q.v.) and the tribes (see CHILDREN OF ISRAEL), and Jesus (q.v.) and Job (q.v.) and Jonah (q.v.) and Aaron (q.v.) and Solomon (q.v.), and as we granted David (q.v.) the Psalms" (q.v.; Q 4:163); "Say, we believe in God and what has been sent down to us and in what was sent down to Abraham, and Ishmael, and Isaac, and Jacob, and the tribes, and in what Moses (q.v.) and Jesus were given, and in what the prophets were given by their lord (q.v.) — we make no distinction between any of them — and to him do we submit"(Q 2:136). The term that binds together these diverse manifestations of revelation is *kitāb* (pl. *kutub*), "scripture":

"O you who believe, believe in God and his messenger and the *kitāb* that he has sent down to his messenger, and the *kitāb* that he sent down before. Whoever disbelieves in God and his angels (see ANGEL) and his *kutub* and his messengers and the last day has already gone far astray" (q.v.; Q 4:136; see also ERROR).

The Qurʾān sees itself as confirming *(muṣaddiq)* the previous revelations (Q 2:41, 89, 91, 97, 101; 3:3, 39, 81; 4:47; 5:48; 6:92; 10:37; 12:111; 35:31; 46:12, 30) in the same way as Jesus came to confirm the Torah (q.v.; Q 3:50; 5:46; 61:6). This raises a difficulty for the notion of verbal inspiration since the actual text of the Qurʾān is not identical to those of the other extant scriptures (see also GOSPEL; SCRIPTURE AND THE QURʾĀN).

Waḥy

The term *waḥy* occurs in Arabic before the rise of Islam (see PRE-ISLAMIC ARABIA AND THE QURʾĀN). In pre-Islamic poetry (see POETRY AND POETS) the word is occasionally used to refer to writing or scriptures (usually with the connotation of the indistinctness of age and foreignness) but more often to describe the message that can be discerned from the traces of an abandoned campsite or the ruins of a habitation (for example, the beginning of Labīd's *Muʿallaqa: kamā ḍamina l-waḥyu silāmuhā,* "as though its rocks contained the message"). Still other uses by the same poets show that the term *waḥy* is equally applicable to communication by sound or gesture. For example, one of the odes of ʿAlqama uses the verbal form *yūḥī* to describe the "speech" of a male ostrich to his nestlings: "He communicates *(yūḥī)* with them in squeaking and clacking sounds, just as the Greeks in their castles speak to each other in an incomprehensible language" (Ahlwardt, *Divans,* 112, v 26). In the poems of the Hudhayl tribe the noun *waḥy* refers to thunder, and the cognate verb *awḥā* is used for the screeching of an eagle (Lewin, *Vocabulary,* 465; for more examples see Izutsu, *God,* 159-60).

Some western scholars have often wanted to see in the term *waḥy* a connection with writing (for example Goldziher, *MS,* ii, 7 and Nöldeke, *GQ,* ii, 1; see ORALITY AND WRITING IN ARABIA). The evidence, however, is far from convincing. Indeed, as will be seen, Muslim tradition has overwhelmingly described the phenomenon of revelation as auditory (even though sometimes accompanied by visions, for example, in the Qurʾān itself: Q 53:4-18; see ORALITY; VISIONS) and very often lacking verbal clarity. Furthermore, the poets' usage of *waḥy* emphasized indistinctness rather than clarity appropriate to a text that declares itself to be in the clear language of the Arabs (q.v.; *lisān ʿarab mubīn,* Q 16:103; 26:195; see also ARABIC LANGUAGE).

In the Qurʾān itself, while *waḥy* is clearly marked as a religious term, three instances of its use remind us that it has a non-religious basis and is not solely a divine activity: Zechariah (q.v.) after being struck dumb gestured *(awḥā)* to his companions that they should give praise (q.v.) to God (Q 19:11; see also Q 3:41, where it is said that Zechariah was only able to communicate *ramzan,* "using signs"); and twice the same verb is used to describe the communication that takes place among the demons (*shayāṭīn,* Q 6:112, 121; see DEVIL; JINN). When the verb is used of divine activity, it most often refers to God's communication with his messengers. Others with whom God communicates are Jesus' disciples (Q 5:111; see APOSTLE), the angels (Q 8:12), Moses' mother (Q 20:38; 28:7) Isaac and Jacob (Q 21:72-3) and Noah (Q 23:27). This verb is also used for God's communication with the bee (Q 16:68), the heavens (Q 41:12; see HEAVEN AND SKY; ANIMAL LIFE) and the earth (q.v.; Q 99:5).

It should be noted that *waḥy,* even when addressed to prophets and messengers, is not by any means confined to the revelation of a scriptural text. Out of the seventy-one occurrences of *awḥā,* only three times each are *kitāb* and *qurʾān* the direct object (or the subject of a passive form). The verb *awḥā* is often used without a direct object: a process of communication takes place but what is communicated is left unstated. At the same time, however, the communication is not devoid of content. In many cases the end result is a concrete instruction to be followed, for example, in God's direction of the prophetic career of Moses (Q 7:117, 160; 10:87; 20:48; 20:77; 26:52, 63; see COMMANDMENTS; BOUNDARIES AND PRECEPTS). On other occasions it is doctrinal content (see CREED; THEOLOGY AND THE QURʾĀN): "Say, 'I am only human like you (see IMPECCABILITY). It is revealed *(yūḥā)* to me that your God is only one God. And whoever there may be who looks forward to the encounter with his lord, let him do good work (see GOOD DEEDS) and associate no one else with his lord in worship" (q.v.; Q 18:110; see POLYTHEISM AND ATHEISM; IDOLATRY AND IDOLATERS).

Izutsu (*God,* 180) and Jeffery (Qurʾān, 190-2) both suggest a development of the idea of *waḥy* in the Qurʾān, from an earlier usage suggesting a general inspiration to say or do something, towards a more technical usage where the term applies very specifically to the verbatim revelation of scripture. There may be some truth to this, but it must also be noted that some of the non-scriptural uses occur in what are generally agreed to be late Medinan sūras (for example Q 5:111; 8:12; see CHRONOLOGY AND THE QURʾĀN).

In the interpretation of *waḥy,* Muslim tradition has guarded the distance between the divine and the human. There are, however, some important indications in the text of a more direct communication. In Q 4:164 it is emphatically stated that God spoke to Moses directly *(wa-kallama llāhu Mūsā taklīman),* though some commentators read the accusative *Allāha,* indicating rather that Moses spoke to God directly. Without mentioning the case of Moses, Q 42:51 outlines three exceptions to the general rule that God does not address people: "It is not granted to any mortal that God should address him *(yukallimahu)* except by *waḥy,* or from behind a veil (q.v.), or that he send a messenger who reveals *(yūḥī)* with his permission what he wills. Surely he is exalted, wise." There seems a clear enough distinction between the first exception and the third: in one case the connection is more direct; in the other, God uses an intermediary. In both cases, however, there is revelatory communication. The verse indicates that the Qurʾān envisages a process of revelation that does not involve an angelic go-between. Perhaps the distinction between direct address *(taklīm)* and the kind of communication that took place with the prophets may be found in pre-Islamic usage of the type already alluded to. A common thread of mysteriousness and indecipherability runs through those uses of *waḥy* and *awḥā.* Often a sense of distance, absence and antiquity are implied. Even when the communication is immediate, however, without an angelic intermediary, it is still incomprehensible to the third-person observer. Recall the poet ʿAlqama's clacking ostrich and incomprehensible Greeks.

Waḥy, then, does not seem to be the simple and unambiguous direct address that Wansbrough takes it to be (*QS,* 34-6), though he is surely right to insist on a measure of demystification (see POST-ENLIGHTENMENT ACADEMIC STUDY OF THE QURʾĀN). Nor does *waḥy* have any necessary connection with written communication as many others have suggested. It indicates a kind of communication that appears impenetrable and perhaps exotic to a third person observing it, yet remains full of meaning for the one receiving it. Given the range of its use, it seems possible, perhaps even preferable, to translate *waḥy* simply as "communication," understanding that it normally refers to divine communication.

The experience of revelation: For the Prophet

The Qurʾān itself tells us little, if anything, about the experience of revelation. The exegetical and historical traditions, on the other hand, have dwelt on the subject in detail, expanding on various suggestive verses of the Qurʾān to piece together a coherent account (see SĪRA AND THE QURʾĀN). The time leading up to the initial experience of revelation for Muḥammad was, according to Muslim tradition, characterized by vivid dreams and portents (Ibn Isḥāq, *Sīra,* 151; Ṭabarī, *Taʾrīkh,* i, 1143-6; id., *History,* vi, 63-7). When the revelation actually begins, one finds a certain vagueness in the tradition about whether the Prophet initially encounters God (as seems to be suggested by Q 53:1-18; see also Ibn Isḥāq, *Sīra,* 150; trans. Ibn Isḥāq-Guillaume, 104-5; Ṭabarī, *Taʾrīkh,* i, 1147; trans. Watt/McDonald, *History,* vi, 67-8, where it is said *al-ḥaqq,* one of the names of God, came to him; see GOD AND HIS ATTRIBUTES) or whether his dealings with the divine are always through the medium of Gabriel. The consensus of the tradition has it that the first words of the Qurʾān to be revealed were the beginnings of sūra 96, when Gabriel came bringing a cloth on which was embroidered the text to be recited. Three times the messenger tells Muḥammad to recite and he answers that he is unable, until finally Gabriel teaches him what to recite, and the words remain with him.

The encounter was physically violent and terrifying to Muḥammad. His reaction of hiding in fear then gave rise to his being addressed by the revelatory voice in Q 74:1 f. (or perhaps Q 73:1 f.). According to some versions, Gabriel first identifies himself and announces Muḥammad's role as messenger before beginning the recitation. In others, it is not until later that the origin and meaning of this terrifying experience is made clear (Ṭabarī, *Taʾrīkh,* i, 1147-50; trans. Watt/McDonald, *History,* vi, 67-72). Commentators distinguish three stages in the life of Muḥammad: *nubuwwa, risāla* and *waḥy* — being a prophet, receiving the commission as a messenger and beginning to receive the revelation he is to pass on. In almost all these accounts there is mention of the Prophet's considering or even attempting suicide (q.v.), either because he thinks he has become a poet or a madman (see INSANITY), or because after the initial encounters the revelations are discontinued (the so-called *fatra*) and he is tempted to think God has rejected him.

The continuing revelations are also depicted in the tradition as often being accompanied by physical effects: a loud ringing sound as of a bell or chain, sweating, pain, fainting, lethargy or trance, turning pale, turning red, becoming physically heavier — perhaps the result of a too literal reading of *qawlan thaqīlan,* "a weighty word," in Q 73:5 (for a listing of traditions referring to these phenomena, see Wensinck/Rippin, Waḥy, 55). It is said in some traditions that the shekhinah (q.v.; *sakīna*) descends upon him in these moments (Fahd, Kāhin, 889).

The Qurʾān itself refers to *waḥy* as sometimes being accompanied by visions. The experience is portrayed as a kind of teaching:

It is nothing other than a revelation *(waḥy)*
that is revealed *(yūḥā)*
One of mighty powers has taught him

one who is vigorous; and he grew clear to view
when he was on the highest horizon
(Q 53:4-7; see also Q 81:23-4).

According to al-Ghazālī (d. 505/1111), one of the differences between the inspiration *(ilhām)* brought by an angel to a mystic (see SAINT; ṢUFISM AND THE QURʾĀN) and the revelation brought to a prophet is that the prophet actually sees the angel (van Ess, *TG*, iv, 621). Al-Bukhārī (d. 256/870; *Ṣaḥīḥ*, iii, 391-2, *Kitāb Faḍāʾil al-Qurʾān, bāb* 1), however, records a tradition to the effect that the angel was also visible on one occasion to Umm Salama, even if Gabriel was not visible to Khadīja (q.v.; Ibn Isḥāq, *Sīra*, 154; see also WIVES OF THE PROPHET).

The experience of revelation: For the people

Apart from the physical effects listed above that the people observed when the Prophet received revelation, there are three important elements to be noted about the people's experience of revelation.

In the first place, the revelation is responsive to the situation in which people find themselves. It does not present itself as a prefabricated text related only in the most general way to the present moment. It is experienced as a living voice, ever on the point of intervening in order to resolve disputes, to clarify issues, to call to faith and to command action. The recurrent pattern "They say x; Say to them y" represents this interactive aspect of the revelation (see for example Q 3:119, 154; 56:47-9; 64:7; 67:25-6). The position of the interlocutors is stated ("they say ..."), followed by the response God wishes the Prophet to deliver (often preceded by the command *qul*, "Say! ..."). Some Companion ḥadīth (see COMPANIONS OF THE PROPHET; ḤADĪTH AND THE QURʾĀN) indicate that it was not uncommon for a qurʾānic verse to be revealed in the middle of a dispute among them or in the Prophet's family (see, for example, Ibn Isḥāq, *Sīra*, 735-6; see FAMILY OF THE PROPHET; PEOPLE OF THE HOUSE).

The second aspect of the hearers' experience is that the words are authoritative. The authority (q.v.) of the Prophet rests on the authority of the word he speaks (see SPEECH). Although there are, in the prophetic biography *(sīra)*, accounts of miracles (q.v.) performed by Muḥammad, the Muslim community has had an ambivalent attitude toward them. They are often seen as either unfounded reports or, if true, extraneous to the essence of his prophecy. The encounter with the revelation elicits faith not because the authority of the Prophet has already been established by some other means, but because of the power of the word itself. The attesting miracle of the Prophet is understood to be nothing other than the Qurʾān (see INIMITABILITY; NAMES OF THE QURʾĀN).

One facet of the word's power, and the third important aspect of the hearers' experience, was its aesthetic force, its sheer beauty. The inimitability *(iʿjāz)* of the Qurʾān has not only an important apologetic role in the Islamic tradition but it signals, as Navid Kermani (Revelation, 223-4; cf. id., *Gott ist schön*) has pointed out, an essential aspect of the Muslim experience of revelation, in the beginning and even now. The sensual nature of this aesthetic dimension is often undervalued because of the more intellectual approach taken to it in apologetics (see RHETORIC AND THE QURʾĀN; FORM AND STRUCTURE OF THE QURʾĀN; LITERARY STRUCTURES OF THE QURʾĀN; NARRATIVES). It remains, however, an ambiguous element. The Qurʾān's repeated insistence (e.g. Q 15:6-7; 21:5; 26:224; 36:69; 37:36; 44:14; 52:29, 30; 68:2, 51; 69:41, 42; 81:22) that the Prophet is neither a possessed poet nor a diviner (see DIVINATION; FORETELLING; SOOTH-

SAYERS) — as well as the *Sīra*'s reference to his considering suicide because he thought he might have become such — indicates that the impression made on the hearers was plausibly comparable to that made by a poet or soothsayer possessed by a spirit.

Yet it is primarily the source of the words, and only to a much lesser extent their literary style (see LANGUAGE AND STYLE OF THE QURʾĀN), that makes the difference between the poet, the soothsayer and the prophet. All are, in a certain sense, visionaries, conveying knowledge of the unseen world *(al-ghayb)*. Indeed, Ibn Khaldūn (d. 780/1379) posits a continuum in the preparedness of human beings to receive heavenly perceptions; the prophets are merely at the highest grade in this respect, but soothsayers, too, receive some genuine though incomplete spiritual perception (Ibn Khaldūn-Rosenthal, i, 207-8). Yet the source for the soothsayer is the *shayāṭīn* or the jinn, while the source for the prophet's knowledge is God. The poets and those who dismiss the Qurʾān as being no more than poetry, soothsaying or invention (see LIE) are challenged repeatedly (Q 2:23; 10:38; 11:13; 17:88; 52:34) to bring something equal to it (see PROVOCATION). The challenge is predominantly interpreted by the tradition in aesthetic terms: there can be no text more eloquent and more beautiful than the Qurʾān (see LITERATURE AND THE QURʾĀN).

The process of revelation: tanzīl

The process of revelation is most commonly characterized by the spatial metaphor of "coming down, sending down" — derivatives of the verbal root *n-z-l*. The causative verb forms *nazzala* (sixty-three finite verbal occurrences, fifteen uses of the *maṣdar*, and two of the participle) and *anzala* (188 finite verbal occurrences, no uses of the *maṣdar*, and seven of the participle) are generally considered to be similar in meaning, "to send down." Although by far the majority of uses of verbs from the root *n-z-l* deal with revelation, there are other objects as well: e.g. mountains (Q 24:43), various kinds of rain (Q 30:49; 31:34; 42:28), manna and quails (Q 2:57; 7:160; 20:80), armies (Q 9:26), and *al-furqān* (Q 2:185; 3:4; 25:1; see PROOF; CRITERION) the meaning of which seems to bear elements of salvation (q.v.) as well as revelation.

In one sense, the notion of sending down itself could be said to be theologically neutral since it is merely spatial. This spatiality implies, however, the theological premise of a two-tiered universe in which the initiative is always in the upper (divine, celestial) tier. Furthermore, the verbal noun *tanzīl* standing by itself (e.g. Q 36:5; 41:2, 42; 56:80; 69:43) is only used to refer to revelation. The activity of sending down is exclusively divine. Humans or angels may bring *(atā bi-)* or recount *(qaṣṣa)* the word of God but only God can send it down.

Although the direction of communication is always downward, tradition has also sought in its development of the story of Muḥammad's ascent to heaven (see ASCENSION) to establish a special prophetic access in the opposite direction. In addition, the first revelations are portrayed as taking place in a cave on Mount Ḥirāʾ to which the Prophet had ascended — in Islamic tradition, no less than in the Jewish and Christian traditions (see JEWS AND JUDAISM; CHRISTIANS AND CHRISTIANITY), the mountaintop enjoys a privileged proximity to heaven.

The mode of sending down scripture is made clear repeatedly. It is oral, in the form of a recitation *(qurʾānan)*; the idea of sending something down in writing is rejected as unlikely to prove convincing (Q 6:7; 4:153). What is sent down is in the vernacular (*ʿarabī*, Q 12:2; 16:103; 20:113;

39:28; 41:3, 44; 42:7; 43:3; see DIALECTS), rather than in a foreign or sacral language (*aʿjamī*, Q 16:103; 41:44; but see FOREIGN VOCABULARY). God never sends a messenger except to speak in the language of the people he is addressing (Q 14:4). The sending down comes gradually (*mufarraqan*, Q 17:106) or, as the commentators say, *munajjaman*, or *najūman* (Suyūṭī, *Itqān*, i, 116-9: *nawʿ* 16, *Fī kayfiyyat inzālihi, masʾala* 1); it comes in response to situations (Q 25:33), rather than as a single, completed pronouncement (*jumlatan wāḥidatan*, Q 25:32).

The difficulty presented by the fact that the Qurʾān was not revealed all at once in an already fixed form is answered in the tradition by patching together, in varying ways, isolated parts of the text in order to outline a coherent schema that could reconcile a preexistent canon with what was clearly an *ad rem* mode of revelation (see COLLECTION OF THE QURʾĀN; CODICES OF THE QURʾĀN). The Qurʾān is presented as already complete in the realm of eternity; the text is preserved on a heavenly tablet (Q 85:22; see HEAVENLY BOOK; PRESERVED TABLET), from which it is sent down whole to "noble scribes" (*safara kirām*, Q 80:15-6) or to the "abode of glory" (*bayt al-ʿizza*, an idea attributed to Ibn ʿAbbās by, among others, Suyūṭī, *Itqān*, i, 116-9: *nawʿ* 16, *masʾala* 1) in the lowest heaven, then transmitted to Gabriel, who in turn parcels it out to Muḥammad according to the situation in which he finds himself (see OCCASIONS OF REVELATION).

The Islamic tradition, in developing its ever more elaborate "topology" of revelation, is certainly careful to maintain the distance between God and humanity (see ANTHROPOMORPHISM). Nevertheless, even if the divine essence remains inaccessible, a genuine unveiling of God's knowledge and manifestation of God's will does take place.

The "occasions" of revelation

The apparently one-directional nature of *tanzīl* is qualified in the exegetical tradition by the notion that each part of the Qurʾān was revealed in a particular context in response to a particular situation. This particularity and contextuality is evident in many parts of the text itself. The term used is *sabab* (pl. *asbāb*), which carries an idea of causality that is somewhat veiled by the usual translation "occasion." Al-Suyūṭī (d. 911/1505; *Itqān*, i, 82-98: *nawʿ* 9, *Maʿrifat sabab al-nuzūl*) quotes Ibn Taymiyya (d. 728/1328): "Knowing the reason for the sending down helps in the understanding of the verse. For knowledge of the cause (*sabab*) yields knowledge of the effect (*musabbab*)."

Because they offer a coherent historical context for individual verses or pericopes and because, taken together, they create a narrative structure for the Qurʾān, the *asbāb al-nuzūl* are among the principal traditional tools of interpretation (see TRADITIONAL DISCIPLINES OF QURʾĀNIC STUDY). The importance of the *asbāb* for exegesis is the recognition of the responsive nature of the revelation that we have already observed. The commentators can, of course, maintain that it is not the verse itself that is occasioned or caused but rather the sending down of that verse, which itself remains preexistent (see ETERNITY; CREATEDNESS OF THE QURʾĀN). Even so, they are still implicitly recognizing that the process of revelation is a divine response elicited by human word and action.

The importance of this dynamic aspect of qurʾānic revelation is not to be underestimated. It is an essential counterbalance to an approach that privileges the idea of an impassive, static pronouncement fixed from all eternity. The God who speaks in the Qurʾān is also described many times as *baṣīr*, *samīʿ* and *ʿalīm* — one who sees and hears and therefore knows the present situation he is addressing (see SEEING AND HEARING).

The role of Gabriel

The Muslim tradition has tended to emphasize those parts of the Qurʾān that suggest that revelation is mediated through Gabriel. The Qurʾān itself does not call Gabriel an angel, though in the tradition there seems to be a conflation of God's spirit (q.v.), the angels and Gabriel. It is explicitly stated in Q 2:97 that it is Gabriel (Jibrīl) who, by God's leave, brings the revelation down upon Muḥammad's heart (q.v.). In an earlier Meccan sūra (Q 53:1-18), however, the most straightforward reading indicates a vision of God (see FACE OF GOD). Muḥammad is described in Q 53:10 as the slave (*ʿabd;* see SERVANT) of the one he sees — a word that could hardly be applied to his relationship with Gabriel: "He revealed to his slave what he revealed."

The biographical tradition, too, shifts between involving Gabriel and speaking as though the revelation were direct. We might deduce from this that the angel plays what we could call the role of a theological safeguard. If the Prophet has dealings only with Gabriel and not with God directly, the absolute transcendence and immateriality of God is safeguarded. Once the point is made, and the theological caveat entered, however, there is little real need to concentrate further on the angel. One finds a similar phenomenon with the role of God's messengers in the Hebrew Bible, for example in the accounts of Moses and the burning bush (*Exod* 3:2-4:17); of Hagar and Ishmael (*Gen* 16:7-14; 21:17-9); of Abraham and his guests (*Gen* 18-19); of Abraham's binding of Isaac (*Gen* 22:11-2); of Jacob (*Gen* 31:11-3; 32:24-30); and of Balaam (*Num* 22-4).

Yet, even though the angel can be understood as in some way bridging the ontological gap between the divine and the human, as Ibn Khaldūn pointed out, there is still a gap between the angelic and the human. The prophet must leave his own state and enter the state of the angels, the highest level of spiritual existence (Ibn Khaldūn-Rosenthal, i, 208). This explains the difficulty prophets experience in the moment of revelation (ibid., i, 201). Ibn Khaldūn's analysis of the phenomenon of prophetic perception reflects the ambiguity of the angelic role. He leaves unresolved the issue of whether angelic agency is necessary to prophecy or whether, when prophets enter the angelic realm, they are just as able as the angels to understand the speech of God. He speaks of it as the realm of direct perception (ibid., ii, 423-4).

Al-Samarqandī (d. 375/985) is reported as saying that there are three opinions about the role of Gabriel in the revelation of the Qurʾān: (1) that he brought both word and meaning *(al-lafẓ wa-l-maʿnā),* having memorized the wording from the Preserved Tablet (q.v.; Q 85:22); (2) that Gabriel brought the meanings *(maʿānī)* and the Prophet expressed *(ʿabbara)* them in Arabic; (3) that it was Gabriel who expressed the message in Arabic — that is how it is recited in heaven — then later brought it in that form to the Prophet (Zarkashī, *Burhān,* i, 228-32: *nawʿ* 12, *Fī kayfiyyat inzālihi*). Some authors would distinguish the second form as being characteristic of the revelation of the sunna (q.v.) rather than the Qurʾān, since the sunna is sometimes thought of as revealed. Whether or not that is accepted, the role of Gabriel has some considerable bearing on the question of verbal inspiration.

Verbal inspiration

The verbal inspiration of the Qurʾān is accepted as virtually axiomatic by the greater part of the Islamic tradition, though the doctrine is recognized even within that tradition as not being without its difficulties. The Qurʾān itself offers no simple answer to the question of the precise relationship between its text and the eternal word of God (q.v.), although some verses have been taken to argue for their being identical. Several times the scripture is announced as a revelation *(tanzīl)* or a revelation of the scripture *(tanzīl al-kitāb)* from God under various of the divine names (e.g. Q 17:106; 20:4; 26:192; 32:2; 39:1; 40:2; 41:2, 42; 45:2; 46:2; 56:80; 69:43; 76:23). In Q 9:6 the Prophet is told to give refuge to any idolater who asks for it "so that he might hear the speech of God *(kalām Allāh)*." Since there is no qualification of this, it seemed to many commentators to offer proof that the Qurʾān is simply equivalent to God's speech. Further support is sought in Q 75:16-8, in which the Prophet is told not to rush ahead of the recitation but to follow it precisely as God recites it.

The reservations about verbal inspiration were based on several factors. There was in the first place the widespread, though not universal, hesitancy about anthropomorphism or anything that blurs the distinction between the divine and the created realms. For God to have produced the actual wording of the scripture would involve him in the use of human language with its sounds, script and grammar, all of which are clearly created (see ARABIC SCRIPT; GRAMMAR AND THE QURʾĀN; ORTHOGRAPHY). Secondly, in the religiously plural context in which the Muslim community lived (see RELIGIOUS PLURALISM AND THE QURʾĀN; COMMUNITY AND SOCIETY IN THE QURʾĀN), it had to be recognized that the other scriptures are not textually identical to the Qurʾān, even though in principle the import of the message should be identical. This led to such distinctions as that made by Ibn Kullāb (d. 241/855?) between *qirāʾa* — the recited wording, which is a material human action — and *maqrūʾ* — what is recited, i.e. what God intends to convey by it (van Ess, *TG*, iv, 615-6; see RECITATION OF THE QURʾĀN). Furthermore, it could not be ignored that there were at least seven recognized readings of the Qurʾān (q.v.) and strong opposition to the idea of canonizing any one of them absolutely. If only the unpointed consonants *(rasm)* were canonized, the way remained open to multiple pronunciations, and therefore multiple versions, based upon it.

For the Muʿtazilīs (q.v.), what we have on earth is never the word of God itself but rather an account or report *(ḥikāya)* of what God said, a kind of indirect speech. The speech of God is created in a physical substrate — for example, the burning bush associated with Moses (cf. Q 28:30). Even in Gabriel it is created. Ibn Kullāb preferred the term *ʿibāra* to the suspect notion of *ḥikāya,* but in the final analysis there was little difference between his and the Muʿtazilī position on this point. Van Ess (*TG,* iv, 622) notes that even the custom of quoting the Qurʾān with the introductory words *qāla llāhu,* "God says," was not always allowed to pass unchallenged for its presumption of identity between the words of the Qurʾān and the word of God.

It should be noted that the belief in the verbal inspiration of the Qurʾān does not necessarily entail a belief in its uncreated nature, as the Muʿtazilīs seemed to fear. It is possible for God to determine the precise wording of the Qurʾān even while knowing the inability of human language fully to express and convey divine thought.

The complexity of the understanding of revelation in the tradition

It is beyond the scope of this article to deal systematically with the doctrines of revelation that developed in the Islamic community over the centuries. Some comments, however, are in order. The discussions of revelation by theologians, commentators and philosophers seem often to conflict (see PHILOSOPHY AND THE QURʾĀN; EXEGESIS OF THE QURʾĀN: CLASSICAL AND MEDIEVAL). Things become clearer, perhaps, if one sees that the discussion has tried to balance a series of tensions. Since the divine is so often defined in negative terms and often through the negation of any similarity to the human, it should not be surprising that theologies of revelation are full of paradox and tension. As Izutsu (*God,* 153-4) put it, the Qurʾān, being God's speech, is divine but it is also speech; it therefore conforms to the models and limitations of all speech.

The tradition wants to assert the immediacy of the revelation to the God who speaks, an immediacy on which it depends for its reliability. At the same time it recognizes the mediation required logically and theologically by the absolute ontological distance between God and creation, and even the relative distance between the human and the angelic.

Through the use of *asbāb al-nuzūl* the tradition focuses on the concrete historicity of the text in its interactions with the Prophet and his hearers. At the same time it argues for its pre-existent, timeless nature.

The text has a very obvious cultural and linguistic particularity and the tradition stresses this in its attachment to and celebration of the Arabic of the Qurʾān. At the same time it insists on its universal appeal and applicability.

The tradition carefully observes the delimited extent and content of the qurʾānic text. At the same time, it asserts the unlimited scope and import of the revelation.

Certain key terms for the understanding and interpretation of the Qurʾān have spatial and temporal significance (the heavenly Preserved Tablet, sending down, abrogation [q.v.], forgetting or causing to forget; see also SATANIC VERSES). At the same time, the tradition is aware of the problematic nature of attributing spatial and temporal characteristics to God.

The tradition maintains the uniqueness of the Qurʾān. Yet, on the other hand, it asserts the Qurʾān's commonality with the earlier revealed scriptures.

The Qurʾān itself and the tradition assert the inprinciple identity of the message to that of the earlier scriptures. At the same time, it is aware that in fact there is a divergence among them (see FORGERY; CORRUPTION; POLEMIC AND POLEMICAL LANGUAGE; APOLOGETICS).

The Muslim tradition insists strongly that the Qurʾān is the sole revealed scripture to have been faithfully recorded and preserved in its original form. At the same time, the fact that only the unpointed consonantal text *(rasm)* is canonized means that in effect the canon is kept open by the many possible pronunciations *(lafẓ)* based on the same *ductus* — some of them doctrinally significant (e.g. Q 2:106).

These tensions are a necessary factor in any theory of revelation because it must account at the same time for the divine and human aspects of the phenomenon. Although Islamic tradition has not succeeded in developing a single coherent theology of revelation, the idea remains central to the religion. God's constancy in revelation shows his engagement with the world, the ceaseless activity of addressing the human situation and providing for human need.

Daniel A. Madigan

Bibliography

Primary: W. Ahlwardt, *The divans of the six ancient Arabic poets. Ennābiga, ʿAntara, Tharafa, Zuhair, ʿAlqama and Imruulqais,* London 1870, repr. Osnabrück 1972; Bukhārī, *Ṣaḥīḥ,* ed. Krehl, iii, 391-2 (66. *K. Faḍāʾil al-Qurʾān, bāb* 1), Fr. trans.

O. Houdas and W. Marçais, *El-Bokhâri. Les traditions islamiques,* 4 vols., Paris 1903-14, iii, 520-1; al-Ghazālī, Abū Ḥāmid Muḥammad, *Iḥyā' 'ulūm al-dīn,* 4 vols., Būlāq 1289/1872, repr. Cairo 1933, i, 244-64 (Bk. 8, *K. Ādāb tilāwat al-Qur'ān*); Fr. trans. G.H. Bousquet, *Ih'ya 'ouloûm ed-dîn ou Vivification des sciences de la foi. Analyse et index,* Paris 1955, 91-4; Eng. trans. (of book 8), M. Abul Qasem, *The recitation and interpretation of the Qur'ān. Al-Ghazālī's theory,* London 1982; Ibn Isḥāq, *Sīra,* ed. Wüstenfeld; Ibn Isḥāq-Guillaume; Ibn Khaldūn-Rosenthal, i, 184-245; ii, 419-24; Ibn Rushd, Abū l-Walīd Muḥammad b. Aḥmad, *Manāhij al-adilla fī 'aqā'id al-milla,* ed. M. Qāsim, Cairo 1964, 208-22; B. Lewin, *A vocabulary of the Hudailian poems. Acta regiae societatis scientiarum et litterarum Gothoburgensis. Humaniora 13,* Göteborg 1978, 465; Suyūṭī, *Itqān,* i, 82-142 (*anwā'* 9-16); id., *Lubāb al-nuqūl fī asbāb al-nuzūl,* Beirut 1978; Ṭabarī, *Ta'rīkh,* ed. de Goeje; trans. W.M. Watt and M.V. McDonald, *The history of al-Ṭabarī.* vi. *Muḥammad at Mecca,* Albany 1988; Wāḥidī, *Asbāb;* Zarkashī, *Burhān,* ed. Ibrāhīm, Cairo 1957. Secondary: N.H. Abū Zayd, *Critique de discours religieux,* Arles 1999; id., *Mafhūm al-naṣṣ. Dirāsa fī 'ulūm al-Qur'ān,* Cairo 1990, 35-65; M. Arkoun, *Rethinking Islam. Common questions, uncommon answers,* Boulder 1994; id., *The unthought in contemporary Islamic thought,* London 2002; J.-M. Balhan, *Comment il le fit descendre. Traduction commentée du chapitre seizième Jalāl al-Dīn al-Suyūti,* al-Itqān fī 'ulūm al-Qur'ān, Rome 2003; van Ess, *TG,* iv, 179-227, 612-25 (with references — essential for the question of verbal inspiration); id., Verbal inspiration? Language and revelation in classical Islamic theology, in Wild, *Text,* 177-94; T. Fahd, Kāhin, in *EI*², iv, 420-2; id., Sakīna, in *EI*², viii, 888-9; Goldziher, *MS;* W.A. Graham, *Divine word and prophetic word in early Islam,* The Hague 1977; id., The earliest meaning of "qur'ān," in *WI* 23/24 (1984), 361-77; id., "The winds to herald his mercy" and other "signs for those of certain faith." Nature as token of God's sovereignty and grace in the Qur'ān, in S.H. Lee, W. Proudfoot and A. Blackwell (eds.), *Faithful imagining. Essays in honor of Richard R. Niebuhr,* Atlanta 1995, 19-38; Izutsu, *God,* 133-97; A. Jeffery, The Qur'ān as scripture, in *MW* 40 (1950), 41-55, 106-134, 185-206, 257-75; id., *The Qur'ān as scripture,* New York 1952; N. Kermani, *Gott ist schön. Das ästhetische Erleben des Koran,* Munich 1999; id., *Offenbarung als Kommunikation. Das Konzept* waḥy *in Naṣr Ḥāmid Abū Zayds* Mafhūm an-naṣṣ, Frankfurt 1996; id., Revelation in its aesthetic dimension. Some notes about apostles and artists in Islamic and Christian culture, in Wild, *Text,* 213-24; D.B. MacDonald, Ilhām, in *EI*², iii, 1119-20; D.A. Madigan, *The Qur'ān's self-image. Writing and authority in Islam's scripture,* Princeton 2001; Nöldeke, *GQ,* i, 20-57; F. Rahman, *Major themes of the Qur'ān,* Minneapolis 1980; N. Robinson, *Discovering the Qur'ān. A contemporary approach to a veiled text,* London 1996, Washington, DC 2004²; U. Rubin, *The eye of the beholder. The life of Muḥammad as viewed by the early Muslims. A textual analysis,* Princeton 1995, 103-12 (the Khadīja-Waraqa story); G. Schoeler, *Charakter und Authentie der muslimischen überlieferungen über das Leben Mohammeds,* Berlin 1996, 59-117 (the narratives on Muḥammad's first revelation, the *iqra'* narratives); id., Schreiben und Veröffentlichen. Zu Verwendung und Funktion der Schrift in den ersten islamischen Jahrhunderten, in *Der Islam* 69 (1992), 1-43; R. Sellheim, Muhammeds erstes Offenbarungserlebnis, in *JSAI* 10 (1987), 1-16; A. Sprenger, *Das Leben und die Lehre des Moḥammad,* 3 vols., Berlin 1869², i, 293-354; Wansbrough, *QS;* Watt-Bell, *Introduction;* A.J. Wensinck/C.E. Bosworth, Lawḥ, in *EI*², v, 698; A.J. Wensinck/A. Rippin, Waḥy, in *EI*², x, 53-6; S. Wild, Die andere Seite des Textes. Nasr Hamid Abu Zaid und der Koran, in *WI* 33 (1993), 256-61; id., "We have sent down to thee the book with the truth..." Spatial and temporal implications of the qur'ānic concepts of *nuzūl, tanzīl* and *'inzāl,* in Wild, *Text,* 137-53; H.A. Wolfson, *The philosophy of the Kalam,* Cambridge 1976, 235-303; M. Zwettler, A mantic manifesto. The sura of 'The Poets' and the qur'ānic foundations of prophetic authority, in James L. Kugel, (ed.) *Poetry and prophecy. The beginnings of a literary tradition,* Ithaca 1990, 75-119.

Revenge see VENGEANCE

Revision and Alteration

The idea and the charge that the text of the Qur'ān (and the Bible) underwent changes and emendations over time. According to traditional Muslim accounts, the revelations that make up the Qur'ān were originally collected together by the second caliph (q.v.) 'Umar (d. 23/644), under the editorship of Zayd b. Thābit, approximately twenty-five years after Muḥammad's death (see COLLECTION OF THE QUR'ĀN). 'Umar died before the task was completed, however, and the collected sheets were transferred to his daughter

Ḥafṣa (q.v.) for safekeeping (see also WIVES OF THE PROPHET). Around 30/650, ʿUthmān (q.v.) later the third caliph (d. 35/655), drew from this collection when he reinstated the editorial commission started by ʿUmar, established the Medinan recension of the materials as the qurʾānic canon and burned all other versions then circulating (see CODICES OF THE QURʾĀN). Traditional Islam understands this ʿUthmānic codex, as it is called, to be both the version most closely resembling Muḥammad's revelations and the very same version still in use today. Bell notes that the religious authorities, largely not positively disposed toward ʿUthmān, never accuse him of having altered the Qurʾān in any form. Similarly, history does not record any substantial disagreements over the text (see TEXTUAL CRITICISM OF THE QURʾĀN; UNITY OF THE TEXT OF THE QURʾĀN).

This does not mean, however, that Islamic tradition rejected absolutely the idea of the alteration of God's word (see WORD OF GOD). Traditional Sunnī Islam recognizes at least three forms of such revision. The Qurʾān itself (Q 13:39; 87:6-7, etc.) speaks of God as editor, causing Muḥammad to forget some revelations or even deleting verses from the Qurʾān (see also SATANIC VERSES; IMPECCABILITY). Additional divine revision comes in the form of the doctrine of *nāsikh wa-mansūkh*, "abrogating and abrogated" (see ABROGATION). According to this principle, the Qurʾān altered and revised itself in the midst of being revealed; later qurʾānic rulings that appear to contradict earlier statements are, in fact, replacing them, terminating the earlier statements in favor of new decrees (for example, Q 4:11 abrogates Q 2:180, Q 24:2 replaces 4:15-6). Some maintain that Muḥammad acted as the Qurʾān's editor as well. According to this tradition, once a year Muḥammad met with the angel Gabriel (q.v.; Jibrīl) to order, fix and collate the revealed materials coming through him (Suyūṭī, *Itqān*, i, 216). In the process, some parts of the revelation were left out of the final compilation, though these continued to hold authoritative status. Indeed, a number of ḥadīth refer to such omitted verses (see ḤADĪTH AND THE QURʾĀN). One such ḥadīth concerns the famous "stoning (q.v.) verse," an omitted verse which declares that male and female adulterers are to be stoned, a punishment that contradicts the lashing (see FLOGGING) prescribed in the written revelation in Q 24:2 (Bayhaqī, *Sunan*, viii, 210; see BOUNDARIES AND PRECEPTS; ADULTERY AND FORNICATION). In line with this view of prophet as editor, Berque suggests that the original command to Muḥammad, *iqraʾ*, may have been a command to assemble/compile the revealed messages, rather than to read/recite them, as traditionally understood (see ORALITY; ORALITY AND WRITING IN ARABIA; ILLITERACY; REVELATION AND INSPIRATION). By ʿUthmān's time, dialectical oddities had crept into the Qurʾān's language, and a third form of revision took place when ʿUthmān edited these out in favor of a pure Qurashī Arabic (see ARABIC LANGUAGE; DIALECTS).

Some modern scholars have disagreed with this traditional (Sunnī) scenario, maintaining that in addition to the supposed early divine and prophetic revisions, later "regular" human hands also played a part in manipulating the content of the revelations. Watt sees evidence of this in the verses' hidden rhyme schemes, pointing out examples of phrases added in order to give passages the correct assonance and cases in which the rhyme of the sūra changes (see RHYMED PROSE). Watt also lists a host of irregularities and unevenness of style in certain sections of the Qurʾān that testify to later human alteration and revision (see LANGUAGE AND

STYLE OF THE QUR'ĀN). He cites changes in subject matter as further evidence of qur'ānic emendation. Weil similarly claims that a number of pericopes (such as the "night journey" verse, Q 17:1; see ASCENSION) were added to the Qur'ān by later hands for a variety of political and religious reasons and were not part of the original revelations. Furthermore, Jeffery maintains that the differences in pronunciation and in words in the assorted canonical *qirā'a* readings (see READINGS OF THE QUR'ĀN) can likewise be seen as alterations, remnants of the various versions destroyed by 'Uthmān. He notes, however, that these variants later came to be seen by normative Islam as little more than acceptable curiosities (see also MUṢḤAF).

The question of the Qur'ān's alteration and revision takes on a different meaning and significance in the Imāmī Shī'ī context (see SHĪ'ISM AND THE QUR'ĀN). In the Imāmī view, the canonical version of the Qur'ān contains words, verses and even whole sūras that have been added, omitted or changed from the true version (originally in 'Alī's possession; see 'ALĪ B. ABĪ ṬĀLIB) in order to fit Sunnī purposes (see POLITICS AND THE QUR'ĀN; THEOLOGY AND THE QUR'ĀN). Through "falsification" *(taḥrīf)* and "alteration" *(tabdīl)*, claim the Imāmīs, the Sunnīs omitted verses from Sūrat al-Nūr (Q 24, "Light"; in the 'Uthmānic text, this sūra contains 64 verses, while, according to the Imāmīs, it should have more than 100 verses; Imāmīs also claim that the Sunnīs omitted or suppressed Sūrat al-Nūrayn, "The Two Lights"; cf. Ar. text and trans. in Nöldeke, *GQ*, ii, 102-7) as well as other passages that testify to 'Alī's distinct role as Muḥammad's spiritual and political heir. Kohlberg, citing von Grunebaum, points out that the Shī'īs never could ultimately agree on the details of the alleged 'Uthmānic distortion of the Qur'ān's content. Eliash, on the other hand, maintains that the Imāmīs never questioned the accuracy of the text's content but only the ordering of the material. According to Kohlberg, however, the original accusation was of content corruption; only as the Imāmīs began to accept the Sunnī notion of the text's perfection (*i'jāz al-Qur'ān;* see INIMITABILITY), did the charge slowly evolve into the lesser criticism of order. The belief in the Qur'ān's integrity remains the conviction of the overwhelming majority of modern Imāmīs, although echoes of the early dissent do surface from time to time (Kohlberg notes the recent Ḥusayn b. Muḥammad Taqī l-Nūrī l-Ṭabarsī [d. 1320/1905], for example).

Khārijīs (q.v.), too, have accused the Sunnīs of content manipulation. Many found Sūrat Yūsuf (Q 12, "Joseph") problematic because of its erotic and hence inappropriate overtones. The entire chapter, they claim, does not belong in the Qur'ān and, they charge, was likely added later by human hands.

Perhaps the most famous accusation of textual alteration and revision, however, concerns not the qur'ānic text but the Bible. This charge appears in the Qur'ān itself (see CORRUPTION; FORGERY; POLEMIC AND POLEMICAL LANGUAGE). According to the Qur'ān, although the Torah (q.v.) and the Gospels (q.v.) are genuine divine revelations, deriving from the very same source as the Qur'ān, the Jews and the Christians tampered with their texts by engaging in both *taḥrīf* and *tabdīl* (see Q 2:42, 59, 75-9; 3:71, 78; 4:46; 5:13, 41; 6:91; 7:162, among others; see JEWS AND JUDAISM; CHRISTIANS AND CHRISTIANITY). This claim explains why Muḥammad does not appear in either the Hebrew Bible or New Testament, despite the Muslim claim that his arrival and mission had originally been predicted there (see PROPHETS AND PROPHETHOOD). Jewish and Christian alteration of the biblical text also solves the riddle of why, if all three scriptures derived from the same divine source, the qurʾānic versions of accounts often contradict those of the Bible (see NARRATIVES; SCRIPTURE AND THE QURʾĀN). The Muslim charge of biblical alteration eventually coalesced into two forms, *taḥrīf al-naṣṣ*, "distortion of text," and *taḥrīf al-maʿānī*, "(deliberate or non-deliberate) false interpretation." Most Muslim writers on the topic accused the Jews (and Christians) mainly of the lesser offense of intentional problematic misinterpretation. Nonetheless, a frequent charge against the veracity of the Torah claimed that it had been burned and subsequently rewritten (inaccurately) by the prophet Ezra (q.v.; ʿUzayr). This more serious allegation of *taḥrīf al-naṣṣ* forms the basis for one of the most famous and systematic polemics against the Bible, that of the Spanish Ẓāhirī theologian Ibn Ḥazm (d. 456/1064). In his detailed *Iẓhār tabdīl al-yahūd wa-l-naṣārā lil-tawrāt wa-l-injīl*, "Exposure of the alterations by the Jews and Christians to the Torah and Gospel" (preserved in his larger *Milal*), Ibn Ḥazm presents case after case in which he claims that the biblical text must have been intentionally altered and falsified by the Jews and Christians. As described by Lazarus-Yafeh, Ibn Ḥazm bases his claims on what he considers to be chronological and geographic inaccuracies, theological impossibilities and preposterous prophetic behavior, among other things (see MIRACLES). Despite his insistence on the unreliability of the Bible and his rejection of using the Bible to prove the truth of a religion or prophet, Ibn Ḥazm nonetheless insists that certain biblical passages testify to the truth of Muḥammad and his prophecy. This dualistic attitude of rejection of and simultaneous reliance upon the "altered" Bible appears throughout the Muslim literature on the topic.

Shari Lowin

Bibliography

Primary: al-Bayhaqī, Abū Bakr Aḥmad b. al-Ḥusayn, *al-Sunan al-kubrā*, 10 vols., Hyderabad 1925-38; Ibn al-Jawzī, Abū l-Faraj ʿAbd al-Raḥmān b. ʿAlī, *Nāsikh al-Qurʾān wa-mansūkhuhu. Nawāsikh al-Qurʾān*, Damascus 1990; Suyūṭī, *Itqān;* al-Ṭabarsī, Ḥusayn b. Muḥammad, *Faṣl al-khiṭāb fī ithbāt taḥrīf kitāb rabb al-arbāb*, n.p. 1298/1860.

Secondary: C. Adang, *Muslim writers on Judaism and the Hebrew Bible*, Leiden 1996; M.A. Amir-Moezzi and C. Jambet, *Qu'est-ce que le shîʿisme?* Paris 2004, 89-97 (on alteration in Imāmī Shīʿīte thought); R. Bell, *Introduction to the Qurʾān*, Edinburgh 1953; J. Berque, *Relire le Coran*, Paris 1993; J. Burton, *The collection of the Qurʾān*, Cambridge 1977; id., Naskh, in *EI²*, vii, 1009-12; J. Eliash, The Šiʿite Qurʾān. A reconsideration of Goldziher's interpretation, in *Arabica* 16 (1969), 15-24; Ibn Warraq (ed.), *The origins of the Koran. Classic essays on Islam's holy book*, New York 1998; Jeffery, *Materials;* id., Progress in the study of the Qurʾān text, in *MW* 25 (1935), 4-16; E. Kohlberg, Some notes on the Imāmite attitude to the Qurʾān, in S.M. Stern et al. (eds.), *Islamic philosophy and the classical tradition*, Columbia, SC 1972, 209-24; H. Lazarus-Yafeh, *Intertwined worlds. Medieval Islam and Bible criticism*, Princeton 1992; id., Taḥrīf, in *EI²*, x, 111-2; id., Taḥrīf and the thirteen Torah scrolls, in *JSAI* 19 (1995), 81-8; J.D. McAuliffe, The qurʾānic context of Muslim biblical scholarship, in *Islam and Christian-Muslim relations* 7 (1996), 141-58; Nöldeke, *GQ*, i, 234-59; ii, 93-112; R. Paret, Ḳirāʾa, in *EI²*, v, 127-9; N. Roth, Forgery and abrogation of the Torah. A theme in Muslim and Christian polemic in Spain, in *Proceedings of the American Academy for Jewish Research* 54 (1987), 203-36; Watt-Bell, *Introduction;* G. Weil, *Historisch-kritische Einleitung in den Koran*, Bielefeld 1878².

Reward and Punishment

A return or recompense made to, or received by, a person or a group for some service or merit or for hardship endured; and its opposite, judicial chastisement intended to make a person or a group suffer for an offence, whether as retribution or as caution against further transgression. Both terms together merge into a word like "requital."

A central theme in the Qur'ān is the requital of human deeds by divine justice both on earth and in the world to come (see JUSTICE AND INJUSTICE; JUDGMENT; ESCHATOLOGY; GOOD DEEDS; EVIL DEEDS). To those who believe and do good deeds (see BELIEF AND UNBELIEF), God gives some reward on earth and a far greater reward in the hereafter (see PARADISE; BLESSING; GRACE). Unbelievers and evildoers can be punished on earth and have to undergo eternal chastisement in the hereafter (see CHASTISEMENT AND PUNISHMENT; ETERNITY; HELL AND HELLFIRE). The ultimate separation of the two groups will take place on the day of judgment (see LAST JUDGMENT). According to ḥadīth, unbelievers will also be punished in their graves (see ḤADĪTH AND THE QUR'ĀN; DEATH AND THE DEAD).

The relevant qur'ānic terminology

The term *ajr*, "wage, pay, reward," is frequently used in sūras of all periods. It sometimes refers to work or services rendered in everyday human contexts. Pharaoh's (q.v.) sorcerers (see MAGIC) expect payment (Q 26:41); Moses (q.v.; Mūsā) was payed for being a shepherd (Q 28:25-7); wives and girl slaves are entitled to an *ajr* (Q 4:24-5; 5:5; 60:10; cf. 33:50; see WOMEN AND THE QUR'ĀN; SLAVES AND SLAVERY); and divorced wives receive payment (pl. *ujūr*) for nursing the children of their former husbands (Q 65:6; see MARRIAGE AND DIVORCE; WET NURSING; LACTATION). A recurrent motif throughout the Meccan sūras (see CHRONOLOGY AND THE QUR'ĀN) is that the Prophet does not ask a wage for conveying the message (e.g. Q 6:90; 38:86; 68:46; in Q 23:72 with *kharj* and *kharāj*); that is to God's account (e.g. Q 34:47). The same is true for the prophets of the past (e.g. Q 26:109; cf. 36:21; see PROPHETS AND PROPHETHOOD). In most places, and predominantly so in the Medinan sūras, *ajr* is the reward given by God for righteous conduct (see VIRTUES AND VICES, COMMANDING AND FORBIDDING). One may be rewarded in this world, as e.g. Joseph (q.v.; Yūsuf) was (Q 12:56), but nearly always *ajr* refers to the reward in the world to come, i.e. in paradise. The word is never used in the sense of "punishment."

Thawāb, mathūba and cognates occur nineteen times in sūras of all periods, the basic meaning being "recompense, compensation, requital." Only twice are they used in a negative sense (Q 3:153; 83:36); in the other cases they are virtually synonymous with "reward." They always refer to the recompense for human actions from God, either in this world or in the world to come (e.g. Q 3:145, 148). *Jazā'* means "compensation, requital, satisfaction, payment." With its cognates, it occurs frequently throughout the Qur'ān. It refers to both reward and punishment on earth, but far more often in the life to come. In the later sūras the connotation of "punishment" is more dominant. Sometimes the word is embedded in the clausula phrase (see Neuwirth, Form, esp. p. 253): "That is how we recompense the doers of good," which occurs in the later Meccan stories about the prophets (Q 6:84; 12:22; 28:14; 37:105-31; see NARRATIVES) but had already been used in an early evocation of the day of judgment (Q 77:44; cf. also Q 5:85; 39:34) or in the often-repeated phrase: "... so that God may recompense them for the best of their deeds" (Q 9:121; 29:7; cf. 39:35).

Among punishment terms in the Qur'ān, *'adhāb* and cognates are by far the most frequent in all periods. They mean "pain, torment," and more specifically "pain or torment inflicted by way of chastisement; punishment." The flogging (q.v.) of adulterers (see ADULTERY AND FORNICATION) is called *ʿadhāb* (Q 24:2, 8) but otherwise this word mainly refers to the torment in hell. God 'seizes' the sinners with the torment (e.g. Q 23:64; 43:48; see SIN, MAJOR AND MINOR), or the torment is personified: it "seizes" the sinners (Q 11:64; 16:113; 26:156, 158, 189), as does the "cry" (see below under *ṣayḥa*); or torment "covers them from above them and from under their feet" (Q 29:55). In some 150 places, especially in the Medinan sūras, the word is embedded in often-repeated clausula phrases, such as "For them is a painful punishment" (e.g. Q 5:36), or phrases ending with the words "a demeaning (or painful, or severe) punishment," e.g. "he will have a painful punishment" (Q 2:178). About *ʿadhāb al-qabr*, "the punishment in the grave," see at the end of this article.

ʿIqāb is the verbal noun of *ʿāqaba*, a verb which means "to do alternately" and "to punish for crime, sin, fault or offence." It is absent from the earliest, and rare in the middle Meccan sūras. Finite verb forms of the root *ʿ-q-b* occur six times in the Qurʾān and always refer to human activities, meaning both "punishing" and "doing what induces punishment." The frequently used *ʿiqāb* always refers to God's punishment. In Medinan sūras it occurs almost exclusively in concluding clausula phrases, which aim at underlining a command or interdiction, as e.g. "God is severe in punishment" (Q 3:11). Unusually, in Q 5:98 this phrase does not occur at the end of the verse: "Know that God is severe in punishment and that God is all-forgiving." Indeed God's punishment is placed in contrast to his willingess to forgive (see FORGIVENESS) already in late Meccan verses (Q 6:165; 7:167; 13:6; 40:3; 41:43).

The term *intiqām*, "revenge, to avenge oneself, take revenge, to bear a grudge," and cognates are used for the grudge that human beings bear against believers for the very fact that they are believers (Q 5:59; 7:126; 85:8) and enjoy God's blessing (Q 9:74). More frequently they are used to denote God's punishment. From the second Meccan period onward, God presents himself as an avenger. He will take vengeance on the evildoers, both here (Q 43:41) and in the life to come (Q 44:16), as he had done in the past, according to the punishment stories (q.v.; Q 7:136; 15:79; 30:47; 43:25, 55). A few Meccan and Medinan verses end in the clausula phrase "God is mighty and vengeful" (Q 3:4; 5:95; 14:47; 39:37). *Al-muntaqim*, "the avenger," is one of God's "most beautiful names" (see GOD AND HIS ATTRIBUTES).

Additional terminology includes *khizy*, "shame, disgrace, ignominy." From the second Meccan period onward, this word and its cognates are often bracketed with God's punishment (e.g. Q 20:134). Disgrace in this world is terrible, but the torment in the hereafter is worse (Q 39:26). On the day of resurrection (q.v.), God will disgrace the evildoers (Q 16:27), as he had already done in the past, witness several punishment stories (e.g. Q 11:39; 41:16). The stay in hell is, among other things, an ignominy (Q 3:192; 9:63). In Q 5:33, where some heavy physical punishments are enumerated, it is not the pain that is emphasized, but the disgrace. Also the roots *dh-l-l* and *k-b-t* which denote "humiliation" express this aspect of the divine punishment (e.g. Q 10:26; 58:5), as well as the frequent collocation "a demeaning punishment" (*ʿadhāb muhīn;* e.g. Q 2:90). *Mathula*, "exemplary punishment," occurs once in the plural *(al-mathulāt)* in a Medinan sūra, where it refers to an unspecified past time (Q 13:6). *Nakāl* and *tankīl* have a similiar meaning. Punishments meted out to the Jews (see JEWS AND JUDAISM; CHILDREN OF ISRAEL) and to Pharaoh are presented as warnings and exhortations for the God-fearing (Q 2:66; 79:25; see FEAR; PIETY). In a law-giving Medinan verse *nakāl* is used for the cutting off of the hands of thieves (Q 5:38; see BOUNDARIES AND PRECEPTS; THEFT; LAW AND THE QURʾĀN).

Rijz, rijs, rujz: rijz is "abomination, filth, impurity" (see CLEANLINESS AND ABLUTION; RITUAL PURITY; CONTAMINATION). In some punishment stories, however, it denotes a scourge which was sent from heaven (Q 2:59; 7:134-5, 162; 29:34; see HEAVEN AND SKY) and, in the phrase "the punishment of a painful scourge" (Q 34:5; 45:11), it refers to the future. Also the word *rijs* has a twofold meaning: in six places it means "abomination, filth, punishable act"; in three verses "scourge" (Q 6:125; 7:71; 10:100). Both *rijz* and *rijs* occur in late Meccan and Medinan sūras. *Rujz,* in the early verse Q 74:5, is sometimes considered to be identical with *rijz,* "abomination," or is taken to be cognate with Syriac *rūgzā,* "wrath" (Jeffery, *For. vocab.,* 139). Finally, *ṣayḥa,* "cry," occurs in the second and third Meccan periods. In Q 50:42 it is the cry or clamor that announces the resurrection on the day of judgment. Mostly, however, the cry has more than a heralding and warning function (see WARNER): it is the punishment itself, or at least part of it. This is hinted at in Q 38:15 and is more obvious in Q 36:49: "they are only awaiting a single cry to seize them." Elsewhere it is the torment that "seizes" them (see above under *ʿadhāb*). In the punishment stories the cry is destructive. Of Thamūd (q.v.) and al-Ḥijr (q.v.) it is said: "We released upon them a single cry and they became like the dry twigs of a pen-builder" (Q 54:31; cf. 11:67, 94; 15:83), but it also occurs in other stories, e.g. in Q 36:29: "It was but one cry, and behold, they were extinguished."

The eschatological division

A roughly chronological reading of the entire Qurʾān gives a better insight into the qurʾānic system of reward and punishment than does a mere enumeration of the relevant vocabulary (see OCCASIONS OF REVELATION). Both reward and punishment belong to the oldest stratum of the message. On the day of judgment, God will separate the unbelieving evildoers, who are to be punished, from the god-fearing believers, who will be rewarded. The first Meccan sūras describe the guilty as "he who is given his book (q.v.) behind his back" (Q 84:10-12) or "in his left hand" (Q 69:25), as "companions of the left," (Q 56:9; see LEFT HAND AND RIGHT HAND), as "one whose scales are light" (Q 101:8; see WEIGHTS AND MEASURES) and as the one whom "we will brand him upon the muzzle" (Q 68:16). Those who are not condemned are called "companions of the right," (Q 56:8, 27), "he who has been given his book in his right hand" (Q 69:19); he "whose scales shall be weighty" (Q 101:6-7). Finally, reward and punishment are strictly individual: on the day of judgment, no soul will be of help to another (Q 82:19; see INTERCESSION).

Who will be rewarded?

The sūras of the first Meccan period mention those "who purify themselves, remember the lord's name and perform the prayers" (cf. Q 87:14-5; see MEMORY; REMEMBRANCE; PRAYER), those "who give and fear God and believe in the fairest [reward]" (Q 92:5-6; see ALMSGIVING), and "those who believe and do good deeds" (Q 84:25; 85:11; 95:6). The early verses Q 90:13-7 give a short description of the types of deeds that may be rewarded: "freeing a slave; feeding, on a day of famine (q.v.), an orphan near of kin (see ORPHANS; KINSHIP), or a poor person in misery (see POVERTY AND THE POOR)," as well as belonging to the believers, who urge one another to be steadfast and merciful (see TRUST AND PATIENCE; MERCY; COMMUNITY AND SOCIETY IN THE QUR'ĀN). Q 51:17-9 emphasizes asceticism (q.v.): "They used to sleep (q.v.) little and to ask for forgiveness at daybreak (see DAWN; DAY, TIMES OF; DAY AND NIGHT; VIGILS); the beggar and the destitute had a share in their wealth (q.v.)." In short, belief, devotion and responsible social behavior (see SOCIAL INTERACTIONS) are decisive already in the earliest sūras, and they remain so throughout the Qur'ān. Enumerations of rewardable behavior in various Meccan passages specify these good deeds (Q 23:1-9; 25:63-74; 32:15-6; 70:22-34).

A similar Medinan enumeration (Q 3:130-5) explicitly mentions "hastening to obtain forgiveness" as rewardable. God's forgiveness can reduce punishment and tip the scales towards reward. Repentance (see REPENTANCE AND PENANCE) is of course a necessary precondition for obtaining forgiveness (Q 66:8). Another Medinan passage, Q 33:35, makes clear that the good deeds of both men and women will be rewarded. In the Medinan period, donating wealth for military activities *(fī sabīli llāhi)* without making a fuss about it (Q 2:262), or even better, participating in the fight physically (Q 4:95; 9:88-9; 61:11; cf. 4:100) and, eventually, being killed on the battlefield (see MARTYRS) are emphasized (see also PATH OR WAY; FIGHTING; WAR; EXPEDITIONS AND BATTLES). Also the bedouins (see BEDOUIN) will be rewarded, when they take part in fighting (Q 48:16). Other groups that are explicitly promised a reward in the later sūras are those who emigrate to God and his messenger (q.v.; Q 4:100; see also EMIGRATION), the first Emigrants and Helpers (q.v.; Q 9:100) and the believers among the People of the Book (q.v.; Q 2:62; 3:199; 5:69, 85). Occasionally very specific actions are mentioned as meriting reward: not talking loudly in the presence of the Prophet (Q 49:2-3) and not discriminating among prophets (Q 4:152).

Those who are punished

The people on the left who will be punished, according to the Meccan sūras, are primarily those who do not believe in God and deny his signs (q.v.; e.g. Q 90:19-20); who turn away (see ERROR; ASTRAY); who doubt the resurrection and the reality of the day of judgment (Q 56:47); who declare the prophetic message a lie (q.v.; e.g. Q 52:11; 56:51); and who call the Prophet a sorcerer, a madman or a poet (e.g. Q 10:2; 37:36; see OPPOSITION TO MUḤAMMAD; INSANITY; JINN; SOOTHSAYERS; POETRY AND POETS). Concomitant with their unbelief are their deeds, notably involving antisocial behavior. The unbelievers are impudent (Q 79:37-8; see PRIDE; INSOLENCE AND OBSTINACY) and cheat (Q 83:1-3; see CHEATING); they do not look after the poor (e.g. Q 69:34), notably the orphans (Q 89:17; 93:9; 107:2); and they live in luxury (Q 56:45), or heap up fortunes (Q 92:8; 104:2). Furthermore, they "obstruct God's way and make a breach with the messenger" (Q 47:32), persecute the believers (Q 85:10) or even forbid them to pray (Q 96:9-10). In Q 74:43-6, the evil-doers in hell explain to the believers why they are there: "We were not among those who prayed, and we were not among those who fed the destitute; we used to talk nonsense with others (see GOSSIP), and we used to deny the day of judgment...."

The Medinan sūras repeat what has been said before but add some elements that reflect the changed political circumstances (see MECCA; MEDINA; POLITICS AND THE

QUR'ĀN). There is a certain emphasis on the hypocrites (see HYPOCRITES AND HYPOCRISY), who were lukewarm in their allegiance to Muḥammad or became outright disloyal to him. They are as bad as the unbelievers (Q 4:138, 140, 145; 9:101; 48:6; 66:9); they will not be forgiven (Q 63:6); and they are "in the lowest depth of hell" (Q 4:145). Close to them, or even identical with them (Q 9:97, 101), are the bedouins insofar as they are unreliable allies (see BREAKING TRUSTS AND CONTRACTS; CLIENTS AND CLIENTAGE). Since at a crucial moment they failed to participate in military activities, they are threatened with a painful punishment (Q 48:16; 9:90). In Q 9, those who refuse to take part in war are a main preoccupation. Q 9:81-5 promises them hell, but they are punished in this life as well: they will not be invited for future expeditions (which is a disgrace; cf. Q 9:39), and the believers are not supposed to pray for them on their death. Even worse are those who actively try to restrain the believers from warfare (*li-yaṣuddū ʿan sabīli llāhi,* Q 8:36).

Other punishable acts mentioned in the Medinan sūras are, for example, mockery (q.v.; Q 9:79), believing in the Trinity (q.v.; Q 5:73), opposing God's messenger (Q 8:13; 9:61, 63) and killing his prophets (Q 3:21; cf. *Mt* 23:37). Already in Meccan passages apostates (see APOSTASY) had been threatened with punishment (Q 16:106) but are so again with still more emphasis in Medinan passages (Q 2:217; 3:176-7; 9:74). Certain mundane perpetrators, like murderers (Q 4:93; see MURDER; BLOODSHED) and adulterers (Q 25:68-9) are explicitly threatened with punishment in the afterlife.

The nature of the retribution in the hereafter

What exactly awaits humankind in the world to come is made abundantly clear throughout the Qur'ān and is described in detail elsewhere in the present work (see e.g. the various cross-referenced articles). The reward is that the believers will abide in a luscious garden, or gardens (see GARDEN), with rivers flowing underneath, where they are given fine food and drink (q.v.) and costly clothing (q.v.), where they will be served by youths and enjoy the company of attractive women (see HOURIS). The guilty, i.e. the unbelievers, will be punished by being thrown into the hellfire, where they will neither die nor live, where they are skinned and tortured and will burn forever.

Divine recompense on earth

God rewards and punishes not only in the hereafter but in this life as well (Q 3:145, 148; 4:134). To the Emigrants, God will give "a good lodging in this world, but the reward in the world to come is greater, if they only knew" (Q 16:41; cf. 16:30-1; see HOUSE, DOMESTIC AND DIVINE). Those who pledged allegiance under the tree, i.e. at Ḥudaybiya (q.v.), were rewarded "with a victory (q.v.) near at hand" (Q 48:18).

Already in the past God's punishment was imposed on earth. Stubborn individuals and peoples who had not taken heed of the warnings of God's messengers were punished for behavior not unlike that of Muḥammad's environment: unbelief, polytheism (see POLYTHEISM AND ATHEISM), disobedience (q.v.), arrogance (q.v.). The punishment had consisted in destruction by stones thrown from heaven, by earthquakes, wind or rain, or by drowning (q.v.). These stories aim, among other things, at convincing the Prophet's contemporaries that the punishment is imminent and real (see Horovitz, *KU,* 10-32; see also CHASTISEMENT AND PUNISHMENT; PUNISHMENT STORIES).

But these ancient peoples were not the only ones to be punished on earth. Indeed "there is no city but we will destroy it before the day of resurrection, or will punish it terribly" (Q 17:58). Unbelievers (Q 13:34), in particular disaffected hypocrites (Q 9:74) and those who slander married women (Q 24:23), will be punished both now and in the hereafter. An earthly punishment may lead to repentance (Q 32:21). The agony of the unjust on their deathbeds, when the angels of death visit them, is called "the punishment of disgrace" (Q 6:93). Sometimes a twofold punishment is announced: disgrace in this life and a severe torment in the world to come (Q 2:85, 114; 5:41; 22:9; 39:26). Human beings may be the instruments of God's wrath on earth (see ANGER), as in Q 59:5, where they cut down palm trees with God's permission, to disgrace the vicious (see DATE PALM). In the battle of Ḥunayn (q.v.), human fighters were helped by invisible soldiers sent down by God, "and he punished the unbelievers" (Q 9:26).

The imagery of the Qurʾān

With reference to reward and punishment the Qurʾān employs two sets of imagery. One of them is that of commerce (see Torrey, *Commercial-theological terms;* Rippin, Commerce; see also ECONOMICS; CARAVAN; TRADE AND COMMERCE). "God buys from the believers their lives and their wealth in return for paradise" (Q 9:111; cf. 4:74). The transaction with God is also called a loan. On his loan to God, the believer will obtain a good or a double advantage, or even more (Q 2:245; 57:11, 18; 64:17). If the believer does not deliver, his soul (q.v.) is impounded (see PLEDGE): "Every soul is a pledge to what it has earned, except for those of the right hand side" (Q 74:38-9; cf. 52:21). Unbelievers suffer a loss *(khusr):* "Humankind is in the way of loss, save those who believe" (Q 103:2-3).

On the day of resurrection everyone will be confronted with his book (*kitāb;* see Madigan, Book, 243-4) in which his standing is recorded. That day will be the "day of reckoning" (*ḥisāb,* Q 38:16, 26, 53; 40:27), on which the account between God and humanity will be settled. A similar term is *aḥṣā,* "counting, calculating." Both *al-ḥasīb,* "the reckoner," and *al-muḥṣī,* "the calculator," are among God's most beautiful names (see Böwering, God, 319). Another commercial metaphor (q.v.) is that of the scales on which all deeds will be exactly weighed: "We set up the just scales for the day of resurrection, so that no soul shall be wronged anything..." (Q 21:47). For God's payment the late Meccan and the Medinan sūras often use the word *waffā,* "to pay in full, to let someone have his full share," which has a more commercial ring than *jazāʾ* or *thawāb:* "every soul shall be paid in full for what it did; they shall not be dealt with unjustly" (e.g. Q 16:111). In executing his part of the deal with humankind in full, God is not "dealing unfairly" *(ẓalama),* he does not "defraud" or "cheat" *(bakhasa, alata),* nor squander the advantage of man *(aḍāʿa)* — all terms with a commercial connotation.

The other set of imagery is of a judicial nature. In a few verses, the day of judgment reminds us of an earthly court, where the guilty are punished and the innocent are released. "He who is given his book in his right hand... shall go back to his people happily" (Q 84:7-9). "Only the most wretched will roast in the blazing fire; the god-fearing will be kept away from it" (Q 92:15-7). On the day of judgment, however, "guilty" or "not guilty" are not exclusively decisive. Above all, God is merciful and inclined to forgive. Numerous are the places in the Qurʾān where punishment is contrasted not with release, but with mercy: "He punishes whom he will and he has mercy upon whom he will," or "forgives whom he will" (e.g. Q 2:284; 3:129; 5:18, 40; 29:21; 48:14). The divine judge punishes or forgives simply because he is mighty enough to do so (see POWER AND IMPOTENCE): "Should you punish them, [you do so since] they are your servants (q.v.); but should you forgive them, [you do so since] you are the mighty one, the wise one" (Q 5:118; see WISDOM; KNOWLEDGE AND LEARNING). Here is neither an accurate bookkeeper at work, nor an honest judge in some mundane court, but a sovereign and almighty king (see KINGS AND RULERS). Bravmann (Allāh's liberty, 236) has pointed out that such a king-judge resembles the Arabic rulers and grandees that figure in pre-Islamic poetry and early Islamic historiography. The adduced parallels are striking; yet they must be seen in the far wider perspective of divine kingship in the ancient Near East (see PRE-ISLAMIC ARABIA AND THE QURʾĀN; RELIGION).

Reward may then be, in the first place, associated with trade, profit, gain, etc., whereas punishment and release belong to the realm of legal jurisdiction. Mercy still fits into the judicial imagery, when we keep the nature of the judge in mind. But all the images are blended, and each of them is evocative of only one aspect of God's justice. Those who were released in the above quoted Q 74:38 we see in paradise already in the very next verse. Indeed, in the overwhelming majority of verses release from punishment is connected with bliss in paradise.

The measurement of reward and punishment

The insufficiency of all metaphors is perhaps best illustrated by how the Qurʾān deals with the measurement of the requital. Good and evil deeds are requited proportionally and precisely. "He who has a done an atom's weight of good shall see it, and he who has a done an atom's weight of evil shall see it" (Q 99:7-8; see GOOD AND EVIL; MEASUREMENT). Hence, there are various degrees of reward and punishment. "All shall have their degrees, according to what they did" (Q 46:19). For polytheists, murderers and adulterers "punishment shall be doubled... on the day of resurrection" (Q 25:69). Liable to an extra punishment are also "those who obstruct the way of God" (Q 11:19-20; 16:88). The unbelievers in hell even dare to demand double punishment for those who misguided them (Q 7:38; 33:68; 38:61). The measure of the reward is variable as well. The believers among the wives of the Prophet (q.v.; Q 33:31) and the People of the Book (Q 28:54) are promised a double reward. Active fighters (Q 4:95) and early converts (Q 57:10) will be privileged. Yet the Qurʾān more than once promises a double reward without there being an extra merit. It sometimes corresponds to a twofold deed, or two deeds: "except those who believe and do a righteous deed. To those there will be double recompense for what they did" (Q 34:37; cf. 57:28). God may simply leave the account books aside: "if it is a good deed, he will multiply it and give from himself a great reward" (Q 4:40; cf. 4:173). While punishment is proportional, reward may be far more than doubled: "He who comes up with a good deed shall have ten times its like; and he who comes up with an evil deed will only be requited for it once" (Q 6:160). As a matter of fact, there is no point in being arithmetical about all this. The measurements are mere indications of the immeasurable extent of God's mercy, and of the sovereignty of his judgment. (In ḥadīth, however, the idea of "two rewards" is elaborated in a down-to-earth manner; see Wensinck, *Concordance*, i, 20-1, s.v. *ajrān*.)

Reward and punishment in theology

Within the Qurʾān, the various commercial and judicial metaphors are blended but not brought into harmony with each other. In theology (see THEOLOGY AND THE QURʾĀN) they are neither, although attempts have been made to harmonize them. From wherever one may start, the central problem is that of free will (see FREEDOM AND PREDESTINATION). Were people not free to act — at least to some extent — they could not be held responsible for their deeds and consequently there would be no point in retribution. But the more freedom there is for people, the less sovereignty (q.v.) for God. Generally it can be said that in the Qurʾān, in ḥadīth and in Islamic theology God's control over human acts and intentions has been emphasised at the expense of human free will. But this was not always the case (see HERESY).

Three very brief sketches may give an idea of the possible theological viewpoints. The Muʿtazila (q.v.), in the third/ninth century, held that humans have the power to do what God requires of them, hence they are responsible for their deeds and will be rewarded or punished accordingly. By virtue of his justice, God has to be just and can do nothing else than deal out reward and punishment with greatest precision, almost mechanically (Watt, *Islamic thought,* 231-42; van Ess, *TG,* iii, 403-8; iv, 507-12). The orthodox who adhered to ḥadīth and sunna (q.v.), without recourse to speculative reasoning, protested vigorously. Is God not free to punish and to forgive whom he wants? Anything less would impair his omnipotence and sovereignty as a creator (see CREATION), a ruler and a judge. God is not constrained to do anything. This line of thought was adopted by al-Ashʿarī (260-324/873-935), an ex-Muʿtazilī who defended orthodox tenets with arguments of reason. He held that a human "acquires" or "appropriates" *(kasaba)* his acts, which are, however, known, willed and created by God. In this manner he saves God's omnipotence, but the individual remains responsible enough to really deserve his reward or punishment (Ashʿarī, *Maqālāt,* 291-2; McCarthy, *Theology,* 53-8). For al-Juwaynī (d. 428/1085) there is no causal connection between human deeds and divine retribution at all: "According to the true believers, the reward is neither a determined right, nor an obligatory retribution. It is a favor on God's part. The punishment is not necessary either. In so far as it takes place, it is justice on God's part" (Juwaynī, *Irshād,* 381).

The punishment in the grave

A punishment that does not fit into the qurʾānic system of retribution is the torment that will be inflicted on the dead in their graves. It is essentially a theme developed in ḥadīth. Until the day of judgment, the bodies of the deceased lie in their graves, separated from their souls or spirits. In the intermediate state (see BARZAKH) they continue to exist in some way and can feel pressure, pain or pleasure. Although the possible qurʾānic allusions to this state are sparse, ḥadīth and popular texts discuss it in detail (see Wensinck, *Handbook,* s.v. "Graves"; Smith/Haddad, *Understanding of death,* 31-61; van Ess, *TG,* iv, 521-8). Some people receive a special reward immediately after their death. Those who are killed on the battlefield for the cause of God are not dead; rather "they are alive with their lord, well-provided for" (Q 3:169). According to a ḥadīth, prophets, martyrs and innocent children immediately enter paradise (Abū Dāwūd, *Sunan, K. al-Jihād,* 25; Ibn Ḥanbal, *Musnad,* v, 58). Another ḥadīth mentions ten persons by name, including the Prophet and the first four caliphs, who "are [already] in paradise" (Abū Dāwūd, *Sunan, Sunna,* 8; Ibn Ḥanbal, *Musnad,* i, 187-8; for other privileged categories, see Wensinck, *Handbook,* s.v. "Graves [who is free from the trial]"; see CALIPH). Most mortals, however, are subject to interrogation *(musāʾala)* or torment in their graves *(ʿadhāb al-qabr)*. A dead man is made to sit up in his grave and asked to render account of his belief and deeds. If he has done any good deeds, these will answer for him. When the result of questioning is positive, the grave is widened, so that his body feels relief. Otherwise, the torment consists in his being further compressed in the grave, which is made too narrow for the body; he may be beaten, flogged or bitten by a fiery snake. There is also the disgrace of his unbelief becoming publicly known (see *Aḥwāl al-qiyāma,* 39-41; trans. 69-73; Smith/Haddad, *Understanding of death,* 41-50; van Ess, *TG,* iv, 528-34; Wensinck/Tritton, ʿAdhāb al-ḳabr). The torment may be performed by an unknown agent; a single angel, who is sometimes called Rūmān; by two angels, who either remain anonymous or are called Munkar and Nakīr (as early as Muqātil, *Tafsīr,* ii, 193, 405-6; see Wensinck, Munkar wa-Nakīr; id., *Creed,* 117-9, 163-5); or even by four angels (van Ess, *TG,* iv, 528, 531).

The Qurʾān does not explicitly mention the punishment in the grave. Yet, in *tafsīr* works various qurʾānic verses are brought into connection with it. According to Q 9:101, the hypocrites will be punished twice. This could be once in this world and once in the grave (ʿAbd al-Razzāq, *Tafsīr,* i, 253; Ṭabarī, *Tafsīr,* xiv, 444; Zamakhsharī, *Kashshāf,* ii, 211). Muqātil (d. 150/767; *Tafsīr,* ii, 193) considers the earlier punishment to be death: "at the moment of death, the angels beat the faces and backs, and Munkar and Nakīr [do so] in the graves." Similarly in Q 32:21 "the nearer punishment, prior to the greater punishment" may consist either in suffering in this world or in the torment in the grave (Ṭabarī, *Tafsīr,* xxi, 68; Zamakhsharī, *Kashshāf,* iii, 245). In Q 14:27, "God confirms those who believe with the firm word in the present life and in the hereafter," the word "hereafter" cannot refer to paradise, since no support is needed there. Hence several exegetes (see EXEGESIS OF THE QURʾĀN: CLASSICAL AND MEDIEVAL) relate it to the punishment in the grave. ʿAbd al-Razzāq (d. 211/827; *Tafsīr,* i, 296) and al-Zamakhsharī (d. 538/1144; *Kashshāf,* ii, 377) mention it briefly, Muqātil (*Tafsīr,* ii, 405-6) and al-Ṭabarī (d. 310/923; *Tafsīr,* xiii, 142-5) treat it at length. God's guidance apparently also remains in effect in the grave, helping the believers to profess the true creed (see CREEDS; FAITH). This is also Muqātil's comment on Q 47:5 (*Tafsīr,* iv, 45), where he interprets the words "he shall guide them," i.e. those killed at Badr (q.v.), as "to the right guidance, i.e. the confession of God's unity *(tawḥīd)* in the grave." At Q 40:11, "Our lord, you have caused us to be dead twice and brought us to life twice," al-Ṭabarī (*Tafsīr,* xxiv, 31) mentions as one interpretation of which he was aware: "They were made to die in this world, then brought to life in their graves, then were interrogated or spoken to, then made to die in their graves and resurrected in the hereafter." "The punishment other [or: less] than that" in Q 52:47 is also sometimes interpreted as the torment in the grave (ʿAbd al-Razzāq, *Tafsīr,* ii, 201; Ṭabarī, *Tafsīr,* xxvii, 22; Zamakhsharī, *Kashshāf,* iv, 26).

The punishment in the grave was once a much disputed theological issue. According to al-Ashʿarī (*Maqālāt,* 430), the Khārijīs (q.v.) and the Muʿtazila denied its existence, but most Muslims asserted its reality. Notably Ḍirār b. ʿAmr (ca. 110-80/728-96) made a point of denying it, since he did not care for ḥadīth, but later Muʿtazilīs did not follow his opinion (van Ess, *TG,* iii, 52; iv, 529). Several creeds of the believers who stuck to ḥadīth and sunna explicitly state that "the torment in the grave is a reality" (see Wensinck/ Tritton, ʿAdhāb al-ḳabr; Wensinck, *Creed,* index s.v. punishment).

Wim Raven

Bibliography

Primary: ʿAbd al-Razzāq, *Tafsīr,* ed. Qalʿajī; Abū Dāwūd, *Sunan;* anon., *Muhammedanische Eschatologie,* ed. and trans. M. Wolff, Leipzig 1872 (*Kitāb Aḥwāl al-qiyāma:* Ger. and Ar.); al-Ashʿarī, Abū Ḥasan ʿAlī b. Ismāʿīl, *Kitāb al-Maqālāt al-islāmiyyīn wa-khtilāf al-muṣallīn,* ed. H. Ritter, Wiesbaden 1980[3]; Ibn Ḥanbal, *Musnad;* al-Juwaynī, ʿAbd al-Malik Imām al-Ḥaramayn, *Kitāb al-Irshād ilā qawāṭiʿ al-adilla fī uṣul al-iʿtiqād,* ed. M.Y. Mūsā/ A.A. ʿAbd al-Ḥamīd, Cairo 1950; Muqātil, *Tafsīr;* Ṭabarī, *Tafsīr,* ed. Shākir (sūras 1-12); ed. Cairo 1323-9/1905-11 (sūras 13-114); Tirmidhī, *Ṣaḥīḥ;* Zamakhsharī, *Kashshāf,* ed. M.Ṣ. Qamḥāwī, 4 vols., Cairo 1972.

Secondary: Bouman, *Gott und Mensch;* G. Böwering, God and his attributes, in *EQ,* ii, 316-31; M. Bravmann, Allāh's liberty to punish or forgive, in *Der Islam* 47 (1971), 236-7; R. Eklund, *Life between death and resurrection according to Islam,* Uppsala 1941; van Ess, *TG;* Horovitz, *KU;* Izutsu, *Concepts;* id., *God;* Jeffery, *For. vocab.*; D. Madigan, Book, in *EQ,* i, 242-51; R.J. McCarthy, *The theology of al-Ashʿarī,* Beirut 1953; A. Neuwirth, Form and structure of the Qurʾān, in *EQ,* ii, 245-66; F. Rahman, *Major themes of the Qurʾān,* Minneapolis 1980; A. Rippin, The commerce of eschatology, in Wild, *Text,* 125-35; J. Schacht, Adjr, in *EI²,* i, 209; J. Smith and Y. Haddad, *The Islamic understanding of death and resurrection,* Albany 1981; C.C. Torrey, *The commercial-theological terms in the Koran,* Leiden 1892; A.S. Tritton, Djazāʾ, in *EI²,* ii, 518-9; W.M. Watt, *The formative period of Islamic thought,* Edinburgh 1973; Wensinck, *Concordance;* id., *Handbook;* id., Munkar wa-Nakīr, in *EI²,* vii, 576-7; id., *The Muslim creed,* Cambridge 1932; id. and A.S. Tritton, ʿAdhāb al-ḳabr, in *EI²,* i, 186-7.

Rhetoric and the Qurʾān

The Qurʾān has been judged in Islamic tradition as inimitable; indeed a dogma emerged in the third/ninth century holding that the Qurʾān is, linguistically and stylistically, far superior to all other literary productions in the Arabic language (q.v.; see also LITERATURE AND THE QURʾĀN). Although the belief in the "inimitability of the Qurʾān" (*iʿjāz al-Qurʾān,* see INIMITABILITY) does not rely exclusively on formal criteria, it has been widely received as a statement about the literary qualities of the Qurʾān both in traditional scholarly literature on Arabic rhetoric (see Heinrichs, Rhetoric and poetics) and in modern scholarship (cf. Bint al-Shāṭiʾ, *al-Iʿjāz al-bayānī lil-Qurʾān*). Kermani *(Gott ist schön)* has contextualized and traced this claim of inimitability for the Islamic scripture, which was a later development in qurʾānic poetics, back to the early strata of Muslim collective memory. As against that, some recent scholars have completely dismissed the notion of *iʿjāz* as being rooted in the event of the Qurʾān. Some have done so based on the assumption of the impossibility of proving that the entire qurʾānic corpus is genuine, and thus maintain that the Qurʾān does not admit of any conclusions drawn from its self-referential statements. Others have — on the basis of a close reading of the so-called challenge verses *(āyāt al-taḥaddī)* — reached the conclusion that the qurʾānic challenges should be viewed as part of the indoctrination of the believers rather than a genuine polemic (see PROVOCATION; BELIEF AND UNBELIEF). The qurʾānic arguments viewed from such a perspective appear topical rather than real, the interlocutors of the qurʾānic speaker being reduced from real to merely imagined, fictitious adversaries (Radscheit, *Die koranische Herausforderung;* see OPPOSITION TO MUḤAMMAD). That assumption, presupposing a strict separation between the biography of the Prophet and the Qurʾān, sets a decisive epistemic course, particularly in a case where matters of prophetic self-image are at stake (see SĪRA AND THE QURʾĀN; PROPHETS AND

PROPHETHOOD): What may have been an existentially significant self-testimony of the Prophet, when read as a true challenge cast against real adversaries, is reduced to a merely rhetorical pattern, an instance of boasting about doctrinal achievements attained.

In view of the internal evidence, enhanced by external evidence (see for new discoveries concerning the interaction between the Prophet and his doctrinal and political adversaries as attested in secular literature, Imhof, *Religiöser Wandel*), the author of this article does not share the pessimism of those qurʾānic scholars who totally negate the legitimacy of drawing connections between the biography of the Prophet and the Qurʾān, provided this biography is not understood in the limited sense of a history of the Prophet's personal development. A close reading of the qurʾānic texts — not as a collection of literary remains left by a no longer feasible charismatic figure and later framed as apologetic-polemic discussions by the redactors (see COLLECTION OF THE QURʾĀN; POST-ENLIGHTENMENT ACADEMIC STUDY OF THE QURʾĀN), but as a sequence of testimonies to an ongoing and progressive communication process (see FORM AND STRUCTURE OF THE QURʾĀN) between the Prophet and his audience(s) — promises insights into a development of rhetorical phenomena discernible in the process of the qurʾānic genesis.

The extraordinary Islamic claim of inimitability *(iʿjāz)* will be revisited in the context of a synopsis of some particularly striking qurʾānic stylistic phenomena. In view of the scanty scholarly work done in the field of qurʾānic rhetoric, the following article is limited to an outline of diverse aspects that deserve to be studied. As such, it aims at tracing developments in the rhetorical self-expression of the qurʾānic message rather than assembling comprehensive exemplative material. It will therefore not attempt to study the rhetorical character of the diverse qurʾānic subgenres such as story-telling (see Welch, Formulaic features; see also NARRATIVES; LITERARY STRUCTURES OF THE QURʾĀN), polemic-apologetic debate (see Radscheit, *Die koranische Herausforderung;* McAuliffe, Debate with them; see also DEBATE AND DISPUTATION; POLEMIC AND POLEMICAL LANGUAGE), or hymnal sections (see Baumstark, Jüdischer und christlicher Gebetstypus), nor will it examine the qurʾānic style as such (see Nöldeke, Zur Sprache des Korans; Müller, *Untersuchungen;* see also LANGUAGE AND STYLE OF THE QURʾĀN). Rather, the following will try to contextualize striking rhetorical phenomena in the text within the qurʾānic communication process. The discussion will proceed from an examination of the stylistic implications of the early allegation that qurʾānic speech should be the speech of a soothsayer or seer (*kāhin,* pl. *kuhhān* or *kahana;* see SOOTHSAYERS), to an inquiry into the relationship between qurʾānic speech and that of a poet (*shāʿir,* pl. *shuʿarāʾ;* see POETS AND POETRY), with particular emphasis on the stylistic characteristics of the early Meccan sūras (q.v.; see also CHRONOLOGY AND THE QURʾĀN). In the third part it will turn briefly to the rhetorical issues of the later — more biblically inspired — parts of the Qurʾān (see JEWS AND JUDAISM; CHRISTIANS AND CHRISTIANITY; PEOPLE OF THE BOOK; CHILDREN OF ISRAEL; SCRIPTURE AND THE QURʾĀN).

The Qurʾān and its local literary forerunners: Kāhin *and* shāʿir *speech*

Already at the time of the Prophet, controversy over the new liturgical communication arose among its listeners, as to the character of the speech recited by the Prophet. Early sūras transmit various insinuations raised against the Prophet and refuted in the text, the most general and unspecified being that he is a *kāhin,* a "soothsayer" (Q 52:29: *fa-dhakkir fa-mā anta bi-niʿmati rabbika bi-kāhinin wa-lā majnūnin*), a poet (Q 52:30: *am yaqūlūna shāʿirun, natarabbaṣu bihi rayba l-manūni*), or a madman, *majnūn* (Q 68:2: *mā anta bi-niʿmati rabbika bi-majnūnin*), i.e. a person possessed by (inspiring) demons (jinn) in general (see INSANITY; JINN). Another kind of denunciation motivated by the refusal to accept particular messages consisted in calling his recitations fabrications (Q 52:33: *am yaqūlūna: taqawwalahu, bal lā yuʾminūna*), tales or legends (Q 83:13: *asāṭīr al-awwalīn*), all of which could equally well have been produced by other humans or were no more than repetitions of earlier-told tales (Boullata, Rhetorical interpretation; see GENERATIONS; LIE; FORGERY). Whereas the latter-mentioned verdict may simply be explained as resulting from the desire not to be bothered with the new message, the references to the two types of public spokesmen, soothsayer and poet, appear more serious (see PRE-ISLAMIC ARABIA AND THE QURʾĀN). They are not totally arbitrary since a number of sūras employ artistic devices that are usually associated with the speech of inspired individuals.

This concerns particularly the speech of the pre-Islamic *kāhin,* a religious functionary about whom we know very little (Wellhausen, *Reste*). The *kāhin* was a man with occult powers that he exercised as a profession and for which he received a remuneration. He gave his utterances in a particular rhythmic form known as *sajʿ* consisting in a sequence of short pregnant sentences, usually with a single rhyme (see RHYMED PROSE).

All speech-act that had its origin in the unseen powers, all speech-act that was not a daily mundane use of words, but had something to do with the unseen powers, such as cursing (see CURSE), blessing (q.v.), divination (q.v.), incantation, inspiration and revelation (see REVELATION AND INSPIRATION), had to be couched in this form.... The magical words uttered by a competent soothsayer are often compared in old Arabic literature to deadly arrows shot by night which fly unseen by their victims (Izutsu, *God,* 183 f.; see MAGIC).

The specimens of *kāhin* sayings that have been transmitted in early Islamic literature are, however, not always assuredly genuine. In some cases, they even appear to be modeled after qurʾānic verses, such as parts of the Satīḥ-story (Neuwirth, Der historische Muhammad) transmitted by Ibn Isḥāq (d. 150/767; *Sīra,* i, 10-11) and adduced by Izutsu (*God,* 174). The literary form of this sparse material has, furthermore, never been studied systematically. It is difficult, therefore, to draw secure conclusions about the relationship between pre-Islamic *kāhin* speech and stylistic phenomena in the Qurʾān. Yet, the identification that is found in traditional literature (Ṭabarī, *Taʾrīkh,* i, 1933 f.) of certain sections of the qurʾānic text with *kāhin* speech has been widely accepted in scholarship; this identification has even led to the assumption that some qurʾānic sūras represent the most reliable evidence for *kāhin* speech itself (Wellhausen, *Reste,* 135). What can be asserted, however, is the similarity between *kāhin* speech and the qurʾānic device of rhymed prose, of *sajʿ*. Rhymed prose in the strict sense of the word — consisting of clusters of very short and thus syntactically stereotyped speech units, marked by rhymes of a phonetically striking pattern — is characteristic of the early sūras.

But though the old traditional form of supernatural communication is used, it serves as a vehicle for conveying a new content, no longer for the purpose of releasing the magical power of words, nor as a form in which to couch "prophecy" in the sense of foretelling (q.v.) future events (Izutsu, *God*, 184).

Sajʿ is given up completely in the later sūras where the rhyme makes use of a simple *-ūn/-īn* — scheme to mark the end of rather long and syntactically complex verses. In these verses, the rhyming end-syllable has ceased to be the truly relevant closing device; that function is transferred to a particular syntactic structure, the clausula or rhyming cadenza (see below; see also FORM AND STRUCTURE OF THE QURʾĀN). *Sajʿ* style is thus exclusively characteristic of the early sūras, those texts that aroused — and therefore explicitly transmit — the impression in some listeners that they were related to *kāhin* speech. In the following, the relationship between *kāhin* speech and the early sūras will be elucidated by focusing on a group of initiatory sections that in western scholarship have been associated with *kāhin* speech, namely the introductory oaths (q.v.) of a series of early Meccan sūras. These introductory oaths (though never studied in context) have traditionally been considered dark, obscure, enigmatic.

The "kāhin-*model*": *Oath clusters, idhā/yawma-clause-clusters, etc.*

The introductory oaths that in twenty-one cases initiate a sūra, and in six cases mark the beginning of a new section, are completely devoid of legal connotations (see LAW AND THE QURʾĀN; CONTRACTS AND ALLIANCES; COVENANT). Several formal characteristics prove their exclusively literary function, the most striking being the multiplicity and diversity of the objects conjured. A second characteristic is their complex formulaic character: they either appear in the form *wa*-X or *lā uqsimu bi*-X, in most cases (eighteen times, all of them early Meccan) continued by further oaths amounting to extended oath clusters. The oaths are usually followed by a statement worded *inna* A *la*-B. Though the oaths most frequently refer to inanimate objects and thus do not appeal to a superior power whose revenge has to be feared, they do convey a particularly serious mood since the objects conjured in some cases project a catastrophic situation; in other cases they pose disquieting enigmas to the listeners. The oath clusters in the Qurʾān may be classified as follows (see Neuwirth, Images):

(1) Oath clusters of the type *wa-l-fāʿilāt* that conjure a catastrophic scenario: Q 37:1-3; 51:1-4; 77:1-5; 79:1-5; 100:1-5 (see APOCALYPSE; PUNISHMENT STORIES)
(2) Oath clusters alluding to particular sacred localities: Q 52:1-6; 90:1-3; 95:1-3 (see PROFANE AND SACRED; SACRED PRECINCTS)
(3) Oath clusters calling upon cosmic phenomena and certain time periods of the day or the night: Q 85:1-3; 86:1, 11-2; 89:1-4; 91:1-7; 92:1-3; 93:1-2 (see WEATHER; COSMOLOGY; DAY AND NIGHT; DAY, TIMES OF)

A few representative examples will be discussed.

Oath clusters that do not explicitly name their objects but only refer to them as unknown, frightening and rapidly approaching phenomena (feminine participles of words of motion or sound appear as harbingers of a catastrophe) have been considered to be the most intricate both by traditional exegetes (see EXEGESIS OF THE QURʾĀN: CLASSICAL AND MEDIEVAL) and by modern scholars, e.g. Q 100:1-5, 6-11:

Wa-l-ʿādiyāti ḍabḥā/fa-l-mūriyāti qadḥā/fa-l-mughīrāti ṣubḥā/fa-atharna bihi naqʿā/fa-wasaṭna bihi jamʿā/inna l-insāna li-rabbihi la-kanūd/wa-innahu ʿalā dhālika la-

shahīd/wa-innahu li-ḥubbi l-khayri la-shadīd/a-fa-lā ya'lamu idhā bu'thira mā fī l-qubūr/wa-ḥuṣṣila mā fī l-ṣudūr/inna rabbahum bihim yawma'idhin la-khabīr
By the panting runners/striking fire in sparks/storming forward in the morning/their track a dust-cloud/that finally appear in the center of a crowd/verily humankind is to its lord (q.v.) ungrateful/verily, he to that is witness/and verily he for the love of good *(al-khayr)* is violent/does he know? When what is in the graves is ransacked (see BURIAL; DEATH AND THE DEAD)/and what is in the breasts is extracted/verily, their lord that day will of them be well informed.

The five oaths depict a kind of canvas or "tableau" of one and the same object viewed in several successive stages of a continuous and rapid motion: a group of horses, whose riders are carrying out a raid, *ghazwa* (Q 100:3: *al-mughīrāt;* see EXPEDITIONS AND BATTLES; FIGHTING; WAR). The progression of their movement (Q 100:1, 5: *al-'ādiyāt/fa-wasaṭna*), which ends with a sudden standstill at its destination in the camp of the enemy, is stressed by the particle *fa-*. The movement is directed towards a fixed aim: to overcome the enemy by surprise, perhaps even while still asleep (Q 100:3: *ṣubḥan*).

On closer examination the tableau depicted in the oath cluster appears incomplete, its immanent tension unresolved. The description is interrupted at the very point where the attack on the enemy camp would be expected to start. Instead, a general statement about human ingratitude to God (see GRATITUDE AND INGRATITUDE), their obstinacy (see INSOLENCE AND OBSTINACY) and greediness (see AVARICE) is made — a focus on two vehement human psychic movements that may be taken to echo the violent movements of the horses (see VIOLENCE). The statement leads up to a rhetorical question about human knowledge of their eschatological fate (Q 100:9 f.; see ESCHATOLOGY) which again extends into a description of the psychic situation of humanity on that day (see LAST JUDGMENT; RESURRECTION). At this point the imagery of the interrupted panel of the *ghazwa* is continued: the eschatological scenery (structured in a likewise ecstatically accelerating form of an *idhā*-clause cluster: Q 100:9 f.: *idhā bu'thira mā fī l-qubūri/wa-ḥuṣṣila mā fī l-ṣudūri*) presents a picture that precisely presupposes a violent attack leading to the overturn of everything, since it portrays devastation: the awakening and dispersal *(bu'thira)* of the sleepers *(mā fī l-qubūri),* the emptying of the most concealed receptacles (Q 100:10: *mā fī l-ṣudūri*). The attack presupposed here has already been presumed prototypically by the panel of the *ghazwa*-riders portrayed in the oath cluster. The threatening scenario of the introductory sections, whose effect is enhanced through the equally frightening associations conjured by the *kāhin* speech style, thus relies on a deeper subtext: the panel of Bedouin (q.v.) attackers taking the enemy by surprise after a rapid and violent ride — perhaps the fear-inducing scenario *par excellence* in the pre-Islamic context — reveals itself as an image of the last day (see SYMBOLIC IMAGERY). It serves as a prototype, easily understandable for the listeners as it derives from genuine social experience, for the as yet not-experienced incidents leading up to the last judgment.

The oath cluster in Q 77:1-6, though usually interpreted as a reference to angels in their various activities (see ANGEL), refers "to the winds bringing up the storm-clouds which give the picture of approaching doom" (Bell, *Qur'ān,* ii, 626; see AIR AND WIND). Once more we are confronted with a tableau of violently moving beings — from the time of their earlier use in Q 100 feminine plural participles in qur'ānic speech have a catastrophic connotation — that prototypically anticipate the eschatological events to be expected. Although the eschatological topic itself is not raised until the end of the sūra, the matrix of images created by the oath cluster remains continuously effective. The refrain repeated ten times throughout the text: "woe that day to those who count false!" (see CHEATING; WEIGHTS AND MEASURES; MEASUREMENT) serves to make audible something of the recitation, the reminder (*dhikr;* see REMEMBRANCE), meant to be a warning, which was part of the appearance of the enigmatic beings projected in the oath cluster (Q 77:5: *fa-l-mulqiyāti dhikrā*). This type of oath cluster soon goes through a change. In the somewhat later text Q 51:1-4, again presenting a panel of clouds that signal a rainstorm, the structural function of the introductory oath clusters has changed. Though it still introduces a prototypical tableau of imminent eschatological incidents, the sense of an "enigma" that had marked the early cases, has now disappeared, and the anticipation of the explicit mention of eschatological phenomena is immediately dissipated. By this stage, the listener is sufficiently accustomed to the prototypical representation of the last day that he or she can immediately translate.

A further step towards the demystification of enigmatic speech is achieved in Q 37:1-5, a sūra of the second Meccan period where an oath cluster of the type *wa-l-fāʿilāt* appears for the last time. Here, the objects conjured no longer belong to the empirical sphere of human experience but to the realm of celestial beings, angels. On the formal side there is a change, too: The usual semantic caesura between the oath formulae and the ensuing statement has vanished, and both textual units display a strong conceptual coherence: the oath cluster involving angels singing hymns (Q 37:3: *fa-l-tāliyāti dhikrā*) is continued by a statement that itself presents the text of that angelical recitation (Q 37:4: *inna ilāhakum la-wāḥidun*). With this last *wa-l-fāʿilāt*-cluster, the earlier function of the oath clusters, i.e. to depict a prototypical panel of the eschatological events, has ceased to operate.

The second and third kinds of oath clusters are less enigmatically coded: they are phrased either *wa-l*-X or *lā uqsimu bi*-X. A group of these clusters alludes to sacred localities. An early example is Q 95:1-3:

wa-l-tīni wa-l-zaytūn/wa-ṭūri sīnīn/wa-hādhā l-baladi l-amīn/la-qad khalaqnā l-insāna fī aḥsani taqwīm/thumma radadnāhu asfala sāfilīn/illā lladhīna āmanū wa-ʿamilū l-ṣāliḥāti fa-hum ajrun ghayru mamnūn/fa-mā yukadhdhibuka baʿdu bi-l-dīn/a-laysa llāhu bi-aḥkami l-ḥākimīn

By the fig and the olive/by Mount Sinai/ and this land secure/surely, we have created man most beautifully erect/ then have rendered him the lowest of the low/except those who have believed and wrought the works of righteousness for them is a reward rightfully theirs/what then, after that will make you declare false in regard to the judgment?/is not God the best of judges?

The first oaths invoke a pair of fruits (resp. fruit-bearing trees; see AGRICULTURE AND VEGETATION; TREES), followed by another pair mentioning two localities (see GEOGRAPHY). The ensuing statement takes a different semantic direction, speaking about human instability from the time of their creation and their falling back, after perfection, into the decrepitude of old age (see BIOLOGY AS THE CREATION AND STAGES OF LIFE). From this bipartite argument — Q 95:6 should be considered a later addition, and not part of the sūra's discourse — the conclusion *(fa-)* is drawn, clad in a rhetorical question, that the truth of the last judgment can no longer be denied. The discursive thread that holds the three verse groups together becomes visible through a close look at the imagery of the oath cluster. The two kinds of trees may simply be taken as signs of divine bounty granted with creation (q.v.); the ensemble of fig and olive, however, suggests a symbolic meaning, advocated already by the traditional Muslim exegetes who read the two verses as an allusion to al-Shām, the biblical holy land (see SYRIA). Of the two localities that follow in the next oath pair, the first recalls the theophany (q.v.) on Mount Sinai (q.v.) granted to Moses (q.v.), whereas the second alludes to Mecca (q.v.), and is associated with its sanctuary, its *ḥaram*. Theophanies symbolize divine communication and ultimately the divine instruction granted to people that marks the true, significant beginning of human time (q.v.). Though physical time (Q 95:4) that runs in a cyclical way ultimately causes humanity's downfall, within the paradigm of salvation (q.v.) history human longevity is secured. For human beings, historical salvific time eclipses the cyclical movement, running linearly towards the point where the pledge (q.v.) of divine instruction is to be rendered, i.e. toward the last judgment (see HISTORY AND THE QUR'ĀN). The oath cluster referring to creation (nature being an allusion to the divine preservation of humanity) and instruction (theophany-localities symbolizing divine communication with people) serves to arouse the listeners' anticipation of the dissolution of both: the dissolution of creation in physical annihilation at the end of "natural time," and the closure wrought by rendering account for the received instruction at the end of "historical salvific time," on judgment day. The solution of the enigma posed in the oath cluster is fulfilled only at the very end of the sūra where God is praised as the best judge (see JUDGMENT) and the tenor of the sūra returns to the hymn-like tone of the beginning (see NATURE AS SIGNS; PSALMS).

A parallel case is Q 90:1-3, where the introductory oaths again raise the two ideas of creation and instruction, arousing the expectation of a closure that presents the rendering of the pledge of instruction at the last judgment. The somewhat later Q 52, however, starting with a complex oath cluster made up of diverse objects like two sacred sites, the holy scripture (see BOOK) and the — perhaps apocalyptically — turbulent sea: "by the mount/ and a book written/in parchment unrolled (see SCROLLS)/by the house frequented/ by the roof upraised/by the sea filled full," attests a development. Here the statement (Q 52:7-8) about the imminence of the punishment (see CHASTISEMENT AND PUNISHMENT; REWARD AND PUNISHMENT) immediately starts to resolve the tension in the listeners' minds, their expectation — prompted by the initial introduction of symbols of divine instruction (sacred sites and scripture) and allusions to the dissolution of nature (sea filled full) — of the explication of eschatological fulfillment, of human rendering of the pledge of divine instruction (see ERROR; ASTRAY). An eschatological scene constituted by a *yawma*-clause-cluster (Q 52:9-10) follows immediately. This leads to a diptych portraying the blessed and the cursed in the beyond (Q 52:23-8), thus completing the fulfillment of the listeners' anticipation of the eschatological account (see HELL AND HELLFIRE; GARDEN; PARADISE).

All of the oath-cluster sūras demonstrate a similar development of the oath clusters and their ensuing statement: from functional units exhibiting a tension between each other, to purely ornamental elements without any sensible semantic caesura between the two parts and thus without the power to build up a structure of anticipation (see Neuwirth, Images, for a detailed discussion of the sūras introduced by references to celestial phenomena, i.e. Q 81:15-9; 89:1-30; 90:1-11; 91:1-15; 92:1-21; and of phases of day and night, i.e. Q 51:7-9; 75:1-22; 85:1-7; 86:1-17; see PLANETS AND STARS). The sūras with introductory oath clusters still closely associated with the tradition of earlier Arabian sacred language (see SOUTH ARABIA, RELIGION IN PRE-ISLAMIC) certainly deserve to be considered as a type of their own, in view of the immanent dynamics that dominates them. This effect — that scholarship has neglected completely (see e.g. Welch, Ḳurʾān) — is formally due to the accumulation of parallel phrases in the introductory section, which creates a rhythm of its own. It is structurally due to the anticipation of a solution for the enigma aroused in the listeners' minds by the amassed metaphorical elements, not immediately comprehensible or at least plausible to them. The "dynamization" of the entire composition produced by the introductory section is the main characteristic of this very early text group and has remained exemplary for the structure of the sūra as such.

Yawma/idhā-*clause-clusters, isolated oaths and later* kitāb-*annunciations*

There are introductory sections in the Qurʾan that are closely related typologically, especially the eschatological scenes with their clusters of *yawma/idhā-l-*X-*faʿala*-phrases, that build up a comparably strong rhythmical incipit. Many of these clusters, however, have the tension resolved immediately in the closely following apodosis; with only a few extended clusters is the solution suspended (e.g. Q 56:1-6; 81:1-3; 82:1-4; see Neuwirth, *Studien,* 188 f.). Yet, in no case of the *yawma/idhā-l-*X-*faʿala*-clusters does the tension affect the entire sūra. It is different with the oath clusters. In the case of the *wa-l-fāʿilāt*-clusters, the anticipation of an explication of the enigma posed in the cluster — the translation of the events presented metaphorically, through their empirically known prototypes, into their eschatological analogues — is fulfilled only at the end of the sūra or of its first main part. The immediate fulfillment of the anticipation roused in the oath cluster occurs only in the later texts where oath clusters have lost their tension-creating function.

It is not merely by coincidence that the standard incipit, characteristic of so many later sūras, emerges from these powerful oath-cluster introductions. In the end, among the originally numerous images projected in the oath, only that of the book, of *al-kitāb* (or *al-qurʾān*), remains in use. This is the most abstract of all the different symbols used, essentially no more than a mere sign. Six sūras start with an oath by the book: Q 36:2; 38:1; 43:2; 44:2; 50:1; 52:2. The book is thus the only relic from among a complex ensemble of manifold accessories of revelation used as objects of oaths, originally comprising cosmic (Q 51:1-4; 77:1-5 [clouds]; 51:7; 53:1; 74:32; 85:1; 86:1; 91:1-2 [celestial bodies]), vegetative (Q 95:1), topographic (Q 52:1, 4; 90:1; 95:2-3), cultic (Q 52:3; 68:1) and social (Q 90:2) elements. The book as the symbol of revelation *par excellence* thus acquires, already in early Meccan times, but particularly during the later Meccan periods — *hādhā/dhālika l-kitāb* becomes the standard initial sign of nearly all the later sūras — the dignity which it has preserved until the present day, i.e. that of representing the noblest emblem of the Islamic religion.

Further rhetorical characteristics of early sūras

An early device introduced to arouse attention is the twofold rhetorical question, the "Lehrfrage" (cf. Neuwirth, *Studien*, 132 f.) attached to a newly introduced but enigmatic term. The new notion is named (*al*-X) and is immediately followed by its echo in simple and then extended question form (*mā l*-X? *Wa-mā adrāka mā l*-X?) — leading to an explanatory gloss, as in Q 101:1-3: *al-qāriʿa/mā l-qāriʿa?/ Wa-mā adrāka mā l-qāriʿa?/yawma takūnu*... (for a stylistic evaluation of the entire sūra, see Sells, Sound and meaning; further examples are Q 69:1-3; 83:7-9, 18-20; 90:11-13; 101:9-11; 104:4-6). A new term — particularly a threatening indirect evocation of the imminent eschatological events — can thus be impressed onto the minds. The *mā-adrāka*-question remains limited to early sūras; after having changed into a simple *al*-X *mā l*-X? at a later stage (Q 56:27 f., 41-2) it disappears completely from the qurʾānic rhetorical spectrum.

Repetition of elements is characteristic of the early texts. It ranges from the repetition of a completely identical phrase (as in Q 94:5-6: *inna maʿa l-ʿusri yusrā/inna maʿa l-ʿusri yusrā*, "So, verily, with every difficulty, there is relief, verily, with every difficulty, there is relief") to repetitions of structural elements, thus the isocolon is frequent: Q 88:12-6: *fīhā ʿaynun jāriya/fīhā sururun marfūʿa/wa-akwābun mawḍūʿa/wa-namāriqu masfūfa/wa-zarābiyyu mabthūtha*, "Therein will be a bubbling spring (see SPRINGS AND FOUNTAINS)/therein will be thrones raised on high/goblets (see CUPS AND VESSELS) placed and cushions set in rows/and rich carpets spread out." Of course, the oath cluster relies on the repetition of strictly parallel elements: *wa-l-shamsi wa-ḍuḥāhā/wa-l-qamari idhā talāhā/wa-l-nahāri idhā jallāhā/*..., "By the sun (q.v.) and his splendor/ by the moon (q.v.) as she follows him/ by the day as it shows up its glory...." (Q 91:1-3). Equally, the *idhā*-clause-cluster is made up of identical structures forming a series of parallelisms or even isocola, as in Q 81:1-13:

idhā l-shamsu kuwwirat/wa-idhā l-nujūmu nkadarat/wa-idhā l-jibālu suyyirat/wa-idhā l-ʿishāru ʿuṭṭilat/wa-idhā l-wuḥūshu ḥushshirat/wa-idhā l-biḥāru sujjirat/wa-idhā l-nufūsu zuwwijat/wa-idhā l-mawʾūdatu suʾilat/bi-ayyi dhanbin qutilat/wa-idhā l-ṣuḥufu nushirat/wa-idhā l-samāʾu kushiṭat/wa-idhā l-jaḥīmu suʿʿirat/wa-idhā l-jannatu uzlifat

When the sun is wound round/and when the stars fall/and when the mountains are made to pass away/and when the pregnant she-camels are neglected/and when the wild beasts are gathered together/and when the seas overflow/and when the souls are joined/and when the infant buried alive is questioned/for what sin was she killed (see INFANTICIDE)/and when the pages are laid open/and when the heaven is stripped off (see HEAVEN AND SKY)/and when hellfire is set ablaze/and when paradise is brought near/[then...]

It is noteworthy that in these clusters, the conditional clauses that normally would be *idhā faʿala l*-X display the inverted syntactic sequence *idhā l*-X *faʿala*, otherwise familiar only from poetry.

In Arabic, etymologic repetitions in morphologically different shape are particularly frequent in *maṣdar*-constructions (see GRAMMAR AND THE QURʾĀN); paranomasias of this type appear in early sūras (cf. Q 52:9-10: *yawma tamūru l-samāʾu mawrā/wa-tasīru l-jibālu sayrā*, "On the day when the firmament will be in dreadful commotion and the mountains will fly hither and thither," and frequently elsewhere).

It is evident that, from the perspective of the transmission of information, many of these devices are not efficient, since they are apt to suspend rather than to convey information; their function is revealed, however, once the text is performed orally (see RECITATION OF THE QUR᾿ĀN). The Qur᾿ān, abounding in imperatives addressed to the Prophet and/or the believers (see EXHORTATIONS): to recite (Q 96:1: *iqra᾿*, and often) or to chant (Q 73:4: *rattili l-qur᾿āna tartīlā*, and often) the text, to recall by reciting (Q 19:16: *udhkur*, or Q 88:21: *dhakkir*, and often; see MEMORY) the text, itself presents the claim of being an oral communication (see ORALITY; ORALITY AND WRITING IN ARABIA). Navid Kermani (*Gott ist schön*, 197) has gone so far as to claim:

If a text is explicitly composed for recitation, fulfilling its poetic purpose only when recited or — more generally speaking — performed, it should be viewed as a score, not as a literary work, as Paul Valéry once said of the poem. Although a score can be read or hummed quietly in private, it is ultimately intended to be performed.

The frequency of appellative expressions presupposing the presence of addressees is particularly striking in the beginnings of early sūras, where the attention of the listeners is sometimes aroused directly through an imperative (Q 73:1-2; 74:1-2; 87:1; 96:1, calling to proclaim), or a related form (Q 106:3, with a preceding address). Polemic introductory parts start with a *waylun li-*, "woe to-," exclamation (Q 83:1-3; 104:1-2; cf. Q 77:24 f.; 107:4-7) or a curse-formula (Q 111:1 *tabbat yadā* X, "may the hands of X perish"), or with a deictic formula, also familiar from interior sections of sūras (Q 107:1: *a-ra᾿ayta lladhī*, "did you see him who…").

It might, on first sight, appear that the hymnic introductory sections stand by themselves. They are strongly reminiscent of biblical models and, more precisely, of liturgical texts such as the Jewish *berākhōt* that are likewise made up of relative clauses *(bārūkh attā adonai asher…)*. In three instances both creation and divine instruction are recalled as is the case in the *berākhōt:* Q 87:1-5, *sabbiḥi sma rabbika l-a'lā/lladhī khalaqa fa-sawwā…;* Q 96:1-5, *iqra᾿ bi-smi rabbika lladhī khalaq/khalaqa l-insāna min 'alaq/iqra…;* and Q 55:1-3, *al-raḥmān/'allama l-qur᾿ān/khalaqa l-insān/'allamahu….* Equally biblically-tuned are hymnic sections in the interior of sūras, like Q 85:13-6 and, particularly, Q 53:43-9, which seems to echo the famous hymn from 1 Samuel 2:6. In the same vein, a number of sūras conclude with a final exclamation clad in an imperative that in most cases calls for a liturgical activity: Q 96:19 (call for prostration; see BOWING AND PROSTRATION), Q 69:52 (call for divine praise; cf. Q 56:74; see also LAUDATION; GLORY; GLORIFICATION OF GOD; PRAISE), Q 52:48 f. (call for patience; see TRUST AND PATIENCE), Q 84:24 (announcement of punishment); see also the final exclamations of Q 53:62 (prostration), Q 93:11 (recitation), Q 94:7-8 (segregation from unbelievers), Q 86:15-7 (patience), Q 51:60 (exclamation of woe); only the final exclamation in Q 55:78 takes the shape of a doxology (see Baumstark, Gebetstypus): *tabāraka smu rabbika*, "blessed is the name of your lord." But in view of the composition of most early sūras made up of diverse elements, it appears problematic to attempt an unambiguous distinction between texts imprinted by ancient Arabian literary traditions and others more biblically styled.

The "poet-model": similes and metaphors, structures of discourse

The allegation that the Prophet was a poet would likely have been based less on particular stylistic evidence than on the general similarity between qur᾿ānic diction and other genres of elevated, non-ordinary speech (cf. Gilliot, Poète ou prophète?, 380-8: "Prophétie contre poésie. De la construction d'un prophète"). It is true that the early sūras, which — though not metrically bound nor carrying a monorhyme — prompted that particular accusation, are highly poetic (for a study in their stylistic devices, see Sells, Sound and meaning, and id., Sounds, spirit and gender). Indeed, the "*kāhin*-model" of speech is only a special case of poetic diction. As Kermani has shown, a high degree of "poeticity" ("Poetizität") cannot be denied to the Qurʾān as a whole. Not only does the entire Qurʾān morphologically and syntactically adhere closely to what has been termed poetic *ʿarabiyya* (see GRAMMAR AND THE QURʾĀN), but it also makes extensive use of a selected vocabulary that — lending itself easily to the demands of the familiar meters — had established itself as poetic (Bloch, *Vers und Sprache*). J.J. Gluck (Is there poetry) has tried to trace rhetorical devices employed by poets. Above all, the priority given in most qurʾānic texts to adornments of speech and devices of appeal to the listeners that are completely unnecessary for the raw transmission of information is a convincing proof of its proximity to the realm of poetry. (For a discussion of the medieval learned debates about the relation between Qurʾān and poetry, see Kermani, *Gott ist schön*, 233-314; von Grunebaum, *A tenth century document*.)

Similes (q.v.; *tashbīh*) and metaphors (*istiʿāra;* see METAPHOR) are, of course, the most striking evocations of poetic speech. A modern survey of these tropes in the Qurʾān — as achieved for pre-Islamic poetry by Renate Jacobi (*Studien zur Poetik*, 115-27, 153-67) and Thomas Bauer (*Altarabische Dichtkunst*, 181-204) — is still to be done. T. Sabbagh *(Le métaphore dans le Coran)* is only an inventory; his classification of metaphorical usages does not consider the contexts in which the words are used, nor the fields of their metaphorical application. More research has been done on the theologically controversial aspect of *tashbīh*, namely the cases of qurʾānic anthropomorphism (q.v.), e.g. God's cunning (*makr*, e.g. Q 3:54; 4:142) and the like (see van Ess, Tashbīh wa-tanzīh; see THEOLOGY AND THE QURʾĀN). Since the appearance in 1892 of the study by C.C. Torrey, *The commercial theological terms in the Koran*, that provides a thorough survey of a number of words touching on commerce and their often metaphoric use in the Qurʾān, commerce had been identified as one major realm of images in the Qurʾān. Torrey, and later scholars following him, suggested that the words and metaphors from the commercial realm form a cluster of terms derived from commercial applications which have taken on theological overtones in the Qurʾān (see e.g. REWARD AND PUNISHMENT; also, ECONOMICS; WEIGHTS AND MEASURES; TRADE AND COMMERCE). As against Torrey who "assumed a mercantile background of Muḥammad and Mecca and then found evidence for that in the Qurʾān" (Rippin, Commerce, 128), Andrew Rippin (The commerce of eschatology) presents a reversal of the commercial-background-theory. He demonstrates that Torrey's terms are employed in three contexts in the Qurʾān, in speaking about the prophets of the past, in legislating the Muslim community and in descriptions of eschatology. Inverting Torrey's argument, he concludes that the

> symbolism of eschatology is partially derived from the image of the foundations of a moral and flourishing society, the symbolism resolves the seeming iniquities of life as it is actually lived — the presence of suffering and injustice as basic facts — by reflecting a divinely-ruled society in which

evil gets its proper reward. The symbolism gives a higher meaning to history by relating it to transcendental mythic patterns (Rippin, Commerce, 134; see ETHICS AND THE QUR'ĀN; GOOD AND EVIL; SIN, MAJOR AND MINOR; OPPRESSION; OPPRESSED ON EARTH, THE).

Rippin advocates utmost caution in attempting a historical contextualization of the symbolism of the text, which he regards as a product of later Muslim readings tailored towards particular ideological ends. A comparative study juxtaposing qur'ānic and poetic similes and metaphors is still a desideratum.

The qaṣīda *and the sūra*

Though the allegation identifying qur'ānic speech with poetical speech arises from observations made on the basis of the earliest texts, it is noteworthy that an intriguing relationship between Qur'ān and poetry can be discerned. This relationship relies less on small isolated speech units — such as the various tropes in both canonical corpora (that still await a comparison) — than on the overall structure of both *qaṣīda* and sūra (see SŪRAS). At a certain stage in the qur'ānic development, the sūra as a literary unit seems to reflect the structure of the dominating poetical genre, the *qaṣīda*. The *qaṣīda* was the standard form of pre-Islamic poetry consisting of a sequence of three sections, each conveying a different mood: a nostalgic *nasīb*, lamenting the loss of stability by recalling the disrupted relation between the poet and a beloved, was followed by the description of a movement in space, a journey (q.v.), *raḥīl* or, more often, a description of the riding camel (q.v.) used by the poet — a section that portrayed the poet regaining his self-consciousness and reattaching himself to the world through recalling instances of his past activities, his interfering with reality through exploitation of the *"kairos,"* the crucial moment for achieving a change. After evoking his heroic achievements, the poet concluded his poem with an evocative *fakhr*, a self-praise or praise of the collective confirming the heroic virtues of tribal society. The social status of the recitation of these poems, as Andras Hamori (*The art of medieval Arabic literature*, 21 f.) stressed, must have come close to that of a ritual:

> The extreme conventionality, repetitiousness, and thematic limitation of the *qaṣīda* need not astonish us.... Already in the sixth century, before the coming of Islam, these poems, rather than myths or religious rituals, served as the vehicle for the conception that sorted out the emotionally incoherent facts of life and death, and by the sorting set them at the bearable remove of contemplation. *Qaṣīda* poets spoke in affirmation of a model they shared, their poetry tended to become a shared experience, all the more as the affirmation was through the replay of prototypal events which the model so successfully charted.

The poet, then, is located in the center of the poem; the one who establishes the model for identification through his word, is at the same time the figure standing in the center of the artifice. Looking at the fully developed (most often) tripartite sūras of the middle and late Meccan periods (see Neuwirth, Rezitationstext) we can trace a comparable structure: The sūra starts with a section that draws on various standard themes such as hymns, lists of virtues or vices (see VIRTUES AND VICES, COMMANDING AND FORBIDDING), polemic against unbelievers and affirmations of the divine origin of the message; most of these themes also serve to furnish the final part which should, ideally, be concluded with the topic of affirming the revelation. The center of the sūra, however, is fixed over a longer period of qur᾽ānic development. It contains one or more stereotyped narratives about prophets, portraying them in their struggle to achieve an ideological reorientation in their communities, announcing that the *"kairos,"* the unique moment to gain salvation, has come, thus exemplifying the chance granted to Muḥammad's listeners in the light of history. Functioning both as a fixed part in the liturgy of the community and as a mirror of contemporary history, these sūras provide ritualized memory and at the same time real experience. In view of the structure of the extremely powerful genre of the *qaṣīda,* where the poet appears at once as the protagonist in and the transmitter of the message that contains the rules of what should be, it is perhaps not surprising to find the figure of the Prophet — or a whole group of representatives of this type — as the protagonist of the drama and the bearer of the word (see WORD OF GOD) again in the middle part of the sūra. The Prophet is thus, like the *qaṣīda* poet in the poem, the exemplary figure and the speaker in one person. Here, as in the case of the ancient *kāhin* speech, it appears that an earlier genre has been absorbed to shape the foundation of a new sacred canon.

This suggestion does not imply that the stance taken in the Qur᾽ān towards poets should have developed positively. In Q 26:224-6 we read: *wa-l-shuʿarāʾu yattabiʿuhumu l-ghāwūna/a-lam tara annahum fī kulli wādin yahīmūna/wa-annahum yaqūlūna mā lā yafʿalūna,* "And the poets, the beguiled follow them/do you not see that in every wadi they err about madly in love/and that they say what they do not do?" These verses should be distinguished from the later addition of Q 26:227 (see Neuwirth, Der historische Muḥammad, 103) that reflects a late Medinan development. In Q 26:224-6 the poets are accused of not coming up to the high claims raised in their poetry ("to do what they say") and thus of being incapable of functioning as spokespeople of their collective. The spokesperson of society is no longer the poet but the prophet. The Medinan addition Q 26:227 excludes from the verdict those poets who have actively sided with the community, which, as an *ecclesia militans,* cannot afford to have itself satirized (see Imhof, *Religiöser Wandel*).

The Qur᾽ān and the Bible: Refrains and cadenzas

Although the Qur᾽ān contains no explicit allegations that it is modeled on biblical speech, some accusations that he was taught by a mortal (Q 16:103: *innamā yuʿallimuhu basharun*) were raised against the Prophet and are refuted in the Qur᾽ān. It is, however, much more relevant that the Qur᾽ān as a message communicated in the Arabian peninsula of late antiquity necessarily draws from both pagan and monotheistic traditions. The qur᾽ānic message soon presented itself as a re-narration of the earlier biblical scriptures and one serving analogous purposes, namely to provide a liturgical base for the communication between God and humanity. We can even locate in the Qur᾽ān the decisive turn from the communication of a divine message to the celebration of liturgy with the memory of salvation history (i.e. biblical stories) placed in its center (see Neuwirth, Referentiality). Those middle and late Meccan sūras that appear to constitute complex liturgies resembling roughly those of the older monotheistic religions are comprised of the following: an introductory section, reading from the scriptures, and a closing section. The presentation of the biblical story is sometimes explicitly introduced by an announcement, as if a pericope to be read in church were being announced: Q 15:51, "Bring them news (q.v.) about the guests of Abraham" (q.v.; *nabbiʾhum ʿan ḍayfi*

Ibrāhīm; cf. Q 19:2: *dhikru raḥmati rabbika ʿabdahu Zakariyya,* "This is a recital of the mercy [q.v.] of your lord to his servant Zechariah [q.v.]"). Qurānic re-narrations of biblical texts are enough to fill a comprehensive reference book (see Speyer, *Erzählungen*). It is particularly in this stage of Meccan development that liturgical formulae familiar from Judaism and Christianity become frequent in the Qurʾān, like Q 27:59: *al-ḥamdu lillāhi wa-salāmun ʿalā ʿibādihi lladhīna ṣṭafā,* "Praise be to God and peace be on his elected servants" (cf. *doxa en hypsistois theō kai epi gēs eirēnē en anthrōpois eudokias,* Luke 2:14; see for the Christian doxology and the Jewish *berākhā* reflected in the frequent qurʾānic exclamations *al-ḥamdu lillāh* and *subḥāna rabbinā/llāhi,* Baumstark, Gebetstypus; a complete introitus may be identified in the Fātiḥa [q.v.], see Neuwirth and Neuwirth, Fātiḥa).

The question, however, of the stylistic and rhetorical impact of biblical texts on the Qurʾān has not yet been studied. Only a few isolated parallels strike the eye, such as the pronouncedly biblical sounding hyperboles in Q 7:40: *inna lladhīna kadhdhabū bi-āyātinā wa-stakbarū ʿanhā lā tufattaḥu lahumu abwābu l-samāʾi wa-lā yadkhulūna l-jannata ḥattā yalija l-jamalu fī sammi l-khiyāṭi,* "To those who reject our signs (q.v.) and treat them with arrogance (q.v.), the gates of heaven will not open for them, nor will they enter the garden, until the camel can pass through the eye of the needle" (cf. Matthew 19:24; Mark 10:25; Luke 18:25; see PARABLES) or Q 39:67: *wa-l-arḍu jamīʿan qabḍatuhu yawma l-qiyāmati wa-l-samāwātu maṭwiyyatun bi-yamīnihi,* "And on the day of resurrection (q.v.) the whole of the earth (q.v.) will be grasped by his hand and the heavens will be rolled up in his right hand" (cf. Isaiah 34:4, 40:12; see for further examples Speyer, *Erzählungen;* see LEFT HAND AND RIGHT HAND).

A more prominent stylistic issue shared by the Bible and Qurʾān is certainly the refrain which appears four times in the Qurʾān (Q 26, 54, 55, 77), again mostly in middle Meccan sūras where the focus has shifted from the ancient Arabian tradition to the biblical. Although there are instances of anaphors and even longer speech units repeated in pre-Islamic and *muḥaḍram* poetry (i.e. poetry that spans the pre-Islamic and the Islamic eras), a refrain appearing with the frequency of the verse *fa-bi-ayyi ālāʾi rabbikumā tukadhdhibān,* "Then which of the benefits of your lord will you two deny?" (e.g. Q 55:13) is not found in poetry (see BLESSING; GRACE). That refrain has, however, a close counterpart in the refrain *kīle-ōlām ḥasdō* in Psalm 136, a text that in many respects resembles the sophisticated composition of Sūrat al-Raḥmān ("The Merciful," Q 55) and must have been well known in monotheistic circles since it plays a major role in Jewish liturgy (see Neuwirth, Qurʾānic literary structure). We can conclude that refrains in the Qurʾān may have been inspired by the Psalms (q.v.) or else by liturgical poetry shaped after the model of the Psalms.

Another major rhetorical phenomenon that appears to have a strong biblical imprint is the clausula — or the cadenza, as it might be termed in analogy to the final part of speech units in Gregorian chant — which, through their particular sound pattern, arouse the expectation of an ending as, for example, the concluding colon of the later Meccan and Medinan long verses of the Qurʾān (see Neuwirth, *Studien,* 157-70; see also FORM AND STRUCTURE OF THE QURʾĀN). In the Qurʾān the cadenza relies less on an identical musical sound than on a widely stereotyped phrasing. It is easily identifiable as an end marker since it is semantically distinguished from its context: it does not partake in the main theme of the discourse but adds a moral, polemic or hymnal comment to it. Although it is true that not all multipartite verses bear such formulaic endings, cadenzas may be considered characteristic of the later Meccan and all the Medinan qurʾānic texts. On a social level, they betray a novel narrative pact between the speaker and his audience, the consciousness that there is a basic consensus not only on human moral behavior but also on the image of God as a powerful co-agent ever-present in human interaction (see GOD AND HIS ATTRIBUTES; POWER AND IMPOTENCE; FATE; DESTINY). But cadenzas achieve even more in terms of constructing a new identity: they provide markers of the sacred that transform narrative events into stages of salvation history, changing the ordinary chronometric time of the narratives into signifying time. An observation of Aziz al-Azmeh (Chronophagous discourse, 193 f.) is useful to illuminate this point:

The vacuous syntagms of ordinary time is the instrument of a finalist paradigm whose instances punctuate the course of this flow at certain loci of accentuation that enclose values of sacredness, lending a sense of sacredness to historical succession. These values are, primarily, an integrality of divine order which reigned with the creation of Adam (see ADAM AND EVE), the imperative of its complete restoration in paradise and the intermittent attempts to calque this order in the history of prophecy.

It goes without saying that the cadenzas owe their aesthetic effect to their widely predictable sound. Their stereotypical appearance, which is due to the morphological and syntactical constraints imposed by the rhyme (see Müller, *Untersuchungen*) would, in a written text, appear awkward. In the recited text, however, the double-edged style of the long verses, consisting of naturally flowing prose merging into artificial, sacred, speech in the formulaic conclusion, powerfully reflects the bi-dimensionality of qurʾānic speech which evokes simultaneously world and hereafter, time (q.v.) and eternity (q.v.).

Angelika Neuwirth

Bibliography

Primary: Ibn Isḥāq, *Sīra*, ed. Wüstenfeld; Ibn Qayyim al-Jawziyya, *Tibyān;* Ṭabarī, *Tafsīr*, ed. Būlāq, 30 vols., Cairo 1323/1905; id., *Taʾrīkh*, ed. de Goeje.

Secondary: H. Abdul-Raouf, *Qurʾān translation. Discourse, texture and exegesis*, London 2001; A. al-Azmeh, Chronophagous discourse. A study of the clerico-legal appropriation of the world in Islamic tradition, in F.E. Reynolds and D. Tracy (eds.), *Religion and practical reason in the comparative philosophy of religions*, Albany 1994, 163-211; Th. Bauer, *Altarabische Dichtkunst. Eine Untersuchung ihrer Struktur und Entwicklung am Beispiel der Onagerepisode*, 2 vols., Wiesbaden 1992; A. Baumstark, Jüdischer und christlicher Gebetstypus im Koran, in *Der Islam* 16-18 (1927-9) 229-48; Bell, *Qurʾān;* Bint al-Shāṭiʾ (ʿĀ. ʿAbd al-Raḥmān), *al-Iʿjāz al-bayānī lil-Qurʾān wa-masāʾil Nāfiʿ b. al-Azraq*, Cairo 1971; A. Bloch, *Vers und Sprache im Altarabischen. Metrische und syntaktische Untersuchungen*, Basel 1946, 1970; I.J. Boullata, The rhetorical interpretation of the Qurʾān. Iʿjāz and related topics, in Rippin, *Approaches*, 139-57; J. van Ess, Tashbīh and Tanzīh, in *EI*[2], x, 341-4; Cl. Gilliot, Poète ou prophète? Les traditions concernant la poésie et les poètes attribuées au prophète de l'islam et aux premières générations musulmanes, in F. Sanagustin (ed.), *Paroles, signes, mythes. Mélanges offerts à Jamal Eddine Bencheikh*, Damascus 2001, 331-96; J.J. Gluck, Is there poetry in the Qurʾān? in *Semitics* 8 (1982), 43-89; G.E. von Grunebaum, *A tenth century document of Arabic literary theory and criticism*, Chicago 1950; S.M. Hajjaji-Jarrah, The enchantment of reading. Sound, meaning, and expression in *sūrat al-ʿādiyāt*, in I.J. Boullata (ed.), *Literary structures of religious meaning in the Qurʾān*, London 2000, 228-54; A. Hamori, *The art of medieval Arabic literature*, Princeton 1974; W. Heinrichs, Rhetoric and poetics, in J. Meisami and P. Starkey (eds.), *Encyclopedia of Arabic literature*, London 1998, ii, 651-6; A. Imhof, *Religiöser Wandel und die Genese des Islam. Das Menschenbild altarabischer Panegypriker im 7. Jahrhundert*, Ph.D. thesis (unpub.), Bamberg 2002; Izutsu, *God;*

R. Jacobi, *Studien zur Poetik der altarabischen Qaside,* Wiesbaden 1971; N. Kermani, *Gott ist schön. Das ästhetische Erleben des Koran,* München 2000; Th. Lohmann, Die Gleichnisse Muhammeds im Koran, in *Mitteilungen des Instituts für Orientforschung* 12 (1966), 75-118, 241-87; J.D. McAuliffe, "Debate with them in the better way." The construction of a qurʾānic commonplace, in A. Neuwirth et al. (eds.), *Myths, historical archetypes and symbolic figures in Arabic literature. Towards a new hermeneutic approach,* Beirut 1999, 163-88; F.R. Müller, *Untersuchungen zur Reimprosa im Koran,* Bonn 1969; A. Neuwirth, Das islamische Dogma der "Unnachahmlichkeit des Korans" in literaturwissenschaftlicher Sicht, in *Der Islam* 60 (1983), 166-83; id., Der historische Muhammad im Spiegel des Koran — Prophetentypus zwischen Seher und Dichter? in W. Zwickel (ed.), *Biblische Welten. Festschrift für Martin Metzger zu seinem 65. Geburtstag,* Göttingen 1993, 83-108; id., Images and metaphors in the introductory sections of the Makkan suras, in Hawting and Shareef, *Approaches,* 3-36; id., Qurʾānic literary structure revisited, in S. Leder (ed.), *Story-telling in the framework of non-fictional Arabic literature,* Wiesbaden 1998, 388-420; id., Referentiality and textuality in *sūrat al-Ḥijr.* Some observations on the qurʾānic "canonical process" and the emergence of a community, in I.J. Boullata (ed.), *Literary structures of religious meaning in the Qurʾān,* London 2000, 143-72; id., Vom Rezitiationstext über die Liturgie zum Kanon. Zu Entstehung und Wiederauflösung der Surenkomposition im Verlauf der Entwicklung eines islamischen Kultus, in Wild, *Text,* 69-105; id., *Studien;* id. and K. Neuwirth, *Sūrat al-fātiḥa* — Eröffnung des Text-Corpus Koran oder Introitus der Gebetsliturgie? in W. Groß, H. Irsigler and Th. Seidl (eds.), *Text, Methode und Grammatik. Wolfgang Richter zum 65. Geburtstag,* St. Ottilien 1991, 331-57; Th. Nöldeke, Zur Sprache des Korans, in *Neue Beiträge zur semitischen Sprachwissenschaft,* Straßburg 1910, 1-30, trans. G. Bousquet, *Remarques critiques sur le style et la syntaxe du Coran,* Paris 1953; M. Radscheit, *Die koranische Herausforderung. Die tahaddī-Verse im Rahmen der Polemikpassagen des Korans,* Berlin 1996; G. Richter, *Der Sprachstil des Korans,* Leipzig 1940; A. Rippin, The commerce of eschatology, in Wild, *Text,* 125-36; id., The poetics of qurʾānic punning, in *BSOAS* 57 (1994), 193-207; T. Sabbagh, *Le métaphore dans le Coran,* Paris 1943; M. Sells, A literary approach to the hymnic sūras of the Qurʾān. Spirit, gender, and aural intertextuality, in I.J. Boullata (ed.), *Literary structures of religious meaning in the Qurʾān,* London 2000, 3-25; id., Sound and meaning in *sūrat al-qāriʿa,* in *Arabica* 40 (1993), 403-30; id., Sounds, spirit and gender in *sūrat al-qadr,* in *JAOS* 111 (1991), 239-59; M. Sister, Metaphern und Vergleiche im Koran, in *Mitteilungen des Seminars für Orientalische Sprachen/Westasiatische Studien* 34 (1931), 104-54; Speyer, *Erzählungen;* Ch.C. Torrey, *The commercial-theological terms in the Koran,* Leiden 1892; A.T. Welch, Formulaic features of the punishment-stories, in I.J. Boullata (ed.), *Literary structures of religious meaning in the Qurʾān,* London 2000, 77-116; id., Ḳurʾān, in *EI*[2], v, 400-29; J. Wellhausen, *Reste altarabischen Heidentums,* Leipzig 1887, Berlin 1961[2].

Rhyme

see RHYMED PROSE; POETRY AND POETS

Rhymed Prose

The common English translation of *sajʿ,* an ancient form of Arabic composition used in proverbs, aphorisms, orations, descriptions of meteorological phenomena, and soothsayers' oracular pronouncements before the advent of Islam and in sermons, book titles, introductions, anecdotes, belletristic epistles, chancery correspondence, *maqāmāt,* histories and other literary works in the Islamic period. In its simplest form, *sajʿ* consists of groups of consecutive cola sharing a common rhyme and meter. The meter of *sajʿ* is accentual, determined by the number of words *(kalima, lafẓa)* in each colon (*sajʿa,* pl. *sajaʿāt; qarīna,* pl. *qarāʾin; faṣl,* pl. *fuṣūl;* or *fiqra,* pl. *fiqar*), rather than the patterns of long and short syllables that characterize quantitative meter, with word accents providing the feet or beats. In the most common form of *sajʿ,* adjacent *sajʿa*s are rhythmically parallel *(muʿtadil),* containing an equal number of beats. Attempts to describe *sajʿ* rhythm solely in terms of syllables are therefore inadequate. *Sajʿ* regularly exhibits *muwāzana,* repetition of a set morphological (and necessarily syllabic or quantitative) pattern in the colon-final word or final foot (*sajʿ,* pl. *asjāʿ; qarīna,* pl. *qarāʾin;* or *fāṣila,* pl. *fawāṣil;* cf. Suyūṭī, *Itqān,* 693-714/iii, 332-60 [chap. 59]; id., *Muʿtarak,* i, 29-31, 31-2: "Is there rhymed prose in the Qurʾān?"; Ḥasnāwī, *al-Fāṣila,* 19-27; 31-100; 103-50) of adjacent cola. In addition, *sajʿ* regularly involves the concentrated use of syntactic and semantic parallelism, alliteration, paronomasia and other rhetorical figures. Given that the characteristic features of *sajʿ* are end-rhyme, accent-based meter, and *muwāzana,* the designation "rhymed prose," reflecting only the first of these three, is something of a misnomer. "Rhymed and rhythmical prose" is an improvement, but it is more accurate to label *sajʿ* a type of accent poetry. Goldziher and others have suggested that *sajʿ* is the oldest poetic form in Arabic (see ARABIC LANGUAGE; LITERATURE AND THE QURʾĀN) and some, noting the importance of parallelism and other similar features in Akkadian, Ugaritic and Hebrew poetic forms, above all in biblical poetry, have argued that *sajʿ* in a sense represents the Ur-poetry of the Semites.

Medieval Muslim theologians, rhetoricians and commentators have disagreed concerning the presence of *sajʿ* in the Qurʾān. This debate reflects a strong concern to distance the Qurʾān, as the primary miracle of the prophet Muḥammad's mission (see PROPHETS AND PROPHETHOOD; MIRACLES), from ordinary human types of composition such as *jāhilī* poetry (see AGE OF IGNORANCE) or the *sajʿ* pronouncements of pre-Islamic soothsayers (q.v.). After all, the Qurʾān itself denies accusations that the prophet Muḥammad was a poet (*shāʿir,* Q 21:5; 52:30; 69:41; see POETRY AND POETS) or soothsayer (*kāhin,* Q 52:29). Theologians such as al-Ashʿarī, (d. ca. 325/937), al-Rummānī (d. 384/994) and al-Bāqillānī (d. 403/1013) held that the Qurʾān does not contain *sajʿ*. Their reasoning is that in the Qurʾān, meaning dominates form, whereas in *sajʿ*, form dominates meaning (see FORM AND STRUCTURE OF THE QURʾĀN; LANGUAGE AND STYLE OF THE QURʾĀN). Therefore, the Qurʾān cannot be *sajʿ*. The second position, held by early Muʿtazilī (see MUʿTAZILĪS) theologians such as al-Naẓẓām (d. 220-30/835-45) and taken up by later rhetoricians such as Ḍiyāʾ al-Dīn b. al-Athīr (d. 637/1239) and al-Qalqashandī (d. 821/1418), admits that the Qurʾān contains *sajʿ* and that many sūras of the Qurʾān are composed entirely in this form. Such authors identify specific sūras, such as Sūrat al-Najm (Q 53, "The Star"), Sūrat al-Qamar (Q 54, "The Moon") and Sūrat al-Raḥmān (Q 55, "The Merciful"), as being composed entirely in *sajʿ*. The third position, represented by the majority of late medieval literary critics and scholars of the qurʾānic text such as Jalāl al-Dīn al-Suyūṭī (d. 911/1505), holds that while to term the Qurʾān *sajʿ* is unacceptable or disrespectful, it nevertheless exhibits many formal features of *sajʿ* style. In fact, the overwhelming majority of the examples given of *sajʿ* composition in manuals of rhetoric are qurʾānic. This controversy resulted in the use of two sets of terms for the features of qurʾānic as opposed to extra-qurʾānic or ordinary *sajʿ*. Critics referring to rhyme in the Qurʾān use the terminology "identical letters" (*ḥurūf mutamāthila* or *ḥurūf mutajānisa*) rather than "rhyme" *(qāfiya),* too closely associated with poetry. The rhyme word in *sajʿ* is designated by the term *sajʿ* (pl. *asjāʿ*) itself, but in qurʾānic studies, the terms *fāṣila* (pl. *fawāṣil*) and *raʾs* (pl. *ruʾūs*) are used. The colon or period in *sajʿ* is usually termed *sajʿa, faṣl* or *qarīna* but with reference to the Qurʾān, *fāṣila* or *āya* appears.

The Qurʾān's debt to pre-Islamic *sajʿ* is obvious, particularly in the early Meccan sūras (q.v.; see also CHRONOLOGY AND THE QURʾĀN). The evidence suggests that the Qurʾān contains a great deal of *sajʿ* and that many sūras are composed entirely in *sajʿ*, but Paret and others are wrong to state that the Qurʾān is entirely in *sajʿ*, for many sections of the Qurʾān do not maintain the rhythmical parallelism *sajʿ* requires. This is particularly clear in the longer sūras, where successive verses, despite end-rhyme, are so long and of such unequal length as to preclude any sustained meter, whether quantitative or accentual. The extent to which qurʾānic style maintains or departs from the styles of pre-Islamic *sajʿ*, a matter of some controversy, is difficult to gauge because extant examples of pre-Islamic *sajʿ* all date from later centuries and many are in fact pastiches of a style associated with paganism and magic (q.v.; see also PRE-ISLAMIC ARABIA AND THE QURʾĀN; SOUTH ARABIA, RELIGION IN PRE-ISLAMIC). The best working hypothesis is that the Qurʾān's sūras drew on many of the stylistic features, content and conventions of several genres of pre-Islamic *sajʿ*, particularly divination (q.v.) and oratory, but modified these features to fit into the biblical, monotheistic framework of Islam's message (see SCRIPTURE AND THE QURʾĀN).

According to one estimate, 86% of the verses in the Qurʾān exhibit end rhyme. A lower percentage of the qurʾānic text is actually *sajʿ*, for many passages that exhibit end-rhyme do not exhibit the rhythmical parallelism characteristic of *sajʿ*. Conversely, some passages exhibit the rhythmic parallelism characteristic of *sajʿ* without exact or even near rhyme. The rhyme word regularly observes *taskīn*, ending on a consonant through the suppression of a final short vowel. While this sort of rhyme also occurs in poetry, poetic rhymes regularly end in a long vowel and final short vowels are usually lengthened rather than suppressed. As in poetry, *-m* and *-n* rhyme. Near rhyme between consonants is also common, frequent combinations being *l/r* (e.g. Q 25:1-62) and *b/d/q* (e.g. Q 111; 113). Geminate consonants are regularly reduced: *wa-tab* < *wa-tabba* (Q 111:1); *mustamir* < *mustamirrun* (Q 54:2); *wa-lā jān* < *wa-lā jānnun* (Q 55:39, 56, 74). Rhyme words with final CC (double consonant) occur in several passages but these should probably be treated as CvC (consonant — vowel — consonant) rhymes: an interstitial half or full vowel should be assumed, as in Q 86:11-2, where the rhyme words *al-rajʿi* and *al-ṣadʿi* should probably be read *al-rajʿ*, *al-ṣadʿ*, or Q 89:1-5, where the rhyme words *l-fajri, ʿashrin, l-watri, yasri, ḥijrin* should probably be read *l-fajr, ʿashr, l-watr, yasr, ḥijr*. The long vowels *-ū-* and *-ī-* rhyme, as in poetry, and the short vowels *-a-, -i-, -u-* also rhyme. The indefinite accusative marker *-an (alif-tanwīn)* is regularly voiced as *-ā* in rhyme position. A final long vowel *-ī* is often suppressed: the first person singular possessive pronominal suffix in *dīn* < *dīnī* (Q 109:6), etc., the first person singular objective pronominal suffix in *aṭīʿūn* < *aṭīʿūnī* (Q 26:108, 110, 126), etc., and the endings of definite defective nouns in *al-mutaʿāl* < *al-mutaʿālī* (Q 13:9); *yawma l-talāq* < *yawma l-talāqī* (Q 40:15); *yawma l-tanād* < *yawma l-tanādī* (Q 40:32); and *kallā idhā balaghati l-tarāq* < *kallā idhā balaghati l-tarāqiya* (Q 75:26). Many other modifications of colon-final words for the sake of rhyme occur. Although some sūras include many rhymes, the tendency to maintain mono-rhyme is quite strong in the Qurʾān, and the most common rhyme by far is *-ūn/-ūm/-īn/-īm*. Sūrat al-Muʾminīn (Q 23, "The Believers") with 118 verses, Sūrat al-Naml (Q 27, "The Ants") with ninety-three verses and Sūrat Yā Sīn (Q 36, "Yā Sīn") with eighty-three verses all maintain complete mono-rhyme. At the other extreme, Sūrat al-ʿĀdiyāt (Q 100, "The Coursers") has four distinct rhymes in only eleven verses.

Medieval rhetoricians classified examples of *sajʿ* according to length of cola, and the fact that they did so in terms of words confirms that the meter of *sajʿ* is essentially accentual. Ibn al-Athīr distinguishes short *sajʿ*, in which the phrases include two to ten words each, from long *sajʿ*, in which the *sajʿa*s have eleven or more words. Al-Qazwīnī (d. 739/1338) names three categories: short, medium and long, but does not give exact numerical definitions. The length of the colon in qurʾānic *sajʿ* varies from two words — *wa-l-mursalāti ʿurfā/fa-l-ʿāṣifāti ʿaṣfā* (Q 77:1-2) — to nineteen. In certain cases, discussed below, a *sajʿa* of one word is possible as part of a more complex rhythmic structure, as in the first cola of the opening of Sūrat al-Raḥmān (Q 55:1-4; "The Merciful"): *al-raḥmān/ʿallama l-qurʾān/khalaqa l-insān/ʿallamahu l-bayān/*. Al-Qalqashandī states that the following verses, with nineteen words each, represent the longest example of *sajʿ* in the Qurʾān:

idh yurīkahumu llāhu fī manāmika qalīlan wa-law arākahum kathīran la-fashiltum wa-la-tanāzaʿtum fī l-amri wa-lākinna llāha sallama innahu ʿalīmun bi-dhāti l-ṣudūr/ wa-idh yurīkumūhum idh iltaqaytum fī aʿyunikum qalīlan wa-yuqallilukum fī aʿyunihim li-yaqḍiya llāhu amran kāna mafʿūlan wa-ilā llāhi turjaʿu l-umūr (Q 8:43-4)

The average length is much less, particularly in the Meccan sūras. The medieval critics agree that short cola are more effective and eloquent than long cola.

Cola are arranged in groups that I have termed "*sajʿ*-units," unified by a common rhyme and meter or rhythmic pattern. The number of cola in a *sajʿ*-unit varies widely, ranging from two through more than ten. In the Meccan sūras, units of two, three and four *sajʿa*s are common but Sūrat al-Takwīr opens with a *sajʿ*-unit of fourteen parallel *sajʿa*s (Q 81:1-14): *idhā l-shamsu kuwwirat/wa-idhā l-nujūmu nkadarat/wa-idhā l-jibālu suyyirat/wa-idhā l-ʿishāru ʿuṭṭilat/wa-idhā l-wuḥūshu ḥushirat/wa-idhā l-biḥāru sujjirat/wa-idhā l-nufūsu zuwwijat/wa-idhā l-mawʾūdatu suʾilat/bi-ayyi dhanbin qutilat/wa-idhā l-ṣuḥufu nushirat/wa-idhā l-samāʾu kushiṭat/wa-idhā l-jaḥīmu suʿʿirat/wa-idhā l-jannatu uzlifat/ʿalimat nafsun mā aḥḍarat/*.

An important feature of *sajʿ*, both qurʾānic and extra-qurʾānic, is the introductory phrase, which falls outside the ordinary prosodic structure of the *sajʿ*. The introductory phrase is in effect a separate entity and the *sajʿa* proper begins after that phrase. This feature, which I have termed *maṭlaʿ*, distinguishes *sajʿ* from poetry, where nothing falls outside the metrical scheme of a poem's verses. The *maṭlaʿ* in the Qurʾān is most often shorter than the following *sajʿa*, on occasion equal in length, and rarely longer. Examples include the following, where the *maṭlaʿ* is enclosed in parentheses:

(al-ḥamdu lillāhi) rabbi l-ʿālamīn/al-raḥmāni l-raḥīm/māliki yawmi l-dīn (Q 1:2-4)
(a-fa-lā yaʿlamu idhā) buʿthira mā fī l-qubūr/wa-huṣṣila mā fī l-ṣudūr (Q 100:9-10)

Recognition of this feature, which has misled many critics from Abū Hilāl al-ʿAskarī (d. after 395/1005) on, is extremely important for the prosodic analysis of *sajʿ* texts. *Sajʿ* cola form groups — I have termed them "*sajʿ*-units" — that share a rhyme and adhere to a common meter or alternative metrical pattern. *Sajʿ* units in the Qurʾān exhibit five main structural patterns. In the first pattern, parallel *sajʿa*s within a *sajʿ* unit are of equal length:

fa-ammā l-yatīma fa-lā taqhar/wa-ammā l-sāʾila fa-lā tanhar (Q 93:9-10)
wa-l-ʿādiyāti ḍabḥā/fa-l-mūriyāti qadḥā/fa-l-mughīrāti ṣubḥā (Q 100:1-3)

This is the most common form of *sajʿ*, in which the feature of rhythmical parallelism, which medieval Muslim critics termed *iʿtidāl*, "balance," is most obvious. While in later Arabic literature, units consisting of paired rhyming phrases are the norm, in the Qurʾān units of three, four, five and more *sajʿas* are frequent.

The second pattern has a unit of roughly parallel *sajʿas*, with following *sajʿas* slightly longer than the preceding ones. As an example of this, Ibn al-Athīr cites the following three verses, which contain eight, nine, and nine words respectively:

bal kadhdhabū bi-l-sāʿati wa-aʿtadnā li-man kadhdhaba bi-l-sāʿati saʿīrā/
idhā raʾathum min makānin baʿīdin samiʿū lahā taghayyuẓan wa-zafīrā/
wa-idhā ulqū minhā makānan ḍayyiqan muqarranīna daʿaw hunālika thubūrā
(Q 25:11-3)

A third type has a final *sajʿa* in a group of parallel *sajʿas* slightly shorter than the preceding ones. The medieval critics disapprove of this type of *sajʿ* but it nevertheless appears in the Qurʾān occasionally:

min sharri l-waswāsi l-khannās/alladhī yuwaswisu fī ṣudūri l-nās/mina l-jinnati wa-l-nās
(Q 114:4-6)

The last verse, with three words, is shorter than the first two, with four and five words, respectively.

A fourth pattern, which I have termed the "quatrain" *(rubāʿī)* form, has two *sajʿas* of equal length followed by a third roughly equal in length to the previous pair combined, resulting in a pattern resembling a quatrain of rhyme scheme *a-a-b-a*. Examples include:

lam yalid wa-lam yūlad/wa-lam yakun lahu kufuwan aḥad (Q 112:3-4)
khudhūhu fa-ghullūhu/thumma l-jaḥīma ṣallūhu/thumma fī silsilatin dharʿuhā sabʿūna dhirāʿan fa-slukūhu (Q 69:30-2)

The fifth pattern is a pyramidal form, where length in successive *sajʿas* within a *sajʿ* unit increases steadily:

wa-l-ḍuḥā/wa-l-layli idhā sajā/mā waddaʿaka rabbuka wa-mā qalā (Q 93:1-3)

Here, the successive *sajʿas* are of one, three and five words. In the Qurʾān, this construction often appears in *sajʿ* units of three *sajʿas*, especially at the beginnings of sūras.

Sajʿ units are joined together in various ways to form larger structures. For the qurʾānic material, particularly the short sūras, this larger block is often the sūra itself. One classical term for the structure which *sajʿ* units form is *faṣl* (pl. *fuṣūl*). Change in rhyme is used quite often in the formation of larger structures:

wa-l-ʿādiyāti ḍabḥā/fa-l-mūriyāti qadḥā/fa-l-mughīrāti ṣubḥā/
fa-atharna bihi naqʿā/fa-wasaṭna bihi jamʿā/
inna l-insāna li-rabbihi la-kanūd/wa-innahu ʿalā dhālika la-shahīd/ wa-innahu li-ḥubbi l-khayri la-shadīd/
(a-fa-lā yaʿlamu idhā) buʿthira mā fī l-qubūr/wa-ḥuṣṣila mā fī l-ṣudūr/inna rabbahum bihim yawmaʾidhin la-khabīr (Q 100:1-11)

This sūra is made up of four distinct *sajʿ*-units, each with a different rhyme *(-ḥā; -ʿā; -ūd/-īd; -ūr/-īr)* and sustained syntactic parallelism. The *sajʿ*-units are also distinguished by length, the first containing cola of two words, the second three-word cola, the third four-word cola and the fourth three-word cola, with the exception of the final *sajʿa* of five words. Rhyme, however, is not the only grouping principle in *sajʿ*. Insertion of an introductory phrase *(maṭlaʿ)*, for example, begins a new unit. In addition, a change in *sajʿa* length without a change in rhyme would also mark a division between *sajʿ* units, and this is very frequent in the Qurʾān:

(qul aʿūdhu) bi-rabbi l-nās/maliki l-nās/ilāhi l-nās/
min sharri l-waswāsi l-khannās/alladhī yuwaswisu fī ṣudūri l-nās/mina l-jinnati wa-l-nās
(Q 114:1-6)

This sūra, though maintaining the same rhyme throughout, breaks up into two distinct *sajʿ*-units of three *sajʿa*s each. The first *sajʿ*-unit has *sajʿa*s of two words each but the second *sajʿ*-unit has longer *sajʿa*s: four, five and three words. A less common structural device is a refrain, as found in Sūrat al-Raḥmān (Q 55; "The Merciful"), where the verse *fa-bi-ayyi ālāʾi rabbikumā tukadhdhibān* is repeated thirty-one times, marking off twenty-eight couplets and three tercets within the sūra.

The last word of the *sajʿa* is termed *fāṣila* (pl. *fawāṣil*), *maqṭaʿ* (pl. *maqāṭiʿ*), *qarīna* (pl. *qarāʾin*), or *sajʿ* (pl. *asjāʿ*). Medieval critics considered it important that the final words in neighboring *sajʿa*s be of the same morphological pattern *(wazn)* and classified *sajʿ* according to the presence or absence of this property. In *sajʿ muṭarraf*, "lop-sided" or "skewed" *sajʿ*, the final words rhyme but do not have the same pattern. The qurʾānic example given by al-Qalqashandī and many other critics is the following:

(mā lakum lā) tarjūna lillāhi waqārā
wa-qad khalaqakum aṭwārā (Q 71:13-4)

Although *waqārā* and *aṭwārā* rhyme, they are not of the same morphological pattern. The critics consider this type of *sajʿ* inferior to *sajʿ mutawāzī*, "parallel *sajʿ*," in which final words both rhyme and exhibit identical pattern:

(fīhā) sururun marfūʿa
wa-akwābun mawḍūʿa (Q 88:13-4)

The terms *izdiwāj*, "pairing," and *muwāzana*, "matching in morphological form," refer to a type of composition which conforms to all the characteristics of *sajʿ* except that of strict end-rhyme. In this type of composition, the final words have identical pattern but do not rhyme. Some critics consider *muwāzana* a type of *sajʿ* itself, especially if it has inexact rhymes, and they term it *sajʿ mutawāzin*. Others, such as al-ʿAskarī, do not consider it *sajʿ* but deem it slightly inferior to *sajʿ* in literary merit. In the following qurʾānic example,

wa-namāriqu maṣfūfa/wa-zarābiyyu mabthūtha
(Q 88:15-6)

the rhythmical parallelism and basic structure of *sajʿ* is maintained, despite the fact that the rhyme consonants are *f* and *th*.

While in *muwāzana*, quantitative parallelism is restricted to the last word in a *sajʿa*, critics prize *sajʿ* that exhibits more sustained internal rhyme and morphological parallelism between corresponding words in parallel cola. Al-Qalqashandī and others call this type of composition *tarṣīʿ* or *sajʿ muraṣṣaʿ*, "proportioned *sajʿ*." Al-ʿAskarī calls it *sajʿ fī sajʿ*, "*sajʿ* within *sajʿ*" and considers it the best type of *sajʿ*. Qurʾānic examples include:

inna ilaynā iyābahum/thumma inna ʿalaynā ḥisābahum (Q 88:25-6)
inna l-abrāra la-fī naʿīm/wa-inna l-fujjāra la-fī jaḥīm (Q 82:13-4)

In these examples, all the words in the parallel *sajʿa*s rhyme and match in morphological pattern, except for the difference of pattern of *abrār* and *fujjār* in the second example. Syllable lengths are exactly the same, if *thumma* in the second *sajʿa* of the first example and *wa-* in the second *sajʿa* of the second example are discounted.

The desired effect of syllabic or morphological parallelism is to enhance the accentual meter with quantitative regularity, particularly when approaching the end of the *sajʿa,* producing matching cadences resembling the clausulae of Latin oratory. Examination of the qurʾānic text shows the frequent use of clausulae, such as those which involve the double epithets of God (*al-asmāʾ al-ḥusnā;* see GOD AND HIS ATTRIBUTES) — *inna llāha ghafūrun raḥīm* (Q 2:199); *wa-kāna llāhu ghafūran raḥīmā* (Q 4:96); *innahu huwa l-ghafūru l-raḥīm* (Q 28:16; see FORGIVENESS; MERCY) — or other general statements concerning God's favor or disfavor (see GRACE; BLESSING; LOVE) — *inna llāha lā yuḥibbu l-muʿtadīn* (Q 2:190); *innahu lā yuḥibbu l-musrifīn* (Q 6:141). Rhythm, in addition to rhyme, is a crucial feature of these clausulae. The most common rhythmical patterns in the penultimate and ultimate feet of a colon include ^ — —/ ^ — — and — ^ — —/— ^ — — (overlong syllables scan as long-long). It seems that there is a strong tendency toward a reduplicative rhythm, where the quantitative pattern of the penultimate foot is repeated in the ultimate.

The structural, grammatical and rhetorical effects of end-rhyme and rhythmical parallelism on the qurʾānic text are far-reaching, and further research into the relationship of *sajʿ* to elements of qurʾānic style, incorporating both classical Muslim and contemporary scholarship, is a much needed desideratum (cf. Ḥasnāwī, *al-Fāṣila;* Rāzī, *Nihāya,* 142-3; Nuwayrī, *Nihāya,* vii, 103-5; Mehren, *Rhetorik,* 166-8; Garcin de Tassy, *Rhétorique,* 154-8). Many qurʾānic verses exhibit deviations from ordinary style in order to bring about end-rhyme, yet many commentators on the Qurʾān, either unaware of or determined to ignore the poetic character of the text, propose tortuous arguments to explain grammatical and syntactic features that are due primarily to rhyme. Müller *(Reimprosa)* has discussed this sort of "poetic license," though with limited recourse to medieval Islamic texts. Among the best analyses of this topic within the tradition is *Iḥkām al-rāy fī aḥkām awākhir al-āy,* "The establishment of sound opinion on the rules governing verse endings," by Shams al-Dīn Muḥammad b. ʿAbd al-Raḥmān b. al-Ṣāʾigh al-Ḥanafī (d. 776/1375). This work, summarized by al-Suyūṭī in his *Itqān,* presents forty types of "rules" (sing. *ḥukm*), essentially deviations from ordinary style, which occur in the qurʾānic text in order to produce what he terms "matching" *(munāsaba),* essentially end-rhyme. On the level of the word, deviations which occur include the alteration of word endings — *sīnīn* (Q 95:2) for *saynāʾ,* "Sinai" (q.v.; Q 23:20); *ilyāsīn* (Q 37:130) for *ilyās,* "Elias" (Q 6:85; 37:133; see ELIJAH) — and the use of one morphological pattern with the meaning of another — *taḍlīl* (Q 105:2) for *ḍalāl,* "error (q.v.), loss" (passim; see also ASTRAY); *lāghiya* (Q 88:11) for *laghw,* "idle talk" (Q 19:62; 56:25; 78:35; see GOSSIP); *amīn* (Q 95:3) for *āmin,* "safe" (Q 14:35, etc.); *ṣamad* (Q 112:2) for *ṣāmid* or *ṣamūd,* "enduring" (see ETERNITY), etc.

Other deviations involve the use of feminine forms where masculine forms would be expected, such as *dhālika dīnu l-qayyima* (Q 98:5) for *dhālika l-dīnu l-qayyim,* "that is the right religion" (q.v.; Q 9:36; 12:40; 30:30; cf. 30:43), or the use of an imperfect verb where a perfect would be expected, as in *istakbartum fa-farīqan kadhdhabtum wa-farīqan taqtulūn* (Q 2:87), "You behaved arrogantly (see ARROGANCE): one group you denied (see LIE), and one group you kill (see MURDER)," when logic and parallelism would dictate *qataltum,* "you killed." Word order is also affected, as, for example, in Q 20:70, *qālū āmannā bi-rabbi Hārūna wa-Mūsā* ("They said: We believe in the lord of Aaron [q.v.] and Moses" [q.v.]), when a rhyme in *-ā* is required, as opposed to the usual order *Mūsā wa-Hārūn,* "Moses and Aaron" (Q 7:122; 10:75; 26:48; 37:114, 120) or *iyyāka naʿbudu wa-iyyāka nastaʿīn,* "You we worship and from you we seek help" (Q 1:5), rather than *naʿbuduka wa-nastaʿīnuk** ("We worship you and seek help from you"). Prepositional phrases are often made to precede the adjectives, nouns, or verbs on which they depend, as in *inna l-insāna li-rabbihi la-kanūd* ("verily humankind is to its lord ungrateful"; Q 100:6; see GRATITUDE AND INGRATITUDE) where the ordinary order would be *inna l-insāna la-kanūdun li-rabbih** ("verily humankind is ungrateful to its lord"), or in *wa-llāhu baṣīrun bimā yaʿmalūn* ("God is watchful over all that they do"; Q 2:96) in a context requiring the rhyme *-ūn* and *wa-llāhu bimā taʿmalūna baṣīr* ("God is over all that you do watchful"; Q 3:156) in a context requiring the rhyme *-īr/-ūr.* As mentioned, Ibn al-Ṣāʾigh al-Ḥanafī distinguishes forty features such as these. Many other "deviations" are so common within the Qurʾān as to become standard features of qurʾānic style. The verb *kāna* "was" and its derived forms often appear in contexts where the past tense is not appropriate. In these cases it appears to be pleonastic, used primarily to produce the required end-rhyme in *-ā,* since its predicate requires the accusative, without altering the meaning significantly. This occurs often in the final clausulae that end in double divine epithets, such as *wa-kāna llāhu ghafūran raḥīmā* ("God was forgiving and merciful"; Q 4:96, 100, 152, etc.) in an environment requiring *-ūnā/-īnā* rhyme, which seems equivalent in meaning to *inna llāha ghafūrun raḥīm,* "God is forgiving and merciful" (Q 2:173, 182, 199, etc.). Similar is the common periphrasis *min* with a following definite plural for the indefinite singular, as in *wa-innī la-aẓunnuhu min al-kādhibīn,* "I think that he is indeed of the liars" (Q 28:38), which may be equated with *wa-innī la-aẓunnuhu kādhiban,* "I think that he is indeed a liar" (Q 40:37), and the use of the compound past imperfect *(kānū yafʿalūn)* with the meaning of the perfect *(faʿalū),* as in *fa-yunabbiʾuhum bimā kānū yaʿmalūn,* "and he will inform them of what they were doing/used to do" (Q 6:108), which appears equivalent to *fa-yunabbiʾuhum bimā ʿamilū,* "and he will inform them of what they did" (Q 24:64).

Devin J. Stewart

Bibliography

Primary: Abū Hilāl al-ʿAskarī, al-Ḥasan b. ʿAbdallāh, *Kitāb al-Ṣināʿatayn,* Cairo 1952; Bāqillānī, *Iʿjāz;* Farrāʾ, *Maʿānī;* Ibn Abī l-Iṣbaʿ, *Badīʿ,* 108-9; Ibn al-Athīr, Ḍiyāʾ al-Dīn Abū l-Fatḥ Muḥammad b. Muḥammad, *al-Mathal al-sāʾir,* 4 vols., Cairo 1959-65; Ibn al-Naqīb, *Muqaddima,* 471-5; Jāḥiẓ, *Bayān;* al-Nuwayrī, Shihāb al-Dīn Aḥmad b. ʿAbd al-Wahhāb, *Nihāyat al-arab fī funūn al-adab,* 33 vols., Cairo 1923-98, vii, 103-5; al-Qalqashandī, Abū l-ʿAbbās Aḥmad b. ʿAlī, *Ṣubḥ al-aʿshā fī ṣināʿat al-inshā,* 13 vols., Cairo 1964; al-Qazwīnī, Abū ʿAbdallāh Muḥammad b. ʿAbd al-Raḥmān, *al-Īḍāḥ fī ʿulūm al-balāgha,* 2 vols., Cairo 1949; id., *Talkhīṣ al-miftāḥ,* Cairo 1904; Rāzī, *Nihāyat al-ījāz fī dirāyat al-iʿjāz,* ed. B.Sh. Amīn, Beirut 1985; Rummānī et al., *Rasāʾil;* Suyūṭī, *Itqān,* ed. A. Sprenger et al., 1 vol., Calcutta 1852-4, 693-714; ed. M.A.F. Ibrāhīm, iii, 332-60 (chap. 59: *Fī fawāṣil al-āy*); id., *Muʿtarak al-aqrān fī iʿjāz al-Qurʾān,* ed. ʿA.M. al-Bijāwī, 3 vols., Cairo 1969-72; Zarkashī, *Burhān,* ed. Ibrāhīm.
Secondary: A. Ben Abdesselem, Sadjʿ, 3. In Arabic literature of the Islamic period, in *EI²,* viii, 734-8; R. Blachère, *Histoire de la littérature arabe des origines à la fin du Xᵛᵉ siècle de J.-C.,* Paris 1964; id., *Introduction;* P. Crapon de Crapona, *Le Coran. Aux sources de la parole oraculaire,* Paris 1981; L. Edzard, Perspektiven einer computergestützten Analyse der qur'anischen Morpho-Syntax und Satz-Syntax in kolometrischer Darstellung, in *Arabica* 50 (2003), 350-80; T. Fahd, *La divination*

arabe. Études religieuses, sociologiques, et folkloriques sur le milieu natif de l'Islam, Leiden 1966, 150-62; id., Sadjʿ, 1. As magical utterances in pre-Islamic Arabian usage, in *EI²,* viii, 732-4; D. Frolov, *Classical Arabic verse. History and theory of ʿarūḍ,* Leiden 2000; J.H. Garcin de Tassy, *Rhétorique et prosodie des langues de l'Orient musulman,* Paris 1873, repr. Amsterdam 1970, 154-8; I. Goldziher, *Abhandlungen zur arabischen Philologie,* Leiden 1896; M. Grünbaum, Beiträge zur vergleichenden Mythologie der Hagada, in *ZDMG* 31 (1877), 183-359; M. al-Ḥasnāwī, *al-Fāṣila fī l-Qurʾān,* Aleppo [1977]; W. Heinrichs, Sadjʿ, 2. Outside *kahāna* before Islam, in *EI²,* viii, 734; B. Hrushovski, Prosody, Hebrew, in *Encyclopaedia Judaica,* Jerusalem 1975, xiii, 1195-1240; A.F. Mehren, *Die Rhetorik der Araber,* Copenhagen/Vienna 1853, 167-8; M. Messadi, *Essai sur le rhythme dans la prose rimée en arabe,* Tunis 1981 (rev. and enl. Ar. ed.: *al-Īqāʿ fī l-sajʿ al-ʿarabī. Muḥāwalat taḥlīl wa-taḥdīd,* Tunis 1996); F.R. Müller, *Untersuchungen zur Reimprosa im Koran,* Bonn 1969; Neuwirth, *Studien;* Nöldeke, *GQ,* 36-43; R. Paret, The Qurʾān — I, in A.F.L. Beeston (ed.), *Cambridge history of Arabic literature. Arabic literature to the end of the Umayyad period,* Cambridge 1983, 186-227; D.J. Stewart, *Sajʿ* in the Qurʾān. Prosody and structure, in *JAL* 21 (1990), 101-39 (Arabic trans. with comm. by M. El-Bereiri in *Fuṣūl* 12/3 [1993], 7-37); K. Vollers, *Volkssprache und Schriftsprache im alten Arabien. Philologische Untersuchungen zur klassischen arabischen Sprache, mit besonderer Berucksichtigung der Reime und der Sprache des Qorans,* Strassburg 1906; W.G.E. Watson, *Traditional techniques in classical Hebrew verse,* Sheffield 1994; Watt-Bell, *Introduction;* A. Welch, Ḳurʾān, in *EI²,* v, 400-28; M.J. Zwettler, *The oral tradition in classical Arabic poetry,* Columbus, OH 1978.

Rhythm see RHYMED PROSE; LANGUAGE AND STYLE OF THE QURʾĀN; FORM AND STRUCTURE OF THE QURʾĀN

Rich(es) see WEALTH; MONEY; PROPERTY

Ridicule see MOCKERY

Right Hand see LEFT HAND AND RIGHT HAND

Righteous(ness) see PIETY; FEAR; GOOD DEEDS

Rites see RITUAL AND THE QURʾĀN

Ritual and the Qurʾān

Following a brief discussion of ritual in modern academic discourse which proposes a functional typology of rituals both within and involving the Qurʾān, and taking into account the context in which certain rituals occur and are performed, this article will then explore the treatment of qurʾānic rituals in works of Islamic jurisprudence (see LAW AND THE QURʾĀN). Those rituals which employ verses of the Qurʾān — written or spoken, individually or collectively — in various ceremonial, talismanic and therapeutic contexts will also be examined. This article does not deal extensively with those rituals specifically mentioned in the Qurʾān, as they are more fully explained under the relevant entries in this encyclopedia (see e.g. the articles WITNESS TO FAITH; PILGRIMAGE; PRAYER; RAMAḌĀN; FASTING; and RITUAL PURITY, in addition to the other entries which are cross-referenced below).

Ritual is the cornerstone of the Islamic faith and, as such, assumes a primary role in the Qurʾān by making manifest a tangible, sacramental expression of God's design for humankind. In comparing Islam to other religions, the Dutch scholar D.C. Mulder (Recitation) observed that Islam "is not very rich in ritual." But Mulder identified only three primary forms of ritual: prayer *(ṣalāt),* pilgrimage *(ḥajj)* and recitation of the Qurʾān (q.v.; *tilāwa*). Those ritual forms found in the Qurʾān and in the ḥadīth (see ḤADĪTH AND THE QURʾĀN) are not as numerous as those found in the Talmud, a cornerstone of rabbinical Jewish law which includes archaic rituals no longer practiced by Jews after the destruction of the second temple in 70 C.E. It might be argued, however, that the number and diversity of ritual forms, practices and observances within Islam are as prolific, variegated and complex as those in

Judaism and Christianity. Furthermore, those rituals which observant Muslims perform — from simply invoking the divine name (see GOD AND HIS ATTRIBUTES; REMEMBRANCE) to more elaborate ritual forms such as supererogatory prayer, supplication and recitation of verses from the Qurʾān — emphasize the richness and diversity of rituals and ritual practice in Islam (see PRAYER FORMULAS; PIETY).

Ritual (from Latin *ritualis*) is a religiously defined and prescribed set of actions whose enactment symbolizes humankind's encounter with and reverence for the divine. Anthropologists and scholars of religion have defined it in various ways, including as "a universal category of human experience" (Bell, *Ritual theory*, 14) or "those conscious and voluntary, repetitious and stylized symbolic bodily actions that are centered on cosmic structures and/or sacred presences" (Zuesse, Ritual, 405; see PROFANE AND SACRED). Jonathan Z. Smith (Bare facts, 125) defines ritual as "a means of performing the way things ought to be in conscious tension to the way things are in such a way that this ritualized perfection is recollected in the ordinary, uncontrolled, course of things." In other words, ritual consists of structures of formalized and sometimes spontaneous behavior which emerge from a setting of reverence for and engagement with the divine in its diverse manifestations. The definition of ritual may be broadened to include rites of passage at which scripture is invoked or displayed such as at births and funerals (see BIRTH; BURIAL), indeed in virtually all aspects of daily life.

The following is a typology of the rituals in Islamic societies that are associated with the Qurʾān. (Most of these rituals — as seen in the overlap among the ten categories — are not mutually exclusive.)

(1) Transformative rituals (see also Rituals of purification, below): the performance of these has the effect of transforming one's spiritual, physical and mental state. Transformative rituals may be prescriptive, as in the five pillars, or may be pious practices *(muʿāmalāt)* or rules of etiquette *(adab)*. A transformative ritual may also have the effect of transforming the state of a sacred or venerable object. Often such rituals are performed in fulfillment of a religious precept, as in the case of prayer, but also in anticipation of receiving "blessing" *(baraka)*. In this category may be included: the testament of faith *(shahāda);* ritual prayer *(ṣalāt);* pilgrimage *(ḥajj);* entering *(dukhūl)* and sitting *(quʿūd)* in a mosque (Ibn al-Ḥājj, *al-Madkhal*, i, 13); fasting (*ṣiyām*, Q 2:183-5, 187, 196); almsgiving *(zakāt);* loyalty (q.v.) to the imām (q.v.; *walāya*); reading/reciting the Qurʾān *(dhikr, tilāwa);* seeking *baraka* from a qurʾānic codex (*tabarruk;* see MUṢḤAF; CODICES OF THE QURʾĀN); kissing *(taqbīl)* the qurʾānic codex; weeping (q.v.; *bukāʾ*) when the Qurʾān is read; ritual purification (*ṭahāra;* as a category it often includes *wuḍūʾ, ghusl, tayammum;* see CLEANLINESS AND ABLUTION); vows (*nadhr, naḥb;* Q 76:7; see VOW); vigils (q.v.; *tahajjud* — spending the night in prayer, praying the night prayer, reciting the Qurʾān nightly); and humbling oneself before God *(taḍarruʿ)*.

(2) Rituals of purification, which are performed prior to prayer or coming into contact with the sacred. They employ the use of water and other substances (sand, dust). Included in this category is *ṭahāra* (ritual purity; Q 5:6), which includes *wuḍūʾ* (ritual ablutions), *ghusl* (ritual immersion; Q 4:43, 5:6), *tayammum* (ritual ablutions with fine sand or dust; Q 4:43; 5:6), *ṭahāra* (ritual purity; i.e. as in Abraham's purification and re-consecration of the house of God; cf. Q 2:125; see ABRAHAM; HOUSE, DOMESTIC AND DIVINE; KAʿBA).

(3) Rituals which mark the fulfillment of religious obligation (*muʿāmalāt;* see GOOD DEEDS; ETHICS AND THE QURʾĀN; see also Obligatory rituals, below), such as marriage (*nikāḥ;* see Rites of passage, below; see MARRIAGE AND DIVORCE) and the ritual slaughtering of animals for food (*taḥlīl,* cf. Q 5:2; see CONSECRATION OF ANIMALS; SLAUGHTER).
(4) Rites of passage, such as birth *(mīlād),* including the naming ceremony; death (*mawt,* cf. Q 3:185, 193; 4:78; 21:35; 33:19, 23; 44:56; 47:27; 56:60, 84-87; 63:10; 75:29; see DEATH AND THE DEAD); marriage (*nikāḥ,* cf. Q 2:187; 25:54, etc.); and the pilgrimage *(ḥajj).*
(5) Obligatory rituals in the Qurʾān, namely: prayer *(ṣalāt),* including prostration *(sujūd)* and bowing (*rukūʿ;* see BOWING AND PROSTRATION); testament of faith *(shahāda);* almsgiving *(zakāt);* pilgrimage *(ḥajj);* and fasting *(ṣiyām).*
(6) Rituals of abstinence (q.v.), which include fasting *(ṣiyām)* and vows (*nadhr* or *nudhūr, naḥb;* Q 33:23: *man qaḍā naḥbahu*). The vow involves making a dedication to God, usually in the form of a sacrifice (q.v.). In a historical context, Muslims, like adherents to other faiths, make vows to engage in or refrain from particular actions. Abstinence from certain practices and *ḥajj* rites, such as eating food and shortening one's hair are valid forms of *nadhr.* In the qurʾānic context, God fulfills vows (cf. Pedersen, Na<u>dh</u>r, for a discussion of the pre-Islamic and Islamic context of *nadhr;* see also CONTRACTS AND ALLIANCES; COVENANT; OATHS).
(7) Rituals of sustenance (q.v.), health (see ILLNESS AND HEALTH), longevity (see also Protective rituals, below), which include consuming food and drink from plates and cups inscribed with qurʾānic verses; consuming food on which qurʾānic verses are inscribed; and seeking *baraka* from the Qurʾān (*tabarruk;* see POPULAR AND TALISMANIC USES OF THE QURʾĀN; EVERYDAY LIFE, THE QURʾĀN IN).
(8) Protective rituals, among which are counted a number of activities. The mere act of bringing out a codex at a public gathering is a means to invoke the protection (q.v.) of God through his words (see WORD OF GOD). Other rituals include reciting the *basmala* (q.v.; i.e. invoking the name of God) orally or silently over somebody or before undertaking an activity; reading/reciting the Qurʾān; seeking *baraka (tabarruk)* from the qurʾānic codex by physically touching it or reciting verses from it; carrying a qurʾānic codex to ward off disease, illness, plague, bodily harm, evil, etc.; wearing a garment with qurʾānic verses inscribed on it (usually a tunic or talismanic shirt on which the ninety-nine names of God and verses from the Qurʾān are inscribed); wearing a necklace, amulet (see AMULETS) or talisman with qurʾānic verses and related expressions or a miniature Qurʾān in a *muṣḥaf* pendant of a precious metal, usually gold (children or adults may engage in this practice; a popular practice is for women and girls to wear amulets); eating or drinking from a vessel with verses of the Qurʾān inscribed; and in Turkey there is the practice of writing the word *mashallah,* literally "what God wants," on an amulet and placing it on the person of a newborn child (see the illustrations of POPULAR AND TALISMANIC USES OF THE QURʾĀN for some examples of the rich variety of material objects employed in protective rituals that involve the Qurʾān).
(9) Rituals acts meant to inflict harm or spread evil. Such rituals appear in a limited historical context. The only known instance in the Qurʾān is the "blowing on knots" (*al-naffāthāt fī l-ʿuqad,* Q 113:4; see MAGIC), but this appears in a negative sense in that the verse alludes to women who

failed in their objective to cause harm to Muḥammad by blowing on knots (see OPPOSITION TO MUḤAMMAD).
(10) Rituals that promote social cohesion and group solidarity, such as prayer *(ṣalāt),* Friday prayer (q.v.; Q 62:9), or prayer in a mosque (q.v.); pilgrimage *(ḥajj);* collectively carrying scriptures in hand while walking in procession at times of crisis, drought and epidemics. This last named function exemplifies the human need to repel imminent danger and disease. Such historical episodes underscore the social function of the Qurʾān in a group environment (see COMMUNITY AND SOCIETY IN THE QURʾĀN; POLITICS AND THE QURʾĀN).

As seen from this typology, the word "ritual" in the Islamic context cannot be expressed by a single word found either in the Qurʾān, the prophetic traditions, or in works of jurisprudence. The closest approximation to "ritual" is *ʿibādāt* (sing. *ʿibāda,* lit. "obedience, submission, humility, devout worship"; see WORSHIP) which is also related to *ṭāʿa* (lit. "obedience, submission"; see OBEDIENCE). In the first instance, *ʿibādāt* refers to religious practice and devotion to God (Q 2:21; 51:56) and is commonly applied to the five pillars *(arkān)* of Islam: *shahāda* (testament of faith; Q 3:19-20; 6:19; 63:1), *ṣalāt* (prayer; e.g. Q 2:45; 9:103; 51:18; 70:22-3; 75:31; 96:10; 108:2), *zakāt* (almsgiving; e.g. Q 2:43, 83, 277), *ṣiyām* (fasting; Q 2:183-4), and *ḥajj* (pilgrimage; e.g. Q 2:189, 196). The Semitic root *ʿ-b-d* from which *ʿibādāt* derives captures the relationship between the devotee as the slave of God whose inner and outer natures surrender to God, the exclusive object of worship (e.g. Q 1:5; see SERVANTS; SLAVES AND SLAVERY). "Ritual" also may be applied to modes of religious behavior and experience, and physical and mental states not classified as *ʿibādāt* by jurisprudents and theologians, such as *taḍarruʿ* (Q 6:42, 43), through which believers are urged to reflect upon the lessons of the past and humble themselves before God as did those before them (see OPPRESSED ON EARTH, THE; TRUST AND PATIENCE; TRIAL; PUNISHMENT STORIES; GENERATIONS; HISTORY AND THE QURʾĀN). During the fifth/eleventh and sixth/twelfth centuries, the very act of remembrance of God (*dhikr,* Q 2:152, 200; 3:41; 7:205; 18:24; 33:41; 72:25) became enshrined in elaborate Ṣūfī rituals and ceremonies that became widespread throughout the Islamic world (see ṢŪFISM AND THE QURʾĀN).

All devotional acts *(ʿibādāt)* require of those who undertake them to declare clearly their intention (q.v.; *niyya*). In *Kitāb al-Arbaʿīn fī uṣūl al-dīn,* al-Ghazālī (d. 505/1111) provides a succinct discussion of *ʿibadāt,* which when performed properly, lead to the perfection of both the outer and inner self in fulfillment of one's religious duties. In his elucidation of the ten primary principles of religion (ritual prayer; almsgiving and charity; fasting; pilgrimage; recitation of the Qurʾān; *dhikr,* remembrance of God; seeking what is permitted, i.e. *ḥalāl;* upholding the rights of other Muslims and maintaining proper companionship with them; enjoining right and forbidding wrong; following the sunna of the Prophet), al-Ghazālī states that he does not mean undertaking only the etiquette *(ādāb)* of the ritual acts, but everything associated with them (p. 68). The object in performing ritual acts is human certitude in the remembrance of God in order to attain the hereafter and withdraw from the worldly life (p. 76). Invoking this work, the north African Mālikī theologian Ibn al-Ḥājj (d. 737/1336) regards *niyya* and *ʿamal* (i.e. the actual performance of the act) as complete ritual devotion *(bi-himā tamām al-ʿibāda)* and *niyya* as the best of the two parts (*al-Madkhal,* i, 13). For without the intention, the believer's ritual is deemed invalid and the threat of divine punishment becomes implicit (see REWARD AND PUNISHMENT; CHASTISEMENT AND PUNISHMENT). According to Eliade (*Patterns,* 370-1), the division between the realms of the sacred and the profane "serves the purpose of preserving profane man from the danger to which he would expose himself by entering it without due care. The sacred is always dangerous to anyone who comes into contact with it unprepared, without having gone through 'gestures of approach' that every religious act demands."

Rituals in the Qur'ān

Rituals in the Qur'ān can be classified according to four primary categories: (1) Prescriptive rituals include prayer *(ṣalāt),* almsgiving *(zakāt),* testament of faith *(shahāda),* fasting during the month of Ramaḍān *(ṣiyām),* undertaking the pilgrimage *(ḥajj)* and ritual purity (*ṭahāra,* Q 5:6); (2) rituals of devotion and remembrance, such as *dhikr* and *tahajjud* (night vigil spent in prayer); (3) rites of passage, including birth, marriage and death; (4) rituals that are time and place specific and that refer to a particular historical event or incident or are otherwise related to the prophets before Muḥammad (see PROPHETS AND PROPHETHOOD), like Abraham and Ishmael (q.v.) ritually purifying the house of God (Q 2:125), women's use of black magic against the Prophet by blowing on knots (Q 113:4) and the allusions to the — proscribed — prostration (bowing) of the Israelites to the sun (q.v.) and moon (q.v.; e.g. Q 41:37).

Ritual prayer *(ṣalāt)* represents the ritual enactment and re-enactment of the Qur'ān par excellence. Several prophetic traditions indicate this, including "The difference between *kufr* (infidelity; see BELIEF AND UNBELIEF) and Islam is *ṣalāt,*" and "Only those who pray have my protection" (cf. Muslim, *Ṣaḥīḥ,* bk. 1, chap. 35, no. 134).

Sunnī and Shīʿī (see SHĪʿISM AND THE QUR'ĀN) works of jurisprudence *(fiqh)* differentiate between *ʿibādāt* and a closely related word — *muʿāmalāt,* which refers to the rules governing human behavior —, and almost invariably discuss the former before the latter. Bousquet recognizes that *fiqh* is a deontology for *ʿibādāt,* the statements of the whole corpus of duties or acts whether obligatory, forbidden or recommended, etc., which is imposed upon people (Bousquet, ʿIbādāt; cf. id., *Les grandes pratiques,* 9). Apart from the five pillars, the question of which rituals are to be classified under *ʿibādāt* is not always clearly delineated in the organization of jurisprudential works. In the Qur'ān one finds mention of such rituals as marriage (*nikāḥ;* e.g. Q 2:220; 33:49) which Bousquet properly indicates should be classified as a pious practice rather than placed among the *ʿibādāt.* The same might be said of other practices, not specifically mentioned as an obligation in the Qur'ān, such as circumcision (q.v.; *khitān*), or qur'ānic recitation *(tilāwa).* Unlike circumcision, however, which is not a qur'ānic prescription but a socially and religiously prescribed ritual and rite of passage, recitation is usually considered among the *ʿibādāt.*

In the ḥadīth collections and in legal and theological discussions of the sunna (q.v.) of the Prophet (see THEOLOGY AND THE QUR'ĀN), qur'ānic and extra-qur'ānic rituals are further elaborated. Various ḥadīth collections do not categorically separate *ʿibādāt* from other ritual forms, though *ʿibādāt* generally are grouped at the beginning of such works. In al-Bukhārī's (d. 256/870) *Ṣaḥīḥ,* for instance, one finds *wuḍū'* (ritual ablution), *ghusl* (ritual immersion), *tayammum* (ritual ablution with fine dust or sand), *ṣalāt* (prayer), *janā'iz* (funerals), *zakāt* (almsgiving), and *ḥajj* (pilgimage). The *Ṣaḥīḥ* of Muslim (d. ca. 261/875) follows a different order and includes *ṭahāra* (ritual purity), *ṣalāt* (prayer), *zakāt* (almsgiving) and *ṣawm* (fasting).

The Shīʿī theologian Sallār b. ʿAbd al-ʿAzīz al-Daylamī (d. 448/1056), the author of *al-Marāsīm fī l-fiqh al-imāmī,* essentially divides his work into *ʿibādāt* and *muʿāmalāt,* the latter of which he subdivides into *ʿuqūd* (contracts, the performance of which does not necessitate the declaration of intention; see CONTRACTS AND ALLIANCES; BREAKING TRUSTS AND CONTRACTS) and *aḥkām* (rules governing conduct within society, e.g. inheritance laws; see INHERITANCE; SOCIAL INTERACTIONS). Al-Muḥaqqiq al-Ḥillī (d. 676/1277) delineates in his *Sharāʾiʿ al-Islām fī l-fiqh al-islāmī l-Jaʿfarī* four primary categories of ritual which formed the basis for the categories found in later Shīʿī works of jurisprudence: *ʿibādāt, aḥkām, ʿuqūd,* and *īqāʿāt* (legally valid pronouncements which require only one party to transact).

One of the most detailed expositions of *ʿibādāt* can be found in the Shāfiʿī jurist al-Nawawī's (d. 676/1277) *al-Tibyān fī ādāb ḥamalat al-Qurʾān.* Al-Nawawī's work is unique for its discussion of those rituals in which the Qurʾān is invoked, the times at which it is efficacious to recite certain verses or chapters of the Qurʾān, when it is necessary to prostrate oneself upon hearing particular verses, and the proper etiquette for carrying and displaying a codex and according it reverence. Al-Nawawī was particularly concerned that Muslims display proper etiquette and reverence for the Qurʾān. For instance, he observes that such practices as putting the codex under the head as a pillow are to be forbidden (Nawawī, *Tibyān,* 190-1). Perhaps some believed that it would facilitate the acquisition of knowledge or protect them from harm as they slept. Such beliefs are attested to in late nineteenth century Iran: Serena (*Hommes,* 333; cf. Massé, *Popular beliefs,* 21) observed that the qurʾānic codex was placed beneath the head of the newborn as a pillow.

The Ḥanbalī theologian Ibn Taymiyya (d. 728/1328) defines *ʿibāda* — more broadly than the traditional delineation of jurisprudential works — as "a collective term [which encompasses] all that God loves and [that] pleases him *(kull mā yuḥibbuhu wa-yarḍāhu)* from the words and inner and external actions, like prayer, alms, fasting, *ḥajj,* veracious speech, keeping a trust, and reverence for one's parents (q.v.) and close relatives (see KINSHIP)." In a treatise on *ʿibādāt* the modern Shīʿī scholar Jaʿfar al-Sijānī (*ʿIbāda,* 20) argues that Ibn Taymiyya has confused *ʿibādāt* with acts of nearness to God *(taqarrub)* by regarding them as synonymous. In Sijānī's view, acts such as giving alms, respecting one's parents, and the *khums* (a tax among the Shīʿa which was originally applied to the fifth of the spoils of war belonging to the ruler; see BOOTY) necessitate *qurbā* to God but are not *ʿibādāt.*

The modern-day scholar and theologian Aḥmad al-Ḥuṣarī (*Mina l-fiqh,* 142) defines *ʿibāda* as "the obedience *(ṭāʿa)* which the [divine] law-giver *(shāriʿ)* has required his slaves to carry out." Al-Ḥuṣarī distinguishes between three categories of *ʿibādāt:* (1) Purely physical rituals *(ʿibādāt badaniyya)* for which one person is not permitted to substitute for another, like prayer, fasting; (2) rituals for which one person is permitted to substitute for another, like almsgiving *(zakāt);* and (3) physical rituals which require the expenditure of property (q.v.; with the stipulation that, in the case of another's substituting, one must be incapable of undertaking them on one's own), like the *ḥajj* (ibid., 144).

The Shīʿī scholar Muḥammad Saʿīd al-Ṭabāṭabāʾī (d. 1982) includes in his *Minhāj al-ṣāliḥīn* the following categories among the *ʿibādāt: ṭahāra* (ritual purity), *ṣalāt* (prayer), *ṣawm* (fasting), *iʿtikāf* (pious retreat in a mosque which is generally associated with the month of Ramaḍān; see FESTIVALS AND COMMEMORATIVE DAYS), *zakāt* (almsgiving), *khums*, and *al-amr bi-l-maʿrūf wa-l-nahy ʿan al-munkar* (enjoining others to do what is commendable and to refrain from what is reprehensible; cf. Q 3:104, 110; 22:41; see VIRTUES AND VICES, COMMANDING AND FORBIDDING).

The most important Ṭayyibī-Mustaʿlī Ismāʿīlī work of jurisprudence which serves as the basis for ʿIsmāʿīlī law and which contains a detailed exposition of *ʿibādāt* is al-Qāḍī l-Nuʿmān's (d. 363/974) *Daʿāʾim al-Islām*, "Pillars of Islam." Al-Nuʿmān, the chief qāḍī under the Fāṭimid caliph al-Muʿizz li-Dīn Allāh (r. 344-65/952-75), includes the following seven *ʿibādāt: walāya* (devotion to the imām), *ṭahāra* (ritual purity), *ṣalāt* (ritual prayer), *janāʾiz* (funerals), *zakāt* (alms tax), *ṣawm* (fasting), *ḥajj* (pilgrimage), and jihād (q.v.; holy war). Immediately following *ṣawm*, al-Nuʿmān discusses *iʿtikāf*.

Esoteric interpretations of ʿibādāt

In *Taʾwīl al-daʿāʾim*, al-Qāḍī l-Nuʿmān stresses the importance for the Ismāʿīlī believer of not only performing the *ʿibādāt*, but also of understanding their esoteric meaning *(bāṭin)*. After providing an esoteric interpretation of *walāya* (affirming the doctrine of belief in and devotion to the imāms), al-Qāḍī l-Nuʿmān explains the *ʿibādāt* as follows: Ritual purity *(ṭahāra)* refers to "purifying oneself through knowledge *(al-taṭahhur bi-l-ʿilm)* and what it necessitates with respect to the impurities of the soul *(bi-mā yūjibuhu l-ʿilm min aḥdāth al-nufūs)*" (*Taʾwīl*, i, 72). In addition to knowledge, wisdom facilitates purification of the soul. Declaring one's intention *(niyya)* in performing *ʿibādāt* is like *walāya* (ibid., i, 85). Al-Qāḍī l-Nuʿmān states that the performance of the ritual prayer *(ṣalāt)* is symbolic of the Prophet's action in making these particular prayers and postures obligatory (ibid., i, 86). The inner meaning of *zakāt* is that the act of giving purifies *(taṭhīr)* one's personal wealth (q.v.; ibid., ii, 87). *Zakāt* is not only associated with ritual purity, but also with righteousness *(ṣalāḥ)* and growth (*numuww;* ibid., ii, 87-8). Al-Nuʿmān quotes several verses to support his interpretations (including Q 9:34, 103; 73:20; 87:14, 15; 91:9, 10). A deeper meaning of *zakāt* is that it represents the one who purifies *(muzakkī)* the people *(al-nās)* — in this case, the foundations *(usus)* and the proofs *(ḥujaj)* who are the vicegerents of the prophets (ibid., ii, 88).

The Ismāʿīlī scholar Abū Yaʿqūb al-Sijistānī (fl. fourth/tenth century) expounds the *ʿibādāt* as follows: Water which represents knowledge purifies the soul from doubt and uncertainty (q.v.). *Walāya* signifies devotion to the imāms. *Ṣalāt* (ritual prayer) signifies devotion to the *awliyāʾ* (the friends of God, i.e. the imāms; see CLIENTS AND CLIENTAGE; FRIENDS AND FRIENDSHIP). *Zakāt* signifies that those who possess knowledge (i.e. the imāms) should send forth guides to the people (see KNOWLEDGE AND LEARNING; KINGS AND RULERS). The lower ranks become *zakāt* for the higher ranks. Fasting *(ṣawm)* means observing silence and not revealing any secrets (q.v.) to the uninitiated (see also HIDDEN AND THE HIDDEN). *Ḥajj* represents the believer having an audience with the imām, who symbolizes the house wherein knowledge of God resides (Sijistānī, *Iftikhār*, chaps. 13-7; especially useful is Poonawala's commentary: see Poonawala/Husayn, *Biobibliography*, 417-29; cf. Poonawala, Ismāʿīlī taʾwīl, 219). Today, Nizārī Ismāʿīlī prayer consists of supplications, but unlike Sunnī and Ithnā ʿAsharī *ṣalāt*, does not include the same sequence of bowing *(rukūʿ)* and prostration *(sujūd)*. Usually prayer is performed in a sitting position.

Ṣūfī works like al-Hujwīrī's *Kashf al-maḥjūb* place importance on understanding and implementing the esoteric and exoteric interpretations in the practice of *ʿibādāt*. In the chapter on ritual purity, al-Hujwīrī emphasizes that while prayer requires purification of the body, gnosis requires purification of the heart (Hujwīrī, *Kashf*, 291). In the chapter on prayer, he stresses the importance of humility, awe, abasement and the annihilation of one's attributes. The chapter on alms links the giving of *zakāt* to poverty in this world, but the giver should also aim to give for the blessings of health, mind and body and infinite blessings should be rendered with infinite thanks to God (see BLESSING; GRACE; GRATITUDE AND INGRATITUDE). In the chapter on fasting, al-Hujwīrī mentions that fasting is abstinence which includes the whole method of Ṣūfism. In the chapter on the pilgrimage, the true meaning of *ḥajj* involves the casting off of the worldly life, sensual desires, the attributes of one's humanity, and the complete submission of the believer to God.

Ritual purity

The Qurʾān itself is described as being contained "in books held greatly in honor, exalted, and pure" (*muṭahhara*, Q 80:13-4; see BOOK; SCROLLS; PRESERVED TABLET). Ritual purity *(ṭahāra)* is the foundation of the *ʿibādāt* upon which the performance of other rituals depends. The north African Mālikī theologian Ibn al-Ḥājj interprets *ṭahāra* as interior ritual purification *(al-ṭahāra al-bāṭina)*. He invokes a tradition of the Prophet (*al-Madkhal*, i, 30): "Supplication *(duʿāʾ)* is the essence of ritual devotion *(ʿibāda)*" and refers to Q 2:222, which mentions ritual purity. Likewise, Ibn al-Ḥājj interprets other ritual acts such as *wuḍūʾ* and *zakāt* as purifying humans from sin, base elements and negative attributes associated with the worldly life. Ritual purity (Q 5:6) and the pure water (q.v.; Q 25:48; cf. 8:11) with which it is associated are referred to in the Qurʾān. The acts of ritual purity practiced by the pre-Islamic Arabs included *iḥrām* (ritual consecration) before entering Mecca (q.v.) and forbidding menstruating women (see MENSTRUATION; PRE-ISLAMIC ARABIA AND THE QURʾĀN) from undertaking the pre-Islamic pilgrimage there. In Islamic times menstruating women were allowed to perform the *ḥajj*, although they were allowed to circumambulate the Kaʿba and undertake the running between Ṣafā and Marwa only when they had achieved a ritually pure state (cf. Howard, Some aspects, 41).

A person in a ritual state is described as *ṭahūr* or *ṭāhir* (Ḥillī, *Tadhkirat*, 7). Bousquet (*Les grandes pratiques*, 16) divides his discussion of the state of ritual impurity into two major categories, which are further elaborated: (1) Minor ritual impurity such as *ḥadath*, which refers to minor emissions from the openings of the body or contact with an impure substance, and which invalidates prayer, circumambulation around the Kaʿba, and touching the Qurʾān; (2) Major ritual impurity *(janāba)* from sexual intercourse (see SEX AND SEXUALITY) and menstruation *(ḥayḍ)*, as a result of which it is generally forbidden to perform prayer, to recite the Qurʾān, to enter a mosque, or to perform the *ḥajj*.

Sunnī and Shīʿī legal sources usually divide the category "ritual purity" *(ṭahāra)* into three sub-categories: *wuḍūʾ* (ablutions), *ghusl* (ritual immersion), and *tayammum* (making ablutions with pure sand or dust; e.g. Ḥillī, *Tadhkirat*, 7, defines *ṭuhūr* as water). Sources usually distinguish between these three forms of ritual purity and discuss the various states of ritual impurity and the conditions under which it is necessary or permitted to undertake ritual purification. They also elaborate upon the physical movements and gestures of the body, as well as the oral formulae which are to be performed.

Wuḍūʾ is necessary for prayer, making *ṭawāf* (circumambulation around the Kaʿba), touching the text of the Qurʾān and for other rituals (cf. Ḥillī, *Tadhkirat,* 8). Similarly, *ghusl* may be made for any one of these three categories in addition to residing in mosques, for producing amulets or talismans for the curing of diseases *(ʿazāʾim)* and for obligatory fasting, etc. *Tayammum* is required for prayer or for the ritually impure person (*junub,* literally "precluded from ritual practice"), and in order to set out for a mosque (ibid.). For a ritually impure person *(junub, muḥdith, ḥāʾiḍ)* to carry a qurʾānic codex or to touch its pages or its writing is a reprehensible act (*makrūh;* Ḥillī, *Tadhkirat,* 241).

Being in a state of ritual purity is required for anybody who touches, reads or recites the Qurʾān. On the basis of Q 56:79, "none shall touch it [the Qurʾān] save for those who are ritually pure *(al-muṭahharūn),*" al-Ḥillī deems it reprehensible for a ritually impure person to touch the Qurʾān. Abū l-Qāsim al-Khūʾī (d. 1992) mentions that the one who is in a state of ritual impurity is not permitted to touch the writing of the codex or the vocalization signs (see RECITATION OF THE QURʾĀN; ORNAMENTATION AND ILLUMINATION; GRAMMAR AND THE QURʾĀN), nor the name of God or the ninety-nine "beautiful names." According to al-Nawawī, other books which contain verses from the Qurʾān are to be treated in the same manner if the qurʾānic text they contain is significantly greater in length than the rest of the text, e.g. a brief gloss or commentary. Thus, it is forbidden for the ritually impure person to touch and carry them (Nawawī, *Tibyān,* 194).

Theological and legal discussions focus on the etiquette *(adab)* of what is permitted and forbidden (q.v.; see also LAWFUL AND UNLAWFUL). For instance, the Qurʾān should be treated with reverence as should, more generally, books which contain the name of God and Qurʾān writing boards used by schoolboys (see TEACHING AND PREACHING THE QURʾĀN). In a related cultural practice, a scribe does not leave a book he is consulting on the ground for fear an animal or person would walk over it, thus divesting the writing of efficacy (Westermarck, *Pagan survivals,* 134). A state of ritual purity is also required when one writes a talisman which includes verses from the Qurʾān or the ninety-nine beautiful names of God, for it is as if a scribe were copying a codex.

Oaths

Oaths (sing. *qasam, ḥalf*) that are sworn on the qurʾānic codex are seldom attested to in pre-modern sources. Unlike in Christianity or Judaism, where the oath upon a physical copy of scripture is presently a requirement, there is no legal requirement that the Qurʾān need be present or that one place one's right hand on a codex in order to validate an oath. Legal sources discourage the taking of oaths by anything apart from God or his ninety-nine beautiful names (cf. Nawawī, *Tibyān*). The eighth/fourteenth century traveler Ibn Baṭṭūṭa mentions that Damascenes made debtors and those against whom they had a claim swear *(yuḥlif)* on the ʿUthmānic codex of the Qurʾān at the congregational mosque (Ibn Baṭṭūṭa, *Riḥla,* i, 105).

In Ibn Taghrībirdī's *al-Nujūm al-zāhira,* a chronicle of the Mamlūk dynasty of Egypt, two references are made to emirs taking oaths. In the first, an emir takes an oath on a *muṣḥaf* (*ḥalafa ʿalā l-muṣḥaf,* Ibn Taghrībirdī, *Nujūm,* ed. Cairo, x, 32, for 742/1341). In the second instance, an emir holds the codex in his hand and takes an oath (*fa-tanāwala l-muṣḥaf al-sharīf bi-yadihi wa-ḥalafa lahum yamīnan,* trans. Popper, *History of Egypt,* xxiii, 80, for 871/1466). A type of oath is the oath of allegiance *(bayʿa)* which the Quraysh (q.v.) swore when they pledged their fealty to the prophet Muḥammad and which also became the standard for the election of a new caliph (q.v.; Q 48:10, 18).

Today certain courts and administrative bodies in western countries have required that when Muslims swear oaths, they place their right hand on the codex. Some consider placing the right hand on the Qurān to be forbidden *(ḥarām),* especially when one is not in a ritually pure state. During the early twentieth century C.E., Tewfik Canaan observed that oaths by the Qur᾽ān *(wa-l-muṣḥaf)* were quite common throughout Palestine (Canaan, Modern Palestinian beliefs, 77). Modern day legal opinions commonly regard swearing by the Qur᾽ān *(al-ḥalf bi-l-muṣḥaf)* as tantamount to swearing by God since the Qur᾽ān is God's words. The Azharī ʿAbdul ʿAzeem al-Matʿani has issued a legal ruling that taking an oath on the Qur᾽ān is not valid unless one clearly states one's intention *(niyya)* that in doing so one is swearing by God (Fatwā, IslamOnline.net, Fatwa id=77191: "Swearing by the Qur᾽ān"). Certain court rulings discuss the expiation (see FORGIVENESS; REPENTANCE AND PENANCE) of one who has not carried out an oath sworn by placing the right hand on the *muṣḥaf.*

Rituals and the Qur᾽ān

Among the rituals that are discussed at length in legal sources are rituals of purification which are required in order to pray and also those ritual practices which are required before touching or reciting the Qur᾽ān (see above). Beyond such rituals, there are those which require physical contact with the Qur᾽ān or particular verses.

Certain highly commendable practices include reciting particular qur᾽ānic verses at different times. Before going to sleep each night, the Prophet would cup his hands together, blow into them and recite over them Q 112 ("Sincerity," Sūrat al-Ikhlāṣ), Q 113 ("Daybreak," Sūrat al-Falaq) and Q 114 ("People," Sūrat al-Nās), and would rub his hands three times over the "permitted" parts of his body (cf. Bukhārī, *Ṣaḥīḥ,* vi, book 61, no. 35).

Kissing the Qur᾽ān

Upon holding the Qur᾽ān in the right hand, Muslims often kiss its cover and raise the Qur᾽ān above their heads in order to derive *baraka.* Although this devotional act is not generally deemed controversial, the Ḥanbalī position as expounded by the eighth/fourteenth century theologian Ibn Taymiyya maintains that there is no basis for this practice in the sunna of the Prophet or in the deeds of the righteous ancestors *(al-salaf).* Ibn Taymiyya discusses this practice in conjunction with other practices, such as standing up *(qiyām)* for, or in the presence of the *muṣḥaf,* though he does quote a tradition of ʿIkrima b. Abī Jahl in which he used to put his face to the qur᾽ānic codex and say: "[These are] the words of my lord *(kalām rabbī);* [These are] the words of my lord" (Ibn Taymiyya, *Fatāwā,* i, 49). Elsewhere, Ibn Taymiyya (*Jāmiʿ,* 109) argues that it is only permissible to touch and kiss the two "Yemeni" stones (i.e. the black stone in the eastern corner of the Kaʿba and that in the south-west corner of the Kaʿba; *lā yushraʿu li-aḥad an yastalima wa-yuqabbila ghayr al-ruknayn al-yamāniyyayn*).

Although no early traditions attest to kissing the qur᾽ānic codex or kissing it and wiping it over the eyes and face, Wahhābīs consider this a heretical innovation *(bidʿa)* which, based upon a legal ruling of the Permanent Committee on Scientific

Research and Religious Rulings, Saudi Arabia (*Bid῾a,* 549: question 12 of *fatwā* no. 1472), they discourage.

Weeping

Weeping at the recitation of the Qur᾿ān is commended by God (Q 17:109). Al-Ghazālī states: "Read the Qur᾿ān and cry; if you do not cry, force yourselves to weep. Weeping is the sixth rule." A Muslim should also weep upon hearing the words *ṣubḥān Allāh,* "Glory be to God" (see GLORIFICATION OF GOD) and Q 17:107-9 (Quasem, *Recitation,* 34).

Resolving conflict

A number of historical incidents are recorded in which verses from the Qur᾿ān were invoked for the purpose of arbitration (q.v.). The words of the sacred text were used to bring about a desired result or resolution to war (q.v.), conflict (see FIGHTING) or oppression (q.v.; see also JUSTICE AND INJUSTICE). But — apart from the famous battles of Ṣiffīn (see ṢIFFĪN, BATTLE OF), wherein Mu῾āwiya and his partisans reportedly raised a copy of the Qur᾿ān upon spears as a stratagem, and of the Camel, where ῾Ā᾿isha asked that the Qur᾿ān be brought for the purpose of arbitration (see ῾Ā᾿ISHA BINT ABĪ BAKR) — only a single incident involves the qur᾿ānic codex itself in a particular historical event: in 851/1447, presumably after failing to pay a 1/10 levy on their merchandise, the Kārimī merchants were deemed renegades by the Mamlūk sultan Juqmuq. The Kārimīs took the extraordinary measure of holding hostage the preacher of the mosque in Mecca and raised the qur᾿ānic codices above their heads and requested a *fatwā* concerning the legality of the 1/10 tax (*῾ushr;* ῾Abbās, *Ta᾿rīkh,* 127).

Recitation of the Qur᾿ān

The general, though by no means universal, consensus among Sunnī and Shī῾ī theologians is that qur᾿ānic recitation *(tilāwa)* is not included among the *῾ibādāt.* Al-Nawawī does not specifically classify recitation *(tilāwa)* under *῾ibādāt.* But, unlike al-Nawawī, the mystic al-Ghazālī in the eighth chapter of *Iḥyā᾿ ῾ulūm al-dīn,* "Revivification of the religious sciences," cites a prophetic tradition on the basis of which he justifies the inclusion of the recitation of the Qur᾿ān among devotional acts (*῾ibādāt;* Quasem, *Recitation,* 22). In the second chapter of the eighth book of *Iḥyā᾿ ῾ulūm al-dīn,* al-Ghazālī mentions rules for the oral recitation of the Qur᾿ān, and in the third chapter he enumerates the associated mental or esoteric tasks (*al-a῾māl al-bāṭina;* ibid., 21).

According to a prophetic tradition narrated by al-Ghazālī, "[One of] the best devotional acts *(῾ibādāt)* of my community is the recitation of the Qur᾿ān" (ibid., 22; this tradition is also mentioned in al-Bāqillānī's *Inṣāf*). The mere act of looking at a codex while reciting the Qur᾿ān is also an act of devotion to God (*῾ibāda;* Quasem, *Recitation,* 52-3).

There is no consensus about reciting the Qur᾿ān over the deceased. Al-Nawawī mentions Q 36 (Sūrat Yā Sīn) or Q 2 ("The Cow," Sūrat al-Baqara) as chapters of the Qur᾿ān to be recited. For up to three days after the funeral, the male and female mourners would gather to mourn separately at the house of the deceased (Massé, *Persian beliefs,* 91-3). There they would engage in the ceremonial recitation of the entire Qur᾿ān *(khatm al-Qur᾿ān).* The qur᾿ānic codex, which would be written in thirty or sixty separate notebooks and which was part of a *waqf* legacy, would be distributed to mourners. Near the Qur᾿ān, a repository (*raḥl,* i.e. for storing the various parts of the codex read by the mourners) would be placed.

A practice found among some mendicant Ṣūfīs (sing. *faqīr*) elicited the rebuke of Ibn Taymiyya (*Fatāwā,* i, 53). Ibn Taymiyya observed that a group of *faqīr*s who met regularly to ritually remember God and to recite a portion of the Qurʾān, would bare their heads and humble themselves *(yataḍarraʿūna)* for the sake of getting near to God *(ʿalā wajh al-taqarrub)*. Ibn Taymiyya labels this practice as reprehensible *(makrūh),* especially if it is regarded as a devotional practice *(ʿibāda)*.

Healing and curing

The healing properties associated with the Qurʾān and the efficacy of reciting specific verses for particular ailments are widely recognized among Muslims; its curative power lies in the belief in God's words (cf. Nawawī, *Tibyān,* 183). Among the most widely recounted prophetic traditions in this regard is that whenever the Prophet became ill, he would recite Q 113 ("Daybreak," Sūrat al-Falaq) and Q 114 ("People," Sūrat al-Nās), then blow his breath over his body. When he was unable to do so, ʿĀʾisha would take and rub his hands over his body hoping for their blessings (Bukhārī, *Ṣaḥīḥ,* vi, book 61, no. 535; see MEDICINE AND THE QURʾĀN).

Donning a garment with verses from the Qurʾān and reciting certain verses and chapters or other segments of the Qurʾān, such as the *muʿawwadhatayn* ("the two chapters against evil"), are efficacious for protecting its wearer from harm and curing illness. According to al-Nawawī, the Qurʾān is more effective than the ḥadīth when one is ailing (Nawawī, *Tibyān,* 183).

Talismanic and amuletic uses of the Qurʾān and talismanic objects

Talismanic uses of the Qurʾān fall under the heading of *mujarrabāt;* practices, methods, objects and rituals employed in humankind's encounter with their fellows and with the divine that are tried and proven through personal experience or the experience of others. Such practices may include the recitation of the Qurʾān in order to cure an illness. According to Ibn Taymiyya (*Fatāwā,* i, 49-52), however, the practice of predicting the future with the qurʾānic codex *(fatḥ al-faʾl)* is reprehensible *(makrūh)* and should be forbidden as it did not exist among the pious ancestors *(salaf)*.

When admiring a child, Egyptians would invoke Q 113 (Lane, *Manners,* 259). In Iran when naming a child, the father or the eldest member of the family randomly places slips with names between the pages of the Qurʾān. Those present recite the opening chapter of the Qurʾān, the Fātiḥa (q.v.) and the father or eldest male present chooses a name (Massé, *Persian beliefs,* 25-6).

Verses from the Qurʾān such as from Q 106 were also engraved on the surface of cups and bowls. Those who utilized them were protected from harm (Lane, *Manners,* 263-4), and these vessels were also employed by magicians to reveal the unseen (Q 21, 50; cf. Lane, *Manners,* 279). Amulets containing certain verses from the Qurʾān (Q 6, 18, 36, 44, 55, 67, 78) were placed under articles of clothing such as caps in order to protect the wearer from the devil (q.v.) and all evil jinn (q.v.).

Among the popular Shīʿī beliefs and practices which have parallels among Sunnīs is the inscription of certain passages from the Qurʾān with a variety of writing substances (e.g. saffron, water, kohl) in a number of media. Verses are pronounced over or dissolved in natural substances such as earth, water, or sand. They are employed to realize certain objectives, such as to affect a cure and alter the physical and mental states of the initiator or other persons. Among the innumerable examples of talismanic verses are the following: Q 11:41, which is inscribed on an Indian oak board blackened at its beginning (Maghniyya, *Mujarrabāt,* 18). Concerning Q 12 (Sūrat Yūsuf): "Whoever records it and buries it in his house and after three days takes it out of the house from its exterior, will experience that the sultan's messenger is calling out to grant him victory and he will become important. Whoever writes a verse and drinks it (i.e. its ink) it will ensure prosperity." Other chapters and verses are inscribed on strips of silken white cloth which are affixed to the upper arm of an infant to protect it from harm and evil. Writing certain verses in saffron and giving them as a drink for a woman who has difficulty lactating, will make her lactate. Whoever writes a certain verse from Q 15 and puts it in his pocket or chest pocket will prosper in his transactions and in his livelihood. If Q 16 is written on the wall of an orchard, trees that do not bear fruit will produce an abundance of ripe fruit. Its invocation also ensures prosperity (Maghniyya, *Mujarrabāt,* 19). Certain verses are efficacious for relieving poverty, such as Q 104:1 which is to be recited at the time of the obligatory prayer.

Q 21 is often recited for the protection of an unborn infant. The verses are to be written on an animal skin and then hung up during the first forty days of pregnancy. During the month in which the mother is due to give birth, she carries it on her person to ensure a successful birth. Marriage will be facilitated for the unmarried person who, every month, reads verses from Q 21 twenty-one times, fasts for three days and supplicates God (Maghniyya, *Mujarrabāt,* 20). When written on a green silken cloth which is hung up, other chapters (like Q 23) prevent individuals from drinking wine. When placed on one's bed, Q 24 prevents one from dreaming. Q 24 is also believed to be efficacious in treating animal ailments: if written in a copper basin from which a sick beast of burden is given to drink, and also if water from the basin is sprinkled on the animal, it will be healed. When Q 26:1 is read over a handful of soil, which is thrown in the enemy's face, God will defeat and forsake the enemy (ibid., 20; see ENEMIES). Other verses constitute forms of sympathetic magic which are intended to alter the physical state of individuals or groups. Q 22 ("The Pilgrimage," Sūrat al-Ḥajj) is employed to defeat one's political rivals, leaders, judges, etc. Other verses are efficacious for the prevention of infidelity and adultery (e.g. ibid., 20-1; see ADULTERY AND FORNICATION). Q 36 is efficacious against jinn and the evil eye (ibid., 21), Q 38 enables one who wears (a strip of cloth with it) on his forearm to become popular among the people (ibid., 22), and Q 41 is efficacious for ailments of the eye: it is written with rainwater and erased, and kohl is then ground into the water and applied to the eye (ibid., 22).

Women in modern day Morocco and elsewhere carry miniature copies of the Qur'ān or select verses of it on their persons. Amulets are also prescribed for various illnesses. Prescriptions may include dissolving a piece of paper with verses from the Qur'ān into water which the patient is instructed to drink (Buitelaar, Between oral traditions, 235-6). Among the popular Shī'ī customs attested to in the modern era is the raising of the Qur'ān over travelers or soldiers going to war in order to protect them from harm.

When visiting the Prophet's tomb in Medina, Shī'ī pilgrims — and, previously, Sunnī pilgrims — would make gifts in charity *(ṣadaqa)* referred to as *najwā*. Such gifts are based on Q 58:12: "O you who believe! When you consult the apostle in private, spend something in charity before your private consultation. That will be best for you and most conducive to purity [of conduct]. But if you find not [the wherewithal], God is oft-forgiving, most merciful." According to al-Ṭabarī (d. 310/923) and al-Nasafī (d. 710/1310) the first person to institute this practice was 'Alī b. Abī Ṭālib (q.v.; Ṭabarī, *Tafsīr,* xxviii, 19-20; Nasafī, *Tafsīr,* iii, 434). In Fāṭimid Egypt, *najwā* was a gift which was collected by

Ismāʿīlīs attending doctrinal teaching sessions (Maqrīzī, *Musawwada*, 92-4).

Rituals of group cohesion and solidarity

Among the qurʾānic rituals which promote group cohesion is the Friday prayer (*ṣalāt al-jumʿa;* cf. Q 62:9) and more generally, congregational prayer at mosques where believers are urged to come together to remember God. The qurʾānic codex also plays an important role in promoting group solidarity. In times of crisis Muslims, Jews and Christians turned to scriptures which they publicly displayed as they walked in procession (Meri, *Cult of saints*, 115). In Damascus in 543-4/1148, the ʿUthmānic codex was brought out in order to ward off an imminent Crusader attack. Men, women and children gathered around it in supplication and the attack was averted. In 680/1282, the ʿUthmānic codex and other venerable copies of the Qurʾān were once again invoked in several Syrian cities in order to ward off a Mongol invasion (ibid., 115-6). The Qurʾān was again used as a weapon against oppression in 711/1312 when the people of Damascus marching in procession with the ʿUthmānic codex and the sandal of the Prophet and the caliphal standards confronted the governor of Damascus about oppressive taxes (ibid., 116).

Josef W. Meri

Bibliography

Primary: Bāqillānī, *al-Inṣāf fī-mā yajibu ʿtiqāduhu wa-lā yajūzu l-jahl bihi*, ed. M. al-Kawtharī, on http://www.alwaraq.com (where the work is incorrectly identified as that of its editor, Muḥammad al-Kawtharī); al-Baṭalyawsī, Abū Muḥammad ʿAbdallāh b. Muḥammad b. al-Sīd, *al-Inṣāf fī l-tanbīh ʿalā l-asbāb allatī awjabat al-ikhtilāf*, ed. A.Ḥ. Kāḥil and Ḥ.ʿA. al-Nashartī, Cairo 1978; Bukhārī, *Ṣaḥīḥ;* al-Ghazālī, Abū Ḥāmid Muḥammad b. Muḥammad, *Iḥyāʾ ʿulūm al-dīn*, trans. M.A. Quasem, *The recitation and interpretation of the Qurʾān. al-Ghazālī's theory*, London 1982; id., *Kitāb al-Arbaʿīn fī uṣūl al-dīn*, Beirut 1979; al-Ḥillī l-ʿAllāma, Ḥasan b. Yūsuf b. ʿAlī b. al-Muṭahhar, *Kitāb al-Sharāʾiʿ fī masāʾil al-ḥalāl wa-l-ḥarām*, ed. ʿA.M. ʿAlī, 4 vols., Najaf 1969; id., *Tadhkirat al-fuqahāʾ fī talkhīṣ fatāwī l-ʿulamāʾ*, 13 vols., Qom 1414/1993-4; al-Hujwīrī, Abū l-Ḥasan ʿAlī b. ʿUthmān al-Jullābī, *Kashf al-maḥjūb*, St. Petersburg 1899, repr. Tehran 1993; Ibn Baṭṭūṭa, Abū ʿAbdallāh Muḥammad b. ʿAbdallāh, *Riḥla [Tuḥfat al-nuẓẓār fī gharāʾib al-amṣār wa-ʿajāʾib al-asfār]*, ed. ʿA. al-Khattānī, 2 vols., Beirut 1975; Ibn al-Ḥājj, Muḥammad b. Muḥammad b. Muḥammad al-ʿAbdarī al-Fāsī, *al-Madkhal ilā tanmiyat al-aʿmāl bi-taḥsīn al-niyyāt wa-l-tanbīh ʿalā baʿḍ al-bidaʿ wa-l-ʿawāʾid allatī ntaḥalat wa-bayān shanāʿatihā*, ed. T. Ḥamdān, 2 vols., Beirut 1995; Ibn Taghrībirdī, Abū l-Maḥāsin Jamāl al-Dīn Yūsuf, *al-Nujūm al-ẓāhira fī mulūk Miṣr wa-l-Qāhira*, ed. W. Popper, 9 vols., Berkeley, CA 1909-30; 16 vols., Cairo 1963-72; trans. W. Popper, *History of Egypt*, 1382-1469 A.D., 7 vols., Berkeley, CA 1954-; Ibn Taymiyya, *al-Fatāwā l-kubrā*, ed. M.ʿA. ʿAṭā, 4 vols., Beirut 1998; id., *Jāmiʿ al-Masāʾil*, ed. M.ʿU. Shams, Mecca 1424/2003; al-Maqrīzī, Abū l-ʿAbbās Aḥmad b. ʿAlī, *Musawwadat Kitāb al-Mawāʿiẓ wa-l-iʿtibār fī dhikr al-khiṭaṭ wa-l-āthār*, London 1995; Muḥammad b. Ḥabīb, Abū Jaʿfar, *Kitab al-Muḥabbar*, ed. I. Lichtenstädter, Hyderabad 1942; Muslim, *Ṣaḥīḥ;* Nasafī, *Tafsīr*, 5 vols., Beirut 1973; Nawawī, *al-Tibyān fī ādāb ḥamalat al-Qurʾān*, ed. M. al-Ḥajjār, Beirut 1996; al-Nuʿmān b. Abū ʿAbdallāh Muḥammad b. Manṣūr b. Aḥmad b. Ḥayyān al-Tamīmī (al-Qāḍī), *Daʿāʾim al-Islām*, ed. ʿĀ. Tāmir, 2 vols., Beirut 1995; trans. Asaf A.A. Fyzee, rev. ed. I.K.H. Poonawala, *The pillars of Islam*, Delhi 2002; id., *Taʾwīl al-Daʿāʾim*, ed. M.Ḥ. al-Aʿẓamī, 3 vols., Cairo 1969-72; al-Shāfiʿī, Muḥammad b. Idrīs, *al-Umm*, ed. M. Maṭrajī, 9 vols., Beirut 1993; al-Sijistānī, Abū Yaʿqūb Isḥāq b. Aḥmad, *Kitāb al-Iftikhār*, ed. I.K.H. Poonawala, Beirut 2000; Suyūṭī, *Itqān*, ed. F.A. al-Zamarlī, 2 vols., Beirut 1999; Ṭabarī, *Tafsīr*, ed. ʿAlī et al.; Zayd b. ʿAli b. al-Ḥusayn b. ʿAlī b. Abī Ṭālib, *Musnad al-Imām Zayd*, Beirut 1966.

Secondary: I. ʿAbbās, *Taʾrīkh bilād al-Shām fī ʿahd al-Atābika wa-l-Ayūbiyyīn*, 490-650, Amman 1998; S.A. Ashraf, The inner meaning of the Islamic rites. Prayer, pilgrimage, fasting, jihād, in S.Ḥ. Nasr (ed.), *Islamic spirituality. Foundations*, London 1987, 111-30; C. Bell, *Ritual theory, ritual practice*, Oxford 1992; G.-H. Bousquet, Ghusl, in *EI²*, ii, 1104; id., ʿIbādāt, in *EI²*, iii, 647-8; id., La pureté rituelle en Islam. Étude de fiqh et de sociologie religieuse, in *Revue de l'histoire des religions* 138 (1956), 53-71; id., *Les grandes pratiques rituelles de l'Islam*, Paris 1949; M. Buitelaar, Between oral traditions and literacy. Women's use of the holy scriptures in Morocco, in *BSA* 9-10 (1994), 225-39; T. Canaan, Modern Palestinian beliefs and practices relating to God, in *Journal of the Palestine Oriental Society* 14 (1934), 59-92; E. Chaumont, Wuḍūʾ, in *EI²*, xi, 218-9; F.M. Denny, Exegesis and recitation. Their development as classical forms of qurʾānic piety, in F.E. Reynolds and Th.M. Ludwig (eds.), *Transitions and transformations in the history of religions. Essays in honor of Joseph M. Kitagawa,* Leiden 1980, 91-123; id., Islamic ritual, in R.C. Martin (ed.), *Approaches to Islam in religious studies,* Tucson, AZ 1985, 63-77; M. Douglas, *Purity and danger. An analysis of ritual and taboo,* London 2002; M. Eliade, *Patterns in comparative religion,* London 1958; W.A. Graham, Islam in the mirror of ritual, in R.G. Hovannisian and Sp. Vyronis Jr. (eds.), *Islam's understanding of itself,* Malibu, CA 1983; id. Qurʾān as spoken word, in R.C. Martin (ed.), *Approaches to Islam in religious studies,* Tucson, AZ 1985, 63-77; I.K.A. Howard, Some aspects of the pagan Arab background to Islamic ritual, in *Bulletin of the British Association of Orientalists* 10 (1978), 41-8; A. al-Ḥuṣarī, *Mina l-fiqh al-islāmī,* Beirut 1988; IslamOnline.net; M.H. Katz, *Body of text. The emergence of the Sunni law of ritual purity,* Albany, NY 2002; R. Kriss, and H. Kriss-Heinrich, *Volksglaube im Bereich des Islam,* 2 vols., Wiesbaden 1962; E.W. Lane, *An account of the manners and customs of the modern Egyptians,* London 1860⁵, repr. Cairo/New York 2003; M. Maghniyya, *al-Mujarrabāt al-imāmiyya,* Beirut 1996; H. Massé, *Persian beliefs and customs,* trans. Ch.A. Messner, New Haven, CT 1954; J.W. Meri, *The cult of saints among Muslims and Jews in medieval Syria,* Oxford 2002; D.C. Mulder, The recitation of the Qurʾān, in *Nederlands Theologisch Tijdschrift* 37 (1983), 247-52; J. Pedersen, Na<u>dh</u>r, in *EI²*, vii, 846-7; The Permanent Committee for Islamic Research and *Fatāwā* (Saudi Arabia), *al-Bidʿa wa-l-muḥdathāt wa-mā lā aṣla lahu;* I.K. Poonawala [I.Q. Husayn], *Biobibliography of Ismaʿili literature,* Malibu, CA 1977; id., Ismāʿīlī *taʾwīl* of the Qurʾān, in Rippin, *Approaches,* 199-222; A.K. Reinhart, Impurity/No danger, in *History of religions* 30/1 (1990), 1-24; J.J. Rivlin, *Gesetz im Koran Kultus und Ritus,* Jerusalem 1934; J.B. Ruska/B. Carra de Vaux/C.E. Bosworth, Tilsam, in *EI²*, x, 500-2; E. Savage-Smith (ed.), *Magic and divination in early Islam,* Aldershot 2004; E. Savage-Smith and F. Madison, *Science, tools, and magic,* 2 vols., London 1997; C. Serena, *Hommes et choses en Perse,* Paris 1883; J. al-Sijānī, *al-ʿIbāda, ḥadduhā wa mafhūmuhā,* Qom 1412/1991; http://www.imamsadeq.org/book/sub4/al-abida; J.Z. Smith, The bare facts of ritual, in *History of religions* 20 (1980), 53-65; M.S. al-Ṭabāṭabāʾī, *Minhāj al-ṣāliḥīn,* Kuwait 1998; al-Ṭabbāʿ al-Miṣrī, *Fatḥ al-Karīm al-Mannān fī ādāb ḥamalat al-Qurʾān,* Cairo 2000 (also on http://www.alwaraq.com/index2.htm?i=1094&page=1), 5; A.J. Wensinck, Nāfila, in *EI²*, vii, 978-9; id., Taha<u>djdj</u>ud, in *EI²*, x, 97; E. Westermarck, *Pagan survivals in Mohammedan civilization,* London 1933; E.M. Zuesse, Ritual, in *ER,* xii, 405-22.

Ritual Purity

A state of heightened cleanliness, symbolic or actual, associated with persons, activities and objects in the context of ritual worship (q.v.; see also CLEANLINESS AND ABLUTION; CONTAMINATION). The Qurʾān imposes a specific, two-tiered requirement of ritual cleansing before prayer (q.v.) and this is its most direct and detailed — and perhaps its only — regulation of ritual purity in the narrow sense. More general notions of purity and impurity extend, however, to a fairly wide array of persons, objects and activities in contexts that are mostly not, strictly speaking, connected with discrete rituals. These range from qualities of substantive impurity affecting persons and foods (see FOOD AND DRINK), to the idea of purity as an ethical concept (see ETHICS AND THE QURʾĀN), to the use of a concept of purity simply to denote what is good or desirable.

Terminology

Words derived from the root *ṭ-h-r* (compare Heb. *ṭoharot*) denote the requisite state of ritual purity for prayer as well as one of the processes by which that state is achieved. Major impurity in the context of prayer is denoted exclusively by the term *junub*. There is no qurʾānic term for minor impurity but such impurity (or perhaps more accurately, the transient lack of requisite purity) must be remedied prior to praying by a combination of wiping *(m-s-ḥ)* and washing *(gh-s-l)* of the body's extremities. Major impurity is removed by purification (*ṭ-h-r*, interpreted by jurists to refer to a major washing). Words derived from the roots *z-k-y* and *ṭ-h-r* are occasionally used synonymously to refer to purity in a non-technical sense. Also, *ṭayyib* may denote the substantive purity of certain foods in some contexts; its antonym is *khabīth*. The words *najas, rijs, rijz* and *rujz* can also denote substantive impurity, though it should be emphasized that the Qurʾān does not exhibit a rigorously developed notion of substantive impurity.

Ritual cleansing for prayer (Q 4:43; 5:6)

The Qurʾān mandates that persons who undertake to pray must first complete a ritual cleansing. The details and requirements of this cleansing appear at Q 4:43 and Q 5:6, two partly overlapping passages that are important, difficult to interpret and central to the formation and classical expression of the Islamic law of ritual purity (see Paret, *Koran*, and id., *Kommentar*, for the following translations; for the subsequent discussion, see generally Katz, *Body of text;* see also LAW AND THE QURʾĀN):

O you who believe: When you undertake the prayer, then wash your faces (see FACE) and your hands (q.v.) to the elbows, and wipe your heads and your feet [q.v.; or: and wash your feet] to the ankles. If you are in a state of major impurity, then purify yourselves. If you are sick (see ILLNESS AND HEALTH), on a journey (q.v.), or one of you has come from the privy, or you have touched women (see SEX AND SEXUALITY), and you do not find water (q.v.), then seek out a clean, elevated place, and wipe your faces and your hands therefrom. God does not want to impose hardship on you but rather he wishes to purify you and to complete his favor (see GRACE; BLESSING) towards you. Perhaps you will be thankful (Q 5:6; see GRATITUDE AND INGRATITUDE).

O you who believe: Do not approach prayer while you are intoxicated (see INTOXICANTS; WINE), until you understand what you are saying, and not [while you are] in a state of major ritual impurity, unless you are [merely] passing by, until you have cleansed yourselves. *If you are sick, on a journey, or one of you has come from the privy, or you have touched women, and you do not find water, then seek out a clean, elevated place, and wipe your faces and your hands.* God is forgiving and pardoning (Q 4:43; see FORGIVENESS).

(The italics indicate the overlap with Q 5:6 but note that Q 5:6 contains one additional word, *minhu*, rendered above as "therefrom.") The overlap in wording notwithstanding, Q 5:6 contains the more complete statement of the purity requirements for those intending to pray, with mostly supplementary details being supplied by Q 4:43. The major exception to the basic requirements set forth at Q 5:6 appear, with virtually identical wording, in both passages. The passages pose several problems, though their general structure emerges clearly enough. Q 5:6 sets forth the following requirements: Prior to praying, certain areas of the body must be wiped *(m-s-ḥ)* and washed *(gh-s-l)*. In case of major impurity *(junub)*, persons are required to "purify" themselves *(ṭ-h-r)*, though the procedure for accomplishing this is not spelled out. Then, the passage sets forth an apparent exception — wiping *(m-s-ḥ)* of specified areas of the body — for certain enumerated situations in which no water is available. The exception appears to apply in lieu of the requirements for the ordinary cleansing (wiping and washing) mentioned at the verse's outset since it neatly substitutes wiping of the faces and hands for the washing of them. Thus, the exception would, in the enumerated situations in which water is not available, allow for the symbolic wiping of the face and hands, and by implication also of the head and feet.

To the foregoing requirements, Q 4:43 adds only the injunction not to pray while intoxicated and the exception that persons merely passing by the mosque (q.v.) need not cleanse themselves of major ritual impurity. A state of intoxication seems to vitiate intent ("until you understand what you are saying") rather than the requisite degree of ritual purity. To the extent that this rule, by negative implication, suggests that intoxicants are licit (apart from the context of prayer), Muslim jurists considered it abrogated by subsequent denunciations of wine *(khamr)* elsewhere in the Qur'ān (see e.g. Abū ʿUbayd, *Nāsikh,* 87-8; Q 2:219 and Q 5:90-1; also below; see ABROGATION). The exceptive reference to persons merely passing by the mosque was understood to refer to travelers (e.g. ʿAbd al-Razzāq, *Tafsīr,* i, 163, ad Q 4:43), who, as noted, were subject only to the requirement of the substitute symbolic wiping, *tayammum.*

Scholarly and juristic interpretation combined with ritual practice to introduce several interpretive wrinkles into this complex of rules (for the following, see Katz, *Body of text,* chapter 2). The interpretation of the first sentence of Q 5:6 differs fundamentally between Sunnīs and Shīʿīs (see SHĪʿISM AND THE QURʾĀN). The most syntactically plausible reading of the Arabic (see ARABIC LANGUAGE; GRAMMAR AND THE QURʾĀN) would be "wash your faces and your hands to the elbows, and wipe your heads and your feet to the ankles," in which washing faces and hands is parallel to wiping heads and feet. This is, however, the minority, Shīʿī interpretation. The majority Sunnīs, by changing one vowel, make "feet" a third object of the verb to wash, thereby making the verse read "wash your faces and your hands to the elbows, wipe your heads, and (wash) your feet to the ankles" (see READINGS OF THE QURʾĀN). It should be noted that, according to generally accepted principles of Islamic law, invalid ablutions lead to an invalid prayer, so the legal consequences of this minor dispute over vocalization can, in theory, have serious consequences for individual believers' salvation (q.v.).

There is also the question of how the majority Muslim sect came to have a practice at variance with the grammatically most probable vocalization of its scripture. One possibility is that the Shīʿī understanding of the passage represents a survival of the earliest practice of the Muslim community as a whole (for other claims of sectarian practice representing authentic ancient survivals, see Crone, *Roman, provincial and Islamic law,* e.g. 21; and generally, Crone and Hinds, *God's caliph;* see COMMUNITY AND SOCIETY IN THE QURʾĀN). Another possibility is that ritual practice in the period of the conquests simply evolved on its own away from, or even independently of, the explicit text of the Qurʾān (see RITUAL AND THE QURʾĀN). Once the pace of conquest had slowed sufficiently to allow Muslim communities and their scholars to engage in the intensive study of a canonized qurʾānic text (see TEXTUAL CRITICISM OF THE QURʾĀN; TRADITIONAL DISCIPLINES OF QURʾĀNIC STUDIES), the discrepancy was noted, and perhaps the discrepancy in practice frozen, for reasons that remain obscure, along emerging sectarian lines (see Katz, *Body of text,* 75-86; on the date of the Qurʾān's canonization, see Crone, Two legal problems; see COLLECTION OF THE QURʾĀN; CODICES OF THE QURʾĀN; POLITICS AND THE QURʾĀN).

Q 5:6 and Q 4:43 generated other exegetical debates as well. The phrase in Q 5:6 "when you undertake to pray" seems to suggest that ritual cleansing is required at every performance of the prayer, though this is not how the rule has traditionally been interpreted. Instead, ablutions performed for the first prayer of the day suffice unless one has had an intervening polluting bodily function *(ḥadath)*. What constitutes a polluting bodily function was inferred from subsequent clauses in the rule that refer, or were assumed to refer obliquely, to elimination of waste and sexual activity. The phrase "when you undertake to pray" was also read to mean "when you arise [from sleep] to pray" and so to require ritual cleansing after sleep (q.v.), making sleep — like the enumerated bodily functions — into something that vitiates ritual purity (Katz, *Body of text,* 60-75).

A phrase common to both Q 5:6 and 4:43, "or [if] you have touched women" *(aw lāmastum al-nisāʾa)* also generated exegetical debate (see EXEGESIS OF THE QURʾĀN: CLASSICAL AND MEDIEVAL). Does the verb "to touch" *(lāmasa)* here refer to mere touching or does it refer euphemistically to sexual intercourse? How one answered this question had deeper implications for the meaning of the passage as whole. If mere touching was meant, a literal reading of the verse could produce the result that in cases of simply touching of women — that is, in cases where ablutions were vitiated but no major impurity incurred — substitute wiping with dust *(tayammum)* would be allowed if no water were available. By negative implication, then, major ritual impurity could not be cured by such substitute wiping. On the other hand, if *lāmasa* referred to sexual contact with women, then its mention in the clause in question entailed the possibility that major ritual impurity could be cured by substitute wiping with dust (Katz, *Body of text,* 86-96).

It should be noted that the phrase *tayammamū ṣaʿīdan ṭayyiban,* "seek out a clean, elevated place," in Q 5:6 likely originally referred to the seeking out of an appropriate place to perform substitute ablutions but the verb *(tayammama)* eventually acquired the technical legal sense of performing substitute ablutions or cleansing with sand (Paret, *Kommentar,* 116).

Neither Q 5:6 nor Q 4:43 provide details about what constitutes major impurity, apart from giving it a name, *junub,* in Q 5. The term *junub* and its triliteral root *j-n-b* have a connotation of being set apart or being a stranger (Lane, 466-7) and the connotation of being an outsider is perhaps reinforced by resonances from cognate languages (e.g. Hebrew *gannab,* "thief"; see STRANGERS AND FOREIGNERS; THEFT; FOREIGN VOCABULARY). Despite the potentially broad implications of the term's semantic range, however, Muslim jurists in general recognized only two varieties of this more serious degree of ritual pollution, or rather, two sorts of occurrences that necessitated the more extensive ritual washing: sexual activity and menstruation (q.v.). Sexual activity was defined by Muslim jurists in the first instance as seminal emission but also as any sexually related or induced emission, whether by a man or woman (Ibn Rushd, *Bidāyat,* i, 40).

Menstruation *(ḥayḍ, maḥīḍ),* on the other hand, is addressed in the Qurʾān in several passages, in regard to determinations of paternity (Q 65:4; cf. 2:228) and also as a disability entailing impurity:

> They ask you about menstruation *(al-maḥīḍ)*. Say: "It is a disability *(adhā),* so sequester women during menstruation and do not approach them until they become pure *(ḥattā yaṭhurna)*. Once they have purified themselves *(idhā taṭahharna),* then approach them in the manner that God has commanded you." God loves the penitent (see REPENTANCE AND PENANCE), and he loves those who purify themselves (Q 2:222).

Although this verse does not mention any particular ritual act the performance of which is impeded by menstruation, Muslim jurists identified menstruation as a variety of major ritual impurity that triggered the more stringent prayer-related cleansing requirements of Q 5:6. Presumably the references in Q 2:222 to purification — denoted by words derived from the root *ṭ-h-r* — drew the jurists' attention and led them to read the requirement of purification in Q 2:222 as parallel to that for major impurity *(junub)* in Q 5:6. A consequence of reading these two verses together is that human states of impurity and associated cleansing requirements were understood to have a limited and specific ritual purpose and therefore to be relatively easily curable. Ritual impurity in human beings was not seen as a general state of substantive uncleanness. Given the lack of references to specific rituals in Q 2:222, it would have been possible, alternatively, to deem menstruation a form of substantive impurity, but that is not the route taken by Islamic law (Reinhart, Impurity/No danger, 15; Katz, *Body of text,* 194-201). On the other hand, Muslim jurists also consider menstruation a bar not only to prayer but also to fasting (q.v.), circumambulation of the Kaʿba (q.v.) and sexual intercourse (Ibn Rushd, *Bidāyat,* i, 49).

Performance of the minor cleansing prior to prayer may have represented an important symbolic act undertaken by converts to Islam in the time of Muḥammad. It is reported (albeit in a very stylized manner) that some of the very first Medinese (see MEDINA) to accept Muḥammad's mission uttered the *shahāda* (see WITNESS TO FAITH), performed the minor cleansing and then prayed (Ṭabarī, *Taʾrīkh,* iii, 1215-6; see also Katz, *Body of text,* 159 n. 42).

Other ritual contexts

Apart from prayer and the varieties of pollution that bar one from performing a valid prayer, the Qurʾān makes no express requirement of ritual purity in connection with other rites. On the other hand, persons undertaking the pilgrimage (q.v.) are considered to be in a special or sacred state (pl. *ḥurum*) and are subject to restrictions in connection therewith (see FORBIDDEN; PROFANE AND SACRED). The Qurʾān suggests that hunting land animals could vitiate this state (Q 5:1, 96) but not fishing (Q 5:96; see HUNTING AND FISHING), though a more likely interpretation of these restrictions would be that the animals in question enjoy a consecrated (taboo) status because of their presence in the sacred precinct (*ḥaram;* see CONSECRATION OF ANIMALS). In addition, some jurists considered the minor cleansing associated with prayer a necessary prerequisite for circumambulation of the Kaʿba and also for touching the Qurʾān (e.g., Ibn Rushd, *Bidāyat,* i, 36-7). Finally, although the Qurʾān imposes no specific requirement of cleansing in connection with fasting, sexual intercourse *(rafth)* is expressly forbidden during the daily fasting period of Ramaḍān (q.v.; cf. Q 2:187).

Substantive impurity

The Qurʾān indicates substantive impurity by the terms *najas,* "unclean," *rijs,* "filthy," *rijz,* "abomination," and *rujz* (see below). The first of these is used only once but the latter appear in a number of passages (see Izutsu, *Concepts,* 240-1).

Even in the context of modern studies of ritual purity and pollution that emphasize the symbolic nature of such concepts (Douglas, *Purity,* 3-4; Katz, *Body of text,* 13-24; Reinhart, Purity/No danger, 18-24), the qurʾānic notion of substantive impurity appears particularly abstract and ideological rather than matter-driven. The Qurʾān labels persons who are portrayed as opposed in one way or another to right religion (q.v.) as unclean. In Q 9:28 the Qurʾān provides that non-monotheists *(al-*

mushrikūn) are *najas,* "unclean," and that they should therefore "not approach the sacred mosque," their fundamental quality of uncleanness precluding them from entry to a sacred site (see BELIEF AND UNBELIEF; POLYTHEISM AND ATHEISM; RELIGIOUS PLURALISM AND THE QURʾĀN). Sometimes, God is said to endow certain impious persons with the quality of *rijs,* or to add to their *rijs* (see Q 6:125; 7:71; 9:125; 10:100; 33:33). In one passage, uncooperative Bedouin (q.v.) are said to be *rijs* (Q 9:95). Finally, in another passage, God desires to expunge *rijs* from Muḥammad's family (or the people of the Kaʿba, *ahl al-bayt;* see PEOPLE OF THE HOUSE; FAMILY OF THE PROPHET) and to purify them (*yurīdu llāhu li-yudhhiba ʿankumu l-rijsa ahla l-bayti wa-yuṭahhirakum taṭhīran,* Q 33:33). In this verse, *rijs* is connected with practices labeled as *jāhilī* (see AGE OF IGNORANCE), and these practices are, in the same verse, opposed to the most fundamental aspects of Muslim practice: prayer, almsgiving (q.v.) and obedience (q.v.) to God and his messenger (q.v.; see also AUTHORITY; KINGS AND RULERS). In all these passages, *rijs* can be understood to refer to a condition in which pre-existing commitments of one kind or another (but above all, pre-Islamic Arabian beliefs and practices; see PRE-ISLAMIC ARABIA AND THE QURʾĀN; SOUTH ARABIA, RELIGION IN PRE-ISLAMIC) interfere with receptivity to Islam (see e.g. Izutsu, *Concepts,* 31).

The term *rijz* differs slightly from *rijs* in its connotations. In several passages, it refers to something punitive that comes from God, perhaps in the nature of a plague or a pestilence that descends from heaven (e.g. Q 2:59; 7:134-5, 162; 29:34; meaning punishment in general: Q 34:5; 45:11; see REWARD AND PUNISHMENT; CHASTISEMENT AND PUNISHMENT). In two other passages, however, it seems to denote a general condition of uncleanness that can be remedied by purification. In Q 8:11, God causes rain to descend from the heavens (see HEAVEN AND SKY; WATER) in order to purify *(ṭ-h-r)* persons and to drive away from them the *rijz* of Satan (see DEVIL). In Q 74:4-5, Muḥammad is urged to purify *(ṭ-h-r)* his garment and to avoid *al-rujz,* a word of disputed meaning. Its proximity to an injunction to purify something suggests that it could refer to a variety of (figurative) pollution, and this possibility is recognized by the exegetical literature. Al-Bayḍāwī (d. prob. 716/1316-7; *Anwār,* ii, 367), for example, paraphrases the verse as urging avoidance of divine punishment by avoiding "abominations" *(qabāʾiḥ).* Commentators also connect it with polytheism *(shirk)* and idol-worship (*awthān;* see IDOLATRY AND IDOLATERS; IDOLS AND IMAGES) as well as with divine punishment (*ʿadhāb;* e.g. ʿAbd al-Razzāq, *Tafsīr,* iii, 361; Farrāʾ, *Maʿānī,* iii, 201; Bayḍāwī, *Anwār,* ii, 367). Paret (*Kommentar,* 163, 184, 493) opines that *rijs,* "Unreinheit," and *rijz/rujz,* "Strafgericht," have been used interchangeably in several passages, even though they are different words with distinct meanings. Jeffery (*For. vocab.,* 139) agrees with those who see *rujz* as a Syriac borrowing of *rugzā,* "wrath," i.e. God's wrath. This last possibility fits with the traditional interpretation of the word as meaning *ʿadhāb* but also raises the question of whether both *rijz* and *rijs* in certain passages (e.g. Q 7:134 and Q 7:71, respectively, both noted above) might not also derive ultimately from *rugzā.*

In other passages, what is substantively unclean divides into sinful conduct and forbidden foods. Wine and certain games of chance (see GAMBLING; DIVINATION) are *rijs* (Q 5:90) as are carrion (q.v.), blood (see BLOOD AND BLOODCLOT) and pork (Q 6:145; see Rivlin, *Gesetz,* 82-3). Muslims are also enjoined to "avoid the *rijs* of idols" (Q 22:30), a phrase which follows closely on the heels of a general provision of dietary law ("livestock are made lawful for you except for that which is recited to you [as being unlawful]"; see Wansbrough, *qs*, 72). Perhaps the reference is to food sacrificed to idols (compare Q 2:173 and similar passages, in which Muslims are forbidden to eat sacrifices made to other than God; ʿAbd al-Bāqī, 738, entry *ḥ-l-l;* see SACRIFICE). These passages could, together with some of those discussed above that refer to persons, be understood as a general denunciation, in terms of ritual purity, of pre-Islamic Arabian cultic practices.

Another group of prohibitions that overlap partly with notions of substantive purity and impurity receive attention in the Qurʾān under the rubric "lawful and unlawful" (*ḥalāl* and *ḥarām;* see LAWFUL AND UNLAWFUL). For example, the list of prohibited foods identified as *rijs* at Q 6:145 are, in the same passage, declared unlawful or forbidden, *muḥarram*. In addition, as with the division of *najas* and *rijs* primarily into persons and things, so too certain persons (e.g. in regard to marriage; see MARRIAGE AND DIVORCE; PROHIBITED DEGREES) and things (especially foods, but some conduct as well) may be declared lawful or unlawful (see VIRTUES AND VICES, COMMANDING AND FORBIDDING). The concept of unlawfulness — the quality of being *ḥarām* — entails simultaneously a sense of taboo and of sacredness, probably originally in connection with ritual-related restrictions on certain activities (see Heninger, Pureté; Izutsu, *Concepts*, 237-41).

Connected with both the above sets of notions — uncleanness, and lawful and unlawful — is the use of the terms *ṭayyib* and *khabīth*, "good" and "bad" (see GOOD AND EVIL). *Ṭayyib* connotes in particular something that is pleasing to the senses, but it is sometimes expressly associated with what is lawful, especially foods, as is *khabīth* with what is unlawful (e.g. Q 7:157) and both also have an ethical dimension (see Izutsu, *Concepts*, 235-6). In this connection, the lone occurrence of the verb *dhakkā* in Q 5:3 may be noted: The passage in question forbids *(ḥurrimat ʿalaykum)* certain enumerated foods "except for those that you purify" *(dhakkaytum)*. Presumably the term refers to a purifying ritual slaughter for animals that are in the throes of a ritually suspect death (the verb *dhakkā* may be borrowed from Aramaic; cf. Jeffery, *For. vocab.*, 135).

Note that persons are, in general, neither substantively impure nor contagious under the qurʾānic purity regime and also not under general principles of Islamic law (Reinhart, Purity/No danger, 19), although the labeling of polytheists as unclean at Q 9:28 has been read literally by Shīʿī jurists (Katz, *Body of text*, 48). It has been suggested that the rubric lawful-unlawful was more important to the pre-Islamic Arabs than that of clean-unclean (Wellhausen, *Reste*, 168). In the very earliest period of Islam, however, it seems that some regarded substantive impurity as related, or equivalent, to major ritual impurity *(junub)*. Under this view, substantive impurity would be polluting or contagious and so require a major cleansing. By analogy, then, major ritual impurity would also be contagious. This view was rejected at a relatively early date, though, and substantive impurity and major ritual impurity were held distinct. Thus, ritual impurity, of both the major and minor variety, remained confined to individuals and so not directly or indirectly communicable (Katz, *Body of text*, 150-1 and chapter 4).

General declarations of purity and impurity

In addition to its declarations concerning the purity-status of worshippers and the inherently unclean and so unlawful nature of certain items and actions, the Qurʾān also identifies various persons, objects and actions as pure or impure in a general, non-technical manner. Although these notions do not in strict terms delineate or supplement rules governing the purity-status of believers, they nevertheless form an ethical discourse which inhabits, as it were, the periphery of the Qurʾān's more expressly normative passages regulating matters of ritual purity.

A prominent theme of the Qurʾān's purity rhetoric concerns God's rendering persons pure: He does this to whom he will (Q 4:49; 24:21), though he also sends messengers to purify persons, especially in conjunction with the teaching of "the book (q.v.) and wisdom" (q.v.; Q 2:129, 151; 3:164; 62:2). Conversely, God disdains to purify those who break their troth (Q 3:77; cf. 2:174; see COVENANT; BREAKING TRUSTS AND CONTRACTS). The foregoing passages employ the verb *zakkā* and seem to be of general applicability. God's purification of individuals is also accomplished using the verb *ṭahhara* but when that verb is employed, the context seems more specific. He has angels (see ANGEL) inform Mary (q.v.) that she has been purified (Q 3:42) and it is said to those who will pray (Q 5:6) and to Muḥammad's family (or his wives, or the people of the Kaʿba) that God wishes to purify them (Q 33:33). He sends rain to purify persons from Satan's iniquity (Q 8:11; see SIN, MAJOR AND MINOR) and he also purifies Jesus (q.v.) from those who disbelieve (Q 3:55).

In several passages, certain persons are variously identified as pure or purified. Moses (q.v.), for example, accuses Khiḍr (see KHAḌIR/KHIḌR) of killing a pure (or innocent) soul (*nafs zakiyya*, Q 18:74) and Mary is told that she is to receive a pure youth (*ghulāman zakiyyan*, Q 19:19). Several of these passages suggest, perhaps, that a state of ritual purity is intended: The believers' spouses in paradise (q.v.) will be purified (*azwāj muṭahhara*, Q 2:25; 3:15; 4:57; see HOURIS) and Lot's (q.v.) followers purify themselves (or hold themselves out as pure, Q 7:82; 27:56). A mosque worthy of being prayed in contains persons who love to purify themselves (*an yataṭahharū*, Q 9:108).

The ideas of charitable giving and self-purification are connected in the Qurʾān by the fact that the root *z-k-y* can signify either or both. The connection between charity and self-purification is frequently explicit, as in Q 9:103, in which it is said that taking alms *(ṣadaqa)* from people's property will purify them *(tuzakkī, tuṭahhir)* or, Q 92:18, in which those who donate property purify themselves (*alladhī yuʾtī mālahu yatazakkā;* see GIFT AND GIFT-GIVING). Other examples are more ambiguous and may intend both senses — purification and charity — at once (e.g. Q 91:9; 87:14; 20:76 and elsewhere; see ʿAbd al-Bāqī, 331, *z-k-y;* on *z-k-y* as a borrowing from Jewish Aramaic in the sense of "alms," see Zysow, Zakāt).

Certain items, especially if connected with the divine, are also identified as pure or purified in the Qurʾān. The pages of revelation *(ṣuḥuf)* are called purified *(muṭahhara)* at Q 80:13-4 and Q 98:2 (see SCROLLS; SHEETS). Abraham (q.v.) and Ishmael (q.v.) were commanded to purify *(ṭ-h-r)* the Kaʿba (Q 2:125; cf. 22:26). God sends pure rain (*māʾan ṭahūran*, Q 25:48, the likely source of the idea that ritual cleansing should be performed with water) and also gives the inhabitants of paradise a pure draught (*sharāban ṭahūran*, Q 76:21).

Finally, notions of purity are expressly connected with ethical (and especially chaste) conduct and passages expressing this idea employ the comparative form, derived from either *ṭ-h-r* or *z-k-y* (see CHASTITY). Adherence to certain rules regulating marriage, for example, is "more pure" (*azkā, aṭhar*, Q 2:232), as is adherence to the principle that one not enter another's home without permission (*azkā*, Q 24:28; see HOUSE, DOMESTIC AND DIVINE). For male believers, it is more pure (*azkā*) not to stare (at women, presumably) and also to cover their private parts (Q 24:30; see MODESTY). Similarly, it is more pure (*aṭhar*) to talk with Muḥammad's wives while separated from them by a curtain (Q 33:53; see VEIL; WIVES OF THE PROPHET; SOCIAL INTERACTIONS). Finally, Lot announces that his daughters would be more pure (*aṭhar*) for his community (Q 11:78; that is, a chaste alternative to their licentiousness; see ADULTERY AND FORNICATION).

It should be noted, that, although the Qurʾān may be said to partake, in certain (but not all) respects, in the generally misogynistic mood of late antiquity (see PATRIARCHY), its notion of substantive impurity does not, and was not interpreted to, relegate women to a special and inherently problematic ritual status (Katz, *Body of text*, 201; see WOMEN AND THE QURʾĀN; GENDER).

Islamic law's approach to ritual purity

The technical terms employed by Islamic law to denote the various aspects of ritual purity discussed above are mostly non-qurʾānic. Ritual purity in general is known as and discussed in books of *fiqh* under the rubric of *ṭahāra*. *Ṭahāra* does not appear in the Qurʾān, though it seems likely to be originally a technical term, given its fundamental etymological and semantic congruence with Hebrew *ṭoharot* (see generally Reinhart, Ṭahāra). Minor or transient impurity entailing the minor cleansing is generally denoted by *ḥadath*, an "event," with a slightly negative connotation (see Lane, 528), though it can also refer to both degrees of ritual impurity (e.g. Ibn Rushd, *Bidāyat*, i, 40). The qurʾānic term *junub* is used for major ritual impurity, though it is an adjective and so the non-qurʾānic noun *janāba* is also employed. The minor cleansing is referred to as *wuḍūʾ*, "ablutions," and the associated verb is *tawaḍḍaʾa* (for further discussion, see CLEANLINESS AND ABLUTION and Chaumont, Wuḍūʾ). The term *ghusl* denotes the major cleansing. None of these three terms occurs in the Qurʾān but they are commonplace in the ḥadīth (see ḤADĪTH AND THE QURʾĀN).

Books of *fiqh* always begin with a chapter on ritual purity, *ṭahāra*. Discussions of *ṭahāra*, in turn, often start with a discussion of what does and does not defile water used for ablutions (see e.g. Shāfiʿī, *Umm*, i, 16-25). Major and minor states of impurity and their causes are discussed, as well as the procedures for remedying them, namely ablutions (*wuḍūʾ*) and the major washing (*ghusl*) and the exception allowing substitute wiping with sand (*tayammum*). Menstruation usually merits a separate and detailed treatment in the chapters on *ṭahāra*. Some authors also include information on cleansing after elimination of waste and possibly other matters affecting the body, such as personal grooming and also circumcision (q.v.). Finally, the category of the substantively impure may receive attention, though the forbidden quality of certain foods may be treated in a separate chapter on food and beverages, outside the *ṭahāra* rubric.

Conclusion

As discussed, the Qurʾān's most basic rules governing ritual purity, at Q 5:6 and Q 4:43, are embedded in a context of covenantal themes (see COVENANT), constituted in particular by references to God's bounty (*niʿma*) and human obedience (*al-samʿ wa-l-ṭāʿa;* Katz, *Body of text*, 32-58). Additionally, the theme of mobilization of the community, especially for war (q.v.), seems to be associated with such passages, suggesting that the purity strictures serve (or served originally) also to demarcate the (early) Muslims from outsiders and to delineate community boundaries (ibid., 53-7). Another covenantal theme sounds in those pronouncements concerning the purity or licitness of certain foods, which are bestowed by God as part of his bounty (see e.g. Gräf, *Jagdbeute,* 4-69). This contextual setting of pronouncements on purity and licitness reinforces the impression that the Qurʾān's purity regime is connected with the demarcation of the Muslims as a distinct community, constituted by a unique and reciprocal relationship with the divine (see Katz, *Body of text,* 58).

The relative lack of systematic concern in the Qurʾān with substantive impurity and contamination suggests further, however, that the principal focus of its purity regime is on the immediate human relationship with the divine and not with the hierarchical understanding of society in accordance with exclusivist principles of holiness, mapped on to the body as cleanness. The highly symbolic, qurʾānically-mandated wipings and washings contrast, for example, with other more intensive and intrusive modes of inscribing and ritualizing the body, such as circumcision. Yet this tendency contrasts with the asserted covenantal aspects of the Qurʾān's purity regime. Thus, a fruitful tension obtains between the appropriation of the body as a symbol of a community specially situated relative to the divine and a lack of danger-symbolizing, boundary-constituting purity strictures.

Fundamental to modern studies of ritual (im)purity is the recognition that notions of purity and pollution do not necessarily concern dirt and its removal but rather symbolic ways of arranging the world. Thus, it has famously been observed that, in the context of ritual purity, dirt is "matter out of place," matter that upsets a familiar pattern (Douglas, *Purity,* 3-4, 35, 40). To the extent that it forms a system, the qurʾānic purity regime centers almost entirely on the purity status of persons performing prayer. Thus, what it seeks to organize, at one level of theological abstraction (see THEOLOGY AND THE QURʾĀN), is a mode of human contact with the transcendent by signifying the worshipper's reassertion of bodily control, a theme developed further by Muslim jurists (Reinhart, Purity/No danger, 20). Readiness for the holy is all.

Barriers to effective contact include the symbolic (and occasionally the actual) residue of the most basic, and mundane, of human bodily functions, urination, defecation, menstruation, sexual intercourse and even (as a result of post-qurʾānic juristic elaboration) prolonged sleep (Katz, *Body of text,* 13-24; Reinhart, Purity/No danger, 18-24). In this regard, the purity-related practices mandated by Islamic law — noteworthy for their conspicuous grounding in the qurʾānic text — have been interpreted as gaining "their resonance not from the recapitulation of ontology but in the anticipation of its reversal" (Katz, *Body of text,* 203) as a symbolic prefiguration of the recapture of the solidity and permanence of the near-divine, heavenly, or paradisiacal state (see ESCHATOLOGY; COSMOLOGY).

Joseph E. Lowry

Bibliography
Primary: ʿAbd al-Razzāq, *Tafsīr,* ed. M.M. Muḥammad; Abū ʿUbayd, *Nāsikh;* Bayḍāwī, *Anwār;* Farrāʾ, *Maʿānī;* Ibn Rushd, Abū l-Walīd Muḥammad, *Bidāyat al-mujtahid,* 2 vols., Cairo n.d.; trans. I.A.K. Nyazee, *The distinguised jurist's primer,* 2 vols., Reading 1994, i, 1-95 (on ritual purity); al-Shāfiʿī, Muḥammad b. Idrīs, *Kitāb al-Umm,* 8 vols. in 5, Beirut 1410/1990; al-Shīrāzī [Ech-Chirâzî], Abū Isḥāq, *Kitâb et-Tanbîh ou Le Livre de l'admonition,* trans. and annot. G.-H. Bousquet, 4 vols., Algiers [1949], i, 11-26 (on ritual cleansing for prayer); Ṭabarī, *Taʾrīkh,* ed. de Goeje.
Secondary: ʿAbd al-Bāqī; E. Chaumont, Wuḍūʾ, in *EI²,* xi, 218-9; P. Crone, *Roman, provincial and*

Islamic law. The origins of the Islamic patronate, Cambridge 1987; id., Two legal problems bearing on the early history of the Qurʾān, in *JSAI* 18 (1994), 1-37; id. and M. Hinds, *God's caliph. Religious authority in the first centuries of Islam,* Cambridge 1986; M. Douglas, *Purity and danger,* London 1966; E. Gräf, *Jagdbeute und Schlachttier im islamischen Recht. Eine Untersuchung zur Entwicklung der islamischen Jurisprudenz,* Bonn 1959; J. Heninger, Pureté et impureté, in H. Cazelles and A. Feuillet (eds.), *Supplément au Dictionnaire de la Bible,* ix, cols. 460-70 (Arabie), Paris 1973; Izutsu, *Concepts;* Jeffery, *For. vocab.;* M. Katz, *Body of text. The emergence of the Sunnī law of ritual purity,* Albany 2002; Lane; Paret, *Kommentar;* id., *Koran;* A.K. Reinhart, Impurity/No danger, in *History of religions* 30 (1990-1), 1-24; id., Ṭahāra, in *EI²,* x, 99; J. Rivlin, *Gesetz im Koran. Kultus und Ritus,* Jerusalem 1934; Wansbrough, *QS;* J. Wellhausen, *Reste Arabischhen Heidentums,* Berlin 1961 (repr.); A. Zysow, Zakāt, in *EI²,* xi, 406-22.

Rivers see WATER; PARADISE

Road see PATH OR WAY

Roast(ing) see FIRE; HELL AND HELLFIRE

Robber(y) see THEFT; BOUNDARIES AND PRECEPTS

Rock see STONE; STONING

Rod

Staff or stick upon which one leans for support or uses as a tool. In the Qurʾān, the Arabic word for rod, *ʿaṣā,* which is mentioned twelve times, is used in the possessive form when speaking of Moses (q.v.), that is, *ʿaṣā Mūsā,* "the rod of Moses." It is used in a singular form *(ʿaṣā)* when related to Moses and in a plural form *(ʿiṣiyya)* with reference to Pharaoh's (q.v.) sorcerers (see MAGIC). Events involving the word *ʿaṣā,* which has a variety of features in the Qurʾān, have been presented in support of its being one of the two great miracles of Moses (see MIRACLES; MARVELS). The qurʾānic commentators narrate various stories of how Moses received the rod (see EXEGESIS OF THE QURʾĀN: CLASSICAL AND MEDIEVAL). Some relate that the prophet Shuʿayb (q.v.), the father-in-law of Moses, gave him the rod and that Adam brought it from heaven when he was compelled to leave (see ADAM AND EVE; FALL OF MAN). It was entrusted to Shuʿayb, who then passed it on to his son-in-law Moses (Ṭabarī, *Tafsīr,* xx, 67; *Jalālayn,* 511).

The word first appears in the Qurʾān in connection with a great need for water (q.v.). On this occasion, the rod works as a miraculous instrument to bring water from the bottom of a rock. The verse says, "When Moses asked for water for his people, we said, 'Strike with your rod the rock, and there will gush out from the rock twelve springs'" (Q 2:60; 7:160). On another occasion, the same rod works to swallow sorcerers' false snakes. Q 7:117 states, "And we inspired Moses, saying 'Throw your rod,' and thereupon it swallowed up their lying show." Moses' rod, on this occasion, has been transformed into a giant snake, to swallow up those of the opposing sorcerers. Moses understood that the power of the sorcerers was demonic, which is why they were defeated by his powerful and miraculously-bestowed rod. The Qurʾān refers to the rod of Moses in a conversation between Moses and God. Moses seems unaware of the actual nature of his rod: "'And what is that in your right hand, O Moses?' He said, 'This is my rod, whereon I lean, and wherewith I beat down branches for my sheep, and wherein I find other uses.' He said, 'Cast it down, O Moses.' So Moses cast it down, and immediately it became a gliding snake." The end of the verse suggests that Moses was told to catch the snake and not to be afraid because God would transform it to its original state (Q 20:17-21; cf. 27:10). A mystical interpretation claims that God blamed Moses because he had related the rod to himself in his presence, when he was supposed to acknowledge that everything belonged to God (see ṢŪFISM AND THE QUR'ĀN; GRATITUDE AND INGRATITUDE; POWER AND IMPOTENCE; POSSESSION). Accordingly, God asked him to throw his rod, so that Moses could show God that he was not the actual owner of the rod (Qurṭubī, *Jāmi'*, xi, 186; for additional comments, see ibid., vii, 258; Ibn Kathīr, *Tafsīr*, ii, 237). Clearly Moses was entrusted with such a miraculous rod so that he could respond to the taunts of Pharaoh's sorcerers. They had magical rods and were able to challenge Moses and his message. They said, "by the glory of Pharaoh, we will be victorious" (Q 26:44; cf. 20:66; see VICTORY).

The Qur'ān presents the rod of Moses as instrumental in opening a way in the sea to help the Israelites (see CHILDREN OF ISRAEL) escape from Pharaoh's oppression (q.v.). This miraculous event appeared at a time when Moses and his followers were chased by Pharaoh's troops. "Then we inspired Moses, saying 'Strike the sea with your rod,' and it parted. Each part was as a mountain vast" (Q 26:63). Al-Qurṭubī (d. 671/1272) comments that the rod was a simple instrument in this case; the one who parted the sea was actually God himself (*Jāmi'*, xiii, 15).

Another word used in the Qur'ān to signify a rod is *minsa'a*, which refers to the rod of Solomon (q.v.). Q 34:14 states, "And when we decreed death for him (Solomon), nothing showed his death to them (the jinn), save a creeping creature of the earth, which gnawed away his rod." The verse indicates that the jinn (q.v.) were unaware of the world of the unseen *(ghayb)*. Since Solomon died while leaning on his rod, they did not know he was dead until his rod decayed, allowing him to fall (see HIDDEN AND THE HIDDEN).

One can argue that the qur'ānic emphasis on the rod of Moses has resulted in the idea that, in Arab culture, carrying a rod has become a sign of faith (q.v.) and an imitation of the prophets (see PROPHETS AND PROPHETHOOD; although there is no mention of Jesus' [q.v.] rod in the Qur'ān, al-Ṭabarī [*Tafsīr*, iii, 285], an early qur'ānic commentator, narrates that Jesus also had a rod). The prophet Muḥammad used to carry a rod and lean on it during the Friday sermon (Qurṭubī, *Jāmi'*, xi, 188; Bayhaqī, *Sunan*, iii, 206; see FRIDAY PRAYER). The rod of the Prophet remained significant, even after his death. It is known that the rod was entrusted to 'Abdallāh b. Mas'ūd, one of his great Companions (see COMPANIONS OF THE PROPHET). He was given the honorary title Holder of the Rod of the Prophet (*ṣāḥib 'asā l-nabī*, Qurṭubī, *Jāmi'*, xi, 189). In Islamic culture, the use of a rod has been viewed as a symbol of spiritual transition among Ṣūfīs. Al-Qurṭubī narrates that an ascetic (see ASCETICISM) was asked why he carried the rod despite the fact that he was not sick or old. He answered, "This reminds me that I am a traveler in this world" (Qurṭubī, *Jāmi'*, xi, 189; see JOURNEY).

Zeki Saritoprak

Bibliography
Primary: al-Bayhaqī, Aḥmad b. Ḥusayn b. 'Alī, *al-Sunan*, ed. 'A. 'Atā, Mecca 1994; Ibn Kathīr, *Tafsīr*, Beirut 1980; *Jalālayn*; Qurṭubī, *Jāmi'*; Ṭabarī, *Tafsīr*, Beirut 1984.
Secondary: B.M. Wheeler, *Prophets in the Qur'ān. An introduction to the Qur'ān and Muslim exegesis*, London 2002.

Romans see BYZANTINES

Ruby see METALS AND MINERALS

Rugs see PARADISE; GARDENS; MATERIAL CULTURE AND THE QUR'ĀN

Ruin(s) see GEOGRAPHY; GENERATIONS; REMNANT

S

Saba᾽ see SHEBA

Sabaeans see SHEBA

Sabbath

Saturday, technically, Friday evening to Saturday evening. While related etymologically to the Aramaic and Hebrew words for the Sabbath (in which tradition it connotes the day of "rest"), the Arabic term *(sabt)* was provided with an appropriate Islamic sense by the Qur᾽ān and later Muslim interpretation.

The Qur᾽ān uses the word *sabt* six times (plus once as a verb, *yasbitu,* "to keep the Sabbath," in Q 7:163) and clearly draws a relationship between the Jews, the Sabbath and not working on that day of the week, in keeping with the Jewish tradition (see JEWS AND JUDAISM). The day was imposed upon the Jews at Sinai (q.v.) according to Q 4:154 through the statement from God, "Do not transgress the Sabbath!" Some Muslim traditions suggest that this regulation was a punishment on the Jews for their refusal to worship (q.v.) on Friday (see FRIDAY PRAYER), the day designated for such activities by God; God would accept the Sabbath as long as the Jews ceased from any work on that day (see Ṭabarī, *Tafsīr,* ii, 167-8). On the other hand, traditions can be found which legitimize all of Friday, Saturday and Sunday as days of worship (e.g. Muslim, *Ṣaḥīḥ, K. Jumʿa* 22). Q 16:124 focuses on disputes over the observance of the Sabbath, "The Sabbath was appointed only for those who were at variance thereon; surely your lord will decide between them on the day of resurrection (q.v.), touching their differences." This perhaps reflects earlier Jewish-Christian debates over the proper day of worship (see CHRISTIANS AND CHRISTIANITY; QIBLA). The breaking of the law of the Sabbath attracts the most attention with three passages, Q 2:65, Q 4:47, and Q 7:163 (where the root *s-b-t* is used twice), speaking of those who transgressed the Sabbath being cursed and transformed into "despised apes" (Q 2:65, 7:166; also see Q 5:60; see BOUNDARIES AND PRECEPTS; LAW AND THE QUR᾽ĀN). Opinion varied as to whether this transformation was to be understood literally or metaphorically, for example as something that happened to Jewish hearts (see HEART; METAPHOR; POLYSEMY). Modern scholarship has not reached a consensus on the origins of this story.

The Qur᾽ān restates the biblical notion

that there were six days of creation (q.v.; Q 7:54; 10:3; 11:7, etc.) but denies the biblical implication that God "rested" from creation and that this is to be commemorated through keeping the Sabbath as a day of rest. God says after his experience with creation, "Weariness did not touch us" (Q 50:38). Thus the exegetical problem arose of how to explain that the seventh day of the week was called *sabt* while not implying that the word conveyed that sense of "rest." The answer was contained in the derivation of the word *sabt* from the verb *sabata* restricted in its meaning to senses of "ceasing" or "being still," without conveying an implication of "rest"; the word *subāt* was still seen to have that meaning, however, as was necessitated by Q 25:47 and Q 78:9, where sleep is termed a "rest." (See also DREAMS AND SLEEP; ANTHROPOMORPHISM; POLEMIC AND POLEMICAL LANGUAGE.)

Andrew Rippin

Bibliography
Primary (in addition to other classical qurʾānic commentaries ad Q 7:163-7): Ṭabarī, *Tafsīr,* ed. Shākir, xiii, 179-207.
Secondary: I. Goldziher, Die Sabbath Institution in Islam, in M. Brann and F. Rosenthal (eds.), *Gedenkbuch zur Erinnerung an David Kaufmann,* Breslau 1900, 86-105, including the Arabic text of al-Ṭabarī's *tafsīr* on Q 50:38; part. Fr. trans., G. Bousquet, Études islamologiques d'Ignaz Goldziher, in *Arabica* 7 (1960), 237-40; Horowitz, *KU,* 96; I. Lichtenstadter, "And become ye accursed apes," in *JSAI* 14 (1991), 153-75; Speyer, *Erzählungen,* 312-4, 340.

Sabians

A religious community mentioned three times in the Qurʾān. The Sabians *(ṣābiʾūn)* should not be confused with the Sabaeans, the inhabitants of Sabaʾ, the biblical Sheba, a famous ancient nation in south Arabia (see SHEBA; BILQĪS; PRE-ISLAMIC ARABIA AND THE QURʾĀN; SOUTH ARABIA, RELIGION IN PRE-ISLAMIC). The identity of the Sabians has puzzled both medieval and modern scholarship.

Q 2:62 states: "As for those who have believed and those who have professed Judaism and the Naṣārā and the Sabians: those who believed in God and the last day and did good, they shall have their recompense with their lord (q.v.) and there shall be no fear (q.v.) upon them, nor shall they grieve" (see JEWS AND JUDAISM; REWARD AND PUNISHMENT; FAITH). Q 5:69 is nearly identical with the verse just quoted, apart from the fact that the Sabians are mentioned before the Naṣārā. Q 22:17 states: "As for those who have believed and those who professed Judaism and the Sabians and the Naṣārā and the Magians (q.v.; *al-majūs,* i.e. Zoroastrians) and those who have associated, verily God shall distinguish among them on the day of resurrection" (q.v.). The first two verses mentioned here seem to be imply that the Sabians, like the believers (Muslims), the Jews and the Naṣārā (generally understood to mean Christians; see CHRISTIANS AND CHRISTIANITY, but see de Blois, Naṣrānī and ḥanīf), are at least potential candidates for salvation and enjoy the status of People of the Book (q.v.). None of the three verses, however, says anything specific about the beliefs of the Sabians or gives any other indication as to who they actually were.

The classical Muslim exegetes (see EXEGESIS OF THE QURʾĀN: CLASSICAL AND MEDIEVAL) offer a large number of conflicting suggestions. Some of these are purely abstract, for example, "they are between the Magians and the Jews" (Ṭabarī, *Tafsīr,* ad Q 2:62), but a few are more concrete. One account (not mentioned in al-Ṭabarī's *Tafsīr* but cited by some of the later commentators) identifies the Sabians with a pagan community in Ḥarrān, generally described as star worshippers (cf. Shahrastānī, *Mafātīḥ*, i, f. 168b f.; id., *Milal*, 248-51; Fr. trans. in *Livre des religions*, ii, 167-72). In fact, the polytheists of Ḥarrān did call themselves *ṣābiʾūn*, at least when writing in Arabic, but among Muslim authorities the view was widespread that these people had appropriated the qurʾānic name "Sabians" merely so as to be able to claim the status of "People of the Book" and thus to avoid Muslim persecution (cf. de Blois, Sabians). A few authors claim that the "real Sabians," i.e. the Sabians of the Qurʾān, are a sect living in the swamps of southern Iraq. Ibn al-Nadīm's (d. ca. 385/995) *Fihrist* (Eng. trans. of this passage in de Blois, Sabians, 53-60) gives a fairly detailed account of these "Sabians of the swamps," who, he claims, were "numerous" in his own time (late fourth/tenth century), from which description their identity as a remnant of an early Christian sect, the Elchasaites, emerges. And, at a later date, the name "Sabians" was also applied to a different community in southern Iraq, the non-Christian Mandaeans.

In 1856 the Russian scholar Chwolsohn observed, correctly, that Ibn al-Nadīm's "Sabians of the swamps" were Elchasaites but, erroneously, identified the latter with the modern Mandaeans, concluding that the Mandaeans are the Sabians of the Qurʾān. It is unfortunate that western students of Islam almost unanimously accepted this unfounded conclusion for a long time. It is now clear that the Ḥarrānians, Elchasaites and Mandaeans are three different religious communities. It is most unlikely that the original Muslim community in western Arabia had any knowledge of these isolated religious groups in the Tigris-Euphrates area. From the context in which they are mentioned in the Qurʾān, it is also improbable that the qurʾānic Sabians were either polytheist nature worshippers (like the Ḥarrānians) or a community that defined itself in stark contrast to the Judeo-Christian prophetic tradition (like the Mandaeans); if, on the other hand, they were Elchasaites, one could ask why they were not included among the Naṣārā. It seems rather that the Muslim tradition very early lost any recollection of who was intended by the qurʾānic term and that "Sabians," consequently, became a convenient label for a variety of small religious communities seeking refuge from potential Muslim persecution.

On the assumption that the qurʾānic term refers to some community that is likely to have existed in Mecca (q.v.) or Medina (q.v.) and is not covered by other qurʾānic names (associators, Jews, Naṣārā, Magians; see POLYTHEISM AND ATHEISM), the present author has suggested tentatively that the Sabians might have been Manichaeans, i.e. those whom Muslims writers on pre-Islamic Arabia called the *zanādiqa* among the Quraysh (q.v.). In this case, the Arabic *ṣābiʾ* (or *ṣābī*) would not be a Babylonian dialect form of the Aramaic *ṣābiʿ*, "baptizing," as previously proposed (linking it either to the Elchasaites or the Mandaeans, both of whom placed great emphasis on baptism), but an Arabic participle from *ṣabā*, "to turn towards," here with the sense of "to convert to a different religion," as was proposed by some of the medieval Arabic philologists.

François de Blois

Bibliography

Primary: Ibn al-Nadīm, *Fihrist*, ed. Flügel, 344-5; ed. Tajaddud, 606; Muqātil, *Tafsīr;* Qurṭubī, *Jāmiʿ*, ed. al-Bardūnī; Shahrastānī, *Mafātīḥ al-asrār wa-maṣābīḥ al-abrār*, 2 vols., Tehran 1989; id., *Milal*, ed. Cureton; trans. J. Jolivet and G. Monnot, *Livre des religions et des sects*, 2 vols., Paris 1993; Ṭabarī, *Tafsīr*, ed. Shākir (Q 1:1-14:27); ed. ʿAlī (Q 14:27 on).

Secondary: D. Chwolsohn, *Die Ssabier und der Ssabismus,* 2 vols., St. Petersburg 1856; F. de Blois, *Naṣrānī* (...) and *ḥanīf* (...). Studies on the religious vocabulary of Christianity and Islam, in BSOAS 65 (2002), 1-30 (esp. 26; this article contains an assessment of previous studies and further bibliography); id., The "Sabians" (Ṣābiʾūn) in pre-Islamic Arabia, in AO 56 (1995), 39-61 (this also contains an assessment of previous studies and further bibliography); T. Fahd, Ṣābiʾa, in EI², viii, 675-8; J. Hjärpe, *Analyse critique des traditions arabes sur les Sabéens Ḥarraniens,* Uppsala 1972; J.D. McAuliffe, Exegetical identification of the Ṣābiʾūn, in MW 72 (1982), 95-106; G. Monnot, Les Sabéens de Šahrastānī, in J. Jolivet and G. Monnot (trans.), *Livre des religions et des sects,* 2 vols., Paris 1993, ii, 3-123; id., Sabéens et idolâtres selon ʿAbd al-Jabbar, in MIDEO 12 (1974), 13-48, repr. in id., *Islam et religions,* Paris 1986, 207-27; M. Tardieu, Ṣābiens coraniques et "Ṣābiens" de Ḥarrān, in JA 274 (1986), 1-44.

Sacred

see PROFANE AND SACRED; FORBIDDEN; SACRED PRECINCTS

Sacred Precincts

Areas considered holy, often associated with places of worship or religious rituals. Sacred precincts are treated in the Qurʾān on two levels: Israelite and Arabian (see CHILDREN OF ISRAEL; PRE-ISLAMIC ARABIA AND THE QURʾĀN; SOUTH ARABIA, RELIGION IN PRE-ISLAMIC). On the Israelite level, a sacred precinct is mentioned, to begin with, in the story of Moses' (q.v.) vocation. In Q 20:12, Moses stands before the burning bush and God tells him that the *wādī,* "valley," i.e. precinct, he is standing in is of "multiple sacredness" *(al-wādī l-muqaddas ṭuwan);* therefore he must take off his shoes. The same description of that sacred precinct is repeated in Q 79:16. The sacredness of the place is conveyed by the Arabic form *muqaddas,* "holy." As for *ṭuwan,* which can be rendered as "multiple," some Muslim exegetes suggested that it stands for the name of that precinct.

The same scene is described in detail in Q 28:30: "And when [Moses] came to [the burning bush], a voice was heard from the right-hand *(ayman)* bank of the valley in the blessed spot *(fī l-buqʿati l-mubārakati)* of the bush, saying: 'O Moses, surely I am God, the lord of the worlds'." This time, the sacredness of a given precinct is conveyed by the Arabic adjective *mubārak,* "blessed (by God)." Besides, the right-hand side of the precinct is singled out, which is another way of saying that this was the most blessed zone of the place (see LEFT HAND AND RIGHT HAND). The same designation is repeated in Q 19:52, where the scene takes place on the "right-hand *(ayman)* side of the mountain *(al-ṭūr).*" The mountain is evidently Mount Sinai (q.v.). This is also the place where God later makes a covenant (q.v.) with the Children of Israel as is indicated in Q 20:80. Here again the right-hand side of the mountain is explicitly mentioned.

The terms *muqaddas* and *mubārak* reappear in relation to the holy land (*al-arḍ al-muqaddasa;* see JERUSALEM; SYRIA; GEOGRAPHY AND THE QURʾĀN). As for *muqaddas,* this is how the Qurʾān describes the holy land into which the Children of Israel are requested to go (Q 5:21): "O my people, enter the holy land which God has prescribed for you...." But the holy land is described more often as a precinct, which God has blessed *(bāraka).* Thus in Q 21:71 the land which God has blessed for all people *(al-arḍi llatī bāraknā fīhā lil-ʿālamīn)* appears as the destination of Abraham (q.v.) and Lot (q.v.), whereas in Q 21:81 it is the place to which the wind is taking King Solomon (q.v.). In Q 7:137, the eastern and western parts of the land which God has blessed are said to have been given by God to the Children of Israel. Specific places are also described as blessed (see also BLESSING). Sometimes they are described as towns *(al-qurā),* as in Q 34:18, where they are said to have been frequented by the merchants of Sheba (q.v.). And finally, the farthest mosque (q.v.) which is located in the precinct blessed by God (*al-masjid al-aqṣā lladhī bāraknā ḥawlahu,* Q 17:1) is identified by the exegetes as the Temple in Jerusalem *(bayt al-maqdis).*

On the Arabian level, sacred precincts are mainly those found in and around Mecca (q.v.). This town is said to have been made sacred *(ḥarramahā)* by God (Q 27:91; see PROFANE AND SACRED; FORBIDDEN). The axis around which its sacredness revolves is the figure of Abraham, which means that the Arabian sphere runs parallel to that of the holy land. In fact, God's blessing and the figure of Abraham are combined in Q 3:96-7 into a common framework for the sacredness of the Kaʿba (q.v.), or *al-bayt,* "the house," as it is called here (see HOUSE, DOMESTIC AND DIVINE): "The first house appointed for people is the one at Bakka, blessed *(mubārak)* and a guidance for all people. In it are clear signs (q.v.), the standing place of Abraham (*maqām Ibrāhīm;* see PLACE OF ABRAHAM), and whoever enters it shall be secure...." The passage ends with a statement to the effect that everyone must perform pilgrimage (q.v.) to the house.

The exegetes explain that Bakka is a name for Mecca and that the passage asserts that the Kaʿba was established on earth forty years before the Temple in Jerusalem *(bayt al-maqdis).* Such an interpretation indicates that the sacredness of the Kaʿba was indeed shaped on the model of Jerusalem, with a view to providing the former with superiority over the latter. The Kaʿba is in fact considered a reflection of a celestial house, an idea found in the commentaries on Q 52:4, which speaks about an "inhabited house" *(bayt maʿmūr).* The exegetes explain that the house is "inhabited" in the sense that angels always frequent it (see ANGEL).

The "standing place of Abraham" *(maqām Ibrāhīm)* is mentioned also in Q 2:125. Here the "house" appears again as a destination for pilgrimage and as a place of security, and the believers are requested to appoint for themselves a place of prayer (q.v.) at the *maqām Ibrāhīm.* Islamic tradition contains vivid details about the history of the sacred stone bearing this name, which is found in the vicinity of the Kaʿba to this very day. Q 2:125 ends with the assertion that Abraham, as well as his son Ishmael (q.v.), were commanded by God to purify God's house for the pilgrims and the believers (see also Q 22:26; see BELIEF AND UNBELIEF). Abraham and Ishmael are also the ones who in Q 2:127 "raise" the foundations of the house.

Abraham is credited not only with the foundation of the house but also with the prosperity of the people living in its vicinity. Their prosperity is the outcome of Abraham's prayer as recorded in Q 14:37: "Our lord, I have settled a part of my offspring in a valley unproductive of fruit near your sacred *(muḥarram)* house, our lord, that they may keep up prayer; therefore make the hearts of some people yearn towards them and provide them with fruits; haply they may be grateful" (see GRATITUDE AND INGRATITUDE). In another version of the same prayer Abraham refers to the "town" *(balad)* in general and not specifically to the house (Q 2:126). The house is mentioned in further passages with no specific allusion to Abraham, while its elevated status is conveyed by a straightforward epithet denoting sacredness, namely, *ḥarām:* In Q 5:97, *al-bayt al-ḥarām* is explicitly the title given to the Kaʿba and in Q 5:2 it features as the destination of sacrificial animals (see SACRIFICE; CONSECRATION OF ANIMALS). The ritual functions of the house come out also in Q 22:33, which refers to the "ancient house" *(al-bayt al-ʿatīq),* near which sacrifice takes place. In Q 22:29, the believers are instructed to perform circumambulation *(ṭawāf)* around the "ancient house," and in Q 8:35 pagan rituals performed in front of the house are denounced (see POLYTHEISM AND ATHEISM).

The most explicit manifestation of the ritual functions of the Meccan sacred precincts is provided by the title *al-masjid al-ḥarām,* "the sacred mosque," by which the Qurʾān refers to the Meccan sanctuary. It usually stands for the entire complex encompassing the Kaʿba and in which some rites of the pilgrimage, such as the *ṭawāf* around the Kaʿba, take place. The title "sacred mosque" occurs, to begin with, in a passage (Q 9:28) asserting that the idolaters are nothing but unclean; therefore they should not approach the sacred mosque (see CLEANLINESS AND ABLUTION; RITUAL PURITY). The need to preserve the purity of this precinct is closely associated with the idea that entering it (during pilgrimage) entails ritual preparations such as shaving one's head or cutting one's hair (Q 48:27). The guardians of the mosque are sometimes mentioned, whom the exegetes identify as the Quraysh (q.v.; Q 9:19; cf. Q 8:34). These guardians must guarantee for all believers free access to the mosque but they fail to do so, for which they are repeatedly deplored (Q 22:25; see also Q 2:217; 5:2; 8:34; 48:25). Because of its utmost sacredness, pacts and covenants concluded at the sacred mosque bear special solemnity, as implied in Q 9:7 (see CONTRACTS AND ALLIANCES; BREAKING TRUSTS AND CONTRACTS).

The sacred mosque is the starting point of the Prophet's nocturnal journey to the "farthest mosque" (Q 17:1), which indicates certain parallelism between the two mosques (see ASCENSION). Indeed, the Qurʾān (Q 2:144, etc.) prescribes that it should become the Islamic direction of prayer *(qibla)* and, according to tradition, this substituted a previous *qibla* (q.v.) that was directed towards Jerusalem.

Sacred precincts outside the sacred mosque are the two foothills, al-Ṣafā and al-Marwa (q.v.), which are mentioned in Q 2:158. The Qurʾān declares them to be among God's *shaʿāʾir* (sing. *shaʿīra*), i.e. his prescribed pilgrimage stations, and permits the believers to perform *ṭawāf* around them. The site of ʿArafāt (q.v.), another station of the pilgrimage situated outside the sacred territory *(ḥaram)* of Mecca, is mentioned in Q 2:198. The Qurʾān states that when performing the rite named *ifāḍa* — going in crowds from one place to another — from ʿArafāt, the pilgrims should come to the "sacred station" *(al-mashʿar al-ḥarām)* and mention God's name there. The exegetes explain that by the "sacred station" the site of Muzdalifa is meant or, more specifically, the mountain Quzaḥ, where the pilgrims stay during the night before proceeding to Minā on the tenth of Dhū l-Ḥijja.

The Meccan precincts are not only sacred but also secure. In fact, sacredness and security go hand in hand, as indicated in passages (Q 28:57; 29:67) stating that God has provided the inhabitants of Mecca with a territory sacred and safe *(ḥaram āmin)*. Therefore they are requested to worship the lord (q.v.) of the house who has fed them against hunger (see SUSTENANCE; FOOD AND DRINK) and gave them security against fear (q.v.; Q 106:3-4). God has actually made the house a place of resort *(mathāba)* for all men and a place of security (*amīn,* Q 2:125). Therefore, whoever enters it shall be secure (Q 3:97). Security is the underlying idea also in the title *al-balad al-amīn,* "the town made secure," by which Mecca is referred to in Q 95:3. The outcome of the combination of sacredness and security is the prohibition of waging war (q.v.) in the vicinity of the sacred mosque, as indicated in Q 2:191. The security of Mecca, much like its sacredness, is traced back to Abraham who is said to have prayed to God to provide this town with security and prosperity (Q 2:126; 14:35-7; see WEALTH).

One particular sacred precinct in the vicinity of Medina (q.v.) is mentioned in Q 9:108, namely, "a mosque founded on piety (q.v.; *al-taqwā*) from the very first day. [...] In it are men who love to be purified." The Prophet is advised to go there rather than to the mosque that was built "to cause harm" (*ḍirār,* Q 9:107; see MOSQUE OF DISSENSION). The exegetes usually identify the mosque of piety with the one built in Qubāʾ, a district of Medina.

The Qurʾān also mentions places of sporadic worship (q.v.) whose sacredness is derived from the rites performed therein, mainly the mentioning of God's name (see BASMALA; GOD AND HIS ATTRIBUTES). They are usually called "mosques" *(masājid),* in the sense of sanctuaries. In Q 72:18 these mosques are defined as belonging to God alone, not to any other claimed deity, and therefore idolaters *(mushrikūn)* cannot visit them (Q 9:17-8; see IDOLATRY AND IDOLATERS). On the other hand, preventing believers from entering God's mosques is a grave sin, as stated in Q 2:114 (see SIN, MAJOR AND MINOR). According to this verse, no one is more unjust (see JUSTICE AND INJUSTICE) than he who prevents the believers from entering the mosques of God and strives to ruin them. Some exegetes hold that this refers to the Temple in Jerusalem and to the Romans who destroyed it, but other exegetes believe that the verse deals with the sacred mosque in Mecca.

The sporadic sanctuaries are also called "houses" *(buyūt),* as in Q 24:36. In Q 10:87 the Children of Israel are requested to turn their homes into a *qibla,* i.e. to use them as sanctuaries and, according to the exegetes, they had to do so because their synagogues were destroyed. Monotheistic non-Islamic places of worship are listed in Q 22:40 (see JEWS AND JUDAISM; CHRISTIANS AND CHRISTIANITY): cloisters (*ṣawāmiʿ;* see MONASTICISM AND MONKS), churches (*biyaʿ;* see CHURCH), synagogues *(ṣalawāt)* and mosques *(masājid).* The Qurʾān states that only God protected them from being pulled down. The word *miḥrāb* (pl. *maḥārīb*), "praying chamber," is another term used in the sense of a sanctuary, being mainly part of the Temple in Jerusalem. It is mentioned in passages dealing with King David (q.v.; Q 38:21), King Solomon (Q 34:13) and Zechariah (q.v.; Q 3:37, 39; 19:11).

Uri Rubin

Bibliography

Primary: al-Azraqī, Abū l-Walīd Muḥammad b. ʿAbdallah, *Akhbār Makka,* in F. Wüstenfeld (ed.), *Die Chroniken der Stadt Mekka,* 2 vols., Göttingen 1858, repr. Beirut, n.d., vol. i; Ibn al-Murajjā al-Maqdisī, *Faḍāʾil Bayt al-Maqdis wa-l-Khalīl wa-faḍāʾil al-Shām,* ed. O. Livne-Kafri, Shfaram 1995.
Secondary: G.E. von Grunebaum, *Muhammadan festivals,* London 1976; G.R. Hawting, The disappearance and rediscovery of Zamzam and the "well of the Kaʿba," in *BSOAS* 43 (1980), 44-54; id., The origins of the Muslim sanctuary at Mecca, in G.H.A. Juynboll (ed.), *Studies on the first century of Islamic society,* Carbonsdale 1982, 23-47, 203-10; id., "The sacred offices" of Mecca from Jāhiliyya to Islam, in *JSAI* 13 (1990), 62-84; M.J. Kister, Sanctity joint and divided. On holy places in the Islamic tradition, in *JSAI* 20 (1996), 18-65; Y.D. Nevo and J. Koren, The origins of the Muslim descriptions of the jāhilī Meccan sanctuary, in *JNES* 49 (1990), 23-44; U. Rubin, The Kaʿba — Aspects of its ritual functions, in *JSAI* 8 (1986), 97-131; R.B. Serjeant, Ḥaram and ḥawṭah. The sacred enclosures in Arabia, in A. Badawi (ed.), *Mélanges Taha Husain,* Cairo 1962, 41-58.

Sacrifice

The act of making an offering to a deity or the offering itself. In Arabic, these are commonly rendered by the roots, *ḍ-ḥ-y,* *q-r-b* and *dh-b-ḥ.* The first root, which in the second form can mean to sacrifice an animal during the period of daylight called *al-duḥā*, is not attested in the Qurʾān, though *ʿīd al-aḍḥā*, "feast of the sacrifice," has become the primary name for the one great sacrificial ritual in Islam, occurring during the daylight hours of the tenth of the month of *dhū l-ḥijja* (see MONTHS; DAY, TIMES OF; NOON) as a part of the major pilgrimage (q.v.; *ḥajj*).

In contemporary usage, some Muslims refer to this feast as *ʿīd al-qurbān* or, in Turkish, *qurbān bayram*, and this word occurs in the Qurʾān three times. Q 3:183: "... those who say: God has covenanted with us that we not believe in a messenger until he brings for us a *qurbān* that fire [presumably from heaven] will eat," and Q 5:27: "Relate to them the true story of the two sons of Adam (see ADAM AND EVE; CAIN AND ABEL), when they [each] offered a sacrifice *(idh qarrabā qurbānan)*," a reference to the narratives found in 1 Kings 18 and Genesis 4. The root of *qurbān* is common in Arabic, Hebrew and Aramaic/Syriac (in which *"qūrbānā"* is the term for the Christian Eucharist; see CHRISTIANS AND CHRISTIANITY) as well as Assyrian and Ethiopian but the morphology of the word suggests a NW Semitic origin. The third locus, Q 46:28, is a difficult verse (see DIFFICULT PASSAGES). Some commentators understand it to mean something like "mediators" (Zamakhsharī, *Kashshāf*, iii, 526) but this seems to ignore syntactical and contextual aspects of the verse (see GRAMMAR AND THE QURʾĀN; EXEGESIS OF THE QURʾĀN: CLASSICAL AND MEDIEVAL).

Dh-b-ḥ occurs in three qurʾānic contexts in the sense of sacrifice (as opposed to, simply, "slaughter" in Q 2:49; 14:6; 27:21; 28:4; see SLAUGHTER). In Q 2:67 and 71, Moses (q.v.) tells the Israelites (see CHILDREN OF ISRAEL) that God commands their sacrifice of a cow, which they do in a sequence that recalls the "red heifer" of Numbers 19:2 (see CALF OF GOLD; NARRATIVES). Q 5:3 forbids making sacrifice on stone altars typically used for dedication to an idol (*ʿalā l-nuṣub;* see IDOLS AND IMAGES). Q 37:102 and 107 occur in the story of Abraham's (q.v.) intended sacrifice of his son. Abraham informs his son that he will sacrifice him (*annī adhbaḥuka*, Q 37:102). Later we are told that God redeemed the son with a magnificent sacrifice as a substitute (*wa-fadaynāhu bi-dhibḥin ʿaẓīmin*, Q 37:107). This is the "intended sacrifice" *(al-dhabīḥ)* that is today commemorated in the "feast of the sacrifice" mentioned above, though neither the Qurʾān nor early tradition literature (see ḤADĪTH AND THE QURʾĀN) makes this connection (Ṭabarī, *Tafsīr*, xxiii, 81-8).

The related word, *uhilla* (fourth form of the root *h-l-l*), is taken by some commentators to refer to slaughter but most understand it to mean invoking the name of God upon an animal when slaughtering it (Ṭabarī, *Tafsīr*, ii, 85-6; Ṭabarsī, *Majmaʿ*, i, 331; Qurṭubī, *Jāmiʿ*, ii, 150-1; see BASMALA; CONSECRATION OF ANIMALS). In all cases the Qurʾān forbids doing so in the name of anything other than God (Q 2:173; 5:3; 6:145; 16:115).

Tradition, then, understands the Qurʾān to prescribe invoking the name of God when slaughtering and that God rather than anything other is the object to which sacrifice is to be made. Q 22:27-37 places both within the context of the pilgrimage. Ritually fit animals are to be slaughtered as the name of God is invoked over the act. They are then eaten and shared with the poor and unfortunate (see POVERTY AND THE POOR; ALMSGIVING; COMMUNITY AND SOCIETY IN THE QURʾĀN). Perhaps because this ritual act of eating a communal meal represented a change from a system in which sacrificial offerings were left for the gods, the section concludes with the statement (Q 22:37): "Neither their flesh nor their blood will reach God, but your religious devotion (*al-taqwā minkum;* see PIETY) will reach him."

Reuven Firestone

Bibliography
Primary: Bukhārī, *Ṣaḥīḥ*, ed. M.M. Khan, 9 vols., Lahore 1983[6] (rev. bilingual ed.), vii, 297-9 *(K. al-Dhabāʾiḥ wa-l-ṣayd);* ed. Krehl, iv, 420, trans. O. Houdas and W. Marçais, *El-Bokhâri. Les Traditions islamiques,* 4 vols., Paris 1903-14, iv, 33 *(K. al-Dhabāʾiḥ wa-l-ṣayd,* 8-9*); Lisān al-ʿArab,* 14 vols., Beirut n.d.; Qurṭubī, *Jāmiʿ,* 21 parts in 11 vols., Beirut 1996; Ṭabarī, *Tafsīr,* Beirut 1984; Ṭabarsī, *Majmaʿ,* 5 vols., Beirut n.d.; Zamakhsharī, *Kashshāf.*
Secondary: R. Firestone, *Journeys in holy lands. The evolution of the Abraham-Ishmael legends in Islamic exegesis,* New York 1990, 94-103; 107-51; Jeffery, *For. vocab.;* A. Kamal, *al-Riḥla al-muqaddasa. The sacred journey. Being pilgrimage to Makkah [...],* New York 1961 (bi-lingual ed.); M. Labīb al-Batanūnī, *al-Riḥla al-ḥijāziyya,* Cairo 1911.

Sadness see JOY AND MISERY

Ṣafā and Marwa

Two low hills near the Kaʿba (q.v.) in Mecca (q.v.) between which the pilgrim engages in a brisk walk or trot called "the running" *(al-saʿy)* during the pilgrimage (q.v.; *ḥajj* and *ʿumra*). This running is an obligatory station (*mansik*, pl. *manāsik*) among the various ritual activities during the ten days of the *ḥajj* pilgrimage ritual at Mecca (see RITUAL AND THE QURʾĀN).

The root meaning of *ṣafā* is to be clear or pure, from which comes the familiar name *muṣṭafā,* meaning "elected" or "chosen" (see NAMES OF THE PROPHET; ELECTION), but may also designate smooth stones. Lexicographers define *marwa* as "a bright, glittering stone that may produce fire." These words have been used since pre-Islamic times as the names for the two Meccan hills and are mentioned once in the Qurʾān (Q 2:158): "al-Ṣafā and al-Marwa are among the ritual ceremonies *(shaʿāʾir)* of God. Therefore, whoever makes the *ḥajj* or the *ʿumra* to the house [the Kaʿba] incurs no sin by making the circuit between them *(an yaṭṭawwafa bi-himā).* God knows and is thankful to whoever voluntarily does a good deed (see GOOD DEEDS)."

This passage attests to the antiquity of the ritual circumambulation between Ṣafā and Marwa. The act, referred to in post-qurʾānic literature as *al-saʿy,* is one of many religious rituals that emerged in the pre-Islamic period in relation to the sacred sites in and around Mecca, which were absorbed into Islam (see PRE-ISLAMIC ARABIA AND THE QURʾĀN; SOUTH ARABIA, RELIGION IN PRE-ISLAMIC). It is possible that the old practice was an independent act of divine worship but it was eventually absorbed into a series of ritual activities that make up the *ḥajj* and *ʿumra.* The tenor of the Qurʾān indicates some ambivalence regarding the ceremony.

Two positions emerged early on with respect to the duty to engage in the ritual. One understands the verse to mean that it is not required in Islam because the qurʾānic expression, "there is no sin in doing it" implies legal neutrality (*mubāḥ;* see SIN, MAJOR AND MINOR; LAW AND THE QURʾĀN). The second position, one that quickly became the norm, assumes that the ritual is obligatory. The latter position required additional support, however, which it found in the sunna (q.v.) of the Prophet. The argument, as put forth on the authority of Muḥammad's wife ʿĀʾisha (see ʿĀʾISHA BINT ABĪ BAKR), was that if the rite were not required, the verse would have read, "Whoever makes the *ḥajj*... incurs no sin by not making the circuit between them."

The origin of the running ritual is uncertain and two sets of traditions have evolved to explain it. The oldest explains that in pre-Islamic times pilgrims who were engaged in the "running" would touch two sacred stones erected on the two hills, images of the gods Isāf and Nāʾila. The two stones were once human lovers who had engaged in sexual intercourse in the sacred Kaʿba for which they were turned into stone. Their petrified images were later set in place on the two hills in order to warn pilgrims against improper conduct in the sacred places. Over the years, the origin of these stones was forgotten and people began to worship them as idols (see IDOLS AND IMAGES). Lazarus-Yafeh (Religious dialectics) suggests that this legend attests to the ancient Near Eastern cultic practice of ritual prostitution practiced at one time in Mecca.

A second set of traditions authenticates the ritual by associating it with Abraham (q.v.). Al-Ṭabarī (d. 310/923) includes the suggestion that it was one of the stations of pilgrimage *(manāsik al-ḥajj)* that Abraham prayed God would teach him and Ishmael (q.v.) as they raised up the foundations of the "house" (*bayt*, Q 2:127-8; see HOUSE, DOMESTIC AND DIVINE). A variation of the Abraham theme found more consistently in the sources places the origin in Abraham's act of leaving Hagar and Ishmael in the location of the future sacred area of Mecca (Q 14:37, read with Genesis 21 as subtext). According to a number of variants attributed to Ibn ʿAbbās (d. 68/686-8), Sarah's jealousy of Hagar after the birth of Ishmael caused such strife in the family household that the two women had to be separated. Abraham therefore personally brought Hagar and her son to Mecca and left them near the location of the Kaʿba. Before leaving them, Abraham recited Q 14:37: "O lord! I have made some of my offspring live in an uncultivated *wādī* by your sacred house, in order, O lord, that they establish regular prayer (q.v.). So fill the hearts of some with love toward them, and feed them with fruits so that they may give thanks." Hagar and Ishmael's water soon ran out and the infant Ishmael began to die of thirst. In desperation, Hagar climbed the nearby hills of Ṣafā and Marwa seeking a better vantage point in her search for water and ran between them seven times. Her running is usually described in some way that will shed light on how one should "run" the *saʿy* of pilgrimage. When she returned to Ishmael, she found him with an angel, sometimes identified as Gabriel (q.v.), who scratched the earth with his heel or wing to bring forth water, thereby saving the progenitors of the future northern Arabs. This legend also serves as an etiology for the sacred Zamzam spring in Mecca (see WELLS AND SPRINGS).

Each of these two traditions provided an acceptable etiology and, therefore, justification, to continue practicing a religious ritual within Islam that was clearly associated with idolatrous practices in the pre-Islamic period. The specific qurʾānic verse referring to Ṣafā and Marwa occurs shortly after verses treating the controversy over the proper *qibla* (q.v.), or direction of prayer (Q 2:142-5). This suggests that the qurʾānic redactors may have understood Q 2:158 as supporting an Arabization of emerging Islam as adherents of the new monotheism strove to understand their particular religious system in relation to Judaism and Christianity on the one hand and indigenous Arabian religious practice on the other.

Reuven Firestone

Bibliography

Primary: al-Azraqī, Abū l-Walīd Muḥammad b. ʿAbdallāh, *Akhbār Makka*, in F. Wüstenfeld (ed.), *Die Chroniken der Stadt Mekka*, 2 vols., Göttingen 1858, repr. Beirut n.d., i, 24-5, 74-5; al-Ghazālī, Abū Ḥāmid Muḥammad b. Muḥammad, *Iḥyāʾ ʿulūm al-dīn*, 4 vols., Cairo 1289/1872, i, 252-8

(book 7, ch. 3, section 2); Ibn al-Kalbī, *Kitāb al-Aṣnām*, Cairo 1924, 9, 29; *Lisān al-ʿArab*, 15 vols., Beirut 1990, xiv, 462-4; xv, 275-6; Ṭabarī, *Tafsīr*, Beirut 1984, ii, 43-52 (ad Q 2:158); viii, 229-30 (ad Q 14:37); Yāqūt, *Buldān*, Beirut 1990, iii, 467; v, 136-7.
Secondary: M.L. al-Batanūnī, *al-Riḥla al-ḥijāziyya*, Cairo 1911; Burton, *Collection*, 12-3, 30-1; R. Firestone, *Journeys in holy lands. The evolution of the Abraham-Ishmael legends in Islamic exegesis*, New York 1990, 63-71; G. von Grunenbaum, *Muhammadan festivals*, New York 1951; A. Kamāl, *al-Riḥla al-muqaddasa. The sacred journey*, bilingual edition, New York 1961; H. Lazarus-Yafeh, The religious dialectics of the hadjdj, in H. Lazarus-Yafeh, *Some religious aspects of Islam*, Leiden 1981, 22-4; F.E. Peters, *The hajj. The Muslim pilgrimage to Mecca and the holy places*, Princeton 1994; U. Rubin, The Kaʿba. Aspects of its ritual functions and position in pre-Islamic and early Islamic times, in *JSAI* 8 (1986), 97-131.

Safety see PEACE; SACRED PRECINCTS

Saint

Person marked by divine favor, holiness. The idea of special, chosen people, "saints," is alien to the Qurʾān (for the closest qurʾānic attestation of this concept, see ELECTION). The word *walī* (pl. *awliyāʾ*) used later for these people, though occurring very frequently, does not designate special people distinguished by striking qualities but the faithful as such, who are devout (*ṣāliḥūn, muttaqūn;* see GOOD AND EVIL; PIETY). This makes them friends of God and he is their friend (see FRIENDS AND FRIENDSHIP; CLIENTS AND CLIENTAGE). Satan (see DEVIL), who is the enemy *(ʿaduww)* of God and the faithful, also has his followers and friends (see ENEMIES; PARTIES AND FACTIONS). God loves his friends and they love (q.v.) him (Q 5:54-5). Therefore they do not need to fear the last judgment (q.v.): "The friends of God, they need have no fear (q.v.) and will not be sad (see JOY AND MISERY). The good news (q.v.) is theirs in this world and the next" (Q 10:62-4).

Once the idea of specially distinguished people had formed in the second/eighth century, these two verses in particular were taken as documentary evidence and the "friends of God" became "saints," special people chosen by God and endowed with exceptional gifts, such as the ability to work miracles (see MIRACLES). They were loved by God and developed a close relationship of love to him. The origin of the idea is unclear; ancient Christian and Jewish elements can be identified (Mach, *Der Zaddik*, 134-46; see JEWS AND JUDAISM; CHRISTIANS AND CHRISTIANITY). A system of concepts associated with this holiness *(wilāya/walāya)* was developed in the second half of the third/ninth century by al-Ḥakīm al-Tirmidhī (d. prob. bet. 295/907 and 300/912). Later authors, such as for instance Ibn al-ʿArabī (d. 638/1240) simply had to expand on al-Tirmidhī's ideas. Among other things al-Ḥakīm al-Tirmidhī developed rudimentarily the concept of a hierarchy of saints/friends of God. Although the names of the individual ranks were later stipulated more precisely, his terminology fluctuates: besides *awliyāʾ* he also uses *ṣiddīqūn* (a term which, with the singular *ṣiddīq*, occurs five times in the Qurʾān; cf. Heb. *ṣaddīq;* see Ahrens, Christliches, 19), *abdāl* (a non-qurʾānic term), *umanāʾ* (the singular form of which appears in the Qurʾān, and is applied to the messenger and to God), and *nuṣaḥāʾ* (this term and its singular appear four times in the Qurʾān, although not in the mystical sense). For the concept of "sanctity" and "sacred" as applied to places, states or things, see e.g. PROFANE AND SACRED; FORBIDDEN; SACRED PRECINCTS.

B. Radtke

Bibliography
Primary: Ibn al-ʿArabī, Muḥyī l-Dīn, *al-Futūḥāt al-makiyya,* Cairo 1911; al-Ḥakīm al-Tirmidhī, *Kitāb Sīrat al-awliyāʾ,* in B. Radtke (ed.), *Drei Schriften des Theosophen des Tirmiḏ,* Beirut 1992, 1-134.
Secondary: K. Ahrens, Christliches im Quran. Eine Nachlese, in *ZDMG* 84 (1930), 15-68, 148-90; M. Chodkiewicz, *Le sceau des saints,* Paris 1986; van Ess, *TG,* see Index, s.v. *"w-l-y";* B. Radtke, *Drei Schriften des Theosophen von Tirmiḏ,* 2 vols., Beirut/Stuttgart 1992, 1996; id. and J. O'Kane, *The concept of sainthood in early Islamic mysticism,* London 1996; R. Mach, *Der Zaddik in Talmud und Midrasch,* Leiden 1957; I. Goldziher, Die Heiligenverehrung im Islam, in Goldziher, *MS,* ii, 275-378.

Sajʿ see RHYMED PROSE

Sakīna see SHEKHINAH

Ṣalāt see PRAYER

Ṣāliḥ

A messenger (q.v.) sent to the people of Thamūd (q.v.), named nine times in the Qurʾān. His story is dealt with in a number of passages (Q 7:73-9; 11:61-8; 26:141-59; 27:45-53; 54:23-31; 91:11-5), and in other verses mention is made of the people of Thamūd and their fate.

The Qurʾān does not contain a complete narrative of the story of this messenger and the events that led his people to punishment and destruction, but it does mention (and occasionally repeats some details of) his mission among his people. Particular attention is given to the words of Ṣāliḥ when summoning his people to faith in God (Q 7:73 f.; 11:61 f.; 26:142 f.; 27:45 f.). Despite his urgings, they refuse to abandon the faith of their fathers (Q 11:62). When introducing the various versions of the speech of the messenger (q.v.) to his people, Ṣāliḥ is described as their "brother" (Q 7:73 and passim; see BROTHER AND BROTHERHOOD). A chronological setting for these people and the story of Ṣāliḥ is clearly given when it is said that the Thamūd were the successors of the ʿĀd (q.v.). The Qurʾān describes the Thamūd as a prosperous people with castles, impressive buildings and gardens; one passage suggests that they rejected various messengers (Q 26:141).

The story of Ṣāliḥ proper is introduced with the statement that he was sent with a she-camel as a sign (Q 7:73; 11:64; 26:155; see SIGNS; CAMEL), a test (Q 54:27; see TRIAL), or a proof (q.v.; i.e. Q 17:59) from God. This camel variously has the right to drink (Q 26:155; 91:13), or the water has to be shared between her and the Thamūd (Q 54:28). In the meantime, Ṣāliḥ's calls to faith prove fruitless, with the exception of a few followers. The haughty elders refuse to believe (Q 7:75) and openly challenge Ṣāliḥ, accusing him of being a simple man like themselves (Q 26:154; 54:24; see IMPECCABILITY) and even of being bewitched (Q 26:153; see INSANITY). The destruction of these unbelievers (see BELIEF AND UNBELIEF) is precipitated when they hamstring the she-camel (Q 7:77; 11:65; 26:157; 91:14) as an act of resistance and rebellion, particularly on the part of one individual among them (Q 54:29). That malevolent act made punishment inevitable (see PUNISHMENT STORIES; CHASTISEMENT AND PUNISHMENT). It took the form of an earthquake that seized them (Q 7:78) or a thunderbolt that left them all dead. The end was, in fact, announced by Ṣāliḥ himself when he became aware of what had been done to the camel: he stated that the punishment would be upon them in three days (Q 11:65). In some passages allusion is made to the punishment by the expression that the Thamūd were overtaken by a shout (or cry) sent by God (Q 11:67; 54:31), which left them prostrate in their dwellings (Q 11:67). Ṣāliḥ and those who believed were naturally placed in safety (Q 11:66; 27:53). Finally, it should be noted that the version in Q 27:45-53 differs almost completely from that given in the other passages, excluding details such as the she-camel, or a description of the type of event that caused the destruction of their houses.

Commentators on the Qurʾān (see EXEGESIS OF THE QURʾĀN: CLASSICAL AND MEDIEVAL) and authors of literature on the prophets add further particulars to the portrait given here. For instance, some state that Ṣāliḥ started his prophetic mission when he was forty years old, as did Muḥammad; it is also said that he died in Mecca (q.v.) when he was fifty-eight. There are differing reports about Ṣāliḥ's genealogy and about the manner in which the she-camel was killed; sometimes the names of the torturer of the she-camel and his collaborators are given. The punishment that destroyed the Thamūd was announced three days in advance: first their faces turned yellow, then red, then black, and on the fourth day they were all dead. A report going back to the Prophet (see ḤADĪTH AND THE QURʾĀN) mentions the case of one individual of the Thamūd who had escaped death because he was in the holy territory of Mecca when the destruction took place. This man, named Abū Righāl, did not, however, escape punishment after he left the holy territory.

Though the Thamūd are known from other sources, pre-Islamic attestations of the name Ṣāliḥ are very rare (see Rippin, Ṣāliḥ). Moreover, the story of Ṣāliḥ and the she-camel has no parallel in other religious traditions.

Roberto Tottoli

Bibliography
Primary: Ibn Kathīr, *Bidāya,* i, 130-8; Ibn Qutayba, Abū Muḥammad ʿAbdallāh b. Muslim al-Dīnawarī, *Kitāb al-Maʿārif,* ed. Th. ʿUkāsha, Cairo 1960, 29-30; Kisāʾī, *Qiṣaṣ,* 110-7; al-Majlisī, Muḥammad Bāqir, *Biḥār al-anwār,* ed. Jawād al-ʿAlawī, Muḥammad Ākhundī et al., 110 vols., Tehran 1956-72, Beirut 1983², xi, 370-94; Muqātil, *Tafsīr,* i, 46-7; Muṭahhar b. Ṭāhir al-Maqdisī, *al-Badʾ wa-l-taʾrīkh,* ed. C. Huart, 6 vols. in 2, Paris 1899-1919, iii, 37-41; Quṭb al-Dīn al-Rāwandī, *Qiṣaṣ al-anbiyāʾ,* Beirut 1989, 95-100; al-Rabghūzī, Naṣr al-Dīn b. Burhān, *Qiṣaṣ al-anbiyāʾ,* ed. and trans. H.E. Boeschoten, J. O'Kane and M. Vandamme, *Stories of the prophets,* 2 vols., Leiden 1995, ii, 77-92; Suyūṭī, *Durr,* 8 vols., Cairo 1983, iii, 489-94; Ṭabarī, *Tafsīr,* Cairo 1968, viii, 224-34; id., *Taʾrīkh,* ed. de Goeje, i, 244-52; al-Ṭarafī, Abū ʿAbdallāh Muḥammad b. Aḥmad b. Muṭarrif, *Qiṣaṣ al-anbiyāʾ,* in R. Tottoli (ed.), *The stories of the prophets of Ibn Muṭarrif al-Ṭarafī,* Berlin 2003, 55-7 (Ar. sect.), 50-2 (Eng. sect.); Thaʿlabī, *al-Kashf wa-l-bayān ʿan tafsīr al-Qurʾān,* ed. A.M. b. ʿĀshūr, 10 vols., Beirut 2002, iv, 251-8; id., *Qiṣaṣ,* 57-63.
Secondary: Horovitz, *KU,* 123; D. Marshall, *God, Muhammad and the unbelievers,* Richmond, Surrey 1999; G.D. Newby, *The making of the last prophet,* Columbia 1989, 58-64; Rippin, Ṣāliḥ, in *EI²*, viii, 984; R. Tottoli, *Biblical prophets in the Qurʾān and Muslim literature,* Richmond 2002, 47-8; B.M. Wheeler, *Prophets in the Quran. An introduction to the Quran and Muslim exegesis,* London 2002, 74-82.

Salt see FOOD AND DRINK

Salvation

Preservation from destruction or failure; in eschatology, deliverance from sin and eternal damnation. Salvation has many meanings in the Qurʾān. Contrary to the final Christian salvation *(khalāṣ),* which supposes deliverance from sin and death for reconciliation and communion with God, the qurʾānic "supreme success" (*[al-]fawz [al-]ʿaẓīm,* Q 4:13, 73; 5:119; 9:72, 89, 100, 111; 10:64; 23:71; 37:60; 40:9; 44:57; 48:5; 57:13; 61:12; 64:9), sometimes called "the great success" (*al-fawz al-kabīr,* Q 85:11) or "the manifest success" (*al-fawz al-mubīn,* Q 6:16; 45:30), is always the ultimate purpose of human life. Therefore the believers "are the successful" (*hum al-*

fā'izūn, Q 9:20; 23:111; 24:52; 59:20) because they enjoy God's pleasure *(riḍwān Allāh).*

This enduring and definitive success is also called *falāḥ* and it is hopefully proposed by the *adhān,* which calls to prayer (q.v.; *ṣalāt*): "Come to success" *(ḥayya ʿalā l-falāḥ).* It is well-known that all who are on "the right path" *(al-hudā, al-sirāṭ al-mustaqīm;* see FREEDOM AND PREDESTINATION; ASTRAY; ERROR; PATH OR WAY) will be "the successful" *(al-mufliḥūn).* Eleven times, the Qurʾān repeats "so that you may be successful" *(laʿallakum tufliḥūn;* see VICTORY), and warns "the unjust" (Q 6:21, 135; 12:23; 28:37; see JUSTICE AND INJUSTICE), "the criminals" (Q 10:17; see SIN, MAJOR AND MINOR), "the sorcerers" (Q 10:77; 20:69; see MAGIC), and "the disbelievers" (Q 23:117; 28:82; see BELIEF AND UNBELIEF) that they shall never be successful *(lā yufliḥūn,* cf. Q 23:117). "The successful" are those "who have repented (see REPENTANCE AND PENANCE), believed and done righteousness" (Q 28:67; see GOOD DEEDS), who "are on true guidance from their lord" (q.v.; Q 2:5; 31:5), who are "enjoining good deeds and forbidding evil" (Q 3:104; see GOOD AND EVIL; VIRTUES AND VICES, COMMANDING AND FORBIDDING), "whose scale will be heavy" (Q 7:8; 23:102; see WEIGHTS AND MEASURES), "who follow the light (q.v.) which has been sent down" (Q 7:157; see REVELATION AND INSPIRATION; NAMES OF THE QURʾĀN), "for whom are the good things" (Q 9:88; see GOOD NEWS; REWARD AND PUNISHMENT), "who say: we hear and we obey" (Q 24:51; see SEEING AND HEARING; OBEDIENCE), "who seek God's countenance" (Q 30:38; see FACE OF GOD), and "are the party of God" (Q 58:22; see PARTIES AND FACTIONS; SHĪʿA). Finally, "whosoever is saved from his own covetousness" (Q 59:9; 64:16; see ENVY) and "purifies himself" (Q 87:14; see RITUAL PURITY; CLEANLINESS AND ABLUTION; JIHĀD) shall achieve success and will be a *mufliḥ.*

But there is a first salvation during life on earth for those whom God has chosen as his prophets (see PROPHETS AND PROPHETHOOD) or representatives among people. Sometimes the verb *anqadha,* "to save" (four times), is used for deliverance from the fire (see HELL AND HELLFIRE): "You were, it is said, on the brink of a pit of fire (q.v.) and he saved you from it" (Q 3:103). God is proclaimed to be the only savior, as when Abraham (q.v.) proclaims that the idols (see IDOLS AND IMAGES) or false deities could not save him (Q 36:23). A similar case is that of Noah's (q.v.) people (Q 36:43). Is the word *fidāʾ* or *fidya,* "ransom," used for redemption (Q 2:184, 196; 47:4; 57:15)? It seems to be only used for human "ransom" from captivity (see CAPTIVES) or from the marriage bond (see MARRIAGE AND DIVORCE), but sometimes it also means "ransom of punishment" (Q 70:11; see CHASTISEMENT AND PUNISHMENT). Nevertheless, it is the root *n-j-w* which mainly means salvation from perils and deadly events, with its two verbal forms *najjā* (thirty-seven times) and *anjā* (twenty-three times). In history (see HISTORY AND THE QURʾĀN), God has always saved each of his prophets "and those who believed with him": Hūd (q.v.; Q 7:72; 11:58), Ṣāliḥ (q.v.; Q 11:66), Abraham (Q 29:24), Shuʿayb (q.v.; Q 11:94), Lot (q.v.; Q 7:83; 27:57), Jonah (q.v.; cf. Q 6:63), Moses (q.v.; "We saved you from great distress," Q 20:40) and the Children of Israel (q.v.; Banū Isrāʾīl: "When we delivered you from Pharaoh's [q.v.] people," Q 2:49). To escape "from the unjust people" (Q 28:25; see OPPRESSION), to be "released" (Q 12:45), to be "delivered from" the enemy (e.g. Q 2:50; 7:141; 20:80; see ENEMIES), this is the "salvation" of people who believed in God. Therefore the Qurʾān proposes to the believers to repeat the prayer of the ones who were saved by God, as did Pharaoh's wife: "My lord! Save me from the unjust people" (Q 66:11), and Moses himself: "Save us by your mercy (q.v.) from the disbelieving folk" (Q 10:86). So salvation *(najāt)* is always God's gift granted to faithful people in the present time and in the hereafter. See also ESCHATOLOGY.

Maurice Borrmans

Bibliography
Primary: Rashīd Riḍā, *Manār;* Rāzī, *Tafsīr.*
Secondary: ʿA.Y. ʿAlī, *The glorious Qurʾān,* Riyadh 1973; Arberry; L. Gardet, *Dieu et la destinée de l'homme,* Paris 1967, esp. 335-51; D. Gimaret, *La doctrine d'al-Ashʿarī,* Paris 1990, esp. 487-500; Pickthall, *Koran.*

Ṣamad see GOD AND HIS ATTRIBUTES

Samaritans

A tiny sect claiming to be Israelite, found today principally in Nablus, biblical Shechem, in the Palestinian territories; and in Holon in Israel. The Samaritans call themselves *Shomᵉrim,* "observant ones," from Hebrew *shamar,* "to observe." 2 Kings 17:24-9, the earliest reference to them, calls them *Shomronim* or "Samarians," alleging that they were pagan peoples settled in Samaria by the Assyrians after the deportations of 722 B.C.E. Enmity between Judaeans and Samaritans flared up with the return of Judaean deportees from Babylon in 539 B.C.E. and continued up to and beyond the time of Jesus. Like Jerusalem, Gerizim, the mountain in Nablus holy to the Samaritans, was captured by the Roman armies and the emperor Hadrian built a pagan temple on its summit. During the Roman and Byzantine periods the Samaritans took part in numerous rebellions, provoked by both their strong separatism and the repressive legislation of the imperial authorities.

The only unequivocal reference to Samaritans in the Qurʾān is to al-Sāmirī, the man who in Q 20:85-95 tempted the Israelites (see CHILDREN OF ISRAEL) in the desert, inducing them to throw their ornaments into a fire and producing a live calf (see CALF OF GOLD). Moses (q.v.) condemned him to saying, "do not touch me" (Q 20:97) for the rest of his life. The Samaritans relate this qurʾānic expression of al-Sāmirī, "do not touch me" *(lā misāsa),* to a covenant (q.v.; see also CONTRACTS AND ALLIANCES) that they claim Muḥammad made with them, saying: "In your lifetime you can indeed say 'Let no one touch me.' You have a pledge (see OATHS). Do not violate it (see BREAKING TRUSTS AND CONTRACTS). Look to your God whom you are still loyally following." That Muḥammad had some knowledge of Samaritans and their beliefs (see RELIGIOUS PLURALISM AND THE QURʾĀN) is suggested by Q 2:96, which defends Solomon's (q.v.) piety (q.v.) — impugned by the Samaritans — against unnamed detractors.

The Samaritans appear to have viewed the Muslim army that invaded Syria in 12/632-3 as liberators from Byzantine oppression (see BYZANTINES). In the view of some early Muslim authors, they were exempted from paying the *kharāj,* or land tax, and subjected only to the *jizya,* or poll tax (q.v.; "four dirhams and a feed-bag of barley"), because of the assistance they rendered the invaders. The only Samaritan mention of the Umayyad caliphate to survive is a reference by the Samaritan chronicler Abū l-Fatḥ al-Sāmirī b. Abī l-Ḥasan (fl. 750/1350) to a devastating earthquake in the time of Marwān II (r. 127-32/744-50). The wars between the last of the Umayyads and the ʿAbbāsids are recorded in Samaritan chronicles, as are the consequences for the Samaritans of the

ʿAbbāsid victory and of the wars that followed the death of Hārūn al-Rashīd (d. 193/809). The Samaritans appear to have been treated well by the first Fāṭimid caliphs of Egypt, al-Muʿizz (r. 344-65/952-75) and al-ʿAzīz (r. 365-86/976-96), and during the crusades they enjoyed relative prosperity. The fall of Nablus to the Mongols (657/1259), combined with the Egyptian Mamlūks' destruction of Christian towns and strongholds throughout Syria (between 658/1260 and 690/1291), led to the suffering of the Samaritans, along with that of the other inhabitants.

Numerous Muslim sources attest to a Samaritan presence in the post-qurʾānic Islamic milieu. Muslim geographers like al-Yaʿqūbī (fl. later third/ninth cent.), al-Masʿūdī (d. 345/956), al-Idrīsī (d. ca. 560/1165), al-Iṣṭakhrī (fl. fourth/tenth cent.), the polymath al-Bīrūnī (d. ca. 440/1048) and the historian of religions al-Shahrastānī (d. 548/1153) all describe some aspect of Samaritan life and culture from the third/ninth to the sixth/twelfth centuries. Finally, even though the Qurʾān does not mention the Samaritans in this context, the jurists (*fuqahāʾ*; see LAW AND THE QURʾĀN) include them, along with Christians (see CHRISTIANS AND CHRISTIANITY), Jews (see JEWS AND JUDAISM), Magians (q.v.) and Sabians (q.v.), among the unbelievers (see PEOPLE OF THE BOOK; BELIEF AND UNBELIEF) who, following Q 9:29, must be fought until they pay the *jizya* (see JIHĀD; FIGHTING; WAR; TOLERANCE AND COMPULSION; TAXATION).

Paul Stenhouse

Bibliography

Primary: Abū l-Fatḥ al-Sāmirī b. Abī al-Ḥasan, *The* Kitāb al-taʾrīkh *of Abū l-Fatḥ*, trans. P. Stenhouse, Sydney 1985.
Secondary: J. Finkel, Jewish, Christian and Samaritan influence on Arabia, in *Macdonald presentation volume*, Princeton 1933, 145-66; Cl. Cahen, Djizya (i), in *EI²*, ii, 559-62; id., Kharādj (i), in *EI²*, iv, 1030-4; A.D. Crown, History, in A.D. Crown, R. Pummer and A. Tal (eds.), *A companion to Samaritan studies*, Tübingen 1993, 123-8; H.A.R. Gibb and J.H. Kramers (eds.) *Shorter encyclopaedia of Islam*, Leiden 1974, s.v. "Djizya," "Kharādj," and "al-Sāmirī"; B. Heller/A. Rippin, al-Sāmirī, in *EI²*, viii, 1046; J.A. Montgomery, *The Samaritans. The earliest Jewish sect. Their history, theology and literature*, Philadelphia 1907; L. Richter-Bernburg, St. John of Acre — Nablus — Damascus. The Samaritan minority under Crusaders and Muslims, in *Hallesche Beiträge zur Orientwissenschaft* 22 (1996), 117-30; H. Schwartzbaum, *Biblical and extra-biblical legends in Islamic folk-literature*, Walldorf-Hessen 1982, 14-7 and footnotes (contains a complete bibliography).

Samson

Biblical figure present in Islamic tradition and qurʾānic commentary, but not the Qurʾān. Called Shamsūn in Arabic, this name is not mentioned in the Qurʾān but is briefly mentioned in exegetical and historical works. His story is embellished with miraculous anecdotes. Many reports on him are cited by al-Ṭabarī (d. 310/923), who narrates them mainly from Wahb b. Munabbih (on whose authority Samson is portrayed as an extreme and austere ascetic: for example, he is said to have put out his eyes so as not to be diverted from the worship of God, and to have castrated himself so as to avoid the temptation of women; cf. Khoury, *Légendes*, 80-1 for Ar. text; see also Schwarzbaum, *Biblical*, 64). Al-Ṭabarī's historical work places Samson immediately before the coming of St. George (Jirjīs), suggesting that Samson lived in the Christian era.

Although he was born in a community of unbelievers (see BELIEF AND UNBELIEF) — other sources suggest a community of idolaters (see IDOLATRY AND IDOLATERS; POLYTHEISM AND ATHEISM) — Samson is portrayed as a strong and powerful man of great faith (q.v.). An inhabitant of a Roman city, he dedicated his life to serving God's cause, which often meant fighting the enemies (q.v.) of God (see PATH OR WAY; JIHĀD). God guided him because of his moral probity and piety (q.v.). Samson is also portrayed as a great fighter (see WAR; FIGHTING) who fought and defeated his people in battle, frequently fighting on his own.

He is reported to have received divine assistance, especially during battles. Sweet water would spring forth from stones to quench his thirst. Samson's enemies soon realized that they could only overcome him through his wife. Bribed by his enemies, she agreed to help them capture her husband. They gave her a strong rope and told her to tie his hands to his neck when he fell asleep. She tried several different ways to tie him down, even with an iron ring tied to his neck, but each time he would break free. When Samson questioned his wife as to why she tied him down, she claimed that she was testing his strength.

Samson had long hair. He confided to his wife that he could only be overcome if his hair was tied. She tied his hands to his neck with his hair while he was sleeping and alerted his enemies. The enemies captured him, pierced his eyes, cut off his nose and ears before bringing him to a local minaret for public display. When he was captured, Samson pleaded with God to let him emerge victorious over those who had captured him (see VICTORY). God miraculously restored his eyesight and the parts of his body that had been mutilated. With his strength restored, Samson was commanded to grasp and pull two of the main pillars on which the minaret rested. As the people jeered, the minaret came crashing down, and the king and all those around him perished.

The discussion on Samson to be found in qurʾānic commentary is closer to the Christian than the biblical account of his life (cf. Rippin, Shamsūn; see Judges 13:5 f., where Samson's mother is told by an angelic messenger that her son is to be consecrated to God from the day of his birth [cf. Numbers 6:2-8] — a passage that likely influenced the later Christian tradition, in which he is depicted as an extreme ascetic; cf. Schwarzbaum, *Biblical*, 156: n. 162 of p. 64). In Islamic tradition, no immoral deeds (see EVIL DEEDS), lust, or acts of self-destruction (cf. e.g. Judges 16:1-31) are mentioned in the exegetical stories about him (see EXEGESIS OF THE QURʾĀN: CLASSICAL AND MEDIEVAL): rather, Samson is depicted as an upright person and a great fighter who is betrayed by a treacherous wife.

Liyakat Takim

Bibliography
Primary: Ḍamīrī, *Ḥayāt*, 2 vols., Cairo 1887, i, 226, l. 7-24; Ṭabarī, *Taʾrīkh*, 8 vols., Beirut 1983; Thaʿlabī, *Qiṣaṣ*, trans. and annot. W.M. Brinner, *ʿArāʾis al-majālis fī qiṣaṣ al-anbiyāʾ or "Lives of the prophets,"* Leiden 2002, 726-7; Yaʿqūbī, *Taʾrikh*, 2 vols., Beirut n.d.
Secondary: R.G. Khoury, *Les légendes prophétiques dans l'Islam*, Wiesbaden 1978, 80-2; A. Rippin, Shamsūn, in *EI²*, ix, 300; H. Schwarzbaum, *Biblical and extra-biblical legends in Islamic folk-literature*, Walldorf-Hessen 1982; R. Tottoli, *Biblical prophets in the Qurʾān and Muslim literature*, Richmond, Surrey 2002.

Samuel

While not mentioned by name in the Qurʾān, there is little doubt that the prophet (*nabī*; see PROPHETS AND PROPHETHOOD) referred to anonymously in Q 2:246-8 is the biblical Samuel, the last of the "Judges" who administered the transition of Israel to a kingdom (see KINGS AND RULERS). This important historical detail is significantly preserved in the short qurʾānic passage treating Samuel, "Have you not looked to the chiefs of the Children of Israel (q.v.) after Moses (q.v.) when they said to a prophet among them, 'Appoint for us a king that we may fight in the way of God'" (Q 2:246; see PATH OR WAY). In contradistinction with the biblical version of the story, however, the qurʾānic account does not present the Israelites as disappointing God with their request for a king (cf. i.e. I Samuel 12:12: "... you said to me, 'No, but a king shall reign over us,' though the lord your God was your king"); nor does the Israelites' request for a king carry any negative connotation in subsequent Islamic prophetology (e.g. al-Kisāʾī, *Qiṣaṣ*, 270: "Samuel humbled himself before God in order that a king might be appointed from among them").

The principal themes of Q 2:246-8, the verses in which this anonymous prophet of the Children of Israel appears, are: the Children of Israel's request for a king; encouragement to fight according to divine prescription (see FIGHTING; WAR); questioning of Saul's (q.v.) legitimacy as the appointed king due to his lack of resources and influence; and description of the resultant sign (see SIGNS) of Saul's kingship, i.e. the return of the ark (q.v.) of the covenant (q.v.). The anonymous prophet, identified with Samuel, is asked by the Children of Israel to furnish them with a king; he says that God has appointed Saul as their king, and to their protestations, he replies that "God gives authority (q.v.) to whom he wills" (Q 2:247; see POWER AND IMPOTENCE). Finally, in Q 2:248, the unnamed Samuel tells of the sign of Saul's authority *(āyat mulkihi)* that will come as a sign *(āya)* for those who believe (see FAITH; BELIEF AND UNBELIEF), namely the ark of the covenant, containing the "shekhinah (q.v.) of your lord."

Exegetical tradition and "stories of the prophets" literature

Identification of this anonymous prophet of Q 2:246-8 is rendered variously in the mainstream exegetical tradition (see EXEGESIS OF THE QURʾĀN: CLASSICAL AND MEDIEVAL). Most commonly he is *Shamwīl;* also *Ashmawīl* (occasionally transcribed *Ishmawīl*), *Ashmāwīl* and *Shamwāʾīl* (the Protestant Arabic translation of the Bible has rendered the name *Ṣamūʾīl;* and the holy burial site of *Nebi Samwīl* preserves a further slightly distinct form). Although this form does not occur in Islamic literature, the properly Arabicized form of the name "Samuel," i.e. that closest to the Hebrew morphology, is Samawʾal. Note, for example, the Jewish pre-Islamic chieftain of Taymāʾ, Samawʾal b. ʿĀdiyāʾ (d. ca. 560 C.E.) or, more incidentally, the Jewish vintner described in a celebrated *khamriyya* by Abū Nuwās (d. ca. 198/814); and especially Samuel's namesake, the Jewish mystic and convert to Islam, Samawʾal b. Yaḥyā al-Maghribī (520-69/1126-74), who describes at the outset of his autobiography, *Ifḥām al-Yahūd,* how his mother, as a result of the manner in which she conceived her child, identified with Hanna, the biblical Samuel's mother, and named her son after him (Shamwāʾīl) "...which is rendered in Arabic al-Samawʾal."

Commenting on Q 2:246, al-Rāzī (d. 606/1210) finds specifying the identity of the unnamed prophet to be less essential than ascertaining the actual point of the short passage in which he occurs (*Tafsīr,* ad loc., second *masʾala*), averring that the multifarious names, even identities, put forward for Samuel detract from the essential message: "...for the intent [of the verse] is [simply] to encourage people to jihād *(al-targhīb fī bāb al-jihād).*" Al-Rāzī distrusts the *isnāds* in the traditions of identification (see ḤADĪTH AND THE QURʾĀN) and vigorously rejects the claim (*pace* Qatāda) that the prophet was Joshua (based on the fact that the prophet of Q 2:246 is described as coming "after" Moses: the temporal preposition "after" is ambiguous and should not override the consensus of historical chronology). Yet even al-Rāzī, the most sophisticated of the classical exegetes, is not impervious to confusion: he cites anonymously those who offered the identity as Ashmawīl b. Hārūn, "which is Ismāʿīl [sic] in Arabic." His claim that this is the majority view is dubious: it is clear that the more consensual patronymic is Ashmawīl b. Bālī. All commentators attribute to al-Suddī the identification of the prophet as Shamʿūn (Simeon); this itself has given rise to further confusion (cf. al-Fasawī who, in *Badʾ al-khalq,* relates separate stories for Shamʿūn and Ashmwāʾīl, as if they were two distinct men with overlapping biographies; yet in al-Ṭabarī's *Taʾrīkh,* Shamʿūn and Ashmwāʾīl are used interchangeably, apparently as variants of the same name). Identification of Samuel with Shamʿūn may be due to interference from the "story of Leah, Jacob's wife, who called her son Simeon, 'because the Lord hath heard that I am hated' (*Gen* 29:33)" (cf. Katsh, *Judaism,* 162). It is thus the story of Samuel's conception that is the source of confusion in prophetic lore. In modern times, Sayyid Quṭb (d. 1966; *Ẓilāl,* i, 266) concurs with al-Rāzī's disinterest in the question of identity, deeming it irrelevant (cf. also, for example, the fifth/eleventh century mystic al-Qushayrī in *Laṭāʾif al-ishārāt* who omits mention of Samuel when discussing Q 2:246).

In the "stories of the prophets" *(qiṣaṣ)* accounts of Samuel, to be found in *tafsīr* and elsewhere, it is clear that there are distinctly Jewish, Islamic and even Christian (see CHRISTIANS AND CHRISTIANITY) elements (see e.g. Katsh, *Judaism,* 160-1 regarding accounts of the prophet's conception and birth). Noticeable discrepancies between I Samuel and the Qurʾān include details of his divine calling: in I Samuel (3:1-9) when he hears the voice of his lord addressing him, he goes to Eli (three times), whereas in the Islamic tradition it is to his father that he repairs, and only then is he sent to Eli. Further, the qurʾānic recognition of Saul by Samuel follows a quasi-folkloric narrative pattern absent from the Bible, to wit: the bubbling of Samuel's oil-horn in the presence of Saul who has come to him in search of his father's lost asses. If, interpretatively, such a theme can be considered a subtext of Q 2:246-8, it shades meaningfully into the leitmotif of sūra 2: that concealed things will come to light (see HIDDEN AND THE HIDDEN). Even the story of "the cow" (Q 2:67-80), and its facilitating the unmasking of a murderer (see MURDER), forces the surrounding theme about the recognition of true and authentic scripture (see BOOK) and prophecy.

Finally, in addition to the exegetical discussion of Q 2:246-8, there are references to apparitions of Samuel in dreams (see DREAMS AND SLEEP), tales which go beyond the qurʾānic account and involve him further in the life of Saul. Regarding Saul's struggles against his enemies, al-Kisāʾī (*Qiṣaṣ,* trans. Thackston, 277-8) relates how Saul consults Samuel: having summoned him in a dream, he is scolded for having relied upon himself, never having acted upon the advice of Samuel while he lived. The deceased prophet disappears from sight and Saul awakens, frightened, from this terse encounter. While this censorious view of Saul attenuates the argument that he is a type for Muḥammad (see below, under *A revisionist reading*), it must be recognized that this kind of prophetic lore postdates the Qurʾān and may therefore be independent of the latter's own rhetorical agenda (see RHETORIC AND THE QURʾĀN).

A revisionist reading

In the light of a recent account of these verses that cogently situates them within the complex agenda of Q 2 (see FORM AND STRUCTURE OF THE QURʾĀN), some attention must also be devoted here to Q 2:249-51, verses which pay particular attention to Saul (Ṭālūt). N. Robinson has identified four issues as crucial to their interpretation, as "what matters is not the historical detail but the relevance of the narrative to Muhammad's situation" (Robinson, *Discovering*, 217-8; see OCCASIONS OF REVELATION; SĪRA AND THE QURʾĀN; HISTORY AND THE QURʾĀN). The first is refusal to fight, which may reflect "the situation in Yathrib (see MEDINA), where there was a widespread recognition of the need for a strong military leader but a general reluctance to do battle with the superior forces of the Meccans" (see MECCA; POLITICS AND THE QURʾĀN). The second is Saul's lack of sufficient wealth (q.v.) to justify his selection as king (Q 2:247); this is distinct from the biblical account in I Samuel, where it is Saul's problematic descent from Benjamin (q.v.) that is questioned, by Saul himself. The third is the return of the ark as a sign of Saul's sovereignty (Q 2:248). Again, distinction with the biblical account is noted: "According to the biblical account the Philistines returned the Ark to the Children of Israel before Saul was made king (*I Sam.* 6-7)." Robinson maintains that if the qurʾānic Saul is indeed a figure for Muḥammad, this particular treatment of the ark of the covenant "probably foreshadows the Kaʿba (q.v.); those who questioned Muḥammad's fitness to rule over them would change their minds when, as a result of his leadership, the Kaʿba came to their possession." The fourth is the similarity of the qurʾānic account of Saul's selection of his troops with the test of the biblical Gideon (cf. Judges 7): Robinson observes (re Q 2:249) that this selection of troops is "... probably mentioned in the present context because it reinforces one of the keynotes of the legislative sections (of sūra 2; see LAW AND THE QURʾĀN): the need to be in control of one's appetites in order to be fit to engage in Jihad" (see JIHĀD). It is noticeable that, according to this reading, the qurʾānic Samuel is eclipsed in importance in favor of Saul the king who may thus emerge as a figure for Muḥammad. Use of the verb *iṣṭafā* for God's selection of Saul in Q 2:247 supports this view and the differentiation between Samuel and Saul in the Qurʾān — that is, the quiet privileging of the latter over the former — is mirrored by the twin roles of Samuel and Muḥammad in the recounting of the sixth/twelfth century Samawʾal b. Yaḥyā al-Maghribī's conversion to Islam (cf. Reynolds, *Interpreting*, 91-2).

Intertextuality?

Some modern Western commentaries on Q 2:249 observe interference from the biblical accounts about Gideon; Wherry, for example, commenting on Sale's translation, wrote disrespectfully in the nineteenth century: "The garbled rendering of Israelitish history in this verse and those following illustrates at once Muḥammad's ignorance of the Bible story, and his unscrupulous adaptation of Jewish tradition to the purposes of his prophetic ambition" (Wherry, *Comprehensive commentary*, i, 379, ad loc). Yet this may overlook the significance of the following cognate details in the life of Samuel as developed in Jewish lore, details that expand on I Samuel 7:6 (Ginzberg, *Legends*, iv, 63-4):

In the midst of the defeats and other calamities that overwhelmed the Israelites, Samuel's authority grew, and the respect for him increased, until he was acknowledged the helper of his people. His first efforts were directed toward counteracting the spiritual decay in Israel. When he assembled the people at Mizpah for prayer, he sought to distinguish between the faithful and the idolatrous, in order to mete out punishment to the disloyal. He had all the people drink water, whose effect was to prevent idolaters from opening their lips.

Considering also that when Gideon was asked to rule the people he directed them back to their lord, saying, "… the lord shall rule over you," it is possible to detect an important point of reference that distinguishes the changed situation in the time of Samuel. This may also explain the (deliberate?) faint resonance of Gideon in the qurʾānic account of Samuel and Saul.

Philip F. Kennedy

Bibliography
Primary (in addition to classical works of exegesis on Q 2:246-8): al-Fasawī, Abū Rifāʿa ʿUmāra b. Wathīma al-Fārisī, *Badʾ al-khalq,* ed. G. Khoury, Wiesbaden 1978, 80 f.; Kisāʾī, *Qiṣaṣ,* trans. W.M. Thackston, *The tales of the prophets of al-Kisaʾi,* Chicago 1997, 270-8; Masʿūdī, *Murūj,* ed. Pellat, § 98; M. Perlmann (ed. and trans.), *Samawʾal al-Maghribī. Ifḥām al-yahūd, "Silencing the Jews",* New York 1964; Qushayrī, *Laṭāʾif;* Quṭb, *Ẓilāl al-Qurʾān,* 6 vols., Beirut 1973; Rāzī, *Tafsīr;* Ṭabarī, *Taʾrīkh,* trans. W.M. Brinner, *The history of al-Ṭabarī. iii. The Children of Israel,* 129-39; Thaʿlabī, *Qiṣaṣ,* ed. Cairo 1954, 262 f.; annot. trans. W.M. Brinner, *Lives of the prophets,* Leiden 2002, 439-44 (Eli and Samuel), 445-60 (Saul).
Secondary: M. Ayoub, *The Qurʾan and its interpreters,* Albany 1984, 236-45; R. Ebeid and L. Wickham, Al-Yaʿqūbī's account of the Israelite prophets and kings, in *JNES* 29 (1970), 81-2; L. Ginzberg, *The legends of the Jews,* 6 vols., Philadelphia 1941, iv, 57 f.; A.I. Katsh, *Judaism and the Koran,* New York 1962, 161-3; Ph.F. Kennedy, Abū Nuwās, Samuel and Levi, in *Medieval and modern perspectives on Muslim-Jewish relations* [Studies in Muslim-Jewish relations, vol. 2], London 1995, 109-25; D.F. Reynolds (ed.), *Interpreting the self. Autobiography in the Arabic literary tradition,* Berkeley 2001; N. Robinson, *Discovering the Qurʾān,* London 1996, 217-8; E.M. Wherry, *A comprehensive commentary on the Quran, comprising Sale's translation and preliminary discourse with additional notes and emendations,* 4 vols., London 1882.

Sanctity and the Sacred see SACRED PRECINCTS; PROFANE AND SACRED; FORBIDDEN; SAINT

Sanctuary see SACRED PRECINCTS

Sand

Loose granular material resulting from the disintegration of rocks. The most common Arabic word for sand is *raml,* which is not found in the Qurʾān. There are, however, some other terms for sand in the Arabic language, such as *kathīb* and *ḥāṣib*. These two words are used in the Qurʾān, in a variety of verses. The former is mentioned explicitly only a single time in the Qurʾān (Q 73:14). Referring to the final hour *(qiyāma),* the verse says, "On the day when the earth and the hills rock, and the mountains become *kathīb*." The word *kathīb* can be interpreted as meaning "a huge amount of sand" (*qiṭʿa ʿaẓīma min al-raml;* Ḥaddād, *Kashf,* vii, 105; see also *Lisān al-ʿArab,* i, 235). On the interpretation of the same word, al-Shawkānī (d. 1250/1834), a Muslim commentator and jurist, says that after the final earthquake, the mountains will become like moving sand (Shawkānī, *Tafsīr,* iv, 371; see APOCALYPSE; LAST JUDGMENT).

The word *ḥāṣib* is mentioned in four verses in the Qurʾān (Q 17:68; 29:40; 54:34; 67:17). On the meaning of the word there are several interpretations by qurʾānic commentators. Ibn Kathīr (d. 774/1372), a prominent commentator (see EXEGESIS OF THE QURʾĀN: CLASSICAL AND MEDIEVAL), interprets the word in a way that can be understood as "a rainy sandstorm." It comes as a punishment for those who disbelieve God's message (see BELIEF AND

UNBELIEF; CHASTISEMENT AND PUNISHMENT; PUNISHMENT STORIES). The people of Lot (q.v.) were punished in such a way (Q 54:34; Ibn Kathīr, *Tafsīr,* iv, 328). Some commentators believe that the army of Abraha (q.v.), who had attempted to destroy what is now the holy shrine of Islam in Mecca (q.v.), was destroyed in such a sandstorm (Shawkānī, *Tafsīr,* vii, 317-8, 553-4). The word is also interpreted as "a strong wind which carries pebbles" (Ḥaddād, *Kashf,* vii, 46).

The two words *kathīb* and *ḥāṣib* are mentioned in reference to the punishment by God of those who deny the message of the prophets (see PROPHETS AND PROPHETHOOD). The Qurʾān threatens its immediate audience, i.e. the Arabs (q.v.), that, if they fail to listen to God's messenger (q.v.), they will be punished like the ancient disbelievers. A verse says: "Have you taken security from him, who is in the heavens (see HEAVEN AND SKY), that he will not send upon you the *ḥāṣib*" (Q 67:17). It is interesting to note how the Qurʾān threatens its initial audience with disasters with which they were already familiar. In the interpretation of the word *ḥāṣib,* al-ʿĀlūsī (d. 1270/1854), a prominent nineteenth-century qurʾānic commentator, says that the destructive storm on the land is called *ḥāṣib*. A similar storm on the sea is called *qāṣif* (ʿĀlūsī, *Rūḥ,* xv, 117).

The Prophet used the word *raml* in an allegorical sense (see METAPHOR; SIMILES). Speaking of the attributes of God (see GOD AND HIS ATTRIBUTES), and commenting on the qurʾānic verse, "the one who forgives all sins, the most forgiving one" (Q 39:53), the Prophet mentions that anyone who says a certain prayer before going to bed, will be forgiven by God for all of her/his sins, even if they are as numerous as sand (Tirmidhī, *Ṣaḥīḥ,* 470; see also ʿĀlūsī, *Rūḥ,* xxx, 259; see ḤADĪTH AND THE QURʾĀN; RITUAL AND THE QURʾĀN; POPULAR AND TALISMANIC USES OF THE QURʾĀN; EVERYDAY LIFE, THE QURʾĀN IN; SIN, MAJOR AND MINOR; FORGIVENESS).

Zeki Saritoprak

Bibliography

ʿĀlūsī, *Rūḥ;* al-Ḥaddād, Abū Bakr b. ʿAlī, *Kashf al-tanzīl,* ed. M.I. Yaḥyā, 7 vols., Beirut 2003; Ibn Kathīr, *Tafsīr; Lisān al-ʿArab;* Shawkānī, *Tafsīr,* ed. F. ʿAlwān, 4 vols., Riyadh 1999; Tirmidhī, *Ṣaḥīḥ.*

Satan(s) see DEVIL

Satanic Verses

Name given by western scholarship to an incident known in the Muslim tradition as "the story of the cranes" *(qiṣṣat al-gharānīq)* or "the story of the maidens." According to various versions, this is the assertion that the prophet Muḥammad once mistook words suggested to him by Satan as divine revelation (see REVELATION AND INSPIRATION; DEVIL); that is to say, as verses of the Qurʾān — the words reportedly interpolated by Satan are called the "satanic verses." The historicity of the satanic verses incident is strenuously rejected by modern Islamic orthodoxy, often on pain of *takfīr* (being declared an unbeliever; see BELIEF AND UNBELIEF).

The satanic verses incident is reported in the *tafsīr* (qurʾānic exegesis; see EXEGESIS OF THE QURʾĀN: CLASSICAL AND MEDIEVAL) and the *sīra-maghāzī* literature (epic prophetic biography; see SĪRA AND THE QURʾĀN) dating from the first two centuries of Islam. While the numerous reports on the incident differ in the construction and detail of the narrative, they may be broadly collated as follows. The incident is generally dated to the fifth year of Muḥammad's mission, when the small Muslim community in Mecca (q.v.) was under persecution by the leaders of Quraysh (q.v.; the dominant tribe in Mecca), the most vulnerable of Muḥammad's followers having fled for safety to Abyssinia. The reports indicate that in these circumstances, Muḥammad hoped to achieve reconciliation with Quraysh. At this time, Sūrat al-Najm (Q 53, "The Star"), was revealed to Muḥammad, who recited the chapter to a gathering of Quraysh (see OCCASIONS OF REVELATION; RECITATION OF THE QURʾĀN). When Muḥammad reached Q 53:19-20, with their reference to the female deities worshipped by Quraysh — "Have you considered al-Lāt, al-ʿUzzā, and Manāt, the third, the other?" — Satan was able to cast two verses into Muḥammad's recitation which Muḥammad took to be divine revelation and duly recited; in some reports, Muḥammad is portrayed as being drowsy and inattentive when he committed the error. These are the "satanic verses": "Indeed they are the high cranes/the high maidens *(al-gharānīq/al-gharāniqa l-ʿulā)*, and indeed their intercession is to be desired." (The precise wording of the satanic verses varies with the different reports; a version of the satanic verses is also reported as a pre-Islamic *talbiya* or ritual invocation of Quraysh; see PRAYER FORMULAS; RITUAL AND THE QURʾĀN.) The Quraysh were greatly pleased at Muḥammad's praise of their deities and at his having accorded them a place in the theology of his revelation, to the point that when Muḥammad recited the closing verse of the sūra, Q 53:62: "So: prostrate yourselves to God and worship [him]" — the unbelievers present prostrated themselves alongside the Muslims (see BOWING AND PROSTRATION). Later, however, Gabriel (q.v.) came to Muḥammad and apprised him of his error; in some reports, Muḥammad is depicted as realizing the error on his own. The Prophet was greatly distressed, so God sent down to him Q 22:52-4, comforting him and explaining to him what had happened:

We have not sent before you a messenger (q.v.) or a prophet (see PROPHETS AND PROPHETHOOD), but that when he desired/recited (*tamannā;* the verb means both "to desire" and "to recite"), Satan cast into his desire/recitation *(umniyyatihi),* so God eliminates *(yansakh)* that which Satan casts, then God establishes his own signs [q.v.; *āyāt*] clearly — and God is all-knowing, all-wise (see GOD AND HIS ATTRIBUTES) — to make that which Satan casts a trial (q.v.) for those in whose hearts is sickness and for those whose hearts are hardened (see HEART) — truly the wrong-doers are in deep dissension — and so that those who have been given knowledge (see KNOWLEDGE AND LEARNING) may know that it is the truth (q.v.) from your lord (q.v.), so that they might believe in it, and that their hearts may submit to it — truly, God guides those who have faith (q.v.) to the straight path (see PATH OR WAY).

Muḥammad then acknowledged his error and recanted the satanic verses, thereby provoking the renewed hostility and persecution of Quraysh (see OPPOSITION TO MUḤAMMAD). Some of the reports cite Q 53:21-2, "Would you have sons, and for him daughters? That, indeed, would be a crooked division," as having been revealed in place of the satanic verses, while others link the incident with the revelation of Q 17:73, "And they strove to tempt you away from that [with] which we inspired you, that you might fabricate against us something other than it;... and had we not made you firm, you would have inclined to them a little." Generally, though, the incident is cited as the "occasion of revelation" *(sabab al-nuzūl)* for Q 22:52, although in some commentaries it appears in the exegesis on Q 53:19. It is also widely reported that the news of the Quraysh prostrating themselves alongside the Muslims made its way to Abyssinia (q.v.), prompting some of the Muslim refugees — understanding Quraysh to have converted to Islam — to return to Mecca, only to have to leave again (see EMIGRATION).

The satanic verses incident is reported in the respective *tafsīr* corpuses transmitted from almost every Qurʾān commentator of note in the first two centuries of the *hijra* (see CALENDAR): Saʿīd b. Jubayr (d. 95/714), Mujāhid b. Jabr (d. 104/722), al-Ḍaḥḥāk b. Muzāḥim (d. 105/723), ʿIkrima the client *(mawlā)* of Ibn ʿAbbās (d. 105/723), Abū l-ʿĀliya al-Riyāḥī (d. 111/729), ʿAṭiyya b. Saʿd al-ʿAwfī (d. 111/729), ʿAṭāʾ b. Abī Rabāḥ (d. 114/732), Muḥammad b. Kaʿb al-Quraẓī (d. 118/736), Qatāda b. Diʿāma (d. 118/736), Abū Ṣāliḥ Bādhām al-Kūfī (d. 120/738), Ismāʿīl al-Suddī (d. 128/745), Muḥammad b. al-Sāʾib al-Kalbī (d. 146/763), ʿAbd al-Malik b. Jurayj (d. 150/767), Muqātil b. Sulaymān (d. 150/767), Maʿmar b. Rāshid (d. 154/770), Yaḥyā b. Sallām al-Baṣrī (d. 200/815). Several of these relate the incident on the authority of ʿAbdallāh b. ʿAbbās (d. 68/687; see EXEGESIS OF THE QURʾĀN: CLASSICAL AND MEDIEVAL). The incident also appears in the respective *sīra-maghāzī* works transmitted in the first two centuries from ʿUrwa b. al-Zubayr (d. 94/713), Muḥammad b. Shihāb al-Zuhrī (d. 124/742), Mūsā b. ʿUqba (d. 141/748), Muḥammad b. Isḥāq (d. 150/767), Abū Maʿshar al-Sindī (d. 170/786) and Muḥammad b. ʿUmar al-Wāqidī (d. 207/823). Thus, the satanic verses incident seems to have constituted a standard element in the memory of the early Muslim community about the life of Muḥammad (q.v.). The incident continued to be cited and its historicity accepted by several Qurʾān commentators and authors of *sīra-maghāzī* works throughout the classical period, including authors of important commentaries, such as Muḥammad b. Jarīr al-Ṭabarī (d. 310/923), Abū Isḥāq al-Thaʿlabī (d. 427/1035), Abū l-Ḥasan al-Māwardī (d. 450/1058), al-Wāḥidī al-Nīsābūrī (d. 468/1076), al-Ḥusayn b. al-Farrāʾ al-Baghawī (d. 516/1122), Jār Allāh al-Zamakhsharī (d. 538/1144), Jalāl al-Dīn al-Maḥallī (d. 864/1459) and others.

Strong objections to the historicity of the satanic verses incident were, however, raised as early as the fourth/tenth century — as evidenced in *al-Nāsikh wa-l-mānsūkh* of Abū Jaʿfar al-Naḥḥās (d. 338/950) — and continued to be raised in subsequent centuries, to the point where the rejection of the historicity of the incident eventually became the only acceptable orthodox position (see ABROGATION; THEOLOGY AND THE QURʾĀN). From among the many important Qurʾān commentators who rejected the historicity of the satanic verses incident, the respective opinions of Abū Bakr b. al-ʿArabī (d. 543/1148), Fakhr al-Dīn al-Rāzī (d. 606/1210), Abū ʿAbdallāh al-Qurṭubī (d. 671/1273), Abū Ḥayyān al-Gharnāṭī (d. 744/1345) and ʿImād al-Dīn b. Kathīr (d. 773/1373) have been regularly invoked by their successors down to the present day. Probably the most authoritatively cited refutation of the incident, however, appears in the *al-Shifāʾ* of al-Qāḍī ʿIyāḍ al-Yaḥṣubī (d. 544/1149), a work written in demonstration of the superhuman qualities of Muḥammad (see NAMES OF THE PROPHET; but see also MIRACLES; MARVELS).

The historicity of the incident is rejected on two bases. First, the satanic verses story portrays Muḥammad as being (on at least one occasion) unable to distinguish between divine revelation and satanic suggestion. This was seen as calling into question the reliability of the revelatory process and thus the integrity of the text of the Qurʾān itself (see INIMITABILITY; CREATEDNESS OF THE QURʾĀN). The incident was thus viewed as repugnant to the doctrine of *ʿiṣmat al-anbiyāʾ*, divine protection of the prophets from sin and/or error, as it developed from the third/ninth century onwards, all theological schools coming eventually to agree that God protected prophets from error in the transmission of divine revelation (see IMPECCABILITY). The satanic verses incident was conceived to be an especially egregious instance of error since the praise of the deities of Quraysh uttered by Muḥammad in his recitation of the satanic verses would have been tantamount to the cardinal sin of *shirk* (associating divinity with an entity other than God; see POLYTHEISM AND ATHEISM). The claim that the Prophet could have committed *shirk* was denounced as *kufr* (unbelief). The doctrine of *ʿiṣma* has been most forcefully and consistently upheld by the Shīʿa (q.v.; see also SHĪʿISM AND THE QURʾĀN), for whom it is a central tenet. It therefore appears that no Shīʿī of any school has ever accepted the satanic verses incident. Those Sunnī scholars who did accept the incident had a slightly, but very significantly, different understanding of *ʿiṣma:* like Taqī l-Dīn b. Taymiyya (d. 728/1328), some of them held that prophets were not protected from error in the transmission of divine revelation, but rather from persisting in error after commission (Ahmed, Ibn Taymiyyah).

The historicity of the satanic verses incident is also rejected on the basis of the *isnād*s, the chains of transmission that carry the numerous reports of the incident. In the standard Islamic methodology developed by the scholars of ḥadīth (see ḤADĪTH AND THE QURʾĀN) for assessing the veracity of reports, a report is judged by the reputation for truthfulness of the individual transmitters who constitute a complete *isnād* that goes back to an eyewitness. The satanic verses incident is not carried by *isnād*s that are complete and sound *(ṣaḥīḥ);* at best, some of the *isnāds* are *ṣaḥīḥ mursal,* meaning that while the transmitters are bona fide, the chains are incomplete and do not go back to an eyewitness. Thus, the reports are viewed as insufficiently reliable to establish the factuality of the incident. The incident is not cited in any canonical ḥadīth collection, although it does appear in some non-canonical collections. Those scholars who acknowledged the historicity of the incident apparently had a different method for the assessment of reports than that which has become standard Islamic methodology. For example, Ibn Taymiyya took the position that since *tafsīr* and *sīra-maghāzī* reports were commonly transmitted by incomplete *isnād*s, these reports should not be assessed according to the completeness of the chains but rather on the basis of recurrent transmission of common meaning between reports (*al-tawātur bi-l-maʿnā;* Ahmed, Ibn Taymiyyah).

Other scholars accepted the idea that the fact of widespread transmission meant that the reports about the satanic verses incident could not be rejected outright but also took the position that the equal fact of the *ʿiṣma* of Muḥammad meant that the incident could not have taken place in the specific manner narrated. To reconcile the apparently contradictory epistemological claims of widespread transmission on the one hand and *ʿiṣma* on the other, scholars such as Ibn Ḥajar al-ʿAsqalānī (d. 852/1505) applied the principle of *taʾwīl* — what could be called rehabilitative interpretation — to the satanic verses reports so as to bring the narrative of the incident within the parameters of the permissibly conceivable. These scholars took the position that since Muḥammad simply could not have been deceived by Satan and have uttered the satanic verses himself, it must have happened that when the Prophet recited Q 53:19, he paused for breath and at this juncture Satan, or one of the unbelievers present, seized on the opportunity to utter the blasphemous verses (see BLASPHEMY) while imitating the Prophet's voice, with the result that those around assumed that the Prophet had uttered them. (None of the early reports actually presents the incident in this way.)

Islamic modernity has been especially forceful and consistent in its rejection of the historicity of the satanic verses incident. The modern *locus classicus* is probably the article "Masʾalat al-gharānīq wa-tafsīr al-āyāt" published by Muḥammad ʿAbduh in *al-Manār* in 1905; but widely-circulated refutations of the incident have also been authored by other influential moderns, including Muḥammad Ḥusayn Haykal (d. 1376/1956) in *Ḥayāt Muḥammad*, Sayyid Quṭb (d. 1387/1967) in *Fī ẓilāl al-Qurʾān*, Abū l-Aʿlā Mawdūdī (d. 1399/1979) in *Tafhīm al-Qurʾān*, and Muḥammad Nāṣir al-Dīn al-Albānī (d. 1420/1999) in *Naṣb al-majānīq li-nasf al-gharānīq* (see EXEGESIS OF THE QURʾĀN: EARLY MODERN AND CONTEMPORARY). Orientalists (see POST-ENLIGHTENMENT ACADEMIC STUDY OF THE QURʾĀN), including the most widely-read biographers of Muḥammad — such as William Muir, D.S. Margoliouth, W. Montgomery Watt, Maxime Rodinson and F.E. Peters — have tended (with few exceptions) just as forcefully to accept the historicity of the incident, the orientalist logic having been epitomized by Peters: "This is the indubitably authentic story — it is impossible to imagine a Muslim inventing such an inauspicious tale." The widespread acceptance of the incident by early Muslims suggests, however, that they did not view the incident as inauspicious and that they would presumably not have, on this basis at least, been adverse to inventing it.

The rejection — or simple omission from *tafsīr* and *sīra* works — of the satanic verses incident having become routine in modern Islamic thought, the incident was somewhat rudely re-introduced to the larger Muslim consciousness through the publication of Salman Rushdie's novel *The satanic verses* in 1988. While the hostile Muslim reaction had less to do with Rushdie's adoption of the satanic verses incident for his titular phrase and central scene than with other offensive motifs in the novel, it is nonetheless noteworthy that Rushdie's publication did not re-open the debate among Muslims over the historicity of the satanic verses incident. Its only result was reiteration of the orthodox view.

Shahab Ahmed

Bibliography

Primary: Abū Ḥayyān, *Baḥr*, ed. Cairo 1911, vi, 380-4; Baghawī, *Maʿālim*, ed. M. ʿAbdallāh al-Nimr et al., 8 vols., Riyadh 1993, v, 393-6; Ibn al-ʿArabī, *Aḥkām*, iii, 1286-91; Ibn Ḥajar al-ʿAsqalānī, *al-Kāfī fī takhrīj aḥādīth al-kashshāf*, Beirut 1966, 114; Ibn Kathīr, *Tafsīr*, 4 vols, Beirut 1966, iv, 655-8; ʿIyāḍ b. Mūsā, *Shifāʾ*, Amman 1986, ii, 275-310; *Jalālayn*, Cairo 1966, 312-3; Māwardī, *Nukat*, iv, 34-7; vi, 397-9; Qurṭubī, *Jāmiʿ*, xii, 79-88; Quṭb, *Ẓilāl*, vi, 3418-22; Rāzī, *Tafsīr*, Cairo 1933, xxiii, 48-55; Ṭabarī, *Tafsīr*, ed. ʿAlī et al., xvii, 186-95; Thaʿlabī, *al-Kashf wa-l-bayān ʿan tafsīr al-Qurʾān*, MS Topkapı Sarayı, Ahmet III, Tefsir 76/3, f. 41b-42a (ed. M. b. ʿĀshūr, 10 vols., Beirut 2002, vii, 29-30); Wāḥidī, *Asbāb*, 319-21; Zamakhsharī, *Kashshāf*, Beirut 1947, iv, 19.
Secondary: M. ʿAbduh, Masʾalat al-gharānīq wa-tafsīr al-āyāt, in *al-Manār* 4/3 (1905), 81-99; Sh. Ahmed, Ibn Taymiyyah and the satanic verses, in *SI* 87 (1998), 67-124; id., *The problem of the satanic verses and the formation of Islamic orthodoxy* (forthcoming); id., *The satanic verses incident in the memory of the early Muslim community. A study of the early* riwāyahs *and their* isnāds, Ph.D. diss., Princeton 1999; M. Nāṣir al-Dīn al-Albānī, *Naṣb al-majānīq li-nasf al-gharānīq*, Damascus 1952; J. Burton, Those are the high-flying cranes, in *JSS* 15 (1970), 246-65; M.Ḥ. Haykal, *Ḥayāt Muḥammad*, Cairo 1935, 140-5; D.S. Margoliouth, *Mohammed and the rise of Islam*, London 1906, 170-5; Mawdūdī, Abū l-Aʿlā, *Tafhīm al-Qurʾān*,

6 vols., Lahore 1958-62, iii, 237-45; Muir, *Mahomet,* ii, 149-59; al-Naḥḥās, Abū Jaʿfar Aḥmad b. Muḥammad, *al-Nāsikh wa-l-mansūkh fī kitāb Allāh ʿazza wa-jalla wa-khtilāf al-ʿulamāʾ fī dhālik,* ed. S. al-Lāḥim, 3 vols., Beirut 1991, i, 429-31, 448-51; ii, 527-9; F.E. Peters, *Muhammad and the origins of Islam,* Albany, NY 1994, 160-1; M. Rodinson, *Mohammed,* Harmondsworth 1971, 106-8; S. Rushdie, *The satanic verses,* London 1988; W.M. Watt, *Muhammad at Mecca,* Oxford 1953, 100-9.

Saul

Israelite king mentioned in both the Qurʾān and the Bible. Called Ṭālūt, the "tall one," in the Qurʾān, Saul is mentioned briefly in Q 2:246-51. After Moses (q.v.), the Israelites (see CHILDREN OF ISRAEL) asked an unnamed prophet (see PROPHETS AND PROPHETHOOD) — identified in qurʾānic commentaries as Ashmawīl or Shamwīl, Samuel (q.v.) — that God appoint a king so that they could fight in his path (see KINGS AND RULERS; PATH OR WAY). They were surprised to find that Saul was appointed, especially since he was a poor water-carrier. The Israelites considered themselves more worthy than he to exercise authority. The prophet assured them, however, that God had chosen him and had granted him knowledge and stature (see KNOWLEDGE AND LEARNING; AUTHORITY).

Saul came with a divine sign, the ark (q.v.) of the covenant (q.v.), which contained the *sakīna,* "tranquility" (see SHEKHINAH), and relics left by the family of Moses and Aaron (q.v.). Before fighting Goliath (q.v.; Jālūt), the Israelites were tested in a river (see TRIAL). They were prohibited from drinking water, and were allowed only to take small sips with their hands. Most of the warriors disqualified themselves from the army by ignoring this prohibition. After they crossed the river, Saul and his small band were frightened by the size of Goliath's army. Some within his army, however, assured others of the ability of a small army to triumph over a larger force. As they proceeded to fight, Q 2:251 states that, with God's help, David (q.v.) slew Goliath. God then granted David the kingdom and wisdom (q.v.), and taught him what he wished.

The exegetes greatly embellish the story of Saul and in doing so differ on many points. Citing different versions from various sources, al-Ṭabarī (d. 310/923; *Taʾrīkh,* i, 549-50; Eng. trans. Brinner, *History,* iii, 131) states that initially the Israelites rejected Saul because he was a descendant of Benjamin (q.v.) and was from the house of neither prophethood nor kingship. Saul was chosen as king because his height corresponded exactly to the length of his staff.

Some commentators state that Saul brought back the ark after the Amalekites had captured it during a battle. This was a sign from God (see SIGNS). The *sakīna,* which Saul brought back, is identified in some sources as the head of a dead cat, whereas in others it is a fragrant wind with a human face. According to al-Ṭabarī (ibid.), the *sakīna* was a basin of gold in which the hearts of the prophets were washed (see HEART). The modern Shīʿī commentator Ṭabaṭābāʾī (d. 1982; *Mīzān,* ad loc.; see SHĪʿISM AND THE QURʾĀN) sees the *sakīna* as "tranquility of the heart, firmness of purpose, and peace of mind."

The remains that Saul brought are identified as the sandals of Moses and the turban and staff of Aaron. Alternative understandings are that the remains refer to knowledge and the Torah (q.v.). The commentators also differ on the number of soldiers in Saul's army. Some claim that up to eighty thousand soldiers were asked not to drink from the river, which is identified as the river Jordan.

Most sources agree that David killed Goliath with a sling, although others say that David threw a stone. Saul became envious of David as he grew more popular. Before the battle, Saul promised to give his daughter in marriage to David if he killed Goliath. When David triumphed, Saul regretted his earlier promise and now stipulated that David slay three hundred more enemies. When David fulfilled this condition, too, Saul sought to have him killed, resulting in David's fleeing to the mountains.

Most commentators identify David's wisdom with the prophethood that he inherited from Samuel. Some state that God taught him the Psalms (q.v.) and the art of judging between people (see JUDGMENT; JUSTICE AND INJUSTICE). He also taught him the language of birds and ants.

Liyakat Takim

Bibliography

Primary: Kisāʾī, *Qiṣaṣ,* trans. W.M. Thackston, *The tales of the prophets of al-Kisa'i,* Boston 1978, 270-8; Ṭabarī, *Taʾrīkh,* ed. de Goeje; trans. W. Brinner, *The history of al-Ṭabarī.* iii. *The Children of Israel,* Albany 1991; Ṭabaṭābāʾī, *Mīzān,* 20 vols., Qom n.d.; Thaʿlabī, *Qiṣaṣ,* trans. W.M. Brinner, *ʿArāʾis al-majālis fī qiṣaṣ al-anbiyāʾ or "Lives of the prophets,"* Leiden 2002, 445-53; Yaʿqūbī, *Taʾrīkh,* 2 vols., Beirut n.d.

Secondary: M. Ayoub, *The Qurʾān and its interpreters,* 2 vols., Albany 1984; Jeffery, *For. vocab.,* 204 (on the form and etymology of "Ṭālūt"); M. Klar, *A popular retelling of Islamic stories. Job, Saul, David and Noah as portrayed in Thaʿlabī's* ʿArāʾis al-majālis, PhD thesis, Oxford 2002 (esp. chap. 7 on Saul); Speyer, *Erzählungen,* 364-71; R. Tottoli, *Bibical prophets in the Qurʾān and Muslim literature,* Richmond, Surrey 2002; B. Wheeler, *Prophets in the Qurʾān. An introduction to the Qurʾān and Muslim exegesis,* London 2002.

Sawda see WIVES OF THE PROPHET

Scholar

A learned person who has engaged in advanced study and acquired knowledge, generally in a particular field. The term *ʿālim,* most commonly used to designate "scholar" in Islamic societies, appears in the Qurʾān only as a description of God, in the sense of "knowing." The plural *ʿālimūn* is applied sometimes to God (cf. Q 21:51, 81) and sometimes to human beings (cf. Q 12:44; 29:43; 30:22), while the plural form *ʿulamāʾ,* which appears twice in the Qurʾān (cf. Q 26:197; 35:28), refers only to human beings. The Qurʾān also denotes knowledgeable or learned human beings by a number of phrases, including *ūlū l-ʿilm,* "those possessed of knowledge," *alladhīna ūtū l-ʿilm,* "those to whom knowledge has been given" and *alladhīna yaʿlamūn,* "those who know."

As the numerous appearances of the root *ʿ-l-m* suggest (Rosenthal, *Knowledge,* 19-22; cf. 30-1), the concept of knowledge *(ʿilm)* is central to the qurʾānic text (see KNOWLEDGE AND LEARNING). Knowledge appears as one of the principal divine attributes (see GOD AND HIS ATTRIBUTES). God's knowledge has no limits: God is "knowing of the hidden and the manifest" (*ʿālim al-ghayb wa-l-shahāda,* Q 6:73; 9:94, 105; 13:9; 23:92; 32:6; 39:46; 59:22; 62:8; 64:18; see HIDDEN AND THE HIDDEN); he "comprehends all things in mercy (q.v.) and knowledge" (Q 40:7), and "encompasses all things in knowledge" (Q 65:12). Like the term *ʿālim,* the word *ʿallām,* "most knowledgeable," is reserved for describing God (Q 5:109, 116; 9:78; 34:48) and *ʿalīm,* "most knowing," refers in most instances to God, who is frequently described as "most knowing and most wise" (*ʿalīm ḥakīm,* cf. Q 2:32; 4:11, 17, 24, 26, 92, 104, 111, 170; 6:83, 128, 139; 8:71; 9:15, 28, 60, 97, 106, 110; 12:6, 83, 100; 15:25; 22:52, 59; 24:18, 58, 59; 27:6; 33:1, 51; 43:84; 48:4; 49:8; 51:30; 60:10; 66:2; 76:3; note, however, among other exceptions, the use of *ʿalīm* in Q 12:55 to describe the prophet Joseph [q.v.] as *ḥafīẓ ʿalīm*).

God's knowledge is of an incalculably

superior order to that possible for human beings. Yet all knowledge derives from God, and he may choose to bestow a degree of understanding on some of his creatures (see, for example, Q 20:114, "Say: Lord! Increase me in knowledge"). Among those to whom God grants a portion of knowledge are his angels (see ANGEL), who assert, "We have no knowledge except what you have taught us" (Q 2:32), and prophets (see PROPHETS AND PROPHETHOOD): to Lot (q.v.), Joseph, Moses (q.v.), David (q.v.) and Solomon (q.v.), God gives judgment (q.v.; *ḥukm*) and knowledge (*ʿilm*, Q 12:22; 21:74, 79; 28:14; on the sense of *ḥukm* and *ḥikma* in the Qurʾān, see Rosenthal, *Knowledge*, 35-40). The Sunnī commentator al-Bayḍāwī (d. ca. 685/1286) glosses these paired gifts as "wisdom" (q.v.) and "prophethood" since "knowledge is appropriate for prophets" (Bayḍāwī, *Anwār*, i, 620, ad Q 21:74; cf. *Anwār*, ii, 78, ad Q 28:14). Moreover, God increases Saul (q.v.) "in knowledge and in body" (Q 2:247), a text taken by some Imāmī Shīʿī (see SHĪʿISM AND THE QURʾĀN) scholars as a proof that among the conditions for the imāmate is that the imām (q.v.) be the most learned among his subjects and the most excellent among them in good qualities (Ṭūsī, *Tibyān*, ii, 292).

The qurʾānic concept of knowledge is often closely connected to ideas of religious understanding and faith (q.v.; Rosenthal, *Knowledge*, 22-32; Rahman, *Major themes*, 34; Gilliot, ʿUlamāʾ). For example, the Qurʾān refers to "those given knowledge and faith" (*alladhīna ūtū l-ʿilm wa-l-īmān*, Q 30:56; see Māwardī, *Nukat*, iv, 323) and it states that "those who believe know it is the truth from their lord" (Q 2:26; for further examples, see Q 58:11, discussed below; Q 6:97-9; Ṭūsī, *Tibyān*, iv, 229-32; Rosenthal, *Knowledge*, 28-32). It is in this sense that the Qurʾān notes that most people lack knowledge (Q 6:37; 7:131, 187; 8:34; 10:55; 12:21, 40, 68; 16:38, 75, 101; 21:24; 27:61; 28:13, 57; 30:6, 30; 31:25; 34:28, 36; 39:29, 49; 40:57; 44:39; 45:26; 52:47), although they will come to know at the time of judgment (Q 15:3, 96; 19:75; 25:42; 29:66; 37:170; 40:70; 43:89; 72:24; 78:4, 5; see LAST JUDGMENT).

Yet the Qurʾān also indicates that some human beings other than prophets may be endowed by God with a measure of knowledge and understanding. The terms and phrases by which such persons are described have sometimes been understood by later commentators as references to those who pursue scholarship and, in particular, religious learning. For example, the Qurʾān states that "Only the knowledgeable ones (*ʿulamāʾ*) among God's servants (*ʿibād*) fear God" (Q 35:28; see further Māwardī, *Nukat*, iv, 471); and "[In these things] are signs for the knowing" (*al-ʿālimīn*, Q 30:22), a reference, according to the Sunnī jurist al-Māwardī (d. 450/1058), to jinn (q.v.) and humans, or to the *ʿulamāʾ* (Māwardī, *Nukat*, iv, 306; for similar verses, see Q 6:97, 98; 7:32; 9:11; 10:5; 29:43, 49). The Qurʾān refers in several instances to "those who know" (*alladhīna yaʿlamūn*; Q 39:9 asks, "Are those who know and those who do not know equal?"); it also recognizes "people who understand" (*qawm yafqahūn*, Q 6:98) and "people who know" (*qawm yaʿlamūn*, Q 2:230; 6:97, 105; 7:32; 9:11; 10:5; 27:52; 41:3); "those who have been given knowledge" (*alladhīna ūtū l-ʿilm*, Q 16:27; 17:107; 22:54; 28:80; 29:49; 30:56; 34:6; 47:16; 58:11), and "the possessors of knowledge" (*ūlū l-ʿilm*, Q 3:18; see also Q 12:76). In Q 16:27, where the context is eschatological (see ESCHATOLOGY), the phrase "those given knowledge" (*alladhīna ūtū l-ʿilm*) refers, according to al-Bayḍāwī, to prophets and the *ʿulamāʾ* or alternatively to the angels (Bayḍāwī, *Anwār*, i, 513); for the Imāmī Shīʿī scholar al-Ṭūsī (d. 460/1067), the phrase refers to "those given knowledge and cognizance *(maʿrifa)* of God" (Ṭūsī, *Tibyān,* vi, 374). In other cases, the same qurʾānic phrase connotes the recognition of divine revelation and the preservation of it from error and alteration (Q 17:107; 29:49; 34:6; cf. Bayḍāwī, *Anwār,* ii, 99, ad Q 29:49; see REVELATION AND INSPIRATION; CORRUPTION; FORGERY). The Qurʾān also recognizes knowledgeable persons among earlier religious communities (see RELIGIOUS PLURALISM AND THE QURʾĀN); for example, Q 26:197 refers to "the learned ones *(ʿulamāʾ)* of the Banū Isrāʾīl" (see CHILDREN OF ISRAEL) and at Q 4:162, the phrase "those who are firm in knowledge" (*al-rāsikhūn fī l-ʿilm*) is sometimes taken as a reference to knowledgeable Jews (see JEWS AND JUDAISM), such as ʿAbdallāh b. Salām and his companions (Ṭūsī, *Tibyān,* iii, 389; Bayḍāwī, *Anwār,* i, 241). The verse Q 58:11 ("God will raise by degrees those among you who believe and those to whom knowledge has been given") is taken by al-Bayḍāwī as a reference to the *ʿulamāʾ,* who will be especially elevated for their combination of knowledge *(ʿilm)* and action *(ʿamal)*. In support of this interpretation, the commentator cites the well-known ḥadīth according to which the virtue of the scholar exceeds that of the worshipper (Bayḍāwī, *Anwār,* ii, 320; for the ḥadīth, see references in Wensinck, *Concordance,* v, 160; see ḤADĪTH AND THE QURʾĀN). Similar interpretations are recorded in some of the exegetical literature for several other qurʾānic passages, including "We raise by degrees whom we please" (Q 6:83; cf. Māwardī, *Nukat,* ii, 139; Bayḍāwī, *Anwār,* i, 298), and "those possessed of knowledge" (*ūlū l-ʿilm,* Q 3:18; cf. Abū l-Futūḥ Rāzī, *Rawḥ,* i, 529, although here the Shīʿī author states his preference for taking the phrase as a reference to ʿAlī; see ʿALĪ B. ABĪ ṬĀLIB).

The qurʾānic phrase "those possessed of authority among [you]" *(ūlī l-amri min[kum])*, which occurs twice in the Qurʾān (Q 4:59, "Obey God, obey the messenger [q.v.] and those possessed of authority [q.v.] among you" and Q 4:83, "If they had referred it to the messenger and to those possessed of authority among them, then those who formulate ideas among them would have known it"; see OBEDIENCE; KINGS AND RULERS), has also sometimes been interpreted as a reference to the *ʿulamāʾ*. This interpretation, supported by a number of ḥadīths, is already recorded by al-Ṭabarī (d. 310/923), who nevertheless endorses the more commonly expressed Sunnī view that the phrase refers to the holders of political authority (see POLITICS AND THE QURʾĀN), to whom obedience is due insofar as their commands are in accordance with God's (Ṭabarī, *Tafsīr,* viii, 495-504). Similar assessments appear in the works of al-Māwardī (*Nukat,* i, 499-500, 511), al-Zamakhsharī (d. 538/1144; *Kashshāf,* i, 535-6) and al-Bayḍāwī (*Anwār,* i, 214-5, 221). By contrast, Sunnī exegetes Fakhr al-Dīn al-Rāzī (d. 606/1209; *Tafsīr,* x, 143-8) and Ibn Kathīr (d. 774/1373; *Tafsīr,* ii, 326) prefer to interpret the phrase *ūlī l-amr* as a reference to the *ʿulamāʾ*. The Imāmī Shīʿī commentators al-Ṭūsī (d. 460/1067) and Abū l-Futūḥ Rāzī (d. 538/1144) interpret the phrase as a reference to the imāms of the family of Muḥammad (Ṭūsī, *Tibyān,* iii, 236, 273; Abū l-Futūḥ Rāzī, *Rawḥ,* i, 784; ii, 15; see FAMILY OF THE PROPHET; PEOPLE OF THE HOUSE).

Another qurʾānic verse that has contributed much to discussions of knowledge and scholarship is Q 3:79, in which the Qurʾān summons its audience to be "masters" *(rabbāniyyīn)* in the teaching of scripture and study (variant readings of the latter part of the verse are presented in the exegetical literature; see READINGS OF THE QURʾĀN). This qurʾānic text has figured with particular prominence in Ṣūfī theories of knowledge (Böwering, *Mystical,* 226-30; Chittick, *Knowledge,* 149; see ṢŪFISM AND THE QUR'ĀN). For the term *rabbānī,* the classical commentators record several interpretations, most of which emphasize the pursuit of religious knowledge, although a number of secondary interpretations imply social and political leadership (Māwardī, *Nukat,* i, 405; Ṭūsī, *Tibyān,* ii, 511; Abū l-Futūḥ Rāzī, *Rawḥ,* i, 593).

Louise Marlow

Bibliography

Primary: Abū l-Futūḥ Rāzī, *Rawḥ,* 5 vols., Qom 1983; Bayḍāwī, *Anwār;* Ibn Kathīr, *Tafsīr,* 7 vols., Beirut 1966; *Lisān al-ʿArab,* Cairo n.d., xi, 140-8; xv, 310-16 (entries *ʿ-r-f, ʿ-l-m*); Māwardī, *Nukat;* Rāzī, *Tafsīr,* 32 vols., Cairo 1934-62; Ṭabarī, *Tafsīr,* ed. Shākir; Ṭūsī, *Tibyān;* Zamakhsharī, *Kashshāf,* 4 vols., Cairo 1966.

Secondary: Böwering, *Mystical;* W.C. Chittick, *The Sufi path of knowledge,* Albany 1989; Cl. Gilliot, ʿUlamāʾ (1), in *EI²,* x, 801-5; R.P. Mottahedeh, *Loyalty and leadership in an early Islamic society,* Princeton 1980; F. Rahman, *Major themes of the Qurʾān,* Minneapolis 1994; F. Rosenthal, *Knowledge triumphant. The concept of knowledge in medieval Islam,* Leiden 1970; Wensinck, *Concordance.*

Science and the Qurʾān

In his anthropological history of India, Abū Rayḥān al-Bīrūnī (d. ca. 442/1050), one of the most celebrated Muslim scientists of the classical period, starts a chapter "On the configuration of the heavens and the earth according to [Indian] astrologers," with a long comparison between the cultural imperatives of Muslim and Indian sciences. The views of Indian astrologers, al-Bīrūnī maintains,

> have developed in a way which is different from those of our [Muslim] fellows; this is because, unlike the scriptures revealed before it, the Qurʾān does not articulate on this subject [of astronomy], or any other [field of] necessary [knowledge] any assertion that would require erratic interpretations in order to harmonize it with that which is known by necessity (Bīrūnī, *Taḥqīq,* 219).

The Qurʾān, adds al-Bīrūnī, does not speak on matters which are subjects of hopeless differences, such as history (see HISTORY AND THE QURʾĀN). To be sure, Islam has suffered from people who claimed to be Muslims but retained many of the teachings of earlier religions and claimed that these teachings are part of the doctrines of Islam. Such, for example, were the Manichaeans, whose religious doctrine, together with their erroneous views about the heavens (see HEAVEN AND SKY; PLANETS AND STARS), were wrongly attributed to Islam (Bīrūnī, *Taḥqīq,* 220). Such attributions of scientific views to the Qurʾān are, according to al-Bīrūnī, false claims of un-Islamic origins. In contrast, all the religious and transmitted books of the Indians do indeed speak "of the configuration of the universe in a way which contradicts the truth which is known to their own astrologers." Driven, however, by the need to uphold the religious traditions, Indian astrologers pretend to believe in the astrological doctrines of these books even when they are aware of their falsity. With the passage of time, accurate astronomical doctrines were mixed with those advanced in the religious books, leading to the confusion one encounters in Indian astronomy (Bīrūnī, *Taḥqīq,* 220-1; see Fig. VI for a later example of such "confusion" — in this case, an Indian map of the world that is replete with details derived from legends surrounding Alexander the Great, including also some qurʾānic details of the life of Dhū l-Qarnayn; see ALEXANDER; MYTHS AND LEGENDS IN THE QURʾĀN).

Although not all Indian religious views contradict the dictates of the astronomical profession, the conflation of religious and astronomical knowledge undermines Indian astronomy and accounts for its errors and weaknesses. And this conflation of scripture and science is contrasted by al-Bīrūnī with the Islamic astronomical tradition which, in his view, suffers from no such shortcomings (although scripture and science may not have been conflated in the classical Islamic period, see the *qibla* [q.v.] compass as depicted in Figs. IV and V for evidence of a type of complimentary relationship between the two that dates to the early centuries of Islam; see also SCRIPTURE AND THE QUR᾿ĀN; THEOLOGY AND THE QUR᾿ĀN). In al-Bīrūnī's view, therefore, the Qur᾿ān does not interfere in the business of science nor does it infringe on the realm of science.

Far from al-Bīrūnī's contentions, contemporary Islamic discourse on the Qur᾿ān and science abounds with assertions of the relationship between the two. This presumed relationship is construed in a variety of ways, the most common of which are the efforts to prove the divine nature of the Qur᾿ān through modern science. These efforts cover a wide range of activities including the establishment of institutions, holding conferences, writing books and articles, and the use of the internet to promote the idea of the scientific miracles of the Qur᾿ān (see MIRACLES; MARVELS; EXEGESIS OF THE QUR᾿ĀN: EARLY MODERN AND CONTEMPORARY). For example, a recent website search listed slightly fewer than two million occurrences on Islam and science, most of which assert that the Qur᾿ān's prediction of many of the theories and truths of modern science is evidence of its miraculous nature and its divine origins (Muẓaffar Iqbal, Islam and modern science, 15, 38; see INIMITABILITY; REVELATION AND INSPIRATION). Such contentions are not just part of folk belief but are also reflected in the work and writings of many contemporary Muslim intellectuals. As a manifestation of the popularity of this idea, the Muslim World League at Mecca formed in the 1980s the Committee on the Scientific Miracles of the Qur᾿ān and the Sunna (traditions of the Prophet; see SUNNA; ḤADĪTH AND THE QUR᾿ĀN). The Committee has since convened numerous international conferences and sponsored various intellectual activities, all aimed at exploring and corroborating the connections between science and the Qur᾿ān. A recent meeting of this Committee in Cairo, reported in the mass media, urged Muslims to employ the "scientific truths which were confirmed in the verses of the Qur᾿ān and which, only recently, modern science has been able to discover" as a corrective to the current misunderstanding of Islam. These truths prove that "Islam is a religion of science." The current president of the Committee, Zaghloul El-Naggar, asserts that it was

> only after man entered the age of scientific discoveries, possessed the most accurate instruments of scientific research, and was able to mobilize armies of researchers from all over the world... that we began to understand the meaning of God's word, may He be exalted, "a time is fixed for every prophecy; you will come to know in time" (Q 6:67).

This verse, according to El-Naggar, refers to the scientific truths that are in the Qur᾿ān that would be discovered in modern times, centuries after the revelation, and would "astound the contemporary scientists and thinkers of the world" (*al-Sharq al-Awsaṭ*, 5 Sept. 2003). According to him, these scientific miracles of the Qur᾿ān are the only weapon with which contemporary Muslims can defend the Qur᾿ān and the only convincing language in this age of science and materialism (ibid., 23 Sept. 2003).

The qur'ānic attitude towards science, in fact, the very relationship between the two, is not readily identifiable and the discordance between the classical and modern Islamic views on this subject is substantial (see TRADITIONAL DISCIPLINES OF QUR'ĀNIC STUDY). To be sure, almost all sources, classical and modern, agree that the Qur'ān condones, even encourages the acquisition of science and scientific knowledge, and urges humans to reflect on the natural phenomena as signs of God's creation (q.v.; see also NATURE AS SIGNS; REFLECTION AND DELIBERATION; KNOWLEDGE AND LEARNING). In fact, a survey of the material culture produced in the Islamic world (see MATERIAL CULTURE AND THE QUR'ĀN) manifests a plethora of "scientific" instruments inscribed with qur'ānic citations (see e.g. Figs. I and III). Most sources also argue that doing science is an act of religious merit and, to some, even a collective duty of the Muslim community. Yet, as actual debates of the Qur'ān and science show, the points of contention are far more significant than this one general convergence. More than any other place, these debates can be traced in interpretations of the Qur'ān, and in several other writings in which specific uses of the Qur'ān are promoted or where a qur'ānic framework and philosophy of science is adduced. Therefore, the starting point for the study of the Qur'ān and science is not the Qur'ān itself since, as we will see, there are considerable differences in the interpretation of the verses that may have a connection to science or the natural phenomena. For this reason, it is not useful to try to ascertain a particular qur'ānic position on science. Rather, it is more productive to look at the way in which the relationship between science and the Qur'ān has been viewed by various Muslim thinkers, albeit with varying degrees of authority. The main source in which qur'ānic paradigms of science are articulated is the genre of qur'ānic exegesis (*tafsīr,* plural *tafāsīr;* see EXEGESIS OF THE QUR'ĀN: CLASSICAL AND MEDIEVAL). Much as they insist on grounding themselves in the immutable text of the Qur'ān, exegetical works are repositories of larger cultural debates and reflect the views prevailing in their times and places. Rather than identifying one fixed qur'ānic paradigm of science, the task then becomes one of tracing the evolution of the Islamic discourse on the Qur'ān and science and adducing some of the factors that shaped this evolutionary process.

Classical qur'ānic exegetical works contain much material of possible scientific import. Despite the contemporary interest, however, in the Qur'ān and science, this aspect of exegesis has not received much scholarly attention. One possible reason for this neglect is that, collectively, these traditional materials do not add up to what might be legitimately called a scientific interpretation of the Qur'ān. Traditional interpreters did not present themselves as engaging in such an interpretive exercise. A minority of medieval scholars, notably Abū Ḥāmid al-Ghazālī (d. 505/1111) and Jalāl al-Dīn al-Suyūṭī (d. 911/1505), maintained that the Qur'ān is a comprehensive source of knowledge, including scientific knowledge (Dhahabī, *Mufassirūn,* ii, 454-64). The basis of the contentions of al-Ghazālī and al-Suyūṭī are such verses in the Qur'ān as "for we have revealed to you the book (q.v.) as an exposition of every thing" (Q 16:89). It should be noted, however, that the same verse starts with "Remind them of the day when we shall call from every people a witness against them, and make you a witness over them" (see WITNESSING AND TESTIFYING; LAST JUDGMENT). After describing the book as an exposition of everything, the verse continues to say "and as guidance and grace (q.v.) and happy tidings for those who submit" (see ERROR; ASTRAY; BLESSING; MERCY; GOOD NEWS). Therefore, the likely reference in this verse to the exposition of knowledge is connected to knowledge of what would happen in the hereafter and the fate of believers (see BELIEF AND UNBELIEF; REWARD AND PUNISHMENT; ESCHATOLOGY; FAITH). Despite their claims, neither al-Ghazālī nor al-Suyūṭī proceeds to correlate the qurʾānic text to science, in a systematic interpretive exercise. Moreover, there are no instances in which these two or other exegetes claim authority in scientific subjects on account of their knowledge of the Qurʾān. Perhaps the most relevant reason for the absence of an articulation of a qurʾānic paradigm of science in premodern times is that there was no need for such an articulation in the absence of the counter-claims of a hegemonic culture of science and the ideological outlook that accompanied the rise of modern science (Iqbal, Islam and modern science, 30).

To be sure, scientific subjects do come up in many medieval qurʾānic exegetical works, but their treatment in these sources is radically different from their contemporary counterpart. The contemporary uses of some of the commonly cited "scientific" verses will be discussed below but, first, I will examine the meaning attributed to these verses in classical commentaries, including some in which such scientific discourse is most pronounced, namely the works of scholars such as al-Zamakhsharī (d. 583/1144) and Fakhr al-Dīn al-Rāzī (d. 606/1210).

The instances of scientific discourse in the classical qurʾānic commentaries are invariably mixed with other kinds of discourse that have no connection to science. Qurʾān commentators had a distinct conception of what constitutes the main thematic emphasis of the Qurʾān and they often, though not always, presented their detailed discussions of specific subjects within this framework. Thus, for example, in his commentary on Q 7:54, al-Rāzī spells out the four themes around which the various discussions of the Qurʾān revolve *(madār amr al-Qurʾān)*. Significantly, the verse in question relates to the natural order. It reads

> Surely your lord (q.v.) is God who created the heavens and the earth (q.v.) in six days, then assumed the throne (see THRONE OF GOD; ANTHROPOMORPHISM). He covers up the day with night which comes chasing it fast (see DAY AND NIGHT); and the sun (q.v.) and the moon (q.v.) and the stars are subjugated by his command. It is his to create and command. Blessed be God, the lord of all the worlds.

Before embarking on a lengthy discussion of this verse, al-Rāzī lists the four overriding qurʾānic themes: the oneness of God (see GOD AND HIS ATTRIBUTES), prophethood (see PROPHETS AND PROPHETHOOD), resurrection (q.v.) and the omnipotence of God (see POWER AND IMPOTENCE) or the related question of predestination (Rāzī, *Tafsīr,* xiv, 96 f., ad loc.; see also Abū Ḥayyān, *Nahr,* i, 809-11; see FREEDOM AND PREDESTINATION); all other themes, including the ones in this verse, ultimately underscore one of these four essential motifs. Al-Rāzī proceeds to explain the manner in which this seemingly unrelated verse does indeed relate to the oneness and omnipotence of God — and lists several interpretations that confirm this correlation. One is to argue that the heavens and the earth are created with a particular size, while their natures do not preclude the possibiliy of having a larger or smaller size. This shows that a willing maker chose to give them this specific size and no other, thus proving the existence of a free and willing creator (Rāzī, *Tafsīr*, xiv, 96-7). Alternatively, the creation at a specific time of the heavens and the earth, when they could have been created at an earlier or a later time, is an act of choice by God, and not due to the inherent nature of either. The same thing also applies to the configurations and the positions of the various parts of the universe relative to each other, and so on (ibid., 97-8). After a lengthy digression to disprove the attribution of place and direction to God (ibid., 98 f.; see SPATIAL RELATIONS; TIME), al-Rāzī returns to the first theme, albeit from a different perspective. He enumerates the benefits that result from the succession of day and night, again as proof that God creates the world in a specific fashion in order to maximize the benefit for humans from this world (ibid., 117). He then undertakes a linguistic exploration, typical of qurʾānic commentaries of all kinds (see GRAMMAR AND THE QURʾĀN), of the meaning of the word "subjugated" *(musakhkharāt)*. The sun, he reports, has two motions: one cyclical rotation is completed in a year, and another in a day. The cycle of night and day, however, is not due to the motion of the sun but to the motion of the great orb, which is also the throne (ibid., 117-8). Moreover, each heavenly body or planet has an angel assigned to it to move it when it rises and sets (ibid., 118-9), and God has endowed the throne, or the great outer orb, with the power to influence all the other orbs, thus enabling it to move them by compulsion from east to west, i.e. in the opposite direction to their west-to-east slow motion (ibid., 119-20). This, according to al-Rāzī, is the meaning of "subjugation": that orbs and planets are organized by God in a particular order for no inherent reason of their own, so that they produce optimal benefit for humans (ibid., 120; see GRACE; BLESSING).

Al-Rāzī's approach is typical of many other commentators, both in its linguistic turn, and in its emphasis on the benefits of creation to humans as evidence of the existence of the willing creator. Commentators often focus not just on the meaning and appropriateness of using certain terms but also on the logic of the order of their appearance in the Qurʾān. Such, for example, is one of the main arguments raised in al-Rāzī's commentary on Q 2:22: "[It is he] who made the earth a bed for you, the sky a canopy, and he sends forth rain from the skies that fruits may grow as food for your sustenance (q.v.). So, do not make another the equal of God knowingly" (see POLYTHEISM AND ATHEISM; IDOLS AND IMAGES). In this verse, al-Rāzī maintains, there are five kinds of signs (q.v.) or proofs (see PROOF) that reinforce belief in God: two from within the self *(dalāʾil al-anfus)* and three from the external world (*dalāʾil al-āfāq;* Rāzī, *Tafsīr*, ii, 101). Since people are more likely to appreciate signs from within themselves and since self-knowledge is clearer than other kinds of knowledge, the Qurʾān first refers to the creation of humans. An added reason for beginning with this proof is that all of God's gifts to humanity presume the prior creation of humans in order to benefit from these gifts (see GIFT-GIVING; GRATITUDE AND INGRATITUDE); in this way the Qurʾān accounts for the creation of humans before accounting for the creation of that from which they benefit. Al-Rāzī also suggests another reason for starting with the creation of humankind, namely that all the signs of the heavens and the earth have their counterparts in humans, whereas the reverse is not true; the unique traits created in human beings include life (q.v.), power, desire (see WISH AND DESIRE), intellection (see INTELLECT) and so on. Elsewhere al-Rāzī explores the reasons why the word "heavens" occurs before the word "earth" in most cases where they occur together in the Qur᾽ān (see PAIRS AND PAIRING). Among the virtues of the heavens is that they are ornamented by God with the bright stars, the sun and the moon as well as the throne, the pen (see INSTRUMENTS; WRITING AND WRITING MATERIALS) and the Preserved Tablet (q.v.). God also uses complimentary names to refer to the heavens in order to underscore their high status. Other merits of the heavens are that they are the abode of angels (see ANGEL) where God is never disobeyed (see OBEDIENCE; DISOBEDIENCE; FALL OF MAN; DEVIL), that prayers are directed to them (see PRAYER), hands are raised towards them in supplication and they have perfect color and shape. The one advantage of the heavens over the earth which invokes a scientific view common at the time is the notion that the heavenly world influences the sub-lunar world, whereas the earth is the passive agent that is acted upon. Al-Rāzī also lists some of the merits of the earth according to those who prefer it to the heavens, including the fact that prophets are sent in it and mosques (see MOSQUE) for the worship (q.v.) of God are built in it (ibid., 106-7). The noticeable feature in this comparison is the absence of any discussion of a natural superiority of heaven over earth, a point to which we will return. Suffice it here to note that rather than using the Qur᾽ān to elucidate science or science to extract the proper meaning of the qur᾽ānic text, quasi-scientific discussions often aim at explaining the order of words in qur᾽ānic verses and at demonstrating the linguistic, rhetorical miracles of the Qur᾽ān (see RHETORIC AND THE QUR᾽ĀN; ARABIC LANGUAGE; LANGUAGE AND STYLE OF THE QUR᾽ĀN). Indeed, it is not just the creation of a perfect and wondrous world that is underscored in the commentaries, but also the fact that God refers to this creation by using words that cannot be emulated by the most eloquent humans (ibid., 105).

The marvel of creation is a recurrent theme of qur᾽ānic commentaries. These marvels are viewed as signs of God and proofs that he exists, is all-powerful and all-knowing, and is the willing creator of all being. The frequent summons in the Qur᾽ān for humans to observe and reflect on the heavens and the earth (e.g. Q 10:101) are seen by many commentators as evidence that there is no way to know God directly and that he can only be known by contemplating his signs (e.g. Rāzī, *Tafsīr,* xvii, 169; Abū Ḥayyān, *Nahr,* ii [pt. 1], 49; also Zamakhsharī, *Kashshāf,* i, 32). At a basic level, such reflection leads to the conclusion that there is order and wisdom in creation, which in turn means that a wise maker must have created it. The complex "secrets" of creation also lead humans to recognize the limits of human comprehension and its inability to grasp the infinite knowledge and wisdom (q.v.) of God. The more one delves into the details of creation, the stronger the belief one develops in the wisdom behind it (Rāzī, *Tafsīr,* xiv, 121, ad Q 7:54).

One of the commonly cited verses which urge contemplation of the signs of the heavens and the earth is Q 3:190-1:

> In the creation of the heavens and the earth, the alteration of night and day, are signs for the wise. Those who remember God (see REMEMBRANCE), standing or sitting or lying on their sides, who reflect on and contemplate the creation of the heavens and the earth, [say]: Our lord, not in vain have you made them. All praise (q.v.) be to you, preserve us from the torment of hell (see HELL AND HELLFIRE).

In his commentary on this verse, al-Rāzī contends that the human mind is incapable of comprehending the manner in which a small leaf on a tree is created, how it is structured or how it grows; needless to say, the larger task of discovering God's wisdom in the creation of the heavens and the earth is completely impossible. One must therefore concede that the creator is beyond full comprehension. Consequently, one should admit the utmost wisdom and great secrets (q.v.) of creation, even if there is no way of knowing what these are (see HIDDEN AND THE HIDDEN). Ultimately, when people reflect on the heavens and the earth, they will come to realize that their creator did not create them in vain but for a remarkable wisdom and great secrets and that the intellects are incapable of comprehending them (Rāzī, *Tafsīr,* ix, 128-41). This means that the ultimate purpose of reflection is to establish the limitations of human knowledge and its inability to comprehend creation, not to establish a scientific fact and demonstrate its correspondence with the Qurʾān. Moreover, as understood in these commentaries, the contemplation for which the qurʾānic text calls lies outside the text, in nature, and does not move back to the text — nor does it follow or correspond to any particular qurʾānic scheme. As such, contemplation does not imply a correlation between science — whether natural philosophy (see PHILOSOPHY AND THE QURʾĀN), astronomy, or medicine (see MEDICINE AND THE QURʾĀN) — and the Qurʾān. The Qurʾān, according to these commentaries, directs people to reflect on the wisdom of the creation of nature but provides no details on the natural order or on ways of deciphering it; these details, if and when they appear in classical qurʾānic commentaries, are drawn from the prevailing scientific knowledge of the time. This overview of the mode in which the commentators invoke creation as evidence of God and his traits illustrates the fundamental divide between science and the Qurʾān.

As noted above, the qurʾānic signs of creation are often classified into those from within the self *(dalāʾil al-anfus)* and those from the external world *(dalāʾil al-āfāq)*. Alternatively, the qurʾānic signs are classified into signs in the heavens, on earth, or in what falls in between. The heavenly signs include the movements of the celestial orbs, their magnitudes and positions, as well as signs specific to different components of the heavens, such as the sun, the moon and the planets. The earthly signs include minerals, plants and humans (e.g. Qurṭubī, *Jāmiʿ,* ii, 191-202; Abū Ḥayyān, *Nahr,* i, 156 f.; Rāzī, *Tafsīr,* ii, 101 f.; ix, 137; xvii, 169; see METALS AND MINERALS; AGRICULTURE AND VEGETATION). The most striking feature of the discussions of these signs, especially the heavenly ones, is the mixing of some information drawn from astronomy and natural philosophy with a wealth of other non-scientific material. Thus, for example, one of the benefits of the rising and setting of the moon is that, while its rising helps night travelers find their way, its setting shelters fugitives trying to escape from their enemies. Additionally, among the signs of the heavens is the fact that the shooting stars or meteors serve as missiles that drive devils away and keep them from spying on the angels in the heavens (Rāzī, *Tafsīr,* ii, 108-9; cf. ibid., xv, 76; xvii, 37; Qurṭubī, *Jāmiʿ,* vii, 230 f.; viii, 38; Zamakhsharī, *Kashshāf,* i, 291, 354-5; Abū Ḥayyān, *Nahr,* i [pt. 2], 7; ii [pt. 1], 49-50). Another common feature of the commentaries on what is often referred to as the "sign verses" (see PORTENTS) is that, while the complexity and perfection of creation is, in and of itself, a sign of the wise creator, the primary proof is not just in the creation of a complex natural order but in the benefits to humanity from this creation. A typical commentary thus focuses on the specific way in which various aspects of the natural phenomena are arranged in order to maximize the benefits to humanity from them. Since there is no inherent reason for the universe to be arranged in a particular fashion, then there must be a willing maker who chose to create it as such. Thus, it is the benefit to humans that ultimately proves the existence of a wise and willing creator. To be sure, the subjugation by God of all creation in the service of human beings serves both their needs for survival and their independence without which they cannot worship God; as such, benefit lies both in this world and in the hereafter (Zamakhsharī, *Kashshāf*, i, 43; Abū Ḥayyān, *Nahr*, i, 54). But benefit and utility are not the ultimate purposes of creation; rather, benefit is what induces people to reflect on God's creation, recognize the magnitude of his power and then believe in him.

While material benefit serves as a secondary objective of creation, the primary objective is the religious benefit in the world to come, which results from belief in God. Such, for example, is the gist of a commentary on the above-mentioned verse Q 2:22: "[It is he] who made for the earth a bed for you, the sky a canopy, and sends forth rain from the skies that fruits may grow as food for your sustenance. So, do not make another the equal of God knowingly." According to one commentator, the term bed *(firāsh)* in this verse means a place on which people could walk and settle; and all parts of the earth play a role in making human life on earth possible (Qurṭubī, *Jāmi'*, i, 227 f.). The ultimate meaning of the verse, however, is that God made humans independent of the rest of creation so that they should not compromise, out of need, their exclusive worship of God. Alternatively, Ṣūfīs argue that this verse teaches the way of poverty *(faqr)* and self-denial by directing people to sleep in the open, with the earth as bed and the sky as cover (ibid., 229-31; see ASCETICISM; ṢŪFISM AND THE QUR'ĀN; POVERTY AND THE POOR). Other verses occasion more detailed debate of the meaning of benefit, as in the commentaries on Q 2:29: "He made for you all that lies within the earth, then turned to the firmament. He proportioned seven skies; he has knowledge of every thing." Al-Qurṭubī (d. 671/1272) reports that some people argue that this verse proves that the rule with regard to all created things is that they are licit unless there is clear textual evidence that prohibits or regulates them (see FORBIDDEN; LAWFUL AND UNLAWFUL). Benefit here is understood as making use of all created things. Without questioning this notion of permissibility or licitness, al-Qurṭubī maintains that the verse means that all things are created for human beings so that they may reflect on the miracle of creation and thereby believe in God, which is the ultimate benefit for human beings (Qurṭubī, *Jāmi'*, i, 250-2; also Zamakhsharī, *Kashshāf*, i, 43; Abū Ḥayyān, *Nahr*, i, 54).

Classical commentaries often introduce elaborate discussions of scientific subjects to illustrate the idea of God's wise choice of creation as a way of maximizing human benefit. For example, in his commentary on Q 2:22 mentioned above, al-Rāzī outlines the prerequisites for making the earth a bed *(firāsh)*. After asserting that one of these prerequisites is that the earth does not move, al-Rāzī proceeds to prove his contention (Rāzī, *Tafsīr*, ii, 101 f.). If the earth were to move, its motion would be either linear or circular. If it were linear, it would be falling. But since heavier objects move faster than slower ones, the earth would fall at a faster speed than the people living on its surface, with the result that they would be separated from the surface of the earth and hence could not use it as a bed. If, on the other hand, the earth's motion were circular, the benefit for humans from it would not be complete since a person moving in a direction opposite to its motion would never reach his destination. Al-Rāzī then surveys the evidence adduced by various scholars to prove that the earth is stationary. What follows is a quasi-scientific discussion which draws on but does not privilege science as the authoritative reference on this subject. Some, al-Rāzī reports, argue that the earth is bottomless and thus has no bottom to move to, which is why it does not move. This view, al-Rāzī contends, is wrong because all created bodies are finite. The finitude of created bodies, it should be noted, is asserted on theological and not scientific grounds. Others concede the finitude of objects but argue that the earth is still because it is a semi-sphere whose flat bottom floats on the surface of water. Al-Rāzī rejects this argument on the grounds that even if this were true, both the earth and the water on which it floats could be moving. Moreover, al-Rāzī wonders, why would one side of the earth be flat and the other round? Again, while al-Rāzī could have invoked arguments for the sphericity of the earth which are more in line with the sciences of the time, his response is notably general and not grounded in science. A third argument which al-Rāzī rejects is that the orbs attract the different parts of the earth with equal forces from all directions; these equal forces would cancel each other at the center, which is where the earth is located. This theory is rejected because lighter objects, and those farther away from the center of the earth, would be attracted faster than those which are heavier or closer to the center and this would mean that the atoms that are thrown out, away from the center, would never fall back to the surface. Irrespective of how scientific these arguments appear to us, from our modern perspective of science, they do not reflect the prevalent scientific view of al-Rāzī's time. The closest he gets to engaging the then-prevalent understanding of science is when he reports, and rejects, the Aristotelian argument that the earth, by nature, seeks the center of the universe. This, al-Rāzī rightly notes, is the view of Aristotle and the majority of his followers among the natural philosophers. Al-Rāzī objects to this view on the grounds that the earth shares the trait of physicality with all other bodies in the universe and its acquisition of a specialized trait that makes it stationary is by necessity logically contingent. Thus, it is the free volition of the maker, and not any inherent nature, that accounts for the stillness of the earth. If anything, al-Rāzī adds, the nature of the earth is to sink in water and God reverses its nature so that it does not submerge in water in order to maximize the human benefit and to make it a place over which they can reside (Rāzī, *Tafsīr,* ii, 102-4).

This elaborate, quasi-scientific discourse which draws freely on the scientific knowledge of the time is evidently not aimed at upholding a particular scientific view of nature, nor does it strive to make positive contributions to the accepted body of scientific knowledge. Rather, its primary purpose is to argue the contingency of the created order and its ultimate dependence on God (see COSMOLOGY). Nowhere in this and other classical commentaries does one encounter the notion that a certain scientific fact or theory is predicted or even favored by the Qur᾿ān. Instead, these commentaries emphatically reject explanations of qur᾿ānic verses that are grounded in the notion of a natural order. The sign verses serve as evidence of the creator not in the particular knowledge that they convey about nature but in the ultimate conclusion in each and every verse that there is a choice in creation and thus a creator who makes this choice, that the "world is created with perfect management, comprehensive determination, utter wisdom, and infinite omnipotence" (ibid., 109).

Inevitably, any discussions of nature in a medieval Islamic context must invoke the question of causality and the natural order, widely debated among intellectuals of the period. The clearest articulation of the traditional Islamic view on this subject is Abū Ḥāmid al-Ghazālī's *Tahāfut al-falāsifa,* "The incoherence of the philosophers," but it was also addressed in *tafsīr*. As the above examples already suggest, the tendency in *tafsīr* literature is to attribute the natural phenomena to direct creation by God, rather than to intermediary causes which, once God creates and sets them in motion, become autonomous causes in their own right. For example, in the commentary on Q 2:22 which speaks of God who "sends forth rain from the skies that fruits may grow...," one commentator states outright that this reference to the growth of fruit due to the rain from the sky is figurative and that the real cause is not rain but the creator of all species (Abū Ḥayyān, *Nahr,* i, 40 f.). Al-Rāzī's comments on this verse are more exhaustive (Rāzī, *Tafsīr,* ii, 110): irrespective of whether the cause of the growth of fruit is rain from the sky or direct creation by God, the existence of a wise maker is a necessity. Thus, right from the beginning, he admits both views within the realm of possibility. He goes on to say, in conscious opposition to the late *mutakallimūn* (speculative theologians), that God's omnipotence would not be affected whether he creates the fruit from nothing or through the intermediacy of the affective and receptive powers in bodies. He also points out the possible wisdom inherent in creating intermediaries: if creation were direct, then the role of the maker would be all too obvious; whereas in the case of intermediaries, people would have to reflect on the intricacies of the process of creation to deduce the existence of a creator. The second process of reflection, according to al-Rāzī, is more difficult and merits more reward for the person who undertakes it.

A similar, perhaps even more pronounced recognition of causality is reflected in al-Nīsābūrī's (fl. ninth/fifteenth cent.) portrayal of nature in his *Gharā'ib al-Qur'ān.* Al-Nīsābūrī's work is the only *tafsīr* work which has been systematically examined for its portrayal of nature and for its relationship to science (Morrison, Portrayal of nature). In his commentaries, al-Nīsābūrī draws on astronomy and natural philosophy and provides descriptions of the natural phenomena which are not restricted to appearances but assume the reality of the phenomena in question. Al-Nīsābūrī thus recognized the existence of a chain of real secondary causes in nature (Morrison, Portrayal of nature, 3, 13 f.). As the study of al-Nīsābūrī illustrates, however, this acceptance was somewhat tempered by the notion that these real causes "operated under God's direct control, when God chose to use them" (ibid., 5-9). The concept employed by al-Nīsābūrī is that of *taskhīr* (subjugating), as opposed to *tafwīḍ* (entrusting or commissioning), of the power of the intermediary, which implies the immediate role of God in controlling these causes (ibid., 13). Moreover, regardless of his acceptance of intermediary causes, al-Nīsābūrī's discussion of the natural phenomena conforms to the general outlines of other classical commentaries in two main respects. First, he does not use the Qur'ān as a source of knowledge about nature. Second, his exposition of various scientific theories and explanations is seldom done for the purpose of favoring one over the others. Rather, this exposition is usually undertaken to suggest that there are multiple possible explanations, on which the Qur'ān is neutral.

Asserting the multiplicity of possible explanations of natural phenomena is hardly compatible with the positivism of the scientific outlook. Classical *tafsīr* works, however, are full of such assertions. Most of the commentaries on the sign verses contain multiple interpretations, of which only some are connected to science. While some of these "scientific" interpretations are rejected, many are allowed as acceptable possibilities. In many cases, information culled from scientific discourse is countered, rather than confirmed, by what are considered acceptable alternative interpretations. One example among many is the commentary on Q 15:16-7: "We have placed the signs of the zodiac *(burūj)* in the sky and adorned it for those who can see (see SEEING AND HEARING). And we have preserved it from every accursed devil." Al-Qurṭubī (*Jāmi*ʿ, x, 9-10) contends that the word *burūj* means palaces and mansions as well as the signs of the zodiac. In the latter case, he adds, the reference to the science of the stars might be because the Arabs (q.v.) at the time of revelation held the zodiac in high esteem. As usual, al-Rāzī has more to say on this subject. The signs of the zodiac, he argues, serve as proofs of the existence of a willing maker because, as authorities on astrology agree, the natures of these signs vary. The celestial orb is thus composed of many components of varying essences. This in turn means that the celestial orb is a composite entity and, as such, is in need of a composer to put its different fragments together in accordance with God's choice and higher wisdom (Rāzī, *Tafsīr*, xix, 168, ad Q 15:16; see Fig. II for an example of the persistence of pre-Islamic depictions of the signs of the zodiac in Islamic times). Both al-Qurṭubī and al-Rāzī also maintain that the preservation of the skies occurs by unleashing meteors to drive away devils. What is characteristic of such commentaries is that the little explanation that is drawn from common scientific knowledge is embedded in a wealth of other material that contradicts the common scientific knowledge of the time. A similar example occurs in the commentary on Q 36:38: "While the sun moves to its resting place *(wa-l-shamsu tajrī li-mustaqarrin lahā)*. That is the dispensation of the mighty, all-knowing [God]." Contemporary translations usually render the first part of this verse as "While the sun keeps revolving in its orbit" and this translation is not totally foreign to the classical understanding of the verse. In fact, the focus of most of the commentaries is on the possible meanings of the word *mustaqarr*. These include a location beyond which the sun cannot go, such that once it reaches that location it starts heading back to where it came from; this is obviously the sense in which the word means orb (Qurṭubī, *Jāmi*ʿ, xv, 278; Rāzī, *Tafsīr*, xxvi, 71, ad Q 36:38). Other meanings of equal possibility, however, are also listed, including the possibility that *mustaqarr* means a resting point under the throne where the sun prostrates (see BOWING AND PROSTRATION) before it is commanded to rise again and go back from where it came; or the day of judgment, after which the sun will no longer move; or a specific location, and so on (Qurṭubī, *Jāmi*ʿ, xv, 278; Rāzī, *Tafsīr*, xxvi, 72). Al-Rāzī, however, is not impartial to all of these interpretations. His preferred understanding of the word *mustaqarr* is as a locality beyond which the sun can not go. This, he continues, corresponds to the highest as well as lowest points in the daily rotation of the sun. Significantly, however, al-Rāzī does not base his choice on simple observation but on the fact that this rotation of the sun generates the day and the night, both of which are essential for maximizing benefit to human beings. Once again, despite references to science, the guiding principle for the exegetical exercise is a theological one, and not a scientific one which stands outside the text itself.

In a move that further clarifies his exegetical strategy, al-Rāzī notes in the commentary on the same verse that most commentators agree that the sky is a plane and has no edges or peaks (Rāzī, *Tafsīr*, xxvi, 75-6). In response, however, he maintains that there is nothing in the text of the Qurʾān which suggests with certainty that the sky has to be flat and not spherical. On the other hand, al-Rāzī adds, "sensory evidence indicates that the sky is actually spherical, so it must be accepted." After giving some of this sensory evidence to illustrate his point, he adds that such evidence is abundant and its proper place is in the books of astronomy. To al-Rāzī, therefore, the authority on this matter is the science of astronomy and not the Qurʾān, however understood. The only reason he gets into this extra-qurʾānic discussion is to undermine the claims of other commentators who wrongly extend the authority of the Qurʾān outside its proper realm.

Another aspect of al-Rāzī's exegetical strategy with regard to the sign verses is also revealed in his commentary on the same verse. This time, however, he takes issue with astronomers, and not the commentators. The astronomers maintain that celestial orbs are solid spherical bodies, but al-Rāzī contends that this is not necessarily the case. The basis for his objection is that it is not impossible, from the standpoint of astronomy, to have an orb which is a circular plate or even an imaginary circle which the planet traces in its motion. Furthermore, it is not beyond God's power to create any of these configurations (Rāzī, *Tafsīr*, xxvi, 76; see also Morrison, Portrayal of nature, 20-2, for the different views of al-Nīsābūrī). While al-Rāzī's interest in these quasi-scientific subjects exceeds those of other commentators, it still reflects a pervasive attitude found in classical commentaries. Scientific knowledge is freely invoked, and occasionally challenged in these commentaries. Yet the purpose of rejecting some scientific views is not to promote alternative ones or to assert the authority of the Qurʾān at the expense of the various fields of scientific knowledge. In the absence of a clear statement in the Qurʾān, one seeks answers to scientific questions in their respective fields. The contrary, however, is not true, since the qurʾānic text is not science. When there is an apparent conflict between a qurʾānic text and a scientific fact, the commentators do not present the qurʾānic text as the arbiter. Rather, they simply try to explore the possibility of alternative scientific explanations and thus suggest that scientific knowledge on such points of contention is not categorical. This, for example, is the case in al-Rāzī's discussion of the numbers of celestial orbs. After presenting a "summary and cursory overview" of the prevalent astronomical views on the subject, al-Rāzī maintains that it is not beyond God's power to create the heavens in this particular configuration. He adds, however, that there is no evidence that this is the only possible order of the heavens (Rāzī, *Tafsīr*, xxvi, 77).

It follows from the above that religious knowledge and scientific knowledge are each assigned to their own compartments. This would justify the pursuit of science and even the use of scientific discourse in commenting on the Qurʾān but it would also limit this use. A case in point is al-Rāzī's contention that some ignorant people may object to his unusual use of the science of astronomy in explaining the book of God. In response, he asserts that God has filled his book with proofs of his knowledge, power and wisdom which are inferred from the conditions of the heavens and the earth. If exploring these subjects and reflecting on them were not permissible, God would not have so frequently urged humans to reflect on these signs. "The science of astronomy," he adds, "has no other meaning than reflection on how he ordered the [heavens] and created its [different parts]" (Rāzī, *Tafsīr,* xiv, 121). The purpose of this exercise is not to establish correspondence between scientific verities and the Qurʾān, but simply to reflect and hence to reinforce belief in the creator of the awe-inspiring universe. This kind of reflection in the service of belief does not produce knowledge about the natural order. Despite all of his talk about the permissibility of using astronomy in exegesis, al-Rāzī asserts that all creation is from God, that the planets have no influence on the sub-lunar world, and that the "assertion of natures, intellects, and souls in the manner advocated by philosophers and diviners is invalid" (ibid., 122-3; see SOUL). These statements are, however, directed primarily at fellow religious scholars and not at scientists. When discussing the religious import of the Qurʾān, commentators are urged to stay within the realm of the text and not to try to impose astronomical knowledge on it or, for that matter, feign a qurʾānic understanding of astronomy. The qurʾānic text to which al-Rāzī wants to restrict himself and his fellow commentators does not have a scientific import and does not translate into binding scientific facts. It underscores the wisdom and power behind creation but says nothing about the exact order of the created world. The complexity and wondrous nature of the world reinforce belief in God but this is not contingent on the adoption of any particular scientific view. In fact, scientific facts and theories in themselves do not provide evidence of the oneness of the creator. Rather, it is the very fact that other natural orders are possible that points to a willing maker who chooses one of these possibilities (e.g. Rāzī, *Tafsīr,* xxii, 161-2, ad Q 21:33). According to this logic, everything in nature, however explained, as well as all scientific discoveries and facts, irrespective of their certainty, serve as proofs for the existence of the maker. And this is the fundamental reason why the scientific and unscientific could appear side by side in the commentaries on the Qurʾān (for example, ibid., 163).

As the above overview suggests, al-Bīrūnī's view was in conformity with the prevalent view within the discursive culture of qurʾānic exegesis. This confluence of attitudes between scientists like al-Bīrūnī and qurʾānic exegetes further suggests a conceptual separation of science and religion in the mainstream of classical Islamic culture. The same, however, cannot be said of modern Islamic discourse on science and religion and on contemporary Islamic views of the relationship between the Qurʾān and science. Ironically, when Muslims were the main producers of science in the world, they did not advocate the idea of the marriage of science and religion, while the contemporary call for such a marriage is concurrent with the dwindling Muslim participation in the production of the universal culture of science. As the above cursory overview suggests, classical commentators on the Qurʾān never even hinted that the miracle of the Qurʾān lies in its prediction of scientific discoveries that were made centuries after the coming of the revelation. Nor did these commentators advocate an understanding of the Qurʾān as a source of scientific knowledge. Yet both claims abound in contemporary Islamic discourse.

Questions of science and religion are approached in manifold ways in modern Islamic discourse. But by far the most common treatments of this subject maintain

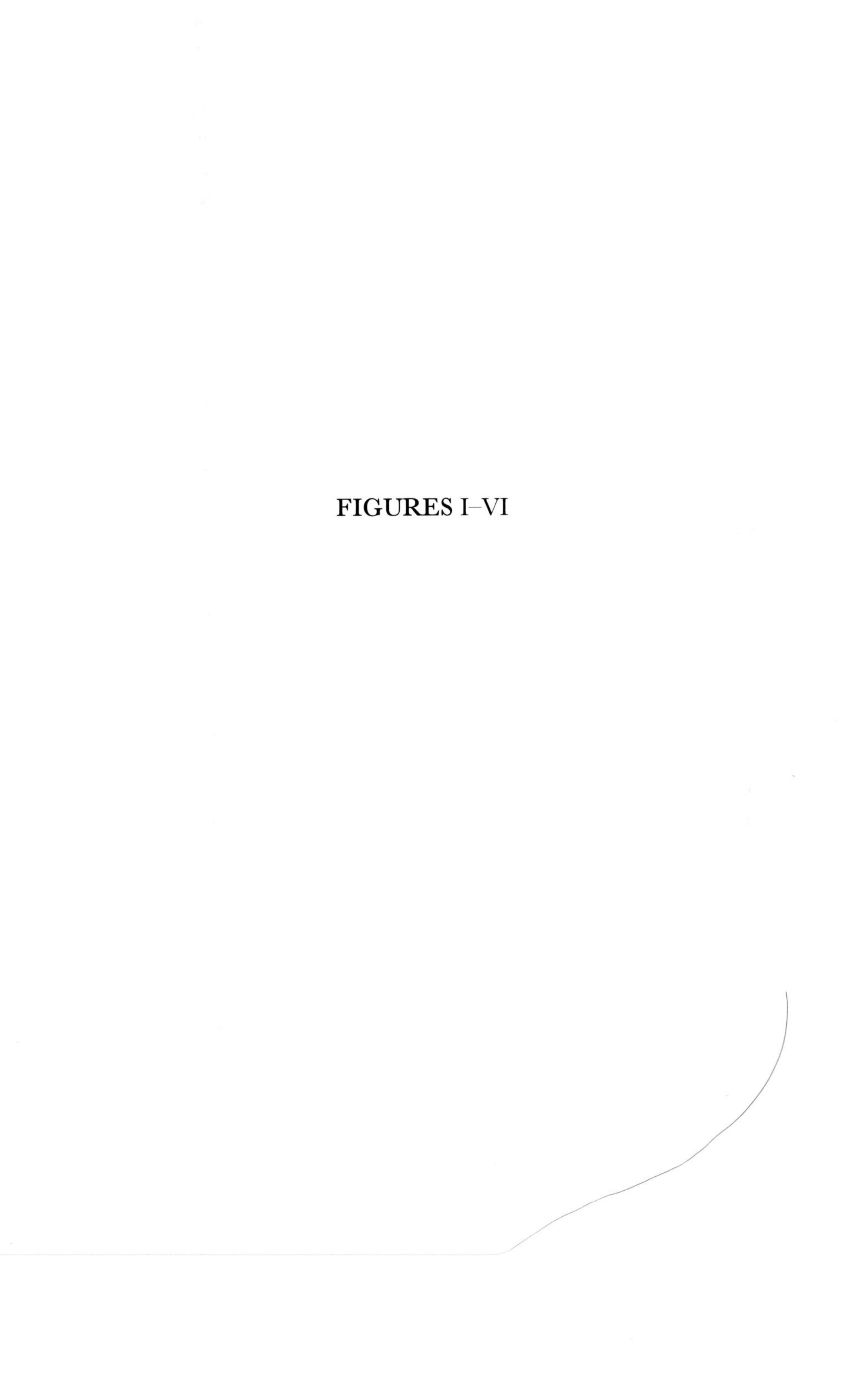

FIGURES I–VI

[I] Nilometer (*miqyās*), interior, with measuring column in foreground: Cairo, 241/867. Built after the Arab conquest in order to measure the annual flooding, it consists of three tunnels extending from the Nile, at various levels, which feed into the east side of a stone-lined pit, in which the measuring column is found. Each of the four sides of the pit, which extends below the level of the Nile, contains a pointed-arch vault, constructed three centuries before any Gothic example of the same. For a detailed description of the Nilometer, see pp. 383-4 of K.A.C. Creswell, *A short account of early Muslim architecture* (rev. ed. Aldershot 1989). See E. Dodd and Sh. Khairallah, *Image of the word* (Beirut 1981), ii, 171-2 for the qur'ānic verses that are inscribed on the *miqyās*. Courtesy of the Ashmolean Museum, Creswell Archives, Oxford (E.A., CA. 2484).

[II] Zodiac plate (ceramic): Iran, 971/1563-4. The twelve circles depicting the twelve signs of the zodiac are a pre-Islamic pictorial tradition that persisted into Islamic times. Courtesy of the Staatliche Museen, Berlin (I. 1292). Photograph: Karin März.

[III] Astrolabe (brass): Iran, early twelfth/eighteenth century. The cartouche in the center of the *kursī* (i.e. the top of the astrolabe) is inscribed with "His throne extends over the heavens and the earth" (Q 2:255). Courtesy of the Museum of the History of Science, Oxford (inventory no. 37940; image no. 153307).

[IV] *Qibla* compass and sundial, open: Istanbul, 1161/1748. This complex device, termed an "equatorial circle" (*dāʾirat al-muʿaddil*) by its ninth/fifteenth century Egyptian inventor, combines a *qibla* compass with a sundial. Courtesy of the Nasser D. Khalili Collection, London (SCI 270).

[v] *Qibla* compass and sundial, view of dial: Turkey, late twelfth/eighteenth century. The religious purpose of this instrument is demonstrated by the depiction of the Kaʿba and some of the other monuments of the *ḥaram* of Mecca. Courtesy of the Nasser D. Khalili Collection, London (SCI 49).

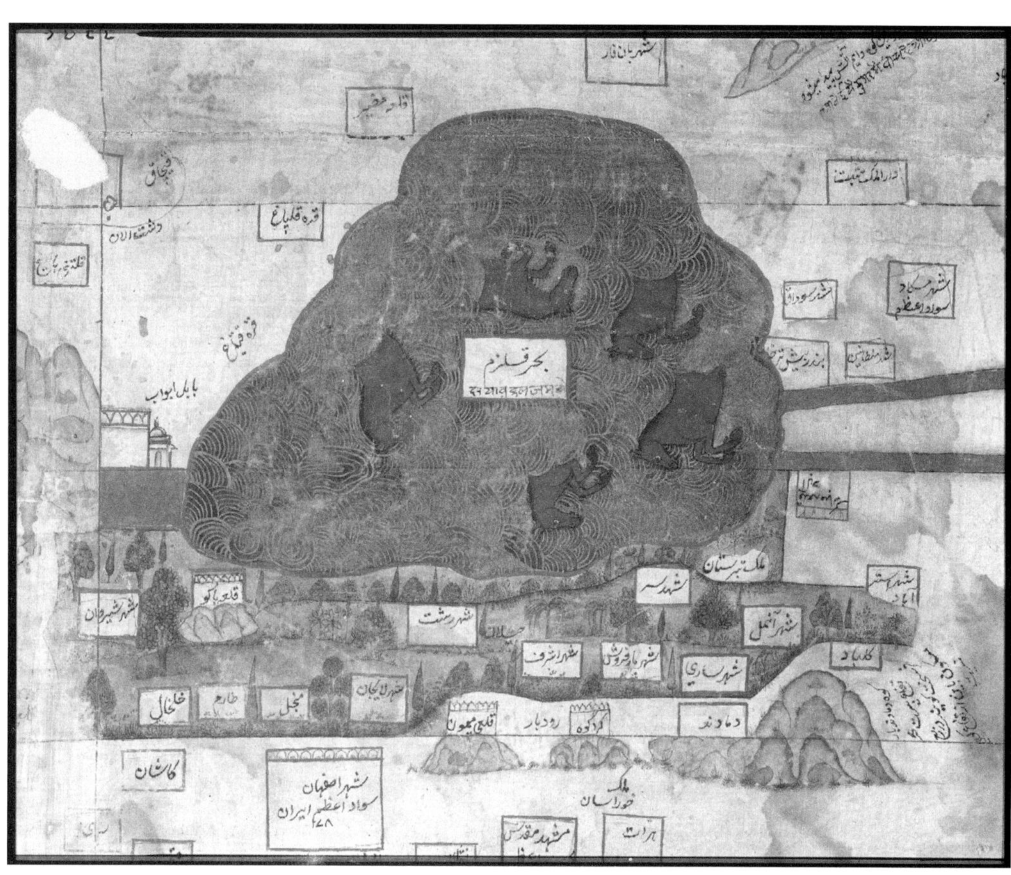

[VI] Map of the world, detail showing horses swimming in the Caspian Sea: India late twelfth/eighteenth century. The map, the primary explanatory details of which are in Arabic, contains images from the stories surrounding Alexander the Great (Dhū l-Qarnayn), such as the wall he built against the people of Gog and Magog (cf. Q 18:94). Courtesy of the Staatliche Museen, Berlin (I. 39/68).

that many modern findings of science have been predicted, or at least alluded to, in the Qurʾān, and that these predictions constitute evidence of what is referred to as the scientific miracle *(iʿjāz)* of the Qurʾān (for example, Nawfal, *Qurʾān wa-l-ʿilm*, 24). To be sure, this view is articulated in more than one way. In one form, this understanding maintains that, in contrast to other scriptures, the Qurʾān does not make any statements which contradict the findings of modern science. The most famous proponent of this argument is the French physician Maurice Bucaille. Bucaille's book *The Bible, the Qurʾān and science. The holy scriptures examined in the light of modern knowledge*, in its many translations and editions, has been extremely popular and has inspired an almost cultic following among large numbers of Muslims all over the world. Bucaille argues that the Qurʾān is full of discussions of scientific subjects, including "[c]reation, astronomy, the explanation of certain matters concerning the earth,... the animal and vegetable kingdoms, [and] human reproduction." In contrast to the Bible, whose treatment of these subjects is full of "monumental errors," Bucaille asserts that he "could not find a single error in the Qurʾān." In fact, Bucaille asserts, the Qurʾān does "not contain a single statement which is assailable from a modern scientific point of view" — which led him to believe that no human author in the seventh century could have written "facts" which "today are shown to be in keeping with modern scientific knowledge" (Bucaille, *The Bible*, 120-1, viii). Bucaille also articulates in this book an idea which is current among modern commentators on this subject, namely that "modern scientific knowledge... allows us to understand certain verses of the Qurʾān which, until now, it has been impossible to interpret" (ibid., 251). The two main points of this argument, therefore, are the miraculous conformity between qurʾānic statements and science, and the possibility, in fact need, for a scientific interpretation of the Qurʾān in the light of the findings of modern science.

Once a correlation between the Qurʾān and science is asserted, it only takes a small extension of the same logic to embark on an arbitrary exercise of collecting extra-qurʾānic facts and discoveries, and mining the Qurʾān for statements that seem to correspond to them. That these new scientific discoveries have nothing to do with the Qurʾān never hinders some modern commentators who proudly present these theories as evidence of the qurʾānic miracle. The qurʾānic text is read with these so-called scientific facts in mind without any recognition that this reading is itself an interpretation of the text which is conditioned by the assumptions of the interpreters and by the restricted focus of their textual examination. In extreme cases, this approach borders on the cultic, as in the widely circulated genre known as the *iʿjāz raqamī* or *ʿadadī* (numerical *iʿjāz*) of the Qurʾān. This form of numerology (q.v.) assigns an order to the occurrence of certain terms in the Qurʾān, which is seen as yet another numerical miracle. Thus, for example, one author maintains that the term "sea" is mentioned thirty-two times in the Qurʾān, and the term "land" thirteen times; the ratio thirteen to thirty-two, the author asserts, is equal to the actual ratio of land to water on the surface of the earth (Suwaydān, *Iʿjāz al-Qurʾān*, passim; and Abū al-Suʿūd, *Iʿjāzāt ḥadītha*, passim). This is by no means an isolated view, as is reflected in the scores of books published on this subject, as well as the hundreds of electronic postings on the web. Another extreme to which this argument is carried, again not without wide popularity, is to present the Qur'ān as a source of knowledge, a book of science of sorts and in some cases even as the comprehensive source of all forms of knowledge, including science.

The verses most frequently cited as instances of the qur'ānic anticipation of modern science include references in the Qur'ān to mountains as stabilizers for the earth which hold its outer surface firmly to prevent it from shaking (e.g. Q 21:31). This "scientific fact" of the Qur'ān, according to the current head of the Committee on the Scientific Miracles of the Qur'ān and Sunna, and author of a whole book on this subject, was only discovered in the middle of the nineteenth century and was not fully understood until the second half of the twentieth (Naggar, *Sources*, passim). The qur'ānic references to the stages of development of the fetus are often quoted as another example in which the Qur'ān is said to have miraculously predicted the discoveries of the modern science of embryology (see BIOLOGY AS THE CREATION AND STAGES OF LIFE). In 1983, Keith Moore, the author of a textbook on embryology, published a third edition of his book under the auspices of the Committee on the Scientific Miracles of the Qur'ān and Sunna, with "Islamic additions" by Abdul Majeed Azzindani, the first head of that Committee. The title of this new edition reads: *The developing human: Clinically oriented embryology. With Islamic additions: Correlation studies with Qur'ān and Ḥadīth, by Abdul Majeed Azzindani*. More recently, the most ambitious of all claims of scientific miracles is that the references in the Qur'ān to the heavens and the earth being originally an integrated mass before God split them (e.g. Q 21:30), are nothing short of a condensed version of the big bang theory (for example, Sa'dī, *Athār*, 41; also Nawfal, *Qur'ān wa-l-'ilm*, 24).

The origins of the school of scientific interpretation of the Qur'ān can be traced back to the nineteenth century. After the sweeping European takeover of most Muslim lands, Muslim intellectuals often attributed European superiority to scientific advancement. Science was, of course, also part of the ideology of the conquering Europeans, who often portrayed themselves as the superior carriers of the culture of reason and science. Faced with the post-Enlightenment ideology of science as well as the effects of European military technologies, Muslim intellectuals generated an apologetic discourse which either internalized European claims about science or simply claimed that the European values of science were not foreign to Muslims. The famous response of the nineteenth century Muslim scholar and activist Jamāl al-Dīn al-Afghānī (d. 1897) to the French Orientalist Ernest Renan (d. 1892) addresses the very question of the compatibility of science and Islam (Keddie, *Islamic response*, 130-87). Other Muslims focused on the promotion of an understanding of Islam which is in conformity with science. The notable example of this trend is Sayyid Aḥmad Khān (d. 1898), who juxtaposed the Qur'ān, the word of God (q.v.), and nature, the work of God, as two manifestations of the same reality that cannot be in conflict. With his positivistic understanding of science, however, Khan maintained that in cases of apparent contradiction between the word and the work [of God], the latter takes precedence while the former should be interpreted metaphorically (Khan, *Tafsīr*, passim; see METAPHOR).

In addition to Afghānī and Khān, both of whose assertions of harmony between the Qur'ān and science served very different political agendas, most discussions by Muslims on this subject were for the purpose of establishing the adequacy of their religion in the age of science and reason and to encourage Muslims to pursue the sciences. Many of the leading Muslim intellectuals of this period wrote on this or related themes, including Muḥammad Iqbal (d. 1938) of India and Muḥammad ʿAbduh (d. 1905) of Egypt. The writings of these intellectuals did not, however, elaborate on the details of the relationship between the Qurʾān and science and were largely restricted to the realm of generalities. Iqbal, for example, passionately argued that the rise of Islam marked the birth of inductive reasoning and experimental methods, but he did not present the Qurʾān as a repository of scientific knowledge nor did he suggest that one can arrive at scientific facts through the Qurʾān (cf. Iqbal, *Reconstruction,* 114-31). Still, a more elaborate discourse on this subject was produced as early as the late nineteenth century by Muslims who wanted to claim a role for their scripture and belief system in the making of the modern culture of science. One major proponent of this approach was Said Nursi (1877-1960), whose interpretations were rather simplistic but had the notable effect of influencing a large group of Turkish students and followers. Nursi's scientific interpretations included the assertion that the qurʾānic story of the prophet Solomon (q.v.; Sulaymān; i.e. Q 34:12) predicts the invention of aviation (see FLYING), and that the light (q.v.) verse (Q 24:35) is an allusion to the future invention of electricity (Kalin, Three views, 52-5; also Nursi, *Sözler,* passim). Unlike earlier apologetics, Nursi's efforts had the added objective of establishing the truthfulness of the Qurʾān on the basis of the findings of modern science. Another work that marks a turning point in the same direction is Ṭanṭāwī Jawharī's twenty-six volume *tafsīr* entitled *al-Jawāhir fī tafsīr al-Qurʾān al-karīm.* Jawharī made a point which is frequently repeated in the contemporary discourse on the Qurʾān and science, namely that the Qurʾān contains 750 verses pertaining directly and clearly to the physical universe, while it has no more than 150 verses on legal matters (see LAW AND THE QURʾĀN). Jawharī thus called on Muslims to reverse the order of interest and to give priority to the scientific verses, especially since they were now living in the age of science (Jawharī, *Tafsīr,* ii, 483-4).

The early attempts to interpret the Qurʾān and verify it in light of the discoveries of modern science received added impetus in the last decades of the twentieth century, when efforts were made to articulate the theoretical foundations of a new mode of *tafsīr* which aims not just at providing a scientific interpretation of the Qurʾān but also at illustrating its scientific miracles. The main proponent of this theorizing effort is Abdul Majeed Azzindani, the first head of the Committee on the Scientific Miracles of the Qurʾān and Sunna, as noted above. While many writers wrote on specific correspondences between the Qurʾān and aspects of modern science, Azzindani wrote a separate work, *al-Muʿjiza al-ʿilmiyya fī l-Qurʾān wa-l-sunna,* in which he identities the rules of the new science of the Qurʾān, the science of *iʿjāz al-Qurʾān.* This new science, Azzindani maintains, is the fruit of the "kind of *tafsīr* which is known to Muslim scholars who are cognizant of the secrets of creation" and is different from the scientific interpretation of the Qurʾān (Azzindani, *Muʿjiza,* 23). The latter occurs when a commentator makes use of the latest developments in "cosmic knowledge" *(al-ḥaqīqa al-kawniyya)* in order to interpret a verse of the Qurʾān. Scientific *iʿjāz,* however, is the "very cosmic truth to which the meaning of the verse points." At the time when the manifestation of the truth of the verse is witnessed in the universe, the interpretation of the verse settles at that truth.

Additional aspects of the universe may become known with time, leading in turn to further confirmation of the "depth and comprehensiveness of the scientific *i'jāz*" just as the cosmic order *(al-sunna al-kawniyya)* itself becomes clearer (Azzindani, *Mu'jiza*, 23-4). Therefore, there are several steps in the unfolding of this process of *i'jāz*. First, a universal cosmic truth, already expressed in the Qur'ān, though not necessarily understood, is suddenly revealed by means of the experimental sciences. After much waiting, Azzindani asserts, humanity has now been able to develop the technical skills that would finally "reveal the secrets of the universe, only to realize that what researchers are discovering, after much research and study using the most complex modern instruments, has been established in a verse or a ḥadīth fourteen centuries ago" (ibid., 27; also see Sa'dī, *Athār*, 11). This discovery or revelation then puts an end to the multiplicity of interpretations when the meaning of the verse finally reaches its resting place *(mustaqarr);* more discoveries in the future can only corroborate this fixed interpretation and thus deepen the sense of *i'jāz* (Azzindani, *Mu'jiza*, 24-5). Azzindani also maintains that, if there is a contradiction between the certain, unequivocal implication of a qur'ānic text *(dalāla qaṭ'iyya lil-naṣṣ)* and a scientific theory, then this theory should be rejected; whereas if there is conformity between the two, then the text serves as proof of this theory. If, on the other hand, the text is ambiguous (q.v.), and the scientific theory is certain, then the text should be interpreted in accordance with the theory (ibid., 26). Azzindani says nothing about the case when both text and theory are certain and unequivocal. What is clear, however, is that the text serves as the final authority in science and not just in religion, ethics or metaphysics (see ETHICS AND THE QUR'ĀN). It is important to note here a distinction between two levels of authority that are attributed to the qur'ānic text: according to Azzindani, the text attests not just to the validity of a scientific discovery but also to its invalidity. The former function is limited and serves to highlight the miraculous nature of the Qur'ān without positing it as a source of scientific knowledge, while in the latter case the Qur'ān stands above science in its own realm. In fact, Azzindani adds, Muslim scientists can find leads in the Qur'ān that would facilitate their future scientific research (ibid., 35), presumably by identifying research projects or finding answers to pending scientific questions.

The way Azzindani deals with instances of conflict between qur'ānic statements and scientific theories marks the main difference between his modern school of interpretation and the classical ones. In such cases of conflict, Azzindani insists on the ultimate authority of the Qur'ān in determining the validity or invalidity of scientific theories. In contrast, classical commentators would typically note the possibility of multiple scientific explanations and theories without deploying the qur'ānic authority in favor of any of these theories, as was noted above. The effect of this recurrent strategy is to guard the autonomy of qur'ānic authority in the realm of religious doctrine without infringing on the autonomy of science in its own realm. In classical commentaries, the Qur'ān and science were separate.

Modern discourse on Islam and science is not restricted to the above attempt to establish instances of scientific miracles in the Qur'ān. Two additional approaches have been influential recently in academic circles. The first focuses on the epistemological critique of modern science and situates scientific knowledge in its historical and cultural contexts (Sardar, *Explorations;* id., *Islamic futures*). In opposition to the claims of universal truth by modern science, this approach underscores the cultural specificity of all forms of knowledge. This critique of science, in its manifold expressions, has been very influential among philosophers of science and, the desire to propose an Islamic epistemology notwithstanding, there is nothing specifically Islamic about it. Moreover, the content of this proposed Islamic epistemology remains undefined (Kalin, Three views, 57-62). The second approach questions the fundamentals of the metaphysical framework within which modern science operates and attempts to articulate an alternative Islamic framework. This approach, best represented by the writings of S.H. Nasr, posits a dichotomy between ancient and modern sciences and contends that the ancient sciences shared conceptions of the sacredness and unity of knowledge (Kalin, Three views, 63 f.; see PROFANE AND SACRED). Yet if the distinctive mark of this ancient metaphysical framework is in the sacredness and unity of knowledge, then it is not clear how Islamic science would be different from, for example, pagan Hellenistic science. Furthermore, as in the epistemological approach, the content of the Islamic metaphysical framework remains unclear. To be sure, both approaches are serious intellectual exercises: Even when they strive to cite verses of the Qurʾān, however, they remain largely extra-qurʾānic. Neither one of these approaches systematically engages the qurʾānic text as a whole or the cultural legacy which endowed the text with its specific historical meanings.

In all its varieties, the newly constructed Islamic discourse on science is not rooted in a historical understanding of the relationship between the Qurʾān and science. On one level, this is understandable. However defined, modern science has and continues to engender multiple and intense responses among Muslims and non-Muslims alike. The challenges posed by the modern culture of science had no parallel in pre-modern societies. It is thus understandable that Islamic attitudes towards modern science would have to confront challenges that were not addressed in the classical period of Islam. But the desire to articulate contemporary critical concerns about science in Islamic language cannot conceal the radical departure of these modern articulations from the classical ones. In contrast to the contemporary readiness to strain and twist and, in effect, manipulate, the qurʾānic verses to endow them with a scientific meaning, classical commentators refused to subordinate the Qurʾān to an ever-changing science. In insisting on the possibility of multiple scientific explanations of the natural phenomena, classical Qurʾān commentators were able to guard the autonomy of qurʾānic, religious knowledge not through the co-option of science but by assigning it to a separate and autonomous realm of its own.

Ahmad Dallal

Bibliography

Primary: Abū Ḥayyān al-Andalusī, *al-Nahr al-mādd min al-Baḥr al-muḥīṭ*, ed. B. Ḍinnāwī and H. Ḍinnāwī, 2 vols. in 3, Beirut 1987; al-Bīrūnī, Abū Rayḥān, *Taḥqīq mā lil-Hind min maqūla maqbūla fī l-ʿaql aw mardhūla*, Hyderabad 1958; Dhahabī, *Mufassirūn* (esp. ii, 454-96); S.A. Khān, *Tafsīr al-Qurʾān*, Lahore 1994; Nīsābūrī, *Tafsīr;* Qurṭubī, *Jāmiʿ*, Cairo 1952-67; Rāzī, *Tafsīr*, Cairo 1352/1933; Zamakhsharī, *Kashshāf*, ed. Būlāq, 4 vols., Cairo 1864.
Secondary: W. Abū l-Suʿūd, *Iʿjāzāt ḥadītha ʿilmiyya wa-raqamiyya fī l-Qurʾān*, Beirut 1991; Ḥ. Aḥmad, *al-Tafsīr al-ʿilmī lil-āyāt al-kawniyya fī l-Qurʾān*, Cairo 1980[3]; A. Azzindani (ʿAbd al-Majīd al-Zindānī), *al-Muʿjiza al-ʿilmiyya fī l-Qurʾān wa-l-sunna*, Cairo n.d.; M. Bucaille, *The Bible, the Qurʾān and science. The holy scriptures examined in the light of modern knowledge*, English trans. A.D. Pannell and the author, Indianapolis 1979; Muḥammad Iqbal, *The reconstruction of religious thought in Islam*, Lahore

1982; Muẓaffar Iqbal, Islam and modern science. Questions at the interface, in T. Peters, M. Iqbal and S. Nomanul Haq (eds.), *God, life, and the cosmos. Christian and Islamic perspectives,* Burlington, VT 2002, 3-41; Ṭ. Jawharī, *al-Jawāhir fī tafsīr al-Qurʾān al-karīm,* 26 vols., Cairo 1340-1351/1921-32; I. Kalin, Three views of science in the Islamic world, in T. Peters, M. Iqbal and S. Nomanul Haq (eds.), *God, life, and the cosmos. Christian and Islamic perspectives,* Burlington, VT 2002, 43-75; N. Keddie, *An Islamic response to imperialism. Political and religious writings of Sayyid Jamal al-Din al-Afghani,* Berkeley 1983; K. Moore, *The developing human. Clinically oriented embryology. With Islamic additions: Correlation studies with Qurʾān and ḥadīth, by Abdul Majeed Azzindani,* Jeddah 1983[3]; R. Morrison, The portrayal of nature in a medieval Qurʾān commentary, in *SI* 94 (2002), 1-23; Z.R. El-Naggar, *Sources of scientific knowledge. The geographical concepts of mountains in the Qurʾān,* Herndon, VA 1991; ʿA. Nawfal, *al-Qurʾān wa-l-ʿilm al-ḥadīth,* Cairo 1959; S. Nursi, *Sözler,* Istanbul 1958; D.S. al-Saʿdī, *Āthār al-kawn fī l-Qurʾān,* Beirut 1420/1999; Z. Sardar, *Explorations in Islamic science,* London 1989; id., *Islamic futures,* London 1985; *al-Sharq al-awsaṭ,* 5 Sept. 2003 (report on the Cairo meeting of the Committee on the Scientific Miracles of the Qurʾān and Sunna); ibid., 23 Sept. 2003 (report on a lecture delivered by Zaghloul El-Naggar, current president of the Committee on the Scientific Miracles of the Qurʾān and Sunna); L. Stenberg, *The islamization of science. Four Muslim positions developing an Islamic modernity,* Lund 1996; Ṭ. Suwaydān, *Iʿjāz al-Qurʾān al-karīm. Min al-iʿjāz al-ʿadadī fī l-Qurʾān,* n.p. n.d.

Sciences of the Qurʾān

see TRADITIONAL DISCIPLINES OF QURʾĀNIC STUDY; GRAMMAR AND THE QURʾĀN; EXEGESIS OF THE QURʾĀN: CLASSICAL AND MEDIEVAL

Scourge

see FLOGGING

Scribe(s)

see ORALITY AND WRITING IN ARABIA

Scripture and the Qurʾān

Addressing the issue of "scripture" in relation to the Qurʾān is at once a straightforward and a complicated venture. It is straightforward because in many respects the Qurʾān itself puts forward a generic concept of scripture that is consistent with that widely used today in the general study of religion. It is complicated because it raises numerous questions of historical, sociological and theological import for any understanding of either Islamic scripturalism or the relation of Islamic scripturalism to that of other religious traditions (see THEOLOGY AND THE QURʾĀN). In short, the meaning of "scripture" generally and its use specifically in the Islamic context are important but not as straightforward as might be assumed.

The generic concept of scripture

First, the history and phenomenology of scripture as both a generic concept and a global reality has only begun to be written and only in recent decades has it become the object of serious scholarly investigation and reflection (Cf. Smith, *What is scripture;* Graham, Scripture; id., *Beyond;* Levering, *Rethinking scripture;* Leipoldt and Morenz, *Heilige Schriften*). In particular, we are still in the process of understanding how "scripture" as a conceptual category has developed and expanded in the past few centuries from its specific (Christian or Jewish) sense, referring to one's own most sacred and authoritative text(s), to a more generic sense, referring to any text(s) most sacred to, and authoritative for, a given religious community.

Second, "scripture" as a particularistic concept seems to have first developed most fully in Jewish and Christian contexts and it was in later phases of these and, most recently, in secular contexts primarily within the Western world (especially those of the modern academy) that generic use of the term was subsequently developed to refer commonly not only to particular Jewish or Christian biblical texts but also to the sacred texts of other religious communities. (For a discussion of the historical emergence of scripture as an important element in religious life, see Smith, Scripture as form.) The earliest such documented usage found by the present author is that of Peter the Venerable (d. 1156 C.E.) in his *Summa totius haeresis saracenorum* (cited in Kritzeck, *Peter the Venerable,* 206), where the *nefaria scriptura* of the Qurʾān is contrasted to the *sacra scriptura* of the Bible. This is not to say that in other religious traditions there are no analogous concepts that might be adduced (most obviously that of *kitāb* in the Islamic case; see below); rather it is to note that the inclusion of the Qurʾān (or Veda or Lotus Sutra) under the rubric of the Latinate word "scripture" is not terribly old historically and was relatively infrequent until the past century or so (at least since the 1879-1894 publication of Max Müller's edited series, *Sacred books of the east*). Such generic usage is now much more common but scripture as a phenomenon occurring in diverse religious contexts and traditions is still something that has only begun to be studied comparatively and globally in any adequate way.

Third, "scripture" as a concept must be understood to be relational, not absolute, in nature. It needs still to be freed to a greater degree from its etymological background and not taken to refer simply to documentary texts or "books" (see ORALITY AND WRITING IN ARABIA). What we mean by "scripture" in the present discussion is very different from and very much more than what we mean by "text." "Scripture" is not a literary genre but a religio-historical one. No text is authoritative or sacred apart from its functional role in a religious community and that community's historical tradition of faith. The sacred character of a book is not an *a priori* attribute but one that develops and achieves widespread recognition in the lives of faithful persons who perceive and treat the text as holy or sacred (see e.g. RITUAL AND THE QURʾĀN). A text only becomes "scripture" when a group of persons value it as sacred, powerful and meaningful, possessed of an exalted authority, and in some fashion transcendent of, and hence distinct from, other speech and writing. In other words, the "scriptural" characteristics of a text belong not to the text itself but to its role and standing in a religious community. A given text may be "scripture" for one person or group and merely another "book" or ordinary "text" for others. It is possible to study the Qurʾān either as text or as scripture but to study the Qurʾān as text is generally very different from studying it as "scripture," just as to read and respond to it only as another book is very different from reading and responding to it as the verbatim word of God (q.v.).

The qurʾānic concept of scripture

Such a generic and relational understanding of "scripture" as that now common in the study of religion is largely compatible with the Qurʾān's own frequent use of *kitāb,* "writing, book, what is laid down or ordained" (see BOOK) and its plural, *kutub,* to refer to scriptural revelation(s) given by God to previous prophets or messengers (see PROPHETS AND PROPHETHOOD; MESSENGER), especially Noah (q.v.), Abraham (q.v.), and their descendants (see CHILDREN OF ISRAEL), before the bestowing of the Qurʾān upon Muḥammad as his *kitāb* (on *kitāb/kutub* generally, see Madigan, *Qurʾān's self-image,* passim). In the Qurʾān, these earlier revelations are clearly considered to belong to the same general religio-historical category ("scripture") as the definitive revelations to Muḥammad (see REVELATION AND INSPIRATION). Jews (see JEWS AND JUDAISM) and Christians (see CHRISTIANS AND CHRISTIANITY; and a group identified as the *ṣābiʾūn;* see SABIANS) in particular are referred to as *ahl al-kitāb,* "people of scripture" (see PEOPLE OF THE BOOK). The Qurʾān conceives of itself as a revelation intended to confirm the truths and set right the distortions in the earlier scriptures. Here we have already in the seventh century C.E. the use of a generic concept of scripture that is arguably unique among major scriptures of the world in its explicit recognition of the sacred texts of other communities as belonging to the same category as the qurʾānic revelations themselves — the category of *kitāb/kutub* (see RELIGIOUS PLURALISM AND THE QURʾĀN; although early Christian Arabic texts name the Qurʾān and Bible as "books of God," *kutub Allāh,* the exact signification of such terminology has yet to be determined; cf. e.g. Sinai Arabic MS 434, f. 181 v., where, in the conclusion to his responses to a Muslim interlocutor that are replete with biblical and qurʾānic allusions, a Melkite [monk?] states: "The answers are finished — abbreviated — since the testimonies of the books of God are abundant"; see similar allusion to the "books of God" in Theodore Abū Qurra's *Debate with Muslim theologians in the majlis of the caliph al-Maʾmūn,* esp. pp. 95, 98, 107-8, 110-1).

It is, however, important to note that *kitāb* can have other senses in qurʾānic usage, notably that of a personal book of destiny in which each person's deeds, good and evil (see GOOD DEEDS; EVIL DEEDS), are written down and will be brought as testimony on the day of judgment (e.g. Q 17:71; 39:69; see LAST JUDGMENT) or that of a heavenly book (q.v.) with God in which everything in the world is written before time (e.g. Q 6:59; 11:6; 35:11). The qurʾānic concept of scripture as a general phenomenon appears to be based on the latter meaning of *kitāb* — especially when it is used to refer to an original, heavenly scripture with God from which all of the earthly scriptures, or *kutub,* have been drawn (see PRESERVED TABLET). One example of this sense is found in Q 10:37: "This recitation *(qurʾān)* is not such as could be invented save by God. Rather it is a confirmation of what came before it and an exposition of the scripture *(al-kitāb)* about which there is no doubt, from the lord of all beings." Sometimes the term *umm al-kitāb,* literally "the mother of scripture" in the sense of the essence, source, or prototype of scripture, "the original scripture," also occurs (Q 13:39; 43:4; see NAMES OF THE QURʾĀN). This further reinforces the notion of a divine *kitāb* that resides with God.

It is, however, the generic use of *kitāb/kutub* to refer to earlier scriptures and to the Qurʾān itself that is special, or even unique, about the qurʾānic notion of scripture. Typically, the other sacred texts of the world's religions that we call "scriptures" were not written with any similar consciousness of belonging themselves to a category of texts called "scripture." Most if not all great scriptural texts other than the Qurʾān are unconscious of being even potentially "scripture," for "scripture" or any analogous concept is usually a category developed ex post facto and then applied to a text or texts that a community has experienced as sacred, and consequently given special treatment. Thus the Vedic texts of India do not speak about themselves as *śruti,* nor the Jewish or Christian Bible about itself as "scripture" (although the Christian New Testament does treat the earlier Hebrew scriptures as scripturally authoritative); it is rather later generations and their texts that recognize them as "scripture." The texts of the religious prophet Mani are possibly one pre-qurʾānic exception to this (Smith, Scripture as form, 35-6) and of course some later Buddhist sutras such as the Lotus Sutra present themselves as the word of the Buddha *(buddhavacana);* but there seems to be no major scriptural text before the Qurʾān that uses a generic concept of "scripture" as a category to which it also claims to belong.

The Qurʾān, for its part, is self-consciously explicit about its own function as scripture, *kitāb,* and about being the latest, culminating revelation in a long line of scriptural revelations from the lord of all beings to previous prophets and their peoples. This notion of a succession of prophets *(anbiyāʾ)* or messengers *(rusul)* to each of whom God gave revelations is gradually fleshed out in the sequence of qurʾānic revelations and is the leitmotiv of the qurʾānic *Heilsgeschichte.* In qurʾānic perspective, the fundamental pattern of history is God's sending a messenger or prophet with revelatory guidance (see ASTRAY; ERROR) to nation after nation. The revealed scriptures that embody this guidance include the "pages" revealed to Abraham (see SCROLLS), the Psalms (q.v.) given to David (q.v.), the Torah (q.v.) vouchsafed Moses (q.v.), and the Gospel (q.v.) sent to Jesus (q.v.), as well as the Qurʾān revealed to Muḥammad. What followed each of these prophetic or apostolic missions was the creation of a new community of those who heard and responded in obedience (q.v.) to God's message (see COMMUNITY AND SOCIETY IN THE QURʾĀN). The Qurʾān, however, seems to hold that while the earlier, successively revealed *kutub* represent scriptures derived from these earlier divine revelations, the communities who preserved them did not succeed in doing so scrupulously enough. Each community that had received revelation previously let its scriptural text be partially lost or changed and thus debased over time (see CORRUPTION; FORGERY; REVISION AND ALTERATION; POLEMIC AND POLEMICAL LANGUAGE) — hence the need for the qurʾānic revelations in "clear Arabic" to rectify such lapses (see ARABIC LANGUAGE; LANGUAGE AND STYLE OF THE QURʾĀN). The Qurʾān portrays itself as a renewed and presumably final revelation of God's word in the scriptural series. It was revealed through the "seal of the prophets," Muḥammad (see NAMES OF THE PROPHET), and is intended to reiterate what has been lost or corrupted in the previous revelations to other prophets or messengers: "This is a blessed scripture *(kitāb)* that we sent down to you, confirming that which came before it..." (Q 6:92).

Thus it is arguable that the Qurʾān is the first sacred text of a major religious tradition to offer a developed understanding of itself as part of a larger scriptural history. With the Qurʾān, scripture as a category provides a clear context in which the Muslim scripture could be revered as the final revelation but also understood to be the recapitulation of all previous revelations from God (and presumably from his heavenly *kitāb*).

The Qurʾān as a discourse of signs

The Qurʾān's own presentation of itself is foundational in preparing the way for its role as "the scripture" *(al-kitāb)* for Muslims ever afterward. It presents itself, and by extension all earlier divine revelations, as, first, a reminder of the manifold signs (q.v.) of God in nature and in history and, second, a compilation of divine words that are themselves signs of God given by him in his revelations. The key word for "sign" here is *āya* (pl. *āyāt*), which in the qurʾānic text can mean (as in the first case above) simply a "sign," or, as in the second, a qurʾānic pericope or "verse" itself (see VERSES).

Both senses of the word are never far away when *āya* or *āyāt* occurs in the Qurʾān, especially in the later revelations when its manifold connotations have been fully developed (see CHRONOLOGY AND THE QUR᾿ĀN). We need only consider a qur᾿ānic *āya* such as Q 38:29, which, addressing Muḥammad, speaks of the Qur᾿ān as "a scripture *(kitāb)* that we sent down to you, a blessed one, in order that they might ponder its *āyāt* and in order that those of intelligence might be reminded" (see INTELLECT; KNOWLEDGE AND LEARNING; REFLECTION AND DELIBERATION). Here one sees that the ambiguities of the word *āyāt* allow for reading it as the signs of God in nature and history or as the signs of God as the verses of scripture. In general, the qur᾿ānic discourse is one in which scriptural words and divine signs in creation can be referred to with the same term since both are ultimately the clearest "signs" of the one God in mundane reality (see NATURE AS SIGNS; HISTORY AND THE QUR᾿ĀN).

The Qur᾿ān conceives itself (and, by extension, every previous scripture) as first and foremost a vehicle for reminding human beings of God's miraculous works in nature and history (see MIRACLES; MARVELS), both of which contain the physical and temporal *āyāt* that alone should convince anyone of good sense that there is one God alone who is worthy of worship (q.v.) and obedience. Second, it views itself as a full-blown verbal miracle of God's direct revelation, his "signs" or *āyāt* as words of revealed wisdom (q.v.) and guidance: "A revelation from the all-merciful compassionate [one], a scripture the *āyāt* of which have been made distinct as an Arabic recitation *(qur᾿ānan ʿarabiyyan)* for a people of knowledge" (Q 41:2-3). Here we see the purpose of the constant qur᾿ānic emphasis upon the clarity, explanatory power and unambiguous force of its message: namely, to stress that even after providing such clear signs in his handiwork and activity in the world, God has also spoken his message in clear human language, so that no doubt can linger. Thus the pointed question in Q 3:101: "How can you reject [faith] when God's *āyāt* are recited to you, and his messenger is among you?" (see FAITH; GRATITUDE AND INGRATITUDE).

What the "sign" language of the Qur᾿ān offers is the unfolding of a sophisticated and consistent understanding of God's revelatory activity in the created world. This is an understanding that dovetails logically and functionally with the piecemeal nature of the Qur᾿ān's own revelations, its episodic and referential style, its didacticism (see RHETORIC AND THE QUR᾿ĀN; FORM AND STRUCTURE OF THE QUR᾿ĀN), and its fundamentally oral character (see ORALITY) as a "reciting" of *āyāt*. It is based upon the Qur᾿ān's generic understanding of divine revelation and scripture as key elements of a *Heilsgeschichte* that culminates in Muḥammad's prophetic mission and the qur᾿ānic revelations of that mission themselves. When Q 6:109 commands Muḥammad, "Say, *āyāt* belong to God" *(innamā l-āyātu ʿinda llāhi)*, the implication is that all the miraculous signs in nature and history and all the miraculous signs of revelation could come solely from one omnipotent lord (q.v.), the creator and sustainer of the universe (see POWER AND IMPOTENCE; CREATION; SUSTENANCE). The God who speaks in the Qur᾿ān (see SPEECH) is the one who throughout history has never left his human creatures without clear signs and tokens, whether in the natural world, in human affairs, or, most explicitly, in his revealed word. Scripture is a discourse of God's signs, the set of divine *āyāt* that recount and call attention to God's other miraculous works; it is the verbal recital of his signs, tokens, or miracles in the created world and its history, a recital that is itself a kind of miracle.

The Qurʾān as scripture

The Qurʾān has functioned as scripture for Muslims from the inception of Islam as a communal reality. If we take the traditional Muslim reports of Islamic origins and the codification of the qurʾānic text as a written codex at anything like face value, the successive revelations to Muḥammad were apparently promulgated and accepted as divinely revealed words from the early days of his prophetic mission, probably well before the time they were codified as a composite text of the many individual revelations (see COLLECTION OF THE QURʾĀN; CODICES OF THE QURʾĀN). Even from a more skeptical viewpoint regarding the traditional accounts of the lifetime of Muḥammad (see SĪRA AND THE QURʾĀN; ḤADĪTH AND THE QURʾĀN), the origin of the Qurʾān, and the development of the early Muslim *umma,* the Qurʾān must have functioned as scripture from almost the same time that the Muslim community achieved some kind of distinct identity over against Jewish, Christian and other religious groups (see POST-ENLIGHTENMENT ACADEMIC STUDY OF THE QURʾĀN). What we understand under the rubric of "Qurʾān as scripture" are its multifarious roles in Muslim life across the centuries and around the world, from the earliest days of Islam down to the present moment. It is the cumulative history of these manifold roles of the Qurʾān in Muslim communities and individual Muslim lives, not the history of the text, its genesis, or its codification, that we study when we consider the Qurʾān as scripture.

These multiple roles of the qurʾānic scripture involve perduring notions among Muslims about (1) the status of the Qurʾān as the word of God, (2) the concomitant question of whether the Qurʾān is created or uncreated (see CREATEDNESS OF THE QURʾĀN), (3) the felt necessity that the Qurʾān be perfect and free from all possibility of human corruption or tampering (see INIMITABILITY), (4) the crucial character of the Qurʾān as a word revealed in Arabic rather than other languages (see FOREIGN VOCABULARY), (5) the exaltation of the word of God by elaborately artistic calligraphic and oral recitative embellishment (see CALLIGRAPHY; ORNAMENTATION AND ILLUMINATION; MANUSCRIPTS OF THE QURʾĀN; ARABIC SCRIPT; RECITATION OF THE QURʾĀN), and, finally, (6) the possibilities for Muslims' employment of the authority of their scripture for both good and evil purposes. These six issues demand individual consideration in what follows, and the central and pervasive presence of the Qurʾān in Islam to which they testify demands that we conclude by reemphasizing (7) the permeating force of the Qurʾān as scripture in the lives of Muslims across the centuries and around the world (see EVERYDAY LIFE, THE QURʾĀN IN).

The Qurʾān as the word of God

The theological centrality of the Qurʾān as Muslim scripture is hard to exaggerate. While the Torah's massive importance in Jewish life comes closest to this kind of overwhelming centrality, the eventual Muslim emphasis upon the Qurʾān as God's speech *ipsissima vox* — perfect and complete — is unique. For Muslims, God's speech is found verbatim in the Qurʾān and the concomitant of this is the overwhelming emphasis over the centuries since Muḥammad on the perfection of the qurʾānic text, the inerrancy of its transmission, and the direct experience of the divine through the recitation, memorization and reverent study of its text (see TRADITIONAL DISCIPLINES OF QURʾĀNIC STUDY). The records of the words and actions of the Prophet and his Companions (see COMPANIONS OF THE PROPHET), known individually and collectively as the ḥadīth, are also often accorded the status of sacred texts in Islam but always as a secondary order of divinely-inspired text and always under the rubric of texts to be transmitted "according to the sense" *(bi-l-maʿnā),* not "verbatim" *(bi-l-lafẓ)* like the Qurʾān.

The issue of scriptural authority was already being debated in the first few Islamic centuries in the question of the status of the ḥadīth as a source of divinely sanctioned authority alongside the Qurʾān. A recent study of this issue shows that, for example, in works ranging from the second/eighth to the fifth/eleventh century, by al-Shāfiʿī (d. 204/820), Ibn Qutayba (d. 276/890) and al-Khaṭīb al-Baghdādī (d. 463/1071), we find evidence of ongoing Sunnī debate as to whether or not the Qurʾān alone or the Qurʾān supplemented by the prophetic ḥadīth should be considered the final authority/ies for Muslim life (see AUTHORITY; LAW AND THE QURʾĀN). While the latter point of view won out, this debate has never completely died and is experiencing a new life today, not least on the internet (Musa, Study of attitudes; see also COMPUTERS AND THE QURʾĀN; MEDIA AND THE QURʾĀN). Even, however, in the prevailing Sunnī view that the ḥadīth represent a second source of revealed guidance for Muslims alongside the qurʾānic word of God, the preeminence of the latter has never been seriously challenged. In Muslim view, the Qurʾān stands alone in its perfection and precision of expression as the literal word of God directly revealed in recitative units during his messenger's lifetime (see OCCASIONS OF REVELATION).

This unique scriptural status of the Qurʾān is the expression of the strong Muslim consciousness of being in the presence of God's living voice and active, ever-present guidance whenever the words of "the reciting" are being rehearsed or read (see RECITERS OF THE QURʾĀN; TEACHING AND PREACHING THE QURʾĀN). In a real sense, the primary locus of the divine-human encounter in the Muslim view is God's revealed word, the Qurʾān. This is the reason that numerous modern scholars trying to capture the force of this fact have suggested that for Muslims the true analog of the Christ as the instantiation of the "word of God" for Christians is the Qurʾān; the Bible is not commensurate in Christian theological perspective with the Qurʾān in the Muslim theological universe. It is in their scripture that Muslims most directly experience God's presence and mercy (q.v.), however much the person and life of their prophet Muḥammad also testifies to both. Thus it is arguable that it is recitation of God's word that corresponds in Muslim practice to participation in the Eucharist in Christian practice (Söderblom, *Einführung,* 117; Graham, *Beyond,* 217 n. 3; Kermani, *Gott,* 465 n. 195). C. Geertz (Art as a cultural system, 1490) catches something of this in his strong claim that in chanting the Qurʾān, a Muslim ideally "chants not words about God, but of him, and indeed as those words are his essence, chants God himself."

The uncreatedness/eternality of the Qurʾān

This kind of ascription of divine ontological status to the qurʾānic scripture as God's verbatim speech was from at least the early second/eighth century an issue of considerable moment in Muslim theological discussions. Those philosophical theologians *(mutakallimūn)* who wanted to safeguard the oneness of God (notably the Muʿtazila) argued that the Qurʾān could not be uncreated *(ghayr makhlūq)* without being a second reality co-eternal with God and therefore a dualistic threat to God's oneness (see POLYTHEISM AND ATHEISM), omnipotence (see POWER AND IMPOTENCE), and unique transcendence as well as an anthropomorphic ascription of the human attribute of speaking to God (see ANTHROPOMORPHISM; GOD AND HIS ATTRIBUTES; ETERNITY; MUʿTAZILĪS). Their notion of the creation of the Qurʾān was, however, severely contested by those like Aḥmad b. Ḥanbal (fl. third/ninth cent.) and others of the ḥadīth specialists, or *muḥaddithūn,* who insisted on both the speaking of God as a proper eternal attribute of the divine and therefore on the uncreatedness of the Qurʾān as a safeguard of the eternality of God's speech as a divine attribute. Ultimately the traditionalist and ʿAsharī insistence on the uncreatedness of the Qurʾān won the day among most Muslims, thus underscoring the eternality of the Qurʾān as God's word, but the very existence of the debate itself gives some indication of the importance ascribed to the Qurʾān's status as God's word in the context of Islamic thought — an importance not unlike that ascribed to the doctrine of the virgin birth or the trinity (q.v.) in Christianity (and productive of similarly bitter controversy).

The perfection of the Qurʾān

The axiomatic nature of the Qurʾān's sublimity as the very speech of God is perhaps most vividly seen in the post-qurʾānic, apparently third/ninth-century, development of the notion of the *iʿjāz,* "(miraculous) inimitability" of the Qurʾān. This was evidently an expression of the felt need to substantiate the divine origin and perfection of the Qurʾān in its uniquely powerful style and content by asserting that no mere human author could write anything remotely as sublime as the miraculous qurʾānic word of God. This concept led to the designation of the Qurʾān by the *mutakallimūn,* among others, as a divine *muʿjiza,* or "miracle," a divinely given wonder, the like of which could not be reproduced by human effort (see PROVOCATION; PARODY OF THE QURʾĀN). The Qurʾān has also been treated in the literature on Muḥammad and the prophets as the special "proof" *(ḥujja)* for his prophetic mission — the particular miracle (one was said to be given to every genuine prophet) granted him by God as the ultimate guarantee of the truth of his prophethood (see PROOF). It can even be argued that the chief motivation for the later, classical Muslim doctrine of Muḥammad's "protection" *(ʿiṣma)* from sin or major errancy was probably ultimately developed to safeguard the Qurʾān from any impugning of its *iʿjāz:* had the messenger not been divinely preserved from at least major sins, how could one be certain he did not make errors with regard to the reception and transmission of God's sacred word? (Graham, *Beyond,* 207 n. 18; see also IMPECCABILITY).

The Qurʾān as the Arabic scripture

A corollary of the Qurʾān's miraculous perfection is understandably the special character of its language. From its early days, Islam became not just an Arab faith (see ARABS) but ever more an international one. Yet even down to the present moment, the fact of the Qurʾān's being revealed in Arabic has remained a centrally important dimension of the text's function as scripture for Muslims of all nations and races and language communities. While it can be argued legitimately that the faith that began with Muḥammad and a largely Arab community became one ultimately made great largely by non-Arabs, the Arabic language has remained highly significant to Muslims whether or not they speak or read the Arabic language. In a practical sense, for Muslims God's final revelation came in the language of the Arabs and its very perfection as God's verbatim word has demanded that Muslims protect and venerate its Arabic form. The Qurʾān itself speaks of the "clear Arabic tongue" (*lisān ʿarabī mubīn*, Q 16:103; 26:195) in which God speaks in the revelations of the Qurʾān. One dimension of the history of the Qurʾān as scripture has been the generally observed axiom (to which the Ḥanafī legal school has been an exception: Pearson, Translations, 429) that one cannot translate the Qurʾān and have it remain the Qurʾān (see TRANSLATIONS OF THE QURʾĀN). Interlinear translations and glosses have existed in numerous languages other than Arabic for hundreds of years but even today there is a hesitancy about letting translations threaten to take the place of the pristine "Arabic reciting" (*qurʾān ʿarabī*, Q 12:2; 20:113, etc.), even as more and more translations appear. The entitling of the popular Muslim translation by M. Pickthall as *"The meaning of the glorious Koran"* is a good example of the attempt to signal that any translation is an interpretation, not God's word itself.

The most vivid consequence of this emphasis upon the importance of the language of scripture has been the insistence in Muslim legal interpretation that a performance of the daily worship of ritual prayer (q.v.; *ṣalāt*) is only ritually valid if some portion, however brief, of the Arabic Qurʾān is recited at the appropriate points in the ritual performance. In particular, the memorization and recitation of the Fātiḥa (q.v.), the first sūra (q.v.) of the Qurʾān, is essential to the performance of the *ṣalāt*. This is a key legal distinction between God's word and the ḥadīth of the Prophet since recitation of the latter (even those ḥadīth containing a non-qurʾānic divine word, or *ḥadīth qudsī*, reported on Muḥammad's authority) would not validate one's *ṣalāt* (Graham, *Divine word*, 55-6). A reflex of this necessity for the presence of the Arabic "reciting" in worship is surely the centuries-long insistence of Muslims around the world that the *adhān*, or "call to worship," can only be given in Arabic. The brief attempt of the 1920s in republican Turkey to substitute a Turkish call to worship ended in failure before this deeply ingrained assumption about retaining the Arabic language of the call to worship God as he would be worshipped.

The Qurʾān has also served, along with pre-Islamic and early Islamic Arabic poetry (and to a lesser degree, other early Islamic texts; see POETRY AND POETS; PRE-ISLAMIC ARABIA AND THE QURʾĀN), but more emphatically, as the standard and proof-text for classical Arabic literary grammar, precisely because it is the divine model of linguistic perfection. Even a *hapax legomenon* in the qurʾānic text becomes a proof of proper grammatical usage because it occurs in the speech of God. Qurʾānic eloquence set the standards used also in Arabic literary criticism. The *iʿjāz* of the Qurʾān means that no other Arabic composition can attain its eloquence and its words and phrases have accordingly permeated Arabic writing and speaking and remained models of Arabic eloquence (see GRAMMAR AND THE QURʾĀN; LITERATURE AND THE QURʾĀN). The evidence provided, from the earliest centuries of Islam, of qurʾānic pericopes found in political speeches and on state identification documents such as coins, papyri or glass weights — both within and outside of the Arabic speaking Islamic world — attests to this elevated status (cf. Dähne, Qurʾānic; al-Qāḍī, Impact; see NUMISMATICS; SLOGANS FROM THE QURʾĀN).

The visual and oral exaltation of God's word

An index of the central role of the Qurʾān as scripture in Muslim life is the lavish overt attention devoted to the special forms of reverent and creative embellishment aimed at exaltation of the scriptural word in both its written and oral forms. Like its Jewish and Christian cousins, the Islamic tradition has seen the highest development of calligraphic art in the preparation of magnificently lettered and illuminated copies of the qur'ānic text. Unlike either Judaism or Christianity, however, it has also seen the development of an almost ubiquitous tradition of stunning monumental epigraphic inscriptions from the Qur'ān on Islamic edifices, religious and otherwise (see EPIGRAPHY AND THE QUR'ĀN; ART AND ARCHITECTURE AND THE QUR'ĀN; ARCHAEOLOGY AND THE QUR'ĀN). Muslims have focused — in part because of their tendency to iconoclasm (q.v.) — almost exclusively on the calligraphed words of the Qur'ān themselves and made them the major form of visual representation in Islam. Furthermore, this has been the case not only in specifically religious contexts such as those of mosques (see MOSQUE), but also as a dominant artistic mode of expression throughout the various sectors and milieux of Islamic cultures more broadly (see also MATERIAL CULTURE AND THE QUR'ĀN).

At least as spectacular has been the immense level of effort directed at the embellishment of the qur'ānic word in the popular practice and professional oral artistry of memorization and recitation. As no other of the world's great scriptures, the Muslim scripture has been the object of a mnemonic and recitative tradition that has saturated and sustained not only Muslims' devotional life and worship, but also the quotidian life in Muslim societies large and small around the globe with the rich, melodic, and moving strains of the recitation of God's word. From the very beginning, as evidenced in the very name Qur'ān, the qur'ānic revelations were rehearsed, memorized and recited, not only as a part of the *ṣalāt* and other worship observances, but also as the highest form of popular entertainment. The recitation of the Qur'ān, whether as an almost ubiquitous personal practice, a requisite component of the universal performance of *ṣalāt*, or a public-performance art across the Muslim world, has been a characteristic of Muslim societies. The technical discipline of Qur'ān recitation has further been one of the central disciplines of Muslim scholarship, and its high level of technical sophistication and development reflects the massive importance placed upon qur'ānic recitation *(tilāwa, tajwīd)* in Muslim learning as well as everyday life (see Nelson, *Art*).

Use and misuse of the qur'ānic scripture

Like religion itself, scripture is subject to the failings as well as the strengths of the human beings involved with it. Thus the Qur'ān has been both well used and also misused by its adherents. There is a good argument to be made for the Qur'ān being the inspiration for whatever spiritual greatness Muslims have achieved but also for some of the saddest excesses of religious fanaticism Muslims have suffered (see POLITICS AND THE QUR'ĀN). The greatest Muslim religious minds have used their scripture as the touchstone of their faith and yet other Muslims have used a narrow and selective, sometimes mindlessly literal, interpretation of the Qur'ān to justify actions and norms that belied and betrayed the sweeping religious vision that the Qur'ān brought to the period of its revelation. In these things, the Muslim scripture has been no different than any other scripture in any other religious community: even if one were to accept that a given scripture is divinely inspired, human beings can use it to evil or perverted, as well as to noble or spiritual, purposes. Religious people, Muslims among them, have used and do use their scriptures for diverse purposes, from bibliomancy, talismanic help (see POPULAR AND TALISMANIC USES OF THE QUR'ĀN), and divination (q.v.; see also FORETELLING) to legal argumentation, mystical speculation (see ṢŪFISM AND THE QURʾĀN) and theological reasoning. For this reason, the formal and informal interpretation of the Qurʾān, like that of other scriptures, has been and remains a constantly changing and dynamic dimension of the Qurʾān's role as scripture, both for good and ill (see EXEGESIS OF THE QURʾĀN: CLASSICAL AND MEDIEVAL; EXEGESIS OF THE QURʾĀN: EARLY MODERN AND CONTEMPORARY). The vast range and extent of interpretations accorded individual portions of the Qurʾān are indices of its immense influence as scripture in Islam: when the Qurʾān or any other scriptural text achieves such massive authoritative and sacred status among its adherents, it will be appropriated to justify and explain any and everything that a person or group may want to do, for it will be understood to deliver divine sanction to actions taken to be in accord with its message. From the point of view of the history of religion, one might reasonably argue that the Qurʾān, like any of the world's major scriptures, has been much more frequently used to good than to evil ends — otherwise, it could not long have sustained so great and influential a tradition as that of Islam.

The permeating force of scripture in Muslim life

As the foregoing suggests, it is difficult to overemphasize the degree to which Islamic societies, both those of Muslim-majority countries and those of Muslim minorities in non-Muslim countries, have been saturated in most aspects of everyday life with the presence of the qurʾānic scripture and informed in a variety of specialized disciplines and fields by focus on the Qurʾān as scripture. It is the very fact of its being venerated as scripture, looked to for authoritative guidance as scripture, and received as the direct and powerful presence of the divine working in the world through scripture that has placed the Qurʾān at the center of what it is to be Muslim.

For an adequate understanding of the Qurʾān in its function as scripture, one has to look to the centuries-long, defining impact of this text on Muslims in multiple dimensions of their lives. The full extent of this impact can only be adumbrated here by noting briefly some of the most salient instances of qurʾānic influence beyond those already mentioned above. These include the central role of the qurʾānic scripture as a source for personal and communal norms, legal justification, and religious guidance (see VIRTUES AND VICES, COMMANDING AND FORBIDDING). They include also the Qurʾān's preeminent role in personal spirituality and piety (q.v.), in popular superstition and bibliolatry, in high culture, in education and moral guidance, in liturgical and ritual use, and in inspiration for (as well as justification of) religious faith and dogma. These dimensions of the Qurʾān's roles as scriptural authority and source of divine power cannot be adequately pursued in the compass of the present article; for a fuller sense of the extent and depth of the Qurʾān's role as scripture, see inter alia MEDICINE AND THE QURʾĀN; SHĪʿISM AND THE QURʾĀN; AMULETS; CONTEMPORARY CRITICAL PRACTICES AND THE QURʾĀN; COSMOLOGY; GEOGRAPHY; DEBATE AND DISPUTATION; LITERARY STRUCTURES OF THE QURʾĀN; MUṢḤAF; MYSTERIOUS LETTERS; NUMEROLOGY; PERSIAN LITERATURE AND THE QURʾĀN; AFRICAN LITERATURE; SOUTH ASIAN LITERATURE AND THE QURʾĀN; SOUTHEAST ASIAN LITERATURE AND THE QURʾĀN; TURKISH LITERATURE AND THE QURʾĀN; PRINTING OF THE QURʾĀN;

READINGS OF THE QUR'ĀN, in addition to the articles already cross-referenced above.

William A. Graham

Bibliography

Primary: Baqillānī, *Iʿjāz;* Ibn Ḍurays, *Faḍāʾil;* Ibn Kathīr, *Faḍāʾil;* Ibn Taymiyya, *Muqaddima;* Jeffery, *Muqaddimas;* Jurjānī, *Dalāʾil;* Nasāʾī, *Faḍāʾil;* Sinai Arabic MS 434, ff. 171r-181v; Suyūṭī, *Itqān;* Thaʿālibī, *Iʿjāz;* Theodore Abū Qurra, *La discussion d'Abū Qurra avec les ulemas musulmans devant le calife al-Maʾmūn,* ed. I. Dick, Aleppo 1999; Zarkashī, *Burhān.*

Secondary: M. Ayoub, *The Qurʾān and its interpreters,* Albany, NY 1984, i, 1-40 (Introduction); D. Brown, *A new introduction to Islam,* Blackwell 2004; id., *Rethinking tradition in modern Islamic thought,* New York 1996; S. Dähne, Qurʾānic wording in political speeches in classical Arabic literature, in *Journal of qur'anic studies* 3 (2001), 1-14; A. von Denffer, *ʿUlūm al-Qurʾān. An introduction to the sciences of the Qurʾān,* Markfield, UK 1983; F. Denny, Exegesis and recitation. Their development as classical forms of qurʾānic piety, in F. Reynolds and T. Ludwig (eds.), *Transitions and transformations in the history of religions (J. Kitagawa Festschrift),* Leiden 1980, 91-123; C. Geertz, Art as a cultural system, in *Modern language notes* 91 (1976), 1473-99; Graham, *Beyond;* id., The earliest meaning of *Qurʾān,* in *WI* 23/24 (1984), 361-77; id., Qurʾān as spoken word, in R. Martin (ed.), *Approaches to Islam in religious studies,* Tucson 1985, 23-40; id., Scripture, in *ER,* xiii, 133-45; Ihsanoglu, *Translations;* J. Jomier, *L'islam vécu en Égypte,* Paris 1994; id., La place du Coran dans la vie quotidienne en Égypte, in *IBLA* 15 (1952), 131-65; N. Kermani, *Gott ist schön. Das ästhetische Erleben des Koran,* Munich 1999; J. Kritzeck, *Peter the Venerable and Islam,* Princeton 1964; J. Leipoldt and S. Morenz, *Heilige Schriften. Betrachtungen zur Religionsgeschichte der antiken Mittelmeerwelt,* Leipzig 1953; M. Levering (ed.), *Rethinking scripture. Essays from a comparative perspective,* Albany, NY 1989; D. Madigan, *The Qurʾān's self-image. Writing and authority in Islam's scripture,* Princeton 2001; A. Musa, *A study of early and contemporary Muslim attitudes toward ḥadīth as scripture,* PhD diss., Harvard U. 2004; K. Nelson, *The art of reciting the Qurʾān,* Austin, TX 1985; J.D. Pearson, Translations of the Ḳurʾān, in *EI²,* x, 429-32; W. al-Qāḍī, The impact of the Qurʾān on early Arabic literature. The case of ʿAbd al-Ḥamīd's epistolography, in Hawting and Shareef, *Approaches,* 283-313; W.C. Smith, Scripture as form and concept. Their emergence for the western world, in M. Levering (ed.), *Rethinking scripture. Essays from a comparative perspective,* Albany, NY 1989, 29-57 (repr. as chap. 3 of id., *What is scripture?,* Minneapolis 1993); id., *What is scripture? A comparative approach,* Minneapolis 1993; N. Söderblom, *Einführung in die Religionsgeschichte,* Leipzig 1920; H.M. Vroom and J.D. Gort (eds.), *Holy scriptures in Judaism, Christianity and Islam,* Amsterdam/Atlanta 1997.

Scrolls

A roll of paper or parchment for writing a document. The Qurʾān refers to scrolls (*ṣuḥuf* and *zubur* — see also PSALMS; for the different terminology for writing as vehicle of divine command, see Ghedira, Ṣaḥīfa, and Madigan, *Qurʾān's self-image,* 131-2) as written documents (and thus conflated to *kutub,* e.g. Q 98:1-2; see BOOK) that contain God's edicts (cf. Schoeler, Writing), especially his judgments against former nations (see Ṭabarī, *Tafsīr,* ad Q 20:133; see JUDGMENT; GENERATIONS; HISTORY AND THE QURʾĀN). The idea of scrolls is thus meant to be a clear sign *(bayyina)* to Muḥammad's audience of the consequences they will face if they persist in their ingratitude (see GRATITUDE AND INGRATITUDE) and resistance to the divine communication (for scrolls as a sign of religious authority see Madigan, *Qurʾān's self-image,* 7; see SIGNS; AUTHORITY; PROVOCATION; OPPOSITION TO MUḤAMMAD). The demand for scrolls by Muḥammad's audience (Q 74:52; Ṭabarī, *Tafsīr,* ad loc. gives the report of Qatāda and Mujāhid that people wanted to know who specifically was being addressed by God; for demands that Muḥammad produce a book, see Q 4:153; 6:7; 17:93) is met with the claim that there is evidence *(bayyina)* of God's will in previous scrolls (i.e. scripture; see SCRIPTURE AND THE QURʾĀN) given to Adam (i.e. the first scrolls, Q 20:133; 26:196; see ADAM AND EVE) and to Moses (q.v.) and Abraham (q.v.;

Q 53:36-7; 87:16-9; see also PROPHETS AND PROPHETHOOD; MESSENGER). The conclusion is drawn that these prophetically conveyed scrolls, having caused division and ingratitude among former nations, will also be met with disagreement — now as an authoritative sign of Muḥammad's mission (Q 98:1-4; Ṭabarī, *Tafsīr,* ad Q 98:2 gives the report of Mujāhid that Muḥammad is no mere prophet within the Judeo-Christian heritage and that he has been given evidence of divine truth, making disagreement over it henceforth impossible; see TRUTH). The demand for scrolls is thus turned into an opportunity to accuse people of disdain for the next world and a warning for them to take heed (see WARNER; ESCHATOLOGY; REWARD AND PUNISHMENT). Indeed, the Qurʾān expresses surprise that people have not heard the news contained in scrolls about the fate of former nations (Q 53:36 f.; see PUNISHMENT STORIES).

The point is clear: socio-political prosperity (see POLITICS AND THE QURʾĀN; COMMUNITY AND SOCIETY IN THE QURʾĀN), i.e. avoiding destruction by God, depends on obedience (q.v.) to God's edicts promulgated in scrolls via messengers of God. It is thus in an eschatological tone that mention is made of the scrolls which will divulge human deeds on judgment day (Q 81:10; Ṭabarī, *Tafsīr,* ad loc. associates scrolls with a record of human deeds to be published on judgment day; see LAST JUDGMENT; HEAVENLY BOOK) — rhetorical encouragement for Muḥammad's audience to choose the next world over this one by recalling the stories contained in the scrolls (Q 80:12-7; Ṭabarī, *Tafsīr,* ad Q 80:13 associates them with the "preserved tablet" [q.v.], *al-lawḥ al-maḥfūẓ,* that the angels have periodically recited as scripture to various prophets; see ANGEL), i.e. the destruction met by former nations (*umam khāliya,* not mentioned but clearly assumed, see Ṭabarī, *Tafsīr,* ad Q 20:133) for refusing to accept God's judgment (cf. Q 87:16-9). Those who accuse Muḥammad of lying about the source of his message should recall that the same accusation was faced by previous messengers of God who came with evidence, scrolls and the illuminating book (Q 3:184; 35:25), in which it is recorded that God caused the earth to swallow up people who did not give heed to former prophets (Q 16:43-5). In short, the idea of scrolls is a rhetorical tool used by the Qurʾān to signify that the record of human deeds has been well documented and should be taken as a warning to those who do not give heed to the divine reminder (Q 54:51-3; see INSOLENCE AND OBSTINACY), making the notion of scrolls an important element in understanding the qurʾānic conception of scripture.

The idea that revelation was not disclosed at once (Q 25:32-3) corresponds to the fact that scrolls containing verses of the Qurʾān were not initially recorded in a single text (see Burton, *Collection,* 119, 139, 141), giving to qurʾānic textual material a fluidity in its earliest form (i.e. pre-ʿUthmānic recension; see COLLECTION OF THE QURʾĀN; CODICES OF THE QURʾĀN; MUṢḤAF) and thereby enabling Muslim scholars to posit an incomplete qurʾānic text *(muṣḥaf)* as reason to explain occasional conflict between Qurʾān and sunna (q.v.; see Burton, *Collection,* 105-13). It is the idea of an open-ended qurʾānic revelation that can help us to understand the early recourse to scrolls as extra-qurʾānic scriptural authority (e.g. Baghdādī, *Taqyīd,* 54-7; the first written collection of prophetic reports, allegedly by ʿAbdallāh ʿAmr al-ʿĀṣ [d. 63/682], was called "the true scroll," *al-ṣaḥīfa al-ṣādiqa;* see SHEETS). The possibility of confusing non-qurʾānic prophetic material in written form with qurʾānic textual material resulted in strong warnings in certain circles against writing down such material (see

Cook, The opponents). Indeed, the concept of scrolls as divine revelation recorded in writing has caused considerable ambiguity over the value of books as vehicle for the transmission of prophetic material (see Heck, Epistemological problem; cf. Melchert, Ibn Mujāhid). See also GOSPEL; TORAH; REVELATION AND INSPIRATION; INSTRUMENTS; WRITING AND WRITING MATERIALS; ORALITY AND WRITING IN ARABIA; MANUSCRIPTS OF THE QURʾĀN.

Paul L. Heck

Bibliography

Primary: al-Baghdādī, Abū Bakr Aḥmad b. ʿAlī al-Khaṭīb, *Taqyīd al-ʿilm,* ed. Y. al-ʿIshsh, n.p. 1975; Ṭabarī, *Tafsīr.*
Secondary: Burton, *Collection;* M.A. Cook, The opponents of the writing of tradition in early Islam, in *Arabica* 44 (1997), 437-530; A. Ghedira, Ṣaḥīfa, in *EI²*, viii, 834; P.L. Heck, The epistemological problem of writing in Islamic civilization. Al-Ḫaṭīb al-Baġdādī's (d. 463/1071) *Taqyīd al-ʿilm,* in *SI* 94 (2002), 85-114; D.A. Madigan, *The Qurʾān's self-image. Writing and authority in Islam's scripture,* Princeton 2001; Ch. Melchert, Ibn Mujāhid and the establishment of seven qurʾānic readings, in *SI* 91 (2001), 5-22; G. Schoeler, *Écrire et transmettre dans les débuts de l'Islam,* Paris 2002.; id., Writing and publishing. On the use and function of writing in the first centuries of Islam, in *Arabica* 44 (1997), 423-35.

Sea see WATER; NATURE AS SIGNS

Seal [of the Prophets] see MUḤAMMAD; NAMES OF THE PROPHET

Seasons

Each of the four divisions of the year (spring, summer, autumn, and winter), marked by particular weather patterns and daylight hours. Arabia, the cradle of Islam, has different seasons, notably a suffocatingly hot summer, while in the higher places it can be bitterly cold during the winter. In spring and autumn many days are mild. There is no word for season in the Qurʾān. The word *mawsim* (pl. *mawāsim*) occurs in ḥadīth (see ḤADĪTH AND THE QURʾĀN) in the sense of market or fair, mostly combined with a pilgrimage (q.v.; *ḥajj*) to a sanctuary, like those held in various places in pre-Islamic and early Islamic Arabia (see PRE-ISLAMIC ARABIA AND THE QURʾĀN). Because these markets (q.v.) took place at a fixed season, the word has also assumed this latter meaning.

In the Qurʾān most references to season are related to the calendar (q.v.). In Islam the calendar is based on a purely lunar year, but in pre-Islamic Arabia this was not the case. Because various names of the Arabian months (q.v.), in so far as these are clear, are related to seasons, it is commonly thought that the old Arabian year was a solar year. For instance, the name Ramaḍān (q.v.), the only name of these months mentioned in the Qurʾān (Q 2:185), is derived from a root that indicates the heat of the summer. From Q 10:5 and Q 36:39, however, it can be concluded that shortly before the advent of Islam the "stations" *(manāzil)* of the moon (q.v.) were used as a measure of time. Because in the period prior to Islam the annual Meccan *ḥajj* (pilgrimage plus market) had to take place in a suitable season of the solar year, it became necessary to prolong the lunar year by intercalating a month every three years to correct the discrepancy between the lunar and the solar year and thus make the lunar month of the *ḥajj* fall within the same season every year. This intercalation *(nasīʾ)* is mentioned in Q 9:37, which characterizes it as "an increase in unbelief" and consequently forbids this practice. Since then, a purely lunar year has been the standard in Islam and consequently the various months of the lunar year move independently of the seasonal year (Wellhausen, *Reste,* 87, 94-8).

In only two cases in the Qurʾān do the

names of a particular season occur, namely in Q 106:2, where the winter and summer journey (q.v.; *riḥlat al-shitāʾi wa-l-ṣayfi*) of the Quraysh (q.v.) are mentioned. Usually this winter journey is interpreted as a trade caravan (q.v.) heading from Mecca (q.v.) to the Yemen (q.v.) in the cold season, while the summer journey is identified with the trade caravan from Mecca towards Syria (q.v.) in the hot season. Q 106 in its entirety should be understood as a sign of God's benevolence towards the Quraysh since, after the rise of Mecca as sacrosanct territory (see PROFANE AND SACRED), the city had become the most important center of pilgrimage and trade in Arabia, as a consequence of which the Quraysh were no longer forced to endure the hardships of the seasonal trade journeys to support themselves (Rubin, Īlāf, 175).

Nico J.G. Kaptein

Bibliography
P. Crone, *Meccan trade and the rise of Islam,* Princeton 1987; P. Kunitzsch, al-Manāzil, in *EI²*, vi, 374-6; A. Moberg, Nasīʾ, in *EI²*, vii, 977; U. Rubin, The *īlāf* of Quraysh. A study of sūra cvi, in *Arabica* 31 (1984), 165-88; J. Wellhausen, *Reste arabischen Heidentums,* Berlin 1897.

Seat [of God] see THRONE OF GOD; GOD AND HIS ATTRIBUTES

Sechina see SHEKHINAH

Secretaries of Muḥammad see COMPANIONS OF THE PROPHET; TEXTUAL CRITICISM OF THE QURʾĀN; COLLECTION OF THE QURʾĀN

Secrets

Hidden matters. Broadly conceived, secrets as a concept relevant to the Qurʾān may include the "unconnected letters" (*ḥurūf muqaṭṭaʿa;* cf. Rāzī, *Tafsīr,* ii, 3; see MYSTERIOUS LETTERS) and the hidden or inward meanings *(bāṭin)* of the qurʾānic passages, which are different from their literal or outward meanings (*ẓāhir;* see POLYSEMY). Some of the mystics and Shīʿī thinkers (see ṢŪFISM AND THE QURʾĀN; SHĪʿISM AND THE QURʾĀN) claim this way of thinking, which is often supported by a ḥadīth report (see ḤADĪTH AND THE QURʾĀN) regarding the fourfold sense of the qurʾānic text (cf. Böwering, *Mystical,* 139-42; Mullā Ṣadrā, *Mafātīḥ,* 39; cf. Böwering, Scriptural "senses"; Lazarus-Yafeh, Are there allegories). Different kinds of secret knowledge are also subsumed under the divine mystery *(ghayb),* which no one knows except God (cf. Q 27:65; see HIDDEN AND THE HIDDEN).

The word *ghayb* implies exclusively divine secrets to which human senses are unable to gain access. On the other hand, the word *sirr,* "secret," refers to hidden matters in general and, in particular, to matters that human beings keep secret in their minds. Different verbal forms of the root *s-r-r* are utilized as signifying the act of hiding and concealing together with the words derived from the roots *kh-f-y* and *k-t-m*. The words derived from these three roots are often used in a similar way, as found in Q 2:77 *(s-r-r),* Q 2:284 *(kh-f-y)* and Q 2:33 *(k-t-m).*

The Qurʾān stresses that God knows everything regardless of whether human beings make it hidden or evident, simply because he is the master of the worlds (see LORD). Since the heavens and the world include human beings as well as their external conduct and psychic characteristics, the master of the worlds naturally governs human beings and their souls (see SOUL). Such different characteristics of the soul as virtue (q.v.), evil (see GOOD AND EVIL), faith (q.v.), unbelief (see BELIEF AND UNBELIEF), love (q.v.) and anger (q.v.) may be expressed in their bodily and verbal acts or may remain hidden. God's final judgment (see LAST JUDGMENT) is always based on the inward aspects of the soul that form the basis of external conduct, be they apparent or hidden, as understood in the context of Q 2:225, Q 2:283 and Q 17:36 (cf. Q 2:284 and Ṭabāṭabāʾī, *Mīzān,* ii, 435-7). The doctrine of religious dissimulation (q.v.; *taqiyya*), which is based on Q 16:106 (also cf. Q 3:28), presupposes the qurʾānic notion of divine omniscience (see KNOWLEDGE AND LEARNING; POWER AND IMPOTENCE), through which God perceives the believer's true intention hidden behind an outward statement made against his will.

Because the words *sirr* and *khafī (akhfā)* in the Qurʾān seem to refer to something secret or to hidden aspects of human consciousness, Ṣūfīs have incorporated them in their theories of the inner subtleties *(laṭāʾif),* a type of religious psychology that analyzes the structure of human inward consciousness. For example, in his *Risāla* (46, 48), a well-known compendium of mysticism, al-Qushayrī (d. 465/1072) presents a four-dimensional structure of human consciousness, which consists of soul (q.v.; *nafs*), heart (q.v.; *qalb*), spirit (q.v.; *rūḥ*) and inmost consciousness/secret *(sirr)*. The *sirr*, the last and deepest dimension of human consciousness, is characterized by a place of contemplation *(mushāhada)* and realization of divine unification *(tawḥīd)*. Although different thinkers present different schemes of *laṭāʾif,* many of the Ṣūfīs and mystical philosophers locate *sirr* at the deepest dimension in the human consciousness, where they realize enlightenment with a divine encounter.

Shigeru Kamada

Bibliography

Primary: Qushayrī, *al-Risāla al-qushayriyya,* Cairo 1959; Rāzī, *Tafsīr;* Ṭabāṭabāʾī, *Mīzān.*

Secondary: Böwering, *Mystical;* id., The scriptural "senses" in medieval Ṣūfī Qurʾān exegesis, in J.D. McAuliffe, B.D. Walfish and J.W. Goering (eds.), *With reverence for the word. Medieval scriptural exegesis in Judaism, Christianity and Islam,* New York 2003, 346-65; R. Gramlich, *Die schiitischen Derwischorden Persiens IIi. Glaube und Lehre,* Wiesbaden 1976; id. (trans.), *Das Sendschreiben al-Qušayrīs über das Sufitum,* Wiesbaden 1989; S. Kamada, A study of the term *sirr* (secret) in Sufi *laṭāʾif* theories, in *Orient. Report of the Society for Near Eastern Studies in Japan* 19 (1983), 7-28; H. Lazarus-Yafeh, Are there allegories in Ṣūfī Qurʾān interpretation? in J.D. McAuliffe, B.D. Walfish and J.W. Goering (eds.), *With reverence for the word. Medieval scriptural exegesis in Judaism, Christianity and Islam,* New York 2003, 366-75; Mullā Ṣadrā, Ṣadr al-Dīn Muḥammad al-Shīrāzī, *Mafātīḥ al-ghayb*, ed. M. Khājavī, Tehran 1984; M. al-Tahānawī, *Kitāb Kashshāf iṣṭilāḥāt al-funūn,* 2 vols., Calcutta 1862.

Sect

see SHĪʿA; PARTIES AND FACTIONS

Sedition and Public Disorder

see CORRUPTION; DISSENSION; POLITICS AND THE QURʾĀN

Seeing and Hearing

The action of the eyes (q.v.), and of the ears (q.v.), respectively. Seeing and hearing are understood to be attributes of God and the terms are used literally as human bodily senses as well as metaphorically in the senses of "to know," "to understand," and "to learn" (see KNOWLEDGE AND LEARNING; GOD AND HIS ATTRIBUTES; HEARING AND DEAFNESS; VISION AND BLINDNESS; METAPHOR).

Baṣīr, "the one who sees, the all-seeing," is an attribute of God mentioned forty-two times in the Qurʾān, ten times immediately following "hearing" or "all-hearing," *samīʿ*. The sequencing of these two attributes probably reflects the constraints of the rhyme scheme of the sūras (q.v.) in which this refrain is found rather than a presumed privileging of one sense over the other (see FORM AND STRUCTURE OF THE

QUR'ĀN; LANGUAGE AND STYLE OF THE QUR'ĀN). Nine times the adjective *baṣīr* is used in reference to humans, including the statement, "We [i.e. God] made him hearing, seeing" (Q 76:2) and "The likeness of the two parties is as the man blind and deaf, and the man who sees and hears; are they equal?" (Q 11:24); the other seven instances contrast sight and blindness. The sense of "sight" as the noun *baṣar* (pl. *abṣār*) is a human trait only, the word often meaning the physical eye, as in, "It is not the eyes *(al-abṣār)* that are blind" (Q 22:46) and "They cast down their eyes" (*abṣārihim,* Q 24:30-1). The physical "eye" is also referred to thirty-six times with the word *ʿayn* (pl. *aʿyun*), which is used of both humans and God as in Q 11:37, "Make the ark (q.v.) under our eyes!" and Q 52:48, "You are before our eyes." The related verbal usage "seeing" as conveyed through *abṣara* and its derivatives (used thirty-six times), predominates in qur'ānic mentions of humans and their ability to perceive: "They have eyes *(aʿyun)* but perceive not *(lā yubṣirūna)* with them" (Q 7:179). *B-ṣ-r* (and its derivatives) is sometimes used in opposition to being blind and, at other times, is used rhetorically (see RHETORIC AND THE QUR'ĀN), as in "Will you [or they] not see?" (e.g. Q 28:72; 32:27). The verb is also used on a few occasions in reference to God, as in Q 18:26, "God knows how long they [the men of the cave; q.v.] stayed; to him belong the unseen in the heavens and the earth (see HIDDEN AND THE HIDDEN). How well he sees *(abṣir)!* How well he hears!"

More common words for dealing with human perception are related to *naẓara,* which is used over one hundred times in the Qur'ān. This root incorporates a broad range of usages, including the imperative, where it is usually translated as "Behold!" Here, the sense is turning one's attention to something, making it the focus of one's gaze. Among the instances of the use of this root is the famous passage Q 75:22-3, "Some faces on that day will be radiant, upon their lord they will be gazing *(nāẓira),*" which created significant theological controversy by suggesting that God could be perceived physically in the hereafter (see FACE OF GOD; ANTHROPOMORPHISM; THEOLOGY AND THE QUR'ĀN).

Ra'ā, on the other hand, is the most widely used root suggesting "seeing" and it conveys a sense of seeing with the eyes but with a strong tendency towards "thinking" as well, especially in the rhetorical, "What do you think *(a-ra'aytum)?*" and variations thereon (Q 6:46; 11:28, 63; 53:19; 96:9, etc.). Moses (q.v.), however, "saw *(ra'ā)* a fire" (q.v.; Q 20:10) and "saw *(ra'ā)* [his staff] quivering like a serpent" (Q 27:10; see ROD). The word is also used of God but infrequently, as in "Surely I will be with you [Moses and Aaron], hearing and seeing *(arā)*" (Q 20:46; see AARON); the fact that the rhyme of this section of the Qur'ān (see RHYMED PROSE) is long "a" undoubtedly dictated this usage of *arā* rather than the more common *baṣīr* in reference to God. Other instances include Q 9:94, 105, and Q 96:14 in which God sees what people do, once again a sensation more often invoked by *baṣīr,* as in Q 3:15, 156, 163, etc.

Fundamentally, the use of all these words suggests that the metaphor of sight as "insight" is well entrenched in Arabic and the Qur'ān. This metaphor appears in many cultures and time periods and reflects what is often termed the prejudice of sight as the "queen of the senses." This becomes especially clear when it is contrasted to the way in which the word for "hearing" is used. "Hearing" *(samīʿ)* is less fully metaphorized in the Qur'ān compared to sight, but on occasion clearly tends towards "learn," suggesting a somewhat more passive action than the active sense "insight" suggests. This applies to God as well, with the frequent conjunction of the "all-hearing, all-knowing" (*ʿalīm*) and the descriptive "hearing, knowing," which occur thirty-two times in total (e.g. Q 2:127, 137, 181, 224; 3:34; 29:5; 29:60; 41:36; 44:6; 49:1; etc.). Such a combination highlights the physicality of knowledge — hearing in order to learn — as compared to the greater inner sense of "insight" through focused seeing; however, as mentioned above, God is both the all-hearing and the all-seeing. Once again, given the predominance in the qurʾānic rhyme scheme of "m" rather than "r," it is not surprising that "all-knowing" (*ʿalīm*) should gain quantitative preference over "seeing" (*baṣīr*) when used in the rhyme position.

In a physical sense, God "hears" petitions from believers (Q 3:38; 14:39) and hears human speech as in Q 58:1, "God has heard the words of her that disputes with you about her husband." Overall, the literal sense of "hearing" is strong in the Qurʾān, often emphasizing the aspect of the orality (q.v.) of the Qurʾān itself in conveying the message. Believers must listen to the Qurʾān (see RECITATION OF THE QURʾĀN; RECITERS OF THE QURʾĀN). The ear (*udhun*, pl. *ādhān*) is clearly indicated as the physical part of the body associated with the sense of hearing, being named eighteen times in the Qurʾān; Q 2:19 suggests putting fingers in one's ears in order not to hear, for example.

Islamic law worked out the metaphorical implications of the conceptions related to "seeing" and "hearing" in the Qurʾān in the realm of Muslim practice (see LAW AND THE QURʾĀN). Blindness and deafness were seen as bodily defects that could disqualify a person from certain legal duties. This is inherent in the Qurʾān when it suggests, for example, that "blindness" is associated with doubt (see UNCERTAINTY), error (q.v.), dark (see DARKNESS), lacking understanding (see IGNORANCE) and sickness (see ILLNESS AND HEALTH), as when the heart (q.v.) is metaphorically linked to blindness in Q 22:46, "What, have they not journeyed in the land so that they have hearts to understand with or ears to hear with? It is not the eyes that are blind, but blind are the hearts within the breasts." While there are many statements in the Qurʾān which suggest that the blind and the seeing are equal (as are the deaf and the hearing), the negative connotations that were carried through the metaphorical usages tended to influence the definition of a full human being. For example, in most law schools a judge (*qāḍī*) must be of sound sight and hearing but such strictures did not prevent many unsighted people from becoming famous in the classical and modern Islamic world, a world where blindness was, and continues to be, a significant sociological fact.

Other aspects of "seeing and hearing" can be considered in relationship to the Qurʾān and its mode of existence and production in the world. That is, Muslims have seen the interaction of both of these human senses with the text of the Qurʾān as vitally important. The Qurʾān has been produced in a manner most pleasing to the sense of sight (see CALLIGRAPHY; ORTHOGRAPHY; MANUSCRIPTS OF THE QURʾĀN; ORNAMENTATION AND ILLUMINATION) and the recitation of the text is designed to produce an aural effect on the person. The privileging of the aural/oral results more from dogmas related to the transmission and preservation of the text of the Qurʾān (which likely evolved in contexts of inter-religious polemic; see COLLECTION OF THE QURʾĀN; CODICES OF THE QURʾĀN; POLEMIC AND POLEMICAL LANGUAGE; MUṢḤAF) than from the appreciation of one range of sense data over another.

Andrew Rippin

Bibliography
van Ess, *TG*, iv, 387-392, 411-5; D. Gimaret, *La doctrine d'al-Ashʿarī*, Paris 1990, 329-44; id., *Les noms divins en Islam. Exégèse lexicographique et théologique*, Paris 1988, 262-8; A. Rippin, Blindness in the Qurʾān, in M. Khaleel and A. Rippin (eds.), *Coming to terms with the Qurʾān* [tentative title] (forthcoming).

Self

see SOUL; SPIRIT

Selling and Buying

see TRADE AND COMMERCE; ECONOMICS AND THE QURʾĀN; CARAVAN; MARKETS

Semantics of the Qurʾān

see LANGUAGE AND STYLE OF THE QURʾĀN; GRAMMAR AND THE QURʾĀN; RHETORIC AND THE QURʾĀN; POST-ENLIGHTENMENT ACADEMIC STUDY OF THE QURʾĀN

Semiotics and Nature in the Qurʾān

see NATURE AS SIGNS; POST-ENLIGHTENMENT ACADEMIC STUDY OF THE QURʾĀN

Sense(s)

see SEEING AND HEARING; VISION AND BLINDNESS; HEARING AND DEAFNESS; SMELL; EARS; HANDS; FACE

Serpent

see ANIMAL LIFE

Servants

Creatures bound in service to God. In over 100 places, the Qurʾān describes prophets (see PROPHETS AND PROPHETHOOD), believers (see BELIEF AND UNBELIEF), jinn (q.v.; cf. Q 51:56) and angels (see ANGEL) as servants (*ʿabd*, pl. *ʿibād*, *ʿabīd;* also *ʿābid*, pl. *ʿābidūn*) of God. Human beings in general are also described as God's servants, though they may be currently worshipping Satan (see DEVIL) or another false god (e.g. the *ʿabada l-ṭāghūt* in Q 5:60, the only occurrence of this plural form; see IDOLS AND IMAGES; POLYTHEISM AND ATHEISM). The relationship of master and servant is one of the key metaphors (see METAPHOR) used by the Qurʾān to describe God's relationship to his creatures (see CREATION).

In classical Arabic, *ʿabd* has two primary meanings: slave to a human being (see SLAVES AND SLAVERY) and servant of a divine being. The Qurʾān, however, nearly always uses *ʿ-b-d* in the sense of divine service or worship (q.v.). The five or six places where this root refers to slaves are usually marked by semantic qualifiers, such as *ʿabd mamlūk* in Q 16:75. The qurʾānic commentary known as *al-Jalālayn* (ad loc.) explains: "*[Mamlūk]* is an adjective which distinguishes [the slave] from the free [servant], who is 'the servant of God.'" As discussed below, the Qurʾān sometimes plays off these two meanings in explaining the proper role for God's servants. The medieval distinction, however, between plurals of *ʿabd* (*ʿibād* for servants, *ʿabīd* for slaves; see *Lisān al-ʿArab*, iii, 271) does not obtain in the Qurʾān, where with one exception both refer to servants. This change in meaning accords with the semantic range of Semitic cognates (Jeffery, *For. vocab.*, 209-10; Dandamaev, *Slavery*, 85n).

One can identify four distinct categories for servants in the Qurʾān. First, all human beings are God's servants, whether they recognize this fact or not. For example, Q 19:93 states: "There is no one in the heavens and earth but comes to the all-merciful as a servant." Unbelievers are also explicitly described as God's servants in Q 25:17, where God gathers together the false gods and says: "Was it you that misled these my servants *(ʿibādī)* or did they stray from the path (see ERROR; ASTRAY; PATH OR WAY)?" There are also statements that could refer to all humankind or to believers, such as numerous refrains describing

God as generous, all-seeing, or not unjust to his servants (e.g. *Allāhu raʾūfun bi-l-ʿibādi* in Q 2:207; see GIFT-GIVING; SEEING AND HEARING; JUSTICE AND INJUSTICE; GOD AND HIS ATTRIBUTES).

A second category comprises those who explicitly believe in God. A partial definition of what this service entails is found in Q 25:63-8, which describes the *ʿibād al-raḥmān* as those who speak peacefully (see PEACE), pray (see PRAYER), spend money moderately, and do not call on other gods, kill or commit adultery (see MURDER; ADULTERY AND FORNICATION). God's servants are also described in several places as *mukhliṣ/mukhlaṣ* (sincere, pure in faith; alternatively, chosen; see ELECTION), and in Q 38:82-3 Iblīs threatens God that he will lead astray all except his sincere servants. In Q 37:40 f., these sincere servants are promised paradise (q.v.).

The title *ʿabd Allāh*, "God's servant" (var. *ʿabdī, ʿabduka, ʿabduhu*, etc.) forms a third category, usually reserved for God's prophets, specifically Muḥammad (q.v.), Jesus (q.v.), Zechariah (q.v.), Job (q.v.), Solomon (q.v.), David (q.v.), Aaron (q.v.), Moses (q.v.), Joseph (q.v.), Lot (q.v.), Abraham (q.v.) and Noah (q.v.). Moses' companion in Q 18:65, often identified in the commentaries as Khaḍir/Khiḍr (q.v.), is also *ʿabd min ʿibādinā*. Several times, Muḥammad is referred to obliquely as "my/his/our servant" (e.g. Q 2:23; 17:1; 18:1; 25:1) or even "a servant" in Q 96:10. The restriction of this usage suggests a special relationship between God and his prophets.

The final category of servants in the Qurʾān includes angels and other creatures, some of whom may have been worshipped by human beings. For example, Q 7:194 is generally understood to refer to idols when it states, "those on whom you call apart from God, are servants *(ʿibād)* the likes of you." In contrast, Q 17:5 refers to "servants belonging to us and possessing great strength," which most commentators connect to various armies or warriors from biblical stories (see SCRIPTURE AND THE QURʾĀN; NARRATIVES; FIGHTING; WAR). Many qurʾānic verses refer to angels and Q 43:19 states directly that angels are *ʿibādu l-raḥmāni*. The commentators, however, clarify that angels are absolutely obedient to God's will (see OBEDIENCE; FREEDOM AND PREDESTINATION), unlike human servants who may go astray.

Several contexts are useful in making sense of these various meanings. First, service to deities was something well known in seventh-century Arabia, as evidenced by theophoric names. For example, the great-great-grandfather of the Prophet, ʿAbd Manāf, was so called "because his mother Ḥubbā offered him to Manāf, the greatest of the idols of Mecca (q.v.), to show her devotion *(tadayyunan)* to it" (Ṭabarī, *Taʾrīkh*, ii, 254, trans. in Watt, *Muḥammad*, 19). Other attested names were ʿAbd al-ʿUzza, ʿAbd Shams and ʿAbd Manāt. This form of naming, and the attendant right to service, has a long history in Near Eastern cultures (Dandamaev, *Slavery*, 82-5; and Herrenschmidt, Bandaka, iii, 684). But the claims of the gods to service extended only to their devotees, not to humankind in general.

A second, more distant context, that of the Hebrew scriptures, accords more readily with the qurʾānic conception of God as universal lord (q.v.), though the language of servanthood is more restricted. As in the Qurʾān, various prophets are occasionally described, or describe themselves, as God's servant (Hebrew *ʿeved*), such as Abraham, Isaac, Caleb, Joshua and Samuel. But Moses is God's servant par excellence in the Bible, and is designated dozens of times as such. God's people, the Children of Israel (q.v.), are also described as his servants (e.g. *Lev* 25:55), but, in the Bible, this term is nowhere universalized to encompass all humankind as in the Qur'ān. Neither are angels explicitly called God's servants, though they clearly carry out his will.

The Christian scriptures are even more reticent to designate someone a servant of God, and when this term does appear, it usually echoes the Hebrew scriptures (Luke 2:29; Acts 2:18). Two innovative uses, however, are worth noting. In Revelation 19:9-10, John prostrates himself to an angel, who responds, "You must not do that. I am a fellow servant with you and your brethren" (also *Rev* 22:8-9). This is the only naming of angels as God's servants in the Bible, and the accompanying command not to worship angels finds a parallel in the Qur'ān. Second, while the teachers of the early church were not called servants of God, they were referred to as "servants (Gr. *douloi*, sing. *doulos*) of Christ" (Rom. 1:1; James 1:1, 2; Peter 1:1; etc.). Martin sees this title as an attempt to raise these men to the status of Moses and the prophets (Martin, *Slavery*, 54-6), but it may also be seen as a claim about the divine status of Jesus.

That title continued to be used in the Christian church, and it may have provided the context for Q 3:79 which states: "It is not for a human being *(bashar)* that God should give him the book (q.v.), judgment (q.v.), and prophethood, and then he should say to people, 'Be my servants, apart from God *(kūnū ʿibādan lī min dūni llāh)*.' Rather, 'Be you masters *(rabbāniyyīn)* by knowing the book and studying" (see KNOWLEDGE AND LEARNING; SCHOLAR). The commentators gloss *bashar* here as Jesus and cite the following occasion of revelation (see OCCASIONS OF REVELATION): "It was revealed when a Christian from Najrān (q.v.) said that Jesus ordered them to take [himself] as a lord *(rabb)*, and when [the Christian] demanded that some Muslims prostrate to [Jesus]" (*Jalālayn*, ad Q 3:79; see also Wāḥidī, *Asbāb*, ad loc.; see CHRISTIANS AND CHRISTIANITY; BOWING AND PROSTRATION). This is just one example in which the Qur'ān sets up its theology of servanthood in contrast to servants of other religious traditions.

The Qur'ān explicitly rejects local conceptions of what it means to be a servant when Muḥammad is instructed to say, "I am not serving *(ʿābid)* what you serve" (Q 109:4; see POLEMIC AND POLEMICAL LANGUAGE). Further correction of contemporary misconceptions is found in Q 51:56-7: "I created jinn and humankind only to serve me *(li-yaʿbudūnī)*. I do not desire provisions from them, nor do I wish them to feed me." This idea of "feeding" God might be a reference to pre-Islamic sacrifices to idols (see SACRIFICE; CONSECRATION OF ANIMALS), although most commentators understand it as a metaphor for God's self-sufficiency. For example, al-Rāzī (d. 606/1210) imagines these words in God's mouth "I am not like a [human] master in demanding service, for [masters] profit from the service [of their slaves]" (Rāzī, *Tafsīr*, xxviii, 234, ad Q 51:56-7). In other ways, however, God's relationship to his servants is seen as precisely cognate to the master-slave relationship. In Q 5:118, Jesus addresses God, saying, "If you chastise them (see CHASTISEMENT AND PUNISHMENT), they are your servants; if you forgive (see FORGIVENESS) them, you are the almighty."

In these passages, important theological distinctions are expressed in the language of servitude (see THEOLOGY AND THE QUR'ĀN). Human beings are servants and God is their master but, unlike human masters, God is utterly self-sufficient and does not benefit from the service of the believers; nonetheless, he retains rights over them much as a master has over a slave. For their part, human believers are not to think of themselves as servants of anyone or anything else but rather are to gain mastery through knowledge *(ʿilm)*, usually understood as knowledge of the law (see LAW AND THE QURʾĀN). Therefore it is through their righteous actions that Muslims exhibit their service to God.

As regards God's special servants, his prophets, the Qurʾān seems to speak in a Judeo-Christian idiom. It is primarily interested in extending the rank of prophet to Muḥammad and in reducing Jesus and other local deities to the rank of servant. For example, Q 4:172 states: "The Messiah will not disdain to be a servant of God, neither the angels who are near [to God]. Whoever disdains to serve him, and waxes proud (see PRIDE; ARROGANCE), he will compel all of them to come before him." Jesus' statement from the cradle that he is God's servant *(ʿabdu llāhi)* in Q 19:30 is also a rejection of Christian conceptions of Jesus as the son of God (Anawati, ʿĪsā, 83).

While the religious implications of the lord-servant relationship were well established in Arabia, this metaphor gained additional meaning from the local practice of slavery (see PRE-ISLAMIC ARABIA AND THE QURʾĀN). For example, Q 16:71 states: "God has preferred some of you over others in provision; but those that were preferred should not relinquish their provision to their slaves to make them equal; do they deny God's blessing?" In what appears to be a straightforward regulation of slavery, some commentators see an allegorical polemic explaining why God does not accept worship of idols. For example, al-Qurṭubī (d. 671/1272) writes: "If you do not allow your slaves *(ʿabīdukum)* to be equal with you, then how can you make my servants *(ʿabīdī)* equivalent to me?" (*Jāmiʿ*, x, 141, ad Q 16:71; cf. Ṭabarī, *Tafsīr*, ad loc.). Such a statement depends on a culture with clear class distinctions between master and slave to make sense (see COMMUNITY AND SOCIETY IN THE QURʾĀN; CLIENTS AND CLIENTAGE). On the other hand, slaves were treated as members of the family and could even serve as the master's agent in business affairs. Such practices provide a context for explaining that God's sincere servants are also granted a level of intimate contact, and that God's prophets serve as his representatives in reminding and warning humankind (see REMEMBRANCE; WARNER).

In the modern world, where slavery has been nearly eradicated, the prominent qurʾānic metaphor of master-servant may seem authoritarian and restrictive. Yet medieval commentators found this metaphor to be a rich source for describing the believer's relationship to God. In the introduction to his *Revivication of the religious sciences*, al-Ghazālī (d. 505/1111; *Iḥyāʾ*, i, 11) demonstrates the range of "the desirable characteristics by… which the servant can gain the favor of the lord of the worlds," devoting hundreds of pages to ten main characteristics, such as repentance (see REPENTANCE AND PENANCE), patience (see TRUST AND PATIENCE), and thankfulness (see GRATITUDE AND INGRATITUDE). Ṣūfīs and other devotees were pleased to call themselves slaves of God, and female Ṣūfīs even gained a measure of worldly freedom by devoting themselves entirely to God (Cornell, *Early Sufi women*, 54-9; see ṢŪFISM AND THE QURʾĀN). Muslims continue to demonstrate their devotion to God by taking on typical names, such as ʿAbdallāh or ʿAbd al-Raḥmān.

Recent translations of the Qurʾān by Muslims steeped in this tradition sometimes prefer to translate *ʿabd* as slave instead of servant (e.g. Pickthall, al-Ḥilālī and Khān; see TRANSLATIONS OF THE QURʾĀN). Such a translation reflects the Qurʾān's propensity to use the human master-slave relationship to explain the believer's relationship to God; but in a world where slavery is rightly condemned as an objectionable practice, it can also hide the rich variety of meanings inherent in the Qurʾān's conception of God's servants. See also SLAVES AND SLAVERY.

Jonathan E. Brockopp

Bibliography
Primary: al-Ghazālī, Abū Ḥāmid Muḥammad b. Muḥammad, *Iḥyāʾ ulūm al-dīn*, 5 vols., Beirut 1991 (repr.); M. al-Hilālī and M. Khān, *Interpretation of the meanings of the noble Qurʾān in the English language*, Riyadh 1972, 1994[4] (rev. and enl. ed.); *Jalālayn; Lisān al-ʿArab;* Pickthall, *Koran;* Qurṭubī, *Jāmiʿ;* Rāzī, *Tafsīr;* Ṭabarī, *Tafsīr;* id., *Taʾrīkh*, ed. de Goeje; trans. W.M. Watt, *The history of al-Ṭabarī. vi. Muḥammad at Mecca*, Albany 1988; Wāḥidī, *Asbāb*.
Secondary: G. Anawati, ʿĪsā, in *EI*², iv, 81-6; J.E. Brockopp, *Early Mālikī law. Ibn ʿAbd al-Ḥakam and his major compendium of jurisprudence*, Leiden 2000; R. Cornell, *Early Sufi women*, Lexington 1999; M.A. Dandamaev, *Slavery in Babylonia (626-331 B.C.)*, trans. V.A. Powell, DeKalb, IL 1984; C. Herrenschmidt, Old Persian Bandaka, in *Encyclopedia Iranica*, London 1982-, iii, 684; Izutsu, *Concepts;* id., *God and man in the Koran. Semantics of the koranic Weltanschauung*, Tokyo 1964; Jeffery, *For. vocab.;* D.B. MacDonald, Malāʾik, in *EI*², vi, 216-9; D. Martin, *Slavery as salvation. The metaphor of slavery in Pauline Christianity*, New Haven 1990; B. Wheeler, *Prophets in the Qurʾān. An introduction to the Qurʾān and Muslim exegesis*, London 2002.

Seven Sleepers see MEN OF THE CAVE

Sex and Sexuality

The act by which humans procreate, and the sum total of those attributes that cause an individual to be physically attractive to another. While the Qurʾān does criticize lust for women as an example of man's infatuation with worldly pleasures (cf. Q 3:14), it does not categorically condemn sex as a cause of evil and attachment to the world. The Qurʾān does recognize sex as an important feature of the natural world and subjects it to legislation in a number of passages (see LAW AND THE QURʾĀN). It accepts sex as a natural and regular part of human existence, specifically authorizing sexual pleasure and not simply condoning sex for the sake of procreation. It restricts sex to the institutions of marriage and slavery (see MARRIAGE AND DIVORCE; SLAVES AND SLAVERY), and condemns incest, adultery, fornication (see ADULTERY AND FORNICATION), prostitution, promiscuity, lewdness (see CHASTITY; MODESTY), and male homosexual sex (see HOMOSEXUALITY), while defining marriage and divorce in ways which modified and restricted the variety of unions found in pre-Islamic Arabian practice (see PRE-ISLAMIC ARABIA AND THE QURʾĀN). Sex also plays an important role in several narratives (q.v.) related to the biblical tradition, including the stories of Adam and Eve (q.v.), Lot (q.v.), Joseph (q.v.), and Mary (q.v.), as well as in descriptions of paradise (q.v.).

Licit sex in the Qurʾān is designated by the term *nikāḥ*, "intercourse, marriage" and its derivatives (Q 2:221, 230, 232, 235, 237; 4:3, 6, 22, 25, 127; 24:3, 32, 33, 60; 28:27; 33:49, 50, 53). Illicit sex or sexual infractions are termed *fāḥisha* (Q 3:135; 4:15, 19, 22, 25; 7:28, 80; 17:32; 24: 19; 27:54; 29:28; 33:30; 65:1), pl. *fawāḥish* (Q 6:151; 7:33; 42:37; 53:32), usually referring to specific instances of adultery, fornication, or other sexual offenses, or the collective term *al-faḥshāʾ* (Q 2:169, 268; 7:28; 12:24; 16:90; 24:21; 29:45). Adultery or fornication is designated by the term *zinā* and the related verb *zanā, yaznī;* adulterers are *al-zānī* and *al-zāniya* (e.g. Q 17:32; 24:2, 3; 25:68; 60:12), which is related to Hebrew *zonah*, "prostitute," and perhaps derives ultimately from the biblical tradition (see SCRIPTURE AND THE QURʾĀN). The most frequent terms for both male and female genitals are *farj*, pl. *furūj*, literally "cleft, opening"

(Q 21:91; 24:30, 31; 33:35; 66:12; 70:29) and *sawʾa, sawʾāt* "pudenda, bad part" (Q 7:20, 22, 26, 27; 20:121).

Naturally occurring pairs are an important part of the order of the universe which the Qurʾān cites again and again as evidence for God's existence and unity (see PAIRS AND PAIRING; GOD AND HIS ATTRIBUTES). Pairs appear in the example of the animals brought onto Noah's (q.v.) ark (q.v.; Q 11:40; 23:27), fruit trees on earth (q.v.) and in paradise (Q 13:3; 55:52; see ANIMAL LIFE; AGRICULTURE AND VEGETATION), and generally: "He created the pair, male and female" (Q 53:45); "We have created everything in pairs, that you might reflect" (Q 51:49; see CREATION; REFLECTION AND DELIBERATION; NATURE AS SIGNS). This general principle applies to humans as well: "And [God] made from it [a drop of sperm] the pair, the male and the female" (Q 75:39); "O humankind! We have created you male and female, and have made you nations and tribes, that you may know one another..." (Q 49:13; see TRIBES AND CLANS); "God created you from dust, then from a sperm-drop, then he made you pairs..." (Q 35:11; see BIOLOGY AS THE CREATION AND STAGES OF LIFE); "Among his signs (q.v.) is that he created for you mates from yourselves so that you might find tranquility in them, and he put love (q.v.) and mercy (q.v.) between you. Therein are indeed signs for folk who reflect" (Q 30:21). One understands from such statements that pairs occur by divine design and that the bond between sexual partners is therefore natural and subject to divine sanction. This view is corroborated by a number of passages elaborating an idea found in post-biblical Jewish texts and in Plato, that men and women are attracted to each other naturally by virtue of having been created out of a single original being: "Humankind! Fear (q.v.) your lord (q.v.), who created you of a single soul, and from it created its mate, and from the pair of them scattered abroad many men and women" (Q 4:1); "He it is who created you from a single soul, and made from it its mate, so that he might find tranquility in her..." (Q 7:189); "He created you from a single soul, then from it made its mate" (Q 39:6). The Qurʾān avoids the hierarchy involved in viewing Eve as created from Adam's rib, a story the Qurʾān does not include, and a ḥadīth (see ḤADĪTH AND THE QURʾĀN) describes women as *shaqāʾiq* "slices, or split halves" of men. The Qurʾān stresses that the sexual bond is intended as a comfort for both partners: "They [women] are a garment for you, and you a garment for them (see CLOTHING)... So lie with them *(bāshirūhunna)*, and seek what God has prescribed for you" (Q 2:187). Marriage is understood to prevent sexual frustration and temptation to sin (Q 4:25; see SIN, MAJOR AND MINOR). The command to marry is general; all who can afford it are enjoined to do so (Q 24:32). Celibacy is not regarded as a virtue, and a well-known ḥadīth of the Prophet states, "There is no monasticism in Islam" (see ABSTINENCE; ASCETICISM; MONASTICISM AND MONKS). The Prophet is also reported to have advised, "Whoever is well-off, let him marry; he who does not marry is not one of us"; "O assembly of young men! Whoever among you can afford to, let him marry, for it is more effective in lowering one's gaze and keeping one's genitals chaste. Whoever cannot, should fast; it has the effect of restraining lust."

The Qurʾān conceives of marriage as a legal contract, one of God's fundamental laws (*ḥudūd Allāh*, Q 2:187, 229-30; 4:12-4; 65:1; see BOUNDARIES AND PRECEPTS; CONTRACTS AND ALLIANCES). The relatives with whom sexual relations would be considered incest are listed as follows (see PROHIBITED DEGREES): "Forbidden (q.v.) to you are your mothers, your daughters, your sisters, you father's sisters, your mother's sisters, your brother's daughters, your sister's daughters, your foster-mothers, your foster-sisters, your mothers-in-law, your step-daughters who are under your protection (born) of your wives unto whom you have gone in — but if you have not gone in unto them, then it is no sin for you (to marry their daughters) — and the wives of your sons from your own loins. It is forbidden that you should take two sisters together, except what has already happened in the past. God is forgiving and merciful" (Q 4:23; see KINSHIP). First cousins are acceptable mates (Q 33:50). Qurʾānic legislation prohibits what were evidently pre-Islamic Arabian practices including the inheriting of wives or marrying women formerly married to one's father (cf. Q 4:19, 22) and effecting a divorce by *ẓihār*, that is, for a man to repudiate his wife by uttering the traditional oath, "You are to me like my mother's back" (Q 58:2-3). The number of wives has traditionally been limited to four on the basis of the verse "marry the women who are pleasing to you — in twos, threes, or fours — and if you fear that you cannot be fair, then one, or those that your right hands possess" (Q 4:3). The suggestion here is that while it is permissible to have four wives, one wife is preferable in some cases. The prophet Muḥammad is known to have had more than four wives, but this is explained as a special dispensation for prophets (cf. Q 33:50; see WIVES OF THE PROPHET). Muslim men and women are forbidden to marry idolaters (Q 2:221; see IDOLATRY AND IDOLATERS). It is permitted for masters to have sex with their slave-women, "what your right hands possess," and this is recommended as an appropriate alternative for men who cannot afford a regular marriage and fear that they will be tempted (Q 4:3, 24, 25; 23:6; 70:30). The *mahr* or *ṣadāq*, "dower," is an essential feature of the marriage contract; it is specified as a payment to the bride herself, and not to her father or guardian (cf. Q 4:4; see BRIDEWEALTH). The *shighār*, by which two men agree to marry their wards to each other in order to avoid paying the *mahr*, is condemned in ḥadīth and the legal tradition, though it does not appear in the Qurʾān (Ibn Rushd, *Bidāyat al-mujtahid*, ii, 43). The legality of temporary or fixed-term marriage *(mutʿa)* in return for payment is a complex issue and is a matter of controversy (see TEMPORARY MARRIAGE). For example, the Shīʿites claim that the second caliph (q.v.), ʿUmar, banned the practice and that it is condoned by the qurʾānic verse, "Those of (the women) from whom you seek contentment *(fa-mā stamtaʿtum bihi minhunna)*, give to them their payments *(ujūr)* as an obligation" (Q 4:24; see SHĪʿISM AND THE QURʾĀN). Sunnī authorities argue that the Prophet banned the practice shortly before his death, though it had been condoned during his mission, and that this verse refers to the *mahr* in a regular marriage (Ibn Rushd, *Bidāyat al-mujtahid*, ii, 43).

According to tradition, marriage must be publicized: a feast or celebration *(walīma)* is thought to be necessary. A well-known ḥadīth report states, "What distinguishes the lawful from the unlawful is the drum and shouts of the wedding" (see LAWFUL AND UNLAWFUL). Accepting an invitation to a wedding feast is strongly encouraged.

The Qurʾān does not restrict sexual positions, and specifically permits husbands to take their wives as they wish: "Your wives are a field for you. Come at your field from where you will" (Q 2:223). The commentaries specify that this verse was directed at the Jews' (see JEWS AND JUDAISM) condemnation of vaginal intercourse from behind, which they claimed would produce cross-eyed children (Nasāʾī, *ʿIshrat al-nisāʾ*, 56-7). Sex during menstruation (q.v.) is forbidden

(Q 2:222). Though not mentioned in the Qurʾān, anal sex is forbidden in the ḥadīth and the legal tradition; a few ḥadīth reports allow it (Nasāʾī, *ʿIshrat al-nisāʾ*, 57-71). *Coitus interruptus (ʿazl)* is sanctioned in the ḥadīth; this ruling is presented as a correction of Jewish tradition (Nasāʾī, *ʿIshrat al-nisāʾ*, 93-9). Some authorities stipulate that a husband must have a wife's permission to do this, in contrast to his treatment of a slave-woman; others hold that it is reprehensible though not forbidden. Tradition also recommends invoking God's blessing before sex, "In the name of God. Oh God, keep Satan away from us, and keep away from Satan what you have granted us." This is supposed to protect any offspring conceived from being harmed by Satan (Tirmidhī, *Ṣaḥīḥ*, no. 1098; Nasāʾī, *ʿIshrat al-nisāʾ*, 74-5; see DEVIL). One should have some sort of cover over both partners' buttocks during sex; it is improper to be completely nude and exposed (Nasāʾī, *ʿIshrat al-nisāʾ*, 73; see NUDITY). Men are advised to wait until their partners are satisfied during sex before terminating (Tijānī, *Tuḥfat al-ʿarūs*, 113-4). The Prophet is supposed to have advised, "One among you should not fall upon his wife as a beast does. Let there be between you a messenger." He was asked, "What is that, O messenger of God?' He answered, "Kissing and talk" (Tijānī, *Tuḥfat al-ʿarūs*, 114). Some reports, particularly sex manuals, stress that the Prophet condoned making excited noises during sex *(ghunj)*, including grunting and snorting. These texts connect such sexual noises with the qurʾānic term *rafath*, which is forbidden during the pilgrimage (q.v.; Q 2:187, 197). The term is taken either to be a euphemism for intercourse or to mean sexually explicit talk in general or making noise or engaging in sexually explicit talk during sex (Tijānī, *Tuḥfat al-ʿarūs*).

Some passages stress the symmetry of the sexual and marital relationship, but other passages make it clear that the rights of men and women concerning sex differ (see GENDER; WOMEN AND THE QURʾĀN). The Qurʾān regularly addresses men primarily regarding sex, marriage, and related issues (see PATRIARCHY). Men have the prerogative of polygamy and repudiation, and the main purposes of marriage, judging from the presentation of its rules, are to satisfy male sexual needs and to allow procreation while preserving accurate male genealogy. Women, though, have an understood right to conjugal duties; we may understand this as not only the opportunity to conceive and procreate, but also that for sex and companionship. The Qurʾān condemns the Prophet's withholding of sexual relations with his wives (Q 66:1), and leaving wives alone in their beds is deemed a punishment for rebelliousness (Q 4:34). In addition, *īlāʾ*, a husband's oath foreswearing sex with his wife, was held to dissolve the marriage contract if they did not resume after four months (cf. Q 2:226).

Prostitution is condemned, particularly as directed toward slave-women (cf. Q 7:33; 16:90; 24:33). A ḥadīth holds that the Prophet outlawed three fees customary in pre-Islamic Arabia: the fee *(mahr)* of a prostitute, the price *(thaman)* of a dog, and the honorarium *(sulwān)* of a soothsayer (see SOOTHSAYERS). Promiscuity and lewdness are also condemned. The Qurʾān praises devout women who preserve the "secret" or "mystery" of sex: "Good women are obedient and guard in secret that which God has guarded" (Q 4:34). Believers are entreated to exhibit what is termed *iḥṣān* or *taḥaṣṣun* (cf. Q 4:24, 25; 5:5; 21:91; 24:4, 23, 33; 59:2, 14; 66:12), the basic meaning of which is to guard, preserve. Mary the mother of Jesus (q.v.) is described as having "guarded" her genitals (Q 21:91; 66:12); this is parallel to verses which use the verb *ḥafiẓa, yaḥfaẓu* and its derivatives to describe both men and women as "guarding" or "preserving" their genitals (Q 23:5; 24:30, 31; 33:35; 70:29). Married persons, those with a licit sexual partner, are termed *muḥṣan, muḥṣana,* "guarded, fortified." Adultery and fornication are forbidden, but the punishments prescribed vary (see CHASTISEMENT AND PUNISHMENT). The punishment is set at one hundred lashes for both men and women in one passage (Q 24:2); another verse instructs that women are to be confined in their houses until death (Q 4:15); the punishment for a false accusation of adultery against a married woman is eighty lashes (cf. Q 24:4; see FLOGGING). Slave-women are to receive half the punishment of free, married women (Q 4:25); the Prophet's wives are to receive double (Q 33:30). The punishment of stoning (q.v.) for married adulterers, which became a standard feature of Islamic law, is based on the sunna (q.v.), including a report that the Prophet ordered that a man be stoned after he confessed to adultery, and the claim, attributed to ʿUmar b. al-Khaṭṭāb, that the Qurʾān originally included a command to stone adulterers *(āyat al-rajm)* that was subsequently lost (Shāfiʿī, *Kitāb al-Umm,* vi, 133-5). The Qurʾān is silent on certain other sexual infractions, including lesbianism *(saḥq, siḥāq),* bestiality, and masturbation *(istimnāʾ, nikāḥ al-yad, jald ʿUmayra).*

Adam and Eve's recognition, at Satan's urging, of their nakedness and shame, at which they cover their pudenda *(sawʾāt)* with leaves of the garden (q.v.) is apparently to be understood as an awareness of sex (Q 7:20-2; 20:121). As confirmation, we may cite one passage that, though it does not mention Adam or Eve by name, refers to the original man's "covering" the original woman and the resulting pregnancy: "It is he who created you from a single soul and made from it its mate, that he might take rest in her. Then, when he covered her, she bore a light burden, and went on her way with it, but when it became heavy they call to God, their lord: If you give us an upright (child?), we shall indeed be thankful" (Q 7:189; see GRATITUDE AND INGRATITUDE). In the story of Lot, the inhabitants of the "sinning cities" *(al-muʾtafika/al-muʾtafikāt),* corresponding to the biblical Sodom and Gomorrah, are clearly addicted to pederasty, later called *liwāṭ* or *lūṭiyya,* which derive from *(qawm) Lūṭ,* "Lot's people," but referred to in the text as an abomination *(fāḥisha)* or lusting after men rather than women. Furthermore, the inhabitants of these cities habitually rape male wayfarers. This is denounced in no uncertain terms, and appears to be the main cause for the cities' destruction. The Lot story includes a morally difficult passage for the commentators (see EXEGESIS OF THE QURʾĀN: CLASSICAL AND MEDIEVAL), where Lot offers his daughters to the crowd clamoring outside his door to deter them from raping his male guests. This seems to be done on the logic that heterosexual sex is a much lesser infraction. The commentators want to avoid attributing such an act to Lot and insist, on little evidence, that he intended to offer his daughters to them in marriage, and not just for sex. In any case, his assailants refuse the offer, confirming their obstinate pursuit of Lot's male guests (Q 7:80-2; 11:77-9; 15:67-71; 27:54-5; 29:28-9).

Perhaps the most dramatic sexual passage in the Qurʾān is the story of Joseph and Potiphar's wife (identified as Zulaykhā in later tradition, but unnamed in the Qurʾān), referred to as the wife of al-ʿAzīz (Q 12:22-35). She tries to seduce Joseph and then accuses him of attempted rape, but he is exonerated and she is rebuked for her misbehavior. The qurʾānic version of the story makes it clear that Joseph is indeed tempted, and would have succumbed had it not been for God's guidance: "She desired him, and he would have desired her had it not been that he saw the sign *(burhān)* of his lord (see PROOF). Thus it was, that we might ward off from him evil and lewdness..." (Q 12:24). His master's wife is clearly driven by lust incited by Joseph's incredible beauty, and she is vindicated when the women who had accused her of improper behavior cut their hands upon witnessing Joseph before them. She is thus excused, to some extent, for her lust, and the commentary tradition portrays her as repenting and being married to Joseph in the afterlife. Sex also plays an important role in the story of Mary, serving to emphasize the miraculous nature of Jesus' birth and the difficult position in which she found herself. Mary fears that the angel (q.v.) sent to announce Jesus' birth is going to rape her. After Jesus is born, she is also accused of being a harlot (*baghiyy*, cf. Q 19:20, 28), but the infant Jesus himself speaks up to defend her (cf. Q 19:30 f.).

Descriptions of the afterlife involve elements of sexual fantasy (see ESCHATOLOGY). The believers are promised beautiful female companions to whom they will be wed in paradise. These companions are large-eyed (*ʿīn*, sing. *ʿaynāʾ*), with marked contrast between the whites and the dark pupils (*ḥūr*, sing. *ḥawrāʾ*) and fair-skinned, being likened to pearls and eggs (see HOURIS). They are "of modest gaze" and virgins, not having been touched before by men or jinn (q.v.; Q 37:48-9; 38:52; 55:56, 72; cf. 44:54; 52:20; 56:22). The believers are to be served in paradise by beautiful boys *(ghilmān, wildān)* as well, also likened to pearls (Q 52:24; 76:19; cf. 56:17).

Devin J. Stewart

Bibliography
Primary: Bukhārī, *Ṣaḥīḥ;* al-Ghazālī, Abū Ḥāmid Muḥammad, *Iḥyāʾ ʿulūm al-dīn,* 5 vols., Beirut 1998; Ibn Rushd, *Bidāyat al-mujtahid,* 2 vols., Cairo n.d.; Muslim, *Ṣaḥīḥ;* Nasāʾī, *ʿIshrat al-nisāʾ,* ed. ʿA.-M.Ṭ. Ḥalabī, Beirut 1997; al-Shāfiʿī, Muḥammad b. Idrīs, *Kitāb al-Umm,* 8 vols., Beirut 1973; Suyūṭī, *Shaqāʾiq al-utrunj fī raqāʾiq al-ghunj,* ed. M.S. al-Rifāʿī, Damascus 2001; id., *al-Wishāḥ fī fawāʾid al-nikāḥ,* ed. Ṭ.Ḥ. ʿAbd al-Qawī, Damascus 2001; al-Tijānī, Muḥammad b. Aḥmad Ibn Abī l-Qāsim, *Tuḥfat al-ʿarūs wa-nuzhat al-nufūs,* Cairo 1987; Tirmidhī, *Ṣaḥīḥ.*
Secondary: A. Bouhdiba, *Sexuality in Islam,* trans. A. Sheridan, London 1985; G.-H. Bousquet, *La morale de l'Islam et son éthique sexuelle,* Paris 1953; A. Gribetz, *Strange bedfellows. Mutʿat al-nisāʾ and mutʿat al-ḥajj. A study based on Sunnī and Shīʿī sources of tafsīr, ḥadīth and fiqh,* Berlin 1994 (good bibliography); S. Haeri, *Law of desire. Temporary marriage in Shīʿī Iran,* Syracuse, NY 1989; W. Heffening, Mutʿa, in *EI²,* vii, 757-9; M.H. Katz, *Body of text. The emergence of the Sunnī law of ritual purity,* Albany 2002; F. Mernissi, *Beyond the veil. Male-female dynamics in a modern Muslim society,* Cambridge, MA 1975, Bloomington, IN 1987 (rev. ed.), repr. London 2003; Ṣ. al-Munajjid, *al-Ḥayāt al-jinsiyya ʿinda l-ʿArab,* Beirut 1958; B. Mussalam, *Sex and society in Islam. Birth control before the nineteenth century,* Cambridge, UK 1983; E. Rowson, *Homosexuality in traditional Islamic culture,* forthcoming; J. Schacht, Nikāḥ. A. In classical Islamic law, in *EI²,* viii, 26-9.

Shade see DARKNESS

Shāfiʿīs see LAW AND THE QURʾĀN

Shahāda see WITNESS TO FAITH

Shayṭān see DEVIL

Sheba

Name of the land in south Arabia whose people developed a prosperous trading civilization in the middle of the first millennium B.C.E., marked by the creation of a kingdom alongside other local states: Maʿin, Qatabān and Ḥaḍramawt. Famous for its caravan (q.v.) traffic and trade in incense and rare spices exported to Babylonia, Egypt and the Mediterranean, the region was called "Arabia Felix" by historians of classical antiquity like

Ptolemy, Strabo or Pliny the Elder. The very existence of the inhabitants of Sheba, the Sabaeans — not to be confused with the Sabians (q.v.), who are discussed in the context of their disputed religious practices (cf. Q 2:62; 22:17; 27:22) — is first attested in the Hebrew Bible (1 *Kgs* 10:18-20 and 2 *Chron* 9:17-9) which reports the meeting between Solomon (q.v.; ca. 970-932 B.C.E.) and the legendary Queen of Sheba, known by the name Bilqīs (q.v.) in qurʾānic exegesis and Islamic sacred history (see HISTORY AND THE QURʾĀN; EXEGESIS OF THE QURʾĀN: CLASSICAL AND MEDIEVAL). The New Testament also evokes this "event" in Luke 11:31. In the Qurʾān, a whole sūra (q.v.) bears the name of "Sheba" (Q 34). It specifically refers to the urban and trading culture of the Sabaeans (Q 34:15-9) for which, in fact, the archeology bears witness through buildings, steles, altars and inscriptions (see ARCHAEOLOGY AND THE QURʾĀN). The latter attest the local language affiliated with Arabic, designated by the terms "south Semitic" or "south Arabian," from which many qurʾānic names and nouns derive (see FOREIGN VOCABULARY). This language resisted the regional spread of Aramaic until the rise of Islam, when it was replaced by Arabic. Q 34:15-6 point out the wealth of the country of Sheba, with its skillfully domesticated landscape endowed with two luxurious gardens and irrigation systems (see GARDEN), as God's sign (see SIGNS). Verse 16, in particular, alludes to the flood caused by the break of the dam of al-ʿArim (q.v.; see also PUNISHMENT STORIES) that occurred circa 542 C.E. in the Yemeni city of Mārib (see PRE-ISLAMIC ARABIA AND THE QURʾĀN).

The Qurʾān provides the Sabaeans with a religious status comparable to that of the Jews and Christians (see JEWS AND JUDAISM; CHRISTIANS AND CHRISTIANITY), for some of them became believers (Q 34:20; see BELIEF AND UNBELIEF) as did their queen (Q 27:44). Q 27 (Sūrat al-Naml, "The Ant") tells the story of the Queen of Sheba's conversion during her reception by Solomon in his fabled palace with a transparent glass floor (see MYTHS AND LEGENDS IN THE QURʾĀN). This qurʾānic narrative (see NARRATIVES; PARABLES) yielded abundant commentaries and stories related in the books on the history of the prophets (Rāzī, *Tafsīr,* xxiv, 200; Ṭabarī, *Taʾrīkh,* i, 684; id., *Tafsīr,* xix, 472-5, ad Q 27:44; Thaʿlabī, *Qiṣaṣ,* 312-3; see PROPHETS AND PROPHETHOOD). These texts evince a particular concern with the illusion effected by the enigmatic glass device, when it appeared to be a pool with which Solomon (q.v.) tested the queen in order to lead her to convert (see TRIAL). Contemporary exegesis demonstrates how the aesthetic cognitive function of the narrative of the Queen of Sheba's conversion complements its main religious message (Gonzalez, *Le piège,* 26-32; id., *Beauty and Islam,* 26-31).

Finally, further details of Sheba are also known through an early (but post-qurʾānic) account related by the historian and commentator Wahb b. Munabbih (d. 110/728 or 114/732) and preserved in Ibn Hishām's (d. ca. 213/828) *Kitāb al-Tījān fī mulūk Ḥimyār.* His report assimilates the kingdom of the Ḥimyarites, who were ruling south Arabia in the third century C.E., to the Sabaeans and descendants of the prophet Hūd (q.v.). In the Qurʾān, Hūd was sent to the Arab tribe of the ʿĀd (q.v.) before Muḥammad, but they rejected him (Q 7:65-72; 11:50-60; 22:42; 26:123-39; 38:12-4).

Valérie Gonzalez

Bibliography
Primary: Ibn Hishām, ʿAbd al-Malik, *Kitāb al-Tījān fī mulūk Ḥimyār,* Hyderabad 1928-9; Kisāʾī, *Qiṣaṣ,* trans. W.M. Thackston, *Tales of the prophets*

of al-Kisa'i, Boston 1978, 309-17; Rāzī, *Tafsīr*, Beirut 1981, 1985³; Ṭabarī, *Tafsīr*, ed. Shākir; id., *Taʾrīkh*, ed. de Goeje; Thaʿlabī, *Qiṣaṣ*, trans. W.M. Brinner, *ʿArāʾis al-majālis fī qiṣaṣ al-anbiyāʾ or "Lives of the prophets,"* Leiden 2002, 519-37; Yaʿqūbī, *Taʾrīkh;* Yāqūt, *Buldān*, 5 vols., Beirut 1955-7.
Secondary: W. Daum, *Yemen. 3000 years of art and civilization in Arabia Felix*, Innsbruck 1988; *Dictionnaire du Judaisme. Encyclopaedia universalis*, Paris 1998, 721-2 (s.v. Sémites); V. Gonzalez, *Beauty and Islam. Aesthetics in Islamic art and architecture*, London 2001 (esp. 26-41); id., *Le piège de Solomon. La pensée de l'art dans le Coran*, Paris 2002; Jeffery, *For. vocab.;* J. Lassner, *Demonizing the Queen of Sheba. Boundaries of gender and culture in post-biblical Judaism and medieval Islam*, Chicago 1984; Y. Moubarac, Éléments de bibliographie sud-sémitique, in *REI* 23 (1955), 121-6; id., Les études d'épigraphie sud-sémitiques et la naissance de l'Islam. Éléments de bibliographie et lignes de recherches, in *REI* 25 (1957), 13-68; id., Les noms, titres et attributs de Dieu dans le Coran et leurs correspondants en épigraphie sud-sémitique, in *Muséon* 68 (1955), 93-135, 325-68; H. Rabin, The origin of the subdivisions of Semitic, in D.W. Thomas and W.D. McHardy (eds.), *Hebrew and Semitic studies presented to G.R. Driver*, Oxford 1963, 104-15; E. Renan, *Histoire générale des langues sémitiques*, Paris 1855; Ch. Robin and B. Vogt (eds.), *Yémen. Au pays de la reine de Sabaʾ. Exposition présentée à l'Institut du monde arabe (25 octobre 1997-28 février 1998)*, Paris 1997 (esp. 64-6: C. Gilliot, "La reine de Sabaʾ. Légende ou réalité?" and 89-93: Ch. Robin, "Fondation d'un empire. La domination sabéenne sur les premiers royaumes"); H. Schwarzbaum, *Biblical and extra-biblical legends in Islamic folk literature*, Walldorf-Hessen 1982.

Sheep see ANIMAL LIFE

Sheets

Flat writing support, made of papyrus *(bardī)*, parchment *(raqq, riqq)*, leather *(adīm, jild)* or, since the late second/eighth century, paper *(kāghadh)*, and used for recording mostly religious, legal and historical texts during the pre- and early Islamic periods (see AGE OF IGNORANCE; PRE-ISLAMIC ARABIA AND THE QURʾĀN). The term "sheets" (*ṣuḥuf*, sing. *ṣaḥīfa*) extends to the (whole or partial) texts thus recorded, synonymous with *kitāb* (pl. *kutub;* see BOOK), *daftar* (pl. *dafātir*) and *kurrāsa* (pl. *karārīs*). Etymologically derived from South Semitic *ṣaḥafa*, "to write," *ṣaḥīfa* literally means "[a thing] written upon" (Nöldeke, *GQ*, ii, 24 n. 4; for qurʾānic attestations of terms relating to the various media used in writing, see SCROLLS; WRITING AND WRITING MATERIALS; INSTRUMENTS).

Like *qirṭās* and *waraq* ("sheet, leaf"), *ṣaḥīfa* does not designate a specific writing material; but unlike both these terms, it also does not specify quantity. Instead, it denotes anything from a single to multiple sheets, the latter rolled up as a scroll *(darj, majalla)* or folded and sewn together as a notebook (Abbott, *Studies I*, 22-3, 57-9, 66). Sheets were kept in scabbards or gathered in bundles, bags, boxes, and other containers. Bound between two covers *(lawḥān, daffatān)* they become a codex (*muṣḥaf;* q.v.), a term early restricted to the Qurʾān. In the plural, *ṣuḥuf* may comprise the complete Hebrew or Muslim scripture or a scholar's collected papers.

In pre-Islamic times, a *ṣaḥīfa* might contain a letter, a legal contract, a poem, an oration, or a collection of sayings. In the Qurʾān, *ṣuḥuf* refer to the Hebrew scripture (see SCRIPTURE AND THE QURʾĀN), the Qurʾān itself, and metaphorically to the divine records of human deeds (see HEAVENLY BOOK). According to tradition, the first redaction of the Qurʾān was comprised of *ṣuḥuf* written by the Prophet's secretary Zayd b. Thābit (d. ca. 42-56/662-76) and preserved by ʿUmar's daughter Ḥafṣa (q.v.); they formed in turn the core for the official redaction led by the same Zayd at the behest of ʿUthmān (see COLLECTION OF THE QURʾĀN; CODICES OF THE QURʾĀN). Ibn Hishām's *Sīra* attributes ʿUmar's conversion (in one of two accounts) to his reading of a *ṣaḥīfa* containing Q 20 (Sūrat Ṭā Hā; Ibn Hishām, *Sīra*, i,

334-5). In the sunna (q.v.), *ṣaḥīfa* refers not only to the Qurʾān but also to early ḥadīth collections (see ḤADĪTH AND THE QURʾĀN) by Companions (see COMPANIONS OF THE PROPHET) and Successors, written ordinances by the Prophet (both of which were handed down in families from one generation to the next) and other writing (Wensinck, *Concordance*, s.v.). Ḥadīth collections such as that of Ibn ʿAbbās (d. 68/687), or the *ṣaḥīfat al-ṣādiqa* of ʿAbdallāh b. ʿAmr b. al-ʿĀṣ (d. 65/684), were numerous (Goldziher, *MS*, ii, 9-11, 194-6; Sezgin, *GAS*, i, 84-90; Motzki, *Anfänge*, 191 n. 588; Azami, *Studies*, 43-4). The Umayyad caliphs ʿUmar II (r. 99-101/717-20) and Hishām (r. 105-25/724-43) made the first efforts to collect these with the assistance of the traditionist al-Zuhrī (d. 124/742). *Ṣuḥuf* further served to record historical accounts (*akhbār;* see HISTORY AND THE QURʾĀN) about the creation (q.v.), pre-Islamic legends (see MYTHS AND LEGENDS IN THE QURʾĀN), the life of the Prophet (see SĪRA AND THE QURʾĀN), and the early Muslim community (see e.g. Abbott, *Studies I;* see COMMUNITY AND SOCIETY IN THE QURʾĀN) as well as works of linguistics and poetry (see GRAMMAR AND THE QURʾĀN; POETRY AND POETS). The earliest extant specimens of such works on papyrus and paper date to the late second/eighth and third/ninth century (see ʿAbdallāh b. Wahb, d. 197/812; cf. Abbott, *Studies I*); others survive independently in later copies (Hammām b. Munabbih, d. 101/719; cf. Azami, *Studies*, appendix) or as part of larger collections, as, for instance, Ibn Ḥanbal's (d. 241/855) *Musnad* (see LAW AND THE QURʾĀN).

A *ṣaḥīfa* served to jot down information as an aid to memory (see ORALITY AND WRITING IN ARABIA). It played an important part in the practice of teaching and transmission, which followed procedures such as in-class audition *(samāʿ)* with subsequent recording at home, in-class dictation *(imlāʾ),* reading an existing copy back to the teacher for correction *(ʿarḍ)* or receiving from him a written copy (*munāwala;* cf. al-Samʿānī, *Adab al-imlāʾ;* see TEACHING AND PREACHING THE QURʾĀN; RECITATION OF THE QURʾĀN). Preserved *ṣuḥuf* of the late second/eighth century show a concern for precision in the use of diacritics, vowel markers, *muhmal* signs, symbols for ḥadīth division and annotations (see Abbott, *Studies I,* document 6 and *Studies II,* document 6; see ORNAMENTATION AND ILLUMINATION; MANUSCRIPTS OF THE QURʾĀN). Typologically the unstructured *ṣaḥīfa* belongs to the formative period of Arabic-Islamic book culture; it precedes the epistle as well as the larger ḥadīth collection *(jāmiʿ),* organized by topic *(muṣannaf, mubawwab)* or source *(musnad),* which some scholars prepared for their students from the late second/eighth century onward. Nonetheless, the term is occasionally applied to a student's whole or partial copy of a thematically organized work (equivalent to *nuskha, juzʾ*). Only from the third/ninth century, with its mass production of manuscript books in the proper sense with title, preface, overall plan, cross references, and addresses of the reader is the *ṣaḥīfa* truly superseded (Schoeler, *Écrire*, 102-7).

Repeated bans on the writing down of ḥadīth by the Prophet and the four "rightly guided" caliphs *(rāshidūn),* as well as the Umayyad caliphs, together with the claims of some scholars of never having used books, conflict with the more frequently cited permission to do so, as well as accounts about the use of writing beginning with Muḥammad's generation (Baghdādī, *Taqyīd;* see ILLITERACY). Political motives aside (see POLITICS AND THE QURʾĀN), underlying this apparent contradiction is a bimodal, interconnected use of memory (q.v.) and writing for mutual correction, with the latter increasing in importance over time (Rāmahurmuzī, *Muḥaddith,* nos. 370-417). This notwithstanding, oral performance and teaching never ceased com-

[1] Notebook of sewn papyrus sheets, resembling the medium of some of the earliest Qur'ān *maṣāḥif*. Taken from A. Grohmann, *Arabische Paläographie*, vol. 1 (Vienna 1967), pl. IX, 2. Courtesy of Harvard University (LSoc 386.3).

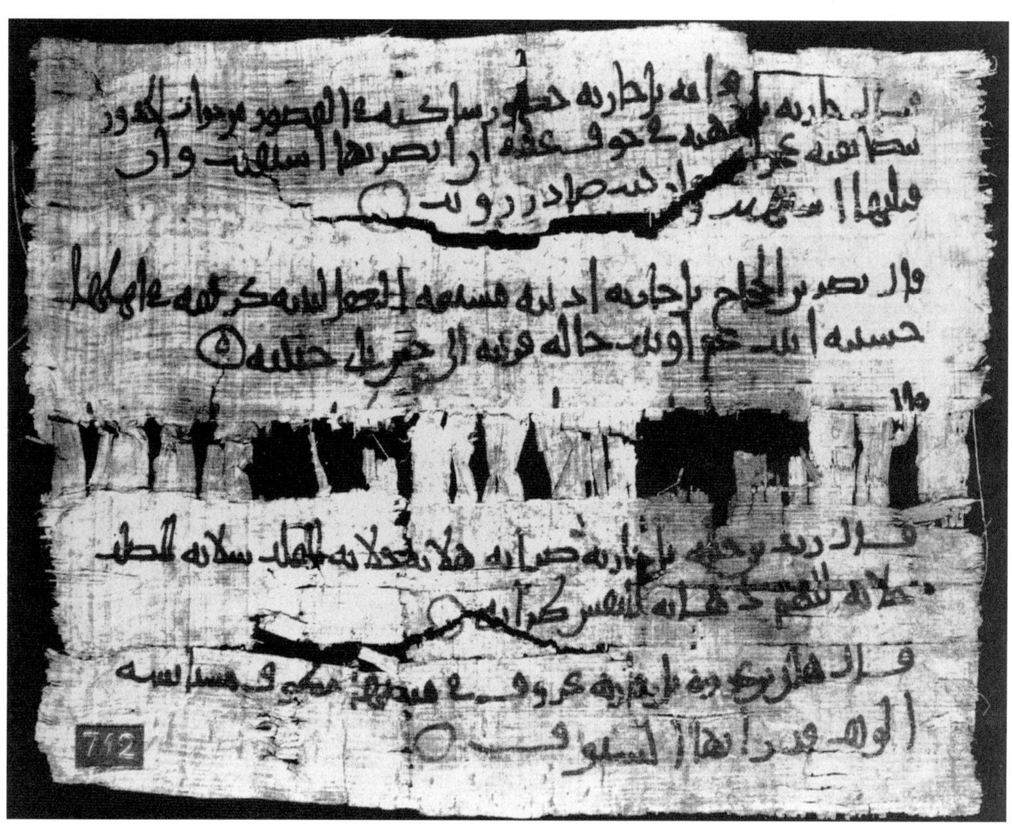

[II] Fragment of papyrus sheet, similar to those upon which early Qurʾān manuscripts would have been inscribed, mid second/third quarter of the eighth century. The specimen depicted here contains a speech of ʿAmr b. al-ʿĀṣ and descriptions of the ideal maiden. Taken from Abbott, *Studies*, iii, document 3, pl. 4. Courtesy of Harvard University (OL 19038.26f).

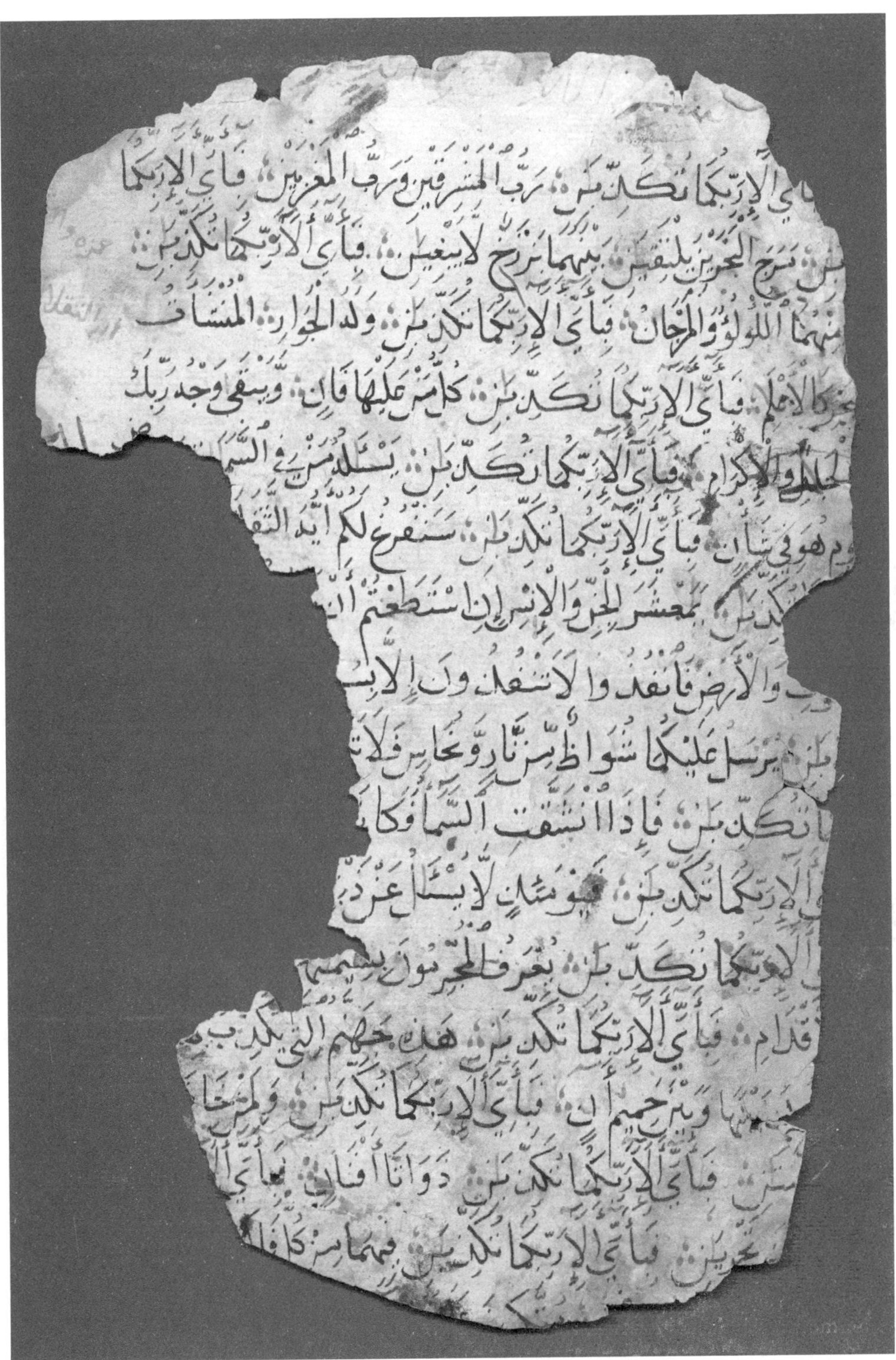

[III] Folio from the Qaṣr Qurʾān containing Q 55:16-53, with marginal notes: Egypt, early twelfth/eighteenth century or before. Courtesy of F. Leemhuis, Groningen University (D03.007b v).

[IV] Folio from the Qaṣr Qurʾān containing Q 55:54-56:17, with marginal notes: Egypt, early twelfth/eighteenth century or before. Courtesy of F. Leemhuis, Groningen University (D03.007b r).

pletely and a good memory continued to be an adornment for a scholar in religion, law and philology. Conversely, a student who learned only from written notes risked being branded a *ṣuḥufī*, i.e. someone who misunderstood and mispronounced his texts for lack of an accompanying oral transmission (Schoeler, *Écrire*, 40, 120-1; see READINGS OF THE QURʾĀN).

As the earliest source for the sunna, *ṣuḥuf* have received great attention. No preserved *ṣaḥīfa*, however, antedates the late second/eighth century, and the authentic survival of the *ṣuḥuf*'s ḥadīth content and notably the chains of transmitters (*isnād*, pl. *asānīd*) in later literature has been challenged in the critical studies of I. Goldziher and J. Schacht (see response by Azami, *Studies*, 215-67) and, more recently, in those of J. Wansbrough, P. Crone and M. Cook. Taking account of the latter scholars' reservations, H. Motzki and G. Schoeler have proposed careful reviews of the sources for jurisprudence and historiography, respectively (on this debate, see Motzki, *Anfänge*, 22-49; Schoeler, *Charakter*, 5-24).

Beatrice Gruendler

Bibliography
Primary: ʿAbdallāh b. Wahb, *Le Jāmiʿ d'Ibn Wahb I-II*, ed. and com. J. David-Weill, 3 pts. in 2 vols., Cairo 1939-48; Abū Dāwūd, ʿAbdallāh b. Sulaymān al-Sijistānī, *al-Maṣāḥif*, ed. A. Jeffery, Cairo 1936, in Jeffery, *Materials;* al-Baghdādī (al-Khaṭīb), *Taqyīd al-ʿilm*, ed. Y. al-ʿUshsh, Damascus 1949; Hammām b. Munabbih, *Sahifa (sic) Hammām b. Munabbih*, intro. and ed. M. Hamidullah, trans. M. Rahimuddin, Paris 1979; Ibn Ḥanbal, *Musnad*, Cairo 1895; Ibn Hishām, *Sīra*, ed. M.F. al-Sarjānī, 2 pts. in 4 vols., Cairo n.d.; al-Rāmahurmuzī, al-Ḥusayn b. ʿAbd al-Raḥmān, *al-Muḥaddith al-fāṣil bayna l-rāwī wa-l-wāʿī*, ed. M.ʿA. al-Khaṭīb, Cairo 1971; al-Samʿānī, ʿAbd al-Karīm b. Muḥammad, *Adab al-imlāʾ wa-l-istimlāʾ* ("Die Methodik des Diktat kollegs"), ed. M. Weisweiler, Leiden 1952; Suyūṭī, *Itqān*.
Secondary: N. Abbott, *Studies in Arabic literary papyri*, 3 vols.: *I. Historical texts. II. Qurʾānic commentary and tradition. III. Language and literature*, Chicago 1957-69; M.M. Azami [Azmi], *Studies in early ḥadīth literature with a critical edition of some early texts*, Beirut 1968, repr. Indianapolis 1978 (see appendix for *ṣuḥuf* of Suhayl b. Abī Ṣāliḥ, d. 138/755, Nāfiʿ the *mawlā* of Ibn ʿUmar, d. 117/735, and al-Zuhrī, d. 124/742); A. Ghédira, *Ṣaḥīfa*, in *EI²*, viii, 834-5; Goldziher, *MS*, repr. Wiesbaden 1961; A. Grohmann, *From the world of Arabic papyri*, Cairo 1952; G. Juynboll, *Muslim tradition. Studies in chronology, provenance and authorship of early ḥadīth*, Cambridge 1983; R.G. Khoury, *ʿAbdallāh b. Lahīʿa (97-174/715-790). Juge et grand maître de l'école égyptienne*, Wiesbaden 1986; id., *Wahb b. Munabbih*, 2 vols., Wiesbaden 1972; H. Motzki, *Die Anfänge der islamischen Jurisprudenz. Ihre Entwicklung in Mekka bis zur Mitte des 2./8. Jahrhunderts*, Stuttgart 1991; Nöldeke, *GQ*, repr. Wiesbaden 1981; J. Schacht, *Origins of Muhammadan jurisprudence*, Oxford 1950; G. Schoeler, *Charakter und Authentie der muslimischen Überlieferung über das Leben Mohammeds*, Berlin/New York 1996; id., *Écrire et transmettre dans les débuts de l'islam*, Paris 2002; id., Mündliche Thora und Ḥadīṯ. Überlieferung, Schreibverbot, Redaktion, in *Der Islam* 66 (1989), 213-41; id., Writing and publishing. On the use and function of writing in the first centuries of Islam, in *Arabica* 44 (1997), 423-35; Sezgin, *GAS*, i; M.Z. Siddiqi, *Ḥadīth literature. Its origin, development and special features*, rev. ed. A.H. Murad, Cambridge 1993; Wensinck, *Concordance*.

Shekhinah

The earthly manifestation of God's presence, a concept common to the Bible and the Qurʾān. Occurring in six verses, *al-sakīna* derives from God and is usually "sent down" to Muḥammad and/or his fellow believers. The Arabic root, *s-k-n*, denotes "stillness, quiet, calm, being motionless," as in Q 6:96: "[God] has made the night [for] stillness/quiet" (see also Q 10:67; 27:86; 28:72; 40:61, etc.), with a secondary meaning (sometimes expressed in the causative fourth form) of "to settle down, to dwell in a habitation" (Q 2:35; 14:37; 17:104, etc.). This parallels the Hebrew/Aramaic/Syriac triliteral root *sh-k-n*, "to settle down, or dwell." The Arabic term *sakīna* also parallels the Hebrew/Aramaic *shᵉkhīnā (shᵉkhīntā)* both linguistically and semantically. Both represent, in the general sense, a divine "in-dwelling."

All qur'ānic renderings of the term *sakīna* occur within militant contexts (see FIGHTING; WAR; EXPEDITIONS AND BATTLES). In Q 2:246-8, the Israelites (see CHILDREN OF ISRAEL) asked their unnamed prophet to raise up a king to lead them in battle (cf. 1 *Sam* 8 f.; see KINGS AND RULERS; PROPHETS AND PROPHETHOOD). When he informs them that God has chosen Saul (q.v.; Ṭālūt), they object because of his lowly stature. In order to prove Saul's divinely chosen status, "Their prophet said to them, the sign of his kingship will be that the ark (q.v.) will come to you containing a *sakīna* from your lord (q.v.) and a remnant of what the family of Moses (q.v.) and the family of Aaron (q.v.) left behind" (cf. *Exod* 25:8).

In three cases, *sakīna* is associated with invisible armies that God sends down from heaven (see HEAVEN AND SKY). In Q 48:4 (after God has just given Muḥammad a clear military victory [q.v.] in a preceding verse: *fatḥ mubīn*, Q 48:1), "He [God] is the one who sent down the *sakīna* into the hearts of the believers (see HEART; BELIEF AND UNBELIEF) to add faith (q.v.; or, *īmān*[an]?) to their faith. To God are the armies of the heavens and the earth...." In Q 9:26, after victories followed by defeat, "Then God sent down his *sakīna* to his messenger (q.v.) and onto the believers and sent down armies you could not see...." In Q 9:40, "... So God sent down his *sakīna* to him [presumably Muḥammad] and supported him with armies that you cannot see...."

In Q 48:18, "God was pleased with the believers when they swore allegiance to you [Muḥammad] beneath the tree (see CONTRACTS AND ALLIANCES; OATHS), and he knew what was in their hearts. So he sent down the *sakīna* to them and rewarded them with an approaching victory." Q 48:26 follows within the same general context of warring and of tension with unbelievers: "When those who disbelieve established scorn in their hearts, scorn of the Age of Ignorance (q.v.; *jāhiliyya*), then God sent down his *sakīna* to his messenger and onto the believers, but required of them a word of piety (q.v.; *al-taqwā*). They were worthy of it and fit for it; and God knows everything."

Traditional Muslim scholarship generally holds that *sakīna* means "quiet" or "tranquility" in most of these verses, based on the Arabic root and buttressed especially by Q 48:26; but because this explanation clearly does not fit Q 2:248 and remains problematic in all but Q 48:26, the exegetes (see EXEGESIS OF THE QUR'ĀN: CLASSICAL AND MEDIEVAL) also rendered it as *naṣr*, meaning "aid," "victory," or even "conquest." Western scholarship considers the term to have derived from the rabbinic concept of *sh*[e]*khīna*, based on Q 2:248, but has had difficulty fitting such a concept into all the other verses.

In every context the *sakīna* is sent down in order to demonstrate God's support for his chosen agent (Saul or Muḥammad) in the face of unbelief, sometimes even among the agent's followers (see OPPOSITION TO MUḤAMMAD; HYPOCRITES AND HYPOCRISY). The contextual meaning of the term therefore denotes divine aid and proof of the authenticity of God's agent in the face of disbelief and adversity, and this aid or proof (or divine presence) comes in the form of divine victory in battle or its potentiality. This representation would fit all qur'ānic contexts.

It is not clear whether *sakīna* in its qur'ānic loci is abstract or has a concrete, tangible existence. In the secondary literature, however, it is clearly represented as the latter. Al-Azraqī (d. ca. 250/865; *Akhbār Makka*, 28) defines the *sakīna* as *rīḥ khajūj lahā raʾs,* "a gale wind with a head," in reference to the extraordinary being that led Abraham (q.v.) to Mecca (q.v.; cf. *Babylonian Talmud, Megilloth,* 29a: "Wherever [Israel] was exiled, the *sheкhīna* went with them"). We find the same and alternative, occasionally sometimes quite fanciful definitions of a sometimes frightening but benevolent being in other works as well (e.g. Ṭabarī, *Taʾrīkh,* i, 275; id., *Tafsīr,* ii, 611; Thaʿlabī *Qiṣaṣ,* 87; Ibn al-Athīr, *Kāmil,* i, 106; *Lisān al-ʿArab,* xiii, 213). *Sakīna* is attested in pre-Islamic sources as meaning quiet and calm, and this may have been associated also with a wind (see AIR AND WIND). The Islamic legends therefore describe an incarnate wind that had become associated with the concept of the *sheкhīna* as the latter became integrated into Arabian culture (see PRE-ISLAMIC ARABIA AND THE QURʾĀN; SOUTH ARABIA, RELIGION IN PRE-ISLAMIC). In the Arabian context, this incarnate and divinely sent *sakīna* wind took on martial power in order to protect its human beneficiaries and bring aid and even victory, especially against the doubters (see UNCERTAINTY) or unbelievers. Finally, al-Bukhārī (d. 256/870) records a tradition that associates this divine presence with the recitation of the Qurʾān (q.v.; cf. *Ṣaḥīḥ,* bk. 61 *[K. Faḍāʾil al-Qurʾān],* no. 531).

Reuven Firestone

Bibliography

Primary: al-Azraqī, Abū l-Walīd Muḥammad b. ʿAbdallāh, *Akhbār Makka,* ed. F. Wustenfeld (as *Chroniken der Stadt Mecca*), 2 vols., Leipzig 1858, repr. Beirut n.d., i, 27-9; *Babylonian Talmud, Megilloth;* Bukhārī, *Ṣaḥīḥ* (on http://64.233.161.104/search?q=cache:1PzZoTtfooAJ:www.balaams-ass.com/alhaj/bukhar61.htm+sakina+quran+hadith&hl=en); Ibn al-Athīr, *Kāmil,* Beirut 1965-7, i, 106; *Lisān al-ʿArab,* xiii, 211-8; Ṭabarī, *Tafsīr,* Beirut 1984; id., *Taʾrīkh,* ed. de Goeje, i, 274-7; trans. W. Brinner, *The history of al-Ṭabarī.* ii. *Prophets and patriarchs,* New York 1987, 69-72; Thaʿlabī, *Qiṣāṣ,* Cairo 1954, 87.

Secondary: R. Firestone, *Journeys in holy lands. The evolution of the Abraham-Ishmael legends in Islamic exegesis,* New York 1990, 68-71, 82-91; I. Goldziher, La notion de Sakîna chez les Mohamétans, in *RHR* 28 (1893), 1-13, repr. in *Ignaz Goldziher Gesammelte Schriften,* ed. J. Desomogyi, 6 vols., Hildesheim 1967-73, iii, 296-308; J. Horovitz, Jewish proper names and derivatives in the Koran, in *Hebrew Union College annual* 2 (1925), 208-9; Jeffery, *For. vocab.;* A.J. Wensinck, The ideas of the western Semites concerning the navel of the earth, in *Verhandelingen der Koninklijke Akademie van Wetenschappen* [N.S.] 17 (1916), repr. in *Studies of A.J. Wensinck,* New York 1978, 60-5.

Shīʿa

Literally, "party/followers." The term *shīʿa* occurs eleven times in the Qurʾān, with the first use in Sūrat al-Anʿām (Q 6, "The Cattle") and the last in Sūrat al-Qamar (Q 54, "The Moon"). The word itself is lexically derived from the Arabic verb *shāʿa, yashīʿu,* meaning "to spread, disseminate, divulge, publicize or become known," and in this sense occurs once, in Q 24:19: "Those who love to spread *(an tashīʿa)* scandal among the believers…." The primary meaning of the term *shīʿa* (pl. *shiyaʿ* and *ashyāʿ*) that is conveyed in the Qurʾān is that of factions, communities, people with similar views and faith, followers and supporters, as portrayed in Q 37:83, "Verily Abraham (q.v.) was surely among the followers [of Noah; q.v.]" *(wa-inna min shīʿatihi la-Ibrāhīm;* see PARTIES AND FACTIONS).

Q 6:65 speaks of God's power to reduce humankind to factions *(aw yalbisakum shiyaʿan),* with exegetes offering varying opinions as to whether *shiyaʿ* meant the Jews and Christians in particular or the consequence of arbitrary human conflict (see JEWS AND JUDAISM; CHRISTIANS AND CHRISTIANITY; RELIGIOUS PLURALISM AND THE QURʾĀN). Al-Qummī (fl. mid fourth/tenth cent.; *Tafsīr,* ad loc.) alludes to religious differences and ʿAlī b.

Muḥammad b. al-Walīd (d. 612/1215; *Tāj*, ad loc.) to community dispute after the Prophet. Q 6:159 refers to those who split their religion and become disparate groups *(kānū shiyaʿan)*, and Q 30:31-2 exhorts believers not to be part of them (see RELIGION; BELIEF AND UNBELIEF). Q 28:4 addresses Pharaoh (q.v.) who arrogantly created divisions among his people *(wa-jaʿala ahlahā shiyaʿan)*. The plural form *ashyāʿ* in Q 34:54 as interpreted by al-Ṭabarī (d. 310/923; *Tafsīr*, ad Q 54:51), refers to those who had intensely questioned the truth (q.v.), while Q 54:51 addresses the polytheists (see POLYTHEISM AND ATHEISM) among Quraysh (q.v.), warning them about how communities in the past had been destroyed (*kamā fuʿila bi-ashyāʿihim;* see PUNISHMENT STORIES).

Q 15:10, on the other hand, employs the term to portray communities to whom messengers (see MESSENGER) had been sent: "Indeed, we sent [messengers] before you among communities of the past" *(arsalnā min qablika fī shiyaʿ al-awwalīna)*. Twice in Q 28:15 it is used for Moses (q.v.), exegetes agreeing that *shīʿatihi* meant the religion of Moses, just as they explain *min shīʿatihi* in Q 37:83 as Abraham following Noah's religion. In Ibn al-Walīd's *Tāj al-aqāʾid*, these verses appear inter-textually to reflect religion as affection for ʿAlī (see ʿALĪ B. ABĪ ṬĀLIB) alongside the prophetic tradition regarding Noah's ark (q.v.), which states that true believers are henceforth called *shīʿa*.

Thus, in four instances (Q 6:65, 159; 28:4; 30:32), the term *shīʿa* has been used to convey the meaning of factions while on four other occasions the word is applied to ancient communities of faith to whom prophets were sent (q.v.; Q 15:10; 28:15 twice; 37:83; see PROPHETS AND PROPHETHOOD). When the Qurʾān speaks of *shiyaʿ al-awwalīn* and *shīʿatihi*, it essentially refers to previously rightly-guided communities (see GENERATIONS), but *kānū shiyaʿan* is used in the divisive sense, while the plural *ashyāʿ* is applied to formerly erring people (see ERROR; ASTRAY), and *min kullī shīʿatin* in Q 19:69 means communities in general.

In post-qurʾānic Arabic writings, the word *shīʿa* can be used in either a qualified or unqualified form, as definite or indefinite. The word can be used in a construct phrase to indicate the "followers" of a particular individual: *shīʿat Muʿāwiya*, for example. Invariably, when the term is found with the definite article *(al-)* and no other qualifier, the followers of ʿAlī are meant: *al-shīʿa* are the "followers [of ʿAlī]" *(shīʿat ʿAlī)*, those who, as described in Abū Ḥātim al-Rāzī's (d. ca. 322/934) *Kitāb al-Zīna*, were intimate with ʿAlī during the lifetime of the Prophet (see also SHĪʿISM AND THE QURʾĀN; FAMILY OF THE PROPHET; PEOPLE OF THE HOUSE; POLITICS AND THE QURʾĀN).

Arzina R. Lalani

Bibliography

Primary: Abū Ḥātim al-Rāzī, Aḥmad b. Ḥamdān, *Kitāb al-Zīna*, ed. in ʿAbdallāh al-Sāmarrāʾi, *al-Ghuluww*, Baghdad 1972; Bayḍāwī, *Anwār;* Ibn al-Walīd, ʿAlī b. Muḥammad, *Tāj al-ʿaqāʾid wa-maʿdin al-fawāʾid*, Beirut 1967; Jaʿfar b. Manṣūr al-Yaman, *Kitāb al-Kashf*, ed. R. Strothmann, London 1952; Naṣr b. Muzāḥim Abū l-Faḍl al-Minqarī, *Waqʿat Ṣiffīn*, ed. ʿA.M. Hārūn, Cairo 1962, 1981[3]; Qummī, *Tafsīr;* Ṭabarī, *Tafsīr;* id., *Taʾrīkh;* Yaʿqūbī, *Taʾrīkh;* Zamakhsharī, *Kashshāf.*
Secondary: M.M. Bar-Asher, *Scripture and exegesis in early Imāmī Shiism*, Leiden 1999; S.H.M. Jafri, *Origins and early development of Shiʿa Islam*, London 1979, 2000[2]; A.R. Lalani, *Early Shīʿī thought. The teachings of Imam Muḥammad al-Bāqir*, London 2000; W. Madelung, *The succession to Muhammad. A study of the early caliphate*, Cambridge 1997; W.M. Watt, *The formative period of Islamic thought*, Edinburgh 1973, Oxford 1998[2]; J. Wellhausen, *The religio-political factions in early Islam*, ed. R.C. Ostle, trans. R.C. Ostle and S.M. Walzer, Amsterdam/New York 1975.

Shīʿism and the Qurʾān

At present, the Shīʿīs, who differ from the Sunnī majority concerning the legitimacy of the political and spiritual succession to Muḥammad, comprise about ten percent of the Islamic community. Like the Sunnīs, they enjoy a rich tradition of scholarship in Islamic sciences, including both ḥadīth collection and classification as well as qurʾānic exegesis. Just as their conception of the legitimate leadership of the Muslim community evolved differently from that of their Sunnī counterparts, so, too, did their understanding of the Qurʾān itself. The following, therefore, will discuss, first, the attitude of the Shīʿa towards the Qurʾān and then provide an overview of the principles and methods of Shīʿī exegesis. It will conclude with a presentation of some of the major Shīʿī exegetes and their works.

The attitude of the Shīʿa to the Qurʾān

One of the bones of contention between Sunnī and Shīʿī Islam concerns the integrity of the Qurʾān. The Shīʿa (q.v.) disputed the canonical validity of the ʿUthmānic codex, the *textus receptus,* of the Qurʾān (see COLLECTION OF THE QURʾĀN; CODICES OF THE QURʾĀN) and cast doubt on the quality of its editing, alleging political tendentiousness on the part of the editors — namely, the three first caliphs (see CALIPH), particularly the third of them, ʿUthmān b. ʿAffān (r. 23-35/644-56). Shīʿī (mainly Imāmī) criticism of the qurʾānic text was most severe in the first centuries of Islam (see POLITICS AND THE QURʾĀN; TEXTUAL CRITICISM OF THE QURʾĀN). The editors were accused of falsification *(taḥrīf)* of the qurʾānic text by both the omission of some phrases and the addition of others (see REVISION AND ALTERATION). Moreover, the claim that the Qurʾān had been falsified is one of the principal arguments to which early Shīʿī tradition resorted to explain the absence of any explicit reference to the Shīʿa in the Qurʾān.

In Shīʿī qurʾānic commentaries many traditions are found accusing the Companions of the Prophet (q.v.) of violating the integrity of the qurʾānic text. In one of these traditions, cited in the commentary *(tafsīr)* ascribed to the Imām Ḥasan al-ʿAskarī (d. 260/873-4), it is stated that "Those whose ambitions overcame their wisdom (*alladhīna ghalabat ahwāʾuhum ʿuqūlahum,* i.e. the *ṣaḥāba*) falsified *(ḥarrafū)* the true meaning of God's book and altered it *(wa-ghayyarūhu)*" (ʿAskarī, *Tafsīr,* 95; cf. Kohlberg, Some notes, 212 and n. 37). A treasure trove of such traditions is *Kitāb al-Qirāʾāt* (known also as *Kitāb al-Tanzīl wa-l-taḥrīf*) by Aḥmad b. Muḥammad al-Sayyārī (fl. late third/ninth century), of which an annotated edition is in preparation by M.A. Amir-Moezzi and E. Kohlberg. A similar tradition — which, however, does not blame the Companions of the Prophet for the falsification — is found in the Qurʾān commentary of al-ʿAyyāshī (d. ca. 320/932): "Had the book of God not been subject to additions and omissions, our righteousness would not have been hidden from any [person] of wisdom" (*lawlā annahu zīda fī kitāb Allāh wa-nuqiṣa minhu mā khafiya ḥaqqunā ʿalā dhī ḥijan;* ʿAyyāshī, *Tafsīr,* i, 25). In a similar tradition it is stated: "The [Qurʾān] contained the names of [various] persons, but these names have been removed" (*kānat fīhi asmāʾu l-rijāl fa-ulqiyat;* ibid., i, 24). The commentator does not attempt to validate this general claim with examples of texts that, in his opinion, have been altered.

Just how unspecific these traditions are can be demonstrated by an account ascribed to Imām Jaʿfar al-Ṣādiq (d. 148/765), cited in relation to verse Q 2:79: "On leaving the house of the [caliph] ʿUthmān, ʿAbdallāh b. ʿAmr b. al-ʿĀṣ met the Commander of the Faithful [ʿAlī; see ʿALĪ B. ABĪ ṬĀLIB] and said to him: 'O ʿAlī, we have spent the night on a matter with which we hope God will strengthen this community.' ʿAlī answered him: 'I know how you spent the night: you have falsified, altered and changed *(ḥarraftum wa-ghayyartum wa-baddaltum)* nine hundred letters/words *(ḥarf);* falsified three hundred letters/words, changed three hundred letters/words and altered three hundred letters/words. [And then ʿAlī added this verse, Q 2:79]: Woe to those who write the book (q.v.) with their hands and then say, 'this is from God'" *(fa-waylun lilladhīna yaktubna l-kitāba bi-aydīhim thumma yaqūlūna hādhā min ʿindi llāhi;* ibid., i, 66). It is obvious that the figures quoted here are not to be taken at face value, just as the three different verbs used to describe the editorial activity (*ḥarrafa, ghayyara* and *baddala*) in no way indicate discrete falsification techniques (see FORGERY; CORRUPTION).

Numerous Shīʿī utterances refer to the nature of the original text of the Qurʾān prior to its alleged corruption by the Sunnīs. In a well-known tradition, which appears in the writings of most early Imāmī commentators, Imām Muḥammad al-Bāqir (d. ca 114/732) declares: "The Qurʾān was revealed [consisting of] four parts: One part concerning us [the Shīʿa], one part concerning our enemies, one part commandments (q.v.) and regulations (*farāʾiḍ wa-aḥkām;* see VIRTUES AND VICES, COMMANDING AND FORBIDDING; BOUNDARIES AND PRECEPTS; LAW AND THE QURʾĀN) and one part customs and parables (*sunan wa-amthāl;* see PARABLE). And the exalted parts of the Qurʾān refer to us" (*wa-lanā karāʾim al-Qurʾān;* ibid., i, 20 and 21 where a tripartite division is suggested; cf. also the following sources, in which allusion is made to division into either three or four parts: Sayyārī, *Qirāʾāt,* tradition no. 11; Furāt, *Tafsīr,* 1, 2; Kulaynī, *Kāfī,* ii, 627-8; Goldziher, *Richtungen,* 288). Other accounts refer to the length of the original Qurʾān. It is believed to have contained 17,000 verses (q.v.; Sayyārī, *Qirāʾāt,* tradition no. 16). Q 33 is given as an example of a text that in the original Qurʾān was two and two-third times longer than Sūrat al-Baqara ("The Cow," Q 2; ibid., tradition no. 418; see SŪRAS), which in turn was longer than the version in the ʿUthmānic codex (ibid., tradition no. 421).

The discrepancy between the qurʾānic text and the Shīʿī viewpoint is not necessarily one that a "correct" interpretation can remedy. This discrepancy results from a textual gap between the incomplete qurʾānic text found in the possession of the Sunnīs and the ideal text that, according to Shīʿī belief, is no longer in anyone's possession but will be revealed by the Mahdī in the eschatological era (see ESCHATOLOGY).

Later, beginning in the fourth/tenth century, in the wake of the political and social changes that Shīʿism underwent, a tendency to moderation became apparent, and some of the criticism became muted. Imāmī-Shīʿī scholars — among them Muḥammad b. al-Nuʿmān, better known as al-Shaykh al-Mufīd (d. 413/1022), al-Sharīf al-Murtaḍā (d. 436/1044), Abū Jaʿfar al-Ṭūsī (d. 460/1067), one of the eminent Imāmī-Shīʿī exegetes, and Abū ʿAlī l-Faḍl b. Ḥasan al-Ṭabarsī (d. 548/1153) — held that although the text of the Qurʾān as we have it is incomplete, it does not contain any falsifications. In other words, what is found in the ʿUthmānic codex is the truth but not the whole truth since it does not include all the revelations made to Muḥammad (see REVELATION AND INSPIRATION). (On the various positions taken by Imāmī-Shīʿīs on this question, see Kohlberg, Some notes.)

Despite the moderate views expressed by these and other Shīʿī scholars, the opinion that the Qurʾān was falsified has been perpetuated throughout the history of Shīʿism and persists to this day. Prominent scholars in Iran during the Ṣafavid period — including Muḥammad b. Murtaḍā al-Kāshānī, known as Muḥsin al-Fayḍ (d. 1091/1680), Hāshim b. Sulaymān al-Baḥrānī (d. 1107/1693 or 1109/1697), and Muḥammad Bāqir al-Majlisī (d. 1110/1699 or 1111/1700) — revived the debate about the integrity of the Qurʾān, basing their anti-Sunnī polemics upon traditions extant in the early Shīʿī corpus of *tafsīr* and ḥadīth (see ḤADĪTH AND THE QURʾĀN).

One of the most radical works ever written on this matter is the *Faṣl al-khiṭāb fī taḥrīf kitāb rabb al-arbāb* by the eminent Shīʿī scholar Ḥusayn Taqī Nūrī l-Ṭabarsī (d. 1320/1902). In this work Nūrī brought together a great number of traditions referring to the question of the falsification of the Qurʾān. A recurrent tradition on which Nūrī bases his argument in favor of *taḥrīf* draws an analogy between the Shīʿīs and the Jews (a notion that in itself is very common in Shīʿī literature): "Just as the Jews and the Christians (see JEWS AND JUDAISM; CHRISTIANS AND CHRSITIANITY; PEOPLE OF THE BOOK) altered and falsified the book of their prophet [sic; see PROPHETS AND PROPHETHOOD] after him, this community [i.e. the Muslims] shall alter and falsify the Qurʾān after our Prophet — may God bless him and his family — for everything that happened to the Children of Israel (q.v.) is bound to happen to this community" *(inna l-yahūd wa-l-naṣārā ghayyarū wa-ḥarrafū kitāb nabiyyihim baʿdahu fa-hādhihi l-umma ayḍan lā budda wa-an yughayyirū l-Qurʾān baʿda nabiyyinā ṣallā llāh ʿalayhi wa-ahlihi li-anna kulla mā waqaʿa fī banī Isrāʾīl lā budda wa-an yaqaʿa fī hādhihi l-umma;* Nūrī, *Faṣl*, 35; whence Brunner, The dispute, 439; see COMMUNITY AND SOCIETY IN THE QURʾĀN). It should be stressed, however, that Nūrī's extreme anti-Sunnī tone was criticized even by the Shīʿī scholars of his day. Nevertheless, the question of *taḥrīf* never ceased to be a burning issue in Shīʿī-Sunnī discourse, to the point that "there is hardly a new book on the general subject of the qurʾānic sciences whose author can afford not to include a long chapter dealing with *taḥrīf*" (Brunner, The dispute, 445; see TRADITIONAL DISCIPLINES OF QURʾĀNIC STUDY).

Significant as it may be, the claim of forgery — i.e. that issues relating to the Shīʿa were deliberately omitted from the Qurʾān — is not the sole argument used by Shīʿī authors to explain the absence of any explicit mention of the *ahl al-bayt*/Shīʿa in the Qurʾān (see PEOPLE OF THE HOUSE). Two additional arguments are (a) the Qurʾān contains hidden meanings, which the exegete should decipher (see POLYSEMY) and (b) the Qurʾān teaches principles while tradition expounds their details.

The most common approach explaining the absence of references to the Shīʿa in the Qurʾān asserts that it is in the nature of the Qurʾān to speak in symbols and codes (see METAPHOR; SIMILES; SYMBOLIC IMAGERY) and according to this approach it should come as no surprise that the Qurʾān does not mention the Shīʿa explicitly: those who know how to read between the lines can decipher the passages that allude to the Shīʿa. This is the principle underlying the broad attempt to interpret many obscure qurʾānic verses *(mubhamāt)* as well as some quite clear ones, as referring to the Shīʿa. Even a cursory reading of the early Shīʿī *tafsīr*s reveals how wholeheartedly this approach was embraced by Shīʿī commentators.

The other approach — that the Qurʾān

teaches principles while tradition expounds their details — is expressed, for example, in the answer al-Bāqir gave to one of his disciples concerning the reason ʿAlī is not mentioned in the Qurʾān:

Say to them [i.e. to those who put this question to you]: God revealed to his messenger [the verses about] prayer (q.v.) and did not [explicitly] mention three or four [prayers] until this was interpreted by the messenger. So also he revealed [the verses about] the pilgrimage (q.v.), but did not reveal the injunction "encircle [the Kaʿba (q.v.)] seven times." So too is the meaning of the verse [Q 4:59] "Obey God and obey the messenger and those in authority (q.v.) among you." This verse was revealed in relation to ʿAlī, Ḥasan and Ḥusayn (ʿAyyāshī, *Tafsīr,* i, 276; see OBEDIENCE; KINGS AND RULERS).

According to this tradition, the reason ʿAlī and his disciples are not mentioned explicitly in the Qurʾān is that the Qurʾān, by its very nature, restricts itself to general principles; it presents religious laws and general rulings yet does not go into details, a prerogative reserved for the interpreter. This tripartite argumentation in no way suggests that these were three separate approaches to the problem, each exclusive of the other. Rather, the three together demonstrate the problems that Shīʿī exegetes faced and the attempts they made to resolve them.

Principles and methods of Shīʿī exegesis

Shīʿī exegetes, perhaps even more than their Sunnī counterparts, support their distinctive views by reference to qurʾānic proof-texts (see EXEGESIS OF THE QURʾĀN: CLASSICAL AND MEDIEVAL). A major distinction is that the Shīʿī exegetes attempt to find in the Qurʾān explicit references to such themes as the imāms' (see IMĀM) supernatural and mystical qualities, their authority to interpret the Qurʾān and other religious scriptures, or such major Shīʿī doctrines as the duty of loyalty (q.v.) to the imāms *(walāya)* and dissociation from their enemies *(barāʾa)*.

A fundamental principle of Shīʿī exegetical tradition is that the authority to interpret the Qurʾān is reserved for ʿAlī and his descendants, the imāms. In a well-known ḥadīth, cited in both Sunnī and Shīʿī sources, Muḥammad is said to have declared: "There is one among you who will fight for the [correct] interpretation of the Qurʾān just as I myself fought for its revelation, and he is ʿAlī b. Abī Ṭālib" (*inna fī-kum man yuqātilu ʿalā taʾwīl al-Qurʾān kamā qātaltu ʿalā tanzīlihi wa-huwa ʿAlī ibn Abī Ṭālib;* ʿAyyāshī, *Tafsīr,* i, 27; Shahrastānī, *Milal,* 189; and cf. Gimaret and Monnot, *Livre,* i, 543, and n. 231, where further sources are cited; also Poonawala, Ismāʿīlī *taʾwīl,* 209-10). This idea of ʿAlī and (implicitly) also his descendants being presented by the Prophet himself as interpreters of the Qurʾān is also deduced from other traditions, the most famous of which is "the tradition about the two weighty things" *(ḥadīth al-thaqalayn),* i.e. the two things that Muḥammad is reported to have bequeathed to his believers. There are significant differences between the Sunnī and Shīʿī exegetical traditions regarding both the identity of these two "things" and the interpretation of the ḥadīth. According to one version, they are the book of God *(kitāb Allāh)* and the Prophet's practice (*sunnat nabiyyihi,* Ibn Isḥāq-Guillaume, 651; see SUNNA). Other versions of this tradition, recorded in both Sunnī and Shīʿī works, mention as the *thaqalān* the Qurʾān and the family of the Prophet (q.v.; *ahl al-bayt*). The explanation given in Shīʿī sources as to the discrepancy between the two versions of this tradition is that while in Sunnī exegesis the practice of the Prophet is considered a tool for interpreting the Qurʾān (and is therefore mentioned in conjunction with the book itself), in Shīʿī tradition the family of the Prophet plays the equivalent role: only through the mediation of the imāms, the descendants of the Prophet, are both the exoteric *(ẓāhir)* and the esoteric *(bāṭin)* meanings of the qurʾānic text revealed to believers. The *thaqalān* are further viewed as being forever intertwined with each other *(lan yaftariqā)* or, in the words of al-Ṭūsī (d. 460/1067): "This tradition proves that [the Qurʾān] exists in every generation, since it is unlikely that [Muḥammad] would order us to keep something which we cannot keep, just as the family of the Prophet, and those we are ordered to follow, are present at all times" (Ṭūsī, *Tibyān*, i, 3-4). The distance from here to the creation of the metaphor describing the imāms as "the speaking book of God" *(kitāb Allāh al-nāṭiq)* is short indeed (see e.g. Bursī, *Mashāriq*, 135; Ayoub, The speaking Qurʾān, 183, n. 17; Poonawala, Ismāʿīlī *taʾwīl*, 200).

The authority of the imāms as interpreters of the Qurʾān is reiterated in many traditions other than the *ḥadīth al-thaqalayn*. One tradition defining the many functions of the imāms includes their role as interpreters of the Qurʾān: "We know how to interpret the book [i.e. the Qurʾān] and how to speak clearly" *(naʿrifu taʾwīl al-kitāb wa-faṣl al-khiṭāb*; ʿAyyāshī, *Tafsīr*, i, 28).

These as well as numerous other traditions have but one purpose — to make clear that those qualified to interpret the Qurʾān are the imāms, and that this right was bestowed upon them directly by God. In the absence of the imāms, the duty of the text's interpreters is restricted to preserving traditions in their name and making these available to believers (see TEACHING AND PREACHING THE QURʾĀN). The interpreters are thus no more than a vehicle and, at least theoretically, are not authorized to pronounce their own views (ibid., i, 27; Qummī, *Tafsīr*, ii, 397).

Among Shīʿīs, as among other religious circles and groups operating on the fringes of society, allegory, typology and secret codes became favorite methods of interpreting the Qurʾān. Nevertheless, only heterodox factions such as the Nuṣayrīs and the Druze (see DRUZES) went so far as to view the inner meaning of the Qurʾān as the exclusive, binding authority. At times such techniques derive from an elitist outlook, one which maintains that religious secrets (q.v.; see also HIDDEN AND THE HIDDEN) should be concealed from the masses and be the unique privilege of the elect. Sometimes it derives from an existential necessity: religious and ideological minorities may find themselves in danger as a consequence of overt and careless expression of ideas unpalatable to the ruling majority (see HERESY; THEOLOGY AND THE QURʾĀN). And indeed, the fact that many Shīʿī factions throughout their history flourished under Sunnī rule required the use of survival techniques both in everyday life and when committing their religious doctrines to writing. Shīʿī scholars had to walk a fine line: on the one hand, they wished to give whenever possible expression to their real intentions; on the other hand, they had to make sure that the expression of such ideas did not arouse the wrath of their Sunnī opponents. This is one of the clearest manifestations of the doctrine of precautionary dissimulation (q.v.; *taqiyya*).

An illustration of the allegorical approach *(taʾwīl)* of Shīʿī Qurʾān exegesis may be seen in the interpretation of the night journey of Muḥammad referred to in the first verse of Q 17 (Sūrat al-Isrāʾ, "The Night Journey"; see ASCENSION). Although aware of the conventional interpretation of this verse as referring to an actual journey during which the Prophet was borne from Mecca (q.v.) to Jerusalem (q.v.), Ismāʿīlī as well as Nuṣayrī authors interpreted this passage as a symbol of the spiritual progress of the imāms or other persons within the divine realm. (For the Ismāʿīlī approach, see e.g. al-Qāḍī l-Nuʿmān, *Asās al-taʾwīl,* 337; for the Nuṣayrī interpretation, see the epistle of the Nuṣayrī author Abū ʿAbdallāh al-Ḥusayn b. Hārūn al-Ṣāʾigh [fl. fourth/tenth century] in Bar-Asher and Kofsky, *The Nuṣayrī-ʿAlawī religion,* 89-97.)

Ismāʿīlīs tend to employ allegory to, *inter alia,* interpret Muslim law. Thus, for example, "the pillars of Islam" are given in Ismāʿīlī writings symbolic meanings: the five obligatory prayers correspond to the five divine ranks *(ḥudūd)* in the Ismāʿīlī hierarchical system; almsgiving (q.v.; *zakāt*) means that those with knowledge should provide reliable mentors to guide the people (see KNOWLEDGE AND LEARNING); fasting (q.v.; *ṣawm*) entails observing silence and not betraying religious secrets to the uninitiated; pilgrimage to Mecca, the house of God (see HOUSE, DOMESTIC AND DIVINE), symbolizes an audience with the imām, since God's knowledge resides with him (Poonawala, Ismāʿīlī *taʾwīl,* 218, paraphrasing *Kitāb al-Iftikhār,* 240 f., by the prominent Ismāʿīlī *dāʿī* Abū Yaʿqūb al-Sijistānī [d. ca. 361/971]). It is worth mentioning that this tendency, prevalent in Ismāʿīlism, is shared by Ghulāt groups such as the Nuṣayrīs and the Druzes. A significant difference, however, should be noted. Moderate allegorists — e.g. Imāmī Shīʿī and most Ismāʿīlīs — maintained that the allegorical interpretation that extracts the true meaning of the Qurʾān does not aim to invalidate the plain meaning of the text (see e.g. Bar-Asher, *Scripture and exegesis,* 122-4). Heterodox groups, in contrast, often held that allegory was the only correct interpretation and thus belittled and even ignored the revealed meaning of the texts.

This distinction became especially glaring with regard to legal matters. Consistent allegorical interpretation led its practitioners, more often than not, to adopt antinomian attitudes toward the religious precepts of the Qurʾān, and once a law assumed a symbolic meaning its literal meaning, according to these circles, was no longer binding. A blatant antinomian interpretation of the pillars of Islam is offered e.g. by the fourth epistle of the Druze canon (*al-Kitāb al-Maʿrūf bi-l-naqḍ al-khafī;* an unpublished critical edition of this epistle is offered by Bryer, *The origins,* ii, 31-50; cf. De Sacy, *Exposé,* ii, 673).

Shīʿī Qurʾān exegesis is further characterized by a radical anti-Sunnī bias. Many qurʾānic verses whose apparent meanings have a negative connotation or refer generally and vaguely to evil or to evildoers (see GOOD AND EVIL; EVIL DEEDS; OPPRESSION) are taken, through allegorical or typological interpretation, to refer to specific historical luminaries of Sunnī Islam. Negative qurʾānic terms such as *baghy* (insolence; see INSOLENCE AND OBSTINACY; ARROGANCE; PRIDE), *faḥshāʾ* (indecency; see ADULTERY AND FORNICATION; CHASTITY; MODESTY), *munkar* (dishonor), *al-fujjār* (the wicked), *al-mufsidūn fī l-arḍ* (corrupters on earth; see CORRUPTION; OPPRESSION), *al-shayṭān* (Satan; see DEVIL), *al-maghḍūb ʿalayhim* (those against whom [God] is wrathful; see ANGER), *al-ḍāllūn* (those who are astray; see ERROR; ASTRAY) and the like are interpreted as referring to the enemies of the Shīʿa in general or to specific persons among them, in particular the first three caliphs, two of Muḥammad's wives (ʿĀʾisha and Ḥafṣa [q.v.], the daughters of the first and the second caliphs, respectively; see also WIVES OF THE PROPHET; ʿĀʾISHA BINT ABĪ BAKR), the Umayyads and the ʿAbbāsids. In an utterance attributed to al-Bāqir he goes so far as to state that "every occurrence in the Qurʾān of the words 'Satan says' is [to be understood as referring to] 'the second' [namely the caliph ʿUmar b. al-Khaṭṭāb]" *(wa-laysa fī-l-Qurʾān [shayʾ] wa-qāla al-shayṭān illā wa-huwa al-thānī;* ʿAyyāshī, *Tafsīr,* ii, 240). In another tradition, cited in the same source, a more general formulation of this idea is also attributed to this imām. To Muḥammad b. Muslim (d. 150/767), one of his disciples, the imām said: "Whenever you hear God [in the Qurʾān] mentioning someone of this nation in praise, it refers to us [i.e. the Shīʿa]; and when you hear God denigrating people who flourished in the past, it refers to our enemies" *(idhā samiʿta llāha dhakara aḥadan min hādhihi l-umma bi-khayrin fa-naḥnu hum wa-idhā samiʿta llāha dhakara qawman bi-sūʾin mimman maḍā fa-hum ʿaduwwunā;* ibid., i, 24; see CHASTISEMENT AND PUNISHMENT; PUNISHMENT STORIES; REWARD AND PUNISHMENT).

Secret language in Shīʿī exegesis is evident on two levels. The first level, the exegetes believe, is found in the Qurʾān itself; it underlies such obscure or general qurʾānic expressions as *al-jibt wa-l-ṭāghūt* (see IDOLS AND IMAGES; JIBT), *al-faḥshāʾ wa-l-munkar* and many others. The second level is added by the Qurʾān commentator himself. When tracing the exegete's method of unraveling the meaning of obscure expressions one often discovers that the exegete not only avoids disclosing the secrets of the text but actually further conceals them. The commentator never claims explicitly that expressions such as those just mentioned refer to Abū Bakr, ʿUmar or other enemies of the Shīʿa; rather, he resorts to code words such as "the first" *(al-awwal)* and "the second" *(al-thānī), ḥabtar,* "fox" (usually applied to Abū Bakr "because of his cunning and fraudulence" (*li-ḥilatihi wa-makrihi,* Majlisī, *Biḥār,* lith., 4, 378; 9, 65) and *zurayq,* "shiny-eyed" or "blue-eyed" (referring to ʿUmar; e.g. Furāt, *Tafsīr,* 69; see also PRE-ISLAMIC ARABIA AND THE QURʾĀN). This physical feature was considered unfortunate by the ancient Arabs (q.v.) and finds an echo in Q 20:102, according to which the wicked will rise on the day of resurrection (q.v.) with shiny (or blue) eyes (q.v.; for these and other derogatory appellations, see Goldziher, Spottnamen, 295-308; Kohlberg, Some Imāmī Shīʿī views, esp. 160-7; Bar-Asher, *Scripture,* 113-20). In other words, the transition from the covert stratum in the Qurʾān to the overt stratum of the interpretation is not direct but undergoes a further process of encoding. The underlying assumption is that every Shīʿī is familiar with these code words which are an integral part of his religious-cultural upbringing.

In other cases Shīʿī exegesis is designed to support the Shīʿī doctrine of the imāmate and concepts derived from it, examples being *ʿiṣma* (see IMPECCABILITY), or the immunity of prophets and imāms from sin (see SIN, MAJOR AND MINOR) and error; the intercession (q.v.; *shafāʿa*) of prophets and imāms on behalf of their communities; *badāʾ* (the appearance of new circumstances that cause a change in an earlier divine ruling); and, in the case of the Ismāʿīlī, Druze and Nuṣayrī factions, such additional concepts as the cyclical creation (q.v.) of the world and the transmigration of souls (q.v.).

Another current feature of early Shīʿī (mainly Imāmī) exegesis is the use of variant readings *(qirāʾāt)* of the qurʾānic text or, in certain cases, the addition of words believed to have been omitted from it (see READINGS OF THE QURʾĀN). Such textual alterations are based on the assumption that the qurʾānic text is flawed and incomplete. Scholars who held the view that the Qurʾān is corrupt believed that the Mahdī will eventually reveal the true text and uncover its original intention. Examples of these alterations are the common textual substitution of *aʾimma* (imāms) for *umma* (nation or community) or slight changes to the word "imām" itself. The implication of these variants is that the institution of the imāmate and other principles associated with it originate in the Qurʾān. For example, for Q 3:110 most early Shīʿī exegetes read: "You are the best leaders [leg. *aʾimmatin* rather than *ummatin,* nation] ever brought forth to humankind" *(kuntum khayra aʾimmatin ukhrijat lil-nās);* or in Q 2:143: "Thus we appointed you midmost leaders" *(wa-kadhālika jaʿalnākum aʾimmatan wasaṭan),* etc. (For the first verse, cf. Qummī, *Tafsīr,* i, 110; ʿAyyāshī, *Tafsīr,* i, 218; for the second, cf. Qummī, *Tafsīr,* i, 63.)

Prominent among the other type of alterations is the insertion of certain words generally proclaimed to be missing from the ʿUthmānic codex of the Qurʾān. These are primarily (a) the words *fī ʿAlī* (concerning ʿAlī) in various qurʾānic verses, among them Q 2:91: "Believe in what God has revealed to you [+ concerning ʿAlī]" *(āminū bi-mā anzala llāh [+fī ʿAlī])* or Q 4:166: "But God bears witness to what he has revealed to you [+ concerning ʿAlī]" *(lākinna llāh yashhadu bi-mā anzala ilayka [+fī ʿAlī]);* or (b) the words *āl Muḥammad* (the family of Muḥammad) or occasionally *āl Muḥammad ḥaqqahum* ([deprived] of their rights) as the object of a verb from the root *ẓ-l-m* (to do an injustice to/to usurp), which appear often in the Qurʾān. Shīʿī commentators believe that this addition stresses that the injustice (see JUSTICE AND INJUSTICE) referred to by words and verbs derived from the root *ẓ-l-m* alludes specifically to the injustice perpetrated against the family of the Prophet and his offspring, i.e. the Shīʿa. The same method is applied with regard to other doctrines. The insertion of the words *fī walāyat ʿAlī* (concerning the [duty of] loyalty to the house of ʿAlī) in several places in the Qurʾān is intended to provide scriptural authority to the doctrine of *walāya,* as the addition of the words *ilā ajalin musamman* (for a given time) to the *mutʿa* verse (Q 4:24), is meant to emphasize the temporary nature of *mutʿa* marriage (see MARRIAGE AND DIVORCE; TEMPORARY MARRIAGE; SEX AND SEXUALITY). Less known is the addition of the word *mutʿa* in Q 24:33: *wa-l-yastaʿfifi lladhīna lā yajidūna nikāḥan [+bi-l-mutʿa] ḥattā yughniyahumu llāhu min faḍlihi,* "And let those who find not the means to enter into a *[+ mutʿa]* marriage be abstinent till God enriches them of his bounty" (Sayyārī, *Qirāʾāt,* tradition no. 372; see ABSTINENCE).

The differentiation between variant readings and additions by the commentators or their sources inheres primarily in terminology. In many places where the commentator introduces a Shīʿī version of a qurʾānic verse, he does so by using typical formulas. The Shīʿī version is preceded by such utterances as (a) *nazala Jibrīl [*or *Jibrāʾīl] bi-hādhihi l-āya hākadhā ʿalā Muḥammad,* "thus the verse was revealed to Muḥammad by [the angel] Gabriel" (q.v.; see e.g. ʿAyyāshī, *Tafsīr,* ii, 353; and for similar versions, ibid., i, 63; Qummī, *Tafsīr,* ii, 111); or followed by (b) *hākadhā nazalat,* "thus [the verse] was revealed" (see e.g. Qummī, *Tafsīr,* i, 142, 297; ii, 21); at other times it is stated that the version cited was the reading of one of the imāms (e.g. ʿAyyāshī, *Tafsīr,* i, 217, 218; Qummī, *Tafsīr,* i, 389). At times even stronger expressions are used to stress that certain passages in the canonical text are incorrect. These include statements formulated in the negative such as (a) *ʿalā khilāf mā anzala llāh,* "[the version in the *textus receptus*] contradicts the form in which it was revealed" (see e.g. Qummī, *Tafsīr,* i, 10, which cites Q 3:110 or Q 25:74 as examples of such verses); or (b) *fīmā ḥurrifa min kitāb Allāh,* "[This verse] is one of those falsified [or altered] in the book of God" (Qummī, *Tafsīr,* ii, 295).

In the absence of such a firm declaration it is difficult to decide whether the alteration is a mere commentary or whether the exegete is in fact suggesting an alternative reading to the canonical text despite the absence of such typical expressions as those mentioned above.

On the basis of such a rejection of the "Sunnī" text one might have expected the Shīʿa to insert these alternative versions and additions into the text of the Qurʾān or at least to implement them when the text is read on ritual occasions (see RITUAL AND THE QURʾĀN; RECITATION OF THE QURʾĀN). In reality, however, almost no action was taken by the Shīʿa to canonize their variant readings. One exception is a late attempt reflected in a manuscript of the Qurʾān, said to have been discovered in the city of Bankipore, India, in which, besides the Shīʿī alternative versions to some of the qurʾānic verses, two apocryphal sūras were also included: *sūrat al-walāya,* "the sūra of divine friendship (i.e. between God and ʿAlī; see FRIENDS AND FRIENDSHIP; CLIENTS AND CLIENTAGE)" and *sūrat al-nūrayn,* the *sūra* of the two lights (i.e. Muḥammad and ʿAlī; on this issue, noted by scholars as early as the nineteenth century, see Amir-Moezzi, *Le guide divin,* 200-27; *The divine guide,* 79-91, 198-206; see LIGHT).

This behavior of the Shīʿa reveals a paradox. On the one hand, Shīʿīs are certain that the true version of the Qurʾān is that known to them; on the other hand, not only do they not reject the canonical codex, they actually endorse it (see e.g. Goldziher, *Richtungen,* 281). This contradiction is typical of the Shīʿa: on the one hand an uncompromising position of superiority was adopted on the theoretical-doctrinal level; on the other hand the constant fear of persecution from the hostile Sunnī environment brought about, on the practical level, a pragmatic attitude that included the adoption *de facto* of the ʿUthmānic codex. This tension and paradox is reflected in the many Shīʿī exegetical traditions in which Shīʿī *qirāʾāt* are mentioned. In some of them one finds the following situation: A disciple of the imām is reading from the (canonical) Qurʾān in the presence of the imām, who tells him that it was revealed in a different version. The imām then proceeds to read the "true" (i.e. the Shīʿī) version. As, however, against such accounts, which underrate the importance of the ʿUthmānic codex, an opposing tendency is sometimes revealed: Someone is reading from the Qurʾān in the presence of one of the imāms, and inserts in his reading the Shīʿī version of the verse. At this point he is stopped by the imām, who instructs him to read according to the version followed by the people (i.e. the *textus receptus*) until such time as "the righteous savior" *(al-qāʾim)* shall come with the correct version of the Qurʾān, identical with the one that ʿAlī possessed and bequeathed to his daughter, Fāṭima (q.v.), whence its title *muṣḥaf Fāṭima,* "the codex of Fāṭima" (see MUṢḤAF).

Other methods of Shīʿī exegesis are based on the word and letter order and calculations of the numerical value of letters (see NUMEROLOGY). In his interpretation of Q 108 (Sūrat al-Kawthar), al-Sijistānī presents a transposition of the words and letters of the sūra, thus reading into it the Shīʿī tenet of *waṣāya,* the rank of plenipotentiary among the imāms (Poonawala, Ismāʿīlī *taʾwīl,* 218-9). The technique of numerical calculation of letters is primarily applied to the mysterious letters (q.v.; *fawātiḥ al-suwar*) appearing at the head of twenty-nine sūras. For example, the letters *alif, lām, mīm, ṣād* (the total numerical value of which is 161) at the head of Q 7 (Sūrat al-Aʿrāf, "The Heights"; see PEOPLE OF THE HEIGHTS) allude, according to an account attributed to al-Bāqir, to the year 161 of the *hijrī* calendar (777 C.E.), a year which had been (incorrectly) predicted as the one in which the fall of the Umayyad dynasty would occur (ʿAyyāshī, *Tafsīr,* ii, 7-8).

It should further be noted that Shīʿī, and particularly Ismāʿīlī, exegesis is characterized by the use of a secret script designed to encrypt information — mainly names of persons — that the author wishes to conceal for precautionary reasons. Numerous examples of this practice are found in the *Kitāb al-Kashf* by the *dāʿī*, Jaʿfar b. Manṣūr al-Yaman (fl. first half of fourth/tenth century), and *Mizāj al-tasnīm* by the Yamamite Ismāʿīlī Sulaymānī *dāʿī*, Ismāʿīl b. Hibat Allāh (d. 1184/1770).

Major Shīʿī exegetes and their works

The earliest Imāmī-Shīʿī Qurʾān commentaries known to us are from the end of the third/ninth century. These include the works of Furāt b. Furāt b. Ibrāhīm al-Kūfī *(Tafsīr Furāt al-Kūfī),* al-ʿAyyāshī *(Tafsīr)* and al-Qummī *(Tafsīr),* all of whom flourished in the last decades of the third/ninth century and the beginning of the fourth/tenth century, that is, prior to the Great Occultation *(al-ghayba al-kubrā)* of the twelfth imām, which occurred in the year 329/941. Somewhat later is Muḥammad b. Ibrāhīm b. Jaʿfar al-Nuʿmānī (d. ca. 360/971), to whom is ascribed a treatise constituting a sort of introduction to the Qurʾān (Majlisī, *Biḥār,* xc, 1-97). Other compositions are the two commentaries ascribed to the sixth and eleventh imāms, respectively: *Ḥaqāʾiq al-tafsīr al-qurʾānī,* a small exegetical treatise of a Ṣūfī character (see ṢŪFISM AND THE QURʾĀN) attributed to Imām Jaʿfar al-Ṣādiq and *Tafsīr al-ʿAskarī,* a comprehensive commentary of a legendary-mythical nature on the first two sūras of the Qurʾān attributed to Imām Ḥasan al-ʿAskarī (d. 260/874; on which see Bar-Asher, al-ʿAskarī). The most outstanding *tafsīr*s of the post-*ghayba* period are al-Ṭūsī's *Tibyān,* al-Ṭabarsī's *Majmaʿ* and the *Rawḍ al-jinān wa-rūḥ al-janān,* a Qurʾān commentary in Persian by Abū l-Futūḥ Ḥusayn b. ʿAlī al-Rāzī (fl. first half of the sixth/twelfth century). Some very comprehensive Imāmī-Shīʿī *tafsīr* works, which are mainly compilations of early sources, were composed in Ṣafavid Iran. The most prominent among these are *Taʾwīl al-āyāt al-ẓāhira fī faḍāʾil al-ʿitra al-ṭāhira* by Sharaf al-Dīn ʿAlī l-Ḥusaynī l-Astarābādī (fl. tenth/sixteenth century), *Kitāb al-Ṣāfī fī tafsīr al-Qurʾān* by Muḥsin al-Fayḍ and *Kitāb al-Burhān fī tafsīr al-Qurʾān* by Hāshim b. Sulaymān al-Baḥrānī. Representative of modern Imāmī-Shīʿī Qurʾān exegesis are Ṭabāṭabāʾī's *Mīzān* and *Min waḥy al-Qurʾān* by Muḥammad Ḥusayn Faḍl Allāh. Needless to say, exegetical material other than Qurʾān commentaries per se proliferates in all genres of Imāmī-Shīʿī literature. (For a detailed survey of Shīʿī *tafsīr* works, see Ṭihrānī, *Dharīʿa,* iii, 302-7; iv, 231-346.)

Ismāʿīlī doctrinal writings include a vast amount of exegetical material but little is known of specific Ismāʿīlī exegetical works. Among the few that have come down to us are *Kitāb Asās al-taʾwīl* by the *dāʿī* al-Qāḍī l-Nuʿmān b. Ḥayyūn Maghribī (d. 363/973) and *Kitāb al-Kashf* by Jaʿfar b. Manṣūr al-Yaman. (For other Ismāʿīlī exegetical works, see Poonawala, *Biobibliography,* index, s.v. *tafsīr* and *taʾwīl.)*

The Zaydī exegetical tradition remains largely unexplored and most Zaydī works of *tafsīr* are still in manuscript form. The Zaydī imāms al-Qāsim b. Ibrāhīm Rassī (d. 246/860), al-Nāṣir lil-Ḥaqq al-Uṭrūsh (d. 304/917) and Abū l-Fatḥ Nāṣir b. Ḥusayn al-Daylamī (d. 444/1052) are among those credited with a *tafsīr* (Ṭihrānī, *Dharīʿa,* iv, 255, 261; Abrahamov, *Anthropomorphism).* A Qurʾān commentary is also ascribed to Ziyād b. Mundhir Abū l-Jārūd, the eponym of the Zaydi-Jārūdī sub-sect, the Jārūdiyya (Ṭihrānī, *Dharīʿa,* iv, 251). The work is not extant; excerpts of it are, however, incorporated in al-Qummī's *Tafsīr* (Bar-Asher, *Scripture,* 46-56, 244-7). Another outstanding Jārūdī scholar who is credited with a *tafsīr* is Aḥmad b. Muḥammad Hamadhānī, better known as Ibn ʿUqda (d. 333/947; cf. Ṭihrānī, *Dharīʿa,* iv, 251). Finally, there is the *tafsīr* by Shawkānī (d. 1250/1834), one of the best known and most prolific authors of the late Zaydiyya.

There is no evidence that Qurʾān commentaries were written by members of Ghulāt groups (such as the Druzes and the Nuṣayrīs), although the Qurʾān is widely cited and often commented on in their sacred writings. See also PERSIAN LITERATURE AND THE QURʾĀN.

Meir M. Bar-Asher

Bibliography

Primary: al-Astarābādī, Sharaf al-Dīn ʿAlī al-Ḥusaynī, *Taʾwīl al-āyāt al-ẓāhira fī faḍāʾil al-ʿitra al-ṭāhira,* Qummī 1407/1986; ʿAyyāshī, *Tafsīr;* Baḥrānī, *Burhān;* al-Bursī, Rajab b. Muḥammad, *Mashāriq anwār al-yaqīn fī asrār amīr al-muʾminīn,* Beirut n.d.; M. Faḍl Allāh, *Min waḥy al-Qurʾān,* Beirut 1405-10/1985-90; Furāt b. Furāt b. Ibrāhīm al-Kūfī, *Tafsīr Furāt al-Kūfī,* Najaf 1354/1935; new ed. M. Kāẓim, Tehran 1410/1990; al-Ḥasan al-ʿAskarī (attrib.), *Tafsīr al-ʿAskarī,* Qummī 1409/1988; Ibn Hibat Allāh, Ḍiyāʾ al-Dīn Ismāʿīl, *Mizāj al-tasnīm* [Abhandlungen der Akademie der Wissenschaften in Göttingen 31], ed. R. Strothman, Göttingen 1948; Ibn Isḥāq-Guillaume; Jaʿfar b. Manṣūr al-Yaman, *Kitāb al-Kashf,* ed. R. Strothmann, London 1952; Jaʿfar al-Ṣādiq (attrib.), *Ḥaqāʾiq al-tafsīr al-qurʾānī,* ed. A. Zayʿūr, Beirut 1413/1993; al-Kashānī, Muḥammad b. Murtaḍā, *Kitāb al-Ṣāfī fī tafsīr al-Qurʾān,* Beirut 1389/1979; Kulaynī, *Kāfī;* al-Majlisī, Muḥammad Bāqir, *Biḥār al-anwār,* Iran 1305-15/1887-98 (lith.); ed. J. al-ʿAlawī et al., 110 vols., Tehran 1956-72, Beirut 1403/1983[2]; al-Nuʿmānī, Muḥammad b. Ibrāhīm b. Jaʿfar (attrib.), *Tafsīr,* in Majlisī, *Biḥār,* ed. Beirut, xc, 1-97; Nūrī al-Ṭabarsī, Ḥusayn Taqī, *Faṣl al-khiṭāb fī taḥrīf kitāb rabb al-arbāb,* [Tehran] 1298/1881 (lith.); al-Qāḍī al-Nuʿmān b. Ḥayyūn Maghribī, *Asās al-taʾwīl,* ed. ʿA. Tamer, Beirut 1960; Qummī, *Tafsīr,* Najaf 1387/1967; al-Rāzī, Abū l-Futūḥ Ḥusayn b. ʿAlī, *Rawḍ al-jinān wa-rūḥ al-janān,* Tehran 1349 Sh.; al-Sayyārī, Aḥmad b. Muḥammad, *Kitāb al-Qirāʾāt* (or *Kitāb al-Tanzīl wa-l-taḥrīf*), ed. M.A. Amir-Moezzi and E. Kohlberg (forthcoming); Shahrastānī, *Milal,* ed. F. Muḥammad; trans. D. Gimaret and G. Monnot, *Livre des religions et des sectes,* 2 vols., Paris/Louvain 1986, i, 543; Shawkānī, *Tafsīr;* al-Sijistānī, Abū Yaʿqūb, *Kitāb al-Iftikhār,* ed. I.K. Poonawala, Beirut 2000; Ṭabarsī [Ṭabrisī], *Majmaʿ;* Ṭabāṭabāʾī, *Mīzān;* al-Ṭihrānī, Āgha Buzurg, *al-Dharīʿa ilā taṣānīf al-shīʿa,* Najaf 1355-95/ 1936-75; Ṭūsī, *Tibyān.*

Secondary: B. Abrahamov, *Anthropomorphism and interpretation of the Qurʾān in the theology of al-Qāsim ibn Ibrāhīm. Kitāb al-mustarshid,* Leiden/New York/Cologne 1996; M.A. Amir-Moezzi, *Le guide divin dans le shiʿisme originel. Aux sources de l'ésotérisme en Islam,* Paris 1992, 200-27; trans. D. Streight, *The divine guide in early Shiʿism. The sources of esotericism in Islam,* New York 1994, 79-91, 199-206; id. and C. Jambet, *Qu'est-ce que le shîʿisme?* Paris 2004, 89-97 (on the Qurʾān), 139-78; M. Ayoub, The speaking Qurʾān and the silent Qurʾān. A study of the principles and development of Imāmī Shīʿī tafsīr, in Rippin, *Approaches,* 177-98; M.M. Bar-Asher, The Qurʾān commentary ascribed to the Imām Ḥasan al-ʿAskarī, in JSAI 24 (2000), 358-79; id., *Scripture and exegesis in early Imāmī Shiism,* Jerusalem/Leiden 1999; id., Variant readings and additions of the Imāmī-Šiʿa to the Quran, in IOS 13 (1993), 39-74; id. and A. Kofsky, *The Nuṣayrī-ʿAlawī religion. An enquiry into its theology and liturgy,* Leiden 2002, 89-97; R. Brunner, *Die Schia und die Koransfälschung,* Würzburg 2001; id., The dispute about the falsification of the Qurʾān between Sunnīs and Shīʿīs in the 20th century, in S. Leder et al. (eds.), *Studies in Arabic and Islam. Proceedings of the 19th Congress, Union Européenne des Arabisants et Islamisants (Halle 1998),* Leuven/Paris 2002, 437-46; D.R.W. Bryer, *The origins of the Druze religion. An edition of Ḥamza's writings and an analysis of his doctrine,* 2 vols., DPhil. diss., U. Oxford 1971, ii, 31-50; J. Eliash, The Šiʿite Qurʾān. A reconsideration of Goldziher's interpretation, in *Arabica* 16 (1969), 15-24; Goldziher, *Richtungen,* 263-309; id., Spottnamen der ersten Chalifen bei den Schiʿiten, in id., *Gesammelte Schriften,* ed. J. Desomogyi, 6 vols., Hildesheim 1967-73, iv, 295-308; E. Kohlberg, Authoritative scriptures in early Imami Shīʿism, in E. Patlagean and A. Le Boulluec (eds.), *Les retours aux écritures. Fondamentalismes présents et passés,* Louvain-Paris 1994, 295-312; id., Some Imāmī Shīʿī views on the *ṣaḥāba,* in JSAI 5 (1984), 143-75; repr. in id., *Belief and law in Imāmī Shīʿism,* Aldershot 1991, chap. 9; id., Some notes on the Imāmite attitude to the Qurʾān, in S.M. Stern, A. Hourani, and V. Brown (eds.), *Islamic philosophy and the classical tradition. Essays presented to Richard Walzer,* Oxford 1972, 209-24; B.T. Lawson, Note for the study of a 'Shīʿī Qurʾān,' in *JSS* 36 (1991), 279-95; H. Modarressi, Early debates on the integrity of the Qurʾān, in *SI* 77 (1993), 5-39; I.K. Poonawala, *Biobibliography of Ismāʿīlī literature,* Los Angeles 1977; id., Ismāʿīlī *taʾwīl* of the Qurʾān, in Rippin, *Approaches,* 199-222; W. al-Qāḍī, *al-Kaysāniyya fī l-tārīkh wa-l-adab,* Beirut 1974; S. de Sacy, *Exposé de la religion des Druzes,* 2 vols, Paris 1838; W. St. Clair Tisdall, The Shīʿah additions to the Koran, in *MW* 3 (1913), 227-41.

Ships

Means of transportation over water. The terms for ship in the Qurʾān are three: *fulk,* which occurs twenty-three times; *safīna,* four times and *jāriya* (pl. *jāriyāt, jawārī*) also four times. The first is probably Greek *(epholkion),* while the third is a purely descriptive term, "the (mellifluously) moving one." In addition to being the most frequently employed, *fulk* is the most significant in qurʾānic thought.

Ships in the Qurʾān appear as an important sign of God's providential care for humankind, an element in the divine economy (see GRACE; BLESSING). It is through the employment of ships that humankind catches fish for food (see HUNTING AND FISHING) and acquires marine ornaments (sing. *ḥilya*); the ship is the means of transportation in maritime commerce, beneficial to humankind (Q 2:164; 16:14; 30:46; 35:12).

In the Qurʾān, ships are associated with four prophets; Noah (q.v.; Nūḥ), Moses (q.v.; Mūsā) and Jonah (q.v.; Yūnus) and, by implication, with Solomon (q.v.; Sulaymān; Q 34:12). The most significant of the references are to Noah, especially Q 11:36-48. Humankind was saved from extinction through his *fulk* (see ARK), the only ship described with some detail à propos of its construction, its planks *(alwāḥ)* its nails *(dusur)* and the mountain *(al-Jūdiyy;* see JŪDĪ) on which it finally rested after the flood, described in Q 11:44, which has been rightly considered one of the summits of qurʾānic literary excellence (see INIMITABILITY). Less significant are references to the ship *(safīna)* that Moses boarded with the "servant of God" (Q 18:65, 71, 79; see KHAḌIR/KHIḌR) and the *fulk* that Jonah boarded, whence he was ejected (Q 37:140).

During the lifetime of the prophet Muḥammad, ships re-entered the framework of the divine economy on two important occasions. When the Kaʿba (q.v.), the house that Abraham (q.v.) and Ishmael (q.v.) built (see HOUSE, DOMESTIC AND DIVINE), was burnt down sometime before Muḥammad's prophetic call, it was rebuilt by a certain Bāqūm, possibly a Copt, and either a carpenter or the ship's captain. The wood came from a Byzantine ship which had run aground at al-Shuʿayba, Mecca's port at that time. And when some members of the nascent Muslim community in Mecca (q.v.) emigrated to Ethiopia (q.v.; see also ABYSSINIA; EMIGRATION), it was ships that transported them and, later, brought most of them back. Thus, ships twice performed a crucial function in saving the believers (see BELIEF AND UNBELIEF), in diluvial and post-diluvial times.

The many references to ships and to their element, the sea, especially to striking specificities involving them, and to human conduct and behavior during sea-voyages, strongly suggest that the Meccans had personal experience of sailing the sea. This sea can only have been the Red Sea, which some of the Meccan merchants must have crossed on their way to its African side, well known for its attractive products and exotica. This is valuable qurʾānic confirmation of what the sources say on commercial intercourse between Mecca and Ethiopia and it has important implications for qurʾānic studies, especially if the prophet Muḥammad himself was one of those who crossed over to the African side, sometime in the period which antedated his call around 610 C.E. (see also CARAVAN; TRADE AND COMMERCE).

Irfan A. Shahīd

Bibliography
Primary: al-Azraqī, Abū l-Walīd Muḥammad b. ʿAbdallāh, *Akhbār Makka*, ed. R.S. Malḥas, 2 vols. in 1, Mecca 1965, i, 157-67; Ṭabarī, *Taʾrīkh*, ed. Cairo, ii, 329, 343.
Secondary: ʿAbd al-Bāqī (s.vv. *fulk, safīna, jāriya, baḥr, rīḥ*); W.W. Barthold, Der Koran und das Meer, in *ZDMG* 83 (1929), 37-43; A.F.L. Beeston, Ships in a quranic simile, in *JAL* 4 (1973), 94-6; L. Casson (trans.), *The Periplus Maris Erythraei*, Princeton 1989; Jeffery, *For. vocab.*, 229-30 (s.v. *fulk*); A.J. Wensinck, *The ideas of the Semites concerning the navel of the earth*, Amsterdam 1916 (for the post-qurʾānic tradition); M. Zemouli, La navigation maritime chez les arabes à travers les textes du Coran et la poésie arabe, in *Graeco-Arabica* [Prodceedings of the 7th International Congress on Graeco-Oriental and Graeco-African Studies, Nicosia, 30 April-5 May 1996] 7-8 (2000), 605-22.

Shirt see CLOTHING

Shout see APOCALYPSE

Shuʿayb

Name of a messenger mentioned eleven times in the Qurʾān. His story is dealt with in a few passages (Q 7:85-93; 11:84-95; 26:176-91; 29:36-7) where his vicissitudes with his people are described. According to the Qurʾān, Shuʿayb was sent to Madyan (Q 7:85; 11:84; 29:36; see MIDIAN). He exhorted his people (to whom, it is stated, a sign was sent; cf. Q 7:85; 11:88; see SIGNS) to believe in God (see BELIEF AND UNBELIEF) and he urged them not to cheat people by altering weights and measures (q.v.; Q 7:85; 11:84-5; 26:181-2; see also CHEATING). He also summoned them not to engage in corrupt behavior (see CORRUPTION) nor to lurk on any road with the intent to threaten people (7:85-6; see THEFT). The Qurʾān does not give further information about the acts to which these exhortations refer. The haughty elders of his people arrogantly refused, in the name of the religion of their fathers — even accusing Shuʿayb of being bewitched (see INSANITY) and challenging him and his followers to renounce their faith or be thrown out (Q 7:88). Elsewhere, in another verse, the people state that they refrain from stoning (q.v.) the prophet only out of respect for his family (Q 11:91). Shuʿayb obviously rejected their injunctions and invoked God to judge them and thereby establish who was on the correct path (Q 7:89; see PATH OR WAY). The judgment went in his favor, while those who opposed him were tragically punished. An earthquake seized them (Q 7:91; 26:37), a clamor (*al-ṣayḥa*, Q 11:94) or a black cloud (Q 26:189) befell the unbelievers within their habitations (see PUNISHMENT STORIES). Shuʿayb and those who believed were placed in safety (Q 11:94; see PROTECTION).

Q 11:89 gives an approximate chronology for Shuʿayb's mission, for in his preaching, Shuʿayb urges his people not to follow the fate of the peoples of Noah (q.v.), Hūd (q.v.) and Ṣāliḥ (q.v.), adding "the people of Lot (q.v.) are not far away from you [i.e. his people]." The Qurʾān does not contain any other details of great significance that relate to the setting for Shuʿayb's life, with the exception of the name "al-Ayka" (also read as "Layka"; see READINGS OF THE QURʾĀN; ORTHOGRAPHY) that is found at the start of a passage that tells of Shuʿayb (Q 26:176). This term is thus understood to be the name of the people to whom he was sent. This term should not be confused with the "people of al-Ayka" cited in other passages (Q 15:78; 50:14; cf. 38:13), who appear to be a different group than the people of Madyan. Both expressions have, however, remained rather puzzling to the exegetes who have proposed various explanations (see below; see also PEOPLE OF THE THICKET).

None of the elements listed above permit the identification of Shuʿayb with any other known personage. Madyan, on the other hand, is related to the biblical Midian and to the story of Jethro and Moses (q.v.), and this is confirmed by the fact the name is also cited in the Qurʾān in connection with those events (Q 20:40; 28:22-3, 45). The identification, however, of Shuʿayb in later traditions with Jethro finds no confirmation in the sacred text. "Tales of the prophets" *(qiṣaṣ al-anbiyāʾ)* traditions expanded the qurʾānic content adding further particulars. Depending upon the contrasting and unclear qurʾānic passages stating that he was sent to Madyan and to al-Ayka, some exegetical reports maintain that Shuʿayb was sent to two different peoples. The name al-Ayka also finds various explanations based mainly on the meaning of the word, usually given as "thicket" or "grove of palms." Further reports describe with full details the punishment that erased Shuʿayb's people or, for example, state that the tombs of Shuʿayb and of his followers are around the Kaʿba (q.v.). All these elements have also prompted various interpretations by Western scholars, especially in connection with the origin of the names Shuʿayb and al-Ayka (for further details see Bibliography).

Roberto Tottoli

Bibliography
Primary: Abū l-Layth al-Samarqandī, *Tafsīr,* i, 554-6; ii, 223; Farrāʾ, *Maʿānī,* ii, 91; Ibn Kathīr, *Bidāya,* i, 185 f.; Kisāʾī, *Qiṣaṣ,* 190 f.; al-Maqdisī, Abū Zayd Aḥmad b. Sahl al-Balkhī, *al-Badʾ wa-l-tarīkh,* ed. C. Huart, 6 vols., Paris 1899-1919, iii, 75-7; Muqātil, *Tafsīr,* ii, 48-50, 434-5; Suyūṭī, *Durr,* 8 vols., Cairo 1983, iii, 500-5; vi, 318-20; Ṭabarī, *Tafsīr,* Cairo 1968, viii, 237-40; ix, 1-6; xii, 98-109; xiv, 47-8; id., *Taʾrīkh,* ed. de Goeje, i, 365-71; al-Ṭarafī, Abū ʿAbdallāh Muḥammad b. Aḥmad b. Muṭarrif, *Qiṣaṣ al-anbiyāʾ,* ed. R. Tottoli, *The stories of the prophets of Ibn Muṭarrif al-Ṭarafī,* Berlin 2003, 52-4; al-Thaʿlabī, Abū Isḥāq Aḥmad b. Muḥammad b. Ibrāhīm, *al-Kashf wa-l-bayān ʿan tafsīr al-Qurʾān,* ed. A.M. b. ʿĀshūr, 10 vols., Beirut 2002, iv, 260-3; id., *Qiṣaṣ,* 145-7; trans. W.M. Brinner, ʿArāʾis al-majālis fī qiṣaṣ al-anbiyāʾ *or "Lives of the Prophets" as recounted by Abū Isḥāq Aḥmad b. Muḥammad b. Ibrāhīm al-Thaʿlabī,* Leiden 2002, 274-7.
Secondary: C.E. Bosworth, Madyan Shuʿayb in pre-Islamic and early Islamic lore, in *JSS* 29 (1984), 53-64; id., The qurʾānic prophet Shuʿaib and Ibn Taimiyya's Epistle concerning him, in *Muséon* 87 (1974), 425-40; F. Buhl/C.E. Bosworth, Madyan Shuʿayb, in *EI²*, v, 1155-6; A. Geiger, *Judaism and Islam,* Madras 1898, 137-42; Horovitz, *KU,* 93-4, 119-20; Speyer, *Erzählungen,* 249-54; C.C. Torrey, *The Jewish foundation of Islam,* New York 1967 (1933), 71; R. Tottoli, *Biblical prophets in the Qurʾān and Muslim literature,* Richmond 2002, 48-50.